MODERN ADMIRALTY LAW

With Risk Management Aspects

Cavendish
Publishing
Limited

London • Sydney

MODERN ADMIRALTY LAW

With Risk Management Aspects

Aleka Mandaraka-Sheppard, LLM, PhD, Solicitor
Director of the London Shipping Law Centre
University College London

Cavendish
Publishing
Limited

London • Sydney

First published in Great Britain 2001 by Cavendish Publishing Limited, The Glass House, Wharton Street, London WC1X 9PX, United Kingdom
Telephone: + 44 (0)20 7278 8000   Facsimile: + 44 (0)20 7278 8080

Email: info@cavendishpublishing.com
Website: www.cavendishpublishing.com

Mandaraka-Sheppard, Alexandra, 1949–
Modern admiralty law
1 Admiralty law – Great Britain
I. Title

343.4'1'096

ISBN 1 85941 531 8

Printed and bound in Great Britain

Knowing the law is the beginning of a battle; knowing how to apply it is winning the battle; and knowing how to practise legal risk management is winning the war.

To the young generation of shipping law and practice
And to Emmanuel-John Sheppard

FOREWORD

Anyone with knowledge of the boundless enthusiasm and apparently inexhaustible energy displayed by Dr Aleka Mandaraka-Sheppard in the conception and evolution of the London Shipping Law Centre is unlikely to be surprised at her successful achievement of another daunting goal, namely to publish a new and comprehensive work on shipping law.

There is of course nothing radical in itself about the idea of a modern work in this field. As the author rightly acknowledges, several valuable works on individual aspects of the general topic have been published in recent years, but there has long been the need for a comprehensive work from which both the student (at various levels) and the practitioner can gain a general perspective as well as concrete and detailed information. Perhaps the late Professor Cadwallader, to whom the author pays tribute, could if spared have tackled the task, but his former student has produced a volume of which he would have been proud, the more so given the striking expansion in volume of the law relating to ships and the sea which has occurred since his day. Even a glance at the table of contents will show the extent of the author's grasp of contemporary legal issues, and the thoroughness with which they have been explored.

In addition to the general merits of this book there is one particular theme which calls for particular mention. That is, the emphasis laid on risk management. In recent years this has become a commonplace of business law and practice in many areas, but with a few notable exceptions it has been an absentee from study and practice in the maritime world. Fortunately this is now changing, and Dr Mandaraka-Sheppard's focus on the subject will, it may be hoped, stimulate interest and promote a wider appreciation of its cardinal importance.

Shelves now groan under the weight of legal textbooks, and inches of shelf-room are at a discount, but place must be made for *Modern Admiralty Law*, whose dimensions belie its approachability whilst evidencing its scope. This is a book for the library, the study and the office. I welcome it, and am sure that readers will do the same.

MJ Mustill
June 2001

PREFACE

This book provides a comprehensive analysis of principles as derived from important decisions, statutes, and other legislation, as well as Government consultation papers and regulations, directives and recent proposals of the European Commission, on the subject of admiralty law and marine safety. It approaches the subject from a modern perspective and includes advice on legal risk management where it is called for. It does not include contracts of affreightment used for the carriage of goods by sea, which is a subject meriting a separate volume. Although aspects of environmental pollution are looked at, as far as recent trends and developments are concerned, it is not within the scope of this book to include detailed provisions of the liability convention for damage resulting from oil pollution, which is an area of marine environmental law.

Admiralty law is not static. Technological developments in the running of ships, public concern for protection of the environment, international regulations for safety at sea, the campaign for quality shipping and insurance concerns have all influenced the development of admiralty law.

In the last decade, there were fundamental changes in the law and practice of admiralty law and marine safety, both nationally and internationally. There have been new international conventions and amendments to existing ones, as well as domestic legislation. Just to mention a few: the 1989 Salvage Convention – (brought into force internationally on 14 July 1996); the Oil Pollution Preparedness, Response and Co-operation Convention 1990 enacted by a statutory instrument in 1998; the amendment to the CLC and Fund for Oil Pollution Damage by the 1992 Protocols; the amendment to the SOLAS Convention 1974 to include the International Safety Management Code (ISMC) being in force since 1 July 1996; further bombardment by new regulations and proposals of the European Commission, having a parallel purpose to the international regulations on safety at sea in European waters; the Convention for the Arrest of Sea-going Ships 1999; the revision of the Brussels Convention on Civil Jurisdiction and Enforcement of Judgments, following the passing of the Amsterdam Treaty 1999, by a Council regulation, which will come into force on 1 March 2002; the Bunkers Convention signed on 23 March 2001. As far as domestic legislation is concerned, apart from a number of regulations and statutory instruments with regard to safety, there have been revolutionary changes, first with regard to arbitration procedures, by the Arbitration Act 1996, and even more so with regard to the doctrine of privity of contract, by the Contracts (Rights of Third Parties) Act 1999. Finally, a fundamental reform has been brought to the Civil Procedure Rules, by the Woolf reforms 1999, which encourage alternative dispute resolution.

A detailed and comprehensive book on all topics of pure admiralty law has long been needed. I recall from my time of studying for my LLM degree, at University College London in 1976, that the late Professor Cadwallader was being urged by students to develop his detailed and informative notes of teaching into a book. Time, however, has moved on and so has the development of admiralty law. The same demand for such a book has continued in the present time and I was encouraged by my students at the University of London (whom I have been teaching since 1993) to write this book. It has been developed from my teaching material, which the students enthusiastically receive, and further thoughts inspired by students' questions for which I acknowledge my deep appreciation.

Admiralty law belongs to the general subject of maritime law and includes: admiralty jurisdiction; ownership, management and mortgages of ships; shipbuilding, sale and purchase; collisions at sea; salvage of ships from danger; towage contracts; ports and pilotage; limitation of liability. Each of these topics deserves a book on its own, and there are such commendable books covering each topic separately. The purpose of this book is to bring the law of these topics together in a cohesive whole, looking beyond what may appear a rudimentary area of law. The subject matter is treated from the point of view of English common law, statutes and relevant international conventions. Since most of the international conventions have been enacted or are reflected in English admiralty law, this book should be of value to both national and international lawyers. In addition, England is the jurisdiction that is chosen by most contracting parties in their contracts concerning shipping transactions for the resolution of their disputes, either by the English courts or by arbitration. It is hoped that the procedural and the substantive law covered in this book will assist in the handling of such disputes.

The book is primarily intended for post-graduate students of shipping law, although it goes much further than what they need to know in this subject as students. It will also be useful to practitioners of shipping law, trainees, in-house lawyers, shipowners and managers, financial institutions and accountants, traders, consultants of shipping companies, claims' managers of protection and indemnity clubs and a wide range of professionals within the shipping industry.

The title of this book indicates that I shall also be dealing with risk management, which is an area that has fascinated me for some years. The phrase 'risk management' is, nowadays, frequently used in different contexts and an explanation is given in the 'Epilogue' of this book. Knowledge of how things did go wrong in previous cases with regard to the application of both the substantive and procedural law will, hopefully, increase awareness of how to avoid the same circumstances.

The reason why I consider discussion of risk management important is twofold: first, I would like students of shipping law to develop an awareness of managing legal risks, so that as shipping managers, or in-house lawyers, or insurance managers, they may be able to advise their principals or clients on how to prevent disputes or protracted litigation. Secondly, in my view, a systematic practice of risk management is a kind of an invisible investment, which will assist in the development of a healthy culture and the economic prosperity of a business.

For reasons of volume and size, it was not possible to include the text of the relevant conventions in this book. I do, however, rest assured that readers can easily find most of the relevant conventions in the Schedules to the Merchant Shipping Act 1995.

I have approached the writing of this book by concepts. Although the law is dry, there seemed to be a glimpse of fun, on some occasions, from the facts of cases and the witty comments of learned judges and counsel. The intellectual stimulation of writing it, however, has been immense but the time constraints frustrating.

General outline of the book

Part I, 'Admiralty Jurisdiction and Procedure', deals with the principles and case law of admiralty jurisdiction' and has been divided into seven chapters. This Part is intended to complement the book on *Admiralty Jurisdiction and Practice* of my learned friend Nigel Meeson, which has now been updated, although the present book expands many admiralty concepts and offers a different perspective. Historical aspects of the admiralty jurisdiction are dealt with in Chapter 1, with an analysis of the nature of jurisdiction in Chapter 2. A workable interpretation of *The Indian Grace* and its impact on various procedural and liability issues is offered (Chapter 3). This chapter deals also with beneficial ownership in a ship and risk management with respect to corporate structures. Chapter 4 deals with procedural matters. Chapters 5 and 6 concentrate on restrictions imposed upon the Admiralty Court, by conventions and doctrines, in exercising or maintaining jurisdiction. Important issues of how the Brussels/Lugano Conventions prevent or resolve conflict of jurisdictions are examined in detail. Finally, in this Part, Chapter 7, there is an overview of anti-suit injunctions.

Part II is titled 'Acquiring Ownership in Ships' and is divided into four chapters. Chapter 8 encompasses principles under English law in relation to ownership of British ships and management. It conveniently deals with management contracts and potential liabilities of owners and managers, particularly in the light of the ISMC (including criminal liability). Chapter 9 deals with the law of mortgages. Chapter 10 covers current law and issues pertaining to shipbuilding contracts. Chapter 11 concludes with ship sale and purchase and primarily intends to raise buyers' awareness in risk management; it includes aspects of freezing injunctions, as well as potential liability of classification societies to buyers.

Part III, 'Safety Regulations in Navigation and Liabilities' comprises one large Chapter 12: it includes liabilities of owners, managers, and officers for negligence, and is divided into three sections. Section A deals with the collision regulations; Section B with criminal liability arising from breach of statutory provisions; and Section C deals with civil liability and damages arising from a collision at sea caused by breach of duty of care, or lack of good seamanship.

Part IV, 'Specialised Contracts in Admiralty Law', is divided into three chapters: Chapter 13 has condensed the law of salvage and deals with recent developments; Chapter 14 is concerned with the law of towage contracts; and Chapter 15, with the law of harbours and pilotage, which is currently undergoing fundamental changes in order to ensure safety in port operations and navigation.

Part V, 'Miscellaneous', contains 'Tonnage Limitation' in Chapter 16. This chapter is concerned with a conceptually independent subject and briefly explains the principles of limitation of liability of shipowners and others with regard to maritime claims. Issues arising from the ISMC and its impact on limitation are discussed, as well as problems surrounding the compensation of victims of ferry disasters are briefly summarised. Chapter 17, titled 'Recent Proposals by the European Commission to the European Parliament and Council' summarises the measures taken by the Commission on Maritime Safety, following the sinking of the oil tanker *The Erika*.

Part V also includes the Epilogue of the book, dealing with issues of risk management generally in the context of the infrastructures that underpin its process at a particular shipping company.

Aleka Mandaraka-Sheppard
April 2001

ACKNOWLEDGMENTS

I received encouragement from my publishers for the completion of this book in no little measure. I am grateful to Jo Reddy, Cara Annett and the expert team of Cavendish Publishing for their patience and appreciation of the difficulties involved in the lonely process of writing a book of this type in addition to other duties.

I am obliged to the members of the London Shipping Law Centre, whose contributions enabled UCL to engage a research assistant at the first stages of this book, although the vast amount of material needed I was able to have available in my computer through 'Context', Lawtel EU interactive and the internet, which saved me a lot of time. My thanks are also due to the Steering Committee, co-director, and executive manager of the Centre, Gerard Mathews, for their support. I owe my gratitude to the Dean and Head of the Law Faculty, Professor Jeffrey Jowell, for permitting me to take leave from teaching for a year to write this book, and to those who took part in the teaching of the LLM courses in my absence, namely: Bernard Eder QC, Nicholas Legh-Jones QC, Nigel Meeson, Jonathan Loftus, Professor Robert Grime and Jessica Killner. My reliable secretary, Deborah Harris, was able to take on administrative duties of the courses in my absence. Without the help of all, this book would have taken longer to reach print.

I am especially grateful to Alison Clarke, senior lecturer at UCL, for her valuable suggestions on the first draft of the mortgages chapter. I would also like to thank Michael Howard QC, who made useful comments to my first draft relating to the evolution of the action *in rem*, Herry Lawford of the UK Club for providing me with information about the Baltic and International Maritime Council new SHIPMAN forms and Pandi Embiricos of Andros Maritime Agencies Ltd, for providing me with a copy of the EC's report on *The Erika*. I should like to acknowledge that the work of the Centre, through its contributors, has been an extra source of information that makes some parts of this book especially market orientated. It is an honour that Lord Mustill, to whom I am most grateful, has agreed to write the foreword.

My deep appreciation and thanks are also due to Chandris Shipping for, had it not been for the scholarship granted to me in 1976 to study shipping law, I would not have been in shipping today!

Finally, this book would not have been possible without the generous encouragement offered to me and patience endured, throughout a year and a half, by my husband, Colin Sheppard, and our young son, Emmanuel-John, who were concerned with my very long working hours. Proof-reading of first drafts by Colin, in between his numerous other engagements, was immensely reassuring. In addition, his skilful home management and cooking saved me a lot of time. Emmanuel-John, who is preparing for his Common Entrance Examination, has shown a great interest in shipping, without undue fascination about regulations preventing collisions. He would prefer, however, if the book contained some naval battles and had the title he offered:

'The Law of the Waves', which would, undoubtedly, make a suitable title for a more interesting book than a legal text!

While my appreciation for comments made to some drafts of the manuscript has been immense, the responsibility remains mine. The text contains the law as I believed it to have been on 31 January 2001 for judgments and as at 7 March 2001 for recent developments in regulations and proposed legislation.

CONTENTS

PART I ADMIRALTY JURISDICTION AND PROCEDURE

Contents

PART II
ACQUIRING OWNERSHIP IN SHIPS

Contents

Contents

PART III
SAFETY REGULATIONS IN NAVIGATION AND LIABILITIES

Contents

PART V
MISCELLANEOUS

TABLE OF CASES

TABLE OF STATUTES

TABLE OF STATUTORY INSTRUMENTS

TABLE OF EUROPEAN LEGISLATION

TABLE OF INTERNATIONAL LEGISLATION

PART I

ADMIRALTY JURISDICTION AND PROCEDURE

INTRODUCTION

This part deals with the nature of Admiralty Jurisdiction, its extent, the types of maritime claims that can be enforced in the Admiralty Court, arrest of ships and the aftermath including the priorities of claims to be paid out of the fund from the sale of the ship by the Admiralty Marshal. The function of statutory rights in rem and maritime liens are also considered. How the jurisdiction of the court is affected by International Conventions and other doctrines, such as the *'forum non-conveniens'* are a paramount consideration. While the jurisdiction of the court is quite wide, there has been a gradual abandonment of jurisdictional chauvinism by English judges. This has occurred in the recent years with the evolution of the European Jurisdiction Conventions – which limit to a certain extent the jurisdiction of the English Court. There has also been a gradual judicial acceptance that the courts of other countries are competent to adjudicate on a matter. It must be shown that a court of another country is the natural or an appropriate forum to which the parties are amenable and justice can be done for the interests of all parties.

Chapter 1 contains introductory elements. Chapter 2 examines the nature of the admiralty jurisdiction. Chapter 3 deals with the mode of exercise of jurisdiction in Admiralty cases with particular emphasis on the nature of the 'action *in rem*'. Chapter 4 briefly outlines an overview of procedure, arrest of ships and the aftermath of sale of the ship by the court, priorities of claims and conflict of laws. Chapter 5 sets out rules and doctrines pertaining the restrictions of the jurisdiction to adjudicate on the merits of a case, and in particular if a stay of proceedings is warranted on grounds of *forum non conveniens* or jurisdiction agreements which are not within the scope of the Brussels Convention on civil jurisdiction and judgments. Chapter 6 examines jurisdiction bases provided by International Conventions separately and deals in particular with the Brussels/Lugano Conventions. It also refers specifically to delegation of jurisdiction to other Conventions by the rules of the Brussels/Lugano Conventions and examines whether or not the Convention rules permit the application of the doctrine of *forum non conveniens* for a stay of proceedings. It also examines the consequences of breach of a jurisdiction agreement to which the Convention rules apply. Issues of anti-suit injunctions whether for breach of contract cases or otherwise are dealt with in Chapter 7.

CHAPTER 1

INTRODUCTORY ELEMENTS

1 THE JURISDICTION OF THE ADMIRALTY COURT – HISTORICAL OVERVIEW

Whether or not the admiralty jurisdiction in England originated from Saxon times, or from the times of Henry I, the authority of the Crown to administer justice in respect of piracy or spoil and other offences committed upon the sea was undisputed by the reign of Edward III.[1] The High Court of Admiralty was an instrument of the Lord High Admiral and had jurisdiction to hear all offences and disputes within the Admiral's jurisdiction. The judge of the court was a deputy of the Lord High Admiral. This jurisdiction was separate from that of the common law courts. However, apart from possessing criminal jurisdiction, the Admiral began, gradually, to hear disputes also in all civil matters connected with the sea. This resulted in usurping the jurisdiction of the common law courts in matters arising in inland tidal waters.[2] The encroachment of the Admiral's jurisdiction upon the common law courts' jurisdiction caused indignation and became intolerable to common law lawyers in the 13th and 14th centuries. The authority of the Admiral to determine disputes involving seizure at sea was denied by the Common Pleas in 1296.[3] Later a statutory restriction of the Admiral's jurisdiction was obtained by the Admiralty Jurisdiction Act 1389,[4] in the reign of Richard II. In addition, by the subsequent statute, the Admiralty Jurisdiction Act 1391, matters of contracts, pleas and quarrels, which arose within the body of a country, whether on land or water, were removed from the jurisdiction of the Lord Admiral and were only triable in common law courts.[5]

In the years that followed, common law lawyers still employed devices to enable them to adjudicate maritime matters, which were actually within the jurisdiction of the Admiralty Court. Attempts by the Lord High Admiral to proceed in the Admiralty Court, either by arresting the person of the defendant or seizing his goods within the jurisdiction (known as the *maritime attachment)* in order to compel the defendant to appear, had been thwarted by

---

1   *Halsbury's Laws*, Vol 1(1), 1989, para 301.
2   *Ibid.*
3   Marsden, *Select Pleas*, Vol 1.
4   This Act was finally repealed in 1879.
5   See details of this background in Wiswall, FL (Jr), *Development of Admiralty Jurisdiction Since 1800*, 1970, CUP.

common law writs of prohibition.[6] The last known instance of admiralty jurisdiction by the arrest of the person was in 1780.[7]

The long conflict between the Admirals and the superior common law courts led to the decline of the Admiralty Court. Eventually, at the end of the reign of William IV in the 1830s, the jurisdiction of the Admiralty Court was retained in matters such as droits of admiralty (wrecks at sea which were the Admiral's property rights) collisions, salvage, possession of ships, bottomry and seamen's wages.[8] During this time, Dr Lushington, who was also a Member of Parliament, succeeded Sir John Nicholas as judge of the High Court of Admiralty in 1838. He promulgated the passing of the Admiralty Court Act (ACA) 1840. This Act effectively abolished the restrictions of Admiralty Court imposed by the Acts of Richard II and extended the court's general jurisdiction, but it did not restore it to jurisdiction enjoyed in the ancient times in questions of contract, freight and charterparties. The new jurisdiction conferred by the Act included cognisance of mortgages on ships, questions of legal title and the division of proceeds of sale on suits of possession, and any claims in the nature of salvage services, provision of necessaries to a ship, as well as claims for towage. It was made clear, however, that none of this jurisdiction was exclusive, but concurrent with that of the courts of law and equity.[9]

From a historical viewpoint, it is interesting to note comments made by Esher LJ and Fry LJ in *The Zeta*[10] explaining what followed:

Esher LJ: In certain cases specified in s 6 of the ACA 1840 (3 & 4 Vict c 65), the jurisdiction was extended so as to enable the court to adjudicate upon claims where the ship was within the body of a county, but there was no remedy *in personam* until in 1854, by s 13 of the 17 & 18 Vict c 78, the obsolete proceedings *in personam* were revived, and the Admiralty Court had power to proceed by way of monition; but the effect of these two Acts was only to enable the jurisdiction to be exercised in the body of a county, and did not give any greater jurisdiction in respect of subject matter than the court had before.

Under s 7 of the ACA 1861 (24 Vict c 10), jurisdiction was given over any claim for damage done by any ship. Dr Lushington (cited in this case) was of the opinion that the Act did not empower him to allow a citation *in personam* to issue against a pilot by whose alleged incapacity, whilst in charge of the vessel,

---

6   *Op cit*, Wiswall, fn 5, p 5.

7   See *The Clara* (1855) Swa 1 (arrest of a person for civil liability was considered out of order. Perhaps, the prohibition of such arrest marked the beginning of protection of human rights and liberties.)

8   *Halsbury's Laws*, Vol 1, para 301.

9   *Op cit*, Wiswall, fn 5, pp 40–41. The author also explains, p 42, how Dr Lushington lost his seat in Parliament, which was a price he had to pay for the passing of the 1840 Act. An opponent of Dr Lushington insisted that a clause was inserted in the Act disqualifying the admiralty judge from sitting in Parliament.

10 *The Zeta* [1892] P 285, pp 297–301.

damage had been done to another vessel. The effect of s 35 of the same Act (ACA 1861), which gave the Admiralty Court jurisdiction either by proceedings *in rem* or *in personam*, was only to enable proceedings *in personam* to be taken where the case was an admiralty suit, so that proceedings *in rem* would have lain against the ship, or against the owners or persons identified in interest with the ship.

Dr Lushington for a time was inclined to give the full literal meaning to the Acts of Parliament, and thought that anything done at sea, or anything done anywhere by a ship, was to be considered as within the admiralty jurisdiction. Sir Robert Phillimore (cited) was more imbued with the idea that the Admiralty Court had all the jurisdiction which it ever had. He was of opinion that that Court had jurisdiction over every tort committed on the high seas.

Fry LJ: [He] considered that the admiralty jurisdiction, which existed in the year 1868 was of a double character. There was the original jurisdiction, which existed in the ancient Court of Admiralty, the jurisdiction of the Lord High Admiral, and there was the enlarged jurisdiction given by the statute 3 & 4 Vict and by the statute 24 Vict. Those statutes professed to enlarge and did enlarge the jurisdiction of the Admiralty Court. Those statutes, for the first time, gave admiralty jurisdiction within the body of a county. It requires no very great stretch of imagination to imagine rafts of timber, or some such structure, getting permanently attached to a coral reef, or rocks, or a sand bank, and to imagine a collision between that object upon the high seas and some vessel. Supposing such an occurrence had happened, would it have been within the jurisdiction of the Lord High Admiral? In the first place, it is to be observed that no case of prohibition of jurisdiction in any such case can be found in the books. On the other hand, it is to be observed that the undoubted jurisdiction of the Lord High Admiral was over everything happening upon the high seas. It has been described as a general power, taking cognisance of all maritime cases. That would in itself go a considerable way towards shewing that the court must have had jurisdiction in these cases; but in my judgment other considerations lead to the same conclusion. It has been doubted whether the jurisdiction of the Admiralty Court or of the Lord High Admiral arose in the reigns of Edward III, or Richard I, or Henry I; but, whenever it arose, it arose at a time when the distinction did not exist between local and transitory actions.

The admiralty jurisdiction as expanded by the Acts of 1840 and 1861 enjoyed exclusively the advantage of the proceeding *in rem*. Maritime law developed in a separate court, but it derived from law expounded in other courts. At the time of Sir Robert Phillimore's judgeship, the Royal Commission, which inquired into the structure of the court, reported in 1869 that the root cause of the need to extend the admiralty jurisdiction was the imperfection of the procedures of the common law system. The recommendations of the Royal Commission were enacted by Parliament by the first Supreme Court of Judicature Act 1873, which consolidated all courts, including the High Court of Admiralty, into the Supreme Court of Judicature. This Court was divided into Her Majesty's High Court of Justice and Her Majesty's Court of Appeal to exercise appellate jurisdiction. The High Court was sub-divided into five divisions: Queen's Bench, Common Pleas, Exchequer, Chancery, and Probate, Divorce and Admiralty (PDA or Admiralty Division).[11] By 1875, any imperfections of the Act were corrected and the long struggle between the Lord Admiral's jurisdiction and the common law courts ended. It was mainly done to foster the development of common concepts between these divisions of courts. The development of admiralty law has continued to be influenced by changes in concepts of common law and vice versa. The reform of the judicature system transformed the attitude of common law lawyers. The admiralty jurisdiction was as readily extended, as it was in the early days when it was in the hands of the civilian admiralty judges. There were frequently transfers of actions, which were not triable at common law, from the Queen's Bench division to the Admiralty Court.[12]

Subsequent enactments modified the Judicature Acts and this led to the consolidation of all statutes by the Supreme Court of Judicature (Consolidation) Act 1925. In addition to the basic jurisdiction of the Admiralty Court, claims for necessaries supplied to any foreign ship anywhere and questions of title arising in suits of necessaries, claims for damage done to any ship (inclusive of personal injury and death), claims for salvage services (including life salvage) rendered anywhere and claims in the nature of towage were added.[13]

The admiralty jurisdiction was later affected by two subsequent Acts: the Crown Proceedings Act 1947 (concerned with limitation of liability and immunity from suit *in rem* of Crown vessels and aircraft); and the Civil Aviation Act 1949 (concerned with claims for salvage of or by an aircraft).

An opportunity for further judicial expansion of the admiralty jurisdiction was given by the Administration of Justice Act 1956. This Act confirmed the jurisdiction the court already possessed and incorporated some provisions of the International Convention for the Arrest of Sea-going Ships 1952 (ratified in this country in 1959, but not all its provisions were introduced into English law).

---

11 *Op cit*, Wiswall, fn 5, pp 100–02.
12 *Op cit*, Wiswall, fn 5, p 128.
13 Supreme Court of Judicature (Consolidation) Act 1925, ss 18 and 22.

2 ADMIRALTY JURISDICTION AT THE PRESENT TIME

The sources of admiralty jurisdiction can be found in statutes,[14] Conventions, rules of court and judicial doctrines. The present statute is the Supreme Court Act (SCA) 1981. The provisions of this Act will be examined in detail later. Conventions,[15] as enacted by various Acts of Parliament, play a major part in the expansion or restriction of admiralty jurisdiction. The rules of court can be found[16] in the Civil Procedure Rules (CPR) 1999 and new Practice Directions. These are the result of the Woolf Reform of Civil Justice[17] and relate only to procedure. The philosophy behind these rules is to encourage parties to a dispute to settle as early as possible and, should they have to litigate, an obligation is imposed upon them and their lawyers to prosecute and defend their proceedings efficiently and without unnecessary delays. The overriding objective is to make the procedures simple and easily understood by laymen and lawyers. There are some dramatic changes particularly in language, for example, latin terms are eliminated. So, apart from the words *'in rem'* and *'in personam'* for which no replacement could be found, the word 'writ' has been replaced with 'claim form'. 'Plaintiff' has become 'claimant', 'pleading' has become 'statement of case', 'discovery of documents' has become 'disclosure', 'Mareva injunction' is now called 'freezing injunction' and 'Anton Piller order' is a 'search order'. 'Leave of the court' is substituted with 'permission'. There will be a cultural change, too, in that speed is required in the management of cases and the judges take a very active role in the process of disposing litigation more efficiently. The intention is to curtail an unnecessary increase in legal costs. The role of expert witnesses has also changed in an attempt to prevent them from taking a partisan role. The court may direct that expert evidence, on particular issues, be given by a 'single joint expert.[18]

---

14 The first statute was the ACA 1840 which gave statutory rights of arrest *(in rem* jurisdiction); this *in rem* jurisdiction was expanded by the Supreme Court of Judicature Acts 1873 and 1875, as consolidated in the Supreme Court of Judicature Act 1925. The Administration of Justice Act 1956 was passed mainly to give effect to two International Conventions: the Convention for the Arrest of Sea-going Ships 1952 and the Convention for the Prevention of Collisions at Sea 1952. The 1956 Act was amended and superseded by the present statute, the SCA 1981.

15 These include: the Arrest Convention 1952, the Convention for the Prevention of Collisions 1952, the International Salvage Convention 1989 (the Salvage Convention), Foreign Immunity 1978, the Brussels/Lugano Conventions 1968 and 1988, respectively, the Athens Convention on Carriage of Passengers and their Luggage by Sea 1974, the Limitation of Liability Convention 1976 (International Convention relating to the Limitation of Liability of Owners and Others of Sea-going Ships), the Convention and Protocol for the Prevention of Pollution Damage 1992.

16 Prior to 1999 these rules were embodied in the so called 'White Book' for the practice in the High Court and in the 'Green Book' for the County Court's practice.

17 For the effect of the Woolf reforms upon the Admiralty and Commercial Court there is a transcription of the speeches by Clarke LJ and Rix J delivered at the third lecture in memory of Professor Cadwallader, the London Shipping Law Centre, 1999.

18 See a short summary of the new CPR in [1999] LMCLQ 321.

The old terms are used here in the discussion of cases decided before the new CPR were implemented.

3 FOREIGN ASPECTS AND EXTENT OF ADMIRALTY JURISDICTION

Admiralty law has developed from sources common to many maritime nations. Thus, through the ratification of International Conventions, the internal municipal laws of different countries show greater similarity to one another. The jurisdiction extends to all ships, hovercrafts[19] or aircraft,[20] British or foreign, wherever the residence or domicile of the owners[21] may be,[22] but it is limited by Crown and foreign sovereign immunity rules.[23] It applies to all maritime claims whenever arising.[24] Its extent is also subject to rules governing the mode of exercise of such jurisdiction and, in the case of collisions, the jurisdiction is restricted where the action is *in personam*.[25] In certain circumstances, the court may have to stay or decline its jurisdiction upon application of other rules and doctrines,[26] such as the European Convention on Civil Jurisdiction and Judgments[27] and the doctrine of *forum non-conveniens*. On the other hand, the expertise that exists in England in maritime matters encourages parties to choose English jurisdiction in their contracts or submit to English jurisdiction.

4 THE CIVIL LAW AND COMMON LAW APPROACHES

In civil law systems, there are three distinct rules provided in civil procedure codes: rules for a provisional pre-trial remedy (for example, conservatory measures to obtain security for a claim, called, in French, *saisie conservatoire*); rules relating to establishing jurisdiction on the merits, which may be based

---

19 Hovercraft Act 1968, s 2(1).

20 Where legislation provides; see *Glider Standard Austria* [1965] 2 Lloyd's Rep 189.

21 Provided the jurisdiction does not conflict with the provisions of the Civil Jurisdiction and Judgments Acts 1982, 1991, or the owners of the relevant property are not the Crown or a foreign State using the ship or cargo for public purposes.

22 SCA 1981, s 20(7)(a).

23 As apply by the Crown Proceedings Act 1947 and the State Immunity Act 1978.

24 SCA 1981, s 20(7)(b).

25 SCA 1981, ss 21 and 22.

26 See Chapter 5, below.

27 The Brussels Convention 1968 as amended and the Lugano Convention 1988, enacted by the Civil Jurisdiction and Judgments Acts 1982 and 1991, respectively (European Civil Jurisdiction Conventions); see Chapter 6, in which reference is made to the amending Regulation EC/44/2001 that will come into force on 1 March 2002 and will replace the Brussels Convention.

on a substantive link between the claim and the particular jurisdiction; and codified rules relating to the status of some claims as preferred claims over unsecured creditors.

By contrast, in the common law jurisdictions, commencing the *in rem* (action) claim and the arrest of the ship merges all three distinct functions. Namely, it has the consequence of obtaining security for the claim; of establishing jurisdiction on the merits[28] (even if there is no substantive link between the claim and the jurisdiction other than the presence of the arrested ship in the jurisdiction); and of securing the position of statutory maritime claimants as preferred creditors over unsecured ones by the issue of the proceedings *in rem*. Art 7 of the Arrest Convention 1952 adopted a middle way between common law and civil law, in that, where the arrest was made, that court should have jurisdiction on the merits, if its own domestic law permitted it, but allows the parties to agree another jurisdiction.

The SCA 1981 provides the means of enforcing those maritime claims specifically mentioned in s 20(2). They are statutory rights *in rem*. The prerequisite is, however, that there must exist a substantive cause of action.

5 UNIQUE ASPECTS OF THE ADMIRALTY JURISDICTION

The distinction between the action *in rem* and the action *in personam* (now renamed '*in rem* claim' and '*in personam* claim' by the new CPR, in force since April 1999) is unique and is not familiar to other European jurisdictions.

The action *in rem* was originally founded on the notion of maritime liens. Enforcement of judgment was allowed against the property arrested, on the theory that a maritime lien attached to the property from the moment of the creation of such a claim. Such an action became known as an action *in rem*.[29] The right to enforce a maritime lien by an action *in rem* was confined to the property by which the damage was caused, or in relation to which the maritime lien arose, even if the property was in the hands of an innocent purchaser.[30] Later, this jurisdiction was extended to other maritime claims provided by the statutes regardless of whether the claims gave rise to maritime liens.

It should be noted that, historically, a claimant had to secure an entry in the action book kept in the Admiralty Registry stating his name and giving a description of the ship to be sued and the amount of the claim. Shortly

---

28 Whether the court will exercise its jurisdiction will depend on there being no other court claiming to have exclusive jurisdiction based on either Convention rules, or a prior agreement between the parties to a dispute. See Chapter 6, below.

29 *Halsbury's Laws*, Vol 1, para 305.

30 *The Ripon City* [1892] P 226, pp 241–42.

thereafter, he had to execute an affidavit to lead a warrant of arrest of the ship. This particular procedure developed in 1801.

Apart from proceedings against the ship, there was also the availability of proceedings against the person interested in the property, by arresting the person or his property (the maritime attachment). The common law courts vehemently disapproved of the proceeding to arrest the person and caused it to become obsolete. The power of arrest was only retained in relation to property if it was the subject matter of the dispute.[31] Wiswall explains[32] that the procedure of maritime attachment was similar in outline to that of the action *in rem* and, because it involved seizure of a vessel, it was often referred to as a proceeding *quasi in rem*. But maritime attachment was a device designed to compel the appearance of the defendant in an action *in personam* and it was by no means an action *in rem*.

The distinguishing feature of the action *in rem* has always been the ability of the maritime claimant to proceed against the ship directly, which was regarded as the defendant, the ship being personified. If the person interested in defending the claim appeared in the proceeding or acknowledged service of the writ *in rem*, the action would become, also, an action against the person. The procedural theory (in that, the *in rem* action aimed to bring the person liable for the claim in the proceedings) developed. It will be seen later, in Chapter 3, how this theory evolved and the effect of the House of Lords decision in the *Indian Grace* upon the action *in rem*.

A new procedure *in personam* was founded by the ACA 1854 and paralleled that of a suit *in rem*, in which the defendant appeared collaterally to defend the *res*. The High Court of Admiralty was empowered to entertain proceedings commenced by personal service upon the owners of the property, which was the subject matter of the dispute. It was particularly useful when the property had been lost. Subsequently, s 35 of the ACA 1861 confirmed the Admiralty Court's jurisdiction by proceedings either *in rem* or *in personam*.

The *in rem* claim can be brought into effect by service on, or arrest of, the relevant ship when she comes within the jurisdiction of the English court. When a claim attracts a maritime lien, the property to be arrested includes the cargo on board the particular ship and the freight due, in relation to the cargo and voyage of the ship arrested.

The *in rem* proceedings can even be brought simply to obtain security for claims referred to arbitration, or for claims for which a court, other than the Admiralty Court, has jurisdiction on the merits.[33] In the realm of the European Civil Jurisdiction Conventions, the action *in rem* has caused some debate but, recently, both the European Court of Justice and the House of

---

31 *Op cit*, Wiswall fn 5, pp 12–17.

32 *Ibid*, p 165.

33 *The Bazias* [1993] 1 Lloyd's Rep 101.

Lords have resolved the matter.[34] The result of the House of Lords' decision in the *Indian Grace*,[35] which will be discussed later,[36] seems to have caused a complete overhaul of the *in rem* (action) claim.

English procedural rules do not require any connection between the claim and the jurisdiction. With regard to actions *in personam*,[37] jurisdiction is established by the service of the proceedings or claim form upon the person within the jurisdiction. However, in maritime or commercial claims, when, in most cases, the defendants are a company registered abroad, other rules have developed to serve them out of the jurisdiction, provided the claim comes within certain defined categories.[38]

6 THE ADMIRALTY COURT

The Administration of Justice Act 1970 (s 2(1)) abolished the PDA division of the High Court and provided for the constitution of the Admiralty Court of the Queen's Bench Division of the High Court. Section 6 of the SCA 1981 replaced this and further provided, by sub-s 2, that the judges are puisne judges of the High Court, nominated by the Lord Chancellor.[39] The Admiralty Marshal performs the arrest, appraisement and sale of a ship or property – being the subject of the *in rem* claim. The Admiralty Registrar carries out the functions of the Queen's Bench Master. The nautical assessors, known as Elder Brethren of Trinity House, who express their opinion in nautical matters, may assist the judge in technical cases. Their expert evidence is admissible in all courts on all issues of fact about seamanship.[40] The nautical assessor is not to be confused with the expert witness; he is not subjected to cross-examination, but the judge has discretion to choose between the opinion of differing nautical assessors.[41]

The SCA 1981 governs the jurisdiction of the Admiralty Court, ss 20–24.

The old Ord 75 of the Rules of the Supreme Court (RSC), relating to procedure in admiralty cases, has been replaced with CPR Pt 49 and Practice Direction 49F (PD 49F).

---

34 See Chapter 6, para 1.6, below.
35 *Republic of India v India Steamship Co Ltd (No 2)* [1994] 3 WLR 818 (HL).
36 See Chapter 3, below.
37 For the advantages of the action *in rem* over the action *in personam*, see Chapter 3, below.
38 See Chapter 5, below.
39 SCA 1981, s 6(1)(b), (2)
40 *The Clan Lamont* (1946) LlL Rep 522.
41 *The Australia* (1926) LlL Rep 142.

7 LIMITS OF EXERCISE OF ADMIRALTY JURISDICTION

An *in rem* claim is not allowed to be brought against ships of the Crown nor against those owned by foreign States. Section 38 of the Crown Immunity Act 1947 states that 'His Majesty's ships' means ships of which the beneficial interest vested in His Majesty, or ships which are registered as Government ships, or which are, for the time being, demised or sub-demised to or in the exclusive possession of the Crown; except that, the said expression does not include any ship in which His Majesty is interested, otherwise, than in right of His Government. By s 29 of the same Act, no proceedings *in rem* shall be brought for any claim against the property of the Crown whether a ship, cargo or aircraft. Section 24(2) of the SCA 1981 preserves that position. The jurisdiction may be exercised *in personam* against the Crown in accordance with the provisions of the Crown Immunity Act 1947.

Similarly, under s 10(1)(2)(3) of the State Immunity Act 1978, a foreign sovereign is immune[42] from either action *in rem* against a ship or a sister ship belonging to that State, or *in personam* for enforcing a claim in connection with such a ship unless, when the cause of action arose, the ship was (or, in a case of a sister ship, both ships were) in use, or intended for use, for commercial purposes. As regards claims *in rem* against cargo belonging to a foreign State, the immunity will apply if both ship and cargo carried on board were not used, or intended for use, for commercial purposes, s 10(4)(a). An action *in personam* will be allowed for claims against the cargo belonging to the State, if the ship carrying it was used, or intended for use, for commercial purposes, s 10(4)(b).

8 WHAT IS A SHIP?

One might possibly take the position of the gentleman who dealt with the elephant by saying that he could not define an elephant but he knew what it was when he saw one, and it may be that this is the foundation of the learned judge's decision, that he cannot define 'ship or vessel' but he knows that this thing is not a ship or vessel.[43]

---

42 *Congresso del Partido* [1978] 2 QB 500, pp 537–38; and *Kuwait Airways Corp v Iraq Airways Co* [1995] 2 Lloyd's Rep 317 (HL).

43 *Merchant Marine Insurance Co Ltd v North of England P&I Assoc* (1926) 26 LlL Rep 201 (CA), p 203, *per* Scrutton LJ.

8.1 Why is it important to define it?

Defining a ship is important in many areas of shipping law (including marine insurance) in order to determine whether the provisions of various statutes, which are intended to apply to ships, are applicable to structures other than those which are obviously a ship. A decision whether a particular structure is a ship or not will determine the basis of liability. For example, if a collision occurs between a floating beacon[44] and a ship, the provisions of the Merchant Shipping Act (MSA) 1995 in relation to apportionment of liability (the admiralty law rule) will not apply, because they only apply if there is a collision between two or more ships. Instead, common law principles will apply. Unlike the admiralty law rule of division of loss in accordance with the degree of blame, the common law did not allow for apportionment of blame between two wrongdoers, prior to the Law Reform (Contributory Negligence) Act 1945. It was, therefore, very important to determine whether a collision between a skiff with oars and a rowing boat involved a collision between two ships.[45]

Whether a subject matter will be referred to the jurisdiction of the Admiralty Court, again will depend on whether a ship was involved in the incident which gave rise to the cause of action. Limitation of liability will also depend on whether the 'thing' that gave rise to liability was a ship under the meaning of the MSA 1995. For the purpose of salvage, the new Salvage Convention 1989 has extended the subject matter, which can be subject to salvage.[46]

8.2 Old definition

The definition of a ship has baffled the courts for more than a century. The problem arose from the circular definition in s 742 of the MSA 1894, which stated:

> ... 'vessel' includes any ship or boat, or any other description of vessel used in navigation; 'ship' includes every description of vessel used in navigation not propelled by oars.

That a vessel includes a ship and a ship includes a vessel does not help much by way of definition. One has to search for the origin of the word 'vessel' which comes from latin *vascellum* meaning a 'vas' and connotes something hollow, a kind of a container. Once this is understood, then the definition in s 742 made three points: first, that the word 'vessel' was all embracing and

---

44 It has been held that this is not a ship: *The Gas Float Whitton* [1897] AC 337 (HL).
45 See *Edwards v Quikenden and Forester* [1939] P 261.
46 See Chapter 13, below.

was wider than the word 'ship', in that it was not limited by the requirement not to be propelled by oars[47]. Secondly, that the physical appearance was important; and thirdly, the use of it ought to be determined.

An interesting explanation of the definition of a ship was given by Blackburn J in *Ex p Ferguson*[48] which is worth quoting, for it would be useful even today (apart from the reference to oars, which has been eliminated from the present definition, for which see later).

It involved a collision between a steamer and a fishing coble, which had oars, but, when fully loaded with fish and wet nets, it did not use the oars at that time. In deciding whether or not the fishing coble was a ship (under s 2 of the MSA 1854), the judge said:

> The chief argument against that proposition [that it was a ship] is by referring to the interpretation clause ... [meaning s 2] which says: '"ship" shall include every description of vessel used in navigation nor propelled by oars'. And the argument against the proposition is one which I have heard very frequently, viz. Where an Act says certain words shall include a certain thing, that the words must apply exclusively to the which they are to include. That is not so; the definition given of a 'ship' is in order that 'ship' may have a more extensive meaning. Whether a ship is propelled by oars or not, it is still a ship, unless the words 'not propelled by oars' exclude all vessels which are ever propelled by oars. Most small vessels rig out something to propel them, and it would be monstrous to say that they are not ships. What, then, is the meaning of the word 'ship' in this Act? It is this, that every vessel that substantially goes to sea is a 'ship'. I do not mean to say that a little boat going out for a mile or two to sea would be a ship; but where it is its business really and substantially to go to sea, if it is not propelled by oars, it shall be considered a ship for the purpose of the Act. Whenever the vessel does go to sea, whether it be decked or not decked, or whether it goes to sea for the purpose of fishing or anything else, it would be a ship.

The fishing coble was, therefore, a ship.

Many old cases dealt with the method of propulsion (which is not relevant any longer), the purpose or use of the structure, or even the area she was used (which are relevant criteria still today under the present statutes). In *The Gas Float Whitton (No 2)*, a boat-shaped gas float, moored in tidal waters to give light, was held not to be a ship for the purpose of salvage.[49] Lord Herschell said:[50]

---

47 Such a requirement has now been eliminated from all relevant statutes which define a 'ship'.

48 (1871) LR 6 QB 280, p 291.

49 Under Art 1 of the Salvage Convention 1989, a gas float like this will be subject to salvage coming within the wide definition of vessel or property and being in any waters whatsoever (see Chapter 13 and, particularly, Brice, G, *Maritime Law of Salvage*, 3rd edn, 1999, Sweet & Maxwell, pp 211–12).

50 [1897] AC 337, p 343.

It was not constructed for the purpose of being navigated or of conveying cargo or passengers. It was, in truth, a lighted buoy or beacon. The suggestion that the gas stored in the float can be regarded as cargo carried by it is more ingenious than sound.

8.3 Modern definitions

The Concise Oxford English Dictionary defines vessel as: 'a hollow receptacle, especially for liquid, a ship or boat', while Collins English Dictionary gives a broader definition: 'any object used as a container, esp for a liquid, or a passenger or freight-carrying ship, boat, etc.' Both refer to its Latin origin. The Oxford English Dictionary gives a conventional broad definition of 'vessel' as 'a craft or ship of any kind now usually one larger than a rowing boat and often restricted to sea-going craft or those plying on the larger rivers or lakes'; it defines a 'ship' as 'a large sea-going vessel (opposed to boat)'.

When the conventional appearance and use of an object lead the mind to perceive that the object is a ship there is no need for a definition, as Scrutton LJ put it so lucidly.[51]

Section 313(1) of the MSA 1995 defines a ship to include every description of vessel used in navigation.[52] The same definition is given by the SCA 1981 s 24(1), which also includes a hovercraft in the definition. The purpose of being 'used in navigation' is important and these words have been carried forward from the old definition. Thus, two elements are considered in the definition of an object as a ship: its physical appearance and its use in navigation.

8.3.1 Physical appearance

It is relevant to quote what Sheen J said, in a fairly recent decision, (*Steedman v Scofield*)[53] concerning a jet ski which was involved in a collision with a speed boat:

> To my mind the word 'boat' conveys the concept of a structure, whether it be made of wood, steel or fibreglass, which by reason of its concave shape provides buoyancy for the carriage of persons or goods. Thus, a lifeboat differs from a liferaft in that the boat derives its buoyancy from its shape, whereas a raft obtains its buoyancy from some method of utilizing air receptacles.

---

51 In *Merchant Marine Insurance v North of England P&I* (1926) 26 LlL Rep 201 (CA).

52 The requirement in the old statutes of 'not being propelled by oars' was excluded quite recently by the Merchant Shipping (Registration) Act 1993, which was consolidated by the present MSA 1995.

53 [1992] 2 Lloyd's Rep 163, pp 165, 166.

The jet ski cannot be boarded until it has reached a speed – at which it is stable enough for a rider to pull himself aboard out of the water.

A person cannot sit in a jet ski, which is stopped in the water, as he can in a boat. The manufacturers do not describe it as a boat, but as 'personal watercraft'. Giving the word 'boat' its ordinary and natural meaning, I do not think it encompasses a jet ski.

He referred to *Dependable Marine Co Ltd v Customs and Excise Commissioners*,[54] in which Roskill J had to decide whether a ski craft was exempt from purchase tax being 'a boat or other vessel large enough to carry human beings':

Whether this craft was a boat or vessel depended on first impressions. The clear primary purpose was to tow skiers and to enable them to have the benefit of a craft to move them without having to use a conventional motorboat together with some person to drive it. It was true that it was physically capable of carrying a human being, who could control the engine. But it had no navigation aids – no rudder, and the only method of changing direction was for the skier or passenger to shift his weight. The phrase 'boats and other vessels' conveyed an element of carriageability – ability to carry either passengers or goods. Those words conveyed something different from the mere physical ability of a craft to support a passenger. It is doubtful whether the average person would have said that this was a boat or vessel capable of carrying passengers in the normal sense of that phrase. Further, it was doubtful if the craft could be said to be a boat or vessel since it was designed to tow skiers and the ability to carry passengers was merely incidental to that primary function. Accordingly, this craft was not a boat or vessel ...

As to 'vessel', Sheen J said that it is usually a hollow receptacle for carrying goods or people. In common parlance, 'vessel' is a word used to refer to craft larger than rowing boats and it includes every description of watercraft used or capable of being used as a means of transportation on water.

8.3.2 Used in navigation

The phrase 'used in navigation' requires that the navigation occurs in navigable waters. If navigation occurs within an enclosed sheet of water, it will not normally be held to be navigable waters. A small artificial lake was held not to be navigable in *Southport Corp v Morris*,[55] while a non-enclosed canal which communicated via locks to the sea with vessels passing up and down was held to be navigable waters in *Weeks v Ross*.[56] The question whether a reservoir was 'navigable waters' and could be used by dinghies for navigation depended on whether vessels were proceeding from an originating place A to a terminus B for the purpose of discharging people or cargo at the

54 [1965] 1 Lloyd's Rep 550, p 553.
55 [1893] 1 QB 359.
56 [1913] 2 KB 229.

destination point, in which case there was navigation. Henry J applied the previous two cases in *Curtis v Wild*, quite recently.[57] This is consistent with some old cases, which dealt with the area and the object of the work.[58]

In *Steedman v Scofield*,[59] Sheen J said it might be possible to navigate a jet ski but it was not a vessel used in navigation.[60]

> ... what is meant by 'used in navigation'? Navigation is the nautical art or science of conducting a ship from one place to another. The navigator must be able (1) to determine the ship's position and (2) to determine the future course or courses to be steered to reach the intended destination. The word 'navigation' is also used to describe the action of navigating or ordered movement of ships on water. Hence 'navigable waters' means waters on which ships can be navigated. To my mind the phrase 'used in navigation' conveys the concept of transporting persons or property by water to an intended destination. A fishing vessel may go to sea and return to the harbour from which she sailed, but that vessel will nevertheless be navigated to her fishing grounds and back again.

> 'Navigation' is not synonymous with movement on water. Navigation is planned or ordered movement from one place to another. A jet ski is capable of movement on water at very high speed under its own power, but its purpose is not to go from one place to another.

It can be concluded that when an object has the shape of a vessel and is used in navigation in navigable waters, in the sense discussed, it will be a ship for the purpose of the MSA 1995 and for the purpose of jurisdiction of the Admiralty Court.

Old cases which do not fit within this interpretation are not good law any longer, but if a pontoon is used to transport goods from one place to another, thus, being like a dumb barge,[61] it may be a ship, provided it is not just a floating crane.[62]

---

57 See *Curtis v Wild* [1991] 4 All ER 172, in which it was held that sailing dinghies used in a reservoir were not used in navigation and, in particular, that 'navigable waters' meant waters used by vessels going from point A to point B, not simply for pleasure purposes, even though this involved steering.

58 *The Mac* (1882) 7 PD 126; *The Mudlark* [1911] P 116.

59 [1992] 2 Lloyd's Rep 163.

60 *Cf* the Court of Appeal in Florida has recently held that a jet ski is a pleasure craft that meets the definition of 'vessel' under the Limitation Act, 55 F Supp 2d 1367 (SD Fla) 1999.

61 Dumb barges have been held to be ships: *The Mudlark* [1911] P 116; *The Harlow* [1922] P 175; barges with small sails intended to be towed from port to port with captain and crew, steering gear and anchors, are held to be ships: *St John Pilot Commissioners v Cumberland Rly & Coal Co* [1910] AC 208; even a 'blower boat' shaped like a ship, but having a flat bottom and flat ends, with the purpose of having barges to lay alongside and only being towed from time to time, was a ship: *Cook v Dredging and Construction Co Ltd* [1958] 1 Lloyd's Rep 334.

62 *Marine Craft Constructions Ltd v Erland Blomquist (Engineers) Ltd* [1953] 1 Lloyd's Rep 514.

Whether a drilling unit could be embraced under this meaning is more difficult to answer. The relevant words in the definition of 'ship' and 'vessel' in the MSA 1995, 'used in navigation', relate to actual use and not the purpose, or main purpose, of the builders, as some authorities seemed to suggest.[63] Drilling units have to cross the waters and, thus, be navigable, and are intended to do their work on the seas, even though at one place at a time. While a definite answer depends on the facts of a particular case, it would seem quite possible that the definition of a ship would apply to drilling vessels, meaning those not attached to the seabed.[64]

In a recent Scottish case, **Global Marine Drilling & Co v Triton Holdings Ltd (The Sovereign Explorer)**,[65] a mobile offshore drilling unit was arrested for the purpose of obtaining security in relation to a dispute under a sub-charter party, which was referred to arbitration. An application by the defendant to set aside the arrest on the ground that the *Sovereign Explorer* was not a ship was refused by Lord Marnoch on 12 November 1999. There was an appeal to the Scottish Court of Session regarding the adequacy of the security offered for her release from arrest and this issue was not questioned.

---

63 *Merchant Marine Insurance Ltd v North of England P&I* (1926) 25 LlL Rep 446 (where it was said that the floating pontoon was designed and adapted to float and to lift and not to navigate, so it was not a ship); similar words were used in the *Gas Float Whitton* [1897] AC 337 (HL).

64 See Chapter 13, para 5.3, below.

65 [2001] 1 Lloyds Rep 60.

CHAPTER 2

NATURE OF THE ADMIRALTY JURISDICTION

1 INTRODUCTION

At the time of writing this book, a new Arrest Convention 1999 was approved by a Diplomatic Conference, which – if enacted by the UK – will have the effect of enlarging the list of claims that can be enforced in the Admiralty Court.[1] Until then, a detailed list of the heads of maritime claims which are within the admiralty jurisdiction of the High Court are found in s 20 of the Supreme Court Act (SCA) 1981.

It should be borne in mind that the Act provides the means for the enforcement of maritime claims against the relevant ship. A cause of action must have arisen. Section 20 outlines the extent of the court's jurisdiction to entertain such claims on their merits. Section 21 specifies the mode of bringing a maritime claim in the Admiralty Court by commencing a claim either *in personam* (s 21(1)) or *in rem* (s 21(2), (3), (4), (5), (6), (7) and (8)).

There are four jurisdictional heads under s 20(1), namely:

- jurisdiction to hear and determine any of the questions and claims mentioned in sub-s (2);
- jurisdiction in relation to any of the proceedings mentioned in sub-s (3), which comprises applications under the Merchant Shipping Act (MSA) 1995 and any action to enforce a claim for damages, loss of life or personal injury arising out of a collision between ships, or non-compliance with collision regulations;
- any other admiralty jurisdiction which it had immediately before the commencement of the Act; and
- any jurisdiction connected with ships or aircraft which is vested in the High Court apart from this section and is, for the time being, by rules of court made or coming into force after the commencement of this Act, assigned to the Queen's Bench Division and directed by the rules to be exercised by the Admiralty Court.

---

1   See Gaskell, N (Prof), 'Explanatory note of the new Convention'(1999) 6(4) *International Maritime Law*, May; and Gaskell, N and Shaw, R, 'The Arrest Convention 1999' [1999] LMCLQ 470, pp 470–90, including an attached appendix of the Convention.

Section 20(2)–(6) elaborates on these heads. The individual heads of jurisdiction provided under s 20(2) are examined under para 3, below, with analysis of decided cases following the alphabetical order of the sub-section. Most of these are rudimentary, but essential in the understanding of the nature of jurisdiction and the construction of the words used in the statute by the courts.

Before the individual heads of claims, which are enforceable in the Admiralty Court, are set out, it is important to refer briefly to the nature of maritime liens, as it is relevant to the discussion of cases that follow, in para 3, below.

2 MARITIME LIENS[2] CONTRASTED WITH OTHER STATUTORY RIGHTS *IN REM*

A maritime lien is a privileged charge on maritime property and arises by operation of law. It does not depend on possession of the property or on agreement. It accrues from the moment of the event which gives rise to a cause of action, and travels with the property. A maritime lien is invisible because it is not subject to any scheme of registration. It survives into the hands of a *bona fide* purchaser for value without notice, and is enforceable by an *in rem* claim.

This concept was first defined by Sir John Jervis in *The Bold Buccleugh*[3] in which it was said that:

> ... a maritime lien is well defined ... to mean a claim or privilege upon a thing to be carried into effect by legal process ... that process to be a proceeding *in rem* ... This claim or privilege travels with the thing into whosoever possession it may come. It is inchoate from the moment the claim or privilege attaches, and, when carried into effect by legal process by a proceeding *in rem*, relates back to the period when it first attached.

A maritime lien has an advantage over a statutory right *in rem* in that the latter depends on the issue of the *in rem* claim form to crystallise on the property, while a maritime lien does not depend on the legal process for its attachment, although the legal process will bring it into effect. This was illustrated in *The Tolten*.[4]

> The essence of the privilege was, and still is, whether, in continental or English law, that it comes into existence automatically, without any antecedent formality, and simultaneously with the cause of action, and confers a true

---

2   For details, read Thomas, R, 'Maritime liens', in *British Shipping Laws*, 1980, Stevens, Vol 14.

3   [1851] 7 Moo PC 267, p 284.

4   [1946] 2 All ER 372, p 379.

charge on the ship and freight of a proprietary kind in favour of the privileged creditor. The charge goes with the ship everywhere, even in the hands of a purchaser for value without notice, and has a certain ranking with other maritime liens, all of which take precedence over mortgages.

Although a maritime lien is similar to a mortgage, in that both are charges on the ship and can be enforced against the owner and any subsequent purchaser, it is quite distinct from it for the following reasons: first, unlike a maritime lien, a mortgage is created by an agreement in a form prescribed by statute; second, a mortgage needs registration which functions as a notice to third parties and the date of registration determines its priority over subsequent registered mortgages; third, while a mortgage has priority over other statutory rights *in rem*, a maritime lien has priority over all other maritime claims; fourth, a maritime lien travels with the ship from the moment of its creation, even when the ship is transferred to a *bona fide* purchaser without notice.

A maritime lien is further distinguishable from the common law possessory lien, which is a right to retain possession of a chattel pending payment of an outstanding obligation for services rendered. Once possession is released, the right to lien is lost. This right is available to ship-repairers and, if possession is retained, it can take priority over later created liens or mortgages.[5]

Another type of lien is called 'equitable lien' which is created by implication of law and does not depend on possession of the thing. It can, however, be lost by a sale of the thing to a *bona fide* purchaser for value without notice.

Under English law, the claims recognised as giving rise to maritime liens are:

- damage done by a ship;
- salvage;
- seamen's wages;
- master's wages and disbursements;
- bottomry bond[6] (which is not in use any longer).

It suffices at this point to quote what **Scott LJ** said in *The Tolten*[7] about the nature and security element of maritime liens:

> The maritime lien is one of the first principles of the law of the sea, and very far-reaching in its effects. In the *Bold Buccleugh*, Sir John Jervis delivering the judgment of the Privy Council, said this: 'Having its origin in this rule of the civil law, a maritime lien is well defined by Lord Tenterden, to mean a claim or

---

5   See Chapters 4 and 9. On whether a maritime lien is a procedural or substantive right, see Jackson, DC, *Enforcement of Maritime Claims*, 2nd edn, 1996, LLP, pp 391–94; see, generally, about maritime liens, Chapters 17 and 18 of the 3rd edn, 2000.

6   See para 3.18, below.

7   [1946] P 135 (CA), pp 144–46.

privilege upon a thing to be carried into effect by legal process; and Mr. Justice Story ... explains that process to be a proceeding *in rem*, and adds, that wherever a lien or claim is given upon the thing, then the Admiralty enforces it by a proceeding *in rem*, and indeed is the only court competent to enforce it. A maritime lien is the foundation of the proceeding *in rem*, a process to make perfect a right inchoate from the moment the lien attaches ...

In *The Sara*, Lord Macnaghten said:

'A "maritime lien", as was observed in the *Two Ellens* ... must be something which adheres to the ship from the time that the facts happened which gave the maritime lien, and then continues binding on the ship until it is discharge ... It commences and there it continues binding on the ship until it comes to an end.'

In the *Ripon City*, Gorell Barnes J reviewed the history of the maritime lien in our law in a long judgment from which, so far as I know, there has been no subsequent dissent. The following extracts describe the essential characteristics. He said:

'The definition of a maritime lien as recognized by the law maritime given by Lord Tenterden has thus been adopted. It is a privileged claim upon a thing in respect of service done to it or injury caused by it, to be carried effect by legal process.'

Later on, Scott LJ continued:

The result of my examination of these principles and authorities is as follows: the law now recognizes maritime liens in certain classes of claims, the principal being bottomry, salvage, wages, masters' wages, disbursements and liabilities, and damage. According to the definition above given, such a lien is a privileged claim upon a vessel in respect of service done to it, or injury caused by it, to be carried into effect by legal process. It is a right acquired by one over a thing belonging to another – a *jus in re aliena*. It is, so to speak, a subtraction from the absolute property of the owner in the thing.

On p 244 is an important passage indicating the learned judge's view of the proper judicial attitude in considering doubtful questions of law to the public interest in encouraging prudent navigation, on the one hand, and the proper protection to the party injured by negligent navigation, on the other:

In my opinion, it is right in principle and only reasonable, in order to secure prudent navigation, that third persons whose property is damaged by negligence in the navigation of a vessel by those in charge of her should not be deprived of the security of the vessel ...

In most actions *in rem* for damage, the ship is released on bail, but cases may occur where the liens or rights *in rem* against the ship are so heavy as to exceed the ship's value to her owners, who, in such case, will probably not enter an appearance and obtain the ship's release on bail. The lien consists in the substantive right of putting into operation the Admiralty Court's executive function of arresting and selling the ship, so as to give a clear title to the purchaser and, thereby, enforcing distribution of the proceeds amongst the lien creditors in accordance with their several priorities, and subject thereto rateably. I call that function of the court 'executive' because, once the lien is admitted, or is established by evidence of the right to compensation for damage suffered through the defendant ship's negligence, there is then no further judicial function for the court to perform, save that in the registry where priorities, quantum and distribution are dealt with.

Maritime liens can be enforced, as all other maritime claims, by an *in rem* claim brought in accordance with the provisions of the SCA 1981, which is dealt with in Chapter 3. Priorities of maritime claims and conflict of laws issues, in the enforcement of maritime claims when a maritime lien is created under foreign law, follow later.[8]

3 MARITIME CLAIMS UNDER s 20(2) OF THE SCA 1981

3.1 (a) Any claim to the possession or ownership of a ship or to the ownership of a share therein[9]

The power of the court to determine questions of title in the ship, ownership or possession is inherent and was conferred to the Admiralty Court for the first time by statute in the Admiralty Court Act (ACA) 1840, s 4. The same provision was carried forward in the subsequent Acts, but it was slightly restricted by the Administration of Justice Act (AJA) 1956 and this was followed in s 20(2)(a) of the SCA 1981. Any omissions are dealt with by the sweeping up provision, s 20(1)(c), which refers to the inherent jurisdiction of the court existing prior to statute. The extent of this power was exemplified in *The Bineta*,[10] in which the court had jurisdiction to make a declaration as to which party was entitled to be registered as the legal owner of a ship.

The registered owner of *The Bineta* sold her to G, who was then registered as owner, but the seller retained possession pending payment of the purchase price. Following the failure of G to pay the purchase price to the seller, the latter exercised his statutory lien of retention and resold *The Bineta* to X. A declaration by the court was necessary to allow X, as claimant, to obtain registration in place of the first purchaser, G, which was granted.

---

8   In this respect, see Chapter 4 and Chapter 9 (on mortgages).

9   *The Glider Standard Austria* [1965] P 463: no application to aircraft.

10 [1966] 3 All ER 1007, or [1966] 1 WLR 121; see, also, *The Cape Don* [2000] 1 Lloyd's Rep 388, in which the Australian Federal Court construed the equivalent provision of the Australian Admiralty Act 1988 as including a dispute concerning whether or not a sale contract about a ship had been concluded.

Questions of possession or ownership, both legal and equitable, regardless of the nationality or domicile or residence of the person who claims to be the owner of the ship – of which the ownership or possession is disputed – are within the admiralty jurisdiction of the court, unless the claim involves impleading a foreign sovereign State.

The Jupiter (No 2)[11]

By a contract of sale made in London, an English company purported to sell, on behalf of the Soviet Government, the steamship *Jupiter* to the defendants, an Italian company. The vessel had belonged to a Russian company, but the Soviet Government asserted that, by a decree of nationalisation, all vessels of the Russian mercantile marine had become State property and that the company had ceased to exist. The Russian company had moved its business to France, and an action *in rem* was brought in its French name, and in the name of the persons appointed by the French courts to administer its affairs, against 'the steamship *Jupiter*', claiming possession. The Italian company entered an appearance and moved to set aside the writ – *inter alia* – on the following ground: that as the action was between foreigners for the possession of a foreign ship, and had been instituted without the consent of the defendants or any request from the representative of the foreign State of which either of the parties was a national, the court had no jurisdiction, or, in the alternative, ought not to entertain the action.

The Court of Appeal held that there was no established rule that the Admiralty Court would not entertain possession suits in respect of foreign vessels, except at the request of the parties or with the consent of the accredited representative of the country to which the vessel belongs. The matter is one for the discretion of the court. The Lords Justice exercised that discretion and did not set the writ aside. The foreign sovereign was not impleaded in this case since the Soviet Government had sold the vessel.[12]

Atkin LJ said,[13] in particular, that:

> The first question is as to the jurisdiction of the court to entertain this claim for possession by one foreigner against another foreigner in respect of a ship that is within the territorial jurisdiction. It appears to me now reasonably plain that there is jurisdiction in the court to entertain such a claim. I think there was jurisdiction before the Admiralty Act of 1840, and in my opinion there is statutory jurisdiction given by that Act.

---

11 [1925] P 69.

12 In the earlier decision of the Court of Appeal concerning a writ *in rem* against the same ship by a French company claiming possession rights, *The Jupiter (No 1)* [1924] P 236, it had been held that the Soviet Government was impleaded by the action *in rem* and the court decided not to exercise its jurisdiction. At that time, the Soviet Government had claimed an interest in the ship and applied to set aside the writ on the ground of foreign immunity.

13 *The Jupiter (No 2)* [1925] P 69, p 77.

The only question that is left is whether or not there is a discretion in the court to decline to exercise jurisdiction in such cases, and, if so, whether that jurisdiction ought to be so exercised in this case. As to that the law seems to me still to obtain that the court in such a case has a discretion as to whether it will exercise its jurisdiction or not, and in cases where the parties both belonging to a foreign State have merely taken the occasion of the ship being temporarily here to get a question of title, which depends on the municipal laws of another country, determined by the courts of this country, the court may in the exercise of its discretion decline to do so. But, in the facts of this case, there seems to me to be no reason why the court should not exercise its discretion and entertain the suit. The vessel has been in this country for a period of years and the question arises in respect of her disposition by a contract entered into in this country by a limited company of this country, the Arcos Shipping Company, Ltd, and although questions may arise as to the right of title of the vendors to the defendants, yet it appears to me to be a case which can properly be tried in this country, and I see no reason for interfering with the discretion of the learned President in that respect.

The English courts, in some cases, may regard another forum as being more appropriate for the particular dispute, as it did in *The Lakhta*,[14] in which the case was in every way connected with Russia (see Chapter 5).

The Court has always had power under s 30 of the MSA 1894, now Sched 1, para 6 of the MSA 1995, to order an injunction prohibiting the dealings with a ship on the application of an interested party made under s 20(2)(a), when there is a dispute. Schedule 1, para 6(1) provides:

The High Court or in Scotland the Court of Session may, if they think fit (without prejudice to the exercise of any other power), on the application of any interested person, make an order prohibiting for a specified time any dealing with a registered ship or share in a registered ship.

This is a substantive right not a procedural right, which can be enforced in the Admiralty Court. An 'interested person' extends only to a person with a proprietary interest in the ship, or at least to a person having a claim against the ship leading to a proprietary right.[15] It does not include personal, non-secured, creditors. This was made clear in *The Mikado*,[16] in which a financial institution having lent money for the construction of a yacht without obtaining a mortgage, was not considered to be an interested person under this provision for the purposes of preventing further dealings with the ship.

---

14 [1992] 2 Lloyd's Rep 269.
15 *The Siben* [1994] 2 Lloyd's Rep 420.
16 [1992] 1 Lloyd's Rep 163.

3.2 (b) Any question arising between the co-owners of a ship as to possession, employment or earnings of that ship

The purpose of this provision is to curb the obstinacy of some part owners from damaging the rights and interests of their co-owners. It derived from s 8 of the ACA 1861 which provided:

> The High Court of Admiralty shall have jurisdiction to decide all questions arising between the co-owners, or any of them, touching the ownership ... of any ship registered at any port in England or Wales, or any share thereof and ... may direct the said ship or any share thereof to be sold, and may make such order in the premises that it shall seem fit.

It includes the power of the court to settle any accounts outstanding between the parties in relation to the ship and to direct that the ship, or any share therein, be sold, or to make any order the court thinks fit (s 20(4)).

In practice today, the relations between part owners will normally be regulated by an agreement. In the event that there is no particular or clear provision about the employment of the ship, or there is a breach of any provision having been made in this connection, there is a remedy to be enforced under this sub-paragraph. If, for instance, the majority shareholders wish to employ the ship in a particular way which the minority object to, the latter may seek to restrain the majority by arresting the ship until security to the full value of the minority's interest in the ship is provided (see Chapter 8).

In *The Vanessa Ann*,[17] the minority shareholders were granted an equitable mortgage in return for the release of the ship from arrest. Once security is provided, the ship is released to perform the voyage at the risk, expense and profit of the majority owners.

In the reverse situation, where the minority are in possession and wish to send the ship to sea against the wishes of the majority, the latter may enforce their rights by bringing an action for possession.

The court also has power to exercise its discretion and order the sale of the ship when there is a co-ownership dispute. In *The Nelly Schneider*,[18] the minority applied to the court for sale of the ship, to recover damages from the majority and settle outstanding accounts, which was opposed by the majority owners.

Sir Robert Phillimore held:

> The court has full power to decree a sale of the ship, but it will be very reluctant to do so at the instance of part owners not possessing a majority of the shares. The defendants have the option allowed to them of purchasing such shares at the amount fixed at valuation. If the defendants do not exercise the option within a fortnight, the ship must be appraised and sold by the

---

17 [1985] 1 Lloyd's Rep 549.
18 (1878) 3 PD 152.

Marshal. The court had to consider whether the sale would be in the interests of all parties.

However, caution is exercised by the court in making an order of sale against the wishes of the majority. It may do so in exceptional circumstances. In *The Hereward*,[19] Bruce J said:

> ... that power may be exercised on the application of a minority of part owners; and it seems to me that, when part owners of the ship are unable to agree as to what is to be done with their common property, and there appears to be no way of preventing the sacrifice of the property except by a sale, the court ought to direct a sale.[20]

3.3 (c) Any claim in respect of a mortgage of or a charge on a ship or any share therein

This provision covers all mortgages and charges, notwithstanding whether they are registered or not, legal or equitable, including those created by foreign law (s 20(2)(c) and (7)(c) of the SCA 1981).

The concept of a mortgage is examined in Chapter 9. Briefly, under English law, a mortgage is a statutory charge on a registered British ship for the security of a debt and must be in a statutory form. The rights and obligations of the lender (mortgagee) are regulated by the MSA 1995 and regulations issued pursuant to the Act. When a mortgage is not in the required statutory form, or not registered, it is an equitable mortgage, which does not enjoy the protection of the statute, but it is, nevertheless, protected by equitable principles.

Most ships, nowadays, are registered abroad under the laws of a particular State carrying the flag of that State. Other than the Commonwealth States and former British colonies, foreign systems of law do not recognise the concept of equitable mortgages. So, if the mortgage is unregistered under the system of the law in the State in which the ship is registered, such a mortgage cannot be enforced by an *in rem* claim against the ship, although the mortgagee will be able to sue the borrower (mortgagor) *in personam* and enforce his claim against any insurance proceeds of the ship, provided he has obtained an effective assignment of the insurance proceeds or policy of the ship. A very good example of this situation occurred in the following case.

---

19 [1895] P 284.
20 *Ibid*, p 285.

The Angel Bell[21]

This concerned a Panamanian ship and mortgage. The substantive law governing the mortgage was the law of the flag of the ship, Panamanian. The mortgagee omitted to register his mortgage within six months after the provisional registration as was required by statute. The result of this was to deprive the mortgagee from his rights *in rem* against the ship. He never became a legal mortgagee under the statute. (Unlike English law, Panamanian law does not recognise equitable mortgages.) It had been agreed that the mortgagee would obtain assignments of the hull and machinery insurance policies and each policy would contain a 'loss payable' clause. The ship sank. The owners of the cargo on board the ship began proceedings against the defendants (shipowners) claiming damages for the loss of their cargo. They applied and were granted a Mareva injunction restraining the defendants from dealing with their assets within the jurisdiction, which were the insurance proceeds of the vessel. The mortgagee intervened in the action claiming that his claim as a lender was secured on the proceeds of the insurance policies. The issue was whether the mortgagee was a secured creditor by way of proper assignment of the insurance policies, so as to entitle him to obtain judgment and execute it upon the insurance proceeds.

Donaldson J examined the matter from various angles. It suffices to mention the two substantive reasons of his decision which seem to lay down a general principle on the issue of assignment. (a) The effect of the loss payable clause; it was accepted that such a clause would not have an effect unless it also constituted or evidenced an assignment of the assured's rights under the policy. Regardless of the fate of the Panamanian mortgage at the time of the renewal of the insurance policies, the mortgagee was under English law – by virtue of the oral agreement to obtain a mortgage on the ship governed by English law – an equitable mortgagee. Therefore, the wording of the loss payable clause in the renewed policies referring to him as 'interested in this insurance as mortgagees' (instead of as assignees) did not defeat the effect of the clause. (b) The effect of assignments under notices of assignment endorsed on the policies; although the notices had not been signed, there was evidence that undated notices are acceptable in the market. So, the mortgagee was an assignee of the policy in the customary manner.

In conclusion, the mortgagee was a secured creditor on the proceeds of the hull and machinery policies.

A charge in the context of this section means a charge in the nature of a mortgage. It does not cover a charge in its wider sense nor a lien for wages.[22] The word did not exist in the old statutes, but it was added in the AJA 1956. It was, perhaps, included for two reasons: (a) to ensure that those who have

---

21 [1979] 2 Lloyd's Rep 491.
22 *The Acrux* [1965] 1 Lloyd's Rep 565.

security on the ship by way of hypothecation,[23] under foreign law, which is a charge in the nature of a mortgage, can enforce their claim under this head; (b) to ensure that equitable mortgages are within this provision.

In this connection, it is relevant to mention that matters of procedure, remedy and priorities are governed by the *lex fori*[24] (the law of the place where the matter has been submitted for adjudication), while questions of validity of a mortgage or charge are determined by the *lex loci contractus* (the law of the place in which the contract was made).

3.4 (d) Any claim for damage received by a ship

This head includes damage done to a ship by something other than a ship, such as a pier head, or a claim against the manufacturer whose defective equipment caused damage to the ship. There is no guilty ship to arrest. This ground of claim is omitted from the provision of s 21 of the SCA 1981, which defines the mode of enforcement of maritime claims against ships. Thus, it prevents enforceability of this claim by an *in rem* claim simply because the ship that receives the damage will be the plaintiff (ship damaged cannot bring a claim against itself), as it was explained by Lord Diplock in *The Eschersheim*.

The Eschersheim[25]

The plaintiff could not invoke the admiralty jurisdiction by an action *in rem* against their own ship. The action must be in connection with a ship. That ship must be the ship specified in the Arrest Convention as the particular ship in respect of which the maritime claim arose – and, therefore, the inclusion of this head of claim could not lead to an action *in rem*.

3.5 (e) Claim for damage done by a ship

3.5.1 Extent of the nature of this claim

Lord Diplock put it succinctly in **The Eschersheim**:[26]

> The figurative phrase 'damage done by a ship' is a term of art in maritime law whose meaning is well established by authority: *The Vera Cruz* (1884) 9 PD 96 [(1884) 10 App Cas 59 (HL)]; *The Currie v M'Knight* [1897] AC 97. To fall within 'damage done by a ship' not only must the damage be the direct result or natural consequence of something done by those engaged in the *navigation of*

---

23 Reference to it is made in the Arrest Convention 1952.

24 See, further, conflict of laws and priorities of maritime claims, Chapter 4, para 9 and Chapter 9, para 7, below.

25 [1976] 2 Lloyd's Rep 1, p 9.

26 [1976] 1 WLR 430 (HL), p 438 (emphasis added).

the ship, but the ship itself must be *the actual instrument* by which the damage
was done. But physical contact between the ship and whatever object sustains
the damage is not essential, a ship may *negligently* cause a wash by which some
other vessel or ... property on shore is damaged (emphasis added).

In this case, a collision took place off the coast of Spain between a Sudanese
ship, *The Erkowit*, and a German ship, the Dortmund, as a result of which the
engine room of *The Erkowit* was holed and became flooded. The tug, *Rotesand*,
went to her aid and a salvage agreement on the Lloyd's Open Form (LOF) was
signed. By the salvors' negligence in beaching *The Erkowit*, she was delivered
in a sinking condition and became total loss. Most of her cargo and the crew's
personal effects were lost or damaged. As some of her cargo was insecticide in
drums, they were washed away causing pollution along the Spanish coast
with consequential interference with fishing in that area. Various actions
commenced; first, the owners of *The Erkowit*, her crew and the owners of the
cargo on board commenced proceedings against the German ship. However,
the respective lawyers of the above claimants had the foresight to protect the
time limit for commencing an action against the salvors in the event they
could not establish a cause of action for the damages suffered against the other
ship. The claimants arrested two sister ships of the tug *Rotesand*, *The Jade* and
The Eschersheim. Indeed, the proceedings against the German ship failed
because the cause of action arising from the collision had been broken by the
subsequent negligence of the salvors.

Various issues arose which will be examined later under each sub-
paragraph of the statute in which they fell.[27] The issue under this head was
whether the claims against the salvors came within the admiralty jurisdiction,
or should be referred to arbitration by virtue of the terms of the salvage
agreement. The House of Lords decided that:

> The act of casting off *The Erkowit* in such a way as to beach her upon an
> exposed shore was something done by those engaged in the navigation of the
> Rotesand, as a result of which *The Erkowit* and her cargo were left exposed to
> the risk of being damaged by wind and wave if the weather worsened before
> she could be removed to a more sheltered position.[28]

Both shipowners' and cargo-owners' claims fell under this sub-paragraph as
well, although they were regarded to be a borderline case, being more
appropriate for the one under (h) to be discussed later.

By virtue of s 20(5)(a)(b), this provision is extended to cover any claim in
respect of liability incurred under the MSA 1995, Sched 4 for pollution
damage. The International Convention for Civil Liability arising from
Pollution Damage 1969 (CLC) has been superseded by the CLC 1992, the 1992

---

27 At the time of these actions, the claims were enforced in the Admiralty Court under the
    previous statute (the AJA 1956), therefore, the claim for damage done by a ship was
    numbered under the letter (d).

28 [1976] 2 Lloyd's Rep 1, p 8.

Protocol. It came into force on 30 May 1996 and it was enacted into English law by ss 152–70 of the MSA 1995. In *The Eschersheim*, it was also held that pollution caused through escaping oil following the negligent beaching of the ship whilst being salved can be enforced under sub-para (e).

3.5.2 Does it cover enforcement of claims for pure economic loss?

A question arose in 1988 whether a claim for pure economic loss can be enforced under (d). In *The Dagmara and The Ama Antixine*,[29] the defendants' vessel A was being dangerously navigated around vessel D belonging to the plaintiffs, in a deliberate attempt to drive the D away from the fishing grounds. For fear of their safety, the master and crew of ship D, left the fishing grounds. The plaintiffs claimed in tort for damages in respect of damage suffered in the form of financial loss. Sheen J, referring to the judgment of the House of Lords in **Currie v M'Knight**, held as follows:

> The judgment of Cairns LJ establishes that damage may be done by a ship, not only without direct physical contact, such as a collision, but also without any transmitted physical force, such as a wash.

It was held that the plaintiffs had a valid cause for an action in tort to be enforced under this head. In this connection, it is important to refer to the factual situation of the *Currie v M'Knight*,[30] in which the principle for enforcement of claims under this sub-paragraph was laid down.

A heavy gale was raging when the vessel D and the vessel E were lying alongside one another in the port. In an attempt to put D out to sea, her crew cut off the ropes of E, so that the latter drifted ashore and was damaged. The question in the action was whether the wrongful act of D's crew was sufficient to create a maritime lien for the damage to E.

Lord Halsbury stated:

> ... the phrase that 'it must be the fault of the ship itself' is not a mere figurative expression, but it imports, in my opinion, that the ship against which a maritime lien for damages is claimed is the instrument of mischief, and that, in order to establish the liability of the ship itself to the maritime lien claimed, some act of navigation of the ship itself should either mediately or immediately be the cause of the damage.[31]

It was held that the act was a wrongful act of self-preservation, but was not an act of navigation, even though other ships were damaged. The section requires the act not just to be an act of the crew, but one in the course of their navigation. This act was done for the purpose of removing an obstacle, which

---

29 [1988] 1 Lloyd's Rep 431.
30 [1897] AC 97.
31 *Ibid*, p 101.

prevented D from starting her voyage. The doctrine of maritime liens could not be extended to cover such a case.

A claim for damage done by a ship gives rise to a maritime lien[32] and it can be enforced as such under s 21(3) of the SCA 1981.

3.6 (f) Any claim for loss of life, personal injury ...

... sustained in consequence of any defect in a ship, her apparel or equipment, or in consequence of the wrongful act, neglect or default of:

  (i) owners, charterers or persons in possession or control of a ship;or

  (ii) the master[33] or crew of a ship, or any other persons whose wrongful acts, neglects or defaults the owners, charterers or persons in possession or control of a ship are responsible,

being an act or default in the navigation or management of a ship in the loading, carriage or discharge of goods on, in or from the ship, or in the embarkation of persons on, in or from the ship.

3.6.1 Origins of this provision

This sub-paragraph is very wide. The AJA 1956 borrowed the same provision from the Arrest Convention 1952. *In personam* jurisdiction for such claims existed even before the ACAs 1840 and 1861. Section 7 of the 1861 Act provided that there should be jurisdiction 'over any claim for damage done by any ship'.[34]

Sir Robert Phillimore explained in *The Sylph*[35] (in which a diver engaged in diving in the River Mersey, was caught by the paddle-wheel of a steamer and suffered considerable injury):

That this court had originally jurisdiction in such a case as the present, I have no doubt whatever. It is given by the terms of the patent under which I hold my office; and it is clear from the old authorities on the subject that the court had jurisdiction over all torts and injuries done within the ebb and flow of the tide, as well as upon the high seas. The whole law is collected in the judgment delivered by Story J in the case of *De Lovio v Boit*. This judgment, in truth, exhausts all the learning upon the subject. I will only observe that the exercise of jurisdiction in this case is supported, among other authorities, by that of the Black Book of the Admiralty, to which Lord Stowell on various occasions

---

32 The nature of maritime liens, para 2, above.

33 Under SCA 1981, s 24(1), master includes every person, except the pilot, having command of the ship.

34 In *The Sylph* (1867) LR 2 A&E 24 and in *The Beta* (1869) LR 2 PC 447, it was held that a personal injury claim can be enforced by an action *in rem*.

35 (1867) LR 2 A&E 24, pp 26–27.

referred as a repertory of the common law and customs of the sea, and of the jurisdiction of the Admiralty Court.

There is no doubt that in, and before, the reign of Edward III, the plaintiff would have had his remedy here for this tort. This original power has been, however, curtailed in various respects by statute law, and by prohibitions by which, at one time, the jealousy of the common law courts thwarted and confined the jurisdiction of a court whose proceedings were founded upon the civil law.

In *The Beta*,[36] the Privy Council Committee had affirmed that a personal injury claim was within 'damage done by a ship' and Lord Romilly expounded without doubt that:

> The words of the 7th section of the Admiralty Court Act, which had been referred to, clearly include every possible kind of damage. Personal injuries are undoubtedly within the words 'damage done by any Ship'. The case of *The Sylph*, which has been referred to, and in which it was so held, had not been appealed from. There was every reason for the Legislature enacting that which the judgment of the court below holds to have been enacted.

Much later, the Maritime Conventions Act 1911 clarified what should be understood as being included in the word 'damage' referred to in any statute, which conferred jurisdiction to the court for such claims. Section 5 provided that:

> Any enactment which confers on any court admiralty jurisdiction in respect of damage shall have effect as though references to such damage included references to damages for loss of life or personal injury, and accordingly proceedings in respect of such damages may be brought *in rem* or *in personam*.

The Supreme Court of Judicature (Consolidation) Act (SCJ(Con)A) 1925 repealed and replaced s 5 of the MCA with s 22. Thus, jurisdiction for loss of life and personal injury was always included in the provision of 'damage done by a ship'. Under the present Act, the provision has been separated from 'damage done by a ship' and has been expanded in order to include jurisdiction for incidents other than just those occurring by negligent navigation.

Consistently with all other maritime claims, such jurisdiction is statutory for the purpose of enforcement of those claims. Claims which result from damage done by a ship are amongst the list of maritime liens.[37] The substantive right of a maritime lien arises upon the incident of the mischief done by a ship, while statutory rights *in rem* crystallise on the ship upon commencement of the proceeding *in rem*[38] and are otherwise known as

---

36 (1869) LR 2 PC 447, p 449.
37 *The Bold Buccleugh* (1851) 7 Moo PC 267.
38 See *The Monica S* [1967] 2 Lloyd's Rep 113.

statutory liens. A question has arisen whether claims for personal injury or loss of life attract a maritime lien,[39] or are just statutory rights *in rem*. Jackson proposes that, if claims for loss of life or personal injury are regarded as an extension of the 'damage lien', it may be argued that the maritime lien attracted to 'damage done by a ship' is extended by analogy to the statutory extension of jurisdiction with respect to these claims. But, if the jurisdiction is seen as a novel jurisdiction, or that a new action is created, such claims will suffer the fate of other novel claims created by statute and will be relegated to a statutory lien.

Thomas[40] has no doubt that there is a maritime lien for personal injury claimants, but not with regard to claimants, who claim under the Fatal Accidents Act (FAA) 1976[41] in respect of loss of life of a relative, as the jurisdiction is solely statutory. In other words, a new action is created by statute,[42] (Jackson's second proposal). However, such a distinction may be artificial because such claims were not created by the FAAs, which gave only statutory authority to an existing right of action for negligence (see *Davidson v Hill*, para 3.6.5, below). The FAAs assisted relatives of the deceased to sue the wrongdoer in England. The separation (from damage done by a ship) in the SCA 1981, was done for the purpose of clarification of the incidents that can give rise to such claims that can be enforced in the Admiralty Court. Whether the jurisdiction is statutory or not is irrelevant to the consideration of whether there is a substantive right of a maritime lien. The incidents referred to in para (f) are obviously still within the broad category 'damage done by a ship', whether that damage was due to negligent navigation or due to defects in the ship. It is submitted that personal injury and loss of life claims ought to be treated as an extension of the 'damage done by a ship lien' (Jackson's first proposal). There is no reason in terms of principle or policy why these claims, if they arise from the same incident, damage done by a ship, should be placed in the same position as all other statutory lien holders. In terms of priority, this would mean that a property damage claimant would enjoy the priority of a maritime lien while personal claims would rank in priority lower than the property claims. At least, a maritime lien should attach on these claims when the cause of their occurrence is negligent navigation, as this would clearly be consistent with the treatment of other claims, which fall within 'damage done by a ship' under para (e).

It should be noted that the International Convention for Maritime Liens and Mortgages 1993 classifies both types of claims for loss of life and personal injury amongst maritime liens, but the Convention is not in force.

---

39 *Op cit*, Jackson, fn 5, pp 33–34.
40 On maritime liens; see *op cit*, Thomas, fn 2.
41 As amended by the AJA 1982.
42 See an explanation of its origin given by Brandon J in *The Esso Malaysia* [1975] QB 198.

3.6.2 Wrongful act, neglect or default in the navigation or management of a ship

The reason why this sub-paragraph is separate from the provision of 'damage done by a ship' under para (e) is that it includes negligence, not only in the navigation, but also in the management of the ship and any defect in the ship, her apparel or equipment, which may cause loss of life or personal injury, whether on board the ship or outside. It was the 1981 statute that extended it to defects of a ship and defaults of certain persons. The Arrest Convention 1952 covers such claims only if caused by any ship or by her operation, which is much narrower than the SCA 1981; but neither the Convention nor the Act preclude loss occurring outside the ship.

3.6.3 Incidents that occurred on board another ship

The Radiant and *The Maid of Kent* are good examples of how the courts have approached such situations. They involve defect in equipment of a guilty ship, other than the one on which the injured person was carried.

The Radiant[43]

This case concerned personal injury sustained by the skipper of a motor fishing vessel.*The Radiant*, was owned by the first defendant, the skipper's employer, of which the second defendant was managing director. The skipper's feet were amputated by a tow rope, which had wrapped around the skipper's legs when the tow rope was thrown out by a sister ship, the *Margaret Hamilton*, which was towing *The Radiant* after it had grounded due to the negligence of the sister ship. It was found that the cause of the accident was the grounding and the inadequacy of ropes in the *Margaret Hamilton*. It was held that defective equipment of one vessel could give rise to a cause of action at the suit of a person on board another vessel. There was no proof of contributory negligence on the part of the skipper.

The Maid of Kent[44]

A North Sea pilot was about to climb a ladder from the pilot launch to board the port side of the ship 'DS'. At the time, *The Maid of Kent* passed the DS too near and too fast, causing a wash, which struck the launch and caused her to roll violently against the DS. The pilot was crushed between the port side of the DS and the launch as a result. He fell into the sea and died. His administratrix based the claim on the FAAs, claiming that the owners of *The Maid of Kent* were liable for damages.The claim was dismissed by the learned

---

43 [1958] 2 Lloyd's Rep 596, p 608.
44 [1974] 1 Lloyd's Rep 434.

trial judge, holding that liability had not been established. On appeal, the Court of Appeal held that on the evidence, those in charge of *The Maid of Kent* were negligent, in that they failed to see the effect which the wash from their ship might have had on a small craft. The accident was foreseeable. The claim could be enforced under this statutory provision (s 20(2)(f) of the SCA 1981), as the words 'wrongful act or neglect or default' are very broad to cover such claims arising in connection with a ship.

3.6.4 Defect in a ship, her apparel or equipment under para (f)

As explained earlier, a claimant must first be able to rely on an actionable substantive cause of action, which he may then seek to enforce by invoking the admiralty jurisdiction. The words used in the provisions of the SCA are construed by the courts to the extent of clarifying the ambit of that jurisdiction. The Statute only provides a link between that cause of action and the *in rem* jurisdiction of the court. For example, in a case of a collision, or in the cases mentioned above, the cause of action is easily identifiable as a breach of the common law duty of care. In other cases, which will be examined in this chapter, the cause of action may lie in breach of contract. There are, also, situations in which the cause of action may lie in a statute. Such statutes are, for the present purposes, the Employers' Liability (Defective Equipment) Act (EL(DE)A) 1969 or the FAAs (currently 1976), or the Occupiers' Liability Act 1957, or the MSA 1995. The case below is apt to explain this point.

The Derbyshire[45]

The action was brought by the personal representatives of the deceased who was employed as a third engineer on board this ship by the defendants, owners of this ship. During a voyage from Canada to Japan, the vessel sank with loss of all the lives on board.The plaintiffs, who were the administrators of the estate of the third engineer, brought an action to recover damages on behalf of his estate and for the benefit of his widow and daughter who were dependent on him. They contended that the design and construction of the vessel were defective and such defects rendered the vessel unseaworthy causing her to break in two. They brought their claim under the EL(DE)A 1969, on the basis that the deceased lost his life in the course of his employment. It was argued that his death was caused by a defect in equipment provided by the employer in the course of his business. Such equipment for the business was the vessel, regardless that the defect was attributable to a third party, the shipbuilder. The issue was whether the vessel constituted 'equipment' within the meaning to be given to that word in the EL(DE)A 1969. The House of Lords answered the question in the affirmative

---

45 [1988] 1 Lloyd's Rep 109.

(reversing the decision of the Court of Appeal). **Lord Oliver** explained[46] the origins of this provision:

My Lords, it is common ground that the 1969 Act was introduced with a view to rectifying what was felt to be the possible hardship to an employee resulting from the decision of this House in *Davie v New Merton Board Mills Ltd* ([1959] 2 Lloyd's Rep 587; [1959] AC 604). In that case, an employee was injured by a defective drift supplied to him by his employers for the purpose of his work. The defect resulted from a fault in manufacture but the article had been purchased by the employers without knowledge of the defect from a reputable supplier and without any negligence on their part. It was held that the employers' duty was only to take reasonable care to provide a reasonably safe tool and that that duty had been discharged by purchasing from a reputable source an article whose latent defect they had no means of discovering. Thus, the action against them failed, although judgment was recovered against the manufacturer. Clearly, this opened the door to the possibility that an employee required to work with, on or in equipment furnished by his employer and injured as a result of some negligent failure in design or manufacture might find himself without remedy in a case where the manufacture and the employer were, to use the words of Viscount Simonds, pp 590 and 620–21, 'divided in time and space by decades and continents' so that the person actually responsible was no longer traceable or, perhaps, was insolvent or had ceased to carry on business. Parliament, accordingly, met this by imposing on employers a vicarious liability and providing, in a case where injury was due to a defect caused by the fault of the third party, that the employer should, regardless of his own conduct, be liable to his employee as if he had been responsible for the defect, leaving it to him to pursue against the third party such remedies as he might have whether original or by way of contribution.

The purpose of the Act, as set out in the long title, is:

... to make further provision with respect to the liability of an employer for injury to his employee which is attributable to any defect in equipment provided by the employer for the purposes of the employer's business; and for purposes connected with the matter aforesaid.

The relevant provisions of the Act, for present purposes, are contained in sub-ss (1) and (3) of s 1 and are as follows:

(1) Where after the commencement of this Act – (a) an employee suffers personal injury in the course of his employment in consequence of a defect in equipment provided by his employer for the purposes of the employer's business; and (b) the defect is attributable wholly or partly to the fault of a third party (whether identified or not), the injury shall be deemed to be also attributable to negligence on the part of the employer (whether or not he is liable in respect of the injury apart from this sub-section), but without prejudice to the law relating to contributory negligence and to any remedy by way of contribution or in contract or otherwise which is available to the employer in respect of the injury ... (3) In this section – 'business' includes the activities carried on by any public body; employee' means a person

---

46   [1988] 1 Lloyd's Rep 109, pp 111–15.

who is employed by another person under a contract of service or apprenticeship and is so employed for the purposes of a business carried on by that other person, and 'employer' shall be construed accordingly; 'equipment' includes any plant and machinery, vehicle, aircraft and clothing; 'fault' means negligence, breach of statutory duty or other act or omission which gives rise to liability in tort in England and Wales or which is wrongful and gives rise to liability in damages in Scotland; and 'personal injury' includes loss of life, any impairment of a person's physical or mental condition and any disease.

My Lords, if sub-s (1) stood alone without such assistance as provided by sub-s (3), I would not, for my part, have encountered any difficulty in concluding that, in the context of this Act, a ship was part of the 'equipment' of the business of a shipowner. In the Court of Appeal, O'Connor LJ, pp 412 and 1100, expressed the view that the word in its natural meaning denoted something ancillary to something else and an echo of this is to be found in the judgment of Glidewell LJ. Thus, both Lords Justices would, I think, regard machinery attached to a ship as 'equipment', because it would be ancillary to the main object, the vessel, but both regarded the word as inappropriate to describe the vessel itself. I do not doubt that the word is frequently and quite properly used to describe the appurtenances of some larger entity, but I can see no reason either in logic or as a matter of language why its use should be so confined. Indeed, there is nothing in the entry in the *Oxford English Dictionary* quoted by O'Connor LJ which necessarily imports that 'equipment' is restricted to parts of a larger whole. The meaning is given as:

> ... anything used in equipping; furniture; outfit; warlike apparatus; necessaries for an expedition or voyage.

Moreover, your Lordships are concerned not with the meaning of 'equipment' simpliciter but of the composite phrase, 'equipment provided by his employer for the purposes of the employer's business'. Speaking for myself, I can think of no more essential equipment for the setting up and carrying on of the business of a shipowner than the ship or ships with which the business is carried on. This involves, in my judgment, no misuse of language ...

In my judgment, a shipowner's fleet of ships is properly described as the equipment of his business. They are, in truth, the tools of his trade and I can see no ground for treating the word 'equipment' in sub-s (1)(a) – leaving aside for the moment the more difficult questions posed by sub-s (3) – as excluding this particular type of chattel as opposed to other articles, of whatever size or construction, employed by a trader in carrying on his trade.

With regard to sub-s (3), Lord Oliver had some difficulty in its construction, but he came to the same conclusion as the dissenting Lloyd LJ of the court below, that the wording of the sub-section intended to be clarifying rather than limiting the application of the section only to any plant and aircraft, but not ships.

Lord Goff added:[47]

The real difficulty in the case, as it seems to me, arises from the fact that the word 'equipment' is defined in s 1(3) of the Act, and that the definition expressly includes any vehicle and aircraft, but makes no mention of ships or vessels … it seems to me that, in the case of ships, the distinction between the equipment on the ship and the structure of the ship is not only very difficult to draw in practice, but is artificial in the extreme. In any event, the duty of care imposed under the Occupiers' Liability Act 1957 may apply not only in respect of vessels, but also in respect of vehicles and aircraft: see s 1(3)(a). I have therefore come to the conclusion in agreement with my noble and learned friend, and with Lloyd LJ in the Court of Appeal, that the definition of equipment in s 1(3) of the Act of 1969 must have been included in the Act for the purpose of clarification only, and that the mere fact that ships and vessels were not expressly included in the definition cannot have been intended to have the effect of cutting down the ordinary meaning of the word 'equipment' by excluding ships or vessels from that word.

3.6.5 (f) Claims in the Admiralty Court by foreigners against a foreign ship for a tort committed on the high seas

Assume that a collision occurs between foreign ships in international waters resulting in damage to property, loss of life or personal injury. Being a tort of negligence committed outside of this jurisdiction, claimants would be restricted from suing the defendant *in personam* in the English High Court, unless the conditions of s 22(2) of the SCA 1981 were satisfied. These conditions are:

- the defendant has his habitual residence or a place of business within England or Wales; or
- the cause of action arose within inland waters of England or Wales; or
- an action arising out of the same incident, or series of incidents, is proceeding in the court or has been heard and determined in the court.

The claimants, however, would be able to issue a claim form *in rem* and wait until the ship came within the English jurisdiction to arrest her by a warrant of arrest. Unlike the *in personam* claim, there would be no need for a substantive link between the jurisdiction and the claim other than the presence of the ship within the jurisdiction. If the dependants of the deceased, in the above example, wished to arrest the ship, they could found their claim on the FAAs.

---

47   [1988] 1 Lloyd's Rep 109, p 115.

The following case dealt with the issue of whether these statutes applied to foreigners.

The Esso Malaysia[48]

As a result of a collision on the high seas between a trawler, registered in Latvia, and *The Esso Honduras*, registered in Panama and owned by the defendants, a Panamanian company, 24 Russian seamen lost their lives. The plaintiff, as administrator of the estates of the Russian seamen, brought an action against *The Esso Malaysia*, a sister ship of *The Esso Honduras*, under the FAAs 1846 to 1959, for the benefit of the dependants of the deceased seamen.

There was a preliminary issue whether the FAAs 1846 to 1959 imposed on the defendants a liability in damages in respect of the deaths of the deceased seamen. It was put by the defendants that the answer to the question whether the Acts applied to death in international waters in circumstances where no British ship was involved, depended on the construction of the Acts and there was a presumption that the statute did not have extra-territorial effect.

It was held by Brandon J, that the plaintiff, as personal representative of the deceased seamen, had a good cause of action against the owners of the Panamanian ship for damages under the FAAs 1846 to 1959.

He applied the previous decision of Kennedy J in *Davidson v Hill*,[49] in which it had been made clear that:

> The basis of the claim to which they [the FAAs] give statutory authority is negligence causing injury, and that is a wrong which I believe the law of every civilized country treats as an actionable wrong. They create, no doubt, a new cause of action ... for previously the relatives of the deceased could not in England sue the wrongdoer.

The decision, being undisturbed by higher authority, has settled the issue that the dependants of a deceased killed by the wrong of a ship, whether foreign or not, and whether or not the incident occurred in territorial waters, can sue in England. The enforcement of such a claim or right against the ship can be in the Admiralty Court by virtue of para (f) or, if any of the conditions of s 22(2) of the SCA 1981 are satisfied, by a claim *in personam*.

3.7 (g) Any claim for loss of or damage to goods carried on a ship

Paragraph (g) permits the arrest only of the ship in which the goods (lost or damaged) were carried, or her sister ship, or any other ship beneficially owned by the person (the carrier) who would be liable for the claim *in*

---

48 [1975] QB 198, pp 205–06.
49 [1901] 2 KB 606.

personam.[50] If the cargo-owner chooses to arrest the non-carrying ship, which might have caused the damage, he must rely on another sub-paragraph of s 20(2). So it was decided in *The Eschersheim* (see under 3.5.1) in which the cargo-owners arrested the sister ship of the tug claiming loss of their cargo carried on board the ship being salved, which was lost by the negligence of the salvors. The claim against the carrying ship will be subject to exclusion or limitation of liability under the contract of carriage, where the carriage by sea Conventions apply.[51] With regard to damage resulting from collision due to negligent navigation, cargo-owners may enforce their claim against the non-carrying ship under sub-para (e): damage done by a ship. The liability of the colliding ships is apportioned on the basis of their respective faults and includes liability incurred to third parties. The limitation of liability provisions applicable by the International Convention 1976 will affect the amount recoverable.[52]

3.8 (h) Any claim arising out of an agreement relating to the carriage of goods[53] on a ship or to the use or hire of a ship

3.8.1 General principle

This sub-section is wide enough to encompass claims in contract and tort arising out of any agreement relating to the carriage of goods in a vessel. It is not necessary for the claim in question to be directly connected with the agreement of the kind referred to in this sub-section, or that it be the agreement made between the two parties to the action themselves.

The St Elefterio[54]

The plaintiffs were holders of the bill of lading for a cargo of cattle cake on board the defendants' steamship. They had bought the cargo from the shippers, who were also the charterers of the vessel, and had later resold the cargo to other purchasers. The bills of lading were endorsed in blank by the shippers and presented to the plaintiffs, but, on presentation to the purchasers of the cargo, the purchasers claimed a right to reject the goods on the grounds that the bills were wrongly dated. It appeared that the goods had not been shipped on the day it was so stated they had been shipped. The plaintiffs sought to enforce their claim against the ship under para (h) of the AJA 1956 for the loss they would sustain if the purchasers were held entitled to reject

---

50 See conditions of arrest, in Chapter 3, below.

51 Hague Rules, Hague-Visby Rules or Hamburg Rules.

52 See Chapter 16, below.

53 A cif (cost, insurance, freight) contract for the sale of goods was not a contract relating to the carriage of goods on a ship: *The Maersk Nimrod* [1991] 1 Lloyd's Rep 269.

54 [1957] PD 179.

the goods. The defendants contended that the court had no jurisdiction to entertain the action and, in particular, under this paragraph. Willmer J said:

> In my judgment, the words of s 1(1)(h) of the Act of 1956, which I agree are different, and materially different, from the corresponding clause in the Act of 1925, are nevertheless wide enough to cover claims whether in contract or in tort arising out of any agreement relating to the carriage of goods in a ship.[55]

The phrase 'arising out of' does not mean 'arising under' an agreement and it has been given a broad meaning which can be equivalent to the phrase 'connected with' it, as was held in the following case by the House of Lords.

The Antonios P Lemos[56]

By a sub-time charter between the plaintiffs, as charterers, and the defendants as disponent owners, the plaintiffs sub-chartered the defendants' ship for one time chartered trip with liberty to sub-let. The plaintiffs entered into a voyage charterparty with A to carry cargo from the USA to Egypt. In the voyage charterparty, the plaintiffs guaranteed that the vessel's maximum arrival draught was 32 feet, as it had been stated in the sub-time charterparty by the disponent owners of the ship. However, when the vessel arrived at Alexandria, her draught exceeded 32 feet and she was unable to berth until her draught was reduced. This caused delay and expenses. The plaintiffs had to pay the costs of lightening and incurred certain other expenses and losses resulting from the breach of the guarantee under their contract with the voyage charterers. They issued a writ *in rem* and arrested the vessel in order to recover such losses from the owner. The defendants sought to set aside the writ and warrant of arrest on the ground that the High Court had no admiralty jurisdiction in respect of the plaintiff's claim, since it did not fall within s 20(2) of the SCA 1981. The main issue was whether for the claim to fall under para (h), the 'agreement' in question should be between the plaintiffs and the defendants, or any agreement in relation to the carriage of goods in a ship or the use or hire of a ship, which could be within the chain of chartering. The learned trial judge held that the claim did not fall within s 20(2)(h), but Parker LJ at the Court of Appeal held:

> Section 20(2)(h) contains no words of limitation restricting the agreements mentioned to agreements between the plaintiff and the defendant. It would have been simple so to limit them if any such limitation had been intended. The Convention contains no words of limitation either. I am unable to find any sufficient reason for importing such words, and would only do so if compelled by authority. In the absence of such authority, I would accordingly hold that, if the plaintiff can establish that his claim arises out of an agreement of the relevant kind, that is, an agreement relating to the carriage of goods in a ship

---

55 [1957] PD 179, p 183.
56 [1985] AC 711 (HL).

or to the use or hire of a ship, then even if such agreement is not one between himself and the defendant, that claim falls within para (h).

It is sufficient for the purposes of this appeal to say that on the ordinary meaning of the words the plaintiffs' claim is, in my view, a claim arising out of the relevant agreement notwithstanding that such agreement is not between the plaintiffs and the defendants, and on that simple ground I would allow this appeal.[57]

The defendants appealed. Lord Brandon at the House of Lords agreeing with the construction given by the Court of Appeal, said further:

I would readily accept that in certain contexts the expression 'arising out of' may, on the ordinary and natural meaning of the words used, be equivalent of the expression 'arising under' and not that of the wider expression 'connected with'. In my view, however, the expression 'arising out of' is, on the ordinary and natural meaning of the words used, capable, in other contexts, of being the equivalent of the wider expression 'connected with'. Whether the expression 'arising out of' has the narrower or the wider meaning in any particular case must depend on the context in which it is used.[58]

Thus, it was sufficient for the claim to be enforced under this paragraph, that the claim arose out of an agreement which, although it was not between the parties to the litigation, was nevertheless connected with it.

3.8.2 Claims in negligence or deceit for ante-dated bills of lading

The Sennar[59]

In June 1973, the plaintiffs purchased groundnut expellers from a Swiss company. It was an express term of the contract of sale that the cargo was to be shipped not later than August 1973.The Swiss company presented the shipping documents to the plaintiffs, which showed the groundnut expellers as having been loaded on board the Sennar on 30 August 1973. In truth, the cargo had not been loaded on board the vessel until September 1973, but the servant of the shipowners had wrongly dated the bill of lading. After arbitration proceedings in London, the plaintiffs were ordered to make payment to the company which purchased the cargo from them, but were unable to get their money back from the Swiss company because it had gone bankrupt. The plaintiffs, therefore, issued a writ in rem against The Sennar and

---

57   [1985] AC 711, pp 717, 719, quoting Parker LJ.

58   Ibid, p 727.

59   [1983] 1 Lloyd's Rep 295.

other ships belonging to the defendants for a claim of indemnity or damages for fraud, breach of duty or negligence, in connection with the shipment of the cargo. The defendants' vessel was arrested and they gave a letter of undertaking to get the vessel released and filed an acknowledgment of service to the writ.[60] It was held that, in the ordinary meaning of the words in para (h), the claim here did arise out of an agreement relating to the carriage of goods in a ship.

3.8.3 Claims under an agreement for the mooring and unmooring of a vessel

The Queen of the South[61]

The plaintiffs were watermen carrying on the business of ship mooring amongst other things. *The Queen of the South*, belonging to the defendants, was employed as a passenger vessel at the time for day trips from London to Glasgow. It was agreed by contract that the plaintiffs should moor and unmoor the ship at her berth in London and convey her crew between the ship and the shore. The plaintiffs rendered the services but the sum due to them under the contract remained unpaid. They issued a writ *in rem* to recover the cost of services, served the writ and arrested the ship. They moved for judgment, appraisal and judicial sale in default of appearance by the defendants. The Port of London Authority intervened and purported to seize the ship under their statutory powers in order to enforce payment of unpaid port dues. One of the questions was whether the plaintiffs' claim entitled them to bring an action *in rem* against the ship. The plaintiffs contended that their claim arose out of 'an agreement relating to the use or hire of a ship'. They argued that their services were rendered by the use of their motor boats suitably manned for the work to be done. Therefore, their claim came under this sub-para (h). Counsel for the interveners in the action sought to draw a distinction between an agreement relating to the rendering of services, in the course of which a ship was used, and an agreement relating to the use of a ship. This claim, he argued, came within the first category, hence not within sub-para (h). Obviously, this fine distinction was not convincing to the judge. Brandon J said:[62]

> I did not think that his argument based on this distinction was convincing. I can see that there might be an agreement for services, in the course of which there was only some incidental and minor use of a ship, which it might be inappropriate to describe as an agreement relating to the use of a ship. In the present case, however, it seems to me clear, on the written and oral evidence before me, that the whole of the services rendered by the plaintiffs were based

---

60 Later, the defendants sought to stay the proceedings, withdrew their acknowledgment of service and entered a conditional appearance in order to contest the jurisdiction of the court. It was held that the acknowledgment of service of the writ had to be treated as a submission to the jurisdiction of the court in this action because the defendants' solicitors had not applied to set aside within the required time period.

61 [1968] P 449.

62 *Ibid*, pp 456–57.

on the use of motor boats owned and operated by them. It is true that in some cases the men engaged in mooring and unmooring did their work on a quay or on a buoy. But they were landed on the quay or on the buoy from a motor boat and taken off again by the same means.

3.8.4 Claims against salvors for negligence during the salvage services

The Eschersheim[63]

The question was whether the claims of both the owners of the vessel salved and the owners of the cargo on board for damages caused due to salvor's negligence could be enforced under sub-para (h). It was held that, in deciding whether it was an agreement relating to the use of a ship, the courts should look at the substance of the matter. There was an agreement by which *The Rotesand* (tug) was to tow *The Erkowit*, to a place of safety. This was considered to be an agreement for the use of a ship (that is, the tug) in the ordinary and natural meaning; thus, the claim was within this sub-paragraph.

Lord Diplock said:[64]

> The salvage agreement was entered into by the master of *The Erkowit* on behalf of the cargo-owners as well as the shipowners. The primary contractual obligation of the salvor under the agreement in Lloyd's Open Form is to use his best endeavours to bring the vessel and her cargo to a place of safety, providing at his own risk, in the time honoured phrase, 'all proper steam and other assistance and labour'. The only possible way in which the salvors could perform their contract was by taking *The Erkowit* in tow and using the tug that had been sent to the scene of the casualty for that very purpose – *The Rotesand*.

While, in this case, it was accepted that the agreement was for the use of the tug, in the following case, the judge did not look at the matter in the same way.

The Tesaba[65]

The vessel sailed with a cargo of steel coils and general cargo *en route* to Mediterranean ports. She ran aground shortly after setting sail and her owners entered into an agreement with the plaintiffs, well known salvors, to salve the vessel and her cargo. The agreement was on the standard terms of Lloyd's form of salvage agreement, containing a clause which provided that the owners of the vessel shall use their best endeavours to ensure that security is provided by the cargo interests before the discharge of the cargo from the ship. The plaintiffs were successful in refloating the vessel. At the end of the

---

63 [1976] 2 Lloyd's Rep 1.
64 *Ibid*, p 7.
65 [1982] 1 Lloyd's Rep 397.

services, the plaintiffs made demands for security from the owners of the ship and the cargo.The owners provided security for the amount due for salvage of the ship, but the owners of the cargo did not provide security and the cargo was discharged at Istanbul. The plaintiffs issued proceedings in the Admiralty Court claiming damages from the defendants (shipowners) on ground of breach of their obligation under the salvage agreement. The defendants moved to set aside the writ on the ground that the claim did not fall within any of the paragraphs under this sub-section of the 1956 Act and they succeeded.

Sheen, J held that there was no reason for not giving the words in para (h) their ordinary wide meaning. However, the plaintiffs' claims arose out of a breach by the defendants of the terms of the salvage agreement which was an agreement to salve *The Tesaba* and her cargo. The agreement was not in relation to the carriage of goods in *The Tesaba* nor was it an agreement for the use or hire of *The Tesaba*, but for the use or hire of the tugs.[66]

It seems that the judge has unnecessarily limited the scope of this paragraph. In both, *The Eschersheim* and *The Tesaba*, there was a use or hire of a tug for the purpose of salvage. The respective claims in both cases were based on a breach of obligations under the salvage agreement. The only difference was that, in the former, the claim was by the owner of the salved against the salvor, while, in the latter, it was the other way round. Arguably, this fine distinction may not be followed in future cases, as is seen in a similar example below. Such claims have been included in the Arrest Convention 1999.

3.8.5 Claims for indemnity against a shipowner under a towage contract for the loss of a tug

By contrast to the interpretation given by Sheen J in *The Tesaba*, Brandon J, in the following case, preferred a wide interpretation of para (h).

The Conoco Britannia[67]

Under a towage contract containing the usual indemnity clause in favour of the supplier of a tug, the plaintiff supplied the defendant with a tug owned by a third party. The tug sank due to a collision with the defendant's ship, causing loss and damage. The plaintiff proceeded *in rem* against the defendant claiming indemnity under the towage contract for liability incurred by him to

---

66 This decision seems to contradict the decision of Brandon J in *The Queen of the South* [1968] P 449, in which the claim of watermen for the costs of the services against the ship which was moored and unmoored with the assistance of the plaintiffs' boats was held to be within 'an agreement for the use or hire' of the boats. The only difference between the two was that the claim of the watermen was for a debt, while the claim of the tug in *The Tesaba* was in damages for breach of the agreement.

67 [1972] QB 543 or [1972] 1 Lloyd's Rep 342.

the tug owners, or for payment direct to the tug owners, or damages for failure to indemnify. The claim was brought under s 1(1)(h) of the old statute, the 1956 Act, being equivalent to the present para (h).

Brandon J held that the words relating to the use or hire of a ship were wide enough to cover hire of the tug under a towage contract. It could be given a wide interpretation because the spirit of the Act and history of jurisdiction was to widen jurisdiction and incorporate claims under the Arrest Convention 1952.

Apparently, apart from Sheen J in *The Tesaba*, a wide interpretation of the words and application of para (h) was preferred by other judges.

3.8.6 Claims for wrongful detention of goods

The Gina[68]

The plaintiffs in this case, having received an order from a company in Saudi Arabia for shipment of three containers of aerosols, instructed their forwarding agents to arrange shipment. The agents arranged for shipment in the defendants' vessel. Eventually, only two containers were presented to the receivers at the port of discharge and the latter refused to obtain delivery – withholding payment of the freight. The defendants refused to return the containers, claiming a lien upon the goods for freight. Contending that it was the defendants' fault that only two containers reached destination, the plaintiffs issued a writ *in rem* against *The Gina* for wrongful detention of their goods, contending that their claim came under para (h) of the Act. It was held that the vessel was properly arrested under that paragraph and the plaintiffs were entitled to use the procedures of an admiralty action *in rem* in order to obtain security for their claim.

3.9 Excluded claims from para (h)

3.9.1 Non-payment of insurance premiums or brokerage

While the words of para (h), 'relating to the use or hire of a ship', were given a wide interpretation, as discussed earlier, the House of Lords chose a narrow construction of the words 'an agreement relating to the carriage of goods in a ship', in the context of the following case:

---

68   [1980] 1 Lloyd's Rep 398.

Gatoil International Inc v Arkwright-Boston Manufacturers Mutual Insurance Co (The Sardina)[69]

The respondents, six insurance companies and an insurance broker, brought an action against the appellants claiming payment of premiums on a policy taken out by the appellants over a cargo of oil shipped from Iran, Kharg Island, to various destinations. In order to found jurisdiction against the appellants, a Panamanian company, and obtain security for their claim, they arrested *The Sardina*, which was lying in the Shetland Islands. It is to be remarked that there was no question of *The Sardina*, or any other ship owned by the appellants, having been concerned with the carriage from Kharg Island of the oil cargo which was the subject of the insurance policy.

The issue was whether the claim came within s 47(2)(e) of the AJA 1956, which applied in Scotland and had equivalent provisions as the English AJA 1956. Paragraph (e) provided:

> ... any agreement relating to the carriage of goods in any ship whether by charterparty or otherwise ...

This provision was similar in effect to s 20(2)(h) of the SCA 1981. After reviewing the relevant authorities, the House of Lords held that for an agreement to come within that section, it must have a reasonably direct connection with the carriage of goods in a ship and not merely a remote connection. A contract of insurance was not connected with the carriage of goods in a sufficiently direct sense to be capable of falling within that paragraph. The 1956 Act was passed in order to enable the UK to ratify and comply with the provisions of the 1952 Arrest Convention. In particular, Lord Wilberforce referred to the proceedings of the conference, which led to the 1952 Convention. In that conference, The Netherlands had proposed the addition of insurance premiums due to underwriters as part of the claims justifying the arrest of a ship. The conference had expressly refused to include claims for insurance premiums among the maritime claims justifying arrest. The legislative intention behind the Convention must be treated as being the same as under the 1956 Act adopting its provisions.

Lord Keith, in particular, referring to the first case on this issue said:[70]

> There is one Scottish decision directly in point. That is, *The Aifanourios* 1980 SC 346, where an insurance association had arrested the defenders' ship on the dependence of an action claiming payment of release calls under a contract of marine insurance over the ship and its cargo. Lord Wylie held that such a contract did not come within the provisions of either para (d) or (e) of s 47(2) of the Act of 1956, and that the arrestment was therefore incompetent.

Lord Wylie said, pp 349–50:

---

69   [1985] AC 255 (HL).
70   *Ibid*, pp 269–70.

Counsel for the pursuers submitted that the provisions of these two paragraphs fell to be broadly interpreted. 'Any agreement relating to the use ... of a ship' was any agreement connected with the use of a ship. The provision was not confined to an agreement 'for' the use of a ship, and it could not be said that an agreement for the insurance of a ship, or for the insurance of its cargo, did not come within the broad terms of the statutory provisions. Put in these simple terms the argument is attractive, but these provisions have to be construed in the light of other provisions of the sub-section as a whole. In addition to claims arising out of damage done to or by any ship, claims in respect of salvage, towage or pilotage, they include claims arising out of the supply of goods or materials to a ship for her operation or maintenance, the construction, repair or equipment of a ship, liability for dock charges and master's disbursements, to take but a few examples of the kind of claims covered by the sub-section. If the provisions of para (d) fell to be as broadly construed as was contended for, it is difficult to see how any of these provisions could fail to come within the ambit of the provision. A claim, for example, arising out of the supply of goods to a ship for her operation or maintenance or arising out of her repair would certainly appear to arise from an agreement relating to the use of a ship. I am accordingly driven to the view that a more restricted construction is called for than that which, in isolation, the words might otherwise bear. Moreover, it is clear that the insurance of a vessel is a matter directed to the convenience or protection of the owner, and is not essential for the operation of the vessel as such.'

Lord Keith then continued:

It is necessary to attribute due significance to the circumstance that the words of the relevant paragraphs speak of an agreement 'in relation to' not 'for' the carriage of goods in a ship and the use or hire of a ship. The meaning must be wider than would be conveyed by the particle 'for'. It would, on the other hand, be unreasonable to infer from the expression actually used, 'in relation to', that it is intended to be sufficient that the agreement in issue should be in some way connected, however remotely, with the carriage of goods in a ship or with the use or hire of a ship, and I think there is much force in the view expressed by Lord Wylie, in *The Aifanourios* 1980 SC 346, as to the inference to be drawn from the presence of certain other paragraphs in s 47(2). There must, in my opinion, be some reasonably direct connection with such activities. An agreement for the cancellation of a contract for the carriage of goods in a ship or for the use or hire of a ship would, I think, show a sufficiently direct connection. It is unnecessary to speculate what other cases might be covered. Each case would require to be decided on its own facts. As regards the contract of insurance founded on in the instant appeal, I am of opinion that it is not connected with the carriage of goods in a ship in a sufficiently direct sense to be capable of coming within para (e).

I consider that, in *The Sonia S* [1983] 2 Lloyd's Rep 63, there was likewise an insufficiently direct connection between the agreement for the hire of containers and the carriage of goods in a ship. There is clear fallacy in the reasoning of Sheen J in the latter part of his judgment, where he equates the use to which the containers were to be put with the use to which the salvage vessel was to be put in *The Eschersheim* [1976] 1 WLR 430. The salvage vessel there was a ship which was to be used under the salvage agreement. The containers were not a ship. In my opinion that decision was wrong and should be overruled.

Once it had been thought that a claim for insurance premiums due under an insurance contract for the hull of a ship or for third parties liabilities covered by a mutual insurance (P&I), would come under this sub-paragraph. However, the decision of the Scottish Court of Session in *The Aifanourios*,[71] mentioned above, shattered the hopes of P&I clubs. It took 19 years for the wheel to turn round and so to include such claims in the list of claims provided by the new Arrest Convention 1999. The new Arrest Convention 1999 has incorporated in the list of maritime claims claims for insurance premiums and brokerage, including claims by a P&I club for unpaid calls. Such claims will qualify for an arrest of a ship to be made once the Convention comes into force, or is enacted by the UK.

3.9.2 Non-payment of container hire or damage to containers under a container leasing agreement

This has been subject to interesting decisions. In reality, containers are supplied to shipowners under a long lease agreement. The container supplier is usually not aware of which particular ship will carry his containers, unless a specific mention is made in the agreement. When a dispute arises under the lease agreement, either for outstanding payment of hire of, or for damage to containers, the container supplier may sue the shipowner *in personam*, but he will not be able to arrest a ship. Such claims can not be considered as 'arising out of any agreement relating to the carriage of goods in a ship'. So was held by Clarke J, in *The Lloyd Pacifico*[72] in which he followed Lord Keith's reasoning in *The Sardina* that 'in relation to' does not mean 'for the carriage of goods in a ship' under sub-para (h). The containers must be provided to a particular ship as they were in *The Hamburg Star*,[73] in which containers with goods were shipped on this ship and some were lost. Whether such claims can be enforced under sub-para (m), will be examined later.

In the new Arrest Convention 1999, a claim arising from the provision of containers for use in a ship is included in the list of maritime claims provided they are supplied to a particular ship.

3.9.3 The enforcement of an arbitration award obtained in relation to a charterparty dispute

In *The Bumbesti*,[74] in which two awards had been obtained in the Constantza Court of Arbitration with regard to a repudiation of a charterparty, the

---

71 [1980] 2 Lloyd's Rep 403.
72 [1995] 1 Lloyd's Rep 54.
73 [1994] 1 Lloyd's Rep 399, p 406.
74 [1999] 2 Lloyd's Rep 481.

claimant detained two ships of the defendant in Constantza by the order of the court for the enforcement of the awards. Later, the claimant arrested *The Bumbesti*, belonging to the defendant, in England again for the enforcement of the awards in case the value of the other two ships was not sufficient. The *in rem* proceedings were issued pursuant to s 20(2)(h) of the SCA 1981 and the issue was whether the claim came within the wording of this paragraph. It was held that:

> The claim in this case was the action on the awards and clearly arose out of the agreement to refer to arbitration the disputes that had arisen under the bareboat charter; but that agreement to refer disputes was not, itself, an agreement in relation to the use or hire of a ship since the arbitration agreement to refer was a contract that was distinct from the principal contract, that is, the bareboat charter.

The agreement to refer to arbitration disputes that had arisen under a charterparty must be agreements that were indirectly 'in relation to the use or hire of a ship', but they were not agreements that were sufficiently directly 'in relation to the use or hire of a ship'; the arbitration agreement was, at least, one step removed from the 'use or hire' of a ship; the breach of contract, relied on to found the present claim, had nothing to do with the use or hire of a ship, it concerned the implied term to fulfil any award made pursuant to the agreement to refer disputes; and the breach of contract relied on when suing on the award did not have the reasonably direct connection with the use or hire of the ship that was necessary to found jurisdiction.

On the proper construction of para (h), an action on an award was not within an agreement which was 'in relation to the use or hire of a ship'; and the court had no jurisdiction to consider the claim under s 20(2)(h) of the SCA 1981.[75] Although this seems to produce an odd and unjust result, security for enforcement of an arbitration award can be obtained under s 26 of CJJA 1982 and s 11 of the Arbitration Act (AA) 1996 (Chapter 4, para 5.3).

3.10 (j) Any claim under the Salvage Convention 1989[76]

> (ii) under any contract for or in relation to salvage services;[77] or (iii) in the nature of salvage not falling within (i) or (ii) above; or any corresponding claim in connection with an aircraft.[78]

---

75 The judge applied *The Beldis* (1936) 53 LlL Rep 255.

76 See Chapter 13 on salvage for its definition and elements.

77 The reference to salvage services includes services rendered in saving life from a ship and the reference to any claim under any contract for or in relation to salvage services includes any claim arising out of such a contract whether or not arising during the provision of the services: s 20(6)(b) of the SCA 1981, as amended.

78 The reference to a corresponding claim in connection with an aircraft is a reference to any claim mentioned in sub-para (i) or (ii) of para (j) which is available under Civil Aviation Act 1982, s 87: SCA 1981, s 20(6)(c).

The predecessor to this paragraph referred only to 'claims in the nature of salvage', so it did not cover a claim against salvors for negligence, which was covered under para (h) above (see *The Eschersheim*). It did not cover a claim for breach by a shipowner of cl 4(b) of the LOF 1980 or cl 5 of the LOF 1990 for salvage. (These clauses provide that the shipowner should use his best endeavours to ensure that security is provided by the cargo interests in favour of the salvor prior to the discharge of the cargo from the ship.) Thus, Sheen J had held in *The Tesaba*[79] that the plaintiffs' claim was not a claim in the nature of salvage within para (j). It was a claim for damages for breach of the agreement and not for a salvage reward, which was enforceable under sub-para (j). His reason was that such a breach did not occur until after the termination of the salvage services. Now, apart from the considerable extension of this paragraph, there are explanatory provisions in s 20(6) of the Act which specifically refer to the inclusion of any claims whether or not arising during the provision of salvage services. The new Arrest Convention 1999 also has now widened the scope of salvage claims that will be enforced by an action *in rem* by including any claims arising from any salvage agreement and for special compensation arising under Art 14 of the Salvage Convention 1989. Damage to the environment is also included as a ground for arrest, as are claims for wreck and cargo recoveries.

Claims for salvage give rise to a maritime lien.

3.11 (k) Any claim in the nature of towage in respect of a ship or aircraft

Only when the aircraft is waterborne, does its towage come within this provision.

Unlike salvage, towage does not give rise to a maritime lien.[80]

3.12 (l) Any claim in the nature of pilotage in respect of a ship or an aircraft

Pilotage charges or dues are claims for which an arrest of a ship can be made, but such claims do not give rise to a maritime lien.

---

79 See para 3.8.4, below.
80 See details of towage in Chapter 14, below.

Again an aircraft must be waterborne when pilotage service is rendered for such a claim to be within this provision.

3.13 (m) Any claim in respect of goods or materials supplied to a ship for her operations or maintenance

Containers have been regarded as goods supplied to a ship for her operation. However, unless they are supplied to a particular ship, any claim arising from a lease agreement with respect to containers will not be enforceable by *in rem* proceedings.

The House of Lords in *The River Rima*[81] made a distinction between the kind of contract which expressly provides that goods are required for the use of a particular ship, identified, or to be identified, when the contract comes to be performed, and the kind of contract which makes no reference to a particular ship, leaving the shipowner to make his choice later. Claims arising under the first category of contract are enforceable under this paragraph. The crucial words are 'supplied to a ship' which require identification of the ship on which the containers will be placed. The reason for this decision was that upon a historical analysis of the jurisdiction of the court regarding the provision of necessaries supplied to a ship, the identity of a ship was an essential ingredient.

The case involved a vessel owned by the Nigerian National Shipping Line (NNSL). NNSL had a number of contracts whereby they leased containers from their owners including the plaintiffs at a daily rate. The plaintiffs claimed conversion of certain containers and breach of an obligation by NNSL under the contract to maintain the containers in good condition and repair. They issued a writ *in rem* and arrested *The River Rima* belonging to NNSL. The issue before the court was whether the action could be maintained as an action *in rem*. The House of Lords held that the action did not come within s 20(2)(m) as the contract did not specify in which ship the containers were to be used, and the contracts were therefore merely contracts for the supply of containers to the shipowner. Paragraph (m) was derived from s 1(1) of the AJA 1956 and an essential ingredient of such a claim was that it should relate to necessaries supplied to a particular and identified ship.

As discussed earlier, one would expect that such claims could be considered as 'arising out of any agreement relating to the carriage of goods in a ship' under s 20(2)(h). However, Clarke J (as he then was) rejected such a submission in *The Lloyd Pacifico*, mainly because the containers must be provided to a particular ship. Although the Arrest Convention 1999 has included such claims arising in relation to the supply of containers, the

---

81　[1988] 2 Lloyd's Rep 193.

provision states also that the containers must be supplied to a particular ship. Unfortunately, this will not help the container company which supplies containers under a long term lease agreement, unless a provision is made in the contract naming the particular ship which will receive them at a time. This, of course, is neither possible nor practical.

Ship's agents are within this category:

The Kommunar (No 1)[82]

The sub-agents of entities in South America were alleged to have supplied goods and materials under two agreements to a number of named vessels belonging to the defendants. Their invoices were presented to the plaintiffs who paid for them. The plaintiffs sought to recover the amount paid and the interest due from the defendants under the agreements with them. They brought an action *in rem* under s 20(2)(m) and (p) of the SCA 1981. The defendants alleged that the court had no jurisdiction because, under the agreements, the plaintiffs' duty was the provision of finance to the shipowners. Therefore, they were merely financiers and not entitled to bring their claim under s 20(2) of that Act. The defendants also alleged that the case did not fall within s 21(4) of that Act. The sub-agents were appointed for the purpose of supplying the goods and services to the defendants and it was the plaintiffs' responsibility to pay for the invoices tendered and later charge them to the defendants' account. It was held that, the fact that the claim was on a general account, did not, by itself, lead to the conclusion that the claim was not a claim in respect of goods or materials supplied to a ship. Clarke J held, thus:

> ... in my judgment, they were not simply acting as bankers, they were not advancing moneys to the shipowner for the shipowner to purchase supplies. By the terms of the contract, it was their responsibility to pay for necessaries supplied by the supplier of the necessaries. I can see no reason why it should not be held that the claim to recover those moneys is in respect of the goods and materials supplied to the ship for her operation or maintenance.[83]

The Arrest Convention 1999 clarifies the position of agents of a ship.

This paragraph also covers advances made by a ship's chandler for payment of crews' wages and the supply of bunkers.[84]

No maritime lien attaches under this head.

---

82 [1997] 1 Lloyd's Rep 1.
83 *Ibid*, p 7.
84 *The Fairport (No 4)* [1967] 1 Lloyd's Rep 602.

3.14 (n) Any claim in respect of the construction, repair or equipment of a ship or dock charges or dues

Claims by shipbuilders and ship-repairers, port dues and charges are within this paragraph. No maritime lien attaches to these claims but the ship-repairer will have a right to detain the ship in his yard until payment of his charges is made. This is a common law right, known as 'possessory lien', which is different from the nature of the maritime lien. It depends on possession of the ship.

Fuel is not within the term 'equipment', but it is covered under the previous para (m).

The D'Vora[85]

An order had been made for the appraisement and sale of *The D'Vora*. The ship was sold and the proceeds were under arrest. The plaintiffs issued their writ and started proceedings claiming a sum for oil supplied to the vessel at Haifa. They claimed that the supply of fuel oil to an oil burning ship was covered by 'equipment' and the claim could, thus, be brought under this paragraph. They contended that equipping meant 'making the ship ready to sail'. Willmer J rejected this contention and stated:

> In my judgment, there is an important difference between 'equip' and 'supply', 'supply' being a word which is appropriate for use in connection with consumable stores,such as fuel oil, whereas 'equip', to my mind,connotes something of a more permanent nature than consumable stores. I can well understand that anchors, cables, hawsers, sails, ropes and such things may be said to be part of a ship's equipment, and that, nonetheless, although they may have to be renewed from time to time; but such things as fuel, coal, boiler water and food-consumable stores – seem to me to be quite a different category.[86]

3.15 (o) Any claim by master or crew of a ship for wages

Various questions about seamen's wages have been brought before the courts. It is important to know what is included in wages because they attract a maritime lien and this will affect the priority of payment out of the proceeds of sale of a ship when there are many claimants (see Chapter 4). The seamen's and master's lien for wages arises independently of contract for services rendered to a ship and are quantified in accordance with the terms of the contract (*The Ever Success*).[87]

---

85 [1952] 2 Lloyd's Rep 404.
86 *Ibid*, p 405.
87 [1999] 1 Lloyd's Rep 824.

3.15.1 The breadth of seamen's wages

What is included in wages was thoroughly and comprehensively analysed by Brandon J in the following case.

The Halcyon Skies[88]

It concerned a claim by a seaman for employees' and employers' contribution to a pension fund. The first issue was whether the right to such payments was part of wages since it arose from a special contract (that is, to be paid contributions to a special fund) and not from the general seaman's contract for wages. The second issue was whether the claims were in debt or in damages, and if it was the latter, could they still be part of wages so as to come within the admiralty jurisdiction. The third issue was, which depended on the answer to the second, whether the claims attracted a maritime lien.

A British Merchant Navy officer was employed by Court Line on board this ship. His contract provided that Court Line would pay employers' contributions to the Merchant Navy pension fund. Such contributions had not been paid when a petition to the Companies' Court was made for the winding up of Court Line and a liquidator was appointed. By an action *in rem*, brought by the second mortgagee of the ship, the ship was appraised and sold by the order of the Admiralty Marshal. The officer brought an action – with the leave of the Companies' Court – against the proceeds of sale claiming priority over the mortgagee's, claiming that he had a maritime lien in respect of the outstanding contributions.

Brandon J first considered the issue of employees' contributions[89] and said:

> So far as a cause of action is concerned, the plaintiff has, in my opinion, a good claim in debt. He had under his contract of employment given Court Line authority to deduct such contributions from his pay and pay them to the fund. Court Line had acted on the first part of that authority but not on the second. In these circumstances the plaintiff was entitled to revoke the second part of the authority, namely for payment of the sums deducted to the Fund, and to require Court Line to pay such sums to him instead. This he did by issuing his writ in the present action. So far as the nature of the claim is concerned there can, I think, be no doubt that the sums concerned, having been deducted from the plaintiff's pay in the first place, were part of his wages for the purpose of s 1(1)(o) of the 1956 Act. I also think ... that he had a maritime lien in respect of the claim.

As regards the disputed item of employer's contributions he examined the history of the court's jurisdiction and previous authorities about seamen's wages as follows:[90]

---

88 [1976] 1 Lloyd's Rep 461.

89 *Ibid*, p 463.

90 *Ibid*, pp 464, 465, 467.

Although, both according to the law administered by the High Court of Admiralty before 1861 and by the express terms of s 10 of the 1861 Act and s 22(1)(a)(viii) of the 1925 Act, the admiralty jurisdiction over claims for wages was limited to wages earned on board the ship, this concept was very broadly interpreted. In particular, the jurisdiction was regularly exercised, both before and after 1861, not only in respect of claims in debt for unpaid wages in the strict sense, but also in respect of claims in damages for wrongful dismissal, including claims for wages lost and for the cost of repatriation (viaticum).

There were other extensions of the wages concept. The claims covered by it were held to include emoluments other than wages in the strict sense, which were payable direct to the seaman, such as victualling allowances and bonuses: *The Tergeste* [1903] P 26; *The Elmville (No 2)* [1904] P 422. This approach was in accordance with s 742 of the MSA 1894, which defined 'wages' as including 'emoluments'.

It was further held in one case that the jurisdiction in wages extended to claims for damages for breach of a seaman's contract of employment during its subsistence. *The Justitia* (1887) 12 PD 145. That was a strange case, in which seamen recovered, in an admiralty action *in personam* for wages, general damages for hardship suffered and risks run when they were obliged to remain on board a ship while she was being used, contrary to the articles on which they had been engaged, as an armed cruiser in support of insurgents.

It is to be observed that, when the admiralty jurisdiction over claims for wages was redefined by Parliament in 1956, the requirement that wages should have been 'earned on board ship' was removed. This was in accordance with the description of the corresponding 'maritime claim' in para (1)(m) of Art 1 of the 1952 Brussels Ship Arrest Convention, which refers simply to claims arising out of 'wages of Masters, Officers, or crew'.

In *The Arosa Star* [1959] 2 Lloyd's Rep 396, the Supreme Court of Bermuda (Chief Justice Worley) held that a foreign seaman could recover, in an admiralty action *in rem* for wages and with the priority accorded by a maritime lien, full pay during sick leave and employer's contributions for social insurance, as being emoluments in the nature of wages to which he was entitled under his contract of employment.

In *The Arosa Kulm (No 2)* [1960] 1 Lloyd's Rep 97, Hewson J held that a foreign master and crew could recover, in an admiralty action *in rem* for wages, social benefit contributions said to be similar to National Insurance contributions, which were payable by the shipowners under their contracts of employment.

In *The Fairport* [1965] 2 Lloyd's Rep 183, Hewson J held that a foreign master could recover, in an admiralty action *in rem* for disbursements, notional deductions from unpaid seamen's wages in respect of insurance and pension contributions payable under their contracts of employment. He further expressed the opinion that the seamen themselves, who had already recovered their wages net of such contributions in an earlier action, would have been entitled to include the amounts of such contributions in their own wages claim.

In *The Fairport (No 3)* [1966] 2 Lloyd's Rep 253, the question arose whether the master's maritime lien for disbursements extended to the amounts recovered by him in respect of insurance and pension contributions under the judgment in the preceding case. Karminski J held that his lien did so extend, on the ground that such contributions formed part of the seamen's wages.

In *The Westport (No 4)* [1968] 2 Lloyd's Rep 559, Karminski J held that a foreign master could recover, in an admiralty action *in rem* for disbursements, firstly, sums which he was bound to pay in respect of deductions from seamen's wages for insurance, pension, provident and union contributions; and, secondly, sums which he was bound to pay jointly with the owners in respect of owners' own insurance and other contributions. The ground of the decision seems to have been that all the contributions concerned were emoluments of the seamen under their contracts of employment or according to their national law.

Then Brandon J examined whether the claim was in debt or in damages and continued:

It was argued for the first defendants that the plaintiff's only cause of action was in damages for breach of contract. It was argued for the plaintiff, on the other hand, that he had a cause of action in debt, on the basis that it was an implied term of his contract of employment that, if Court Line did not pay the employer's contributions to the fund, they would pay them to him instead. In my opinion it is not necessary to imply the term contended for in order to give business efficacy to the contract and it would not therefore be right to do so. The true view, I think, is that the failure of Court Line to pay the employer's contributions was a breach of contract for which the plaintiff is entitled to recover damages at law. It follows that his cause of action in respect of such contributions is in damages and not in debt. It seems that, if damages were not an adequate remedy, the plaintiff could seek the alternative equitable remedy of specific performance: *Beswick v Beswick* [1968] AC 58.

Does it make any difference that the plaintiff's claim is not, if I am right in my answer ... above, a claim in debt for the contributions themselves, but a claim in damages for breach of contract in failing to pay them? In my judgment, it does not, because the admiralty jurisdiction in wages has long extended, as I explained earlier, to claims founded in damages as well as debt. Further, that extended jurisdiction has not only been exercised regularly in respect of claims for damages after termination of the contract of employment by wrongful dismissal, but also at least once prior to 1951 in respect of a claim for damages for breach of such contract during its subsistence. Indeed, it may well be that the reason why the judges, who decided the group of further cases from 1951 to 1968 referred to above, did not pause to analyse the precise cause of action on which the claims in respect of employer's contributions succeeded was that they did not think it mattered, so far as the seaman's right to recover was concerned, whether such cause of action was in debt or in damages.

With regard to the third issue, whether these claims attracted a maritime lien his answer was affirmative.

The next case (referred to already in the judgment of Brandon J) made an important point and is worth discussing.

3.15.2 Wages in lieu of notice, when a seaman is wrongly dismissed, and emoluments

The Arosa Star[91]

There were claims by various plaintiffs to the proceeds of the sale in the steamship *Arosa Star*. The vessel had been arrested first at the suit of oil companies claiming for bunkering services. There were claims by the port authorities for port dues incurred during the period when the vessel was under arrest; also claims for the cost of repatriating passengers who had been on board the vessel; claims by the master and crew for unpaid wages and damages for breach of contract; and for unredeemed mortgages and interest due thereunder. The priorities of all these claims was in issue. The amounts due to the master, officers and crew of the ship included wages earned on board and damages for breach of contract up to the expiration of the notice of dismissal. The question was whether or not the whole of the amounts due to them would rank in priority over the mortgagees' interest. It was contended on behalf of the mortgagees that the maritime lien for wages due and unpaid did not cover any part of the sum awarded as damages for breach of contract, as it would not come strictly within the relevant head. In substance, the question was whether the plaintiffs were claiming wages, which remained unpaid under their respective contracts, or whether they were claiming damages for breach of contract after the termination of the contract.

It was held that there was merely a breach of the contract by the employer (by his default in not paying the wages) and the contract subsisted and could be made the subject of a simple claim for wages; that there was no repudiation of the contract accepted by the seamen which would have put an end to the contract and given rise to a claim for damages;[92] and that, therefore, the master and crew had a maritime lien in respect of the whole of the amounts of their judgments and the whole sum would be preferred to the claims of the mortgagees. It was further held that most seamen were engaged on special contracts which provided for notice of termination of service, paid leave, sick leave, bonuses, and so on, which could be and were properly regarded as additions to wages, additions which the mariner could 'be fairly said to have earned by his services'.

---

91 [1959] 2 Lloyd's Rep 396 (Supreme Court of Bermuda).

92 Damages for repudiation of contract after its termination by wrongful dismissal have been included in the admiralty jurisdiction as part of wages: see reference to it in *The Halcyon Skies* [1976] 1 Lloyd's Rep 461.

Although the court here seems to have restricted the damages for breach of contract to those when the contract is still in subsistence, for example, when the seamen have not accepted the conduct of their employer as a repudiation, the judgment of Brandon J, in the previous case, expanded the scope of a claim for damages by seamen.

Under English law, a maritime lien is not limited to wages earned on the last voyage and includes emoluments.

The Westport (No 4)[93]

Pursuant to an action *in rem*, the vessel *Westport* was sold by order of court.The first plaintiff, the master of *The Westport*, asked for judgment on behalf of himself, his officers and crew, in respect of outstanding wages due, pension fund contributions, disbursements and repatriation expenses.In particular, the master was asking for income tax deductions, which he had to make to the Greek tax authorities and also deductions for a pension fund, compensation for the termination of his contract and a claim for repatriation. There were deductions also made by the officers being contributions to various funds and union dues. The principle laid down in *The Arosa Star* was followed, that when a mariner's contract is under consideration, it is construed on the basis that the mariner is entitled to the benefit of the doubt. One important matter was whether or not the deductions made were to be considered as part of the emoluments of the officers and crew. 'Emoluments' was defined as generally covering something, which is received by a member of a ship's company 'as recompense for the execution of his duty'. It was held that the master's claim would be allowed and payment was ordered.

3.15.3 Severance payments (redundancy pay) were not considered to be part of wages

The Tacoma City[94]

The shipowners announced that they were ceasing trade at the end of May 1985. The first mortgagees (the bank) issued a writ *in rem*, arrested the vessel and it was sold by order of the court. There was a second mortgagee ranking immediately behind the bank. The plaintiffs were 20 officers, who had served aboard the ship. They claimed maritime liens for severance payments and wages in lieu of notice against the proceeds of sale of the ship, in priority to the claim of the second mortgagee. The question was whether severance payment agreements could fairly be regarded as the development of new terms in special contracts, which are as much 'additions to wages' as, for example, damages for wrongful dismissal or wages payable during sick leave.

---

93 [1968] 2 Lloyd's Rep 559.
94 [1991] 1 Lloyd's Rep 330.

Sheen J gave a number of reasons in support of his conclusion that this type of claim is not within wages, which included: (i) a severance payment is not payable 'for service to the ship', because it may be payable to one officer, who is declared surplus, and not to another who is not; (ii) a severance payment is 'compensation' for losing employment and is not part of the emoluments of employment; (iii) it is not paid for services rendered but because services are no longer required; (iv) the essence of a severance payment is a reward for long service payable as compensation for having had the service cut short.

At the Court of Appeal, **Gibson LJ** said:[95]

> I do not think it is possible to formulate a principle based upon any of those reasons and to demonstrate that it is supported by any particular authority. The cases show a development of the concept of 'wages' based upon a liberal approach and a determination to do what is fair and just in order to secure to the seaman what he has earned by service to and in the ship.

> The reasons for his conclusion given by Sheen J represent, I think, a description of aspects of these severance payments which together exclude them from the concept of wages rather than the formulation of any rule or principle. Thus, there is, in my view, no conclusive force in the fact that a severance payment may be payable to one officer who is declared surplus and not to another who is not. That would be true of a claim to damages for wrongful dismissal and the cost of repatriation: a seaman would not be deprived of his claim merely because other seamen have not been wrongfully dismissed. Further a claim to wages during sick leave, as was allowed in *The Arosa Star*, is normally available to one officer and not to another.

> Further, I do not find anything conclusive in the fact that a severance payment is 'compensation for losing employment' or that it is paid 'because services are no longer required'. Damages for wrongful dismissal are paid because employment has been lost and wages during sick leave are paid because services cannot be rendered.

> Sheen J viewed with concern the fact that, if the plaintiffs' claims to maritime liens were held to be good, the security provided by a mortgage on the ship would be greatly diminished, because those serving in the ship would have contingent rights to large sums of money by way of severance payments which would become due if the officers became surplus to the requirements of the owners at the end of service in the ship. Miss Bucknall has submitted that that is an irrelevant consideration. I accept that it is of no real weight. Those who lend money on ships are, no doubt, aware of the priority of a maritime lien for wages and can either require information as to the maximum risk for wages and for the payments and limit their lending accordingly or require the provision of sufficient security, by insurance or otherwise, against the risk.

> I am, however, quite unable to accept the full extent of Miss Bucknall's argument, namely that any sum is 'wages' and gives rise to a maritime lien, if

---

95 [1991] 1 Lloyd's Rep 330, pp 344–45.

it is promised to be paid in consideration of service in a ship. If, for example, the payment of a pension upon retirement age was promised by a shipowner by terms incorporated in a crew agreement, to be taken as a lump sum or by future periodical payments, I do not accept that that lump sum, or the value of the pension, or even the sums which have fallen due at the time of the termination of employment in the ship, would fall within the concept of 'wages', for which the law would give a lien. Such claims would not, in my judgment, be 'wages', even though the immediate consideration for the promised pay was service by the seaman in the ship coupled with prior service to the shipping company or to other companies.

All the additions to wages, payable under special contracts, 'which the mariner can be fairly said to have earned by his services' (*per* Worley CJ in *The Arosa Star*, p 403) which have been accepted as giving rise to liens, have been claims which can be regarded as items in the quantification of the value of the current service in the ship by the seafarer. Pension, as contrasted with contributions towards a pension fund, is not part of the agreed value of the current service but, in substance, is the reward for past service.

Legatt LJ stated:[96]

Since wages include 'emoluments', they are not confined to periodic payments. In its natural meaning of severance payment it does not constitute remuneration, because it is not paid for services rendered or for services that would have been rendered ... It is paid when a seaman who has been continuously employed for at least two years is dismissed by his employer. In other words, it is a payment made not for services to a ship, but to compensate the seaman for the termination of his employment after a reasonably long period of service to the same employer. It is not paid for past service, even though the amount of the payment is calculated by reference to the length of it. In my judgment severance pay does not constitute wages.

And Dillon LJ added:[97]

... the severance pay is to be calculated by reference to the whole of his service with the company or group in question. It is not paid as extra remuneration, or deferred remuneration on a contingency, for his services merely during the voyage in his last ship when he becomes surplus to requirements. Indeed, it is not paid as remuneration for his services at all; it is paid as compensation for the loss of the expectation he would otherwise have had that because of his long service he would have been offered further employment by the company or group after the end of what was in the event his final voyage in his last ship for the company or group.

It was held, therefore, that the appellants' claim for severance pay was not the subject of a maritime lien. The distinction made between damages for wrongful dismissal, on the one hand, and compensation to the seaman for being made redundant, on the other hand, was that the former is for services

---

96 [1991] 1 Lloyd's Rep 330, p 346.
97 *Ibid*, p 348.

rendered or to be rendered under the seaman's contract, while the latter is for loss of expectation of further work, because he had already served the minimum of two year's employment. In other words, a loss of certainty of employment qualifies for a maritime lien while a loss of an expectation does not. Similarly, as Gibson LJ explained, a lump sum of pension or future periodic payments upon retirement for old age does not fall within the concept of wages.

Payment of wages to a ship agent on account of the crew under a contract of employment, which had been agreed to be paid to the agent with the consent of the crew as wages for their services were not for the account of the agent. Thus, the payment attracted a maritime lien.[98]

3.16 (p) Any claim by a master, shipper, charterer or agent in respect of disbursements on account of a ship

The Sea Friends[99]

The plaintiffs were Lloyd's brokers who incurred a liability to Lloyd's underwriters in respect of premiums for hull insurance on the vessel. A writ *in rem* was issued and they intended to arrest the ship as soon as it arrived within the jurisdiction.The question was whether their claim could come under s 20(2)(p), entitling them to arrest the vessel on its arrival. Therefore, it was necessary to consider whether the plaintiffs' insurance brokers could be regarded as 'agents' for the purpose of this sub-section. Both the Admiralty Registrar and the trial judge held that the plaintiffs were not entitled to arrest the vessel under s 20(2)(p).On appeal to the Court of Appeal, it was reminded that the House of Lords in *The Sardina*[100] had clearly shown that the legislative intention behind both the 1956 and the 1981 Acts was to exclude claims for insurance premiums from the list of maritime claims. They could, therefore, not be subtly included under para (p). According to Lloyd LJ:

> Put in simple and non-technical language, bunkers are, to take just one example, a disbursement within (p) because bunkers are needed to keep the ship going. But insurance is not needed to keep the ship going. Insurance is needed to reimburse the shipowners in case a ship is lost or damages. The ship

---

98 *The Turidu* [1998] 2 Lloyd's Rep 278; see voluntary payments of wages by third parties, and assignment of the wages claim in Chapter 4, para 11.

99 [1991] 2 Lloyd's Rep 322.

100 [1985] AC 255.

could very well sail uninsured, although, of course, it never, in fact, does. The disbursement in this case is, in my view, no more a disbursement on account of the ship than it would have been if the premium were in respect of insurance on freight.[101]

It was held that the disbursement must be something, which would ordinarily be regarded as a master's disbursement, whether that disbursement be incurred by the master himself or by the shippers or the charterers or the agents. Insurance premiums are not ordinarily included within the description of master's disbursements.

At common law, no maritime lien was attached to master's disbursements incurred on account of the ship (*The Castelgate*).[102] A statutory maritime lien was, however, given by statute (MSA 1970, s 18) which is now found in s 41 of the MSA 1995 and states:

> ... the master of the ship shall have the same lien for his remuneration and all disbursements or liabilities properly incurred by him on account of the ship, as a seaman has for his wages.

Such a maritime lien does not extend to others who incur expenses on account of the ship (shippers, charterers, ships' agents). They, as all maritime claimants, can enhance their position by issuing *in rem* proceedings pursuant to their statutory rights *in rem* under the SCA 1981, whereupon they become secured creditors irrespective of the subsequent winding up of the defendant company by petition to the Companies' Court. The following case illustrates the position.

The Zafiro[103]

The plaintiffs made necessary disbursements on account of the vessels *Oro* and *Zafiro*, both of which were owned by the defendant. Subsequently, the defendant proposed a resolution for voluntary winding up of the company. The plaintiffs issued a writ *in rem* against *The Zafiro* claiming disbursements on account of the ship and arrested that vessel. The creditors of the company passed a resolution that the company should be wound up and appointed a liquidator. *The Zafiro* was sold and the proceeds paid into court. In the first motion, the plaintiffs moved for a judgment in default of defence against the defendants and/or the proceeds of sale claiming payment of the sum due to them. In the second motion, the defendants moved for an order that the action be stayed on the ground that, since the issue of the writ, the resolution for the voluntary winding up of the defendant's company had been passed and that, before the issue of the writ, the plaintiffs had been given notice of the meeting at which such resolution was to be proposed. The defendant further sought an order that the proceeds of sale of *The Zafiro* be paid out to him after the

---

101 [1991] 2 Lloyd's Rep 322, p 324.
102 [1883] AC 38 (HL).
103 [1960] P 1.

satisfaction of the claim of the owners of another vessel, who had previously obtained judgment against *The Zafiro* in a collision action.

It was held that:

- the arrest of a vessel was not an 'execution' within the meaning of s 326 of the Companies Act 1948 and, accordingly, the plaintiffs were entitled to the benefit of the arrest of *The Zafiro* as against the liquidator in spite of the prior notice of the meeting at which a resolution for the winding up of the defendant company was to be proposed;
- by arresting *The Zafiro*, the plaintiffs had become secured creditors;
- the general practice of the court was to stay all actions against the company after the commencement of the voluntary winding up of the company, save in special circumstances. This was an action for necessary disbursements, in which the writ had been issued prior to the commencement of the winding up.[104]

3.17 (q) Any claim arising out of an act which is claimed to be a general average act

The elements of a general average act derive from s 66(2) of the Marine Insurance Act 1906 and the York-Antwerp Rules 1974 as amended in 1994. Briefly, for general average to qualify as such, there must be some intentional or voluntary sacrifice or expenditure reasonably made with regard to the ship or cargo in time of peril or danger for the common safety of the adventure. There is no maritime lien for general average claims. The shipowner has a possessory lien over the cargo for its proportionate contribution to general average, enforceable against the consignee of the cargo, notwithstanding that – at the time of the general average act – he may not be the owner of the cargo.[105]

3.18 (r) Any claim arising out of bottomry

Bottomry bonds were contracts in the nature of a mortgage of a ship where the owner borrowed money while the ship was at sea to enable him to fit her as needed. He had to pledge the keel or the bottom of the ship as security for repayment. Such bonds are no longer in use today, but they gave rise to a maritime lien when used.[106] The new Arrest Convention has deleted it from the list of maritime claims.

---

104 For the provisions of the Insolvency Act 1986 and their effect upon statutory rights *in rem* and secured maritime creditors, see Meeson, N, *Admiralty Jurisdiction and Practice*, 2nd edn, 2000, LLP, pp 95–107. (There is now a new Insolvency Act 2000.)

105 *Castle Insurance v Hong Kong Island Shipping* [1984] AC 226 (HL).

106 The last reported case was *The Conet* [1965] 1 Lloyd's Rep 195.

3.19 (s) Any claim for the forfeiture or condemnation of a ship or for the restoration of a ship or goods after seizure or for droits of admiralty

The old MSA 1894 and the current Act 1995 have provided for occasions of forfeiture of a ship in case of contravention of the Acts by her owner or master. Some grounds of forfeiture are mentioned as examples below, where:

- a false declaration is made as to qualification to ownership of a British vessel, under s 3(1) of the MSA 1995, except where the false declaration is made for the purpose of escaping capture by an enemy of war (MSA 1995, s 3(2));
- the British character of the ship is concealed (MSA 1995, s 3(4) and (5));
- dangerous goods are shipped without marks or without notification. (MSA 1995, s 87(1));
- there is contravention of Customs and Excise requirements.[107] A ship will be liable to forfeiture for contravening the Customs and Excise Management Act 1979. Examples of contravention include: exporting stores contrary to a prohibition or restriction (s 68); shipping coastwise contrary to regulations (s 74); concealing goods (s 88); jettison or destruction of cargo to prevent seizure (s 89); inability of the master of a ship to account for missing cargo (s 90).

Droits of admiralty are abandoned property at sea which can be claimed by the Crown. Historically, this right of the Crown existed in the old MSA 1894 and now in the 1995 Act. Such property includes: jetsam, flotsam, lagan and derelict found at sea, which are not claimed by their owner 'in due time' (within a year and a day). It also includes goods and ships taken from pirates (but, apparently not property in the possession of pirates and belonging to others).

Presently, ss 241–44 of the MSA 1995 provide that Her Majesty is entitled to all unclaimed wrecks found in territorial waters in any part of Her Majesty's dominion. A good example of the territorial requirement of these provisions is found in *The Lusitania*.[108]

4 FURTHER JURISDICTION OF THE ADMIRALTY COURT IS GIVEN BY s 20(1)(b) AND (3)

This section includes:

- any application to the High Court under the MSA 1995;

---

107 *The Skylark* [1965] 3 All ER 380.
108 [1986] QB 384.

- any proceedings to enforce a claim for damage, loss of life or personal injury arising out of: (i) a collision between ships; or (ii) the carrying out of or omission to carry out a manoeuvre in the case of one or more ships; or (iii) non-compliance on the part of one or more ships with the collision regulations.
- any action by shipowners or other persons for limitation of their liability under the MSA 1995.

Also, s 20(1)(c) has preserved any other admiralty jurisdiction which the court had immediately before the commencement of this Act, otherwise known as the 'sweeping up' provision encompassing the court's inherent jurisdiction and such jurisdiction as the court had under the old ACAs 1840 and 1861. Examples of the court's inherent jurisdiction include jurisdiction over acts done on the high seas and power to award interest, which is now also statutory by virtue of s 35A of the SCA 1981.

Under s 20(1)(d), any other jurisdiction connected with a ship or aircraft which is vested in the High Court after the commencement of the SCA 1981 will be within the jurisdiction of this court.

5 POWER OF THE COURT TO GRANT INJUNCTIONS

Such power of the court existed since the Judicature Act 1873, s 25(8), which was re-enacted by s 45 of the SCJ(Con)A 1925. An injunction would be granted when the court thought it was just or convenient. Now the court's power to grant injunctions can be found in s 37(1) of the SCA 1981 which has replaced s 45.[109]

However, the general rule, before 1975, was that a plaintiff, as a mere putative judgment creditor, could not obtain an injunctive order to prevent a defendant dealing with his own assets before judgment was obtained[110] (unless the assets belonged to the plaintiff – whereupon he would have a tracing or proprietary claim). Lord Denning MR, in 1975, sitting in the Court of Appeal, innovated an injunction – relying on s 45 of the SCJ(Con)A 1925 – upon an *ex parte* application by a shipowner to restrain a charterer from disposing or removing his assets from the jurisdiction before a judgment for unpaid hire was obtained.[111] Again, in the same year, Lord Denning MR (sitting in the Court of Appeal) granted the same injunction to shipowners in *The Mareva v International Bulcarriers*,[112] hence the name of this injunction

---

109 For details of such injunctions refer to specialist books: Gee, S, *Mareva and Anton Pillar Orders*, 1998, Sweet & Maxwell; also, a brief summary is provided in *op cit*, Jackson, 3rd edn, fn 5, Chapter 16.

110 *Lister v Stubbs* (1890) 45 Ch D 1.

111 *Nippon Yusen Kaisha v G&J Karageorgis* [1975] 2 Lloyd's Rep 137 (CA).

112 [1975] 2 Lloyd's Rep 509.

became known as a 'Mareva' injunction. Under the new Civil Procedure Rules, it is now named 'freezing' injunction. Although its validity has been endorsed by s 37(3) of the SCA 1981, it is not a statutory remedy.[113]

Briefly, a 'freezing injunction' is an interim remedy in the form of an order to restrain a party from removing his assets located within the jurisdiction, or to restrain a party from dealing with any assets whether located within the jurisdiction or not.[114] The claimant must show that he has a good arguable case, that is, a better than 50% chance of success[115] of an accrued – not a future – cause of action,[116] that the defendant has assets within the jurisdiction and there is a real risk[117] that such assets will be dissipated before a judgment can be enforced. The question of risk of disposal of assets is a question of fact judged from the surrounding circumstances, such as evidence of dishonesty or attempts by the defendant to remove or dissipate assets.[118]The applicant must make a full and frank disclosure in his affidavit of all facts and circumstances[119] and give an undertaking in damages to the court, the effect of which is that the defendant can only ask the court to enforce it, should he suffer any loss by the issue of the order.[120] He should also give an undertaking to indemnify third parties who might be affected by the injunction and incur expenses.

Since its judicial innovation in the late 1970s,[121] it has been expanded by case law, practice directions and legislation. The applicant (claimant), however, is not in the same position as a secured creditor and he has no proprietary claim to the assets which are subject to the injunction. Thus, his position greatly differs from the security provided by the arrest of a ship. The purpose of the injunction is to preserve assets of the defendant for execution of a judgment or the enforcement of an award obtained subsequently.[122] In

---

113 *Mercedes-Benz AG v Leiduck* [1995] WLR 718 (PC), p 728, *per* Lord Mustill.

114 CPR, r 25(1)(f), Pt 25; *Interim Remedies of the Civil Procedure Rules 1999*, 2nd edn, 1999, Blackstone's.

115 *Ninemia Maritime Corp v Trave Schiffahrtsgesellschaft* [1983] 1 WLR 1412 (affirmed by the Court of Appeal [1983] 2 Lloyd's Rep 660).

116 *Veracruz Transportation Inc v VC Shipping Co Inc* [1992] 1 Lloyd's Rep 353 (CA).

117 *Third Chandris Shipping Corp v Unimarine SA* [1979] QB 645, p 669.

118 *Aiglon Ltd v Gau Shan Co Ltd* [1993] 1 Lloyd's Rep 164; see further cases in *op cit*, Gee, fn 109, pp 189–200.

119 See *op cit*, Gee, fn 109, Chapter 8, and a recent case concerning a non-sufficient disclosure: *The Giovana* [1999] 1 Lloyd's Rep 867.

120 *Op cit*, Gee, fn 109, Chapter 9.

121 *Mareva Compania Naviera v International Bulkcarriers* [1975] 2 Lloyd's Rep 509.

122 The defendant may, upon application to the court, obtain a variation of the order if he can show that he needs to cover ordinary living expenses, or, if the defendant is a company, allowance may be made to use some of the assets for business expenses: *The Angel Bell* [1981] QB 65; see, also, Mareva injunctions and third parties, *op cit*, Gee, fn 109, Chapter 15; and Devonshire (1999) 62(4) MLR 539, pp 539–63.

principle, there can be no objection to a defendant being allowed by the court to employ such assets for the purpose of his business or, where appropriate, to pay living expenses or legal fees, or to seek in good faith to repay loans in the ordinary course of business.[123]

A similar power has been given to the court by the old provision, s 30 of the MSA 1894, now Sched 1, para 6 of the MSA 1995. However, unlike the Mareva (freezing) injunction, which is an interim relief, an application under section 30 has been held to be a substantive right of relief, not being ancillary to any other cause of action.[124]

Originally, the Mareva injunction was limited to English proceedings in which the claimant was claiming a substantive relief against a foreign based defendant and the injunction was sought to ensure that the defendant did not remove assets out of the English jurisdiction before judgment. It was also available in aid to arbitration proceedings by s 12(6)(f) and (h) of the AA 1950,[125] which has now been replaced by s 44 of the AA 1996. But, an injunction could not be granted when the only factor connecting the case with England was the presence of assets within the jurisdiction because it was ancillary to a pre-existing cause of action triable in England.[126] Thus, a claimant who was seeking to serve a defendant out of the jurisdiction would need to show that his cause of action fell within the provisions of court rules for service out of the jurisdiction (Ord 11 r 1) in order for the injunction to be granted.[127] In other words, that the substantive cause of action was triable in the English court.

However, the Mareva or Freezing injunction has been subject to dramatic changes in recent years. It has gradually gained much wider scope applying to domestic or foreign proceedings, English or foreign defendants, English or foreign assets. The combination of changes brought by case law,[128] statute[129]

---

123 *The Angel Bell* [1980] 1 Lloyd's Rep 632; *Derby v Weldon (Nos 3 and 4)* [1990] Ch 65 (CA); *The Coral Rose* [1991] 1 Lloyd's Rep 563 (CA).

124 See *The Mikado* [1992] 1 Lloyd's Rep 163 and *The Siben* [1994] 2 Lloyd's Rep 420.

125 *The Rena K* [1979] QB 377.

126 *The Siskina* [1979] AC 210 (HL); see, also, Chapter 11, para 8.

127 The Privy Council left the matter open as to whether there could be a free standing injunction in *Mercedes Benz v Leiduck* [1996] AC 284; see, further, a paper on Mareva injunctions delivered by Gee, S (QC), the London Shipping Law Centre, 1999 (available from the Centre's office, UCL Law Faculty).

128 *Channel Tunnel Group Ltd v Balfour Beatty Constructions Ltd* [1993] AC 334 (HL), in which it was accepted that there was jurisdiction to grant an interlocutory injunction, although the English proceedings were stayed in favour of foreign arbitration.

129 Civil Jurisdiction and Judgments Act 1982, s 25; AA 1996, s 44 repeats (with necessary variations applicable to arbitration) Art 24 of the Brussels Convention. A straightforward interpretation of the meaning of provisional or protective measures under Art 24 was given by the European Court of Justice in *Mario Reichert and Others v Dresdner Bank AG* (Case C-261/90) (1992): 'In matters within the scope of the Convention, provisional measures are intended to preserve a factual or legal situation so as to safeguard rights, the recognition of which is sought elsewhere, from the court having jurisdiction as to the substance of the matter.' Article 24 of the Convention expressly provides that a [contd]

and statutory instrument[130] have allowed a free standing freezing injunction and the 'Siskina barrier' for service out of the jurisdiction of originating process seeking a free-standing interim relief has been removed.[131]

Further recent changes have also enabled claimants to obtain a worldwide freezing injunction. The first step towards this direction was made in 1987 when the question whether the court had jurisdiction to grant an order requiring the disclosure of foreign assets in support of a domestic Mareva injunction was negatively answered.[132] In 1990, however, three Court of Appeal decisions recognised a jurisdiction to grant injunctions against assets outside the jurisdiction, thus, permitting it to have extra-territorial effect.[133] More recently, the Court of Appeal held in *Credit Suisse Fides Trust SA v Cuoghi*[134] that a worldwide relief can be granted in proceedings whether or not these are domestic or foreign, under s 25 of the Civil Jurisdiction and Judgments Act (CJJA) 1982, or in aid to foreign arbitration.

---

129 [contd] court has jurisdiction under its national law to grant an application for provisional or protective measures, even if it does not have jurisdiction as to the substance of the matter. An order for interim payment of contractual consideration delivered by a court not having jurisdiction under the Convention as to the substance of the matter is not a provisional measure capable of being granted under Art 24: *Hans-Hermann Mietz v Intership Yachting Sneek BV* (Case C-99/96) [1999] ECR I-2277.

130 The CJJA 1982 (Interim Relief) Order 1997 (SI 1997/302)

131 RSC Ord 11 has been amended by the inclusion of r 8A.

132 *Ashtiani v Kashi* [1987] 1 QB 888.

133 *Babanaft International Co SA v Bassatne* [1990] 1 Ch 13; *Republic of Haiti v Duvalier* [1990] 1 QB 202; and *Derby v Weldon* [1990] 1 Ch 48.

134 [1997] 1 WLR 871.

CHAPTER 3

MODE OF EXERCISE OF JURISDICTION

1 INTRODUCTION

Thus far, we have seen that the admiralty jurisdiction is statutory, with specific heads of subject matter. It entertains both claims *in rem* and claims *in personam*. The *in rem* claim which, until recently, was known as the action *in rem*, has had a long history. It has been mentioned in the introduction of Chapter 1 that the conflict between the common law courts and the Admiralty Court was settled first, by permitting the Lord Admiral to determine disputes in matters that concerned exclusively what happened at sea, such as collisions and salvage, as well as matters that involved mortgages on ships, questions of possession of, or title in a ship. The Lord Admiral was allowed to proceed with a suit only *in rem* against the ship. This perhaps marked the genesis of the truly *in rem* causes, which involved claims concerned with proprietary rights on the ship and maritime liens and, in which, the defendant was the ship. The concept that the ship was the defendant in maritime claims was used to extend the jurisdiction of the court. The Admiralty Court Acts (ACA) 1840 and 1861 extended the admiralty jurisdiction to other maritime claims, which were not all concerned with proprietary rights in a ship, or maritime liens, the non-truly *in rem*. The merger of these additional claims with the truly *in rem* claims, coupled with the merger of all courts by the Judicature Acts (JA) 1873–75 brought a fusion of truly *in rem* claims with the non-truly *in rem*. Actions *in rem* and actions *in personam* could be tried in the same courts. The distinction, however, between truly and non-truly *in rem* claims and *in rem* or *in personam* proceedings has always been maintained in the mode of exercise of jurisdiction and can be found in the present statute, as will be seen later. Briefly, the truly *in rem* claims can be brought against the relevant ship without considerations of who would be liable *in personam* for the claim, or who is the beneficial owner of the ship to be arrested. The maritime lien is attached to the ship, the mortgage is a legal or equitable right in a ship, claims of ownership or possession of a ship are rights in a ship. By contrast, considerations of ownership, or liability *in personam*, are taken into account when a non-truly *in rem* claim is brought against the relevant ship. Before examining these considerations in detail, it is important to understand, first, what are the nature and the functions of *in personam* and *in rem* claims, respectively. An examination of the effect of *The Indian Grace* on the nature of the *in rem* claim follows, after an analysis of how non-truly *in rem* claims can crystallise on the ship by institution of suit.

2 CLAIMS *IN PERSONAM* –
s 21(1) OF THE SUPREME COURT ACT 1981

As the latin tag indicates, these are claims against the person, or the company being the beneficial owner or the demise charterer of the ship. By s 22(1) of the SCA 1981 a claim *in personam* may be brought in the High Court in all cases within the admiralty jurisdiction of that court. The proceedings may be brought, either by a claim form *in personam,* or through an *in rem* claim. Since shipping companies are normally incorporated abroad, personal service of the *in personam* claim form cannot be effected, unless the claim falls within certain categories of claims for which permission of the court can be obtained in accordance with the Rules of Court.[1] An *in personam* claim form may also be served out of the jurisdiction, where the defendant has agreed to submit to this jurisdiction, or the claim is about salvage for services rendered within the jurisdiction.[2]

There are, however, certain restrictions on jurisdiction imposed by other statutes or Conventions, such as the Brussels/Lugano Conventions, in the event of multiple proceedings, which will be examined later. There is also a limitation to commencing *in personam* proceedings in collision cases,[3] unless the defendant submits to this jurisdiction. Section 22(2) provides that the High Court shall not entertain such actions unless:

(a) the defendant has his habitual residence or place of business within England or Wales; or

(b) the cause of action arose within the inland waters of England or Wales or within the limits of a port of England or Wales; or

(c) an action arising out of the same incident or series of incidents is proceeding in the court, or has been heard and determined in the court.

There are two major weaknesses of the *in personam* proceedings:

First, it may be difficult sometimes to obtain permission to serve the defendant out of the jurisdiction; second, unlike the *in rem* claim, the *in personam* does not provide security for the claim, so that a judgment, if obtained, will be an empty shell unless a quasi-security is obtained for satisfaction of the judgment, by means of a freezing injunction. However, as was explained in the previous chapter, a freezing injunction is not a form of a certain security, in the same sense as when the ship is arrested, first because the asset made subject to the injunction may not be sufficient to satisfy the

---

1   See, eg, *The Manchester Carriage* [1973] 1 Lloyd's Rep 386; *The Craiova* [1976] 1 Lloyd's Rep 356; Ord 11, Sched 1 to the CPR and PD 49F, para 3.1(2)(c).

2   PD 49F, para 3.1(2)(a)(b).

3   *The World Harmony* [1969] 1 Lloyd's Rep 350; contrast *The Fagerness* (1927) 28 LlL Rep 261; PD 49F, para 3.1(1).

claim and, second, because the defendant can obtain a variation of the injunction by which the asset may be used for his business expenses.

3 THE *IN REM* CLAIM (OR THE OLD ACTION *IN REM*)

3.1 The origins of non-truly *in rem* claims

Statutory rights by way of an action *in rem* were first created by the ACA 1840. It is illustrative to use the words of Brandon J, in *The Monica S*:[4]

> Such rights were given by s 6 in respect, firstly, of claims for towage, and, secondly, of claims for necessaries supplied to foreign ships, whether within the body of a country or on the high seas. Further rights of the same kind were created by the ACA 1861. Such rights were given by s 4, in respect of claims for building, equipping or repairing a ship, if at the date of institution of the cause the ship or its proceeds were under arrest of the court; by s 5, in respect of claims for necessaries supplied to any ship elsewhere than in the port to which she belonged, unless at the time of institution of the cause any owner or part-owner was domiciled in England or Wales; by s 6, in respect of claims by holders of bills of lading of any goods carried into any port in England or Wales for damage to such goods, subject to the same proviso as to domicile of any owner or part-owner; and by s 10 in respect of masters' claims for disbursements. Section 35 further provided that the jurisdiction of the Admiralty Court could be exercised either *in rem* or *in personam*.

Later the Judicature (Consolidation) Act 1925 expanded the list of claims which could be enforced by an action *in rem*, and further extension was achieved by the Administration of Justice Act (AJA) 1956, and the present statute, the Supreme Court Act (SCA) 1981 (as has already been seen).

3.2 Functions of the *in rem* proceedings

At its commencement, the *in rem* claim is against the property, such as the relevant ship or cargo or freight, as the case may be (see para 5). It requires the relevant ship or property to be within the jurisdiction for it to be arrested, unless the defendant submits to jurisdiction and provides security in lieu of arrest. The uniqueness of an *in rem* claim under English procedural law lies on its triple function, namely: it assists the claimant (a) to obtain security for the claim; (b) to invoke the jurisdiction of the English court on the merits of the claim; and (c) regarding 'non-truly *in rem*' claims, to have his right *in rem*

---

4   [1967] 2 Lloyd's Rep 113, pp 118–19, *per* Brandon J.

crystallised on the property from the time of issue of the *in rem* claim form.[5] Functions (a) and (b) are discussed in Chapter 4. The origins of function (c) are examined next.

3.2.1 The crystallisation of non-truly in rem claims on the property

The crystallisation of the non-truly *in rem* claim on the ship (against which proceedings *in rem* have been issued) was established in 1967 by the decision of Brandon J, in *The Monica S*. This decision has had far reaching effect upon purchasers of ships who bought a ship after the issue of the writ. It has remained unchallenged. It will later be examined whether or not the effect of this decision has been undermined by the recent decision of the House of Lords in *The Indian Grace*.[6]

The Monica S[7]

The cargo-owners of the cargo on board this ship claimed damages to their cargo and issued a writ *in rem*. At the time of the issue, the ship was named *Monica Smith* and was owned by S. Before the writ was served, *Monica Smith* was transferred to T and was renamed *Monica S*. The writ was subsequently amended, accordingly, to describe the name and the defendants as 'the owners of the ship formerly called *Monica Smith* and now known as *Monica S*' and was served on the ship. The new owner T entered conditional appearance and applied by motion to set aside the writ or the service. After the service, T sold the ship to someone else. T claimed, *inter alia*, a declaration that no lien or charge arose against *Monica S* by reason of issue of the writ or service on grounds that (1) T was not the owner of the vessel at the date of issue, or when the cause of action arose; (2) T would not be liable *in personam*; (3) the claim gave no rise to a maritime lien or charge on the ship. He claimed that the plaintiff had only a statutory right of action *in rem* under the AJA 1956, which was enforceable against the *res* if (i) the *res* was arrested while still owned by the person liable *in personam*, or (ii) the writ had been served before change of ownership.

Brandon J had to decide the issue whether a change of ownership of the ship, occurring after institution of proceedings but before service of process or arrest, defeated the statutory right of action *in rem*. He reviewed all previous authorities being relevant to the question and held:

> T was the owner of the vessel at the time of service of writ and had an interest in defending it. As a matter of principle, if creation of a substantive right could occur on arrest then it could occur at date of action brought. There was a preponderance of authority to show that the defendants' contention (that

---

5   *The Monica S* [1967] 2 Lloyd's Rep 113.
6   [1998] 1 Lloyd's Rep 1.
7   [1967] 2 Lloyd's Rep 113.

under the pre-1956 law a change of ownership after issue of writ, but before service or arrest, defeated a statutory right of action *in rem*) was wrong. There was no reason why, once the plaintiff had properly invoked jurisdiction under the 1956 Act by bringing an action *in rem*, he should not, despite a subsequent change of ownership of the *res*, be able to prosecute it through all its stages, up to judgment against the *res* and payment out of the proceeds.

The motion of the defendant, T, was dismissed. Brandon J referred to the following decisions, some of which, he thought, supported his view, although he accepted that none of them was exactly on the point, while others were conflicting. In *The Pacific*,[8] in which there was competition between a claim by a mortgagee and a claim for necessaries supplied to the ship, Dr Lushington had stated:

> The material(s) man …by the mere fact of his supplying necessaries, in no case obtains the ship as a security until he institutes his suit in this court… [he] has not a maritime lien; for a maritime lien accrues from the instant of the circumstances creating it, and not from the date of the intervention of the court.

In *The Princess Charlotte*,[9] in which the sale of the ship took place the day after the institution of the cause and on the same day as the arrest, Dr Lushington again expounded that:

> I am of the opinion that the mere transfer of a foreign ship to a British owner does not bar the remedy … and, moreover, in this case, the title (of the new owner) did not commence till after the suit was instituted.[10]

In the subsequent case, *The Troubadour*,[11] Dr Lushington repeated his view expressed in his previous decision, *The Pacific*, that the necessary man did not acquire a lien on the ship until institution of suit, so the necessary man, again, came in priority after a mortgagee whose mortgage had been registered before institution of suit. In *The Two Ellens*,[12] the Privy Council – construing s 5 of the ACA 1861 – approved the decision in *The Pacific* and confirmed that the *res* did not become chargeable with the debt for necessaries until the suit was actually instituted. It was the institution of suit, Brandon J explained, commenting on another decision of the Privy Council (*The Pieve Superiore*),[13] that gave a claimant the right to arrest and the arrest gives him security. This case, however, did not absolutely support the judge's point of view, but he gave it a liberal interpretation.

---

8   (1864) 1 Brown 7 Lush 243, p 246.

9   (1864) LJ Adm 188.

10 But, at that time, it had been thought that a claim for necessaries conferred a maritime lien, which view was overruled by the House of Lords in *The Heinrich Bjorn* (1886) 11 App Cas 270 (HL) (see below).

11 (1866) LR A&E 302.

12 (1872) LR 4 PC 161.

13 (1874) LR 5 PC 482.

Next he examined *The Aneroid*,[14] in which, however, Sir Robert Phillimore had said that a necessary man would have no cause of action if the sale of the ship preceded the arrest of the ship. Brandon J thought that, even if the judge in that case had put his mind to this point, it must have been *obiter*, as it was not relevant to the case, because the sale had occurred before the institution of the proceedings *in rem*.

What persuaded Brandon J most in his judgment, was the statement of Lord Watson in *The Heinrich Bjorn*,[15] who had said:

> The position of a creditor who has a proper maritime lien differs from that of a creditor in an unsecured claim in this respect – that the former, unless he has forfeited the right by his own laches, can proceed against the ship, notwithstanding any change in her ownership, whereas the latter cannot have an action *in rem* unless, at the time of *its institution*, the *res* is the property of his debtor.

In an earlier passage, however, Lord Watson had said that:

> The attachment of the ship by process of the court had the effect of giving the creditor a legal nexus over the proprietary interest of his debtor, as from the date of *the attachment*.[16]

The plaintiffs in *The Monica S* argued that this passage was directed to the time from which the security, when obtained, took effect, and not to the time when the right to obtain it accrued. This interpretation was not accepted by Brandon J, because Lord Watson in the next case referred to by Brandon J, *The Sara*,[17] had approved what Dr Lushington had said about the effect of institution of suit in *The Pacific*.

In *The Cella*[18] case, at first instance, the judge referred to the correctness of *The Pacific*, but the Court of Appeal (Esher and Fry LJJ), having approved the first instance decision, used the word 'arrest' of the ship as being the critical time offering the greatest security for obtaining substantial justice. Esher LJ also referred to the alternative time of the service of the writ. Lopes LJ, however, said that, from the time of arrest, the ship is held by the court to abide the result of the action and the rights of the parties must be determined by the institution of the action and cannot be altered by anything which takes place subsequently. Brandon J preferred the words used by Lopes LJ, in that, it is from the institution of suit that the rights of the parties are determined. *The Cella* concerned the right *in rem* of a ship-repairer, who had issued a caveat against release of the ship (which had previously been arrested by its master)

---

14 (1877) 2 PD 189.
15 (1886) 11 App Cas 270, p 276 (emphasis added).
16 *Ibid*, p 276 (emphasis added).
17 (1889) 14 App Cas 209: this case is now wrong on the point that the master does not have a maritime lien for disbursements on account of the ship.
18 (1888) 13 PD 82.

as against the liquidator of the shipowning company. Brandon thought that, because of the caveat, neither Esher LJ, nor Fry LJ put their mind to the effect of the issue of the writ. In a much later decision, *The Zafiro*,[19] (to which Brandon J referred), the court upheld the claim of a necessary man secured on the ship by arrest against the liquidator of the company.[20] A further two decisions, *The James W Elwell*[21] and *The Colorado*,[22] seem to stress the incident of arrest of the ship as having the effect of creating security on the ship for a non-maritime lien claimant. Brandon J commented about these decisions that the point of distinction between issue of writ and arrest of he ship was not in issue.

Finally, Brandon J asserted that Sir Boyd Merriman, in *The Beldis*,[23] supported his view. He was, in fact, commenting on the contrast being made by the House of Lords' decision, in *The Heinrich Bjorn*, between the security aspect of maritime liens, which does not depend on bringing a suit, and other maritime claims which need the institution of suit in order to be attached on the ship.

Brandon J concluded that seven of these decisions supported or tended to support his view, six were against and one was neutral. On closer examination, however, bearing in mind that some of these decisions were strained in their interpretation by Brandon J, only six[24] of them seemed to support his view that the institution of suit causes a statutory right *in rem* to accrue on the ship. Three[25] decisions were not clear, or were not deciding the point and seemed to equate arrest with institution of suit. Five[26] referred

---

19 [1960] P 1.

20 However, when maritime creditors are in competition with the creditors of the company, there must have been an arrest of the ship belonging to the company prior to the commencement of the winding-up proceedings for maritime claims, other than maritime liens and mortgages, to be given priority over the company's unsecured creditors. Otherwise. the arrest will be void for being equivalent to 'sequestration' under s 128(1) of the Insolvency Act 1986. The discretion of the judge in the company court is very important in this context. Issue of a caveat against release of the ship which has been arrested by another maritime claimant, will have the same effect, provided it is issued before the commencement of the winding-up proceedings: Re Aro Co Ltd [1980] Ch 196 (CA); for the extent of the discretion of the court, which will depend on the circumstances of each case, see *The Bolivia* [1995] BCC 666.

21 [1921] P 351.

22 [1923] P 102 (CA).

23 [1936] P 51.

24 *The Pacific* (1864) 1 Brown 7 Lush 243; *The Princess Charlotte* (1864) LJ Adm 188; *The Troubadour* (1866) LR A&E 302; *The Two Ellens* (1872) LR 4 PC 161; *The Sara* (1889) 14 App Cas 209; *The Cella* (1888) 13 PD 82: but, in the Court of Appeal the arrest or service was mentioned.

25 *The Pieve Superiore* (1874) LR 5 PC 482; *The Heinrich Bjorn* (1886) 11 App Cas 270 (CA) and (HL); *The Beldis* [1936] P 51 (CA).

26 *The Cella* (1888) 13 PD 82 (CA); *The Aneroid* (1877) 2 PD 189; *The James W Elwell* [1921] P 351; *The Colorado* [1923] P 102 (CA); *The Zafiro* [1960] P 1.

directly to the incident of arrest and one[27] was neutral. One can hardly argue that there was a preponderance of opinion in favour of the judge's view.

It is important, however, to note that the procedure of the court between 1859 until 1874 (at which time the decisions that supported Brandon J's view were decided) required that a cause was instituted by having the cause written in the book. If the cause was *in rem*, a warrant for the arrest of the *res* was taken out, served and executed. In practice, arrest followed very soon, usually within one or two days of institution and there was not then any separation between service of process and arrest, both being carried out simultaneously.[28] There should be no surprise, therefore, that, in some of the decisions referred to by Brandon J, the issue of the writ and the arrest seemed to be equated by the judges. However, these authorities had been decided before the AJA 1956 and Brandon J was more concerned with the construction of the 1956 Act than previous authorities.

The judge thought that the passing of the Act made his argument stronger by reason of the statute's express requirements. In particular, s 3(4) provided:

> In the case of any such claim as is mentioned in para (d) to (r) of s 1(1), being a claim arising in connection with a ship, where the person who would be liable on the claim in an action *in personam* was, when the cause of action arose, the owner or charterer of, or in possession or in control of, the ship, the admiralty jurisdiction of the High Court ... may be invoked by an action *in rem* against (a) that ship, if at the time *the action is brought*, it is beneficially owned as respects all the shares therein by that person ... [emphasis added].

Thus, the critical time under the Act was when the 'action was brought' against the relevant ship, which caused the statutory right *in rem*[29] to accrue upon it irrevocably and, hence, be enforced against that ship, even if it had, in the meantime, been transferred to a *bona fide* purchaser, who bought the ship for value and without knowledge of the issue of the writ at the time.[30] In essence, the gist of Brandon J's decision is that, with the institution of suit *in*

---

27 *The Igor* [1956] 2 Lloyd's Rep 271.

28 Summary given by Brandon J in *The Monica S* [1967] 2 Lloyd's Rep 113, p 119 (see above).

29 The judge also preferred the expression 'statutory right of action *in rem*' to the expression 'statutory lien', for it seemed to him to be a more accurate description of the right in question. But, he also thought that 'statutory lien' was a convenient expression if it was used to mean no more than an irrevocably accrued statutory right of action *in rem*.

30 It has been the practice of solicitors involved in the sale and purchase of ships to conduct a search in the Admiralty Registry, as part of the due diligence exercise, to see whether there are any outstanding claims *in rem* issued against the ship to be bought. Unfortunately, Pt 5 of the CPR provides that members of the public may only search for claim forms which have been served. This places purchasers at a considerable disadvantage, unless an exception to this rule is made for this purpose (*per* Clarke LJ: 'The civil justice reform, its impact on maritime litigation, the maritime industry and London', lecture in memory of Professor Cadwallader, 1999, the London Shipping Law Centre, UCL Law Faculty.

rem, a contingent right of security is created upon the ship which will be brought into effect by the arrest of the ship, regardless of change of ownership between the issue and the arrest. That was, he thought, the intention of the statute as derived from the words 'action is brought', and he disregarded persuasive arguments by the defendants' counsel about the meaning of previous authorities and the need to protect innocent purchasers. On balance, Brandon J preferred to protect maritime claimants, because a purchaser would be able to rely on the contractual indemnity obtained from the seller, if he did not become insolvent by the time it was discovered that the ship bought was encumbered by either maritime liens[31] or statutory rights *in rem*.[32]

3.2.2 Does 'action brought' mean institution of claim?

The foundation of *The Monica S* may crumble if the words 'action brought'[33] in the statute do not mean only the issue of the writ, but also the service or the arrest. Brandon J said on this point that:

> It seems to me that it would be strange if a statutory right of action *in rem* only became effective, as against a subsequent change of ownership of the res, upon arrest of the *res*, and yet, by the same statute, as conferred the right of action, arrest was in many cases prohibited.[34]

This is a very powerful judicial statement of a very experienced admiralty judge (as he then was), with an insight into the realities of shipping practices, in that shrewd shipowners would, of course, sell a ship, against which a writ *in rem* had been issued for a substantial maritime claim, to avoid the consequences. It seems that policy considerations were very important in his decision, which has remained unchallenged since 1967.[35]

---

31 Maritime liens cannot be registered, so there is no means of finding out about them from a public record, unless the purchaser inspects the log books of the ship, in case there are incidents recorded which might have given rise to maritime liens

32 See fn 30.

33 The construction of these words under the Warsaw Convention for the Unification of Certain Rules relating to International Carriage by Air was given a broader meaning by the Court of Appeal in *Milor Srl and Others v BA plc* [1996] QB 702, in which Phillips LJ said: 'I accept that, in the appropriate context, the expression "to bring an action" can naturally mean "to commence an action". To find such a context, one need look no further than the next article of the Convention. Article 29 provides: "The right to damages shall be extinguished if an action is not brought within two years, reckoned from the date of arrival at the destination, or from the date on which the aircraft ought to have arrived, or from the date on which the carriage stopped." Plainly in Art 29 "brought" means "instituted or commenced". The natural meaning of "brought" will, however, depend upon its context. If a litigant says, "I brought a successful action", the natural meaning of "brought" embraces both the initiation and the pursuit of the action. In my judgment, the context of Art 28 is one in which "brought" naturally has the latter meaning, rather than meaning no more than "instituted".'

34 *The Monica S* [1967] 2 Lloyd's Rep 113, p 131.

35 The decision was approved by the Court of Appeal in *Re Aro Co Ltd* [1980] 1 Ch 196, where it was held that a plaintiff by commencing an action *in rem* against a ship, even if the writ has not been served or the ship has not been arrested, puts himself in a position of a secured creditor.

It remains to be seen whether his decision will remain unchallenged in the future.

It should be noted that, shortly after the decision of Brandon J, the phrase 'the jurisdiction may be invoked' of s 3(4) of the 1956 Act (which preceded the words 'when the action is brought') was construed by the Court of Appeal in *The Banco*.[36] Megaw LJ thought that the jurisdiction was invoked when the writ was served on the one ship chosen, and not at its issue (when more than one ship can be named in the writ). Lord Denning MR, in the same case, said that it was when the writ was served and a warrant of arrest was executed, because it was an action against the very thing itself. Cairns LJ was in the minority and agreed with what Brandon J said in *The Monica S*. Brandon J, in his subsequent decision, *The Berny*,[37] observed that, in the context of s 3 of the AJA 1956, the expressions used 'when the action is brought' and 'when the jurisdiction is invoked' were not intended to be the same thing. To support this, he drew a *prima facie* inference from the statute, which used both phrases in different parts of the sub-sections. Relying on older authorities,[38] he said that the jurisdiction of the court was invoked by the service and not by the issue of the writ.

It has since been established (see *The Duke Yare* and *Freccia del Nord*) (but this will be correct until 1 March 2002)[39] that the court's jurisdiction, whether *in personam* or *in rem*, can only be invoked or be seised by the service of proceedings. It should be observed that the draftsman of s 21 of the SCA 1981, which replaced s 3 of the 1956 Act, has used the words 'action may be brought'[40] in all sub-sections. To avoid confusion, the words 'jurisdiction may be invoked' have been eliminated.

Before any conclusion can be drawn about the 'status' of *The Monica S* at the present time, it is essential to examine who has been regarded as the defendant *in rem* proceedings.

3.3 Who is the defendant in the *in rem* proceedings?

Historically, there have been two schools of thought. One school has viewed the *in rem* action (claim) as a means of compelling the defendant liable for the claim to appear in court and defend the claim personally (known as 'the procedural theory'). In other words, an *in rem* claim really aims at the person

---

36 [1971] P 137.

37 [1977] 2 Lloyd's Rep 533.

38 *Sociate Generale de Paris v Dreyfus Brothers* (1885) 29 Ch D 239 and *The Hagen* [1908] P 189.

39 Prior to *The Duke Yare* [1991] 2 Lloyd's Rep 557 (CA) (discussed later), it had been thought that the court was seized of jurisdiction at the issue of the proceedings. It will be seen in Chapter 6 that the new Regulation amending the Brussels Convention reverts to the issue of proceedings.

40 In the new PD 49F, para 6.2(4)(b)(iii), the word 'issued' instead of 'brought' is used.

who is interested in the ship, who will – after appearance – be personally liable, beyond the value of the ship, if the claim exceeds its value.[41]

The other school has viewed it as being against the *res* and has developed from the concept of maritime liens, which attach on the ship from the moment of the incident that gave rise to the claim. In other words, the *res* has been considered to be the 'personified' defendant, hence, the name attributed to this theory is known as the 'personification theory'.[42]

The procedural theory gradually gained preponderance amongst English judges over the personification theory, particularly since 1892, when Sir Francis Jeune decided *The Dictator*,[43] which, in fact, concerned the enforcement of a maritime lien claim for salvage, that is, a truly *in rem* claim. The owners of the ship had put up bail, but the sum awarded exceeded the bail. The question was, whether the owners were personally liable for the balance of the judgment, which exceeded the bail amount, and it was held that they were.

The decision was severely criticised by Wiswall,[44] who claimed with audacity that Sir Francis Jeune did not cite any authority for his proposition, which was in complete contradiction to what was thought at the time by other eminent judges. In particular, it has been argued by Wiswall that Jeune J confused the action *in rem* with the maritime attachment,[45] which was a procedural device designed to compel the appearance of a defendant in an action *in personam* (a jurisdiction *in personam*), if he was absent, by seizing his property. This was by no means a proceeding *in rem*. 'It is this crucial distinction,' the author says, 'which was so deftly grasped by Sir John Jervis,[46] and so unfortunately ignored by Sir Francis Jeune'.[47] However, the procedural theory prevailed and, but for two decisions,[48] which concern truly *in rem* claims and seem to be against it, there have been no other authorities that are inconsistent with *The Dictator*.[49]

---

41 *The Dictator* [1892] PD 304, *per* Jeune J.

42 This derived from *The Bold Buccleugh* (1850) 7 Moo 267, p 282, in which the Privy Council (Sir John Jervis) had held that the action *in rem* was not a procedural device for obtaining personal jurisdiction over shipowners, but a unique proceeding directly against the ship.

43 [1892] PD 304.

44 See Wiswall, FL (Jr), *Development of Admiralty Jurisdiction Since 1800*, 1970, CUP.

45 See Chapter 1, para 1, above.

46 In *The Bold Buccleugh* (1850) 7 Moo 267.

47 See *ibid*, Wiswall, Chapter 6, 'The evolution of the action *in rem*', p 165.

48 *The Longford* (1889) 14 PD 34, which was not cited in argument, nor was it considered by the Court of Appeal in *The Gemma* [1899] P 285, which approved *The Dictator* [1892] PD 304. In *The Burns* [1907] P 137, Moulton LJ repudiated the procedural theory and in effect overruled Jeune J's decision on the point.

49 *Ibid*, Wiswall, p 198.

Before examining how the House of Lords recently treated *The Dictator* in *The Indian Grace*, first, it is important to outline the features of the *in rem* proceedings as had prevailed up to this latter decision. Later, it will be seen to what extent *The Indian Grace* has affected the features of the *in rem* claim.

3.4 Nature and features of the *in rem* claim prior to *The Indian Grace (No 2)*[50]

(a) The *in rem* proceeding (whether the claim is truly *in rem* or not) is primarily a vehicle of obtaining security for the claim.

(b) It is also a vehicle of founding jurisdiction on the merits of the claim by the arrest of the ship within this jurisdiction (subject to certain limitations and restrictions, which will be examined later).

(c) With regard to maritime liens, the *in rem* proceeding gives effect to an already accrued maritime lien on the ship, which dates back to the date of its creation. The maritime lien is enforceable against the relevant ship, notwithstanding the change of ownership, either prior to, or after the issue of the proceeding, or liability *in personam*.

(d) With regard to non-truly *in rem* claims, the *in rem* proceeding causes a statutory right *in rem*, or lien, to accrue on the ship from the time of issue of the *in rem* proceeding. From that time, the *in rem* claim is enforceable against the ship, regardless of a subsequent transfer of ownership to a *bona fide* purchaser without notice.

(e) Whether truly or non-truly *in rem* claims, the value of the ship had always been the limit for the satisfaction of maritime claims, unless the defendant acknowledged service of the *in rem* proceeding, or otherwise submitted to the jurisdiction unconditionally, whereupon the action became also *in personam*.[51]

(f) In the absence of acknowledgment of service or submission to jurisdiction, the *in rem* proceeding, as far as domestic law was concerned, remained solely *in rem* and no personal jurisdiction over the owner, or the person liable *in personam*, would be created by service. However, the *in rem* proceeding forced the defendant interested in the ship to 'appear' and either defend the claim or contest jurisdiction over him.

(g) A court sale by the admiral marshal, consequent to judgment in the action *in rem*, extinguishes all encumbrances on the ship and gives a clean title to the purchaser.

---

50 [1998] 1 Lloyd's Rep 1

51 *The Nordglimt* [1988] QB 183; *The Maciej Rataj (sub nom The Tatry)* [1992] 2 Lloyd's Rep 552 (CA): after acknowledgment the action continued as a hybrid action, being both *in personam* and *in rem*, but without losing its previous *in rem* character; in *The Anna H* [1995] 1 Lloyd's Rep 11 (CA) the same principle was followed.

3.5 The nature of the *in rem* claim after *The Indian Grace (No 2)*

3.5.1 The decision

The House of Lords, in *The Indian Grace*, has brought some changes which may have drastically affected some features of the action *in rem*, or *in rem* claim, if the decision is correct.

It was held that the action *in rem* is against the owners of the ship from the moment of service of the writ (now claim form). The reasoning of this decision is first examined and, then, an attempt is made to explore its consequences and effect on the features of the *in rem* claim, as seen above.

3.5.1.1 Factual background

A cargo of munitions was carried on board the vessel from Sweden to Cochin, India. During the voyage, fire broke out in No 3 hold, necessitating her to divert to the nearest port for inspection. Some shells and charges had to be jettisoned. The remaining cargo was repacked and re-stowed. Some of the boxes of the cargo showed damage but the vessel resumed her voyage and, finally, discharged the cargo at destination on 4 September 1987. The Ministry of Defence, on behalf of the Indian Government, wrote to the defendants claiming a total loss of £2.6 m. Eventually, on 1 September 1988, a claim was made in India seeking damages only for the undelivered (that is, jettisoned) cargo for £7000, on the ground of negligence and carelessness of the defendants while the cargo was in transit.

On 25 August 1989 (before judgment in the Indian action), the claimants brought an action *in rem* in England. On 16 December 1989, judgment was delivered in India. On 4 May 1990, *The Indian Endurance*, a sister ship of *The Indian Grace*, was arrested. The owners submitted to English jurisdiction, provided security for the claim and the ship was allowed to sail. The claimants amended their claim, claiming damages for £2.6 m. (in respect of the damaged cargo in hold No 3) on the ground of breach of contract to make the ship seaworthy and failure to take reasonable care in the stowage and carriage. The owners pleaded, originally, issue estoppel as a defence, and were later allowed to amend their defence to rely on s 34 (*res judicata*) of the Civil Jurisdiction and Judgments Act (CJJA) 1982. Only s 34 is relevant here.

The judge struck out the English action because the cause of action was the same as that on which the claimants relied when they obtained a judgment in India. Section 34 was an absolute bar to it. The Court of Appeal dismissed an appeal by the claimants. At the House of Lords,[52] it was raised for the first time that the judgment of the Indian Court was not a judgment between the

---

52   *The Indian Grace (No 1)* [1993] 1 Lloyd's Rep 387, or [1993] AC 410.

same parties, as the parties in the *in rem* action. Thus, the case was remitted to the judge to determine this issue. Clarke J held that the *in rem* action was against the ship, while the Indian action was *in personam*. Therefore, s 34 did not apply to bar the English *in rem* action. The Court of Appeal reversed this decision on the ground that, the owners of the vessel served with the action *in rem* were the same person as the defendants in the Indian action. The owners appealed.

One of the questions for the House of Lords, this time round, was whether a judgment obtained against the owners of the ship in India for shortage of cargo was a bar to the *in rem* claim brought by the claimants in England by virtue of s 34, which provides that:

> ... no proceedings may be brought by a person in England and Wales ... on a cause of action in respect of which a judgment has been given in his favour in proceedings between the same parties, or their privies ... in a court of an overseas country, unless that judgment is not enforceable or entitled to recognition in England and Wales.

Thus, the issue was whether the action *in personam* in India was between the same parties as the action *in rem* in England for the purpose of s 34.[53]

3.5.1.2 Ratio decidendi

It was held that for the purpose of s 34, an action *in rem* was an action against the owners from the moment the Admiralty Court was seised with jurisdiction. The court was seised, or its jurisdiction was invoked, by the service of the writ, or where the writ was deemed to be served, as a result of acknowledgment of the issue of the writ by the defendant before service. From that moment, the owners were parties to the proceedings *in rem* and s 34 was a bar to the action *in rem*.[54]

3.5.1.3 The reasons

Lord Steyn, who delivered judgment, sought support for this conclusion from previous authorities, starting from a historical perspective[55] of the action *in rem*, as follows:

---

53 *Indian Grace (No 2)* [1998] 1 Lloyd's Rep 1 (HL). See, also, Chapter 6, para 2.3.4.4, below.

54 Clarke J, at first instance – who followed Moulton LJ in *The Burns* [1907] P 137 (above): that 'the action *in rem* is against the ship itself' and Hobhouse J, in *The Nordglimt* [1988] QB 183 (above): that 'the action *in rem* is against the ship until the defendant acknowledges service of the proceeding' – held that s 34 was inapplicable because the parties in the two sets of proceedings were different at the inception of the proceedings and before acknowledgment of service.

55 For a more extensive historical perspective, see, also, Chapter 1, above.

The historical background

During the struggle for power between the common law courts and the High Court of Admiralty, the common law courts effectively blocked the assumption by the High Court of Admiralty of *in personam* jurisdiction. This was done by writs of prohibition, which did not, however, extend to the admiralty jurisdiction over the ship. Admiralty practitioners and judges used the concept that the ship was a defendant in an action *in rem*, as a means of defending and extending the jurisdiction of the High Court of Admiralty. An enlarged view was taken of what constituted a maritime lien. The personification theory flourished. But, this struggle for power was ended by the JAs in 1873–75. Although the ship was still regarded as both the source and limit of liability, the personification theory fell into decline after these Acts. Four reasons contributed to this decline (he said): first, the action *in rem* was permitted in new categories of claims not just maritime liens. Second, there was a new procedure introduced in 1883 by which the owners of the vessel were named as defendants. It was easier to regard an action *in rem* as an action against the owners of the vessel, thus, he said:

> ... the procedural theory stripped away the form and revealed that, in substance, the owners were parties to the action *in rem*.[56]

Third, until the JAs, it was not possible to combine actions *in rem* and *in personam*. Fourth, judges of the Admiralty Court, with its non-common law roots, were more sympathetic to the personification theory than those trained in the common law. But the breakthrough, Lord Steyn said, came with *The Dictator*[57] and quoted the well known passage of Sir Francis Jeune, in that:

> ... the action *in rem* ...not only determines the amount of the liability, and in default of payment enforces it on the *res*, but is also a means of *enforcing against the appearing owners, if they could have been made personally liable* [emphasis added] in the Admiralty Court, the complete claim of the plaintiff, so far as the owners are liable to meet it.

Lord Steyn was convinced of the change in the character of the action *in rem* and said:

> ... since *The Dictator*, the law has been that once the owners enter an appearance (or in modern phraseology when they acknowledge issue of the writ) there are two parallel actions: the action *in personam* and the action *in rem*. From that moment the owners are defendants in the action *in personam*.[58]

To complete the historical perspective, he referred to all other cases supporting *The Dictator*. For example, he referred to Scrutton LJ in *The Tervaete*[59] who had affirmed the procedural view, thus:

---

56 *The Indian Grace (No 2)* [1998] 1 Lloyd's Rep 1, pp 6, 7.
57 [1892] P 304, p 320
58 *The Indian Grace (No 2)* [1998] 1 Lloyd's Rep 1, p 7.
59 (1922) 12 LlL Rep 252, p 254.

... the action *in rem* was not based upon the wrongdoing of the ship personified as an offender, but was a means of bringing the owner of the ship to meet this personal liability by seizing his property.[60]

Further, he stressed that the Court of Appeal, in *The Gemma*,[61] endorsed *The Dictator*, which prevailed, despite the support of the personification theory by Moulton LJ in another Court of Appeal case, *The Burns*.[62] In addition, he said the House of Lords, in *The Cristina*,[63] unambiguously rejected the personification theory and adopted the view that, in an action *in rem*, the owners were the defendants.[64]

The sovereign immunity cases

Lord Steyn next relied on the sovereign immunity cases, such as *The Parlement Belge*,[65] *The Cristina*[66] and *The Arantzazu Mendi*,[67] which, he said, established that the sovereign is directly impleaded by the service of the action *in rem* on its vessel. Therefore, the sovereign immunity principle then applied.

Recent decisions

Referring to more recent cases, he quoted Lord Brandon, in *The August 8*:[68]

... once a defendant in an admiralty action *in rem* has *entered an appearance* in such an action, he has submitted himself personally to the jurisdiction of the court, and *the result of that is that, from then on, the action continues against him not only as an action in rem but also as an action in personam* ...

Furthermore, in the context of the European Civil Jurisdiction Conventions (ECJCs),[69] he drew support from *The Deichland*,[70] in which the Court of Appeal held that the owner of the vessel who is served with the proceedings *in rem* is 'sued' for the purpose of Art 2 of the Brussels Convention. Also, in this context, the European Court of Justice (ECJ) ruled in *The Maciej Rataj* (*sub nom The Tatry*)[71] that an action *in rem* and an action *in personam* involved the

---

60 This passage harks back to the maritime attachment which was possible through an action *in personam* mentioned by Wiswall, *op cit*, fn 44.

61 [1899] P 285, p 291.

62 [1907] P 137, p 149.

63 (1938) 60 LlL Rep 147.

64 Lord Steyn qualified the position with regard to maritime liens to which the procedural theory would not be appropriate, but, since this case was not concerned with a maritime lien, he put this issue to one side.

65 (1880) 5 PD 197.

66 [1938] AC 485 (HL).

67 (1939) 63 LlL Rep 89.

68 [1983] 1 Lloyd's Rep 351, p 355 (emphasis added).

69 This topic is discussed in Chapter 6 with the relevant cases.

70 [1989] 2 Lloyd's Rep 113.

71 [1995] 1 Lloyd's Rep 302 (ECJ).

same cause of action and the same parties for the purpose of Art 21 of the Brussels Convention 1968.

Against this background, Lord Steyn concluded that, since Art 21 and s 34 had similar wording, it would be curious if one were to give a different meaning in interpreting the words 'between the same parties', which appear in both provisions. He said that given the decision of the ECJ in *The Tatry, The Nordglimt*, on which Clarke J relied, at first instance, of *The Indian Grace*, was no longer good law.

3.5.2 Criticisms of the decision in The Indian Grace (No 2)

While the *ratio decidendi* of this decision does not seem to give rise to any objections, insofar as s 34 is concerned, the reasoning of Lord Steyn's judgment appears to go further than that. It would be sufficient for the purpose of s 34, which was the issue in this case, if he had only relied on judgments that dealt with the application of Art 21 of the Brussels Convention, which has a similar wording to s 34 of CJJA 1982. There was no need to overhaul the action *in rem*, as has been known in domestic English procedural law. What is wrong with this decision is now examined.

3.5.2.1 The misapplication of the procedural theory decisions

There is no doubt that, despite the origin of the action *in rem*, which was distinct from the old procedure of the maritime attachment (by which the defendant was compelled to appear in court in an action *in personam*), the procedural theory of an action *in rem*, as developed since the decision of Jeune J. in *The Dictator*, prevailed. But the problem arising from *The Indian Grace* does not stem from whether or not the procedural theory applies to *in rem* claims. It stems from the misapplication of the cases that advocated this theory.

All the cases upon which the House of Lords relied, in *The Indian Grace*, consistently referred to the 'appearance' of the defendant in the action *in rem* as being the trigger of creating a personal jurisdiction against the defendant. The procedure of 'appearance' used in the past is now equated to the procedure of 'acknowledgment' of service, or of the issue of the proceedings under the present rules.[72]

The House of Lords, in *The Indian Grace*, instead of applying the *ratio decidendi* and the *dicta* quoted from those authorities, which expressly referred to the 'appearance' of the defendant, interchanged this word for the word 'service' of the writ or equated the word 'appearance' only with 'acknowledgment of issue of the writ', in modern phraseology. While the service of the proceedings may compel the defendant to appear, at that time, he has not yet taken a step to become a party to the proceedings, unless he

---

72 It will be seen under para 3.7 how Nigel Meeson deals with this aspect of the decision.

had already chosen to acknowledge the issue of the proceedings, which would have been a 'deemed' service.

The fact that there was a consistent reference in the old decisions to the 'appearance' of the defendant, which was regarded as the incident creating personal jurisdiction over him, is clearly shown from the following extracts of the relevant judgments:

In particular, Smith LJ had pointed out, in *The Gemma* that:

> ... if the defendants had not appeared, and the proceedings had throughout been solely *in rem*, the judgment ... according to the practice of Admiralty Court, would have been not ... condemning the defendants ... but would have condemned the ship alone.[73]

And in *The Beldis*,[74] Sir Boyd Merriman said that:

> It is true that, unless the defendant appears to an action *in rem*, satisfaction of the judgment is limited to the value of the *res*, but if the defendant appears, the action proceeds *in personam*, as well as *in rem*. In such a case, as where the action is brought *in personam* in the first instance, execution can issue against any property of the defendant, including any surplus value of the *res* over and above the amount for which bail has been given.

Moulton LJ, in *The Burns*,[75] commented on *The Dictator* and *The Gemma* as follows:

> They both of them treat the appearance as introducing the characteristics of an action *in personam*. In other words, it is not the institution of suit that makes it a proceeding *in personam*, but the appearance of the defendant.

In the same vein of thinking, Hobhouse J, in *The Nordglimt*,[76] pointed out the time at which the action *in rem* would be enforceable also *in personam*, and said:

> Unless and until anyone appears to defend an action *in rem*, the action proceeds solely as an action *in rem* and any judgment given is solely a judgment given against the *res*. It is determinative and conclusive as against all the world in respect of the rights in the *res*, but does not create any rights that are enforceable *in personam*. An action *in rem* may be defended by anyone who has a legitimate interest in resisting the plaintiff's claim on the *res*. Such a person may be the owner of the *res* but, equally, it may be someone who has a different interest in the *res* which does not amount to ownership, or, again, it may be simply someone who also has a claim *in rem* against the *res* and is competing with the plaintiff for a right to the security of a *res* of an inadequate value to satisfy all the claims that are being made upon it ...Unless and until a person liable *in personam* chooses to defend an action *in rem*, the action *in rem* will not give rise to any determination as against such person of any personal

---

73 [1899] P 285, p 291.
74 [1936] P 51, pp 75–76.
75 [1907] P 137, p 148.
76 [1987] 2 Lloyd's Rep 470.

liability on his part, nor will it give rise to any judgment which is enforceable *in personam* against any such person.[77]

Apparently, this was consistent with the authorities on which Lord Steyn relied in *The Indian Grace*, but, nevertheless, Lord Steyn declared that *The Nordglimt* was no longer good law.

3.5.2.2 The sovereign immunity cases[78] – an inappropriate parallel

These deal with specialised statutes, the aim of which is to protect a foreign sovereign from being compelled to come to this court. Thus, neither in personam nor in rem proceedings are permitted even to be issued against a foreign sovereign, if its ships do not trade for commercial purposes. Scrutton LJ had explained, in *The Jupiter*,[79] the position of a foreign sovereign by referring to the old practice of the Admiralty Court:

> The appearance of a person interested in property used to be enforced, either by seizing him to make him appear, or by seizing his ship, or by seizing his property other than his ship; but, the object of all the processes of seizing was to make the man appear, so that he might be a personal defendant to the action. *If he did appear, he at once became personally liable to the judgment of the court* [emphasis added]. If he did not appear, the court, having given him the opportunity of appearing, might take away his property ... The foreign government, which does claim a right or interest in the ship, must do one of three things. First, it may appear to defend, but it cannot be compelled to appear; secondly, if it were not to appear and let the action go on, the court might feel able to forfeit the property of a foreign sovereign; thirdly, it can come to the court and say: 'I am not going to discuss what my title is; I say I am a foreign sovereign; I claim a right in this property, and you cannot compel me to come to your court to show you that I have good cause for saying that it is my property.'

Whether it is the issue of proceedings, or the service, or the arrest of a ship of a foreign sovereign that impleads it, the foreign immunity cases are not concerned with when the foreign State becomes a party to the *in rem* proceedings.[80] They are concerned with the fact that 'the writ commands an appearance to be entered' and that alone would constitute impleading of the foreign sovereign.[81] In any event, in most cases referred to by Lord Steyn, the 'appearance' of the foreign sovereign, rather than the service of process upon it, was more relevant to the issue of impleading. There is ample evidence of this in this group of decisions, as well as, for example, in the above citation

---

77 [1987] 2 Lloyd's Rep 470, p 482.

78 *The Parliament Belge* (1880) 5 PD 197; *The Cristina* (1938) 60 LlL Rep 147; *The Arantzazu Mendi* (1939) 63 LlL Rep 89.

79 [1924] P 236, p 243.

80 See, also, in this respect a critique of *The Indian Grace* by Teare, N (QC), 'The admiralty action *in rem* and the House of Lords' 1998 LMCLQ 33, p 39.

81 *The Cristina* [1938] AC 485 (HL), *per* Lord Wright.

and in the speeches of both Lord Atkin and Lord Wright in *The Cristina*[82] (in which the ship had been arrested). In particular, Lord Atkin said:

> In any case, when they do appear as defendants, and as such I conceive that they are impleaded. And when they cannot be heard to protect their interest unless they appear as defendants, I incline to hold that … they are by the very terms of the writ impleaded.

3.5.2.3 The service of proceedings is important in the context of the Brussels/Lugano Convention

Under Art 21 of the Brussels Convention, when it has to be determined which of the courts of the two Contracting States – in which proceedings involve the same cause of action and are between the same parties – is seised first, the time of service is important. The court seised second of the matter[83] is obliged to stay its proceedings until the jurisdiction of the court first seised is determined.[84] (It should be noted, however, that the amending Regulation (44/2001/EC), which will replace the Brussels Convention when it comes into force on 1 March 2002, provides in Art 30 that a court shall be deemed seised at the time when the document instituting the proceedings is lodged with the court.)

In *The Deichland*,[85] in which one of the issues was whether the rules of the Brussels Convention applied to actions *in rem*, it was explained by Sir Denys Buckley that before unconditional appearance in the *in rem* proceedings, the defendant did not become liable *in personam*.[86] Neil LJ also said that 'it is Deich who is interested in contesting liability and against whom the plaintiff would wish to proceed *in personam* if an *appearance is entered*'.[87] Only for the purpose of the Convention, was it held that it was impossible to conclude that Deich was not being sued, even though, at that time, the proceedings were solely *in rem*. So, the action *in rem* and the action *in personam* were regarded as being between the same parties from the time of service. However, it was recognised that the action *in rem* had special characteristics, but that its characteristics could not affect the application of the rules of the Brussels Convention. Neil LJ said in this context:

> By English law an admiralty action *in rem* has special characteristics …I do not consider, however, that the rules relating to such actions and governing the rights of a plaintiff to levy execution can affect the substance of the matter

---

82 [1938] 60 LlL Rep 147, pp 157 and 163.

83 See, later, *The Duke Yare* [1991] 2 Lloyd's Rep 557 (CA) and *The Freccia del Nord* [1989] 1 Lloyd's Rep 388.

84 See Chapter 6.

85 [1990] 1 QB 361, the Court of Appeal held that the owner of the vessel, which is served with the proceedings *in rem*, is 'sued' for the purpose of s 2 of the CJJA 1982.

86 *Ibid*, p 389.

87 *Ibid*, p 373 (emphasis added).

when the court is faced with an international convention designed to regulate the international jurisdiction of national courts.[88]

The incident of service, which causes the jurisdiction of the court to be seised, is distinct from the defendant's unconditional submission to jurisdiction.

The cases concerned with the ECJCs aim to provide a consistent interpretation of the Convention rules and, therefore, no importance is to be attached to the fact that the proceedings may be of a different nature under the civil procedural law of one or other of the States concerned.[89] Thus, it is submitted, that no general principle can be drawn from these cases that can affect the nature of the *in rem* proceedings (that is, up to the incident of appearance, or, in the modern phraseology, the acknowledgment of either the service or the issue of the proceedings).

Similarly, since *The Indian Grace* concerned the application of s 34 of the CJJA 1982, which has similar wording to Art 21 of the Brussels Convention, the principle drawn from this case ought to be limited to what was in issue. Namely, whether an *in rem* claim in England or Wales was barred by s 34 after judgment was given *in personam* in favour of the claimant in the foreign court on the ground that, if the respective actions concerned the same cause of action and persons, *res judicata* would apply. In other words, no new trial would be permitted afresh. Logically, therefore, the remaining *dicta* in the decision, which were not strictly relevant to determining this issue, ought to be disregarded, particularly because they are remarkably wrong. If this conclusion is not correct, the potential consequences of the decision are analysed below.

3.5.3 Consequences of The Indian Grace[90]

It has been trite procedural law that the acknowledgment of service of the *in rem* proceedings (or, as was previously, the 'appearance' by the defendant) renders him personally involved in the proceedings, so that payment of any unsatisfied balance of the claim over and above the value of the ship can be enforced against him (if he is found liable) by a writ of execution, *fieri facias*.[91] Seizure of another ship in his fleet by the sheriff would be possible only as a means of execution of judgment which is different from an arrest of the ship by a warrant of arrest.

If, indeed, the service of the *in rem* proceedings – regardless of lack of acknowledgment of service or submission to jurisdiction by the defendant – was to have an effect beyond the scope of s 34, the following consequences might result.

---

88 [1990] 1 QB 361, pp 373–74.
89 *The Tatry* [1995] 1 Lloyd's Rep 302 (ECJ), *per* Advocate General.
90 *Op cit*, Teare, fn 80.
91 See, eg, *The Gemma* [1899] P 285.

3.5.3.1 The Indian Grace may have indirectly undermined The Monica S

It is important to note that this decision was not referred to at the hearing in the House of Lords, although it was at first instance. The long standing principle of *The Monica S* has been that, by the issue of the *in rem* proceeding, a statutory right *in rem* irrevocably accrues on the ship[92] and the ship can be arrested, even if she has subsequently been transferred to a *bona fide* purchaser without notice.[93]

There may be two consequences of *The Indian Grace* upon this decision:

(a) Since it held that the *in rem* action is against the owner of the ship from service, a claimant, who has issued *in rem* proceedings, but did not obtain security, may arguably not be allowed to pursue those proceedings by arresting the relevant ship after a foreign judgment on the same issues has been given. That was the sequence of events in *The Indian Grace*. However, for the purpose of obtaining security, such an argument should not be correct, because, on the facts of *The Indian Grace*, albeit that the ship was not sold to a *bona fide* buyer after the issue of the writ, the claimant arrested the ship after the Indian judgment had been obtained for the purpose of retrying the same issues. It is arguable, therefore, that, if the arrest is made only for the purpose of obtaining security to satisfy the judgment, the principle of *The Monica S* is not undermined. If this were correct, the arrest of the ship in the hands of the purchaser for this purpose should not be barred by s 34 (see para 3.6).

(b) Another matter which ought to be clarified is this: bearing in mind the principle of *The Monica S*, assume the following scenario. A ship, heavily burdened with claims for which *in rem* claim forms have been issued, is sold to a *bona fide* purchaser, who owns a fleet of ships registered in the name of the same company that bought this ship. After the transfer of the ship, a claim form is served and the ship is arrested. The 'sins of the forefathers' are visited upon the new purchaser. Hoping to get an indemnity from the seller, he decides not to acknowledge service in order to save legal costs. The court proceeds with judicial sale. Prior to

---

92 In a question before the court whether a maritime claimant becomes a secured creditor against the ship from the issue or the service of the writ, vis a vis the creditors of the shipowning company, which is faced with winding-up, the Court of Appeal held, unanimously, in *Re Aro Co Ltd* [1979] 2 WLR 150, that, regardless of whether the plaintiffs had invoked the jurisdiction of the Admiralty Court prior to the winding-up, they should be considered as having the status of secured creditors because, after the issue of the writ, they could have served it and could have arrested *The Aro* with the result that the vessel would effectively be encumbered with their claim. Brightman LJ stated at p 465: 'The service of the writ adds nothing to the status of the claimant vis a vis the vessel sued. This is established by the issue of the writ. As between the plaintiff and the defendant, service merely causes time to commence running within which the defendant must enter appearance in order to avoid being a respondent to a motion for judgment by default.'

93 This decision was not cited to the court, so the Lords did not put their mind to it.

The Indian Grace, the action would remain solely *in rem* and the owner, or the person interested in the ship, who did not acknowledge service of the proceeding *in rem*, would not be a party to the proceedings. If the service of the proceedings *in rem* were to render the person interested in the ship personally liable after *The Indian Grace*, what would the buyer's position be with regard to an *in rem* judgment obtained in default? Would his other ships be at risk if the judgment exceeded the value of the ship arrested? It is submitted that they would not for the following reason.

The Monica S dealt with the accrual of a security interest in the ship from the issue of the *in rem* proceedings, while *The Indian Grace* dealt with personal jurisdiction over the relevant defendant created from the time of service of the *in rem* proceedings for the purpose of *res judicata*. The effect of *The Indian Grace* is to make the previous owner only, who would be interested in defending the claim, bound by the proceedings personally[94] from the time of the service, and not the *bona fide* buyer of the ship.

A risk of arrest of the ship bought by an innocent purchaser existed, anyway, prior to *The Indian Grace*. Upon service of the proceedings *in rem* on the ship, the new owner in the above scenario may acknowledge service conditionally to contest personal jurisdiction over him on the ground that he was not the person liable *in personam* for the relevant claim.[95] He could do this, also, before *The Indian Grace*. The claimant, in reality, is after the person liable *in personam* hoping that, if he still exists, some pressure exercised upon him by the buyer will compel him to put up security for the claim through his P&I insurer.

If the seller exists, then the buyer will be able to enforce his remedy for an indemnity or damages under the sale contract and, presumably, the seller's liability insurer would put up security in respect of the buyer's claim. If he does not exist, the ship will still be the limit of liability for the claims against the ship. In the latter case, the risk of the buyer will be, as always has been, that, in the event the proceeds of sale of the ship are exhausted to satisfy the claimants, he will have lost his asset and will be unable to obtain indemnity from the non-existing seller. The issue of an indemnity from the previous owner is a separate matter and a risk that buyers should always bear in mind. It may be worth considering insuring against such a risk, or obtaining a bank guarantee from the seller in the event the ship is encumbered with liens and debts or the risk of being arrested.[96] Obtaining some form of insurance or security for such a risk is even more important after the new Civil Procedure Rules (CPR). While, prior to CPR, the buyer's lawyer was able to check in the

---

94 In *The Dictator* [1892] PD 304, it was stressed that the action *in rem* was against 'the *appearing owner if he could be made personally liable*' (emphasis added).

95 This conclusion may be inferred from the actual judgment of Lord Steyn in *Indian Grace (No 2)* [1998] 1 Lloyd's Rep 1 (HL), p 9.

96 See Chapter 11.

Admiralty Court Book whether a writ had been issued against the ship intended to be bought, after the CPR he may only search for claims which have been served.[97]

From the point of view of the claimant, however, if a statutory right *in rem* does not accrue from the issue, but from the service, of the *in rem* proceeding, the transfer of ownership before service would defeat the right *in rem*, except in the case of truly *in rem* claims. As was discussed earlier, (para 3.2.2) the words 'action brought' in s 21 of the SCA 1981, which regulates the mode in which the jurisdiction of the Admiralty Court can be exercised, mean, according to Brandon J in *The Monica S*, 'institution of suit', which does not include service. This principle has never been challenged[98] and it was not raised as an issue in *The Indian Grace*.

3.5.3.2 The effect of The Indian Grace on other assets of the defendant who would be liable in personam

Prior to *The Indian Grace*, if the relevant person, who would be liable *in personam* for the claim, did not acknowledge service of the *in rem* proceeding, or did not submit to jurisdiction unconditionally, judgment obtained in the action would be executed only against the ship arrested, even if the amount adjudged exceeded the value of the ship.

If the decision in *The Indian Grace* is intended to have a wide application, it has certainly affected the extent of liability of owners and demise charterers of the ship in connection with which the claim arose. Other ships in the fleet of the beneficial owner or demise charterer of the arrested ship, whether or not they acknowledge service of the *in rem* claim form, will now be exposed to a risk of execution of judgment, if the ship is served with the *in rem* proceedings when she comes within the jurisdiction.

Morally, there is nothing wrong with that effect of the decision.

3.5.3.3 Risk management issues

If the relevant ship, or a sister ship, was not yet due to come within the jurisdiction, so as to be served with the *in rem* claim form, it would obviously be unwise if solicitors acting for shipowners or demise charterers accepted service of the *in rem* claim form.

Despite what has been noted in the previous paragraph, in practice, *The Indian Grace* may not make any difference to personal liability, if the person

---

97 Under CPR, Pt 5, members of the public may only search for claim forms that have been served, so he will not be in a position to find out whether a writ has been issued (see fn 30). In the past, if his solicitors had omitted to check the Admiralty Registry, perhaps he could have an action in damages against them.

98 See reference to it by the Hong Kong Court of Final Appeal in *The Tian Sheng (No 8)* [2000] 2 Lloyd's Rep 430, p 432.

who would be liable *in personam* did not have any other assets than the ship of the one-ship company. In most cases, security is provided to a claimant who threatens to serve the *in rem* proceeding when the ship is about to come to the jurisdiction. In the event that the person interested in the ship provides or procures the provision of an undertaking for security of the claim – in consideration of no arrest or re-arrest of the relevant ship or any other ship in the same or associated ownership or management – it may be prudent to include that any judgment or award obtained will not be enforceable against the person liable for more than the amount given in the undertaking. If this is possible to be agreed, the person concerned (that is, the company) will have to be included as a party to such an undertaking, which is usually signed by the liability insurer.

The decision's possible effect on personal liability is also ameliorated when the person liable constitutes a limitation fund in accordance with the provisions of the Limitation Conventions. Since the fund will be the limit of liability, presumably no judgment obtained for a claim that may be raised against the fund will be enforced against the person liable, for, if it were otherwise, it would be contrary to the philosophy behind the Limitation Convention.[99]

3.6 Extent to which the features of the *in rem* action are affected by *The Indian Grace*

Most of the features of the *in rem* action (mentioned under para 3.4, above) should still remain the same: that is, it is a means of obtaining security for the claim, judgment, or arbitral award, by arresting the ship; it gives effect to the inchoate right of a maritime lien, which can be enforced irrespective of change of ownership; it creates a security right on the ship from the moment of its issue for claims non-truly *in rem*; sale of the ship by the admiralty marshal wipes out all encumbrances or claims on the ship. The decision may, however, have an impact upon personal liability of the defendant who would be liable *in personam*. In particular:

(a) In theory, the value of the ship will no longer be the limit of liability for the satisfaction of maritime claims, which arose in connection with the ship, once the *in rem* claim form is served, whereupon the action becomes also *in personam* from that moment, whether or not the defendant chooses to acknowledge service.

Except in the case of a *bona fide* buyer of the ship, as explained earlier, personal liability of the owner or demise charterer (that is, the person

---

99 Limitation Convention 1976, Art 13(2), see Chapter 16.

liable *in personam*) will arise if the value of the ship is not sufficient to satisfy all the claims.

(b) Although the House of Lords, in *The Indian Grace*, stated that the case before it did not concern maritime liens, nevertheless, it proceeded to support its reasoning by relying on authorities concerned with truly *in rem* claims. Bearing in mind, however, that maritime liens can be enforced either as maritime liens under s 21(3) regardless of personal liability of the owner, or as statutory rights *in rem* under s 21(4) of the SCA 1981, the result would arguably be the same as in non-truly *in rem* claims. Depending on who would be liable *in personam*, for example, in a collision, the owner or demise charterer, that person will inevitably be involved personally in the action from the service of proceedings, whether or not he chooses to acknowledge service. What is important, in the context of s 34 of the CJJA 1982 and Art 21 of the Brussels Convention, is who is the person interested in defending the claim. The maritime lien could be enforced against the ship to the extent of realising the security attached on the ship for such a claim, of which see below.

(c) *The Indian Grace* decided, at least, that for the purpose of s 34, the parties to a foreign judgment *in personam* will be the same as the parties to English *in rem* proceedings (concerning the same cause of action as the foreign judgment) from the time of the service of the *in rem* proceedings.[100] Could, then, the enforceability of a maritime lien, which by its nature is enforceable against the *res*, regardless of liability *in personam*, be barred by s 34 when a foreign judgment on liability has been obtained and remains unsatisfied? Although the House of Lords did not have to decide this, it is submitted that the answer would be in the negative for the following reasons: the old rule of no merger between a judgment *in personam* and proceedings *in rem* was necessary to protect maritime lien claimants,[101] who were concerned to realise their security

---

100 The same principle applies to *in rem* and *in personam* proceedings brought in Contracting States to the Brussels/Lugano Conventions in the context of Art 21: *The Deichland* [1990] 1 QB 361; *The Maciej Rataj* [1995] 1 Lloyd's Rep 302, see Chapter 6, para 2.3.4.4, below.

101 The issue whether s 34 of CJJA 1982 has abolished the old rule: 'That an unsatisfied foreign judgment obtained *in personam* is no bar to an action *in rem*, which had been established in cases of maritime liens', was not decided by the House of Lords in *The Indian Grace*. The rule was thought to be ancient and strange and Lord Steyn did not wish to extend it beyond the limits laid down by authority. There was discussion at the hearing that the rule of no merger would be irrelevant in cases of non-maritime liens when the ship has been transferred to a new owner after judgment because, in any event, it would not be possible to establish personal liability for the claim under the SCA 1981, s 21(4). Nigel Meeson, in *Admiralty Jurisdiction and Practice*, 2nd edn, 2000, LLP, discusses (pp 82–84) how *The Indian Grace* has not affected truly *in rem* claims, so a judgment in a claim truly *in rem* is not a bar to a subsequent claim *in personam* and vice versa. The author of the present book submits that *The Indian Grace* dealt with the issue of *res judicata* under the CJJA 1982, s 34 and was not concerned with the enforcement of maritime liens, or an accrued right of security on the ship, or the mere right of a maritime claimant to obtain security against which a foreign judgment could be enforced (see Chapter 4, paras 5.5.2–5.5.3).

by arresting the ship if security had not been obtained. In old cases, when a claimant could not recover the fruits of his judgment at common law because the judgment remained unsatisfied, he was permitted to proceed *in rem*. In Dr Lushington's decisions, *The Bengal*[102] (master's wages) and *The John and Mary*[103] (collision case), the issue was one of realising the security attached on the ship, the maritime lien, and not an issue of a cause of action, or jurisdiction on the merits. The clear effect of *The Indian Grace* is that the person who has obtained a foreign judgment in his favour will be barred from relitigating the same cause of action afresh through *in rem* proceedings, unless the judgment is not enforceable or entitled to be recognised in England and Wales or, as the case may be, in Northern Ireland. Even if the judgment is partly in his favour, no retrial of the same issues will be permitted unless the judgment cannot be recognised or enforced. It follows that if the claimant has lost in the foreign proceedings, the section will have no application, although the principles of estoppel should operate to prevent a second action.[104] The decision has not touched the issue whether a claimant can realise his security by arresting the ship. In other words, a distinction must be made between invoking jurisdiction on the merits and seeking the assistance of the court with the view to obtaining security. It is submitted that s 34 should not be a bar to *in rem* proceedings used only for the latter purpose and not for the retrial of the same cause of action. This should be applicable to both truly *in rem* claims and to statutory liens *in rem*.[105] Such an analysis is strengthened by the fact that, since s 26 of the CJJA 1982 has been in force, assistance is provided to all maritime claimants to arrest a ship to obtain security, even if the jurisdiction on the merits of a case is arbitration or another court abroad. Alternatively, execution of an unsatisfied judgment *in personam*, after its recognition, can be effected by seizure of the defendant's assets by the sheriff.

---

102 (1859) Swab 468.

103 (1859) Swab 471.

104 See Briggs, A and Rees, P (eds), *Civil Jurisdiction and Judgments*, 2nd edn, 1997, LLP, p 358 (see, now, 3rd edn, 2001); the authors also state, p 359, that the effect of s 34 is not to impose the technical characteristics of the doctrine of merger upon a foreign judgment. Rather, the section operates to give a defence to the defendant, unless he can be estopped from relying on this statutory defence.

105 Clarke J, who discussed these issues in *The Indian Grace* [1994] 2 Lloyd's Rep 331, p 351, was of the view that, although the old rule of no merger was developed in maritime lien cases, he could not see any reason why the general principle of permitting a maritime claimant to realise his security by *in rem* proceedings could not apply to non-maritime lien cases.

3.7 Another point of view

Meeson[106] interprets *The Indian Grace* making a noble attempt to rewrite the judgment because of the ambiguities it has created. He is saying that Lord Steyn's judgment can only be directed to 'quasi-*in rem*' claims because the decisions that troubled him involved those claims, and not truly *in rem*. The writer does not explain, however, why most of the judgments relied upon by the House of Lords were concerned with truly *in rem* claims. For example, *The Terveate*, *The Gemma*, *The Parlement Belge* were concerned with collision claims; *The Dictator* was a salvage case; *The August 8* dealt with master's wages and disbursements; *The Jupiter*, *The Cristina*, *The Arantzazu Mendi* were concerned with claims for possession of a ship. Meeson accepts, however, that the sovereign immunity cases referred to by Lord Steyn do not support his decision.

He has reworded the decision as follows: 'The House of Lords held that, for the purpose of s 34, a 'quasi-*in rem*' claim was a claim against the owners of the ship, so that it was between the same parties as an *in personam* claim.' At first sight, the suggestion may sound plausible. However, were it to be correct, one would need to explain this: why is it that. in relation to Art 21 of the Brussels Convention, the service of the *in rem* proceeding (whether it concerns truly or quasi-*in rem*) would operate to determine *lis pendens* in a contracting state,[107] while with regard to res judicata the service would operate only with regard to 'quasi-*in rem*'? He seems to suggest that, because of the nature of the truly *in rem* claims, *res judicata* would be inappropriate. But, is it not the case that the legislative object of both Art 21 and s 34 is the same, namely to avoid irreconcilable judgments by prohibiting multiproceedings, or relitigation, of the same cause of action between the same parties? Moreover, Lord Steyn's argument that the procedural change in 1883 brought about a change in substance and influenced the reasons of judges in subsequent cases, which were, in fact, truly *in rem*, seems to suggest that he wished to embrace all *in rem* claims under a uniform rule, at least for the purpose of s 34.

Meeson further says that. if the distinction between truly *in rem* and quasi-*in rem* is kept in mind. the criticisms of the decision fall away. However, the author does not dispute that the reasoning in the case appears to go further than that. If, according to Lord Steyn, the service was the relevant point in time at which the *in rem* claim was against the defendant *in personam*, Meeson would appear to be making a slip by his reference that the quasi *in rem* claims

---

106 *Op cit*, Meeson, fn 101, pp 86–84.
107 See, in Chapter 6, that when the new EC Regulation replacing the Brussels Convention comes into force in March 2002, the court of a Contracting State will be seised of the matter from the issue of the proceedings not the service.

remain solely *in rem* until acknowledgment of service,[108] unless he means that *The Indian Grace* has no application outside the scope of s 34.

3.8 Conclusion

The service of the *in rem* proceedings has been considered important by decisions in the context of Art 21 of the Brussels/Lugano Conventions.[109] These have established that, the time from which the court is 'seised' of the matter, is the time of service. This will be correct until 1 March 2002, assuming that the UK opts to the new EC Regulation (see Chapter 6). The concern of the courts, in such cases, has been to avoid irreconcilable judgments, which might be given by different courts of the Contracting States. The conclusion in *The Indian Grace* that the court is seised with jurisdiction from the service of the writ for the purpose of s 34 of the CJJA 1982 is in line with these decisions.

Therefore, it could be argued that this judgment has perhaps a limited application. Such a suggestion can be derived from the conclusion of the judgment, in which Lord Steyn stated:

> ... it is now possible to say that, for the purpose of s 34, an action *in rem* is an action against the owners from the moment the Admiralty Court is seised with jurisdiction.[110]

It is submitted, however, that, in the context of the issues involved in this case, no broad principle can be drawn from it that it creates a personal jurisdiction over the defendant in all cases of *in rem* proceedings from the time of service.

In summary, it is suggested that the following proposals may iron out the difficulties created by this decision.

(a) As regards a *bona fide* purchaser of a ship without notice of the issue of the *in rem* claim form,[111] or of a maritime lien, service of the *in rem* claim form does not create a personal jurisdiction over him because he is not the person liable for the claim. As far as enforcement of the security by arresting the ship is concerned, the claim would remain solely *in rem*, for this purpose, if another form of security has not been obtained.

---

108 *Op cit*, Meeson, fn 101, pp 81, 98.

109 *The Dresser v Falcongate (sub nom The Duke Yare)* [1991] 2 Lloyd's Rep 557 (CA), pp 563–70, in relation to actions *in personam*, and in relation to actions *in rem*, *The Freccia del Nord* [1989] 1 Lloyd's Rep 388, which, however, will cease to be good law after 1 March 2002, see fn 107, p 39.

110 *The Indian Grace (No 2)* [1998] 1 Lloyd's Rep 1 (HL), p 10; whether for the purpose of s 34, the court will be seised of a matter from the issue of the proceedings (as it will be for the purpose of the lis pendens provisions of the EC Regulation as from 1 March 2002, will be an issue for further judicial consideration.

111 Pursuant to the new CPR, Pt 5, an inspection of the Court's Record is only allowed to the public after service of the claim form, see para 3.5.3.1, above.

(b) On the other hand, the service of the *in rem* claim form creates a personal jurisdiction against the person who is interested to defend the claim on the merits, such as the owner or the demise charterer of the relevant ship. The issue of obtaining security for the claim, however, is a separate issue. Confusion frequently arises under English law (unlike under civil law systems) because the procedure of arresting a ship has a dual function, namely to enable the claimant to obtain security for the claim, on the one hand, and, on the other, to establish jurisdiction on the merits.

(c) The point of service of *in rem* proceedings is only relevant to the *res judicata* issue. Thus, the defence of s 34 should not be a bar to *in rem* proceedings (whether they are concerned with truly or non-truly *in rem* claims), if they are brought only for the purpose of obtaining security, or realising the security attached on the ship (that is, maritime liens and crystallised rights *in rem*), unless sufficient security has already been obtained (see Chapter 4). The claimants in *The Indian Grace* commenced the *in rem* proceedings in the Admiralty Court to relitigate the same issues and were, in fact, claiming higher damages than what they claimed in India.

If such interpretation is acceptable, then the problems canvassed can be resolved.

4 THE RELEVANT CONDITIONS OF BRINGING IN REM CLAIMS

The rights *in rem* have been divided into two categories:

(a) those which, in themselves, are regarded as having proprietary characteristics, the truly *in rem* claims, such as maritime liens, and those which are relevant to rights of owners or mortgagees of a ship, as well as those concerned with forfeiture of a ship and droits of admiralty (s 20(2)(a), (b), (c), (s));

(b) all other statutory rights *in rem* under s 20(2)(e)–(r), the 'non-truly *in rem*' claims.

4.1 No conditions in truly *in rem* claims

It will be seen shortly that s 21(4) of the Act treats these categories separately with regard to the mode of exercise of jurisdiction and different conditions apply to each category when an action *in rem* is brought.

By s 21(2) and (3), an action *in rem* can be brought against the ship without considering who is the owner of the ship at the time the claim form is issued, or who would be liable *in personam* when the cause of action arose. So, it is said that these claims are truly *in rem*.

In the second category, however, there is a requirement of a link between the claim and liability of the relevant person *in personam*, and considerations of ownership when the *in rem* proceeding is issued. These considerations are examined below.

4.2 Non-truly *in rem*: *in personam* link when the cause of action arose

An *in rem* claim form regarding claims within paras (e)–(r) may be brought under s 21(4) of the SCA 1981 where:

(a) the claim arises in connection with a ship; and

(b) the person who would be liable on an action *in personam* (the relevant person) was, when the cause of action arose, the owner or charterer or person in possession or in control of, the ship.

The section requires that, for claims from para (e)–(r) of s 20(2), the claimant must identify first who would be liable *in personam*, if he were sued *in personam*. That person must have been either the owner, or demise charterer, or the person in possession or control of the ship when the cause of action arose.

'Owner' means the registered owner. Lord Donaldson opined, in *The Evpo Agnic*,[112] that, on a true construction, the word in s 21(4)(b), which refers simply to 'owners', is to be contrasted with 'beneficial owner' in sub-paras (i) and (ii). The Arrest Convention 1952 looks to ownership and registered ownership as one and the same. Registered owners appear in the registers of shipping, they are nominal owners, but in real commercial life, registered owners can be both legal and beneficial owners of all the shares in the ship:

> ... in real commercial life ... registered owners, even in one-ship companies, are not bare legal owners. They are both legal and beneficial owners of all the shares in the ship and any division between legal and equitable interests occurs in relation to the registered owner itself, which is almost always a juridical person. The legal property in its shares may well be held by A and the equitable property by B, but this does not affect the ownership of the ship, or of the shares in that ship. They are the legal and equitable property of the company.[113]

---

112 [1988] 2 Lloyd's Rep 411 (CA).

113 *Ibid*, p 415; see, also, *Haji-Ioannou v Frangos* [1999] 2 Lloyd's Rep 337, that ownership of a ship for the purpose of the admiralty jurisdiction means legal ownership, except in those provisions where the word is qualified by the adjective 'beneficial'; *The Tian Sheng* [2000] 2 Lloyd's Rep 430 (HK Court of Final Appeal), in which it was explained that, in the general run of things, registration would be virtually conclusive, unless there was a fraudulent procurement of registration.

'Charterer' was then thought by Lord Donaldson, in the same case, to refer only to the demise charterer. However, later decisions contradicted him and the prevailing judicial view is that 'charterer' can include either a charterer by demise, or time, or even a voyage charterer. This is derived from a true construction of the statute, in that, if the intention was to be restricted to the demise charterer only, the statute would have spelled that out. 'Person in possession or control' refers to a person in the position of a demise charterer. Such a person could be a manager and operator of the ship, or a salvor, or a mortgagee who has taken over the possession and management of the ship from the owner in the event of default of the loan conditions.

The Permina[114]

By a time charterparty, *The Ibnu* was chartered by the appellants (charterers) and the charter hire was to be paid monthly. The respondents (owners) contended that the appellants had failed to pay hire due and, therefore, arrested the charterers' vessel *Permina*. The charterers, applied to set aside the writ and the warrant of arrest on the ground that the claim asserted in relation to the charter of *Ibnu* had no connection with the *Permina* and that the word 'charterer' meant charterer by demise. At first instance, in Singapore, their motion was dismissed and the charterers appealed. They lost on appeal in which it was held that the ordinary meaning of the word 'charterer' did not mean only 'by demise'. If the legislature had intended to limit the operation of the sub-section to charterers by demise only, it would have expressly added those words.

This was affirmed by the English Court of Appeal in the following case.

The Span Terza[115]

The owners of the ship *N* issued a writ *in rem* and applied for a warrant of arrest against the vessel *S*, belonging to the time charterers. The application was made in respect of their claim to damages pursuant to a breach of the time charter of the ship *N* by the charterers. The application was turned down by the High Court, but on appeal to the Court of Appeal, the arrest was allowed. In the reasoning of the Court of Appeal, 'charterer' in that provision must include 'time charterer'. If it was meant to be construed only as a 'demise charterer', then the word 'demise' would have been inserted. Alternatively, the word 'charterer' could have been omitted and 'a person in possession or control of the ship' would have automatically included a demise charterer. Therefore, 'charterer' must be taken to mean both demise and time charterers and the time charterers' ship could be arrested for the claim against both.

---

114 [1978] 1 Lloyd's Rep 311 (Singapore CA).
115 [1982] 1 Lloyd's Rep 225 (CA).

It is now clear that 'charterer' includes even a voyage charterer, as has recently been decided in **The Tychy**,[116] with regard to a slot charterer, in which Clarke LJ said:

> ... the purpose of the 1981 Act was to ensure that, before a person's ship could be arrested in respect of a maritime claim, that person had some relationship with the ship in connection with which the maritime claim arose; there was no reason, in principle, why a time or a voyage charterer of the ship should not have been regarded as having a sufficient relationship and no reason to narrow the scope of that relationship by giving the words of s 21(4) other than their ordinary and natural meaning; and, in the case of a sister ship, the ship being arrested must be wholly beneficially owned by the person liable *in personam*; the expression 'the charterer' in s 21(4) was not confined to a demise charterer. If a charterer included a time charterer, it must include a voyage charterer; and it included a voyage charterer of part of a ship.'

The liability must have arisen when the owner or charterer or the person in possession or in control of the ship had that status at that particular time. Rix J said in a recent case, **The Fajal**,[117] that the words of the statute require looking at the status of the relevant person at the relevant time, namely when the cause of action arose.

4.3 Non-truly *in rem*: ownership criteria when action is brought

> Subject to the above requirement, s 21(4) further provides that the action may (whether or not the claim gives rise to maritime lien on that ship) be brought against,
>
> (i) that ship, if at the time when the action is brought the relevant person is either the beneficial owner of that ship as respects all the shares in it or the charterer of it under a charter by demise; or
>
> (ii) any other ship which, at the time when the action is brought, the relevant person is the beneficial owner as respects all the shares in it.

The expression 'or the charterer of it under a charter by demise' was not in s 3(4) of the AJA 1956, but it was added to s 21(4) of the 1981 Act.

4.3.1 Beneficial ownership and arrest
of the relevant ship or a sister ship

It was seen earlier that s 21(4) of the SCA 1981 requires that the arresting claimant must identify first the relevant person who would be liable *in personam* when the cause of action arose. That person can be either the owner, or the charterer, or the person in possession or control of the ship in connection with which the claim arose. The same section also requires that, at

---

116 [1999] 2 Lloyd's Rep 11 (CA).
117 [2000] 1 Lloyd's Rep 473.

the time of issuing the claim form *in rem* for the arrest of that ship, the relevant person must be the beneficial owner of all shares in the ship, or the demise charterer. If the ship to be arrested is other than the one in connection with which the claim arose, the relevant person must be the beneficial owner of that other ship at the time of issuing the proceedings. For example, if the person liable when the cause of action arose was the demise charterer and it is not possible to arrest the ship in connection with which the claim arose (if, for example, she was lost after a collision incident), any ship beneficially owned by the demise charterer would be a target for arrest under s 21(4)(ii).

Ownership under English law includes rights of exclusive enjoyment, destruction and alienation.[118] While 'owner' refers to the registered owner of the ship, and charterer includes also time and voyage charterers, beneficial ownership, which is not a term included in the Arrest Convention 1952, had originally been thought to include the person in possession or control of the ship. This had been decided in the following case, which, however, is not now followed.

The Andrea Ursula[119]

This case concerned the meaning of the expression 'beneficially owned', as used under s 3(4) of the AJA 1956 which stated 'beneficially owned as respects all the shares therein'. The issue was whether the phrase 'beneficial owner' was wide enough to include a demise charterer. Repairs had been carried out on the vessel under the instructions of the demise charterers and prospective owners of the vessel. Upon repudiation of the contract for repairs by the demise charterers, the repairs remained uncompleted and the plaintiffs, the shiprepairers, accepted the repudiation. Exercising their right of a possessory lien for unpaid costs, they detained the vessel and started *in rem* proceedings. At the time of issue of the writ, the defendants were still the demise charterers of the vessel, but had not yet bought the ship. The question for the court was whether the requirements of s 3(4) of the Act had been satisfied. This Act did not include 'demise charterer' in the requirements for arrest. In deciding whether the court had jurisdiction to entertain the action *in rem* for this claim, Brandon J held:

> There is no definition in the Act of the expression 'beneficially owned' as used in s 3(4). It could mean owned by someone who, whether he is the legal owner or not, is in any case the equitable owner. That would cover both the case of a ship, the legal and equitable title to which are in one person, A, and also the case of a ship, the legal title to which is in one person, A, but the equitable title to which is in another person, B. In the first case, the ship would be beneficially owned by A, and in the second case by B. Trusts of ships, express or implied, are, however, rare and the words seem to me to be

---

118 *Halsbury's Laws*, 4th edn, Vol 35, para 1227.
119 [1973] QB 265, or [1971] 1 Lloyd's Rep 145.

capable also of a different and more practical meaning related not to title, legal or equitable, but to lawful possession and control with the use and benefit which are derived from them. If that meaning were right, a ship would be beneficially owned by a person who, whether he was the legal or equitable owner or not, lawfully had full possession and control of her, and, by virtue of such possession and control, had all the benefit and use of her which a legal owner would ordinarily have.[120]

It was held that 'beneficially owned' could, thus, include a demise charter.

However, beneficial ownership was considered differently by Goff J, in the following case, the definition of which has been widely accepted. The issue was whether the operator or manager of a ship was a beneficial owner.

Congresso del Partido[121]

Goff J said:

In my judgment, the natural and ordinary meaning of these words is that they refer only to such ownership as is vested in a person who, whether or not he is the legal owner of the vessel, is in any case the equitable owner ... Furthermore, on the natural and ordinary meaning of the words, I do not consider them apt to apply to the case of a demise charterer or indeed any other person who has only possession of the ship, however full and complete such possession may be, and however much control over the ship he may have ... such words are only appropriate when describing ownership in the ordinary sense of the word, and not possession which is concerned with a physical relationship with the vessel founded on control and has nothing to do with shares in the vessel. A demise charterer had, within limits defined by contract, the beneficial use of the ship, he does not however have the beneficial ownership as respects all the shares in the ship.

In *The Father Thames*,[122] the above definition was adopted.

The vessel was under a demise charter for a period of two years to B Ltd and the owners had completely divested themselves of all control and possession of the vessel. During the demise charter, the ship collided with another. After the collision, the benefit and liabilities of the demise charter were assigned to P Ltd. A writ *in rem* was issued and *The Father Thames* was arrested. The owners claimed that there was no jurisdiction to proceed against their vessel because, at the time the cause of action arose (the collision), they were not liable for the negligent navigation and damage done. Under a demise charter, the crew were employees of the demise charterer. The problem was that the 1956 Act did not provide for the alternative requirement that the person who would be liable *in personam* could be the demise charterer when the writ was issued. The owners urged the court to follow the decision

---

120 [1973] QB 265, p 269, or [1971] 1 Lloyd's Rep 145, p 147.
121 [1978] 1 All ER 1169, pp 1201–02.
122 [1979] 2 Lloyd's Rep 364.

of Justice Brandon, in *The Andrea Ursula*, in that a beneficial owner included a demise charterer and, in this case, that charterer had changed when the writ was issued. It was held, however, that 'beneficially owned' did not apply to a demise charterer; the decision in *Congresso del Partido* was followed. However, although the person who would be liable *in personam* was not the beneficial owner of the ship, the writ *in rem* was not set aside because a maritime lien (due to the collision damage) attached on the ship from the time of the incident.

For the arrest of the ship concerning claims under s 20(2)(a)–(c) and (s), and those attracting maritime liens, there is no need to identify the person who would be personally liable, nor to consider ownership criteria at any time (s 21(2) and (3)). The same applied under s 3(2) and (3) of the 1956 Act. The change brought by the 1981 Act is under s 21(4), in which the term 'charterer by demise' has been added in relation to actions *in rem* under s 20(2)(e)–(r), some of which, it will be observed, concern maritime liens. So, the claim form *in rem* may be brought against that ship, if at the time the action is brought, the relevant person is the beneficial owner of all shares in the ship or a charterer by demise.

A question may sometimes arise as to whether the demise charter had already been terminated at the time of the issue of the proceedings. This was an issue in a recent decision of the New Zealand High Court of Admiralty in *Rangiora, Ranginui and Takitimu*.[123] These three ships were owned by Deil shipowners and were chartered by demise to South Pacific Shipping (SPS) in 1995. Due to outstanding areas of hire, the owners decided to terminate the charter arrangements and formal notices to that effect were given by Deil to SPS on approximately 16.00 hours, on 18 February 1998. The next day, a shareholders' resolution for voluntary winding up of SPS was passed. On 20 February, a stevedoring company commenced proceedings *in rem* against the vessel *Ranginui* for monies owed to it by SPS with regard to services rendered during the time of the demise charter. On the same day, Mobil Oil New Zealand commenced *in rem* proceedings against the *Rangiora*. The owners of the ships applied to set aside the proceedings, on the ground that the person who would be liable *in personam*, SPS, were no longer the demise charterers at the time the proceedings were issued. The claimants argued that the notices of termination of the charter did not have an immediate effect, but were notices of future intention, and that, in accordance with the construction of the charterparties, the charters were still in existence. So, SPS were still the demise charterers at the date of the issue of the writ. The court decided that the contractual status remained on foot until the owners took steps to proclaim recovery of possession of the ships from the charterers. Under German law,

---

123 [2000] 1 Lloyd's Rep 36.

which applied to the contracts, a demise charter is brought to an end upon physical delivery. The owners' application was dismissed.

An interesting example of a company structure by which the arrest of the ship was successfully evaded can be observed in a recent decision of the highest appellate Court of Hong Kong in *The Tian Sheng (No 8)*.[124]

The owners (TSI) had chartered this ship by demise to T&R, who, in turn, chartered her on a time charter to Tiansheng Ocean, who were the carriers of the cargo and, on their behalf, the bill of lading was signed. The ship deviated and the cargo was sold by court order. The ship was sold to a company IRI before the issue of the writ by the cargo-owners who claimed damages for loss of their cargo carried on board. The ship, whose name was changed to *Resourse I*, was arrested and her new owners contested jurisdiction having obtained her release by putting up bail. Both the judge and the Court of Appeal (HK), suspecting that the documents were fabricated to disguise the real ownership of the person liable *in personam*, Ocean, held that the arrest was valid. The highest appeal Court of Hong Kong reversed the decision because neither the owner nor the demise charterer were the person liable when the cause of action arose. So, when the writ was issued in Hong Kong the person who would be liable was neither the beneficial owner, nor the charterer by demise of the ship for it to be arrested.

The facts of this case, as indeed of other cases involving a series of charterparties and the creation of companies, in order to distance the owner and the demise charterer from direct contractual arrangements with cargo-owners, may give cause for one to 'raise eyebrows'. However, since the company structure, in the eyes of the law, shields the person who would really be liable *in personam*, the decision is within the bounds of the law.

When under s 21(4), a ship other than the one in connection with which the claim arose is to be arrested, that other ship must be, at the time of issuing the writ, beneficially owned in all shares by the relevant person who was identified as the person who would be liable *in personam*. Since s 21(4) covers claims within (e)–(r), maritime liens can also be enforced this way. So, a sister ship can be arrested, but the maritime lien will obviously be lost. By contrast, there can be no sister ship arrest for claims under (a), (b), (c) and (r).

As discussed earlier, 'beneficially owned' refers to equitable ownership, whether or not accompanied by legal ownership. 'Equitable ownership' is meant to cover an owner for whose benefit the legal owner holds the shares in the ship under the English law concept of trust. Thus, the adjective 'beneficial' before owner ensures that, if the ship is operated under the cloak of trust, she can still be arrested for maritime claims. The commercial reality is that registered owners of ships are not just legal owners of bearer shares. They are both legal and beneficial owners of all shares in the ship. Any division

---

124 [2000] 2 Lloyd's Rep 430.

between the legal and equitable interest in the ship occurs in relation to the registered ownership itself. For example, the legal property in the shares may be held by A and the equitable by B.

4.3.2 Minority shareholding in a ship not sufficient for the purpose of arrest

For the purpose of arrest, it is not enough that the beneficial owner owns a fraction of 64 shares in the ship and not all of them. This was confirmed by the Federal Court of Canada in the following case.

The Looiersgracht[125]

This ship was arrested in respect of maritime claims, which arose in connection with her and five other vessels, which were believed to be her sister ships. The defendants claimed that security to be posted should not include security for alleged damage to cargo carried on the other five vessels, as they did not beneficially own all the shares therein. From the Lloyd's Register of Shipping, it was clear that the defendants were managing agents for many vessels and had minority ownership of some of them. Most of the vessels were owned by either one or more limited partnerships. The plaintiffs alleged that there was a common ownership based on the management of the fleet by the defendants, and, also on the part-ownership of the defendants in the shares of the ships. The defendants admitted minority ownership interest in some of them, but maintained that each vessel-owning limited partnership was made up of a different group of participants. Canada is not a signatory to the 1952 Arrest Convention. It has, however, enacted parallel legislation, the Federal Court Act 1992, which is similar to the English statute, save for no reference to all shares in the ship with regard to beneficial ownership. The trial judge of the Canadian Federal Court, Hargrave J, stated:

> Under our legislation, it is not sufficient to show merely some beneficial interest. Our legislation requires that the sistership be 'beneficially owned by the person who is the owner of the ship that is subject of the action'. To come within the Canadian sister ship provisions, there must be common complete ownership of both vessels by the same owner or owners, for that is the plain and ordinary meaning of our legislation. It is not enough to be an owner, but rather it must be the owner, that is a similar complete ownership of both vessels.[126]

The judge also held that this was an instance in which a series of one-ship companies were not a sham to defeat legislation, but had been established for legitimate reasons.

---

125 [1995] 2 Lloyd's Rep 411.
126 *Ibid*, p 415.

4.3.3 Investigation of who is the real beneficial owner: is it permitted?

Under an old English authority, *Salomon v A Salomon & Co Ltd*,[127] the concept of legal personality given to a corporation means that, no matter who the shareholders are, the company is a separate person owning its own assets. One could not pierce the incorporated entity to pursue the shareholders and persons controlling the company for liabilities of the company. It is not uncommon for a ship owned by one company to be transferred *bona fide* to another company (both of which are controlled by the same person), before a claim has arisen, or a claim form been issued. In such a case, the requirements of s 21(4) of the SCA 1981 will not be satisfied for an arrest of that ship, or her sister ship, to be effectively made. The question that arises in relation to one-ship companies is whether the corporate veil could be pierced, so as to trace ownership from the registered owner of the ship to the owner *de facto*. This is restricted to special circumstances, which indicate a mere facade concealing the true facts.[128]

The Court of Appeal, in a non-shipping case, *Adams v Cape Industries* (see below) delineated the circumstances that would constitute a facade. It gave guidelines that the court would pierce the corporate veil when a defendant had attempted by the device of a corporate structure to evade: (i) limitations imposed on his conduct by law; (ii) such rights of relief against him as third parties already possess, but not rights that may be acquired in the future. The veil would not be pierced, even if it was necessary to achieve justice.[129] This principle has prevailed ever since the Salomon case and there has been recognition of the separate legal identity of companies within a group.

Adams v Cape Industries[130]

Cape was the parent company in the case. It owned four subsidiary companies Capaso, NAAC, E and Casap, for its mining and marketing activities for the USA and worldwide. One of its subsidiaries owned the asbestos mines from which came the asbestos dust used by its customers. One such customer was PCC, which purchased the asbestos and used it in its factory for 10 years, until the factory closed. People later became aware of the long term damage caused by the use of asbestos and personal injury claims began to mount in court, from 1974 to 1979, by both factory workers and those who lived in the neighbourhood of the factory. Cape and her subsidiaries were defendants in the action, as it was alleged that they had been responsible for the supply of the asbestos used in the factory. The allegation against them was that, notwithstanding their knowledge about the dangers of asbestos,

---

127 [1897] AC 22 (HL).
128 *Woolfson v Strathclyde RC* 1978 SLT 159 (HL).
129 *In re Company* [1985] 1 BCC 99.
130 [1991] 1 All ER 929.

they failed to give adequate warning. It was alleged that this amounted to negligent acts and omissions and breaches of implied and express warranties. Judgment in default was entered in the action against Cape and her subsidiary Capaso in September 1983, in Texas. Capaso was the subsidiary, which organised the sale of asbestos worldwide, to those who used it for industrial purposes. Both Cape and Capaso had been incorporated in the UK and some of the plaintiffs sought to enforce the judgments, entered against these defendants, in this country. At the trial for enforcement, the question was whether the foreign court, in Texas, had jurisdiction to give a judgment which was sought to be enforced in the UK. After the first set of proceedings had been heard in the US, the subsidiary NAAC was wound up and another subsidiary AMC was formed to continue trade in the USA. Another company CPC was to act as agent for AMC. The plaintiffs claimed that, although the defendants were incorporated in the UK, they were residents in the USA, at the time of the commencement of the proceedings. The presence of any of Cape's subsidiaries incorporated in the USA was sufficient to give the US court jurisdiction. The trial judge rejected this submission and the plaintiffs appealed. The plaintiffs claimed that Cape/Capaso and NAAC constituted one single commercial unit. Therefore, in relation to AMC and her agent CPC, the corporate veil should be pierced, so that their presence in the USA could also be treated as the presence of Cape and Capaso. The Court of Appeal re-emphasised the doctrine that every company is a separate legal person that cannot be identified with its members. Slade LJ stated:

> Our law, for better or worse, recognises the creation of subsidiary companies, which, though in one sense are the creatures of their parent companies, will nevertheless under the general law fall to be treated as separate legal entities with all the rights and liabilities which would normally attach to separate legal entities. In deciding whether a company is present in a foreign country by a subsidiary, which is itself present in that country, the court is entitled, indeed bound, to investigate that relationship between the parent and the subsidiary. In particular, that relationship may be relevant in determining whether the subsidiary was acting as the parent's agent and, if so, on what terms ... However, there is no presumption of any such agency. There is no presumption that the subsidiary is the parent company's *alter ego* ... If a company chooses to arrange the affairs of its group in such a way that the business carried on in a particular foreign country is the business of its subsidiary and not its own, it is, in our judgment, entitled to do so. Neither in this class of case, nor in any other class of case, is it open to this court to disregard the principle of *Salomon v A Salomon & Co Ltd*, merely because it considers it just so to do.[131]

The courts have held that it is not permissible to pierce the corporate veil unless there is evidence of a sham transfer of the legal ownership of the ship.

---

131 [1991] 1 All ER 929, pp 1019–20.

For this purpose, the court can order evidence to be produced, in certain circumstances, to investigate the beneficial ownership in order to determine whether there has been a sham transfer.[132] However, it is legitimate for shipowners to arrange their affairs by running a series of one-ship companies as a group and cause them to use their individual assets to their mutual advantage. There is no reason why they should not do so without any risk of the arrangement being held to be a sham.[133]

The Evpo Agnic[134]

The plaintiffs were the cargo-owners of cargo laden on board the vessel *Skipper*, which sank. The plaintiffs issued a writ *in rem* against 'the owners of that ship, or the ship *Evpo Agnic*', for breach of duty in loading and handling of their cargo. The latter ship was owned by a separate company from that which owned *The Skipper*, but both companies were owned and controlled by the same shareholder and president, Mr Pothitos. According to the plaintiffs, the owners of the vessel *Evpo Agnic* were, at all times, the owners of the vessel *Skipper*. The defendants moved to set aside the writ *in rem* and the warrant for the arrest of the *Evpo Agnic*. Sheen J, in the lower court, ordered the defendants to disclose all documents relating to the ownership of both vessels. The defendants appealed against this order on the basis that the two vessels were owned by two separate 'one-ship' companies. It was held that there was no evidence that the holding company of the two sister companies was the beneficial owner of all the shares in *Evpo Agnic* or her demise charter. Lord Donaldson MR refused to pierce the corporate veil and defined owner to mean the registered owner with no rights on the assets of a sister company. He said:

> I would be most reluctant to interfere with the exercise of judicial discretion in an admiralty action by a judge of the experience of Sheen J and there can be no doubt that discovery can be ordered, if there is any real indication that this may uncover a situation which will confirm, or for that matter negative, the court's jurisdiction. But, there has to be some real indication that further facts may exist which will affect the issue.[135]

Unlike flexible jurisdictions on arrest of ships, such as South Africa and probably France, under English law and in those jurisdictions which follow it (for example, Hong Kong) the controlling shareholders of two sister companies, each owning one ship, will not be sufficient evidence to pierce the corporate veil of a legitimate one ship company for the purpose of arresting the asset belonging to the other sister company, unless there is fraud. Mr

---

132 See *The Aventicum* [1978] 1 Lloyd's Rep 184, under para 4.3.5, below.
133 Lord Donaldson in *The Evpo Agnic* [1988] 2 Lloyd's Rep 411.
134 *Ibid*.
135 *Ibid*, p 415.

Pothitos' companies were legitimate, said Lord Donaldson, and he was not regarded the beneficial owner of the ships owned by the separate corporate structures.

In some circumstances, however, a transfer of ownership in a ship will be an illegitimate method, if the purpose is to evade third party rights already accrued, examples of which are shown below.

4.3.4 When the corporate veil has been pierced

The court can pierce the corporate veil in situations where there has been a 'sham' transfer of the ship to another company in an attempt to avoid liability for claims. The definition of a 'sham' was given by Diplock LJ in a case concerning hire purchase,[136] as follows:

> ... it means acts done or documents executed by the parties to the 'sham' which are intended by them to give to third parties or to the court the appearance of creating between the parties legal rights and obligations different from the actual legal rights and obligations (if any) which the parties intend to create. But, one thing, I think, is clear in legal principle, morality and the authorities (see *Yorkshire Rly Wagon Co v. Maclure and Stoneleigh Finance Ltd v Phillips*), that for acts or documents to be a 'sham,' with whatever legal consequences follow from this, all the parties thereto must have a common intention that the acts or documents are not to create the legal rights and obligations which they give the appearance of creating. No unexpressed intentions of a 'shammer' affect the rights of a party whom he deceived.

In shipping cases, the facts of the following cases illustrate what would not be regarded in the eyes of the law as a genuine single-ship company but only used to conceal the true ownership of a ship to evade liability to creditors.

The Saudi Prince[137]

In 1976, a cargo of ceramic tiles was carried on the ship A. At the time, the vessel was owned by Mr Orri, a Saudi businessman, who traded the ship under the company SEL. The cargo suffered damage before delivery and the cargo-owners claimed such damages from the carriers. When the Saudi Prince, also belonging to SEL, being a sister ship of A, came into the jurisdiction in August 1979, a writ *in rem* against her was issued and she was arrested. Mr. Orri sought to have the writ set aside on the ground that before the writ was issued the legal ownership of the SP had been transferred to another company (SSST) in which he owned 80% of the shares, while his two daughters owned 20%. Even if it was permissible to regard the shareholders of the company as the beneficial owners of the SP, Mr Orri argued, he was not

---

136 *Snook v London and West Riding Investments Ltd* [1967] 2 QB 786, p 802.
137 [1982] 2 Lloyd's Rep 255.

the beneficial owner of all shares therein. On the evidence, however, it was not shown that the vessel had been transferred to this company for value. There was no convincing evidence that his children paid money for the shares. The shares were just put in their name as nominees of Mr Orri to divest himself of shares, in name only. In any event, the company had not properly been incorporated in accordance with Saudi Arabian law. Therefore, it was held that an investigation of the true beneficial ownership of SP showed that Mr Orri was, at the time of the issue of the writ, the true beneficial owner of the vessel.

The Tjaskemolen[138]

The defendants, Bayland Navigation Inc (B), was a company being part of a group of companies which were formed for the purpose of owning this ship T. B entered into a charterparty with the plaintiffs (charterers) for the carriage of steel from Rotterdam to Korea under which B warranted that the ship's certificates of class and seaworthiness were in order. The charterers in turn had contracted with D to sell and transport cargo of steel to Korea. When the notice of readiness for loading of the cargo was tendered by the charterers, the classification certificate was not on board. As a result, the charterers were unable to load and cancelled the charterparty. Consequently, the buyer of the steel D cancelled the sale contract. The charterers arrested the ship, seeking security in respect of their claim in damages, which had been submitted to arbitration. The defendants B applied for the release of the ship from arrest on the grounds that, at the time of the issue of the writ, she was not owned by them, nor was she chartered by demise to the person who would be liable for the claim *in personam*. They submitted that they had transferred legal and beneficial ownership to another company in the group, G, before the issue of the writ. The plaintiffs alleged that the agreement was a sham and that neither legal nor beneficial ownership could have passed until the vessel was deleted from the Register of Ships in Panama. This event did not occur until after the issue of the writ. On evidence, it was shown that, at the time the memorandum of agreement for the sale of the ship was signed, G did not exist and was not incorporated until afterwards. In addition, there was never any intention that G should pay a full price for the ship. It was held that the whole arrangement was a sham made only for the purpose of ensuring that the vessel was not made subject to security for any arbitration award.

By contrast to the above case, Toulson J, in *The Rialto (No2)*,[139] a case concerning a Mareva injunction, refused to pierce the corporate veil on the ground that the court could not treat the director of a company of brokers, Mr Yamvrias, retrospectively as a party to a charterparty. Mr Yamvrias as a

---

138 [1997] 2 Lloyd's Rep 465.
139 [1998] 1 Lloyd's Rep 322.

chartering broker had signed a charterparty on behalf of the contracting party, the charterers, who eventually repudiated it and the owners of the chartered ship claimed damages. On evidence, it was shown that Mr Yamvrias had control of the chartering company and, on the day of the repudiation of the charterparty, he had caused the transfer of money from the account of the charterers to other companies controlled by him, in order to protect the money from the owners' claim in damages. The judge distinguished the previous case from this one on the basis that, at the time of the transfer, liability had not yet arisen following the principle laid down in the Adams case seen earlier. This case shows that the technicality of the law can sometimes overrule common sense. It could not have been a more obvious deliberate evasion of liability by the charterers than the transfer of the money from the company's account on the day of the repudiation, regardless that, technically, liability arose a few hours later on the same day.

The Ocean Enterprise[140]

The sale of a ship by a director of the owning company, who had no authority from the board of directors and the sale was in breach of his fiduciary duty, was declared invalid and fraudulent on the company. The beneficial ownership in the ship remained with the company. The buyer was not a *bona fide* purchaser for value and without notice of the defect in the title. On the facts, the director of the purchasing company was involved in a covering up for the seller in a series of sham sales and registration of the ship. He was ordered by the court to pay damages to the plaintiff (the defrauded company) for conversion of its property.

4.3.5 When the corporate veil was not pierced

The Courts are, sometimes, prepared to look behind the corporate veil (which is known as 'lifting the veil' to peep behind it), in order to determine whether there is a genuine link between corporate structures which may reveal that the corporate veil ought to be pierced, for treating the liabilities of the relevant company as the liabilities of its shareholders or directors.[141]

Staughton LJ said, in **The Coral Rose**,[142] that, like all metaphors, the corporate veil can sometimes obscure reasoning rather than elucidate it. He explained, relying on the Adams case, that there were two senses in which the phrase is used, which needed to be distinguished:

---

140 [1997] 1 Lloyd's Rep 449.

141 It seems that the distinction between 'lifting' and 'piercing' the corporate veil was made by Slade LJ in *Adams v Cape Industries* [1991] 1 All ER 929.

142 [1991] 1 Lloyd's Rep 563, p 571 (concerning a Mareva injunction).

> To pierce the corporate veil is an expression that I would reserve for treating the rights or liabilities or activities of a company as the rights or liabilities or activities of its shareholders. To lift the corporate veil or look behind it, on the other hand, should mean to have regard to the shareholding in a company for some legal purpose.

Thus the court may order evidence to be adduced for this purpose as is shown in the following cases.

The Kommunar (No 2)[143]

The plaintiffs applied for the appraisement and sale of the vessel K, which they had earlier arrested for reimbursement of sums owed to them with regard to services for the supply of goods and materials to the ship.[144] The services were provided to various Russian fishing vessels, which at the time were managed by an entity called POL. This entity was a state enterprise under the control of the Russian Ministry of Fisheries through the medium of another state enterprise, S. S had arranged for the plaintiffs to provide agency services to these vessels in Central and South America. POL was privatised in 1993 and became a public joint stock company limited by shares. It was no longer an emanation of the Ministry and it was renamed AOL. The plaintiffs, thus, alleged that AOL had taken over the debts of POL, including the debt owed to the plaintiffs. AOL applied for the arrest to be set aside on the grounds that, at the time the cause of action arose, they were not the owners, or charterers, nor in possession or control of the ship. They also submitted that, although they owned the vessel K, they were not the same legal person as POL. It was held that once there was discontinuity of legal personality, no amount of statutory transfer of assets or liabilities by means of legal succession could satisfy the provisions of s 21(4) of the SCA 1981. Colman J held that the wording of the legislation dealing with privatisation was significantly more consistent with discontinuity of legal personality than with continuity. Also, the kind of legal entity created in AOL differed fundamentally from the kind that existed up to that time. The creation of a joint stock company out of an unincorporated State enterprise was more than a mere change of name. The defendant's motion succeeded because the conditions of s 21(4) were not strictly satisfied.[145]

---

143 [1997] 1 Lloyd's Rep 8.

144 For discussion of this case see, previously, Chapter 2, para 3.1.3, with regard to s 20(2)(m) of the SCA 1981; *Kommunar (No 1)* [1997] 1 Lloyd's Rep 1.

145 See, also, para 4.3.6, below.

The Aventicum[146]

Three separate companies were part owners and controlling shareholders of another company, which, in turn, owned two subsidiaries, one of which owned the ship *Aventicum* (A).

The plaintiffs, consignees of cargo, claimed damages for breach of contract and/or duty in the loading/handling of the cargo carried on board the vessel A in 1976. They issued a writ on 5 May 1977 and arrested the vessel in respect of their claim on 11 August 1977. The defendant owners of the vessel applied to have the writ, service of writ and all subsequent proceedings set aside, on the ground that the court had no jurisdiction over the vessel or her owners. The matter, which had to be decided, was who owned the ship when the cause of action arose and whether that person was also the beneficial owner of all the shares in the ship when the writ was issued. At the time the cause of action arose, the vessel belonged to a company Armadora, which was a subsidiary of company Scalotas. Scalotas was owned by three separate parent companies. After the cause of action had arisen, the ship was transferred to a sister company of Armadora, Longan. This company, with the ship, was later bought by Anglo Norse and a new subsidiary company was set up, Loquat, to which the ship was transferred again. The plaintiffs argued that the company Longan, which owned the ship by August 1976, belonged to Anglo Norse. At the time the writ was issued, the vessel was owned by Loquat, which also belonged to Anglo Norse. In this manner, it could be said that Anglo Norse was, therefore, beneficial owner of both companies and still the beneficial owner of the shares in the ship. Although there had been changes in the registered ownership of this vessel, it was argued that the real owners had, throughout, remained the same and, if one looked at all the connecting links between these companies, the beneficial owners were the same person. The defendants urged the court not to lift the corporate veil, but to take matters at face value. Slynn J disagreed and ordered evidence to be adduced:

> I think that it is wrong and that where damages are claimed by cargo-owners and there is dispute as to the beneficial ownership of the ship, the court in all cases can and in some cases should look behind the registered owner to determine the true beneficial ownership ... I have no doubt that on a motion of this kind it is right to investigate the true beneficial ownership. I reject any suggestion that it is impossible 'to pierce the corporate veil' ... it is plain that s 3(4) of the Act intends that the court shall not be limited to a consideration of who is the registered owner, or who is the person having legal ownership of the shares in the ship; the directions are to look at the beneficial ownership.[147]

It was permitted, therefore, to look behind the corporate veil. However, on the evidence, the plaintiffs could not prove that the beneficial owner of the ship

---

146 [1978] 1 Lloyd's Rep 184.
147 *Ibid*, p 187.

arrested was the same person with the person liable *in personam*. That was a smart way of avoiding claims already accrued, although the successive transfers of the ship from one company to another commenced after the claim had arisen. Perhaps, if the evidence had been more carefully scrutinised, a trace back to the person liable *in personam* could have been made. By contrast to this complex corporate structure, the following case concerned a simple structure of a parent and a subsidiary company.

The Maritime Trader[148]

The plaintiffs, owners of the vessel *Antaios*, time chartered her to MTO and claimed outstanding payment of hire. MTO was a parent company of MTS, which owned the vessel *Maritime Trader*. The plaintiffs, believing that MTO had financial difficulties, issued a writ against *The Maritime Trader* and arrested her. The question was whether, at the time the action was brought, *The Maritime Trader* was beneficially owned in respect of all shares therein by MTO, the person who would be liable on the claim *in personam*.

It was held that it could not be said that *The Maritime Trader* was beneficially owned by MTO, unless the corporate veil was to be lifted. Without evidence of fraud, the court would not pierce the veil. There was no evidence of sham as the vessel had been owned by MTS ever since she was built, which was over four years before the charterparty contract was entered into between the plaintiffs and MTO.

In *The Glastnos*,[149] where there was a genuine transfer of the ship within a group of distinct legal entities for legitimate reasons, Steyn J (as he then was) said:

> My conclusion is that all the companies in the Tolteca Group were distinct legal entities: to describe any as sham is simply not correct. I accept that Mr Farias resorted to the device of incorporation to attain the benefits of limited liability. That is, of course, why the shipping trade is structured on the basis of one-ship companies, but by itself it affords no basis for piercing the corporate veil, and the evidence before me certainly does not justify an inference that the companies were vehicles for the commission of fraud ...
>
> The companies in question were Tolteca SA, Tolteca Inc and, possibly, Marbank. One can readily accept that ultimate control rested with Mr Farias. A great many shipping groups, structured in one ship companies, are ultimately controlled by one individual or family. By itself that proves nothing. What matters is how business and affairs are carried on.

---

148 [1981] 2 Lloyd's Rep 153.
149 [1991] 1 Lloyd's Rep 482, pp 490, 491.

4.3.6 Beneficial ownership and privatisation of State owned corporations

The question, whether a given corporate entity can be said to be the same legal personality as some previous legal entity,[150] is, perhaps, best answered by investigating the different legal characteristics of the two to see whether continuity has been broken or maintained.[151]

The Nazym Khikmet[152]

The plaintiffs were owners or parties interested in a cargo of tobacco, damaged on a voyage on board this ship. *NK Blasko*, a State enterprise, was a managing company of a fleet for the Ukraine Government, in possession and control of the N. Thus, when the cause of action arose, Blasko was the person who would be liable *in personam*. The plaintiffs arrested Z, a sister ship of NK, and claimed that Blasko was the beneficial owner of Z, at the time the action was brought. Both Blasko and the Republic of Ukraine contended that at the time of the issue of the writ, Z was not beneficially owned by Blasko, but by the Republic. Upon conclusive evidence, Clarke J held that, although Blasko had some rights of ownership, it did not have full rights to dispose of or mortgage the ship without the consent of the Government. The Court of Appeal affirmed his decision and Sir Thomas Bingham MR, stated:

> The evidence makes plain that the process of liberalisation, which took place in the Ukraine once it became independent, has involved a devolution of commercial authority to trading enterprises; this process has led to a loosening of the bonds of State control, but not to a severance of them. The State has retained its ownership of the income earning assets of enterprises such as Blasko, and had retained the right and power of ultimate decision over the use and exploitation of those assets.[153]

At a later stage, however, as is shown in the following case, Blasko was thought to have taken over ownership rights by having power to mortgage the ship, which was arrested in respect of a claim of bunker suppliers. Nevertheless, it was held by the Court of Appeal that it only had the status of a demise charterer.

Guiseppe di Vittorio[154]

The plaintiffs supplied bunkers, on two occasions, to the ship G, which was operated by Blasko.[155] Remaining unpaid, the plaintiffs issued a writ *in rem*

---

150 For a summary of State reconstruction in Russia and its effect on arrest of ships bought by the new entity, see Thomas, R, 'State reconstruction and ship arrest' [1998] IJSL 236.

151 *The Kommunar (No 2)* [1997] 1 Lloyd's Rep 8, p 16, *per* Colman J.

152 [1996] 2 Lloyd's Rep 362.

153 *Ibid*, p 374.

154 [1998] 1 Lloyd's Rep 136.

155 See *The Nazym Khikmet* [1996] 2 Lloyd's Rep 362.

arrested her and applied for an order that the vessel be sold *pendente lite*. The Republic of Ukraine intervened, claiming that it was the beneficial owner of the ship and not Blasko. Therefore, it contended that since it was a successor state of the USSR, the ship was not subject to arrest under the SCA 1981. The State Immunity (Merchant Shipping (USSR) Order 1978 applied to a ship owned by it and it was immune from liability. The plaintiffs submitted that at the time the cause of action arose, Blasko was the beneficial owner, or demise charterer, of the vessel and there had been a transfer of property in the vessel to Blasko before the issue of the writ. They relied on a mortgage agreement by which it appeared that Blasko had power to mortgage the ship. The plaintiffs argued that this was an act consistent with Blasko being the legal and beneficial owner of the vessel. Although, at first instance, the judge held that it was, the Court of Appeal held that, on the evidence, there was no suggestion of a transfer either by Blasko's representatives, or by the Ministry of Transport. On the issue whether Blasko could be described as a demise charterer of the ship, the court held that there need not be a document which records a consensual agreement between the owner and the charterer, before the statutory definition of 'demise charterer' can be satisfied. The terms on which Blasko held the vessel were set out in a document described as a 'charter' and had the effect that Blasko could sell or mortgage its vessels, provided necessary government or State consent was obtained. Evans LJ held that Blasko's position vis a vis the Republic could be interpreted as a demise charterer and, as such, the provision of s 21(4) for the arrest of the ship was satisfied.

In situations of privatisation of State enterprises, a transfer of the whole undertaking of a fleet of ships from one corporation to another will be done effectively if continuity is broken, so that it can be said that the new corporation is a new entity. The Russian State had successfully broken that continuity as has been shown in *The Kommunar (No 2)*.[156]

Russian fishing vessels, which were managed by a State enterprise and controlled by the Ministry of Fisheries, were transferred by privatisation of the managing company. It involved a conversion into a public joint stock, a company limited by shares, and change of its name. The conversion occurred after claims arose, but before the arrest of the ship in connection with which the claim arose. The beneficial owner, therefore, at the time of the issue of the writ was not the person who would be liable *in personam* when the cause of action arose. The ship was released from arrest.

---

156 [1997] 1 Lloyd's Rep 8.

4.3.7 Beneficial ownership and risk management

These cases illustrate that there are various ways of structuring the owning companies of ships, some of which are legitimate in the eyes of the law but others are illegitimate, if the intention is to avoid liabilities already accrued.[157] For purpose of risk management, a shipowner can legitimately arrange his affairs in such a way so that the exposure of his assets is limited. Forming one-ship companies provides one legitimate method of limiting liability;[158] parent and, a series of subsidiary companies, is another. A genuine transfer of a ship from one sister company to another, before a suspected claim has arisen, may provide a shield to reaching the beneficial owner when the *in rem* claim form is issued. Similarly, the ship can be chartered down the line and the carrier of cargo, for example, can be a subsidiary company of the owning companies, which acts as a time charterer, signing bills of lading as carrier, but who does not own ships. So, although he would be liable personally for a cargo claim, the ship in connection with which a claim might arise cannot be arrested because he would neither be the beneficial owner of that ship nor the charterer by demise. If the carrier/charterer does not beneficially own ships itself, no other ship can be arrested under s 21(4) of the SCA 1981. In some cases, however, the claimant may be able to base his claim in tort against the owner of the ship, in which case the ship could be arrested.

If an arrest of the ship or 'other' ship is difficult, the claimant may be able to locate where the freight or hire is to be paid and apply for a freezing injunction, but that is often difficult.

It has already been mentioned that, unlike the arrest of a ship, which is available as of right, an application to the court for an injunctive relief depends on judicial discretion. 'The eye of equity' can look behind the corporate veil in order to do justice.[159] Thus, the court may peep through the corporate status of a company as a legal entity and will consider who are the shareholders, or the people who direct and control the activities of a company, where the character of a company, or the nature of persons controlling it, is a relevant feature.[160]

---

157 *Yukong Lines Ltd P of Korea v Rendsburg Investment Corp (The Rialto (No 2))* [1998] 1 Lloyd's Rep 322.

158 *Bakri Bunker Trading Co Ltd v The Owners of Neptune* [1986] HK LR 345. Single-ship companies and legal consequences have been examined by Christodoulou, D, *The Single-Ship Company*, 2000, Sakkoulas, which provides an interesting comparative study of the subject matter, particularly in relation to the position of creditors. The author examines the circumstances in which the courts in England, USA and Greece pay regard or disregard the corporate personality, as well as the conditions of ship arrest under the more flexible legal systems, such as in France and South Africa. The viability of financial security for creditors is also examined and the reasons why the single-ship companies are justified.

159 *The Coral Rose* [1991] 1 Lloyd's Rep 563, p 569, *per* Neill LJ.

160 *Merchandise Transport Ltd v British Transport Commission* [1962] 2 QB 173, p 206.

Furthermore, the English court has recently broken new ground in the piercing of the corporate veil on an issue arising under s 51 of the SCA 1981, relating to Court's discretion to order any party to pay the costs of English proceedings. In *The Ikarian Reefer*,[161] it was held that the director of a company, a non-party to previous proceedings brought by the assured (the company) against the hull underwriters of the ship for a total loss, was liable to pay the outstanding legal costs of those proceedings in which the assured had lost at the Court of Appeal on the ground of willful misconduct.

Whether or not the Court of Appeal decision against the company was correct (and it is submitted that it was not), the result of this case may be alarming to shareholders or directors of one-ship companies who support litigation financially. Even if they are domiciled in a European Union State, they may be sued in the court seised of the original proceedings under Art 6(2) of the Brussels Convention,[162] which provides for an alternative to the domicile rule, a special jurisdiction against a third party in any third party proceedings.

5 PROPERTY AGAINST WHICH AN IN REM CLAIM MAY BE BROUGHT

The ship – in connection with which the maritime claim arose – and/or her sister ship are the primary property against which an *in rem* claim can be brought, provided the conditions laid down in s 21(4) of the SCA 1981 are satisfied. A sister ship is a ship owned by the same company, which owns the ship in connection with which the claim arose. For claims enforceable under s 21(2) and (3), however, there is no provision for a sister ship arrest. But, since the claims attracting maritime liens are also included in s 21, para (4), a sister ship arrest is allowed under this paragraph. The consequence of arresting a sister ship for a claim which attracts a maritime lien will, however, be the loss of the privilege of maritime lien because the sister ship is not the property on which the lien has attached.[163] If the ship is under a time charter, the bunkers on board the ship belong to the charterer.[164] So, if a mortgagee arrests the ship, the charterer can intervene in the action[165] and the proceeds of sale of the bunkers, if the ship is sold by a court order, will be paid to the charterer.[166]

The cargo on board the ship, or freight earned, may be subject to arrest only if there is a maritime lien attached, for example, when there have been

161 *National Justice Compania Naviera SA v Prudential Assurance Co Ltd (The Ikarian Reefer (No 2))* [2000] 1 Lloyd's Rep 129 (CA).
162 See Chapter 6.
163 *The Leoborg (No2)* [1964] 1 Lloyd's Rep 380.
164 *The Span Terza (No 2)* [1984] 1 Lloyd's Rep 119 (HL).
165 *The Saint Anna* [1980] 1 Lloyd's Rep 180.
166 *The Eurostar* [1993] 1 Lloyd's Rep 106; *The Pan Oak* [1992] 2 Lloyd's Rep 36.

salvage services rendered to save ship and cargo. The same would apply to the bunkers on board, which do not belong to the shipowner. An aircraft can only be the subject of arrest, if it is waterborne and there has been salvage, or towage, or pilotage of the aircraft as per ss 21(3), (4) and 24(1).

CHAPTER 4

PROCEDURE (OVERVIEW)

1 ISSUE OF THE *IN REM* CLAIM FORM

An *in rem* claim form can be issued naming more than one ship, or separate *in rem* claim forms may be issued against different ships belonging to the same owner for the same claim, but only one ship can be arrested.[1] The claimant must elect which ship to arrest.[2] In practice, the claimant waits until one of the ships named comes within the jurisdiction, whereupon he amends the claim form and serves it on that ship.

The Berny[3]

This case involved claims in relation to cargo of sugar that was carried from Dunkirk to Dar-es-Salaam on the defendant's ship, *The Berny*. The plaintiffs/cargo-owners brought actions for shortage of bags of cargo delivered.One was *in rem* against a number of sister ships of *The Berny*, another was against *The Berny* and a third was *in personam* against the defendants. As neither *The Berny* nor any of her sister ships visited a port within the jurisdiction and the time of the validity of the writs was about to expire, the plaintiffs applied for their renewal, which they obtained. A sister ship entered jurisdiction and the shipowners/defendants, at the request of the plaintiffs, provided a letter of undertaking to nominate solicitors to accept service. Later, the writ in the action against *The Berny* was served upon her and the shipowners entered a conditional appearance, but they contended that the action should be stayed on the ground that, when it was begun, the cargo-owners had already invoked the jurisdiction of the court in respect of a sister ship. Therefore, the court had no jurisdiction to entertain the action against *The Berny*.

It was held that the cargo-owners were entitled to institute proceedings *in rem* against more than one ship, provided they only served proceedings or arrested only one of such ships. The shipowner's contention was rejected. Instead, it was held that the Administration of Justice Act 1956 gave the cargo-owners the option to invoke the admiralty jurisdiction of the court *in rem*, against either *The Berny* or any other sister ship. The right course of action for the court was to compel them to elect against which of such ships they wished

---

1   *The Banco* [1971] 1 Lloyd's Rep 49; also s 21(8) of the SCA 1981.
2   *The Berny* [1977] 2 Lloyd's Rep 533.
3   *Ibid*.

to continue. If they elected to continue against *The Berny*, the sister ship writ was to be set aside. It would not be right to compel them to continue against one of the sister ships rather than against *The Berny*, simply on the ground that the writ against a sister ship was issued first and the one against *The Berny* second.

If an *in rem* claim form has been wrongly served on a ship, which is mistakenly thought to be the one against which the claim could be brought, the right ship can be arrested by a subsequent action.[4] The parties may be described and not named, for example, 'the owners of the ship X' or 'the owners of the cargo laden on board the ship X'. A full and concise statement of the nature of the claim and the remedy sought should be contained in the claim form.[5] If particulars of the claim are not served with the claim form, they must be served within 75 days of the service of the claim form.[6]

2 EFFECT OF ISSUE

Unless the principle established by *The Monica S* has been undermined by *The Indian Grace* (as discussed in Chapter 3), the effect of the issue of the claim form is the crystallisation of the claimant's statutory right *in rem* against the relevant ship. The consequence of this is that, in the event of ownership transfer even to a *bona fide* purchaser of the ship before service of the claim form, the claim will still be enforceable against the ship by service and arrest. Therefore, prompt issue of the *in rem* claim form is essential.

3 SERVICE OF THE *IN REM* CLAIM FORM

The service can be effected[7] either upon the property, by affixing the claim form (or a copy) on the outside of the property in a position where it may reasonably be expected to be seen; or upon the defendant's solicitor who has authority to accept service. The service does not constitute arrest without a warrant of arrest, which must be issued upon a separate application and executed by the admiralty marshal or his substitute. The effect of service or arrest is that the jurisdiction of the court is invoked[8] and, in addition,

---

4   *The Stephen*[1985] 2 Lloyd's Rep 344.
5   CPR, Pt 16, r 2.1(a), (b).
6   See PD 49F, para 2.1(2).
7   See PD 49F, para 2.1(6).
8   *The Freccia del Nord* [1989] 1 Lloyd's Rep 388.

following *The Indian Grace*, the person named in the claim form, as the person who would be liable *in personam*, becomes a party to the proceedings.[9]

The *in rem* claim form cannot be served out of the jurisdiction (the ship must come within the jurisdiction) nor can an order for substituted service be made.[10] In most cases, in practice, however, when an undertaking is given by way of security for the claim to the claimant in an acceptable form prior to the service of proceedings and in lieu of arrest, there is a condition of that undertaking that solicitors will be appointed by the defendant to accept service unconditionally. The solicitors then accept service by endorsing on the claim form such acceptance, which amounts to submission to the jurisdiction of the court by the defendant. Alternatively, the defendant may choose to acknowledge the issue[11] of the claim form, which will amount to submission to jurisdiction. If he wishes to contest the jurisdiction of the court, he may acknowledge service conditionally,[12] since unconditional acknowledgment will amount to submission.

An important change by the new Civil Procedure Rules (CPR), Pt 5, is that members of the public may only search the record for claim forms which have been served.[13]

4 ARREST BY ISSUE AND EXECUTION OF A WARRANT

The service of the *in rem* claim form on the ship does not constitute arrest. A separate application must be made for the issue of a warrant of arrest. Only the admiralty marshal or his substitute may effect the arrest of property.[14] An application to arrest (containing an undertaking to pay the marshal's fees) may be made by filing an application notice in the admiralty and Commercial Registry. Before the application is made, the applicant must carry out a search in the caveat book in order to ascertain whether there is a caveat against arrest. Then he must file a declaration in the prescribed form (ADM 5) containing the particulars of the claim, the property, the amount of the security and show that the requirements of s 21(4) of the Supreme Court Act (SCA) 1981 are met. The declaration must be sworn as an affidavit,[15]

---

9   But the claim also continues to be a claim *in rem*, PD 49F, para 2.5. See conclusion on *The Indian Grace*, Chapter 3, para 3.8.

10 *The Good Herald* [1987] 1 Lloyd's Rep 236.

11 PD 49F, para 2.4.

12 By acknowledging service, the right to dispute the court's jurisdiction is not lost (PD 49F, para 2.7).

13 In the past, they could check the Admiralty Registry for any claims *in rem* issued, which was very useful to a person who was about to buy a particular ship.

14 PD 49F, para 6.4.

15 PD 49F, para 6.2(4).

containing statements of information and belief about the particulars and sources thereof stated. The Admiralty Court may issue a warrant of arrest even if the declaration does not contain all the particulars.[16] The claimant no longer needs to make full and frank disclosure of all material facts, provided the requirements of PD 49F, paras 6.1 and 6.2 are complied with. He must, however, correct any inaccuracies promptly. Issue of an arrest warrant is as of right, that is, the court no longer has a discretion, as it used to prior to the decision in *The Varna*.[17]

The admiralty marshal, or his substitute, will serve the warrant on the ship or property to be arrested.[18] To prevent arrest, a caveat against arrest may be filed in the Admiralty and Commercial Registry accompanied by an undertaking to file an acknowledgment of service and to give sufficient security to satisfy the claim with interest and costs. The entry of a caveat against arrest shall not be treated as a submission to the jurisdiction of the English court and property may be arrested, notwithstanding a caveat against arrest. Where a defendant constitutes a limitation fund, in accordance with Art 11 of the Limitation of Liability Convention 1976, and desires to prevent the arrest of his property, he may file a caveat against arrest.[19] If the property is already under arrest, any other person claiming to have a right *in rem* against the property under arrest may file a caveat against its release.[20]

5 THE AFTERMATH OF ARREST

5.1 Rights of third parties

Once the ship or property arrested is under the custody not the possession of the admiralty marshal. A pre-arrest right or remedy of a third party based on possession is not affected, such as a statutory right of detention of a port authority. The marshal can apply to court for directions. In *The Queen of the South*[21] the port authority's right to detain the ship, which was under the custody of the marshal, was preserved. The port authority was allowed to receive payment for its outstanding dues from the proceeds of sale of the ship by the marshal before other maritime claimants. Third parties whose rights

---

16 PD 49F, paras 6.1 and 6.2.

17 [1993] 2 Lloyd's Rep 253.

18 For a useful outline of the procedure of arrest by the admiralty marshal see *The Johnny Two* [1992] 2 Lloyd's Rep 257, *per* Sheen J.

19 PD 49F, para 6.3.

20 PD 49F, para 6.5(2).

21 [1968] P 449.

are adversely affected by the arrest can intervene but any other interference with the arrest is a contempt of court being subject to committal.[22] If the port operations are affected the court has inherent jurisdiction to give directions to the marshal as it thinks it may be appropriate.

The Mardina Merchant[23]

In this case, there was an application by the port authority to the admiralty marshal for direction to move a ship from her place of arrest to another place. The vessel had been arrested by various claimants and remained under arrest for a while, causing interference to the working of the port, thus, causing financial loss to the port and the owners of the berth. Under the rules of court, a third party could intervene only if it could show that it had an interest in the property arrested. Unless the court, could exercise its inherent jurisdiction, the port authority, of course, could not show an interest. Brandon J held:

> I am of the opinion that there must be an inherent jurisdiction in the court to allow a party to intervene if the effect of an arrest is to cause that party serious hardship or difficulty or danger ... In all such cases it seems to me that the court must have power to allow the party who is affected by the work of the system of law used in admiralty actions *in rem* to apply to the court for some mitigation of the hardship or the difficulty or danger.If it were not so, then there would be no remedy available for such persons at all.[24]

Any other person interested in the property under arrest, or its proceeds of sale, whose interests are affected by any order sought or made, may be made a party to any claim *in rem* against the property or proceeds of sale where the court considers it would be just and convenient, and on terms the court may think fit.[25] If the ship is under arrest, but cargo on board her is not, and those interested in the cargo wish to secure its discharge, they may request the marshal to take the appropriate steps, provided the applicant gives a written undertaking satisfactory to the marshal to pay on demand the marshal's fees and expenses to be incurred by him in taking the desired steps. The marshal will apply to court for the appropriate order. Alternatively, they may intervene in the action. The same rules apply when the cargo is under arrest but the ship is not.[26]

---

22 CPR Sched 1, RSC Ord 52.
23 [1975] 1 WLR 147.
24 *Ibid*, p 149.
25 PD 49F, para 6.8.
26 PD 49F, paras 6.10 and 6.11.

5.2 Provision of security for the claim and release from arrest

The owner of the property may arrange for security to be placed for the amount of the claim plus interest and costs in lieu of the release of the ship from arrest. There are standard letters of undertaking provided either by the owner's P&I club, or by his bank, which include an undertaking that solicitors will be instructed to accept service on the owner's behalf and the owners will submit to jurisdiction. There is no requirement, as yet, for an undertaking in damages to be given by the arresting party to the shipowner in case of wrongful or unjustified arrest.[27] The amount of security for release of a ship must be reasonable and its assessment approximate.

The Moschanthy[28]

A consignment of second hand machinery was shipped on the defendants' motor vessel *A*, at London for carriage to Tripoli, to be delivered to the plaintiffs' order. When the discharge was completed at Tripoli, the machinery was placed with the defendants' agents, who claimed a lien for unpaid freight. An application to the Lebanese court for an order of delivery of the goods against a bank guarantee was rejected. Later, the plaintiff issued a writ *in rem* in the English Court against the *M*, a sister ship of *A*, claiming damages or the value of the goods plus damages, and *M* was arrested in Liverpool. A high amount of security was requested for the release of the ship from arrest on the ground that the plaintiff expected to make a 100% profit from the sale of the goods. The defendants, who in the meantime had commenced an action in Lebanon claiming freight due, applied to stay the proceedings in the English Court on the ground, *inter alia*, that the security given was excessive and should be reduced. It was held that having regard to the value of the goods, and also the amount of interest and costs, which would ultimately be payable if the plaintiffs succeeded, any assessment of a reasonable figure for security could only be approximate. The amount requested fixed was not excessive.

Contrast the criteria applied in the following case.

The Tribels[29]

While the plaintiffs' vessel was entering into the harbour, she took to the ground due to a strong northeasterly wind. The master employed the defendants' harbour tugs on the standard Lloyd's form of Salvage Agreement. The salvors, pursuant to the contract, demanded security in the sum of £3,323,000. The plaintiffs asked for an injunction to prevent the salvors from

27 When the new Arrest Convention 1999 is enacted by the UK, there will be such a provision therein.

28 [1971] 1 Lloyd's Rep 37.

29 [1985] 1 Lloyd's Rep 128.

demanding security, exceeding £1m. The salved value was probably about £16,150,000. It was an implied term of the salvage agreement that the contractor would not ask for unreasonably high security.It was held that security in the sum of £1m gave a very ample margin of protection in respect of whatever sum the arbitrator would award after the salvage. Taking the case at its most favourable to the salvor, the sum provided an ample margin of protection.

5.3 Release in particular circumstances

(a) Where a shipowner constitutes a limitation fund in accordance with the Merchant Shipping Act (MSA) 1995 and the Rules of Court,[30] he will be entitled to the release of the ship as of right, if the prerequisites of Art 13(2)(3) of the Limitation of Liability Convention 1976 are satisfied.[31]

(b) When a claim is subject to an arbitration agreement and *in rem* proceedings have commenced, the court will stay the proceedings upon the application of the defendant, and may order the release from arrest, provided sufficient security for the claim is given (s 26 of the Civil Jurisdiction and Judgments Act (CJJA) 1982). Prior to s 26, a vessel could be arrested for the purpose of provision of security to satisfy a judgment and not an arbitration award. If the proceedings were stayed in favour of arbitration pursuant to s 1 of the previous Arbitration Act (AA) 1975, the court had a wide discretion whether or not to maintain the arrest. If the court took the view that the proceedings would result in a judgment, the arrest could be maintained as security for that judgment.[32] Such a wide discretion is no longer needed. Section 26 of the 1982 Act, coupled with s 11 of the AA 1996, give the court power either to maintain the arrest as security for the arbitration award, or to order the release from arrest upon provision of security for the satisfaction of any such award. The following case confirmed that position, even before the AA 1996 was enacted.

The Bazias[33]

The plaintiffs were the bareboat charterers of two vessels, *B1* and *B2*,which were owned by the defendants. They chartered the vessels under time charters to Sally Line Ltd, (the time charterers) who employed the ships for cross-channel ferry services. The defendants withdrew their vessels from the services to plaintiffs on grounds of failure by the plaintiffs to pay hire and for other breaches of the bareboat charters. Sally Line gave notice to the plaintiffs

---

30 PD 49F, para 9.
31 If a limitation decree is granted, any proceedings arising out of the occurrence may be stayed: PD 49F, para 9.3(1)(a).
32 *The Tuyuti* [1984] 2 All ER 545.
33 [1993] 1 Lloyd's Rep 101; see, also, *The Jalamatsya* [1987] 2 Lloyd's Rep 164.

ending the time charters, as they could no longer perform under the contract. The defendants in this action commenced arbitration proceedings against the plaintiffs, claiming unpaid hire and damages. The plaintiffs counterclaimed for loss of profits with respect to the remaining period of the bareboat charters and, in order to obtain security for their counterclaim, they issued proceedings *in rem* against the vessels; due warning had been given that they intended to arrest. Meanwhile, the defendants had already entered into bareboat charters with Sally Line Ltd, so that the cross-channel ferry service continued. *The Bazias* was arrested by the plaintiffs. The defendants applied for a stay, under s1 of the AA 1975, on the ground that the dispute was referred to arbitration, and sought to set aside the warrant of arrest. All parties agreed that the defendants were entitled to a mandatory stay under the above section. The question in issue was whether the court still had a discretion to release the vessel according to pre-existing practice without requiring equivalent security, especially in the light of s 26 of the CJJA 1982. Counsel for the defendants argued that s 26 preserved the pre-existing wide discretion of the court in arbitration cases and the manner in which it was exercised. It was held that the reason for the wider discretion exercised by the court previously had gone with the advent of the CJJA 1982. This Act was drafted to cover all classes of cases. The usual practice was that the vessel would only be released on the provision of sufficient security to cover the amount of the claim plus interest and costs. Therefore, a stay was granted and it was ordered that the vessel remained under arrest until a further order of the Admiralty Court.

5.4 Wrongful arrest

The Arrest Convention 1952 has left the matter of remedies in case of wrongful arrest to the State parties. Under English law, the shipowner or demise charterer has to show that the arresting party was guilty of *mala fides* or *grossa negligentia* when they arrested the ship which ought not to have been arrested.[34] The 1999 Arrest Convention, by Art 6, permits the court to require the claimant, as a condition of arrest, to put up security in the event of wrongful, or unjustified arrest, or when excessive security has been demanded and provided.[35]

---

34 *The Evangelismos* (1858) 12 Moo PC 352; *Walter D Wallett* [1893] P 202; this issue was eloquently and forcefully argued by Eder, B (QC), a seminar held by the London Shipping Law Centre in 1998 (the paper is available from the office of the Shipping Law Centre, UCL Law Faculty).

35 See comments by Gaskell, N and Shaw, R, 'The Arrest Convention 1999' [1999] LMCLQ 470, pp 470–90.

5.5 Can there be a re-arrest?

The authorities on this issue, although not consistent, can conveniently be divided into four categories. There is no overall principle that can be derived from them, but the result seems to depend on the facts of each case. It can be observed that the approach reflects an instinctive attitude of judges as to what would be fair and just in the circumstances.

5.5.1 Prior to judgment on liability there can be re-arrest with the leave of the court

Before judgment on liability has been given, the court has power to direct measures to be taken to do full justice to the claimant and re-arrest may be allowed, if the bail given is not sufficient.[36] However, Dr Lushington had held previously in *The Kalamazoo*,[37] that the bail represented the ship and it would be absurd to contend that you could arrest a ship, take bail to any amount, and afterwards arrest her again for the same cause of action. He repeated the same in *The Wild Ranger*[38], when he said: 'Now bail given for a ship in any action is a substitute for the ship; and whenever bail is given, the ship is wholly released from the cause of action and cannot be arrested again for that cause of action.'

In *The Hero*,[39] Dr Lushington commented on his two previous decisions that, if the expressions in those cases were literally interpreted, it would indicate that he did not have power to grant a re-arrest for the same cause of action after property had been released on bail. But, he explained that, what he said in those earlier cases must be read subject to the facts that formed the ground of the decisions. In each of those cases, the cause of action had passed into *res judicata*.

Following these decisions, Bateson J made a pragmatic comment in *The Point Breeze*,[40] in which bail had been given for a collision liability and the ship was re-arrested after judgment (that is, *res judicata*) the amount of which exceeded the bail. Disallowing the re-arrest, he said:

> If the plaintiffs are right in their contention that they are entitled to arrest this ship, it seems to me that it will open the door to the re-arrest of vessels, or arrest after getting bail, whenever a party thinks that his claim may be more than he originally thought it was. No immunity from arrest will be obtained by giving bail, and the result of that, on the question of maritime liens, might be very serious.

---

36 Dr Lushington in *The Hero* (1865) B&L 447.
37 (1851) 15 Jur 885, p 886.
38 (1863) Lush 553; (1862) 1 New Rep 132.
39 (1865) B&L 447, p 448.
40 (1928) 30 LlL Rep 229, p 231.

The 1952 Arrest Convention allows only one arrest (Art 3(3)) in respect of any maritime claim. The 1999 Arrest Convention (Art 5) entitles the claimant to re-arrest only in the following circumstances:

(1) where, in any State, a ship has already been arrested and released, or security has already been provided to secure a maritime claim, that ship shall not thereafter be rearrested or arrested in respect of the same maritime claim unless:

    (a) the nature or amount of the security in respect of that ship already provided in respect of the same claim is inadequate, on condition that the aggregate amount of security may not exceed the value of the ship; or

    (b) the person who has already provided the security is not, or is unlikely to be, able to fulfil some or all of that person's obligations; or

    (c) the ship arrested or the security previously provided was released either upon the application or with the consent of the claimant acting on reasonable grounds, or because the claimant could not by taking reasonable steps prevent the release;

(2) with regard to any other ship, which would otherwise be subject to arrest in respect of the same maritime claim, arrest shall not be allowed unless the nature or amount of the security provided in respect of the same claim is inadequate; or the provisions of (1)(b) and (c) above are applicable.

5.5.2 No re-arrest after a judgment on liability has been given

In *The Kalamazoo* and *The Wild Ranger* (mentioned above), in which the bail given for a collision claim was found to be insufficient after judgment, Dr Lushington set aside a warrant of arrest to obtain further security. This principle, based on the notion that the cause of action had become merged in the judgment, therefore *res judicata*, was accepted to be correct in later decisions, *The Point Breeze*[41] and *The Alletta*.[42]

All the authorities were reviewed by Mocatta J, in the **The Alletta**.

A claim arose out of a collision incident, security was provided in lieu of arrest of *The Alletta* and her owners submitted to the jurisdiction. A judgment for damages was obtained against the defendants, who were not able to limit their liability. It appeared later that the amount of the security was not enough to satisfy the full claim amount. Seven years later, the ship was sold and she was renamed, *The Tarmac I*. In the hands of her new owner, she was threatened to be arrested by the plaintiffs. The buyers knew nothing about the claim prior to delivery; subsequently, they claimed an indemnity from the

---

41 (1928) 30 LlL Rep 229.
42 [1974] 1 Lloyd's Rep 40.

previous owner (the first defendant in this action) and joined the action seeking an order for warrant of arrest to be set aside. It was argued that the plaintiffs' right to arrest, either by way of enforcing a maritime lien or a statutory right *in rem*, had been lost (i) by laches, or (ii) by the fact that the plaintiffs had obtained judgment against the first defendants. The laches point was not accepted, but on the second point, Mocatta J applied the previous authorities and stated a broad principle:

> If a ship may be arrested after judgment on liability has been obtained against her and she is by the date of the arrest the property of a third party, which had bought her without knowledge of the maritime lien, grave injustice may be done. The third party may have no right of indemnity or, which is less unlikely supposition, his indemnity may be worthless. His vendor may, through lack of adequate funds, incompetent legal advice or other reason, not properly and fully have contested the issue of liability ... The position would be quite different from that obtaining when an arrest is effected after transfer of the *res* to such a third party, but before there had been judgment on liability. The third party can then intervene.[43]

It was held that the plaintiff's right of arrest was lost because it had become merged in the judgment.

This decision was criticised by the Singaporean court in **The Daien Maru**,[44] which did not follow *The Alleta*. The Singaporean court held that the plaintiff, who had instituted an action *in rem* against the ship to enforce a maritime lien for services provided to the ship, but had not obtained security, was entitled to arrest the ship for the same cause of action, even after he had obtained judgment. The facts were unusual. The ship was originally arrested by her owners for a claim of possession they had against the charterers. The crew, who had a claim for unpaid wages against the owners, issued a caveat against release of the ship and proceeded to judgment. Thereafter, the owners persuaded the court to release the ship from arrest they had effected themselves. Then the crew arrested the ship to obtain security and execute judgment against it. The judge said that, although once a judgment has been obtained in an action the claim was merged in the judgment, it did not follow and there was no authority supporting the view that the right to security in the ship was lost or extinguished by such merger. The plaintiff who has instituted an action to enforce a maritime lien must be entitled to arrest the ship in the same action, even after he has obtained judgment, provided always that, in such a case, no bail has been previously put up for the ship in that action.

On the facts of this case, it would be unfair if the arrest of the ship was not permitted after judgment in the same action for execution of the judgment against security.[45] This situation is clearly different from a case of arresting or

---

43   [1974] 1 Lloyd's Rep 40, pp 50–51, *The Point Breeze* [1928] P 135 was applied.

44   [1986] 1 Lloyd's Rep 387.

45   See, also, Chapter 3, para 3.6.

re-arresting the ship to relitigate the same issues that have merged with the judgment.[46] By contrast, *The Alleta*, in which security had been provided and the enforcement of judgment by arrest in the hands of an innocent purchaser took an unusually long time after judgment, is clearly distinguishable.[47]

An interesting question arises as to whether the new admiralty Practice Direction 49F, para 6.7(3)(b), which expressly permits re-arrest so as to obtain further security up to the full value of the property, has reversed *The Alletta*. This was voiced by the admiralty judge, in a recent decision, **The Ruta**.[48] He approached the matter on the basis that permission will be judged on criteria of oppression or unfairness.

When a domestic judgment *in rem* has been obtained after bail has been given, which has the effect of submission to jurisdiction by the defendant,[49] but the bail is not sufficient to satisfy the total amount of judgment, the judgment can be executed by seizure and sale of the ship or goods (belonging to the defendant) by the sheriff under a writ of *fieri facias*.[50] By submitting to the jurisdiction, the *in rem* proceedings become also *in personam* and any surplus of the judgment over and above the bail amount can be executed against property belonging to the defendant by a writ of execution, which is different from the *in rem* proceedings.

In conclusion, a re-arrest, after a judgment has been given, will not be permitted unless the re-arrest is for the purpose of enforcement of a maritime lien or a statutory lien *in rem*, when security had not been obtained, or, insufficient security had been provided and when upon the court's discretion, there was no oppression or unfairness.

5.5.3 A foreign in rem judgment can be executed by re-arrest in this jurisdiction

When a foreign *in rem* judgment has been obtained and is not satisfied, the duty of the English court, founded on international comity and on interest of

---

46 In the writer's view, the same could be said with regard to the effect of *The Indian Grace*, in that the right to security in the ship belonging to the defendant is not lost by virtue of s 34 of the CJJA 1982, which operates as a defence to a claim on the merits of the same cause of action being brought afresh when there has already been a judgment in favour or partly in favour of the claimant (see, also, Chapter 3, paras 3.6 and 3.8, above).

47 That the claimant cannot re-arrest the vessel after judgment, having previously obtained bail up to her full value, was also held in: *The Freedom* (1871) LR 3 A&E 495; *The Gemma* [1899] P 285; *The Ioannis Vatis* [1922] P 213: '... having received bail in the full value of the defendants' vessel, the plaintiffs could not arrest her *in rem*, but could proceed *in personam* and were entitled to a declaration that the amounts due in respect of interest and costs were enforceable by seizure and sale of the vessel by a sheriff under a writ of *fi fa*.'

48 [2000] 1 Lloyd's Rep 359.

49 When bail is provided, it is linked with an undertaking given by the defendant to submit to jurisdiction: *The Prinsengracht* [1993] 1 Lloyd's Rep 41. Bail could be given under protest if there are grounds for the defendant to contest the jurisdiction of the Court: *The Anna H* [1994] 1 Lloyd's Rep 287 (CA), *per* Hobhouse LJ.

50 CPR 1999, Sched 1, Ords 46 and 47.

justice with respect to execution of a foreign judgment based upon a maritime lien, had been established since 1608.[51] Sir Phillimore in **The City of Mecca**[52] allowed a judgment obtained *in rem* in Lisbon in respect of a collision damage to be enforced by an action *in rem* in England.[53] It should be noted that the case concerned a foreign judgment for which security had not been provided.[54]

In a 20th century, Sheen J confirmed this principle in **The Despina GK**,[55] which concerned a cargo claim. The plaintiffs arrested the ship at a Swedish port and commenced an action in the Admiralty Court in Stockholm, which gave judgment and awarded a maritime lien on the vessel for the sum adjudged. Sheen J said:[56]

> There is, of course, a distinction between those claims which give rise to a maritime lien and which may, therefore, be enforced against the ship, notwithstanding a change of ownership, and those claims which may only be enforced by an action *in rem* if the person who would be liable *in personam* is still the owner of the ship at the time when the writ is issued.

> Likewise, there is the further distinction between an action *in rem*, which may be brought in the High Court against the ship, and execution of a judgment obtained in such an action …

> A judgment creditor who has obtained a final judgment against a shipowner by proceeding *in rem* in a foreign Admiralty Court can bring an action *in rem* in this court against that ship to enforce the decree of the foreign court *if that is necessary to complete the execution* of that judgment, provided that the ship is the property of the judgment debtor at the time when she is arrested.[57]

5.5.4 Prohibition of re-arrest by s 21(8) of the SCA 1981

Re-arrest of the ship or a sister ship is not allowed by s 21(8) of the SCA 1981 for claims mentioned in s 20(2)(e)–(r) with regard to proceedings in this country,[58] and by Art 3(3) of the Arrest Convention 1952, insofar as multiple proceedings *in rem* are concerned in contracting States. Under the new Arrest Convention 1999, Art 5 permits re-arrest in order to obtain an increase of the

---

51 Sir Phillimore explained in *The City of Mecca* (1879) 5 PD 28.

52 *Ibid*.

53 The judgment was reversed by the Court of Appeal (1881) 6 PD 106, as it appeared from a further affidavit that the facts upon which the decision was based were different from the facts proved. But the principle laid down by Sir Phillimore regarding enforcement of a judgment *in rem* by way of execution was not undermined (see Sheen J's comments in *The Despina GK* [1982] 2 Lloyd's Rep 555).

54 See, also, Chapter 3, paras 3.6 and 3.8, above.

55 [1982] 2 Lloyd's Rep 555.

56 *Ibid*, pp 558–59.

57 Emphasis added. The action must be for the purpose of execution (as the judge stressed) and not for the trial of the matter.

58 *The Kommunar (No 2)* [1997] 1 Lloyd's Rep 8; the section emphasises that in this jurisdiction one ship should be arrested only (see *The Banco* [1971] 1 Lloyd's Rep 49).

security already provided. Similarly PD 49F, para 6.7(3)(b) permits re-arrest for this purpose (*supra* 5.5.2).

5.5.5 Re-arrest and risk management

In most cases in practice, security is provided by agreement and, in consideration of that agreement, the claimant releases the ship from arrest and promises not to re-arrest this, or any other ship, in the same ownership, etc. A further arrest would not only be in breach of the agreement, but would also be against good faith, unless there were circumstances in which the agreement was rendered inoperative.[59] It is important to bear in mind, however, that any agreement, by which the claimant promises not to re-arrest a vessel in return of security, should expressly be made, not only between the claimant and the entity providing the security, but also between the claimant and the shipowner, or demise charterer, as the case may be.[60]

There have been instances in which a ship has been arrested or re-arrested, in consequence of the bail becoming insolvent.[61] The rule that the bail represents the ship, so there should be no re-arrest, is not without exceptions. The justification for the rule is, and always has been, to avoid oppression and unfairness.[62] The same would apply where the security given is not bail, but consists of a personal undertaking such as a guarantee where proper reasons are shown for it.[63] The discretion of the court is broad and the judges adopt a pragmatic approach.

---

59 *The Christiansborg* (1885) 10 PD 141; see, also, *Westminster Bank Ltd v West of England Association* (1933) 46 LlL Rep 101, in which it was said that, when there has been a mistake about the amount of bail, or there is a question of solvency of the surety, the bail question may re-opened. Also, when the security given is by way of a personal guarantee which may prove to be inoperative, further arrest may be allowed.

60 A suggestion made by Clarke LJ in his speech on the subject ('The civil justice reform, its impact on maritime litigation, the maritime industry and London', lecture in memory of Professor Cadwallader, the London Shipping Law Centre, 7 July 1999; the text of the speeches on the new CPR can be obtained from the office of the Shipping Law Centre, UCL Law Faculty).

61 *The City of Mecca* (1879) 5 PD 28, *per* Sir Robert Phillimore.

62 Lloyd LJ, in *The Arctic Star* (1985) *The Times*, 5 February; the same view was held recently by Steel J, in *The Ruta* [2000] 1 Lloyd's Rep 359.

63 *Westminster Bank Ltd v West of England Steamship Owners' P&I Association Ltd* (1933) 46 LlL Rep 101, *per* Roche J.

5.6 Appraisement and sale by the court

5.6.1 When it can be ordered

If there is no acknowledgment of service and/or defence to a claim *in rem* within the time required, the claimant may apply for a judgment in default by filing an application, a certificate proving proper service of the claim form and evidence proving the claim to the satisfaction of the court. There is a presumption of good service if the claim form was served by the Court.[64] The property under arrest will be appraised and sold by court order. Appraisement is an official valuation of the property by a court appointed valuer. An order for sale before judgment may only be made by the admiralty judge.[65]

5.6.2 Sale by the admiralty marshal and effect

The admiralty marshal can sell either by private treaty or public auction advised by brokers. The effect of sale by the admiralty marshal is that all encumbrances, including maritime liens, are extinguished. Private negotiations for sale by the owner, or a third party, after a court order is made will be in contempt of court.

The APJ Shalin[66]

In a dispute arising under a shipbuilding contract, the plaintiffs alleged default in payment under the contract. The defendants' vessel came within the English jurisdiction and the plaintiffs issued a writ *in rem* and arrested her. The defendants applied for the writ and the arrest to be set aside, claiming that the vessel was valueless to the plaintiffs as security because there were other claims ranking in priority to that of the plaintiffs. They also sought an order giving them liberty to sell the vessel privately, subject to the supervision of the admiralty marshal. It was held that it would not be right for the court to order the release of the ship, without security being given, against the wishes of the creditor, who had properly exercised his right to arrest the ship. The issue of priority was to be determined when all the actions had proceeded to judgment. It was also held that while a ship was under arrest, it was in the custody of the admiralty marshal. The shipowners could only sell the vessel, if they could find someone willing to buy her under arrest, but it would remain under arrest. However, where an order for sale was made by the court, there could not be a private sale because such a transaction would be open to abuse.

---

64 PD 49F, para 7.1.
65 PD 49F, paras 8.1, 8.2 and 8.3.
66 [1991] 2 Lloyd's Rep 62.

The Cerro Colorado[67]

The plaintiff lent a substantial amount of money to the defendants, secured by a mortgage upon the ship. They obtained judgment and the court ordered that the ship be appraised and sold by the admiralty marshal. Earlier, solicitors for the master and crew of that ship had requested the entry of a caveat against the release of the ship, on the grounds that they had a right of action *in rem* against the ship, pursuant to s 20(2)(o) of the SCA 1981, for various claims for wages, severance pay and interest. A writ had not been issued against the ship on their behalf. When an order for the sale was made, the Spanish Embassy in London sent a note to the effect that a purchaser of the ship would find himself subject to substantial claims by the crew for unpaid wages, which had been incurred by the previous owner. An article in the Lloyd's List, published soon thereafter, contained the same warning. Upon an application by the admiralty marshal to the court for directions, it was held that a sale by the admiralty marshal gave the purchaser a title free of all liens and encumbrances. It was also held that the articles published could be treated as a contempt of court, tending to interfere with the administration of justice. The master and crew were given 28 days in which to make a claim *in rem* against the ship, or the proceeds of sale if they so wished.

The admiralty marshal cannot sell the ship for less than the appraised value without an order of the court.

The Halcyon The Great[68]

The mortgagees of the ship proceeded by an action *in rem*. During the trial, they applied for an order for the appraisement and sale of the vessel. After her appraisal, the admiralty marshal invited bids. Even the highest of the bids made was substantially below the appraised value. The commission of appraisement and sale required that the admiralty marshal did not sell below the appraised value. He applied to the court for an order to sell below the appraised value. The plaintiffs opposed the application and were supported by various creditors and other parties interested in the action. The court considered that there was a risk that there might not even be a bid as good as the one offered at that time, if the application of the marshal to sell below the appraised value was refused and the ship was re-offered. However, the judge agreed to grant the request made by the plaintiffs and the other parties, on the condition that they undertook to indemnify the court against any loss, which could result from refusing the marshal's application. On receiving the undertaking, the judge held that the marshal was, thus, denied liberty to sell the ship for less than the appraised value without further order of the court.

---

67 [1993] 1 Lloyd's Rep 58.
68 [1975] 1 Lloyd's Rep 525.

The proceeds of sale will be kept in court until all claimants, who have obtained judgment against the ship, apply to be joined in the list for payment. The court will determine the priorities of the various claimants (see para 8).

5.6.3 Sale pendente lite

Appraisement and sale of the ship may be ordered pending action (*pendente lite*) in certain circumstances.

The Myrto[69]

The plaintiffs were mortgagees of the defendants' vessel. They arrested the vessel for the amount due and owing to them under a registered mortgage. Many other claimants had also entered caveats against release of the vessel. The charterers of the ship intervened in the action claiming that the arrest of the ship was an unlawful interference with their contractual rights. The plaintiffs applied for the appraisement and sale of the vessel *pendente lite*, which was resisted by both the owners and charterers. It was held that, on the evidence, it was unlikely that the owners would have sufficient resources either to pay off the claims against the ship or to complete the voyage, which had been seriously disrupted already by the events that had taken place leading up to the arrest of the vessel. No purpose would be served by releasing the ship from her present arrest.[70]

On the question of whether an order for appraisement and sale of the ship under arrest should be made, the court held that such a situation only arises where there is a default of appearance or defence. If the defendants appear, they usually obtain release from arrest by giving bail or providing security. The court would make such an order (on the plaintiff's application) in a situation where the security of the plaintiff's claim was imperiled to be diminished by the continuing costs of maintaining the arrest to the disadvantage of all those interested in the ship, including the defendants themselves, if there was still a residual interest left to them.

Brandon J said:

> I accept that the court should not make an order for the appraisement and sale of a ship *pendente lite* except for good reason, and this, whether the action is defended or not. I accept further that, where the action is defended and the defendants opposed the making of such an order, the court should examine more critically than it would normally do in a default action the question whether good reason for the making of an order exists or not ... It would, in my view, be unreasonable to keep the ship under arrest at great expense for

---

69 [1977] 2 Lloyd's Rep 243.
70 For further information on this point, and possible interference with the contractual rights of third parties, see Chapter 9 on mortgages.

seven months or more, with the result that, if the bank succeeded in their claim, the amount of their recovery would be reduced by the costs incurred. If the owners were prepared to hear or contribute to those costs for the time being in order to prevent a sale, different considerations might apply.[71]

The Gulf Venture[72]

The plaintiffs applied for the appraisement and sale of *The Gulf Venture*, which had been earlier arrested. They claimed that the vessel was a wasting asset and ought to be sold for the benefit of all the creditors, as the cost of maintaining her under arrest would exceed £5,000 per month. The owners and the second mortgagees disputed the application. The court considered whether the plaintiffs had a reasonably arguable case, that the defendants would be liable on the claim in an action *in personam*. There was no dispute as to the amount it would cost to maintain the vessel under arrest. The court examined and reaffirmed the principles laid down in *The Myrto*.[73] It was held that the plaintiffs had a probable case on liability and, also, it was probable that if judgment was obtained in their favour, it would not be satisfied by the defendants personally. The plaintiffs would still have to obtain an order for the sale of the ship. Concerning the second mortgagees, it was in their interest that they should intervene to enforce their security at the present time, rather than later, seeing that the security available one year later after the adjudication would be about £60,000 or less. The sale of the vessel was therefore ordered.

Brokers may advise the admiralty marshal to order that repairs be effected on the vessel before it is sold, in order to achieve a better price.

The Westport (No 2)[74]

The case concerned the supply of necessaries to the defendants' ship by the plaintiffs, who claimed the price of 245 tons of fuel plus interest. The court had already ordered a sale of the vessel *pendente lite*. In a motion for judgment in default of defence, the plaintiffs applied for an order that the feed waterpump of the ship was repaired. The brokers advised that it would be good commercial practice to repair the ship, so that she might be sold at a better price than if the pump remained unrepaired. The court held that in order to safeguard the interests of all the claimants, including those of the owners, the advice of the brokers would be taken and the ship was duly repaired.

---

71 *The Myrto* [1977] 2 Lloyd's Rep 243, pp 260–61.
72 [1985] 1 Lloyd's Rep 131.
73 [1977] 2 Lloyd's Rep 243.
74 [1965] 1 Lloyd's Rep 549.

6 COMPETITION OF CLAIMS BROUGHT IN ADMIRALTY AND COMPANY COURTS[75]

There are occasions when there are company creditors who may petition to the court dealing with company matters (Chancery Division of the High Court) for the winding up of the company. At the same time, maritime claimants may exercise their right *in rem* either by the issue of a claim form or by the arrest of the company's asset, the ship. A question that arises, in such circumstances, is this: which class of creditors should be permitted to proceed with enforcement of their rights against the company's assets? On the one hand, the policy of the insolvency legislation aims to protect the company's assets for the benefit of the company's creditors and, on the other hand, the policy of the Admiralty Court is to protect secured maritime creditors. Secured maritime creditors, such as maritime lien holders and mortgagees, may be allowed to proceed in the Admiralty Court to realise their security, only with the leave of the Companies' Court. Such leave will be given, even if the secured maritime creditors issue their *in rem* claim after the winding up order is made against the company (s 130(2) of the Insolvency Act 1986 and equivalent provisions of the new Insolvency Act 2000). Maritime claimants, other than maritime lien holders and mortgagees, are not secured creditors, unless they issue their *in rem* claim form before the commencement of the winding up of the company.

Re Aro Co Ltd[76]

An unregistered Liberian shipping company was ordered to be wound up compulsorily in the Commercial Court, following a petition by a P&I club to which the company was indebted to the sum of $134,912.37. The company had no assets in the UK and the only asset it had was the vessel, *Aro*, which had been laid up for years for lack of employment. The vessel's value was only about $300,000 and there were numerous other claims against the vessel, including that of the plaintiffs. The plaintiffs' claim was for damages in respect of damage to cargo of oil carried by the vessel and estimated to be about $60,000. There was also a debt owed to the admiralty marshal, incurred after the arrest of the vessel. The plaintiffs had issued a writ in the Admiralty Court with respect to their claim, prior to the commencement of the winding up, but they had not served it, nor had they arrested the vessel because she was already under arrest by S Ltd. They merely entered a caveat on the same day, so that, even if the arrest was lifted, the petitioners could not have her removed without notice to the plaintiffs. The plaintiffs applied for leave

---

75 For details of the statutory provisions of the insolvency legislation and how the issue of an *in rem* claim form or the arrest of the ship has been interpreted in the context of that legislation, see Meeson, N, *Admiralty Jurisdiction and Practice*, 2nd edn, 2000, LLP, pp 95–107.

76 [1980] 2 WLR 453.

pursuant to s 231 of the Companies Act (CA) 1948 to continue their action against the vessel and the Liberian company pending in the Admiralty Court, notwithstanding the winding up order. The trial judge held that the plaintiffs remained unsecured creditors because they had not served the writ or arrested the vessel. The Court of Appeal overturned this decision and held that regardless of whether the plaintiffs had invoked the jurisdiction of the Admiralty Court prior to the winding up, they were considered as having the status of secured creditors because, after the issue of the writ, they could have served it and could have arrested *The Aro,* with the result that the vessel would effectively be encumbered with their claim.

Also, that it had been a long established practice to issue a caveat against release of a vessel under arrest, rather than cause multiple arrests. Relief under s 231 of the CA 1948 could not be confined to a case of a claimant who had served a writ on the ship, as distinct from one who had issued his writ but not served. According to Brightman LJ:

> The service of the writ adds nothing to the status of the claimant vis a vis the vessel sued. This is established by the issue of the writ. As between the plaintiff and the defendant, service merely causes time to commence running within which the defendant must enter appearance in order to avoid being a respondent to a motion for judgment by default.[77]

He further said that the rights of a plaintiff suing *in rem* have points of similarity with legal or equitable mortgagees or charges. The similarity has been carried forward by the decision in *The Monica S* where it was held that the burden of the statutory right *in rem* ran with the ship, so as to enable the plaintiff to arrest the ship, notwithstanding the transfer of ownership since the writ was issued.[78]

7 PRIORITIES IN PAYMENT OF
CLAIMS OUT OF THE COURT FUND

Once the arrested ship is sold by court order the fund of the proceeds of sale remains under the control of the admiralty marshal who will distribute the fund on the basis of established priorities. The court still maintains discretion. Priorities are a matter of procedure and are subject to the law of the forum, *lex fori.* However, some rights, which lie on special powers of arrest and detention, fall outside the scheme of priorities and are considered first as they affect the order of priorities. These are as follows.

---

77 [1980] 2 WLR 453, p 465.
78 See Chapter 3.

7.1 Statutory powers of port authorities for detention and sale

The Harbours Docks and Piers Clauses Act (HDPCA) 1847 empowers the port authorities to arrest and sell any vessel or wreck within the precincts of the port for unpaid port dues or damage done to its premises by the ship. A question of law that has been disputed has been whether the port authorities' statutory right is preserved after surrender of the ship to the admiralty marshal and whether, after a court sale of the ship, the claim of the port authority is transferable to the court fund retaining its preferential treatment over and above other preferential claims.

7.1.1 Effect of sale by the admiralty marshal upon the right of the port authority

The Court of Appeal in *Emilie Millon*[79] held that the statutory right of the port authority could not be transferred to the court fund.

While the ship was in the docks at Liverpool, the master and crew arrested her for unpaid wages earned. Judgment was given and the admiralty marshal ordered the sale of the ship by auction. Sale by auction failed and the ship was sold by private treaty. The court was asked to sanction the sale and deliver the ship to the purchaser, free of all encumbrances. At this time, the appellants (the port authority) were asserting their right under statute to detain the ship until tonnage rates being due were paid. The judge sanctioned the sale and ordered that any right of the port authority to payment of their charges in priority over other claimants be preserved, as against the fund in court. The port authority appealed against this order. The Court of Appeal reversed the order on the ground that the judge ignored the right given by the statute to the port authority to detain the vessel until they were paid and said:

> While the port's dock tonnage rates remained unpaid in respect of any vessel liable, the Board would cause such vessel to be detained until all such rates were paid. Such a right given by the statute was paramount, notwithstanding that the master and crew of the vessel had a maritime lien upon her for wages due before she entered the dock. Therefore, the court could not, in such an action, make an order for the sale and delivery of a ship to a purchaser which would deprive a dock authority of its statutory right of detention without its consent; and that such a right was not transferable to the court fund representing the ship.

This decision was followed by subsequent decisions concerning the same issue of preserving the port authority's statutory right of detention and sale over the marshal's jurisdiction to deal with the *res* and the priorities of other claims. However, conflicting legal and practical issues arising from this decision are shown in the decisions below.

---

79   [1905] 2 KB 817.

In *The Sea Spray*,[80] Dean J resolved the question of priorities between the port authority for their expenses incurred in respect of raising the wreck of this ship (which sank after a collision with a barge) and the claim of the barge for damages suffered due to the collision, by allowing the port authority (who intervened in the action) to sell the ship, pay itself and deposit the balance of the proceeds with the court. The main reason of this decision was that, had it not been for the port authority, which raised the wreck, there would be no *res* for the marshal to sell. The decision did not deal with the question whether the purchaser from the port authority would buy the ship free from encumbrances. Willmer J, in *The Ousel*,[81] followed *The Sea Spray* by upholding the motion of the Harbour Board as interveners (claiming wreck removal expenses) in the arrest of the ship by salvors exercising their maritime lien on the cargo on board, so that the Board could proceed with its statutory power of detention and sale and reimburse itself out of the proceeds. The judge did not decide, but accepted that it was not disputed, that the sale by the port authority in the exercise of its statutory power would give title free of encumbrances. The motion requiring the marshal to withdraw from the arrest was not opposed. Although, the judge did not decide the issue of whether the port authority could give title free of encumbrances, his *obiter* comments in this respect should be disregarded in the light of a recent decision.[82]

In *The Spermina*,[83] again, there was a motion, this time by the Manchester Ship Canal Company, as interveners in a mortgagees' action, requesting that the marshal be directed to withdraw from possession of the steamer *Spermina*, or, alternatively, that the warrant of arrest be set aside to enable the interveners to exercise their statutory right of sale of the vessel. Hill J held that, while the Canal Company were in a preferential position to be paid for outstanding dues in priority to the mortgagees' claim, it might be disastrous if the Canal Company sold, because they could not give a clean title, whereas the marshal could in a sale by him.

7.1.2 Effect of constituting limitation fund on the right of the port authority

In a similar question, namely whether the statutory claim by the port authority was transferable to the limitation fund set up by the shipowner who was, by statute, entitled to limit his liability, the House of Lords held (by majority of 3:2) in *The Countess*,[84] that the claim by the port authority for damage done to the port by the ship, permitted the port to be paid first out of the limitation fund, provided it had exercised its right of detention.

---

80 [1907] P 133.
81 [1957] 1 Lloyd's Rep 151.
82 See *The Blitz* [1992] 2 Lloyd's Rep 441 (para 7.1.5, below).
83 (1923) 17 LlL Rep 17.
84 *Mersey Docks and Harbours Board v Hay* [1923] AC 345.

Overruling the majority of the Court of Appeal and the President of the Admiralty Court, it held that the Board's claim, having the status of a statutory possessory lien conferred by the statutory power to detain, remained effective against the fund, although the harbour authority parted with possession of the ship. The right was not extinguished. The court, in distributing the statutory amount of the shipowners' liability rateably among the claimants, ought to have regard to the priorities as well as to the amounts of the claims; that, consequently, the whole of the fund should be paid out to the Board as its special right was not adjunct to the right to participate in the distribution of the limitation fund.

Although the majority of the Lords agreed with the Court of Appeal in *Emilie Millon* that the right of detention of the port authority was paramount, because the authority did not have a charge on the ship or any other protection, it could not see how the problem could be resolved if the port authority was not paid first, but kept the ship under detention.[85]

7.1.3 The Scottish approach

The Scottish Court of Session, in **The Sierra Nevada**,[86] applied the reasoning of the House of Lords in the above case and held that the port authority's right would be transferable to the proceeds of sale where the ship was sold by the court with the consent of the port authority, on the understanding that its priority was preserved. Although it distinguished the *Emilie Millon* decision on the facts, in that it concerned a private sale and that the harbour authority had intervened before the sale had been sanctioned by the court, it criticised the decision as being inconsistent with the view taken of the matter by the majority in the House of Lords. Clyde Navigation Trustees in the Scottish case, were, therefore, entitled to enforce their right of detention in the competition and to a preference over the first mortgagees in the distribution of the proceeds of sale.

7.1.4 Reconciliation of approaches

Since the House of Lords did not have to decide whether the admiralty marshal can proceed with the sale of the ship, but only dealt with the situation of claims when a limitation fund is constituted and the preservation of the right of the port authority, Brandon J, in **The Queen of the South**, tried to

---

85 Lord Sumner (dissenting) did not think that the port should have priority over other claimants as the right to detain was not equivalent to an arrest or proceeding *in rem*. If the port continued to detain the ship after the money owed was deposited with the court, the owner would have an action in detinue. Further, he said, that, apart from pressure put upon the owner, detention may lead to nothing.

86 (1932) 42 LlL Rep 309 (Ct Sess).

bridge the gulf between the Scottish and the English approach by reconciling the two.[87] If the matter were free from authority, he said, he would have followed the Scottish approach which, as was indicated by Lord Fleming in *The Sierra Nevada*, allows the court to sell, free of rights, while transferring equivalent rights with equivalent priority to the proceeds of sale in court, whether or not the dock or harbour authority consents. However, he recognised that this area was a disputed area in law and he preferred not to express a final decision, since he did not have to as there was a simpler solution. English authorities, he said, allow the marshal to incur expenditure on the ship where it is for the benefit of all interested in her. So, the court, if it thinks fit for the benefit of all, Brandon J proposed, has power to pay off the claims of the intervening port authority and then include such expenditure to his expenses of sale. In future cases, he suggested, the marshal could ask all interested parties whether they objected to such a solution; if all interested parties consented, the marshal would apply to the registrar to give such authority. If, on the other hand, one or more parties objected, the registrar should determine the matter himself or apply to the judge.[88] In the case before him, Brandon J decided:

> In my judgment, on the facts of this case, it would be for the benefit of all those interested in *The Queen of the South* that the interveners' claims for rates should be paid off, so that the marshal can sell the vessel free of the interveners' rights of detention and sale, whether already exercised or capable of being exercised hereafter. If the marshal cannot sell the ship free of such rights, he may be unable either to find a purchaser at all, or at any rate to find one willing to pay a proper price. If the interveners are to be paid off in this way, however, it must be on the basis that they give a written undertaking to the court not to exercise their rights of detention or sale in respect of the rates concerned.[89]

7.1.5 Port authorities' statutory right of sale and risk management

In a fairly recent decision, the court held that a sale by the harbour authority will give a purchaser title free only of all mortgages on the ship but not of prior maritime liens:

The Blitz[90]

A mortgage for a loan granted in connection with this ship was duly registered, but the debt remained unpaid. The vessel was arrested for unpaid harbour dues and, pursuant to s 44 of the HDPCA 1847, the harbour authority sold the vessel to the defendant. The mortgagee claimed the money due under

---

87 [1968] P 449; if the port authority does not exercise its power of detention, its right will be lost: *The Charger* [1966] 2 Lloyd's Rep 670.

88 [1968] P 449, pp 462–66.

89 *Ibid*, p 465.

90 [1992] 2 Lloyd's Rep 441.

the mortgage and the question was whether the sale of the vessel pursuant to s 44 of the HDPCA 1847 was a sale free from encumbrances, so that a *bona fide* purchaser obtained a title, free of the mortgage, on the ship.

Sheen J held that the harbour authority could give a title free from any mortgage, because the purchaser could not be expected to investigate the registry of interests on the ship before buying from a harbour authority. If the harbour authority was required to find out whether there was a mortgage and advertise for sale subject to that mortgage, it would not be possible to sell the vessel. If that was allowed, the owner of a ship could effectively deprive a harbour authority of its remedy under s 44 by mortgaging the ship for her full value. The risk of non-payment should be borne by the person who, voluntarily and unwisely, lends a large amount on the security of a ship, rather than by a harbour authority, or an innocent purchaser without notice of the mortgage.

The conclusion to be drawn from these decisions is that the port authority is justified by statute to exercise its right of detention for payment of outstanding dues or other charges or a claim for damage caused to its property by a ship, but a sale of the ship by the authority does not have the same effect as the sale by the admiralty marshal, so as to give a title free from all encumbrances. The port authority should be co-operative to give up its detention of the ship, in lieu of payment by the marshal, in priority over other claimants, once the proceeds of sale are materialised by a court sale. If it is not co-operative, the court should make an appropriate order in those terms. Purchasers from the port authority should be aware that they will not get a title free from all encumbrances.

7.2 The ship-repairers' lien and risk management

This type of lien arises at common law and commences as soon as the ship enters the yard but continues only by retaining possession of the ship. It means that, as long as the ship-repairer retains possession, he is entitled to a priority of payment for the cost of repairs. In particular, the ship-repairer has priority over all other claims, except for maritime liens created before he exercised his possessory lien.

The Russland[91]

After stranding of this vessel on the rocks, she was assisted by salvors to get off and was placed in the dock for temporary repairs. A salvage action commenced and an action by the ship-repairer claiming that the sum for the repairs due to him should be allowed over the salvors' claim. The court

---

91   [1924] P 55.

ordered that a ship repairer's claim ranked after maritime liens already accrued and there was no basis on which the ship repairer's claim could be preferred to those of the salvors, even taking into consideration that the repairs benefited the salvors.[92]

The repairer's right to lien is lost if it is not exercised, or if possession of the ship is given up. Even if a ship-repairer enjoys a maritime lien under the substantive law of the country in which the repairs were done, such as in the USA, the ship-repairer, as it will be seen later, ought to consider getting paid before letting the ship leave his yard, in the event of arrest of the ship by the mortgagee in a jurisdiction which applies English law for the enforcement of maritime claims.

Were possession and control to be surrendered to the admiralty marshal, when other maritime claimants exercise their right *in rem* by arresting the ship, the lien holder would like to know whether his right would be preserved. A line of old authorities show that the English court has recognised and preserved the priority of the possessory lien holder over other maritime claims, even maritime liens that arose after the ship entered the shipyard.

In *The Immacolata Concezione*,[93] there was a competition between claims of a necessaries man, the master and crew, and the shipyard in which the ship had entered before the other claims arose. Some wages for the crew had already accrued. Butt J said:

> But for *The Gustaf*,[94] I should not feel quite clear that [the claim of the repair yard] had not priority over a maritime lien, but, by that decision of Dr Lushington, I am bound. I shall, therefore, give priority to Carter [repair yard] over all the other claimants, except the mariners, so far as regards the claim of the latter for wages [already accrued before the ship entered the yard]. *The Gustaf* is a clear decision to the effect that the claim of the mariners has priority over the shipwrights' common law possessory lien up to the time of the beginning of such lien, and therefore, as I have said, the seamen's wages must have priority over the other claims. With regard to the rest of the wages claim, it will rank after Carter's claim.

Following this principle, the judge held, in *The Tergeste*,[95] that a possessory lien holder who surrenders the ship to the admiralty marshal should be put in exactly the same position as if he had not surrendered the ship:

> The Italian steamship *Tergeste* was arrested by the marshal of the court in an action for wages and disbursements brought by the master on behalf of himself and the crew. At the time she was arrested, the ship-repairers claimed to have a common law possessory lien on the ship for work which they had done. The ship was sold in the wages action, and, as the proceeds in court

---

92 See, also, *The Katingaki* [1976] 2 Lloyd's Rep 372.
93 (1883) 9 PD 37, p 42.
94 Cited by Butt J.
95 [1903] P 26.

were insufficient to meet the total amount of both claims, the question that arose, between the master and crew, on the one side, and the ship-repairer, on the other, was as to which should have priority.

Phillimore J, relying on previous authorities, stated as follows:

> The view which the Admiralty Court took with regard to conflicting claims by shipwrights having a possessory common law lien, and claims which have been sustained by process in the Admiralty Court, has been well established, and has been accepted by this Division of the High Court of Justice. It is that it is the duty of the material man not to contend with the admiralty marshal; to surrender the ship to the officer of the court, and let the officer of the court, under the order of the court, remove and sell her; but when he has done that, the court undertakes that he shall be protected, and that he shall be put exactly in the same position as if he had not surrendered the ship to the marshal. The court has further decided in the case of *The Gustaf* that the possessory lien of a shipwright is subject to maritime liens attaching prior to the ship being taken into the shipwright's yard. If there is a possessory lien, that possessory lien takes precedence of all maritime liens for claims which accrue after the date when the possessory lien begins. The only doubt that Butt J had in the case of *The Immacolata Concezione* was whether *The Gustaf* was not too favourable to the claimants under a maritime lien. There is no doubt here when the possessory lien began; it began when the ship was put into dry dock. It is perfectly true that for some days there was no money in respect of which the lien would operate; but if Messrs Rait and Gardiner had such possession as to give them a possessory lien at the date when the ship was taken by the admiralty marshal, they had it for the price of the whole of the work which they had done up to that time.
>
> It is said that they had no possessory lien, because the master and crew were on board; if that were the rule a great number of shipwrights' liens would be disturbed. That man has a lien who has such control of the chattel as prevents it being taken away from his possession. He may admit other persons or workmen to access to the chattel, and other tradesmen may claim a possessory lien over the chattel or part of it, but if it cannot be got out of the dock or yard without the consent of the owner of the dock or yard, the owner of the dock will have a possessory lien, though perhaps not the only one, on the chattel, which he can enforce, and which the Court has taken upon itself to enforce for him as against subsequent claims. I have no doubt in this case that Rait and Gardiner had an ample possessory lien.

The priority of a possessory lien holder could arguably be subject to maritime claims for which an *in rem* claim form had been issued before the commencement of the possessory lien (for example, before the ship entered a shipyard for repairs), since the issue of the proceedings, according to *Monica S*, results in the crystallisation of the right *in rem* on the ship. However, it may be deduced from the tenor of the above decisions, although they were decided a long time prior to The *Monica S*, that only maritime liens accrued before the possessory lien began are given priority over the possessory lien holder. In any event, a ship-repairer should bear this risk in mind, so that he may consider obtaining contractual security for his costs of repairs.

8 DISTRIBUTION OF THE COURT FUND BY THE COURT

The court will determine the distribution following the order of priorities (s 21(6) of the SCA 1981) but there are no strict rules of ranking. The court has discretion. Payment will be made only to judgment holders as follows:

(a) The admiralty marshal's costs.

(b) Claimant's costs.

(c) Maritime lienees: if all the liens are in the same category, they rank *pari passu*,[96] except in relation to salvage, where the last in time takes priority. If they are different categories of maritime liens, the lien of the person who preserved the *res* (salvor) takes priority in order to encourage saving of maritime property. It must be the latest in the time of all other liens created (including all other salvage and damage liens)[97] in order to take priority. When a claimant has a damage lien subsequent to the lien that preserved the *res*, he will take priority over that salvage lien in the interests of careful navigation.[98]

The Lyrma (No 2)[99]

The ship encountered bad weather and began to list. Her master sent out a signal and the ship *A* responded to the call for assistance. By the time the *A* reached *The Lyrma*, the weather conditions had become worse. After much difficulty, *The Lyrma* was towed with her cargo to safety. The salvors brought an action for remuneration, so the ship and cargo were arrested. The crew of the ship had remained in the service of the ship until quite a long time after this incident and, therefore, brought an action *in rem* against the ship, claiming unpaid wages, emoluments and other disbursements. The owners did not enter an appearance. The court gave an order for the sale of the ship. The master and crew claimed wages earned, before and after the salvage was rendered, and repatriation expenses. It was held that there was no distinction in priorities between wages earned before or after salvage, as against a salvor's claim. It was a long established principle that a salvor's lien took priority over all earlier liens, including those of wages claimants.

---

96 *The Steam Fisher* [1926] P 73.

97 *The Inna* (1938) 60 LlL Rep 414.

98 *The Veritas* [1901] P 304.

99 [1978] 2 Lloyd's Rep 30.

The Veritas[100]

The vessel was safely towed into the Mersey Docks by salvors when her engines had broken down. Another vessel ran to her assistance, thereafter, and, to prevent her sinking into deep water, second salvors tried to beach her with the result that she came into contact with and damaged a landing stage belonging to the Dock Board. The Board removed the vessel under its statutory powers, as she was obstructing the waterway. The vessel was sold and, after expenses were taken out, the remaining sum was paid into court. The proceeds were insufficient to meet the claims of the two salvors and the Dock Board for the damage done. It was held that the Board's statutory lien took first priority, overriding the prior salvage liens. Between the two salvors, the claim of the second salvor took precedence, being the one that preserved the *res* for the benefit of the earlier claimants.

The issue whether a damage claimant has priority over a wages' claimant or vice versa was recently decided by the admiralty judge, David Steel, in *The Ruta*[101] in favour of the wages maritime lien. The judge said, in particular:

Although there was a suggestion in some of the textbooks that there was a rule whereby a damage lien had priority over a wages' lien, it was clear that questions of priority were not capable of being compartmentalised in the form of strict rules of ranking.

The decisive factor in resolving the present issue was the fact that the wages' claimants had no alternative forms of redress; the owners of *Ruta* were insolvent; and where the only remedy open to the wages' claimants was recovery from proceeds of sale, consideration of public policy justified, according to them, a very high level of priority; any preferment of the damage lien to the wages' lien would encourage crews to refuse to disembark from vessels under arrest so as to try and force other claimants to pay off their claims and this was likely to exacerbate their plight at least in the short term and in any event not be conducive to the efficient dispatch of business when vessels were under arrest.

The maritime lien which attaches to the ship in connection with which the claim arose may lose its normal priority over other claims *in rem*, if a sister ship, and not that ship, is arrested, but the right will remain in the class of the statutory rights *in rem*.

The Leoborg[102]

The plaintiffs, who were the first mortgagees of the ship, applied to the court for a determination of the priorities and payment out of the fund

---

100 [1901] P 304.
101 [2000] 1 Lloyd's Rep 359.
102 [1964] 1 Lloyd's Rep 380.

available in court after the sale of the vessel *L*. The chief engineer of the vessel had a claim for unpaid wages while in service on board the *L*. He also had a claim for unpaid wages while serving on *L*'s sister ship *H*, which he made against the *L*, also. The mortgagees argued that his claim for wages in the service of *H* did not carry a maritime lien and should rank below the mortgagees' claim. The court held that in order of priorities, the claim for wages for service on board the *L* took priority over the first mortgagees' claim, while the claim relating to service on the *H* came after the mortgagees' claim.

(d) Mortgagees in the order of registration, equitable mortgagees having last priority.

(e) Claimants who become secured creditors by the issue of the *in rem* claim form (statutory liens *in rem*). As, between themselves, they run *pari passu*.

(f) Claimants who have obtained a judgment *in personam* against the shipowner of the *res* will be last. For the execution of the judgment, a judgment creditor will seek the issue of a writ of *fieri facias*[103] and the sheriff will seize any property of the company in England. Since most shipowning companies are foreign, the sheriff will execute such a writ upon a ship when it comes within the jurisdiction. If the sheriff seizes the ship before the issue of an *in rem* claim form by maritime claimants (other than maritime lien holders) and prior to mortgagees, it is likely that the *in personam* creditor will be able to have his judgment executed against the seized ship.[104]

(g) The balance, if any, will be paid to the owner of the ship.

9 APPLICABLE LAW TO MARITIME LIENS AND CONFLICT OF LAWS[105]

The concept of maritime liens originated in English law from the following.

The Bold Buccleugh[106]

> The claim or privilege travels with the thing, into whosoever possession it may come. It is inchoate, from the moment the claim or privilege attaches, and when carried into effect by legal process, by a proceeding *in rem*, relates back to the period when it first attached.

It has already been seen, in Chapter 2, that a maritime lien attaches to a ship and cannot be extinguished until a court sale. It follows the vessel even into the hands of a *bona fide* purchaser for value. Under English law, claims which

---

103 See CPR, Sched 1, RSC Ord 46.
104 *The James W Elwell* [1921] P 351.
105 See, also, Chapter 9 on mortgages.
106 [1851] 7 Moo PC 267, p 284.

attract maritime liens are: damage lien, salvage, crew's accrued wages, master's wages and disbursements.

There are, however, other maritime claims, which are assigned the status of a maritime lien by the law of the country in which they arose or the contract was made. As a ship moves from one jurisdiction to another, there is a risk that the priority of a mortgagee may be affected. This raises a conflict of laws problem when the court has to determine the validity of the foreign lien before it determines priorities of claims for the distribution of the proceeds of sale of a ship.

English law, and the laws of countries following it, recognise the priority of a mortgage over other statutory rights *in rem*, but not over a maritime lien. In the USA, however, there are US contract maritime liens (necessaries) which include repairs to a ship, supply of bunkers, other supplies, stevedores' claims, claims under towage, even damage to cargo carried under US contract and charterers' liens. All these are, in English law, statutory rights *in rem* which would become statutory liens *in rem* from the issue of the claim form, while in USA they would have priority, even over a US preferred mortgage, if they entered into before the filing of the mortgage. But, they would not be preferred to a US mortgage, if they entered into after the filing of the mortgage. However, foreign ship mortgages that are not guaranteed under Title XI of the Merchant Marine Act 1936 have lower priority to US preferred contract liens.[107]

For the purpose of priorities, a very important question is whether or not the recognition of a maritime lien should be decided by applying the law of the State where the claim arose (the *lex causae*),or the law of the forum deciding the matter of priorities (the *lex fori*). If the maritime lien is regarded as a substantive right, given by the *lex causae*, then it should be enforceable in another jurisdiction where the claims against the vessel are being tried and it should be afforded the priority that it commands by its nature. On the other hand, if it is a mere procedural remedy, then its enforcement will depend on the procedure of the forum of the court that determines priorities.

This issue was decided by the Privy Council (3:2 majority) in *The Halcyon Isle*.[108] The case involved the priority of claims between a mortgagee, an English bank, granted under English law and an American ship-repair yard, which carried out repairs to the vessel in New York. It should be noted that the mortgage at this time was not registered. Knowing that his right of enforcement was protected under US law, the ship-repairer let the vessel sail without payment of his cost of repairs. Later the mortgage was registered. The

---

107 See Tetley, W, *Maritime Liens and Claims*, 2nd edn, 1998, pp 872–76; and Tetley, W, *International Conflict of Laws (Common, Civil and Maritime)*, 1994, International Shipping, pp 540.
108 [1981] AC 221 (PC).

ship was diverted by the mortgagees to Singapore and was arrested by them. Subsequently, she was sold by the order of the High Court of Singapore. The Singaporean court, in the exercise of its admiralty jurisdiction, applies English law. When the proceeds from the sale were insufficient to satisfy all claims, the question was whether the claim of the mortgagees should take priority over the claim of the ship-repairers. Since the latter's claim gave rise to a maritime lien under US law, the judge decided in favour of the ship-repairer, which was reversed on appeal. Upon further appeal to the Privy Council, the issue was which law should be applied, the *lex loci contractus*, or the *lex fori*.

By a majority of 3:2, it was held that a maritime lien was a remedy and, therefore, subject to the law of the forum, English law, which regarded the claim of the ship repairer as a statutory right *in rem* ranking after mortgages. Lord Diplock (delivering the majority judgment) stated:

> As explained in the passage from *The Bold Buccleugh* ... any charge that a maritime lien creates on a ship is initially inchoate only; unlike a mortgage, it creates no immediate right of property; it is, and it will continue to be, devoid of any legal consequences unless and until it is 'carried into effect by legal process, by a proceeding *in rem* '. Any proprietary right to which it may give rise is thus dependant upon the lienee being recognised as entitled to proceed *in rem* against the ship in the court in which he is seeking to enforce his maritime lien. Under the domestic law of a number of civil law countries, even the inchoate charge to which some classes of maritime claims give rise is evanescent. Unless enforced by legal process within a limited time, for instance, within one year or before the commencement of the next voyage, it never comes to life. In English law, while there is no specific time limit to a maritime lien, the right to enforce it may be lost by laches.[109]

There are some flaws of this judicial statement: it cuts through the very essence of maritime liens and misinterprets the word 'inchoate' used in *Bold Buccleugh*; in addition, it disregards principles applicable to conflict of laws. The recognition of a right created by foreign law should be a matter of substance to be determined by applying that law and not a matter of procedure to be determined according to *lex fori*. Once the validity is determined according to foreign law, then it would be a matter of determining its ranking, the procedure of priorities, in accordance with the law of the forum.

Clearly, this decision was based on policy considerations in order to protect the security of mortgagees by avoiding uncertainty in the law regarding the enforcement of their security rights over the ship. It was thought to be necessary, particularly, because of the law in USA where more maritime claims than those under English law are treated as giving rise to a maritime lien. This problem was highlighted very succinctly by the minority view in the Privy Council in answering the question: should English and

---

109 [1981] AC 221, p 234

Singaporean laws recognise a foreign maritime lien, where none would exist, had the claim arisen in England or Singapore?

> Whatever the answer, the result is unsatisfactory. If in the affirmative, maritime States may be tempted to pass 'chauvinistic' laws conferring liens on a plurality of claims, so that the claimants may obtain abroad a preference denied to domestic claimants; if in the negative, claimants who have given the ship credit in reliance upon their lien may find themselves sorely deceived. If the law of the sea were a truly universal code, those dangers would disappear. Unfortunately, the maritime nations, though they have tried, have failed to secure uniformity in their rules regarding maritime liens.[110]

In the view of the minority, the balance of authorities, the comity of nations, private international law and natural justice, all answer this question in the affirmative. If this was correct, they said, the lex fori, English law, should give the maritime lien created by the lex loci contractus precedence over the mortgagees' mortgage. If it were otherwise, injustice would prevail because the American ship-repairer relied on his lien, valid as it appeared to be throughout the world and, unlike an English ship-repairer, who would keep possession of the ship, he gave up his possession. The nature of a maritime lien, therefore, should be determined by the lex loci contractus and the priority by the lex fori.[111]

A number of commentators have criticised the judgment of the majority.[112] Its correctness has now been seriously undermined by the Rome Convention 1980, which was enacted in English law by the Contracts (Applicable Law) Act 1990 and has been in force since 1 April 1991. The decision has, nevertheless, been followed in other jurisdictions.[113] But, the Supreme Court of Canada, in a case decided prior to *The Halcyon Isle*, had a different view.

---

110 [1981] AC 221, p 244; see, also, Berlingieri, F, 'An analysis of the issues and difficulties involved in the ratification of the International Conventions of Maritime Liens and Mortgages, 1926, 1967, 1993' [1995] LMCLQ 57.

111 Lord Diplock espoused the view of the Bermuda court in *The Christine* (1974) AMC 331.

112 See Jackson, DC, *Enforcement of Maritime Claims*, 3nd edn, 2000, LLP, p 393; *op cit*, Tetley, 1994, fn 107 and Chapter 9, below.

113 See the South African case of *The Andrico Unity* [1987] 3 SALR 794; New Zealand, Australia, Singapore, Malaysia, Cyprus and Israel followed *The Halcyon Isle*; China applies the law of the forum pursuant to its Maritime Code; European countries have their own codified systems, but the Rome Convention 1980 must now be the guide to conflicts. For details of relevant cases in different jurisdictions, see the useful references in *op cit*, Tetley, 1994, fn 107; also Chapter 9 on mortgages, below.

The Ioannis Daskalelis[114]

The vessel, a Panamanian ship, was subject to a Greek registered mortgage. Ship-repairers rendered necessary repairs to the vessel in New York. The ship left the shipyard without paying the cost of repairs and was diverted by the mortgagees to a port in Vancouver, Canada, where they arrested her. The question for the Supreme Court of Canada was whether the shipyard's claim had priority over the mortgage. Ritchie LJ, quoted with approval from Cheshire's *Private International Law* (8th edn, p 676), thus:

> Where, for instance, two or more persons prosecute claims against a ship that has been arrested in England, the order in which they are entitled to be paid is governed exclusively by English law.

> In the case of a right *in rem* such as a lien, however, this principle must not be allowed to obscure the rule that the substantive right of the creditor depends upon its proper law. The validity and nature of the right must be distinguished from the order in which it ranks in relation to other claims. Before it can determine the order of payment, the court must examine the proper law of the transaction upon which the claimant relies in order to verify the validity of the right and to establish its precise nature.[115]

The court recognised the ship-repairer's maritime lien applying US law because it held that the lien was a substantive right governed by the law of the country in which it was created. Thus, applying its own procedural law on priorities, it held that it had priority over the mortgagee's claim. It relied on the English decision in *The Colorado*,[116] which the Supreme Court interpreted as being the authority for the contention that, where a right in the nature of a maritime lien exists under foreign law which is the proper law of the contract, the English courts will recognise it and will accord it the priority which a right of that nature would be given under English procedure.[117] The German necessary man in this case did not take priority over the French mortgagee, not because the English court disregarded the proper law of the contract, but because the necessaries had been supplied in England and, as such, the claim

---

114 [1974] 1 Lloyd's Rep 174; so Canada recognises foreign maritime liens.

115 *Ibid*, p 177.

116 [1923] P 102.

117 [1974] 1 Lloyd's Rep, pp 177–78. It was also explained that *The Colorado* decision was clouded by the fact that the judges purported to follow the cases in *The Milford* (1859) Swa 362 and *The Tagus* [1907] P 44, which were concerned with foreign seamen's wages and the English court disregarded the proper law of the contract, which restricted their lien to the last voyage only. The Supreme Court of Canada also interpreted *The Zigurda* [1932] P 113, as having been misunderstood, but that a closer examination would reveal that it did not really support the contrary proposition. The German necessary man argued that, if the ship was under arrest in Germany, he would have had rights analogous to those given by a maritime lien and, therefore, would rank in priority to other claimants. In fact, on evidence called in proof of German law, it was not shown that his claim would be recognised in Germany as being equivalent to an English maritime lien. In the result, the English court treated him as an ordinary creditor.

did not give rise to a maritime lien, while under French law it was accorded the status of a maritime lien.

In the light of the conflict that exists in this area, the mortgagee usually protects its position in the deed of covenants requiring the owner to provide information about the movements of the ship in case she calls at a port of a jurisdiction where *The Halcyon Isle* has been applied. There is also insurance cover for such a risk. At the time of enforcement of his security, the mortgagee usually considers the jurisdiction in which to proceed, although this necessitates forum shopping. As regards a ship-repairer, he could protect his rights by demanding payment before giving up possession of the ship.

10 EXTINCTION OF MARITIME LIENS

For details in this topic the reader is referred to Jackson[118]. The space in this book allows only a list of the circumstances in which the lien can become extinct:

- immunity from suit (in cases of foreign State immunity and Crown ships, the maritime lien may lie dormant until the ship is transferred out of government ownership);
- delay of suit to enforce the lien by an *in rem* claim;
- stay of proceedings upon provision of security;
- provision of bail, payment into court, or provision of security by way of an undertaking or guarantee;[119]
- establishment of limitation fund under the Limitation Convention;
- waiver, or general principles of estoppel;
- destruction of the property;
- judgment on liability, although the lien must continue until satisfaction of the claim by arrest of the property;
- judicial sale.

11 ARE MARITIME LIENS TRANSFERABLE BY ASSIGNMENT OF THE CLAIM TO, OR PAYMENT BY, A THIRD PARTY?

11.1 Assignment

Whether a lien can effectively be assigned depends on principles of assignment applicable to 'choses in action', which are rights enforceable by

---

118 *Op cit*, Jackson, fn 112, Chapter 18, pp 472–80.

119 The Canadian court in *The Birchglen* [1990] 3 CF 301, cited in *The Ruta* [2000] 1 Lloyd's Rep 359, held that, whether or not a maritime lien continues, or is revived, or is extinguished when security has been put up, is determined according to the facts of each particular case and the requirements that full justice and equity be applied.

litigation. An assignment of a bare right of litigation (for example, not being ancillary to an assignment of a property right or interest, or without a genuine commercial interest of the assignee) is not valid. This principle has been laid down in *Trendtex Trading Corp v Credit Suisse*:[120]

> If the assignment is of a property right or interest and the cause of action is ancillary to that right or interest or if the assignee had a genuine commercial interest in taking the assignment and in enforcing it for his own benefit, the assignment of a chose in action is valid.

For the purpose of assignment of a maritime lien, however, which is considered to be a chose in action, an assignment of the claim does not mean that it carries with it the maritime lien, if the right reflected in the claim is not assignable.[121]

Wages' lien cannot be renounced by any agreement, as provided by s 39 of the MSA 1995. Could an assignment of the claim to a person who pays the wages voluntarily be seen as falling foul of this section? This question came before the court in Hong Kong recently, for the first time, in *The Sparti*[122] and the judge considered the equivalent statutory provision to s 39 under the Merchant Shipping (Seafarers) Ordinance, s 93(1).

Briefly, on the facts of this case: the owners of the vessel were in financial difficulties and asked the assignee who was acting as the agent of the vessel in Colombo, to pay the crew. Although the assignee was under no legal duty to do so, he agreed to pay the crew taking appropriate assignments from them. Each of the assignments from the members of the crew was in the same form and provided, *inter alia*:

> In consideration of the payment by you to me of US$ ... in respect of wages and other amounts due for my employment on board *MV Sparti*, I hereby assign to you all my rights against the owners of the vessel or the vessel itself.

No written notice of the assignment was given by the crew or the assignee to the owners of the vessel, so that the assignments were equitable assignments. Both, the mortgagee and the agent of the ship obtained judgments for their respective claims against the ship, and the ship was sold by court order. Since the court fund was insufficient to satisfy the claims in full, the issue was one of priorities.

The mortgagee's counsel argued that the assignment was invalid because it meant the renouncement of the maritime lien. The judge disagreed because the assignment of wages to the assignee in this case was not an inequitable agreement and could not be characterised as renouncement of the lien or the remedy for recovery of wages. The owner's obligation to pay wages was not in any way abandoned by the crew by their making the assignment. As a

---

120 [1981] 3 All ER 520, p 531.
121 *Op cit*, Jackson, fn 112, p 470.
122 [2000] 2 Lloyd's Rep 618.

matter of construction, the judge held that s 93(1) did not itself present a bar to the transfer of the crew's wages lien by the assignment to the assignee. However, he regrettably granted priority to the mortgagee, on the basis that a maritime lien, being personal in nature, was incapable of being transferred in law by an assignment. Nothing could be read in the judgment of Hill J, he said, in *The Petone*,[123] who left the matter of assignability of maritime liens open, indicating otherwise.

11.2 Voluntary payment of claims

A voluntary payment by a third party of claims to which a maritime lien has attached will not transfer the lien to that party unless the payment is made with judicial consent or is ordered by the court.[124]

This is relevant in particular to payment of crew wages by the ship's agents or mortgagees.

In *The Sparti*,[125] Waung J dealt with this issue as understood by the British and Hong Kong courts. By contrast to Scottish law[126] and USA law[127] under which a person, who pays off the crew wages in a foreign port, is put into the shoes of the seaman whose wages he had paid, he held that the weight of English authorities was strongly against this doctrine.

What are the restrictions or limitations of the exercise of jurisdiction on the merits is examined in the next chapter.

---

123 [1917] P 198.

124 *Ibid*.

125 [2000] 2 Lloyd's Rep 618; the decision is important, also, from a comparative perspective because it refers to how the courts in other jurisdictions have dealt with this issue (such as Canada and New Zealand where the maritime lien is not assignable).

126 *Clark v Bowring* (1908) SC 1168.

127 *The President Arthur* (1928) 25 F (2d) 999, in which public policy applied in favour of the payor of wages.

CHAPTER 5

RULES AND DOCTRINES RESTRICTING THE JURISDICTION OF THE ADMIRALTY COURT TO ADJUDICATE ON THE MERITS OF A CASE

1 INTRODUCTION

Although the jurisdiction of the Admiralty Court is very wide (see Chapter 1), there are some limits and restrictions which the court will consider in exercising its discretion to determine its own jurisdiction. For example, as mentioned in Chapter 1, para 7, the jurisdiction of the Admiralty Court cannot be assumed in circumstances provided by the Crown Immunity Act 1947 and the State Immunity Act 1978. Convention rules or other doctrines also restrict the scope of exercising or maintaining jurisdiction on the merits of a case, as will be seen in this and in the following chapters. On the other hand, the court may, by an anti-suit injunction, restrain a foreign court from continuing in a matter if there are grounds for asserting, or protecting, its own jurisdiction (see Chapter 6).

2 JURISDICTION BASES

There are two broad types of jurisdiction bases under English procedural law: the jurisdiction base by way of 'service of process' and the 'Convention' jurisdiction base. While, in both types of asserting jurisdiction, a claim form is issued to initiate the proceedings, which is then served, as regards the former jurisdiction base there has traditionally been no need for substantive connecting factors between the jurisdiction and the claim. It is sufficient that, subject to certain exceptions, in claims *in personam*,[1] the claim form is served upon the defendant, or as is otherwise provided by the procedure rules, within the jurisdiction, unless he voluntarily submits to jurisdiction. In collision damage claims, pursued *in personam*, special rules apply (see Chapter 3, para 2). In claims *in rem*, the claim form must be served on the property within the jurisdiction.

As far as claims *in personam* are concerned, exceptions to the general rule of no connecting factors with the English jurisdiction are the occasions described by the Civil Procedure Rules for service out of the jurisdiction (Ord 11, now found in Sched 1 to the CPR). A substantive connecting factor must be

---

1   PD 49F, para 3.1.

shown for the court to give leave to the claimant to serve the defendant out of the jurisdiction.

As far as claims *in rem* are concerned, once the ship is within the jurisdiction, she can be served with the *in rem* claim form.[2] Except, as is otherwise provided in the practice directions, after acknowledgment of service has been filed, the procedure relating to the claim shall be the procedure applicable to a claim *in personam*, but the claim also continues to be a claim *in rem*.[3]

In accordance with Convention jurisdiction bases, founding jurisdiction depends on specified substantive links with the jurisdiction required by Conventions, which have been enacted, or reflected, into English law.

In the following paragraphs, the occasions in which the court has discretion whether or not to exercise, or maintain its jurisdiction are examined.

3 OCCASIONS WHEN JURISDICTION MAY NOT BE EXERCISED OR BE MAINTAINED

(a) On an issue of time bars applicable for instituting proceedings.
(b) On grounds relating to service out of the jurisdiction. This applies only to a claim brought *in personam* when the defendant is outside the jurisdiction and the cause of action does not fall within any of the prescribed rules of Ord 11, which would allow the English court to assume jurisdiction.
(c) On the ground of *forum non-conveniens*; when a forum other than England is shown to be more appropriate for the claim which, on balance, has substantive links with the other forum.
(d) On the ground of a foreign jurisdiction agreement.
(e) On the ground of an arbitration agreement.
(f) On the ground of *res judicata* (as seen in Chapters 3 and 4).
(g) On the ground of Convention jurisdiction provisions, which allocate jurisdiction according to special rules of a particular Convention. Some of these rules are mandatory and the court will be bound to decline its jurisdiction, others give the court discretion whether or not to do so.

The topics from (a) to (e) will be examined in this chapter. The topic under (g) (Convention rules) and, in particular, the rules under the Brussels/Lugano Conventions will be discussed in Chapter 6.

---

2 PD 49F, para 2.1.
3 PD 49F, para 2.5.

3.1 Discontinuance of proceedings on ground of time bars

There are statutory and consensual time limits within which a claim may be brought. Delay in bringing suit may bar the remedy or, in exceptional cases, the claim, unless an extension of time has been obtained either by agreement, or by an order of the court.

The CPR also provide for certain time limits regarding procedures. The court has power to strike out proceedings for failure by the litigants to observe a rule, or practice direction, or a court order. Inexcusable delays may amount to an abuse of process. Once proceedings have started, case management under the new rules[4] is intended to assist the parties in taking the required procedural steps without delay and has, in a way, curtailed the strict approach of the court to strike proceedings out under the old rules.

As a general rule, under English law, a time bar is a procedural remedy and is governed by the law of the forum, unless the substantive matter is governed by foreign law, when limitation will also be treated as a matter of that law in accordance with the Foreign Limitation Periods Act 1984. In addition, the Contracts (Applicable Law) Act 1990 (which enacted the Rome Convention) has affected the classification of time bars as procedure. It provides that matters of extinguishing obligation, prescription and limitation of action, are matters of the applicable law to the contract.

The general time limits are contained in the Limitation Act (LA) 1980, as amended by the Latent Damage Act (LDA) 1986, which does not apply where other statutes dealing with particular matters prescribe limitation. In maritime claims, particularly for collision damage or salvage or personal injury claims, limitation provisions of Conventions, as enacted into English law, have been consolidated in the Merchant Shipping Act (MSA) 1995, which are referred to below. Limitation of time, with regard to contracts to which the Hague-Visby rules apply by force of law, is governed by those rules.

3.1.1 Cargo claims against the carrying ship or her owners

When there is a contract to which the Hague-Visby Rules (HVR) do not apply, or when they do not apply by force of law but by agreement, there is usually a contractual time limit,[5] which may be extended by agreement. When the HVR

---

4   CPR, Pt 3.
5   A specifically negotiated clause is likely to take precedence over the merely incorporated, but clear words are required for a time bar, so that, in a case of doubt or ambiguity, the conflict must be resolved in favour of a longer time limit: *Finagra (UK) Ltd v OT Africa Line Ltd* [1998] 1 Lloyd's Rep 622. It should also be noted that, under the Arbitration Act 1996, the arbitrators have power to consider whether a time limit should be extended; s 12(2) limited the right to seek an extension to circumstances 'after a claim had arisen and after exhausting any available arbitral process for obtaining an extension of time'. This new provision postpones formally any right to apply to the court for an extension under any scheme of arbitration giving the arbitrators the right to [contd]

apply by force of law, Art III, r 6 provides: 'Subject to para 6 *bis* (referring to indemnity claims) the carrier and the ship shall, in any event, be discharged from all liability whatsoever in respect of the goods, unless suit is brought within one year of their delivery, or of the date when they should have been delivered. This period may, however, be extended if the parties so agree after the cause of action has arisen.'

The wording of this Article makes time bar mandatory and the court does not have power to extend it.[6] The effect of lapse of time, without prior agreement to extend it, is that it extinguishes the claim and no reliance on it can be made, by way of defence, or a set off, in accordance with the view of the majority of the House of Lords in *The Aries*.[7]

Lord Wilberforce clearly stated the effect of Art III, r 6:

> This amounts to a time bar created by contract. But, I do not think that sufficient recognition to this has been given by the courts below; it is a time bar of special kind, viz, one which extinguishes the claim ... not one which, as most English statutes of limitation ... and some international conventions do, bars the remedy while leaving the claim itself in existence ... The charterers' claim, (in this case) after May 1974 and before the date of the writ, had not merely become unenforceable by action, it had simply ceased to exist, and I fail to understand how a claim which has ceased to exist can be introduced for any purpose into legal proceedings, whether by defence or (if this is different) as a means of reducing the respondents' claim, or as a set off, or in any way whatsoever. It is a claim which, after May 1974, had no existence in law, and could have no relevance in proceedings commenced, as these were, in October 1974.[8]

The severe consequences of loss of the claim right by limitation can occur even if a claim form has been issued within time, but is not served within the time of the validity of the 'claim form'. Under the CPR, r 7.5, a claim form *in personam* is valid for service for four months, unless it is to be served out of the jurisdiction, when it is valid for six months. An application to extend the time of service must be made within the period of service (CPR, r 7.6). If the application is made out of time, the court has discretion to extend the time if the claimant has taken all reasonable steps to serve, but has been unable to do so and if he acted promptly in making the application (r 7.6(3)). In a recent case, *Pirelli v United Thai*,[9] the court was lenient to extend the time for

---

5   [contd] extend time; it would, therefore, be the arbitrators who may determine whether or not any time bar applied, before deciding whether to grant an extension: *The Seki Rollete* [1998] 2 Lloyd's Rep 638.

6   *The Antares* [1987] 1 Lloyd's Rep 424.

7   [1977] 1 WLR 185 (HL).

8   *Ibid*, p 188.

9   [2000] 1 Lloyd's Rep 663; the case is also relevant to stay of proceedings on ground of a foreign jurisdiction discussed under para 3.4, below.

issuing a concurrent 'writ'[10] under the Rules of the Supreme Court (RSC) (Ord 6 r 8), which had not been issued within the validity of the original writ, as provided by the old rules. In order to cure this defect, the original writ was deemed to be extended for six months. An *in rem* claim form is valid for 12 months (PD 49F, para 2.1(6)).

It should also be noted that an amendment to the claim form would not be permitted, once the time bar has expired, to include a defendant not named in the original claim form, which was issued against another defendant within time.[11]

Under the Gold Clause Agreement (GCA) 1950, as amended in 1977, the time for bringing suit for a cargo claim may be extended. The GCA is an agreement entered into between insurers, certain cargo interests and shipowners. Clause 4 provides that, upon the request of any party representing the cargo, whether made before or after the expiry of the one year period, the shipowners will extend the time for bringing suit for a further 12 months provided notice of the claim, with the best particulars available, has been given within the one year period.

3.1.2 Indemnity claims for liability to cargo owners

Allocation of liability for cargo claims, as between owners and charterers (contracted under a New York Produce Exchange (NYPE) time charter which incorporates the Inter-Club NYPE Agreement), in respect of cargo carried on board under bills of lading to which the HVR are incorporated, is subject to a two year time limit.

The HVR, by Art 6 *bis*, also provide that indemnity claims can be brought, even after the expiration of the year provided for in Art 6, if brought within the time allowed by the law of the court seised of the case. However, the time allowed shall not be less than three months commencing from the day when the person bringing such action for indemnity has settled the claim, or has been served with process in the action against himself.

The Privy Council gave the interpretation of this provision in *The Xingcheng and Andros*[12] in which it held that:

> Rule 6 *bis* of Art III created a special exception to the generality of r 6; r 6 *bis*, in a case to which it applied, had a separate effect of its own independently of r 6; the case to which r 6 *bis* applied was a case where shipowner A, being under actual or potential liability to cargo-owner B, claimed an indemnity by way of damages against ship or shipowner C; if that claim was made under a contract of carriage to which the HVR applied, then the time allowed for bringing it

---

10 Apparently, the new CPR do not refer to the issue of a concurrent claim form under Pt 7.
11 *The Jay Bola* [1992] 2 Lloyd's Rep 62.
12 [1987] 2 Lloyd's Rep 210.

was that prescribed by r 6 *bis* and not r 6; there was no requirement in r 6 *bis* that the liability to shipowner A should also arise under a contract of carriage to which the HVR applied and there was no reason why such a requirement should be implied.

3.1.3 Claims for loss of life or personal injury against the carrying ship

Claims for loss of life or personal injury of persons carried on the ship, except when the Athens Convention applies (see para 3.1.4, below), occasioned by negligence are subject to the Fatal Accidents Act 1976,[13] in respect of claims by the dependants of a deceased, and the LA 1980. The time limit against the carrying ship is three years, commencing from the date of the incident, which gave rise to the cause of action. The period may not commence until the claimant has knowledge of the injury.[14]

3.1.4 Claims of passengers carried on passenger vessels

Claims for loss of life or personal injury or loss of luggage of passengers carried on passenger ships are subject to two years time limit, commencing from a date as specified by Art 16 of the Athens Convention 1974, when it applies. The commencement date depends on the particular claim made. The date of disembarkation is the relevant date for personal injury claims, or the date of death for loss of life when death occurred after disembarkation of an injured passenger, provided that the time should not exceed three years from the date of disembarkation. The date of disembarkation or the date when disembarkation should have taken place is relevant for damage to, or loss of, luggage. These time limits may be extended either by a written declaration of the carrier or by agreement of the parties after the cause of action has arisen.

3.1.5 Property or personal injury/loss of life claims against another ship at fault

Under s 190(1)(3) of the MSA 1995, the time limit to bring any claim against owners or ship, in respect of damage or loss caused by the fault of that ship to another ship, its cargo or freight, or any property on board it, or for damages for loss of life or personal injury caused by the fault of that ship to any person on board another ship, is two years from the date of the incident causing the damage or loss. This may be extended on grounds of reasonableness.[15]

---

13 As amended by the Administration of Justice Act 1982.
14 Limitation Act 1980 (ss 11, 12, 13) as amended by the Latent Damage Act 1986.
15 *The Berny* [1979] 2 Lloyd's Rep 533.

3.1.6 Claims for contribution

Claims for contribution by one ship against the other ship at fault, in respect of liability to third parties for loss of life or personal injury, are subject to a one year time limit, commencing from the date of payment under s 190(4) of the MSA 1995. But, contribution claims for liability incurred to third parties concerning damage to property are subject to a two-year time limit, commencing from the date of payment under s 1 of the Civil Liability (Contribution) Act 1978.

3.1.7 Salvage claims

Under Art 23 of the Salvage Convention 1989, any claim for payment under the Convention shall be time barred, if judicial or arbitral proceedings have not been instituted within a period of two years. The limitation period commences on the day on which the salvage operations are terminated. The person against whom the claim is made may extend this period by making a declaration to the claimant. An action for indemnity by a person liable may be instituted, even after the expiration of the aforesaid limitation period, if brought within the time allowed by the law of the State where proceedings are instituted.

3.1.8 Claims for wages

The LA 1980 provides for a six year time limit to bring claims arising from breach of contract, commencing from the date of the breach. This time limit applies to claims of seamen against their employer for unpaid wages.

3.2 No assumption of jurisdiction if a claim *in personam* is not within Ord 11

Save for cases where the defendant is within the jurisdiction to be served with the claim form, or he has agreed to submit to the jurisdiction of the court, and for those in which the Brussels/Lugano Conventions apply[16] (examined later, in Chapter 6) a claimant will need the permission of the court to serve proceedings out of the jurisdiction (Ord 11 r 1(1) of the RSC. Order 11 has been incorporated in CPR, Pt 6, Section III, rr 6.17–6.31 and CPR, PD 6B). This is only applicable to limited circumstances in which there is a link between the claim and the jurisdiction.[17]

---

16 There is no need to obtain the court's permission to serve a defendant who is domiciled in a Contracting State to the Conventions for a claim to which the Conventions apply (Ord 11 r 1(2)).

17 The reader is referred to CPR, Sched 1, RSC Ord 11 for details.

For example, there may be a contractual link if the contract was made here, or is governed by English law (Ord 11 r 1(1)(d)). Another link with this jurisdiction will be in cases of claims based on tort, where the alleged tort happened within the jurisdiction (Ord 11 r 1(1)(f)).

The grant of permission is discretionary. By Ord 11 r 4, the claimant must state the grounds of the application and show that, in his belief, he has a good cause of action and that there is a real issue to be tried. No permission shall be granted, unless it shall be made sufficiently to appear to the court that the case is a proper one for service out of the jurisdiction.

In circumstances outside the provisions of this order, the court cannot assume jurisdiction if the defendant is foreign, unless there is a convention jurisdiction base, or the parties to a dispute have agreed to this jurisdiction.

It is beyond the scope of this book to deal with this procedural area which requires a book in its own right.

3.3 Stay on the ground of *forum non-conveniens*

Even if English jurisdiction has been properly invoked, the English court has power to exercise its discretion and stay an action before it, when there are grounds of *forum non-conveniens*. For example, when there are connecting factors with the jurisdiction of a foreign court which is amenable to the defendant, the English court will consider, taking also into account all the circumstances of the case, whether that court is more appropriate to determine the matter for the ends of justice and the interests of all parties. The origins and meaning of this doctrine are explained in the following paragraphs. What would constitute connecting factors are explained under para 3.3.5.4, below.

Being originally a Scottish doctrine, *forum non-conveniens* was gradually incorporated into English law in the 1970s. The court's approach before that time is briefly explained below.

3.3.1 Historical perspective and 'the 1936 rule'

Prior to the Judicature Act (JA) 1873, the High Court had power to grant an injunction to restrain proceedings in England. By s 24(5) of the 1873 Act, however, this power to restrain proceedings by an injunction was removed but, in the same sub-section, the court's inherent power to stay proceedings, as it thought fit for the purpose of justice, was recognised.

Section 24 of the JA 1873 was later replaced by s 41 of the Judicature (Consolidation) Act 1925. The court's inherent power to stay proceedings was maintained in the new Act, as it had been in the 1873 Act. However, the rule in the new Act added a provision relating to the court's power to stay its proceedings in cases where there was proof of vexation or oppression on the part of the claimant. But, the power was not limited only to those cases. It is important to note that the rule in the 1873 Act contained no reference to vexation or oppression in relation to the court's power to stay.

In the leading case of **McHenry v Lewis**[18] the Court of Appeal, in a matter involving multiple proceedings in England and America, used the word 'vexatious' as an illustration of the provision. In later decisions,[19] the court followed this principle, but without placing too much weight on the words oppressive and vexatious. The emphasis was on whether the defendant would be subjected to such an injustice, that he ought not to be sued in the court in which the action was brought.

This principle was formulated in the *St Pierre* case, known as 'the 1936 rule'. The criteria of injustice, however, as laid down by Scott LJ, were whether the English action would cause an injustice to the defendant that was 'oppressive or vexatious' to him, or an abuse of the process of the court, which he had to prove.

St Pierre v South American Stores[20]

The action brought in this jurisdiction involved a dispute with regard to a lease of land in Chile. The defendants (English companies) had commenced proceedings in Chile, while the plaintiffs commenced proceedings in England. The defendants applied for a stay of the English action, on the ground that Argentina was a more appropriate forum. Scott LJ held that: (1) a mere balance of convenience was not a sufficient ground for depriving a plaintiff of the advantages of prosecuting his action in England when the English action was, otherwise, properly brought; (2) in order to justify a stay, the defendants had to prove (a) that the continuance of the action in England would cause an injustice that was oppressive or vexatious to him, or would be an abuse of the process of court in some way and (b) that the stay would not cause an injustice to the plaintiff. The burden of proof in both situations was on the defendant.

Thus, if the plaintiff was not acting vexatiously or oppressively, but genuinely believed that England would be to his advantage (despite there being another more appropriate forum), the court would not grant a stay.

The application of the 1936 rule in subsequent cases, until 1973, operated in such a way as to make it extremely difficult for the defendant to obtain a stay of an action. He could not easily satisfy the court that the continuance of the action would work an injustice to him. This was due to the difficulty of proving that the action was oppressive or vexatious in the opprobrious sense, which was a meaning these epithets were generally regarded as having, in the

---

18 (1882) 21 Ch D 202.

19 *Peruvian Guano Co v Bockwoldt* (1883) 23 Ch D 225; *Hyman v Helm* (1883) 24 Ch D 531; *Logan v Bank of Scotland* [1906] 1 KB 141.

20 [1936] 1 KB 382 (CA).

context in which they were used.[21] Such applications were, invariably, dismissed.[22]

3.3.2 Why was the 1936 rule distinct from the doctrine of forum non-conveniens?

(a) It recognised an exceptional power of the court;
(b) the power could be described by reference to vexation or oppression;
(c) the court's discretion was general as is shown in the *Peruvian Guano* case.[23]

An action was brought in this court by an English company against a firm of French merchants for the delivery of the cargoes of certain ships, or in the alternative for damages, and for an injunction and appointment of a receiver.

At the commencement of the action the ships were in British waters, but they had since been removed by the direction of the defendants to ports in France, and the cargoes had been taken possession of by the defendants. Proceedings had been instituted by the plaintiffs in a French court for recovery of the cargoes. The English action comprised a claim for the cargo of one ship which was not claimed in the French action.

A motion, on behalf of the defendants, that the plaintiffs might be ordered to elect whether they would proceed with the English action or with the French proceedings, was refused.

Jessel MR laid down the criteria for a stay, which was rarely granted in those days, as follows:

It is very important in these cases that the court should clearly see that in stopping an action it does not do injustice. Of course, a man brings an action at the peril of costs if the action does not succeed, and as a general rule that is sufficient to protect defendants from ill founded actions. There is another protection, which is that, where the action is vexatious, it may be stayed. Now it may be vexatious on many grounds. It may be so utterly absurd that the judge sees it cannot possibly succeed, and that it is brought only for annoyance, and then the judge has jurisdiction to stay the action. That is pure vexation. Or, it may be vexatious in another way; that is, the plaintiff not intending to annoy or harass the defendant, but thinking he would get some fanciful advantage, sues him in two courts at the same time under the same jurisdiction – two of the Queen's courts. That is vexatious, because whatever the intention of the plaintiff may be he cannot get any benefit in that way, and the defendant is harassed by two suits ...

21 *The Abidin Daver* [1984] 1 All ER 470, p 481, *per* Lord Brandon of Oakbrook.
22 *The Janera* [1928] P 55; *The London* [1931] P 14; *The Madrid* [1937] 1 All ER 216; *The Quo Vadis* [1951] 1 Lloyd's Rep 425; *The Monte Urbasa* [1953] 1 Lloyd's Rep 587; *The Lucile Broomfield* [1964] 1 Lloyd's Rep 324.
23 *Peruvian Guano v Bockwoldt* (1883) 23 Ch D 225.

It may be put, as regards this case, shortly in this way: that it is not vexatious to bring an action in each country where there are substantial reasons of benefit to the plaintiff. He has the right to bring an action, and if there are substantial reasons to induce him to bring the two actions, why should we deprive him of that right? It is very unpleasant, no doubt, to be sued twice – it is unpleasant to many people to be sued once – but still that does not make it vexatious where the plaintiff seeks to get a real substantial advantage.

3.3.3 The gradual incorporation of the Scottish doctrine into English law

The incorporation of the Scottish doctrine of *forum non-conveniens* into English common law was effectively done by *The Abidin Daver* in 1984, but the process started in 1973 with *The Atlantic Star* and it was refined further in *Macshannon*. The trilogy of these decisions (which will be examined shortly) had a great impact on the change of the attitude of English judges, so that a tendency for jurisdictional chauvinism was gradually diminished. The difficulty of showing that the action in England was oppressive or vexatious was for the first time examined by the House of Lords in the following case.

The Atlantic Star[24]

Pursuant to a collision between their barge and the appellants' vessel *Atlantic Star*, in Belgian waters, the respondent Dutch shipowners arrested the *Atlantic Star* in England. By virtue of the arrest, they founded jurisdiction in the English court and obtained security for their claim. The appellants sought a stay of the action in England on the ground that the Belgian court was the more appropriate forum to deal with the claim. The court surveyor in Belgium had already been called to give evidence in court and the conclusion in his report appeared to point to the opinion that the appellants' vessel was not at fault. Therefore, the chances were that, if the action was tried in Belgium, the respondents would fail. The trial judge had held that, although the balance of convenience was heavily in favour of the Belgian court, and the case had absolutely no connection with England, he felt bound by previous authorities to refuse a stay, since it was not proved that the plaintiffs were acting 'vexatiously' or 'oppressively', or in abuse of the process of the court. His decision was upheld by the Court of Appeal in which Lord Denning MR reemphasised that access to the Queen's court, even by a foreign plaintiff, must not be lightly refused and said:

No one who comes to these courts asking for justice should come in vain ... This right to come here is not confined to Englishmen. It extends to any friendly foreigner. He can seek the aid of our courts if he desires to do so. You may call this 'forum shopping' if you please, but if the forum is England, it is a

24 [1973] 2 Lloyd's Rep 197.

good place to shop in, both for the quality of the goods and the speed of service.[25]

Lord Reid later, in the House of Lords, criticised this statement:

My Lords, with all respect, that seems to me to recall the good old days, the passing of which many may regret, when inhabitants of this island felt an innate superiority over those unfortunate enough to belong to other races ... There was a time when it could reasonably be said that our system of administration of justice, though expensive and elaborate, was superior to that in most other countries. But, today we must, I think, admit that as a general rule there is no injustice in telling a plaintiff that he should go back to his own courts ... So, I would draw some distinction between a case where England is the natural forum for the plaintiff and a case where the plaintiff merely comes here to serve his own ends. In the former, the plaintiff should not be 'driven from the judgment seat' without very good reason, but, in the latter, the plaintiff should, I think, be expected to offer some reasonable justification for his choice of forum if the defendant seeks a stay ... I think that a key to the solution may be found in a liberal interpretation of what is oppressive on the part of the plaintiff. The position of the defendant must be put in the scales. In the end, it must be left to the discretion of the court in each case where a stay is sought ... looking to all the circumstances, including the personal position of the defendant.[26]

Lord Wilberforce reviewed the previous authorities and concluded with regard to 'vexatious and oppressive':

These words are not statutory words; as I hope to have shown from earlier cases, they are descriptive words, which illustrate, but do not confine, the courts' general jurisdiction. They are pointers rather than boundary marks. They are capable of a strict, or technical application; conversely, if this House thinks fit, and as I think they should, they can in the future be interpreted more liberally.[27]

Lord Kilbrandon agreed and added:

There are plenty of earlier examples of the use of the words 'oppressive' and 'vexatious' in this context. But the words have, at all events today, certain shades of meaning which make it difficult to accept an uncritical construction ... 'Oppressive' is an adjective which ought to be, and today normally is, confined to deliberate acts of moral, though not necessarily legal, delinquency, such as an unfair abuse of power by the stronger party in order that a weaker party may be put in difficulties in obtaining his just rights. 'Vexatious' today has overtones of irresponsible pursuit of litigation by someone who either knows he has no proper cause of action, or is mentally incapable of forming a rational opinion on that topic. Either of these attitudes may amount to abuse of the process of the court, but in my opinion a defendant moving for a stay

---

25 [1972] 2 Lloyd's Rep 446, p 451.
26 [1973] 2 Lloyd's Rep 197, p 200–01.
27 *Ibid*, p 209.

cannot be compelled to bring the plaintiff's conduct within the scope of these grave allegations.

Thus, the House of Lords rejected the narrow construction of the expressions 'oppressive' and 'vexatious'. It was invited to take the opportunity in this case to bring English law into line with the Scottish doctrine of *forum non-conveniens* and make the plea available in England. It refused to adopt this approach, but upheld the court's residual right to decline to exercise its jurisdiction in appropriate cases. It was for the court to take into account (a) any advantage to the plaintiff in this jurisdiction, and (b) any disadvantage to the defendant by refusing a stay. It was held by majority of 3:2 that the defendants (appellants) had shown that they ought not to be required to litigate in England and the action was stayed.

At this stage, the judgment of Scott LJ in *St Pierre* was still treated as the framework on which the law was built, but the words 'oppressive' and 'vexatious' were no longer to be understood in their natural meaning. However, the House of Lords in the following case eliminated these words from the test.

Macshannon v Rockware Glass Ltd[28]

The plaintiffs were Scotsmen who brought actions against their employers for damages for personal injury or disabilities suffered in the course of employment in a factory in Scotland. It was alleged that the injuries had been caused by the negligence of the employers. The employers were companies with their head offices in England, but their places of business in Scotland. The plaintiffs brought their actions in England, though there was no connection with it, because they were advised that the English court would be likely to award higher damages and more generous party and party legal costs. The Court of Appeal acknowledged that Scotland was the more appropriate forum for the action, but considered that the *ratio decidendi* of *The Atlantic Star* compelled the court to allow the proceedings to continue in England.

In the House of Lords, Lord Diplock examined the *ratio decidendi* in *The Atlantic Star* and said that, although by the modification of the statement of the law, as had been set down by Scott LJ in the *St Pierre* case, the words 'vexatious and oppressive' were given, by the House of Lords in *The Atlantic Star*, a liberal interpretation, these words still caused problems and should be eliminated to avoid confusion, as in the instant case. He then restated the principle of *St Pierre* as follows:

> In order to justify a stay two conditions must be satisfied, one positive and the other negative: (a) the defendant must satisfy the court that there is another forum to whose jurisdiction he is amenable in which justice can be done

28 [1978] 1 All ER 625 (HL).

between the parties at substantially less inconvenience or expense, and (b) the stay must not deprive the plaintiff of a legitimate personal or judicial advantage which would be available to him if he invoked the jurisdiction of the English court.[29]

No reference was made to the burden of proof. Lord Keith added:

Where England is the natural forum for the action, in the sense of being that with which the action has the most real and substantial connection, it is necessary for the defendant, in order to establish injustice to him and no injustice to the plaintiff, to show some very serious disadvantage to him which substantially outweighs any advantage to the plaintiff. Where, however, the defendant shows that England is not the natural forum and that, if the action be continued there he would be involved in substantial (that is, more than *de minimis*) inconvenience and unnecessary expense, or in some other disadvantages, which would not affect him in the natural forum, he has made out a *prima facie* case for a stay, and if nothing follows it may properly be granted. The plaintiff may, however, seek to show some reasonable justification for his choice of forum in the shape of advantage to him. If he succeeds, it becomes necessary to weigh against each other the advantages to the plaintiff and the disadvantages to the defendant, and a stay will not be granted unless the court concludes that to refuse it would involve injustice to the defendant and no injustice to the plaintiff.[30]

Thus, the House of Lords examined the advantages of hearing the action in Scotland viz: the availability of medical and other expert witnesses, who treated the plaintiffs in Scotland, and all the witnesses to the facts in this matter were living in Scotland. The main disadvantage of hearing the action in England would be the inconvenience, not only for the parties, but for all the witnesses concerned. The plaintiffs alleged that the advantage they would be deprived of, if the action was tried in Scotland, was an unsubstantiated, though perhaps *bona fide*, belief of their legal advisers on the advantages of English over Scottish legal process. It was held that the advantage to the plaintiff must be a real one, it must be shown objectively and, on balance of probabilities, that it exists. The defendants had shown that Scotland was the only natural and appropriate forum for the actions, where they could be tried at substantially less inconvenience and expense. The plaintiffs had not shown that they would be deprived of any real personal or judicial advantage. The action was stayed.

In the final case of the trilogy, the doctrine of *forum non-conveniens* was firmly established in English law. The existence of *lis pendens* in a foreign jurisdiction was a factor to be taken into account, but alone was not sufficient to tilt the balance.

---

29   [1978] 1 All ER 625, p 630.
30   *Ibid*, pp 644–45.

The Abidin Daver[31]

This involved a collision, in Turkish territorial waters, between a Turkish ship and a Cuban ship. Both vessels sustained damage. The Turkish parties arrested the Cuban ship and started an action in the Turkish court against the Cubans. Three months later, the Cuban shipowners arrested a sister ship of the Turkish vessel in England. The Turkish owners brought a motion to stay the action in England, giving an undertaking to provide security for any cross-claim that the Cubans may decide to make in the Turkish action. The stay was granted by the trial judge, but his order was reversed by the Court of Appeal. The Court of Appeal held that a mere balance of convenience was insufficient to deprive the plaintiffs of pursuing their action in England. It was also held that a situation of *lis pendens* in another jurisdiction was not, in itself, a bar to the plaintiffs' right to proceed in England.

Lord Keith of Kinkel referred to 'natural forum', having already defined it in *The Macshannon* case as 'that with which the action had the most real and substantial connection'. He said that, in this case, the defendant, if he were required to meet the plaintiff's claim in England, would be involved in substantial inconvenience and expense. Lord Diplock, delivering the main judgment, examined all the factors pointing towards Turkey as the forum in which justice could be done at less inconvenience and expense than in England. Neither party had any connection with England. The connecting factors were: (i) the crew and the pilot were Turkish; (ii) the surveyors were appointed in Turkey; (iii) the collision took place in Turkish waters; (iv) most of the witnesses were Turkish. As far as the Cuban witnesses were concerned, there was little to choose between Turkey and England. Turkey was definitely the natural and appropriate forum for the action, which was already pending there. It was stressed that:

> ... the essential change in the attitude of the English courts to pending or prospective litigation in foreign jurisdictions, that has been achieved step by step during the last 10 years as a result of the successive decisions of this House in *The Atlantic Star*, *Macshannon* and *Amin Rasheed*, is that judicial chauvinism has been replaced by judicial comity to an extent which I think the time is now ripe to acknowledge, frankly, that is indistinguishable from the Scottish legal doctrine of *forum non-conveniens*.[32]

Lord Brandon also added:

> ...the Court of Appeal ... have fallen into error. Mere balance of convenience cannot, of itself, be decisive in tilting the scales; but strong, and *a fortiori* overwhelming, balance of convenience may easily, and in most cases probably will, be so. Similarly, the mere disadvantage of multiplicity of suits cannot of itself be decisive in tilting the scales; but multiplicity of suits involving serious

---

31 [1984] 1 All ER 470.
32 *Ibid*, p 476.

consequences with regard to expense or other matters, may well do so. In this connection, it is right to point out that, if concurrent actions in respect of the same subject matter, proceed together in different countries, as seems likely if a stay is refused in the present case, one or other of two undesirable consequences may follow: first, there may be two conflicting judgments of the two courts concerned; or, second there may be an ugly rush to get one action decided ahead of the other, in order to create a situation, or *res judicata*, or issue estoppel in the latter.[33]

It was also held that there was no evidence that in Turkey, the plaintiffs would be under any disadvantage compared with a plaintiff in England, nor that they would not obtain justice in the Turkish courts.

Thus, from this point in time, the Scottish doctrine of *forum non-conveniens* became part of English law.

3.3.4 The application of forum non-conveniens principles and service out of the jurisdiction under RSC Ord 11

Similarities do exist between the doctrine of *forum non-conveniens* and criteria applicable to applications for service out of the jurisdiction. Their differences are examined under para 3.3.6, below, after discussion of the new formula of *forum non-conveniens*, as was encapsulated by Lord Goff in *The Spiliada*.

Amin Rasheed Corp v Kuwait Ins[34]

The plaintiffs were a shipping company incorporated in Liberia having their place of management in Dubai. They sought to litigate their claim in England against their insurers, who had their head office in Kuwait and a branch office in Dubai. The claim was for a constructive total loss of their ship insured under a hull policy against marine and war risks. The form of policy was based upon the Lloyd's (of London) standard form of marine policy, but Kuwait was stated as the place of issue and the place for the payments of claims. There was no provision as to proper law of the contract. In order to bring their action in England, as opposed to in the Kuwaiti court, the plaintiffs had to bring their case within RSC Ord 11 r 1, to obtain leave to serve the writ out of the jurisdiction on the insurers. Both Bingham J and the Court of Appeal held that there was no jurisdiction to serve the writ on the defendants in Kuwait under that rule. On appeal to the House of Lords, Lord Diplock said:

> ... the jurisdiction exercised by an English court over a foreign corporation which has no place of business in this country, as a result of granting leave under RSC Ord 11 r 1(1)(f) for service out of the jurisdiction of the writ on that corporation is an exorbitant jurisdiction ... [thus] the judicial discretion to

33 [1984] 1 All ER 470, p 485.
34 [1984] AC 50.

grant leave under this paragraph of RSC Ord 11 r 1(1) should be exercised with circumspection in cases where there exists an alternative forum, viz the courts of the foreign country where the proposed defendant does carry on business, and whose jurisdiction would be recognised under English conflict rules. Such a forum in the instant case afforded by courts of Kuwait.[35]

The House went on to examine whether a Kuwaiti court, in addition to having jurisdiction, was also a *forum conveniens* for the dispute. According to Lord Wilberforce:

> In considering this question the court must take into account the nature of the dispute, the legal and practical issues involved, such questions as local knowledge, availability of witnesses and their evidence and expense. It is not appropriate, in my opinion, to embark upon a comparison of the procedures, or methods, or reputation or standing of the courts of one country as compared with those of another ...[36]

After considering the necessary factors, it was held that the Kuwaiti court was an alternative forum where the defendant had its place of business, and where the contract was made and had jurisdiction over the matter in dispute. The plaintiffs had not shown, either that justice could not be obtained, or that it could only be obtained at excessive cost, delay or inconvenience. Therefore, it was held that this case was not a proper one for service out of jurisdiction under the rule.

Thus, *forum non-conveniens* principles can be considered at the time of the application to obtain leave to serve out of the jurisdiction.

3.3.5 The present formula of forum non-conveniens

The principles of *forum non-conveniens* as applied under English law today, were laid down by Lord Goff in the following case.

The Spiliada[37]

The shipowners were a Liberian corporation with part of their management in Greece and the other part in England. Their ship, *The Spiliada*, was chartered to carry a cargo of sulphur from Vancouver to India, the chemicals of which caused damage to the ship. The voyage charter provided for arbitration in London. The shippers and sellers of the cargo carried on business in Canada as exporters of sulphur. The shipowners obtained leave to serve proceedings on the shippers in Vancouver on the ground that it was an action to recover damages for breach of a contract governed by English law. According to them, the cargo was wet when it was loaded and, therefore, caused severe corrosion

---

35 [1984] AC 50, pp 65–66.

36 *Ibid*, p 72.

37 [1987] 1 AC 460 (HL).

to the holds and tank tops of the vessel. The sellers applied to have the *ex parte* order discharged on the ground that the case was not a proper one for service out of jurisdiction under Ord 11 r 4(2). The trial judge, who was at the same time hearing the trial of a similar action involving the same sellers and another ship, *The Cambridgeshire*, dismissed the application. He considered that the availability of witnesses, possible multiplicity of proceedings and the experience of counsel and solicitors, derived from their participation in *The Cambridgeshire* action, would save money and time. On appeal by the shippers, the Court of Appeal allowed the appeal and set aside the writ. It thought that it was impossible to conclude that the factors considered by the judge showed that the English court was distinctly more suitable for the ends of justice. On appeal to the House of Lords, it was held that, in order to determine whether a case was a proper one for service out of the jurisdiction under Ord 11 r 4(2) of the RSC, the court had, as in applications for a stay on the ground of *forum non-conveniens*, to identify in which forum the case would be most suitably tried for the interests of all parties and the ends of justice.

After examining the Scottish authorities on *forum non-conveniens*, and the trilogy of cases referred to above, Lord Goff found the opportunity to consolidate and summarise the law concerned with the doctrine of *forum non-conveniens* as derived from the Scottish doctrine. He laid down the general principle and a two-stage test for the court's approach to applications for a stay on this ground.

3.3.5.1 General principle

A stay will only be granted where the court is satisfied that there is some other available forum, having competent jurisdiction, which is the appropriate forum for the trial and in which the case may be tried more suitably for the interests of all parties and the ends of justice.

3.3.5.2 Burden of proof

In general, the burden of proof rests on the defendant to establish that there is another forum, which is clearly, or distinctly, more appropriate than the English forum for the trial. Where a party seeks to establish some evidence to persuade the court to exercise its discretion in his favour, the evidential burden will rest on that party. If the court finds that another forum is *prima facie* the appropriate forum for the trial, the burden will then shift to the plaintiff to show that there are special circumstances, by reason of which justice requires that the trial should, nevertheless, be held in England.

3.3.5.3 Effect of founding jurisdiction as of right

The fact that the claimant has found jurisdiction as of right in accordance with the law of England and Wales is not in itself an advantage for the claimant that should not be disturbed by the court. However, in cases in which there is no other natural forum (that is, collision on the high seas), the English court will not disturb the jurisdiction so established.

3.3.5.4 Connecting factors (first stage test)

In determining whether there exists another forum clearly more appropriate for the trial, the court will look first to see what factors there are which point in the direction of another forum. It will look at the forum with which the action had the most real and substantial connection. These connecting factors will include, not only those affecting convenience or expense (such as the availability of witnesses), but also other factors, such as the law governing the relevant transaction and the parties' place of residence or business. If the court concludes, at that stage, that there is no other available forum which is clearly more appropriate for the trial, it will ordinarily refuse a stay.

3.3.5.5 Second stage (all the circumstances)

If, however, the court concludes, at that stage, that there is some other available forum which *prima facie* is clearly more appropriate for the trial, it will ordinarily grant a stay, unless there are circumstances by reason of which justice requires that a stay should, nevertheless, not be granted. In this inquiry, the court will consider all the circumstances of the case, including circumstances which go beyond those taken into account when considering connecting factors with the other forum. One such factor, if established objectively by cogent evidence, can be the fact that the plaintiff will not obtain justice in the foreign jurisdiction.

3.3.5.6 Treatment of a legitimate personal or juridical advantage

Other advantages to the plaintiff proceeding in this jurisdiction may be relevant but not decisive. The key to the solution as to the treatment of a legitimate personal or juridical advantage lies in the underlying fundamental principle, which is where the case may be tried suitably for the interests of all the parties and the ends of justice. Typical examples of such advantages are: the award of higher damages; power to award interest; a more generous limitation period. However, even if the plaintiff were to be deprived of an advantage, such as a higher award of damages, a procedural advantage, time bar, and such like, it would not mean that the action should not be stayed. The most important element would be that the court was satisfied that substantial justice would be done in the available forum.[38]

It was held in the *Spiliada* that the trial judge, having identified the correct test, considered the relevant factors and that his exercise of discretion should not be interfered with. The existence of *The Cambridgeshire* action was also a relevant factor to be considered in the exercise of the court's discretion.

---

38   [1987] 1 AC 460 (HL), pp 476–78, 482–84.

In a recent case, ***Lubbe v Cape plc Africa and Others***,[39] concerning claims by employees of South African subsidiaries of the defendant (an English based company) for asbestos related diseases allegedly caused to workers over 20 to 30 years, the *Lubbe* action was stayed by the judge on the ground that South Africa was clearly more appropriate forum than England. The Court of Appeal lifted the stay and there was a petition to the House of Lords which was refused. Thereafter, further actions were commenced on behalf of 1539 claimants (the African writ), neighbours to the South African subsidiaries who alleged they suffered asbestos related damage. The defendants applied for a stay, again, in these new actions. Two reasons were submitted by the claimants against a stay: first, that the South African court did not have experience in group actions with multiple claimants and, second, that the claimants would not be able to obtain legal aid there. It was held by Buckley J that, as the circumstances had changed since the last Court of Appeal decision, the *African* and other actions should proceed as a group in the more appropriate forum, South Africa.

On appeal, the Court of Appeal affirmed the judgment of Buckley J, and Pill LJ said on these issues:

> It is not disputed that South Africa has a legal system of high repute, both with respect to the quality of its judges and its administration. I am entirely unpersuaded by arguments that the South African High Court would be unable to handle these actions efficiently, either on the ground that there are territorial divisions within South Africa, or because there is at present no procedure expressly providing for group actions. It is common ground that the law potentially to be applied is the same throughout South Africa...[40]

> Justice does not in my judgment require the refusal of a stay ... The general rule is that the court will not refuse to grant a stay simply because the plaintiff has shown that no financial assistance will be available to him in the appropriate forum. It may exceptionally be a relevant factor, but the plaintiff has far from established that substantial justice cannot and will not be done in South Africa. I have already referred to the high repute in which the South African courts are held. There is also in South Africa a legal profession with high standards and a tradition of public service, though I do not suggest that lawyers in South Africa, any more than those anywhere else, can be expected to act on a large scale without prospects of remuneration. While I would not be prepared to apply the second stage of *The Spiliada* test, so as to permit English litigation, even in the absence of evidence that legal representation will be available, I am unable to conclude that in the circumstances it would not become available for claims in the South African courts. Moreover, given the accessibility to the wealth of scientific, technical and medical evidence available in this context, I am confident that it could be made available in a

---

39   [2000] 2 Lloyd's Rep 383 (HL) and [2000] 1 Lloyd's Rep 139 (CA).
40   [2000] 1 Lloyd's Rep 139 (CA), p 162.

South African court to the extent required to achieve a proper consideration of the plaintiffs' cases. The action would by no means be novel or speculative.[41]

On appeal to the House of Lords by the plaintiffs, it was held that:

A plaintiff must take a foreign forum as he found it, even if it was in some respects less advantageous to him than the English forum; it was only if the plaintiff could establish that substantial justice would not be done in the appropriate forum that a stay would be refused; and it was not necessary enough to show that legal aid was available in England, but not in the foreign forum.

Whether the issue of delay by the foreign court to deliver judgment would be a factor to be taken into account at the second stage of *The Spiliada* test, Newman J held, in a recent decision,[42] that the court was not satisfied that substantial justice could not be done in India, although it might well be that it would take longer than if the proceedings had remained in England. In addition, the difference in the level of recoverability of costs was not something that denied substantial justice to parties in India.

3.3.6 Order 11 and forum non-conveniens compared

Lord Goff concluded that, although the general principle of *forum non-conveniens* was remarkably similar to the principle applied to cases of the court's discretionary power under RSC Ord 11, as derived from what Lord Wilberforce said in *Amin Rasheed* (see para 3.3.4, above), he identified three differences:

(a) in Ord 11 cases, the burden of proof rests on the plaintiff, whereas in *forum non-conveniens* cases, it rests on the defendant, at least at the first stage;

(b) in Ord 11 cases, the plaintiff is seeking to persuade the court to exercise its discretionary power to permit service on the defendant outside the jurisdiction. Although statutory authority has specified the particular circumstances in which that power may be exercised by Ord 11 r 1, r 4(2) of Ord 11 leaves it to the court to decide whether to exercise such power in a particular case. Permission shall not be granted, unless it shall be made sufficiently to appear to the court that the case is a proper one for service out of the jurisdiction. Special regard must be had to the fact stressed by Lord Diplock in *Amin Rasheed* that the jurisdiction exercised under Ord 11 may be exorbitant, meaning extraordinary;

(c) the importance to be attached to any particular ground invoked by the plaintiff may vary from case to case. For example, the fact that English law may be the putative proper law of the contract may be of great importance in some cases, but of little importance in others.[43]

---

41 [2000] 1 Lloyd's Rep 139 (CA), p 164.

42 *Radhakrishna Hospitality Service Private Ltd and Eurest SA v Eih Ltd* [1999] 2 Lloyd's Rep 249.

43 *The Spiliada* [1987] 1 AC 460 (HL), pp 480–81.

3.3.7 What change did The Spiliada bring to the doctrine of forum non-conveniens?

(a) It made a coherent statement of the principle as had developed from the previous cases and confirmed its uniformity with the Scottish doctrine;

(b) provided a clear guideline for judges, by dividing the test into two stages;

(c) delineated the burden of proof;

(d) clarified the treatment of a legitimate personal or juridical advantage.

In subsequent cases, the principle was easy to apply, although there have been some conflicting decisions on the treatment of a legitimate personal advantage.

In collision cases the appropriate forum would be easily identifiable as the place where the collision occurred, if not on the high seas as, for example, in *The Wellamo*[44] where the collision took place in Swedish territorial waters. The action in England was stayed in favour of the court in Stockholm. If the interests of all parties and the ends of justice are not served, however, the place of the collision will not be the only factor. In *The Vishva Ajay*,[45] despite proof of a natural forum, a stay of the English action was refused. The collision took place in India. However, the circumstances prevailing in India at that time (delay in delivering a judgment, non-realistic award of legal costs) would constitute denial of justice to the plaintiff, who had come to the English courts for justice.[46] By contrast, another judge recently, in *Radhakrishna Hospitality v Eih Ltd*,[47] decided that these factors were not depriving the plaintiff of substantial justice.

The conclusion to be drawn is that the court has wide discretion on the treatment of a juridical advantage of the claimant, which depends on the circumstances of a particular case and the time at which the issue is determined.

Where there is no natural forum the court will refuse a stay.[48]

3.3.8 Forum shopping by way of limitation actions

As has already been seen, prior to 1973, there was an inclination by the English courts towards English jurisdictional chauvinism which culminated with the well known remark of Lord Denning, MR that: 'No one who comes to these courts asking for justice should come in vain provided he acts in good faith ... You may call this forum shopping ... but if the forum is England, it is a good place to shop in, both for the quality of the goods and the speed of

---

44 [1980] 2 Lloyd's Rep 229.

45 [1989] 2 Lloyd's Rep 558.

46 See, also, *The Sidi Bishir* [1987] 1 Lloyd's Rep 42.

47 [1999] 2 Lloyd's Rep 249, see para 2.3.5.3, above.

48 *The Coral Isis* [1986] 1 Lloyd's Rep 413; *The Po* [1990] 1 Lloyd's Rep 418 (CA); [1991] 2 Lloyd's Rep 206.

service.'[49] To which Lord Reid responded in the House of Lords: '... that seems to me to recall the good old days, the passing of which many may regret, when inhabitants of this island felt an innate superiority over those unfortunate enough to belong to other races.'[50]

Until then, it was rare for proceedings brought in England to be stayed, or set aside in favour of a foreign jurisdiction, even if it could have been more appropriate for the particular case.

In a limitation action, which is an action brought by a person seeking to limit his liability in respect of maritime claims, consideration is given by that person to the system of law which provides either low limits (such as the law of the countries following the International Convention for Limitation of Liability 1957), or a more difficult test by which the right to limitation may be broken (such as those countries which have adopted the 1976 Limitation Convention). The latter has been ratified by States holding 43% of the world tonnage, while the former applies to 7.6%; the remaining States adhere to limitation of their own national law.

Outside the European Conventions regime (discussed later), there is flexibility for forum shopping and this has been acceptable in practice. This position seems to have been strengthened by recent decisions.

Caspian v Bouygues[51]

Rix J, having thoroughly reviewed all relevant authorities, held that admission or determination of liability was not a condition precedent to limitation. He said that limitation of liability for loss of a barge under tow (in the port of Cape Town), commenced in England by the owners and time charterers of the tug, could be determined here on the basis of the Limitation Convention 1976, prior to liability actions which had commenced in both South Africa and England. Although there was no connection with England, other than that the towage contract provided for English jurisdiction, the advantage to the applicants for limitation here was that it would be harder for limitation to be broken, while under South African law (which applies the 1957 Convention) it would be easier. In accordance with the second stage of *The Spiliada* test, the judge decided in favour of England despite South Africa being the natural forum for the liability issues. There was nothing unusual in determining a limitation action in a forum different from that of liability, Rix J said. The Court of Appeal[52] allowed the limitation action to continue here and held that the right to limit was a quite separate issue from the issue of liability. The action for damages, by the owners of the tow against the owners of the tug, its

---

49 *The Atlantic Star* [1972] 2 Lloyd's Rep 446 (CA), p 451.
50 *The Atlantic Star* [1973] 2 Lloyd's Rep 197 (HL), p 200.
51 [1997] 2 Lloyd's Rep 507; see Chapter 8 for the facts of the case.
52 [1998] 2 Lloyd's Rep 461.

time charterers and the Cape Town port authorities, was allowed to continue in South Africa.

A similar situation arose in **Caltex Singapore v BP Shipping**.[53] BP's ship collided with the jetty of the plaintiffs (Caltex oil companies) in Singapore. Liability proceedings against BP were brought in England where the limitation under the 1976 Convention was higher than the plaintiffs' claim. Naturally, BP commenced its limitation action in Singapore, (the natural forum for determination of liability) in view of lower limits applicable there under the 1957 Limitation Convention. There was no issue of apportionment of fault. BP also applied for a stay of the English action. Although Clarke J ruled that the appropriate forum for liability was Singapore, he dismissed BP's application for stay of the English proceedings on the basis of the second stage of *The Spiliada* test. He concluded that the interests of both parties and the ends of justice – viewed objectively – would be better served if the plaintiffs were not deprived of the larger limit, since it was proper to regard the 1976 Convention as representing a widely accepted development, and being part of English law, it could be fairly regarded as part of English public policy.

It was that very reasoning that the judge in Hong Kong found difficult to accept in the subsequent decision, **The Kapitan Shvestov**,[54] basically because *The Caltex* judgment seemed to equate the local public policy (being a subjective value judgment) with objective substantial justice, which was a distinct requirement laid down by *The Spiliada* and *De Dampierre v de Dampierre*.[55]

There were similar facts to *The Caltex* in *The Kapitan Shvestov*. A collision between a Russian and a Singaporean ship took place in the dredged channel of the Chao Fhraya river in Thailand, but neither of the shipowners wanted proceedings brought in Bangkok. Instead, the Singaporean owners commenced an action in Singapore and the Russian owners brought an action in Hong Kong. Both applied for a stay of the respective proceedings of each other. An important factor in the applications was that Singaporean law applied the 1957 Limitation Convention, while Hong Kong applied the 1976 Convention. Waung J stayed the Hong Kong action on the ground that – since the parties had displaced the natural forum of the Bangkok court – Singapore was a more appropriate forum than Hong Kong, on the basis of various connecting factors and, also, because the proceedings in Singapore had reached an advanced stage. There, objectively, substantial justice could be done for the interests of all parties and the ends of justice. The judge thought that in *The Caltex* case undue emphasis had been placed on the loss of the advantage to the plaintiffs if their limitation action in England was stayed,

53 [1996] 1 Lloyd's Rep 286.
54 [1998] 1 Lloyd's Rep 199 (HK Ct 1st inst and CA).
55 [1988] 1 AC 92 (HL).

which was not in accord with *The Spiliada* and *De Dampierre* cases. However, the Hong Kong Court of Appeal, by majority of 2:1, reversed this result and decided in favour of the Hong Kong jurisdiction. The majority thought that, since Singapore was not the natural or appropriate forum, the trial there would deprive the Russian owners of a legitimate juridical advantage and, since the Russian ship was more severely damaged, the limitation fund in Singapore would not be sufficient, particularly if the Singaporean ship was found more to blame. An interesting point was raised by the minority in the Court of Appeal, which supported the judge's decision as regards the result. This was that substantial legal costs had already been incurred in the Singaporean proceedings and, given that the expected burdensome additional legal costs which were likely to be incurred to reach the same level of the proceedings in Hong Kong, the possible shortfall in the limitation figure of US\$338,000 could hardly justify a second set of legal proceedings in Hong Kong.

In the subsequent case, **Herceg Novi and Ming Galaxy**,[56] the competing fora were Singapore and England. A collision occurred in the straits of Singapore between the *Ming Galaxy and Herceg Novi*, which resulted in the sinking of the latter. The owners of the former began an action *in rem* in Singapore and the owners of the latter commenced an action in England. The motives of the parties to the actions were, again, the differences in the law of each forum with respect to limitation of liability. The defendants to the English action sought a stay of the action on the ground that England was not the natural or appropriate forum. The plaintiffs' argument was that, were the stay to be granted, they would be deprived of the benefit of the more generous limitation amount under the 1976 Convention. Clarke J was inclined to refuse the stay, bearing in mind this factor, but temporarily granted it until the determination of the liability and quantum issues was resolved in Singapore.

However, the Court of Appeal[57] chose to discourage forum shopping, on the basis of higher limitation applicable by the law of a forum in which jurisdiction is obtained as of right by arrest of a ship, particularly when there is another forum which is more appropriate by being the natural forum, as was Singapore in this case. It was stressed that as the 1976 Convention has not received universal acceptance, the preference for it had no greater justification than the 1957 regime. The Court of Appeal agreed with the first instance judge in *The Kapitan Shvetsov* and with the dissenting judgment of the Hong Kong Court of Appeal in the same case.

Apparently, there is a conflict between two Court of Appeal decisions, *The Caspian*, which encourages forum shopping, if a party chooses to proceed in a jurisdiction where the higher limit of the 1976 Convention applies, and *The*

---

56 [1998] 1 Lloyd's Rep 167.
57 [1998] 2 Lloyd's Rep 454.

Herceg Novi, which discourages such an approach. While there may be an opportunity in the future for that conflict to be resolved by the House of Lords, it is submitted that no general principle can be drawn either way. Each case should be looked upon its own circumstances. Where there is a natural forum, the first stage test of *The Spiliada* can easily be satisfied, although this factor alone will not be decisive. As regards the balancing act of advantages and disadvantages at the second stage, the 1976 Convention limit should not weigh heavy, if the court is satisfied that substantial justice could be done in the alternative more appropriate forum. However, better justice could be done if there is a larger fund in court to satisfy the claims and this reason may justify the separation of the liability from the limitation action.

3.4 Stay on the ground of a foreign jurisdiction agreement[58]

The parties to a contract usually agree where and how any disputes arising out of the contract will be adjudicated. Such agreements may provide either for arbitration, or for the jurisdiction of a competent court, English or foreign. There are occasions, however, when one party to the agreement decides to bring suit in a jurisdiction other than the contractual, in breach of the jurisdiction agreement. In the following paragraphs, both the principles and the approach of the English court with regard to proceedings brought in the English courts in breach of a foreign jurisdiction clause (to which the Brussels/Lugano Conventions do not apply) are examined. With respect to jurisdiction agreements to which the Brussels/Lugano Conventions apply, see Chapter 6.[59] As far as a breach of an English jurisdiction clause or arbitration is concerned, see Chapter 7.

3.4.1 General principle

When there is a breach of a foreign jurisdiction clause to which the Brussels Convention does not apply, the English court, upon the application of the aggrieved party for a stay of the proceedings, is not bound to stay the action, but it has discretion. The court's discretion is exercised in favour of a stay, unless the claimant shows a strong reason or cause for not giving effect to the foreign jurisdiction clause. The English courts have followed this principle consistently.[60] Balancing of all the circumstances of the particular case is

---

58 The issues involved in this area are analysed in detail by Peel, E, 'Exclusive jurisdiction agreements: purity and pragmatism in the conflict of laws' [1998] LMCLQ 182.

59 The rules applicable under the Brussels/Lugano Conventions are different, as are explained at the end of Chapter 6.

60 In *The Cap Blanco* [1913] P 131, p 136, it was said that 'effect must be given, if the terms of the contract permit it, to the obvious intention and agreement of the parties'; *The Fehmarn* [1957] 2 Lloyd's Rep 511; *The Chaparral* [1968] 2 Lloyd's Rep 158; and other, more recent, cases mentioned in this section.

required in order to determine in which forum, the chosen or the English, justice will best be served with less inconvenience and expense. The discretion of the first instance judge should not easily be disturbed by the appellate court, on the basis that the latter disagrees with it, unless it is shown that the judge made an error in principle, or that he took or omitted to take into account matters which he ought not to, or he evaluated the circumstances wrongly.[61]

The following broad factors have been considered in various cases to have been connecting factors with either forum:

(a) where the evidence is available;
(b) with which country either party is closely connected;
(c) whether the law chosen is different from English;
(d) whether the defendant genuinely desires to proceed in the chosen forum, or only seeks a procedural advantage;
(e) whether there are related actions already commenced in one forum;
(f) whether the plaintiff would be prejudiced in the chosen forum, if the claim was time barred, or if he was deprived of security for the claim, or if there was delay in procedures of administration of justice there.

It will be seen that one of these factors alone may not be sufficient to tilt the balance in favour of not granting the stay. In recent years, a less nationalistic attitude of the English courts and more respect for the parties' choice of forum has been shown.

3.4.2 What is a strong cause or reason for the court to refuse stay of proceedings?

By a process of elimination, the circumstances which have not been regarded as constituting a strong cause or reason by the courts for the purpose of staying proceedings, in favour of a foreign jurisdiction clause, will first be examined.

3.4.2.1 Availability of factual evidence in England is not in itself a strong cause

In *The Eleftheria*,[62] an express jurisdiction clause was contained in the bill of lading, which provided that all disputes arising under it were to be decided in the country where the carrier had his principal place of business, applying the law of such country. The principal place of business of the defendants, the shipowners, was in Greece. *The Eleftheria* carried wood intended to be discharged in London and Hull. When she arrived at docks in London, there

---

61 *The Nile Rhapsody* [1994] 1 Lloyd's Rep 382; *Reichhold Norway v Goldman Sachs Int* [2000] 1 WLR 173 (the judge had not misdirected himself).

62 [1969] 1 Lloyd's Rep 237.

was labour trouble and she could only discharge part of the cargo. She sailed for Rotterdam where she discharged the rest, as was allowed by the contract in the circumstances. The plaintiffs claimed the expenses to transship the cargo back to its destination and arrested the vessel in England, alleging breach of contract. In this court, the defendants confined themselves to the application for a stay of the action on the ground that the Greek courts had jurisdiction by express agreement of the parties, which was not disputed. Considering the fact that the parties had agreed the jurisdiction and the law for their disputes, Brandon J held that the inconvenience to the plaintiffs in having to take witnesses to Greece was not insuperable. It was of substantial importance that Greek law governed and it would be more satisfactory for the law of a foreign country to be decided by the courts of that country. He exercised his discretion by granting the stay. The plaintiffs had not shown a strong cause why they should not be held to their agreement and they would not be prejudiced by having to sue in Greece. All the circumstances in each case need to be taken into account.

In *The Makefjell*,[63] the Court of Appeal upheld the decision of the trial judge, Brandon J, in this case, affirming the same principle. At the time, and after *The Atlantic Star*, a more liberal and less nationalistic attitude was being displayed by the English judges.

The case involved Norwegian shipowners, a Canadian shipper and an English receiver of cargo of cheesecakes, which was loaded on *The Makefjell* in Canada for carriage to London. The bills of lading provided for Norwegian law and jurisdiction in the place of business of the carrier, with respect to any disputes arising under the bills. The cargo arrived in London and was partly discharged. Due to some difficulties in further discharge of the cargo, the rest of it was left in a non-refrigerated shed. Consequently, the cheesecakes thawed. The plaintiffs brought two actions in England, one *in personam* (by serving out of the jurisdiction) and one *in rem* and threatened to arrest a sister ship, which was about to come to England. They also issued summons in the Norwegian court to protect themselves in the event the English action was stayed. The defendants applied for a stay on the ground of the express jurisdiction clause, while the plaintiffs contended that they should not be held to their agreement, because the facts giving rise to their claim arose in England. This, they alleged, was because the factual witnesses were here. As regards the applicable law, Norwegian lawyers who were familiar with English language could give evidence on Norwegian law (which was not materially different from English law).

It was held that the inconvenience of witnesses, if they had to give evidence in the foreign agreed jurisdiction, was not a strong cause to refuse a stay. The existence of factual evidence in England was not, in itself, a decisive factor for not granting a stay.

---

63 [1976] 2 Lloyd's Rep 29.

On the discretion point, the judge (at first instance) thought that English witnesses could very well give evidence in Norway, as it could equally happen the other way around. Two considerations were influential upon exercising his discretion to grant the stay: (a) the key point was, in his view, whether the circumstances that the bulk of the evidence was to be found here, was something of such an exceptional character as to afford strong reasons for allowing the plaintiffs to depart from their contract. The answer to this, in his view, was that, while this may be an important factor, there must also be other factors operating against a stay. Besides, a large number of cargo claims involved evidence which would be found in the country of discharge. If all such cases were treated as exceptional, the rule as to enforcement of jurisdiction clauses would be undermined; (b) a broader consideration, which the judge took into account, was the tendency of the courts, both in England and the USA, at that time to adopt a more liberal and less nationalistic attitude to questions of choice of jurisdiction. The Court of Appeal, constituted by the Cairns and Stevenson LJJ and Sir Gordon Willmer, approved the judge's reasoning and conclusion.

3.4.2.2 Time bar in the contractual jurisdiction is not in itself a strong cause

Whether or not the time bar of a claim in the contractual jurisdiction is a strong cause in refusing a stay of the English proceedings has not been treated uniformly by the courts. There exist three possible views: either, against a stay (*Blue Wave*),[64] or in favour of a stay, or that the time bar is a neutral factor. The judge in *Adolf Warski*[65] preferred the second view, but it was *obiter* and the Court of Appeal did not decide the point, although it thought that the time bar might be a neutral factor.

There are a number of interesting recent decisions on the issue. Rix J in *The MC Pearl*,[66] chose a robust approach. In this case, the claim in the contractual jurisdiction, South Korea, had become time barred. He considered the authorities and conflicting views on this issue and distinguished cases concerning *forum non-conveniens*. He held that, as regards jurisdiction clauses, the time bar point alone would not have assisted the plaintiff to continue their case here, if he did not have a strong cause for it separately.[67] He was not

---

64 [1982] 1 Lloyd's Rep 151.

65 [1976] 2 Lloyd's Rep 241.

66 [1997] 1 Lloyd's Rep 566.

67 The strong cause was multiplicity of proceedings, of which see later. Previously, Sheen J (in *The Blue Wave* [1982] 1 Lloyd's Rep 151) had decided that a time bar in the contractual jurisdiction would be an important factor for refusing a stay of the English action, unless the plaintiff acted unreasonably and his conduct showed that, without good reason, he deliberately allowed the time limit to expire without instituting alternative proceedings. Lord Goff, *obiter*, in *The Spiliada* [1987] 1 AC 460, seemed to support that view. The Court of Appeal, in *The Adolf Warski* [1976] 2 Lloyd's Rep. 241, thought that it was a neutral factor to considerations of a stay with regard to jurisdiction clauses.

prepared to find that the existence of a limitation defence in South Korea saved this action, or caused him even to stay it, only on terms that the South Korean limitation defence was waived.[68] Even where the plaintiff did have a strong cause for jurisdiction in England, the fact that he had allowed the time bar to go by default in the contractual jurisdiction always required some consideration or explanation.[69] Although Rix J agreed with Colman J, who stated the law in *Citi-March v Neptune*[70] as derived from previous cases, he stressed his disagreement with the following proposition of Colman J that:

> In a case where, however, but for the time bar, strong cause in favour of England could not be shown, a plaintiff may be able to rely on the prejudice to him by reason of the time bar in the contractual forum if he can show that he did not act unreasonably in failing to issue protective proceedings in order to prevent time running against him ... At the end of the day, the court must consider whether in the interests of justice it is more appropriate to permit a plaintiff to proceed in England, although he has omitted to preserve time in the contractual forum, and although England is not clearly the more appropriate forum, than to deprive him of all opportunity of pursuing his claim in any forum.[71]

Such a soft approach was not acceptable to Rix J, who preferred a hard line attitude to deprive a litigant of pursuing his claim, if he let the time limit in the contractual jurisdiction expire.

In some cases, however, a plaintiff may be unable to obtain an extension of time under the law of the country of the chosen jurisdiction, either by waiver, or through the discretion of the court, which would, in effect, result in rendering the exclusive jurisdiction clause invalid. In such a case, the Court of Appeal held, recently, that the action commenced here as protective measures, should not be stayed. It reversed its previous, not finalised, order by which a stay had been granted on ground of *forum non-conveniens* and on the condition that the defendants gave an undertaking to waive the time bar point in the contractual jurisdiction, Pakistan. At this hearing it was shown that it would be very difficult under the local statute to obtain a waiver of the time bar.[72]

A warning to litigants, who deliberately let a time limit lapse in the contractual jurisdiction in order to proceed in another forum, was given in the strongest terms by Godfrey J sitting in the Court of Appeal of Hong Kong,

---

68 [1997] 1 Lloyd's Rep 566, p 576, 2nd col: to that extent he differed from the view expressed by Colman J in *Citi-March v Neptune* [1997] 1 Lloyd's Rep 72.

69 [1997] 1 Lloyd's Rep 566, p 576; Rix J thought that this case was on all fours with *Citi-March Ltd v Neptune Orient Lines Ltd* [1997] 1 Lloyd's Rep 72, in which Colman J summarised the principles derived from previous cases.

70 [1997] 1 Lloyd's Rep 72.

71 *Ibid*, p 77, 1st col, *per* Colman J. (The above statement does not seem to be in accord with the general principle stated by Colman J in the previous paragraphs of his judgment.)

72 *Baghlaf Al Zafer Factory Co v Pakistan National Shipping Co (No 2)* [2000] 1 Lloyd's Rep 1.

which was cited with approval by Lord Goff at the Privy Council in the same case, *The Pioneer Container*.[73] Godfrey J said:

> If you find yourself bound to litigate in a forum which is more expensive than the one you would prefer, deliberately to choose the latter rather than the former seems to me …to be forum shopping in one of its purest and most undesirable forms. And, if in pursuance of your deliberate decision to litigate here, instead, you let time run out in the jurisdiction in which you are bound to litigate, without taking the trouble (because of the expense) even to issue a protective writ there, you are not, as I think, acting reasonably at all; you are gambling on the chance of a stay being refused here and you cannot complain if you then lose that gamble. That may seem to you at the time a justifiable commercial risk to take. But that, in the context of the litigation, does not make your decision a reasonable one.

On a voyage from Taiwan to Hong Kong, the vessel in this case sank off the coast of Taiwan. Despite the Taiwan exclusive jurisdiction clause contained in the bill of lading, the cargo-owners, plaintiffs, allowed the time limit to expire deliberately and commenced an action in Hong Kong. An application for a stay by the defendants, shipowners, was successful on appeal, as it was found that, apart from the time bar point, there was strong connection of the case with Taiwan.

The circumstances that could constitute a strong cause or reason are examined next.

3.4.2.3 Expert evidence in England would be a strong cause

Evidence of experts appointed in England was regarded as an exceptional factor for not granting a stay. The same judge and the Court of Appeal in the following case decided against a stay. It is worth noting the factors, which were decisive in the exercise of their discretion.

The Adolf Warski[74]

The plaintiffs, cargo-owners, started actions *in rem* against the shipowners for damages to cargo carried on two of their Polish ships from South America to England. There were two bills of lading issued which contained similar jurisdiction clauses in favour of the Polish courts and, also, provided that Polish law was to apply. The claims in Poland had, however, become time barred and the defendants had refused to agree an extension of time. The defendants provided security for the claims and applied for a stay of the English proceedings. The plaintiffs objected on the grounds that the receivers were English companies and the evidence was more readily available in England. They pleaded two further important factors: their claim had become

---

73 [1994] 1 Lloyd's Rep 593.
74 [1976] 2 Lloyd's Rep 241.

time barred in Poland and, if it were necessary to call witnesses from Chile, the port of loading, there could be political difficulties in obtaining visas for them to visit Poland. The trial judge came to the conclusion that the court should exercise its discretion by refusing a stay and allowing the actions to proceed in England. Looking at all aspects of the main evidence necessary to enable claims to be decided justly, there was a strong balance of argument in favour of a trial in England, rather than Poland. The Court of Appeal held that the judge was entitled to exercise his discretion that way. Cairns LJ stated:

> The judge was not satisfied that there was any factor in favour of the plaintiffs arising from their connection with England as against the defendants' connection with Poland. He considered that the jurisdiction clauses were reasonable, but that this did not mean that it would be right to enforce them irrespective of the circumstances ...There was no evidence of any difference between the English and Polish law, and nothing to show that the English court would have difficulty in applying Polish law. He considered that expert evidence was the most important factor in this case, and as the damaged goods had been surveyed on both sides by English surveyors, and both sides had consulted English experts ... it would be difficult to put the evidence in a satisfactory form before the Polish court. He attached some, but no great, weight to possible difficulties in calling Chilean witnesses.[75]

On the question as to what made this case exceptional, or different from the previous one, Cairns LJ said, having approved the judge's approach, that it was the necessity of calling English expert witnesses on a highly technical matter.[76]

Similarly, in *The El Amria*,[77] a stay of the English proceedings, which were commenced despite the Egyptian jurisdiction clause, was refused because, on balance, there was a significant or strong cause shown for refusing the stay. That was, again, the evidence of expert witnesses in England (surveyors and agronomists) who had examined the cargo during and after discharge, and the evidence relating to the slowness of discharge. Such evidence, being at the centre of the dispute, was more readily available in England and there would be considerable difficulty in conveying – through interpreters to the Egyptian judge or court – expert technical evidence which the surveyors and agronomists would be called to give.

3.4.2.4 Multiplicity of proceedings is a strong cause

Another factor, which the Court of Appeal in *The El Amria*, unlike the judge in the same case, found to be not just a matter of convenience, but of great importance, was the existence of another action in this jurisdiction by the same claimant against another party (Mersey Docks and Harbour Company). In this

---

75 [1976] 2 Lloyd's Rep 241, p 244.
76 *Ibid*, p 246.
77 [1981] 2 Lloyd's Rep 119.

action, many of the issues were the same as the action between the claimants and the defendants with regard to the cargo claim for which a stay was sought in favour of the chosen jurisdiction, Egypt. It would be a potential disaster if these actions were not tried together, because of the inherent risk that the same issues might be determined differently in the two countries, said the Court of Appeal. Although it approved the judge's application of the general principle, it criticised him in three respects for his reasons in refusing the stay: (a) he had misapprehended the potential importance of oral evidence which the defendant might reasonably have wished to call from Egypt; (b) he had failed to take into account the close connection of the defendants with Egypt; (c) he had taken into account a factor which he should not have, namely a supposed inferiority of the procedures used by the Egyptian court. On the whole, there were strong conflicting considerations in favour of either court. However, the two factors stressed by the Court of Appeal: the expert evidence and the parallel action in England led it to refuse the stay. In addition, the fact that the defendants did not just ask for a stay merely for a procedural advantage, (since security for the claim had been provided) added a weight in favour of England.

Multiplicity of proceedings is, undoubtedly, a strong cause as has clearly been stated in more recent decisions, *Citi-March v Neptune*[78] and *The MC Pearl*,[79] in which Colman J and Rix J (respectively) applied *The El Amria*, having considered that the strong cause was the multiplicity of suits in England. This was a paradigm, Rix J said, for the concentration of all relevant parties' disputes in a single jurisdiction.

Occasionally, however, there may be a clash of jurisdiction clauses contained in separate contracts, which involve disputes of related issues and may give rise, unintentionally, to multiplicity of proceedings in different jurisdictions. Such a clash arose in a recent case, *Sinochem v Mobil Sales*,[80] in which Rix J decided in favour of each exclusive jurisdiction clause contained in the individual contracts, which provided for jurisdiction in Hong Kong and England, respectively. The mere possibility of multiplicity of proceedings, when no proceedings had yet commenced in Hong Kong under the separate contract, was not a strong reason why, in the interests of justice, Sinochem London should be relieved of its bargain to litigate disputes under its English contract in England.

The El Amria case, which has been applied by judges in subsequent decisions, insofar as jurisdiction agreements are concerned, represents the school of thought of 'broad judicial discretion'. In particular, in determining whether or not a stay should be granted, it allows judges to consider which would be the appropriate forum (England or the chosen one) for the ends of

---

78 [1997] 1 Lloyd's Rep 72.
79 [1997] 1 Lloyd's Rep 566.
80 [2000] 1 Lloyd's Rep 670.

justice and the interests of parties, which is almost identical to the doctrine of *forum non-conveniens*. Sometimes, the agreement of the parties as to jurisdiction may play, relatively, a less important role. The 'broad judicial discretion' school of thought has, however, been criticised for allowing *forum non-conveniens* principles to assist, instead of preventing, a party to an agreement breaking his bargain. Since *The Angelic Grace*[81] – which involved a breach of an arbitration clause – there has emerged a school of thought supporting the view that there should be a 'narrow judicial discretion' when there is a contractual choice of jurisdiction. In particular, the Court of Appeal, in this case, stressed, in strong terms, that a choice of forum by parties to a contract should be respected. The differences between these two strands are examined in Chapter 7, in the context of anti-suit injunctions.[82]

3.4.2.5 The Spiliada connecting factors provide a strong cause[83]

In the following case, connecting factors, which were important at the first stage of *The Spiliada* case, pointed towards the chosen jurisdiction as being the most appropriate forum.

The Rothnie[84]

The plaintiffs, an English company, were the demise charterers of the vessel R. The defendants were an English company carrying on business as a shipyard and ship-repairer in Gibraltar. The parties entered into a contract to repair the vessel in drydock in Gibraltar. The contract expressly provided that 'the agreement shall be governed by and construed in accordance with the laws of Gibraltar and the parties hereto submit to the non-exclusive jurisdiction of the courts of Gibraltar'.

Subsequent to a dispute concerning the work carried out on the vessel, the plaintiffs issued a writ in England on 17 July 1995. The defendants, who had not been paid served proceedings in Gibraltar, on 19 July 1995, and applied for a stay of the English proceedings. They contended that the effect of the non-exclusive jurisdiction clause, by which the parties acknowledged the jurisdiction of the courts of Gibraltar, combined with the defendant's commencement of proceedings there, created a strong *prima facie* case that the

---

81 [1995] 1 Lloyd's Rep 87; see also *Reichhold Norway v Goldman Sachs* [2000] 1 WLR 173; stay of related proceedings in England was granted pending determination of arbitration in Norway.

82 Consistency in the treatment of foreign and domestic jurisdiction clauses is needed. Other than those cases concerning breach of an arbitration agreement, or a jurisdiction agreement which is within Art 17 of the Brussels Convention, where special rules apply, all other cases of breach of a jurisdiction agreement, whether the application is for an anti-suit injunction, or for a stay of proceedings, should be treated in the same way: see, further, Chapter 7.

83 *The El Amria* [1981] 2 Lloyd's Rep 119.

84 [1996] 2 Lloyd's Rep 206.

jurisdiction of Gibraltar was an appropriate one. The plaintiffs contended that both parties were English companies and jurisdiction had been founded by right in the English High Court. Moreover, the wording of the jurisdiction clause imposed no obligation to litigate in Gibraltar. After summarising the principles laid down by Lord Goff in *The Spiliada*,[85] the learned trial judge held that the defendant had satisfied the court that there was another available forum which was *prima facie* the appropriate forum for the trial of the action. The jurisdiction agreement in the parties' contract created a strong *prima facie* case that the jurisdiction of Gibraltar was an appropriate one. The action had its most real and substantial connection with Gibraltar, having regard to all the relevant factors, such as the place where the work was completed, the law, witnesses resided there, and such like. There were no circumstances by reason of which justice required that a stay should not be granted, after considering all the circumstances of the case.

3.4.2.6 Forum shopping in breach of a jurisdiction agreement and risk management

In the light of these decisions, careful consideration should be given to the circumstances, which have been regarded by the courts to constitute a strong cause, before litigants embark in wasted litigation. The burden of proof is on the claimant to show why a stay of the English proceedings should not be granted in favour of the agreed jurisdiction, by contrast to cases of a stay on ground of *forum non-conveniens* in which the burden of proof, at the first stage of *The Spiliada* test, is on the defendant to show why the stay should be granted. There seems to be, in some respects, a great similarity between the two approaches, with regard to the factors taken into account. For this reason, the courts, in some cases, tend to conflate the principles and assimilate *forum non-conveniens* when considering a stay on the ground of foreign jurisdiction agreements.[86] Such an approach, however, leads to inconsistent results given that, in other cases, the courts have distinguished the doctrine of *forum non-conveniens per se* from considerations applicable to a stay in favour of a foreign jurisdiction agreement and approached the matter with caution in order to keep the parties to their bargain[87] (see, further, below). Whether reasons of judicial comity, respect to the jurisdiction of the court chosen, should be taken into account, giving a broader application of the principles as stated in the *Patel v Airbus* on issues of anti-suit injunctions, are discussed in Chapter 7.

However, jurisdiction clauses will not be upheld if the HVR apply to the bill of lading contract by force of law and the foreign law chosen by the

---

85 [1987] 1 AC 460 (HL).

86 *The El Amria* [1981] 2 Lloyd's Rep 119; *The Nile Rhapsody* [1992] 2 Lloyd's Rep 399 and [1994] 1 Lloyd's Rep 382 (CA); see, *op cit*, Peel, fn 58.

87 *The MC Pearl* [1997] 1 Lloyd's Rep 566; *The Pioneer Container* [1994] 1 Lloyd's Rep 593; *The Angelic Grace* [1994] 1 Lloyd's Rep 168; [1995] 1 Lloyd's Rep 87 (CA) (see Chapter 7).

foreign jurisdiction clause confers less liability upon the carrier than the liability under the HVR – unless the defendant undertook to take no advantage of the lower limit.[88] If not, then the foreign jurisdiction will be null and void by virtue of Art 8 of the HVR.[89]

Sometimes, a jurisdiction clause may not be exclusive but optional, or may be obligatory upon one party to the agreement only, or it may not be effective.[90]

An attempt by one party to the agreement to oust the jurisdiction clause, by issuing proceedings in a jurisdiction other than the chosen one on the ground of *forum non-conveniens*, will be futile, if the clause provides for an exclusive jurisdiction which is a question of construction of the agreement. Whether or not an agreement provides for an exclusive jurisdiction, guidance has been given by the courts in further two cases. In the case below, Webster J took the view that a plea of *forum non-conveniens* would not be open to the parties when their agreement was freely negotiated and it was not just a standard term incorporated by reference. Although this case concerned a breach of an English jurisdiction clause, the remedies for which are discussed in Chapter 7, it is relevant in this context as well.

Aerospace v Dee Howard[91]

DHC was a company incorporated and carrying on business in the USA. BAE was an English company carrying on business in England. Both parties entered into an agreement known as TAA, whereby BAE agreed to provide DHC with assistance and information in connection with a re-engineering programme that DHC was undertaking. Their contract provided that the courts in England should have jurisdiction and for each party to provide an address in England for service of documents, in the event of proceedings being commenced. In December 1991, DHC stopped further work on the grounds that BAE had totally failed to perform its obligations under the TAA agreement. DHC commenced proceedings in the Texas court, USA, and service was made on BAE in England. BAE applied to have the Texas proceedings dismissed on the grounds (a) that they were in breach of the jurisdiction clause in the agreement and (b) *forum non-conveniens*. It was held that, whether or not the clause was one of exclusive jurisdiction was a question of construction, irrespective of whether or not the word 'exclusive' is used. The jurisdiction clause stated:

---

88 *Pirelli v United Thai* [2000] 1 Lloyd's Rep 663.
89 *The Morviken (sub nom The Hollandia)* [1983] 1 Lloyd's Rep 1 (HL).
90 *Insurance Co Ingosstrakh Ltd v Latvian Shipping Co* [2000] IL Pr 164.
91 [1993] 1 Lloyd's Rep 368.

This agreement shall be governed by and be construed and take effect according to English law and the parties hereto agree that the courts of law in England shall have jurisdiction to entertain any action in respect hereof ...

It was also held that, since the parties here had expressly agreed on English law, there would be no need to agree expressly that the English courts should have exclusive jurisdiction. The use of the word 'shall' was apposite to create the language of an obligation. Furthermore, the words 'any action' clearly do mean all actions. This clause was, under English law, an exclusive jurisdiction clause. It was not open to the defendant to start arguing about the relative merits of fighting an action in Texas as compared with England, where the factors relied upon would have been eminently foreseeable at the time of the contract. Adopting that approach, he thought it was not permissible to displace England based on such factors as inconvenience of witnesses, the location of documents, timing of the trial, and so on, in favour of Texas.

Sinochem v Mobil Sales[92]

Litigants should also note from this recent case that, while in the context of jurisdiction agreements the party suing in the non-chosen jurisdiction must show a strong cause why he should not be held to the agreement, the judge said that matters of convenience are, at any rate, largely, if not entirely, irrelevant. With regard to the determination of whether or not the clause was an exclusive jurisdiction one, the judge said that, not only did the clause in the Hong Kong contract provide for Hong Kong law to apply, but also that the Hong Kong courts 'are to have jurisdiction to settle any disputes' between the parties and that the parties 'submit to the jurisdiction of those courts'. In the judge's view, such a clause, as well as the clause under the London contract, provided for exclusive jurisdiction. 'It has all the indicia of such a clause,' the judge said. 'It is mutual, it refers to "any disputes" ... and the language "are to have jurisdiction"... is a language of obligation and not an option.'[93]

To the extent that proceedings are brought to obtain security for the claim, the English court has power, under s 26 of the Civil Jurisdiction and Judgments Act (CJJA) 1982, to retain the arrest of a ship until sufficient security is provided to satisfy a judgment of a foreign court of competent jurisdiction, which had been chosen by the parties in their contract to have exclusive jurisdiction.[94]

---

92 [2000] 1 Lloyd's Rep 670, p 677, *per* Rix J; see, also, *Ingosstrakh Ltd v Latvian Shipping Co* [2000] IL Pr 164 (CA).

93 *Ibid*, p 676.

94 *The Havhelt* [1993] 1 Lloyd's Rep 523.

3.5 Stay on the ground of an arbitration agreement

3.5.1 General principles under s 9 of the Arbitration Act 1996

The stay of court proceedings on this ground is discretionary, with regard to domestic arbitration, and mandatory, in respect of non-domestic arbitration.

By s 9(1) of the Arbitration Act (AA) 1996, a party to an arbitration agreement against whom legal proceedings are brought in respect of a matter, which under the agreement is to be referred to arbitration, may (upon notice to the other parties to the proceedings) apply to the court in which the proceedings have been brought to stay the proceedings, so far as they concern the matter. Section 9(4) provides that, upon an application under this section, the court shall grant a stay, unless satisfied that the arbitration agreement is null and void, inoperative, or incapable of being performed.[95]

The grant of a stay in non-domestic arbitration has been mandatory since the previous AA 1975, by s 1, which is reflected in s 9(4) of the 1996 Act. Section 86 of the 1996 Act expressly states that s 9(4) does not apply to domestic arbitration. This reflects s 4 of the AA 1950, which was applicable to domestic arbitration and the court had discretion whether or not to stay court proceedings brought in breach of an arbitration agreement. Although, generally, the intention of the new Act is not to distinguish between domestic and non-domestic arbitration, the distinction exists with regard to stay of court proceedings, in that the stay is mandatory when a non-domestic arbitration is involved, while it is discretionary in domestic arbitration. Once such a distinction is abolished, s 86 will be repealed and s 88 gives the Secretary of State power to repeal or amend s 86.[96]

A significant difference between s 9 and the equivalent s 1(1) of the 1975 Act is that the latter had specifically provided that, if there was, in fact, no dispute between the parties with regard to the matter referred to arbitration, a stay would not be granted. In such a case, an Ord 14 of the old RSC application would be made to the court to give a judgment where it was shown that there was no arguable defence. The words of s 1(1) of the 1975 Act referred to above have been omitted from s 9. If one party to the agreement commences English proceedings, a stay of those proceedings is mandatory by

---

95 The House of Lords, in *Inco Europe Ltd v First Choice Distribution and Others* [2000] 1 Lloyd's Rep 467, decided whether an appeal lay to the Court of Appeal from a decision of a first instance court made under s 9, which is silent on the point. It held that, where a section was silent about an appeal from a decision of the court, no restriction was intended.

96 See Merkin, R, *The Arbitration Act 1996: An Annotated Guide*, 1996, LLP, pp 25 and 120.

s 9, even when the party who has resorted to the court argues that there is 'in fact no dispute'.[97]

The intention of the new AA is to limit, as much as possible, the involvement of the courts in matters of jurisdiction under an arbitration agreement. In place of such a limitation, the Act has extended the powers of the arbitrators.

3.5.2 Application of principles in recent cases

There have been a few very important decisions about the court's approach in applications for a stay under s 9, particularly with reference to s 30 of the AA 1996 and its interrelationship with the new CPR. In *Al-Naimi v Islamic Press*,[98] concerning a building contract, the subject matter of the court proceedings was whether the dispute between the parties was covered by the arbitration agreement of the main contract, or arose under a separate oral contract not being subject to arbitration. The Court of Appeal approved the approach of his Honour Judge Lloyd QC in s 9 applications as correct (in *Birse Construction Ltd v David Ltd*),[99] in a situation in which what was in dispute was not whether a clause existed at all, but what it precisely covered.[100] It is pertinent, therefore, to refer to extracts of the judge's approach and then add the comments made by Waller LJ in the *Al-Naimi case*.

Per Humphrey Lloyd QC in *Birse Construction*:

The following courses are open to me:

1   To determine, on affidavit evidence that has been filed, that an arbitration agreement was made between the parties, in which case the proceedings will be stayed in accordance with s 9 of the AA 1996.

2   To stay the proceedings but on the basis that the arbitrator will decide the question of whether or not there is an arbitration agreement since s 30 of the AA 1996 provides: '(1) unless otherwise agreed by the parties, the arbitral tribunal may rule on its own substantive jurisdiction, that is, as to (a) whether there is a valid arbitration agreement ...(c) what matters have been submitted to arbitration in accordance with the arbitration agreement. (2) Any such ruling may be challenged by any available arbitral process of appeal or review.' This sub-section refers to s 67 of the Act about challenging the award.

---

97   *Halki Shipping Corp v Sopex Oils Ltd (The Halki)* [1998] 1 Lloyd's Rep 465 (CA) where it was held that there was a dispute once money was claimed, unless and until the defendants admitted that the sum was due and payable. If a party refused to pay a sum, which was claimed or denied that it was owing, then, in the ordinary language, there was a dispute between the parties.

98   [2000] 1 Lloyd's Rep 522 (CA).

99   [1999] BLR 194.

100   Although his decision was later reversed by the Court of Appeal, on the point that the parties had failed to make it clear to him that he should decide the question on affidavit evidence alone, it was understood that his approach was not disapproved of.

3   Not to decide the question immediately but to order an issue to be tried. Under the old procedure rules, RSC Ord 73 r 6(2) provided, 'in a question whether an arbitration agreement has been concluded or whether the dispute which is the subject matter of the proceedings falls within the terms of such agreement, the court may determine that question or give directions for its determination, in which case it may order the proceedings to be stayed pending the determination of that question'.

4   To decide that there is no arbitration agreement and dismiss the application to stay.

The judge held that the power of the arbitrator under s 30 is not mandatory. The Act does not require a party who maintains that there is no arbitration agreement to have that question decided by the arbitral tribunal. The existence of the power does not mean that the court must always refer a dispute, which concerns whether or not an arbitration agreement exists, to the tribunal whose competence to do so is itself disputed. The judge then referred to another decision (*Azon Shipping Co v Baltic Shipping Co*),[101] which supported the approach that the court ought to decide questions relating to the existence or the terms of the arbitration agreement, for there may, otherwise, be a real danger that there will be two hearings: the first, before the arbitrator under s 30 of the Act and, the second, before the court on a challenge under s 67 of the AA 1996.

In the *Al-Naimi v Islamic Press* case, Waller LJ entirely supported the above approach, particularly in relation to an application under the old rules Ord 73 r 6(2) and added the following:

If the court decides that it is the court which should determine whether the matters, the subject of the action, are the subject of an arbitration clause, unless the parties were agreed that the matter should be resolved on affidavit, then, if there is a triable issue, directions should be given for trying that issue. It may be helpful to add that the equivalent of Ord 73 r 6(2) appears in the CPR Pt 49, para 6.2 in almost identical terms and it would seem that the approach should, thus, be the same. It is right to point out that under the CPR the court has a wider discretion to rule what evidence it needs to decide any particular point...

The only other comment I would like to make, so far as the above approach is concerned, is that it must not be overlooked that the court has an inherent power to stay proceedings. I would in fact accept that on a proper construction

---

101 [1999] 1 Lloyd's Rep 68, *per* Rix, J: that there was an interest in encouraging parties to put their arguments on jurisdiction before the arbitrator himself under s 30; in many cases where there was simply an issue as to the width of an arbitration clause and no issue as to whether a party was bound to the relevant contract in the first place, the arbitrator's view might be accepted; where, however, there were substantial issues of fact as to whether a party had made the relevant agreement in the first place, then, even if there had already been a full hearing before the arbitrator, the court, upon a challenge under s 67, should not be placed in a worse position than the arbitrator, for the purpose of determining the challenge.

of s 9 it can be said with force that a court should be satisfied (a) that there is an arbitration clause and (b) that the subject of the action is within that clause, before the court can grant a stay under that section. But a stay under the inherent jurisdiction may in fact be sensible in a situation where the court cannot be sure of those matters but can see that good sense and litigation management make it desirable for an arbitrator to consider the whole matter first.[102]

3.5.3 The scope of s 11 of the AA 1996

Section 11 of the 1996 Act re-enacts s 26(1) of the CJJA 1982. insofar as an order for security to be provided and an order to stay the court proceedings in favour of the arbitration clause are concerned.

It has already been discussed[103] that, before the enactment of s 26, when a ship was arrested for the purpose of obtaining security in satisfaction of an arbitration award, the court had a *wide discretion* either to release the ship from arrest by setting aside the warrant of arrest, or to maintain the arrest until security was provided for the arbitration award, if the plaintiff showed that an arbitration award in his favour would be unlikely to be satisfied by the defendant.[104] If the discretion was exercised in favour of ordering security to be provided, the plaintiff would thereafter pursue the action *in rem*, to enforce the security.

Such a wide discretion was abolished by s 26 of the CJJA 1982 and now by s 11 of the AA 1996. Section 26 is, naturally, wider than s 11, in that it empowers the court to make the same orders when the dispute should be submitted to another court, either in the UK or overseas. Both sections provide that, where admiralty proceedings are stayed on the ground that the dispute in question should be submitted to arbitration, and property has been arrested, the court may: (i) order that the property, or security provided, be retained for the satisfaction of the award; or (ii) order that the stay of the proceedings be conditional on the provision of equivalent security for the satisfaction of any such award. The maintenance of arrest is discretionary.[105]

Section 26(2) of the CJJA 1982, which allows the court to attach any other conditions as it thinks fit when it makes the orders referred to sub-section (1) – such as the prompt commencement of the arbitration – has been omitted from s 11 of the AA 1996. This was necessary because its inclusion would have caused difficulties with regard to non-domestic arbitration to which the New York Convention applies, which prevents the grant of a stay being made subject to any conditions.[106]

---

102 Waller LJ in *Al-Naimi v Islamic Press* [2000] 1 Lloyd's Rep 522 (CA), p 525.
103 Chapter 4, para 5.3.
104 *The Rena K* [1978] 1 Lloyd's Rep 545; *The Vasso* [1984] 1 Lloyd's Rep 235 (CA); *The Tuyuti* [1984] 2 Lloyd's Rep 51 (CA).
105 *The Bazias* [1993] 1 Lloyd's Rep 101.
106 See, further, *op cit*, Merkin, fn 96.

CHAPTER 6

CONVENTION JURISDICTION BASES AND MULTIPLE PROCEEDINGS IN ADMIRALTY

1 INTRODUCTION

It has already been explained in the previous chapter that under English procedural law there are two broad types of jurisdiction bases by which the jurisdiction of the court can be invoked on the merits. The one depends merely on service of the proceedings on the defendant, without requiring substantive connecting factors between the claim and the jurisdiction, subject to certain exceptions (see Chapters 3, 4 and 5). The other is known as the 'convention jurisdiction' bases, which depends on jurisdiction rules as provided by International Conventions. Examples of International Conventions relating to maritime claims providing jurisdiction are briefly given in this Chapter, while the main emphasis is placed upon the European Civil Jurisdiction Conventions (ECJC). It will be shown how the jurisdiction of the English court may be restricted to determine the merits of a case and how conflict of jurisdictions is resolved by Convention rules.

1.1 The Athens Convention 1974

This provides a liability regime for the carriage of passengers and their luggage, which has been directly enacted by the UK. It is included in Sched 6 to the Merchant Shipping Act (MSA) 1995. Article 17 provides for jurisdiction of the court of (a) the place of permanent residence or principal place of business of the defendant; or (b) the place of departure or destination; or (c) the place of the domicile or permanent residence of the claimant, if the defendant has a place of business there and is subject to that jurisdiction; or (d) the place of the contract if the defendant has a place of business there and is subject to the jurisdiction of that State.

1.2 Convention relating to Contracts for International Carriage of Goods by Road 1956 (CMR)[1]

It deals with liability for contracts of international carriage of goods by road. Article 1 makes the Convention applicable to the whole of the carriage, if the

---

1   As enacted into English law by the Carriage of Merchandise by Road Act 1965.

vehicle containing the goods is carried over part of the journey by sea, rail, inland waterways, or air and the goods are not unloaded from the vehicle. However, when the loss, damage or delay is caused by an event during the sea transport, and the carrier by road is also the carrier by sea, the carrier's liability is to be determined as if the contract was for the carriage of goods by sea (Arts 2 and 10(2)). By Art 31(1), jurisdiction is allocated to a court of a Contracting State designated by agreement of the parties to a contract. In addition, in the courts of a country where (a) the defendant is ordinarily resident, or has principal place of business, or the branch or agency through which the contract of carriage was made; or (b) the place where the goods were taken over by the carrier, or the place designated for delivery is situated; and in no other courts or tribunals.

1.3 The International Convention on Civil Liability for Oil Pollution Damage 1992

The 1969 Civil Liability Convention for oil pollution damage was enacted by the UK in 1971, and was revised by the 1992 Protocol, known as the Civil Liability for Oil Pollution Damage Convention 1992, which came into force at the end of May 1996. Its provisions have been made part of English law, ss 152–70 of the MSA 1995. Actions for compensation may only be brought in courts of Contracting States where pollution damage occurred or preventative measures were taken to prevent or minimise such damage.

1.4 The International Convention Relating to the Arrest of Sea-going Ships 1952

The Arrest Convention was ratified by the UK in 1959 but it was previously partly enacted through s 3 of the Administration of Justice Act 1956 (now ss 20 and 21 of the Supreme Court Act (SCA) 1981). Article 7 of the Arrest Convention provides that the court of the country where the arrest was made has jurisdiction to determine the case on its merits, if the domestic law of that country gives jurisdiction to that court. It will be seen later how this provision interrelates with the provisions of the Brussels Convention. The new Arrest Convention 1999 has altered s 7 but it is not yet in force.

1.5 The International Convention on Civil Jurisdiction in matters of Collisions 1952

The International Convention on Certain Rules Concerning Civil Jurisdiction in Matters of Collisions 1952 (the Collision Convention) is not enacted into

English law, but the UK is a party to it. Article 1 of the Collision Convention relating to jurisdiction is reflected in s 22 of the SCA 1981 in relation to jurisdiction in actions *in personam*.

Article 1 provides for the jurisdiction of the court in a country where: (a) the defendant has his habitual residence, or place of business; or (b) the arrest was made; or (c) arrest could have been effected but bail, or other security, has been furnished; or (d) the collision took place. The claimant may choose any of the above bases, unless the parties involved agree the place of jurisdiction, or refer the matter to arbitration (Art 2). Counterclaims or multiple proceedings may be brought in the court first seised (Art 3).

1.6 The Brussels and Lugano Conventions

The European Community Convention on Civil Jurisdiction, Recognition and Enforcement of Judgments in Civil and Commercial Matters 1968 (the Brussels Convention) – as amended by the Accession Conventions 1978,[2] and 1989 (the San Sebastian Convention)[3] – was enacted into English law by the Civil Jurisdiction and Judgments Act (CJJA) 1982. It came into force in the UK on 1 January 1987.

In addition, there is a parallel Convention on the same matters entered into between the members of the European Community (EC) and the six members of the European Free Trade Association (EFTA)[4] dated 1988 (the Lugano Convention). It came into force in the UK on 1 May 1992 and it is to be found in Sched 1 to the CJJA 1991. The Lugano Convention is substantially identical to the post-San Sebastian version of the Brussels Convention, but it is separate from it. It may have a limited expectation of life once all the EFTA countries join the EC and adhere to the Brussels Convention.[5] They are dealt with, in this part, jointly and only insofar as they affect the admiralty jurisdiction of the English court. For ease of reference, they are referred to in this book as the ECJCs.

Since by virtue of Art 57 of those Conventions, jurisdiction conferred by other specialised Conventions is not affected, there will be reference to both the Arrest and the Collision Conventions, as they affect admiralty jurisdiction.

Revision of the Brussels Convention was recently undertaken by the European Commission, as it was considered essential. The reasons for this

---

2   This Accession Convention brought the UK into the Brussels Convention when the UK, Ireland and Denmark joined the EC.

3   The San Sebastian Convention incorporated Spain and Portugal into the scheme of civil jurisdiction and judgments when they joined the EC. When Greece joined the EC, this was done by the Greek Accession Convention, which was signed on 25 October 1982, but made no other changes to the Brussels Convention.

4   Norway, Sweden, Finland, Iceland, Austria and Switzerland.

5   Briggs, A and Rees, P, *Civil Jurisdiction and Judgments*, 2nd edn, 1997, LLP, Chapter 1, p 6.

have basically been the following: to make the rules of jurisdiction highly predictable; to clarify the domicile of a legal person, so as to make the common rules more transparent and avoid conflicts of judgments; subject to exclusive grounds of jurisdiction, to preserve the autonomy of the parties to a contract, save for insurance, consumer and employment contracts in which the parties' autonomy is limited; to minimise the possibility of concurrent proceedings and to ensure that irreconcilable judgments will not be given in two Member States by providing a clear and effective mechanism for *lis pendens* cases and related actions; to extend the protection given to consumers; and to ensure effective and swift enforcement procedures.

It had originally been thought that a new Convention would replace the Brussels Convention, but that method of reform would be slow. Thus, as an alternative, it was thought to reform the Brussels Convention by a Council Regulation.[6] A Regulation to this effect was approved by Council on 22 December 2000, EC 44/2001,[7] following the Treaty of Amsterdam, which came into effect on 1 May 1999, amending the Treaty of Rome and the Treaty of European Union.

However, the Regulation is brought into effect under Title IV of the amended Treaty of Rome. Save for the UK, Ireland and Denmark, judicial co-operation in specified matters becomes part of substantive European law, by virtue of Title IV, for all other Member States. But since Denmark, Ireland and the UK are not bound by it, they will have to opt into the amendment, otherwise they will continue to be bound by the provisions of the Brussels Convention. The UK and Ireland have indicated their intention to do so in respect of judicial co-operation in civil matters.[8] Denmark is not participating in the adoption of the Regulation and, therefore, it will continue to be bound by the Brussels Convention.[9] By Art 68 of the Regulation, the Brussels Convention will be superseded by the Regulation, insofar as other Member States are concerned. The Regulation will enter into force on 1 March 2002 (Art 76) and no later than five years after entry into force, the Commission will present a report on the application and, if need be, submit proposals for adaptation.[10]

Since the new Regulation will not be in force until March 2002, the following paragraphs deal with the law as it now stands, as far as maritime claims are concerned and reference is made to the particular articles of the Regulation which will change the present position.

---

6   Com(1999) 348, final 14 July 1999.
7   OJ L12, 16.1.2001, p 1.
8   See para 20 of the preamble to the Regulation; Jackson, DC, *Enforcement of Maritime Claims*, 3rd edn, 2000, LLP, Chapter 3, p 88.
9   See para 21 of the preamble to the Regulation.
10 See para 28 of the preamble to the Regulation.

2 THE ECJCs

The primary purpose of the Conventions was to give effect to Art 220 of the Treaty of Rome, and to ensure the simplification of formalities governing the reciprocal recognition and enforcement of judgments within countries of the EU. To this end, it was necessary to provide a scheme for determining which courts were to have jurisdiction over what matters and avoid conflicting decisions of the courts of different Member States. The scope and basic principle of the Conventions are laid down in Art 1–3. Primarily, the aim is to protect persons, who have their domicile or seat in Community States, from being sued in the courts of States other than where their domicile or seat is established. For this purpose, well defined rules provide for various jurisdictional bases. On the one hand, these rules enlarge the jurisdiction of the English courts and, on the other hand, they inevitably impose restrictions upon such jurisdiction. The basic provisions as they affect the jurisdiction of the English courts are summarised below.

2.1 Application of the Conventions

They apply to civil and commercial matters (Art 1) and to proceedings brought within Contracting States; proceedings brought to enforce a cause of action pursuant to Arts 2–20 (which are Arts 2–26 under the Regulation); or brought in more than one Contracting State to enforce the same or related cause of action (Arts 21, 22, which are Arts 27 and 28 under the Regulation); or brought as a provisional remedy (Art 24, Art 31 under the Regulation); or to recognise/enforce a judgment of a Contracting State)

They shall not apply to

(a) property arising out of matrimonial relationships, wills and succession;
(b) bankruptcy proceedings;
(c) arbitration;
(d) social security.

2.1.1 The domicile rule and allocation of jurisdiction

Article 2, which remains the same under the Regulation, provides:

> Subject to the provisions of this Convention, persons domiciled in a Contracting State shall, whatever their nationality, be sued in the courts of that State. Persons who are not nationals of the State in which they are domiciled shall be governed by the rules of jurisdiction applicable to nationals of that State.

> Persons domiciled in a Contracting State may be sued in the courts of another Contracting State only by virtue of the rules set out in Arts 2–6 of the Convention [and Arts 2–7 under the Regulation] (Art 3). Thus, derogation from

the domicile rule is only allowed as provided by the Convention rules themselves. Some stipulate for mandatory derogation, while others for optional. The optional are alternatives to domicile.

2.1.2 Mandatory versus optional derogation from the domicile rule

The only mandatory exceptions to the general rule of domicile are the following:

(a) exclusive jurisdiction relating to immovable property (Art 16 which will be Art 22 under the Regulation);

(b) jurisdiction allocated to a Contracting State by agreement of the parties to a contract (Art 17)[11] (this will be Art 23 under the Regulation which provides that such jurisdiction shall be exclusive);

(c) when a defendant enters appearance in a court of a Contracting State not just for contesting jurisdiction (Art 18, Art 24 under the Regulation).

Other articles provide for optional allocation of jurisdiction, such option being given to the claimant in certain circumstances to sue in a court of a Contracting State other than that of the defendant's domicile.

The optional derogation from the domicile rule comprises the following categories:

(a) special jurisdiction of a Contracting State as provided by Art 5 (when there is a specific substantive link with the dispute) and by Art 6 (concerning suits with multidefendant parties or counterclaims in the Contracting State of one of the parties or where a claim has been brought);

(b) jurisdiction in relation to insurance contracts (Arts 7–12, which will be Arts 8–14 under the Regulation; the latter provide for specific insurable risks in relation to sea-going ships);

(c) jurisdiction over consumer contracts (Arts 13–15, covered by Arts 5–17 under the Regulation, while Arts 18–21 of the Regulation concern jurisdiction over contacts of employment);

(d) Art 6A, which will be Art 7 under the Regulation, provides for an alternative jurisdiction to domicile of the limitation defendant, to the extent that he has not already commenced a limitation of liability action in the court of his domicile, another Contracting State. If he has not, then the limitation of liability action must be brought in the court which is seised with the liability claim.

---

11 See *Lafarge Plasterboard Ltd v Fritz Peters & Co KG* [2000] 2 Lloyd's Rep 689.

2.1.3 Inapplicability of certain national jurisdictional rules

In Sched 1 of Art 3, certain provisions of national procedural law of Contracting States, which conflict with the basic principles of the Conventions, are declared inapplicable, as against these rules. In particular, as far as UK law is concerned, the following rules which would otherwise enable jurisdiction to be founded are overridden: (a) service upon the defendant during his temporary presence in the UK; (b) the presence of the defendant's property within the UK; (c) the seizure by the plaintiff of property situated in the UK.

It immediately becomes apparent from Art 3(b) that the Admiralty Court would have no jurisdiction to entertain a suit against a ship which came within the jurisdiction, had it not been for Art 57 of the Conventions to which both Arts 2 and 3 are made subject. Article 57 permits a court of a Contracting State to assume jurisdiction in accordance with the rules of specialised conventions to which the Contracting State is a party. This is a convention allocation of jurisdiction by virtue of Art 57, which will be Art 71 under the Regulation.

2.1.4 Convention allocation to other Convention jurisdiction

Article 57(1) provides that the Convention shall not affect any conventions to which the Contracting States are, or will be, parties and which, in relation to particular matters, govern jurisdiction or the recognition or enforcement of judgments. Article 57(2) provides that this Convention shall not prevent a court of a Contracting State, which is a party to a convention referred to in the first paragraph, from assuming jurisdiction in accordance with that convention, even where the defendant is domiciled in a Contracting State which is not a party to that convention. Discussion of this topic will follow (para 3, below).

2.2 Community versus national law concepts

Some concepts are purely community concepts, in that their meaning is to be found in community law. Such as:

(a) civil and commercial matters under Art 1 which must be given a Convention meaning[12] (a distinction has been drawn between private and public law, for example, an action between a public authority, exercising its powers, and a person being subject to private law, is not within the subject matter of the Conventions);

---

12   *LTV GmbH & Compania KG v Eurocontrol* [1977] 1 CMLR 88.

(b) the terms used under Art 21 (*lis pendens*) and its equivalent Art 27 under the Regulation;[13]

(c) exclusive jurisdiction under Art 16, and its equivalent Art 22 under the Regulation;

(d) place of harmful event under Art 5;

(e) sufficient time for defence under Art 20, and its equivalent Art 26 under the Regulation, which contains additional paras 3 and 4 dealing with service of judicial documents within Member States.

Other concepts are left to be determined by the national laws, but some changes will be brought in this respect by the EC Regulation, so that some of the following concepts will be community concepts as at 1 March 2002, as shown below:

(a) The meaning of domicile and seat under Arts 52 and 53: In English law these are defined in ss 41–43 of the CJJA 1982. An individual is domiciled in the UK if, and only if, he is resident in the UK and the nature and circumstances of his residence indicate that he has a substantial connection with the UK (s 41(2)). With regard to corporations, a seat of a corporation shall be treated as its domicile. A corporation has its seat in the UK only if it was incorporated under the UK law, and has its registered office, or official address, in the UK, or its central management and control is exercised in the UK (s 42(1), (3)).[14] Under the new EC Regulation, by Art 60, a Community concept of domicile of a company or a legal person is *to replace the reference to national law*. For the purpose of the Regulation, a company or other legal person is domiciled at the place where it has its statutory seat, or central administration, or principal place of business. There is no difference from the definition of corporate domicile under English law. The Regulation will not apply to a defendant who is domiciled in a Member State which will not be bound by the Regulation, such as Denmark.

(b) The meaning of when the court is seised of jurisdiction under Arts 21, 22 and 23 is at present governed by the rules of national law and for the purpose of the Conventions the action must be definitively pending.[15] The new Regulation will impose a *European definition* of when a court is seised, by Art 30: a court shall be deemed to be seised (i) at the time when the document instituting the proceedings, or an equivalent document, is lodged with the court, provided that the plaintiff has not subsequently failed to take the steps required to have service on the defendant; or (ii) if the document has to be served before being lodged

---

13 *Gubisch v Giulio Palumbo* [1989] ECC 420; *The Maciej Rataj* [1995] 1 Lloyd's Rep 302 (ECJ).

14 In *The Deichland* [1990] 1 QB 361 (see below), the German central management and control of the defendant, a company incorporated in Panama, was accepted as the domicile for the purpose of Art 2.

15 *Zelger v Salinitri* [1984] ECR 2397.

with the court, at the time when it is received by the authority responsible for service, provided that the plaintiff has not subsequently failed to take the steps he was required to take to have the document lodged with the court.[16]

(c) The place of performance of the obligation[17] under Art 5(1) is a matter for national law.

(d) The meaning of cause of action is also a matter for national law.

2.3 Conflicts of jurisdiction – multiple proceedings within Contracting States

When more than one Convention jurisdiction bases are involved, the courts of two Contracting States may be seised of jurisdiction in the same matter at different times. The court seised second has to consider whether to decline jurisdiction, or to stay the proceedings before it. Convention rules provide that, in some instances, the court has an obligation to decline, or stay, its proceedings, while in others it has discretion to do so. Except in cases where the second seised court has exclusive jurisdiction, the court first seised of the same matter does not have power to decline its jurisdiction or stay its proceedings. The purpose of these rules is to reinforce the primary objective of the Conventions, which is to prevent irreconcilable judgments by restricting the determination of the same issues by different courts within Contracting States. By allocating jurisdiction in accordance with accepted Convention rules, a quick recognition and enforcement of judgments will ensue.

2.3.1 When does a court of a Contracting State have an obligation to decline its jurisdiction?

Declining jurisdiction has a more permanent and definite result. An obligation to decline jurisdiction arises under the following articles:

(a) Art 19 – this provides that where a court of a Contracting State is seised of a claim which is principally concerned with a matter over which the court of another Contracting State has exclusive jurisdiction by virtue of Art 16, it shall declare of its own motion that it has no jurisdiction;

(b) Art 20 – which states that where a defendant is domiciled in a Contracting State and is sued in another, provided he has not appeared,

---

16 As to when the English Court is seised of a case, see decisions in this respect in para 2.3.4.2, below. When the UK opts into the Regulation, so that litigants in UK courts are not placed at a disadvantage, the effect will be to revert to the old English decisions.

17 Where there are many obligations to be performed, the place of performance for the purpose of Art 5 is the place of the primary obligation: *Union Transport v Continental Lines* [1992] 1 All ER 161 (HL).

that court shall declare of its own motion that it has no jurisdiction, unless it s jurisdiction is derived from the provisions of this Convention;

(c) Art 21 (*lis pendens*) – there must be multiple proceedings in different Contracting States involving the same cause of action and parties. When the jurisdiction of the court first seised is established, any court other than the first seised shall decline jurisdiction in favour of that court;

(d) similarly, Art 23 – where actions come within the exclusive jurisdiction of several courts, any court other than the court first seised shall decline jurisdiction in favour of that court.

The EC Regulation does not change the substance of these rules apart from the numbers of the articles, which will be Arts 25, 26, 27 and 28, respectively

2.3.2 When does a court of a Contracting State have an obligation to stay its proceedings?

(a) Under Art 20, the court shall stay the proceedings, so long as it is not shown that the defendant has been able to receive the documents instituting the proceedings in sufficient time to enable him to arrange for his defence. Paragraphs 3 and 4 of the equivalent Art 26 of the Regulation refer to a previous Council Regulation ((EC) 1348/2000) on service of process of judicial and extra-judicial documents in civil and commercial matters in the Member States, which shall apply if the document instituting the proceedings had to be transmitted from one Member State to another pursuant to this Regulation. Otherwise, if the aforesaid Regulation on service does not apply, Art 15 of the Hague Convention on the Service Abroad of Judicial and Extra Judicial Documents in Civil and Commercial Matters 1965 shall apply, if the document instituting the proceedings had to be transmitted pursuant to that Convention.

(b) Under Art 21 (new Art 27 of the Regulation), the court, other than the court first seised of proceedings involving the same cause of action and the same parties, shall, of its own motion, stay its proceedings until such time as the jurisdiction of the first seised court is established. Thus, under Art 21 the court second seised has an obligation, first to stay its proceedings until the jurisdiction of the court first seised is established. Then, once such jurisdiction is established the second seised court shall have to decline its jurisdiction.

2.3.3 When does a court of a Contracting State have discretion to decline or stay its proceedings

Only under Art 22, where related actions are brought in the courts of different Contracting States, does any court other than the first seised have discretion to stay its proceedings, while the actions are pending.[18] It may also decline

---

18 Pending actions mean definitely pending without procedural defects: *Grupo Torras* [1995] 1 Lloyd's Rep 374; see, also, *Andrea Mezario Ltd v Internationale Spedition* [contd]

jurisdiction, on the application of one of the parties, if the law of that court permits the consolidation of related actions and the court first seised has jurisdiction over both actions.

2.3.4 How do the Convention rules resolve lis alibi pendens?

2.3.4.1 English lis pendens versus Convention lis pendens

The treatment of *lis alibi pendens* under English law is not uniform, but it depends on the procedural topics in which the issue arises. For example, the law on discretionary stays is different from the law on ant-suit injunctions. In both areas, however, if the foreign proceedings have reached an advanced stage by the time an application is made either for a stay of parallel English proceedings, or for an anti-suit injunction to prevent the continuance of the foreign proceedings, it may then be appropriate to let the foreign proceedings determine the parties' rights. In the absence of an agreement between the parties to a dispute to submit to the jurisdiction of a certain court or tribunal, when the agreement was freely negotiated and it was not just a standard term incorporated by reference, an overall consideration in applications of *lis pendens* is the interests of justice.[19]

By contrast, in the context of the ECJCs, there is a uniform treatment of *lis pendens* by rigid rules based on the civilian systems' approach. Multiple proceedings are an unavoidable result of the fact that there is more than one jurisdiction base provided by the Conventions.

The provisions of Arts 21, 22 and 23 (which deal with *lis alibi pendens*) are paramount guidelines for the second seised court to determine whether to stay its proceedings or to decline its jurisdiction in favour of the first seised court, provided its jurisdiction is not exclusive either by Art 16 or 17.[20]

The rules applying to resolving conflicts of jurisdiction when there are concurrent proceedings in different Contracting States will be examined only with reference to decided cases concerning maritime claims. First, the relevant articles are set out.

Article 21 (actions must involve the same cause of action and be between the same parties) states:

> Where proceedings involving the same cause of action and between the same parties are brought in the courts of different Contracting States, any court other than the court first seised shall of its own motion stay its proceedings until such time as the jurisdiction of the court first seised is established.

---

18 [contd] (2001) unreported, 23 January, transcript (Westlaw) (CA) relating to the International Carriage of Goods by Road Convention 1956, Art 31(2), where it was held that 'pending' means when the proceedings have been served.

19 See, further, *op cit*, Briggs and Rees, fn 5, para 4.12.

20 *Continental Bank NA v Aeakos Naviera SA* [1994] 1 Lloyd's Rep 505.

> Where the jurisdiction of the court first seised is established, any court other than the court first seised shall decline jurisdiction in favour of that court.

The same wording is adopted in Art 27 of the new Regulation.

Article 22 (related actions) provides:

> Where related actions are brought in the courts of different Contracting States, any court other than the first seised may, while the actions are pending at first instance, stay its proceedings. A court other than the court first seised may also, on the application of one of the parties, decline jurisdiction if the law of that court permits the consolidation of related actions and the court first seised has jurisdiction over both actions.
>
> For the purpose of this article, actions are deemed to be related where they are also so closely connected that it is expedient to hear and determine them together to avoid the risk of irreconcilable judgments resulting from separate proceedings.

Article 28 of the new Regulation has not changed the substance of this provision, but has only refined its wording.

Article 23 (exclusive jurisdiction) states:

> Where actions come within the exclusive jurisdiction of several courts, any court other than the court first seised shall decline jurisdiction in favour of that court.

As explained earlier, when Arts 16 and 17 apply, there is no option for the claimant to choose a court other than the one as provided by these articles to have exclusive jurisdiction and, when they apply, the court seised of the matter, otherwise than by virtue of these articles, does not have a discretion, but an obligation, to decline its jurisdiction. As far as Art 17 is concerned, the position has not so far been clear, as will be discussed later, but the new Regulation, by Art 23, makes it clear that such jurisdiction is exclusive, unless the parties agree otherwise. There is no such exclusivity as regards the jurisdiction bases provided by the other Convention rules, mentioned previously. The question then will be which court is seised first.

2.3.4.2 *When is a court seised?*

Prior to the new Regulation mentioned earlier, the answer to this question was referred to the procedural rules of the Contracting States' national law following the decision of the European Court in *Zelger v Salinitri*.[21]

The concept of when a court is 'first seised', or when proceedings are 'definitively pending' before a court, are not terms which had an established meaning in English law. But, in considering Arts 21–23 of the Brussels Convention, the English courts have had to decide when, under English law,

---

21 [1984] ECR 2397.

the court was seised. Art 30 of the new Regulation, however, has made this issue a Community law concept (see para 2.2, below).

While in *Kloeckner v Gatoil Overseas*,[22] the judge had decided that the moment the court is seised was the issue of the proceedings, the Court of Appeal, in the *Duke Yare* case, decided that, in an action *in personam*, the English court was seised of jurisdiction on the merits when the writ or claim form was served.[23] In claims *in rem*, the court is seised either at the time of service, or at the time of arrest of the ship, whichever is the earliest.[24] Article 30 of the Regulation will reverse this position and the law will be as was decided in *Kloeckner v Gatoil*. Although the following decision will not be good law after 1 March 2002, insofar as those Member States which will be bound by the new Regulation, it is worth looking at how the law has been since 1991.

Dresser v Falcongate (sub nom The Duke Yare)[25]

It involved the carriage of electronic goods by Falcongate (the first defendants) from West Germany to Scotland. Falcongate sub-contracted the sea leg of the carriage to an English company (the third defendants) who, in turn, with the fourth defendants arranged for the goods to be shipped from Scheveningen to Great Yarmouth in the second defendant's vessel, *The Duke Yare*. Having been loaded on deck, the goods were lost overboard. The third defendants were the bareboat charterers and their head office was in the UK, but they had an agent acting for them (the fourth defendants), a Dutch company having an office in Scheveningen. The cargo-owners brought an action in the UK against the defendants in tort, not under the bill of lading, which contained a jurisdiction clause in favour of Rotterdam. Only the third and fourth defendants challenged the jurisdiction of the English court, claiming that the court of Rotterdam had jurisdiction. The issue of whether the jurisdiction clause should be given effect by virtue of Art 17 of the Convention was disposed of on the ground that it did not apply to the sub-bailment and the defendants were sued in tort. The other central issue on jurisdiction was whether Art 22 applied. For this purpose, the timing of commencement of the proceedings was important. A writ had been issued in the UK on 15 July 1988, which was served almost a year later, on 13 July 1989. In the meantime, the defendants had commenced limitation proceedings in Rotterdam on 21 February 1989. On 27 February, the court determined the limit of liability of the defendants, who lodged a guarantee in that amount requesting the court to determine the division of the fund, and a meeting of creditors was fixed for August 1989. On 13 June, the plaintiffs lodged a written defence in the limitation proceedings, saying that they had lodged their claim in the English court on 15 July 1988.

---

22 [1990] 1 Lloyd's Rep 177.
23 *The Dresser v Falcongate (sub nom The Duke Yare)* [1991] 2 Lloyd's Rep 557, pp 563–70.
24 *The Freccia del Nord* [1989] 1 Lloyd's Rep 388.
25 [1991] 2 Lloyd's Rep 557.

They also challenged the court's right to limit and its competence, relying on the existence of proceedings before the English court relating to the same claim. On these facts, the main questions before the Court of Appeal were: (a) were the English and the Dutch proceedings 'related' within the meaning of Art 22?; (b) when did the English and the Dutch courts become seised of their respective proceedings? It was plain that these proceedings were related, but the second question raised novel and important issues. Bingham LJ quoted the relevant passage from the decision of the ECJ in the *Zelger v Salinitri* interpreting the words 'the court first seised' under Arts 21–23, which resolve contest of jurisdiction between Contracting States:

> The court first seised is the one before which the requirements for proceedings to become definitively pending are first fulfilled, such requirements to be determined in accordance with the national law of each of the courts concerned.

The ECJ had accepted, in that case, that the procedures of the Contracting States as regards the dates at which the courts are seised were not identical and, hence, a common concept of *lis pendens* could not be arrived at. So, it left it to the national courts to apply the above definition to their own procedure.

Bingham LJ[26] then examined English procedure and concluded:

> Until the UK acceded to the Brussels Convention in 1987, no English court had ever had to consider when it was 'first seised' of proceedings nor when proceedings were 'definitively pending' before it …But Arts 21–23 are now part of English law and s 3(1) of the CJJA 1982 requires us to apply the convention in accordance with principles laid down by the ECJ …We must be wary of adopting and applying any rule developed for different purposes in different circumstances.

Referring to the only English decision on the same issue, *Kloeckner v Gatoil Overseas*[27] (in which Hirst J had decided that the moment an action became pending was the issue of the writ),[28] Bingham LJ preferred to follow the continental and Scottish approach, which had uniformly accepted the moment of service of the proceedings to be the determining factor of when the court is seised. He explained that, although an action commences by the issue of the writ, this causes the time limit to cease to run against a plaintiff, but that alone does not bring the writ to the defendant's attention. A claimant who has not served can discontinue the action. He said:

> It is service of the proceedings, not issue, which ordinarily activates the litigious process and imposes procedural obligations on the parties. Thus, the defendant must acknowledge service within the time limited by Ord 12 r 5 … It would of course be wrong to suggest that the court has no jurisdiction to

---

26 [1991] 2 Lloyd's Rep 557, p 564.

27 [1990] 1 Lloyd's Rep 177.

28 Hobhouse J at first instance, in *The Duke Yare* [1991] 2 Lloyd's Rep 557, had followed the view of Hirst J, which was said to be based on private international law.

make orders against a person until he has been served. Mareva injunctions, Anton Piller orders and other injunctive orders may be and very regularly are granted and made before service. But they may also be granted before issue ... Even if an action is pending on issue of proceedings, it is necessary to consider if it is 'definitively' pending ...[29]

... it is in my judgment artificial, far-fetched and wrong to hold that the English court is seised of proceedings, or that proceedings are decisively, conclusively, finally or definitively pending before it, upon mere issue of proceedings ...[30]

The most obvious exception is where an actual exercise of jurisdiction (as by the granting of a Mareva injunction or the making of an Anton Pillar order or the arrest of a vessel) precedes service: plainly the court is seised of proceedings when it makes an interlocutory order of that kind.[31]

It was held that the English court became seised of the proceedings when the defendants were served.[32] It was then that the plaintiffs and the defendants became bound by the rules of court to perform the obligations laid on them respectively or suffer the prescribed consequences of default.

With the introduction of a Community concept as to when a court is seised of a matter, which will be the time of the issue of the proceedings when the Regulation comes into force, it seems that the decision of the English court in *Kloeckner v Gatoil* will represent the correct approach.

The issue whether obtaining leave to issue and serve out of the jurisdiction could cause the court to be definitively seised of the matter was decided by the Court of Appeal in *The Sargasso*,[33] that it would not amount to the court being seised. However, in the light of the new Regulation, this case may have to be revisited but, in the meantime, it is useful to examine it.

The Sargasso

The shipowners, a Panamanian company, were the registered owners of the Sargasso. The vessel was loaded in Portugal and discharged in Antwerp on May 1991. Some of the cargo was found contaminated. The cargo-owners arrested her in Rotterdam on 1 June 1991, solely to obtain security for the claim. The owners' P&I insurers provided security for the claim. Then, on 20 May 1992, they applied to the English court for leave to issue a concurrent writ *in personam* and serve it on the shipowners (defendants) in Japan. That writ was issued on 22 May and it was served on 17 July 1992, upon the

---

29 *The Duke Yare*, [1991] 2 Lloyd's Rep 557, p 566.

30 *Ibid*, p 569. (The irony is that all these *dicta* will be wrong from 1March 2002!)

31 *Ibid*, p 569.

32 See a commentary by Briggs, A, 'Get your writs out' 1992 LMCLQ 150; there will be no hurry to serve the claim form after March 2002 if the proceedings are issued swiftly and prior to any other proceedings in another Member State.

33 [1994] 2 Lloyd's Rep 6.

defendant's solicitors in England, who acknowledged service subject to the defendants' right to challenge jurisdiction. In the event that the English court might decline jurisdiction, the cargo-owners also issued and served a writ in Rotterdam on 4 June to preserve the validity of the letter of guarantee. The shipowners sought to have the English proceedings stayed on the ground that the court of Rotterdam was first seised of the action (Art 21). The main issue before the court, as far as English procedure was concerned, was: did the English court become seised when leave to issue the writ was granted on 22 May, or on the service of it on 17 July? If it became seised on 17 July, which was a later day than when the Dutch proceedings were served, then the Dutch court would have been first seised. Thus, the English court should decline jurisdiction. Sheen J decided that the English court was seised on 17 July and the Dutch court on 4 June 1992. The plaintiffs appealed, alleging that the judge was wrong not to hold the English court was seised when leave was given to serve the writ out of the jurisdiction on 22 May. They relied on what Bingham LJ said in *Dresser v Falcongate* about the exception to the rule of service in cases of Mareva or Anton Piller orders or provisional measures. The Court of Appeal disapproved and Steyn LJ said:[34]

> For my part I would ... differ from Bingham LJ on what he describes as the exceptional cases. In my judgment a court which grants provisional measures is not by virtue of that fact alone definitively seised of jurisdiction on the merits of the dispute. And I would similarly rule that a court which exercises a jurisdiction merely to order service out of the jurisdiction is not by virtue of that limited exercise of jurisdiction definitively seised of the merits of the dispute. This interpretation fits in with the purpose of the Convention ...
>
> ... the general thrust of the *Dresser* case, involving the rejection of the date of issue of the writ solution ... is correct. But I respectfully disagree that there are any genuine exceptions to the rule that the date of service marks the time when the English court becomes definitively seised of proceedings. That rule is a simple and practical rule, which will readily be understood in England and in other jurisdictions which have to grapple with the question when an English court is seised of the proceedings.

The English court was, thus, obliged to decline jurisdiction in favour of the court of Rotterdam which was seised on 4 June.

Similarly, in claims *in rem*, the law at present is that the court is seised with jurisdiction on the merits either upon service of the writ (claim form) or the arrest of the ship, whichever is the earliest, provided the arrest is not a step just for provisional measures.

---

34   [1994] 2 Lloyd's Rep 6, p 11.

The Freccia del Nord[35]

Pursuant to a collision between the plaintiff's ship S and the defendant's vessel F, the plaintiffs issued a writ *in rem* in England against four ships belonging to the defendants at 16.10 hours on the 25 June 1987. They were unable to serve the writ on that day as no ship belonging to the defendants was within the jurisdiction at the time. On 8 July 1987, the plaintiff's solicitors informed the defendant's solicitors that a ship belonging to the defendants currently within the jurisdiction would be arrested, if they did not provide security. The defendant's solicitors accepted service of the writ on 9 July 1987. On 23 July, they acknowledged service on behalf of the shipowners. Meanwhile, 20 minutes after the writ had been issued on 25 June, the plaintiffs' ship was arrested in Rotterdam by the owners of the F. The writ in the Dutch action was served on 3 July. The central question in the case was: when was the English Admiralty Court seised of jurisdiction in an action *in rem* for the purposes of Arts 21 and 22 of the Convention?

Counsel for the plaintiffs contended that the English court was seised of jurisdiction at the moment when the writ was issued. Counsel for the defendants contended that the English court was not seised of jurisdiction until the writ was served on 9 July. Sheen J held that,

> In respect of any claim within the admiralty jurisdiction of the High Court, an action *in rem* may be brought against only one ship. Nevertheless it is permissible in respect of any one ship to issue a writ naming more than one ship ... After service, the writ should be amended by deleting all but one of the names upon it. So that if on 25 June 1987, one had asked the question: 'Is the court seised of the action?', another question would have arisen, that is to say: 'Against which ship is the action brought?' ... It seems to me that the court cannot be seised of an action *in rem* until the plaintiff has not only made up his mind as to which ship he will arrest, but also has either served the writ upon the ship or arrested the ship ... in my judgment, the court is seised of an action *in rem* from the moment, whichever is the earlier, of service of the writ, or of arrest of the ship.[36]

Again, when the Regulation amending the Brussels Convention comes into force, the court will be seised from the time of the issue of the *in rem* claim form although the claim form may name several ships of the defendant. Since the concept of when the court is seised will be a Community concept, the arrest of a ship, which frequently occurs before the issue of an *in rem* claim form and it has, under English law the effect of invoking jurisdiction on the merits, ought to be deemed as amounting to issue of process for the purpose of *lis pendens* and related actions under Arts 27 and 28 of the Regulation. If it were otherwise, the amending Regulation will certainly cause some unnecessary litigation in this respect.

---

35 [1989] 1 Lloyd's Rep 338.
36 *Ibid*, pp 391, 392.

2.3.4.3 When is there a 'pending action' under the Convention rules?

Pending action means 'definitively pending' – without procedural defects.

Grupo Torras[37]

The plaintiffs, a Spanish company and its English subsidiary, claimed damages for conspiracies and monies due for breaches of directors' duties in which the defendants were involved. The defendants applied to the English court to stay the action in favour of the Spanish court on the ground, *inter alia*, that there were pending proceedings in Spain and the Spanish court was first seised. The English court was urged to decline or stay the proceedings either under Art 21 or 22. Mance J held that, although in any Contracting State the precise procedural formalities reflecting the concept of when proceedings are 'definitively pending' would depend on the national law and be selected by the national court, there must be respect of the general concept of a 'decisive conclusive final or definitive' litigation relationship between the court and the litigant. But, which court was first seised of such proceedings was to be decided by a simple test of chronological priority, ignoring any amendments of the cause of action or parties which might otherwise be treated under national law as having retrospective effect.

In a recent case, *Molins plc v GBSpA*[38] the action was not pending for the purpose of Art 21 when the Italian proceedings had not been served.

2.3.4.4 The 'same cause of action' and 'between the same parties'

The general rule under Art 21 is that the proceedings brought in the courts of two Contracting States must have the same cause of action and must be between the same parties. It may not be too difficult for the court to ascertain whether a matter of which two courts are seised of jurisdiction concerns the same cause of action. Also, in cases where the cause of action is brought by proceedings *in personam* in two Contracting States, the identification of the parties of such proceedings should be of no difficulty. An issue arose regarding the application of Art 21 to the English action *in rem*. Historically, the defendant in an action *in rem* was the ship (see Chapters 1 and 3). Under English procedural rules, *in rem* proceedings are also used to invoke jurisdiction on the merits. In civil law systems, *in rem* proceedings are used for conservatory measures, unless the court has jurisdiction on other grounds. The issue was this: could an English action *in rem* be between the same parties as an action *in personam* for the purpose of Art 21? Both this issue and the issue whether the *in rem* and *in personam* proceedings brought in two Contracting States involved in the same cause of action were first examined in *The*

---

37   [1995] 1 Lloyd's Rep 374.
38   [2000] 2 Lloyd's Rep 234 (CA).

Nordglimt.[39] Although the decision has been overruled in respect of *dicta* in relation to the nature of the action *in rem* (see Chapter 3), it is, nevertheless, an important decision, insofar as the other points stated in the summary are concerned and in explaining the issue in question by way of background.

The Nordglimt[40]

In December 1983, *The Nordkap* loaded barley at Antwerp under two bills of lading for carriage to Jeddah. One of the bills contained false information. Delivery of the cargo took place in January 1984. The plaintiffs, receivers of the cargo, commenced an action against the defendants, shipowners, in Belgium in January 1985, claiming loss of or damage to part of their cargo, but no security was obtained. In April 1987, the plaintiffs began an action *in rem* in England against *The Nordglimt*, a ship in the same ownership as *Nordkap*. She was arrested and security was put up for her release. The defendants applied to have the action struck out and the warrant of arrest set aside on various grounds. One of the grounds was that concurrent proceedings involving the same cause of action and the same parties had commenced in Antwerp, and the English court should of its own motion decline jurisdiction in favour of Antwerp. Three interrelated questions were considered in relation to the arrest proceedings: (a) did Art 21 apply, at all, to an action authorised by the 1952 Convention (that is, jurisdiction by arrest of vessels?); (b) if so, did Art 21 preclude the making of an order under s 26 of the CJJA 1982?; (c) was an admiralty action *in rem*, 'proceedings involving the same cause of action and between the same parties', vis a vis an action *in personam* for the purpose of Art 21? Hobhouse J said that the fundamental question was the first one and stated:

> It is clear both from the text of the 1968 Convention and the Accession Convention and the commentaries of Mr Jenard and Professor Schlosser that the relationship of conventions such as the 1952 Convention to the 1968 Convention is that of the special to the general. Where special provision is made in the special convention it shall govern; where no special provision is made the general provision of the 1968 convention shall apply.[41]

Referring to the interpretation of the conventions and their interrelations he concluded:

> I consider that it is contemplated by the 1968 Convention ... that it is permissible and proper that there should be an arrest of a vessel in one jurisdiction in support of a determination of the merits of a dispute by a court

---

39 At the time, the status of an *in rem* action in a sense of being against the person (and not just against the *res*), who would be liable *in personam* from the time of service for the purpose of Art 21, had not been decided.

40 [1988] QB 183; [1987] 2 Lloyd's Rep 470.

41 *Ibid*, p 480.

of competent jurisdiction in another Contracting State and to provide security for the satisfaction of the judgment given by that court.[42]

As regards the question of the nature of the action *in rem*, the judge said relying on an explicit statement of Moulton LJ in ***The Burns***,[43] that:

> Unless and until anyone appears to defend an action *in rem* the action proceeds solely as an action *in rem* and any judgment given is solely a judgment given against the *res*. It is determinative and conclusive as against all the world in respect of the rights in the *res* but does not create any rights that are enforceable *in personam*. An action *in rem* may be defended by anyone who has a legitimate interest in resisting the plaintiff's claim on the *res*. Such a person may be the owner of the *res* but equally it may be someone who has a different interest in the *res* which does not amount to ownership, or again it may be simply someone who also has a claim *in rem* against the *res* and is competing with the plaintiff for a right to the security of a *res* of an inadequate value to satisfy all the claims that are being made upon it ... The consequence of this is that in my judgment on the correct interpretation of Art 21 an admiralty action *in rem* is not at the time of its inception an action between the same parties as an action *in personam*. It will only become an action between the same parties when and if a shipowner, liable *in personam*, chooses to appear in the action and defend it.[44]

It was held that, although both proceedings concerned the same cause of action, they were not between the same parties. The defendant had not 'appeared' in the action unconditionally. The judge did not think that the action *in rem*, so long as it had the character solely *in rem*, came within the scope of Art 21 in relation to the pending Belgian proceedings *in personam*, but it would, only from the time when the defendant chose to appear in these proceedings. In any event, he said, the arrest should be maintained as that would be consistent with both Art 7(2) of the 1952 Arrest Convention and s 26 of the CJJA 1982. Thus, it was permissible and proper that there should be an arrest of a vessel in one jurisdiction in support of a judgment on liability given by a court of competent jurisdiction in another Contracting State (in this case, Belgium).

In the opinion of the writer, the logical analysis of the law by Hobhouse J in the context of the facts of this case is to be admired but, regrettably, the House of Lords in *The Indian Grace* considered it not good law, as far as the nature of the action *in rem* is concerned, which now, after the latter case, stands to be most confusing. It should be remembered that *The Nordglimt* was really concerned with maintaining the security for the claim, the merits of which were to be determined by another competent court. What was

---

42 [1987] 2 Lloyd's Rep 470, p 481.
43 [1907] P 137, p 149.
44 *Ibid*, pp 200–01.

determined, therefore, in relation to s 26 of CJJA 1982 is still correct.[45] Only insofar as Art 21 of the Convention is concerned has the decision of Hobhouse J been overruled. His view about the nature of the action *in rem* had previously been supported by two decision of the Court of Appeal, in *The Maciej Rataj* (*The Tatry*) and in *The Anna H* (discussed later). Consequently, if *The Indian Grace* was correctly decided and intended to have a wider application than the issue of *res judicata*, it would follow that these decisions have also been indirectly overruled.[46]

The question whether, for the purpose of Art 21, an action *in rem* could be between the same parties as an action *in personam* was referred to the European Court of Justice (ECJ) by the Court of Appeal in *The Tatry*. But an earlier Court of Appeal decision had addressed this question, in *The Deichland* (see para 3.1.1). It had held that the action *in rem* really aimed against the person interested in defending the claim, who was being sued, from the time of the service. In the light of conflicting judicial views domestically, it was proper for the court in *The Tatry* to refer the issue to the ECJ to resolve a matter of interpretation of the Convention.

The Maciej Rataj (sub nom The Tatry)[47]

A cargo of soya bean oil was carried aboard *The Tatry*, a vessel belonging to a Polish shipping company. The voyage was from Brazil to Rotterdam for part of the cargo, and then to Hamburg with the rest of the cargo. The cargo-owners complained that the cargo was contaminated during the voyage with hydrocarbons or diesel. They were split in three groups. Group one obtained security from the owners P&I club in October 1988 and agreed that the Rotterdam court had jurisdiction for their dispute. Groups two and three missed the opportunity to arrest the ship and, although they requested an undertaking for provision of security from the owners' P&I club stipulating for English jurisdiction, their request was ignored. The shipowners commenced proceedings in Rotterdam on 18 November 1988 for a declaration of no liability in relation to groups one and three cargo. On 15 September 1989, groups two and three located *The Maciej Rataj* (a sister ship of *The Tatry*) in Liverpool and arrested her. Security was, then, provided by the P&I club. On 18 September 1989, the owners brought proceedings in Rotterdam, again, for a declaration of no liability against group two cargo-owners. On 26 October 1990, they initiated proceedings in Rotterdam for limitation of their liability under the International Convention of 1957, and also applied to the English court to decline jurisdiction pursuant to Art 21 (*lis pendens*) or

---

45 The decision of Sheen J, in *The Kherson* [1992] 2 Lloyd's Rep 261, on the issue that the plaintiffs were not entitled to arrest the ship for the purpose of obtaining security when there were *in personam* proceedings in Rotterdam is not correct.

46 See comments in Chapter 3, paras 3.6, 3.7, 3.8, below.

47 [1995] 1 Lloyd's Rep 302.

alternatively, pursuant to Art 22 (related actions). The grounds of the application were that, at the date of the English writ, the Rotterdam court was already seised of the proceedings involving the same cause of action and being between the same parties. Alternatively, the Rotterdam court was already seised of related proceedings and it was the appropriate forum.

Sheen J held, *inter alia*, that *in rem* proceedings did not involve the same cause of action with the declaratory proceedings in Rotterdam. The shipowners only commenced those proceedings as a pre-emptive forum seeking. However, the Court of Appeal decided this question as follows:

> For the purpose of Art 21, the declaratory proceedings in Rotterdam and the English proceedings had the same cause of action (that is, the same contractual relationship) and the same subject matter, which was the issue whether or not the cargo on *The Tatry* was contaminated. After an acknowledgment of service had been given an action *in rem* continued as a hybrid; the action became *in personam* but it did not lose its previous character of being an action *in rem*. The guidance of the ECJ was needed in order to determine whether a hybrid action could involve the same cause of action as an action *in personam* at another Contracting State for the purpose of Art 21, and whether the actions were between the same parties for the purpose of Art 21.[48]

The ECJ confirmed what the Court of Appeal had held about the proceedings involving the same cause of action, despite the fact that the Rotterdam proceedings were only concerned with an application for a declaration of no liability. On the question of whether they involved the same parties, it was held that:

> ... in Art 21 of the Convention the terms 'same cause of action' and 'between the same parties' have an independent meaning (see *Gubish v Palumpo* [1989] ECC 420).They must therefore be interpreted independently of the specific features of the law in force in each Contracting State. It follows that the distinction drawn by the law of a Contracting State between an action *in personam* and an action *in rem* is not material for the interpretation of Art 21.[49]

Thus, it was held that where an action *in rem* has subsequently continued both *in rem* and *in personam*, or solely *in personam* (according to the distinctions drawn by the national law of the Contracting State), it did not cease to have the same cause of action and the same object, or to be between the same parties as a previous action brought *in personam*.

---

48 It is interesting to note that Sheen J in both *The Linda* [1988] 1 Lloyd's Rep 175 and *The Kherson* [1992] 2 Lloyd's Rep 261, had decided that the parties of an action *in rem*, in which the defendant had acknowledged service, and of an action *in personam* brought in another Contracting State, were the same. These decisions had been decided before the Court of Appeal had decided *The Tatry*.

49 [1995] 1 Lloyd's Rep 302, p 308.

On the scope of Art 57, the ECJ held that Art 57 precluded the application of the provisions of the Brussels Convention only in matters governed by the specialised Convention. It was stated:

> In those circumstances, when a specialised Convention contains certain rules of jurisdiction but no provision as to *lis pendens* or related actions, Arts 21 and 22 of the Brussels Convention apply.[50]

It should be observed that the question put to the ECJ was purely whether a hybrid action (that is, an *in rem* action which has become also *in personam* by the acknowledgment of service by the defendant) was between the same parties as an action *in personam* in another Contracting State. Thus, the ECJ answered this question from a point of view of the Convention and was not concerned with an action *in rem* in which no acknowledgment of service had been filed. Therefore, the need to answer this last question arose in *The Indian Grace* in the context of *res judicata*.

The Indian Grace (No 2)[51]

The plaintiff's cargo consisting of munitions was carried by the defendants' ship, *The Indian Grace*, from Sweden to India. Fire broke out during the voyage in one of the holds which was extinguished by the crew. Some artillery shells had to be jettisoned. The cargo was repackaged and re-stowed at an intermediate port and the vessel arrived at destination to discharge. It was found that the cargo had suffered damage from the heat and from the water used to extinguish the fire. In September 1988, the Union of India, as plaintiffs, started proceedings in India seeking damages for shortage of cargo. While these proceedings were pending, they brought an action *in rem* in England in August 1989 for total loss of the cargo, which had been damaged by heat. A *judgment was given in India in December 1989*, in the plaintiff's favour. The *in rem* writ was served on a sister ship, *The Indian Endurance*, in May 1990. To avoid her arrest, the owners provided security and submitted to the jurisdiction conditionally. They applied to strike out the English action on various grounds, but the relevant one in this context was that the claim was barred by *res judicata* and relied upon s 34 of the CJJA 1982, which provides:

> No proceedings may be brought by a person in England and Wales or Northern Ireland on a cause of action in respect of which a judgment has been given in his favour in proceedings between the same parties, or their privies, in a court in another part of the UK or in a court of an overseas country, unless that judgment is not enforceable or entitled to recognition in England and Wales.

One of the three main issues was whether the section applied to bar the English proceedings having regard to the fact that it was an action *in rem*.

---

50 [1995] 1 Lloyd's Rep 302, p 307.
51 [1998] 1 Lloyd's Rep 1.

Clarke J thought it did not, since at the time when the action was brought, it was not between the same parties as the action *in personam* in India. The defendants application was refused. The Court of Appeal took the opposite view and reversed the decision. It was held that s 34 must have been intended, like Arts 2 and 21 of the Brussels Convention, to prevent the same cause of action being tried twice over between those who were in reality the same parties. The test under s 34 was satisfied and the action was barred. On appeal by the plaintiffs, the House of Lords approved the decision above saying (p 10):

> For the purpose of s 34 an action *in rem* was an action against the owners from the moment that the Admiralty Court was seised with jurisdiction. The jurisdiction of the Admiralty Court was invoked by the service of the writ, or where a writ was deemed to be served, as a result of acknowledgment of the issue of the writ by the defendant before service. From that moment, the owners were parties to the proceedings *in rem* and s 34 was a bar to the action *in rem*.

As it will be seen next in *The Deichland*, the English judges have taken a realistic view of who is behind *in rem* proceedings for the purpose of the rules of *res judicata* and *lis pendens*. To that extent and that alone, it is submitted, these decisions provide certainty in the application of these principles, bearing in mind the purpose of the ECJCs and s 34 of the CJJA 1982.[52] However, none of these decisions will be a good law after 1 March 2002 when the new regulation replacing the Brussels Convention comes into force as Art 30 provides that the court will be seised from the issue of the proceedings!

3 HOW DO THE CONVENTION RULES DELEGATE JURISDICTION ON THE MERITS?

The primary purpose of the ECJCs is to prevent irreconcilable judgments and, therefore, the Convention rules regulate what is to happen when multiple proceedings have commenced in more than one Contracting States. As it has been seen, clash of jurisdictions is sometimes inevitable due to the existence of more than one jurisdictional bases under the convention regime.

The domicile rule may be overridden by virtue of Art 57[53] which allows specialised conventions to take precedence over the primary jurisdiction base

---

52 See, also, conclusions on the effect of *The Indian Grace (No 2)* [1998] 1 Lloyd's Rep 1, in Chapter 3, para 3.8.

53 Article 57 has become Art 71 in (EC) Regulation 44/2001. The amending article refers only to other conventions to which the Member States are parties and has deleted the previous reference to conventions to which the Member States will be parties. The deletion may not make a difference because the matter will be considered as and when the issue arises. The new Article emphasises that a judgment given by a court in a Member State in the exercise of jurisdiction provided for in a convention on a particular matter shall be recognised and enforced in the other Member States in accordance with the Regulation.

of domicile provided jurisdiction has properly been established under the rules of those conventions. It is important to see the interrelationship between Art 57 and other jurisdiction rules in practice and what the courts have held.

3.1 The window of Art 57

It specifically states:

(1) This Convention shall not affect any conventions to which the Contracting States are or will be parties and which, in relation to particular matters, govern jurisdiction or the recognition of judgments.

(2 This Convention shall not prevent a court of a Contracting State which is party to a convention referred to in the first paragraph from assuming jurisdiction in accordance with that convention even where the defendant is domiciled in a Contracting State which is not a party to that convention. The court hearing the action shall, in any event, apply Art 20 of this Convention.

Save for Arts 16 and 17,[54] Art 57 prevails over other Convention rules. Notwithstanding that Art 57 grants jurisdiction to a court of a Contracting State by the application of the rules of other conventions, the jurisdiction granted is regarded as being within the scope of the Brussels or Lugano Conventions. If the rules of the other conventions allocating jurisdiction do not, however, provide for *lis pendens*, or are not properly invoked, the *lis pendens* provisions of Art 21 and 22 will come into operation.[55] Article 57 is like a window, which permits exit from the jurisdiction bases provided by the ECJC and entry to other convention jurisdiction bases, only if jurisdiction is assumed in accordance with the special provisions of the specialised conventions. If not, then there will be a return to a jurisdiction base according to the provisions of the general rules of the ECJC. It will soon be seen in decided cases how this round flight for jurisdiction turns back to a jurisdiction ground of the ECJC. There are many international conventions with regard to maritime claims, which have jurisdiction provisions.[56]

The relevant conventions that will be referred to below for the purpose of Art 57 and admiralty jurisdiction are the Arrest Convention 1952, Art 7, and the Collision Convention 1952, Art 1.

---

54 Whether the effect of Art 17 is to provide exclusive jurisdiction has not been absolutely clear (see, under para 5, the problems which have arisen in its application). The new Regulation, by Art 23 replacing Art 17, has now made it clear that a choice of jurisdiction is exclusive, unless the parties have otherwise agreed.

55 See, also, *op cit*, Briggs and Rees, fn 5, para 2.32.

56 Arrest of Sea-going Ships Conventions 1952, 1999; Collision Convention 1952; Convention on Civil Liability for Oil Pollution Damage (Protocol 1992) and Fund Convention (Protocol 1992); Hague Rules 1924 and Hague-Visby Rules 1968; Hamburg Rules 1978 (not in force in the UK); CMR Convention 1956, to the extent that it is relevant to carriage of goods by sea, Multimodal Convention 1980; Athens Convention 1974 in relation to Carriage of Passengers; Limitation of Liability Convention for Maritime Claims 1976; Law of the Sea Convention 1982.

3.1.1 The flight to the Arrest Convention 1952

It has been seen earlier that jurisdiction on the merits under this Convention may be invoked by Art 7, which, insofar as it is material here, provides:

> The courts of the country in which the arrest was made shall have jurisdiction to determine the case upon its merits ... If the court within whose jurisdiction the ship was arrested has no jurisdiction to decide upon the merits, the bail or other security given in accordance with Art 5 to procure the release of the ship shall specifically provide that it is given as security for the satisfaction of any judgment which may eventually be pronounced by a court having jurisdiction so to decide; and the court or other appropriate judicial authority of the country in which the arrest is made shall fix the time within which the claimant shall bring an action before a court having such jurisdiction.

The best example of how Art 7 of the Arrest Convention can effectively surpass the domicile rule (and by inference jurisdiction rules other than those conferring exclusive[57] jurisdiction under the Brussels Convention regime) is provided by the following case.

The Deichland[58]

In January 1986, the plaintiffs shipped a cargo of steel coils on board *The Deichland* from Glasgow to La Spezia. At the time, the vessel was under a demise charter to a Panamanian corporation, Deich, which had its central management and control in Germany. The plaintiffs alleged that the cargo was damaged on that journey and, therefore, issued a writ *in rem* against the vessel in January 1987. The writ was served on 27 November 1988, but the vessel was not arrested. By this time, the demise charter to Deich had ended and the vessel was in different ownership. The demise charterers, however, acknowledged service of the writ, put up security for the claim, by way of an undertaking from their P&I club, in consideration of the plaintiffs refraining from arresting the vessel. They refused to submit to the English jurisdiction and later applied to the court seeking a declaration under Ord 12 r 8 that the court had no jurisdiction over them. They argued that they should be sued in Germany, the place of their central management and control, in accordance with Art 2 of the Brussels Convention and s 42 of the CJJA 1982. The plaintiffs contended that Art 2 of the Convention did not apply, because the jurisdiction of the English court was properly exercised by the service of the writ on the ship, and that such jurisdiction remained unaffected by the Convention because of the effect of Art 57, and s 9 of the CJJA 1982. Even if the domicile

---

57 A possible conflict between Arts 57 and 17 will be seen later. Concerning admiralty jurisdiction, there has been only one decision, *The Bergen*, the correctness of which has been doubted given that Art 17 jurisdiction is considered to be exclusive, if the jurisdiction agreement satisfies the criteria of Art 17. The amending Regulation resolves any doubt that might have prevailed over the hierarchy between Arts 57 and 17.

58 [1990] 1 QB 361.

rule was to be applied, the place of domicile was Panama (a non-contracting State) and not Germany.

Sheen J held that the provisions of the CJJA 1982 did not apply to an action *in rem*, when it remained solely *in rem*. The action in the writ was described as an action *in rem* against the ship, *The Deichland*. Therefore, Deich was not a defendant in this action and Art 2 did not apply. The motion was dismissed and the charterers appealed.

In the Court of Appeal, the issues were: (1) whether the provisions of the Brussels Convention incorporated in the CJJA 1982 had any application at all to an admiralty action *in rem*; (2) whether Deich was domiciled in Germany as opposed to Panama; and (3) whether, nevertheless, jurisdiction had been founded under Art 57 of the Convention which gave effect to the provisions of the Arrest Convention. Issues one and three are relevant here – the seat of the corporation (issue two) was straightforward. Neil LJ stated, *inter alia*, that:

> ... the right approach when one is considering the effect of an international convention is to take account of the purpose or the purposes of the convention. Plainly the 1968 Convention was intended, *inter alia*, to regulate the circumstances in which a person domiciled in one Contracting State might be brought before the courts of another Contracting State in civil and commercial matters.

> Accordingly it seems to me that all forms of proceedings in civil and commercial matters were intended to be covered except insofar as some special provisions such as Art 57 might otherwise prescribe. Furthermore it seems to me that para 7 in Art 5, which confers a special jurisdiction in the case of claims for remuneration in respect of the salvage of cargo or freight, contemplates that this special jurisdiction may be exercised by proceedings either *in rem* or *in personam*.

> It is true that in the present case the vessel is no longer chartered to Deich and that jurisdiction to entertain the action *in rem* is based on the provisions of s 21 of the Act of 1981. But looking at the reality of the matter, it is Deich who is interested in contesting liability and against whom the plaintiffs would wish to proceed *in personam* if an appearance is entered ...

> In these circumstances, I find it impossible to conclude that on the proper construction of Arts 2 and 3 of the 1968 Convention, Deich is not being 'sued' in these proceedings, even though at this stage the proceedings are solely *in rem*. Deich is liable to be adversely affected by the result of the proceedings and wishes to contest the merits of the plaintiff's claim. By English law an admiralty action *in rem* has special characteristics ...I do not consider, however, that the rules relating to such actions and governing the rights of a plaintiff to levy execution can affect the substance of the matter when the court is faced with an international convention designed to regulate the international jurisdiction of national courts.[59]

---

59 [1990] 1 QB 361, pp 373–74.

On the issue whether the jurisdiction of the English court had properly been invoked in accordance with the Arrest Convention, the operation of which is not affected by the Brussels Convention, the Court of Appeal also held that, on proper construction of the word 'arrest' in Art 7 of the Arrest Convention, an arrest of the vessel is mandatory to found jurisdiction and mere service of a writ or provision of security is not sufficient. If the ship had been arrested the English court would have had jurisdiction over the merits.

The fact that mere service of the writ or provision of security without arrest will not suffice to establish jurisdiction under Art 7 was stressed by Stuart-Smith LJ, as follows:

> If a plaintiff for some reason is determined to litigate in the English Admiralty Court he can easily secure this: either he arrests the ship, or he secures express agreement by the defendant owner or demise charterer to submit to the jurisdiction of the English court to avoid arrest, no doubt at the same time obtaining security. In the present case the plaintiffs did neither of these things.[60]

3.1.2 How has the trap of The Deichland been prevented?

The words of Stuart-Smith LJ provided sufficient guidance in a subsequent case, *The Anna H*, in which the lawyers acting for the claimants took the appropriate steps to ensure that English jurisdiction was properly invoked by arresting the ship as required under Art 7 of the Arrest Convention, despite the defendants' attempt to avoid that result by filing a caveat against arrest.

The Anna H[61]

In December 1990, *The Anna H* was loaded with cargo of steel coils at Swansea for carriage to Barcelona. During loading, the coils got wet due to rain. The Spanish cargo-owners (consignees of the bills of lading) alleged that since this happened during loading and stowing of the cargo, the shipowners and demise charterers (both Germans) were responsible for the damage. Their solicitors sought to obtain security from the owners' P&I club in September 1991. The shipowners, anticipating that the ship might be arrested, entered a caveat against arrest of the vessel. At the same time they purported to initiate proceedings in Germany against the cargo-owners for a declaration of no liability, but it turned out that the German court did not become seised of the action. In October 1991, the cargo-owners issued a writ *in rem* and on 11 November arrested *The Anna H* for a few minutes only because of the caveat against arrest.[62] She was released without security having been

---

60 [1990] 1 QB 361, p 385.
61 [1995] 1 Lloyd's Rep 11.
62 A caveat against arrest of a vessel does not prevent the issue of a warrant of arrest on that vessel.

obtained. Subsequently, the defendants' P&I club executed a bail bond without protest in respect of any judgment that might be given against the shipowners, not just against the ship. The defendants acknowledged service of the writ and sought an order that the English court set aside or stayed its proceedings, or declined jurisdiction in favour of the court of their domicile in Germany. The plaintiffs contested the shipowners' arguments and relied on (a) Art 57 of the Convention, (jurisdiction could be founded by arresting the vessel), and (b) the fact that the defendants had submitted to the jurisdiction of the English court when they filed the praecipe for the caveat against arrest, or when they acknowledged service of the writ and put up bail as security. The defendants contended that since the CJJA 1982 expressly mentions bail in s 26 and gave the court power to decline jurisdiction where security had been given, the putting up of bail could no longer amount to an irrevocable submission to jurisdiction.

Clarke J (as he then was) held in favour of the plaintiffs on the ground of Art 57 and that there was submission to jurisdiction by the lodging of the bail bond, which could not be affected by the wording of s 26 of the 1982 Act. The Court of Appeal examined the relationship of the Arrest and Judgments Conventions and paid regard to the *travaux preparatoires* which explained the importance of giving heed to jurisdictional rules imposed by other agreements between state parties. Hobhouse LJ said:[63]

> The two Conventions are to be read together. Their relationship is of the special to the general. Where special provision is made in the special convention, it shall govern. Where no special provision is made, the general provision of the judgments convention apply. Accordingly, within its scope, the Arrest Convention governs the jurisdiction of the Admiralty Court and prevails over the provisions of the judgments convention. There is no reason to impose any implicit restriction on the effect of Art 57 ... Further, it is clear that the intention is that the jurisdiction available under the Arrest Convention should be preserved and that it should continue to apply even though the owner of the ship may be domiciled in another Member State.

He continued:

> The Arrest Convention, in the words of Mr Jennard and Professor Schlosser, 'prevails over' the Judgements Convention. The Arrest Convention qualifies and must be read as part of the Judgements Convention. Any supposed difference of policy must be resolved in favour of the Arrest Convention ... Article 57(2) expressly negatives the inference that the jurisdiction is to be excluded because 'the defendant is domiciled in another Contracting State'.

---

63   [1995] 1 Lloyd's Rep 11, pp 18, 20.

3.1.3 Submission to jurisdiction and bail

On the issue of submission to jurisdiction Hobhouse LJ did not have to decide but he said, *obiter*, that as a defendant can acknowledge service without always submitting to the jurisdiction, should he wish to challenge it, equally, he can put up bail conditionally reserving the right to challenge jurisdiction.

However, the lodging of bail had been thought, at first instance, prior to *The Anna H*, to be a clear submission to jurisdiction by Sheen J in the following case.

The Prinsengracht[64]

The plaintiffs issued a writ *in rem* on 15 April 1991 for damage to their cargo laden on the defendant's ship. It could not be served during the remaining months of that year because the ship did not come within jurisdiction. *The Deichland* had just been decided, so the plaintiffs' solicitors wanted to be cautious and wrote to the defendants' solicitors formally asking for appropriate security for the claim and a letter of undertaking submitting to the jurisdiction. In order to avoid the inconvenience of arrest, the defendants, without waiting for the writ to be served, acknowledged its issue and executed a bail bond. The bond was filed into the Admiralty Court and a few minutes later, the plaintiffs arrested the ship to avoid the problem of *The Deichland*. Thereafter, the ship was released on the same day. The defendants contended that, since they had voluntarily given bail as security for the claim, they had deprived the plaintiffs of the right of arrest; the arrest should be set aside, and they should have been sued in The Netherlands which was their country of domicile. The question for the court was this: if shipowners were domiciled in a Contracting State and voluntarily gave bail to avoid the inconvenience of arrest of their ship, was the consequence of putting up bail that this court was deprived of jurisdiction (in a sense that the plaintiffs were deprived of the right to arrest) to hear and determine the plaintiffs' claim?

Bearing in mind that a bail is an undertaking given to the court, Sheen J answered the question in strong terms:[65]

> Contractual security may be given without submitting, or agreeing to submit, to the jurisdiction of this court (as in *The Deichland*) but bail cannot be given without submitting to the jurisdiction ... Under the old procedure relating to appearance, bail could only be given after appearance ...but the defendant who appeared under protest could put in bail ...Under the current procedure a person who desires to prevent the arrest of his property must acknowledge the issue or service of the writ, as the defendants have done ...

---

64 [1993] 1 Lloyd's Rep 41.
65 *Ibid*, pp 45–46.

> It would be absurd and it would bring the law into disrepute, if a defendant could procure a bail bond in which there is a solemn undertaking to satisfy a judgment of the court and then say to the plaintiff 'of course you can not obtain a judgment against me because you cannot arrest my ship and I have not submitted to the jurisdiction of the court'. Fortunately that is not the effect of the decision in *The Deichland*. The defendants have, by acknowledging the issue of the writ, shown their desire to take part in the proceedings. They are free to do so.

It was held that the defendants had clearly submitted to the jurisdiction of the court not only by voluntarily acknowledging the issue of the writ at a time when no action was required of them, but also by putting up bail.

The shipowners in this case fell into two traps: acknowledging issue of the writ and putting up bail without protest.[66] Apart from *obiter* comments by the Court of Appeal in *The Anna H*, that it is possible to put up bail under protest, reserving the right to challenge jurisdiction, there are two first instance decisions (*Anna H* by Clarke J and this one) upholding the view that by lodging a bail bond the defendant submits to jurisdiction. Although bail under protest could be a safeguard for the defendant, it would be of no significant effect if the claimant proceeds with the arrest of the ship for a few minutes only to ensure that jurisdiction is established under Art 7 of the Arrest Convention.

3.1.4 The new Arrest Convention 1999

Under the new Arrest Convention,[67] however, Art 7 has been amended, so that the issues discussed in the above cases will be of no significance if the 1999 Arrest Convention is enacted into English law. Article 7(1) gives jurisdiction to a court of a place where either the arrest has been made or security is provided in lieu of arrest, unless the parties validly agree, or have validly agreed to submit to the jurisdiction of another state, which accepts jurisdiction. However, by para (2), the court which is given jurisdiction either by arrest or by provision of security to obtain release of the ship, will have power to refuse to exercise that jurisdiction if the law of that state allows it and the court of another state accepts jurisdiction. The new Arrest Convention will be more in line with the provisions of the Collision Convention 1952, discussed next.

---

66 Jackson doubts that the provision of bail which is a provisional measure should cause submission to jurisdiction: Jackson, DC, *Enforcement of Maritime Claims*, 2nd edn, 1996, LLP, p 343.

67 For an authoritative commentary of the new Arrest Convention 1999, see Gaskell, N and Shaw, R, 'The Arrest Convention 1999' [1999] LMCLQ 470.

3.1.5 The flight to the Collision Convention 1952

Article 1 of the Collision Convention states that an action for collision between seagoing vessels can only be introduced:

(a) before the court where the defendant has his habitual residence or a place of business; or

(b) before the court of the place where arrest had been effected of the defendant ship or of any other ship belonging to the defendant which can be lawfully arrested, or where arrest could have been effected and bail or other security had been furnished; or

(c) before the court of the place of the collision when the collision has occurred within the limits of a port or in inland waters.

Article 3 provides that any counterclaims arising out of the same collision can be brought before the court having jurisdiction over the principal action (as per Art 1).

The best illustration of this was provided by the following case.

The Po[68]

The Italian vessel of the defendants, *The Po*, collided with an American ship, *The Bowditch*, belonging to the US Navy (plaintiffs), in Rio de Janeiro while at anchor. The operators of the American ship commenced proceedings in the Brazilian court and the vessel was duly arrested. An undertaking was provided by the P&I club of *The Po* for her release. After an inquiry by the administrative agent in the Port of Rio de Janeiro, the proceedings in the Brazilian court were discontinued. Subsequently, the plaintiffs commenced these proceedings in England. A writ *in rem* was served on *The Po* in Southampton and, in order to prevent her arrest, the owners' P&I club put up security for the second time. In the covering letter, the defendants' solicitors reserved the right to challenge the jurisdiction of the English court on the ground of *forum non-conveniens*.

As the decision of the Court of Appeal in *The Deichland* had just been given, the defendants brought a motion asking the court to decline jurisdiction on the ground that under the Brussels Convention the proceedings should have been brought in Italy were the vessel was registered. One of the main questions for consideration was whether this case could be distinguished from *The Deichland*.

The question whether or not England had implemented the Collision Convention or made it part of English municipal law was immaterial.

According to Lloyd LJ:[69]

---

68   [1991] 2 Lloyd's Rep 206.
69   *Ibid*, p 211.

> Article 57 of the 1968 Convention does not depend for its beneficial operation on showing that the Contracting States have implemented the special convention. It is enough that the state is a party to the Convention, which the UK is. The High court indubitably has jurisdiction in accordance with English municipal law in the present case, since the writ *in rem* was properly served on the vessel when she was at Southampton ....This assumption of jurisdiction was not only not contrary to the Collision Convention, but was positively authorised by it, since the vessel could have been arrested and security was duly offered and accepted. In those circumstances, I can not see that it matters whether the Collision Convention as such, or the last part of Art 1(1)(b) are part of English municipal law. Since the assumption of jurisdiction was in accordance with the Collision Convention, it is saved from being contrary to Arts 2 and 3 of the 1968 Convention by Art 57.

He distinguished *The Deichland* on the ground that it was a case decided on Art 7 of the Arrest Convention, the wording of which is stricter than the wording of Art 1 of the Collision Convention.

The issue of the first motion in this case (that is, stay on the ground of *forum non-conveniens*) is discussed later.

3.2 Return to the general Convention ground of jurisdiction

3.2.1 Operation of Arts 21 and 22

It has already been seen in *The Tatry* that proceedings for a declaration of no liability brought in a court of a Contracting State prior to arresting a ship in England would cause the other court to be seised first in accordance with Art 21. It was explained in *The Deichland*, *The Anna H* and *The Prinsengracht*, that if litigants wish to come to an English court they must cause the jurisdiction of the court to be seised by following the correct procedures, even if a few minutes would make a difference. The ECJC provide a scheme, which has become much clearer in the recent years, yet surprises cannot altogether be overruled. On the one hand, the rules of ECJC permit specialised Conventions to take jurisdiction through the window of Art 57 and, on the other, they can claw jurisdiction back[70] if the ship has not, or cannot be arrested, pursuant to Art 7 of the Arrest Convention and, in the meantime, an action for declaration of no liability has been brought in a court of another Contracting State in which the defendant is domiciled.[71] If, in such a case, the court of a Contracting State, which is also a party to the Arrest Convention, does not assume jurisdiction in accordance with Art 7, then Art 21 of the ECJC

---

70 Briggs, A, 'The Brussels convention tames the Arrest Convention' [1995] LMCLQ 163.

71 This problem will be resolved when the new Arrest Convention 1999 comes into force and is enacted in the UK.

will step in to determine the issue of *lis pendens* because there is no special provision about *lis pendens* in the Arrest Convention. The relationship between the Arrest Convention and the ECJC is that of the special to the general and the general provisions of the latter shall govern.

A problem of irreconcilable judgments may also arise when multiple proceedings are brought in different Contracting States, which do not have the same cause of action, but they are related. The ECJC prevent this problem from arising by Art 22. How 'related actions' have been judicially defined is examined next.

3.2.2 Definition of related actions

Article 22 of the Convention provides:

> Where related actions are brought in the courts of different Contracting States, any court other than the court first seised may, while the actions are pending at first instance, stay its proceedings.

> A court other than the court first seised may also, on the application of one of the parties, decline jurisdiction if the law of that court permits the consolidation of related actions and the court first seised has jurisdiction over both actions.

> For the purposes of this Article, actions are deemed to be related where they are so closely connected that it is expedient to hear and determine them together to avoid the risk of irreconcilable judgments resulting from separate proceedings.

Sarrio SA v Kuwait Investment Authority[72]

The plaintiffs brought two identical actions in England claiming damages in tort for negligent misstatements by the defendants, which allegedly induced them to enter into a contract with companies controlled by the defendants for the sale of the plaintiffs' special paper. A year before, the plaintiffs had filed a claim in Spain for a debt against the defendants concerning unpaid sums under the contract and the defendants had duly been served with the Spanish proceedings. For this reason, the defendants applied to the English court for a stay of the action in England on the basis of Art 22 of the Brussels Convention. Unlike the judge, the Court of Appeal held on this point that the case was outside the scope of Art 22 because the primary issues of fact in the English proceedings were distinct from those raised in the Spanish proceedings and there was, thus, no risk of irreconcilable judgments. In its analysis, it drew a distinction between facts necessary to establish a cause of action and other facts and matters on which conflicting decisions might arise. The House of Lords (having approved the decision of Mance J) rejected this analysis. It held

---

72 [1998] 1 Lloyd's Rep 129 (HL).

that the simple wide test laid down in Art 22 should be applied in every case. Lord Saville stated in his analysis of the words used in that article, that:

> The actions, to be related, must be 'so closely connected that it is expedient to hear and determine them together' to avoid the risk of irreconcilable judgments resulting from separate proceedings. To my mind these wide words are designed to cover a range of circumstances, from cases where the matters before the courts are virtually identical (though not falling within the provisions of Art 21) to cases where although this is not the position, the connection is close enough to make it expedient for them to be heard and determined together to avoid the risk in question. These words are required, if 'irreconcilable judgments' extends beyond 'primary' or 'essential issues', so as to exclude actions which, though theoretically capable to giving rise to conflict, are not sufficiently closely connected to make it expedient for them to be heard and determined together.[73] There should be a broad common sense approach to the question whether the actions in question are related, bearing in mind the objective of the article, applying the simple wide test set out in Art 22 and refraining from an oversophisticated analysis of the matter.[74]

The English action was stayed in favour of Spain for the same reasons as held by the judge.

4 CAN PRINCIPLES OF *FORUM NON-CONVENIENS* BE PERMITTED IN THE ECJC REGIME?[75]

4.1 The Convention approach

In cases where the ECJCs apply there is a limited scope for the application of principles of *forum non-conveniens*. A distinction between 'pure' and 'non-pure' convention rules has been drawn.[76] When pure convention rules apply, they leave no room for the application of a discretionary power to bypass the convention rules, even in cases where for the interests of justice a forum other than the one prescribed by the conventions would be more appropriate. Conversely, when non-pure convention rules come into play, English courts have applied principles based on *The Spiliada*, the objective of which is to serve the ends of justice.

---

73 [1998] 1 Lloyd's Rep 129 (HL), p 134.

74 *Ibid*, p 135.

75 This topic is extracted from the author's article '*Forum non-conveniens*, or forum shopping by way of limitation actions (1999) 6(3) *International Journal of Maritime Law*, April, Lawtext.

76 Arts 2 and 3 have been referred to as 'pure' Convention rules by Mance J in *The Sarrio* case, [1998] 1 Lloyd's Rep 129 (HL), and by Clarke J in *The Xin Yang* case [1996] 2 Lloyd's Rep 217, see para 4.2.1, below.

The ECJC regime does not explicitly refer to *forum non-conveniens*, which is a concept not known to continental legal systems.[77] However, **Art 4** of the Convention expressly states that:

> If the defendant is not domiciled in a Contracting State, the jurisdiction of the courts of each Contracting State shall, subject to the provisions of Art 16, be determined by the law of that state.
>
> As against such a defendant, any person domiciled in a Contracting State may, whatever his nationality, avail himself in that State of the rules of jurisdiction there in force, and in particular those specified in the second paragraph of Art 3, in the same way as the national of that State.

Article 4 of the new Regulation remains broadly the same, except that it is made subject to both articles providing for exclusive jurisdiction, namely those that will be equivalent to the present Arts 16 and 17.

English courts have held that Art 4 grants a discretion for staying proceedings on the ground of *forum non-conveniens* although this is disputed by some writers in the field.[78] Thus, Art 4 – by reference to domestic law – allows an indirect application of *forum non-conveniens*, when the defendant is not domiciled in a Contracting State.

Once the domestic law of a Contracting State is permitted to come into play by the ECJC (and that law recognises the doctrine of *forum non-conveniens*), there is no express rule in the ECJC preventing its application save for when there is a choice of jurisdiction in a Member State (Art 17).

In English law, *forum non-conveniens* within the Convention regime is expressly dealt with by **s 49 of the CJJA 1982**, which provides that:

> Nothing in this Act shall prevent any court in the UK from staying, sisting, striking out or dismissing any proceedings before it, on the ground of *forum non-conveniens* of otherwise, where to do so is not inconsistent with the 1968 Convention or as the case may be the Lugano Convention.

What would be inconsistent with the Convention is not absolutely clear. A caution to litigants was given by Professor Schlosser in his report,[79] in that they should not waste their time and money risking that the court concerned may consider itself less competent than another, and the choice of the plaintiff should not be weakened by considerations of *forum non-conveniens*.[80]

---

77 Lord Goff explained, in *Airbus v Patel* [1998] 1 Lloyd's Rep 631, the different approaches between the civil law systems and the common law systems in this respect, see Chapter 7, introduction.

78 *Op cit*, Briggs and Rees, fn 5, p 169; Newton J, 'Forum non-conveniens in Europe (again)' [1997] LMCLQ 337.

79 On the accession of Denmark, Ireland and the UK to the Brussels Convention (1979) OJ C59/7197.

80 However, both Mance J in *The Sarrio* [1998] 1 Lloyd's Rep 129 (HL), and Clarke J in *The Xin Yang* case [1996] 2 Lloyd's Rep 217 (see later) interpreted this to mean that the discouragement by Professor Schlosser for the application of *forum non-conveniens* was only relevant in the context of jurisdiction exercised on pure Convention [contd]

It seems from recent decisions of the English courts that the exercise of discretion to stay proceedings on grounds of *forum non-conveniens* would not be inconsistent with Convention rules if (a) the defendant is not domiciled in a Contracting State irrespective of proceedings being brought in two Contracting States; (b) if the contest of jurisdiction is between non-contracting States, regardless of the defendant being domiciled in a Contracting State. Examples under each category are considered below.

4.2 When the defendant is not domiciled in a Contracting State

4.2.1 The effect of Art 4 of the Conventions

The factual background of *The Sarrio* case, mentioned earlier under Art 22, will illustrate how the English courts have approached this issue.

The defendants (KIA) were established in Kuwait and through various subsidiaries controlled a Spanish company, Grupo Torras (GT) and its subsidiaries. GT was involved in the business of paper packaging. The plaintiffs, Sarrio, a Spanish company, decided to sell off its own special paper business to a subsidiary of GT, Torraspapel (T). Part of the agreement was, *inter alia*, that the plaintiffs would buy shares in T and other subsidiaries of GT and they were also given a 'put option' to require GT to buy back the shares in T from Sarrio. Having exercised the 'put option', Sarrio made a loss out of the deal because GT did not pay the agreed value, went into receivership, and the subsidiary's value fell sharply. Sarrio filed proceedings in Spain against the defendants, claiming sums, which GT had failed to pay under the 'put option'. Subsequently, it also brought two identical actions in England, claiming damages in tort for negligent misstatement made orally during the negotiations which induced it to enter into contracts with these companies controlled by the defendants. The defendants applied for a stay of the action on two grounds. First, under Art 21 and 22 of the Brussels Convention; secondly, under *The Spiliada* doctrine of *forum non-conveniens*, in that Spain was a more appropriate forum. It was not disputed that the defendants were not domiciled in a Contracting State. The plaintiffs contended that where the choice of forum was between two Contracting States, the English court had no power, even in a case of a defendant domiciled outside the EC, to apply the common law principles of *forum non-conveniens*. Mance J[81] rejected this contention and enunciated the principle as follows:

> In the case of a defendant domiciled within a Contracting State jurisdiction was regulated by the pure convention rules negotiated between such States.

---

80 [contd] grounds under Arts 2 or 3, where the Convention lays down a scheme which does not apply to defendants not domiciled in a Convention State.

81 [1996] 1 Lloyd's Rep 650.

The primary rule set out in Art 2 was that suit was to be brought in the court of defendant's domicile. Article 3 referred to situations in which suit may be brought elsewhere and identified a number of national rules which could not as a result survive ...

The position in relation to defendants not domiciled within a Contracting State is quite different. Jurisdiction depends upon national rules: see Art 4 of the Brussels Convention. Insofar as jurisdiction or the exercise of jurisdiction by English courts depends on considering whether England is the appropriate forum, there is nothing in the Convention inconsistent with the English court considering this: see s 49 of the CJJA 1982. The obvious qualification is that it would not be consistent for an English court to insist on exercising jurisdiction on the grounds that it was, applying *The Spiliada* principles and apart from the Convention, the appropriate forum, in circumstances where under Arts 21–23 it would be obligatory or appropriate for it, as the court second seised, to decline or stay the exercise of its jurisdiction.[82]

Evans LJ approved this analysis in the Court of Appeal[83] but, unlike the judge, he did not allow the stay of the English proceedings on the ground that the actions were not related. Upon application of Art 22, however, (see *Sarrio v Kuwait Investments* (under para 2.2 above), the House of Lords restored the judge's decision because the Spanish court had been seised first, and, therefore, the House of Lords declined jurisdiction under Art 22(2). It did not have to consider whether the court had discretion under Art 4 to consider principles of *forum non-conveniens* as applied by national law in appropriate cases, because the issue of jurisdiction was resolved on the basis of Art 22. Thus, the decisions of the courts below have not been overruled on this issue. The same principle was followed in the subsequent case.

The Xin Yang[84]

A collision occurred between two foreign ships in Holland, while one of them was loading cargo alongside a berth, causing damage to both of them and to the jetty as well. The owners of the jetty arrested *The Xin Yang*, which was presumed to be at fault, in Holland to obtain security for damages to the jetty. The owners of the moored ship arrested a sister ship of *The Xin Yang* in England claiming damages. Subsequently, the defendant commenced limitation proceedings in The Netherlands (the place of the collision) and applied to stay the English action on the basis of *forum non-conveniens*. The limitation proceedings in The Netherlands and the action for liability in England were in Contracting States, but the defendants in either proceedings were not domiciled in a Contracting State. Clarke J stayed the English action in favour of Holland, although the English liability action had been commenced before the Dutch action.

---

82 [1996] 1 Lloyd's Rep 650, p 654.
83 [1997] 1 Lloyd's Rep 113.
84 [1996] 2 Lloyd's Rep 217.

Had Clarke J not stayed the English action, the Dutch court (being second seised) would have been obliged to stay the proceedings or decline its jurisdiction in accordance with Arts 21 and 22, if the jurisdiction of the first seised court had been established. Clarke J considered that, as the parties were not domiciled in a Contracting State (and since neither Art 16 or 17 applied) the court was not prevented by pure Convention rules (such as Arts 2 and 3) from staying the proceedings on ground of *forum non-conveniens*. Following the reasoning of Mance J, in *Sarrio v Kuwait* (later approved by the Court of Appeal on this point), he relied on Art 4, which expressly permits domestic law to apply if the defendant is not domiciled in a Contracting State. Since English law includes principles of *forum non-conveniens*, there was no sound basis for holding that the Convention intended to restrict the court in the exercise of its jurisdiction to stay the action on those grounds. Furthermore, the power of the court to stay the action was expressly retained by s 49 of the CJJA 1982. In such circumstances, the court, although it was first seised, was entitled to decline to exercise jurisdiction on ground of *forum non-conveniens*, whether or not the alternative forum was within a Contracting State.[85] Clarke J stated that:

> ... jurisdiction is preserved by Art 4 of the Brussels Convention. There is nothing in the Convention which expressly restricts the way in which or the circumstances in which the English court may exercise that jurisdiction. In particular there is nothing in Art 4 or any other provision of the Convention which restricts the right or duty of the English court (or, indeed, the right or duty of the court of any Contracting State which might otherwise be first seised within the meaning of Art 21) to decline to exercise that jurisdiction on the ground of *forum non-conveniens* or any other discretionary ground.[86]

> The sensible place for the determination of the quantum between the various claimants would be in the Dutch limitation proceedings.

The principle derived from these decisions is that, insofar as the interpretation of Art 4 by English courts is concerned, *forum non-conveniens* principles are permitted as between two Contracting States when the defendant is not domiciled in a Contracting State and even if the jurisdiction is invoked by the arrest of a ship.[87] The appropriate forum for liability and limitation issues was the place of the collision in the *Xin Yang* and in the *Happy Fellow* (see below).

---

85 On this point, the decision of the ECJ in *Overseas Union v Hampshire Insurance* [1992] 1 Lloyd's Rep 204, is distinguishable because it involved Art 21 considerations while neither *The Sarrio* [1998] 1 Lloyd's Rep 129 (HL) nor *The Xin Yang* [1996] 2 Lloyd's Rep 217 did.

86 [1992] 1 Lloyd's Rep 204, p 220.

87 The approach of Clarke J (as he then was) in *The Xin Yang*, has been criticised by an academic writer, *op cit*, Newton, fn 78, p 343, in that the judge disregarded that jurisdiction of the English court was founded on Art 57 which should be a pure convention rule. Although the present author disagrees with this statement, there may be an opportunity in the future for the ECJ to define which are pure and non-pure convention rules.

If a matter which is within the conventions has not been brought before a court of a Contracting State, or is not caught by the jurisdiction rules of another Convention permitted by Art 57, or the exclusive jurisdiction provisions, or is not referred to the national law of the forum by virtue of Art 4, a court which is seised with jurisdiction prior to any other court of a Contracting State cannot decline to hear the matter.

How litigants invent ways to bypass these rules is seen below.

4.2.2 Limitation actions within the Conventions regime and risk management

Although limitation actions provide a fertile field for forum shopping, the courts have recently shown determination to send defendants to the appropriate forum – for determination of liability issues and limitation.

Article 6A of the Conventions provides that:

> Where by virtue of this convention a court of a Contracting State has jurisdiction in actions relating to liability arising from the use or operation of a ship, that court, or any other court substituted for this purpose by the internal law of that state, shall also have jurisdiction over claims for limitation of such liability.

This article will be Art 7 of the amending Regulation to the Brussels Convention. There is no change to this provision other than replacing the phrase 'Contracting State' with 'Member State'.

This article pre-supposes that a court of a Contracting State has jurisdiction in the liability action by virtue of a convention base. 'Use or operation of a ship' clearly includes liability arising from collisions between sea-going ships and by virtue of Art 57, the jurisdiction of a Contracting State may be invoked as provided by Art 1 of the Collision Convention already discussed. Once such jurisdiction is invoked in a court of a Contracting State, Art 6A contains both a discretionary and a mandatory element. The discretion relates to permitting that court to substitute another court for the claim upon criteria of its internal law. (If the court seised is English, it may consider appropriate to apply *forum non-conveniens* principles according to domestic law). The obligation imposed by Art 6A is that the original court, or the substituted one, shall also determine limitation of liability for such claims.

There is, therefore, a restriction upon a defendant to a collision action, who wishes to limit liability, in that, by Art 6A, the limitation action cannot be split from the liability action. However, it seems from decided cases that he may be able to choose a forum of his preference for limitation, if he pre-empts the jurisdiction of that court (should that be the place of his domicile and within a Contracting State), by instituting limitation proceedings there prior to the arrest of his ship involved in the collision. The anomaly created by such pre-emptive action, however, would be that the forum of the domicile may not be the appropriate forum for the collision liability, unless liability is admitted. Once a limitation fund is established, there will be a bar to other proceedings by Art 13 of the Limitation Convention 1976. Alternatively, a defendant may agree with a claimant to invoke the desired jurisdiction for liability issues, whereupon any other action instituted subsequently by other claimants, elsewhere, would have to be stayed pursuant to Art 22 of the Brussels and Lugano Conventions.

In *The Happy Fellow*,[88] where a collision took place near the mouth of Seine, the other ship (*Darfur*) being blamed for the collision was arrested at Le Havre by the owners of *The Happy Fellow*. Seven other French claimants also issued proceedings there. Subsequently, the time charterers of the *Darfur* issued proceedings in England against the owners of this ship claiming indemnity. A few days later, a limitation action commenced in England by the owners of *The Darfur* naming as defendants the time charterers and all the other parties who were proceeding in France. A stay of the limitation action in England was allowed upon application of the operators of *The Happy Fellow* on the ground that the actions 'were related' and Art 22 should apply. The Court of Appeal[89] approved the judge's decision that the French court would conclude that it should deal with limitation issues and, thus, there was a risk of irreconcilable judgments. It disregarded the fact that, before the appeal, the owners of *The Darfur* – hoping to influence the court in exercising its discretion to refuse the stay of the English limitation action – admitted liability in the French proceedings.

In the *Xin Yang*, Clarke J said that it would be permitted by Art 6A to substitute the appropriate court for the claim on grounds of *forum non-conveniens*, as he did by virtue of Art 4.

4.3 When the competing court is in a non-Contracting State

The question here is whether principles of *forum non-conveniens* will be applicable although the defendant is domiciled in a Contracting State.

Two well known cases are very apt to illustrate this situation. In *Re Harrods (Buenos Aires)*[90] the Court of Appeal held that, pursuant to s 49 of the CJJA 1982, it was not inconsistent with the letter or the spirit of the Convention for the English court to stay the proceedings on grounds of *forum non-conveniens*, if the alternative forum was a non-Contracting State. Here,

---

88 [1997] 1 Lloyd's Rep 130 and [1998] 1 Lloyd's Rep 13 (CA).
89 [1998]1 Lloyd's Rep 13.
90 [1992] Ch 72; CA disapproved opposite view held in *Berisford v New Hampshire Insurance* [1990] 2 QB 631 and *Arkwright v Bryanston Insurance* [1990] 2 QB 649.

although the defendant company was registered in a Contracting State (England), its principal place of business was in Argentina.[91]

Re Harrods (Buenos Aires)

The applicant (L), a minority shareholder of Harrods (Buenos Aires Ltd) (H), was a company incorporated in Switzerland. H was incorporated in England and was the subject matter of the proceedings. The majority of shares in H were held by another company incorporated in Switzerland. The business of H was carried on exclusively in Argentina, where the central management and control of the company was established. L alleged that the affairs of the company were being conducted in a manner unfairly prejudicial to L. Therefore, L brought a petition under the Companies Act 1985 for an order that the majority shareholder based in Switzerland purchased the minority share holding or, alternatively, that the English company, H, should be compulsorily wound up. Leave to serve the defendants out of jurisdiction was granted. The majority shareholder applied to set aside the order on the ground, inter alia, that Argentina was a more appropriate forum for the trial.

At the Court of Appeal, the question, at a preliminary hearing, was whether *forum non-conveniens* was excluded by the provisions of the CJJA 1982 incorporating the Brussels Convention. If not, the next question was whether the English court could stay the action, strike out or dismiss proceedings on the ground of *forum non-conveniens* where the defendant in the English proceedings was domiciled in England. It was undisputed that the company was domiciled in both the UK and Argentina.

Section 49 of the CJJA 1982 provides that nothing in the Act shall prevent any court in the UK from staying or striking out proceedings before it on the ground of *forum non-conveniens* or otherwise where to do so is not inconsistent with the Convention. Dillon LJ stated:

> For the English court to refuse jurisdiction, in a case against a person domiciled in England, on the ground that the court of some non-contracting State is the more appropriate court to decide the matters in issue does not in any way impair the object of the Convention of establishing an expeditious, harmonious and, I would add, certain procedure for securing the enforcement of judgments, since *ex hypothesis*, if the English court refuses jurisdiction there will be no judgment of the English court to be enforced in the other Contracting States. Equally, and for the same reasons, such a refusal of jurisdiction would not impair the object of the Convention that there should, subject to the very large exception of Art 4, be a uniform international jurisdiction for obtaining the judgments which are to be so enforced ...
>
> Articles 21 and 22 of the Convention are only concerned with the position where proceedings involving the same cause of action and between the same

---

91 The domicile of a corporation is either at the place of incorporation or where the central management and control is exercised: CJJA 1982, s 42.

parties, or where related action, are brought in the courts of different Contracting States. There is nothing at all in the Convention to deal with the situation where there is one *lis* pending in a court of a Contracting State against a person domiciled in that State and another, and possibly earlier, *lis* pending, in proceedings involving the same cause of action or a related action, in the courts of a non-contracting State.[92]

It was held that as the Brussels Convention is merely an agreement between the Contracting States themselves, and since Art 49 preserved the court's power to stay or dismiss proceedings where to do so was not inconsistent with the convention, the English court had jurisdiction to stay or dismiss the petition on grounds of *forum non-conveniens*, if the English court held that Argentina was the more appropriate forum for the trial.

In *The Po*,[93] where the shipowners were Italian (a Contracting State) and the competing courts were in Brazil and England, the Court of Appeal followed The *Harrods* case, but preserved the English action upon the application of *forum non-conveniens* principles.

Two ships collided in the harbour of Rio de Janeiro. *The Po* was owned by an Italian company. She was later served with a writ *in rem* at Southampton and security was put up by her P&I club to prevent arrest. Through Art 57 of the Convention, the jurisdiction of the English court was established under Art 1 of the Collision Convention 1952. Thus, the defendant's motion that they should be sued in Italy and that the ECJC prevented the court from taking jurisdiction failed in both the court below and the Court of Appeal.[94]

The defendant's second motion that the English proceedings should be stayed in favour of the natural forum, Brazil failed too. But the plaintiffs' argument that the Brussels Convention excluded any discretion of the court to apply *forum non-conveniens* principles was rejected. The Court of Appeal held that – on the basis of *Re Harrods (Buenos Aires)* – such discretion was not precluded when the competing forum was not a Contracting State. Applying the second stage test of *The Spiliada* principles, the court refused the stay because, although Brazil was the natural forum, if the case was tried there, the plaintiff would be deprived of an important juridical advantage which he would enjoy in England. That advantage was concerned with the burden of proof. Unlike Brazilian law, under English law, where a *prima facie* case of negligence had been made out on the basis of *res ipsa loquitur*, as was in this case, the defendant had to disprove negligence.

The view of English courts that the jurisdiction to stay proceedings on grounds of *forum non-conveniens* in favour of a non-contracting State, even though the defendant is domiciled in a Contracting State, was recently upheld

---

92 [1992] Ch 72, *per* Dillon LJ, p 97.
93 [1991] 2 Lloyd's Rep 206 decided after *Re Harrods,* the latter was reported late.
94 See para 3.1.5, above.

again in *Ace Insurance v Zurich Insurance*.[95] The judge said, applying *The Harrods*, that it would be odd if the law were to be that a stay was available to a UK defendant but not to a defendant domiciled in any other Convention State; and it would be even odder, if an agreement to submit to the jurisdiction of a non-contracting State had to be treated as ineffective in any Convention country.

As is shown from these decisions, when 'pure convention' rules are not violated and it is appropriate to apply *forum non-conveniens* principles for the ends of justice, the English courts are prepared to apply them. Although the Convention Jurisdiction must be carefully safeguarded, so that there is certainty and uniformity in the application of Convention rules, the approach taken by the English courts in the above cases is sensible, particularly, when it is considered that it will serve justice to be done and pure Convention rules are not infringed. In the complex infrastructure of the European empire of jurisdictions, an unwarranted rise of EU jurisdictional chauvinism would be contrary to ends of justice.

5 JURISDICTION AGREEMENTS, ART 17

Invariably, a conflict may arise between convention jurisdiction bases. For example, when there is a jurisdiction agreement to which the Brussels Convention applies, the question has been this: can Art 17 take precedence over another convention jurisdiction base and, in particular, the one founded on Art 57? The answer would depend, first, on whether the parties to the agreement intended their choice of jurisdiction to be exclusive; second, on whether Art 17 conferred exclusive jurisdiction over other convention jurisdiction bases (but that begs the question); and, third, on whether the requirements of Art 17 were complied with.

When the amending Regulation comes into force, the position will be much clearer. The equivalent to Art 17 is Art 23 of the Regulation, which provides expressly that a choice of jurisdiction by the parties shall be exclusive, unless the parties agreed otherwise. Until then it is still useful to know how Art 17 has been interpreted by the English courts.

5.1 Is jurisdiction under Art 17 exclusive, in a sense of being mandatory?

Article 17 provides:

> If the parties, one or more of whom is domiciled in a Contracting State, have agreed that a court or the courts of a Contracting State are to have jurisdiction

---

95   [2000] 2 Lloyd's Rep 423.

> to settle any disputes which have arisen or which may arise in connection with a particular legal relationship, that court or those courts shall have exclusive jurisdiction. Such an agreement conferring jurisdiction shall be either: (a) in writing or evidenced in writing, or (b) in a form which accords with practices which the parties have established between themselves, or (c) in international trade or commerce in a form which accords with a usage … in such a trade …
>
> Where such an agreements is concluded by parties, none of whom is domiciled in a Contracting State, the courts of other Contracting States shall have no jurisdiction over their disputes unless the court or courts chosen have declined jurisdiction.

Although Art 17 states that the jurisdiction conferred in accordance with the requirements set out in the article is exclusive, the position has been unclear as to whether such jurisdiction is mandatory,[96] in a sense of having hierarchy over other jurisdiction bases, except Art 16.

English courts have held that the answer depends on the construction of the jurisdiction agreement. In determining this issue, the court asks the following questions: (a) did the parties intend to resolve their disputes in the chosen court?; (b) does the particular dispute fall within the scope of the parties' clause?; (c) have the formal requirements of Art 17 been fulfilled? If the answers to these questions are affirmative, the chosen court has exclusive jurisdiction by reason of Art 17. In other words, if in the context of the particular contract the clause obliges the parties to resort to the relevant jurisdiction, it will be exclusive, irrespective of whether or not the word 'exclusive' is used. So, was held by the Court of Appeal in *Sohio Supply Co v Gatoil USA*.[97] However, Staughton LJ observed that in some types of contracts, such as insurance policies, there is a reason for providing for non-exclusive jurisdiction. It will be seen from the contrast of the following insurance cases that the answer depends on the context of the particular case.

Berisford v New Hampshire[98]

The case concerned a dispute which arose out of two insurance policies taken out by the first plaintiffs (a UK parent company) with the London office of the defendants (insurers, who were incorporated in the USA) through London brokers for the benefit of the second plaintiff (a subsidiary of the first, being incorporated in New York). One policy was made in the usual form used by the Institute of London Underwriters incorporating the Institute Cargo Clauses (A) and expressly bore on its face the words 'This insurance is subject to English jurisdiction'. The other policy covered fidelity risks and there was

---

96 The court held in a recent case, *Lafarge Plasterboard Ltd v Fritz Peters & Co KG* [2000] 2 Lloyd's Rep 689, that the jurisdiction under Art 17 is mandatory if its requirements are fulfilled.

97 [1989] 1 Lloyd's Rep 588 (CA). (See Chapter 7, below.)

98 [1990] 1 Lloyd's Rep 454.

no jurisdiction clause. The second plaintiffs had been the victims of a series of thefts at their premises and claimed under the policies in England. The defendants applied for a stay of the action on the ground that the courts of New York were the appropriate forum. The issues before the court were: (a) whether the jurisdiction clause was an exclusive jurisdiction clause or merely a permissive one; (b) if there was no exclusive jurisdiction clause, whether the provisions of the Convention had any application; and (c) whether the action should be stayed. Was the clause one that on its true construction obliged the parties to resort to the relevant jurisdiction irrespective of whether the word 'exclusive' is used. According to Hobhouse J:

> In the present case, in my judgment, the words used are inapt to create any obligation. If an obligation was intended it could easily have been so stated in clear words ... Under English law where a contract has been placed through brokers it will be very rare indeed that an underwriter will ever have to start an action against an assured. The primary relevance of the clause must be for actions to be brought by the assured against the underwriter. To construe this wording as requiring the assured to sue only in England is to go beyond the natural meaning of the words actually used. Further, to construe the words as declaratory is not to deprive them of significance. It is a statement to the assured, who may be foreign, that the rights that he has under the policy are capable of enforcement in the English courts. Such is an apt interpretation having regard to the legal and commercial relationships created by the document and having regard to the words actually used. Such a clause, even though creating no obligation to sue only in England is a contractual acknowledgment of the jurisdiction of the English courts and a contractual agreement to the invocation of that jurisdiction.[99]

Hobhouse J (as he then was) concluded that the clause was not an exclusive jurisdiction clause. Relying on Art 8, which provides for jurisdiction also of the place where an agency of the insurer is established, he decided that the defendants were deemed to be domiciled in England.

The following case is to be contrasted insofar as the construction of Art 17 is concerned.

Denby v Hellenic Mediterranean Lines[100]

Greek ferryowners took out insurance in the London market against the risk of cancellations of bookings on their ferries, which operated between Greece and Italy. The contract form contained an English jurisdiction clause. The ferryowners brought proceedings under the insurance contract in the Greek court claiming losses arising out of alleged cancellations. The insurers sought to avoid the insurance for misrepresentation and claimed a declaration from the English court that they were entitled to avoid the insurance.

---

99 [1990] 1 Lloyd's Rep 454, p 458.
100 [1994] 1 Lloyd's Rep 320.

The ferryowners applied to stay, dismiss or adjourn the English proceedings in favour of the proceedings commenced by them in Greece. The question was whether the clause in the insurance policy was a jurisdiction clause, which under Art 17 of the Convention amounted to an agreement for exclusive jurisdiction in England. It was held that the slip signed by the underwriters was clearly an agreement in writing or evidenced in writing for such a jurisdiction clause. Article 17 was a self-contained code for deciding whether the parties had, or had not, agreed upon a jurisdiction clause for the purposes of that article. Therefore, the English court had exclusive jurisdiction for claims under this contract for which the ferryowners sued the insurers in Greece. It was also held that Art 17 took precedence over Arts 21 and 22 in all situations, including a situation where the question of there being exclusive jurisdiction under Art 17 was in itself in dispute.

The reasoning of this decision has been preferred in subsequent cases. The *Berisford* case could perhaps be distinguished bearing in mind the fact that there were two insurance contracts, one of which provided for jurisdiction in England and the other did not at all. In the context of those contracts, an inference was drawn that the parties had agreed an optional as opposed to an exclusive jurisdiction.

5.2 Why is the status of Art 17 important?

It is important because were it to have the same status as Art 16, it would not come within the *lis pendens* provisions of Art 21 and 22. A problem of construction, however, exists: if, under the scheme of the Convention, Art 17 was to be regarded as having the same status as Art 16, then it ought to have been mentioned in **Art 19** which states:

> Where a court of a Contracting State is seised of a claim which is primarily concerned with a matter over which the courts of another Contracting State have exclusive jurisdiction by virtue of Art 16, it shall declare of its own motion that it has no jurisdiction.

The new Regulation in Art 25, the equivalent to Art 19, states the same. It would make matters easier, however, if the equivalent article to Art 17 (Art 23) was included in Art 25, bearing in mind that it will have the effect of exclusive jurisdiction. An explanation for this omission, however, may be that the ultimate exclusivity of jurisdiction under Art 23 will depend on the parties' agreement.

The following case was the first to determine that Art 17 took precedence over Art 21, so the issue whether the second seised court (if it is the court agreed upon by the parties) would have to stay or decline its proceedings in favour of the first seised did not arise.

Kloeckner v Gatoil[101]

Both the plaintiffs and the defendants entered into 'book out' contracts in respect of purchase and sales of North Sea crude oil. A large number of purchase and sale agreements were booked out and the plaintiffs submitted invoices for the sums due, which remained unpaid. An exclusive jurisdiction clause provided that the book out agreements shall be subject to the exclusive jurisdiction of the English courts

Further such contracts were entered into between the parties but they were never booked out. In the meantime the price of oil fell sharply and the defendants (Gatoil) failed to pay the sums due. The plaintiffs terminated the contracts and issued proceedings in the English court on 23 November 1988 pursuant to the jurisdiction agreement. They obtained leave to serve the writ out of the jurisdiction and served it on 30 January 1989. In the meantime, the defendants had filed a claim in the German court for a declaration that they were not be liable to the plaintiffs and had served the same upon the plaintiffs on 30 November 1988. They, therefore, challenged the English jurisdiction on the ground that the German court had been seised first. The plaintiffs contended that Arts 21 and 22 were irrelevant because the English courts had exclusive jurisdiction. Hirst J agreed with the plaintiffs' contention and with respect to the interrelationship between Arts 17 and 21 held that:

> Undoubtedly, under Art 21 the priority accorded to the court first seised is important in order to avoid conflicting decisions and to simplify the formalities governing the reciprocal recognition and enforcement of judgments. Equally important, however, is the exclusivity under Arts 16 and 17 of a specified court's jurisdiction ... I do not think it appropriate to downgrade those two articles in favour of Art 21. The absence of any exception in Art 21 does not in my judgment carry great weight when considering a European instrument like the convention ... In my judgment a court with alleged exclusive jurisdiction under Art 16 or 17 must be free itself to examine whether it has exclusive jurisdiction under one or other of those articles, since otherwise it would be sufficient for one of the parties to claim that the contract allegedly according exclusive jurisdiction did not exist, thus depriving this part of the Convention of legal effect.[102]

He, therefore, held that he was free under Art 17 to consider the validity of the English exclusive jurisdiction clause and, if valid, to allow any claims that were covered by it.

The conclusion reached by Hirst J was later approved by the Court of Appeal in the following case in which it was confirmed that if there is an exclusive jurisdiction clause, then Art 17 will override the priority provision

---

101 [1990] 1 Lloyd's Rep 177.
102 *Ibid*, p 195.

in favour of the court first seised[103] and, provided there is no submission to jurisdiction by the defendant pursuant to Art 18, the issue of a stay under Art 21 or 22 will not arise. If it were otherwise, a party to a choice of jurisdiction could frustrate the agreement by bringing contrary proceedings.

Continental Bank v Aeakos Naviera SA[104]

The plaintiff, an American bank with an office in Greece, granted a secured loan facility to the defendant borrowers, who gave to the bank an assignment of freights, other earnings and also a mortgage over the vessel. The loan agreement provided that: 'this agreement shall be governed by and construed in accordance with English law.' It also contained a jurisdiction agreement in the following terms:

> Each of the borrowers ... hereby irrevocably submits to the jurisdiction of the English courts ... but the bank reserves the right to proceed under this agreement in the court of any other country claiming or having jurisdiction in respect thereof.

The borrowers defaulted in repayment of instalments and entered into a rescheduling agreement, which was also made subject to English jurisdiction. Upon further default by the borrowers, the bank claimed the total sums due. On 20 November 1990, the borrowers commenced an action for damages in Greece against the bank claiming that the bank had exercised its rights under the agreement contrary to business morality. The bank issued a writ in England against the borrowers and the guarantors on 4 October 1991 and sought an injunction to restrain the borrowers from continuing the Greek proceedings on the ground of breach of the jurisdiction agreement. In the bank's submission, the jurisdiction clause conferred exclusive jurisdiction on the English courts to try the relevant disputes. The borrowers sought an order that the bank's writ and claim be struck out, or, alternatively, the action should be stayed under Art 21 or 22 of the Convention. The trial judge refused the borrowers' application to strike out the English action. On appeal to the Court of Appeal, it was held that the jurisdiction clause evidenced a clear intention that the borrowers, but not the bank would be obliged to submit disputes in connection with the loan facility to the English courts. Steyn LJ stated:

> In construing the Brussels Convention it is important to put aside pre-conceptions based on traditional English rules. The convention is a radical new regime governing the international legal relationships of the Contracting States. It is intended to eliminate obstacles to the functioning of the common market and to further the evolution of a vast single market: *Jennard Report*

---

103 A court of a Contracting State may be seised first if one party to the agreement brings proceedings in a court of another Contracting State and jurisdiction is based on another Convention ground (which is not mandatory, as is under Art 16).

104 [1994] 1 Lloyd's Rep 505.

(1979) (OJ C59/19). The genesis of the convention is the jurisprudence of the civil law rather than the common law. Since the original states were civil law countries, and the UK played no role in the drafting of the Brussels Convention, this is hardly surprising. Traditionally, English courts assert a discretion to enjoin a party by injunction from pursuing foreign legal proceedings in breach of an exclusive jurisdiction clause. The idea that a national court has discretion in the exercise of its jurisdiction does not generally exist in civilian systems:[105] *Schlosser Report* (1979) (22 OJ C59/97, para 76). Article 17 follows the civilian approach. Article 17 has a mandatory effect. When Art 17 applies it follows that the jurisdiction agreement prorogates (confers) jurisdiction on the courts of the Contracting State chosen by the parties, and that the jurisdiction agreement deprives the courts of other Contracting States of jurisdiction. Indeed, it is the duty of the courts of other Contracting States of their own motion to consider whether Art 17 applies and to decline jurisdiction if it does; *Schlosser Report*, para 22. There is no discretionary power in the Convention itself to override the conclusive effect of an exclusive jurisdiction agreement, which conforms with the requirements of Art 17. It follows that, if Art 17 applies, its provisions take precedence over the provisions of Arts 21 and 22. The structure and logic of the Convention convincingly points to this conclusion.[106]

It was held that since there was an exclusive jurisdiction clause in this case, the English court had exclusive jurisdiction and by virtue of Art 17[107] the Greek courts had been deprived of jurisdiction. The question of a stay under Arts 21 and 22 did not arise.

5.3 Is there a conflict between Arts 57 and 17?

From the foregoing, it could be inferred that there should be no conflict, if the court seised by virtue of Art 57 followed the guidelines of the Court of Appeal in the previous case, *Continental Bank v Aeakos*. In support of this proposal, it is important to examine closely the requirements for the application of Art 17, which are part of the consideration whether its jurisdiction is exclusive, before considering how the English court has dealt with the issue of possible conflict between Art 17 and 57.

---

105 Steyn LJ had also had ample experience of a civil law system when practising as an advocate for many years in the Republic of South Africa.

106 [1994] 1 Lloyd's Rep 505, pp 510–11.

107 The ECJ, in a case concerning an insurance dispute, did not expressly deal with whether Art 17 is included in the concept of exclusive jurisdiction. In the court's view, exclusive jurisdiction was regarded to be the only exception to the obligation normally imposed by Art 21 upon the court second seised: *Overseas Union v New Hampshire* [1992] 1 Lloyd's Rep 204.

5.3.1 When does jurisdiction under Art 17 apply?

As was mentioned earlier (para 5.1), the third factor the court takes into account in deciding whether the jurisdiction under Article 17 is exclusive (in addition to the intention of the parties and whether the dispute falls within the scope of the parties' agreement), is the fulfilment of the following requirements, which are stated in Art 17: (a) if there is a valid agreement between the parties which must be in the form prescribed therein; (b) if, at least, one of the parties is domiciled in a Contracting State (if none is so domiciled, the courts of other Contracting States shall have no jurisdiction over the dispute unless the chosen court has declined jurisdiction); (c) if a court of a Contracting State is the parties' chosen jurisdiction.

Adrian Briggs[108] suggests that: 'Art 17 is slightly misleading when it describes the chosen court as having exclusive jurisdiction;[109] all it does is to exclude the jurisdiction, based upon rules lower in the hierarchy, of courts which would otherwise have had it. It does not operate to confer a jurisdiction, which prevails over those provisions previously discussed.' Such provisions referred to by the author were Art 16 and submission to the court of another Contracting State. It follows that, save for Art 16 and 18, Art 17 is higher in hierarchy than other jurisdiction bases of the convention rules.

In a fairly recent decision, however, *The Bergen* (below) Clarke J (as he then was) held that, when the jurisdiction of the English court was founded on Art 7 of the Arrest Convention, which is brought in through Art 57, it prevailed over Art 17 because Art 17 did not apply to deprive the court of jurisdiction, which it had.

The Bergen[110]

Article 57 is set out here again:

> This Convention shall not affect any Conventions to which the Contracting States are or will be parties and which, in relation to particular matters, govern jurisdiction or the recognition or the enforcement of judgments.

And Art 57(2):

> This Convention shall not prevent a court of a Contracting State which is party to a Convention referred to above from assuming jurisdiction in accordance with that Convention, even where the defendant is domiciled in a Contracting State which is not a party to that Convention.

The plaintiffs were the owners of a cargo of wood carried on the defendants' vessel, B, from the USA to Scotland. The bills of lading incorporated the

---

108 *Op cit*, Briggs and Rees, fn 5, para 2.82.
109 That explains the reason why the new provision in the amending Regulation (mentioned earlier) was needed to clarify the position.
110 [1997] 1 Lloyd's Rep 380.

Hague Rules and the jurisdiction clause provided that any dispute arising would be decided in the courts of the carrier's principal place of business, which, in this case, was Germany. The plaintiffs arrested the vessel in England and brought a claim for alleged loss and damage to the cargo. The defendants challenged the jurisdiction of the English court by virtue of Art 17 of the Brussels Convention relying on the exclusive jurisdiction clause. The plaintiffs contended that Art 17 had no application because the English court was seised with jurisdiction as was permitted by Art 57. Clarke J held:

> Article 7 of the Arrest Convention is preserved by Art 57 of the Brussels Convention. It confers jurisdiction upon the courts of the State in which the arrest is made to determine the case upon its merits in accordance with the domestic law of that state. In the instant case the vessel was properly served and arrested in England. It follows that the English court has jurisdiction to determine the plaintiff's claim on the merits in accordance with English domestic law. As so far understood the position under English domestic law is that the court retains jurisdiction ... even in case where there is an exclusive jurisdiction clause which provides for the determination of the dispute in a foreign court, but the court has a discretion to stay the action, which it will exercise unless strong cause why it should not do so is shown ...
>
> If Art 17 applies and is relied upon, the court will be bound to hold that it has no jurisdiction and will have no such discretion. In that event, the court would not be applying English domestic law in accordance with Art 7 of the Arrest Convention.
>
> It follows that in the absence of authority I would conclude that the plaintiffs are right in their submission that there is a conflict between Art 17 of the Brussels Convention and Art 7 of the Arrest Convention and that, by reason of Art 57 of the Brussels Convention, Art 7 must prevail. That conclusion seems to me to follow logically from the express provisions of Art 57(2).[111]

And he held further:

> The effect of Art 17, where it applies, is ... to deprive the court of original jurisdiction. Accordingly, its effect is not that another court must decline to exercise jurisdiction which it otherwise has, as is the case under Art 21, but that it must decline jurisdiction on the ground that it never had it.[112]

Although the judge accepted that he was bound by the court of Appeal decision in *The Aeakos* (see above), where it was emphasised that Art 17, when it applied, deprives a court of another Contracting State of jurisdiction, he concluded that Art 17 did not apply because the English court had jurisdiction by virtue of Art 7 of the Arrest Convention.

Accepting the plaintiffs' submission that there was a conflict between the Arrest Convention and Art 17, he regarded that the Arrest Convention should take priority by virtue of Art 57(2) for, if it were otherwise, Art 17 would

---

111 [1997] 1 Lloyd's Rep 380, p 383.
112 *Ibid*, p 387.

deprive the court's jurisdiction, which it had pursuant to Art 7. He placed no significance to the submission of the defendants based on *The Maciej Rataj* that Art 57 must be understood as precluding the application of other provisions of the Brussels Convention only when the issue in question is governed by the special convention brought in through Art 57. For example, the Arrest Convention by which the jurisdiction of the English court is invoked does not govern what is to occur when the parties to a maritime claim had already agreed to submit their claims to the jurisdiction of another court. Regardless of this submission, the judge thought that for Art 17 to prevail, the precondition was that the English court had no jurisdiction, which – in the situation before him – it had by virtue of Art 7 of the Arrest Convention brought in through a Convention jurisdiction base, that is, Art 57.

The decision may be criticised on the following grounds.

The judge applied the general principles under English law of staying an action by virtue of a breach of a foreign jurisdiction clause,[113] in which the court has discretion, although he accepted that if Art 17 applied the court would not have such a discretion.

He did not apply the guidelines of the Court of Appeal in *Sohio Supply Co v Gatoil* (see Chapter 7) and in *The Aeakos*, in which it was held that Art 17 has a mandatory effect in relation to other non-mandatory convention provisions. Article 57(2) does not state that it shall have an overriding effect even upon the exclusive jurisdiction provisions of the Brussels Convention, but only over Arts 2 and 3. If it were otherwise, there would be a danger that a party to an exclusive jurisdiction agreement would be allowed by the Convention itself to override Art 17 by pre-emptively arresting a ship in England.

In a reverse situation where, in a recent case, *OT Africa Line v Hijazy*,[114] there was an English jurisdiction clause within the scope of Art 17, Aikens J, following the guidelines of *The Aeakos*, held that Art 17 took precedence over Art 21 and, although the English court was second seised, it did not have to stay its proceedings in favour of the first seised Belgian court.

To overcome the difficulty of a possible conflict between the Arrest Convention (Art 7) and Art 17, it is suggested that, when the parties have chosen the jurisdiction for their disputes, the function of the arrest should be limited to obtaining security for the claim rather than founding jurisdiction on the merits.[115] Support for this proposition is gained, first, from the Arrest Convention itself, under which the arrest has two separate functions: namely, it operates as a means of obtaining security for a claim, or establishing jurisdiction, if the domestic law of the country of the arrest allows it. English

---

113 See the second sentence of the first paragraph of the quotation cited above.

114 [2001] 1 Lloyd's Rep 76; see, also, Chapter 7.

115 A suggestion on similar lines has been made by another author as well: Siig, K, 'Maritime jurisdiction agreements in the EU' [1997] LMCLQ 362.

law allows it, but English law also includes the jurisdictional rules imposed by the Brussels Convention. Second, as far as English law is concerned, further support is found in s 26 of the CJJA 1982, which provides for a stay or dismissal of proceedings, while preserving the security, when a dispute has been agreed to be referred to arbitration, or is submitted for adjudication on the merits to another court either in the UK or overseas.

Ironically, in the runner up to *Bergen (No 1)*, *The Bergen (No 2)*,[116] the same judge arrived at a conclusion, which he ought to have arrived at in the *(No 1)* case, had he accepted that Art 17 applied in the first place. In *Bergen (No 2)* he stayed the English proceedings in favour of the agreed forum, Germany, despite the fact that the claim had become time barred there. He based his decision on *The El Amria* case and *forum non-conveniens* principles, which, strictly speaking, do not apply within the ECJCs, except only in limited circumstances (see para 4, above).

6 AN OVERVIEW OF REMEDIES FOR BREACH OF JURISDICTION AGREEMENTS

As a general rule under English law, when parties to a contract have agreed to refer their disputes to the court or tribunal of their choice, they must be held to their bargain, unless they subsequently agree to vary the agreement or there is a waiver. In the event of breach of that agreement, there are three types of remedies to be obtained by the aggrieved party. He may apply for an order that the English court: (a) stays its proceedings or declines jurisdiction when there is a foreign jurisdiction clause, or arbitration; or (b) issues an anti-suit injunction, if foreign proceedings have commenced in breach of an English jurisdiction clause, or arbitration; or (c) awards damages arising from the breach of the jurisdiction agreement.[117]

The third remedy for breach of a jurisdiction agreement, that is, damages, is not really an effective remedy in practice as the English court has held (see Chapter 7).

The second type of remedy, anti-suit injunctions, is examined generally in Chapter 7, exploring the attitude of the English courts in two different situations: first, when foreign proceedings are brought in breach of an English jurisdiction agreement ('the breach of contract cases') and, second, when foreign proceedings are brought when there is no breach of contract, but there may be questions of the suitability of the forum for the particular case ('the non-contract cases').

---

116 [1997] 2 Lloyd's Rep 710.

117 *The Atlantic Emperor (No 2)* [1992] 1 Lloyd's Rep 624, pp 633–34, in which it was held that an award for damages is not an effective remedy; see, also, *OT Africa Line Ltd v Hijazy (The Kribi)* [2001] 1 Lloyd's Rep 76.

It has been seen in Chapter 5, paras 3.4 and 3.5, above, how the court approaches an application for a stay of English proceedings in cases of breach of a foreign jurisdiction agreement, which is outside the scope of the Brussels Convention, or an arbitration agreement. In the previous paragraph, it was discussed how the courts have approached the issue of breach of a jurisdiction agreement to which Art 17 of the Brussels Convention applies. It should be noted that different principles apply to each category. By way of a contrast, it is emphasised here briefly that, in the case of a breach of a foreign jurisdiction agreement, which is outside the scope of the Brussels Convention, the English court has discretion whether or not to stay its proceedings. It will exercise that discretion unless a strong cause is shown not to do so.[118]

Conversely, in cases to which Art 17 of the Brussels Convention applies, there is no such discretion and a question of a stay under Arts 21 and 22 does not arise. Provided Art 17 applies (if the intention of the parties to the agreement is that the chosen court should have exclusive jurisdiction and the dispute comes within the parties' agreement), the court of a Contracting State, other than the one chosen by the parties, is expected to decline jurisdiction, even if it is seised first, unless Art 16 applies, or Art 17 has been waived by, for example, submission to the non-chosen jurisdiction pursuant to Art 18. The new Regulation by Art 23 purports to clarify the situation with regard to the status of Art 17 by emphasising that it confers exclusive jurisdiction, unless the parties agree otherwise.

In case of breach of an arbitration agreement, there is also no discretion of the court whether or not to stay its proceedings and a stay is mandatory by virtue of s 9 of the Arbitration Act 1996.[119]

Before moving to the next chapter, it is relevant to mention here that the amending Regulation to the Brussels Convention has made substantial changes with regard to recognition and enforceability of a judgment in another Member State. It is provided that a judgment should be enforced immediately (Art 41) upon completion of the formalities and the court in which the judgment is sought to be enforced is not entitled to consider any grounds for non-enforcement, but it must declare that the judgment is enforceable. Only upon appeal by the defendant can grounds of non-enforceability be considered (Arts 43 and 44). By Art 45, a declaration of enforceability shall be revoked only on grounds specified in Arts 34 and 35. Such grounds have been tightened. A judgment shall not be recognised if it is manifestly contrary to 'public policy' of the Member State in which recognition is sought. 'Default of appearance' may be a ground, but it will not be acceptable if the defendant failed to take the appropriate steps to challenge jurisdiction when it was possible for him to do so. Another important ground

---

118 *The El Amria* [1981] 2 Lloyd's Rep 119 (Chapter 5, paras 3.4.2.3 and 3.4.2.4, above).
119 See Chapter 5, para 3.5, above.

is, if the judgment is 'irreconcilable' with a judgment given in a dispute between the same parties in the Member State in which recognition is sought. In addition, there will be a ground of non-recognition if the judgment is irreconcilable with an early judgment given in another Member State, or in a third State involving the same cause of action and between the same parties, provided that the earlier judgment fulfils the conditions necessary for its recognition in the Member State addressed (Art 34). More grounds of non-recognition are provided in Art 35, which include a conflict of the judgment with certain rules of the Regulation, such as s 3, 4 or 6 of Chapter II, or with Art 72. It is also expressly stated that the test of public policy under Art 34 may not be applied to the rules relating to jurisdiction.

These provisions will be very relevant and important when a court considers whether or not to issue an anti-suit injunction, which is the subject of the next chapter.

CHAPTER 7

ANTI-SUIT INJUNCTIONS

1 UNDERLYING PRINCIPLES

Before entering into discussion of this topic, an important distinction must be made between two regimes on jurisdiction: the European Civil Jurisdiction regime and the common law system. The contradistinction was elegantly summarised in this context by Lord Goff in *Airbus v Patel* (the decision is discussed below):

> This part of the law is concerned with the resolution of clashes between jurisdictions. Two different approaches to the problem have emerged in the world today, one associated with the civil law jurisdiction of continental Europe and the other with the common law world. Each is the fruit of a distinctive legal history and also reflects, to some extent, cultural differences ... In the continent of Europe ... the essential need was seen to be to avoid any such clash between Member States ... A system, developed by distinguished scholars, was embodied in the Brussels Convention, under which jurisdiction is allocated on the basis of well defined rules. The system achieves its purpose, but at a price. The price is rigidity and rigidity can be productive of injustice. The judges of this country ... have to accept the fact that the practical results are, from time to time, unwelcome. This is, essentially, because the primary purpose of the Convention is to ensure that there shall be no clash between the jurisdictions of Member States of the Community. In the common law world, the situation is precisely the opposite. There is, so to speak, a jungle of separate, broadly based, jurisdictions all over the world ... But the potential excesses of common law jurisdictions are generally curtailed by the adoption of the principle of *forum non-conveniens*[1] – a self-denying ordinance under which the court will stay (or dismiss) proceedings in favour of another clearly more appropriate forum ... The principle is directed against cases being brought in inappropriate jurisdiction and tends to ensure that, between common law jurisdictions, cases will only be brought in a jurisdiction which is appropriate for their resolution ... It cannot, and does not aim to, avoid all clashes ... Indeed, parallel proceedings in different jurisdictions are not of themselves regarded as unacceptable. In that sense, the principle may be regarded as an imperfect weapon; but it is both flexible and practicable and, where it is effective, it produces a result which is conducive to practical justice. It is, however, dependent on the voluntary adoption of the principle by a State in question ... if one State does not adopt it, the delicate balance which the

---

1   It is of interest that it has also been adopted in Japan, whose system has largely been influenced by German law.

universal adoption of the principle could achieve will, to that extent, break down.[2]

The central question in this chapter is whether the English court has jurisdiction to restrain foreign proceedings and, if it has, what are the circumstances and the limits of such jurisdiction.

The major issues the courts have to grapple with on applications for an anti-suit injunction are whether interference with the foreign court would be justified if the injunction were regarded as impeaching the foreign sovereign's jurisdiction, or were in breach of the public policy of that State, or might be against the provisions of the Human Rights Convention.

An overview of these issues is made here, by pointing out how the court derives its jurisdiction, how the principles have developed and to what extent the jurisdiction is limited. There has been a rapid development of the law in this area and numerous cases. As the space in this book does not permit to include all the decisions, the reader is given general guidance and an opportunity for further research.

It is worthy of note that in a fairly recent decision of the Court of Appeal in *Philip Alexander Securities v Bamberger*,[3] it was held that the practice of the courts in England to grant injunctions to restrain a defendant from prosecuting proceedings in another country may now require reconsideration. The conventional view has been that such an injunction operates only *in personam*, so that the English courts do not regard and have never regarded themselves as interfering with the exercise of jurisdiction by the foreign court. Leggatt LJ raised a very important issue here and continued: 'Where the foreign court regards such injunctions as an infringement of its sovereignty and refuses to permit them to be served, the English court is in a quandary. In cases concerning the European Union, what would best meet the predicament is a directive defining the extent of the recognition, which the orders of the courts of each Member State are entitled to receive, from the courts of other Member States.'

The provisions of recognition and enforcement of judgments between Member States, as have been amended by the new Regulation, mentioned at the end of Chapter 6, may assist English courts to reconsider the exercise of their jurisdiction upon an application for an anti-suit injunction in cases concerning the European Union.

---

2   *Airbus Industrie v Patel* [1998] 1 Lloyd's Rep 631, p 636, *per* Lord Goff.
3   [1997] IL Pr 73.

2 WHEN AN ANTI-SUIT INJUNCTION CAN BE GRANTED

As explained in the previous chapter (para 6), an anti-suit injunction is one of the three remedies that may be granted when there is a breach of a jurisdiction, or an arbitration agreement, that is, a breach of a contractual right to resolve a dispute under a particular contract in the forum agreed by the parties to the contract. It may also be used to restrain a party to litigation from proceeding in a forum where, comparative to another forum, it is considered that justice may not be done.

Four broad categories of anti-suit injunctions are compared here: (i) the breach of contract cases, those concerned with a breach of a jurisdiction, or an arbitration agreement; (ii) the non-breach of contract cases, those not involving a breach; (iii) the convention allocation of jurisdiction in non-contract cases; and (iv) mixture of contract and non-contract cases.

Within the first category, however, there are further sub-categories to which a brief mention is made, after discussion of the general principles. There is no end to the long line of authorities in this area and it is not possible to refer to all. For present purposes, only leading decisions will be referred to under the broad categories, in order to identify the extent to which the principles stated have been consistently applied and whether there are any common considerations or differences between them.

2.1 The 'breach of contract' cases

2.1.1 General principles

Before the Brussels Convention was in force in the UK, the issue of an anti-suit injunction to restrain foreign proceedings in breach of an English exclusive jurisdiction clause was considered by the Court of Appeal in *The Lisboa*,[4] in which Italian proceedings had been brought. Jurisdiction to grant such an injunction was recognised if: (a) the foreign proceedings were vexatious or oppressive, in the sense that there was no ground whatever for making any claim there; and (b) the party seeking the injunction would not be adequately protected by an award in damages. On the facts of this case, the arrest of the ship in Italy, obtained for security measures, was held to be neither vexatious nor oppressive.

A few years later, it was confirmed by the House of Lords in *British Airways Board v Laker Airways Ltd*[5] that, as a general principle, an injunction could be granted if there was a legal right not to be sued in the

---

4   [1980] 2 Lloyd's Rep 546.
5   [1985] AC 58 (HL) (a non-breach of contract case).

foreign proceedings. Such a right would exist when there was an exclusive jurisdiction or a valid arbitration clause.

The reference to 'vexatious and oppressive' was made again by Staughton LJ, as he then was, in *Sohio Supply Co v Gatoil (USA) Inc*,[6] in which he held that to proceed in the foreign court in breach of a contract, which provides for an exclusive English jurisdiction, may well in itself be vexatious and oppressive in a given case.[7]

The foregoing principles were summarised by Rix J, in *The Angelic Grace*[8] (later approved by the Court of Appeal).[9] In this case (where proceedings were brought in Italy in breach of an English arbitration agreement), the court elaborated more specifically on the criteria of granting an anti-suit injunction. Such criteria must be that:

(a) the foreign proceedings are vexatious;

(b) without an injunction the defendant will be deprived of their contractual rights in a situation in which damages will be manifestly an inadequate remedy;

(c) the injunction has been sought promptly and before the foreign proceedings are too far advanced.

The principle was refined further by Clarke J in *A/S D/S Svendborg v Wansa*[10] (later approved by the Court of Appeal), which involved a breach of an English jurisdiction agreement (not being subject to the European Civil Jurisdiction Conventions (ECJC)).[11] He held that, where there is an exclusive jurisdiction clause, the parties should be held to their bargain if:

(a) the application for an injunction has been made promptly; and

(b) there exists no good reason to deny the injunction (such as delay or voluntary submission to the jurisdiction of the foreign court). The judge steered clear from the words 'vexatious and oppressive'. In addition, he clarified the meaning of 'countervailing factors' – used in *The Aeakos* case (see below) – by explaining what would constitute 'good reason' not to grant the injunction.

---

6 [1989] 2 Lloyd's Rep 588 (CA), p 592.

7 The Texan court, in this case, was not obliged to decline jurisdiction in the face of the parties' agreement to sue in England.

8 [1994] 1 Lloyd's Rep 168.

9 [1995] 1 Lloyd's Rep 87 (CA), p 96: Millet LJ said that, 'there was no good reason for diffidence in granting an injunction to restrain foreign proceedings on the clear and simple ground that the defendant has promised not to bring them'.

10 [1996] 2 Lloyd's Rep 559, p 570, affirmed [1997] 2 Lloyd's Rep 87 (CA).

11 Similarly, in *Akai v People's Insurance Co* [1998] 1 Lloyd's Rep 90, the judge was in favour of giving effect to the jurisdiction agreement by an injunction, unless to do so would be contrary to public policy.

It should also be noted that the English Court held very recently that the anti-suit injunction sought in *OT Africa Line Ltd v Hijazy*[12] was not unlawful under s 6 of the Human Rights Act 1998.

2.1.2 Breach of an arbitration agreement

In such a case, the injunction will be granted, unless there is a good reason not to do so. There is no longer great caution not to grant it, as was stated by the Court of Appeal in *The Angelic Grace*.[13]

Good reason not to grant it is narrowly interpreted under this sub-category of breach of contract cases. It could include proof that (i) the foreign court would stay execution on ground of the New York Convention on the Recognition and Enforcement of Arbitral Awards 1958;[14] or (ii) the arbitration provision in the parties' contract did not create a binding agreement to arbitrate in London;[15] or (iii) there has been submission to the foreign jurisdiction; or (iv) delay to apply for an injunction.

Sometimes the validity of an arbitration clause may be disputed by one party to it who issues proceedings at another forum. This was recently dealt with by the English court in *The XL Insurance v Owens Corning*.[16] Toulson J held that, by stipulating for arbitration in London under the provisions of the Arbitration Act 1996, the parties chose English law to govern the matters which fell within those provisions, including the formal validity of the arbitration clause and the jurisdiction of the arbitral tribunal. It is for the arbitral tribunal to rule on the validity of the agreement and its jurisdiction in the event of challenge, unless the matter is referred to the Court. He also held that, although the inconvenience to the challenging party of not being able to sue all their insurers in the same proceedings was recognised, that was a consequence of having different contracts with them and it was not a good reason for depriving the other party of its contractual rights.

He granted the injunction restraining the party who broke the putative arbitration agreement from continuing with litigation it had commenced in Delaware.

---

12 [2001] 1 Lloyd's Rep 76.

13 [1995] 1 Lloyd's Rep 87.

14 The French court was not willing to stay its proceedings in favour of the English arbitration clause in *Toepfer v Societe Cargill* [1998] 1 Lloyd's Rep 379. The question, whether the exception of Art 1.4 of the Brussels Convention extends to proceedings commenced before the English court seeking an injunction restraining the French court from continuing its proceedings and to a declaration that the French proceedings constituted a breach of the arbitration agreement, was referred to the European Court of Justice. However, the case was, in the meantime, settled.

15 *Philip Alexander Securities & Futures Ltd v Bamberger* [1997] IL Pr 73 (CA); see below.

16 [2000] 2 Lloyd's Rep 500.

For the purpose of recognition and enforcement of an anti-suit injunction in the foreign court whose jurisdiction is restrained, however, the injunction may involve an infringement of the foreign sovereignty and this poses a serious problem, particularly if the injunction is considered by that court as a violation of public policy. Such a dilemma for the issuing court is shown in the *Bamberger*[17] case and for this reason, it is important to look at its factual background.

Philip Alexander Securities & Futures Ltd v Bamberger

The dispute involved trading in futures and options by German customers who were recruited in Germany by German brokers to trade through the plaintiff (that is, the applicant for an anti-suit injunction). Liability of the plaintiff for losses in trading was incurred and the customers brought actions in various German courts. The plaintiff's defence was that the dispute should be adjudicated by arbitration in London. While the plaintiff had referred the same matter to arbitration in London and won, some of the German courts gave judgment against him. The plaintiff, therefore, sought interim injunctions and declarations from the English court to restrain the remaining actions in Germany and enforce the arbitration order. Interlocutory injunctions obtained had no effect in restraining the customers from continuing with their actions in Germany. Some German courts refused to serve the orders on the basis that there would be an interference with the German sovereignty. At first instance, Mance J thought that, although it was an appropriate case to grant an injunction, he felt that it was not appropriate to grant it at this stage of the proceedings.

The Court of Appeal held that the rules to which the agreements were subject, gave customers the right to elect to arbitrate. But, since some had not so elected, their case could only be litigated. Consequently, the arbitration agreement would be considered by a Contracting State of the New York Convention, in this case Germany, inoperative. Different factual situations can give different results.[18] It distinguished *The Angelic Grace* case on the facts in that the arbitration proceedings in London had commenced before the Italian court proceedings and the foreign parties submitted to the arbitration proceedings. The Italian proceedings were held vexatious and the Italian court would decline jurisdiction. By contrast, it was clear in this case that the German court was offended and took the view that there was no obligation to stay its proceedings under the New York Convention on the basis of the consumer laws being applied in Germany. The citizens, according to German law, had the right, as consumers, to come to German courts.

---

17 *Philip Alexander Securities & Futures Ltd v Bamberger* [1997] IL Pr 73, or [1996] CLC 1757.
18 *Alfred Toepfer International v Molino Boschi* [1996] 1 Lloyd's Rep 510.

For these reasons the Court of Appeal regarded it inappropriate to grant the anti-suit injunction.

Recognition and enforcement of injunctions, or of any conflicting judgements that might be obtained on the same matters, is a major issue for a court before it grants an anti-suit injunction. Recognition will be subject to the rule of public policy under Art 27(1) of the ECJC.[19] Leggatt LJ, in *The Bamberger* stated that, where a foreign domiciled defendant has notice of an interlocutory injunction issued in England and Wales before obtaining judgment in an action relating to the same cause of action in his home courts, the resultant foreign judgment will be unrecognisable in England under Art 27(1) of the EC Judgments Convention.

Article 34 of the new Regulation (see Chapter 6, para 6) requires a stricter test than Art 27(1); namely, for a judgment not to be recognised, it must be manifestly contrary to public policy in the Member State in which recognition is sought. What would constitute 'manifestly' contrary to public policy will be an issue for interpretation in the context of a particular case.

As public policy varies between legal systems,[20] the English courts have considered that a more universal consideration should be taken into account, such as international rules of justice, or the criterion of the interests of justice in a particular case, rather than the public policy of the foreign sovereign.[21]

It can be deduced from the foregoing that, if the arbitration agreement is determined to be valid by the tribunal which has jurisdiction and power to do so, and in such circumstances the court grants an anti-suit injunction, there should be no issue of public policy with regard to the recognition and enforcement of the injunction in the State in which it is sought to be enforced, provided the application for the injunction was made promptly and it was notified to the other party prior to obtaining judgment in the court of that State.

2.1.3 Breach of an English jurisdiction agreement

This may constitute a breach of two different types of agreement: one, which is within Art 17 of the Brussels Convention, and the other, which is outside the scope of the Convention.

With regard to a breach of Art 17 of the Brussels Convention, where the agreed jurisdiction is England, the Court of Appeal held, in *The Aeakos*,[22] that

---

19 The Court of Appeal in the *Bamberger* case did not have to decide this point because it found that the arbitration clause was not enforceable, but it thought that Art 27(1) of the ECJC would prevent its recognition if it was against public policy.

20 *Akai v People's Insurance Co* [1998] 1 Lloyd's Rep 90.

21 See para 2.7, below.

22 *Continental Bank v Aeakos Naviera SA* [1994] 1 Lloyd's Rep 505 (CA); see, also, *OT Africa Line Ltd v Hijazy* [2001] 1 Lloyd's Rep 76.

an injunction preventing the claimant from continuing the foreign proceedings is the only effective remedy for the purpose of enforcing the exclusive jurisdiction agreement. Without an injunction, the party in breach of contract will persist in his breach and the other party's rights, as enshrined in the jurisdiction agreement, will prove valueless. In the absence of special countervailing factors, this was a paradigm case for the grant of the injunction. The guidelines of this decision to be taken into account in future cases, in which the European Civil Jurisdiction Conventions apply, can be summarised as being fourfold:

(a) a clear breach of an exclusive jurisdiction agreement;
(b) damages for that breach would not be an effective remedy;
(c) there are no special countervailing factors against granting the injunction;
(d) the foreign proceedings amount to vexatious and oppressive conduct.

The same considerations are taken into account when the breach of a jurisdiction agreement is outside the scope of the Convention. The only difference between breach of a jurisdiction agreement falling within Art 17 of the Brussels Convention and a non-Art 17 agreement is that, in the former, the court has limited or no discretion not to grant it, unless there are special factors against it.

Notwithstanding such guidelines, however, questions still arose in subsequent cases with regard to identifying what would constitute 'special countervailing factors' in a particular case. The phrase was later explained by Clarke J in *Svendborg v Wansa* (see above).

Equally the phrase 'vexatious and oppressive[23] conduct' has given cause for definition in the context in which it is used (of which see later under 2.5.1).

2.1.4 Discretion of the judge in 'breach of contract' cases

Jurisdiction agreements which fall within the European jurisdiction regime are governed by special rules. English judges have viewed their jurisdiction in granting the injunction with no diffidence.[24] In cases not falling within Art 17, the English court has a wider discretion whether or not to issue an anti-suit injunction, unless there is a good reason not to do so. That discretion varies in

---

23 These terms have historically different meanings: *Societe Nationale Industries Aerospatiale v Lee Kui Jak* [1987] 1 AC 871 (PC). In *Airbus Industrie v Patel* [1998] 1 Lloyd's Rep 631 (HL), p 637, Lord Goff was inclined to accept the formulation of the principle with regard to injunction jurisdiction based 'simply on the ends of justice' and without reference to vexation or oppression (as the Supreme Court of Canada did in *Amchem Products Inc v Workers' Compensation Board* [1993] 102 DLR (4th) 96).

24 The courts of other Contracting States to the ECJCs are not familiar with the concept of anti-suit injunctions. In the event of breach of a jurisdiction agreement under Art 17, the rules of the Convention provide guidance for the courts of contracting States, as has been seen in Chapter 6.

degree depending on the circumstances of a case. For example, in arbitration cases, the judge will be less cautious in granting it and he has limited discretion not to grant it. In all other cases of breach of an English jurisdiction clause, the discretion not to grant it is wider and caution will be exercised not to interfere with the foreign court's sovereignty. 'Good reason' will be construed widely.

2.2 The 'non-breach of contract' cases and anti-suit injunctions
(requirement of sufficient interest or connection)

While, in the breach of contract category, the courts have taken a robust view for the purpose of holding the parties to their bargain, in the non-breach of contract cases, the issue of interference with foreign courts has been an acute problem, as the examples of cases discussed later will show.

The broad principle underlying the jurisdiction of a court to grant an anti-suit injunction under this category is that it is to be exercised when the ends of justice require it. However, in exercising its jurisdiction, the court must pay regard to comity and so, the jurisdiction is one which must be exercised with great caution.[25] Thus, the jurisdiction of the court is limited by the respect that should be shown to the jurisdiction of other foreign courts, but the ultimate aim is to serve the ends of justice, so that, in certain cases, an interference with foreign courts may be justified.

How this broad principle can be applied was analysed by Lord Goff, in *Airbus Industrie v Patel*,[26] who drew together principles from previous cases; in particular, from his decision in *Societe Nationale Industries Aerospatiale v Lee Kui Jak*,[27] and the Canadian decision, *Amchem Products Inc v Workers Compensation Board*.[28]

2.2.1 Historical overview

Prior to the *Aerospatiale* case, there were two House of Lords decisions on anti-suit injunctions[29] of this category which had determined the issue on the basis of *forum non-conveniens* principles, but the jurisdiction was exercised with caution. The doctrine of *forum non-conveniens* applied only if there were two alternative fora having jurisdiction for a particular claim, one of which was England. But different criteria applied where there was only a single forum, which was a foreign court, with competent jurisdiction to determine the merits of a particular claim. In a case of a single forum, Lord Scarman said in

---

25 *Airbus Industrie v Patel* [1998] 1 Lloyd's Rep 631, p 637, *per* Lord Goff.
26 *Ibid.*
27 [1987] 1 AC 871 (PC).
28 [1993] 102 DLR (4th) 96.
29 *Castano v Brown & Root* [1981] AC 557 and *BA v Laker Airways* [1985] AC 58.

BA v Laker,[30] the English court would only interfere to restrain the foreign proceedings, if the conduct of the claimant was so unconscionable and unjust that, in accordance with English principles of a 'wide and flexible' equity, such conduct could be seen to be an infringement of an equitable right of the applicant. This equitable right not to be sued abroad, he said, arose only if the inequity was such that the English court ought to intervene to prevent injustice. He further said that such cases of anti-suit injunction must be few, because the court should be guided by caution.

In *BA v Laker* (a single forum case), Laker had sued BA in the US courts for protection of their trading interests. An anti-suit injunction, applied for in the English court by BA to restrain those proceedings, was refused because Laker's conduct was not unconscionable and their action could not, in any event, be justiciable in England.

On the other hand, the *Aerospatiale* case belonged to the 'alternative fora' sub-category of the non-contract cases. It is important to summarise the facts of this case for the sake of comparison with the *Patel* case (later), which set the general principle.

Societe Nationale Industries Aerospatiale v Lee Kui Jak

A helicopter, which had been built in France and was operated and serviced by a Malaysian company, crashed at Brunei and a businessman was killed. His widow sued both the Malaysian company and the French manufacturer in the court of Brunei. In addition, she sued the French manufacturers in France (where the action was later discontinued) and, also, sued both defendants in Texas, under the law of which punitive damages and strict liability apply. The Texas court had jurisdiction over the manufacturers because they carried on business there. The widow's action against the Malaysian company in Brunei was settled eventually, but the French manufacturers issued a contribution notice on the Malaysian company in Brunei. The French manufacturers accepted service of a writ issued in Brunei by the owners and insurers of the helicopter seeking an indemnity. In the meantime, their application to the Texas court for a stay in favour of Brunei on the ground of *forum non-conveniens* was dismissed, despite their undertaking to protect the rights of the plaintiff – which she would have if the action continued in Texas. But the widow had also agreed that she would not pursue punitive damages and strict liability in Texas. In these circumstances, the Court of Appeal of Brunei dismissed the appeal by the French against the refusal by the lower court to grant an anti-suit injunction and held that the Texas court had become the natural forum, having regard to the advancement of the proceedings there.

---

30 [1985] AC 58, p95.

On appeal to the Privy Council,[31] Lord Goff, examining the historical development of the court's jurisdiction with regard to anti-suit injunctions, dismissed the application of *forum non-conveniens* principle to the determination of whether or not an anti-suit injunction should be granted, which he thought to be appropriate only to applications for a stay of proceedings. His reasons were twofold: (i) if *forum non-conveniens* principles were applied, there would be a risk that the English court could arrogate jurisdiction only on the basis of England being the natural forum; and (ii) the injunction would indirectly terminate the jurisdiction of the foreign court and the mere fact that Brunei was the natural forum was not enough, of itself, to justify the grant of an injunction. It would only be granted, he said, to prevent injustice, which, in the context of this case, meant that the Texas proceedings must be shown to be vexatious or oppressive.

The elements of vexation or oppression, however, had in this case been neutralised by the plaintiff's agreement not to pursue punitive damages or strict liability in Texas. On the other hand, the fact that the defendant had undertaken to preserve the rights of the plaintiff (obtainable in Texas) in the Brunei proceedings was a factor in favour of Brunei. Therefore, since the advantage the plaintiff would have had in Texas would have been maintained in Brunei, a possible element of injustice to her had been eliminated.

At the end, the most important factors in favour of granting the injunction against Texas proceedings were the claims for contribution and indemnity brought in Brunei. Had the Texas proceedings continued, there would have been multiplicity of actions, which would have to be brought separately for the enforcement of contribution rights sought by the defendants and the indemnity action against the defendants, the French manufacturers. For this reason the injunction was granted.

2.2.2 The new formula – stricter approach having regard to comity

It was Lord Goff again in the next case, *Airbus v Patel*, who clarified the principle with regard to alternative fora cases, as he had previously formulated it in the *Aerospatiale* case. For the first time, he imposed limitations to the granting of the injunction on both categories, alternative fora and single forum cases, on grounds of comity.

2.2.2.1 Brief facts of Airbus v Patel[32]

The aeroplane in this case belonged to Indian Airlines, which flew from Bombay to Bangalore, struck the ground and caught fire on landing at destination. Ninety-two passengers died. The London families of British

---

31   [1987] 1 AC 871.
32   [1998] 1 Lloyd's Rep 631.

citizens carried on board, four of whom died and four who were injured, sued Airbus in Texas. The defendants sought an injunction from the English court to restrain those proceedings on the ground that they were vexatious and oppressive. Colman J refused to grant it. The Court of Appeal granted it, mainly because India was the natural forum. Applying *forum non-conveniens* principles, it regarded Texas as a non-appropriate forum. *Forum non-conveniens* doctrine is not recognised in Texas.

The House of Lords reversed the decision of the Court of Appeal on the basis of the new formula, discussed below.

2.2.2.2 *Airbus v Patel (general principle)*

There is one general non-rigid rule applicable to both, the alternative fora and the single forum cases: namely (a) there must be a sufficient interest or connection between the action and England for an intervention with the foreign court by an anti-suit injunction to be considered (the comity requirement); and (b) such an intervention must be for the ends of justice.[33]

The approach with regard to 'comity' is different in each sub-category. In particular:

(a) in the 'alternative fora' cases, where England is the natural forum and the jurisdiction of a foreign court has been invoked, there is sufficient interest to justify an intervention by the English court in order to protect its jurisdiction. On this basis, there would be no infringement of comity. Thus, the court will examine only whether the interests of justice are served, taking into account the claimant's advantage there and the possible loss of advantage of the defendant in the natural forum. It will also consider whether any possible oppression in the foreign court was neutralised. It will seek to ascertain what the foreign court will be likely to do. Would the foreign court stay its proceedings itself observing judicial comity?;

(b) in the 'single forum' cases, where there is only one foreign court having jurisdiction, but the jurisdiction of another foreign court is invoked, the question for the English court when an application for an anti-suit injunction is made is this: could the English court be asked to guard the jurisdiction of the single forum by issuing an anti-suit injunction? In this situation, the role of comity has been prominent. At first glance, an intervention by the English court would be inconsistent with comity. The court will proceed in two stages. At the first stage, it will examine whether there is sufficient interest or connection with England, which warrants the court's intervention for the ends of justice. Such a

---

33 Generally speaking, Lord Goff said, injustice can occur when the foreign proceedings are vexatious and oppressive and, as he had said in the *Aerospatiale* case, these terms, historically, have had different meanings. From the tenor of his judgment in the *Airbus* case, however, he seemed to prefer no reference to these terms.

connection could be established if the transaction was made here,[34] or there were grounds of public policy. If there is no connection or sufficient interest, the matter will be closed at the first stage by refusing the injunction. If, on the other hand, there was such a connection, the comity requirement would be satisfied, as it would be if England was the natural forum in the 'alternative fora' cases. Then, the court will proceed to the second stage, during which it will examine whether the foreign proceedings against which the injunction was sought were oppressive. If they were, an injunction would be granted because to allow them to continue would be against the ends of justice.[35]

2.3 Jurisdiction allocated by a convention and anti-suit injunctions (in 'non-contract' cases)

An interesting case on this issue was *The Deaville v Aeroflot Russian International Airlines*.[36] It involved a jurisdiction base provided by the Warsaw Convention 1929, as amended by the Hague Protocol 1955. In determining whether or not the injunction should be granted, the judge allowed comity to prevail and refused to grant the injunction against the French proceedings and in favour of the Convention jurisdiction.

Under the Warsaw Convention, Art 28, jurisdiction was allocated to either Russia or England or Hong Kong, that is: (a) where the carrier is ordinarily resident or has his principal place of business; or (b) where the carrier has an establishment by which the contract for carriage was made; or (c) at the place of intended destination, respectively. An Aeroflot flight destined for Hong Kong crashed near Siberia killing all passengers and crew. The dependants of the deceased brought proceedings in France, first against the manufacturers of the plane and Aeroflot. Then, they issued proceedings in England, just to protect time against Aeroflot. Aeroflot challenged the jurisdiction of the French courts and applied here for a declaration that the plaintiffs must comply with Art 28 jurisdiction and, since France was not one such jurisdiction, they also applied for an anti-suit injunction.

The determining factor for the deputy judge, Brice QC, to decide against granting the injunction was that the manufacturers were French and the Warsaw Convention was silent when a claim was not only against the carrier, but also against the manufacturers. While he recognised that the only jurisdiction against the carrier should be as allocated by Art 28, and also that by virtue of Art 57 of the ECJC, the English court was not compelled to decline its jurisdiction, he exercised his discretion against granting the anti-suit

---

34 *Midland Bank plc v Laker Airways Ltd* [1986] QB 689.
35 These approaches are inferred from the conclusion of the analysis by Lord Goff, [1998] 1 Lloyd's Rep 631, p 642.
36 [1997] 2 Lloyd's Rep 67.

injunction for reasons of comity towards the French court. It was more appropriate, he said, to let the French court determine its own jurisdiction than for the English court to make an order preventing some claimants from participating in those proceedings. He placed reliance on the principle that, unless there was a manifest injustice or breach of international law, the foreign court was entitled to give effect to the policies of its own legislation. Comity required a policy of non-intervention.[37]

2.4 Mixture of 'contract' and 'non-contract' cases

A good example of this final category is *Bouygues v Caspian (sub nom BOS-400).*[38] It is a paradigm case of numerous proceedings and court orders, which were issued in two jurisdictions. The battle to maintain English jurisdiction must, undoubtedly, have resulted in wasted legal costs. Hopefully, in the future this will be an example to litigants how to manage legal risks in a more cautious way. It is worth summarising the facts.

BOS-400

By a towage contract, Bouygues, a French company and owners of the tow, *BOS-400*, engaged the services of the tug, *Tigr*, owned by Caspian, a Russian company. The tug was under time charter to Ultisol, which was managed by a Dutch company. As the tow was approaching Cape Town, the tow lines parted in stormy conditions and it was driven ashore to the rocks becoming a total loss. Bouygues claimed damages against Ultisol, Caspian and the Cape Town port authority, Portner. Proceedings were brought in both England and South Africa. Since, in the towage contract, Bouygues and Ultisol had agreed English jurisdiction, an injunction was granted by Clarke J to Ultisol restraining Bouygues from proceeding in South Africa, while such an injunction was refused to Caspian by Morison J. Both Caspian and Ultisol issued third party notices to join Portner in the English proceedings. Colman J refused to set aside these notices on application by Portner. Rix J granted a declaration sought by Ultisol and Caspian to limit their liability in England, where the 1976 Limitation Convention is applicable, providing for a tougher test for breaking limitation, while the 1957 Convention is applicable in South Africa. Walker J refused to set aside the anti-suit injunction and to stay the limitation proceedings. There were appeals against the orders of Clarke, Colman, Rix and Walker JJ.

The Court of Appeal discharged the anti-suit injunction, set aside the joinder of Portner and stayed the liability proceedings in England, in the light of change of circumstances. Since the order had been made by Clarke J, the

---

37 *Re Maxwell Communications Corp (No 2)* [1992] BCC 757, p 765, *per* Hoffmann J.
38 [1998] 2 Lloyd's Rep 461.

action against Portner was substantially advanced in South Africa (called the Portner factor). Also, the fact that Morison J refused an anti-suit injunction to Caspian against Bouygues had radically altered the possibilities of avoiding multiplicity of proceedings, with its attendant risk of conflicting decisions. Thus, the argument that Bouygues should be kept to its contractual bargain with Utisol was counterbalanced. The anti-suit injunction against Bouygues was discharged for a good reason – widely interpreted – that was the existence of proceedings in South Africa involving the same issues and facts between parties not bound by contractual jurisdiction. The Portner factor constituted a special countervailing factor against the anti-suit injunction.

The English liability proceedings were stayed on the ground of *forum non-conveniens*, South Africa being the natural forum for the resolution of the disputes regarding liability. The limitation action, which was considered quite separate from the liability actions, was maintained in England.[39]

2.5 Are there any common considerations applicable to the various categories?

2.5.1 'Vexatious or oppressive' – an offensive element in the pursuit of justice

In most decisions, the courts have considered whether the foreign proceedings were vexatious or oppressive. Historically, since the 19th century, these terms were used in the exercise of the court's jurisdiction whether or not to grant anti-suit injunctions. But, in the context of stay of proceedings on ground of another forum being the more appropriate forum, these terms were effectively abolished by the House of Lords in the *Macshannon*[40] case. This was because of the moral connotations attached to these words and the difficulty for the defendant to prove that there was something wrong in the character of the plaintiff. Although Lord Goff explained, in the *Aerospatiale* case, that these words could have different meaning in different contexts, he was inclined, in the *Patel* case, to agree, albeit *obiter*, with Judge Sopinka in the *Amchem* case, who preferred to use, simply, 'ends of justice'. However, Lord Goff did not expressly abandon these words.

Different meaning has been given to the term 'vexatious and oppressive' by the judges in various authorities when considering whether or not to issue an anti-suit injunction, in both the contract and non-contract categories depending on the context of a particular case:

---

39 It should be noted that since this case did not fall within the ambit of the Brussels Convention, there was no prohibition in separating the limitation from the liability action.

40 *Macshannon v Rockware Glass Ltd* [1978] 1 All ER 625.

(a) in *The Angelic Grace*, it was said that it would be 'vexatious or oppressive' to allow the contract breaker to persist with the breach of contract where damages would be an inadequate remedy;

(b) in *Toepfer v Societe Cargill*,[41] it was said that it would be 'vexatious or oppressive' if the party, who was in breach of an arbitration agreement, was allowed to continue the foreign proceedings – this would be so, if that party could not prove that the foreign court would stay its proceedings under the mandatory provisions of the NY Convention 1958;

(c) in the case of both *Estonian Shipping Ltd v Wansa*[42] and *Akai PTY Ltd v People's Insurance Co Ltd*,[43] the public interest was balanced against the interest of the parties – it was explained by the court that it would be 'vexatious or oppressive', if multiple proceedings were allowed where the plaintiff resorted to the foreign court in order to evade important policies of the English jurisdiction;

(d) in the context of the Texas cases, the non-contract category, the fact that the Texas jurisdiction was so wide and extra-territorial, so as to be contrary to accepted principles of international law, was 'vexatious or oppressive';

(d) if it was shown that the claim in the foreign court was bound to fail, then the making of such a claim could be seen to be frivolous and vexatious (although a case of this kind was thought to be rare).[44]

2.5.2 The second common consideration is 'comity'

As has been shown, comity is part of the general principle limiting the jurisdiction of the court to exercise its jurisdiction by granting an anti-suit injunction in the non-contract cases. Comity has also been considered in the contract cases, in which it has been stressed that the court should exercise its discretion with caution for reasons of comity and, in *The Deaville v Aeroflot* case, where jurisdiction was allocated by convention. In cases which are within the ambit of the European jurisdiction regime, regard to comity, it is submitted, is intermingled with the rules regulating the jurisdiction of the Contracting States. In cases where there is a breach of an arbitration agreement, regard to comity is not negligible. The Court of Appeal, in *The Angelic Grace*, did not say that the question of comity was of little regard. Instead, it said that, in a straightforward case, there was little mileage in a 'ritual incantation' of the doctrine of comity as supporting a general principle that the issue should always be left, in the first instance, to the foreign court whose jurisdiction was invoked in breach of the parties' agreement.[45] In other

---

41 [1998] 1 Lloyd's Rep 379.

42 [1997] 2 Lloyd's Rep 183.

43 [1998] 1 Lloyd's Rep 90.

44 *Shell v Coral* [1999]2 Lloyd's Rep 606.

45 [1995] 1 Lloyd's Rep 87 (CA), *per* Millet LJ, p 96.

circumstances, particularly when there is a question of validity of an arbitration clause under foreign law, comity may require caution.[46]

Sometimes, however, the English courts have contradicted themselves in observing comity, as, for example, in the analogous context of the reverse case of stay of proceedings in favour of a foreign jurisdiction clause. The rule is, similarly, that stay will be granted unless there is a good cause to the contrary. Such a cause may be that there are factors establishing a sufficiently close connection with England (*The Spiliada* factors).[47] Such an approach would only be correct, it is submitted, if it was followed purely for the interests of justice, as was clearly done in the *El Amria* case, and not for reasons of jurisdictional chauvinism. The English courts have, however, shown a tendency, sometimes being overzealous, in allowing their proceedings to continue in breach of a foreign jurisdiction clause, which is paradoxical considering their approach to anti-suit injunctions. If that happens, in the absence of a serious cause to serve the interests of justice, the foreign court might be prepared to restrain the English court from maintaining its jurisdiction, in order to protect its own consensual jurisdiction. The English court would have done so, had it been in the reverse position. Then there would be a problem of enforcement or, indeed, contradictory judgments. Recent cases, however, indicate that judges approach foreign jurisdiction clauses on the basis of construction of the clause, that is, whether an exclusive jurisdiction clause was intended (see Chapter 5, para 3.4.2.6, above).

2.6 Practical considerations and risk management

It is paramount that litigants should give careful consideration before they embark on applications for anti-suit injunctions. Not only is there a risk of non-enforcement of the injunction, if it is considered as an infringement of the foreign court's sovereignty,[48] but there may also be a risk of having to indemnify the party, for its legal costs and expenses, against whom the injunction is obtained.[49]

First, litigants should consider whether an application to the foreign court for a stay of its proceedings would be likely to be granted if the same principles applicable in England were applied there, too. On the other hand, if

---

46 This point was explained by Rix J in *Credit Suisse v MLC* [1999] 1 Lloyd's Rep 767, p 781.

47 *El Amria* [1996] 2 Lloyd's Rep 140; and the cases that have followed it, see Chapter 5, para 3.4, above.

48 German courts seem to be very resistant to give the blessing to English anti-suit injunctions: Harris, J, 'Enforcement of an English anti-suit injunction' (1997) CJQ 283 pp 283–89.

49 *Akai v People's Insurance Co* [1998] 1 Lloyd's Rep 90, *per* Thomas J (on breach of an English jurisdiction clause by proceedings in Australia, the defendant applied for an anti-suit injunction in the Singapore court instead of England. Although the injunction was granted later by the English court, Akai was ordered to indemnify the other party for its expenses to defend the Singaporean injunctive proceedings).

the English court defers its decision as to the granting of the injunction until after the foreign court has considered the matter, but the foreign court does not stay its proceedings, it would be the reverse of comity if the English court then granted an injunction.[50] There must be a balancing act of the advantages and disadvantages, before an application for an anti-suit injunction is made, and promptness in issuing the application, if the circumstances favour such a procedure, is an important factor, as has been shown in the cases discussed.

Second, it is now established by the Court of Appeal that, when there has been a breach of an exclusive jurisdiction clause and the claim being pursued falls within its terms, an anti-suit injunction would not be such an interference with the foreign court's sovereignty, but merely an enforcement of a contractual promise. Application for an anti-suit injunction must be made promptly in breach of contract cases,[51] and should be granted without waiting for the foreign court to determine its jurisdiction.[52] In any case, the foreign proceedings should not have reached an advanced stage before the application is made. If they have, there will be a risk of refusal of the injunction for a good reason,[53] particularly if there has been a submission to that jurisdiction.[54]

Third, there may be an alternative protection to an aggrieved party instead of applying for an anti-suit injunction. If there is no submission to the foreign jurisdiction and, assuming the jurisdiction agreement is valid and enforceable, a judgment obtained abroad will not be enforceable in this country by virtue of s 32 of the CJJA 1982.[55] Thus, the injunction will not be needed, because it will be possible to resist the enforcement of the foreign judgment obtained in breach of a jurisdiction agreement. In this connection, Edwin Peel (in his comprehensive article on the subject)[56] suggests this: as a prerequisite to any award of an injunction to restrain foreign proceedings, the courts should first consider whether s 32 of the CJJA 1982, or damages, or a combination of the two might provide adequate protection to the aggrieved party, who is a party to a valid jurisdiction agreement breached by the other party.

Fourth, another important consideration must be the existence of related multiple actions commenced in various jurisdictions, two of which are contractual, or one is contractual and the other is the natural forum.

---

50 Males, S, 'Comity and anti-suit injunctions' [1998] LMCLQ 543, p 549.

51 It is possible to get it, even if there is only a threatened or anticipatory breach of the jurisdiction agreement: *Shell International Petroleum Co Ltd v Coral Oil Co Ltd* [1999] 1 Lloyd's Rep 72.

52 *The Angelic Grace* [1994] 1 Lloyd's Rep 168.

53 *Toepfer v Molino Boschi* [1996] 1 Lloyd's Rep 510 (no injunction was granted because the Italian proceedings had been well advanced).

54 *The Atlantic Emperor (No 2)* [1992] 1 Lloyd's Rep 624: caution prevented the court from granting the injunction, although the plaintiff was relying on a legal right not to be sued abroad, because he had submitted to the Italian proceedings.

55 This section does not apply to judgments from Contracting States of the ECJCs.

56 Peel, E, 'Exclusive jurisdiction agreements: purity and pragmatism in the conflict of laws' [1998] LMCLQ 182, p 209.

Interference in such cases may be justified, if there are reasons of justice to restrain the foreign proceedings and determine the related actions in England,[57] or to stay the English proceedings in favour of the natural forum, despite the jurisdiction agreement, particularly, when there are parties in the foreign proceedings not bound by any agreement.[58]

2.7 Conclusion

It has been apparent, in all cases, that the judges pondered judicial comity. However, *The Angelic Grace* has been criticised as having relaxed the historical caution that existed before it in the granting of an anti-suit injunction.[59] How can a balance be struck?

From the foregoing analysis, it is submitted that the same principle formulated by Lord Goff[60] in *Patel* is capable of application to all cases, save for those cases governed by the rules of the EJCs and special statutory rules in cases of arbitration agreements.

Lord Goff stressed that, as between common law jurisdictions, there is no system comparable to that enshrined in the Brussels Convention, so that there is no embargo on concurrent proceedings in the same matter in more than one jurisdiction. There are simply two weapons: a stay (or dismissal) of proceedings and an anti-suit injunction.[61]

The rule in *Airbus v Patel* is sound and straightforward. It is suggested that it can be applied to cases across the board (except in the context of the ECJC regime and in arbitration agreements where stringer rules apply). The basic elements of the *Patel* case are the ends of justice and respect to other courts' jurisdiction (comity). These elements are also apparent in the decisions concerned with breach of an English jurisdiction agreement. Save where defined rules are rigid and do not permit discretion of the court, as was highlighted earlier, a connecting factor or sufficient interest exists when there is an English jurisdiction clause, as much as when England is the natural forum. Once this first hurdle is overcome, taking into consideration that the parties should be held to their bargain, the court then would exercise its discretion by making an inquiry whether the ends of justice would be served, if an injunction were not granted.

---

57 See, eg, *Svendborg v Wasna* [1996] 2 Lloyd's Rep 559, where the Sierra Leone proceedings were restrained because of evidence that the party proceeding there was boasting that he could manipulate the legal system in Sierra Leone to obtain justice in his favour.

58 *BOS-400* [1998] 2 Lloyd's Rep 461; *Credit Suisse First Boston (Europe) Ltd v MLC (Bermuda) Ltd* [1999] 1 Lloyd's Rep 767; cf *Donohue v Armco Inc* [1999] 2 Lloyd's Rep 649, while the judge refused the injunction, his order was reversed on appeal by a majority of 2:1, Brook LJ dissenting, [2000] 1 Lloyd's Rep 579.

59 [1994] 1 Lloyd's Rep 168, p 206.

60 Although he did not put his mind to contract cases when he formulated the new principle (see [1998] 1 Lloyd's Rep 631, p 640).

61 *Ibid*, p 637.

With regard to that inquiry, the following non-exhaustive list of factors may be relevant: (a) whether the foreign forum is acting oppressively by not staying its proceedings;[62] or (b) its rules are against international rules of justice;[63] or (c) the jurisdiction clause would operate to defeat mandatory rules of substantive law;[64] or (c) public policy;[65] or (d) it would not serve the interests of justice because there were multiple factors pointing towards the non-agreed forum,[66] unless that was a foreseeable incident of the parties' agreement;[67] or (e) that, in the competing forum, there are related actions which must be tried together.[68] Such an approach marries considerations of comity with the 'ends of justice' part of Lord Goff's principle. It should be observed that Goff's principle has been tacitly applied by most judges in cases of breach of an English jurisdiction agreement, although it has not been formulated in exactly the same terms. If a uniform principle were to be made expressly applicable, there would be less confusion, not only between litigants, but also amongst the judiciary itself, so that contradictory judgments would be avoided.

In short, there should be two categories of anti-suit injunctions, so that clear and distinct principles can be applied to each, namely: (a) the Brussels Convention (Art 17) and arbitration agreements category, in which the court has very limited discretion, and only to the extent of ascertaining the validity of the agreement; and (b) all other cases category, in which the court would determine whether or not the injunction should be granted on the basis of comity and ends of justice.

Finally, it is also submitted that stay of proceedings for breach of a foreign jurisdiction agreement should be treated, subject to construction of that agreement, on the basis of comity, respect of the parties' agreement and the ends of justice factor. Then it could be said that a right balance could be struck. The ends of justice would be an overall consideration. Recent English decisions show a trend that a choice of a foreign jurisdiction should be respected when the parties intended it to be exclusive and their choice was freely negotiated (see Chapter 5, para 3.4.2.6, above).

Having covered in this Part, aspects of jurisdiction and procedure in the Admiralty Court, the remaining parts deal with substantive law.

---

62 As shown in cases referred to above.

63 As in *Societe Nationale Industries Aerospatiale v Lee Kui Jak* [1987] 1 AC 871 (PC).

64 *The Hollandia* [1983] 1 AC 565.

65 *Akai v People's Insurance Co* [1998] 1 Lloyd's Rep 90, but public policy varies between legal systems.

66 These factors have been applied by analogy in the exercise of the court's discretion in a stay of proceedings.

67 *Aerospace v Dee Howard* [1993] 1 Lloyd's Rep 368 (see Chapter 5, para 3.4.2.6, above).

68 See fns 57 and 58, above.

PART II

ACQUIRING OWNERSHIP IN SHIPS

OVERVIEW

This part contains four related chapters, the common element of which is shipowning. Chapter 8 deals with registration of ships and significance of Flag States in the context of a regulatory regime, ownership principles and management of ships. It also explores the legal implications of the International Safety Management Code in liabilities of shipowners, managers and officers, including criminal liabilities. These are discussed in the context of the new regulatory regime imposed by the International Convention for Safety of Life at Sea (SOLAS) 1974, Chapter IX, concerning the enforcement of a safe management and transparent system of ship operations. Chapter 9 highlights important issues of the law relating to ship mortgages, which is an essential part of shipowning. Chapter 10 deals with general legal principles of shipbuilding and Chapter 11 with some aspects of the law relating to ship sale and purchase.

CHAPTER 8

OWNERSHIP, REGISTRATION AND MANAGEMENT OF SHIPS

1 INTRODUCTION

One cannot begin to practise law or any shipping business without putting one's mind to the legal and commercial considerations of ownership structures, the choice and significance of the flags which ships fly, as well as the management and safety aspects of ships. Extreme importance has been attached to these topics by the very fact of the introduction recently of international regulations concerning safety of operations and management of ships which is the most significant event in shipping history in the last two decades for all concerned. This chapter examines the aspects of this development which have had a tremendous impact on how shipowners own and manage their ships, so that a foremost consideration is not just their profit, but the effect their operations might have upon the rest of the world and, indeed, their continuation in business. It begins with the concept of the ship's flag and registration generally, but with particular focus on registration of British ships, questioning the sad decline of British shipping. It continues with management of ships and the changes necessitated by the growing culture of safe ship operation and management brought about by the International Safety Management Code (ISMC), being an attachment to Chapter IX of the International Convention for Safety of Life at Sea (SOLAS) 1974.

1.1. Importance and role of the ship's flag[1]

Ships must possess a national character to be allowed to use the high seas freely. They have the nationality of the State whose flag they are entitled to fly, which is the symbol of the ship's nationality. Individual States fix the conditions for the entry of ships in their registries. Connecting factors between a ship and a State, such as the incorporation of the owning company of the ship in that State, provide a test for the ship's nationality. However, some States may not require the ship to be registered in the records of the State where the owning company is registered. The registration of a ship in the public records of a State attributes the national character of that State to the ship and the documents issued to the ship by the competent authority of that State are evidence of the ship's nationality. The registration of a vessel under

---

1   Ready, N, *Ship Registration*, 2nd edn, 1994, LLP, from which a summary is provided here. He treats the subject from a comparative perspective between British and other well known registers.

the flag of a State implies that her operation will be subjected to the laws and fiscal regime of that country. Jurisdiction over vessels on the high seas will reside with that State. The law of the vessel's flag will govern offences committed on the high seas.[2] Nationality of ships enables them to engage in trade, to enter ports and deal with the authorities of other nations. International law lays down rules regulating how the freedom to sail on the high seas should be used. The Geneva Convention on the High Seas 1958 and the United Nations Convention 1982 on the Law of the Sea require States to exercise effective control over ships flying their flag.

There are various factors that influence shipowners to choose a flag of a particular State. The most important factors are economic considerations and operating costs.

1.2 Flags of convenience

Maritime nations, historically, required a 'genuine link' between a vessel and the State in which the ship was registered. Market forces and attractions offered by 'open registries' known as 'flags of convenience' brought a significant decline of the traditional ship registries since the 1950s.

Subject to international law, States have had freedom to set their own regulations for ships carrying their flag. Some States have been very liberal in the regulations for entry of foreign ships in their ship registers, making it very convenient and opportune for shipowners to register their ships with them. This gave rise to the proliferation of open registers or flag of convenience States which provided attractive advantages.[3] The most important of such advantages have been: the confidentiality of who is the actual beneficial owner of the ship,[4] the allowance of ownership and control of the ship by non-citizens of that State, no income tax (only a registration fee and annual fees), the freedom of manning of those ships by non-nationals. The latter allowed the shipowners to use cheap labour and has been, together with the tax advantages, the greatest stimuli for them to register under a flag of convenience. In addition, Open registries enable the shipowners to distance themselves from the political and economic situation of their country.

---

2 *The Oteri v The Queen* [1977] 1 Lloyd's Rep 105 (PC).

3 The origin of flag of convenience has its roots in the ingenuity of British merchants in the 16th century, who used the Spanish flag to avoid Spanish monopoly restrictions on trade with the West Indies, and later of British fishermen in the 17th to 19th centuries, who tried to avoid fishing restrictions imposed by Great Britain by using either the French or the Norwegian flags: see *op cit*, Ready, fn 1, Chapter 2 and references cited thereto. See, also, Spruyt, J, *Ship Management*, 1990, LLP, pp 50–51.

4 However, the introduction of the ISMC is leading to greater transparency because it requires the identification of the entities responsible for the operation and management of the ship, as will be seen later.

How did they start? Prohibition laws of the USA preventing the sale of liquor signalled the beginning of the use of open registries in the early 20th century. This resulted in the transfer of ships to the Panamanian flag, which at the time had a liberal maritime law to attract foreign tonnage. Another factor contributing to the boost of the Panamanian flag was the worsening of the political situation in Europe in the 1930s and the outbreak of war in 1939. The dissatisfaction with the Panamanian flag, however, was first shown after the Second World War, due to political instability in Panama, and this gave rise to other flags of convenience, such as the Liberian flag.[5] Other nations raised such flags of convenience,[6] some of which have been criticised for being lax in preserving high standards in terms of enforcing safety regulations.

However, safety aspects of sub-standard ships linked to flags of convenience and sub-standard labour conditions on board have led to a campaign against those flags for many years. Moreover, in recent years, the fact that incidents of casualties of ships under flags of convenience have outnumbered the casualties of ships under other flags has alerted the international shipping community to action. The safety aspect has a lot to do with the age of ships, as well as construction and lack of a rigorous system of maintenance, by regular surveys and repairs. Classification societies play a great role here as well.

An attempt to attract European shipowners away from flags of convenience has been pursued by the European Commission, which proposed the establishment of a European Community (EC) ship register (EUROS) in 1989. However, for such a flag to be successful, the incentives offered have to be greater than those offered by the existing flag States.

1.3 The regulatory regime

1.3.1 The Flag and Port State Controls

International law has imposed a duty upon all Flag States to ensure that the necessary steps have been taken, such as regular surveys of ships under their flag and compliance with international regulations relating to safety at sea, prevention of pollution and crew conditions and training. However, there has been a tendency by some Flag States to take this responsibility with less seriousness than do the older maritime States. This phenomenon, coupled with the intense competitive nature of the international shipping industry and overcapacity of ships, leads to a departure of ships from Flag States which

---

5   *Op cit*, Ready, fn 1, pp 20–21.
6   Algeria, Barbados, Belize, Bulgaria, China, Cuba, Croatia, Cyprus, Egypt, Estonia, Honduras, Iran, Lebanon, Liberia, Lithuania, Malta, Panama, Portugal, Romania, St Vincent and Grenadines, Syria, Vanuatu, Ukraine.

take these responsibilities seriously, to those which take them more lightly To counterbalance this deficiency, the Port State Control[7] emerged as a second line of defence. Coastal States have had to harmonise their approach to Port State Control by membership of the Paris Memorandum of Understanding (PMOU)[8] which ensures that ships calling in the ports of a Port State are inspected and, if they have not complied with international safety standards, are detained. However, the Achilles heel of Port State Control is risk analysis, which is the analysis by owners of sub-standard ships being at risk of detention. If the owners undertook a serious risk analysis to prevent detention by the Port State Control, the problem would go away, but, it is a fact of life, that some owners do not.[9] The elimination of a regulatory regime, based upon compliance and evasion, therefore, is not possible, not at least until a safety culture is instilled in the shipping industry in general, not just the shipowners themselves.

Lord Donaldson, who has taken an active role in ship safety, has commented that ship safety – and the consequences of any lack of it – is a topic which is as fascinating as it is complex. His recommendations made after the public inquiry on *The Braer* disaster, which he chaired, are contained in the report *Safer Ships; Cleaner Seas*. The scope of this, he said:

> ... covered every aspect of manning, operation, maintenance, classification and insurance of vessels. It covered Flag State and Port State Controls, surveillance, tracking and identification of vessels. It covered pollution protection and clean-up. It did so in the context of domestic and international law, as well as on a practical, day to day basis.

Remedial action in shipping has to be international in both its application and enforcement. He further said:

> Insofar as there is a regulatory regime, it is to be found in international Conventions evolved through the International Maritime Organisation, a United Nations agency. Primary responsibility for enforcement lies with the States whose flags the vessels fly – Flag State Control. However, coastal States at which vessels call are entitled to take measures to protect themselves from sub-standard shipping – Port State Control. The principal measure consists of detaining ships, which do not come up to the internationally agreed standard

---

7   For details of the evolution of the Port State Control system see Kasoulides, G, *Port State Control and Jurisdiction*, 1993, Kluwer.

8   Membership in the PMOU includes the UK, Belgium, Denmark, Finland, France, Germany, Greece, the Republic of Ireland, Italy, The Netherlands, Norway, Portugal, Spain and Sweden (in Europe) and Canada. There is a similar scheme in Tokyo covering Asia and the Pacific and two other schemes cover the Caribbean and Latin America.

9   See Lord Donaldson's paper, 'The ISM Code: the road to discovery?' [1998] LMCLQ 526, delivered at the first lecture in memory of Professor Cadwallader, 26 March 1998, the London Shipping Law Centre, UCL Law Faculty.

... But Port and Flag States are not the only players in this battle to raise standards. classification societies have a major part to play.[10]

1.3.2 The role of classification societies in the safety of ships

Classification societies have shown a weakness over the years as guardians of ship safety, mainly because they are not authorised, nor are they regulated by statute, for the performance of their functions (one of which is the certification of ships) as is the case in the aviation industry. Competing amongst themselves for business, classification societies are paid by the shipowners. The lack of a statutory regulatory regime of classification societies permits some of them to be more lenient than their competitors in the enforcement of safety aspects upon inspection of ships, so that they can stay in business.

This particular weakness, Lord Donaldson explained,[11] 'has now, to some extent, been cured by the creation of the International Association of Classification Societies (IACS), which imposes and polices the quality of its members' work and prevents owners transferring from one member society to another, simply in order to avoid having to take remedial action required by the first society. However, not all classification societies are members of IACS, although IACS members classify 90% of the world's shipping.

These issues are being tackled by the European Commission, which proposes to amend the present Directive (94/57/EC) on inspection of ships by classification societies, so that more controls of their actions are imposed and classification societies become financially accountable for negligence.[12]

The issue of liability of classification societies for negligence (under English law) to third parties who suffer economic loss due to unseaworthiness of a ship, which was nevertheless certified to be in class by the ship's classification society, is discussed in the context of sale of ships, in Chapter 11, para 9.

1.3.3 The role of the ISMC and further initiatives on safety

What has the Code sought to do? Briefly, it superimposes a safety case regime by which risk analysis by owners, the Achilles heel of the Port State Control,

---

10 See Lord Donaldson, 'Safer ships; cleaner seas – full speed ahead or dead slow?', the Donald O'May (annual memorial) lecture at the Institute of Maritime Law, University of Southampton, 12 November 1997 (published in [1998] LMCLQ 170, pp 171, 172). For a general guide to classification societies, see Lux, J (ed), *Classification Societies*, 1993, LLP (although it needs updating to include recent changes in the law with regard to their liability).

11 *Op cit*, Lord Donaldson, fn 9.

12 See Chapter 17, below.

has become compulsory.[13] It has adopted a new approach to ship operations and management by requiring the shipowners and managers to establish a safety management system (SMS) so that the company's philosophy to safety becomes transparent. It obliges both Flag and Port States to enforce it and has already had a significant effect on surveillance and control of sub-standard ships.

The system includes the maintenance of reports of accidents and non-conformities with the Code, which is monitored and supervised by a Designated Person (DP). In particular, the Code requires of the owners and their personnel the following broad objectives: (i) to provide for safe practices in ship operations; (ii) to provide a safe working environment; (iii) to undertake risk assessment of all identifiable risks; (iv) to commit themselves to continuous improvement of safety management skills.

Certificates of compliance with the requirements of such a system are granted by the Flag State and delegated authorities, which audit whether the system with regard to the company and each of its ships is in place and fully operative. Classification societies are delegated by the Flag States to carry out surveys to ensure compliance. The underlying purpose of this Code, together with its counterpart, the Standard of Training Certification and Watchkeeping (STCW) Convention, as amended in 1995, is to reduce accidents caused by 'human errors'.

Whether or not all problems of ship safety will be solved by the enforcement of this Code, so that there may be 'safer ships and cleaner seas', remains to be seen.

Further measures are being taken for the purpose of tackling sub-standard ships, harmonising levels of inspection and co-ordinating information about the performance of vessels of particular flags, which is monitored and kept in electronic databases. Such a system has been operative and enforceable by the US Coast Guard. The European Commission, in addition to proposing amendments of the Port State Control Directive,[14] initiated the establishment of an electronic data interchange network between the authorities in the Member States for the implementation of the Hazmat Directive,[15] which is also due for amendment.[16] A similar scheme, known as Early Warning

---

13 It has been implemented under Chapter IX of the SOLAS Convention 1974 and has had the force of law in SOLAS States with regard to passenger ships, oil, chemical tankers, gas and bulk carriers and high speed crafts (all of 500 GRT and over) since 1 July 1998. With regard to ro-ro passenger vessels operating on regular service to and from ports of EU Member States, it has been applied since 1 July 1996. It will be enforceable on other cargo ships and mobile offshore drilling units (of 500 GRT plus) from 1 July 2002.

14 95/21/EC, COM(97) 416, re-amended by proposal COM(2000) 850; see Chapter 17, below.

15 93/75/EEC).

16 COM(2000) 802, 6 December 2000; see Chapter 17, below.

System (EWS) for the Baltic Sea, was concluded in 1999.[17] This database information operates through the internet: it is known as the European Quality Shipping Information System (EQUASIS).[18] It will give users a wide range of safety related information. A database of inspections which have led to detention for serious deficiencies is kept for future targeting. From the insurers' perspective, many insurance companies have adopted a quality insurance system (ISO 9002).

1.3.4 The missing link in the equation of safety

So, what can go wrong in the future? It is worth noting the answer given to this question by Lord Donaldson:

> On the face of it, full compliance [with the code] would at a stroke eliminate all shipping accidents and pollution, save only those brought on by unforeseen perils of the seas and unforeseen defects in safety management policies. Sadly, the answer is that quite a lot can and will go wrong. We live in a wicked world and the greater the financial pressure, the wickeder some of us will become. Shipowners are not more wicked than others, but overcapacity (which hopefully the ISMC will help to eliminate), the international nature of competition within the industry and low or negative margins of profit will lead many shipowners into temptation. A few, it has to be said, need no temptation. It just comes naturally. In practical terms, some Flag States will undoubtedly ignore their responsibilities and will be prepared to certify compliance in the teeth of the evidence or in spite of it ...Accepting, as I do, that until some form of discipline can be introduced in relation to Flag States by, for example, an International maritime organisation (IMO) resolution withdrawing the right of offenders to issue internationally accepted certificates, the real burden of making this system work will fall upon Port State Control. However, I hope that classification societies, underwriters, charterers and shippers will provide powerful assistance in their own interests, by withdrawing class, by loading premiums or declining to insure and, in the case of shippers and charterers, by becoming much more selective in the shipping which they use.[19]

Although this observation is fairly accurate, there may be other factors, which have direct or indirect effect on ship safety and have not been tackled by international conventions. If complete safety (CS) were to be represented by a mathematical equation, $CS = ISM + Y$, the search for the missing link, that is, the value of the unknown Y, still continues.

While ships are the obvious and tangible objects when disastrous casualties occur, their owners or Flag States may not always be the operative

---

17 COM(2000) 802, p 9; proposals to improve this system are under discussion and it is intended that the present Directive (93/75/EEC) will be replaced with a new one; see Chapter 17, below.

18 Further details can be found at the office of the London Shipping Law Centre, UCL.

19 See fn 9.

wrongdoers. They sometimes become the scapegoats for the faults of others who are not easily detectable. Equal efforts must be made to detect those who place ships in a position of danger, either by their chartering practices or by loading dangerous cargoes or by exposing ships to unnecessary risks in dangerous ports. In addition, one should not leave out of the equation the practices of some shipyards, in the construction of ships or in the implementation of repairs, which ought to be made accountable for disastrous accidents. Classification societies, too, some of which fail to observe safety standards must be targeted. If the failing ones happen to be members of IACS, the sanction is now disqualification from membership, unless they follow the rules of quality standards. However, this sanction alone may not be sufficient because the problem stems from those societies which are not members of IACS. An effective sanction worth considering may be to render those classification societies obsolete by international law for safety reasons.

There are, however, recent commendable initiatives taken by both the IMO and the EC to implement ways of controlling the activities of both the Flag States and Classification Societies. The Flag State implementation sub-committee at IMO has proposed that IMO should be given power to audit Flag States and lead them to self-assessment about Flag State performance; the EC has proposed to audit classification societies and make them accountable for negligence (on which see Chapters 11 and 17, below).

It has also been recognised by the Quality Shipping Campaign that the role of the shippers/cargo-owners is important and that the successful eradication of sub-standard operations and practices in shipping depends on the co-operation of all links in the responsibility chain.[20] But the role of the shippers has been looked at only from the point of view whether a mechanism can be created by which sanctions can be imposed on them if they use sub-standard ships. Any monitoring, however, in this direction has been rejected on the basis that it would be impracticable and expensive.[21] The questions that have not been asked by the Quality Shipping Campaign are these: (i) to what extent the shippers/cargo-owners and charterers contribute to making ships unsafe and thereby causing pollution at sea?; (ii) how can they be targeted so that sanctions can be imposed upon them for the consequences of rendering ships unsafe?

At a recent seminar on 'The missing link in regulation of shipping',[22] it was concluded[23] that the 'missing link' is lack of transparency within the

---

20 Lisbon Conference on Quality Shipping, 4 June 1998.

21 British Maritime Law Association (BMLA) study on the role of cargo-owners/shippers and marine insurers in the Quality Shipping Campaign, copy available from the office of the London Shipping Law Centre, UCL Law Faculty.

22 The seminar was set as a challenging question to the shipping industry by the London Shipping Law Centre; it was chaired by Lord Donaldson on 18 January 2000; papers are available at the Centre's Office.

23 By Cubbin, A, Director of Policy and Standards, Maritime & Coastguard Agency (ibid).

industry, as well as lack of consistency and effective implementation of international conventions by Flag States. If that were the answer to the value of Y in the equation of safety, it would prove the equation. Such answer is, however, lacking in precision and, therefore, cannot solve a mathematical equation. It is surprising that no initiative has been taken to include in the Quality Shipping Campaign those additional players (mentioned above), who cannot be left out of the complex matrix of maintaining 'safer ships and cleaner seas'. As a suggestion, it may not be impossible or impracticable to include them in the EQUASIS information system, or the new initiative by the EC to improve monitoring of ships and information systems, as discussed in Chapter 17. The IMO should also join this scheme. The owners themselves may, from their experience, volunteer such information, so that the jigsaw puzzle is completed and the equation is proved.

2 STATUTORY OVERVIEW OF OWNERSHIP AND REGISTRATION OF BRITISH SHIPS

The British flag has had a long and good reputation but, unfortunately, has fallen into decline. The Government's attempt to boost British tonnage by statutory reform is examined next.

2.1 The effect of the Merchant Shipping Acts prior to1995

In 1988 the British Government launched a new system of ownership and registration of British ships aiming to encourage foreign investment into British shipping. It took almost 100 years for the Government to realise that the law in Britain concerning ownership of British ships, unlike other foreign laws, was too restrictive to allow foreign capital.

Under the previous Merchant Shipping Act (MSA) of 1894 (s 1) only British subjects (by birth or naturalisation) could own all 64 shares in a British ship. If the owner was a corporation, it should have been registered and have had its principal place of business in Her Majesty's dominion. Although this mechanism permitted foreign capital investment to a certain extent, it was in a way prohibiting, because of the requirement that the company should be established under the laws of some part of Her Majesty's dominions and have its principal place of business there. From a taxation point of view, this was discouraging to investment. Moreover, breach of the statutory provisions would result in forfeiture of the ship to the Crown.[24]

---

24 *The Polzeath* [1916] P 241 (CA): a ship registered as British was owned by a company registered as British under the Companies Acts. Doubts having arisen as to the title of the ship to be registered as a British ship, the Commissioners of Customs and [contd]

The MSA 1988 brought fundamental changes.[25] First, a new U.K. shipping register of ships was created which replaced the old British Empire register. The new register stopped the imposition of UK maritime law on old dependent territories.

Secondly, the 1988 Act introduced, for the first time, the registration of ships in the British Registry as entitlement, instead of as an obligation. It allowed, therefore, 'flagging out' to other registers of a ship which, otherwise, would be entitled to be registered as British. As a result, the definition of a British ship changed from one based on ownership to one based on registration, under the provisions of the MSAs.

Thirdly, the Act introduced flexibility in ownership, in that only the majority interest in a ship of 24 m,[26] or more, in length (instead of all 64 shares in it) had to be British owned. Furthermore, if these persons were not UK residents, then a representative person, being a UK resident, should be appointed, providing the British connection.

Fourthly, by contrast, the Act invented a rigid system for fishing vessels by setting up a separate British fishing register to prevent fishing 'quota hopping' by non-British ships changing to British Registry. Under s 14, the legal ownership, management and control of fishing vessels were required to be British. Unwittingly, this resulted in great controversy with European fishing competitors, which ended up in the European Court of Justice (ECJ) in *The Factortame*,[27] and a change of the statute became necessary later by the Merchant Shipping (Registration, etc) Act (MS(Reg)A) 1993.

It is, therefore, important to summarise this case in this context.

The Factortame

The applicants, companies incorporated under the UK law and their directors and shareholders, most of whom were Spanish nationals, owned between them 95 deep sea fishing vessels registered as British under the 1894 Act. In the light of the change of the statutory regime of registration by the 1988 Act,

---

24 [contd] Excise, pursuant to the provisions of s 51 of the MSA 1906, directed the plaintiff, the registrar of shipping at the ship's port of registry, to require evidence to be given to his satisfaction that the ship was entitled to be so registered. The evidence adduced established that the affairs of the company, from the time the ship was bought and put upon the register, were directed from Hamburg by the chairman of the board of directors, a naturalised British subject of German origin, who held the majority of the shares and resided at Hamburg, both before and after the outbreak of war between Great Britain and Germany. Accordingly, proceedings for forfeiture were instituted in accordance with the provisions of s 76 of the MSA 1894 – since the principal place of business of the company was not within His Majesty's dominions, the ship, therefore, was forfeit to the Crown.

25 See Gaskell, N, 'The Merchant Shipping Act 1988' [1989] LMCLQ 133.

26 Ships below 24 m were dealt with for registration purposes by the MSA 1983, which provided for a small ships register.

27 [1991] AC 603 (HL).

vessels registered as British under the previous Act were required to be re-registered. The 95 vessels in question failed to satisfy the conditions for registration under s 14 of the 1988 Act by reason of being managed and controlled from Spain or by Spanish nationals, or by reason of the proportion of the beneficial ownership of the shares in the applicant companies in Spanish hands. The applicants by an application for judicial review sought to challenge the legality of these provisions of the Act on the ground that they contravened the provisions of the EEC Treaty by depriving the applicants of Community law rights. They also applied for the grant of interim relief until such time as final judgment was given on their application for judicial review. The trial judge decided to stay the proceedings and apply for a preliminary ruling on the issues of Community law raised from the ECJ. He also ordered that, pending judgment, the application of that part of the 1988 Act be disapplied by way of an interim relief as regards the applicants.

Both the Court of Appeal and the House of Lords held that under English law, English courts had no jurisdiction to suspend the application of Acts of Parliament by way of interim relief in advance of any decision by the ECJ. The House of Lords referred this matter of interim relief to the European Court, which held that in a case concerning Community law, if a national court considered that the only obstacle to granting such a relief was a rule of national law, it had to set that rule aside.

Therefore, on reference back to the Lords, it was held that in considering whether an interim relief should be granted, the court had to consider, first whether there was an adequate remedy in damages and, then, if no such remedy existed, the court had to take into account the interests of the public in general to whom the authority enforcing the law owed a duty. The court had discretion and was not obliged to restrain the public authority from enforcing the law, unless it was satisfied that the challenge to its validity was sufficiently and firmly based to justify that exceptional course being taken. The applicants' challenge to the compatibility of the 1988 Act with Community law was *prima facie* a strong one in the light of ECJ cases. Since the substantial detriment to the public interest, that would have occurred if the applicants eventually failed in their challenge, was not sufficient to outweigh the obvious and immediate damage that would continue to be caused to them if interim relief were not granted (in the event that they were ultimately successful), interim relief was granted.

The EJC in its recent decision[28] struck down Greek legislation with regard to registration of ships as being contrary to EC law. It held that Member States should not discriminate on grounds of nationality when exercising their powers to define the conditions on which they will grant nationality in respect of vessels, but ensure that there is a genuine link[29] between State and the ship.

---

28 *Commission v Greece* (Case C-62/96), judgment 28 November 1997.
29 High Seas Geneva Convention 1958, Art 5 and UNCLOS 1982, Art 91.

Qualified persons to own a British ship were defined by s 3 of the MSA 1988, thus: (i) British citizens; (ii) British Crown dependent territories' citizens; (iii) British citizens overseas;[30] (iv) companies incorporated in the UK, or in any of the relevant overseas territories[31] and having their principal place of business in the UK, or in any such territory; (v) persons who were British subjects under the Nationality Act (NA) 1981; (vi) persons who under the Hong Kong (British Nationality) Order 1986 were British nationals (overseas); (vii) citizens of the Republic of Ireland.

Section 5 of this Act encouraged the registration of a ship owned by a foreign company registered in any relevant overseas territory to be registered as British, provided there was a representative in the UK.

2.2 Who can own and register a British ship under the present statute?

2.2.1 Eligibility to own a British ship under the MSA 1995

The provisions of the 1988 Act as to who would be a qualified person to own a British ship were carried forward in the MS(Reg)A 1993.[32] By the 1993 Merchant Shipping (Registration of ships) Regulations (reg 7), the categories of qualified persons outlined above were amalgamated into eight broad categories. The qualifications were extended to EC nationals. Regulation 7(1) provided that qualified persons are:

> British citizens or persons who are nationals of a Member State other than the UK and are established (within the meaning of Art 52 of the EEC Treaty) in the UK; British dependent territories' citizens; British overseas citizens; persons who under the British NA 1981 are British subjects; persons who under the Hong Kong (British Nationality) Order 1986 are British nationals (overseas); bodies corporate incorporated in any relevant British possession and having their principal place of business in the UK or in any such possession; and European Economic Interest Groupings, being groupings formed in pursuance of Art 1 of Council Regulation (EEC) 2137/85 and registered in the UK.

A person who is not qualified under para 1 to be the owner of a British ship may nevertheless be one of the owners of such a ship, if:

(a) a majority interest in the ship (within the meaning of reg 8) is owned by persons who are qualified to be the owners of British ships; and

---

30 Such as in Hong Kong.

31 The Isle of Man, and any of the Channel Islands (included colonies, but that is now out of date).

32 See Gaskell, N and Clarke, A, 'Sailing towards consolidation' [1994] LMCLQ 146.

(b) the ship is registered on Pt I of the Register, which covers ships owned by 'qualified persons', excluding fishing vessels (Pt II) and those registered as small ships (Pt III).

The British connection and majority interest is provided by reg 8. A representative person in the UK for service of documents and notices is an essential requirement preserved by the Act (regs 8,9,18,19). Thus, subject to having a British connection either by residence, or by a representative in the UK, it became possible for a foreign company incorporated in any of the EU States to be able to own a British ship for the first time.

Upon consolidation of all MSAs by the 1995 Act, which came into force on 1 January 1996, Sched 1 to the MS(Reg)A 1993, concerning ownership and registration of ships and mortgages, was transferred in the new Act and the 1993 Regulations issued under the previous Act, as a subordinate legislation, are still applicable. The Secretary of State can review and issue new regulations. With the change of British possession and British territories, it is perhaps time that new regulations were issued.

Thus, the MS(Reg)A 1993 (reg 2) created a new Central Register of British ships[33] available for public inspection, divided into four parts: (a) the large ships register (Pt I) for ships of 24 m in length and over; (b) the register of fishing vessels (Pt II); (c) the small ships register; and (d) the bareboat register (Pt IV).

For the first time, by s 7 of the 1993 Act, now s 17 of the 1995 Act, British bareboat charterers became entitled to register a foreign chartered vessel under the British flag.[34]

2.2.2 Eligibility to own a British fishing vessel

British citizens or nationals of other EU States (resident and domiciled in an EU State) must wholly own the legal and beneficial title of a fishing vessel (regs 12, 13). If the above requirements are not met, but the person has been resident in the UK for a long time, there may be a dispensation of the provisions by the Secretary of State who may determine eligibility (reg 15). In case the owner is a body corporate in any of the EU States there must be a British connection (reg 14).

2.3 The decline of British shipping

The flexibility of registration introduced by the 1988 Act was a noble attempt to encourage the growth of British shipping by lifting the restriction of full British ownership and making registration in the British Registry optional. But by making registration in the UK optional, the Act permitted flagging out

---

33 The register of ships maintained under the 1894 Act, the small ships register maintained under the 1983 Act and the register of fishing vessels under the 1988 Act were closed by s 1 of the 1993 Act.

34 The formalities of registration are dealt with in Pt VI of the 1993 Regulations.

indirectly and the result may have been counterproductive. The lures of foreign registers (even in relevant overseas territories), with a more flexible taxation system, than the UK became an attraction.

The unintended effect of the legislation does not, however, give a full answer to the central question of why British shipping has declined. In the 1850s, the British controlled 82% of the world shipping tonnage, legislation and colonialism having played a great part in this boom.[35] The British islanders of the 20th and 21st centuries seem reluctant to invest in shipping, considering the risks inherent to shipping business, when there are more attractive business opportunities on land. Yet, there must be more to it than just a choice between land and sea. Young people may not regard themselves as belonging to a maritime nation since it does not build ships any longer.

The British Government has offered some reasons for the decline of British shipping, such as unequal competition for the UK shipping industry from flags, which offer lower labour costs when ships are crewed with officers from South East Asia and Russia, and the additional costs of operating UK ships stemming from the regulatory regime, globalisation of the world economy and changing patterns in seaborne trade, which have shifted the focus of growth to the Far East. The Government accepts, however, that such reasons have caused a steeper decline to UK shipping than to other traditional maritime nations.[36] The answer to explaining the decline certainly lies in a combination of factors, which are beyond the scope of this book, and deserves a different type of study.[37]

Two obvious factors for lack of growth of British shipping are pointed out here which have been addressed presently by the British Government: (a) The lack of attractions for young people to choose the sea as the area of their profession; and (b) the lack of Government encouragement to cost-effective investment in shipping business. The first has been attended to by various shipping companies making efforts to train seafarers and direct young people to take up this career. The second, which is linked to the first, has been addressed by the Government with the introduction of the UK tonnage tax. This new legislation of corporate taxation of shipping companies is based on the net tonnage of vessels operated in the UK. It aims to provide incentives for investment in shipping and boost UK shipping by encouraging shipowners to relocate to the UK because their services are very important to the British economy. A UK-resident shipowning company may either elect for tonnage

---

35 It is worth reading the book, Davies, M, *Belief in the Sea, State Encouragement of British Merchant Shipping and Shipbuilding*, 1992, LLP.

36 See DETR, *British Shipping – Charting a New Course*, 16 December 1998, www.detr.gov.uk.

37 Harlafis, G, *Greek Shipowners and Greece 1945–1975*, 1993, Athlone, explains from a historical point of view how familial bonds and kinship greatly assisted the development of a close network in Greek shipping and contributed to the success of a strong shipping enterprise: also, by the same author, *A History of Greek-Owned Shipping*, 1996, London: Routledge.

tax, or be taxed under the normal corporation tax rules.[38] Whether or not the introduction of the tonnage tax will be a factor in boosting British shipping tonnage remains to be seen in the future.

Other countries in Europe, had already initiated similar legislation to increase shipping tonnage, for example, Norway took this route in 1987. The Norwegian system,[39] which created a second register, the offshore national register, did result in a successful increase of the Norwegian tonnage.[40] However, the Norwegian system is quite different, overall, from the British tonnage tax.

One also hopes that, in this century, the number of open registers will decline considerably because of the pressures brought internationally to promote a safety culture. If there is no reform of them, financial institutions and the insurance market will decline to accept sub-standard ships registered under such registers.

3 OWNERSHIP PRINCIPLES

Evidence of ownership rests in the documents of registration and executed bill of sale. However, registration of a ship in the ship registry is not conclusive evidence, but provides *prima facie* evidence of the registered owner being the true owner. The burden of proof shifts to the person alleging to be the owner. The court has jurisdiction to make a declaration as to which party would be entitled to be registered as the legal owner of a ship.[41] In absence of fraud, execution and registration of the bill of sale give good title.[42] The legal person registered to be the owner would be liable for the negligence of those on board the ship,[43] unless the ship has been chartered to a charterer by demise.

The common and voluntary methods of acquiring ownership are discussed in Chapter 10 (regarding new buildings) and Chapter 11 (regarding the commercial purchase of ships). Ownership can also be acquired involuntarily either by inheritance or bankruptcy, which is known as

---

38 Moore Stephens, Greiner, R, 'Off-shore and UK shipping structures, tonnage tax, advantages and disadvantages', delivered in the series of Risk Management Papers, the London Shipping Law Centre, 18 October and 22 November 2000.

39 Briefly, it includes: no taxation of foreign owners; minimum registration fee; no nationality requirements in respect of crew; freedom to negotiate wages; the company may be incorporated outside Norway with a representative in Norway. Thus, the Norwegian register attracts, not only Norwegian ships, but also others.

40 See, *op cit*, Spruyt, fn 3, pp 48–49.

41 *The Bineta* [1966] 3 All ER 1007; see Chapter 3, para 3.1, above.

42 *The Horlock* (1877) 2 PD 243.

43 *Hibbs v Ross* (1866) 1 QBD 534.

transmission. It may be acquired by capture of an enemy ship in times of war, or by judicial sale (discussed in Part I).

The principles applicable to ownership of chattels[44] apply to ownership of ships. When two or more people own a ship jointly, they own it either as 'joint tenants' or as 'tenants in common'. These phrases bear the meaning attributed to them at common law. There can be joint owners of shares in the ship who have a single joint right to possession of the whole chattel. In the absence of any words to the contrary, when a chattel is transferred to two or more people they will hold the chattel as 'joint tenants' with a unity of title. Joint tenants do not have an exclusive right to possession as against their co-owners. When one of them dies, his interest in the ship will automatically accrue to the other.

'Tenants in common', on the other hand, own separate shares in the ship with an undivided interest in the whole of their shares and, therefore, they have several rights to possession in the ship, unless it is otherwise agreed between them. There must be an express intention of the co-owners, in such a case, that they should have separate shares in the ship for them to be tenants in common, otherwise they will be joint tenants. Indications of there being 'tenants in common' will be inferred either from the words used in their agreement, for example, 'they are to have separate interests in the ship in equal shares', or, when the joint owners have contributed to the purchase price in unequal proportions. When one of them dies, his interest in the ship passes to his estate or pursuant to the terms of his or her will.

A tenant in common can dispose of his 'interest' in the ship and the assignee or buyer of it will step in his position, becoming a tenant in common with the others.

If a joint tenant disposes of his 'interest' in the ship by a lifetime gift or assignment, the effect of it will be the severance of the joint tenancy and the third party will become a tenant in common with the other co-owners.

The ownership in the 'whole ship' owned jointly could only be transferred to a third person by the agreement of all co-owners. If one of them purports to sell the absolute interest in the ship without the authority of his co-owners, he cannot pass greater title than he actually has, *nemo dat quod non habet*. So the purchaser will acquire the seller's interest in the ship and become a tenant in common with the other joint owners.

The relationship between co-owners is normally regulated by express agreement. In the absence of an agreement, the rights and remedies between joint owners are governed by common law. For example, if one co-owner wrongfully takes possession of the chattel, or wrongfully disposes of it, or

---

44   Palmer, N and McKendrick, E (eds), *Interests in Goods*, 2nd edn, 1998, LLP, Chapter 10.

refuses to give it back when demanded, he or she will commit the tort of conversion.[45]

When the co-owners disagree about the employment of the ship, the principle in English law is that the will of the majority must prevail, provided that the interest of the dissenting minority can be protected. The court's power of sale may be exercised, even on the application of a minority, if it is for the interest of all parties.

The Hereward[46]

The majority shareholders of a ship formed a limited company to which they transferred their shares. That way, they made it impossible for the ship to be employed profitably, unless the minority shareholders joined the company. Also, that meant that the liability of the minority had been increased and their shares, thus, rendered non-saleable. The minority shareholders moved, in an action of restraint, for the sale of the ship. According to Bruce J:

> ...that power may be exercised on the application of a minority of part-owners; and it seems to me that, when part-owners of the ship are unable to agree as to what is to be done with their common property, and there appears to be no way of preventing the sacrifice of the property except by a sale, the court ought to direct a sale.[47]

It was held that the majority of the co-owners had no right to change the character of the ownership without the consent of all parties. Therefore, in the interests of all concerned, the sale of the whole ship would be decreed.

All part-owners must consent to a voyage, but when the minority shareholders dissent, they will be excluded from any profits or losses of the voyage.

The right of a part-owner holding a minority of shares in a vessel to institute an action of restraint and arrest the vessel is undoubted. Upon sufficient proof being adduced by the minority shareholder that he/she objects to the manner in which the vessel is being employed, the court is bound to order security to be provided by the remaining part-owners for the safe return of the vessel and in the amount of the plaintiff's interest in the vessel.[48] If the court makes the order for security, the minority, though not liable for the expenses of the voyage on which the vessel is engaged, will not be entitled to any share of the profits of the adventure. The right of the minority to arrest the vessel is in no way affected by the fact that the ship's husband, who negotiated the charterparty to which the minority objects, was

---

45 See *Halsbury's Laws of England*, 4th edn, Vol 45.
46 [1895] P 284.
47 *Ibid*, p 285; he applied *The Nelly Schneider* (1878) 3 PD 152.
48 *The Appollo* (1880) 1 Hagg 306.

appointed by the whole body of the co-owners without objection on the part of the objecting part-owner.[49]

The foregoing principles derive from 19th century cases and have been applied by the court up to the present day, unless there is an agreement to the contrary.

The Vanessa Ann[50]

The case involved three part-owners of the fishing vessel, *Vanessa Ann*, which had not yet been registered because of defects of the registration of previous owners. It had been agreed between them that the vessel would be converted to a topsail schooner for use as a pleasure cruiser. In the meantime, one of the part-owners signed a charterparty for the vessel for day cruises from Antigua at $10,000 per week, providing for cancellation of the contract upon 28 days notice. The length of the charterparty was later varied to last for 12 months. The plaintiff, who had already proposed to the other owners to sell his share to them, opposed to the length of the charter and arrested the ship, thus obstructing the commencement of the charter. He applied to court for sale of the vessel *pendente lite*. The main dispute at this hearing was the employment of the vessel.

Staughton J, taking the interests of all parties into account, exercised his discretion and ordered the defendants: (i) to execute an equitable mortgage of the vessel or of their interest therein containing the usual covenants to secure the plaintiff's claims in a form satisfactory to the plaintiff; (ii) to undertake to the court that they would procure the execution and registration of a statutory mortgage as soon as possible; (iii) to undertake to the court that they would perform all the covenants. An equitable mortgage, he said, was the best that could be achieved, for the time being, until the registration of the vessel in the names of the parties had been perfected, bearing also in mind that the plaintiff wished to get out of the partnership.

Even if there is a management agreement signed by all co-owners, by which a third party is authorised to carry out the management of the ship, the minority shareholders can still object (subject to any contrary term) to the way the ship is managed. By an action of restraint,[51] they will be entitled to bail in the value of their shares, but they will obtain no profits nor incur any liabilities concerning a particular voyage.[52] Such an action of restraint cannot,

---

49 *The Talca* (1880) 5 PD 169.

50 [1985] 1 Lloyd's Rep 549.

51 Under the MSA 1995, Sched 1, para 6 (previously, MSA 1894, s 30), upon an application of any interested person in the ship (who has a proprietary right), the court has power to grant an injunction to prevent, for a specified time, any dealing with a registered ship or a share in it.

52 *The England* (1886) 12 PD 32.

however, be sustained if the part-owner is also the mortgagee of the ship who arrests the ship while she is performing a charterparty.[53] Similarly, a purchaser of shares in a ship, which at the time of the sale is on a voyage, will not be entitled to arrest the ship on the ground of objection to the charterparty having already been concluded by the appointed managing owner. The purchaser will be liable for the expenses of the voyage and will be entitled to a share of the freight, but may also be made to pay damages resulting from his wrongful arrest of he ship.[54]

The relationship between co-owners of ships in modern times is primarily governed by agreements, which contain extensive clauses of every aspect of their rights and obligations. The company structures of ownership are complex and they will either be in a form of various limited companies, parent and subsidiaries, each owning one ship, or in the form of public companies, depending on their financial arrangements. One company, for example, in the ownership venture may provide management and operation services, while another may charter the ship on a long bareboat charter and engage chartering brokers for the ship's employment. A different company may deal with the employment of crew, their competence and training, as well as their welfare. As will be shown in para 4, managing companies of a ship or a fleet can be exposed to liabilities and, with the advent of the ISMC, they also have an obligation to establish the operation of a safety management system. Breach of statutory provisions with regard to safe operation of ships will make them accountable to criminal liabilities.

4 MANAGEMENT OF SHIPS

4.1 General overview

The manager of the ship under English law has been known, from old times, as the ship's husband, who is expressly appointed by an agreement to manage the vessel or vessels of a company for its owners and he is not a part-owner.[55] The ship's husband is distinct from a managing owner who may be one of the co-owners.[56]

'Shipbrokers and agents' is a term used to represent the owners' managing agents, which are usually incorporated offshore with a representative office in

---

53 *The Innisfallen* (1886) LR 1 A&E 72; see, further, in Chapter 9, below, to what extent a mortgagee may, or may not, interfere with the rights of a charterer of the mortgaged ship.

54 *The Vindobala* (1887) 13 PD 42.

55 *The England* (1886) 12 PD 32.

56 *The Vindobala* (1887) 13 PD 42, in which the manager was a managing owner.

the UK. It may be a subsidiary or a sister company of the owning company, another offshore company. The company of shipbrokers is delegated with various tasks of management and it may have equity interest in the ships owned by the registered owners. The shipbrokers or agents sign contracts on behalf of the owners as agents only.

The growing complexities and competition in shipping since the late 1970s and, in particular, in the 1980s and 1990s have led to management of ships by independent professionals, who may manage their own ships, as well as those of others, or may provide management services for others only. Traditional and experienced owners, however, prefer to keep all management aspects under their control, by setting up their own management company and engaging the necessary expertise in-house or engaging a professional manager as a consultant. In a traditional integrated system, there is a close link between the officers and crew on a ship and the owner. In this way, a dual or split loyalty of the master, in particular, between owner and manager is avoided.[57]

As John Spruyt says:

> ... most of the large ship-management companies were shipowners before they became dedicated managers of ships for third parties. Most of these owners made a conscious switch into being managers, rather than doing a bit of management on the side. Few of the current leading managers are shipowners in any significant way, that is, in the sense of being involved in an equity risk in ships.[58]

A broad range of activities are undertaken by managers, if the whole management is delegated to them. For example, they supply all the necessary services on board, they carry out shore supervision, they look after the employment of the ship, arrange for a chain of charterparties, and even provide finance for certain debts. The capital finance of the ship is a risk taken by the owners. Finance, marketing and sales have been separate activities delegated to different expertise. Commercial management has included the marketing and chartering, while the technical operation and manning of ships have been kept separately.[59] Some managers provide only crewing management under special agreements. Professional managers are engaged particularly by banks when they take over ships from the owner after default under the mortgage agreement.

---

57 See Willingale, M (ed), *Ship Management*, 1998, LLP (this is the third edition of *op cit*, Spruyt, fn 3).

58 *Ibid*, p 178.

59 See generally, *op cit*, Spruyt, fn 3, and the second edition of this book (1994, LLP); this book has been drastically updated because of many changes in ship management in the late 1990s and the third edition, *ibid*, looks very different from the first two (Willingale is the general editor with other contributors).

4.2 The framework of management of ships

Although most of the agreements are tailor-made, the Baltic and International Maritime Council (BIMCO) has drafted a simple and straightforward ship management form (SHIPMAN), which is all embracing on the basic aspects of management. It was first issued in 1988 and updated in 1998 to reflect the changes brought by the ISMC, with regard to safety aspects of management of ships and contemporary ship management practices. The parties to the contract can agree further details to suit their requirements. There are also two BIMCO standard crew management agreements (CREWMAN A and CREWMAN B) which deal with specific management of crew. It is beyond the scope of this chapter to outline and analyse all management agreement clauses, but some will be mentioned in the appropriate sections later. The standard management agreement broadly includes the following tasks to be performed by the manager:

(a) to engage competent and qualified master and crew for the ship on behalf of he owners;

(b) to provide technical and operational information as required by the owner;

(c) to buy stores and lubricants;

(d) to engage arrange drydocking and surveys for the vessels;

(e) to maintain the ships in class and comply with requirements of class and safety regulations;

(f) to arrange insurance;

(g) to provide chartering services (if not separately provided by the managing owners or shipbrokers);

(h) to provide voyage estimates and accounting;

(i) to subcontract and appoint agents;

(j) to supervise sales and purchases;

(k) to provide budgeting and keep true accounts.

The standard ship management agreement responds to a need for uniformity. SHIPMAN has a widespread usage, providing a self-contained document which is used as a *pro forma* for third party management. It contains clear contractual provisions aiming to strike a fair balance between owners and managers.

The new form divides the management into three main compartments: crew management; technical management; and commercial management (chartering and incidental activities to chartering). Each of these aspects of management can be delegated to one professional managing company or be separated. A general manager may also deal with insurance arrangements, accounting services, sale and purchase, supply of provisions and bunkering. While accounting is part of the duties of any manager, the tasks of insurance, sale and purchase, bunkering and ship's provisions are usually preserved by the managing owner or shipbroker.

An experienced owner has, traditionally, maintained separate companies in his venture structure, each dealing with each aspect of management. With the advent of the ISMC, however, which requires voluminous maintenance of documentation and sophisticated computer systems, the privilege of preserving control of all management aspects within the ownership structure may be in the past for the less experienced owners. There is now more need for reputable professional managers, particularly as the legal implications of non-compliance with the requirements of the Code (as will be seen at the end of this chapter) may be far reaching for the less experienced owners.

4.3 Authority of ship managers and risk management

The authority of the manager is contained in the management agreement, which provides details of the powers of the manager to bind the owner to contracts with third parties and defines his obligations to the owner. Clause 3 of SHIPMAN 1998 makes it clear that the manager acts as the agent for, and on behalf of, the owner.

The manager must act always within the authority granted to him by the owners in accordance with the management agreement or, as the case may be, additional express authority. When the contract is silent about a specific matter, implied authority will arise, only if that matter is reasonably incidental to the execution of the manager's express authority.

Clause 3 of SHIPMAN provides: 'The managers shall have authority to take such actions as they may from time to time in their absolute discretion consider to be necessary to enable them to perform this agreement in accordance with sound ship-management practice.'

If the manager exceeds his authority, he will not bind the owner to contracts with third parties, unless the owner later ratifies the contract, and he will be at risk of being sued by the third party for breach of warranty of authority.

In some circumstances, the conduct of the principal may be such as to have held the agent out as having such authority; this would give rise to an agency by estoppel or apparent authority, in that the principal could be estopped from denying that the agent had authority to bind him to the contract.

Difficulties arise when the third party is not aware of the owner's existence. This is particularly so, because the owner of the ship, that is, the registered owner, is never in the front line. The shipbroking company or agent, which is separate from the registered owner, will usually contract on the owners' behalf, who may or may not be named in the contract.

Sometimes, the agent is made a party to the contract and he may sue on it. The question then arises as to what he can recover. In the leading case, *The Albazero*,[60] it was affirmed that the measure of damages for breach of contract is generally the financial loss which the plaintiff has sustained by reason of the defendant's failure to perform the contract according to its terms. The manager, therefore, who does not come within the exceptions of certain classes of people such as trustees or bailees who can recover the loss suffered by the beneficiary or bailor respectively, must prove his own loss.

It is common practice and knowledge that the shipbroker signs contracts on behalf of his principals, always as agent only. In this connection, particular attention must be given when proceedings are about to be issued for a breach of contract signed by the agent for the owners with the third party (defendant). The proceedings must be issued in the name of the registered owner, the contracting party. Otherwise, if they are issued in the name of the agent (who normally gives the instructions), there may be a professional negligence claim against the lawyer by his client owner for the loss suffered by not being able to claim his loss against the defendant, unless the owner takes part in the proceedings later (provided the claim is not yet time barred) and the claim form is amended accordingly.

The professional manager must also make it clear to the third party that he is acting for his principal, the owner. He will not be liable to the third party, if the third party knew that the manager was acting with authority of his principal. It is common practice for the managers to act as agents for the owners, except in certain circumstances when managers act as principals for the engagement of crew and the crew prefer to see themselves as employees of the managers. Their possible exposure to liability for crew negligence is discussed later.

When the owner is disclosed and named he can enforce the contract against the third party. When he is not named, that is, undisclosed, the intention of the third party becomes important. If, for example, the third party wanted to contract with the manager and no one else, then he is not bound to accept performance by the owner, or even worse for the owner, he may refuse to pay for the performance. Complex questions frequently arise in this respect as to whether the third party has repudiated the contract if his intention to contract with the agent, instead of the owner, is not sufficiently shown.

It is important to summarise the general principles in this respect:[61]

(a) where an agent enters into a contract, oral or written, in his own name evidence is admissible to show who is the real principal, in order to charge him or entitle him to sue on the contract;

---

60 [1977] AC 774.

61 See *Bowstead and Reynolds on Agency*, Sweet & Maxwell, 1996, Chapter 8, Art 78, and Chapter 9, below (on relations between agents and third parties).

(b) an undisclosed principal may sue or may be sued on any contract made on his behalf, or in respect of money paid or received on his behalf by his agent acting within the scope of his actual authority;

(c) an undisclosed principal may also be sued on any contract made on his behalf by his agent, acting within the authority usually confided to an agent of that character, notwithstanding limitations put upon that authority as between the principal and the agent;

(d) subject to the intervention of the principal, the agent can sue on a contract made with a third party when the principal is undisclosed; he is personally liable and entitled to the benefit of it, provided he can prove his loss.

Whether or not the agent has authority is a question of fact in each case. At common law, the manager may pledge the credit of his co-owners who have appointed him, or have acceded to his appointment, or held him out as having their authority. Registration of the manager in the registry does not, in itself, amount to holding out.

Frazer v Cuthbertson[62]

The management of the ship, *Coniscliffe,* was left to Watson (W) after the death of his father and he had been entered in the register as managing owner. The defendant, Cuthbertson (C), was the executor and later became registered owner of some shares in the ship, but he was trying to sell the ship. The defendant was not aware, in fact, that W was so registered as managing owner. W sent the ship on a voyage without the defendant's knowledge and, contrary to the terms of an agreement, made between them. The defendant did not participate in the adventure and had previously informed W that he did not intend to navigate the ship, or take any part in her management. The plaintiffs supplied necessaries for the ship previous to such voyage, upon the order of W, without the knowledge or consent of the defendant. The plaintiffs, doubting W's credit, consulted the register before supplying the goods and found the defendant's name entered as part-owner of the ship and that his record was solvent. W subsequently declared himself bankrupt.

The plaintiffs sued the defendant for the price of the goods and stores and contended that, even though the defendant did not know about the transactions, W had been allowed to navigate the ship by, or on behalf of, the owners. The issue was, whether the non-cancellation of the entry in the register that W was managing owner, amounted to holding W out to third parties as agent to navigate and manage the ship on behalf of the defendant.

Mr Justice Bowen held that, the fact that the defendant had allowed the entry on the register describing W as managing owner to remain unaltered, did not, *per se*, amount to a holding out of W as his agent, so as to render the

---

62 (1880) 6 QBD 93.

defendant liable for the necessaries supplied by the plaintiffs. In as much as W had not, in fact, authority to bind the defendant, the plaintiffs could not recover against the defendant for such necessaries.

He further stated:

> Shipowners to begin with are not necessarily partners. An owner's liability or non-liability for necessaries supplied to a ship depends on the question whether the person who gave the order had his authority to give it. The register no doubt is evidence of ownership of the vessel and the registered owner, until the contrary is shewn, may be presumed to be the employer of those who have the custody of her, and who are engaged in her navigation. But a part-owner, whether registered or not, has no power to bind the other owners without their assent. The question in each case is one of fact, whether he has had such authority committed to him, or if this is not in fact the case, whether he has been allowed to hold himself out as armed with such apparent authority ...
>
> The term managing owner ... is not defined in the Act of Parliament; it is a commercial and not a legal expression. It is perfectly true that a managing owner is a name which frequently and commonly denotes an owner to whom the other owners have delegated the management of a vessel. But I do not think it follows ... that every single other owner must be taken to have joined in the adventure merely because there is an owner called a managing owner. There is no magic in the term managing owner which creates him a plenipotentiary for those owners whose agent he is not in fact.[63]

Unless the management agreement provides that the manager has authority to engage repairers for exceptional repairs needed on the ship, or a specific authority is given in this respect, the manager is only authorised to debit the credit of the owner for ordinary running repairs.

Boston Deep Sea v Deep Sea Fisheries[64]

The plaintiffs carried on the business of management and operation of both their own fishing trawlers, and those of other people. They were the managers of the defendants' vessel, *The Harry Melling*. In pursuance of that management, they had to get the trawler ready for sea which involved provisioning her, providing coal and stores, engaging a skipper and crew, selling the fishing catch and paying off the crew and themselves. At the end of the year, the plaintiffs accounted to the defendants for profits made after all expenses and commission to them had been paid. On a night of bad weather, the skipper could not see well and hit a rock resulting in extensive bottom damage to the trawler. As the periodical five-yearly Lloyd's survey was almost due, the plaintiffs advised the defendants to carry out the survey at the same time as the collision repairs. The total estimated cost of repairs was

---

63   (1880) 6 QBD 93, pp 97, 98.
64   [1951] 2 Lloyd's Rep 489.

£5,800. The plaintiffs employed a firm to do most of the work involved in the Lloyd's survey and did some of it themselves, but the final cost of the work was actually £8,629, £2,829 in excess of what the defendants had been led to believe. The cost of repairing the collision damage was another £2,286, which the insurers paid. Part of the excess was paid out of the profits of subsequent voyages and the bulk of it had been paid previously. Later, the defendants agreed to share half of the proceeds of the profits on voyages with the plaintiffs, but this arrangement did not last and the defendants terminated the agency agreement. In a claim by the plaintiffs for the balance of the amount, the defendants claimed that the plaintiffs had no authority in the first place to order any work above what the Lloyd's surveyor had estimated the costs of the repair to be.

It was held that the management agreement did not of itself cover authority to do these exceptional repairs, that agreement would cover ordinary running repairs. However, on the facts, there was special and express authority from the defendants to do this work and to pay for it. There was no question that the work was not necessary and that the cost was not reasonable.

Moreover, when the bill was presented, there had been no suggestion that the plaintiffs had exceeded their authority. It was also held to be a material fact that there was no complaint to the crediting of the defendants' profits against the bill. Even in the absence of special authority, the defendants, on the facts, ratified what had been done.

Normally the management agreement will provide the particular way in which the parties wish to regulate their affairs. Confidentiality clauses and provision for close co-operation are very much in demand at present times.

SHIPMAN 1998 expressly provides, by cl 3.2, for authority of the manager, if the provision of technical management is agreed, to arrange and supervise drydocking, repairs, alterations and upkeep of the vessel, provided that the manager shall be entitled to incur the necessary expenditure to ensure that the vessel will comply with the law of the flag and the recommendations of the classification society. In addition, it has been incorporated in the new form that the manager shall have authority to fulfil the function of development, implementation and maintenance of a Safety Management System (SMS) in accordance with the ISMC. This is a very important new development in the light of the international regulations imposed upon owners and managers to provide a transparent system of safety. These regulations have made the need of professional managers even more prominent. Some owners would now prefer to have the managers in the front line, but the owners themselves would also have the obligation to provide a clear line of communication with the manager and define the extent of responsibilities and authority delegated to others.

If the crew management is delegated to a manager, the manager has authority and should make sure that the crew supplied should be competent and well trained and comply with the STCW 1995 code.[65] This is clearly the crew manager's obligation.[66] If the technical management is also delegated to managers, cl 4.2 of SHIPMAN 1998 provides that they shall procure that the requirements, or the law of the flag of the vessel, are satisfied and they shall, in particular, be deemed to be the 'Company'[67] as defined by the ISMC. They shall assume responsibility for the operation of the vessel and take over the duties and responsibilities imposed by the code, generally, and, in particular, in respect of the ships' surveys and repairs and whatever is required for their proper maintenance. All incidents must be recorded in the manuals and monitored for the purpose of risk analysis and prevention of accidents. These two aspects of management (crewing and technical) are the cornerstone of the requirements of the code for a safe management system. It should be noted, however, that the fulfillment of the obligations under the Code is a joint operation, between the owner and the manager under the agreement, and depends on what is delegated to the manager.

By cl 5.2 of the agreement, where the managers are not providing technical management, the owners shall procure that the requirements of the law of the flag of the vessel are satisfied and that they, or such other entity as may be appointed by them and identified to the managers, shall be deemed to be the 'Company' as defined by the code, having the responsibilities for the operation, etc.

4.4 Duties arising from the management agreement

Generally, an agent is under a contractual duty to perform his obligations under the contract with his principal with reasonable care and diligence in accordance with the terms of the contract and his principal's instructions. Under cl 4 of the SHIPMAN form, the manager undertakes to use his best endeavours to provide the agreed management services as agent for the owners, in accordance with sound management practice and to protect and promote the interests of the owners in all matters relating to the provision of services agreed in the contract. Best endeavours coupled with emphasis on

---

65 In 1995, the International Convention on Standards Training Certification and Watchkeeping for Seafarers 1978 was substantially revised and amended and entered into force in February 1997. The revised Convention contains explicit new responsibilities for shipping companies and is the 'sister' to the ISMC.

66 Hilton, C, 'Shipman and crewman revisited' (2000) BIMCO Review 57, pp 57–59.

67 ISMC, cl 1.1.2 provides that: 'Company means the owner or any other organisation or person such as the manager, or the bareboat charterer, who has assumed the responsibility for operation of the ship from the shipowner and who, on assuming such responsibility, has agreed to take over all duties and responsibility imposed by the code.'

sound ship-management practice does not mean less than exercising due care in the performance of the services by the manager, who must do his best in accordance with the skill that he professes to possess. Although the phrase 'best endeavours' usually embraces a subjective element in the standard of the duty, such endeavours are measured against the standard of a reasonable manager possessing the same skill and experience. The yardstick is 'sound management practice', which is an objective standard and does not refer to the manager's personal view of what is sound. For example, if the manager was instructed to insure the ship and he failed to do so, causing loss to his principal, he will be in breach of his duty of care and, hence, be liable in damages.[68] But, if he exercised his best endeavours to find an insurer for the ship and no insurer was willing to insure the particular risk, the manager would not be in breach of his duty. Under-insurance of the ship by the ship manager, which causes loss to the principal when the ship becomes total loss, will be a breach of the manager's duty, as it was in *The Maira*.[69]

The manager will also owe a fiduciary duty to his principal owners. This derives from the nature of the agreement, which is one of trust and confidentiality. It includes the duty of the manager not to take advantage of his position or his principal's property in order to acquire benefit for himself and not to act inconsistently with the interests of the owners. An illustration of such a duty was aptly given in *The Borag*, a ship-management case, in which the question was whether the manager's relationship with the shipowner was one of trustee and beneficiary.

The Borag[70]

The owners entered into an agreement by which the managers were appointed to act as technical and commercial managers of the vessel *Borag*. The agreement provided, *inter alia*, that the managers were entrusted with the entire and exclusive management responsibility of the owners' tanker, and that the managers undertook to perform the task with the same zeal and energy as if the vessel were their own, watching over the owners' interests in the spirit of close co-operation. In the course of dealings between the parties, the owners paid the managers US$55,000 to cover the vessels' monthly operating expenses and any balance in favour of the managers would be settled by the owners on receipt of the managers' monthly statement of accounts and vouchers. Disputes later arose between the parties, as regards funds for the drydocking of the vessel, and the manager claimed unpaid balances for one month and advance payment for the other. On the managers' orders, but without the knowledge of the owners, the vessel was secretly sailed into South African territorial waters, were she was arrested by the

---

68 *Turpin v Bilton* (1843) 5 Man & G 455.
69 [1986] 2 Lloyd's Rep 12.
70 [1980] 1 Lloyd's Rep 111.

managers for the sums allegedly owed them by the owners. The vessel was released on the tender of a letter of guarantee. The dispute was referred to arbitration and the umpire stated his award in the form of a special case for the opinion of the court. The owners were claiming that the circumstances of the arrest were such as to constitute breach of contract by the managers. According to the owners, the clause providing for the relationship between the parties had the effect of creating a full relationship of trustee and beneficiary, carrying with it all the incidents attached to such a relationship under English law. The managers claimed that the clause merely stipulated the standard of skill and endeavour they were expected to show, and was not different from any ordinary contract between a manager and a shipowner. Mustill J, as he then was, held that the managers had been in breach of their obligations:

> In my view, its purpose was to prescribe the spirit as well as the letter of the managers' functions. The owners were dependent on the managers' expertise in carrying out the day to day running of the vessel, which had been placed entirely within their control. They were entitled to have confidence in the managers to provide not merely a technically competent performance of their functions, but one which was furnished in a spirit of undivided loyalty to the best interests of the owners. The facts stated in the award make it clear that this confidence was abused. The managers did not, as the contract required, 'watch over' the owners' interests in a 'dedicated' manner. Instead, they watched over their own.[71]

It was also held that the managers could not have been trustees of the vessel in the strict sense, as they had no proprietary interest in the vessel. Although the parties clearly intended to create a fiduciary relationship between them, such a relationship was not identical with that of a trustee and beneficiary. In the light of breach of contract by the managers, the owners would be entitled to claim damages resulting from the provision of the guarantee and wasted running costs and expenses by reason of the vessel's detention if the arrest was wrongful.

A similar case arose recently with regard to breach of the fiduciary duty by the manager in *The Peppy*,[72] which was arrested by the manager for alleged outstanding balance of account. It was held, *inter alia*, that the conduct of the director of the managing company was dishonest, in that he knew that his company was the exclusive chartering manager and was required to fix the vessel at the most favourable terms and to collect the freight and account for them to the owner. As, on the facts, it was found that there was no outstanding balance at the time of the arrest, because there was a variation of the agreement to defer payments until the vessel was sold, the arrest of the

---

71 [1980] 1 Lloyd's Rep 111, p 122.
72 [1997] 2 Lloyd's Rep 722.

vessel was a repudiatory breach by the managers and the owners suffered recoverable loss by reason of the arrest.

4.5 Consequences of breach by the manager and contractual exclusion or limitation of liability

If the manager fails to perform his obligations under the contract, in accordance with sound ship-management practice, he will be exposed to liability, not only towards his principal, but also towards third parties for negligence. Clause 11 of the SHIPMAN form regulates the extent of liability of the manager to the owner. *Force majeure* is stated to be a cause excusing both parties from their mutual obligations to each other, if performance is prevented by reason of any cause whatsoever of any nature or kind beyond their reasonable control.

The manager will be liable to the owner for any loss, damage or delay or expense of whatsoever nature, caused due to his negligence, gross negligence or wilful misconduct, or that of his employees, or agents, or subcontractors employed by him in connection with the vessel. He can limit his liability provided the loss, etc, did not result from his personal act or omission committed with intent to cause same or recklessly and with knowledge that such loss, etc, would probably result. The liability shall not exceed the total of 10 times the annual management fee payable under the agreement (cl 11.2(i)). Such limit is very low, but it takes into consideration that, in reality, the manager's annual income per ship is between $80,000 and $150,000.[73]

If the manager is engaged for crew management, he has an option either to engage the crew as an employer, under BIMCO'S form CREWMAN B 1998, in which case he will be liable for their negligence, for which he can limit his liability, or to engage the crew as agent for and, on behalf of the owner, under CREWMAN A.

The manager shall not be liable for crew negligence, or gross negligence when the employment contract is signed on behalf of the owner, who will be the crew's employer. He may be liable, however, if he supplied uncertificated crew or failed to ensure that the crew had passed medical examination or training in compliance with STCW 1995 regulations and flag requirements (cl 11.2(ii)). In this respect, the manager is entitled to limit his liability.

---

73 Lawford, H (Chapter 6), in *op cit*, Willingale, fn 57.

4.6 Indemnity and 'Himalaya' clauses

An indemnity from the owner with regard to liability to third parties incurred by the manager, his employees, agents or sub-contractors in the course of the performance of the agreement is also granted to the manager by sub-cl 11.3. Such indemnity refers to liability that might be incurred by the manager to third parties and not to the owner, under cl 11.2.

Until very recently, under English law, the doctrine of privity of contract prevented third parties to a contact to take the benefit or protection of exclusion or limitation of liability clauses. Common law had invented a way round this situation, basically for policy reasons rather than strict legal principle. If a special clause was incorporated in the contract of the two main parties, the protection of exclusion or limitation of liability afforded to one contracting party would be extended to his employees or agents.[74] Otherwise, the employees, whose negligence invariably causes loss to the other contracting party, could be sued in tort to circumvent the contractual exclusion or limitation of liability. Such a clause became known as the 'Himalaya' clause having taken the name of the ship in a case in which this issue first arose.[75]

SHIPMAN includes such a clause (11.4), which is designed to afford a wide protection of the managers' employees, agents and sub-contractors.

The case for recognising a contract for the benefit of a third party on the ground of respect to the autonomy of the will of the parties to the contract and, in particular, when the third party has organised its affairs on the faith of that contract, has now been given the blessing of the Contracts (Rights of Third Parties) Act 1999.

The need and reasons for change in the light of the problems that had been created by the privity doctrine, which was seen as undermining commercial contracts, are explained in other recent publications.[76] Now a person, who is

---

74   *New Zealand Shipping Line v Satterthwaite (The Eurymedon)* [1972] 2 Lloyd's Rep 544 (PC); however, it was recently clarified by the Privy Council in *The Mahkutai* [1996] 3 All ER 502, that an exclusive jurisdiction clause did not fall within any of the terms in the bill of lading which purported to confer the benefit of exception or limitation of liability to every servant, agent and sub-contractor.

75   *Adler v Dickson (The Himalaya)* [1954] 2 Lloyd's Rep 267: a passenger of a cruise ship suffered injuries, which were allegedly due to the master's negligence. The contract for the cruise excluded all liability of the shipping company and its employees. The claimant commenced proceedings in tort against the master, who sought to rely upon the exclusion clause in the contract to which he was not a party. The defendant could not rely on the clause. Similarly, in *Scruttons Ltd v Midland Silicones Ltd* [1962] AC 446 (HL), the House of Lords held that the stevedores, by whose negligence the cargo on board the ship was damaged during discharge, were unable to rely upon a contract between the carrier and the consignees by which they had been given immunity from suit at the instance of the consignees. see Carver, *Carriage by Sea*, 13th edn, 1982, Stevens, Vol 1, paras 370–84; see, also, Chapter 14, below.

76   Recommendations for reform by the Law Commission (Report No 242) which resulted in the passing of the Contracts (Rights of Third Parties) Act 1999; and [contd]

not a party to a contract, may, by virtue of this Act, enforce a term of the contract if the contract expressly provides that he may, or the term purports to confer a benefit on him, unless on proper construction of the contract it appears that the parties did not intend the term to be enforceable by the third party.

4.7 Insurance

Potential exposure of the ship manager, for liability to the owners of the vessel managed and to third parties for loss caused due to his or his employees' negligence, is covered by insurance. He needs professional indemnity insurance and protection against third parties and statutory liabilities. The insurance must cover the manager's and his sub-contractors' negligence, breach of warranty of authority and fraud of his employees. The International Transport Intermediaries Club (ITIC) provides professional indemnity insurance of ship agents and shipbrokers. It also covers risks for claims by third parties against the manager when the owner's indemnity is inoperative or the owner has gone into liquidation, as well as legal costs in defending claims or in pursuing claims against others. The manager needs also to be co-assured with the owner, in the owners' insurance for Hull and P&I, because of the nature of the duties he undertakes. If the potential risks that might arise from the performance of such duties were insured separately, the premium would exceed the management fee.[77] Since the owner's duty to his contracting parties to exercise due diligence to make the ship seaworthy is non-delegable, the manager, who has undertaken full management, could be responsible to indemnify the owner for liability incurred due to unseaworthiness of the ship and caused by the manager's negligence.[78]

4.8 Safety aspects and the manager's obligations under the ISMC

As mentioned earlier, the ISMC has had a significant impact on the obligations of both owners and managers – to ensure that a safe system is in operation – as well as on the relationship between owners and managers.

First, the purpose of the Code is to provide an international standard for the safe management and operation of ships and for pollution prevention. The

---

76 [contd] comments on that report: Burrows, A, 'Reforming privity of contract (Law Commission Report No 242)' [1996] LMCLQ 467. See, also, Merkin, R (ed), *Privity of Contract*, 2000, LLP.

77 *Op cit*, Willingale, fn 57, Chapter 6, pp 124 and 131.

78 See, eg, *The Marion* [1984] 2 Lloyd's Rep 2 (HL), where the actual fault and privity of the managers deprived their principal, the owner, from the right to limit liability. However, as both the managers and owner were co-assured in the same P&I club no indemnity was pursued.

cornerstone of good safety management is commitment from the top of the shipowning company (*Preamble*).

Secondly, 'company' under the Code means the owner of the ship or any other organisation or person, such as the manager or bareboat charterer, who has assumed the responsibility for the operation of the ship from the shipowner and who, on assuming such responsibility, has agreed to take over all duties and responsibility imposed by the code (Art 1.1.2, which must be read together with Arts 3.2 and 2.2, providing for the company's responsibilities).

Thirdly, the *objectives* of the Code are generally described in Art 1.2:

(a) to ensure safety at sea, prevention of loss of life or human injury, protection of the environment;
(b) to improve safety management skills of personnel ashore and aboard ships; to establish safeguards against identified risks and to provide safe practices in ship operation;
(c) to ensure compliance with mandatory rules and regulations and that guidelines and standards recommended by the Flag State, classification societies and the marine industry organisations are taken into account.

Furthermore, the following *duties and responsibilities* of the relevant company arise from the Code:

(a) to establish a safety management system and policy and ensure that the policy is implemented and maintained at all levels of the organisation, ship-based and shore-based (Art 2);
(b) to define levels of authority and lines of communication between shore and shipboard personnel, as well as to establish procedures for reporting accidents and non-conformities with the provisions of the code (Art 1.4);
(c) if a manager is appointed, the owner must report full details to the Flag State administration and document the authority and responsibility of all personnel who manage (Art 3, which should be read together with Arts 1.1.2 and 12.6: the management personnel should take timely corrective action on deficiencies found);
(d) to designate a person or persons ashore having direct access to the highest level of management, who should have authority and responsibility to monitor all aspects of safe operation of each ship (Art 4);
(e) to define clearly the master's responsibility and issue instructions and orders in a clear and simple manner (Art 5) and ensure that the ship's personnel are able to communicate effectively in the execution of their duties under the code (Art 6.7);
(f) to maintain the ship and equipment by ensuring that inspections are held at appropriate intervals and corrective action is taken as well as keep record of these activities (Art 10);
(g) to establish and control all documents and data relevant to the Code (Art 11);

(h) to ensure that the ship operated by the company is issued with a document of compliance (DOC) and that every company is issued with a safety management certificate of compliance with the Code (SMC) (Art 13).

The new SHIPMAN form has taken into account the provisions of the Code and provides, if agreed between the parties, who will assume direct responsibility under the Code. It has already been noted that under cl 4.2 of the contract, when the manager undertakes the technical management of the ship, his company will be considered to be the 'company' under the Code, having the duties prescribed by it. On the other hand, if the owner does not delegate the technical management to the manager, cl 5.2 puts an obligation upon the owner to procure whatever is necessary for this purpose and, accordingly, his company will be the 'company' as defined by the Code.

The implementations of the Code have brought enormous changes in management practices, attitude and the interrelations between managers and owners. It does not require much imagination to appreciate the legal and commercial implications of the Code. It is hoped that a safety culture will become second nature in the not too distant future, otherwise the shipping industry may seriously shrink.

The documentation required by the Code, to be maintained by both owners and managers, will provide evidence and – even under the conservative new rules of court disclosure – will be made available under a specific request for disclosure in litigation. Thus, claims in relation to carriage of goods by sea, or claims by the owner or manager under the insurance contract, or for limitation of liability, may be affected, depending on the particular circumstances. Such issues have been discussed elsewhere by the author[79] and others.[80] Some of the points raised in those articles are discussed in the next section, having taken into account recent developments.

---

79 Mandaraka-Sheppard, A, 'The ISMC in perspective' (1996) 10 P&I International.

80 For an excellent up to date review of the Code and its implications, see Anderson, P, *ISM Code: A Practical Guide to the Legal and Insurance Implications*, 1998, LLP, which incorporates the statutory instrument enacting the Code into domestic legislation in 1998, and the opinions of other authors on the subject.

5 LEGAL IMPLICATIONS OF THE ISMC

5.1 Effect of non-compliance

The Code itself does not impose liabilities on the owners and managers of ships in the event of breach of its provisions. Breaches, however, will result in the non-certification of the company or the particular non-compliant ship, which, in turn, may have legal implications in the areas discussed here. SOLAS States that implement the Code into domestic legislation may, however, impose penalties, or criminal sanctions, for non-compliance.

By a 1998 statutory instrument, the Merchant Shipping ISMC Regulations 1998 (SI 1998/1561), the UK Government has effectively enacted the Code into domestic legislation. This statutory instrument provides for offences and penalties in the event of breach of the obligations stated therein, which will be discussed later under the sub-paragraph dealing with criminal liability.

Undoubtedly, the Code will provide a yardstick of conduct against which the shipowner's or manager's performance in operation of ships can be measured by the very reason that the Code requires extensive documentation of all incidents and communications between the designated person and senior management of the respective companies.

Evidence of a transparent system of operation, provided all is reported, may carry adverse consequences for those owners or managers who failed to comply with recommendations or to follow up results of risk assessment. Equally, a non-transparent system will give cause for serious questions to be asked.

There are several areas that this can be relevant in litigation. It is only intended here to examine four of them:[81] Due diligence under the Hague-Visby Rules (HVR); privity of the assured under s 39(5) of the Marine Insurance Act (MIA) 1906; limitation of liability under the Limitation Conventions; and criminal liability of the company.

These aspects become complicated because the owners or managers are not individuals, but companies, and, in each case, one has to identify the person or persons who are making the decisions in the corporate structure. Before entering into discussion of each area mentioned in the previous paragraph, it is appropriate at this point to examine the basis on which liability may be attributed to the company, for acts of persons of the company.

---

81 For further information on other aspects on which the Code will have a bearing, please refer to Anderson's practical guide (*op cit*, fn 80).

5.2 The rule of attribution[82]

The leading authority redefining this rule is *Meridian Global Funds Management Asia v Securities Commission*.[83] In a nutshell, the rule was put in the following words:

> Where a company's rights and obligations could not be determined either by the primary rules of attribution, expressed in its constitution or implied by law (for determining what acts were to be attributed to the company) or by the application of the general principles of agency or vicarious liability, the question of attribution for a particular substantive rule was a matter of interpretation or construction of that rule.

Thus, the sub-divisions of the attribution general theory are these:

(a) the primary rules of attribution of the company itself, which are to be found in the company's articles of association or its constitution, or the majority decisions of the shareholders, or the board's decisions. One will be able to find how the company has allocated responsibility and authority to certain persons, so that the directing mind and will of the corporation will be identified: thus, this theory is known as the 'identification' theory or doctrine;[84]

(b) the rules of attribution based on general principles of agency or vicarious liability for determination of liability of a corporation: The primary rules of attribution are, obviously, not enough to enable a company to go out into the world and do business. Not every act on behalf of the company could be expected to be the subject of a resolution of the board, or a unanimous decision of the shareholders. The company, therefore, builds upon the primary rules of attribution by using general rules of attribution, which are equally available to natural persons, namely, the principles of agency. It will appoint servants and agents whose acts, by a combination of the general principles of agency and the company's primary rules of attribution, count as the acts of the company. And, having done so, it will also make itself subject to the general rules by which liability for the acts of others can be attributed to natural persons, such as estoppel or ostensible authority in contract and vicarious liability in tort. This is known as the 'agency or vicarious liability' doctrine;[85]

---

82 An analysis of the origins and development of the subdivisions of the rule of attribution is given in Chapter 16, para 8.

83 [1995] 3 All ER 918 (PC).

84 *Lennard's Carrying Co Ltd v Asiatic Petroleum Ltd* [1915] AC 705 (HL); *DPP v Kent and Sussex Contractors Ltd* [1944] 1 KB 146; *ICR Haulage Ltd* [1944] KB 551; *Moore v Bresler* [1944] 2 All ER 515; *The Lady Gwendolen* [1965] P 294 (CA); *Tesco Supermarkets Ltd v Nattrass* [1972] AC 153 (HL); *Eurysthenes* [1976] 2 Lloyd's Rep 171 (CA); *The Safe Carrier* [1994] 1 Lloyd's Rep 75 and 589 (HL).

85 *Birmingham and Gloucester Rly Co* (1842) 3 QBD 223; *Great North of England Rly Co* (1846) 9 QBD 315; *Mousell Brothers Ltd v London and North Eastern Rly Co* [1917] 2 KB 836; *Griffiths v Studebakers Ltd* [1924] 1 KB 102 (HL).

(c) the 'special rule of attribution': sometimes, the court, having regard to the policy of a statute (the substantive law applicable to a particular case), may have to devise a special rule of attribution to determine whose act, or knowledge, or state of mind was, for the purpose of that statute or provision, to be attributed to the company. Knowledge of an act of a duly authorised servant or agent, or the state of mind with which it was done, although such person may not be the 'directing mind and will' of the company, would be attributed to the company only where, upon true construction of the relevant substantive provision, the policy behind the substantive rule of law so required.

In all cases, the Privy Council explained, it was a matter of construction for the Court in order to decide how the substantive rule of law was intended to apply. It may be that the rule of law, either expressly or by implication, excludes attribution on the basis of the general principles of agency; or the court might interpret the law as meaning that liability could apply to a company only on the basis of its primary rules of attribution (that is, if the act giving rise to liability was specifically authorised by a resolution of the board or a unanimous agreement of the shareholders).

However, in some cases, insistence on the primary rules of attribution would, in practice, defeat the intention of the substantive rule of law, thus, the court must fashion a special rule of attribution for the particular substantive rule as a matter of interpretation. It has to ask the question: 'Whose act (or knowledge, or state of mind) was, for *this purpose,* intended to count as the act, etc, of the company?' The contrast between this case and the *Tesco*[86] case illustrates the difference between the special rule of attribution and the pure identification doctrine.

On the facts of the *Meridian* case the substantive rule was a statute (New Zealand Securities Amendment Act 1988). A chief investment officer of an investment management company and its senior portfolio manager with the company's authority, but unknown to the directors, used funds managed by the company to acquire shares in a public issuer. So, the company became a substantial security holder in that public issuer. Under s 20(3) of the Act, the company ought to give notice of that holding, which it did not do and, therefore, it was in breach of its duty. The Securities Commissioner prosecuted the company and the question for the court was whether the knowledge of the employees, below the level of directors, could be attributed to the company. It was held that:

> Having regard to the policy of s 20 of the Act of 1988, and upon its true construction, the appropriate rule of attribution to be implied was that a corporate security holder knew that it was a substantial security holder in a public issuer when that was known to the person who had acquired the relevant interest with the company's authority, whereupon the company was

---

86 *Tesco Supermarkets Ltd v Nattrass* [1972] AC 153 (HL); see Chapter 16, below.

obliged to give notice under s 20(3). The knowledge of the transaction by the relevant employee was attributable to the company irrespective of whether he could be described in a general sense as its directing mind and will, and so in failing to give notice the company had been in breach of its duty under s 20(3).

If, on the contrary, the primary rules of attribution were applied, by which only the directors' knowledge would be attributed to the company, the policy of the Act which compelled immediate disclosure would be defeated.

This was contrasted with the ruling of the House of Lords in *Tesco Supermarkets v Nattrass*[87] (the identification doctrine), in which the substantive law for interpretation was the Trade Descriptions Act (TDA) 1968. Tesco were prosecuted under s 11(2) for displaying a notice that goods were being 'offered at a price less than that at which they were in fact being offered'. The shop manager had failed to notice that he had run out of the specially marked low price packets.

The Act requires reasonable precautions to be taken and due diligence to be exercised by the shop owner to avoid commission of an offence under the Act. But, whose precautions counted as those of the company? For the purpose of the TDA 1968, it was sufficient that the board of the company took the precautions and it had taken them. Therefore, the negligence of the manager, who was personally liable, was not attributed to the company.

It should be noted that Lord Hoffmann (in the *Meridian* case) when formulating the rule of attribution, entered a caveat of caution:

> Their Lordships would wish to guard themselves against being understood to mean that whenever a servant of a company has authority to do an act on its behalf, knowledge of that act would for all purposes be attributed to the company. It is a question of construction in each case as to whether the particular rule requires that the knowledge that an act has been done, or the state of mind, with which it was done, should be attributed to the company.[88]

The central question in this part of the chapter is, whose acts or omissions could be attributed to the shipowning or ship-management company and what is the relevance of the ISMC and of the delegated person? Each aspect of the attribution rule mentioned earlier will be considered in the context of the 'due diligence' provision of the HVR, 'privity' of the assured under s 39(5) of the MIA 1906, limitation of liability and criminal liability.

5.3. The due diligence provision of the HVR

It is not the objective of this book to look at this area, about which the reader is referred to other specialist books. It suffices to mention, for the present

---

87 [1971] 2 All ER 127.
88 *Meridian Global Funds Management Asia v Securities Commission* [1995] 3 All ER 918, p 928.

purpose, that the due diligence provision under the HVR is not delegable. In other words, there would be no defence to a cargo claim by the owner that he instructed reputable surveyors or repairers to rectify faults of the ship but which, without his personal fault, were negligently repaired. Consequently, if the cargo carried on the ship is damaged and the cargo-owner proves, not only that the ship was unseaworthy, but also causation, the shipowner then must discharge the burden of proof that he exercised due diligence before and at the beginning of the voyage to make the ship seaworthy, as is required by these Rules.[89] In doing so, he will not be assisted by the fact that he had delegated the repairs of the ship to a reputable independent contractor, whose negligence rendered the ship unseaworthy. The obligation imposed on the shipowner is one of due diligence in the work of repair by whomsoever it might be done, even when the work is delegated to the independent contractor for his technical or special knowledge or experience and the negligence is not apparent to the shipowner.[90] It seems that the policy behind the HVR is not to ask whether or not the directing mind of the company knew about it. A special rule of attribution applies here.

Any failings of the system of operations, selection of crew,[91] or management, which render the ship unseaworthy, will now be more apparent from the safety management manual (SMM), if the proper documentation required by the ISMC is kept. This will supply ammunition to cargo claimants to show a causative link between the cargo damage and the unseaworthiness. Incidents that occur on the ship which are likely to render her unseaworthy will now have to be reported, so that the examples of *The Apostolis*[92] (in which there were no contemporaneous documents showing when the welding, which was alleged to have been the cause of the fire, took place) and *The Toledo*[93] (failure to have proper systems in place for inspecting and maintaining the vessel) ought to be curtailed. Even if the system is not transparent enough, the owner will not be able to explain why the documents are not kept, nor that he had delegated the tasks of monitoring for the purpose of the ISMC to the designated person or the manager.

Since the duty of due diligence is non-delegable, the significance of this for ship-managers is that the owner, who may be found liable to third parties due to negligence of the manager, would seek an indemnity or damages against the manager for breach of the management contract, if the failings rendering the ship unseaworthy were due to the latter's negligence. However, since the manager is normally co-assured in the owner's insurance, the consequence

---

89 HVR, Art III(1).
90 *The Muncaster Castle* [1961] AC 807 (HL), p 836, *per* Viscount Simonds.
91 *The Makedonia* [1962] 1 Lloyd's Rep 316 (inefficient chief engineer rendered the ship unseaworthy).
92 [1996] 1 Lloyd's Rep 475 and [1997] 2 Lloyd's Rep 241 (CA).
93 [1995] 1 Lloyd's Rep 40.

will be that the owner's P&I insurance will respond, unless there are breaches of the insurance contract under the Marine Insurance Act 1906 or of the rules of the P&I Association. An example of this was in *The Marion*[94] case (seen in another context later) – in which the ship-managing company failed to make sure that old charts on the ship were destroyed and up to date ones provided. As a result, the master of the ship – who followed an old chart – caused the fouling of the ship's anchor, resulting in damage to an oil pipe line in berth. Both manager and owner were insured with the same P&I club, under the same policy, and, since the owner could not limit his liability due to the manager's fault and privity, the P&I insurer paid the third party's claim in full. The insurer could not sue (under its subrogated rights) its other assured (the manager) for a claim the owner might have had against him.

As far as breaking limitation of liability under the HVR is concerned, the test is the same as under the 1976 Convention discussed under para 5.5.1, below.

5.4 Privity of the assured under s 39(5) of the MIA 1906

What is said here assumes some knowledge of the subject. In a claim by the assured under an insurance policy contract against the underwriters for an indemnity in respect of a loss or damage to the ship (hull and machinery insurers), or liability to third parties (P&I insurance), the insurers may raise the defence of s 39(5). The burden of proof is on the insurer to show that: (i) the ship was unseaworthy when she was sent to sea; (ii) the assured had positive knowledge of her unseaworthiness or had turned a 'blind eye'[95] to the facts, which rendered her unseaworthy; and (iii) the loss was attributable to that unseaworthiness of which the assured was privy[96] (causation).

Privity is concerned with the assured's state of mind. In a case of a company, the identification[97] of the natural persons who had the relevant state of mind in relation to unseaworthiness is necessary. It is the state of mind of the head man that is taken into consideration, or whoever may be considered to be the *alter ego* of the company, or the directing mind and

---

94 [1984] 2 Lloyd's Rep 1.

95 Eg, if a man is suspicious of the truth and turns a blind eye to it, and refrains from inquiry so that he should not know it for certain: see *The Eurysthenes* [1976] 2 Lloyd's Rep 171, p 179, *per* Lord Denning MR. Recently, the House of Lords held in *The Star Sea* reported [2001] 1 Lloyd's Rep 389 that 'blind eye knowledge ... requires a conscious reason for blinding the eye. There must be at least a suspicion of a truth about which you do not want to know and which you refuse to investigate', *per* Lord Clyde.

96 *The Eurysthenes* [1976] 2 Lloyd's Rep 171; *Thomas v Tyne and Wear Steamship Insurance Association* (1917) 117 LT 55.

97 The 'identification' theory (see, further, Chapter 16, below).

control of the company.[98] Constructive knowledge of the condition of the ship on the part of the directors of the owning or managing company is not sufficient, as is shown in the case discussed below.

In decided cases, it has been difficult for the insurers to discharge this burden, even in *The Star Sea*,[99] the factual background to which, one would have thought, ought to have assisted the insurers to succeed in discharging the burden of proof on the privity point. However, the events happened before the implementation of the ISMC. It is important, therefore, to look at this case in the light of ISMC.

The ship had some history of deficiencies and, in 1990, the Belgian port authority surveyor had found, *inter alia*, that the emergency fire pump was not working. The master was instructed to rectify this and other deficiencies before departure. The chief engineer tried to repair the pump, but failed. In the course of his efforts to do so, he cut the suction pipe passing through the forepeak ballast tank to a non-return valve in the ship's side. The emergency fire pump was, in due course, repaired, but the cut pipe was never repaired. The ship sailed for her next voyage fully loaded. As she approached the Panama Canal, a fire started in the engine room, which spread to other parts and was not finally put out for several days, by which time the vessel had become a constructive total loss (CTL). Two other vessels in the same ownership, the *Centaurus* and the *Kastora*, had become CTL by fire in similar circumstances. When the owners claimed under the insurance policy, the insurers denied liability relying on breach of the duty of utmost good faith and on s 39(5). Only the second defence is relevant here, the grounds of which were the following: (i) by reason of the cut pipe the emergency fire pump was useless when the vessel was laden; (ii) there was ineffective sealing of the engine room; (iii) the master was incompetent in that he was unaware of the need to use the CO_2 system as soon as he realised that the fire could not be fought by any other means and that he did not know how to use it.

Tucky J held that the ship was unseaworthy by reason of the cut pipe and the fact that the master was incompetent in not knowing how to use the CO_2 system, which was the most potent weapon in fire-fighting. On the issue of privity of the assured under this section, the judge held that the directors of the company, the *alter ego*, had a 'blind eye' knowledge of the relevant facts of the ship's unseaworthiness. In particular, he said that:

> With the message staring them in the face that the CO_2 system on *Centaurus* and *Kastora* had not been used so as to prevent those ships from becoming constructive total losses, the assured took no effective steps to ensure that this would not happen again. The incompetence of the master and the state of the

---

98 *The Eurysthenes* [1976] 2 Lloyd's Rep 171, p 179, *per* Lord Denning MR.

99 *The Star Sea* [1995] 1 Lloyd's Rep 651 (1st inst) and [1997] 1 Lloyd's Rep 360 (CA). The hearing of the appeal to the House of Lords was taking place at the time of the completion of this book and the decision was announced on 18 January 2001 during the proofreading stage, later reported [2001] 1 Lloyd's Rep 389.

safety equipment for sealing the engine room, essential to the effectiveness of the CO_2 system on *Star Sea* show only too clearly how ineffective those steps were and how inadequately equipped she was to fight a fire effectively. The assured did not want to know about the competence of the master to use the CO_2 system effectively.[100]

Thus, the assured's claim failed. However, the Court of Appeal thought differently on the issue of privity. Leggatt LJ held that:

> However negligent it may have been not to learn lessons from the previous fires on *Centaurus* or *Kastora*, or to fail to give proper instructions in fire-fighting or whatever, what the defendant underwriters had to establish was a suspicion or realisation in the mind of at least one of the relevant individuals that *Star Sea* was unseaworthy in one of the relevant aspects, and a decision not to check whether that was so for fear of having certain knowledge about it. Thus, on this aspect, and to be precise, to succeed the underwriters would have to establish that one or other of the individuals …suspected that the master was incompetent in lacking the knowledge as to how to use CO_2 and that that rendered *Star Sea* unseaworthy, but that he decided not to check for fear of having certain knowledge and allowed the ship to go to sea anyway. The judge made no such finding. Indeed his finding in this area comes down simply to a finding of negligence, albeit negligence in a high degree.[101]

The Court of Appeal found that the relevant directors of the management company of the assured were involved in the decision making process required for sending the ship to sea. But Leggatt LJ drew a distinction between an allegation that 'they ought to have known' (as the judge thought) and an allegation that 'they suspected or realised but did not make further enquiries'. The former indicates constructive knowledge, while the latter would amount to 'blind eye' privity.

The House of Lords, on 18 January 2001[102] affirmed the decision of the Court of Appeal. Lord Scott explained 'blind eye' knowledge by giving a vivid example: 'Nelson at the battle of Copenhagen made a deliberate decision to place the telescope to his blind eye in order to avoid seeing what he knew he could see if he placed it to his good eye.' Lord Scott continued: 'It is, I think common ground – and if it is not, it should be – that an imputation of blind eye knowledge requires an amalgam of suspicion that certain facts may exist and a decision to refrain from taking any step to confirm their existence.'

This is a very significant decision with respect to the application of the duties of the owners and managers under the ISMC. The factual position of this case is the very situation that the Code intends to prevent. The directors of

---

100 *The Star Sea* [1995] 1 Lloyd's Rep 651, p 664.

101 [1997] 1 Lloyd's Rep 360 (CA), p 377.

102 Transcript, which was kindly provided to the author by Hill Taylor Dickinson, the solicitors acting for the owners; it was subsequently reported [2001] 1 Lloyd's Rep 389.

the managing company, or of the owners, have to make sure that the master is competent in using any systems on the ship as well as to ensure (by an efficient risk assessment) that previous incidents in any of the ships of the group do not recur. Documenting, monitoring and making a risk analysis of all previous incidents, which must be recorded in the company's SMM, can achieve this objective.

An important question that is frequently asked in the light of the ISMC is whether, for the purpose of s 39(5), the knowledge of the DP of deficiencies in the SMS, which he failed to report to the senior management, could be attributed to the company.[103] Although this may be a 'catch 22' situation for the owners, in that a failure by the DP to report could be, if proved, a failure of the SMS of the company in some cases, knowledge of the DP, it is submitted, could not be imputed to the company, unless DP is made, by the primary rules of attribution, a member of the board of directors. However, the directors of the company are now under an increased obligation by the Code to ask questions and make an enquiry of what the DP knows, but for the purpose of s 39(5), it is not what the directors ought to have known but what they suspected or consciously realised by the reported events and did not make further inquiries.

The point in law made by Leggatt LJ and the House of Lords in this case is that, if the insurers could only show constructive knowledge by the directors of the company of the relevant facts, it will not be sufficient for the discharge of the burden of proof under s 39(5).

However, if the insurer still fails to discharge the burden under s 39(5), there is now an alternative way in which he can be discharged from liability. The Institute Clauses for hull insurance 1995 contain a special contractual classification warranty. The warranty in effect side-steps the difficulty of s 39(5). It requires strict compliance by the assured with matters of class and maintenance of seaworthiness during the duration of the policy, failing which the insurer will be discharged from liability as from the date of the breach. The documentation, under ISMC, will assist in the collection of evidence and make owners and managers more vigilant about management practices and incidents, which have or ought to have been reported to class, which, in turn, will assist the insurers to catch the recalcitrant assured under this warranty, if not under s 39(5). Similarly, the amendment to the Inchmaree clause in the 1995 Clauses makes the insured risks under this clause (including crew negligence) subject to the exercise of due diligence not only by the owners and managers, but also by the superintendent and the assured's shore management. If, for example, a loss is caused due to the negligence of the master or crew, this will be a covered peril, provided due diligence had been exercised by the persons mentioned in the clause, not only in the selection procedures of the ship's personnel but also in their supervision and training.

---

103 See, *op cit*, Mandaraka-Sheppard, fn 79.

The documentation required under the Code may enable the insurers to support their defence to a claim made by the assured under the policy.

In any event, even if the 1995 Clauses are not used in a hull policy, the Hull and Machinery insurers, since the implementation of the Code, insist on compliance with the Code by the assured. For this purpose, a clause is inserted in the policy to this effect, expressly requiring the assured to comply with the provisions of the Code, spelling out the consequences of failure. Similarly, with the advent of the Code, P&I clubs have taken care to include an ISMC compliance clause in their rules in the nature of a condition that the owner shall not be entitled to any recovery under the policy in respect of claims arising during the period when the assured was not fulfilling the requirements under the Code.[104] P&I clubs vary in their approach, some have indicated that they will take a hard line and cancel cover automatically, while others are taking a more flexible approach.[105]

5.5 Limitation of liability

5.5.1 From an English law perspective

Limitation of liability is examined in Chapter 16. Only brief reference will be made here to general principles for the purpose of considering the likely effect of the ISMC on the right of the owner or manager to limit liability.

Under the Limitation Convention 1957, following which s 503 of the MSA 1894 was amended by the subsequent MSA 1958, the shipowning company could limit its liability, if there was no 'actual fault or privity' of the owner. The burden of proof was upon the owner seeking to limit liability. 'Breaking' limitation was relatively easy. English law now applies the 1976 Limitation Convention, but some maritime nations still apply the 1957 Convention.

To make a brief contrast between the two, it suffices to mention that, under the old system of limitation, the owner, even if he had delegated the duty of management to a manager, could not limit his liability if the 'actual fault or privity' of the managing director of the managing company was the cause of the casualty. So, it was held in *The Marion*,[106] by the House of Lords, in which the managing director of the managing company had failed to give proper instructions to his subordinates during his absence and to ensure that adequate supervision was exercised over the master of the ship.

---

104 See, eg, the new cl 5K of the UK Club Rules, which is a provision subject to the directors' discretion. Similarly, r 29 of the North of England P&I Club.
105 *Op cit*, Anderson, fn 80, p 160
106 [1984] 2 Lloyd's Rep 1 (see further Chapter 16).

In *The Lady Gwendolen*,[107] the owners were unable to limit liability because the fault of a superintendent was traced upwards to the board of directors for a series of faults in the operating manuals and for not having adequately supervised the operation. In *The Garden City*,[108] again, the owners could not limit liability under the 1957 Convention, as they failed to discharge the burden of proof that the accident was without their fault or privity. The top management of the owning company had failed to ensure that a senior superintendent should be responsible for supervising the quality of navigation and that the vessels in the fleet should be regularly inspected with checklists and written reports.

The facts of these cases echo the philosophy behind the ISMC. Where the 1957 Convention still applies, any failures by the owner or manager in keeping am SMS under the ISMC will provide the evidence of fault or privity, but even prior to the implementation of the Code, it was not that difficult under this Convention for the right to limit to be broken.

By contrast, the 1976 Limitation Convention has a rigid rule of impeaching the right to limit liability. First, the burden of proof is upon the claimant resisting limitation, instead of upon the owner, as it was under the old law. The claimant needs to prove: (i) that the loss claimed resulted from a personal act or omission of the legal persona of the shipowner (it would not be enough that the fault was that of a DP); and (ii) that it was committed, either with intent to cause such loss, or recklessly and with knowledge that such loss would probably result (Art 4 of the Convention).

In other words, the legal persona of the company must have anticipated the likelihood or probability of the loss or damage, but, nevertheless, acted or failed to act regardless of that probability. So, it is no longer a question of simple fault, nor is it sufficient for the act or omission to be that of the manager or DP (such as servants or agents),[109] but it is required to be the personal act or omission of the person who seeks to limit.

Instead of privity, as was necessary under the old English system of limitation, proof of intent to cause such loss is needed, or proof of recklessness coupled with knowledge that such loss would probably result. Since it is hard to discharge the burden required by this new rule, it has been difficult to break limitation.[110] As a *quid pro quo* to bargaining away a test by which it was not previously difficult to break limitation, a much higher limitation figure per ship's ton is provided by this Convention.

---

107 [1965] 1 Lloyd's Rep 335 (see case summary in Chapter 16).

108 [1982] 2 Lloyd's Rep 382.

109 Unlike Art 4 of the 1976 Convention, Art 25 of the Warsaw Convention, as amended providing bar to limitation of liability of airlines, includes acts or omissions of 'servants or agents'.

110 For details of cases that have construed the wording of this rule, see Chapter 16, below.

In applying the rules of attribution for the purpose of Art 4 of the 1976 Convention, it is submitted that it would be a violation of its wording and the policy behind this substantive rule of law, if the act or failure to act by an agent (that is, the DP of the company seeking limitation) unbeknown to the company, was allowed to be taken into account – unless such a person had been made a member of the board of directors.

If, however, the evidence showed that the highest level of management ignored certain facts reported to them by the DP in relation to deficiency of the system leading to non-conformity with the Code, then such evidence would point strongly to recklessness by the legal persona of the company. A person acts recklessly when he acts in a manner which indicates a decision to run the risk or a mental attitude of indifference to its existence.[111] But, for the purpose of breaking limitation, the claimant must also prove that the legal persona of the company seeking limitation acted with knowledge that such loss would probably result[112] from such non-conformity with the Code.

This would involve proof of either (i) a high degree of subjective realisation that damage would probably result, or (ii) a deliberate shutting of the eyes to a means of knowledge which, if used, would have produced the same realisation. Falling short of that test, constructive knowledge of the directors of the company, in a sense that they ought to have known that damage would probably result, would not be in line with the policy behind the respective statutes dealing with limitation of liability and having the wording analysed above.

However, in the light of the ISMC, the person seeking limitation is likely to be questioned as to why he did not make inquiries to ensure that all was in order. Were it to be shown that he made a decision to run the risk and shut his eyes to a means of knowledge staring him in the face by virtue of the ISMC, which, if used, would have produced a conscious realisation that such loss would probably result, the test of Art 4 would be met.

In each case it will be a question of fact with regard to the extent and degree of faults in the SMS of the relevant company and whether a non-corrective approach to those faults amounted to recklessness with knowledge that the kind of loss claimed would probably result.

5.5.2 From a US perspective

A very appropriate example in terms of factual background in this respect is provided by a recent American decision, *The Merchant Patriot*,[113] although

---

111 *Goldman v Thai Airways International* [1983] 1 WLR 1186, p 1194, *per* Eveleigh LJ.

112 These words were construed by the Court of Appeal, in *Goldman* (*ibid* and [1983] 3 All ER 693), as requiring a higher standard than mere recklessness.

113 (2000) transcript of the US District Court of Georgia, 17 February, kindly provided to the author by Herry Lawford of the UK P&I Club.

the facts surrounding the case arose prior to the implementation of the Code. The issue in this decision was limitation under USA law, in particular, the Limitation of Liability Act 1851, 46 USC paras 183–89. So, the test was one of knowledge or privity of the loss-causing negligent act, or unseaworthy condition by the owners or the owners *pro hac vice* of the vessel. The facts of this decision may be relevant in considering the role of the DP and the impact of the ISMC, so it is important to look at the history of the ship and the quality of its management in relation to the casualty.

The ship was carrying steel products of $10 m worth, which was lost during the voyage. The problem started with the deteriorated and wasted condition of certain pipes in the seawater circulating system, which caused the flooding of the engine room, the contamination of the lube oil and, eventually, the shutdown of the main engine which resulted in the abandonment of the ship and the loss of the cargo.

The ship, which had been built in Scotland in 1980 and classed with Lloyd's Register, was bought in 1988 and the management of it was transferred to V Ships, who also managed other vessels of the same owner as agents without ownership rights in the ships. V Ships were not charterers but hired and managed the crew, operated the ship and oversaw her maintenance on an annual budget. The owners paid crew wages, running expenses of the ship and repair costs. The principal of the owners spoke to V Ships personnel about the ships under their management, during every given day, and was meeting with the managing and operations' directors frequently to discuss the status of the ships. V Ships provided the owners with several types of reports pertaining to the condition of the vessels, and the principal of the owners was, interestingly, described as 'a hands-on owner' who would personally attend the vessels and perform his own repairs. V Ships performed their duties through a Safety and Quality Management System, which set out in a series of manuals, policies and procedures what should be followed. The maintenance to the vessels was to be a joint effort by the ship's staff and the office personnel of V Ships who were to conduct periodic inspections of the vessel's structure and systems including the engine room piping, together with V Ships' fleet Superintendents.

V Ships, apparently, had a very similar system of safety management in place to that required now by the ISMC, but it was not as structured and vigorously enforced as the one required by the Code. So, what did go wrong? It was the corroded state of the pipes internally and externally. When the principal of the owners and every senior person in V Ships saw the status of the pipes, it was admitted – with hindsight – that the condition was unacceptable and the pipes ought to have been renewed. Why, then, had they not been renewed? The senior fleet superintendent of V Ships did not call for any renewal or replacement during the vessel's drydocking in April 1997, although six months earlier, when he had performed an inspection, he commented in his report that some engine pipes and valves required replacement, indicating that that should be done at the upcoming drydocking. However, the chief engineer, at about the same time, had reported after conducting visual inspection and hammer tests that the engine room piping was satisfactory. Was this due to human error, incompetence or superficiality in inspection, or due to inadequate mechanical equipment used for the inspection? This background has significant implications on how things can be prevented under the systems imposed by the ISMC. The use of old methods of hammer tests at inspections will be insufficient to satisfy the requirements of the Code.

The court found that the ship was unseaworthy and both the owners and V Ships were privy to the condition that caused the casualty, which could have been averted if those, having managerial responsibility of the vessel, including the fleet superintendents, the managing directors of the companies and the principal of the owning company, had taken reasonable action. The court pointed out the critical acts and omissions of the owners and V Ships which established privity and are important to be summarised here by way of illustrating how such acts and omissions can be averted under the ISMC system:

(a) There was no effective system for creating an historical record of critical information about the seawater pipes and ensuring that those responsible for maintenance were provided with that information. The fleet superintendent had not seen reports of previous failures nor was he aware of them.

(b) There was no planned system in effect for the inspection and maintenance of the seawater pipes. V Ships kept no written records of pipe inspections. The techniques to prevent galvanic corrosion were not employed on the vessel.

(c) No programme was implemented to identify and renew pipes prior to their failure, although there was knowledge possessed by the managing director of V Ships that ferrous seawater pipes fail after five years of service.

(d) There was a failure to effect a permanent repair to the patched aft pipe after more than three years and intervening drydocking. This demonstrated, the court said, either an ineffective follow-up system, or a conscious decision to leave the pipe in place.

(e) The corrosion reports put the owners and the managers on notice that galvanic corrosion was a significant problem with regard to seawater piping.

(f) The type of inspection that the owners and managers employed was insufficient and unreasonable. They conducted only a visual examination of the seawater piping, while the implementation of additional procedures for the inspection and replacement of them was feasible.

(g) Nothing was done to impede the progress of corrosion or galvanic corrosion.

In conclusion, the court found the owners liable for the damage to the cargo on the ground of their failure to exercise due diligence to make the ship seaworthy at the commencement of the voyage, which caused the casualty. The owners could not discharge the burden of proof required under the US limitation statute that they lacked knowledge or privity with regard to unseaworthiness. Under USA law, constructive knowledge of the top management of the owners counts for the purpose of limitation. In other words, 'knowledge is not only what the shipowner knows but what he is charged with discovering in order to apprise himself of conditions likely to produce or contribute to a loss',[114] or knowledge and privity includes constructive knowledge, or what the vessel owner could have discovered through 'reasonable inquiry'.[115] The belief of V Ships that they had an efficient system was not accepted by the court. What mattered was that the system, in fact, was inefficient to detect the defects in the piping system.

The court's finding, in this case, seems to have been the prelude to the ISMC and the safety system which must be in place, which has to be monitored and supervised by the designated person who is the link man between the top management and those on board. In this connection, it is relevant to refer to what Lord Donaldson said at the first Cadwallader Memorial Lecture,[116] considering the role of the DP:

> I regard this as not only one of the central pillars of the code, but also as the errant shipowners Achilles' heel. The 'blind eye' shipowner is faced with a 'catch 22' situation. If he hears nothing from the designated person, he will be bound to call for reports, for it is inconceivable there will be nothing to report. If the report is to the effect that all is well in a perfect world, the shipowner would be bound to enquire how that could be, as the safety management system is clearly intended to be a dynamic system which is subject to continuous change in the light, not only of the experience of the individual ship, and of the company as a whole, but also of the experience of others in the industry. So, there will always be something to report. Quite apart from this, the shipowner can, at any time, be called upon to produce documentary evidence of his internal audit of every area of his system including the work of the designated person.

This observation suggests that any mistakes or personal inattention of the DP will be caught up, if the owner or manager is rigorous in the enforcement of the Code. It also suggests that a fallible nature of human beings will be reversed by the ISMC. To a great extent, it is correct to say that a 'catch 22'

---

114 *Hercules Carriers Inc*, cited in the judgment of *The Merchant Patriot* (2000) transcript of the US District Court of Georgia, 17 February, p 28, see fn 113.

115 *Suzuki of Orange Park Inc v Shubert* [1996] 86 F 3d 1060, p 1064 (11th Cir).

116 *Op cit*, Lord Donaldson, fn 9.

situation has been created by the Code for owners and managers, but the writer is still sceptical about the extent to which, in reality, all will become transparent in the SMS. In the myriad of problems and issues that have to be attended on each ship, it may not always be possible to eliminate all possible faults, even with the most elaborate and carefully structured system of safety being in place. Large multinational companies may face greater problems of communication than small ones, in which there can be more effective communications by close relationship and co-operation between the teams of people delegated with the various tasks.

5.6 Criminal liability

It should be borne in mind that the ISMC does not itself impose criminal liability. It is up to each individual State, which implements the Code, to legislate the extent to which criminal liabilities for breach of the Code by the owner, or manager, or officers delegated with ISMC responsibilities can arise. In this part, the matter is looked upon from the point of view of English law. Criminal sanctions for the unsafe operation of ships had already been imposed by the MSAs 1988 and 1995, before the ISMC was implemented by a statutory instrument SI 1998/1561. Separate criminal sanctions for breaches of the obligations under the Code are now imposed under this statutory instrument. While such offences are clearly defined by statute, the major issue for discussion at the end of this part is criminal liability for involuntary manslaughter by corporations, and the effect of the ISMC.

5.6.1 Statutory offences under the MSAs

The MSA 1995 contains various statutory offences, some of which are relevant here. By s 77, every British ship must keep an official logbook on board (that is an obligation of any ship of any nationality). Destruction of, or obliteration of, entries of the logbook by anyone is a criminal offence punishable with fine on summary conviction.

Section 98, which replaced s 30 of the MSA 1988, makes the owner and master of a dangerously unsafe ship, or any other person who has assumed the responsibility for safety matters (under a charterparty or a management agreement) guilty of an offence liable on summary conviction to fine up to £50,000, or, on conviction on indictment, to imprisonment for up to two years.

Dangerously unsafe is defined in s 94, as amended by the Merchant Shipping and Maritime Security Act 1997:[117] a ship in port is dangerously unsafe if it is unfit to go to sea without serious danger to human life. A ship at sea is dangerously unsafe, if, having regard to the nature of the service for

---

117 See Sched 1, para 1.

which it is being used, or intended, the ship is, by reason of the matters mentioned in sub-s 2, either unfit to remain at sea without serious danger to human life, or unfit to go on a voyage without serious danger to human life.

Incidents of unsafe condition include the unsuitability of machinery or equipment, undermanning, overloading or unsafe loading.

The only defence under this provision is proof by the accused that, at the time of the offence, arrangements had been made to ensure the ship's fitness before she was sent to sea.

Section 100, which replaced s 31 of the MSA 1988, imposes a duty upon the owner, demise charterer or manager of a ship to take all reasonable steps to ensure that the ship is operated in a safe manner, failing which it shall be a criminal offence punishable on summary conviction or on indictment. By contrast to s 98, this section does not extend the liability to the master.

The first decision on unsafe operation of a ship under the predecessor to s 100 was _The Safe Carrier_,[118] which is worth mentioning in some detail to see the extent to which the SMS of the ISMC is likely to prevent the same, or similar, incidents from happening and, if they do, whether the transparency of the system will provide the evidence required for conviction of the owner or manager under this section.

The ship-managers were charged with an offence for failing to ensure that the vessel was operated in a safe manner, particularly by allowing the chief engineer less than three hours to familiarise himself with the ship before sailing. Usually, he would need three days for a newly converted ship. During the next 24 hours, the engines broke down leaving the ship in total black-out to drifting at sea. The service tanks had run dry, because the fuel purifier throughput was inadequate to meet the engine demand. The justices for the city of Newcastle upon Tyne convicted the managers but stated a case for the opinion of the Divisional Court of the High Court, which quashed the conviction. The secretary of State for Transport appealed to the House of Lords.

The issues were these: (i) whether the principle of the _Tesco v Nattrass_ case (that the corporation was criminally liable only for the conduct of those representing its directing mind and will) applied; (ii) whether s 31 provided for strict liability; (iii) whether there was vicarious liability under the section on the part of the manager, if any of his employees failed to comply with the requirements of the section, or was there a crime only if the manager himself or someone whose omission was to be attributed to him failed to comply.

It was held by the House of Lords that to secure a conviction under s 31 the prosecution must prove beyond reasonable doubt that the accused owner, charterer or manager of a ship had failed to take all reasonable steps to secure

---

118 [1994] 1 Lloyd's Rep 589 (HL).

that the ship was operated in a safe manner. The fault of an employee other than senior management in putting the ship to sea with an engineer insufficiently familiar with the ship could not be attributed to the company (the *Tesco* principle applied). There was no evidence as to how it came about that the engineer was only allowed very little time to get familiar with the ship. It further held that it was not helpful to categorise the offence as being or not being one of strict liability. The section provides simply for failure to take steps, which by an objective standard must be reasonable. It is a personal duty and the owner, charterer or manager will not be criminally liable for the acts or omissions of his subordinate employees if he had himself taken all such steps, which were 'reasonable to him'.

Undoubtedly, there should be evidence in the future in the ISMC documentation to show how the engineer of *The Safe Carrier* was allowed only such a short time to become familiar with the ship and who ordered the ship to sail. In any event, if the company is complying with both the ISMC and the STCW regulations, which specifically require that sufficient familiarisation of new personnel on the ship should be given, a casualty such as *The Safe Carrier* should not occur again.

There are also other statutory offences under the MSA 1995 for breach of the collision[119] and pollution regulations which are referred to in Chapter 12.

In connection with the criminal liabilities under the Act, s 277 refers to offences by officers of corporations. It makes a director, manager, secretary or other similar officer of the body corporate or any person who was purporting to act in such a capacity, as well as the body corporate, guilty of the relevant offence punished accordingly, if it is proved that the offence was committed with the consent or connivance of, or attributable to any neglect on the part of any of them.

5.6.2 Criminal liability under SI 1998/1561[120]

This statutory instrument was issued under the powers given to the Secretary of State by s 85 of the MSA 1995. Its regulations apply to UK ships, wherever they may be, and to other ships, while they are within UK waters. Regulation 19 of the SI sets out offences, which may be committed by the company, or the master of the ship, or the DP, when there is an infringement of certain regulations, and provides for penalties. Brief reference is made to these offences, below:

(a) Offences committed by the company: any contravention by the company of regulations dealing with compliance with the ISMC, or the duty to hold a DOC, or the duty to carry on board each ship an SMC, or the

---

119 See Chapter 12.
120 The full text of this statutory instrument can be found in *op cit*, Anderson, fn 80.

obligation to appoint a DP, will be an offence punishable by fine not exceeding the statutory maximum, or, on conviction on indictment by imprisonment, up to two years, or a fine, or both. If no certificate of compliance is carried on each ship, it will be an offence punishable with a fine (regs 19.1 and 19.2). If the company operates a ship when the service has been suspended for breaches of the Code, it shall be guilty of an offence and liable to a fine not exceeding the statutory maximum, or on conviction on indictment, to imprisonment for up to two years, or a fine, or both (reg 19.5).

(b) Offences by the master or the DP: if the master of the ship operates his ship in contravention of the company's SMS, he will be punished, either by a fine not exceeding the statutory maximum, or, on conviction on indictment, by imprisonment up to two years, or a fine, or both. Similarly, if the DP is in breach of his obligations under the Code, he will be punished in the same way (reg 19.3 and 19.4).

(c) Offences by any person: any contravention of reg 18.3 shall be an offence, punishable by a fine not exceeding the statutory maximum, or on conviction on indictment, by imprisonment for no more than six months, or a fine, or both.

Regulation 18.3 is of equal importance, because it may affect any person, including auditors of a company. It provides that no person shall intentionally alter a DOC or a SMC; or, in connection with any audit conducted pursuant to these regulations, knowingly or recklessly shall furnish false information; or, with intent to deceive, uses, lends or allows to be used by another, a DOC or a SMC; or, fails to surrender a DOC or SMC required to be surrendered; or, as far as Scotland is concerned, forges any DIC or SMC.

The company is defined by reg 2 of the SI to be the owner of a ship or any other organisation or person, such as a manager, or bareboat charterer, who has assumed responsibility for the operation of the ship from the owner.

The regulations do not define how to attribute liability to the company. But the MSA 1995 (which gave power to the Secretary of State to issue the SI) provides in s 277 that: 'Where a body corporate is guilty of an offence under this Act or any instrument made under it, and that offence is proved to have been committed with the consent or connivance of, or to be attributable to any neglect on the part of, a director, manager, secretary or other similar officer of the body corporate or any person who was purporting to act in such a capacity, he as well as the body corporate shall be guilty of that offence and shall be liable to be proceeded against and punished accordingly.'

Unfortunately, the section, beginning with the words 'where the corporate is guilty', is clumsily drafted and has a circular effect. It does not clearly define when the corporate can be guilty. A further problem arising from this drafting is that the word 'manager' can mean any manager, of a junior or a senior level.

What this section intends, however, is to make both the officers and the company liable to a fine, so that there may be an effective deterrent.

The drafting difficulties may be resolved by applying the appropriate rule of attribution in accordance with the *Meridian* guidelines. When the court interprets the substantive rule of law, for example, the statute or statutory instrument, it will ask this question: is the intention of the statute to attribute liability to the company only when the directors, that is, the will and mind of the corporate body, are guilty of the particular offence, or even when some one below the board of directors is guilty?

It is submitted that the intention, as can be derived from s 277, is that a special rule of attribution is to be applied. The liability of persons mentioned in the section who are below the status of a director, but not as low as to be below the status of a manager (of a high managerial position) or the company secretary, or persons authorised to act in such capacity, will attribute liability to the company. *The Safe Carrier* is distinguishable because it concerned the offence under s 100 of the Act, which makes the duty 'to take reasonable steps to ensure that the ship is operated in a safe manner' personal to the owner, or charterer, or manager by referring to 'the taking of all such steps as it is reasonable for him to take in the circumstances'.

By contrast, the offences under the regulations of the statutory instrument can be committed by any person referred to therein, so that person and the company can be charged with the offence, unless the defence of reasonable precautions and exercise of due diligence to avoid the commission of the offence is made out (reg 20).

5.6.3 Criminal liability of a company for involuntary manslaughter[121]

This area of law affects many companies operating in the UK, not just shipping companies. Even if a shipping company does not operate in the UK, but a death occurs on board its ship, which happens to be within UK waters, the English court would have jurisdiction over the matter.[122]

It is not within the scope of this chapter to indulge in this fascinating area of criminal law. The intention is to consider whether or not the rules of attribution are of any help in rendering a company criminally liable for involuntary manslaughter when a person has been killed as a result of an alleged failure by the company to put in place sufficient safety measures to

---

121 For a historical analysis of the problems involved in this area and proposals see the Law Commission's Report No 237, 1996.

122 Whether the directors of the foreign based company could be extradited to be tried in the English court, would depend on whether there was an extradition treaty between the UK and the country in which the company is incorporated, or has its principal place of business.

prevent the accident. This is known as gross negligence manslaughter for breach of duty of care.

5.6.3.1 The test for gross negligence manslaughter against individuals

The test for convicting an individual for gross negligence manslaughter was laid down by the House of Lords in *R v Adomako*:[123]

> ... that in cases of manslaughter by criminal negligence involving a breach of duty the ordinary principles of the law of negligence applied to ascertain whether the defendant had been in breach of a duty of care towards the victim; that on the establishment of such breach of duty the next question was whether it caused the death of the victim, and if so, whether it should be characterised as gross negligence and therefore a crime; and that it was eminently a jury question to decide whether, having regard to the risk of death involved, the defendant's conduct was so bad in all the circumstances as to amount to a criminal act or omission.

The difficulty with this offence is, in some cases, the proof of duty of care to the victim. In civil cases, the claimant must prove, in addition to pecuniary loss caused by the death, that A owed a duty to B to take care, that that duty was not discharged and that the default caused the death. If it is proved that A fell short of the standard of reasonable care required by law, it matters not how far he fell short of that standard. In criminal cases, on the contrary, the amount and degree of negligence are the determining factors.[124]

The jury may find gross negligence on proof of: (i) indifference to an obvious risk of injury to health; (ii) or actual foresight of the risk coupled, either with a determination nevertheless to run it, or with an intention to avoid it, but involving a high degree of negligence in the attempt to avoid it; or (iii) inattention, or failure to advert to a serious risk, going beyond mere inadvertence in respect of an obvious and important matter of the defendant's duty demanded of him.[125]

The difficulty of proof by the Prosecution of gross negligence has, in some cases, restrained prosecution. However, prosecutions against individuals may increase in the light of new developments in the area of judicial review. In the recent decision, *R v DPP ex p Jones*,[126] the brother of a deceased dockworker, who was decapitated by a grab bucket while working, brought successful proceedings against the DPP for judicial review to quash the decision of the DPP not to prosecute. The managing director of the company had ignored an

---

123 [1995] 1 AC 171 (HL).

124 *Ibid*, p 184, *per* Lord Mackay.

125 The House of Lords agreed with the definition of gross negligence given by the Court of Appeal in this case.

126 [2000] IRLR 373: reference to this is made with acknowledgment to Elizabeth Gloster QC, who brought the issue to the attention of the London Shipping Law Centre at her lecture on 'Directors' and officers' liabilities', delivered on 17 January 2001.

obvious and clear risk to the safety of the company's workers by making them work near to, or directly under, the open grab bucket.

5.6.3.2 Attributing liability for gross negligence manslaughter of individuals to the company

Interest in the subject of corporate manslaughter has arisen generally since the incidents of a series of recent shipping and non-shipping disasters in which a large number of people were killed. In 1987, there was the King's Cross fire in which 31 people died. The cause was the failure of the various groups and individuals within the overall corporate structure to identify their respective areas of responsibility. In 1987, again there was the infamous Zeebrugge disaster in which the ferry, *Herald of Free Enterprise* capsized killing 192 people. The official inquiry, chaired by Sheen J, found that 'from the top to bottom the body corporate was infected with the disease of sloppiness'. The failure on the part of shore management to give proper and clear directions was a contributory cause of the disaster. In 1988, there was the *Piper Alpha* oilrig explosion, killing 167 people. The alleged causes were 'mundane design faults', human error and unsafe working conditions. In 1989, the *Bowbelle/Marchioness* collision on the Thames caused the deaths of 51 people on the pleasure boat, the public enquiry of which was about to finish at the time of writing. The more recent train disasters, Southall, Paddington and Hatfield crashes have given cause again for a public outcry.[127]

The central question that has occupied legal minds, but baffled non-legal ones, is how to hold a corporation criminally liable for such disastrous results of loss of human life.

Corporations have been held liable for regulatory statutory offences without difficulty. For example, the statutory offences under the MSA 1995 and the new offences relating to breaches by the relevant company under SI 1998/1561, discussed earlier, define expressly the type of offences and the punishment without requiring *mens rea*. The crime is simply the failure to maintain safety standards or to take reasonable precautions, as defined by the relevant Acts.

This is the same as the regulatory crimes under the Health and Safety at Work Act (HSWA) 1974 for infringement of safety regulations.[128]

---

127 The first conviction of a company for involuntary manslaughter by the English court was with regard to a one man company and, therefore, the principle of identification was easy to apply: *Kite and OLL Ltd* (1994) unreported, 8 December (Winchester Crown Court); (1994) *The Independent*, 9 December. '... the company, with the only managing director, stood or fell together', as the trial judge said. A recent decision of conviction concerned again a small company: *Roy Bowles Transport Ltd* (1999) *The Times*, 11 December.

128 See recent decisions under this Act: *R v British Steel* [1995] ICR 586; *R v Gateway Foodmarkets* [1997] ICR 382; *R v Nelson Group Services Maintenance Ltd* [1999] ICR 1004.

The rules of attribution of liability to a corporation were discussed earlier.

A dual system of liability has developed by which a corporation can be liable for criminal offences either vicariously or directly. As explained in the text books of criminal law, vicarious liability generally depends on the relevant offence being construed as one of strict liability. Thus, it is fairly easy to convict a corporation for regulatory offences on the basis of the vicarious liability doctrine, or on the basis of the specific provisions of a particular statute.

Direct liability applies to traditional *mens rea* offences and will render a company liable, only when a director or senior officer of the company has the appropriate knowledge to satisfy the mental element of the offence.[129] The difference between the two approaches, as Lord Reid pointed out in the *Tesco* case, is that: 'The corporation must act through living persons. The person who acts *is not speaking or acting for the company*. He is acting as the company and his mind, which directs his acts, is the mind of the company. There is no question of the company being vicariously liable. He is not acting as a servant, representative, agent or delegate ... If it is a guilty mind, then that guilt is the guilt of the company.'[130]

Manslaughter requires the mental element of gross negligence. The issue with regard to involuntary manslaughter for breach of duty of care by a company is concerned with the need for the prosecution to satisfy the test of gross negligence, which applies in the case of individuals.[131]

The *Herald of Free Enterprise*[132] provides the immediate and much debated example. Briefly what caused the disaster were these facts:

(a) the assistant bosun failed to close the bow doors of the ferry before it sailed;

(b) the chief officer failed to check that the bow doors were shut;

(c) the master, who set off at a maximum speed in an overcrowded boat, was responsible for the safety of the ship, but he had followed the system approved by the senior master;

(d) the senior master failed to co-ordinate practices of different crews on board and to enforce such orders as had been issued;

(e) the board of directors did not appreciate their responsibilities for the safe management of their ships and did not apply their mind to safety issues. In addition, the management had not acted upon reports of previous open door incidents.

---

129 See, eg, Lacey, N and Wells, C, *Reconstructing Criminal Law*, 2nd edn, 1998, Butterworths, p 515.

130 *Tesco v Nattrass* [1972] AC 153 (HL), p 170 (emphasis added).

131 *The Adomako* [1995] 1 AC 171 (HL), see para 5.6.3.1, above.

132 *R v HM Coroner for East Kent ex p Spooner and Others* (1989) 88 Cr App Rep 10 and *R v P&O European Ferries (Dover) Ltd* (1990) 93 Cr App Rep 72; see, also, summary in Chapter 12, para 2.3.

This is the area that the ISMC is now taking care of, but the question still remains whether the company can be convicted for involuntary manslaughter under the present law.

A jury must find a culpable state of mind in order to convict a corporation and that state of mind must be of someone in the senior management of the company.[133]

As seen earlier, the vicarious liability doctrine usually applies in relation to statutory offences when that is the intention of the particular statute.[134] In *The Safe Carrier*, it was elaborated by both the Divisional Court[135] and the House of Lords that it was not the intention behind s 31 of the MSA 1988 (which was enacted to prevent the recurrence of situations like the *Herald* case) to make the company criminally liable for breach of duty of an employee, below the board of directors, as that was not intended by Parliament, regardless of whether or not the section imposed strict liability.

In the *Herald* case, *R v HM Coroner for East Kent ex p Spooner*,[136] Bingham LJ noted that:

> A company may be vicariously liable for the negligent acts and omissions of its servants and agents, but for a company to be criminally liable for manslaughter...it is required that [culpability for] manslaughter should be established not against those who acted for, or in the name of the company but against those who were to be identified as the embodiment of the company itself.

The identification doctrine became the established route to the imposition of corporate criminal liability. However, there are major problems with this doctrine and, over the past decade, there has been a growing realisation that it simply does not reflect modern corporate practice, particularly in larger companies.[137]

In the *Herald* case, it could not be proved that the risk of open door sailing was obvious to any of the crew and to others who testified, nor to any of the senior managers.[138] Accordingly, no *mens rea* could be attributed to the company and it was not acceptable to the court to aggregate the faults of each

---

133 See, further, Wells, C, *Corporations and Criminal Responsibility*, 1993, OUP; Sullivan, GR, 'The attribution of culpability to limited companies' (1996) 55(3) CLJ 515, pp 515–46; *AG's Reference (No 2 of 1999)* [2000] IRLR 417, or [2000] 3 All ER 182 (CA).

134 HSWA 1974; *British Steel plc* [1995] 1 CR 586.

135 [1994] 1 Lloyd's Rep 75, pp 80–82.

136 (1989) 88 Cr App R 10.

137 Clarkson CMV, 'Kicking corporate bodies and damning their souls' (1996) 59(4) MLR 557, p 561; see, also, a very clear analysis of the law in this area in the Law Commission's Report No 237, 1996.

138 At the time of the prosecution, the courts were still applying the recklessness test of criminal liability, ie failure to appreciate an obvious and serious risk of injury, as derived from *The Lawrence* [1982] AC 152, prior to the test of gross negligence of *The Adomako* [1995] 1 AC 171.

of those liable. Turner J acquitted P&O[139] in the criminal proceeding brought against the company, although Sheen J, who chaired the public inquiry, was considerably critical about the conduct of everyone in the company.

The conclusion is that the identification doctrine is unworkable in proving the required mental element of the offence of involuntary manslaughter, because it requires the prosecution to prove that one of the controlling officers of the corporation was personally guilty of gross negligence in respect of his duty of care, in order for the offence to be attributed to the corporation.

The editor of the *Criminal Law Review* has commented that this is a virtually impossible task when the most direct cause of the disaster is usually an operational failure by a lower level employee.[140] Considering of the above requirements, the *Meridian* special rule of attribution does not solve the problem either. While this rule may be appropriate for attributing liability to the company for statutory offences, it is not so appropriate for the common law offence of involuntary manslaughter. The rule still requires the identification of a person who is the embodiment of the company itself, and did the criminal act, before liability can be attributed to the company.[141] Unless clear evidence of gross negligence of a person in that capacity is established, an aggregation of faults of various individuals in the company (who are not in board) cannot satisfy the test required·

There remains the main question: are the implications of the ISMC such as to impute the gross negligence of the designated person to the company for the purpose of convicting the company for involuntary manslaughter? From the above analysis of English law, it can be concluded that the identification of the designated person, whose conduct may amount to gross negligence for the purpose of involuntary manslaughter, will not suffice to attribute that liability to the shipowning company, unless he has been included in the board of directors and represents the embodiment of the company. He, personally, will be exposed to the risk of conviction if the required mental element is proved.

Generally, however, it may now be easier for the prosecution, through the documentation required by the Code, to identify whether the criminal negligence was that of the directing mind and will of the company, so as to impute the criminal negligence of those persons to the company.

---

139 In *R v P&O European Ferries (Dover) Ltd* (1990) 93 Cr App Rep 72.

140 Professor Ian Dennis: [1999] Crim LR6 01 (August).

141 It would be interesting to see, in the near future, whether the prosecution will be able to prove criminal gross negligence of the Railtrack company in the Hatfield train crash. 'Railtrack had been told that the track was in dangerously poor condition, but failed to close the line, replace the track or impose speed restrictions.' (2000) *Observer*, 29 October.

5.6.3.3 The future of corporate manslaughter

The only solution, therefore, would be for the Government to enact the proposals of the Law Commission in 1996[142] for reform of this area of criminal law. The Law Commission proposed three separate offences:

(a) corporate killing when there is a management failure (as opposed to operational negligence of employees). The elements of this proposed offence are that the conduct of the corporation fell significantly below what might reasonably be expected (there will be no need to show that the risk was obvious, or that the company was capable of appreciating the risk); such management failure must have caused the death;

(b) reckless killing; and

(c) killing by gross negligence (by this proposed offence it will be easier to prosecute directors and officers of companies personally as there will be no need to prove that a duty of care was owed to the victim).

All three new offences will replace the common law crime of involuntary manslaughter.

Clarkson put it very poetically that implementation of these proposals would make the conviction of companies a real possibility and perhaps the damning of their corporate souls might stimulate the development of a few more consciences in those companies that have the lives and safety of others on their hands.[143]

There have been some criticisms of the Law Commission's proposal, in that it does not cater for grievous bodily harm, and that, perhaps, the Australian approach should have been adopted, which takes into account the corporate policy or culture test.[144] As far as shipping is concerned, the company policy and safety culture test will be reflected in SMS. Another critic of the Law Commission's proposal says that the approach applicable under the HSWA 1974, which relies on the 'vicarious liability' doctrine, is strong, flexible and tested. Therefore, it should be adopted across the board instead of resorting to new untested concepts of 'management failure'.[145]

Once the Law Commission's recommendation[146] for a statutory offence of corporate killing is passed into a statute, the SMS of a shipping company will constitute the evidence required for the prosecution to prove that there was a failure in the management system, which fell far below what could reasonably

---

142 Law Commission Report No 237 (*Involuntary Manslaughter*, 1996).

143 *Op cit*, Clarkson, fn 137, p 572.

144 Bergman, D, 'Manslaughter and corporate immunity' (2000) 150 NLJ 316.

145 Smith, I, 'Manslaughter and corporate immunity' (2000) 150 NLJ 656.

146 The punishment, however, ought to be such as to act as a sufficient deterrent to the guilty company and to others. Fines paid to the Government would not assist the community that has been inflicted with losses and may not be sufficiently high to send the message home.

be expected and caused the death prosecuted for, regardless of whose fault it was. However, in areas other than shipping, where corporate liability frequently arises, there is no regulatory regime similar to the ISMC. For uniformity purposes, perhaps the same regulatory safety system should be imposed on companies operating in other spheres of business.

The proposals of the Law Commission for legislation on corporate killing were incorporated into a Private Bill, the Corporate Homicide Bill, which was, however, rejected on 18 April 2000. It is envisaged that a new draft Bill will be presented to the Parliament as the Government is seeking consultations from interested groups in the light of the recent train disasters.

CHAPTER 9

SHIP MORTGAGES

1 INTRODUCTION

Success in shipping has largely been due to the ingenuity and courage of those captains and engineers of ships who spent years battling with the waves at sea and were prepared to take risks. Some of them with entrepreneurial talents, having saved some money, sought the assistance of banks for finance to start their business in shipping. They had an invaluable and intangible asset, their immense experience about how ships behaved at sea! Most of them were born and lived close to the sea, such as on Greek islands. Financial institutions saw the benefit of investing in shipping and came into partnership with those islanders, providing the bulk of the money for the purchase of a ship, which provided their primary security, the mortgage on the ship, until repayment of the loan. The lender is known as the mortgagee and the borrower as the mortgagor.

Unlike lenders for the purchase of land, however, the inherent risks involved in a floating object of security necessitated the ship mortgagees seeking special protective measures, that is, insurance cover and collateral securities. The loan agreement contains covenants regulating the conduct of the borrower; the mortgage creates a preferential security interest of the lender on the ship; insurance to protect the interest of the mortgagee on the ship must be obtained in addition to the borrower's insurance against perils of the sea; assignment of the insurance proceeds of the ship, in the event of loss, is provided, as well as assignment of the earnings of the ship. Apart from the risk of accidental loss of the ship, mortgagees are protected by law in the enforcement of their security on the ship and are given priority over other maritime creditors, save for those who claim maritime liens. Given this limitation to their security, mortgagees may seek to obtain personal and corporate guarantees, a general charge over the company's assets, or a pledge on the company's shares. The development of ship mortgages, therefore, is based on these unique characteristics of the nature of the subject matter and the business in which it is used. The main concern of the financier is to balance the risks involved in the trading of ships with the expected return on capital.

Ship mortgages are today distinctive contractual transactions, with voluminous documentation including the loan agreement, the mortgage, deed of covenants, assignments of earnings, assignments of insurance policies, guarantees, pledges or charges on other assets and the like depending on the circumstances of a particular transaction. The sophistication of their development has reached a level, which requires special expertise in financial markets.[1]

The most straightforward transaction is a loan supported by a mortgage on a ship, based on a satisfactory valuation with an assignment of earnings and insurance. The Flag State in which the ship is registered is very important to the mortgagee. Most financiers will insist on a flag that has a good reputation in the enforcement of international regulations of safety. They will also consider the law of the Flag State, which will govern the validity of the mortgage.

With new orders of shipbuilding, a 'project finance' transaction may be suitable in which the assets are the new buildings and the source of repayment of the loan is the cash flow generated by the assets. The construction may be financed through a tax-based scheme (offshore) or through the capital markets; the ships are chartered to a reputable charterer of substance from delivery.[2]

2 WHAT IS THE NATURE OF A SHIP MORTGAGE IN ENGLISH LAW?

There have been two theories about the nature of a ship mortgages, which are worth mentioning in order to understand the principles that derive from each.

2.1 The property transfer theory

Under English common law, chattel mortgage has been regarded as a property transfer by way of security,[3] whereby legal ownership is transferred to the mortgagee and, upon payment of the loan amount with interest, it is re-transferred to the mortgagor.

According to this traditional property transfer analysis, the ship mortgagee acquires legal title regardless of whether or not the mortgage is registered.[4] The registered owner of the ship retains, during the mortgage, an equitable right of redemption. All other subsequent mortgages are necessarily equitable because the shipowner does not have legal ownership to pass to

---

1   Goldrein, I (ed), 'Financing ships and shipping companies', in *Ship Sale and Purchase*, 3rd edn, 1998, LLP, Chapter 5.

2   Frances Steel of Watson Farley and Williams explained the complexities of 'project finance' to the LLM students at UCL, January 2001.

3   For a historical account of the evolution of mortgage, from a pledge to the transfer by way of security, see Bagias, A, 'Legal aspects of ship mortgages in English and Greek Law', unpublished thesis, 1996, Gonville and Caius College, University of Cambridge; he supports the property transfer theory.

4   About the procedure and effect of registration, see para 3, below.

another lender. Once the first mortgage is discharged, the second in line of creation will become legal.

This theory derived from the judgment of Lindley J in *Keith v Burrows*:[5]

> The mortgage to the plaintiffs was in the statutory form, and by it the ship was 'mortgaged' to them. The word 'mortgage' is a well known word, and signifies a transfer of property by way of security ... A mortgage is a transfer of all the mortgagor's interest in the thing mortgaged: but such transfer is not absolute; it is made only by way of security; or, in other words, it is subject to redemption. Unless, therefore, there is any statutory enactment to the contrary, the plaintiffs in this case acquired by their mortgage the whole of the mortgagor's interest in the ship, or, in other words, the legal title to the ship as a security ...
>
> The conclusion, then, to be drawn from the mortgage and the statute, is, that the mortgagee of a ship, like the mortgagee of any other property, acquires an ownership in the ship, viz, such ownership as the mortgagor has to give. A first mortgagee will, thus, acquire the whole ownership in the ship, but only of course as a security for his money. Second and other mortgagees will only acquire the interest left in the mortgagor, or, in other words, his right to redeem. That right will be legal or equitable ... as the time for paying off the first mortgage has not yet arrived or has passed.

The mortgage in this case was unregistered, as to which the judge said:

> ... the only consequence of not registering a mortgage is to postpone it to a subsequent mortgage or transfer which is registered before it.[6]

There is, however, a contradictory element in this view: although it recognises only the first created mortgage to be a legal mortgage, it, nevertheless, accepts that a subsequent mortgage may take priority over the legal mortgagee, if it is registered prior to the first created mortgage, according to statutory requirements. The peculiar effect of the judge's second statement is that it creates an oxymoron to his first statement. The result of this is that a subsequent registered mortgage, which in the judge's view would be equitable because the mortgagor would not be able to pass a title that he did not have, would, nevertheless, take priority over the first legal mortgage by reason of it being registered.

The judge further said:

> The mortgagee, however, is not to be deemed the owner of the ship, except so far as may be necessary for making her a security for the mortgage debt (s 70 of the MSA 1854). This section was inserted for his protection against liabilities which might have attached to him by reason of his interest in the ship; see

---

5   (1876) 1 CPD 722, pp 731–33; (1887) 2 App Cas 636 (HL): no comment was made on this issue by the House of Lords, which decided the rights of a mortgagee in possession of the ship. However, what Lord Cairns said on the rights of mortgagee before possession (pp 645, 646) seems to impinge upon the very foundation of the judge's view of the nature of a mortgage.

6   (1876) 1 CPD 722, p 734. It is submitted that this case would not have been decided in the same way today.

Dickinson v Kitchen; and would have been quite unnecessary if the mortgage transferred no interest in the sense of ownership in her to him; or, in other words, if it created a mere charge on her in his favour.[7]

The definition of a mortgage under general English law was examined quite recently in ***Downsview v First City Corp***,[8] in which Lord Templeman said:

A mortgage, whether legal or equitable, is security for repayment of a debt. The security may be constituted by a conveyance, assignment or demise or by a charge on any interest in real or personal property. An equitable mortgage is a contract which creates a charge on property, but does not pass a legal estate to the creditor. Its operation is that of an executory assurance, which, as between the parties, and so far as equitable rights and remedies are concerned, is equivalent to an actual assurance, and is enforceable under the equitable jurisdiction of the court. All this is well settled law and is to be found in more detail in the textbooks on the subject and, also, in *Halsbury's Laws of England* (4th edn, 1980, Vol 32, p 187, paras 401ff).

The owner of property entering into a mortgage does not by entering into that mortgage, cease to be the owner of that property any further than is necessary to give effect to the security he has created. The mortgagor can mortgage the property again and again. A second or subsequent mortgage is a complete security on the mortgagor's interests subject only to the rights of prior encumbrancers.

Meeson explains that

... the difference between an outright disposition and a mortgage is that the latter is by way of security only. What appears, on its face, to be an absolute transfer of property may be proved by extrinsic evidence to have been intended as a security transaction and will be treated as a mortgage only. The courts will always look to the substance of the transaction and will, where necessary, admit evidence to establish the true nature of any transaction. The burden of proof will be upon the person alleging that a transaction which appears upon its face to be an absolute disposition is, in fact, a security transaction.[9]

2.2 The statutory nature of a ship mortgage perfected by registration

The alternative view of the nature of a ship mortgage is that registration under the Merchant Shipping Acts (MSAs) has created a *sui generis* statutory security perfectible by registration.[10] Mortgages under the Act have ceased to be a

---

7 MSA 1854, s 70 – which was equivalent to s 34 of the 1894 Act – is now MSA 1995, Sched 1, para 10.

8 [1993] AC 295, p 311 (PC).

9 Meeson, N, *Admiralty Jurisdiction and Practice*, 2nd edn, 2000, LLP, Chapter 10, para 10-036.

10 Clarke, A, 'Ship mortgages', in Palmer, N and McKendrick, E (eds), *Interests in Goods*, 2nd edn, 1998, LLP, Chapter 26; she provides a most comprehensive study and a critique of the traditional view of the nature of ship mortgages, which is essential reading.

property transfer. Ownership still remains with the mortgagor as is reflected in MSA 1995 (Sched 1, para 10, being formerly s 34 of the MSA 1894).[11] There are authorities supporting this view. A couple of examples follow:

Barclays Bank v Poole[12]

The managing owner of a ship contracted to sell his shares in the ship to other part-owners who agreed: (i) to apply the purchase money in discharging the vendor's debt to the ship; and (ii) to pay the balance to him. The shares were transferred to the purchasers by a registered bill of sale. After the contract and transfer, but before the purchase money had been paid, the purchasers received notice of an unregistered mortgage existing prior to the contract. The mortgagees applied to court to stop the money being transferred to the purchasers. Section 56 of the MSA 1894 had given the registered owner absolute power, not only to dispose of his interest in the ship in a manner provided by the Act, but also to give effectual receipts for the purchase money. It was held, therefore, that the vendor could give effectual receipts for it and direct how the money should be used. The purchasers had acquired a valid title to the shares, being a registered interest, and their contractual right had priority over the previous unregistered mortgage.

The Two Ellens[13]

The registered vessel was mortgaged to B as security for the repayment of a $5,000 debt. The mortgage was duly registered under the MSA 1854. Subsequently, in February 1868, by order of the master who was also a part-owner of the vessel, ship-repairers did work and provided supplies to the vessel to put her in a seaworthy condition. In July 1868, B transferred the mortgage to C in the prescribed form. This transfer was made without valuable consideration and was not registered.[14] C took possession of the vessel on behalf of B, the registered mortgagee. The ship-repairers instituted an action against the ship to recover the amount due to them for the necessaries supplied and work done on the ship. C (the assignee of the mortgagee) intervened. At the time, however, the vessel was already under arrest by the crew for unpaid wages. When the vessel was sold by court order, the proceeds were insufficient to pay off the mortgage and the debt to the ship repairer. The question was which of the unsatisfied claims took priority. The assignee of the mortgage or the necessaries man (the ship-repairer)?

---

11 *Op cit*, Clarke, fn 10.
12 [1907] 2 Ch 284.
13 (1872) LR 4 PC 161.
14 The effect of this assignment being made, for no valuable consideration, ought to have been questioned as to whether it defeated the right of the original registered mortgagee.

The Privy Council, affirming the judgment of the court below, held that the assignee of the mortgagee was entitled to have his mortgage debt satisfied before the ship-repairer, who did not have a maritime lien, was paid out. Moreover, the assignee of the mortgagee was not liable for necessaries supplied to the ship because the master, who instructed the ship-repairer, was not acting as his agent, but as the agent of the mortgagor who remained the owner of the vessel under the MSA 1854.

The point made in this case was that registration of a mortgage according to statutory provisions created a legal mortgage[15] as opposed to an unregistered one, which is regarded under English law to be equitable.

To understand the transformation of a modern ship mortgage into a statutory form of security, it should be noted that, from a historical perspective, the British ship mortgage originated as a property transfer security and was executed by a bill of sale, which was registered and was subject to a covenant for re-transfer of the ship back to the mortgagor upon the payment of the loan.[16] The passing of the MSA 1854, however, introduced a statutory scheme of registration of a mortgage form, which was maintained by the MSA 1894 and was re-enacted by the present MSA 1995. The bill of sale was no longer used.[17] This statutory system has fundamentally changed the nature of the ship mortgage, which is now more accurately described as a statutory security perfectible by registration.[18] Owner-type rights of a ship mortgagee, which stay dormant until it becomes necessary for him to take possession and exercise his powers given under statute and contract, may not be exercised if the debt is paid as agreed.

In support of the second view, Alison Clarke comments that:

> If registration in the Shipping Registry perfects title so that mortgagors have legal title by virtue of being registered owners, and all legal mortgages are legal by virtue of registration, it is difficult to see how the registered ship mortgage can realistically be described as a property transfer mortgage. Conversely, if ownership and title pass independently of registration, and registration has no effect on the nature or status of an interest, the argument that the MSAs have converted the property transfer mortgage into a statutory charge is considerably weakened.[19]

---

15 However, it may be doubtful whether the subsequent assignment, which was made without valuable consideration and was not registered, was capable of conferring the same rights to the assignee in this case.

16 *Thompson v Smith* (1815) 1 Madd 395.

17 This is mentioned by the judge in *Keith v Burrows* (1876) 1 CPD 722, but he did not think that this change had any impact in the nature of the ship mortgage as a transfer of property.

18 *Op cit*, Clarke, fn 10.

19 *Op cit*, Clarke, fn 10, p 672. She explains the origins of the property transfer theory as existed before the passing of the MSA 1854 and, sensibly, proposes at p 674 some reasons why, bearing in mind the reality of modern ship mortgages, the traditional view ought to be jettisoned.

The traditional analysis of a ship mortgage is no longer appropriate to a registered statutory mortgage under the 1995 Act which allows the registration of second, and subsequent, mortgages and gives them the same legal consequences as a first registered mortgage. A registered ship mortgage is better regarded as a *sui generis* form of statutory security perfected by registration.[20]

The question whether the ship mortgage is a property transfer or statutory security perfected by registration may remain academic, and it is not the scope of this chapter to analyse the issue in depth[21] save for referring to further decisions in the context of the rights of mortgagors and mortgagees which seem to be against the property transfer theory (paras 8, 9). The fundamental question to be asked is: what is the purpose of a ship mortgage and what does it do? The purpose is to give the mortgagee a right against property of the debtor so he is not left only with a personal remedy against him. The effect of the mortgage is that the mortgagee, when he needs to enforce his security, can exercise owner-type rights on the mortgaged property, subject to rights of previous registered mortgages, or maritime liens, to meet the debt and such rights are given by statute and contract.

The view that a ship mortgage is a *sui generis* statutory charge perfected by registration is more in accord with the wording of the provisions in the statute and the modern aspects of ship finance.

3 EFFECT OF THE STATUTORY SCHEME OF REGISTRATION

By the MSA 1854, the transfer of ownership in the ship to the mortgagee by a bill of sale was abolished. Instead, a special mortgage form as prescribed by the statute created the security on the ship and was the instrument to be produced for registration of the mortgage. The subsequent statute, MSA 1894, followed the same statutory scheme and, in particular, s 31 provided:

(1) A registered ship or a share therein may be made as a security for a loan or other valuable consideration, and the instrument creating the security (in this Act called a mortgage) shall be in the form marked B in the First Schedule to this Act ... and on the production of such instrument the registrar of the ship's port registry shall record it in the register book.

---

20 Meeson (*op cit*, fn 9), Chapter 10, para 10-046, agrees (in his second edition) with Clarke (*op cit*, fn 10).

21 See other research on this topic, *op cit*, Clarke, fn 10 (supporting the statutory charge theory) and *op cit*, Bagias, fn 3 (supporting the property transfer) theory.

(2) Mortgages shall be recorded by the registrar in the order in time on which they are produced to him for that purpose, and the registrar shall by memorandum under his hand notify on each mortgage that it has been recorded by him, stating the day and the hour of that record.

A slightly amended version of this wording made only for linguistic purposes – leaving the substance unchanged – was carried forward in the MSA 1988 and later in the Merchant Shipping (Registration etc) Act MS(Reg)A 1993, which was supplemented by the 1993 Regulations still applicable today. These regulations apply only to British ships registered under the Acts and do not apply to small ships or fishing vessels (being subject to simple registration) or to bareboat chartered ships.[22]

The MSA 1995[23] (the consolidating Act), **Sched 1** (Private Law Provisions for Registered Ships) **provides by para 7**:

(1) A registered ship, or share in a registered ship, may be made a security for the repayment of a loan or the discharge of any other obligation.

(2) The instrument creating any such security (referred to in the following provisions of this Schedule as a 'mortgage') shall be in the form prescribed by or approved under registration regulations.

(3) Where a mortgage executed in accordance with sub-para (2) above is produced to the registrar, he shall register the mortgage in the prescribed manner.

(4) Mortgages shall be registered in the order in which they are produced to the registrar for the purpose of registration.

Paragraph 8 deals with priorities of registered mortgages and the effect of priority notices; **para 9** deals with the mortgagee's power of sale when the money falls due.

Paragraph 10, titled 'Protection of registered mortgagees' is important in the scheme of the statutory provisions and provides:

Where a ship or share is subject to a registered mortgage then (a) except so far as may be necessary for making the ship or share available as a security for the mortgage debt, the mortgagee shall not by reason of the mortgage be treated as owner of the ship or share; and (b) the mortgagor shall be treated as not having ceased to be owner of the ship or share.

This paragraph clarifies that the mortgagee, by reason of the exercise of his statutory powers, which give him owner-type rights for the limited purpose of realising his security, shall not be treated as owner. The heading indicates that

---

22   See Chapter 8 on the registration of British ships.

23   The Act is supplemented by the 1993 Registration Regulations issued pursuant to the MS(Reg)A 1993, the provisions of which have been consolidated by the 1995 Act. These provisions have substantially re-enacted the mortgage provisions of the MSA 1894. They enable proprietary interests on ships to be recorded on the Register. MSA 1995, Sched 1, paras 7, 8 and 10 have replaced ss 31, 33 and 34, respectively, of the MSA 1894.

the mortgagee is protected from being exposed to owner-type liabilities during his possession of the ship.

It is also relevant to quote, at this point, **para 1 of Sched 1**,[24] which affirms the most fundamental rights of the registered owner of the ship:

(1) Subject to any rights and powers appearing from the register to be vested in any other person, the registered owner of a ship or of a share in a ship shall have power absolutely to dispose of it provided the disposal is made in accordance with this Schedule and registration regulations ...

(3) The registered owner of a ship or of a share in a ship shall have power to give effectual receipts for any money paid or advanced by way of consideration on any disposal of the ship or share.

Such rights will of course be subject to the terms of the mortgage.

Paragraphs 11 and 12 deal with transfer and transmission of the registered mortgage respectively. **Paragraph 13** provides:

Where a registered mortgage has been discharged, the registrar shall, on production of the mortgage deed and such evidence of the discharge of the mortgage as may be prescribed, cause an entry to be made in the register to the effect that the mortgage has been discharged.

It should be observed that in, this paragraph, there is no mention of a re-transfer of the property back to the mortgagor upon the discharge of the mortgage. If the property transfer theory were correct under the statutory scheme of ship mortgages, it would be expected to find, in this paragraph, and in para 7, a provision from which an intention of property transfer could be inferred.

4 UNREGISTERED SHIPS AND STATUS OF AN UNREGISTERED MORTGAGE

Unlike a registered vessel, there is no prescribed form for a mortgage of an unregistered ship, which does not come within the provisions of the MSA. Therefore, common law will be relevant to determine the status of such a mortgage. No formality is required for a chattel mortgage, as mentioned earlier, thus, the words used become relevant. It has been seen in *Keith v Burrows* that the nature of the common law mortgage[25] is simply a transfer of all the mortgagor's interest in the chattel mortgaged by way of security and is subject to redemption on payment of the debt. The following case is an example of the risk to an innocent purchaser who buys an unregistered ship.

---

24   It has replaced ss 56 and 57 of the MSA 1894.
25   (1876) 1 CPD 722, p 731.

The Shizelle[26]

The operative words were 'hereby mortgages to BCT all that the vessel ... as security for repayment of the said loan'. The plaintiffs (P) were a finance company who lent money to M to finance purchase of the vessel *The Shizelle*. The loan agreement contemplated that the vessel would be registered under the 1894 Act, but neither the vessel nor the mortgage was ever registered. On 18 March, M sold the vessel to D 'free from any encumbrances' and D never had reason to believe that there was a mortgage on the vessel. D was a *bona fide* purchaser without actual or constructive knowledge of the mortgage. On 9 April, D registered the vessel under the Merchant Shipping (Small Ships Register) Regulations 1983, but this did not have the same effect as the 1894 Act. On 2 February 1992, P wrote to D advising him of the outstanding mortgage. D contended that the mortgage was invalid against him as he was a bona fide purchaser of the vessel without notice. P arrested the vessel. It was held that nothing prevented the mortgage executed between the parties from being a legal mortgage, as opposed to an equitable one at common law. The non-registration of the vessel and, hence, of the mortgage did not reduce the legal mortgage to an equitable one. Mr Adrian Hamilton QC stated that: 'I therefore cannot find anything in the 1894 Act, which affects a common law mortgage of an unregistered ship.'[27]

The mortgagee had acquired, by the mortgage, the whole of the mortgagor's interest in the ship by way of security. This was a legal mortgage of an unregistered ship. On the question of the effect on a *bona fide* purchaser without notice of the mortgage, it was held that a legal mortgage at common law was enforceable against such a purchaser, but an equitable mortgage would not be.

The correctness of this decision has been doubted for being out of line with the coherent property system set up by the MSAs.[28] However, since the Act has not made any provisions regarding mortgages of unregistered ships, such mortgages cannot be statutory. This lacuna in the law ought to be rectified for the protection of innocent purchasers of unregistered ships,[29] although such a situation is not very common.

---

26   [1992] 2 Lloyd's Rep 444.
27   *Ibid*, p 449.
28   *Op cit*, Clarke, fn 10, pp 685, 686.
29   The lacuna arises from the fact that all ships are excluded from the scope of the Bills of Sale Act 1878. Although the Act makes provision for registration of certain agreements, ship mortgages fall outside its scope (*op cit*, Meeson, fn 9, para 10-041). So, there is no means of discovering an unregistered mortgage of an unregistered ship, which does not come within the statutory provisions of the MSA 1995.

5 COMPARISON OF A SHIP MORTGAGE WITH OTHER TYPES OF SECURITY

5.1 Charge

A mortgage under the MSA 1995 is different from a charge on a property in that the latter is recognised in equity as an appropriation of property as security for a debt. The chargee can realise his security by judicial process either by appointment of a receiver or court sale. Being equitable, it ranks below legal registered interests, hence, a registered mortgage, and the chargee, unlike the mortgagee, does not have a right to take possession. A charge may be fixed on a specific asset of the debtor, which cannot be disposed of without the permission of the chargee, or payment of the debt. Alternatively, it may be floating on stocks-in-trade, which are changeable. When a default occurs, a floating charge crystallises, in other words, it becomes fixed. A charge is always equitable.

A charge on a ship is not registrable as it does not come within the statutory scheme of the MSA 1995.

A distinction between a mortgage under general law and a charge in equity was made by Buckley LJ, in *Swiss Bank Corp v Lloyds Bank Ltd*:[30]

> The essence of any transaction by way of mortgage is that a debtor confers upon his creditor a proprietary interest in property of the debtor, or undertakes in a binding manner to do so, by the realisation or appropriation of which the creditor can procure the discharge of the debtor's liability to him, and that the proprietary interest is redeemable, or the obligation to create it is defeasible, in the event of the debtor discharging his liability. If there has been no legal transfer of a proprietary interest but merely a binding undertaking to confer such an interest, that obligation, if specifically enforceable, will confer a proprietary interest in the subject matter in equity. The obligation will be specifically enforceable if it is an obligation for the breach of which damages would be an inadequate remedy. A contract to mortgage property, real or personal, will, normally at least, be specifically enforceable, for a mere claim to damages or repayment is obviously less valuable than a security in the event of the debtor's insolvency. If it is specifically enforceable, the obligation to confer the proprietary interest will give rise to an equitable charge upon the subject matter by way of mortgage.

Under the Law of Property Act (LPA) 1925, which deals with mortgages on land, the phrase 'charge by way of legal mortgage' is used in ss 85(1) and 87(1). A legal mortgage on land is created by a deed expressed to be by way of a legal mortgage. The charge is registrable and the chargee will enjoy the

---

30 [1982] AC 584, p 595 (HL): in which the House of Lords approved the judgment and repeated it in this report.

protection of the Act and have the statutory powers of sale and appointment of a receiver, as provided by s 101 of this Act. The charge under the LPA 1925 is different from a charge in equity.

A charge under English law should not be confused with the charge under civil law, which is known as *'hypotheque'* and is registrable. A hypothecation under civil law gives the mortgagee the same rights as the statutory English mortgage exercisable when a default event occurs but excludes the power of the mortgagee to sell the ship, otherwise, than by a court sale.[31] A hypothecation under English maritime law was effected in the past by way of a bottomry bond (charge on the ship) or respondentia (charge on the cargo). Both are, however, now obsolete.

5.2 A pledge

Pledge is the oldest and most fundamental form of chattel security.[32] It arises whenever a person (the pledgor) transfers the possession of goods actually, or constructively by an atttornment or by transferring the means of control, or symbolically by the delivery of documents of title to another person as security for a debt.[33] It is to be distinguished from the other three forms of security relating to chattels, for example, the mortgage, the charge and the lien.

By contrast to a mortgage, possession is essential to a pledgee for the creation of the right, while a mortgagee may enter into possession when his security is impaired. The mortgage is regulated by statute and it is perfected by registration. While foreclosure by the mortgagee (which would operate to defeat the mortgagor's right of redemption) would be another difference between mortgage and a pledge, foreclosure is not consistent with the statutory type mortgage and, besides, the MSAs do not refer to such a right.[34]

Examples of a pledge as an additional security for a mortgagee of a ship are a pledge or charge over the shares in the shipping company, which is common with a single ship company (shares security). When the shares are bearer shares, however, this effectively means that, whoever has the bearer shares, owns the company and, thus, the ship.

---

31 Under Greek law, there is, in addition, another type of ship mortgage the 'preferred ship mortgage' perfected by registration, which is founded by a special statutory instrument (SI 1958/3899) issued pursuant to the Code of Private Maritime Law. This gives the mortgagee practically the same powers as the English ship mortgage, under the statutory provisions of the MSA 1995.

32 Palmer, N, *Bailment*, 2nd edn, 1991, LLP, Chapter 22.

33 Palmer, N and Hudson A, 'Pledge', in Palmer and McKendrick, *op cit*, fn 10, Chapter 24, p 621 and fn 6.

34 *Op cit*, Clarke, fn 10, p. 690.

5.3 Common law possessory lien

This resembles the pledge, in that it depends on possession until the debt is satisfied. But the lien holder does not have a right of sale in the event of default and he will lose his security right if he delivers the chattel, while the pledgee may redeliver the chattel to the pledgor temporarily without losing his security.[35]

6 PRIORITIES OF MORTGAGES

The importance of priorities between various maritime claimants and mortgagees has been discussed in Chapter 4 and will also be seen in the context of conflict of laws in para 7, below.

6.1 Priorities between mortgages

A mortgage is valid from the date of its creation and not from the date of registration, but priorities of mortgages are determined by the date of registration. Despite the traditional view about the nature of a mortgage, held by the judge in *Keith v Burrows*, the statutory provision of priorities of registered mortgages among themselves was unaffected by this judgment.

The series of events leading up to the issues that arose in this case are worth summarising:

(a) On 1 December, M, the registered owner of the ship, Stonehouse, mortgaged his ship to the plaintiff (P) for a loan plus further advances. The mortgage was not registered.

(b) On 4 January and 22 February, the defendants (D) advanced money to M upon an equitable assignment of the cargo by way of security, without notice of P's mortgage after searching the registry. It was arranged that D should sell the cargo and receive the proceeds on account of M.

(c) On 2 February, M again mortgaged the ship to P for further advances.

(d) On 26 February, D was assigned the freight of the ship as security for their advances.

(e) On 2 March, M mortgaged the ship to Harold (H) who registered his mortgage on 3 March.

(f) On 6 March, P registered his mortgage.

(g) On 13 April, the ship arrived and H and P took possession. H's claim was satisfied with the security on the ship, therefore, he did not claim freight.

---

35   *Op cit*, Palmer and Hudson, fn 33, p 622.

On the question of priorities and entitlement to freight, it was held that P had not lost priority over D by virtue of non-registration. By the MSA 1854, an unregistered mortgage was not void, its priority was only postponed to a subsequent registered mortgage.

The effect of H's mortgage was that it had statutory priority, being registered, and could receive freight. However, since H's claim was satisfied, he would hold any surplus for the benefit of subsequent encumbrances. P's mortgage was prior in date to the assignment to D, and P could, thus, take possession and freight against anyone except the registered mortgagee, H.

A registered mortgage takes priority over an earlier unregistered interest even if the registered mortgage had notice of the unregistered interest.

Black v Williams[36]

Debentures were issued by the company in statutory form under a trust deed executed by the mortgagors on 8 November 1889. Mortgages, also in statutory form, were created on three steamers and then registered, on 15 June 1891. Later, two remaining steamships, mortgaged under the debenture deed were transferred to company M and registered. Mortgages were created subsequently in favour of the company M and registered. In accordance with the agreement (debenture deed), the company executed mortgages of the vessels in favour of the trustees. The mortgages, given or transferred to the corporation M, were all registered before the mortgages given to the trustees. It was held that the mortgage in the statutory form, which had been registered, was to be preferred to the title of the debenture holders. The debenture holders had a prior equitable title and were entitled to get that converted into a legal title in the statutory form and be registered, but they had chosen not to do so. Vaughan Williams J gave the rationale of the law as it stood:

> The Act of Parliament was passed for the benefit of commerce, and in order that English ships might be easily dealt with by English shipowners. The legislature has recognised that occasions arise when it is to the interest of the whole community that people should be able to raise money on ships by sale or mortgage, and, in the interests of the general public, it has, therefore, provided that registered titles in the statutory form shall have a priority, thus, enabling those who are disposed to purchase or lend money upon ships to do so with perfect confidence that their titles will not be overridden by priority being obtained by equitable unregistered titles which happen to be prior in point of time, and which for reasons of their own, the owners of those equitable titles have not thought fit to convert into legal form, or to register in the way pointed out by statute.[37]

---

36 (1895) 1 Ch 408.
37 *Ibid*, p 421.

Registration is essential to priority. In an old case, which is unlikely to happen today, a managing owner of a ship mortgaged his share to his bankers, who did not register the mortgage, being persuaded by the owner not to do so. Subsequently, the managing owner sold his share to his joint owners, who were not aware of the mortgage. The bill of sale was duly registered. The mortgagee having an unregistered prior mortgage did not have priority over the purchasers.[38]

The MSA 1995, **Sched 1, para 8** states:

(1) Where two or more mortgages are registered in respect of the same ship or share, the priority of the mortgages between themselves shall, subject to sub-para (2) below,be determined by the order in which the mortgages were registered (and not by reference to any other matter).

(2) Registration regulations may provide for the giving to the register by intending mortgagees of 'priority notices' in a form prescribed by or approved under the regulations which, when recorded in the register, determine the priority of the interest to which the notice relates.

A scheme of priority notices is provided by **reg 59 of the Merchant Shipping (Registration of Ships) Regulations 1993**. By this regulation, a mortgagee may register his intention to register a mortgage and, if he subsequently does register such a mortgage within 30 days (which may be renewed for a further period) of the priority notice, his mortgage is deemed to have been registered at the date of entry of the priority notice.

If no registration takes place within the notice period and, in the meantime, another mortgagee registers his mortgage granted subsequently to the first, the mortgage, which is registered first, takes priority. Registered mortgages, of course, take priority over unregistered ones but, as between unregistered mortgages (otherwise equitable ones), priorities are determined by equitable principles, that is, by the date of creation.

6.2 Further advances

As a general rule, known as the *Hopkinson v Rolt*[39] rule, advances made by the first mortgagee, whose mortgage is taken to secure future advances, cannot take priority over a second mortgagee when such advances were made after he had notice of the second mortgage. Lord Chelmsford stated this rule succinctly as follows:

---

38 *Barclay v Poole* [1907] 2 Ch 284.

39 (1861) 9 HLC 514 (HL); concerning a shipbuilder who granted a mortgage to a bank and, subsequently, to the plaintiff. The bank made the further advances with knowledge of the plaintiff's mortgage.

As the first mortgagee is not bound to make the stipulated further advances, and with notice of a subsequent mortgage he can always protect himself by inquiries as to the state of the accounts with the second mortgagee, if he chooses to run the risk of advancing his money with the knowledge, or the means of knowledge, of his position, what reason can there be for allowing him any priority? ... But, on the other hand, if it be held that he is always to be secured of his priority, a perpetual curb is imposed on the mortgagor's right to encumber his equity of redemption.

It follows that, if the first registered mortgagee does not have knowledge of the second mortgage, the priority of his further advances is not affected.[40] However, it is understood from an earlier decision that the advances must have been made under the registered mortgage and not under a separate unregistered instrument.[41]

In a non-shipping case, the Court of Appeal subsequently held that the doctrine of *Hopkinson v Rolt* applies to further advances made in pursuance of an obligation or covenant on the part of the first mortgagee entered into at the time of the first mortgage.[42]

6.3 Harbour authority claims and risk management by the mortgagee

It is appropriate at this point to refer to what was said about priorities of maritime claims in Pt I, Chapter 4, of this book, that a mortgagee may find himself bound to take his security subject to a harbour authority's right of detention and sale. Moreover, the harbour authority, in exercising its statutory right, may sell the ship and can pass a title to a purchaser of the vessel free of the mortgage, even though the mortgage had been registered.

The Blitz[43]

A loan of £10,000 was secured by mortgage on the vessel and the mortgage duly registered in 1989.

In 1991, the vessel was arrested for unpaid harbour dues and pursuant to s 44 of the Harbours, Docks and Piers Clauses Act 1847, the harbour owners sold the vessel to the defendant. The purchaser was unaware of the mortgage. The question was whether the sale was one free of encumbrances, or whether the mortgagee could enforce his mortgage against the ship after she had been sold by the harbour authority. Sheen J held that a purchaser of the ship from

---

40 *Liverpool Marine Credit Co v Wilson* (1872) 7 Ch App 507, p 512.
41 *Parr v Applebee* (1855) 7 De GM&G 585.
42 *West v Williams* [1899] 1 Ch 132 (CA).
43 (1992) 2 Lloyd's Rep 441.

the harbour authority could not be expected to investigate the register, which may be in some foreign land, and a harbour authority could not be expected to clear any unsatisfied mortgage affecting a ship pursuant to his right under s 44. The risk of non-payment should be borne by the person who voluntarily lends an unwisely large amount on the security of a ship, rather than a harbour authority or an innocent purchaser without notice of the mortgage. The claim of the mortgagee failed.

The decision is based on a construction of a statutory provision and may be correct as a matter of both law and policy. From the point of view of risk management by the mortgagee, he may prevent a sale by the harbour authority from happening by stepping in to pay off the authority's claim, assuming that the value of the ship is sufficient to cover his security and the additional advance.

7 CONFLICT OF LAWS

There are two major issues on the question of conflict of laws:

(a) what law determines the validity of the mortgage;
(b) priorities between foreign liens and mortgages.

7.1 Law governing the mortgage and law of the agreement to grant a mortgage

Prior to the Rome Convention 1980, the proper law of the mortgage was the law of the place of registration of the ship or the law of the flag,[44] unless another choice of law had been expressly stated in the mortgage deed.

The Angel Bell[45]

The owners of the ship, a Panamanian company, approached G for a loan to purchase vessels. In February 1974, it was agreed that G would be granted a mortgage for payment of the loan and have the marine policies assigned to them. The mortgage was granted and was provisionally registered under Panamanian law, which fixed all questions of priority by reference to the date of the registration, provided that there was a definite registration within six months. Time expired without final registration of the mortgage. The vessel sank with all cargo belonging to the plaintiff, who brought an action in

---

44 The law of the flag is unsuitable, as a rule, today because of flags of convenience which render the flag a questionable contact in terms of conflict of laws. It can only be one indicator of contact, among many, in determining the law of the contract: see Tetley, W, *International Conflict of Laws (Common, Civil and Maritime)*, 1994, International Shipping, p 224.

45 [1979] 2 Lloyd's Rep 491.

England, obtained a Mareva injunction against the insurance proceeds restraining the defendant from dealing with his assets within the jurisdiction, or removing them out of the jurisdiction. G intervened in the action on the basis that they were: (a) originally assured under one set of insurance policies; (b) designated loss payees; (c) assignees under another set of insurance policies; or (d) assignees under the notices of assignment endorsed on the policies. The issue was whether G was a secured creditor and, a related question to this issue, was: which law governed the mortgage?

It was held by Donaldson J (as he then was) that, although it was possible to have an English contract for a mortgage of foreign land which would result in the mortgage being governed *inter partes* by English law, *prima facie*, mortgages either of foreign land or ships would be governed by the law of their *situs* or flag, in this case – Panamanian law. There was no contrary evidence to displace that presumption. Thus, the failure of G to register the mortgage under Panamanian law reduced its effectiveness, in that it conferred no *in rem* rights against the ship, but only rights *in personam* against the borrower.

One of the agreements, however, which concerned the granting of a mortgage to G, was governed by English law, meaning that G were equitable mortgagees. (This concept was unknown to Panamanian law). Under that agreement, G could, therefore, rely upon the 'loss payable' clause in the insurance policy, under which money received by the assured would be received on behalf of G. Also, G were held to be assignees of the policies under the notices of assignment. Therefore, G were creditors of the borrower, secured on the proceeds of the hull and machinery policies.

The Rome Convention on the Law Applicable to Contractual Obligations 1980, which was implemented in the UK by the Contracts (Applicable Law) Act 1990, applies to contracts entered into after 1 April 1991. The Convention provides that its rules shall apply to contractual obligations in any situation involving a choice between the laws of different countries, whether or not it is the law of a Contracting State. Essentially, the rules of the Convention will apply to all cases brought in UK courts, provided the dispute falls within the scope of the Convention, save for certain exceptions provided by it.[46] Priority is given to the law chosen by the parties to a contract who can select the law applicable to the whole, or part of it, when the contract is severable (Art 3(1)). The validity of the law chosen is to be determined by the law so chosen (Arts 3(4), 8(1), 9(4)).[47] In absence of choice, Art 4(1) provides that to the extent that the parties have not chosen a law to govern the contract, the law of the country with which the contract is most closely connected shall govern the contract. This is to be determined by reference to presumptions contained in

---

46 See Benjamin's *Sale of Goods*, 4th edn, 1992, Sweet & Maxwell, paras 25-028–25-040.
47 *Ibid*, paras 25-041–25-062.

the article, such as characteristic performance, habitual residence, central administration, principal place of business.[48]

7.2 Priorities between foreign liens and mortgages

At present, there is no uniform international approach to the problem of recognition and enforcement of maritime liens granted by foreign law and attached to a vessel before it leaves the jurisdiction of the law where such liens were created. Different jurisdictions may attach different legal consequences to the same type of claim. This raises a conflict of laws problem when determining priorities in the distribution of the ship's fund to the various creditors. The problem was aptly summarised by Lord Diplock in the *Halcyon Isle*:[49]

> In the case of a ship, however, the classification of claims against her former owners for the purpose of determining priorities to participate in the proceeds of her sale may raise a further problem of conflict of laws, since claims may have arisen as a result of events that occurred, not only on the high seas, but also within the territorial jurisdictions of a number of different foreign States. So the *lex causae* of one claim may differ from the *lex causae* of another, even though the events which gave rise to the claim in each of those foreign States are similar in all respects, except their geographical location; the *leges causarum* of various claims, of which, under English conflict rules, the 'proper law' is that of different States, may assign different legal consequences to similar events. So, the court distributing the limited fund may be faced, as in the instant case, with the problem of classifying the foreign claims arising under differing foreign systems of law in order to assign each of them to the appropriate class in the order of priorities under the *lex fori* of the distributing court.

There was no English authority directly relating to maritime liens and mortgages at the time. There were only cases in which similar incidents had arisen involving other foreign rights.[50]

The decision of the Privy Council in The Halcyon Isle

In this case, the mortgagees were an English bank with a mortgage created in April 1973 and registered in London in May 1974. In March 1974, American ship-repairers carried out repairs to the vessel in New York, and under US law, they were entitled to a maritime lien for the repairs done. The vessel sailed from New York and was later arrested and sold by the order of the High Court

---

48 *Op cit*, Benjamin, fn 46, paras 25-063–25-071 and, further, see Dicey, AV and Morris, JHC, *Dicey and Morris on the Conflict of Laws*, 10th edn, 1980, Stevens.

49 [1981] AC 221 (PC), p 230.

50 See *The Colorado* [1923] P 102 (discussed in Chapter 4, para 7).

of Singapore. When the proceeds from the sale were insufficient to satisfy all claims, the question was whether the claim of the mortgagees should take priority over the claim of the necessaries (repair) men, the latter's claim giving rise to a maritime lien under US law. The practice and procedure of the Singaporean court, in the exercise of its admiralty, jurisdiction applies English law, and such a claim would not give rise to a maritime lien if the event had occurred in England. The court had two options, viz: (1) to accord the claim the legal consequence that would have attached to that event if it had occurred in England, or in Singapore (the *lex fori*); or (2) to accord the claim the legal consequence that would be accorded to it under the *lex causae* (USA).

The question was, thus, whether the maritime lien, which arose by reason of the events in the foreign jurisdiction, was enforceable in the court distributing the fund. Would English law, in circumstances such as these, recognise the maritime lien created by the law of the USA, the *lex loci contractus*, where no such lien existed by its own internal law? English choice of law rules provide that, for a substantive right, the *lex loci contractus* governs the transaction, while for a procedural right, the *lex forum* would govern. It was concluded that the legal nature of the maritime lien was procedural or remedial both under English and Singaporean law, therefore the claim would be classified according to the *lex fori*. Lord Diplock stated:

> ... in principle, the question as to the right to proceed *in rem* against a ship, as well as priorities in the distribution between competing claimants of the proceeds of her sale in an action *in rem* in the High Court of Singapore, falls to be determined by the *lex fori*, as if the events that gave rise to the claim had occurred in Singapore.[51]

This meant that the mortgagee's claim took priority over that of the ship-repairers. The court was not ready to extend the classes of claims recognised in English law (and Singaporean law) as giving rise to maritime liens.[52] Lord Diplock, in particular, stated that:

> As a matter of policy, such a claim might not unreasonably be given priority over claims by holders of prior mortgages, the value of whose security had thereby been enhanced. If this is to be done, however, it will, in their Lordships' view have to be done by the legislature.[53]

The dissenting minority, Lords Salmon and Scarman held that:

> The question is: does English law, in circumstances such as these, recognise the maritime lien created by the law of the USA, that is, the *lex loci contractus*, where no such lien exists by its own internal law? In our view, the balance of authorities, the comity of nations, private international law and natural justice,

---

51 [1981] AC 221, p 235.

52 The International Convention 1993 relating to maritime liens and mortgages has not been ratified. For its contents and scope, see Berlingieri, F, 'The 1993 Convention on maritime liens and mortgages' [1995] LMCLQ 57.

53 [1981] AC 221, p 242.

all answer this question in the affirmative. If this be correct, then English law (the *lex fori*) gives the maritime lien created by the *lex loci contractus* precedence over the mortgagee's mortgage. If it were otherwise, injustice would prevail. The ship-repairers would be deprived of their maritime lien, valid as it appeared to be throughout the world, and without which they would obviously never have allowed the ship to sail away without paying a dollar for the important repairs upon which the ship-repairers had spent a great deal of time and money and from which the mortgagees obtained substantial advantages.[54]

And they continued, comparing a maritime lien with a mortgage as security rights:

A maritime lien is a right of property given by way of security for a maritime claim. If the Admiralty Court has, as in the present case, jurisdiction to entertain the claim, it will not disregard the lien. A maritime lien validly conferred by the *lex loci* is as much part of the claim as is a mortgage similarly valid by the *lex loci*. Each is a limited right of property securing the claim. The lien travels with the claim, as does the mortgage; and the claim travels with the ship. It would be a denial of history and principle, in the present chaos of the law of the sea governing the recognition and priority of maritime liens and mortgages, to refuse the aid of private international law.[55]

The decision of the majority has been criticised by academic writers,[56] particularly as the following decision is regarded by most commentators to be correct in the application of principles of international private law.[57] It should be noted, however, that since the Rome Convention 1980 is binding upon the UK, if a ship were arrested today in the UK in circumstances of the *Halcyon Isle*, the UK court ought to apply USA law. This is because of Arts 3 and 4 of the Convention (mentioned earlier). Thus, 'much of the air has been taken out of the *Halcyon Isle* balloon', as Professor Tetley has put it. He further states that the law of the flag, in respect of contractual liens, seems inconsistent with the basic conflict rules of Arts 3 and 4 of the Rome Convention, which call for the law expressly or implicitly chosen by the parties, or the law having the closest connection with the contract.[58]

The Ioannis Daskalelis[59]

The Canadian Supreme Court was faced with a similar kind of situation as that in *The Halcyon Isle*. The vessel was mortgaged to the defendants in December 1961. In March 1963, the plaintiffs rendered necessary repairs to the

---

54   [1981] AC 221, pp 246–47.
55   *Ibid*, p 250; see, also, Chapter 4, para 7, above.
56   See Chapter 4, para 7, above.
57   Lord Salmon and Lord Scarman applying those principles delivered dissenting judgments in *The Halcyon Isle*.
58   *Op cit*, Tetley, fn 44, Chapter XVII, pp 580–81.
59   [1974] 1 Lloyd's Rep 174.

vessel in New York, but the sum due to them remained unpaid. The vessel sailed to Canada and she was arrested in June 1964. She was sold by a court sale and the question arose again whether the plaintiffs' claim in respect of the repairs had priority over the defendants' mortgage. The ship-repairers were entitled to a maritime lien under US law, but not under the law of Canada, the distributing court. Firstly, the court established that it had jurisdiction. Ritchie J then summarised the law of England (also the applicable law in Canada in this case) and quoted a passage from *Cheshire's Private International Law* (8th edn, p 676) as follows:

> The validity and nature of the right must be distinguished from the order in which it ranks in relation to other claims. Before it can determine the order of payment, the court must examine the proper law of the transaction upon which the claimant relies in order to verify the validity of the right and to establish its precise nature.

The court also followed *The Strandhill*[60] where the principle was clearly established that a maritime lien, acquired under the law of a foreign State, would be recognised and be enforced in Canada. On the question of priorities, the court followed *The Colorado*[61] which was taken as authority for the contention that, where a right in the nature of a maritime lien exists under foreign law, which is the proper law of the contract, the English courts will recognise it and accord it the priority which a right of that nature would be given under English procedure. It was held that the ship-repairer's lien took priority over the mortgagee's claim.

The lack of uniformity in the law of liens between maritime nations continued and still does.

In the following case, the South African court followed *The Halcyon Isle*.[62]

The Andrico Unity[63]

The South African court also had to consider similar circumstances, in a case involving the supply of bunkers to a vessel in Argentina. In a bid to justify the arrest of the vessel, the supplier contended that a 'privileged credit' in the nature of a maritime lien attached to his claim under Argentinean law, and he was therefore entitled to enforce it by an action *in rem* against the vessel. The South African court was required by its law to apply the law which the High Court of Justice of England and Wales would have applied on 1 November 1983, insofar as that law applied. Following *The Halcyon Isle*, the court held that a notional High Court of England would have declined to recognise the

---

60 [1926] 4 DLR 801.
61 [1923] P 102.
62 *The Halcyon Isle* has also been followed in Cyprus, Singapore, Malaysia, Australia; see further authorities in *op cit*, Tetley, fn 44, Chapter XVII.
63 (1987) 3 SALR 794.

Argentinean lien. Marais J discussed the difference between the nature of a maritime lien and a mortgage as follows:

> ... when, therefore, a court dealing with competing claims to priority in the distribution of a limited fund is asked to recognise a foreign maritime lien which would not arise under the court's own system of law, it is being asked to supplant its own law in that regard by a foreign law. When a court is asked to recognise a foreign mortgage, it is not being asked to go as far. It is merely being asked to enforce a contract of mortgage, which the parties have entered into in a foreign jurisdiction.[64]

Marais J saw no conflict between *The Halcyon Isle* and the prior English authority (*The Colorado*). *The Halcyon Isle* was described, simply, as a decision based on readily understandable considerations of policy. In a more recent decision, the South African court followed *The Halcyon Isle* again.[65]

7.3 Proposed solutions and risk management issues

There are no uniform substantive rules governing ship mortgages. Unless the Rome Convention applies, matters relating to creation and perfection will usually be governed by the law of the State of registration, as the legally attributed *situs* of the ship. Matters relating to enforcement will be controlled by the law of the State of enforcement. Priorities under the conflict rules of some countries are treated as substantive and, therefore, are governed by the law of the place of registration, while, in others, will be regarded as procedural and be determined by the *lex fori*.[66]

Could there be a solution to conflicting judicial decisions from different jurisdictions in this area by the ratification of the 1993 Convention on Maritime Liens and Mortgages to ensure certainty and uniformity in the law and prevent forum shopping, or is this issue a political matter reflecting a protectionist approach of individual national interests?

Is there a likelihood that a compromise can be reached? The same questions have been asked since the drafting of the very first Convention for unification of the law in this area in 1926 (which was ratified by non-common law jurisdictions) and later by the subsequent Convention in 1967. The 1993 Convention, which is an improvement of the previous two, remains the thorny issue between ship-repairers and mortgagees. It is unlikely to come into force, because its authors (against strong advice) did not take into account consideration of special legislative rights of various nations. The world needs

---

64   (1987) 3 SALR 794, p 812.

65   *Banco Exterior de Espana SA v Government of Namibia* [1999] 2 SA 434.

66   Goode, R (Sir), 'Battening down your security interests: how the shipping industry can benefit from the UNIDROIT Convention on International Interests in Mobile Equipment', lecture given at the Institute of Maritime Law, University of Southampton, 10 November 1999, published in [2000] LMCLQ 161.

a proper Convention of international maritime liens and mortgages as well as a proper international Convention on conflict of laws.[67]

The only solution, at present, would be for individual parties, whose interests would be likely to be affected adversely by the arrest of the ship in an unfavourable jurisdiction, to prevent such an eventuality from happening. For example, a ship-repairer, whether American or otherwise, should well be advised to exercise its possessory lien before the ship leaves his shipyard, while a mortgagee may be able to control the jurisdiction to which the ship may proceed to, in order to enforce its security there.

8 RIGHTS AND OBLIGATIONS OF THE MORTGAGOR

8.1 The mortgagor is bound by contractual covenants

The rights and obligations of the parties are largely governed by the terms of their contract, which are contained in the deed of covenants. There is usually a long list of covenants stipulating the mortgagor's obligations.

In practice, ship mortgages have developed into a sophisticated system of extensive contractual terms to cover every aspect of the parties' legal relationship, so as to avoid the uncertainties created by common law principles. When there is no deed of covenants, which is unlikely nowadays, the parties' relationship will be governed by the provisions of Sched 1 of the MSA 1995, the 1993 Regulations, issued pursuant to MS(Reg)A 1993. Where there are gaps in the statutory provisions, common law and equity step in.

Broadly the covenants include the following provisions.

8.1.1 An obligation to insure

A Hull and Machinery (H&M) insurance against the physical loss of or damage to the mortgaged ship, third party liability for collision, general average contributions and other losses caused by insured perils must be procured by the mortgagor. A separate war risks cover may be obtained, in circumstances where the ship is likely to enter a war zone. The mortgagor must also ensure that third party liabilities are insured with a P&I club. He is required to pay all premiums and comply with insurance warranties. The mortgagee's interest must be noted in the insurance policies as an assignee or as a co-assured or as a loss payee. The mortgagor must obtain a letter of undertaking from the insurers confirming the status of the insurance and that

---

67   Tetley W, *Maritime Liens and Claims*, 2nd edn, 1998, Blais, p 214.

the mortgagee will be informed in the event the insurance is suspended or terminated for breaches of the insurance contract by the mortgagor.[68]

Lord Hoffmann, in *Colonial Mutual General Insurance Co Ltd v ANZ Banking Group (New Zealand Ltd)*, illustrated the legal effect of the insurance covenant, thus:[69]

> The purpose of a covenant for insurance is to ensure that, if the value of the security should be depreciated by the occurrence of a fire or other insurable risk, the proceeds of the policy will provide a fund to make up the shortfall. This purpose can be achieved only if the covenant gives the mortgagee an interest by way of charge, and no more than an interest by way of charge, in the proceeds. Standard insurance covenants contain various provisions designed to ensure that the mortgagee will be able to retain control of the insurance policy and its proceeds. Insisting that the mortgagee has the right to approve or nominate the insurer, take custody of the insurance policy, be shown receipts for premiums ... are some of the cumulative techniques used for this purpose. So is the requirement that the insurance be effected in the name of the mortgagee. But all these provisions are, in their Lordships' view, intended to protect the mortgagee's interest by way of charge over the proceeds of the policy rather than to create it. That such an interest exists is a fundamental assumption of the covenant. It cannot be destroyed by the mortgagor's failure to comply with one or other of the protective terms.

The insurance covenant is paramount, but it has its limitations. If the assured mortgagor is in breach of the insurance contract, (that is, of the duty of 'utmost good faith' under the Marine Insurance Act (MIA) 1906,[70] which will entitle the insurer to avoid the contract *ab initio*, or in breach of a warranty,[71] which will discharge the insurer of liability from the date of the breach) the mortgagee will not be able to recover the assigned insurance proceeds. The mortgagor may be guilty of wilful misconduct, whereupon it may be proved that the loss of the ship was not proximately caused by a peril insured against.[72]

8.1.2 An obligation to maintain the ship in good condition and repair

Obviously, not only is the mortgagee concerned that its security is not devalued by the deterioration of the ship, but also that accidents are prevented by maintaining the ship in good condition. In addition, this covenant protects the mortgagee from the risk of the ship being detained in a

---

68 The reader is referred to specialist books on marine insurance.
69 [1995] 2 Lloyd's Rep 433, p 436 (PC).
70 See *Pan Atlantic Insurance Co Ltd v Pine Top Insurance Co Ltd* [1994] 2 Lloyd's Rep 427 (HL).
71 See *The Good Luck* [1991] 2 Lloyd's Rep 191 (HL).
72 *Samuel v Dumas* [1924] AC 431 (HL).

port for breaches of the International Safety Management Code (ISMC), which may result in the impairment of his security and prejudice the insurance cover. Connected with this covenant is the covenant to maintain the ship registered and in class. Keeping the vessel always in class by following class recommendations for repairs, complying with the international requirements for safety of ships and safe management (the ISMC compliance) are also paramount obligations for insurance purposes as well. Were the assured, however, unable to recover for the loss of the ship under the insurance for hull and machinery, the mortgagee, as assignee, would not be able to recover either.

In practice, the mortgagee takes out a separate insurance, the mortgagee's interest insurance, to cover himself for any of these eventualities. The law of mortgages is, thus, very much linked to marine insurance law and the reader is referred to specialist books on the subject.[73]

8.1.3 An obligation to notify the mortgagee

Notification to the mortgagee with regard to the movements of the ship is required, in case the ship sails either in war zones, where the security will be exposed to a higher risk or loss, or in jurisdictions in which the law may be unfavourable to the priority enjoyed by the mortgage over other maritime claims, which are not recognised as maritime liens under the law of the mortgage.

Giving information to the mortgagee about any accidents the ship has experienced, which may affect the security, are also included in the covenants as obligations of the mortgagor.

8.1.4 An obligation to discharge claims or liens

In parallel with the previous covenant, the mortgagor has an obligation to discharge all debts and liabilities, which may encumber the ship and can be enforced against the security by arrest, as discussed in Chapter 2. If the ship is arrested, the mortgagor has an obligation to provide security and procure its release.

To pay dues to port authorities and any debts, which may affect the priority of the mortgagee's security, also form part of the covenants.

---

73 See Hodges, S, *Law of Marine Insurance*, 1996, Cavendish Publishing; Merkin, R, *Kluwer's Insurance Contract Law*, loose-leaf, quarterly updated, 2000 edn, Croner.

8.1.5 An obligation not to sell or grant a charge on the ship

During the duration of the mortgage, the mortgagor covenants not to sell, or grant a mortgage or charge to any person without first discharging the debt to the mortgagee.

8.1.6 An obligation of legal trading

Illegal trading will prejudice the insurance policy for breach of the implied warranty of legality under s 41 of the MIA 1906. Furthermore, it will result in detention or confiscation of the ship.

8.1.7 A covenant as to charterparties

Although a long time charter agreed on favourable terms will be a source of revenue for discharging the debt to the mortgagee, the mortgagor may be required to inform the mortgagee prior to engaging the ship for a long term, in case the terms of the charterparty prevent the mortgagee from exercising his rights in case of default by the mortgagor.

The mortgagor must employ the ship in a prudent manner so that the earnings will provide income for payment of the instalments. Assignment of earnings is a collateral security.

8.2 The mortgagor's statutory obligations

It is implicit in the statute (Sched 1, paras 9 and 10 of the MSA 1995) that unless the mortgagor repays the loan, as agreed, or if he is in breach of contract, impairing the security, the mortgagee may take steps, as empowered by the statute, to make the ship available as a security. The statute does not provide for any other obligations leaving the parties to agree the details in their contract, by the deed of covenants.

8.3 The mortgagor's right of ownership of the mortgaged ship

From paras 1 and 10 of Sched 1 of the Act (see above), the ownership rights of the mortgagor are confirmed.

Lord Westbury in *Collins v Lamport*,[74] as far back as 1864, described the position under the statute as follows:

> In my judgment, under the statute, so long as the mortgagee of a ship does not take possession, the mortgagor, as the registered owner, subject to the

---

74 (1864) 4 De GJ&S 500.

mortgage, retains all the rights and powers of ownership, and his contracts with regard to the ship will be valid and effectual, provided that his dealings do not materially impair the mortgagee's security.

The mortgagor's rights of ownership are restricted only when the mortgagee takes possession, a right given by statute and being necessary for the purpose of making the ship available to satisfy the mortgaged debt. Apart from that incident, were the owner not to have retained his powers and rights of ownership, he would be acting as an agent for the mortgagee on the basis of the property transfer theory. Lord Westbury in the same case continued:

> Under earlier statutes the mortgagee, upon the making and registration of the mortgage, became in the eye of the law, the owner of the property, the mortgagor being treated as his quasi agent. The result was, that the mortgagee frequently found himself bound either by the contracts of the mortgagor, or, at all events, by the necessary expenditure and outgoings of the vessel, a result seriously injurious and inconvenient to mortgagees, and one which interposed considerable difficulty in the way of persons desirous of raising money upon this species of security.[75]

It is clear from this statement that the property transfer theory was already a spent force upon the reform of the ship mortgage by the 1854 statute.[76] The mortgagor has all the ordinary incidents of ownership while he is in possession, including the payment of expenses, provision of insurance, entitlement to freight, and the right to enter into contracts which do not materially impair the mortgagee's security. The manner in which he wishes to employ his asset, subject, of course, to his obligations to the mortgagee under the deed of covenants, is up to him.

In this connection, the famous dictum of Lord Cairns, in *Keith v Burrows*,[77] is in sharp contrast to the property transfer theory advanced by the judge at first instance in the same case:

> The question arises with regard to the rights of the mortgagee of the ship taking possession, both generally and also under the circumstances of this case. My Lords, with regard to the general rights as between mortgagor and mortgagee of a ship there cannot, I think, at this time of day be any real controversy. The mortgagee of a ship does not, ordinarily speaking, or by a mortgage such as existed in the present case, obtain any transfer by way of contract or assignment of the freight, nor does the mortgagor of a ship undertake to employ the ship so as to earn freight at all. The mortgagor of a ship may allow the ship to lie tranquil in dock, or he may employ it in any part of the world, not in earning freight, but for the purpose of bringing home goods of his own for his own benefit ... All these acts would be the ordinary

---

75 (1864) 4 De GJ&S 500, p 503.

76 It is submitted that references to Lindley's judgment in *Keith v Burrows* (1876) 1 CPD 722, after what Lord Westbury said, serve only to confuse matters and the case should be taken as having implicitly been overruled.

77 (1887) 2 App Cas 636, p 645.

incidents of the ownership of the mortgagor, who remains the *dominus* of the ship with regard to everything connected with its employment, until the moment arrives when the mortgagee takes possession. If the mortgagee is dissatisfied with the amount of authority which the mortgagor possesses by law, it is for him to put an end to the opportunity of exercising that authority by taking the control of the ship out of the hands of the mortgagor.

Lord Westbury in *Collins v Lamport*[78] summed up the mortgagor's rights to enter into contracts in relation to his ship in the light of the statutory provisions:

> Every contract, therefore, entered into by the mortgagor remaining in possession, is a contract which derives validity from the declaration of his continuing to be the owner, but at the same time, every such contract is a contract into the benefit of which the mortgagee may at any time enter by giving notice to the person who under that contract is to pay to the mortgagor, that he requires the payment to be made to him, the mortgagee.[79]

8.4 The mortgagor's right to redeem the ship

The equitable right of the mortgagor to redeem his property upon payment of the loan is central to the essence of a ship mortgage. The court has inherent equitable jurisdiction to interfere in all ship mortgages in which the terms are unconscionable, or constitute a 'clog or fetter' on the mortgagor's right of redemption. The court of Appeal defined the extent of the court's intervention in *Knightsbridge Estates Trust Ltd v Byrne*[80] concerning a mortgage of real property, in which Sir Wilfrid Greene MR said:

> ... equity may give relief against contractual terms in a mortgage transaction, if they are oppressive or unconscionable, and in deciding whether or not a particular transaction falls within this category the length of time for which the contractual right to redeem is postponed may well be an important consideration ...

> But equity does not reform mortgage transactions because they are unreasonable. It is concerned to see two things – one that the essential requirements of a mortgage transaction are observed and, the other, that oppressive or unconscionable terms are not enforced. Subject to this, it does not, in our opinion, interfere ...[81]

> ... In our opinion the proposition that a postponement of the contractual right of redemption is only permissible for a 'reasonable' time is not well-founded. Such a postponement is not properly described as a clog on the equity of

---

78 (1864) 4 De GJ&S 500.

79 *Ibid*, p 504.

80 [1939] Ch 441.

81 *Ibid*, p 457.

redemption, since it is concerned with the contractual right to redeem. It is indisputable that any provision which hampers redemption after the contractual date for redemption has passed will not be permitted. Further, it is undoubtedly true to say that a right of redemption is a necessary element in a mortgage transaction and, consequently that, where the contractual right of redemption is illusory, equity will grant relief by allowing redemption.[82]

If the mortgagee refuses the mortgage money offered, the court will protect the mortgagor's equity of redemption. An action in damages against the mortgagee would lie, if it were no longer possible to redeem the mortgaged property.

Fletcher & Campbell v City Marine Finance Ltd[83]

The first plaintiff mortgaged the vessel as security for a loan. The second plaintiff was the beneficial owner of the vessel. The first plaintiff executed a collateral deed, which provided for repayment in monthly instalments. In April 1967, there was default in payment by the first plaintiff and the defendants wanted to take possession. The second plaintiffs approached the defendants with the outstanding debt, but the defendants refused to accept payment from the second plaintiff, alleging that they would only accept from the first plaintiff on unconditional terms. The second plaintiffs informed the defendants later that the first plaintiff would send the money to them. However, they sold the vessel a few days thereafter, depriving the first plaintiff (the mortgagor) of his right to redeem. It was held that the tender of the sum due by the second plaintiff was a proper tender and the defendants had acted unreasonably by refusing to accept it. The mortgagor was entitled to recover damages, because his right to redeem was prevented by the wrongful action of the mortgagee. Roskill J quoted from p 16 of Benjamin Constant's book:

> It should be explained that an essential characteristic of a mortgage is the right of the mortgagor to redeem his property at anytime after the date named in the mortgage as the date for repayment of the mortgage debt until the mortgage is foreclosed, or the property is sold, and a term, whether in the mortgage itself or in an independent agreement, which impedes or prevents the mortgagor in the exercise of this right may be a clog on the equity of redemption, and therefore invalid and unenforceable.[84]

The judge further commented that the courts would not, however, intervene in every case of interference with a due exercise of a mortgagor's right to redeem and continued, referring to another relevant passage from the book of the above author:

---

82 [1939] Ch 441, p 456.

83 [1968] 2 Lloyd's Rep 520.

84 *Ibid*, pp 535, 536.

Although a mortgagor retains, even after the date specified in the mortgage as that for the repayment of the mortgage debt, an equitable right to redeem his property, he can do so only by giving the mortgagee six month's notice of his intention or by paying him six month's interest in lieu of notice ... But, where the mortgagee has himself demanded the repayment of his debt, or has taken other steps to realise his security, no question of notice arises, and the mortgagee must accept a tender of his principal with interest to the date of repayment.

Roskill J concluded in this case:

Accordingly, in my judgment, there is, as a matter of English law, a right in the mortgagor of a ship to recover damages against his mortgagee, if his right to redeem is prevented by the wrongful act of the mortgagee. I do not think it matters whether one makes the necessary implication into the collateral deed as a matter of law, or whether one makes the implication therein as arising from the other express terms of the deed or whether one arrives at the same result by the application of basic principles of equity.[85]

A clog on the equity of redemption would be void where the clog was imposed as part of the original transaction of a mortgage, in which it had been arranged between the mortgagor and the transferee that the transferee, in return for the loan, should have an option to purchase part of the mortgaged property. The option to purchase part of the mortgaged property, unless it is given by a separate transaction, would be void as a clog on the equity of redemption for, if it was exercised, it would prevent the mortgagor from recovering the part of the property to which it applied. The court looks at the substance of the matter and not the form in which the bargain was carried out, and inquires into the object and purpose with which the documents were executed.[86]

If the mortgagee has a right under the contract to accelerate his power of sale without notice, even if there is no financial default, such a clause, normally, would be a 'clog' on the right to redemption, if the mortgagee exploited his bargaining strength at the time of the agreement.

However, the Privy Council, recently, adopted a non-intervention approach if, upon construction of the contract, it is found that the parties had sufficiently agreed in their contract how to deal with specific events, notwithstanding the possibility of an unlawful exercise of power of sale without notice. It is important to look at what exactly happened in this case.

The Maule[87]

The plaintiffs lent money to the defendants. As security for the performance of their obligations under the loan agreement, the defendants granted to the

---

85 [1968] 2 Lloyd's Rep 520, p 538.

86 *Lewis v Love* [1961] 1 WLR 261; *Reeve v Lisle* [1902] AC 461 (HL); *Samuel v Jarrah Timber and Wood-Paving Corp Ltd* [1909] AC 323 (HL).

87 [1997] 1 WLR 528 (PC).

plaintiffs a mortgage over their vessel, which was registered in Cyprus. The deed of covenants provided that upon the occurrence of any of the events of default specified in the loan agreement the plaintiffs would be entitled, forthwith, to exercise all the powers possessed by them as mortgagees of the vessel. One such power was to sell the ship, with or without prior notice to the owners and the sale would be deemed to be within the mortgagees' power. Amongst the events of default in the loan agreement was the failure by the borrower to sell a vessel belonging to the group, *The Foresight Driller II*, within 60 days after notice by the mortgagees had been given, in the event that no employment could be found for her. The ship was not sold within the required time limit. Although no instalment was outstanding and the lender had not exercised its power to accelerate repayment of the loan, the defendants' vessel, *The Maule*, was arrested in Hong Kong. *The Foresight Driller II* was eventually sold and its proceeds were used to reduce the indebtedness of the owners in the group to the lender.

The judge held that a power of sale under a mortgage could only be exercised when money was due. The Court of Appeal of Hong Kong dismissed the plaintiffs' appeal. The plaintiffs appealed to the Privy Council and the issue was, whether they were entitled to arrest *The Maule* in the circumstances. If they were not, the shipowners were claiming damages for wrongful arrest. As the ship was registered in Cyprus, the applicable statute was the same in all material respects as the MSA 1894, the relevant sections of which have now been consolidated in the MSA 1995.

The Privy Council, allowing the appeal, held that the rights and duties of the parties to the mortgage of a ship were primarily governed by the contract. On true construction of the relevant clause in the deed of covenants the parties had expressly agreed that the plaintiffs should have power to sell the vessel in the event of a non-financial default, even though no sum of money had become due under the loan agreement. The plaintiffs were, therefore, not obliged to give notice accelerating repayment of the loan before exercising their power of sale. The mere possibility that the power of sale could be exercised in an unlawful manner without notice, so as to defeat the borrowers' right of redemption, did not invalidate the power conferred in this case. Therefore, the plaintiffs were entitled to arrest the vessel pursuant to their power of sale conferred by the contract.

While the Privy Council confirmed the principle derived from the previous case,[88] that any sale without notice would be unlawful and give rise to a claim in damages, it distinguished that position from the facts of the case in question. In this case, the borrowers were aware of the proposed sale and they could seek assistance from the contract under which they could give

---

88 *Fletcher & Campbell v City Marine Finance Ltd* [1968] 2 Lloyd's Rep 520.

seven days notice to repay and thereby redeem the ship.[89] It seems that the decision will have a limited application, but it reinforces, save for the right of redemption, freedom of contact in the loan agreement. It allows the parties to bargain the power of sale beyond the classic events of default known in practice and in law. Skillful drafting, however, would have prevented the borrowers from finding themselves in such an unfavourable situation, unless the bargaining power weighed heavily on the side of the mortgagee.

9 MORTGAGEE'S RIGHTS AND OBLIGATIONS[90]

Once the mortgagee enters into possession of the ship, if the occasion arises for the realisation of his security, he has owner-type rights conferred on him by statute or contract, but only such rights as are necessary for the enforcement of his security. They are exercisable only to the extent that it is necessary for that purpose. The rights and remedies of a registered mortgagee are conferred by statute, essentially by paras 9 and 10. Paragraph 10 not only defines the mortgagee's rights, but it also regulates their exercise.

9.1 The right to take possession

Express provisions in the deed of covenants will specify when the mortgagee can enter into possession. But, independently of contract, the mortgagee has a right at common law to enter into possession when there is default in payment of capital or interest, or a threat to his security. In addition, he can rely on the statutory rights given by the MSAs.

Paragraph 10 of Sched 1 to the 1995 Act, which was previously s 34 of the 1894 Act, gives power to the mortgagee to exercise his rights and remedies and interfere with the mortgagor's possession, control and operation and, insofar as it is necessary to make the ship available as a security, he may be treated as owner.

The mortgagee has no right to take possession of the ship unless there has been default or a threat to his security. If the mortgagee enters into possession in the absence of either of these circumstances, or express contractual

---

89 Clarke, A, in her commentary on this case, [1997] LMCLQ 329, p 337, concluded that: 'Any uncertainties about the power of sale left unresolved by *The Maule* can be avoided by competent drafting.'

90 Restriction or exclusion of mortgagee's liability in the exercise of his rights and remedies are subject to the Unfair Contract Terms Act 1977, if the mortgagee is dealing as a consumer, as is invariably the case with yacht-owners. The Unfair Terms in Consumer Contracts Regulations 1999, which superseded the same of 1994, will apply.

provisions, he may be liable to the mortgagor for costs and substantial damages.[91]

9.1.1 What would amount to default?

Default in payment of instalments of the capital and interest will entitle the mortgagee to take possession, but the totality of the circumstances will be looked at in the context of the contract. Schedule 1, para 9 of the MSA 1995 provides for when the mortgagee could sell the ship and, by implication, he may enter in possession before sale. Before such power can be exercised, para 9 puts a condition that there must be money or any part of it due. In the absence of a variation in the contract, once the date of payment has passed, technically, the mortgagee will be able to exercise his statutory power. The statute does not specify any other default or the extent of default, but gives only a general event of money being due, leaving the parties to agree other reasons of default and any maximum or minimum non-payment. In *The Cathcart*,[92] for example, while the date for payment had passed, the parties had agreed to postpone repayment until freight had been paid. When the mortgagee arrested the ship for non-payment, despite the fact that he had full knowledge that the vessel was about to commence a profitable charterparty, the court held him liable in damages.

9.1.2 When would the security be impaired?

Other than default in payment of instalments by the due date, there may be various events, which indicate that, at the end of the day, the ship's value may be diminished to an extent that it will not be sufficient for the mortgagee to cover his security, thus, a threat to the security may be imminent.

One question that has frequently faced the courts is this: when could it be said that the mortgagee's security is being endangered, or that his security is likely to be impaired? The answer to that question depends on the circumstances of each case and it is a question of fact.[93] The courts usually consider a certain number of factors before coming to the conclusion that the mortgagee was justified in taking possession, if his security was indeed impaired or likely to be impaired, in the absence of default of payment. Examples of some of these circumstances have been an impecunious mortgagor[94] and the prospect of the vessel remaining burdened with maritime liens coupled with financial difficulties of the mortgagor. (This may

---

91 *The Cathcart* (1867) LR 1 A&E 314, *per* Dr Lushington; *The Blanche* (1887) 6 Asp MLC 272; *The Manor* [1907] P 339.

92 (1867) LR 1 A&E 314.

93 *The Myrto* [1977] 2 Lloyd's Rep 243.

94 *De Mattos v Gibson* (1858) 4 De G&J 276.

mean that the vessel remains unrepaired for a long time or uninsured.)[95] An unprofitable charterparty with onerous terms and provisions, which may greatly affect the mortgagee's right to recover his security, may amount to impairment.[96] Sometimes, the mere presence of one of these factors may not be sufficient to entitle the mortgagee to enter into possession, but a combination of them will.[97] Some examples given below illustrate those circumstances.

The Manor[98]

The borrower was in breach of a covenant to pay premium with respect to insurance. (It had been agreed that the mortgagees would pay part of the premium). In addition, the borrower had incurred debts, such as unpaid wages to the crew and master, canal dues, dues for coal. A lot of money was needed for the repair of the vessel. The liabilities would exceed the amount expected to be earned from freight out of a nine-month voyage. Time for the repayment of the mortgage amount was imminent and the mortgagee took possession of the ship. The issue for the court was whether the mortgagee's security would be materially impaired if the ship were left under the control of the mortgagor. The judge came to the conclusion that, on the facts, there was not sufficient impairing of the security to justify the mortgagee in taking possession. The Court of Appeal held that a set of circumstances existed, which did, in fact, impair the security and the mortgagee was entitled to take possession. In particular, Fletcher Moulton LJ said:

> It may well be that to allow a ship to become subject to a maritime lien may not be an infringement of the rights of the mortgagee, even though that maritime lien ranks above claims of the mortgagee ... But, there is an obvious difference between allowing a ship to become burthened with a maritime lien, and allowing her to remain burthened with such a lien, without the power to discharge it, for, to that extent, you have, as in this case, substantially diminished, that is to say, impaired the value of the mortgage security.[99]

Law Guarantee and Trust Society v Russian Bank of Foreign Trade[100]

The plaintiffs were trustees of a debenture trust deed. The deed was entered into by the defendants, British shipowners, to secure the holders of debentures of the shipowning company. By an undertaking of the company, all its

---

95 *Laming & Co v Seater* (1889) 16 Ct of Sess Cas (4th ser) 828.
96 See *The Myrto* [1977] 2 Lloyd's Rep 243; cf *The Maxima* (1878) 4 Asp MLC 21; *The Fanchon* (1880) 5 PD 173.
97 *The Manor* [1907] P 339, *per* Moulton LJ; *The Myrto* [1977] 2 Lloyd's Rep 243, *per* Brandon J.
98 (1907) P 339.
99 *Ibid*, pp 361–62.
100 (1905) 1 KB 815.

property was assigned to the plaintiffs as a security for the payment of the debentures. Three steamships of the company were the 'mortgaged premises'. Mortgages on the steamers were executed in the statutory form and were registered. The trust deed provided that the trustees might enter into possession of the mortgaged premises upon the happening of certain events. In 1904, when Russia was at war with Japan, the defendants entered into charterparties for carriage of cargoes of coal from Barry to Vladivostock in Russia in their three steamers. However, they signed fictitious documents with the knowledge of the charterers, purporting to carry the goods to the neutral ports of Manilla and Shanghai, because there was great risk of the vessels being captured, as Russian ports were blockaded by the Japanese. It was not disputed that the Russian Government was interested in the coal. Insurance premiums against war risks for vessels going to Russian ports were very high at the time, so to insure them for war risks would have left little or no profit on the charterparties. Lord Alverstone CJ, agreeing with the learned judge in the lower court, stated that the mortgagor was not justified to enter into these charterparty contracts, which were, in themselves, such as to imperil the security of the mortgagee and, therefore, the latter was not bound by those charterparties according to the rule in *Collins v Lamport*. Making reference to his previous judgment in *The Heather Bell*,[101] he made an observation on a minor point for clarification:

> ... I did not mean to say [in that case] that non-insurance was not a matter to be considered in connection with such cases, but merely that, if the charterparty was otherwise binding on the mortgagee, the fact that the ship was not properly insured against ordinary perils of the sea might not of itself be sufficient to prevent the charterparty from being binding upon him.[102]

> The mere fact that the ship is about to sail in a jurisdiction in which it may be more difficult for the mortgagee to enforce his security is not a factor in itself to allow the mortgagee to take possession.[103]

The modern deed of covenants in ship mortgages provides extensively for the circumstances in which the mortgagee can enter into possession.[104]

9.2 Mode of exercising his powers

The mortgagee may recover his debt either by instituting an action *in rem* under s 21 of the Supreme Court Act 1981; or by taking actual or constructive possession of the vessel. He may take actual possession by putting his own representative on board the vessel, and constructive possession by simply

101 [1901] P 272.
102 (1905) 1 KB 815, pp 825 and 826.
103 *The Highlander* (1843) 2 W Rob 109.
104 See, eg, *The Maule* [1997]1 WLR 528.

giving notice to the mortgagor and all interested parties, like insurers, charterers and bill of lading holders.[105] When he takes possession, he must take sufficient steps to indicate his intention to enter into possession, which must be clear and unambiguous to the interested parties.[106]

9.3 Mortgagee's rights and obligations in possession

When the mortgagee takes possession of the vessel, he becomes responsible for the mortgagor's contractual obligations under pre-existing binding contracts. Thus, he will be liable to pay the expenses, but he will also enjoy the benefits of such contracts. Once he has taken possession of the vessel, he is entitled to freight, which is being earned.

9.3.1 Right to freight

A mortgagee of the ship, having taken possession of her before any freight had become payable from the charterers to the owners, is entitled to the freight. He takes it, in priority, to an assignee of freight, who took an assignment with knowledge of the mortgage.[107]

Liverpool Marine Credit Co v Wilson[108]

The owners of the ship executed and registered a mortgage in favour of the plaintiffs. Two days later, a second mortgage was executed in favour of the defendants and it was later registered. The owners then gave a lien on the accruing freight to a third party, to which the plaintiffs signed a written consent that this advance would have priority over their own mortgage. As additional security to the second mortgagee, the owners granted the defendants a lien on accruing freight. The plaintiffs with no notice of the defendant's lien on the freight, made further advances to the owners on the security of another mortgage, including all freight already earned, or to be earned under any charterparty entered into during the continuance of the mortgage. The plaintiff's second mortgage was unregistered. All parties who were given a lien on the freight subsequently gave notice of their charge to the charterers. The plaintiffs took possession of the vessel and claimed priority over the defendants to the net proceeds of the sale and to the freight (subject to the sum payable to the third party) for the satisfaction of their second mortgage. The defendants contended that the plaintiffs were not entitled to

---

105 *Rushden v Pope* (1868) LR Ex 269.
106 *Benwell Tower* (1895) 8 Asp MLC 13.
107 *Brown v Tanner* (1868) LR 3 Ch 597 (CA).
108 (1872) LR 7 Ch 507.

the freight as a separate fund in the discharge of their first mortgage. It was held that:

> The first registered mortgagee of a ship, by taking possession of her before the freight is completely earned, obtains a legal right to receive the freight, and to retain thereat not only what is due on his first mortgage, but also the amount of any subsequent charge which he may have acquired on the freight, in priority to every equitable charge of which he had no notice; and it makes no difference that a subsequent incumbrancer was the first to give notice to the charterers of his charge on the freight.

On the right of the mortgagee to the freight, Sir WM James LJ stated:

> It is to be observed that the MSA nowhere deals with charges on freight. They were long before the passing of the Act securities well known in the shipping world, and of ordinary occurrence. And the right of a mortgagee in respect of freight had also been long settled and well recognised. But it was not thought fit to provide by that Act either with respect to the priorities of charges on freight, or with respect to the rights of mortgagees to freight. These were left to be dealt with according to the ordinary principles of law and equity, and the rules and doctrines established by the decisions of the courts. Now, the right of the mortgagee in respect of freight was well established and clear, but somewhat peculiar. He had no absolute right to the freight as an incident to his mortgage; he could not intercept the freight by giving notice to the charterer before payment; but, if he took actual possession, or, according to a recent decision in the Court of Exchequer, if he took constructive possession of the ship before the freight was actually earned, he, thus, became entitled to the freight as an incident of his legal possessory right, just as a mortgagee of land taking actual possession of the land before severance of the growing crops would have the right to sever and take the crops.[109]

His position was like that of the legal mortgagee of any other kind of property who made further advances on the property itself without notice of any intervening equitable interests.

If the mortgagee, however, takes possession before the freight had become payable and, at the time of the possession, still remains unpaid, he will not be entitled to the freight.[110]

9.3.2 Obligation during operation and management

Although the statute does not specifically stipulate this, it should be implicit that when a mortgagee exercises his owner-type rights by taking possession, he may like to continue the operation of the ship and earn the profits to satisfy his security, particularly, if there is a profitable charterparty ongoing. He is not obliged to exercise his power of sale once he enters into possession. As the mortgagee, usually, does not have the expertise to operate or manage

---

109 (1872) LR 7 Ch 507, p 511.
110 *Anderson v Butler's Wharf Co Ltd* (1879) 48 LJ Ch 824.

ships, he will appoint a professional manager. The operation of a ship will entail liabilities and, in practice, it is rarely the case that a mortgagee would wish to get involved in such an exposure, unless the circumstances warrant profitable returns.

Should he decide to trade her, he must use her as a prudent man would use her. Lord Campbell, in *Marriott v The Anchor Reversionary Co*,[111] stated as follows:

> I cannot concur in the unlimited right of the mortgagee to use the ship as the owner might do ... Nor can I lay down the strict rule that the mortgagee can never lawfully employ the ship to earn freight, or that, after taking possession, he must allow her to lie idle till he may prudently sell her ... But, although there may be great difficulty in defining the limits of the power of the mortgagee to use the ship, this, I think, may be laid down with perfect safety and confidence, that if the mortgagee does take possession he can lawfully use the ship as a prudent man would use her, if she were his own property.

A mortgagee has an equitable duty to manage the ship with due diligence, so that he trades her profitably (see para 9.5, below, in the context of a receiver appointed to manage a mortgaged property).

9.4 Power of sale

9.4.1 Source of power

As already mentioned, para 9 is the key to this statutory power. It has slightly varied the power of its predecessor, s 35 of the MSA 1894, in that it specifically requires that there must have been some default in payment. A second or subsequent registered mortgagee cannot exercise the power of sale without the concurrence of every prior mortgagee, except when the order is made by a court of competent jurisdiction (Sched 1, para 9(2)).

An additional source of the mortgagee's power of sale is the contract. Whether or not he takes possession of the ship, he can exercise this power by having the ship arrested and sold by the court.

9.4.2 Role of the mortgagee in the sale of the ship

In exercising his power of sale, the mortgagee is not a trustee of the power of sale for the mortgagor. Salmon LJ restated the principle of the mortgagee's role in the sale of the ship in *Cuckmere Brick Co Ltd v Mutual Finance Ltd*,[112] in which he said:

---

111 (1861) 2 Giff 457.
112 [1971] Ch 949.

It is well settled that a mortgagee is not a trustee of the power of sale for the mortgagor. Once the power has accrued, the mortgagee is entitled to exercise it for his own purposes whenever he chooses to do so. It matters not that the moment may be unpropitious and that by waiting a higher price could be obtained. He has the right to realise his security by turning it into money when he likes. Nor, in my view, is there anything to prevent a mortgagee from accepting the best bid he can get at an auction, even though the auction is badly attended and the bidding exceptionally low. Providing none of those adverse factors is due to any fault of the mortgagee, he can do as he likes. If the mortgagee's interests, as he sees them, conflict with those of the mortgagor, the mortgagee can give preference to his own interests, which of course he could not do were he a trustee of the power of sale for the mortgagor.[113]

With regard to any surplus of value fetched by the sale after satisfaction of the debt to him, he will hold the sum as a constructive trustee[114] for any subsequent mortgagees and for the mortgagor.

9.4.3 Nature of duty of the mortgagee in the exercise of his power of sale

The question has frequently arisen, particularly in land property cases, whether the mortgagee, in the exercise of his power of sale, owes a duty of care to the mortgagor, or must he do no more than just act in good faith. This issue is of great importance because, if the mortgagee is in breach of duty of care, he will be made liable in damages suffered by the mortgagor due to such negligence, while, if he is only required to act in good faith, he will be liable only if he acted recklessly, or fraudulently. When the sale is tainted by fraud, provided relief is sought promptly, the court may, depending on the circumstances of the particular case, set aside the sale.[115] However, the court will also consider the position of the purchaser; if the purchaser had notice of the breach, setting aside the sale may be an appropriate order,[116] but if the purchaser was innocent, damages to the mortgagor may be an alternative remedy.

In *Farrar v Farrars Limited*,[117] the Court of Appeal held that the mortgagee must act *bona fide* for the purposes of realising his security and must take reasonable precautions to secure a proper price.

There were three mortgagees involved. One of them was a solicitor and acted for the other mortgagees. He negotiated a sale in principle and agreed a price with intended purchasers. He subsequently took shares in a company formed by the purchasers to carry the sale into effect. The plaintiffs contended that the sale was by the mortgagee to himself and others, under the guise of a

---

113 [1971] Ch 949, p 965.
114 *Banner v Berridge* (1881) 18 Ch D 254.
115 *Haddington Island Quarry Co Ltd v Alden Wesley Huson* [1911] AC 722 (PC).
116 *Tse Kwong Lam v Wong Chit Sen* [1983] 1 WLR 1349.
117 (1888) 40 Ch D 395.

sale to a limited company. On the nature of a mortgagee's power of sale, Lindley LJ stated:

> A mortgagee with a power of sale, though often called a trustee, is in a very different position from a trustee for sale. A mortgagee is under obligations to the mortgagor, but he has rights of his own, which he is entitled to exercise adversely to the mortgagor. A trustee for sale has no business to place himself in such a position as to give rise to a conflict of interest and duty. But every mortgage confers upon the mortgagee the right to realise his security and to find a purchaser if he can, and, if in exercise of his power, he acts *bona fide* and takes reasonable precautions to obtain a proper price, the mortgagor has no redress, even though more might have been obtained for the property if the sale had been postponed.[118]

There was no impropriety in this case and the mortgagee solicitor did his best to get the best price.

However, other decisions were not consistent on the issue until the Court of Appeal examined them in the *Cuckmere* case mentioned above, in which Cairns LJ summarised the problem as follows:

> I find it impossible satisfactorily to reconcile the authorities, but I think the balance of authority is in favour of a duty of care. That there is such a duty was certainly the view of Kekewich J and of the Court of Appeal in *Tomlin v Luce* (1889) 41 Ch D 573; (1889) 43 Ch D 191; also, of the Judicial Committee in *McHugh v Union Bank of Canada* [1913] AC 299. It also appears to have been the view of Lindley LJ at the time of his judgment in *Farrar v Farrars Ltd* (1888) 40 Ch D 395. That judgment was so interpreted by the judge of first instance in *Kennedy v de Trafford*, but, on the appeal, in that case, Lindley LJ said ([1896] 1 Ch 762, p 772) that, when he had referred in Farrar's case to a mortgagee's duty to take reasonable precautions, he had meant merely that the mortgagee must not act fraudulently or wilfully or recklessly; and, in the House of Lords, [1897] AC 180, p 185, Lord Herschell said that he thought it would be unreasonable to require the mortgagee to do more than act in good faith, that is, not wilfully or recklessly to sacrifice the interests of the mortgagor. These expressions of opinion in the Court of Appeal and in the House of Lords were, however, not necessary to the decision. Lindley LJ said, [1896] 1 Ch 762, p 772, that the mortgagees 'acted from first to last in an honourable and businesslike manner, without in the least sacrificing the interests of the mortgagor'.
>
> Lord Herschell said, [1897] AC 180, p 185: 'My Lords, it is not necessary in this case to give an exhaustive definition of the duties of a mortgagee to a mortgagor, because it appears to me that, if you were to accept the definition of them for which the appellant contends, namely, that the mortgagee is bound to take reasonable precautions in the exercise of his power of sale, as well as to act in good faith, still in this case he did take reasonable precautions.'
>
> I, therefore, consider that *Tomlin v Luce* (1889) 43 Ch D 191 is the stronger authority and I would hold that the present defendants had a duty to take

---

118 (1888) 40 Ch D 395, p 410–11.

reasonable care to obtain a proper price for the land in the interest of the mortgagors.[119]

Salmon LJ dissented, only to the extent of establishing a yardstick for the value to be obtained on sale, and he preferred to use the phrase 'the true market value' instead of 'proper price'; he said:

> ... both on principle and authority, the mortgagee, in exercising his power of sale, does owe a duty to take reasonable precautions to obtain the true market value of the property at the date on which he decides to sell it.[120]

In 1993, it was explained by the Privy Council in the *Downsview Nominees* (see later) that the duty to take reasonable precautions was limited to obtaining a proper price of the mortgaged property and that the *Cuckmere* decision was not an authority for any wider proposition.

There is no fixed rule that a mortgagee exercising his power of sale might not sell the mortgaged property to a company in which he is interested, but he must show that he had made the sale in good faith and had taken reasonable precautions to obtain the best price reasonably obtainable at the time. However, he must not sell to himself as an individual.

Tse Kwong Lam v Wong Chit Sen[121]

The mortgagee, in exercise of his power of sale under a charge, arranged for the property to be sold by public auction. The auction was advertised and at the auction, the mortgagee instructed the auctioneer that the reserve price was to be $1.2 m. Meanwhile, the mortgagee and his wife were directors of a company of which his children were the shareholders. It had been agreed at a directors' meeting of this company that the wife would bid for the property, on behalf of the company, up to $1.2 m. His wife was the only bidder at the auction and at a bid of $1.2 m, the property was sold to the company. The borrower/mortgagor applied to have the sale set aside. The court held that, because of the close relationship between the mortgagee and the company, a heavy onus lay on the mortgagee to show that in all respects, he had acted fairly to the borrower, and used his best endeavours to obtain the best price reasonably obtainable for the mortgaged property.

The Judicial Committee of the Privy Council stated, thus:

> In the result, their Lordships consider that in the present case the company was not debarred from purchasing the mortgaged property but, in view of the close relationship between the company and the mortgagee and in view in particular of the conflict of duty and interest to which the mortgagee was subject, the sale to the company for $1.2 m can only be supported if the

---

119 *Cuckmere Brick Co Ltd v Mutual Finance Ltd* [1971] Ch 949, pp 977–78.
120 *Ibid*, p 968.
121 [1983] 1 WLR 1349.

mortgagee proves that he took reasonable precautions to obtain the best price reasonably obtainable at the time of sale.[122]

In this case, the mortgagee had made no effort to discharge this burden, and there was insufficient evidence to show that this particular auction produced the true market value of the property. However, the sale was not set aside in view of the borrower's delay in pursuing his claim.

The Privy Council in the following case did not extend the duty of the mortgagee and of the receiver in dealing with the asset of the mortgaged property to a general duty of care.

Downsview Nominees v First City Corp[123]

The nature and extent of the duties owed by a mortgagee and his receiver or manager to subsequent encumbrancers and the mortgagor was examined. The first debenture holder (also the first defendant) appointed the second defendant as receiver for the sole purpose of disrupting the receivership under the second debenture belonging to the first plaintiff. The first plaintiff offered to buy the first debenture from the first defendant at a price equivalent to the amounts outstanding and secured under the debenture, but the first defendant refused. There was subsequently gross mismanagement on the part of the defendant's receiver resulting in considerable losses. The question was whether the first debenture holder and his receiver owed any duty to subsequent encumbrancers (the plaintiff) and to the company. The judgment of the Privy Council was delivered by Lord Templeman, who said, with regard to the duty, that it is primarily an equitable duty:

> If a first mortgagee commits a breach of his duties to the mortgagor, the damage inflicted by that breach of duty will be suffered by the second mortgagee, subsequent encumbrancers and the mortgagor, depending on the extent of the damage and the amount of each security ...

> ... when a receiver and manager exercises the powers of sale and management conferred on him by the mortgage, he is dealing with the security; he is not merely selling or dealing with the interests of the mortgagor. He is exercising the power of selling or dealing with the mortgaged property for the purpose of obtaining repayment of the debt owing to his mortgagee. The receiver and manager owes these duties to the mortgagor and to all subsequent encumbrancers in whose favour the mortgaged property has been charged ...[124]

The general duty of care said to be owed by a mortgagee to subsequent encumbrancers and the mortgagor in negligence is inconsistent with the right of the mortgagee and the duties which the courts, applying equitable principles, have imposed on the mortgagee. If a mortgagee enters into

---

122 [1983] 1 WLR 1349, p 1356.
123 [1993] AC 295.
124 *Ibid*, pp 311–12.

possession he is liable to account for rent on the basis of wilful default; he must keep mortgage premises in repair; he is liable for waste. Those duties were imposed to ensure that a mortgagee is diligent in discharging his mortgage and returning the property to the mortgagor. If a mortgagee exercises his power of sale in good faith for the purpose of protecting his security, he is not liable to the mortgagor even though he might have obtained a higher price and even though the terms might be regarded as disadvantageous to the mortgagor. *Cuckmere Brick Co Ltd v Mutual Finance Ltd* [1971] Ch 949 is Court of Appeal authority for the proposition that, if the mortgagee decides to sell, he must take reasonable care to obtain a proper price, but is no authority for any wider proposition. A receiver exercising his power of sale also owes the same specific duties as the mortgagee. But that apart, the general duty of a receiver and manager appointed by a debenture holder, as defined by Jenkins LJ in *In re B Johnson & Co (Builders) Ltd* [1955] Ch 634, p 661, leaves no room for the imposition of a general duty to use reasonable care in dealing with the assets of the company. The duties imposed by equity on a mortgagee and on a receiver and manager would be quite unnecessary if there existed a general duty in negligence to take reasonable care in the exercise of powers and to take reasonable care in dealing with the assets of the mortgagor company.[125]

The receivership of the second defendant was inspired by improper purposes and carried on in bad faith verging on fraud. Lord Templeman continued:

A mortgagee owes a general duty to subsequent encumbrancers and to the mortgagor to use his powers for the sole purpose of securing repayments of the moneys owing under his mortgage and a duty to act in good faith. He also owes the specific duties which equity has imposed on him in the exercise of his powers to go into possession and his powers of sale. It may well be that a mortgagee who appoints a receiver and manager, knowing that the receiver and manager intends to exercise his powers for the purpose of frustrating the activities of the second mortgagee or for some other improper purpose or who fails to revoke the appointment of a receiver and manager when the mortgagee knows that the receiver and manager is abusing his powers, may himself be guilty of bad faith, but in the present case this possibility need not be explored.[126]

The mortgagee can sell to the mortgagor as there is no fiduciary relation between them during the sale. The mortgagee stands in a fiduciary position, only when he holds a surplus of the value after the sale. However, if there is a single mortgagor, he has nothing to do, but redeem by paying the principal, interest and costs. Where there are several mortgagors and one of them agrees to buy from the mortgagee, exercising his power of sale, there is nothing to prevent him.[127]

---

125 [1993] AC 295, p 315.
126 *Ibid*, p 317.
127 *Kennedy v De Trafford* [1896] 1 Ch 762.

In conclusion, it seems to be a clear reconciliation of the English authorities that the duties of the mortgagee to the mortgagor and other mortgagees during the exercise of his power of sale are these: first, the mortgagee owes a duty of care to obtain a proper, or the market, value of the ship, failing which he may be liable in damages to the mortgagor or to subsequent mortgagees, if they have suffered loss by his negligence. Second, he does not owe a general duty of care in any other respect but a duty to act in good faith when he deals with the asset of the mortgaged property.[128] Third, the sale may be set aside only in case of fraud of which the purchaser had notice.

9.4.4 Effect of sale by the mortgagee

A purchaser of the ship from the mortgagee will get good title. However, a private sale will have the effect of extinguishing only such encumbrances on the ship that arose after the mortgage, including mortgages taken with notice of the prior mortgage.[129] Sale by the mortgagee privately does not extinguish maritime liens created at any time. In the light of this disadvantage, which would make it difficult for the mortgagee to find a buyer willing to take such risk, the mortgagee seeks the assistance of the Admiralty Court by arresting the ship, so that the sale can be made by a court order, the effect of which is to extinguish all encumbrances.

9.5 Appointment of a receiver

There may be occasions when the mortgagee does not wish to undertake the liabilities, which would be inherent from his position in possession of the ship or from the exercise of his power of sale. The deed of covenants normally contains an express provision for an appointment of a receiver by the mortgagee who will be deemed to be the agent of the mortgagor.[130] If the deed of covenants does not provide for appointment of a receiver, the mortgagee can apply to court for such an appointment, where the mortgagor is in default or the mortgagee's security is threatened. Where a prior mortgagee has already taken possession of the ship, a subsequent mortgagee may apply to court for the appointment of a receiver subject to the right of the first mortgagee. The court may appoint a receiver in cases where there has been gross mismanagement on the part of the first mortgagee in possession. The function of the receiver is to collect the earnings of the mortgaged

---

128 See, also, *China and South Sea Bank Ltd v Tan Soon Gin* [1990] 1 AC 536 (PC).

129 *Black v Williams* [1895] 1 Ch 408.

130 *Gaskell v Gosling* [1896] 1 QB 669 (CA), p 679, *per* Lord Esher MR, concerning appointment of a receiver by a trustee. The receiver negligently bought goods from the plaintiff after a winding-up order of the company. The receiver acted as agent of the company and was not liable himself to the plaintiff.

property (freight or hire), and pay the necessary expenses until the realisation of the security, or an order from the court.

The nature of the duties owed by a receiver and manager appointed by a debenture holder to act *bona fide* were summarised in the case of *Downsview Nominees v First City Corp* (see above). In the more recent Court of Appeal decision, *Medforth v Blake*,[131] it was held that the extent and scope of any duty of the receiver or manager additional to that of good faith depended on the facts and circumstances of the particular case. While his primary duty in the exercise of his powers of management was to try to bring about a situation in which interest on the secured debt could be paid and the debt itself repaid, the receiver owed a duty to manage the property with due diligence.

9.6 Foreclosure

Foreclosure under the general law means the taking over of the property by the mortgagee, who becomes absolute owner of it in consideration of the mortgage debt. It extinguishes the equitable right of redemption of the mortgagor and, therefore, it is contradictory to that right protected by equity. For this reason, only the court can order it.

With regard to ship mortgages, the MSAs have not envisaged such a right and it is doubtful whether the right exists with regard to registered mortgages of registered ships, because it would be inconsistent with the statutory nature of the ship mortgage. Alison Clarke argues that foreclosure is, essentially, the remedy of a property transfer mortgage. So, in principle, it ought not to be available on the statutory security analysis, since the MSAs, by virtue of which the mortgagee has been a registered mortgagee and not a registered owner since 1854, do not provide for it. She further argues that: 'In a genuine property transfer type mortgage, the mortgagee is already owner and foreclosure is achieved merely by a court of equity declaring that the mortgagor's equity of redemption is at an end. But, even in land mortgages, foreclosure is now obsolete.'[132]

---

131 [1999] 3 WLR 922.
132 *Op cit*, Clarke, fn 10, p 690.

10 EFFECT OF MORTGAGEE'S EXERCISE OF RIGHTS UPON CHARTERPARTIES

10.1 The issues

It has been stated, in the authorities discussed earlier, that the mortgagor as owner in possession is free to employ his vessel in any way in which he wishes provided that his acts do not impair the mortgagee's security, which will necessitate the mortgagee to take possession. This derives from Sched 1, para 10 of the MSA 1995, as discussed. It follows that the mortgagor can enter into charterparty contracts while in possession, which contracts will be binding on the mortgagee provided they do not materially impair his security.

It is a well established principle, as will be seen in the following authorities, that where the charterparty contract is subsequent to the mortgage, the mortgagee may only enter into possession and interfere with the charterparty where his security is threatened, or is materially impaired. But, if the charterparty contract precedes the mortgage, the issue of notice of the charterparty becomes important in determining whether the mortgagee may exercise his rights which will cause the termination of the charterparty.

Has the charterer of the ship any rights himself to restrain the mortgagee from interfering with the performance of the contract after the mortgagee entered into possession to realise his security? Being a third party vis à vis the mortgagee, the question is whether common law or equity will assist the charterer, even if the mortgagee has committed no wrong by seeking to exercise his rights under his contract with the mortgagor.

This is an area where legal issues can be complex and some preliminary points are raised. If the mortgagee exercises his statutory right to enforce his security when he is fully entitled to do so, he will be committing no wrong. If the third party charterer suffers loss in consequence thereof, his cause of action should be against his contracting party, whose conduct with regard to the mortgaged ship gave cause to the mortgagee to take possession and control of the ship. Thus, the charterer should claim damages against the mortgagor for breach of contract unless the mortgagee had taken the mortgage with full knowledge of the terms of the charter. Specific performance would not be possible in the circumstances when the mortgagee has taken possession. On the other hand, if the mortgagee enters into possession unjustifiably, the charterer could either restrain him by seeking an injunction from the court, and/or claim damages for his loss on the basis of the tort of wrongful interference with his contract. Some examples of leading authorities of the two categories of charterparties (subsequent or preceding to the mortgage) illustrate the complexities in this area.

10.2 Charterparty subsequent to the mortgage (leading cases)

Collins v Lamport[133]

After a registered mortgage had been granted on the ship, her owner, who was contemplating the sale of the vessel, chartered her to the prospective buyer's nominee. The mortgagee also contracted to sell the vessel to another buyer free from the charterparty. An application of an injunction to restrain the mortgagee from interfering with the charterparty was made to the court. The question was whether the MSAs gave the mortgagee the power to interfere, at will and at anytime, with everything done by the mortgagor and to take possession of the ship, stripping her entirely of any contract or engagement. Lord Westbury stated:

> As long ... as the dealings of the mortgagor with the ship are consistent with the sufficiency of the mortgagee's security, so long as those dealings do not materially prejudice and detract from or impair the sufficiency of the security comprised in the mortgage, so long as there is Parliamentary authority given to the mortgagor to act in all respects as owner of the vessel, and if he has authority to act as owner he has, of necessity, authority to enter into all those contracts touching the disposition of the ship which may be necessary for him to get the full value and benefit of his property. But, whenever a mortgagee can shew that the act of the mortgagor prejudices or injures his security, he ceases to be bound by the Parliamentary declaration as to the ownership of the mortgagor, and can claim the full benefit of and exercise the rights given to him by his mortgage.[134]

An injunction was granted to restrain the mortgagees from interfering with the performance of the charterparty, as it was not shown that it would prejudicially affect the sufficiency of their security.

The Heather Bell[135]

The defendant was the former owner of the vessel and also the holder of a mortgage on the vessel, as collateral security for purchase money owed to him. The new owners of the vessel entered into an agreement with the plaintiffs to run her on specified daily excursion trips for about six weeks, dividing the profits between themselves after deduction of expenses and advancing monies to liberate part of the machinery held as lien for repairs. The mortgagor was to insure the vessel and the plaintiff was under no obligation to keep the ship in repair. The plaintiff was to have a charge and lien on the boat ranking, in the highest position that the owners were able to fix, having regard to the existing circumstances for the liberation of

---

133 (1864) 4 De GJ&S 500.
134 *Ibid*, p 504.
135 [1901] P 272.

machinery, and other advantages. When an instalment of purchase money fell due, the defendant seized the vessel, alleging that the agreement between the plaintiffs and the owners was not binding upon him, as it postponed his rights as mortgagee and depreciated the saleable value of the vessel. It was held that the agreement was binding upon the mortgagee as it was not prejudicial to the security created by the mortgage, nor was there proof of fraud between the owner and the plaintiff. Lord Alverstone did not believe that the agreement to run the boat at half profits was, under the circumstances, impinging upon the rights of the mortgagee. There could still be an honest expectation that there would be profits and the contract, therefore, could not be considered as materially impairing the security of the mortgagee. The mortgagee could restrain her from going to sea, if she was not fully insured against perils of the sea, but that alone would not justify him to set aside the charterparty.

Where a profitable charterparty has been entered into by the mortgagor in possession of a ship, the mortgagee cannot object to the charterparty being carried out simply upon the ground that the effect of it would be to remove her out of the jurisdiction of the court and to render it difficult for him to enforce his security.[136]

The following decision of Brandon J set down a broad principle of the circumstances in which the mortgagee could exercise his rights without being bound by the charterparty and it is worth looking at the various issues that arose, particularly as they provide a guide for risk management purposes.

The Myrto[137]

The vessel was bought and registered in Liberia. The bank had advanced money to the owners to buy the vessel and it was agreed that the debt was to be secured by a first mortgage on the vessel. The mortgage was executed and, then, the vessel was transferred to the Greek Registry, when it was provisionally registered in Greece. The bank lent further sums to the owners secured by a second mortgage executed under Liberian law, but registered in Greece. The owners then let their vessel on a voyage charterparty. Default of payments under both mortgages occurred and the mortgagees arrested the vessel and applied for her appraisement and sale. One of the grounds on which the owners applied for the release of the vessel was that the arrest was an unlawful interference with their rights to continue with the charterparty.

It was held that the owners had dealt with the vessel in such a manner as to impair the mortgagee's security for the following reasons: (i) the charterparty contract was speculative and improvident; (ii) the mortgagors were impecunious and there was every possibility that the expenses of

---

136 *The Fanchon* (1880) 5 PD 173.
137 [1977] 2 Lloyd's Rep 243.

completing the voyage would exceed the funds expected from the freight; (iii) the vessel had already been under arrest for three weeks at the suit of a creditor in respect of a substantial debt; and iv) the mortgagors had numerous other accrued debts and liabilities, the most important being a large debt to the crew carrying a maritime lien having priority over the bank's mortgages. Brandon J summarised the general principles:

(1) the owner is entitled subject to one exception to deal with the ship as he would be entitled to do if the ship were not mortgaged, that includes employing her under contracts with third parties;

(2) the one exception is that the owner is not entitled to deal with the ship in such a way as to impair the security of the mortgagee. The question whether the contract is such as to impair the mortgagee's security is a question of fact;

(3) when a contract with a third party is not such as to impair the security of the mortgagee and the owner is both able and willing to perform the contract, the mortgagee is not entitled to interfere with the performance of the contract

(4) the mortgagee is, however, entitled to exercise his rights under the mortgage without regard to any such contract where:

(i) The contract is of such a kind and/or the performance of that contract would result in the impairment of the mortgagee's security, or

(ii) Where the owner is unwilling and/or unable to perform the contract. This is a question of fact;

(5) Where the mortgagee exercises his rights in circumstances other than these, he commits a tort or actionable wrong in the nature of interfering with the contractual rights of a third party. In such cases, the remedy available to the third party – depending on the mortgagee's actions – includes: (a) an injunction restraining the mortgagee from selling the ship; or (b) an order for the release of the ship if he has arrested it in an action in *rem*; (c) further or alternatively to (a) or (b), damages;

(6) it is open to a court as a matter of law to find as a fact that a particular contract is such as to impair the mortgagee's security, if evidence shows that the owner is impecunious and that he can only perform the voyage to which the contract relates, if at all, on credit and that the ship is already subject to pressing liabilities and charges.

10.3 Charterparty entered into prior to the mortgage (leading cases)

De Mattos v Gibson[138]

The plaintiff had chartered a ship from its owner, Curry, who subsequently charged the ship to Gibson. Gibson had actual notice of the charterparty and

---

138 (1858) 4 De G&J 276.

its terms. Curry got into financial difficulties and was unable to continue the voyage. Gibson sought to enforce his security by taking possession of the ship and diverted her to another port to sell her. The plaintiff (charterer) claimed an injunction against Gibson restraining him from interfering with the charterparty. The judge refused to grant it. Lords Justice Knight Bruce and Turner, granted an interim injunction on appeal, but on full hearing, Lord Chelmsford LC affirmed the judge's decision that the injunction ought to be refused, only because the owner was unable to perform the charter.

After considering the issue of specific performance against the owner of the ship, the Court of Appeal turned to the main issue whether the mortgagee was justified to do what he did. It was held that the mortgagee had not, in any way, interfered with the performance of the charterparty, until it was evident that Curry was wholly unable to perform it. It was clear that, if the vessel had remained in the possession of the owner (Curry), no repairs would have been effected and without them, the vessel could not put to sea. The actual performance of the contract, as between the plaintiff and Curry, was virtually at an end when Gibson took possession of the vessel and repaired her, Curry being utterly unable to perform the contract.

The well known and much quoted statement of Lord Justice Knight Bruce is said to have established a general principle of law applicable even outside the context of ship mortgages:

> Reason and justice seem to prescribe that, at least as a general rule, where a man, by gift or purchase, acquires property from another with knowledge of a previous contract, lawfully and for valuable consideration made by him with a third person, to use and employ the property for a particular purpose in a specified manner, the acquirer shall not, to the material damage of the person, in opposition to the contract and inconsistently with it, use and employ property in a manner not allowable to the giver or seller. This rule, applicable in general, as I conceive, to moveable and immoveable property, and adopted, as I apprehend, by English law, may, like other general rules, be liable to exceptions arising from special circumstances ... [139]

The remedy of an injunction, suggested in *De Mattos v Gibson*, is equitable and is generally applied in cases where the charterparty precedes the mortgage. Thus, for the mortgagee to be bound by the charterparty he must have had notice of it and its terms.

The Celtic King[140]

This involved a sale of the mortgaged ship being subject to a charterparty. While the steamer was being built, the shipowner entered into an agreement with the defendants (charterers) by which he undertook to fit her for a

---

139 (1858) 4 De G&J 276, p 282.
140 [1894] P 175.

particular trade and run her for five years, as one of the defendants' line. After completion of building and registration of the vessel, the shipowner mortgaged the vessel to the first mortgagees, who had no notice of the agreement with the defendants. A second mortgage was subsequently granted to the plaintiff, who had notice of the agreement between the shipowner and the defendants. After the charterparty had been running upwards of two years in the defendants' line, and was temporarily laid up, her owner died having made default in payment of instalments under the first mortgage. The first mortgagees took possession of the vessel and sold her to the plaintiff (second mortgagee) who, at the time of purchase, had notice of the contents of the agreement between the owner and the defendants. The plaintiff entered into a contract of sale of the ship with a third party and demanded the certificate of registration, which was in the hands of the defendants. The defendants denied the plaintiff's right to the certificate, except on condition that the plaintiff should be restrained from dealing with the ship in derogation of the agreement, and applied for an injunction.

Barnes J held that the certificate was a separate issue from the possible right of the charterer for an injunction to restrain the plaintiff from dealing with the ship without being bound with the charterparty. It was ordered that the certificate should be handed over to those entitled to it, that is, the plaintiff.

In considering the application for an injunction against the plaintiff, it was held that the first mortgagees, having no notice of the prior agreement, were not bound by its terms at the time of their mortgage. That meant that they could sell the ship, free of it, if they chose to enforce their security. On the issue of whether the mortgagee could pass his title free from the charterparty to a purchaser who had notice of it, Barnes J stated:

> ... decisions in equity cases have been cited to me which shew that a purchaser with notice is entitled to rely upon the title of his vendor without notice, because otherwise that vendor would be restricted in his powers of sale.[141]

The main concern of the judge, on the facts of this case, was that the charterparty contract was not an ordinary one. It was such that it would have depreciatory effect on the mortgagee's security, because it was a contract binding the ship for a very long period with various clauses making it difficult for anybody to purchase a ship tied to these terms. Although, it was argued that, since this particular buyer was aware of the terms of the contract and was buying the ship burdened with it, what was significant, the judge thought, was that the vendor, first mortgagee, was not aware of it and he ought to be able to sell the ship free from an onerous contract. Otherwise, he would be unable to sell to the plaintiff, if he was the best purchaser available, and this definitely constituted a fetter in the vendor's right to realise his security. Bearing in mind that the original owner had by then died, it was not

---

141 [1894] P 175, pp 188–89.

certain whether his estate would be, in any event, prepared to continue with this contract and the best remedy for the charterer would be to seek damages from the estate of the deceased.

On those facts, this case was quite unusual. It involved one mortgagee who had no knowledge of the pre-dated charterparty and a subsequent mortgagee with knowledge of it and of its terms (the *De Mattos v Gibson* point). The judge based his decision on the fact that the first mortgagee had no knowledge of the charterparty, thus, he was entitled to deal with the ship free from the contract.

10.4 Can a purchaser of a ship be bound by a pre-existing charterparty? (A related matter)

Whether or not an injunction could be obtained against a new purchaser of the ship, similar principles have been applied.

Lord Strathcona Steamship Co Ltd v Dominion Coal Co Ltd[142]

The owners of a steamship entered into a charterparty with Dominion for 10 consecutive St Lawrence seasons, with an option for continuing for a further period of at least five more seasons. Later, the ship was transferred to various successive owners, who all had notice of the terms of the charterparty agreement and undertook to accept all responsibilities thereunder. The appellants, Lord Strathcona, the new owners of the vessel, refused to perform the charterparty. Following the case of *De Mattos v Gibson*, it was held that an injunction could be granted in such circumstances to compel one who obtains a conveyance, or grants sub-conditions, from violating the condition of his purchase to the prejudice of the original contractor. The Privy Council further stated that the purchaser of a ship who has notice of the terms of a charterparty, entered into for its employment, is in the position of a constructive trustee, and he can be restrained, at the suit of the charterers from employing the ship in a way inconsistent with the charterparty. In order to get the injunction, the plaintiff ought to have a continuing interest in the property, but that, also, a bare contractual right, as opposed to a property interest, was a sufficient interest for this purpose.

Port Line Ltd v Ben Line Steamers Ltd[143]

In this case, Diplock J, sitting then as a judge, thought that *The Strathcona* was wrongly decided on the point of constructive trusteeship.

---

142 [1926] AC 108 (PC); *Lorenzen v White Shipping Co Ltd* (1943) 74 LlL Rep 161 followed it.
143 [1958] 2 QB 146; [1958] 1 Lloyd's Rep 290.

Port Line (the plaintiffs) had chartered a vessel from Silver Line for 30 months which commenced in March 1955. In February 1956, Silver sold the vessel to Ben Line subject to an immediate bareboat charter by Ben to Silver to cover the unexpired term of the plaintiffs' time charter with Silver. The bareboat charter contained a clause providing that, if the Government requisitioned the vessel, this charter would cease. There was no comparable clause in the plaintiffs' charter with Silver. Due to the Suez crisis, the vessel was requisitioned and was put at the Crown's disposition and an agreement was entered between Ben and the Ministry of Transport providing for rates of hire, as compensation during the period of requisition. Silver contended that the time charter with Port Line had been frustrated. Port claimed they were entitled to recover the compensation, or part of it, received by Ben for the requisition on the ground that there was a subsisting contract between them and Silver and, under the Compensation Act 1939, such compensation should be paid to the person entitled to possession or use of the ship. Therefore, Ben to whom compensation was paid was deemed to act as a trustee for Port under this Act and the principle laid down in *Lord Strathcona*.

Ben argued that Port's charter had been frustrated, in any event, and that *The Strathcona* had been wrongly decided, or if not, it applied only when the subsequent purchaser had express notice of the terms of the subsisting charter.

Deciding against compensation, the judge did not follow *The Strathcona* on the constructive trusteeship point. Although, Diplock J was not actually concerned with the question whether Port was entitled to a negative injunction to restrain the tort, he gave an alternative ground for his decision that actual, as opposed to constructive, notice of the terms, not just of the existence of the charter by Ben, was necessary in such a case.

10.5 An injunction on the ground of tort of knowing interference with contractual rights

In the following decision, at first instance, Browne-Wilkinson J, differed from Lord Diplock and held that *The Strathcona* was rightly decided on the issue that Dominion was entitled to an injunction against Strathcona to prevent the latter from interfering with the contract between Dominion and the original charterer, but did not express any view whether or not the Privy Council was correct on the constructive trusteeship point.

It is essential, first to clarify how the House of Lords dealt with the contractual position of the parties involved and then look at how Browne-Wilkinson J, at first instance, gave an overview of the existence of jurisdiction of the Court to grant an injunction on the basis of the tort of interference with a pre-existing contract.

Swiss Bank v Lloyds Bank[144]

The appeal to the House of Lords was concerned with competing claims to a fund of approximately £800,000 held on deposit by Lloyds Bank (Lloyds). It represented proceeds of sale of securities issued by a company incorporated in Israel, FIBI Holdings Ltd, to the respondent, Israel Financial Trust (IFT) There were three issues in the appeal: (1) whether the appellants, Swiss Bank, had a charge over or a proprietary interest in the FIBI securities and, if so, what was the nature of that charge or interest; (2) whether a charge created by IFT over the FIBI securities in favour of Lloyds was valid; (3) (depending on the answers to (1) and (2)) whether the interest of the Swiss Bank had priority over the charge to Lloyds.

The agreement for the loan by the Swiss Bank to IFT had been made subject to conformity with exchange control regulations and to obtaining the consents required. The loan was payable on demand. IFT provided a charge to the Swiss Bank on the sterling cash deposits held by the bank for IFT. In due course, the Swiss Bank advanced Swiss francs to IFT, which were used in the acquisition of the FIBI securities, and were deposited with a parent company of IFT. Subsequently, the parent company ran into financial difficulties and borrowed from Lloyds a substantial sum of money to meet these difficulties on terms that all its subsidiaries, including IFT, would guarantee this loan and grant charges over various assets. IFT, accordingly, executed a memorandum of deposit in favour of Lloyds. Later, in the same year the FIBI securities were sold, with the agreement of Lloyds, and the proceeds of the sale realised the £800,000 mentioned above.

The judge, at first instance, held that the Swiss Bank had an equitable charge and were entitled to these proceeds. The Court of Appeal took the opposite view. It said that the Swiss Bank was not entitled to any charge, or to other proprietary interest. Lord Wilberforce agreed with that view. Upon construction of the documents, there was nothing in the agreement between the Swiss Bank and IFT to repay the loan out of the FIBI securities. The fact that the loan agreement contained an express charge upon the sterling deposits, vitiated any intention to create a charge in the FIBI securities. Therefore, the appellants' claim to any charge or proprietary interest in the FIBI proceeds of sale failed.

With regard to the position of Lloyds, which had obtained an express charge on the securities and were holding them, after deliberating whether the charge was illegal, for being in breach of the Exchange Control Act 1947, their Lordships came to the conclusion, unanimously, that the charge to Lloyds was valid, not illegal and it took priority over the Swiss loan.

---

144 [1982] AC 584 (HL).

This is a paradigm case of how complex financial arrangements can go wrong, particularly due to less than careful drafting. The issue of the appeal was an issue of construction of the documents, but the first instance decision, which was reversed on point of construction of the agreements, is still relevant on the issues discussed here, regarding the principle of the tort of knowing interference with contractual rights. Brief reference to it is therefore important.

After examining all the relevant authorities, Browne-Wilkinson J[145] laid down the principles as follows:

(1) The principle stated by Knight Bruce LJ in *De Mattos v Gibson*, is good law and represents the counterpart in equity of the tort of knowing interference with contractual rights.

(2) A person proposing to deal with property in such a way as to cause a breach of a contract affecting that property will be restrained by injunction from so doing, if when he acquired that property he had actual knowledge of that contract

(3) A plaintiff is entitled to such an injunction, even if he has no proprietary interest in the property: his right to have his contract performed is a sufficient interest.

(4) There is no case in which such an injunction has been granted against a defendant who acquired the property with only constructive, as opposed to actual, notice of the contract. In my judgment, constructive notice is not sufficient, since actual knowledge of the contract is a requisite element in the tort.[146]

When the case was decided, it had already been recognised at common law that it was a legal wrong or tort for someone to interfere with the contractual rights of others.[147] It has subsequently been established that equity would intervene to restrain such a tort and such jurisdiction is frequently exercised at the present day[148] ... It follows that, if at the date of the Lloyds charge, Lloyds had had actual notice of the plaintiff's rights in relation to the FIBI securities and the plaintiff had been informed of IFT's intention to grant the Lloyds charge, the plaintiff could, in my judgment, have obtained an injunction restraining Lloyds from taking the charge since, by so doing, they would have been committing the tort.[149]

On the facts, however, the judge did not find that Lloyds had actual knowledge, which is an essential ingredient of the tort and, therefore, committed no legal wrong. It is to be noted that the judge regarded the principle of *De Mattos* as the counterpart in equity of the tort of knowing interference with contractual rights at common law.

---

145 [1979] 3 WLR 201.

146 *Ibid*, p 226.

147 *Lunley v Gye* (1853) 2 E&B 216.

148 *Sefton v Tophams Ltd* [1965] Ch 140.

149 *Swiss Bank v Lloyds Bank* [1979] 3 WLR 201, p 223, *per* Browne-Wilkinson J.

10.6 Conclusion

Despite the difficulty in reconciling some of these authorities, it seems clear that the general principles are as follows.

10.6.1 A post-mortgage charterparty: the impairment factor

The right of the mortgagor to deal with the mortgaged property – until it becomes necessary for the mortgagee to make the ship available as a security – derives from Sched 1, para 10 of the MSA 1995. Under the deed of covenants, the mortgagor is obliged to inform the mortgagee of the terms of the employment of the ship under a charterparty. The mortgagee can only interfere with the performance of such a charterparty, if there is a serious impairment of his security. If there is no impairment of the security, then the mortgagee will wrongfully interfere with the contractual rights between the mortgagor and the charterer, inducing breach of contract. The charterer's remedy to restrain him from doing so by way of an injunction is both an equitable remedy and a remedy at common law, based on the tort of wrongful interference.[150] If he suffered loss, by reason of the tort, which was reasonably foreseeable, he would have a claim in damages against the mortgagee.[151]

No such remedies will be available if the security is in fact impaired, as the mortgagee will be committing no wrong.

10.6.2 A pre-mortgage charterparty: the knowledge factor

If there was a pre-mortgage charterparty, the mortgagee would, normally, take his security with knowledge of the charterparty. In practice, the distinction between actual and constructive knowledge may be academic because the mortgagee's lawyers ought to have inquired about any pre-existing charterparty and studied its terms. If they did not, they would be exposed to a potential claim in negligence. Assuming that the mortgagee was so advised, it would follow that he could not later turn round and say to the mortgagor or to the charterer: 'I do not like the terms of this charterparty now because it impairs my security,' unless the circumstances in relation to the performance of the charter have changed, or important side letters between the owner and the charterer varying the terms of the charter had not been disclosed to the mortgagee.[152]

---

150 *Collins v Lamport* (1864) 4 De GJ&S 500 and *The Myrto* [1977] 2 Lloyd's Rep 243.

151 *Kuwait Airways Corp v Iraqi Airways Co (No 7)* [2001] 1 Lloyd's Rep 161, pp 248–53 (concerning the test for causation and remoteness of damages in cases of wrongful interference with goods).

152 *The Odenfeld* [1978] 2 Lloyd's Rep 357.

Save as aforesaid, the charterer will have an equitable remedy based on the principle of *De Mattos v Gibson* to obtain an injunction against the mortgagee, if the latter attempts to terminate the charter.[153] The injunction would be an appropriate remedy in equity if the mortgagee took the mortgage with full knowledge of the charterparty, unless the circumstances with regard to it later changed. If the charterer provided evidence of actual knowledge of the terms of the charter by the mortgagee, this would be sufficient ground for the injunction to be granted to prevent the mortgagee from exercising his rights, if his security was impaired, otherwise than in allowing the continuation of the charterparty. If the security was impaired, the mortgagee would be committing no wrong, so the tort of wrongful interference would be of no help to the charterer in such a case, but still equity would assist him because of prior knowledge of the charter by the mortgagee.[154] It seems that the risk is placed on the mortgagee, who having knowledge of the circumstances entered into the loan transaction, unless cumulative factors of the mortgagor's inability to perform would justify an order for sale of the ship by the court, as was decided in *The Myrto*.

10.6.3 Exception to the De Mattos principle

The outcome of the decision in *De Mattos v Gibson* was that, although the mortgagee had actual knowledge of the contractual obligation imposed under the charterparty, he was not prevented from dealing with the ship otherwise than in accordance with the charterparty because there was evidence that the mortgagor was not himself in a position to perform his contractual obligation under the charterparty. Thus, the exception to the principle of *De Mattos v Gibson* is that when there is an accumulation of factors pointing towards inability of performance of the charterparty by the mortgagor, the mortgagee can exercise his statutory rights under his security.[155] In such a case, the charterer should look upon his contracting party for enforcement of his rights and remedies. Demand for performance will be of no practical use if the mortgagor is unable to do so. Under those circumstances, the charterer could not, by an injunction, prevent the mortgagee from exercising his rights just because the charterparty would be interfered with. The charter would have been at an end, in any event, because of the inability of the mortgagor to perform, regardless of the mortgagee's action.

10.6.4 The tort of wrongful interference with a contract

This tort is about inducing breach of contract existing between two parties. For the tort to be committed, not only must there be inducement, absence of

---

153 The mortgagor may also be able to rely on an equitable estoppel by way of a defence, if the mortgagee – having taken the mortgage with knowledge of the charterparty – interferes with the performance of the contract by arresting the ship.

154 That the remedy is equitable in such a case has been stressed by, *op cit*, Clarke, fn 10, pp 693–95; see, also, her previous article '*De Mattos v Gibson* again' [1992] LMCLQ 448.

155 In such a situation, Brandon J was right to conflate the principles as derived from both *Collins v Lamport* (1864) 4 De GJ&S 500 and *De Mattos v Gibson* (1858) 4 De G&J 276 in *The Myrto* [1977] 2 Lloyd's Rep 243.

justification and substantial damages suffered, but also knowledge of an existing contract.[156]

When a mortgagee, or a purchaser, takes over a ship, with actual knowledge of the terms of the contract between the mortgagor and the charterer, he may find that he has committed the tort, if he wrongfully and unjustifiably interferes with its performance. In practice, no wise mortgagee or purchaser would fund, by loan or purchase, a ship without investigating its precise history and its owners' contractual relationships with third parties. Thus, an issue of impairment of the mortgagee's security should not arise. In both equity and common law, an injunction against the mortgagee or purchaser would be a just and practical result for the protection of the charterer, who could not have recourse against his contracting party if that party was not in breach of the charterparty.

In a decision of the House of Lords, *Merkur Island Shipping Corp v Laughton*,[157] albeit in a different shipping context, in which there was a typical chain of charter parties, ITF officials boycotted the performance of a towage contract by persuading the servants of the tugowner, who was performing towage services to assist the ship out of the dock, to stop working in protest of low wages to the ship's crew. The shipowners applied for an injunction on the basis of the common law tort of wrongful interference with the performance of a contract. The contract interfered with was the charterparty and, in turn, the series of charters in the chain. The form of interference was the immobilisation of the ship in port (Liverpool). The judge granted the injunction requiring ITF to lift the blacking of the ship. His decision was approved by both the Court of Appeal and the House of Lords. Lord Diplock, in his decision, summarised the development and extension of this tort and approved the statement of principle, as had been enunciated by Lord Denning MR, previously, at the Court of Appeal in 1969, in *Torquay Hotel Ltd v Cousins*:[158]

> ... there must be interference in the execution of a contract. The interference is not confined to the procurement of a breach of contract. It extends to a case where a third person *prevents or hinders* one party from performing his contract, even though it be not a breach [Lord Denning's emphasis].

This statement of principle, Lord Diplock said, resolved pre-existing doubts, if any, in this matter.

A different but related question arose in a subsequent decision of the Court of Appeal, *Edwin Hill and Partners v First National Finance Corp plc*,[159] which is of importance in this context. It concerned a legal charge on a

---

156 *Halsbury's Laws*, 1999, Vol 45(2), para 691.
157 [1983] 2 All ER 189 (HL).
158 [1969] 2 Ch 106, p 138.
159 [1989] 1 WLR 225.

freehold property as security for the indebtedness of a developer to the bank. The developer was unable to repay the loan or raise further finance to complete the development, for which the plaintiffs had been appointed as architects. The bank agreed to provide the necessary finance, on condition that the plaintiffs were replaced by other architects. So, the developer dismissed the plaintiffs, who sued the bank claiming damages against it for procuring breach of contract. Both the judge and the Court of Appeal decided against the plaintiffs on the ground that the bank's interference with the plaintiffs' contract was justified as being in defence and protection of an equal or superior right of the bank, under the legal charge to be repaid. This case should be distinguished from a case of a ship mortgagee who is in a position to investigate the terms of a pre-existing charterparty before he lends money.

11 RISK MANAGEMENT AND INSURANCE ISSUES OF THE MORTGAGEE

There are an infinite variety of risks that attach to the mortgagee's interest in the ship, which has been financed. As was stressed in the introduction of this chapter, the risks are inherent to the mobility of the mortgaged property and, hence, its exposure, not only to perils that it may encounter on the sea, but also to being exposed to the law and jurisdiction of other nations, which may apply a wide range of maritime liens, or submit the ship to political or war risks, or cause the detention of the ship for any reason. The mortgagee, therefore, will be concerned to balance such possible risks by taking into account the charterparty commitments of the vessel, the reputation of the owners and managers and their respective compliance with the ISMC regulations, the value and condition of the ship, the experience and nationality of the crew and their relations with the owners.

In order to manage or diminish such risks, the mortgagee will seek a combination of contractual, insurance and security mechanisms. He will arrange to obtain as much protection as possible contractually in the deed of covenants (discussed at para 8.1, above).

He will obtain sufficient insurance both as a co-assured and separately by taking a mortgagee's interest insurance (MII), which is designed to protect the mortgagee from the mortgagor's breaches under the insurance contract of which the mortgagee is an assignee or loss payee. But, the MII has its limitations based on its wording and exclusions from liability. The Institute Mortgagee's Interest Clauses 1997 enumerate the perils insured which relate to conduct of the mortgagor for which the underwriters of the H&M or the P&I policies would decline to pay. Indemnity under the MII, would not be recoverable, however, if the mortgagee were privy to that conduct of the mortgagor. Similarly, the MII would not cover the event of termination of the hull or P&I insurance for non-payment of premium. A mortgagee's additional perils policy (MAP) can be obtained to cover exposure of mortgagees to pollution risks, particularly in jurisdictions such as the USA, where the tort law enables third parties to acquire a priority lien over a vessel for liabilities incurred from oil pollution exceeding the convention limits. Pre-existing liens on the ship can also be covered by insurance.[160]

---

160 An interesting paper on these issues can be found in the office of the London Shipping Law Centre, Hill Taylor Dickinson, 'Ship mortgages and insurance issues', delivered in the series of the Centre's lectures, 17 September 1998.

CHAPTER 10

SHIPBUILDING[1]

1 INTRODUCTION

Over the recent years, the shipbuilding market has shown a major shift towards the East, particularly Japan, Korea and China (the last two having attracted a large shipbuilding capacity since the mid-1990s). This movement has prompted the European Commission to issue a proposal for a Council Decision on the signing and conclusion of an International Agreement between the European Community and the Republic of Korea relating to assistance of the world shipbuilding market (Com/2000/263, 3 May 2000 and Com/2000/0130, 26 May 2000). Shipbuilding contracts are, usually, made in the English language and provide for English law and jurisdiction. In this chapter, the basic principles of English law pertaining to shipbuilding contracts are explained with examples of leading cases.

2 NATURE OF SHIPBUILDING CONTRACTS

The contract involves both the construction and the sale of the ship. The question that has frequently arisen in some cases is whether the contract can be categorised as a building contract, or one of sale of goods. The answer to this question is of importance to the extent that, if the contract is one of sale, only the ordinary rules relating to the sale of goods will apply. If it is classified as a building contract, the rules relating to construction and the supply of work and materials will apply, which in many respects are similar to those applying to sale of goods contracts, but they place emphasis on the means of production.

Historically, in older cases, English law treated the shipbuilding contract as one for the sale of goods. For example, in *Lee v Griffin*[2] it was held that:

> ... if the contract be such that, when carried out, it would result in the sale of a chattel, the party cannot sue for work and labour; but if the result of the contract is that the party has done work and labour which ends in nothing that can become the subject of a sale, the party cannot sue for goods sold and delivered.

---

1 There are three authoritative books in this area: Clarke, M, *Shipbuilding Contracts*, 2nd edn, 1992, LLP; Curtis, S, *The Law of Shipbuilding Contracts*, 2nd edn, 1996, LLP; Goldrein, I (ed), *Ship Sale and Purchase*, 3rd edn, 1998, LLP.

2 (1861) B&S 272.

Diplock J, in *McDougall v Aeromarine*,[3] followed the same view and said:

> ... it seems well settled by authority that, although a shipbuilding contract is, in form, a contract for the construction of the vessel, it is in law a contract for the sale of goods.

Naturally, the intention of the parties to the contract was and is always relevant and the result may vary from contract to contract. In *Sir James Laing & Sons v Barclay, Curle & Co Ltd*,[4] the issue was whether the property in a ship under construction, for which payment was by instalments, passed to the buyer bit by bit, at each period of construction and as soon as the work had been inspected by the buyer. The House of Lords considered this question:

> Where it appears to be the intention of the parties to a contract for the building of a ship that the vessel is not to be delivered and finally accepted until after an official trial of a foreign coast, and until after conditions of the contract have been fulfilled as to speed, consumption of coal, capacity, etc, the property in the ship does not pass to the purchaser while the vessel remains uncompleted, although the contract contains stipulations for the price to be paid by instalments at certain periods of construction.

The respondents, a Glasgow firm of shipbuilders, agreed to build two ships for an Italian firm, according to certain specifications and under the superintendence of an agent appointed by the Italian firm, for a certain amount payable by instalments at specified stages of construction; but delivery of the ships was not to be considered to be completed until they had passed trials at Greenock and off the Italian coast. Before the ships were fully constructed, but after several instalments had been paid, the appellants, an English firm of shipbuilders, arrested the ships in Scotland for a debt alleged to be due to them by the Italian company, but on a petition to the First Division of the Court of Session the arrestments were recalled.

> Affirming the decision of the First Division, it was held that no intention was shown in the contract to make delivery of or to pass the property in the ships, before they were completed and that the arrestments were properly recalled.

Whether the contract is one for sale of goods, or a contact for construction and sale, the crucial issue concerns the determination of the parties' accrued rights. This involves three separate questions: (a) does the buyer have a property right to the partly constructed hull? (this is relevant when a third party, that is, a claimant of the buyer, or a receiver appointed to arrange the affairs of the shipbuilder, arrest the semi-constructed ship); (b) could a buyer claim a property right on the material, which had been approved by him but had not

---

3   [1958] 2 Lloyd's Rep 345, p 355: concerning the issue whether the buyer could reject the ship when she was tendered for delivery on the ground of unmerchantable quality. The question whether the ship had become the property of the buyer after payment of an instalment was relevant to the issue of rejection. Since the buyer had not yet become the owner of the ship, his rejection right was not affected.

4   [1908] AC 35.

yet been made part of the hull?; (c) what is to happen to accrued rights of the parties upon cancellation of the contract?

The answer to these questions can be found in the following authorities. The first (for example, buyer's property right to the partly constructed hull) was dealt with by the House of Lords (Sc) in *Seath v Moore*,[5] in which, although Scottish law applied to the contract of a shipbuilding in Scotland, Lord Blackburn illuminated the issue involved by comparing English with Scottish law, thus:

> The law of England does differ from the civil law and those laws founded on it, including the Scotch law, as to what is sufficient to pass the property in a moveable chattel. A contract for a valuable consideration, by which it is agreed that the property in a specific ascertained article shall pass from one to another, is effectual according to the law of England to change the property. It may be that the party who has sold the article is entitled to retain possession till the price is paid, if that was by the contract to precede delivery, but still the property is changed.

> It is essential that the article should be specific and ascertained in a manner binding on both parties, for unless that be so it cannot be construed as a contract to pass the property in that article. And in general, if there are things remaining to be done by the seller to the article before it is in the state in which it is to be finally delivered to the purchaser, the contract will not be construed to be one to pass the property till those things are done.

> But it is competent to parties to agree for valuable consideration that a specific article shall be sold, and become the property of the purchaser as soon as it has attained a certain stage: though if it is part of the bargain that more work shall be done on the article after it has reached that stage, it affords a strong *prima facie* presumption against its being the intention of the parties that the property should then pass ... It is, I think, a question of the construction of the contract in each case, at what stage the property shall pass; and a question of fact, in each case whether that stage has been reached.

> As I understand the civil law, the property is not transferred without delivery, and, consequently, unless there was an actual, or perhaps a constructive delivery, the property remained the property of the seller, and his creditors might seize it.

Lord Watson added:[6]

> The English decisions to which I have referred appear to me to establish the principle that, where it appears to be the intention, or in other words the agreement, of the parties to a contract for building a ship, that at a particular stage of its construction, the vessel, so far as then finished, shall be appropriated to the contract of sale, the property of the vessel as soon as it has reached that stage of completion will pass to the purchaser, and subsequent

---

5 (1886) 11 App Cas 350 (HL), p 370; see, also, *Re Foster v Blyth Shipbuilding and Drydocks* [1926] Ch 494 (see below).

6 (1886) 11 App Cas 350, p 380.

additions made to the chattel thus vested in the purchaser will, *accessione*, become his property. It also appears to me to be the result of these decisions that such an intention or agreement ought (in the absence of any circumstances pointing to a different conclusion) to be inferred from a provision in the contract to the effect that an instalment of the price shall be paid at a particular stage, coupled with the fact that the instalment has been duly paid, and that until the vessel reached that stage the execution of the work was regularly inspected by the purchaser, or some one on his behalf.

Although this case was decided prior to the Sale of Goods Act (SOGA) 1893, it was made sufficiently clear that, under English law, it is the intention of the parties to the contract of sale of ascertained goods that determines, upon construction of the contract, when the property passes to the purchaser. The parties can agree in their contract whether property can pass as soon as it has attained a certain stage. In a shipbuilding contract, the agreement may provide whether property in the ship being under construction can pass before completion.

Whether property in the materials can pass to the buyer before completion (the second question), clear and unambiguous words must be used specifically stating the stages and requirements of appropriation.[7]

For example, a clause in a shipbuilding contract purporting to pass the property in the material to the purchaser as the construction of the vessel proceeded was construed by the House of Lords in *Reid v Macbeth & Gray*[8] against the purchaser, as the parties had failed to express a clear intention to that effect. Since the material had not been affixed to the ship at the time of the bankruptcy of the builder, it could not be regarded as appropriated to the contract.

In *Re Blyth Shipbuilding and Drydocking Co,*[9] Romer J held, on the facts of this case, that although a receiver and manager of the shipbuilder's estate had no right to retain the partly constructed hull, the property of which had passed to the purchaser, he could retain both the unworked and worked material intended for the vessel. The latter portion of that decision was appealed. The Court of Appeal approved Romer's decision and affirmed that certain worked material lying on the yard ready to be incorporated into the hull of the vessel and approved by the purchaser's surveyor, had not been 'appropriated for her' so as to become the property of the purchaser. Thus, in relation to the issue of appropriation of property, although the ship had not been completed, the property in the uncompleted ship excluding the non-affixed material was the property of the purchaser.

---

7   Such a clause can be found in *Workman, Clarke & Co Ltd v Lloyd Brazileno* [1908] 1 KB 968, in which it had been agreed that the property in the material was to pass to the purchaser from payment of the first instalment.

8   [1904] AC 223 (HL).

9   [1926] Ch 494.

The modern view of the nature of a shipbuilding contract is that it has a hybrid nature. The answer to the third question (that is, what is to happen to the parties accrued rights upon cancellation of the contract?) arose in the *Hyundai* cases.[10] The House of Lords declined to apply a rule that there were no accrued rights to be enforced after termination of the contract. There would be no accrued rights if the contract were solely one of sale.[11] The buyer in *Hyundai v Papadopoulos*[12] defaulted in the second instalment and the builder exercised his right under the contract to terminate it. The issue was whether the second instalment was payable by the guarantor. It was held by all courts that it was. Viscount Dilhorne commented that:

> ... in this case the contract was not just for the sale of goods ... It was a contract to 'build, launch, equip and complete' a vessel and 'to deliver and sell' her. The contract price included 'all costs and expenses for designing and supplying all necessary drawings for the vessel ...'. It was a contract which was not simply one of sale but which, so far as the construction of the vessel was concerned, the contract resembled a building contract.[13]

Particular rights of the parties to the contract will be determined, depending on the circumstances of a case, and the issue in question will be addressed by applying either sale or construction principles as may be appropriate, upon proper construction of a particular agreement. A large part of a shipbuilding contract is directed towards the regulation of a substantial and complex construction project in which each party assumes long term obligations to the other and bears significant commercial risks. Although the ultimate purpose of the contract is to transfer the legal title in the ship upon payment of the price, to categorise the contract as belonging to the one or the other category would be misleading.[14]

In a more recent decision, *Stocznia Gdanska SA v Latvian Shipping Co*,[15] Clarke J said that the shipbuilding contract in question was for the construction and sale of the hull. In the same case, the House of Lords, affirming the decision of the judge and reversing the Court of Appeal's decision, answered the question, whether or not an accrued instalment was payable to the yard after termination of the contract, as follows:

> The present case cannot, therefore, be approached by asking the simple question whether the property in the vessel or any part of it has passed to the

---

10   *Hyundai Shipbuilding Heavy Industries Co Ltd v Pournaras* [1978] 2 Lloyd's Rep 502 (HL) and *Hyundai v Papadopoulos* [1980] 2 Lloyd's Rep 1 (HL).

11   Benjamin's *Sale of Goods*, 4th edn, 1992, Sweet & Maxwell: '... in ordinary circumstances, unless the contract otherwise provides, the seller on rescission following the buyer's default, becomes liable to repay the part of the price paid.'

12   See para 10.1.6 for the facts of this case.

13   *Hyundai Heavy Industries Co Ltd v Papadopoulos* [1980] 2 Lloyd's Rep 1, p 5, *per* Viscount Dilhorne (HL).

14   See, also, *op cit*, Curtis, fn 1, p 1.

15   [1995] 2 Lloyd's Rep 592; [1996] 2 Lloyd's Rep 132 (CA); [1998] 1 Lloyd's Rep 609 (HL).

buyers. That test would be apposite if the contract in question was a contract for the sale of goods (or, indeed, a contract for the sale of land) *simpliciter*, under which the consideration for the price would be the passing of the property in the goods (or land). However, before that test can be regarded as appropriate, the anterior question has to be asked: is the contract in question simply a contract for the sale of a ship or is it rather a contract under which the design and construction of the vessel formed part of the yard's contractual duties, as well as the duty to transfer the finished object to the buyers? If it is the latter, the design and construction of the vessel form part of the consideration for which the price is to be paid, and the fact that the contract has been brought to an end before the property in the vessel or any part of it has passed to the buyers does not prevent the yard from asserting that there has been no total failure of consideration in respect of an instalment of the price which has been paid before the contract was terminated, or that an instalment which has then been accrued due could not, if paid, be recoverable on that ground.

I am satisfied that the present case falls into the latter category. This was what the contracts provided in their terms. Moreover, consistently with those terms, payment of instalments of the price was geared to progress in the construction of the vessel. That this should be so is scarcely surprising in the case of a shipbuilding contract, under which the yard enters into major financial commitments at an early stage, in the placing of orders for machinery and materials, and in reserving and then occupying a berth for the construction of the vessel.[16]

Thus, by these two House of Lords decisions (*Hyundai v Papadopoulos* and *Stocznia*) the issue of the nature of the shipbuilding contract has now been settled as being a hybrid contract of construction and sale of a ship.

The preamble to the standard form of the Shipbuilders' Association of Japan (SAJ) form, states that the builder shall 'build, launch, equip and complete' the vessel and, thereafter, 'sell and deliver' her to the buyer. It is a special agreement to sell a ship by description after construction, which is regulated by the specific terms of the contract and the SOGA 1979 as amended by the Sale and Supply of Goods Act (SSGA) 1994.[17] Under the SOGA 1979, contracts for sale are divided into 'sales' outright, in which property in the goods passes to the buyer from the time of the conclusion of the contract (s 2(3)), and 'agreements to sell' (which usually concern future goods). Under an agreement to sell, the property passes to the buyer at a future time or when a condition has been fulfilled (s 2(4)). It is undisputed that shipbuilding contracts relate to the sale of future, rather than existing, goods.[18]

---

16 [1998] 1 Lloyd's Rep 609, pp 619, 620, *per* Lord Goff.

17 The Sale of Goods (Amendment) Act 1995 concerns only the amendments to the law relating to the sale of unascertained goods forming part of an identified bulk and the sale of undivided shares in goods.

18 *Behnke v Bede Shipping Ltd* [1927] 1 KB 649.

3 PRE-CONTRACT STAGE

This stage is particularly important to both parties and it can be time consuming and expensive. Simon Curtis has succinctly explained pre-contract negotiations and procedures in Part 2 of his book,[19] to which the reader is referred. It is important to summarise some of his points, by way of background to what follows next in this chapter. The nature of shipbuilding contracts is such that it entails the need of negotiations in great detail between the buyer and the builder before an agreement can be reached about the form, the substance of the contract and the ship's specification. A very important factor for the buyer in his choice of a builder would be previous business dealings with the shipbuilding yard. Expertise in commercial, technical and legal terms is needed for the success of a building project. Shipbrokers and naval architects are usually crucial at this stage, who may be instructed to approach various shipbuilding yards to obtain information about pricing, timing and specific designs. The shipbuilder may be able to supply a ready made specification, known as Principal Particulars. In other cases, the buyer may already know what he wants and submit to various shipbuilders his own specification and summary of proposed contract terms to obtain competitive bids. This is known as 'an invitation to tender'. If the first method (that is, the builder's specification) is followed, the next stage of negotiations will be less time consuming, while if the second is chosen (that is, the buyer's specification) the builder will need some time to prepare the technical requirements of the tender. Once these have been completed, the parties will execute a 'letter of intent',[20] which is not usually intended to be legally binding unless such an intention is derived from it. It is useful in order to set out the parties' mutual understanding of the proposed project and it imposes a moral rather than a legal obligation. It is an agreement to negotiate in good faith and it is usually made subject to the terms of the shipbuilding contract.

This is the crucial time, which will determine whether or not the parties will proceed to contract. That decision will depend on the ability of the buyer to obtain appropriate finance for the project. Assuming that a willing bank becomes interested in financing the project, an interim or 'bridging' contract may be concluded at this stage so that the builder is assured that the buyer is serious before he engages in substantial work. By the bridging contract, the builder agrees to provide design and technical services for the development of the project in return for a fee.

---

19 *Op cit*, Curtis, fn 1, pp 7–13.
20 For the effect of letters of intent see: *Wilson Smithest & Cape (Sugar) Ltd v Bangladesh Sugar & Food Industries Corp* [1986] 1 Lloyd's Rep 378, concerning sale of goods (c&f (cost and freight) terms).

After the design is submitted, final negotiations take place about the details of the contract and specification. There are standard forms of contract reflecting the strength of the particular shipbuilding yard. The SAJ form 1974 has been widely used and has formed the basis of other standard contracts used by other yards, such as South Korea, Taiwan and China. There is also the AWES (Association of West European Shipbuilders) form 1972, the MARAD form 1980 of the US Department of Marine Administration, and the form of the Association of Norwegian Marine Yards 1981.[21]

4 SIGNIFICANCE OF REPRESENTATIONS DURING NEGOTIATIONS AND RISK MANAGEMENT

It is naturally common for commercial people to use legitimate means and persuasive powers during negotiations to make the other party accept the deal offered. What is not, however, allowed is to make representations, which the party making them knows that they are not true and by making them induces the other party to enter into contract. This is distinguished from mere puffs or expressions of opinion.

Control of what negotiating parties state during negotiations leading up to a contract is imposed by the Misrepresentation Act (MA) 1967, which makes it an absolute duty on the negotiating parties not to state facts which the representor could not later show that he had reasonable ground for believing.

Section 2 of the MA 1967 states:

(1) Where a person has entered into a contract after a misrepresentation has been made to him by another party thereto and as a result thereof he has suffered loss, then, if the person making the misrepresentation would be liable to damages in respect thereof had the misrepresentation been made fraudulently, that person shall be so liable notwithstanding that the misrepresentation was not made fraudulently, unless he proves that he had reasonable ground to believe and did believe up to the time the contract was made that the facts represented were true.

Breach of the provisions of this Act may entitle the other party to damages, which will be assessed as if the misrepresentation were fraudulent.[22] The consequences of negligent misstatements are discussed in the next chapter in the context of sale and purchase of used ships.

---

21   These can be found in *op cit*, Goldrein, fn 1, Appendices.

22   *Howard Marine & Dredging Co Ltd v Ogden & Son (Excavations) Ltd* [1978] 2 WLR 515 (CA); *Royscot Trust v Rogerson* [1991] 2 QB 297 (CA); *Avon Insurance v Swire Fraser* [2000] 1 All ER 573.

5 THE MAKING OF A SHIPBUILDING CONTRACT AND RISK MANAGEMENT

Like any other contract, there must be a binding agreement – an offer and an unconditional acceptance, intention to create legal relations and consideration. Consideration under English law requires that each party has given something of value in return for the other party's promise. There must also be certainty of terms, which define clearly the extent of the duties of each party, particularly as shipbuilding contracts are complex and contain many clauses of technical jargon. Shipbuilding contracts are most challenging for lawyers, either in the drafting or in trying to make sense of what others have drafted when the matter has reached litigation. It cannot be stressed too strongly that this is an area, which requires skilful legal risk management at the stage of negotiations, drafting and at the stage of performance of the contract when, frequently, a need to renegotiate the terms arises. A simple example of such problems may be offered by the decision of Lord Denning MR in *Okura & Co Ltd v Navara Shipping Corp SA*.[23]

The original contract for shipbuilding was between Okura (Japanese contractors) and Navara. But the shipbuilder was Ujina dockyard. Navara were to pay a considerable amount of money by instalments in advance, coming to nearly half the price as the ship was being built. Navara fulfilled that provision. Although the vessel was to be built in 12 months, that time could be extended by reason of *force majeure*, if causes of delay were beyond the builder's control. Another provision in the contract allowed the buyer to cancel the contract and claim repayment of the instalments with interest, if the delivery was delayed by more than 150 days after delivery date. Okura did not manage to keep to the delivery date, because it ran into financial difficulties. Not only were many items unfinished, but also the first trials revealed serious defects in the engines. Navara gave their notice of cancellation. So, this contract came to an end. New negotiations commenced for a new contract. This contract was on a tripartite basis between the shipbuilders under the head contract (Ujina), the Japanese contractors (Okura) and the buyers (Navara). The proposal was that the buyers should take the ship as it was, and do remedial work on the defects in the engines. The shipbuilders should make good the listed unfinished items. But the buyers were not to be bound by the contract until after sea trials had been completed. It was contemplated that there would be a written contract drawn up and signed after the telex sent setting out the telephone negotiations. The issue for the court was whether these negotiations as contained in the telex resulted in a binding contract or were merely the basis for a future agreement. It was a question of construction. Two points arising from the telex were crucial to the

23 [1982] 2 Lloyd's Rep 537 (CA).

construction: (a) it referred to all other terms and conditions as contained in the previous shipbuilding contract to apply in full. The original contract stated that, 'the contract shall become effective as from the date of fulfilment and realisation of all conditions'. Such conditions included the signing of the contract by the buyer and the contractor; (b) it had also been stated in the telex that its items would be incorporated in a memorandum of agreement (MOA) in mutually acceptable manner. It was, therefore, contemplated that an MOA was to be drawn up and the parties conducted themselves on that footing. The buyer's solicitors did draft the MOA reflecting the telex, but included a new clause:

> The parties hereto agree that there shall be no extension of time for delivery of the vessel due to *force majeure* and that the provision of Art III(1) of the contract shall not apply to this agreement.

That clause was inconsistent with the telex by which the parties intended to incorporate all other terms and conditions of the previous contract. In effect, what the buyers were saying was that they wanted absolute compliance with the delivery date, while the builders were saying they wanted an extension of time for *force majeure*. As the parties could not reach agreement about this clause, Navara gave an ultimatum that, unless the builders agreed to it, by a certain time, Navara would withdraw from the contract and ask that all money held by the builders be released. On the other hand, if builders agreed to this clause, Navara were prepared to wait for another week for the contract to be signed. The builders did not accept the clause, so no MOA was signed up and the money was refunded to Navara. The builders sold the vessel elsewhere, but that was not the end of the matter. Later Navara claimed that there was a binding contract, which was repudiated by the builders. The latter issued a writ seeking a declaration that there was no contract, which the buyers contested.

The judge held that there was a binding contract. The Court of Appeal reached a unanimous decision on the issue, reversing the judge.

The reason of Lord Denning MR was that upon construction of the documents the agreement was provisional; the parties were not to be bound unless and until they signed a contract. In addition, the parties did not treat the telex as a binding agreement because all sorts of matters had to be arranged. The refund was asked and was made to Navara.

Other essential terms of the shipbuilding contract without which a contract may not be complete are the following:

(a) ship's description and dimensions with dead weight capacity (DWC). The ship is given a Hull number during construction, which is not, however, regarded as an essential part of her description.[24] The class must also be specified. Details of description and class may be inserted later;

---

24 *The Diana Prosperity* [1976] 2 Lloyd's Rep 621 (HL).

(b) speed and fuel consumption;

(c) price and method of payment;

(e) inspection of work in progress;

(f) modification of agreed description;

(g) nature and conditions of trials;

(h) time and place of delivery;

(i) transfer of title and risk with insurance arrangements;

(j) rectification of defects.

The description, modification of description and transfer of title are the most essential terms of the contract for it to confer the necessary certainty.[25] It can be agreed that the details of other terms may be filled in later. If the parties need more time to consider their position they can agree provisionally on a draft which is made 'subject to contract',[26] which is understood to mean that there is no binding contract until a formal written contract is drawn up or this condition is withdrawn or waived.

The contract may be subject to conditions to be fulfilled by either party before the commencement of the construction. The effect of conditions on the contract depends on the type of the condition. If a condition is to the effect that one party has to do something before the commencement of the contract (condition precedent), there will be no contract until that condition is met. If the condition requires one party to the contract to do something within a certain time after the commencement of the contract (condition subsequent), the non-fulfilment of that condition will operate to discharge the parties from an existing contract. If the condition suspends the operation of the contract until a subsequent agreement on the details or upon the buyer obtaining finance, there is a contract, but its operation is suspended until the condition is met.[27]

The contract will state that the vessel is to be built according to a specification, which is an integral part of the making of the contact.

---

25 *Op cit*, Clarke, M, fn 1, p 3.

26 This phrase has been explained in cases concerning conveyance of land: see *Keppel v Wheeler* [1927] 1 KB 577 (CA); *Law v Jones* [1974] Ch 112 (CA).

27 For the construction of such a condition in the context of the parties' exchanges: see *Fast Ferries One SA v Ferries Australia Ltd* [2000] 1 Lloyds' Rep 534, in which it was held that the parties proceeded on the assumption that approval of finance was a formality; the parties were agreeing in the exchanges to treat the contract effective, but subject to termination if the assumption was unjustified.

6 THE FRAMEWORK OF THE CONTRACT

Taking as an example the SAJ shipbuilding contract, which is more widely used, the basic express terms of the contract are divided into 21 articles and include the following broad provisions:

Article I: description, dimensions, characteristics, classification (rules and regulations), subcontracting and registration.

Article II: contract price, currency, terms and method of payment.

Article III: delivery, speed, fuel consumption, dead weight.

Article IV: approval of plans and drawings, appointment of buyer's representative, inspection by him, liability of builder and responsibility of the buyer.

Article V: modification of specification, change in class, substitution of materials.

Article VI: trials and notice, weather conditions, method of trials; method of acceptance or rejection, effect of acceptance.

Article VII: time and place of delivery, when the buyer has fulfilled his obligations, documents to be delivered to the buyer, tender of the vessel, title and risk.

Article VIII: delays and extension of time, notice of delay, defining what is permissible delay, right to rescind for excessive delay.

Article IX: warranty of quality, notice of defects, remedy of defects, extent of builder's responsibility.

Article X: rescission by the buyer, notice, refunds by builder, discharge of obligations.

Article XI: buyer's default, what is default, interest and charge, effect of default, sale of vessel.

Article XII: builder's obligation to insure and extent of coverage, recoverable losses.

Article XIII: dispute and arbitration (the printed form stipulates for arbitration in Tokyo, but it is usually the case that parties agree London as the seat of arbitration, hence the relevance of English law).[28]

Article XIV: deals with prohibition of assignment of the contract unless prior consent of the other party and approval from the Japanese government are obtained.

Articles XV and XVI: deal with taxes and duties in Japan, patents trademarks, copyright, etc.

---

28 The printed form of NSF 1993 provides for English law and arbitration.

Article XVII: regulates supplies by the buyer and his responsibility for them.

The remaining four articles deal with address of notices, effective date of contract, law and interpretation of the contract, and the guarantee in the event of default by the buyer.

7 TYPES OF CONTRACTUAL TERMS

7.1 General

The contract will contain other important terms, some of which may be conditions, the breach of which under English law will entitle the other party to treat the contract as at an end. Other terms may have been agreed to be warranties, the breach of which will sound in damages, but will not entitle the other party to terminate the contract.[29] There may be other terms, known as intermediate or innominate; the effect of breach of such a term depends on whether the breach goes to the root of the contract, so that the other party is entitled to treat himself as discharged. It will depend on the nature and consequences of the breach.[30] Whether a term is a condition or a warranty or an innominate term does not depend on the use of those words in the contract, but on the construction of the contract as a whole. In the absence of clear words, a term will not be interpreted as a condition, if the result of doing so would be unreasonable.[31] The term 'shipped in good condition' in a sale of goods contract was held by Lord Denning MR in *The Hansa Nord*[32] not to be a condition, but an intermediate term and the buyer would not be discharged from the contract, unless there was a serious and substantial breach of this term.

7.2 Implied terms under the SOGA 1979

Sometimes, the court may imply a term if it is necessary to give business efficacy to the contract and if both parties could reasonably have intended such a term, although they did not expressly say so.

---

29 Contrast 'warranties' under insurance contracts, breach of which discharges the insurer of liability as from the date of the breach (*The Good Luck* [1991] 2 Lloyd's Rep 191 (HL)).

30 *Hong Kong Fir Shipping Co Ltd v Kawasaki Kisen Kaisha* [1961] 2 Lloyd's Rep 478 (CA); *Bunge Corporation v Tradax Export SA* [1981] 2 Lloyd's Rep 1 (HL), p 7, *per* Lord Scarman; *The Aktion* [1987] 1 Lloyd's Rep 283, concerning sale of a ship, see Chapter 11.

31 *The Hansa Nord* [1975] 2 Lloyd's Rep 445 (CA): read Roskill LJ, p 457.

32 *Ibid*, p 451.

7.2.1 Compliance with description (the law before 3 January 1995)

Other important terms are implied by statute. Section 13 of the SOGA 1979 provides that where there is a contract for the sale of goods by description, there is an implied condition that the goods will correspond with the description.

As it was mentioned earlier, a shipbuilding contract is a contract for the construction and sale of a ship by description. If the relevant terms in the description do not conform with the vessel when it is eventually delivered, the buyer is entitled to reject the ship for non-compliance.

An important question, with regard to non-conformity of delivered goods with the contractual description is this: would any non-conformity of whatsoever nature entitle the purchaser to reject the goods whether or not the non-conformity would have caused him loss had he accepted them? Contract law lawyers would say that, historically, English law has treated the term of description strictly. This was emphasised by the decision of the House of Lords in *Arcos Ltd v Ronnasen*.[33]

Arcos Ltd v Ronnasen

Agents for the sale of Russian timber agreed to sell to English buyers a quantity of staves of Russian redwood and whitewood, required by the buyers, as the sellers knew, for making cement barrels. The price was to include cost, freight and insurance from Archangel to the River Thames. With respect to the length, breadth, and thickness, the agreement contained stipulations, which allowed some variation in the length and in the breadth of the staves, but none in the thickness, which in all cases was specified as half an inch. When the goods arrived in London the buyers claimed to reject them on the ground that they did not conform to the description in the contract, in that they were not of the thickness of half an inch.

In an arbitration under the contract, an umpire made an award in the form of a special case for the opinion of the King's Bench Division, in which he found that, in thickness, none of the staves were less than half an inch; about 5% were half an inch; a large proportion were over half an inch, but not more than an inch. The umpire found that the staves were fit for making cement barrels and that, when shipped they were commercially within and merchantable under the specification in the contract.

Wright J in his judgment decided in favour of the buyers, upon the ground that the difference in the sizes was not of such a trivial character as would justify its being disregarded by the court; that the finding as to measurement showed that the goods were not those contracted to be sold and that it was

---

33 [1933] AC 470 (HL).

those goods, and not their commercial equivalent, that the buyers were entitled to demand.

The Court of Appeal affirmed his decision. The House of Lords also held that the buyers were entitled to demand goods answering the description in the contract, and were not bound to accept the goods tendered merely because they were merchantable under that description.

This strict approach to the construction of description clauses by old authorities was questioned by the House of Lords in the 1970s when Lord Diplock adopted a more flexible approach in *Ashington Piggeries Ltd v Christopher Hill Ltd*:[34]

> It is open to the parties to use a description as broad or narrow as they choose. But ultimately the test is where the buyer could fairly and reasonably refuse to accept the physical goods proffered to him on the ground that their failure to correspond with that part of what was said about them in the contract makes them different goods from those he had agreed to buy.

The trend since then has been that the shortcoming of the goods must have been a substantial ingredient of the description of the goods, so that a reasonable person would regard the goods as distinct from what he contracted for. The description must also be seen in the context and purpose of the particular contract. The House of Lords, in the following case, did not regard the number of the hull of the ship delivered under a long term charterparty as a matter entitling the charterers to reject the newly constructed ship when it was delivered to them for chartering services.

The Diane Prosperity[35]

It concerned a charterparty, entered in Shelltime 3 form, with respect to a new building of a tanker constructed in Japan. At the time of construction, the oil market was strong. The description of the vessel was referred to by the owners in the charterparty and in the documents as being built by Osaka Shipbuilding Co (a reputable Japanese builder) with the hull number 354. Due to some difficulties at the Osaka yard the vessel was actually built at Oshima yard (a company in which Osaka owned 50% of shares) and with the hull number 004. All other physical attributes of the vessel corresponded with those required under the charterparty. At the time of delivery to the charterers, the oil market had fallen sharply and the charterers rejected the vessel, contending that the vessel tendered did not correspond with that on the documents. It was held that the hull number of the vessel had no special significance for the parties, so as to raise it to a matter of fundamental obligation. The words 'hull number 354' were not intended to be part of the description of the vessel. The vessel contracted for was the vessel tendered.

---

34 [1972] AC 441, pp 503–04 (HL).
35 [1976] 1 WLR 989 (HL).

The purpose of the hull number in the context of this contract was without a significant meaning, other than to identify the vessel, which had not been constructed nor did it have a name at the time of fixing the charter. Lord Wilberforce said that he was not prepared to accept that the authorities as to 'description' in the sale of goods cases should be extended or apply to the contract in question. He rather thought they ought to be re-examined:[36]

> Some of these cases either in themselves, for example, *Moore v Landauer*,[37] or as they have been interpreted, for example, *Behn v Burness*,[38] I find excessively technical and due for fresh examination in this House.[39]

In his view, the question of importance was whether a particular item in a description of goods – whether in sale of goods, or in other contracts – constituted a substantial ingredient of the 'identity' of the thing and, only if it did, he was prepared to treat it as a condition. He absolutely agreed with what Roskill LJ said in *The Hansa Nord*:[40]

> In principle it is not easy to see why the law relating to contracts for the sale of goods should be different from the law relating to the performance of other contractual obligations, whether charterparties or other types of contract. Sale of goods law is but one branch of the general law of contract. It is desirable that the same legal principles should apply to the law of contract as a whole and that different legal principles should not apply to different branches of that law.

Lord Wilberforce further stressed that the general law of contract had developed along much more rational lines, and, in particular, after the *Hong Kong Fir* case,[41] it has no longer been necessary to adhere to rigid categories of breach which do or do not automatically give right to rescind. It is rather a question of attending to the nature and gravity of a breach, he said. However, it might have been a different matter, if the parties to a construction contract had intended that a particular yard, and no other, should build the ship.

7.2.2 The 'taming' of the SOGA 1979 by the SSGA 1994

In view of extreme consequences that might result, even if the breach is slight, it was thought appropriate to amend the 1979 Act. By s 4 of the Sale and Supply of Goods Act (SSGA) 1994, s 15A was inserted in the 1979 Act. It relates to modification of remedies for breach of a condition in non-consumer contracts and provides:

---

36 [1976] 1 WLR 989 (HL), p 998.
37 [1921] 2 Lloyd's Rep 519.
38 (1863) 3 B&S 751.
39 Following the same lines of argument, Lord Glaisdale and Lord Kilbrandon commented that the cases on the sale of goods may call for reconsideration.
40 [1975] 2 Lloyd's Rep 445, p 458.
41 *Hong Kong Fir Shipping & Co Ltd v Kawasaki Kisen Kaisha* [1961] 2 Lloyd's Rep 478.

(1) where in the case of a contract of sale (a) the buyer would, apart from this sub-section, have the right to reject goods by reason of a breach on the part of the seller of a term implied by ss 13, 14 and 15 ... but (b) the breach is so slight that it would be unreasonable for him to reject them,

... then, if the buyer does not deal as consumer, the breach is not to be treated as a breach of condition but be treated as a breach of warranty.

This section applies unless a contrary intention appears in, or is implied from, the contract; the burden of showing that a breach fell within the above subsection is upon the seller. The test is that of a reasonable purchaser.

The new Act came into force on 3 January 1995, so only contracts entered after that date are affected by it.

7.2.3 The demise of 'merchantable quality'

7.2.3.1 The law until 3 January 1995

Section 14(2) of the SOGA 1979 provided that, where the seller sold goods in the course of a business, there was an implied condition that the goods supplied under the contract were of merchantable quality, except that there was no such condition as regards defects specifically drawn to the attention of the buyer. Goods of any kind would be of merchantable quality within the meaning of this Act,[42] if they were as fit for the purpose or purposes for which goods of that kind were commonly bought, as was reasonable to expect having regard to any description applied to them, the price (if relevant) and all the other relevant circumstances (s 14(6)). The implied condition would be broken, if the defect was so serious that a commercial man would have thought that the purchaser was entitled to reject them. Thus, 'merchantable' quality was made synonymous to 'fitness for purpose' and other aspects of quality were left ambiguous.

7.2.3.2 The law after 3 January 1995

As mentioned in para 7.2.2, s 4 of the SSGA 1994 modified the effect of the consequences of breach of implied terms under the 1979 Act and, by the insertion of s 15A in the 1979 Act, a non-consumer buyer will not have the right of rejection if the breach is slight.

In addition, in recognition of the difficulties created in the interpretation of the term 'merchantable quality', s 1(1) of the SSGA 1994 introduced the term 'satisfactory quality' and substituted s 14(2) of the 1979 Act with the following:

---

42 The definition was adopted from the Supply of Goods (Implied Terms) Act 1973, s 7(2).

Where the seller sells goods in the course of his business, there is an implied term that the goods supplied under the contract are of satisfactory quality. For the purpose of this Act, goods are of satisfactory quality if they meet the standard that a reasonable person would regard as satisfactory, taking into account of any description of the goods, the price (if relevant) and all the other relevant circumstances.

For the purpose of this Act, the quality of the goods includes their state and condition and the following (among others) are in appropriate cases aspects of the quality of the goods:

- the fitness for all the purposes for which goods of the kind in question are commonly supplied;
- appearance and finish;
- freedom from defects;
- safety and durability.

All other references to 'merchantable quality' in the 1979 Act have been substituted, accordingly, by the term satisfactory or unsatisfactory as the case may be.

But, if the goods are sold second hand, then the buyer must judge what is satisfactory for him considering the price he pays, unless there is something radically wrong with them.[43] Whether a defect renders the vessel unsafe or unable to operate in the market for which she was built will be judged in the view of a commercial man.[44] Defective electrical wiring has been considered by the court to be a serious defect affecting the vessel's quality (see *The Raspora*, para 7.3, below).

7.2.4 Fitness for purpose

As much as the description and the quality of the goods, the purpose for which the goods are bought is equally important to the commercial man's decision to purchase the particular goods. Again, when the breach of this implied term is slight there will be no right of rejection by the buyer, by virtue of the new s 15A of the SOGA 1979, as mentioned earlier.

Section 14(3) of the SOGA 1979 provides that:

... where a seller sells goods in the course of a business and the buyer, expressly or by implication, makes known ... any particular purpose for which the goods are being bought, there is an implied condition that the goods supplied under the contract are reasonably fit for that purpose, whether or not that is a purpose for which such goods are commonly supplied, except the circumstances show that the buyer does not rely, or that it is unreasonable for him to rely, on the skill or judgment if the seller.

---

43 *The Hansa Nord* [1975] 2 Lloyd's Rep 445 (CA), p 452.
44 *Op cit*, Curtis, fn 1, p 100.

7.2.4.1 Reliance on the skill and judgment of the seller

The extent of reliance upon the skill and judgment of the seller was in issue at the House of Lords in the following case.

Cammell Laird & Co Ltd v The Manganese Bronze and Brass Co Ltd[45]

A firm of shipbuilders agreed to build for and sell to the UM Company, two sister ships (A and B) designed for carrying petroleum or molasses, with main propelling diesel engines, each ship to be classed A1 at Lloyd's.

The shipbuilders entered into a contract with the MB and B Company, who were makers of ships' propellers out of manganese bronze prepared by a special process, for the manufacture of two propellers for these ships, to be of special Parsons manganese bronze, of a specified diameter, and pitch, each with four blades of a specified total developed area and of a maximum brake horsepower at a specified number of revolutions per minute. Each propeller was to be finished, chipped, and polished in style of the highest class, with boss bored, faced, and keyway cut to the shipbuilders' template, with edges brought up to fine lines, to be true to pitch; all in accordance with the shipbuilders' blue print, to be ready for fitting to the shaft on delivery; and to be to the entire satisfaction of the UM Company's representative and the shipbuilders themselves. They were to be delivered on a certain agreed date. The working drawings gave the information necessary to enable the work to be carried out, including the thickness required along the medial lines of the blades; but beyond this and apart from the direction that the 'edges' were 'to be brought up to fine lines', further details as to the thickness of the blades were left to the skill and judgment of the MB and B Company.

On trials, the propeller fitted unto vessel A made so much noise that the vessel could not be classed A1 at Lloyd's. The propeller which had been fitted onto B, the second vessel, was tried on A and it worked satisfactorily. Without prejudice to the rights of the parties, a second propeller was made for A to the correct specifications and free from fault in other respects, but proved equally unsatisfactory as the first. Finally, a third propeller was made for A (also without prejudice to the rights of the parties) and this one worked quite silently. The shipbuilders sued the engine constructors for delay in executing the work and the expenses incurred as a result of delay. It was found that nothing in the specification or plan could account for the trouble in the propellers or the engines. It seemed reasonable to infer that the problems lay with the finishing which was a matter left to the discretion of the defendants and not given in the plan and particulars.

The House of Lords held that the agreement was a contract of sale of future goods under s 14(1) of the SOGA 1893. Inasmuch as the plaintiffs had

---

45   [1934] AC 402 (HL).

made known to the defendants the purpose for which the propeller was required, and relied upon their skill and judgment, it was not necessary, for the purposes of this sub-section, that the buyer should rely totally and exclusively on the skill and judgment of the seller for every detail in the production of the goods. It was sufficient, if reliance was placed on the skill and judgment of the seller to some substantial extent. In the present case, with regard to that part of the work which was left to the skill and judgment of the sellers, there was a breach of the implied condition that the propeller should be reasonably fit for the purpose for which it was required.

7.2.4.2 Idiosyncrasy of the subject matter

By contrast, there will be no breach of the implied condition of fitness when the failure of the goods to meet the intended purpose arises from an abnormal feature or idiosyncrasy not made known to the seller. *Slater v Finning*[46] is a recent House of Lords' decision on the issue, in which the above case was contrasted.

The defendants were dealers in marine engines. The plaintiffs were owners of a fishing vessel, *Aquarius 11*, which functioned on a caterpillar diesel engine and presented some problems. They called the defendants to replace a new camshaft to the engine of *Aquarius 11*, but the first replacement was not a success. Subsequently, two other camshafts were fitted to the engine, none of them were a success and the engine continued to have problems. Therefore, the plaintiffs sold the engine and installed a new engine with a different design.

The old engine, after an extensive overhaul, but with no replacement to the camshaft by the new owner in South Africa, was fitted into another vessel, *the Ocean Spray,* and it worked for long periods without any problems. The plaintiffs instituted an action against the defendants for breach of the implied condition under s 14(3) of the 1979 Act, contending that the camshafts which were bought for *Aquarius 11* were not reasonably fit for the purpose of her engine, and the defendants had known that the camshafts were to be fitted into *Aquarius 11*.

The House of Lords rejected the plaintiffs' argument and held that there was no breach of the implied condition. It had been found that *Aquarius 11* had an unknown and unusual characteristic, a tendency to create excessive torsional resonance in camshafts. The particular purpose for which the camshafts were required was that of being fitted in the engine of a vessel which suffered from a particular abnormality or idiosyncrasy. The defendants, not being aware of that tendency, were not in a position to

---

46 [1996] 2 Lloyd's Rep 353.

exercise skill and judgment for the purpose of dealing with it. Lord Keith stated:

> As a matter of principle, therefore, it may be said that where a buyer purchases, goods from a seller who deals in goods of that description there is no breach of the implied condition of fitness where the failure of the goods to meet the intended purpose arises from an abnormal feature or idiosyncrasy, not made known to the seller, in the buyer or in the circumstances of the use by the buyer. That is the case whether or not the buyer is himself aware of the abnormal feature or idiosyncrasy.[47]

In the context of a shipbuilding contract, whether or not there has been a breach of the implied term of 'fitness for purpose' will depend on the particular circumstances of the contract. A breach of fitness may be an aspect of quality, thus, it will fall within the previous sub-paragraph. In any event, contracts entered into after 3 January 1995 will be subject to the amendment of the 1979 Act by the SSGA 1994, by which the breach must not be so slight so as to be unreasonable for the buyer to reject the ship.[48]

7.3 Exclusion clauses and the Unfair Contract Terms Act 1977

The Act does not apply to international supply contracts and those contracts in which the parties chose English law to apply, which, otherwise, would be governed by the law of another country (ss 26 and 27, respectively).

Where the Act applies, it provides a statutory prohibition of exclusion or limitation of liability clauses for death or personal injury resulting from negligence. Otherwise, it does not prohibit exclusion or limitation of liability clauses[49] relating to other forms of loss or damage provided they satisfy the test of reasonableness (s 2(1), (2)).

Insofar as consumer contracts of sale of goods are concerned, s 6(2) prohibits exclusion or limitation of liability for breach of the statutory conditions implied by ss 13, 14 and 15 of the SOGA 1979 and s 1 of the SSGA 1994 (referring to description, quality and fitness for purpose). Insofar as non-consumer contracts are concerned, s 6(3), makes such exclusion or limitation subject to the requirements of reasonableness.

In the following case, the building of a powerboat was classed as a consumer contract; it did not fall within the category of an international supply of goods.

In *Rasbora v JCL Marine*,[50] the contract was for the building and sale of a powerboat and included a clause excluding the application of any implied

---

47 [1996] 2 Lloyd's Rep 353, p 358.
48 See, further, *op cit*, Curtis, fn 1, pp 102–03.
49 *The Zinnia, Stag Line Ltd v Tyne Shiprepair Group Ltd* [1984] 2 Lloyd's Rep 211.
50 [1977] 1 Lloyd's Rep 645.

condition or warranty, and liability 'for any loss, damage, expense or injury howsoever arising' except as accepted under the terms of the warranty certificate. Although the builders agreed to build the boat for a private buyer in England (A), the contemplated purchaser was a company registered in Jersey, which was wholly owned by A – this was to avoid paying UK tax. After the sale was completed, the vessel caught fire during a cruise and the plaintiffs, who had now been substituted for the original buyers, claimed damages from the sellers for breach of the implied condition under s 14(2) of the SOGA 1979, that the boat was not of merchantable quality. They contended that the fire was caused by defective electrical installations on the boat. The sellers sought to rely on the exclusion clause.

It was held that by novation, the company, as plaintiffs, were party to the contract originally made between A and the defendants. The substitution was amply supported by consideration. By s 55 of the SOGA 1979, contracting out of the implied term of merchantability was prohibited except in the case of international sales of goods, and in the case of non-consumer sales where the test of reasonableness would be applicable. This was clearly a consumer sale and did not involve an international sale of goods. Therefore, the implied condition could not be excluded when the boat was not of a merchantable quality. It was further held that the sellers could not rely on the exclusion clause in the contract because the seller's breach and the consequences of the breach were fundamental in character.

The majority of shipbuilding contracts, however, are undertaken outside the UK and neither the buyer nor the builder have any connection with the UK. Being characterised as international contracts, the Unfair Contract Terms Act 1977 will have no application, even if the parties choose English law as the law of the contract. In the absence of express or implied choice of law by the parties, the Rome Convention 1980 will apply the law of the country with which there is closest connection.[51]

8 THE SPECIFICATION

A significant part of the contract is the specification, which comprises the second part (the first being the terms of the contract). It covers the details of how the ship is to be constructed and includes the following general items:

(a) a detailed description of the type of ship, her hull and equipment, including the builder's scale plan and drawings;

(b) the materials to be used, depending on the wish of the buyer and the cost he is prepared to pay;

---

51 See the application of the Rome Convention in Chapter 9.

(c) the way in which the ship is to be constructed, configuration of engine and fittings, details of officers' cabins, details of the piping system, method of welding, etc;

(d) the specification must meet mandatory regulations of the country of the ship's intended registration, as well as international regulations of safety imposed by conventions (for example, the International Convention for Safety of Life at Sea 1974) and the regulations of the ship's intended classification society;

(e) sea trials and how they will be carried out.

The specification is of equal significance as the main contract, but in the event of conflict between the two, in the absence of an express agreement, the contract will prevail.[52]

9 INCREASE OF PRICE

The contract must address the risk of price fluctuation in costs of labour and materials.

A cost escalation clause may be included in the contract where extra costs incurred by the builder with respect to fluctuation in prices for labour and materials may make it necessary for the builder to pass on such costs to the buyer. Such clauses are otherwise known as 'contract price adjustment clauses' or 'fluctuation clauses'. For those representing either the buyer's interests or those of the builder, careful drafting of such a clause is needed. The builder will require as wide a clause as possible, while the buyer must be cautious and restrict the width of such a clause with clear words for a cut off point. At the end, it will depend on the market forces, inflation and the parties respective bargaining powers.

If there is no such a clause and the builder unilaterally attempts to increase the price in the course of the building, exercising pressure upon the buyer and threatening to discontinue performance unless the extra price is agreed, he will be faced with the risk of the agreement being unenforceable for lack of consideration, or be set aside for economic duress. Each of these situations is briefly explained, and it is hoped that the parties to a contract will bear in mind the issues involved for the purpose of risk management.

9.1 Lack of consideration and risk management

The agreement may be legally unenforceable for lack of consideration if the builder undertook to perform nothing more than that which he was obliged to

---

52   See, further, *op cit*, Goldrein, fn 1, pp 7, 8.

perform under the existing agreement. By analogous application of the principle, in *Stilk v Myrick*,[53] it could be said that the performance of a pre-existing obligation under a building contract could not be held to constitute good consideration so as to justify increase of the contract price.

In this case, two members of the crew deserted the ship before the return voyage commenced. The captain promised to reward the remaining crew with extra wages if they sailed the vessel safely home. The issue was whether the crew were entitled to that reward. It was held that the deserting two members of the crew made no difference to the duties required of the remaining crew. The latter were performing their obligations under the pre-existing contract of employment, being members of the ship's crew, and had done no extra work to have earned any extra pay. Although the captain had made a promise of extra pay, on which the crew had relied, the court was reluctant to support what was implicitly a form of blackmail or extortion.

In the context of *Stick v Myrick*, the principle clearly emerges that something further is required of one contracting party in order to merit extra payment. The principle of this case, however, having stood for almost 200 years, underwent a radical development in 1990 by the Court of Appeal decision in *Williams v Roffey Bros & Nichols*.[54]

The defendant (main builder) sub-contracted with the plaintiff to carry out carpentry work in a block of 27 flats for an agreed price of £20,000. The plaintiff got into financial difficulty because the agreed price was too low for him to operate satisfactorily and at a profit. The main building contract contained a time penalty clause and the builder worried lest the plaintiff did not complete the carpentry work on time. He, therefore, agreed orally with the plaintiff to pay him an additional sum of £10,300 at the rate of £575 for each flat. Approximately seven weeks later, when the plaintiff had substantially completed eight more flats, the defendants made only one further payment of £1,500 whereupon the plaintiff ceased work on the flats. The plaintiff then sued the defendants for the additional sum promised. The judge held that the agreement for payment of the additional sum was enforceable and did not fail for lack of consideration, because the defendant received a commercial advantage. He gave judgment for the plaintiff.

The Court of Appeal affirmed the judgment and held:

> ... that where a party to a contract promised to make an additional payment in return for the other party's promise to perform his existing contractual obligations and as a result secured a benefit or avoided a detriment, the advantage secured by the promise to make the additional payment was capable of constituting consideration thereof, provided that it was not secured by economic duress or fraud;

---

53 [1809] 2 Camp 317.
54 [1991] 1 QB 1 (CA).

The consideration was avoidance of the detriment of delivering the flats late, which would result in having to pay penalties to the purchasers of the flats, or to buy further building materials and employ labour for the flats to be completed on time.

The refinement and limitation of the principle in *Stilk v Myrick* has gained acceptance in other recent cases. It is worth mentioning an unusual shipbuilding case, **Anangel Atlas Compania Naviera v Ishika Heavy Industries Co Ltd (No 2),**[55] which can be of practical use to both buyers and shipbuilders.

The Angelicoussis group was a long standing customer of a Japanese shipbuilding yard and ordered some new buildings through their agent, a naval architect. During the shipping slump in 1984–85, he and other customers of the yard obtained substantial price reductions for their buildings. Mr Angelicoussis, being a loyal customer, obtained a variation of the original contract and letters were exchanged in which it was stated that the group would be entitled to 'most favoured customer treatment'. The group agreed to take early delivery of the new building, although it did not have to, which would encourage other reluctant customers of the yard to follow suit. However, it was later found out that a friend of Mr Angelicoussis, Mr Goumas, another customer of the yard, had obtained a better reduction in the price from the yard than the reduction granted to his group, and sued the yard for price differential or damages. The issue was whether the aforesaid letters constituted a binding contract. Hirst J held, on the consideration issue, applying *Williams v Roffey*, that whoever provides the services, where there is a practical conferment of benefit or a practical avoidance of detriment for the promisee, there is good consideration, and it is no answer to say that the promisor was already bound. The yard got a clear benefit, or avoided a detriment, since their best customers accepted an early delivery, so that the other customers followed suit.

Similarly, in **The Atlantic Baron,**[56] Mocatta J (see fully below) had held 11 years earlier that the parallel increase of the letter of credit (refund guarantee provided by the builder to the buyer as security) being equivalent to the demanded increase of the contract price to counterbalance the devaluation of the dollar was not merely fulfilling a pre-existing contractual obligation, but an 'increased detriment' constituting good consideration.

---

55 [1990] 2 Lloyd's Rep 526.
56 *North Ocean Shipping Co Ltd v Hyundai Construction Co Ltd (The Atlantic Baron)* [1979] QB 705, or 1 Lloyd's Rep 89.

9.2 Economic duress and risk management

The principle derived from the aforesaid trilogy of cases, however, will not suffice to save the contract, if the agreement is founded on economic duress or fraud, when it may be vitiated by the buyer at his option. In the event that the builder exercises undue pressure on the buyer to pay the extra price, his conduct may amount to economic duress, thus, being subject to the common law rule that the agreement may be held by the court to be voidable.

The Atlantic Baron

Hyundai shipbuilding company entered into a contract by which they agreed to build a tanker for shipowners for a fixed price in US dollars, payment to be made in five instalments. The company agreed to open a letter of credit to provide security for repayment of instalments in the event of their default in the performance of the contract. After the owners had paid the first instalment, the US dollar was devalued by 10%, upon which the company put forward a claim for an increase of 10% in the remaining instalments. The owners, asserting that there was no legal ground on which the claim could be made, paid the second and third instalments without the additional 10%, but the company returned both instalments. The owners suggested that the company should subject their claim to arbitration, but the latter declined to do so, and requested the owners to give them a final and decisive reply to their demand for an increase by a certain date, failing which they would terminate the contract. The owners, who at that time were negotiating a very lucrative contract for the charter of the tanker, replied that, although they were under no obligation to make additional payments, they would do so 'without prejudice' to their rights, and requested that the company arranged for corresponding increases in the letter of credit. The company agreed to do so and the owners remitted the remaining instalments, including the 10%. increase, without protest. After eight months, the owners commenced arbitration claiming the return of the overpayments on two grounds: lack of consideration and economic duress. The arbitrators stated a special case for the opinion of the court.

Mocatta J gave a judgment in favour of the builder on the consideration point (see earlier) and in favour of the owners with respect to economic duress, but for the delay to bring the claim. In particular, he held that:

> ... the company's threat to break the contract without any legal justification unless the owners increased their payments by 10% did amount to duress in the form of economic pressure and, accordingly, the agreement for extra payments was a voidable contract which the owners could either affirm or avoid; that, since there was no likelihood that the company would resile from the contract to build the tanker at the time she was due for delivery, the owners, by making the final payments without protest and, also, by their delay from November 1974 until July 1975 before making a claim for the return of the

extra payments, had so conducted themselves as to affirm the contract and, accordingly, their claim failed.

This is a good example for owners to bear in mind in the future, for the purpose of risk management, should they find themselves in the same situation of making extra payments to the builder under economic duress. However, mere commercial pressure and use of bargaining power by one party to the contract negotiated at arms length will not suffice for the court to declare the contract voidable for economic duress. The Privy Council, in *Pao v Lau Yiu Long*,[57] said that: although the defendants had been subjected to commercial pressure, the facts disclosed that they had not been coerced into the contract of guarantee and, therefore, the contract was not voidable on the ground of duress; in the absence of duress, public policy did not require a contract negotiated at arm's length to be invalidated because a party had either threatened to repudiate an existing contractual obligation, or had unfairly used his dominant bargaining position in negotiating the agreement.

Economic duress was revisited in *Huyton v Cremer*,[58] in which the court redefined its ingredients. These are: illegitimate pressure and deflection, rather than coercion of the will of the innocent party. Mance J said that relief must depend on the court's assessment of the qualitative impact of the illegitimate pressure objectively assessed. He rejected the argument advanced that there was a third essential ingredient of economic duress: that is, 'no practical, alternative course open to the innocent party'. However, he said, relief may not be appropriate if the innocent party decides, as a matter of choice, not to pursue an alternative remedy, which any and, possibly, some other reasonable persons in his circumstances would have pursued.

Examples of factors that may lead the court to find economic duress may be: evidence of the builder's knowledge that the buyer has a charterparty to commence on the date of delivery and, thus, cannot afford to have the ship delivered late; or the builder's knowledge of the buyer's circumstances, by which the latter would have no option but to agree to a sudden price increase.

10 BASIC RIGHTS AND OBLIGATIONS OF THE PARTIES

The relationship between the buyer and the builder is governed by the terms of contract provided for in the Standard Form Contract. The seller has agreed to build a ship for a fixed price made to specification, to perform trials and to deliver on time. The buyer has agreed to pay the contract price by instalments during the process of building, the full agreed price being payable upon

---

57 [1980] AC 614 (PC).
58 [1999] 1 Lloyd's Rep 620; see, also, the present author's 'Commentary' on the case, (1999) *International Journal of Shipping Law*, June, p 137.

satisfactory completion to specification, and to accept delivery of the ship on time.

10.1 Payment, transfer of title and protection of the builder in the event of non-payment

The builder's primary concern is to be paid for the job done. The contract provides details of payment and when property and risk pass to the buyer. Payment by instalments is necessary in this type of contract to commit the buyer more and more to the ship.

10.1.1 Title and risk

The contract provides when property and risk shall pass to the buyer. Art VII.5 of the SAJ form stipulates that the title and risk for loss of the vessel shall pass to the buyer only upon delivery and acceptance thereof, having been completed, as stated in the contract. Until such time, it is expressly stated that title to the vessel and risk for her loss or her equipment shall be in the builder, excepting risks of war, earthquake and tidal waves.

In the absence of express or clear provision in the contract with regard to transfer of title, the usual contract rule in English law concerning specific goods is that the property in them is transferred at such a time as the parties to the contract intend it to be transferred. By s 17(2) of the SOGA 1979, the intention of the parties is ascertained from the terms of the contract, the conduct of the parties and the circumstances of the case.

The rules of ascertaining intention are specified in s 18 of the SOGA 1979. Where there is a contract for the sale of future goods by description, as is the case in the construction and sale of a ship, the property does not pass until the goods are in a deliverable state and are appropriated to the contract either by the seller with the assent of the buyer or by the buyer with the assent of the seller (r 5). However, bearing in mind the hybrid nature of a shipbuilding contract, even if the ship is uncompleted, the property in it (but not in the materials which have not been appropriated to her) may, in some circumstances, pass to the buyer, if the parties have clearly stipulated it in their contract.[59]

10.1.2 Statutory protection of the builder in the event of buyer's default

The ship is the builder's ultimate security. If he is unpaid, his rights are determined in ss 38–43 of the SOGA 1979. He can exercise his statutory lien,

---

59   See *Re Blyth Shipbuilding and Drydocks Co Ltd* [1926] Ch 494 (para 2, above).

provided by s 41, before he gives up possession. Delivery of the ship before being fully paid and without reserving the right of disposal will cause the termination of the lien (s 43). Failure by the buyer to pay an instalment will give rise to a claim in debt (s 49(2) of the SOGA 1979).[60]

10.1.3 Buyer's default and contractual protection of builder

The meaning of default is defined in the contract of SAJ form, first as failure in payment of first, second and third instalments within three days after the due date; second, failure in payment of the fourth instalment, concurrently with delivery of the vessel by the builder to the buyer; and third, failure by the buyer to take delivery of the vessel when the vessel is duly tendered for delivery by the builder (cl XI.1).

The builder is normally protected by a third party guarantee, by which the guarantor guarantees irrevocably and unconditionally due and faithful performance by the buyer of all its liabilities and responsibilities under the contract and any subsequent amendment change or modification made including, but not limited to, due and prompt payment of the contract price by the buyer (see cl XXI of the SAJ form).

The contract also provides what is to happen in the event of buyer's default in payment (cl XI.3 of the SAJ form). The effect of default will automatically postpone the delivery date for a period of continuance of such default by the buyer. But, if any default continues for more than 15 days, the builder has the option to rescind the contract by giving notice of such effect to the buyer. Upon receipt of such notice, the contract shall become null and void and any of the buyer's supplies shall become the property of the builder. In addition, the builder shall be entitled to retain any instalments paid by the buyer to the builder on account.

10.1.4 Repudiation of contract and risk management

Under the contract, default in payment will not excuse the builder from his obligation to continue construction, but it will postpone delivery, unless the default by the buyer constitutes repudiation of the contract (for example, the buyer evinces an intention not to fulfil his obligations under the contract), whereupon the builder has an option whether or not to accept the same as terminating the parties' primary obligations.[61]

The question that has recently arisen in the context of repudiation of contract is whether mere failure to perform a contractual obligation by the aggrieved party is capable of constituting acceptance of anticipatory

---

60 *Workman Clarke & Co Ltd v Lloyd Brazileno* [1908] 1 KB 968 (CA).
61 *Fercometal SARL v Mediterranean Shipping Co SA (The Simona)* [1989] 1 AC 788 (HL); concerning a charterparty cancellation clause and non-readiness of the ship.

repudiation. In other words, whether there can be acceptance of repudiation by conduct. The House of Lords has clarified this issue in *The Santa Clara*,[62] (a sale of goods case), in which it was held that: on repudiation of a contract the aggrieved party could elect whether to accept the repudiation or affirm the contract; an acceptance required no particular form provided the aggrieved party clearly and unequivocally demonstrated to the repudiating party that he was treating the contract as determined, and notification, either personally or by an agent, was not necessary where the fact of election came to the attention of the repudiating party. Failure to perform was capable of signifying to a repudiating party, an election by the aggrieved party to treat the contract as at an end.

However, in the context of a shipbuilding contract, the builder has to be cautious before deciding to discontinue performance on the basis of the buyer's default, because he may be in repudiation of the contract himself, if the contract contains a specific warranty by the builder that the construction of the vessel shall proceed continually until delivery,[63] unless there is a suspension clause for non-payment. The mere commencement of proceedings by the one party to determine his rights does not necessarily mean that he repudiates the performance of the contract in any event. He may submit to perform it, if the court comes to the conclusion that he is bound to perform it, and it cannot be taken to be an absolute repudiation.[64] Wrongful exercise of the contractual right of rescission is not to be treated as a repudiatory breach provided there is no manifestation by conduct of an ulterior intention to abandon the contract.[65]

10.1.5 What is to happen to the vessel on rescission by the builder?

Damages for breach will be assessed with reference to the date at which the other party accepted the repudiation and rescinded the contract.[66]

By cl XI.4 of the SAJ form, the builder would be entitled to sell the ship either uncompleted or to sell it after completion. In either case, he shall apply the proceeds to cover, first, his expenses incurred attending such sale and, then, to payment of all unpaid contractual instalments, plus interest. In either case, any surplus of the proceeds shall be paid to the buyer, provided that such payment does not exceed the total amount of the instalments paid by him and the costs of the buyer's supplies, if any. On the other hand, if the proceeds are not sufficient to pay the expenses and costs of the builder, the

---

62 *Vitol SA v Norelf Ltd* [1996] AC 800 (HL): where a buyer rejected cargo before loading commenced and neither party took further steps to perform the contract.

63 *Hyundai Heavy Industries Co Ltd v Papadopoulos* [1980] 2 Lloyd's Rep 1.

64 *Spettabile Consorzio v Northumberland Shipbuilding Co* (1919) 121 LT 628.

65 *Woodar v Wimpey* [1980] 1 WLR 277 (HL).

66 *Tai Hing Mill v Kamsing Factory* [1979] AC 91 (PC).

buyer shall promptly pay the deficiency to the builder. Sub-clause 4c provides for reimbursement of the builder with respect to his cost of construction up to the incomplete state of the vessel, less the instalments already retained and any compensation to the builder for loss of profit due to the rescission of the contract.[67]

10.1.6 Rights of the builder under the guarantee for payment of instalments

The contract contains a cancellation clause when there is default by the buyer. This is normally linked to a contractual guarantee given to the builder to recoup unpaid instalments from the guarantor, if the cancellation clause became operative. The issue as to the builder's accrued rights of payment prior to cancellation of the contract came before the House of Lords in the following case:

In *Hyundai Heavy Industries Co v Papadopoulos*,[68] the plaintiffs (builders) entered into a contract with buyers for the construction of a vessel. A contract clause gave the builders the right to rescind the contract if an instalment remained unpaid for more than three days after the due date and the builder notified the buyer that, if the default continued for seven days after the builder's notification, he would exercise such a right by giving notice of rescission. Such a right had been agreed to be in addition to any other rights, powers and remedies that the builder might have under the contract, and or at law, at equity or otherwise. The defendants had guaranteed to make payment on all sums due under the contract in default of the buyers. The contract did not state what was to happen with regard to rights, which had accrued prior to cancellation. When the buyers defaulted in payment, the builders rescinded the contract and claimed under the guarantee. The defendants contended that, by exercising the right to rescind before the writ was issued against them, liability to pay instalments which had become due and had not been paid ceased and was replaced by a claim, not in debt, but in damages. The cancellation deprived the builder of his accrued right to payment of the unpaid instalment either from the buyer or the guarantor.

The House of Lords (and the courts below) held unanimously that it was difficult to believe that commercial men could have intended that the guarantor were to be released from their liability for payments already due and in default just because the plaintiff, builders, had used his remedy of cancelling the shipbuilding contract for the future.

---

67 In this connection see: *Neptune Navigation Corp v Ishikawahima-Harima Heavy Industries Co Ltd* [1987] 1 Lloyd's Rep 24.

68 [1980] 2 Lloyd's Rep 1.

The default of the buyer was the very event that gave rise to the liability of the defendants under the letter of guarantee. The defendants' promise that they would forthwith make the payment in default showed that the obligation arose immediately upon default by the buyer and was not merely an obligation to pay any deficiency brought about in the final accounting. The defendants could not be released from their liability for payments already due, just because the plaintiffs exercised their rights of cancellation under the contract. It was also held that the cancellation by the plaintiffs did not release the buyer of his liability under the second instalment. The builder could rely on his remedies at common law.

Viscount Dilhorne, who stressed that the shipbuilding contract is not just a contract for sale, said – distinguishing cases of sale of land or goods, or in which there is total failure of consideration – that the law has been that cancellation or rescission of a contract, in consequence of repudiation, did not affect accrued rights for the payment of instalments of the contract price, unless the contract provided that it was to do so.

These and similar issues came before the House of Lords recently in the following case.

In *Stocznia v Latvian Shipping Co*,[69] contracts were agreed for the construction and purchase of six refrigerated vessels. Under the contracts, payment was structured into four instalments so that: (a) 5% of the contract price was to be paid seven banking days after receipt by the buyer of the bank guarantee to be furnished by the builder; (b) 20% was to be paid within five banking days after the yard had given notice to the buyer of keel laying; (c) 25% was to be paid within five banking days after the builder had given notice of the successful launching of the vessel; (d) the balance of the contract price (50%) was to be paid upon delivery of the vessel. The first instalment was paid for all six vessels. Thereafter, the owners began to have financial problems because of downturn in the reefer market and proposed to the builder a 20% reduction in the price for each vessel, together with a five year deferral of payment of the new reduced price and delayed delivery. Otherwise, the buyers informed the builder during these negotiations, that although they wanted the vessels, taking delivery of them would be impossible. However, the proposal would have disrupted the yard's cash flow and work programme.

The yard did not treat that as repudiation, but completed the keel laying of the first vessel, and served notice claiming the second instalment. The money was not paid and the yard gave notice that they were treating the contract as repudiated. The same thing happened with the second vessel. The keel was laid, the second instalment was demanded, but remained unpaid and the builder served notice treating the contract as being repudiated. Later, he

---

69 [1998] 1 Lloyd's Rep 609.

brought an action claiming instalments of the remaining four vessels on the basis of repudiation by the buyer.

The issues for the House of Lords were these: (1) whether the yard acquired accrued rights to the second instalments of the contract price in respect of vessels 3–6; (2) the impact of the yard electing for contractual rescission on the yard's right to recover the second instalments of the price; (3) whether the yard's action to recover the second instalments of the price must fail because, if recovered, they would have to be immediately repayable on the ground of total failure of consideration.

With regard to the first and second issues, it was held that by exercising the right of rescission under the contract, the yard did not express an intention that they abandoned their right at common law to recover as a debt unpaid instalments of the price, which had already accrued due, and it made no difference whether there was a sale of the ships or not. This right at common law was not inconsistent with the contract terms, and the yard was entitled to recover accrued and unpaid instalments.[70]

As regards the third issue, the fact that the contract had been brought to an end before the property in the vessel or any part of it had passed to the buyers, did not prevent the yard from asserting that there had been no total failure of consideration in respect of an instalment of the price which had been paid before the contract was terminated. To put it differently, an instalment which had then accrued due could not, if paid, be recoverable on that ground. (*Hyundai Heavy Industries Co v Papadopoulos* was applied.)

It was further held that the yard did not have any rights under the contract with respect to non-accrued instalments. The yard was entitled to make an alternative claim in damages for anticipatory repudiation in relation to contracts for vessels 1 and 2.

10.1.7 Acceleration in payment and penalty clauses

In some circumstances, the builder may demand that the payment under the contract is accelerated, or the contract may provide for liquidated damages in favour of the builder in the event of buyer's default. The level of such damages must not amount to a penalty clause. Liquidated damages are a genuine pre-estimate of damages.

In *The Angelic Star*,[71] the plaintiffs, Swedish shipbuilders, agreed to build, sell and deliver this ship to Angelicos Company. The payment of 20% of the contract price was payable in advance and the remaining 80% on delivery by a 'delivery credit', which was to be repaid over eight years by 16 semi-annual

---

70 The decision of the Court of Appeal was reversed on both points.
71 [1988] 1 Lloyd's Rep 122.

instalments and it bore a fixed rate of interest at 8.5%. Upon delivery of the vessel, the buyer was to deliver to the builder 31 bills of exchange covering the capital and interest. By way of security to the builder, the buyer was required to execute a mortgage of the vessel. For this purpose, the shipbuilding contract included complex loan conditions; the relevant condition in this context was the event of default in payment of the loan. This clause provided that:

> The loan together with all other monies due to the lenders by the owners shall immediately become payable and the lender shall forthwith be put in funds to cover all existing and future liabilities under the bills of exchange drawn in connection with the loan, and the security for the loan and such monies shall become enforceable ... if ... (a) the owners fail to make payments of capital or interest ... on due dates.

The buyer failed to make payments of capital and interest, and the issue was whether the above clause was enforceable or whether it amounted to a penalty clause.

The Court of Appeal – following the decision of the House of Lords in *Dunlop Pneumatic Tyre Company Ltd v New Garage and Motor Co Ltd*[72] held:

> Clearly, a clause which provided that, in the event of any breach of contract a long term loan would immediately become repayable and that interest thereon for the full term would not only be still payable but would be payable at once, would constitute a penalty as being 'a payment of money stipulated as *in terrorem* of the offending party' ... But I do not so read condition 13. 'The loan' is the capital sum. 'All other monies due to the lenders by the owners' cannot be construed as 'all other monies which would otherwise become due by the owners in the future'. It means 'all other monies due at the time of the happening of an event of default'. The mere fact that the capital sum becomes immediately repayable upon a failure to comply with the conditions upon which credit was extended cannot constitute a penalty. The provision that the lenders shall forthwith be put in funds to cover all existing and future liability under any outstanding bills drawn in connection with the loan is intended to safeguard the shipbuilders against their potential liability as drawers, should the bills have been negotiated and the purchaser, as acceptor, fail to honour the bills upon maturity ... This again is not a penalty provision.[73]

As regards the justification of non-sanctioning a penalty clause, Gibson LJ said:[74]

> ...it seemed clear to me that there was no basis for holding that the provision for acceleration of capital must be regarded as unenforceable or as excluded from the contract. The doctrine relating to penalties is not a rule of illegality: it is a rule by which the court refuses to sanction legal proceedings for recovery of a penalty sum, a rule which the court had produced and maintained for

---

72 [1915] AC 79 (HL).
73 [1996] 2 Lloyd's Rep 132 (CA), *per* Lord Donaldson MR, p 125.
74 *Ibid*, pp 126–27.

purposes of public policy: see *per* Lord Radcliffe, *Campbell Discount Company Ltd v Bridge* [1962] AC 600, p 622. The rule is, in my judgment, not designed to strike down any more of a lawful contract than is necessary to give effect to the court's purpose of applying public policy; and, moreover, the rule should be applied so as to interfere as little as possible with the proper enforcement of a lawful contract according to its terms. Parties to a contract are free expressly to stipulate not only the primary obligations and rights under the contract but also the secondary rights and obligations, that is, those which arise upon non-performance of any primary obligation by one of the parties to the contract: see *per* Diplock LJ (as he then was): *Robophone Facilities Ltd v Blank* [1966] 1 WLR 1428, p 1446B.

10.2 Builder's guarantee, trials and risk management

Testing whether the performance and condition of the ship are satisfactory and in accordance with the contract is carried out during the trials, which are an important part of the contract terms. Trials give the opportunity to the buyer to verify whether the builder has complied with the specification. The standard forms of contract, SAJ and the Norwegian forms, oblige the buyer either to accept that the ship complies with the specification and requirements of the contract, or to reject her within a short period of time after the completion of the trials.[75]

In this context, the builder's guarantee that certain characteristics and condition of the ship will be met on delivery is very important. Failure by the builder to meet the minimum guaranteed characteristics might cause delay in delivery resulting in loss of profit to both parties. The guarantee is usually linked to a provision for liquidated damages in favour of the buyer as a pre-estimate of the buyer's loss, which will preclude him from relying on common law damages. A neat example of this is provided by the House of Lords' decision in ***Cellulose Acetate***[76] case.

A contract for delivery and erection of an acetone recovery plant provided that, if the work were not completed within a certain time, the contractors should pay to the purchasers by way of penalty a sum of 20*l* for every week that they were in default. The contractors were 30 weeks late in completing the work. In an action by them against the purchasers for the contract price, the defendants counterclaimed 5,850*l*, the actual loss they had suffered through the delay.

It was held that the sum of 20*l* a week was the full amount that the plaintiffs agreed to pay towards compensation to the defendants for delay in completing, and that they were liable for 600*l* and no more.

---

75 *Op cit*, Goldrein, fn 1, pp 19–23.
76 *Cellulose Acetate Silk Co v Widnes Foundry Ltd* [1933] AC 20 (HL).

The fact that a precise pre-estimate is almost impossible will not prevent the sum being liquidated damages.[77]

A builder's guarantee usually provides that, following acceptance by the buyer, if defects in materials and/or workmanship are discovered within 12 or 24 months, the builder shall remedy the defects at his own expense. But, if defects have not been discovered within the guarantee period, there is no remedy for the buyer, particularly when the builder has successfully exempted his liability for any other defects whatsoever. A recent example of the construction of a guarantee clause and the extent of builder's liability is provided by *The Seta Maru*.[78]

The Seta Maru

The guarantee cl IX.1 provided that:

... the builder for a period of 12 months following acceptance by the buyer of the vessel, guarantees the vessel, her hull and machinery ... which are manufactured, furnished or supplied by the builder ... against all defects in material and/or workmanship on the part of the builder.

Sub-paragraph IX.3 (extent of builder's liability) excluded the builder's liability for any defects discovered after the expiration of the guarantee period and for any defects whatsoever, other than the defects specified under cl IX.1. Any other indirect consequential, or special, losses, damages or expenses were also excluded.

Three ships were built by China shipbuilding and were delivered to the buyer. After the expiration of the guarantee period, two of them appeared defective in the erection welding, as result of which they suffered a casualty, involving ingress of water through the shell plating. Following the discovery of these defects, the third vessel was inspected within the guarantee period and the same defects were discovered and corrected by the builder. With regard to the defects in the other two ships the buyer commenced arbitration and claimed from the builder the costs of repairs and depreciation in value as damages.

On a preliminary issue before the arbitrators, it was decided that in view of non-compliance by the builder of the notification procedures for acceptance of the vessels, the terms of the contract did not exempt the builder from liability for the breaches. The builder appealed to the court, which was asked to construe the clause excepting the builder's liability after the quarantine period.

---

77 *Clydebank Engineering v Don Jose Ramos Yzquierdo Castaneda* [1905] AC 6 (HL).

78 *China Shipbuilding Corp v Nippon Yusen Kabukishi Kaisha and Galaxy Shipping PTE Ltd (The Seta Maru)* [2000] 1 Lloyd's Rep 367.

Thomas J held that cl IX.3 was a comprehensive provision forming part of what was a complete code for dealing with defects discovered after the delivery of the vessel. The terms of cl IX provided a guarantee for defects discovered after the buyer accepted delivery of the vessel. Clause IX.3 excluded liability for defects, arising from breaches of the express terms beyond the liability expressly assumed under the guarantee terms. The sending by the builder of a telex notification of readiness was not a condition precedent to the operation of the clause. He remitted the case to the arbitrators.

Naturally, the buyer suffered loss here, which arose mainly from an unfavourable drafting in the contract. In the light of this risk that defects may, and frequently do, appear after the 12 months guarantee, the buyer could perhaps protect his position by seeking to obtain a longer guarantee period. If this cannot be achieved at the stage of negotiations, particularly if the builder is in a stronger bargaining position, the buyer ought to inspect the vessel during the guarantee period for any defects that might exist in the vessel, which could be remedied by the builder under the guarantee, as was done in this case with respect to the third ship.

Ordinary insurance cover may not always protect the buyer to get indemnified for his loss. It will depend on the type of loss and the construction of the insurance contract,[79] unless the buyer obtains a special cover for building defects.

10.3 Default by builder – the buyer's right to reject the ship or rescind the contract

The buyer's remedies are provided for in the standard shipbuilding agreement forms. These are supported by statutory rights and rights at common law. He may reject the ship, or reject and demand remedial work, and/or damages, or claim specific performance.

The buyer's right to reject the vessel may arise in two situations. First, he may reject the ship after the trials, pointing out that there are various defects which need to be remedied.

Second, he may reject the ship where there has been a serious breach of the contract by the builder. In such a situation, the buyer may accept the conduct of the seller/builder as a repudiation and sue in damages.

A breach by the builder does not necessarily mean that the breach amounts to repudiation of the contract by him. It will depend on the magnitude of the defect and its consequences. In *McDougall v Aeromarine*,[80]

---

79 See *The Caribbean Sea* [1980] 1 Lloyd's Rep 338.
80 [1958] 2 Lloyd's Rep 345.

it was held that, if the defect was one that could be remedied within a time, which would still permit the builder to deliver within the period of delivery permitted by the contract, the buyer would not be entitled to treat the contract as repudiated. The buyer could recover damages for delay in the delivery. The SAJ form provides for liquidated damages. However, if the delay has been caused partly by the buyer, he will not be entitled to recover damages. The principle that no liquidated damages for delay can be claimed, if completion was in part delayed by conduct of the employer, would be applicable.[81]

10.4 Delay in delivery and *force majeure*

Events beyond the builder's control frequently occur during the construction of the contract and become a cause of delay in delivery. The builder needs protection and, although it is possible to manage such risks by insurance, it is also sensible to limit his liability for delay in delivery by an exclusion clause in the contract with regard to a range of events, which would be beyond his control. The contract provides a protection for the builder in this respect by the *force majeure* clause (Art VIII of the SAJ form). It enumerates 35 specific events, which may be beyond the builder's control and prevent the work. Upon the occurrence of any of such events, the clause provides that the time for the delivery is extended for certain days, not exceeding the total accumulated time of all such delays, after the builder has given notice to the buyer of any *force majeure* event.[82] The burden of proof is upon the builder to show that such an event has occurred and it is within the clause.

Most common events include act of God, fire, flood, hurricanes, storms or other weather conditions not included in normal planning, earthquakes, intervention of government authorities, war, blockade, strikes, lockouts, labour shortage, explosions, shortage of materials, defects in materials, machinery, equipment (which could reasonably be expected by the builder to be delivered), delays in transportation, delays in the builder's other commitments. There is a sweeping up provision at the end of the clause providing: '... or due to other causes or accidents beyond the control of the builder, its sub-contractors or supplier of the nature whether or not indicated by the foregoing words, irrespective of whether or not these events could be foreseen at the day of signing this contract.'

Industrial action during the construction of shipbuilding is the most common incident of delay. However, as the builder may sometimes be able to

---

81 *The Cape Hatteress* [1982] 1 Lloyd's Rep 518, p 526: the delay to the repairs of the ship had been caused by the conduct of the defendants.

82 For details of *force majeure* and shipbuilding contracts, see McKendrick, E (ed), *Force Majeure and Frustration of Contract*, 2nd edn, 1995, LLP, Chapter 7 (by Curtis), particularly, as to the effect of *force majeure* events, and his comments on the lack of clarity in cl VIII of the SAJ form about the extent of delay.

control the happening of strikes and labour disturbances, this incident may become the cause of a dispute between the builder and the buyer, if the latter considers that the event does not come within the protection of the *force majeure* clause. For example, if the builder acted unreasonably in dealing with the workforce and, therefore, failed to prevent the strike or mitigate its consequences, it will not be regarded as being beyond his control.[83]

With regard to shortage of materials or equipment, the clause restricts the protection of the builder to circumstances in which the builder at the time of ordering could reasonably expect their delivery. Failing delivery, despite the builder's reasonable conduct in ordering from a certain supplier in whom the builder could reasonably rely and expect timely delivery, the question is whether the builder would be obliged to buy in from other sources. Were he obliged to do so, should he do so, instead of relying on the *force majeure* clause, even if the price was much dearer? The House of Lord has held in a non-shipping case that, provided a shortage of supply has been proved, the defendants were entitled to rely on the clause, notwithstanding the existence of an alternative source of supply. But, a mere increase in price would not be sufficient to establish a shortage in supply.[84]

The clause, in para 4 of Art VIII of the SAJ form, provides that the buyer may or may not elect to cancel the contract if the delay exceeds beyond a certain period.[85]

Invariably, a *force majeure* event has a knock-on effect, so that delay of completion of one vessel caused by *force majeure*, may affect completion of other vessels, as was shown in the following case.

Matsoukis v Priestman[86]

The defendants agreed to build and deliver a steamer to the plaintiff on or before 28 February 1913. The contract contained the following exceptions clause: 'If the said steamer is not delivered entirely ready to purchaser at the above mentioned time, the builders hereby agree to pay to the purchaser for liquidated damages, and not by way of penalty, the sum of 10 pounds Sterling for each day of delay and in deduction of the price stipulated in this contract, being excepted only the cause of *force majeure*, and/or strikes of workmen of the building yard where the vessel is being built, or the workshops where the machinery is being made, or at the works where steel is being manufactured for the steamer, or any works of any sub-contractor.'

83   *Channel Island Ferries Ltd v Sealink Ltd* [1988] 1 Lloyd's Rep 323 (CA).
84   *Tennants (Lancashire) Ltd v CS Wilson and Co Ltd* [1917] AC 495.
85   *Harland & Wolff Ltd v Lakeport Navigation Co Panama SA* [1974] 1 Lloyd's Rep 301.
86   [1915] 1 KB 681.

As a result of a general coal strike of 1912, the works from which the defendants obtained their materials for other ships they were building got behind. The ship in turn to be built, before the plaintiff's ship, occupied the berth much longer than otherwise she would have done. The same berth was intended to be occupied by the plaintiff's ship. Consequently, the plaintiff's steamer was late in being laid down. The steamer having been delivered after the contract date, the plaintiff claimed damages.

The court held that the general dislocation of the business of the defendants and of those from whom they obtained materials operating indirectly on the completion of the plaintiff's steamer, by preventing the completion of the vessel prior in turn, constituted a case of *force majeure* within the meaning of the exceptions clause and, therefore, excused the defendants in respect of the delay so caused.

It further held that, apart from delay due to bad weather, the delay due to breakdown of machinery was covered by the exception of *force majeure*.

10.5 Effect of buyer's rescission

It can be observed from cl X (buyer's rescission) and cl XI (builder's rescission) of the SAJ form, as well as from the equivalent provisions of the AWES form (cll 10 and 11, respectively), that there is an imbalance of contractual remedies between the buyer and the builder. Upon rescission by the buyer for builder's default, the buyer is only entitled to a refund of all instalments paid in advance, plus interest, and is discharged from any further obligations. But the contract expressly excludes any claim in damages for losses incurred. The builder, on the other hand, has a contractual right to claim damages for loss of profit due to buyer's default, or damages that he would have had at common law. The Norwegian form is silent about this issue, so presumably, the parties' rights at common law are preserved.

The refund to the buyer must be paid promptly. Apart from the refund the buyer is entitled to claim, the effect of buyer's rescission is to terminate the parties' further primary obligations under the contract. If the buyer has provided supplies, they presumably remain the property of the buyer and therefore returnable, unless the contract stipulates otherwise.

In the event that title in the vessel has passed to the buyer, if the contract provided that it would pass in stages during the building after payment of the first instalment, the buyer has two options: (i) either to revest the title in the builder upon reimbursement of the pre-paid instalments; or (ii) to remove the ship from the yard and terminate the builder's contractual entitlement to continue the completion of the ship. If the builder is in liquidation, however, this issue will have to be decided in accordance with the law of the *lex situs*.[87]

---

87 See *op cit*, Curtis, fn 1, p 164.

In some contracts, it may be provided that the buyer has the right to complete the building work at his own risk and expense. In the light of the risk involved for the buyer in case of rescission and the contractual prohibition against claiming his losses, which may inevitably be loss of bargain, or expenses thrown away, the buyer manages those risks by obtaining insurance cover in the event of delayed delivery or cancellation of the contract.

10.6 Can specific performance be ordered?

Specific performance is a discretionary remedy under English law when a party to a contract does not wish to bring the contract to an end by exercising his option to rescind the contract for breach by the other party. He may seek, therefore, to obtain a remedy of specific performance ordered by the court or tribunal, particularly when an award in damages would not be an adequate remedy to compensate the victim of the breach.[88] Such remedy is available under s 52 of the SOGA 1979 and applies to sale of ascertained goods. The ship under construction, although not yet completed, is ascertainable, insofar as the agreement provides for the end product. It concerns the sale of a future ship and the order of specific performance would be relevant only to the extent that it would be possible for it to be completed for delivery to take place. In this context, therefore, an order for specific performance obtained by the buyer may be useless, if the builder has been unable to complete for financial reasons and his company is in liquidation. Even if he is not in liquidation, there may be problems of enforcing such a court order, if the building is taking place in a foreign yard. Usually, an order for specific performance would not be granted where the remedy required detailed supervision by the courts.

In *Gyllenhammar & Partners Int Ltd v Sour Brodogradevna Split*,[89] the defendants (builders) entered into a shipbuilding contract with the plaintiffs (buyers) which was subject, *inter alia*, to the defendants declaring by telex to the buyer that all necessary permissions and approvals had been obtained. The approvals were to be obtained within 30 days of signing the contract, without which, the contract would be null and void, unless otherwise agreed by both parties. On failing to obtain the necessary approvals, the defendants notified the plaintiffs asserting that the contract had become null and void. The plaintiffs sued them arguing that the defendants were debarred from relying on this clause because, in their view, the necessary approvals were not obtained by reason of (i) the defendants' non-compliance with this clause, and (ii) the defendants' failure to use their best endeavours to obtain the necessary

---

88 *The Ore Chief* [1983] 2 Lloyd's Rep 509.
89 [1989] 2 Lloyd's Rep 403.

permission. They claimed specific performance of the contract, or damages in lieu of that.

Holding that the defendants were entitled to rely on the clause, the court went on to examine the plaintiff's request for specific performance (merely for academic purposes). Hirst J said:

> Here, I need say no more than that the voluminous specification shows that this is a very complex contract requiring extensive co-operation between the parties on a number of matters, in particular modifications, optional variations, and, perhaps most important of all, matters of detail (some by no means unimportant) left undefined in the specification. In my judgment, these factors, coupled with the consideration that the work would take place in a foreign yard outside the court's jurisdiction, would tell strongly against an order for specific performance being in principle appropriate in the present case.[90]

11 INSURANCE AND MANAGEMENT OF RISKS

Unless otherwise agreed in the contract, the builder retains property and risk in the ship until delivery. Even if property is agreed to pass to the buyer gradually during the stages of construction, the risk of total loss of the ship in the yard remains with the builder. He has an insurable interest to insure the ship for damage or loss during construction, either as owner, or as bailee as the case may be. He has a duty under the contract to insure. The buyer will be a co-assured, so he will have to make sure that the contract does not become vitiated for breach of the duty of utmost good faith by the builder, or his broker, when placing the insurance and that the premium is paid by the builder during the currency of the policy. The buyer can also insure separately for other risks in the event of rescission of the contract and the consequential losses, which he will be unable to recover from the builder, if a claim for damages at large is excluded, as is normally the case under shipbuilding contracts. Most importantly, the buyer should obtain cover for any latent defects in the ship which may be discovered after the guarantee period and which will be excluded from the obligation of the builder under his guarantee to correct them, as was shown earlier in *The Seta Maru*.

---

90 [1989] 2 Lloyd's Rep 403, p 422.

12 MANUFACTURER'S OR BUILDER'S LIABILITY TO THIRD PARTIES FOR DEFECTIVE PRODUCTS

English law is now well settled with regard to liability of a manufacturer in tort for physical injury, on the one hand, and on the other for pure economic loss to remote owners of chattels.

The House of Lords, in *Murphy v Brentwood DC*,[91] reached its decision that remote purchasers of a defective building had no claim in tort for economic loss against the Council, which had approved the plans of a building, by analogy with the position of a manufacturer who had no liability in tort for a defective chattel.

Lord Bridge stated the principle quite clearly as follows:[92]

> If a manufacturer negligently puts into circulation a chattel containing a latent defect which renders it dangerous to persons or property, the manufacturer, on the well known principles established by *Donoghue v Stevenson* [1932] AC 562, will be liable in tort for injury to persons or damage to property which the chattel causes. But, if a manufacturer produces and sells a chattel which is merely defective in quality, even to the extent that it is valueless for the purpose for which it is intended, the manufacturer's liability at common law arises only under and, by reference to the terms of any contract to which he is a party in relation to the chattel, the common law does not impose on him any liability in tort to persons to whom he owes no duty in contract but who, having acquired the chattel, suffer economic loss because the chattel is defective in quality. If a dangerous defect in a chattel is discovered before it causes any personal injury or damage to property, because the danger is now known and the chattel cannot safely be used unless the defect is repaired, the defect becomes merely a defect in quality. The chattel is either capable of repair at economic cost, or it is worthless and must be scrapped. In either case, the loss sustained by the owner or hirer of the chattel is purely economic. It is recoverable against any party who owes the loser a relevant contractual duty. But, it is not recoverable in tort in the absence of a special relationship of proximity imposing on the tortfeasor a duty of care to safeguard the plaintiff from economic loss. There is no such special relationship between the manufacturer of a chattel and a remote owner or hirer.

While there is a duty of care owed by a manufacturer or builder to third parties for a reasonably foreseeable physical injury to a person or property caused by a dangerous defect in a chattel, with regard to economic loss, as a general rule, there is no such duty on the part of the manufacturer, unless there is a special relationship of proximity imposing a duty on the manufacturer to safeguard a third party from economic loss. A special relationship of proximity would exist, if the defendant had voluntarily

---

91 [1991] 1 AC 398.
92 *Ibid*, p 475.

assumed a responsibility to act in the matter by involving himself in the claimant's affairs, or by choosing to speak.[93] For example, in the celebrated case of *Hedley Byrne*,[94] the defendant chose to speak and was taken to have assumed responsibility from that fact alone. Reliance by the claimant on the defendant's act or advice would be relevant in determining whether there was an assumption of responsibility and causation.

How can these principles apply in the context of shipbuilding? There is no doubt that, if a dangerously defective part, such as an engine, of a new building (whether it be a ship or an aircraft), which causes explosion resulting in death, will give rise to tortious liability. If the ship, or aircraft, is not new, however, it will be a matter of evidence whether the dangerous equipment, which caused an accident, was due to bad maintenance or developed from a latent defect.

Insofar as economic loss is concerned, the application of the principles is best explained by a recent Court of Appeal decision in the case described below.

The Rebecca Elaine[95]

The appellants owned a number of fishing vessels and contracted with boat builders to build what became *The Rebecca Elaine*. Because of their good experience with Gardner engines, the appellants decided that the new vessel should be fitted with such an engine. The manufacturers did not sell engines direct and there was a chain of contracts between them and the boat builders. The new vessel was commissioned and her new Gardner engine was accompanied by a one year manufacturer's warranty against defects in workmanship or material and a manual which stated that its 'pistons would run for 20,000 hours or more without dismantling and before replacement is necessary'.

Later, the manufacturers of the engine sold their business to the respondents. The sale was of the entire undertaking, property and assets of the business as a going concern, together with the respondents' right to represent that they were carrying on the business in continuation of, and in succession to, the manufacturers. Two years after the building of the boat, the respondents began to receive reports that pistons in Gardner engines had broken or cracked before they should have done. The pistons concerned had all been manufactured by an independent contractor, Wellworthy Ltd. These pistons, as the judge found, were liable to fail after only about one third of the running time stated in the manual. On the judge's unchallenged finding, the respondents were on notice of a very real problem affecting the Wellworthy

---

93 *White v Jones* [1995] 2 AC 207 (HL).
94 *Hedley Byrne & Co v Heller & Partners* [1963] 1 Lloyd's Rep 485 (HL).
95 [1999] 2 Lloyd's Rep 1.

pistons which they realised might cause major engine failure, or worse. However, despite this knowledge the respondents chose not to warn those with engines fitted with such pistons, which the judge held they could have done by contacting known customers, authorised distributors and service agents, or by advertising in trade journals.

When *The Rebecca Elaine* was four miles south west of the Needles, the pistons failed prematurely and the engine seized. Fortunately, the vessel was towed to safety and the only loss was the damage to the engine itself, which cost £25,972 to repair, and loss of earnings, which the judge assessed at £21,344.

The appellants' case could not be made in contract since the warranty had expired and any claim against the boatbuilders would have been successfully met by an exclusion clause in the boatbuilding contract and/or the fact that the appellants did not rely on the boatbuilders' skill or judgment in the supply of the engine. The case against the respondents was put solely in negligence. The essence of the appellants' complaint was that, knowing there was a problem with the Wellworthy pistons, the respondents did nothing to warn operators/owners to carry out inspections more frequently, so as to confine any damage to the pistons themselves and avoid major engine failure of the kind suffered by *The Rebecca Elaine*.

The judge found that, if the respondents had been under a duty to warn, they were in breach of duty and that this was the cause of the appellants' loss because, if they had been given a warning, they would have acted on it.

After a full review of the authorities the judge concluded that for the appellants to establish a duty of care to avoid economic loss they had to show a special relationship of proximity which involved both an assumption of responsibility by the respondents and reliance by the appellants.

He held that the respondents had not assumed any responsibility to safeguard the appellants from economic loss, although they might have assumed responsibility to avoid physical damage to persons or property.

The Court of Appeal approved the first instance decision and considered further whether in such cases there is duty to warn.

Tuckey LJ said:[96]

> Under English law I do not think that there is any basis for putting failure to warn of a known danger into a category of its own … My review of the authorities shows that the general rule is that a manufacturer in the position of the respondents owes no duty of care to avoid economic loss. Exceptionally, he may be under such a duty if he assumes responsibility to his customers in a situation, which is akin to contract. That duty may include a duty to warn, but

---

it would be much more difficult to infer in the case of mere silence than in the case of misrepresentation.[97] Reliance by the customer is relevant to whether there has been an assumption of responsibility and essential as to causation.[98]

---

97 *Banque Keyser Ullman SA v Scandia (UK) Insurance* [1988] 2 Lloyd's Rep 514 (CA): the court had to consider whether the underwriter of the defendant (insurers), who knew that a broker had issued a false cover note to the plaintiff bank, owed a duty of care to warn the bank which lent large sums of money on the security of the cover. Slade LJ, giving the judgment of the court, said, at p 559: 'Can a mere failure to speak ever give rise to liability in negligence under *Hedley Byrne* principles? In our view it can, but subject to the all important proviso that there has been, on the facts, a voluntary assumption of responsibility in the relevant sense and reliance on that assumption. These features may be much more difficult to infer in the case of mere silence than in the case of misrepresentation.'

98 In a Canadian case, *Can-Arc Helicopters v Textron*, cited by Tuckey LJ in *The Rebecca Elaine* [1995] 2 Lloyd's Rep 1, the British Columbia Supreme Court found the manufacturers liable for economic loss for a failure to give adequate warning of a defect in a service bulletin, which they knew their customers relied on.

CHAPTER 11

SHIP SALE AND PURCHASE

1 INTRODUCTION

The sale and purchase of used ships involves various stages in preparation before a contract is signed and before delivery of the ship to the buyer takes place. These stages can be grouped into three main ones. The negotiations and contract stage, the inspections stage and the completion stage.

At the negotiation stage, which is usually carried out by brokers appointed by the respective parties (buyer and seller), there will be telex exchanges with the seller's brokers making an invitation to offer. The parties are mainly concerned initially with the price, the particulars of the ship and lay-days to decide whether the transaction is worthwhile. Price bargaining and negotiations of the main terms of the contract usually follow this initial approach which may be prolonged or may be quickfire exchanges between professional brokers, having experience of many previous dealings and commercial knowledge of the trade. If the parties agree on the basic terms, a recap telex recapitulating the terms discussed is exchanged, being made subject to details to be agreed later. A large number of negotiations can, therefore, be split into negotiation and agreement of the main terms, followed by a similar process regarding details. The 'main terms' and 'details' are, usually, separated by the recap telex setting out the main terms agreed. The question often arises, as will be seen later, whether or not there is a contract at the time of the recap telex.[1] In this respect, the role and experience of the brokers engaged are crucial.

Provided the details are agreed, which may involve numerous back and forth communications, a formal contract for the sale of the ship is later drawn up. This is known as the Memorandum of Agreement (MOA), which usually incorporates a standard form contract like the Norwegian Sale Form, otherwise known as the NSF. Sometimes, the final agreement of the parties may be made conditional upon the drawing or the incorporation of the sale form. Invariably, the contract may still be subject to certain details such as obtaining approvals from directors or shareholders, or licences, or being subject to satisfactory inspection and other checks. It will be seen later in more detail that these 'subjects' indicate that the parties intend to have a conditional contract.

---

1   See Jamieson, A, *Shipbrokers and the Law*, 1997, LLP.

A deposit of 10% of the agreed price is paid by the buyer to commit him to the contract, which is held at an escrow account in the joint names of the parties.

The inspections stage involves: first the inspection of documents, such as the ship's class records, certificates of compliance with regulations, etc; and second, the physical inspection of the ship afloat, as provided for in the contract, by the buyer or his representative surveyor. The physical inspection is usually a superficial one of the ship and its logbook, unless the parties have agreed otherwise. After inspection, the buyer may confirm his commitment to buy by accepting the ship, or he may refuse her.

The third stage, known as the completion stage, involves pre-delivery matters including inspection of underwater parts by the classification society,[2] delivery of documents and the physical delivery of the ship upon payment of the balance of the contract price. There are also post-delivery matters to be taken care of at this stage.

Documents and physical delivery usually occur at different places, depending on where the ship is. The final inspection in drydock, at the port of delivery, is conducted by the surveyor of the classification society, who checks the ship's bottom and underwater parts, so that a clean certificate of class can be given. He may recommend some repairs to be effected at the seller's expense before delivery. Sometimes, in lieu of a drydock inspection, the buyer may appoint a diver, approved by the classification society, to carry out the underwater inspection while the ship is afloat.

The MOA specifies the procedures necessary for the closing meeting. The necessary documents are prepared. Such documents include: the closing memo, minutes of a meeting of the seller's directors and shareholders, a certificate of good standing, power of attorney, the bill of sale, certificate of class, any consents or licences required by government authority, a certificate by the registrar of the ship's registry permitting the sale. The seller must also arrange for the deletion of his name from the registry and the deletion of the ship from her existing flag, if the buyer wishes to change flag. He also cancels the insurance cover; pays off the mortgage and other debts and arranges for the repatriation of his crew from the vessel. When the seller is ready, he serves an advance notice of delivery, Notice of Readiness, on the buyer. If the ship is, indeed, ready, the buyer arranges for payment of bunkers and stores on board, as has been agreed, and instructs his bank, or financial institution, to make arrangements for payment on the actual delivery date.

These broad three stages are examined in turn under Sections A, B, and C.

---

2   The role of the classification societies is to ensure that the ship inspected will not be a danger to life or property at sea. Regular surveys of ships entered with a society aim to enhance safety by making recommendations for repairs. Rules and technical standards vary from society to society, but major societies, which are members of the IACS apply, by and large, similar practices.

SECTION A THE NEGOTIATIONS AND CONTRACT STAGE

2 THE MAKING OF THE CONTRACT AND GOOD FAITH

Unlike non-common law systems, which recognise and enforce an overriding principle of good faith in both the making of and during the performance of contracts, there is no such principle under English law. Bingham LJ, in *Interfoto Picture Library Ltd v Stiletto Visual Programmes Ltd*[3] (concerning the validity of power granted under a purported power of attorney), contrasted the two systems in an exemplary manner:

> In many civil law systems, and perhaps in most legal systems outside the common law world, the law of obligations recognises and enforces an overriding principle that, in making and carrying out contracts, parties should act in good faith. This does not simply mean that they should not deceive each other, a principle which any legal system must recognise; its effect is perhaps most aptly conveyed by such metaphorical colloquialisms as 'playing fair', 'coming clean' or 'putting one's cards face upwards on the table'. It is in essence a principle of fair and open dealing ... English law has, characteristically, committed itself to no such overriding principle, but has developed piecemeal solutions in response to demonstrated problems of unfairness. Many examples could be given. Thus, equity has intervened to strike down unconscionable bargains. Parliament has stepped in to regulate the imposition of exemption clauses and the form of certain hire purchase agreements. The common law has also made its contribution by holding that certain classes of contract require the utmost good faith, by treating as revocable what purports to be agreed estimates of damage but are, in truth, a disguised penalty for breach, and in many other ways.

In a later case, *Walford v Miles*,[4] the House of Lords confirmed in stronger terms that good faith during the negotiation stage of a contract is not compatible with the adversarial position of the parties.

> ... the concept of a duty to carry on negotiations in good faith is inherently repugnant to the adversarial position of the parties when involved in negotiations. Each party to the negotiations is entitled to pursue his (or her) own interest, so long as he avoids making misrepresentations, and to advance those interests they must be entitled, if they think it appropriate, to threaten to withdraw from further negotiations, or to withdraw in fact, in the hope that the opposite party might seek to reopen the negotiations by offering improved terms.

---

3   [1988] 1 All ER 348, pp 352–53.
4   [1992] 2 AC 128, p 138.

If one party has, however, undertaken to use his best, or reasonable, endeavours to negotiate an agreement with the other party in good faith, it is possible to infer a collateral contract. Then, the good faith aspect will have a legal effect representing an undertaking.[5] If the party who undertook to negotiate in good faith withdraws, his withdrawal may amount to a breach of that collateral contract, hence – subject to issues of causation – he may be liable to the other party in damages.

3 THE PARTIES' OBLIGATION TO AVOID MISREPRESENTATIONS

Although there is no general duty of disclosure and the parties are free to make their own investigations about each other's position and the ship intended to be purchased (the *caveat emptor* principle applies in this respect), they should not induce the other party to enter into the contract by making material representations, which they know are not true.

Statements or assurances made during negotiations leading to a contract may be either 'terms', which form the express terms of the contract, or statements, which do not intend to be part of the contract, but help to induce the contract. These are mere representations and, if they are untrue, they are misrepresentations. Mere 'puffs', as, for example, when the broker makes a comment that, if he had the money he would buy that ship, would be so vague as to be without effect.

Depending on whether an untrue statement became a contractual term, or whether it was only intended to induce the innocent party to enter into the contract, and it did so, different remedies are available to the innocent party.

3.1 Untrue statements forming express terms of the contract

If an untrue statement is made an express term of the contract, it will result in a breach of contract. The innocent party may either rescind the contract or claim damages and, depending on the breach, he may elect for both. Unlike the situation of a misrepresentation, which is not part of the contract (see below), the claim for damages on the ground of an untrue statement forming an express term of the contract does not depend on fraud or negligence. If the term is fundamental, or the seriousness of its breach goes to the root of the contract, the innocent party may treat the contract as repudiated by the other party and elect to terminate it, as well as claim damages.

---

5   *The Mercedes Envoy* [1995] 2 Lloyd's Rep 559, p 565.

3.2 Mere representation inducing the contract

By s 2(1) of the Misrepresentation Act (MA) 1967, where a person has entered into a contract after a misrepresentation has been made to him by another party and as a result he has suffered loss, the person making the misrepresentation would be liable in damages, as if the misrepresentation were made fraudulently, unless he proves that he had reasonable ground[6] for believing, and did believe up to the time the contract was made, that the facts represented were true. Where there is room for exercise of judgment, a misrepresentation ought not to be too easily found. The test is whether the representation was substantially correct. For a representation to have induced the contract, there must be material contribution to the decision made by the other party, not just mere support or encouragement.[7]

In the present context, for example, an issue may arise of the effect of a representation made by the seller's agent that the vessel is in class. Would that be a representation as to the condition of the vessel? It was held by Phillips J in *The Morning Watch*[8] that such a representation amounted to no more than a statement of the classification status of the vessel and did not constitute any implicit representation by the maker as to the actual condition of the vessel. (The class records are inspected by the buyer any way at the inspection stage).

Under s 2(2) of the MA 1967, the innocent party would have a right to rescission in lieu of damages, if he entered into the contract in reliance upon an innocent or negligent misrepresentation. The right to rescission may be lost, if the innocent party, upon learning of the misrepresentation, declares to perform the contract, or actually performs some act from which such an intention can be inferred, or where he fails to rescind for a considerable time after discovering the falsity.

Apart from the case of fraudulent misrepresentation, the court is given power by s 2(2) to grant damages in lieu of rescission, if it is equitable to do so having regard to the nature of the misrepresentation, the loss that would be caused if the contract were upheld, and the loss that the rescission would cause to the other party. On the other hand, where the misrepresentation was fraudulent and, as a result of it, the innocent party entered into the contract, the remedy will be both damages and rescission. The principle of measure of damages in such a case is that the claimant must be put in the same position

---

6   The absolute obligation, imposed under the Act, not to state facts which the representor could not show he had reasonable grounds for believing in their truth was stressed in *Howard Marine & Dredging Co Ltd v Ogden & Sons (Excavations) Ltd* [1978] 2 WLR 515 The capacity of barges was misrepresented by the barge-owner before a charterparty was concluded. The charterer had had a right in damages under the Act.

7   *Royscot Trust v Rogerson* [1991] 2 QB 297 (CA); *Avon Insurance v Swire Fraser* [2000] 1 All ER 573.

8   [1990] 1 Lloyd's Rep 547.

he would have been in, had the tort not been committed. In other words, had the misrepresentation not been made, the particular contract would not have been entered into, as it was held on the facts of *The Siben (No 2)*.[9] The recoverable loss is the loss directly caused by the misrepresentation, whether it was foreseeable or not (being subject to mitigation).[10]

In the event that someone other than the contracting party or his agent makes the misrepresentation, the innocent party will not be able to rely on the statutory protection afforded by the above MA 1967. His remedy, however, will lie at common law in damages, if he can establish that the person who made the misrepresentation owed a duty of care to him by reason of a special relationship between them. For a special relationship to exist, in accordance with the negligent misstatement principle, under *Hedley Byrne v Heller & Partners*,[11] three requirements must be fulfilled: (i) that the innocent party relied on the skill and judgment of the representor that he would make careful inquiries; (ii) that the representor knew, or ought reasonably to have known, that the innocent party was relying on his advice or representation; and (iii) that it was reasonable in the circumstances for the innocent party to rely on the representor.

Alternatively, he may sue the other party on the ground of the tort of deceit.

3.3 Brokers' role and risk management

Brokers play a significant role in the negotiations and will use their skills and persuasion to conclude a contract on best terms for their principals. They must be aware, however, of their potential exposure to liability for misrepresentation, if they overstep the mark in their excitement to conclude the contract and induce the other party by false statements. A broker owes a duty of care to his principal. Unless a special relationship of the *Hedley Byrne* type exists between the broker and the third party, the broker does not owe a duty of care to the latter. However, in the event that the buyer is induced to enter into the contract having relied on a misrepresentation made by the seller's broker about the ship, the broker's principal will suffer loss, if the buyer chooses to rescind the contract or claim damages. The principal could claim damages against his broker to recover his loss, if the latter, without the authority of his principal, gave untrue information about the ship in order to induce the contract.

If the broker is a sole broker for both seller and buyer, he will be in a precarious situation of conflict of interest, as he will owe a duty of care to both

---

9   *The Siben (No 2)* [1996] 1 Lloyd's Rep 35.

10   *Smith New Court Securities v Citibank* [1997] AC 254 (HL).

11   [1963] 1 Lloyd's Rep 485 (HL).

principals. In such circumstances the principles applicable to insurance brokers would apply.[12] It is beyond the scope of this book to unravel these issues here.

Another issue which is of importance to brokers' liability is liability arising from a broker having exceeded the limits of his authority. Agency principles have been examined elsewhere in this book.[13]

Brokers protect themselves for such risks under a special insurance cover for errors and omissions, or under mutual liability insurance for professional negligence, as well as for risks arising from breach of warranty of authority.

4 ON THE MAKING OF A BINDING CONTRACT AND RISK MANAGEMENT

4.1 Express your intention clearly

The negotiations stage is the stage during which the parties must exercise care and prevent possible risks, either of not having a firm agreement, or of being found bound to an agreement to which they did not yet wish to be bound.

Generally, in all contractual transactions, the court looks for a firm offer and an unconditional acceptance in determining whether or not a binding contract exists between the parties. It examines the intention of the parties from what they said and the surrounding circumstances.

The striking feature of sale and purchase transactions is that, sometimes, the brokers may have expressed themselves as if there was a final agreement but, upon true construction of their telex exchanges, it may transpire that either one or both parties did not objectively have such an intention. For example, they may not have completed the agreement because they have not agreed some details, or the terms may not have been sufficiently certain. If parts of the agreement, which are considered important by the parties, are left for further negotiations, or are so ambiguous that the ambiguity cannot be resolved by reference to the rest of the contract, the court or arbitrator will not complete an incomplete bargain by adding what might be considered reasonable. Conversely, if both parties believe that there is an agreement, when they have had previous dealings and have left out what would be

---

12 The court, however, has condemned a broker for acting in a dual capacity in a manner contrary to the interests of his principal, in this case the assured: *Vesta v Butcher* [1989] 1 Lloyd's Rep 331 (HL); see, also, *Anglo-African Merchants v Bayley* [1970] 1 QB 311 and *Eagle Star Insurance Co v Spratt* [1971] 2 Lloyd's Rep 116.

13 See Chapter 8, para 4.3.

considered by them as familiar gaps, the court will not destroy a commercial bargain.[14]

The general principles to be applied in deciding whether there has been a concluded contract were summarised by Cresswell J, in a recent case, *The Bay Ridge*,[15] as derived mainly from the judgments of Bingham and Lloyd LJJ in *Pagnan SPA v Feed Products Ltd*.[16] It is important to set out extracts from the summary for easy reference and guidance to brokers:

1 The court's task is to review what the parties said and did and from that material to infer whether the parties' objective intentions as expressed to each other were to enter into a mutually binding contract. The court is not concerned with what the parties may subjectively have intended.

2 There will be some cases where continued negotiations after a contract has allegedly been made will lead to the inference that the parties never in truth intended to bind themselves ... This will the more obviously be so where a term raised by one or other party early in the negotiations had not been the subject of agreement at the time of the alleged contract.

3 Where the parties have not reached agreement on terms which they regard as essential to a binding agreement, it naturally follows that there can be no binding agreement until they do agree on those terms ... But just as it is open to parties by their words and conduct to make clear that they do not intend to be bound until certain terms are agreed, even if those terms (objectively viewed) are of relatively minor significance, the converse is also true. The parties may by their words and conduct make it clear that they do intend to be bound, even though there are other terms yet to be agreed, even terms which may often or usually be agreed before a binding contract is made ... The parties are to be regarded as masters of their contractual fate. It is their intentions which matter and to which the court must strive to give effect.

4 Even if the parties have reached agreement on all the terms of the proposed contract, nevertheless they may intend that the contract shall not become binding until some further condition has been fulfilled. That is the ordinary 'subject to contract' case. Alternatively, they may intend that the contract shall not become binding until some further term or terms have been agreed ... Conversely, the parties may intend to be bound forthwith even though there are further terms still to be agreed or some further formality to be fulfilled ... If the parties fail to reach agreement on such further terms, the existing contract is not invalidated unless the failure to reach agreement on such further terms renders the contract as a whole unworkable or void for uncertainty.

---

14 See Goldrein, I (ed), *Ship Sale and Purchase*, 3rd edn, 1998, LLP, Chapter 2, p 63.

15 [1999] 2 Lloyd's Rep 227, p 240. This case is very important from the point of view of risk management in terms of choosing an experienced broker for the negotiations and a good solicitor for the litigation, if things have gone wrong. The judge's comments in this respect are very interesting; see facts of this case under para 4.4, below.

16 [1987] 2 Lloyd's Rep 601 (CA), pp 610, 611, 619.

5   The relevant principles of the law of contract are of universal application, but the proper inference to draw may differ widely according to the facts of the particular case. One case may concern a protracted negotiation, perhaps conducted in writing through lawyers, between parties who have had no dealings of any kind before. Another may concern a series of quickfire exchanges between professionals, both of them practitioners of the same trade, both having had many previous dealings, and with a wide measure of common experience, knowledge, and understanding between them. One could not sensibly approach these cases in the same way. Inferences which it would be appropriate to draw in one case might be quite inappropriate in the other. But the court's task remains essentially the same: to discern and give effect to the objective intention of the parties.

6   The courts recognise that business terminology and practices may differ from one market to the next. The courts recognise the efficacy of the maritime variant of the well known 'subject to contract'. The expression 'subject to details' enables owners and charterers to know where they are in negotiations and to regulate their business accordingly. The assumption of those in the shipping trade that it is effective to make clear that there is no binding agreement at that stage ought to be respected.[17]

4.2 The effect of non-signing a formal document upon the validity of the contract

Sometimes, an agreement may not be binding until a formal contract has been drawn up. It is, however, important for the parties to use phrases like 'subject to contract' to make it clear to the court and each other that they did not intend to be bound by a firm contract at that stage.

In *The Blankenstein*,[18] **Goff LJ** said:

> ... the court has to decide on the construction of the relevant documents, considered in the light of the surrounding circumstances, whether it was the intention of the parties that the negotiations were not to have contractual force until a formal document was signed.[19]

In this case, the buyer's brokers entered into negotiations with the sellers for the purchase of three vessels, after which a contract was concluded containing all terms of the sale including the price of the vessels. The only detail that was left for a later stage was the name of the purchasing company which was to be nominated in due course. An MOA was drawn up in the NSF for and on behalf of the buyer yet to be nominated. The buyer was required to pay a deposit at 10% of the contract price. By cl 13 of the agreement, the sellers had a

---

17   As in *The Junior K* [1988] 2 Lloyd's Rep 583, p 588 and *The CPC Gallia* [1994] 1 Lloyd's Rep 68, p 74.

18   [1985] 1 Lloyd's Rep 93 (CA).

19   *Ibid*, p 104.

right to cancel the contract, and a right to keep the deposit if the purchase did not go through. The MOA was not signed, and later on, when the buyer's company was nominated, a new MOA was drawn up. By the cancelling date, the agreement was still not signed and no deposit had being paid. The sellers elected to treat the contract as repudiated by the buyers, claimed damages and retained the deposit.

It was held that there was a binding contract between the parties irrespective of the fact that the MOA had not been signed. Fox LJ said:

> I see nothing in the present case to lead me to the conclusion that the parties contemplated the execution of the MOA as a prerequisite to the conclusion of a contract. That they contemplated and indeed agreed upon the execution of a written memorandum I accept. But that, of itself, is not conclusive. It is open to parties to agree to execute a formal document incorporating terms, which they have previously agreed. That is a binding contract. In the present case, on 8 July all the terms of the sale were agreed. And, it seems to me, that all the indications are that they were not intended to be subject to the execution of the memorandum.[20]

Similarly in *The Great Marine (No 2)*[21]

The sale was confirmed by a recap telex, which was not made subject to signing of the MOA. The price was agreed and the contract was to incorporate the terms of the standard form NSF 1987 in the MOA. The vessel was to be delivered on completion of her then voyage, but was delivered outside the agreed period. The buyers claimed damages for breach of contract. One of the issues for the judge was whether a binding agreement had been reached upon the exchange of telexes. It was held that, at the time of the recap telex, the parties were *ad idem* and, having manifested an intention to create binding legal relations, an oral agreement had been reached. The fact that the terms of the standard form of agreement were to be incorporated into the contract did not prevent a binding agreement being reached. The signing of the form was not a condition precedent to the contract. The buyers were entitled to insist on delivery of the vessel at the requisite time.

The phrase, commonly used, 'otherwise NSF to be mutually agreed and to incorporate agreed terms/conditions' was construed in the context of *The Bay Ridge*.[22] The buyer's opening offer was expressed to be a firm offer in a sense that it was based on main terms, but subject to agreement of further terms and conditions. It was held that, until all further terms and conditions had been agreed, there was no concluded agreement.

---

20 [1985] 1 Lloyd's Rep 93, p 97.
21 [1990] 2 Lloyd's Rep 250 (1st inst).
22 [1999] 2 Lloyd's Rep 227.

4.3 The effect of 'buyer to be nominated' on the validity of the contract

Usually a buyer has to form the corporate vehicle by which the ship can be bought. A company may already exist for this purpose, but often, when an opportunity arises for the purchase of a ship, a buyer may not yet be certain about the outcome of negotiations. Thus, the buying interests may not wish to go into expense of incorporating a company until agreement has been reached. In such circumstances, the contract will permit the subsequent nomination of the buyer, whereupon the contract between the original parties will be novated. The nominated company will enter the contract in substitution for the original buyer. By the method of novation, all contractual rights and obligations of the original buyer are transferred to the nominated one and the original buyer is discharged. Novation, however, requires formal consents to be obtained by the sellers and the novated company. The sellers, in addition, may require a specific time by which the nomination can be made and a guarantee to be given by the original buyer that the substituted buyer will perform. The following two cases highlight problems that can arise with novation.

The Blankenstein[23]

The sellers entrusted the task of selling their three vessels, *Blankenstein*, *Bartenstein* and *Birkenstein* to their broker Mr Nebelsiek, while the broker of intending buyers was Mr Panas. Following negotiations between the brokers, a telex was sent on 4 July 1977, containing what was described as an official firm offer for all three vessels at $2 m. The offer was made on behalf of Messrs Raftopoulos and/or for company or companies to be nominated by them in due course.

On 8 July 1977, a concluded contract was reached in which all the terms and conditions of the sale and the price of $2,365,000 were agreed save for the name of the purchasing company or companies which had yet to be disclosed.

There was a further exchange of telexes between the brokers and on 13 July 1977, an MOA was drawn up between the sellers and the buyers, Raftopoulos, for and on behalf of companies still to be nominated. The memorandum was on the NSF and provided that the buyers were to pay a deposit of 10% of the purchase money on signing the contract. By cl 13, it was provided *inter alia* that:

> Should the purchase money not be paid ... the sellers have the right to cancel this contract in which the amount deposited shall be forfeited to the sellers.

---

23 *Damon Compania Naviera v Hapag-Lloyd International SA (sub nom The Blankenstein)* [1985] 1 Lloyd's Rep 93.

The memorandum was not signed by the Raftopoulos brothers or by any company or other person nominated by them.

On 1 August 1977, Mr Panas sent another telex to Mr Nebelsiek in which he stated that the buyers nominated as purchasing company Damon Compania Naviera SA and requested a new MOA to be issued in which the buyers would be Damon. However, at the time the Raftopoulos brothers had not acquired the shares in Damon and it was not until after the nomination that this occurred. The new MOA, recording Damon as buyers, was sent to the buyer's broker, but neither was the agreement signed nor was the deposit paid by the time required. The sellers withdrew from the contract reserving all their rights and claimed damages against Damon, which the arbitrator awarded stating a special case for the court. Damon challenged the award on the ground that the purported novation was never ratified and was ineffectual.

The lower court and the Court of Appeal decided that there was an agreement of which payment of the deposit was a fundamental term. Although Raftopoulos brothers became directors of the company after the nomination, it was highly likely that at the time of the nomination they had authority to make the nomination. It was always understood, Fox LJ said, that the Raftopoulos brothers were not buying the ships in their own name, but that they would eventually nominate a company. But the contract could not be forced on Damon without its agreement. The issue was whether Damon accepted such nomination between the time of the nomination and the repudiation of contract. The Lords Justice accepted that, on the evidence, there was acceptance of the novation by Damon on the footing that the nomination was ratified by two subsequent telexes, sent by one of the brothers with full power to do so, on behalf of Damon. In any event, on the facts, either the original nomination was authorised, or it was ratified afterwards.

By contrast, in *The Action*,[24] the nomination was ineffectual and the original buyers failed to show that the nomination was validly accepted by the nominated company.

Briefly, by an MOA on the NSF, Action Maritime, as sellers, and Kasmas, as buyers, agreed on the sale of *The Action*. The MOA described the buyers to be nominated by Kasmas and later a purported nomination of Lagonissi was made. The deposit was duly paid by Kasmas. At the time of signature of the MOA, the ship was on the high seas. She proceeded to Lisbon and, shortly thereafter, the sellers served notice of readiness of the vessel to the buyers. After inspection by the buyers, defects were found in the vessel, which were notified to the sellers. The latter, in the spirit of good co-operation, were willing to put them right, although they regarded such defects of minor significance. The buyers still insisted that the defects had not been put right

24   [1987] 1 Lloyd's Rep 283.

and refused to take delivery. After many exchanges between the parties, the buyers cancelled the contract and the sellers accepted buyers' conduct as repudiation claiming damages and the forfeiture of the deposit against Kasmas, as the original party, against Lagonissi as the substituted party, and against three Kasmas brothers individually as being the company's undisclosed principals at the time of signing the MOA. Kasmas alleged, *inter alia*, that after the nomination of Lagonissi, the latter became the sole contracting party and Kasmas were absolved of any further obligations under the contract, and were also retrospectively relieved of their former obligation, so that they were entitled to be repaid the deposit.

It was held that the original buyers remained the contracting party.

The truth of the matter was that the buyers wanted to get out of this contract because of the falling market, but they were caught being themselves in a repudiatory breach. This case is relevant also later on, but the point to be made here is what was the effect of the cancellation by the buyers on the purported novation. The facts of *The Blankenstein* were distinguished. The court rejected the submission of the defendants that novation takes place at the moment of the nomination, whatever the nature and the circumstances of the contract. The terms of the contract in this case undermined any possibility of novation prior to the transfer of the vessel. Also a strong factor against Kasmas was that all the telex exchanges, including the cancellation one, were despatched by Kasmas. Since the transfer of the vessel was forestalled by the buyer's cancellation, the Kasmas company remained the contracting party and novation of Lagonissi never in fact occurred.[25]

In terms of risk management, the buyers could well have been better off to stick to the contract rather than cancel it in order to obtain the advantage, as they thought, of the falling market. The result of having to pay damages (the difference in market value) to the sellers and legal costs to defend the case, as well as the costs of the winning party, must have cost them more than the amount they thought they would save by getting out of this contract.

4.4 What do 'subjects' mean?

Where the main terms have been agreed, but there are subsequent details to be discussed, there will be no legally binding agreement until those details have been agreed upon. It is, at best, a conditional agreement. If the recap telex is made 'subject to contract', it is clearly understood that there is no binding agreement, yet. Frequently, however, the parties use the expression 'subject details' or 'subrecon' which are familiar expressions to both chartering and sale/purchase brokers. The question that has arisen in quite a number of chartering and sale of ship cases is whether or not the parties have made their

25 [1987] 1 Lloyd's Rep 283, p 310.

intention to be bound clear to each other. How the courts have approached this issue is shown in the following examples.

The Gladys (No 2)[26]

In this case the buyer's broker, acting on behalf of the Indian Government, indicated acceptance of a firm offer for the purchase of this vessel for scrap. The understanding was that the broker would be supplied with an MOA on the NSF, blank as to details of the vessel; the price and other conditions requiring completion and, without additional clauses added, such blanks and clauses were left for the broker to draft before final agreement and signature. The buyers later withdrew. The sellers claimed that there was a binding contract and, by appointing an arbitrator as provided by the contract, claimed a declaration to that effect and damages for breach, while the buyers disputed the existence of an agreement and, consequently, of the validity of the arbitration agreement. The issue for the court was the construction of the contemporary documents and correspondence between the parties. The court came to the conclusion – having examined the parties' previous dealings – that, on this occasion, no final agreement had been reached. It further held that, it was clear from the facts, that an oral agreement had been reached only in terms which plainly contemplated that there were further terms to be agreed, albeit only matters of detail, before a binding contract was made.

From a risk management aspect, an important point in negotiations which arose in this case was that, on the basis of previous dealings between the Indian Government (which was determining what vessels to buy through a committee) and the owners (sellers) of the vessels, some deals were indicated by the committee to be 'subject of a firm offer' and others 'subrecon'. With respect to this particular vessel there was an exchange of telexes from which the court inferred that the parties had not come to a firm agreement about the price, date of delivery and whether the terms would be on the basis of the sale of previous ships. Thus, the deal was on the basis of 'subrecon', despite the brokers' failure to spell this out in the telex. Just before the final agreement was communicated to the committee, the latter withdrew because, in the meantime, the committee had found out that the ship was a reefer and reefers were not within the purchasing policy of the Indian Government. Although this might have been a matter of detail, particularly with regard to the purchase of a ship for scrap, the buyer was entitled to make its inquiries to check whether the information previously supplied proved to be significantly in error.[27]

---

26 [1994] 2 Lloyd's Rep 402.
27 *Ibid*, p 409.

Therefore, the court concluded – relying on principles derived from a previous authority *Pagnan SPA v Feed Products Ltd*[28] – that the court's task is to review what the parties said and did and, from that material, to infer whether the parties' objective intentions as expressed to each other were to enter into a mutually binding contract. The court was not concerned with what the parties subjectively had intended. The decision of Bingham J in the above case was endorsed by the Court of Appeal where Lloyd LJ, as he then was, added:

> It is for the parties to decide whether they wish to be bound and if so, by what terms, whether important or unimportant. It is the parties who are, in the memorable phrase coined by the judge, 'the masters of their contractual fate'. Of course, the more important the term is, the less likely it is that the parties will have left it for the future decision. But there is no legal obstacle which stands in the way of the parties agreeing to be bound now while deferring important matters to be agreed later.[29]

Lloyd LJ thought that the distinction between essential and non- essential terms was misleading.

In the context of a charterparty negotiations, the meaning of the expression 'subject to details' arose for construction in the following case, which has a bearing upon negotiations in the context of sale and purchase:

The Junior K[30]

Negotiations for a charterparty were concluded by the despatch and receipt of the recap telex in which it was stated that the fixture was 'sub details'. The terms agreed were set out ending with the words 'sub dets Gencon CP', meaning subject to the details of a Gencon charterparty standard form, the details and alternative provisions of which require exercise of choice by the parties. The principal issue was whether there was a binding contract. It was held that no contract had been concluded, in this case, at that stage, since the parties had not made a positive selection of the desired alternative provisions of the form and no discussion had taken place about these options. Against this background, it was clear that the words used conveyed that there was a fixture conditional upon agreement being reached about the details of the Gencon form. Steyn J stated:

> The expression 'subject to details ' enables owners and charterers to know where they are in negotiations and to regulate their business accordingly. It is a device which tends to avoid disputes and the assumption of those in the shipping trade, that it is effective to make clear that there is no binding agreement at that stage, ought to be respected.[31]

---

28 [1987] 2 Lloyd's Rep 601 (CA), p 610.

29 *Ibid*, p 619.

30 [1988] 2 Lloyd's Rep 583.

31 *Ibid*, p 588: the judge referred to previous authorities; *The Solholt* [1981] [contd]

In a couple of later decisions the term 'subject to details' was construed in the same way. The first, **The CPC Gallia**,[32] concerned the carriage of a jet foil from Kobe to Las Palmas under a Conline booking note 'subject to details/logical amendments'. The precise form of the booking note became later the subject of a dispute, particularly a clause with regard to substitution of the vessel and transshipment. CPC line took the view that there was a contract while the shipper CTM held the opposite view. The court held, in favour of the shippers, that the term 'subject to details', despite the additional words 'logical amendments', meant that a contract had still to be drawn up on the basis of the booking note. If the parties intended to restrict the customary effect of the term by the additional words, the words of limitation ought to be made clear in their content and context. 'Logical amendments', therefore, were interpreted as an illustration rather than a limitation.

The next decision is to be contrasted only in terms of the outcome, but the court gave the same interpretation. In **Granits SA v Benship International Inc**,[33] a charterparty was concluded orally and the vessel was to be nominated for the carriage of bulk wheat from France to Bangladesh. Benship later alleged that there was no contract because the negotiations were made 'subject to details' and the parties were not *ad idem* over certain terms. The court accepted the evidence of the Granit, the plaintiffs, that the words 'subject to contract' were not used in the negotiations. The plaintiffs' evidence was that, if there had been no intention to have a binding agreement, these words would have been used. The fact that minor matters remained for an agreement to be reached did not mean that a binding agreement had not been concluded.

Messina v POL[34] is a good demonstration of how negotiations are conducted by numerous exchanges of proposals and counterproposals until an agreement is reached, if, indeed, it is reached. The central issue here was the construction of these exchanges and, in particular, the words that the terms of the NSF were 'subject to appropriate amendments to be mutually agreed'. Until such amendments were agreed, Clarke J, as he then was, held there would be no agreement. This was supported by the fact that the NSF contains 15 printed clauses many of which have gaps, which have to be filled in. Clarke J said:[35]

---

31 [contd] 2 Lloyd's Rep 574 and *The Nissos Samos* [1985] 1 Lloyd's Rep 378 in which there had been some observations, albeit that they did not form part of the *ratio decidendi*, about the meaning of this expression to the effect that there was no contract until the subsidiary terms were agreed. In the USA, however, the judge commented, the details were regarded unimportant if the parties can go back to the printed form. However, it was observed that there has been no uniform approach by the judiciary and arbitrators there.

32 [1994] 1 Lloyd's Rep 68.

33 [1994] 1 Lloyd's Rep 526.

34 [1995] 2 Lloyd's Rep 567, and, in particular, pp 578–81.

35 *Ibid*, pp 578, 579.

These negotiations were approached in the usual way. There were exchanges between the brokers during which different terms were agreed in principle at different times. Once all the terms were agreed, it was contemplated that the board [of the sellers] would give approval and that an MOA would be drawn up setting out all of the agreed terms. I would not expect the parties to have intended that there be a legally binding agreement until then. That conclusion seems to me to be borne out by the terms of the NSF condition, namely that the terms were to be subject to 'appropriate amendments to be mutually agreed'. If one asks what was to happen if there was no mutual agreement, the natural answer is that no NSF would or could be agreed and, if no NSF was or could be agreed, there would be no agreement for the sale of the vessels unless the parties intended that there should be an agreement of sale notwithstanding the absence of an MOA on the terms of the NSF. Yet, I do not see how it could be held that the parties intended that there should be a legally binding contract for the sale of the ships in those circumstances, when the agreement expressly provides that, otherwise, the terms of the NSF subject to appropriate amendment are to be mutually agreed ... A term such as the NSF condition is recognised among brokers as meaning, in effect, that the agreement is subject to contract in the sense that, there is to be no binding agreement, until the MOA is signed.

In this case, the facts that determined that there was no binding agreement were that the NSF was subject to appropriate amendments, and not the fact that the form had not been signed, which in itself would not be a reason to hold that there was no agreement.[36]

The terms made subject to construction by the court in a more recent case, *The Bay Ridge*,[37] were a combination of 'approvals' and 'subjects' the effect of which, as appeared in the exchange of telexes, was examined by the judge in order to determine whether or not there was a binding contract. This is a very interesting decision in which the problems that can arise in this connection are highlighted, and the telex exchanges of the parties are worth reading from a risk management point of view, but it is not possible to quote these lengthy exchanges here.

Briefly, the sellers and the buyers negotiated the sale of this ship through their respective brokers. The exchanges and telephone communications culminated in the recap telex dated 28 June 1995.The issues were:

(a) whether that telex constituted a binding contract. The plaintiffs (sellers) sought a declaration that there was no concluded contract. The defendants (buyers), who had commenced arbitration claiming damages for the difference between the contract and the market value, argued that there was, and that the second defendants were the nominated buyers;

---

36 See *The Blankenstein* [1985] 1 Lloyd's Rep 93 and *The Great Marine (No 2)* [1991] 1 Lloyd's Rep 421 (CA), above.

37 [1999] 2 Lloyd's Rep 227.

(b) if there was an agreement, did the sellers' brokers have authority to conclude a contract on such terms?;

(c) if there was an agreement between the brokers, but no contract was in fact concluded because the sellers' broker did not have authority, were these brokers, who had been joined as a third party, liable to indemnify the buyers for breach of warranty of authority;

(d) alternatively, if a contract were concluded, would the sellers' brokers be liable to the sellers for exceeding their actual authority?

The central questions for consideration in this context,[38] as pleaded by the sellers, were the following:

(1) one of the terms of the buyers was 'sellers warrant vessel approved by all major oil companies' – the sellers never agreed to this term, so the buyers' requirement was left unresolved;

(2) there were two subjects, buyers' inspection and approval of classification records and buyers' inspection and approval of onboard condition survey, which were never lifted;

(3) the statement in the recap, 'buyers right to place two representatives on board *after conclusion/confirmation of sale by telex/fax*' (emphasis added), was inconsistent with the allegation that a contract had already been concluded.

The judge concluded that there was no binding agreement upon the following grounds:[39]

> There was a good commercial sense in seeking to agree main terms first. If main terms could not be agreed there was no point in going further. If main terms were agreed the parties would, thereafter, proceed to seek to agree further terms and conditions (by way of amendments, additions and deletions to NSF–87). There would be no concluded agreement until all further terms and conditions had been agreed.

> Negotiations continued orally and by telex/fax during 28 June. The recap at the end of the day recorded what had been agreed to date as to certain main terms. There was good commercial sense in recording the position reached at the end of the day, but the objective intentions of the parties were that negotiations would continue until all further terms and conditions had been agreed ...

> The words in the recap fax 'otherwise *per* NSF–87 mutually agreed ...' meant in context 'otherwise *per* NSF–87 to be mutually agreed ...'

> The words, 'We are pleased to confirm the sale of the above vessel as follows: ...' must be construed in context. Amendments, additions and deletions to NSF–87 remained to be agreed. The fact that there was no concluded contract of sale at the end of the day on 28 June is confirmed by the

---

38 See, also, under para 4.1, above.
39 See pp 242–43.

words in para 11(c) of the recap, *'after conclusion/confirmation of sale by telex/fax'* (emphasis added) ...

> The common understanding was that this would take place after 28 June. All oral exchanges between the brokers on 28 June proceeded on the basis that main terms would be agreed first (and embodied in a recap to the extent that the same were agreed) and that negotiations would follow as to appropriate amendments, additions and deletions to NSF–87. Thus, the position reflected in para 8 of Oceanbulk's opening offer, ('Otherwise NSF–87 to be mutually agreed and to incorporate agreed term/conditions'), continued throughout. At no stage did these inexperienced brokers consider the detailed provisions of NSF–87. This was to be left to a later stage ...

> On June 28 the parties sought to establish agreement on main terms. There was no intention to create legal relations at the time of the recap. The question of oil majors approval (which had been accorded the status of a main term by Oceanbulk) was still being negotiated at the end of the day. The mutual agreement of amendments, additions and deletions to NSF–87 had yet to take place.

He further held that,

> ... without agreement of the details, the right of buyers to place divers for the underwater inspection would be unworkable. Since the first issue was decided in favour of the sellers, there was no need to consider the remaining issues about the brokers' authority and the possibility of breach of warranty of authority.

These cases illustrate how important it is for the parties and their brokers to be careful at the negotiation stage to record their agreement precisely and express in clear terms whether or not they wish at that stage to be bound by a final contract.

5 CLASSIFICATION OF TERMS OF A CONTRACT AND THEIR IMPORTANCE

5.1 At common law

Although the terms of a contract were explained in the previous chapter, it is pertinent to summarise their significance in the context of this chapter as well. The terms of a contract under English common law are divided into three categories: conditions, warranties and innominate or intermediate terms. Breach of the first will amount to repudiation entitling the innocent party to elect either to terminate the contract and also claim damages, or to go on with the contract and claim damages only. A breach of a warranty (except in insurance contracts in which the insurer is automatically discharged from liability from the date of the breach) does not entitle the innocent party to terminate the contract, but to claim damages. The consequences of a breach of an intermediate or innominate term (lying between a condition and a warranty)[40] will depend on the nature and seriousness of the breach.[41]

Even if the parties describe a term as a condition, it does not mean that it is a condition, it will depend on the construction of the term in the context of the whole contract.[42] An apt example, in this context, is the term which became a cause of a dispute in *The Action*.[43] The ship was to be delivered in the same physical condition as she was when was inspected. The buyers alleged that there were defects when notice was given to them for delivery. Although the sellers agreed to make repairs, the buyers cancelled the contract before the sellers completed the repairs. The court construed the term of the condition of the ship on delivery as an innominate term and not as a condition precedent. If the parties wanted to make it a condition, they should expressly set out in the contract the right to cancel in the event of a breach of a term. There was judgment for the sellers.

In principle, contracts are made to be performed and not to be avoided according to the whims of market fluctuations and, where there is a free choice between two constructions, the court should tend to prefer that construction which will ensure performance and will not encourage avoidance of contractual obligations.[44]

5.2 Under the Sale of Goods Act 1979

Similarly, the Sale of Goods Act (SOGA) 1979 provides, in s 11(2), that where a contract of sale is subject to a condition to be fulfilled by the seller, the buyer may waive the condition, or may elect to treat the breach of the condition as a breach of a warranty and not as a ground for treating the contract as repudiated.

In s 61(1), the Act defines a warranty as a term the breach of which gives rise to a claim for damages, and not to a right to reject the goods and treat the contract as repudiated. Whether a stipulation in a contract of sale is a condition or a warranty, depends in each case on the construction of the contract; and a stipulation may be a condition, though called a warranty in the contract (s 11(3)).

The SOGA 1979, by s 10, does not regard a stipulation as to time of payment as a term of essence of a contract of sale, unless a different intention

---

40 *Bunge Corporation v Tradax Export SA* [1981] 2 Lloyd's Rep 1 (HL).
41 *Hong Kong Fir Shipping v Kawasaki Kisen Kaisha* [1961] 2 Lloyd's Rep 478 (CA).
42 *Schuler v Wickham Machine Tools Sales Ltd* [1973] 2 Lloyd's Rep 53, or [1974] AC 235 (HL).
43 [1987] 1 Lloyd's Rep 283.
44 *Cehave NV v Bremer (The Hansa Nord)* [1975] 2 Lloyd's Rep 445 (CA), p 457, *per* Roskill LJ.

appears from the terms of the contract. Whether any other stipulation as to time is or is not of essence of the contract depends on the terms of the contract.

5.2.1 Sale by description

It has already been seen in the previous chapter that the strict rule under the SOGA 1979 concerning the implied terms that goods sold by description should comply with that description has been amended by s 4 of the Sale and Supply of Goods Act (SSGA) 1994. The effect of the amendment is that where goods have been sold commercially, for example, not to a consumer, a breach of description, or quality, or fitness for purpose will not be treated as a breach of a condition but as a breach of a warranty, if the breach is so slight that it would be unreasonable for the buyer to reject the goods (ship).

It has also been seen in the shipbuilding chapter (Chapter 10) that the SSGA 1994 has replaced the term 'merchantable quality' with the new implied condition of 'satisfactory quality', although this change may not be so relevant to the sale of second hand ships, which will depend on what the parties agreed.

But, is it necessary to describe the ship adequately in the sale contract? The preamble to the saleform contains the classification of the ship, the year in which she was built, the builder, flag, call sign, register number, place of registration and register tonnage. There may not be a misdescription of the ship's year of building or registration if it falls within the *de minimis* rule and the certificate of registry, as well as the builder's certificate provide *prima facie* evidence of the year in which the ship was built.[45]

5.2.2 The passing of property

By s 17(1) of the SOGA 1979, where there is a contract for the sale of specific or ascertained goods, the property on them is transferred to the buyer at such time as the parties to the contract intend it to be transferred. Section 17(2) provides that, for the purpose of ascertaining the intention of the parties, regard shall be had to the terms of the contract, the conduct of the parties and the circumstances of the case.

By s 18, unless a different intention appears, the intention of the parties as to the time at which the property in the goods is to pass to the buyer is ascertained in accordance with five rules depending on the circumstances of the case. Two of these rules are mentioned below, by way of a contrast, the second of which is relevant to the sale of second hand ships.[46]

45　*The Troll Park* [1988] 1 Lloyd's Rep 55, approved by CA [1988] 2 Lloyd's Rep 423.
46　The second rule is also relevant to shipbuilding contracts, see Chapter 10.

Rule 1: where there is an unconditional contract for the sale of specific goods in a deliverable state, the property in the goods passes to the buyer when the contract is made, and it is immaterial whether the time of payment or the time of delivery, or both, is postponed. This rule is relevant to the first category of sale contracts made by s 2 of the SOGA 1979, namely, the sale contract and not the agreement to sell. Section 61(5) defines a 'deliverable state' as being such a state that a buyer would be bound to take delivery under the contract.

Rule 2: where there is a contract for the sale of specific goods and the seller is bound to do something to the goods for the purpose of putting them into a deliverable state, the property does not pass until the thing is done and the buyer has notice that it has been done. This rule refers to an agreement to sell, the second category under s 2 of the Act, where the property passes at a future date.

The sale of second hand ships is normally an agreement to sell, in which the parties provide in the saleform that, in the event of deficiencies found at the inspection stage, the seller will be obliged to carry out repairs and put the ship in a deliverable state. Before notice of delivery, the ship is not yet in a deliverable state and the parties' intention is that property shall pass upon payment on the day of delivery. Property cannot pass when the contract is made, unless the agreement is for a sale 'as is where is', which means that the buyer has chosen an 'outright' sale, if he had already inspected her before the contract was concluded. In such a case, the seller is not required to do repairs on the ship after the conclusion of the contract, but, even in this situation, property shall pass when the parties intended it to pass.

Naamlooze Vennootschap Stoomvaart Maatschappij 'Vredoobert' v European Shipping Co Ltd [47]

An agreement for sale of five second hand ships provided that buyers were to 'buy now'. Before any part of the purchase price had been paid, one of the vessels was sunk by a collision, and the insurance company paid the seller on the policy. The buyer claimed that property had passed to him, and he was, therefore, entitled to the benefit of the insurance policy.

The House of Lords, affirming the decision of the Court of Appeal, held that the words 'buy now' did not mean an immediate transfer of property. This was an agreement to sell and not a sale. Viscount Dunedin remarked that:

> ... using the phraseology of the SOGA 1979, I look on this contract as a 'contract to sell' and not a 'sale' ... in determining whether a contract is a sale

---

[47] (1926) 25 LlL Rep 210.

or an agreement to sell, is to see whether there remains something to be done. Now, here there was certainly something to be done.[48]

6 CONTRACTUAL TERMS UNDER STANDARD FORMS OF THE SALE CONTRACT

The sale contract most frequently used is the NSF 1987, its predecessors being dated 1983 and 1966. The latest edition of NSF, however, is Saleform 1993. The parties must specify at the outset which form is going to be used. Another sale contract of second hand ships is the Nipponsale 1993, which is used by Japanese sellers. Both types of forms concern an absolute sale,[49] which comprises physical possession and transfer of property at the same time in exchange of payment of the contract price. It is not the scope of this book to examine all contracts and all their clauses.[50] Only clauses that have presented problems are examined. Comparisons between clauses of the various forms are made where a situation warrants drawing a comparison.

6.1 When is the deposit payable?

As earlier stated, the buyer is required to pay a deposit of 10% as security for the due performance of the contract. **Clause 2** of both NSF forms (1987 and 1993) provides for the payment of deposit as follows:

> As a security for the correct fulfilment of this contract, the buyers shall pay a deposit of 10% of the purchase money within …banking days from the date of this agreement. This amount shall be deposited with [a bank] and held by them in a joint account for the sellers and the buyers. Interest, if any, to be credited to the buyers. Any fee charge for holding said deposit shall be borne equally by the sellers and the buyers.

Payment of the deposit is a fundamental term of the contract, breach of which entitles the seller to cancel the contract and recover his loss as damages.[51] What is the measure of damages depends on the contract terms. Clause 2 must be read together with cl 13, which has been amended (see para 7.1.1, below). If the buyer fails to pay the purchase money, the seller will be entitled to cancel the contract, and the buyer will forfeit his deposit and all the interest that has accrued on it. In *The Blankenstein*,[52] the contention made by the

---

48 (1926) 25 LlL Rep 210, p 212.
49 Other types of sale are by instalments, or by credit, which may involve a mortgage on the ship granted to the seller as security, or by hire purchase, or judicial sale.
50 Reference will be made to *op cit*, Goldrein, fn 14.
51 *The Selene G* [1981] 2 Lloyd's Rep 180.
52 [1985] 1 Lloyd's Rep 93.

buyers was that, since cl 2 of the NSF provided for payment of the deposit 'on signing' the contract, the deposit never became payable, as the contract was never signed. According to Fox LJ, the situation that existed in this case was that a binding contract had already been entered into, the consequence being that:

(a) the parties became bound to sign the MOA incorporating the agreed terms within a reasonable time; and

(b) the purchaser became bound, upon signing the memorandum, to pay the deposit.

The Court of Appeal also held that the plaintiff (seller) was entitled to recover the amount of the deposit by way of damages for breach of contract, in which cl 13 of the 1966 NSF (which was used in this case) did not specify the kind of damages in case of non-payment of the deposit. It will be seen at para 7.1.1, below, that cl 13 of the 1987 NSF has been amended.

The payment of the deposit is linked to the right of the buyer, as provided by a **new cl 15** of the 1993 NSF, to place two representatives on board the ship for familiarisation purposes and as observers, but without interfering with the operation of the vessel.

Where there is a sale and a sub-sale, the head-buyer may use the sub-sale deposit to pay the seller, but the sale and sub-sale must be back to back. Problems may arise if the buyers' lawyers omit to reconcile the delivery date under both contracts, as is illustrated by the following case.

The Ranger[53]

The contract between the sellers and the head-buyers required the buyers to put up a deposit of 10% of the purchase price and gave the buyers a right to cancel the contract if the vessel was not delivered by 30 June. Upon failure of delivery on the due date by the sellers, the deposit and accrued interest would immediately be released to the buyers. The head-buyers sub-contracted to sell the vessel to the second defendants for the same price and on the same terms, but the delivery and cancelling date for this agreement was 31 May of the same year. The deposit for the first contract was funded by the deposit paid under the second contract, and the amount was paid into an interest bearing account in the joint names of the second defendants (the buyers under the sub-sale) and the head-sellers' agent. Upon non-delivery of the vessel under the sub-sale by the cancelling date, the second defendants cancelled the sub-contract on 1 June. On 13 June, the head-sellers tendered the ship for delivery under the head-contract to the buyer but the latter refused to accept the vessel. Treating the buyers' conduct as a repudiation, the head-sellers cancelled the contract and sought the release of the deposit. The second defendants refused.

---

53 [1970] 1 Lloyd's Rep 32.

It was held that since the second defendants had consented to the use of their names as one of the two parties to the opening of the joint account, the second defendants were ratifying its use as agents for the head-buyers. Therefore, as the head-sellers were entitled to the deposit as against the head-buyers, the sub-buyers had no claim to the deposit as against the head-sellers.

For risk management purposes, the mistake that was made in this case was that the date of delivery under the second contract was earlier than the date under the first contract. It will be seen below and at para 7.1.1 when the deposit can be forfeited to the seller.

SECTION B THE INSPECTIONS STAGE

The relevant contractual terms continue below.

6.2 Inspections by the buyer

At this stage it will be determined whether or not the purchase will become definite, unless there are still other 'subjects' to be confirmed. **Clause 4** of Saleform 1987 provides for two types of inspection: '... the buyer shall have a right to inspect the vessel's classification records and declare whether same are accepted or not ... [within a certain time agreed].' The inspection of the records will reveal the history of ship's maintenance and compliance with the requirements of class.

The clause also provides for the physical inspection of the ship afloat:

... the sellers shall provide for inspection[54] of the vessel at ...The buyers shall undertake the inspection without undue delay to the vessel. Should the buyers cause such delay, they shall compensate the sellers for the losses thereby incurred. The buyers shall inspect the vessel afloat without opening up and without cost to the sellers. During the inspection, the vessel's log books for engine and deck shall be made available for the buyers' examination. If the vessel is accepted after such afloat inspection, the purchase shall become definite – except for other possible subjects in this contract – provided the sellers receive written or telexed notice from the buyers within 48 hours after completion of such afloat inspection. Should notice of acceptance of the vessel's classification records and of the vessel not be received by the sellers as aforesaid, the deposit shall immediately be released, whereafter this contract shall be considered null and void.

The drafting of this clause is reasonably clear and the parties ought to know where they stand in respect of their respective rights and obligations. It gives

---

54 *The Merak* [1976] 2 Lloyd's Rep 250: the sellers have an obligation to provide the vessel for inspection, otherwise they will be in breach of contract.

an unfettered discretion to the buyer whether or not to accept the ship and, at this stage, he has an opportunity to refuse the ship and recover the deposit if he realises that he made a bad bargain because, for example, there has been a fall in the market between the contract and the inspection.[55] It is submitted, however, that his rejection should be based on reasonable grounds, otherwise, he may be at risk of forfeiting the deposit, unless he might be better off commercially looking for another ship than accepting to proceed with this purchase.

The equivalent clause in the **1993 Saleform is cl 4(b)**, which includes three variations: (a) the inspection can be other than afloat – for example, it can be in the drydock; (b) the notice period of acceptance is extended to 72, instead of 48, hours; (c) the deposit together with interest accrued is released by the seller (instead of just the deposit) if the notice is not received within the time provided. An additional clause, cl 4(a) is included which is a confirmation that the ship has already been inspected, if she has been, before the contract was concluded. Either clause should be deleted depending on whether or not the inspection has taken place. This optional clause reflects market practice. The effect of choosing this alternative is an outright sale to the buyer, without the need to give notice of the vessel's acceptance to the seller.

SECTION C THE COMPLETION STAGE

This stage leads up to physical and document delivery. At this time the classification society will perform the pre-delivery inspection in drydock at the port of delivery. The next phases will be pre-delivery, actual delivery and post-delivery. The relevant contractual terms continue below.

6.3 Inspection by classification society (drydocking)

Clause 6 of the 1987 Saleform is usually known as the drydocking clause. A surveyor of the classification society with which the ship is entered carries out inspection under this clause. This inspection is very different from the inspection under cl 4, which is carried out by the buyer.

It is important to set out its provisions:

> In connection with the delivery the sellers shall place the vessel in drydock at the port of delivery for inspection by the classification society of the bottom

---

55 See, *op cit*, Goldrein, fn 14, p 110. The buyer may like to renegotiate the price, if the market has fallen, or to find ways of performing his obligation to accept delivery. If the seller misinterprets the buyer's intention and treats such a conduct as an anticipatory repudiation, he may be found guilty of repudiation himself by re-offering the ship for sale too soon: *The Hazelmoor* [1980] 2 Lloyd's Rep 351 (CA).

and other underwater parts below the summer load line. If the rudder, propeller, bottom and other underwater parts ... be found broken, damaged or defective, so as to affect the vessel's clean certificate of class, such defects shall be made good at the seller's expense to satisfaction without qualification on such underwater parts.

The clause also provides that the tail-end shaft may be inspected, if it is so required by the buyer or the classification surveyor and, if it is found defective so as to affect the issuing of a clean class certificate, it shall be renewed or made good at the sellers' expense at the satisfaction of class. The expense of drawing and replacing of the tail-end shaft is to be borne by the buyer, unless the classification society recommends its renewal, in which event the seller is to bear these expenses.

The expenses of drydocking dues, putting the vessel in and taking her out as well as the classification surveyor's fees, shall be paid by the sellers if the underwater parts are defective, otherwise they shall be paid by the buyer.

During the inspection, the buyer's representative shall have the right to be present, but without interfering with the class surveyor's decisions. The vessel shall be brought to the drydock and then to the place of delivery at the seller's expense.

By comparison with the equivalent clause of the 1993 Saleform, an alternative is provided by the later edition to reflect market practice. The first part provides for inspection by the classification society's surveyor, to be done at the sellers' expense, if defects are found, while the second alternative provides that the vessel shall be delivered without drydocking. However, a diver appointed by the buyers, upon the approval of class, may carry out the underwater inspection at the buyer's expense. The extent and conditions under which this inspection is performed shall be to the satisfaction of class. If the diver (under the diver's inspection) discovers any damage, which cannot be repaired afloat, the sellers must arrange for the ship to be drydocked at their own expense. This new clause is very long and detailed.

If the classification society surveyor decides that the ship is in acceptable condition, the buyer will be bound by that decision. If the classification society makes recommendations for repairs, the seller must make repairs at his own expense; if he does not, he cannot tender the vessel for delivery and could be held in repudiatory breach of contract. The seller's obligation in such circumstances is to make such repairs to the satisfaction of the classification society.

The Great Marine (No 2)[56]

Instead of the NSF 1987 cl 6 provision, the parties had agreed by an additional clause to have a joint inspection by a diver approved by ABS (the classification

---

56   [1991] 1 Lloyd's Rep 421 (CA).

society). If the diver found damage to the ship's hull or underwater parts below the summer load line, leading to a condition of class being placed on the ship, Clause 6 would be reinstated and the ship would be drydocked. Clause 11 provided that the ship would be delivered and taken over 'as she is at the time of inspection fair wear and tear excepted … with present class free of recommendations'. The same clause obliged the sellers to notify ABS of any matters coming to their knowledge prior to delivery which would lead to the withdrawal of the ship's class or to imposition of recommendations relating to her class. In addition, cl 18 provided that the sellers should deliver the ship free of average damage affecting class.

When the underwater inspection was done, the diver discovered that the propeller was seriously damaged. The buyers attempted unsuccessfully to persuade the sellers to report the damage to the classification society, but the sellers contended that the damage did not affect the class of the ship. The buyer's attempt to inform the society of the damage also failed since the society claimed that, prior to delivery, it kept contact with the seller only. However, the buyers took delivery, repaired the propeller themselves and claimed damages against the sellers.

The court gave judgment for the buyers, holding the sellers in breach of their obligation under cll 11 and 18 to notify the classification society and deliver the vessel free of any average damage affecting class. Recoverable damages were the costs incurred by the buyer to make the propeller's damage good by the heating and fairing method. While the sellers accepted they were in breach of their obligation, they disagreed on the method of repairs and, hence, the amount of damages. They appealed. The Court of Appeal held that the sellers' obligation was to deliver the ship with clean certificate from the classification society and that was the contractual measure of quality. The buyers were to be put in the same position as if the sellers had performed their obligations; that was as if the sellers had reported the damage, ABS had made its recommendations and the vessel had been drydocked for carrying out the necessary work to obtain a clean certificate from ABS. Clause 6 required the seller to carry out repairs to the satisfaction of the ship's classification society without qualification.

The standard of repair required was that which would preserve a clean certificate of class; by cropping and grinding in a workshop the sellers would have done what was required of them under the contract, irrespective of whether a loss of efficiency of the propeller resulted. The sellers won by majority of 2:1, so the buyers could not recover their heating and fairing expenses; Lloyd LJ, however, agreed with the judge.

While fair wear and tear is excluded from the requirement of the ship's condition at delivery, what could affect class was interpreted in *The Alfred Trigon*:[57]

> The words 'affecting class' ... meant damage of such a character as either to prevent the vessel being in class or to result in the surveyor, on his becoming aware of the damage, imposing some qualification on class by way of recommendation.[58]

> 'Average damage affecting class' was not just any damage affecting class but damage affecting class of a certain kind and meant damage occasioned by a peril ordinarily covered by insurance as opposed to defects through wear and tear or general old age.[59]

6.4 Notice of readiness and risk management

The notice of readiness is linked to arrangements for payment of the balance of the contract price. Therefore, the seller is anxious to give notice of readiness as soon as he considers that the ship might be ready by the end of the notice period. Sometimes, it may not be ready pursuant to the contract and problems usually arise.

Clause 3 of the NSF 1987 provides:

> The said purchase money shall be paid free of bank charges to ... on delivery of the vessel, but not later than three banking days after the vessel is ready for delivery and written or telexed notice thereof has been given to the buyers by the sellers.

> The notice period for payment expires at midnight of the third day.[60] Banking day is taken to be the business working day for both the principal financial centre in the country of the currency in which the money is payable and the place where the financial closing of the sale is to take place.[61]

The clause is essentially dealing with the buyer's obligation to pay the purchase money within a time limit after the seller has given notice that the ship is ready for delivery. Whether the clause requires the seller to give notice only when the ship is in a deliverable state at the time the notice, or whether prospective readiness would be sufficient, has caused concern in practice and in law. In *The Action*, Hirst J held that it does not. In particular, he said:

> The suggestion that it is necessary for the vessel to be in a fully deliverable state at the time of the notice, as contrasted with the time of delivery, has an air of marked commercial unreality, seeing that it is of no consequence

---

57 *Piccinini v Partrederiet Trigon II (The Alfred Trigon)* [1981] 2 Lloyd's Rep 333.
58 [1981] 2 Lloyd's Rep 333, p 336.
59 *Ibid*, p 338.
60 This is also the position of payment of hire under a time charterparty: *The Afovos* [1983] 1 Lloyd's Rep 335.
61 See, *op cit*, Goldrein, fn 14, p 101.

whatsoever to the buyers whether or not the vessel is in a deliverable state at the earlier date, so long as it is at the latter.[62]

As a matter of construction of the contract, he said, there was no prerequisite to the validity of the notice of readiness that the vessel was actually in a deliverable state on the date it was given.

At first glance it seems that such a construction of cl 3 would be correct, but the wording of the clause creates uncertainty. One would expect that the seller's obligation to have the ship in a deliverable state – save for details and preparation of documentation – on the date of the notice would be a natural prerequisite to the buyer's obligation to make arrangements for payment of the balance of the contract price. If the ship were not ready, there would be little or no time to correct any outstanding matters of the ship's condition in three days, unless such matters were trivial. The buyer would be exposed to risks by releasing his money when the ship might not, practically, be ready by the end of the notice period. The ship's non-readiness would have practical and legal consequences. Such risks the buyer could properly have managed if thought had been given at the stage of negotiations and the drafting of this clause. Bearing in mind that this is the most important part of completion of the parties' respective obligations under the contract, the clause ought to have been drafted in clear and unambiguous language. The notice obligation of the seller ought to be in a separate clause.

In the following recent case, however, cl 3 of the NSF 1987 was given a different construction from that given in *The Action*. The contract had been varied by the parties with the addition of other notice provisions.

Zegluga Polska SA v TR Shipping Ltd (No 2)[63]

The NSF 1987 was used with additions and amendments. But the contract concerned a new building of a bulk carrier, so, in addition to the printed notice of readiness (cl 3), there was added another clause of notices to be given by the sellers to suit the requirements of this contract. Clause 5 provided: 'The sellers shall give the buyers three months and one month approximate notice and a seven days definite notice of readiness for delivery of the vessel.' The sellers did comply with these notices, but the buyers refused to accept the seven days definite notice of readiness contending that the grabs, which formed part of the specification of the vessel, were not in accordance with the specification. They refused to pay the balance of the contract price and obtained an *ex parte* injunction restraining the sellers (who had already given notice of cancellation of the contract) from disposing of the vessel. Colman J ordered specific performance and maintained the injunction until then. On

---

62   [1987] 1 Lloyd's Rep 283, p 295.
63   [1998] 2 Lloyd's Rep 341.

appeal by the sellers, the issue was: when, on the proper construction of the contract, did the buyers become obliged to make payment?

It was held that on a natural reading of cl 3, the notice must be of actual readiness for delivery, when the notice was given, not of any prospective readiness. The notices required under the other clauses were prospective notices. Under cl 5, in particular, it was not required that the vessel should be actually ready for delivery when the seven days definite notice was given, all that the notice appeared to require was a notice by the sellers that the vessel definitely would be ready for delivery after seven days. The giving of actual notice of readiness, if properly given, acted as a trigger and left no room for doubt when the three days began and ended and could not begin to run from any date earlier than the expiry of the seven days' notice. The buyers, therefore, were entitled to insist on the vessel being ready.

It should be noted that the Court of Appeal commented on the construction of cl 3 given by Hirst J in *The Action*, that any support of the view held by the judge would be profoundly uncommercial.[64]

In the light of the problems created by the drafting of the notice provisions in the NSF 1987, which became apparent by the decision in *The Action*, the notice provision in the next edition of the NSF has been amended.

The obligation of the buyer to arrange for the purchase money after notice has been given and the obligation of the seller to give notice when the ship is ready are provided in two separate clauses in the 1993 NSF. **Clause 3 of the 1993 form** provides:

> The said purchase price shall be paid in full free of bank charges to ... on delivery of the vessel, but not later than three banking days after the vessel is *in every respect physically ready for delivery* in accordance with the terms and conditions of this agreement and notice of readiness has been given in accordance with cl 5 [emphasis added].

Clause 5 provides:

> When the vessel is at the place of delivery and *in every respect physically ready for delivery* in accordance with this agreement, the sellers shall give the buyers a written notice of readiness for delivery [emphasis added].

The separation of each party's obligations at delivery is achieved by these two clauses and, it seems that by linking the two, the trigger of buyer's obligation to instruct his bank for payment is the fulfilment by the seller of his obligation to give notice when the ship is in every respect physically ready for delivery. This is emphasised by stressing the obligation of the seller in cl 5 that he shall give notice when the vessel is in every respect physically ready for delivery at the place of delivery. There is no room for construction that there can be prospective readiness. In addition, the consequences of the sellers' failure to comply with this obligation are spelt out in **cl 14 of the NSF 1993,** which provides:

---

64   [1998] 2 Lloyd's Rep 341, pp 344–45.

Should the sellers fail to give Notice of Readiness in accordance with cl 5 or fail to be ready to validly complete a legal transfer by the date stipulated in line 61 the buyers shall have the option of cancelling this agreement provided always that the sellers shall be granted a maximum of three banking days after Notice of Readiness has been given to make arrangements for the documentation set out in clause 8. If after Notice of Readiness has been given but before the buyers have taken delivery, the vessel ceases to be physically ready for delivery and is not made physically ready again in every respect by the date stipulated in line 61 and new Notice of Readiness given, the buyers shall retain their option to cancel. In the event that the buyers elect to cancel this agreement the deposit together with interest earned shall be released to them immediately.

Should the sellers fail to give Notice of Readiness by the date stipulated in line 61 or fail to be ready to validly complete a legal transfer as aforesaid they shall make due compensation to the buyers for their loss and for all expenses together with interest if their failure is due to proven negligence and whether or not the buyers cancel this agreement.

Clause 14 of the 1993 NSF has considerably expanded the same clause of the 1987 NSF. It makes it to be understood that the three days after notice is given are intended for the preparation of the necessary documentation by the seller and not for making the vessel physically ready, which, as derived from cll 3 and 5, should be in every respect physically ready at the date of the notice. The clause also caters for the eventuality that the ship may cease to be physically ready after notice has been given and before delivery, in which case the seller is obliged again to make her physically ready by the date stipulated in the contract. Although the clause requires the seller to give new notice of readiness in such a case, it does not seem to grant a grace period to the seller to make the ship ready again from the date of the new notice. It is inferred from this drafting that the only occasion the seller can deal with the physical aspects of the ship's readiness during the three days period after notice has been given is when something happens to the ship affecting her physical readiness after the date of the notice of readiness. Unless the parties vary this provision to give the seller another three days from the date of the new notice to make the ship physically ready definitely and, also, suspend the buyer's obligation to transfer the purchase money accordingly, it can be inferred from this drafting that the seller has an absolute obligation to rectify any new physical defects by the agreed date of delivery. This is so because the clause expressly provides that the buyer's right of election to cancel is retained. It may, however, be argued that the clause just intends to place the control on the buyer, who may decide to give extra time to the seller, if he wishes, instead of exercising his option to cancel.

6.5 Essential documentation for exchange at delivery

Clause 8 of the 1987 Saleform stipulates:

> In exchange for payment of the purchase money the sellers furnish the buyers with legal bill of sale of the said ship free from all encumbrances and maritime liens or any other debts whatsoever, duly notarially attested and legalised by the … consul together with a certificate stating that the ship is free from registered encumbrances. On delivery of the ship the sellers shall provide for the deletion of the ship from the registry of ships and deliver a certificate of deletion to the buyers. The deposit shall be placed at the disposal of the sellers as well as the balance of the purchase money, which shall be paid as agreed together with payment for items mentioned in cl 7 (bunkers and spares).

> The sellers shall, at the time of delivery, hand to buyers all classification certificates as well as all plans, etc, which are on board the ship. Other technical documentation which may be in the sellers' possession shall promptly upon the buyers' instructions be forwarded to the buyers. The sellers may keep the logbooks, but the buyers to have the right to take copies of same.

Clause 8 of the 1993 Saleform improves on cl 8 of the 1987 form, being clearer about the required documents to be delivered by the sellers. It provides for:

(a) closing meeting ashore;
(b) delivery protocol;
(c) documents for delivery at completion;
(d) documents to be delivered on board.

The form of the bill of sale is determined by the ship's Flag State.[65]

The gist of this clause is the obligation of the seller to furnish a bill of sale of the said ship free from all encumbrances which is linked with the sellers' warranty provided by cl 9 (see later).

It is clear from the clause what are the important documents to be delivered by the sellers in exchange for receiving the balance of the purchase price. The duties of the buyers under this clause are to release the deposit to the seller, to pay the balance and pay for bunkers, lubricants and other items on board.

6.6 Sellers' obligations under cl 9

6.6.1 Sellers' undertaking

Clause 9 of the NSF 1987 stipulates:

> The sellers warrant that the vessel, at the time of delivery, is free from all encumbrances and maritime liens or any other debts whatsoever. Should any

---

65   Insofar as British ships are concerned, see Chapter 8.

claims, which have been incurred prior to the time of delivery be made against the vessel, the sellers hereby undertake to indemnify the buyers against all consequences of such claims.

Clause 9 of the NSF 1993 is a variation of cl 9 of the 1987 form:

The sellers warrant that the vessel, at the time of delivery, is free from all charters, encumbrances, mortgages and maritime liens or any other debts whatsoever. The sellers hereby undertake to indemnify the buyers against all consequences of claims made against the vessel which have been incurred prior to the time of delivery.

This amended clause is, in effect, the same as under the 1987 NSF, but for the additions in the first sentence of the words 'charters' and 'mortgages'. The second sentence is effectively reversed. However, the difficulties in the construction of cl 9, which will become apparent upon careful reading and which arose in the case to be discussed below, have not been removed by the amendment.

6.6.2 Construction of cl 9

It seems that he clause provides for two separate remedies for the buyer under each sentence. Liability for damages will arise in the event of breach of the warranty provided in the first sentence regarding incidents of encumbrances attached on the ship. A liability to indemnify the buyer will arise when the latter incurs losses by reason of claims brought against the ship. What is unclear in the clause is this: what is meant by the phrase 'any other debts whatsoever' in the first sentence, and whether there is an overlap between the two sentences by the words 'all consequences of claims' used in the second sentence.

The Barenbels[66]

The ship was sold under the NSF 1966 in which cl 9 was broadly similar to cl 9 of the 1987 form except that it provided for a guarantee, instead of a warranty, in the first sentence, to deliver the ship free from encumbrances, maritime liens or any other debts whatsoever. Prior to delivery, the sellers owed large sums of money to their agents at Qatar in respects of debts. After delivery of the ship to the buyer, the agents commenced proceedings in the court of Qatar for the purpose of recovering the money due to them from the sellers and the court ordered the detention of the vessel at Qatar. The detention was allowed under Qatar law even though the ship had been transferred to a new owner and no proceedings had been issued against the ship before the transfer. The buyers, having failed to persuade the sellers to provide security or to settle the claim, provided security in the form of a guarantee furnished by their P&I

---

66   [1985] 1 Lloyd's Rep 528.

club for the release of the vessel. The buyers then claimed damages against the sellers for breach of the guarantee under the first sentence of cl 9, or alternatively an indemnity against the consequences of the arrest under the second sentence of the clause.

The arbitrators, by a unanimous award, decided against the claim for damages on the ground that the claim did not fall within encumbrances and maritime liens; they construed 'any other debts', of the same sentence, as inappropriate to embrace indebtedness arising otherwise than in relation to the vessel. With regard to the indemnity claim, they held that the language in the second sentence of the clause was insufficiently clear to embrace a conservatory arrest ordered by the court in Qatar, and the buyers could not show that the claim was a claim against the vessel. The buyers appealed.

Sheen J found in favour of the buyers. He construed the word 'encumbrances' as referring to claims, liens and liabilities attaching to the ship. As to 'any other debts whatsoever', he said, the draftsman had in mind the personification of the ship when claims are made against her. So, the words meant that the sellers guaranteed that, at the time of delivery, the vessel would be free from the risk of being arrested in respect of any debts of the sellers. (Under English law, this risk would arise if a writ or claim form had been issued against the ship or a sister ship before the transfer of the ship to the buyer). On the issue of indemnity under the second sentence, he disagreed with the arbitrators that a conservatory arrest was not embraced within the indemnity provision. The sellers appealed.

The Court of Appeal (with Goff LJ, as he then was, delivering judgment) held that the two sentences of the clause contain separate obligations. The second sentence is not intended merely to express a remedy available to the buyer in the event of breach of the guarantee contained in the first sentence:

> The first sentence is concerned with a guarantee relating to the vessel at the time of delivery, whereas the second sentence is concerned with an indemnity in respect of claims made against the vessel which are plainly intended to refer to claims so made after the delivery of the vessel though incurred prior to the time of delivery.[67]

Then Goff LJ proceeded to construe the effect of the words contained in the two sentences. In the first sentence, 'encumbrances' referred to proprietary and possibly possessory rights over the ship. The sellers' debt to their agents at Qatar at the time of delivery did not constitute an encumbrance.

On construction of the phrase 'free from ... any other debts whatsoever', in the context of the first sentence, he held that:

---

67 [1985] 1 Lloyd's Rep 528, p 532.

... this should be read as relating to any other debts, which at the time of delivery, had given rise to *actual existing rights affecting the property in, or the use of, the ship.*[68]

These words were not wide enough to include debts, which would be capable of rendering the ship liable to be arrested in the future, because this was intended to be covered by the second sentence. On this construction, the debt owed by the sellers to Qatar National (the agent) was not within the guarantee provision under the first limb.

Turning to the indemnity provision, it was held that the claim of Qatar agents in respect of debts owed to them by the sellers was a claim in respect of liabilities, which had been incurred prior to the time of delivery, and the claim was indeed against the ship.

6.6.3 Comments on the wording of cl 9 in the 1987 and 1993 NSF

Although, at first glance, the construction given to the first sentence by Goff LJ seems a little obscure, careful reading reveals the following. The first sentence is referring to proprietary rights in the ship (that is, title in, use or possession of the ship), which are truly *in rem*, actual and existing at the time of delivery. The second sentence includes claims other than the above, which may arise in the future for pre-delivery debts that may render the ship liable to be arrested. Since the clause in the previous form did not include in the first sentence the word 'mortgages', which was added to the 1993 form, the additional phrase 'any other debts whatsoever' was justified in the 1987 NSF. The use of same phrase in the 1993 NSF can be justified only for the purpose of avoiding any doubt with regard to proprietary claims. The insertion of the words 'free from any charters' in the first sentence may be intending to cover the situation in which a charterparty existed at the time of delivery of which the buyer had no notice. If he had notice, he would be bound by it,[69] but that presupposes that he bought the ship with actual knowledge of the charter and its terms.

6.6.4 Judicial interpretation of cl 9 of the NSF 1993

The second sentence of cl 9 of the 1993 NSF became the subject of a dispute and was determined by the Court of Appeal recently. The issues arose because of grammatical problems in its drafting, which had already been commented upon by both the judge and the Court of Appeal in *The Barenbels*. The parties can prevent such litigation risks from arising by making amendments to the standard form. It is unfortunate that cl 9 still remains problematic, even after its amendment in the 1993 NSF. It is hoped that in a

---

68 [1985] 1 Lloyd's Rep 528, p 533 (emphasis added).
69 See similar issues arising when the mortgagee of a ship exercises his right to possession, Chapter 9, para 9.6.

future amendment of the NSF the draftsman takes into account the issues raised in the following case, so that a clear and unambiguous clause results.

In **Rank Enterprises v Gerrard**,[70] the buyers had been able to obtain a company guarantee as a security for breach of cl 9 by the seller. After delivery, claims were made against the vessel, which the seller denied as being invalid and spurious. The issue was the construction of the words, 'should any claims which have been incurred prior to the time of delivery be made', and the meaning of 'claims against the vessel' in both cl 9 and the company guarantee. At first instance, the judge – adopting the expanded version of the clause as interpreted in *The Barenbels* – construed these words as meaning claims in respect of any liability incurred (actual or contingent) prior to delivery, which resulted in a later claim against the vessel. The words did not include the consequences of claims against the vessel such as costs and expense in defending them. He then construed 'claims against the vessel' as involving a demand which carried with it a threat of seizure of the vessel and that the threat must be real and present, but there was no need for there to have been proceedings, or an order of arrest, before there could be said to be a claim against the vessel.

There was an appeal by the buyers and a cross-appeal by the sellers. The issue on appeal was whether the second sentence of cl 9 referred only to claims in respect of which the sellers were actually liable. Liabilities in respect of any claim or demand under the expanded version of the sentence, Mance LJ said, may embrace 'liabilities actual or alleged'. It did not have to be actual or contingent liabilities. One paraphrase of the clause, which seemed to be appropriate, was that the sentence applied to 'any claims exposure', which was incurred prior to delivery and was made against the vessel after delivery'.[71] It was common ground that the clause intends to protect the buyer against adverse consequences, for example, costs and expense of valid claims, but the question was whether it covered such costs and expense resulting from spurious claims. The answer to this was that if cl 9 was read as covering the adverse consequences of claims, good or bad, generated by pre-delivery events, the buyers would be assured of indemnity, provided they acted in a reasonable and business-like way in dealing with such claims. The buyers in reality, as a matter of elementary self-protection and prudence, usually inform the sellers on receipt of any claims and try to co-operate, seeking information and assistance from the sellers, although the clause does not contain any such provision. In conclusion, Mance LJ said:

> ... the judge took too limited a view of the scope of the second sentence of cl 9. The sentence, in my judgment, addresses claims made, the exposure to which stems from pre-delivery events, whether the liability asserted by such claims may prove to exist or not.

---

70 [2000] 1 Lloyd's Rep 403.
71 *Ibid*, p 409.

The buyers' appeal was allowed and the cross-appeal was dismissed.

6.6.5 Risk management in drafting and safeguarding against breach of cl 9

(a) Clause 9 ought to be redrafted, as has already been pointed out. The difference between the two sentences ought to be spelt out. Goff LJ criticised the clause, that it was not grammatically correct in the second sentence, but the same problems of construction, unfortunately, still appear in cl 9 of the 1993 NSF.

(b) It would be more meaningful if the obligation under the first limb of the clause was made a condition entitling the buyer to terminate the contract, if he became aware of the breach at delivery. In some contracts, the parties amend the clause to that effect.[72] While the buyer can find out from the ship's registry whether a registered ship is subject to a registered mortgage,[73] there is no public record for maritime liens. In what ways can the buyer protect himself against such risks? He could examine the accident history of the ship from the logbook to find out whether the ship had caused damage by collision, or received salvage services, or there was any other incident, which would have given rise to a maritime lien. He could question the crew if they have been remunerated. An ownership or possessory right on the ship could be discoverable from the ship's registry.

(c) The buyer could seek to negotiate at the stage of the formation of the contract that security is provided in the event of breach. An unconditional and irrevocable guarantee, backed up by a bank guarantee, could be obtained by which the seller, or the guarantor in default of the seller, would guarantee to pay the buyer on demand for any loss or damages and expenses incurred by him in consequence of breach of cl 9.[74] A provision for the non-release of the deposit to the seller at the delivery stage in the event of breach of cl 9 would be the minimum safeguard for the buyer by way of a self-help remedy, but this would only be useful when encumbrances or claims are discovered at the time of delivery.

(d) In the event of a claim for indemnity under the second sentence, by virtue of the nature of such a claim, the buyer will only be able to claim his loss after he had defended the claim made by the third party against the ship for liability incurred by the seller prior to delivery. By that time, however, the risk the buyer runs is that the seller may no longer be in

---

72   See *op cit*, Goldrein, fn 14, p 141.

73   By contrast, there is no means of registering a mortgage of an unregistered ship (see, eg, *The Shizelle* [1992] 2 Lloyd's Rep 444, Chapter 9).

74   This was achieved in *Rank Enterprises v Gerrard* [2000] 1 Lloyd's Rep 403.

existence. He may negotiate to amend this part of the clause either by obtaining the seller's agreement to take over the claim brought by any third party against the ship after delivery, or by seeking security for such a claim from the seller at the time of the contract by way of a company guarantee backed up by a bank guarantee to be activated if and when a claim by a third party is brought. This is essential as a risk management exercise, particularly, because there is no means of knowing whether there are outstanding claims for debts or liabilities of the seller for which the ship might be arrested. Even a search in the admiralty book for claim forms, which was, in the past, a way of finding out whether a writ had been issued against a ship in England, is no longer available to the public, unless the claim form has been served.[75] If, after delivery of the vessel, the buyer is put in a position to have to defend a claim against a third party, the possibility of losing the opportunity of enforcing an indemnity against a dissolved one-ship company, the seller, will not be a light risk to take.

6.7 Condition of vessel on delivery and risk management

Clause 11 of the 1987 NSF provides:

> The vessel with everything belonging to her shall be at the sellers' risk and expense until she is delivered to the buyers, but subject to the conditions of this contract, she shall be delivered and taken over as she is at the time of inspection, fair wear and tear excepted.

However, the vessel shall be delivered with present class free of recommendations. The sellers shall notify the classification society of any matters coming to their knowledge prior to delivery which, upon being reported to the classification society, would lead to the withdrawal of the vessel's class, or to the imposition of a recommendation relating to her class.

There are three obligations of the seller under this clause:

(a) to deliver the ship in the same condition as she was at the time of inspection – fair wear and tear excepted;

(b) to deliver the ship with her present class maintained, free of recommendation;

(c) to notify the class of any matters within their knowledge prior to delivery which would lead to withdrawal of class or to recommendation relating to class.

The first obligation is an obligation to reconcile the condition at delivery with the condition at the time of inspection. There is an exception for fair wear and

---

75 See Chapter 3, above.

tear to the extent that the class of the ship and normal maintenance matters are not affected.

Naturally, the risk of loss or damage until delivery is still on the seller whose insurance will cover damage or loss caused by an insured peril. The seller's insurance is cancelled immediately post-delivery.

The second obligation means that the ship's certificates must be valid and free from conditions or recommendations. This can simply be satisfied by the seller delivering an original class status certificate to the buyers issued within a few days prior to delivery.

The second sentence of **cl 11 of the 1993 NSF** has significantly been amended in the following respects:

> ... her class maintained without condition/recommendation free of average damage affecting the vessel's class, and with her classification certificate and national certificates, as well as all other certificates the vessel had at the time of inspection, valid and unextended without condition/recommendation by class or the relevant authorities at the time of delivery. 'Inspection' in this cl 11, shall mean the buyers' inspection according to cll 4(a) or 4(b), if applicable, or the buyers' inspection prior to the signing of this agreement. If the vessel is taken over without inspection, the date of this agreement shall be the relevant date.

The additional words in this clause 'free of average damage' are for clarification and they are usually added to the same clause of the 1987 Saleform, when it is used.

The phrase has been held, in *The Alfred Trigon*,[76] to mean:

> ... 'average damage affecting class' is not just any damage affecting class. It is damage affecting class of a certain kind, and means damage occasioned by a peril ordinarily covered by insurance as opposed to defects arising through wear and tear or general old age.[77]

The words 'class maintained' mean that the vessel had to be in class; 'affecting class' means damage of such a character as either to prevent the vessel being in class or to result in the surveyor, on his becoming aware of the damage, imposing some qualification on class by way of recommendation.[78]

It is to be observed that under the 1987 Saleform, the seller has an obligation to notify the classification society of any matter coming to their knowledge, prior to delivery, which may lead to a recommendation against class. This obligation was introduced in the 1983 revision of the NSF as a direct consequence of the gap in the wording, which was considered in *The Buena Trader*.[79] The sellers' obligation to notify class has, however, been

---

76 [1981] 2 Lloyd's Rep 333.

77 *Ibid*, p 338, *per* Goff J; see, also, *The Star of Kuwait* [1986] 2 Lloyd's Rep 641, and *The Great Marine (No 2)* [1990] 2 Lloyd's Rep 250.

78 *The Andreas P* [1994] 2 Lloyd's Rep 183.

79 [1978] 2 Lloyd's Rep 325.

deleted from cl 11 of the 1993 form (see above). With the deletion of this obligation under the 1993 Saleform, the buyer's position is weakened as it reverts back to what it was before 1983. This duty will not be implied into the contract as was held in *The Buena Trader*. It is important to examine this development.

The Buena Trader

Negotiations by telex for the sale of a vessel were concluded in accordance with the provisions of the NSF 1966. It provided that, '... the vessel shall be delivered charter free, class maintained free of recommendation, free of average damage affecting class with all trading certificates clean and valid at the time of delivery': also that, '... the vessel is to be delivered with continuous machinery survey cycle up to date at time of delivery'.

The buyers refused to accept delivery of the vessel on the ground that, among other matters, the continuous machinery survey was not up to date and that the vessel had suffered wear and tear damage, known to the sellers, affecting the maintenance of the vessel's class. They contended that the sellers were, therefore, under an implied obligation to notify the classification society of this fact. The breach of this implied obligation entitled them to refuse to accept delivery of the vessel. The dispute was referred to arbitration.

The arbitrator decided in favour of the sellers and found that 'up to date' only meant that each item would have been examined some time within the last five years. Relying upon evidence as to practice of Lloyd's surveyors, he said that it did not matter that the whole cycle was not evenly spread. He stated a special case for the court to decide the issue whether the buyers were liable to the sellers in damages for their refusal to accept the vessel.

The judge came to the opposite view in that, pursuant to the rules of the class, 20% of the items ought to be examined each year, so that the cycle was evenly spread. Seeing that far fewer were examined, and that the cycle was not up to date, he held in favour of the buyers. The sellers appealed.

Lord Denning MR agreed with the arbitrator, insofar as the interpretation of the rules of the classification society were concerned and, further, considered whether there was an implied term in the contract that the sellers ought to notify the class about wear and tear items. He held that:

> In those circumstances it seems to me that there was no implied term that the owners were to notify Lloyd's of any of these items of wear and tear, which might affect class. As we all know, no terms are to be implied unless they are necessary to carry out and give business efficacy to the contract.[80]

There was no obligation, therefore, upon the sellers to do anything other than do the repairs, which were recommended and outstanding. The ship was

---

80 [1978] 2 Lloyd's Rep 325, pp 329–30.

delivered as she lay at the time of delivery. Thus, the 1966 form had a serious deficiency. Even if the sellers were aware of defects or damage affecting the ship's class, which arose after the buyer's inspection, they were not obliged to report them to the classification society, or to make them known to the buyer. The latter had to rely on the statutory protection if he could prove breach of merchantable quality or fitness for purpose.[81]

To avoid the problems of *The Buena Trader*, the notification obligation was introduced in 1983 and was repeated in the amendment of the form in 1987.

The questions that arose after the amendment of the clause have been, as follows. What matters does it refer to? What is the position with matters that already existed at the time of the buyer's afloat inspection? What is the earliest date when the existence of these matters is of relevance to the sale contract?

In *The World Horizon*,[82] under a contract of sale drawn on the 1983 Saleform, the plaintiffs were the buyers and the defendants were the sellers of the vessel *World Horizon*. Clause 11 of the form provided for the delivery of the vessel with her present class maintained free of recommendations and free of average damage affecting class. It also provided that the sellers shall notify the classification society of any matters coming to their knowledge prior to delivery which upon discovery would lead to the withdrawal of the vessel's class or the imposition of a recommendation. When the vessel was delivered, it was contended that the sellers were in breach of their obligation under cl 11 because they had failed to notify the classification society of two matters which they knew prior to delivery, and which would affect the class of the vessel. These matters were that the spare main/engine piston rod was not yet on board the vessel, and the clamps and supports for the deck piping were in need of repair.

It was found that both these matters were old, as they had existed since the inspection by the buyers and the classification society, and the society had made no recommendations on them. The Court of Appeal held that the obligation under cl 11 related to matters coming to the knowledge of the sellers from the date of the last survey by the classification society or the last inspection by the buyers.

In *The Niobe*,[83] a later Court of Appeal decision, the question was directly in issue. It was held that the obligation referred to matters coming to the sellers' knowledge from the date of the contract. 'Coming' looks to the future from the date of the contract. It reversed the decision of Gatehouse J who had held that it was from the date of the last survey by the classification society before the contract. However, The House of Lords[84] chose a more flexible

---

81 See, also, *op cit*, Goldrein, fn 14, p 144.

82 [1993] 2 Lloyd's Rep 56, p 57.

83 [1994] 1 Lloyd's Rep 487.

84 [1995] 1 Lloyd's Rep 579.

approach than the two earlier Court of Appeal decisions. The question put to the House of Lords was whether the sellers were under an obligation to notify their classification society prior to delivery of matters that affected class and which came to their knowledge, as from (1) the date of the contract, or (2) the date of the last survey of the equipment in question, or (3) from some other date and, if so, what date. The Lords unanimously held that the obligation covered all matters affecting class, whenever such matters might have come to the sellers' knowledge before or after the contract and it did not only refer to the future. According to Lord Mackay of Clashfern LC:

> Grammatically, the phrase 'coming to their knowledge' is an adjectival present principle governing the word 'matters' ... Of course, the phrase may take colour from its context, and in some contexts point only to the future ... But in the present context the adjectival phrase is as apt to cover knowledge acquired before the contract as after. Like 'within their knowledge', it means matters known to the sellers: neither more nor less. It follows that there is no *terminus a quo*, and the sellers are obliged under the contract to inform the classification society before delivery of all matters affecting class whenever such matters may have come to their knowledge. In practice however, it will not usually be necessary to go back beyond the last relevant survey.[85]

From a risk management point of view, the protection afforded to buyers by cl 11 of the 1987 form should not lightly be bargained away. If the 1993 form is used, then an appropriate reinstatement of the reporting requirement should be negotiated.

Sellers' knowledge does not include constructive knowledge, for example, that possessed by the sellers' agents, but it ought to include a 'turning a blind eye knowledge' when a person, suspicious of the truth, deliberately refrains from inquiring and turns a blind eye to the truth.[86]

There are, however, still difficulties in practice as to how the buyer can prove that the sellers knew about defects, since there is no duty of good faith. Presumably, the standard of a reasonable seller would apply depending on the particular case, that is, what would a reasonable person in the position of a seller would have suspected, or believed, to be the situation.[87]

---

85 [1995] 1 Lloyd's Rep 579, p 583.

86 *The Eurysthenes* [1976] 2 Lloyd's Rep 171 (CA), in the context of s 39(5) of the Marine Insurance Act 1906; see *op cit*, Goldrein, fn 14, p 151.

87 This test derives from what the Court of Appeal said in *The Star Sea* [1997] 1 Lloyd's Rep 360 about privity of the owners or managers in relation to the unseaworthiness of a ship.

6.8 The closing meeting

It has already been mentioned that all documents need to be ready for exchange at this meeting which invariably takes place at a different location from the place of the physical delivery, but simultaneously. Representatives of the buyer and seller on board the ship will communicate with the lawyers of the parties at the place of the financial closing, once the pre-delivery inspection is completed and the buyer's representative is satisfied with the condition of the ship. This is the time when either matters go smoothly and the buyer's bank is instructed to release the balance of the money, or heated arguments may ensue if the seller has failed to comply with his obligations discussed previously.

From a risk management aspect, the timing is very important. If the money has already been released and the buyer's representative communicates that the ship should not be accepted, the buyer's lawyers should be on the alert to obtain a freezing injunction against the seller to refrain him from removing the money out of the jurisdiction. At what point in time this can be done will be seen under para 8.2, below.

If the closing proceeds smoothly, the next step is for the seller to communicate with the registrar of the ship's registry to discharge the mortgage and deliver to the buyer the ship's certificates and other documents. An executed discharge of the mortgage would have been lodged with the ship's registry in advance. Upon payment of the money, the seller will transfer title in the ship to the buyer. The buyer will register the ship under the new flag and the buyer's mortgagee will instruct the registrar to register the new mortgage.

The seller must also deliver additional documents, such as minutes of the directors' and shareholders' meeting approving the sale, the company's constitutional documents, and an original certificate of the seller's good standing. An original power of attorney, an original certificate of the ship's classification society, an original certificate of the ship's registry stating that the ship is free from all registered encumbrances and any governmental approvals or consents, that might be needed, must also be delivered. A protocol of delivery with a commercial invoice and an original inventory of the ship's parts, together with the ship's manuals and plans, form part of essential documents for delivery at this stage.

6.9 Post-delivery matters

After the closing meeting the remaining matters for the completion to be finalised are: the cancellation of insurance by the seller and the issue of a new insurance policy in the name of the buyer; the delivery to the buyer of the certificate of permanent deletion from the ship's registry; the issue of a new class certificate by the classification society; the registration of the ship, or the conversion of a preliminary registration to a permanent one by the buyer. Finally, the new crew boards the ship.

7 THE PARTIES' RESPECTIVE REMEDIES FOR DEFAULT

7.1 Buyer's default

7.1.1 The seller's contractual remedies

It has been seen earlier that, under cl 2, the buyer is obliged to establish the deposit within a stated time as a security for his commitment to the contract. This clause does not specify the consequences for breach.

Clause 13 of the NSF 1987 deals with buyers' default in payment either of the deposit or the purchase money and stipulates the consequences of non-payment. It provides:

> Should the deposit not be paid as aforesaid, the sellers have the right to cancel this contract, and they shall be entitled to claim compensation for their losses and for all expenses incurred together with interest at the rate of 12% per annum.

> Should the purchase money not be paid as aforesaid, the sellers have the right to cancel this contract, in which case the amount deposited together with interest earned, if any, shall be forfeited to the sellers. If the deposit does not cover the sellers' losses, they shall be entitled to claim further compensation for their losses and for any expenses together with interest at the rate of 12% per annum.

Clause 13 of the 1993 NSF provides the same, apart from omitting a fixed rate of interest which leaves discretion with the arbitrators to fix it according to market rates, if the parties adjudicate their dispute by invoking the arbitration clause of the contract.

Prior to the 1987 NSF, the 1966 form did not provide for compensation in respect of the seller's loss and for his expenses incurred by reason of the buyer's failure to pay the deposit. In *The Blankenstein*[88] (decided in 1985), failure to pay the deposit was held to be a repudiatory breach of the contract, entitling the sellers to recover the amount of the deposit by way of damages for breach of contract, even though the amount of the deposit exceeded the amount of their loss (that is, the fall in market price). No doubt because this was felt to be an unfair 'windfall' for the sellers, what is now the first

---

88 [1985] 1 Lloyd's Rep 93.

paragraph of cl 13 was added to the 1987 Saleform, giving the sellers the option to cancel the contract and claim compensation for their losses.

Whether the first paragraph of cl 13 – having regard to the second paragraph of the same – precludes the sellers from recovering the deposit as part of 'their losses', if the buyer withdraws from the sale before payment of the deposit, was adjudicated by London arbitrators.[89] The argument in the arbitration was that the ordinary measure of the sellers' loss would be to put them in the same position as if the deposit had been paid. If that were correct, the deposit could be forfeited. The arbitrators decided that the second paragraph of cl 13 is intended to prescribe the only situation in which the deposit can be forfeited. When the deposit has not been paid in breach of cl 2, then the deposit does not exist and, therefore, it cannot be forfeited or claimed as part of the sellers' damages for the buyers' repudiation. Their measure of loss is now spelt out in the first paragraph of cl 13.[90]

As regards the second paragraph of the clause, it simply refers to failure by the buyer to pay the purchase price. However, the buyer may rightfully not pay because of default by the seller to deliver the ship free of defects. It must be implied in the clause that the sellers' right of cancellation arises from a wrongful refusal by the buyer to pay. An example of this has been seen in *The Action*:[91] the list of 12 defects presented to the seller by the buyer's representative were eventually repaired – nevertheless, the buyers withdrew from the contract just before the rectification of the last defect and were held to have wrongfully failed to pay.

7.1.2 The seller's statutory remedies

Equally, the SOGA 1979 affords protection to the seller should the buyer fail to pay the purchase price. Section 50(1) provides that 'where the buyer wrongfully neglects or refuses to accept and pay for the goods, the seller may maintain an action against him for damages for non-acceptance'. Sub-section (2) states that 'the measure of damages is the estimated loss directly and naturally resulting, in the ordinary course of events, from the buyer's breach of contract'. In particular, sub-s (3) provides that 'where there is an available market for the goods in question the measure of damages is *prima facie* to be ascertained by the difference between the contract price and the market or current price at the time or times when the goods ought to have been accepted'. This section will apply when the parties have not dealt with

---

89 Unreported; arbitration awards are not published because of confidentiality unless the parties to the reference consent.

90 See, also, *op cit*, Goldrein, fn 14, p 93.

91 [1987] 1 Lloyd's Rep 283.

damages expressly in the contract. If the parties use either the 1987 or the 1993 NSF, cl 13 stipulates the amount recoverable.

The right to cancel and claim damages must be exercised within a reasonable time by the sellers. What is a reasonable time will depend on the circumstances of a case, but in *The Great Marine (No 1)*[92] the sellers delayed for over a week and that was held to have been too long.

7.2 Seller's default

7.2.1 Delay in delivery or non-delivery as per contract

Clause 14 of the 1987 NSF deals with default of the seller and provides:

> If the sellers fail to execute a legal transfer or to deliver the ship with everything belonging to her in the manner and within the time specified in line 38, the buyers shall have the right to cancel this contract in which case the deposit in full shall be returned to the buyers together with interest at the rate of 12% per annum. The sellers shall make due compensation for the losses caused to the buyers by failure to execute a legal transfer or to deliver the ship in the manner and within the time specified in line 38, if such are due to the proven negligence of the sellers.

The effect of cl 14 is twofold:

(a) the buyer has a right to elect to cancel and claim the deposit back with a fixed rate of interest, if the ship is not delivered as provided by the contract irrespective of negligence by the seller (no fault provision);

(b) in addition, the buyer has a right to claim compensation if it is proved that the seller's failure to deliver the ship according to the contract and within the contractual date was due to his negligence, which caused losses to the buyer[93] (proven negligence provision).

The clause has been made clearer in **cl 14 of the amended NSF 1993**, which provides:

> Should the sellers fail to give Notice of Readiness in accordance with cl 5 or fail to be ready to validly complete a legal transfer by the date stipulated in line 61 the buyers shall have the option of cancelling this agreement provided always that the sellers shall be granted a maximum of three banking days after Notice of Readiness has been given to make arrangements for the documentation set out in cl 8. If after Notice of Readiness has been given but before the buyers have taken delivery, the vessel ceases to be physically ready for delivery and is not made physically ready again in every respect by the date stipulated in line 61 and new Notice of Readiness given, the buyers shall retain their option to

---

92 [1990] 2 Lloyd's Rep 245.

93 *Linett Bay Shipping Co Ltd v Patraicos Gulf Shipping Co SA (The Al Tawfiq)* [1984] 2 Lloyd's Rep 598.

cancel. In the event that the buyers elect to cancel this agreement the deposit together with interest earned shall be released to them immediately.

Should the sellers fail to give Notice of Readiness by the date stipulated in line 61 or fail to be ready to validly complete a legal transfer as aforesaid they shall make due compensation to the buyers for their loss and for all expenses together with interest if their failure is due to proven negligence and whether or not the buyers cancel this agreement

As explained under para 6.4, this clause must be read together with cll 5 and 3 providing for the seller's obligation to give notice of readiness and the buyer's obligation to arrange for payment of the balance of the purchase money respectively when the ship is in every respect physically ready for delivery.

Apart from the clarification in this new clause with respect to the seller's obligation to have the ship actually physically ready and not just prospectively ready when he gives notice of readiness, there are two further differences between the 1987 and the 1993 clauses. (i) When the buyer elects to cancel the contract under the first paragraph of the 1993 clause and claims the deposit, the interest rate is not fixed. Presumably, the arbitrators will determine the interest rate. (ii) When the ship is not ready due to proven negligence by the seller, under the second paragraph of the clause, the buyer can claim compensation, not only for losses so caused, but also for his expenses whether or not he elects to cancel the contract.

For other breaches, the buyer will be entitled to rely on remedies provided either in other terms of the contract or under the general law.

7.2.2 Other breaches by the seller

Generally, and if the contract does not otherwise provide, the buyer would have protection under common law or the provisions of the SOGA 1979 and/or the SSGA 1994 as discussed in the beginning of this chapter and in the previous one. Such protection is afforded for a total or partial failure by the seller to perform. If it is a partial failure, the buyer's remedy will depend on whether the breach is one of a condition of the contract or a statutory condition under the SOGA 1979 and/or the SSGA 1994. If it is a breach of a condition, the buyer will have the option to cancel the contract and claim damages. If it is a breach of a warranty, his remedy will be in damages only, and, if it is a breach of an innominate term, his remedy will depend on the seriousness of the breach.

7.3 Causation and remoteness of loss

Generally, the principle applicable to causation and measure of damages for breach of contract derives from *Hadley v Baxendale*,[94] which contains two rules, thus:

> Where two parties have made a contract which one of them has broken, the damages which the other party ought to receive in respect of such breach of contract should be such as may fairly and reasonably be considered as either arising naturally, that is, according to the usual course of things, from such breach of contract itself, or such as may reasonably be supposed to have been in the contemplation of both parties, at the time they made the contract, as the probable result of the breach of it.

The first rule begins with the word 'either' and the second with the word 'or'.

Buyers and sellers are probably aware that the recoverable loss is the loss that arises naturally, in the usual course of things, from the other party's breach, and this is judged objectively. In addition, there may be a loss that, at the time of the contract, was in the reasonable contemplation of the parties as likely to result from the breach. For example, the seller ought to bear in mind that the buyer, at the time of the contract, might have already fixed the ship for a charterparty to commence at the time of delivery under the sale contract. He may also have been put on notice by the buyer why the latter may need the ship delivered punctually on the date agreed. Conversely, the buyer ought to bear in mind that if he wrongfully withdraws from the contract, the seller might be likely to miss another good buyer, or that the price may fall later.

In particular, in the event of non-delivery by the seller, if there is an available market for the particular ship, the measure of damages for non-delivery of, or failure to transfer the title in, the vessel is *prima facie* the difference between the contract price and the market price, or the current price of the ship at the time when it ought to have been delivered (s 51(3) of the SOGA 1979). If there is no market for this type of vessel, the measure of damages is the estimated loss directly and naturally resulting, in the ordinary course of events, from the seller's breach of contract (s 51(2), the first rule of *Hadley v Baxendale*).

In the event of loss of profit from not having the use of the ship in the meantime, particularly, if there is no readily available market for the type of ship in question, such loss of profit can be added to the difference between the contract and the market price. This interesting point arose in *The Ile aux Moines*,[95] in which the buyers' lawyers had only pleaded damages under s 51(3) in the arbitration. When the case was referred to the court, as a special case on a point of law, namely whether the buyer could claim both the

---

94 (1854) 9 Exch 341.
95 [1974] 2 Lloyd's Rep 502.

difference in the market price and the loss of use suffered in the meantime, the answer was in the affirmative. However, it was by then too late to recover both, because the award had already been made final!

From a risk management perspective, the lesson to be learnt from this case is that the buyers should claim under both paragraphs of s 51(2) and (3). Provided there is no available market at the time of the breach, loss of profit from the date of the breach up to the time of finding a substitute, could be added on the damages measured on the basis of market and contract price.

In this case, it would have been in the reasonable contemplation of the parties at the time of the contract that extra loss could be incurred to the buyer by the non-delivery of the vessel as provided by the contract, hence, the second rule of *Hadley v Baxendale* should apply.

Loss of a lucrative charter, however, cannot be claimed, unless the seller was aware of the intended use of the particular ship.[96]

When there is late delivery, the general principles of measure of damages will apply. If the buyers accept the ship late, they could claim loss of profit being measured on the basis of what they would have been likely to earn during the gap between the specified delivery date and the actual delivery. The buyers are to be put in the same financial position as if the sellers had performed the particular obligation in question.[97]

7.4 Mitigation of loss by the buyer

The Solholt[98]

The question of mitigation of loss arose in *The Solholt*. The contract for sale of this vessel was on the NSF. The purchase price was US$5 m. The contract provided for a specified delivery date being 'not later than 31 August 1979'. In the event of default by the sellers for reasons for which they were responsible, cl 14 gave the buyers the right to cancel, claim the deposit with interest of 5% and compensation for their losses so caused. Fearing late delivery, as the vessel had to complete a charterparty at the time, the sellers sought an

---

96 *Victoria Laundry (Windsor) v Newman Industries* [1949] 2 KB 52 (CA)8, leading authority on remoteness and measure of damages for breach of contract: the defendants, an engineering company, with knowledge of the nature of the plaintiffs' business, having promised delivery by a particular date of a large and expensive plant, could not reasonably contend that they could not foresee that loss of business profit would be liable to result to the purchaser from a long delay in delivery; that although the defendants had no knowledge of the dyeing contracts which the plaintiffs had in prospect, it did not follow that the plaintiffs were precluded from recovering some general, and perhaps conjectural, sum for loss of business in respect of contracts reasonably to be expected.

97 *The Great Marine (No 2)* [1990] 2 Lloyd's Rep 250.

98 [1983] 1 Lloyd's Rep 605 (CA).

extension of time from the buyers, but the latter refused. The vessel arrived at the port for inspection and she was late by only two days. Her market price was US$5 m, but the buyers cancelled the contract. It was agreed that the buyers were entitled to cancel the contract and to recover their full deposit ($500,000). The question was whether they were entitled to a remedy in damages in addition to the return of their deposit, that is, the increase in the market value, and whether the buyers had mitigated their loss.

The judge and the Court of Appeal held that the direct loss of the buyer from the sellers' breach was $500,000, but since there was evidence that the sellers would be prepared to accept an offer from the buyers to buy the ship at the original price, the buyers failed to take reasonable steps to mitigate their loss.

Lord Donaldson MR said with respect to mitigation:

> A plaintiff is under no duty to mitigate his loss, despite the habitual use by the lawyers of the phrase 'duty to mitigate'. He is completely free to act as he judges to be in his best interests. On the other hand, a defendant is not liable for all loss suffered by the plaintiff in consequence of his so acting. A defendant is only liable for such part of the plaintiff's loss as is properly to be regarded as caused by the defendant's breach of duty.[99]

7.5 Currency of loss

The currency in which the loss is claimed may make a significant difference. However, the currency must appropriately reflect the recoverable loss. Disputes arising under sale of ships contracts are expressly made subject to arbitration in London, so, by inference English law would apply. For the purpose of assessing the currency of loss for breach of the contract, however, it would not matter if the proper law of the contract were English law. If neither of the parties to the contract, nor the contract itself, nor the claim had any connection with sterling, it would be a *prima facie* case for giving judgment in a foreign currency.

It is apt to quote in this connection what Lord Wilberforce said in *The Despina R and The Folias*.[100]

> My Lords, in *Miliangos v George Frank (Textiles) Ltd* [1976] 1 Lloyd's Rep 201; [1976] AC 443, this House decided that a plaintiff suing for a debt payable in Swiss francs under a contract governed by Swiss law could claim and recover judgment in this country in Swiss francs. Whether the same, or a similar, rule could be applied to cases where (i) a plaintiff sues for damages in tort, or (ii) a plaintiff sues for damages for breach of contract, were questions expressly left

---

99 [1983] 1 Lloyd's Rep 605, p 608.

100 [1979] 1 Lloyd's Rep 1; see, also, *Transoceanic Francesca and Nicos V* [1987] 2 Lloyd's Rep 155, Chapter 12, para 4.5.

open for later decision. These questions were regulated before *Miliangos* as to tort by *SS Celia (Owners) v SS Volturno (Owners) (The Volturno)* (1921) 8 LlL Rep 449; [1921] 2 AC 544 and as to contract by *Di Ferdinando v Simon, Smits & Co Ltd* [1920] 3 KB 409, which decided that judgment in an English court could only be given in sterling converted from any foreign currency as at the date of the wrong. Now these questions are directly raised in the present appeals.[101]

In the first appeal, the issue in which currency damages were payable when a plaintiff sues in tort arose out of a collision between two ships and the award made for the repairs was held to be in the currency in which the loss was sustained. In the second appeal, the issue of what would be the appropriate currency of damages awarded when a plaintiff sues in breach of contract arose from a collision again, but this time the charterers sued the owners of the ship to recover their loss for money paid in French francs to the cargo-receivers. Lord Wilberforce observed:

> A decision in what currency the loss was borne or felt can be expressed as equivalent to finding which currency sum appropriately or justly reflects the recoverable loss. This is essentially a matter for arbitrators to determine. A rule that arbitrators may make their award in the currency best suited to achieve an appropriate and just result should be a flexible rule in which account must be taken of the circumstances in which the loss arose, in which the loss was converted into a money sum, and in which it was felt by the plaintiff. In some cases the 'immediate loss' currency may be appropriate, in others the currency in which it was borne by the plaintiff. There will be still others in which the appropriate currency is the currency of the contract.[102]

8 LEGAL AND COMMERCIAL RISK MANAGEMENT FOR THE BUYER

8.1 Considerations before exercising the option to reject the ship

First, the buyer should consider whether the breach amounts to failure to perform and whether the contract or the statute gives him the right to cancel. He should also consider, whether the seller's failure is capable of being remedied, and whether the seller is willing to rectify the breach within a reasonable time. If he purports to cancel the contract when the seller is willing to rectify the breach within a reasonable time, the buyer may be in repudiation of contract. Assuming that he has the right to cancel, foremost consideration for the buyer before electing to cancel the contract will be, whether he would be likely to recover damages from the seller, and whether the market for this type of ship has risen. The buyer may have already been committed to

---

101 [1979] 1 Lloyd's Rep 1, p 4.
102 *Ibid*, p 9.

perform a charterparty. He should consider whether the consequence of his waiting until the defects are remedied would be the cancellation of the charter; also, whether he could recover his consequential damages from the seller, who may not be in existence for very long after the transfer of the ship.

8.2 Considerations before applying for a freezing injunction against the purchase money

8.2.1 The underlying principles

The nature of a freezing injunction and what it purports to achieve has already been discussed in Part I of this book. Briefly, it assists a claimant – by obtaining a court order – to prohibit a defendant from disposing of his assets, which are within the jurisdiction (or in exceptional cases out of the jurisdiction), until a judgment or arbitration award is obtained. The injunction does not, however, give a security interest to the claimant as against the assets over which the injunction has been granted, nor priority over other creditors of the defendant.

Not until recently, 1997, has it been possible to obtain a 'free standing' freezing injunction. Before 1997, such an injunction could not be granted by the English court unless it had jurisdiction to determine the main substantive issues of a case for which the order was sought. Consequently, leave to serve a defendant out of the jurisdiction could not be granted by reference only to the need to obtain the order, but only if the cause of action was within the provisions of RSC Ord 11 r 1.[103] There existed one exception to this rule after the enactment of the Civil Jurisdiction and Judgments Act 1982, s 25, which permitted this interlocutory remedy, if the substantive proceedings were in a court of a Contracting State to the Brussels Convention, as amended. With regard to proceedings in a court of any other State in the world, the restriction was lifted by a statutory instrument.[104] In addition, s 44(2)(e) and (3) of the new Arbitration Act 1996 allows such an interim relief to be granted by the court to preserve assets for the purpose of, and in relation to, arbitral proceedings anywhere.

The general requirements for obtaining such an order must first be satisfied. There must be a good arguable case; it must be shown that there is a real risk that the seller will dissipate the assets or remove them from the jurisdiction; the buyer must make a full and frank disclosure of all material facts; and it must be just and convenient that the order should be granted. The

---

103 This restriction (comprised of two rules, in that the cause of action should be triable in England and that the need for the injunction was not itself sufficient to obtain leave to serve out of the jurisdiction), known as 'The Siskina rules' [1978] 1 Lloyd's Rep 1 (HL), has now been lifted (see Chapter 2, para 5).

104 SI 1997/302.

buyer must be prepared to give an undertaking to pay damages to the defendant for any loss suffered by reason of the order; and an indemnity to third parties in respect of costs and liabilities reasonably incurred by them in complying with the order.

8.2.2 Limits of granting such an injunction to a buyer of a ship

Frequently, buyers are in a dilemma whether or not to part with their money when they believe that there might be some defects in the ship on delivery, which the seller, upon receiving full payment, may not be willing to rectify and – being a one-ship foreign company – there may be a risk that the only asset of the seller (the purchase money) will be dissipated or removed from the jurisdiction.

Although the English courts have recognised that a freezing injunction against the seller may be appropriate and just in some cases, they have, however, imposed some restrictions in the granting of this discretionary relief. These are examined next.

8.2.2.1 There must be an accrued cause of action

The first hurdle that the buyer has to overcome is that he cannot obtain the order for an anticipatory breach by the seller, but only for an existing cause of action.[105] For example, he cannot apply to the court in advance of the delivery of the ship in anticipation that the seller will be in breach of contract. He must make out an arguable case of breach by the seller when he makes the *ex parte* application. Until the ship is delivered, unless there is already a late delivery and therefore a breach, the buyer does not have the right to sue for damages in case the ship is delivered in a defective condition.

The Veracruz 1[106] is a very good example of these issues. The ship bought by the plaintiff was under a bareboat charter. Repairs were necessary in the amount of $3 m and a dispute arose between the owners (sellers) and charterers as to who would pay this sum; that dispute was referred to arbitration in Norway. The ship was not ready for delivery on the agreed date. The buyers referred this dispute to arbitration in London.

The buyers were concerned that the purchase price, which would be paid to the sellers in London would be the sellers' only asset within the jurisdiction and that the latter, fearing an adverse award in the London arbitration, would remove the purchase money out of the jurisdiction. The buyers' concern was that there would be no assets against which to enforce the arbitration award. Consequently, when the sellers gave a new notice of intention to deliver the vessel, the buyers applied *ex parte* for a Mareva injunction to restrain the

---

105 This is the third rule derived from *The Siskina* [1978] 1 Lloyd's Rep 1 (HL): ie, that the injunction has an ancillary nature to a substantive cause of action. (See fn 103, the other two rules.)

106 [1992] 1 Lloyd's Rep 353.

sellers from dealing with the purchase money when it was paid over, which was granted. The injunction was not to come into effect until after delivery and payment. The buyers' claim was for damages for late delivery and for damages in respect of defects, as they believed that the repairs had not been fully carried out. On handing over the purchase money, the buyers advised the sellers that it was subject to the injunction.

On appeal *inter partes*, Hobhouse J held that although the plaintiffs had no accrued cause of action for damages for defects in the vessel at the time of the *ex parte* application, they had an accrued cause of action for damages for delay in delivery; and to the extent that the plaintiffs could show an arguable claim for defects which they expected would be present on delivery the court had jurisdiction to grant an anticipatory Mareva injunction:

> He also held that despite the buyers' misrepresentation, when applying for the *ex parte* injunction, of the factual position pertaining to communications between the charterers, the owners and the classification society, which was culpable, in the circumstances this did not justify the total discharge of the injunction but a reduction of the sum over which the injunction was originally granted.

On further appeal, although the Court of Appeal agreed with the judge that the order should not be discharged completely, it felt bound by the decision of the House of Lords in *The Siskina* that the right to obtain an interlocutory injunction was not a cause of action in itself it could only stand in relation to a pre-existing cause of action.

Thus, on the issue of the feared defects, the Court of Appeal held that the learned judge was wrong to grant so much of the relief as related to the plaintiffs' claim to damages for defects which they feared would be present when the vessel was delivered; the plaintiffs could not, before delivery, by means of a Mareva injunction, secure a retention in whole or in part of the purchase price against feared defects; on this issue the defendants' appeal would be allowed.

As regards the breach of delayed delivery, it confirmed the continuation of the injunction.

This case re-affirms the general principle that a buyer may obtain such an injunction provided he could show that he has a good arguable case that a breach has already been committed by the seller and makes a full and frank disclosure of all material facts to the court.[107] This is in conformity with the test for granting an injunction whenever it is just and convenient.[108]

---

107 See, also, on similar issues *The Giovana* [1999] 1 Lloyd's Rep 867: an inchoate right and non-full and fair disclosure disbarred the cargo interests from obtaining the injunction against the owners of the ship.

108 *Rasu Maritima SA v Pertamina* [1977] 2 Lloyd's Rep 397, *per* Lord Denning MR, applying the principle laid down by the House of Lords in *American Cyanamid v Ethicon* [1975] AC 396; *The Niedersachsen* [1983] 2 Lloyd's Rep 660.

However, Saville J had devised previously a conditional injunction in the *A v B* case.[109]

The plaintiffs entered into a contract to buy a vessel from the defendants and pursuant to that contract paid a deposit into an account in the joint names of the plaintiffs and defendants.

The plaintiffs alleged that delivery of the vessel might be in breach of the contract in that the vessel might not be in the order and condition stipulated by the contract.

The defendants had no assets within the jurisdiction and the plaintiffs applied for Mareva relief to freeze the sums in the joint account to await the plaintiffs' claims in the arbitration proceedings which they intended to bring against the sellers.

The plaintiffs had no cause of action against the defendants at that stage because until the vessel was delivered there was no right to sue for damages for delivery of a vessel in a condition which was not in accordance with the contractual stipulations.

It was held that, if the material produced to the court, satisfied the court that it would be appropriate to grant Mareva relief when the cause of action arose, there was no good reason why the court should not grant relief in advance to take effect at that moment; if a conditional Mareva injunction was granted it would give effect to the court's view that it would be appropriate to freeze the sums involved; provided nothing in the order came into effect until the moment of delivery, the authorities ought not to prevent the granting of an order; in the circumstances a conditional order would be granted; the Mareva injunction would come into effect, as and when, the vessel was delivered.

Beldam LJ, however, in *The Veracruz* rejected such an approach and, while considering the reasoning of Saville J, he said:

> Though it may be convenient to the applicant to obtain an order which anticipates his cause of action, the court has to balance any such convenience against the obvious inconvenience to the other party. The defendant seller, obliged by the terms of the contract to carry out repairs to put the ship in a deliverable state, may depend upon the assurance of receiving the purchase price to secure finance to carry out the repairs. The prospect that they may be deprived of the whole or a substantial part of the price by a surreptitious application to the court could impede or prevent them obtaining the means to do so.[110]

With respect to the Court of Appeal, there are two flaws in this comment: first, in the light of an imminent threat to the buyer (provided his case is based on sound reasons and not mere suspicions), it should not be a question of balance

---

109 *A v B* [1989] 2 Lloyd's Rep 423, *per* Saville J.
110 *The Veracruz* [1992] 1 Lloyd's Rep 353, p 358.

of convenience, but what would, in the interests of justice, be fair just and reasonable in the circumstances of a case; second, the seller's obligation to carry out repairs and deliver a ship in accordance with the contract is not conditional upon securing finance from the purchaser in order to do the repairs. The part of his bargain is to deliver a ship without defects in exchange for the purchase money.

Prior to the Court of Appeal decision in *The Veracruz* in 1992, commercial court judges were following the approach of Saville J, because it was expedient to grant the injunction in cases such as the sale of used ships where the accrual of the cause of action was both imminent and, in practical terms, inevitable. A common sense approach was considered, in the interests of justice, to be appropriate. Thus, in special cases judges were prepared to introduce an exception to the general *Siskina* rule applicable to injunctions if, in reality, there was a high probability that the seller had committed a breach, which would, inevitably, become apparent on the day of delivery. The buyer's difficulty has been that he is not able to show before the delivery date that his cause of action has certainly accrued. It is a matter of a technical jurisdiction. This problem was, in fact, recognised by Sir John Megaw in *The Veracruz*, but, in agreement with Nourse LJ, he said that the court's difficulty was that it was not free to deal with the question of jurisdiction without the constraint of binding authority (meaning *The Siskina*). He, nevertheless, regarded the approach of Saville J in *A v B* as being a sensible and desirable approach in commercial cases. He saw no valid reason, in logic or practical convenience in the interests of justice, why jurisdiction should not exist in such cases provided the court order was made on the condition, which Saville J applied, that the injunction should not operate unless and until the anticipated cause of action arose. In the end, he felt precluded by authority from so deciding on the question of technical jurisdiction.[111]

Perhaps, the House of Lords, or legislation, may, in due course, vary the third rule of *The Siskina* in the interests of justice and draw a line between the general rule applicable to the granting of injunctions, generally, and possible exceptions that ought to exist for the interest of justice. Until such time, buyers should bear in mind what Nourse LJ said in *The Veracruz* in connection with applications for such an injunction:

> If there is no cause of action, the want of jurisdiction cannot be supplied by suspending the operation of the injunction until one exists.[112]

What the buyers can do to overcome this difficulty is to have the application ready and apply to the court at the same time as the delivery of the vessel provided that they can show that the anticipated breach has indeed become

---

111 *The Veracruz* [1992] 1 Lloyd's Rep 353, p 361.
112 *Ibid*, p 360.

actionable. In *Ninemia Corp v Trave (The Niedersachsen)*,[113] the buyers did reapply for an injunction on the day of delivery, albeit that their application was rejected on appeal because it was not shown that there was a real risk that a judgment or award would remain unsatisfied. In *The Assios*,[114] the buyers knew from the drydock inspection that the ship's bottom had a good deal of indentation which would require repairs. So, on the day of delivery when the money was exchanged, their solicitors handed over to the sellers, and to the bank, a letter advising them that the deposit was subject to the injunction, which had just been obtained. However, there are further hurdles to be overcome, as is shown below.

8.2.2.2 Obligation to notify the sellers of the application prior to delivery

In addition to the requirement that the buyer must have an accrued cause of action he must also disclose to the court all the circumstances, so that the court can determine whether or not the buyer should undertake to notify the seller of the injunction prior to the closing meeting. The court has wide discretion as to whether or not to order the buyer to notify the seller in advance, which depends on the circumstances of a case. The buyer's failure to make full and frank disclosure, or failure to comply with his undertaking given to the court to notify the seller in advance, will result in the discharge of the injunction.[115] In *The Assios*, the injunction was discharged on the ground that the buyer had not made proper disclosure to the court that the injunction was intended as a trap for the seller to be presented with it at the closing meeting, particularly bearing in mind that the seller had, in any event, undertaken not to remove the deposit out of the jurisdiction except upon giving the buyer two clear days notice.

Although reservation has been shown by the court concerning the buyer's conduct in preparing himself behind the seller's back to deprive him of part of the price, albeit that such a conduct is inherent in this type of *ex parte* application, nevertheless, the Court of Appeal, in *The Niedersachsen*, did not wish to lay down any guidelines. It recognised that in some cases the circumstances might well be such as to justify a freezing injunction even in the face of this factor.[116]

In *A v B*, Saville J required the buyers to give sellers notice of the injunction immediately and the buyers did give an advance notice. Commercial judges, however, are realistic about the risk involved for the buyer when notice of the injunction is given to the seller in advance of

---

113 [1983] 2 Lloyd's Rep 660.

114 [1979] 1 Lloyd's Rep 331

115 *The P* [1992] 1 Lloyd's Rep 470, in any event the injunction was discharged for want of an accrued cause of action; Evans J was bound by *The Veracruz* [1992] 1 Lloyd's Rep 353.

116 *The Niedersachsen* [1983] 2 Lloyd's Rep 660, p 615, *per* Kerr LJ.

delivery. Therefore, when the circumstances warrant caution, advance notice may not be required as Leggatt J explained in *The Great Marine (No 1)*:[117]

> If when application is made for such an injunction, the court is not told of the intention to use it to block payment of purchase money, any injunction granted will be discharged for non-disclosure.
>
> Provided that the court is told the facts, it can decide whether to grant an injunction subject to an undertaking that notice of the intention to serve it will be given to the sellers before completion of the sale so that they may consider, before there are assets of theirs within the jurisdiction to which the injunction can apply, whether there are grounds open to them for not completing the sale. Although such an order may be appropriate in some cases, in others it may seem more just to allow the trap to be laid so that a one-ship foreign company is not enabled to divest itself not only of the ship but also of the proceeds of sale before a *bona fide* claim advanced against it can be satisfied.[118]

Buyers may negotiate with the seller to obtain an undertaking from the latter that the money will not be removed from the jurisdiction without prior notice to the buyer. To a great extent, however, such co-operation will depend on the reputation of the seller.

9 CIVIL LIABILITY OF CLASSIFICATION SOCIETIES TO BUYERS AND OTHER THIRD PARTIES

It should be noted that the role of the classification societies is to enhance safety of life and property at sea. This is purported to be achieved by each classification society, which surveys ships entered as members of it in order to verify whether they comply with the society's own technical rules and regulations, which may vary from one society to another but, by and large, societies which are members of the International Association of Classification Societies (IACS) apply the same rules. A classification society issues or renews the classification certificate, or may make recommendations to member owners to carry out repairs, either straight away or within a certain time, and may impose certain conditions shown on the certificate. Unlike in the aviation industry where the relevant authority empowered under statute may issue a certificate of airworthiness in relation to an aircraft, the classification certificate issued by a classification society is not a certificate of seaworthiness. There is usually a misunderstanding by the public that the classification society is responsible to make sure that a ship is seaworthy. That obligation is upon the shipowner who has a non-delegable duty to make his ship seaworthy. When a classification society performs its classification or statutory work, it does not

---

117 [1990] 2 Lloyd's Rep 245.
118 *Ibid*, p 250.

design, build, install, supervise, own, control, manage, operate, repair, maintain, or derive the commercial benefits from the ship it surveys. Complying with the classification society's technical rules and regulations is an element of seaworthiness. For a ship to be seaworthy, or safe, it has to be substantially sound, but it also has to be properly crewed, maintained, operated and navigated. These factors fall outside the scope of classification.[119]

There is a contract between a shipowner and the classification society that surveys the ships entered with it. There would be a breach of contract if the society did not perform its contractual duties but, if the owner made a claim against the society for a loss suffered and allegedly caused by the negligence of the society's surveyor, the outcome would depend on causation. Invariably, there is a year gap between one survey to another, thus, maintenance of the ship in a good condition during the year is the owner's responsibility which would affect causation.

An important question that has reached the House of Lords[120] has been whether a classification society of a vessel owes a duty of care to third parties, who may suffer economic loss, when a vessel being in class, causes damage to property on board. The same question has arisen in the context of purchase of ships when buyers – relying on a clean class certificate – suffer economic loss by reason of defects in the ship. Since there is no contractual relationship between a buyer of a ship and its classification society, which acts independently and is, normally, appointed by the seller, the matter has to be examined in tort. The general principles of tortious liability as developed in recent years are briefly summarised below.

Since 1990,[121] the English courts have applied a three stage incremental approach to the question whether a duty of care exists. This is comprised of three ingredients: (i) foreseeability of damage; (ii) a relationship of proximity between the parties; and (iii) that in all circumstances it is fair, just and reasonable to impose a duty of care upon the defendant. With regard to liability of classification societies, there has been a trilogy of cases:

The Morning Watch[122]

The owners requested that the classification society carried out a special survey of their yacht which was to be sold early in the next season. A full time

---

119 Extracts from a paper delivered by Harrison, J, of Lloyd's Register, 'Accountability of classification societies', seminar held by the London Shipping Law Centre, 21 February, 2001.

120 *Mark Rich and Co AG v Bishop Rock Marine Co (The Nicholas H)* [1995] 2 Lloyd's Rep 299, or [1996] AC 211 (HL).

121 *Caparo Industries plc v Dickman* [1990] 2 AC 605 (HL); *Murphy v Brentwood DC* [1991] 1 AC 398 (HL).

122 [1990] 1 Lloyd's Rep 547.

senior yacht surveyor of the defendants (the classification society) carried out the special survey and issued an interim certificate. The vessel passed the special survey, subject to listed repairs, which were duly effected by the owners. The vessel was later purchased by the plaintiffs. The plaintiffs contended that the vessel proved to have serious defects that rendered her unseaworthy and that these defects should have been discovered by the defendant's surveyor. They claimed against the Classification Society (Lloyd's) damages for economic loss suffered as a consequence of relying on the misstatements negligently made.

The court examined the principles and cases in this area under English law and held: a duty of care would only arise where: (1) it was reasonably foreseeable to the defendant that the plaintiff was liable to rely upon his statement; (2) there was the necessary proximity between the plaintiff and the defendant; and (3) it was just and reasonable in all circumstances to impose a duty of care on the part of the defendant to the plaintiff.

On the facts, since Lloyd's had been informed that the plaintiff was interested to buy the vessel after the survey was carried out, the first requirement was established.

However, the court was not prepared to accept the general proposition that Lloyd's owed a duty of care to those foreseeably liable to suffer economic loss in consequence of reliance on the negligent classification of a vessel. To accept such a proposition, it would be to make a substantial further advance in the law of negligence. Therefore, the plaintiffs had failed to show that the defendants owed them a duty of care either when the special survey was carried out, or on the issue of the interim certificate.

While Phillips J (as he then was) accepted the plaintiff's submission that, as Lloyd's deliberately maintained a system whereby parties other than the owners of classified vessels would be likely to rely on the fact that a vessel was maintained in class and that this system provided an assurance that the vessel was maintained in good condition, he made the following observation:

(i) The primary purpose of the classification system is, as Lloyd's rules make plain, to enhance the safety of life and property at sea, rather than to protect the economic interests of those involved, in one role or another, in shipping.

(ii) Insofar as negligence in relation to classification is liable to harm economic interests, I can see no general ground for distinguishing between the economic interests of the charterer, the mortgagee and the purchaser. All are foreseeably liable to rely upon the class status of the vessel – often to the extent of making the maintenance of class a contractual obligation – and all are at risk of being caused economic loss if classification surveys are not carried out with proper skill and care.

Does English law impose a duty of care upon a classification society towards those whose economic interests are like to be harmed?[123]

Referring to *Caparo v Dickman*, he considered the relationship between the classification society and purchasers of ships and stated:

> The relationship does not reflect any statutory scheme to protect purchasers ... There is no relationship akin to contract. There is no voluntary assumption of responsibility to potential purchasers of shares ... There is no greater proximity between Lloyd's and a potential purchaser than between Lloyd's and the bank that may advance the purchase price on the security of a mortgage on the vessel ...[124]

Applying the three stages of the incremental approach, the second and third requirements were not satisfied in the circumstances. In effect, the third requirement that it must be fair, just and reasonable in all circumstances has restricted the law of negligence, unless the principle to be applied is clearly that of assumption of responsibility.[125]

The three stage approach is now to be applied universally in cases concerned with the recovery of damages for either economic loss or physical damage, for example, whatever is the nature of the harm sustained by a plaintiff. It is an overarching formula within which can be found all cases of recognised duties of care.[126] However, recognition is given to some categories in which it is obvious that, as a matter of common sense, and justice, a duty should be imposed. The difference between categories lies on the fact that it may be more difficult to satisfy the three stage test in cases of pure economic loss than in straightforward cases of physical damage.[127]

The duty of care was not imposed upon a classification society for physical damage to cargo on board a ship and consequential economic loss, mainly for policy considerations, by the majority of the House of Lords in the following decision.

The Nicholas H[128]

The vessel was loaded with the plaintiffs' cargo of lead and zinc for a voyage from Chile to Italy and the USSR. She had to deviate and call at a port in Europe because a crack was found in her hull. Further cracks later developed. A surveyor from the vessel's classification society boarded her and

---

123 [1990] 1 Lloyd's Rep 547, p 559.

124 *Ibid*, p 560.

125 As developed by *Hedley Byrne v Heller* [1964] AC 465.

126 *The Nicholas H* [1995] 2 Lloyd's Rep 299 (below).

127 See, also, a paper delivered by Gross, P (QC), at a lecture held by the London Shipping Law Centre, March 1997, available at the Centre's office.

128 *Mark Rich and Co AG v Bishop Rock Marine Co* [1995] 2 Lloyd's Rep 299, or [1996] AC 211 (HL).

recommended permanent repairs at the nearest port with such facilities. The owners, however, persuaded the surveyor that temporary repairs should be carried out at anchor because permanent repairs would have involved drydocking and unloading of the cargo. The surveyor then reversed his initial recommendation, allowed temporary repairs and the vessel proceeded to the discharge port where the repairs would be further examined after discharge. The next day, while on the voyage, the welding of the temporary repairs cracked. Six days later, the vessel sank with the loss of all cargo. The cargo claim was settled between the cargo interests and the shipowner at the limitation amount in accordance with the Hague-Visby Rules which were applicable to the contract of carriage. The cargo interests claimed the balance of their claim against the classification society on the ground of breach of duty of care owed to them, which caused the loss to their cargo.

The case reached the House of Lords on a preliminary point: assuming there was negligence of the surveyor (which the classification society denied), did a classification society owe a duty of care to a third party – the owners of the cargo laden on the vessel – for the careless performance of a survey resulting in the vessel being allowed to sail and subsequently sink with her cargo. Counsel for the cargo-owners contended that, since the case involved physical damage to property in which the plaintiff had a proprietary or possessory interest, the only requirement was proof of reasonable foreseeability and, therefore, the additional requirements of proximity and considerations of whether it was fair, just and reasonable to impose a duty of care were inapplicable.

The House of Lords by a majority rejected this argument. It was held that the elements of foreseeability, proximity, fairness, justice and reasonableness were relevant to all types of harm sustained by the plaintiff. The majority of their Lordships considered that there was a sufficient degree of proximity to fulfil the requirement for the existence of a duty of care. However, it was held that the recognition of a duty would be unfair, unjust and unreasonable based on considerations of policy. Lord Steyn stated:

> I conclude that the recognition of a duty would be unfair, unjust and unreasonable as against the shipowners who would ultimately have to bear the cost of holding classification societies liable, such consequence being at variance with the bargain between shipowners and cargo-owners based on an internationally agreed contractual structure. It would also be unfair, unjust and unreasonable towards classification societies, notable because they act for the collective welfare and, unlike shipowners, they would not have the benefit of limitation provisions. Looking at the matter from the point of view of cargo-owners, the existing system provides them with the protection of the Hague Rules or Hague-Visby Rules. But that protection is limited under such rules and by tonnage limitation provisions. Under the existing system any shortfall

is readily insurable. In my judgment, the lesser injustice is done by not recognising a duty of care.[129]

Unlike the judge at first instance, who did not think that there were any considerations of policy which would justify the application of the criterion of 'fair, just and reasonable', both the Court of Appeal and the House of Lords dismissed the claim on application of this criterion. However, Lord Lloyd (dissenting) agreed with the judge and said:

> We are not here asked to extend the law of negligence into a new field. We are not even asked to make an incremental advance. All that is required is a straightforward application of *Donoghue v Stevenson* ...

> In physical damage cases, proximity very often goes without saying. Where the facts cry out for the imposition of a duty of care between the parties, as they do here, it would require an exceptional case to refuse to impose a duty on the ground that it would not be fair, just and reasonable. Otherwise, there is a risk that the law of negligence will disintegrate into a series of isolated decisions without any coherent principles at all, and the retreat from *Anns v Merton* will turn into a rout.[130]

However, the majority were influenced by three important factors: (a) the assumed negligence of the class surveyor had not involved the direct infliction of the physical damage to the cargo; (b) the class played a subsidiary role in matters of seaworthiness as compared to the shipowner; (c) a recognition of a duty would cause an imbalance with the Hague-Visby Rules. It would be a different situation if the classification society assumed a responsibility towards a third party, for example, a buyer of a ship by giving advice on which the buyer relied and the society knew, or ought reasonably to have known, that the buyer would rely on their advice before he/she decided to buy the ship. [131]

The trilogy of English decisions in this area is completed by another recent decision, in **Reeman v DOT and Others**,[132] concerned with the certification of a fishing vessel by a surveyor of the Department of Trade (DOT) performing

---

129 [1995] 2 Lloyd's Rep 299, pp 316–17.

130 *Ibid*, p 309.

131 On the basis of the *Hedley Byrne v Heller* principle; in a case involving duty owed by auditors of a company to third parties, *Galoo Ltd v Bright Grahame Murray* [1994] 1 WLR 1360, the Court of Appeal held that, although mere foreseeability that a potential bidder for shares in, or lender to, a company might rely on the company's audited accounts did not impose on the auditor a duty of care to the bidder or lender, such a duty would arise if the auditor were expressly made aware that a particular bidder or lender might rely on them or other statements approved by the auditor without independent inquiry and intended that he should so rely; that, since it was not alleged that the defendants knew or intended that the third plaintiff would rely on their accounts for the purpose of making loans, or for the purpose of calculating the purchase price under the supplemental share purchase agreement, the pleaded facts disclosed no cause of action against the defendants on those issues.

132 [1997] 2 Lloyd's Rep 648 (CA).

regulatory functions under the Merchant Shipping Acts (MSAs). The DOT was sued by a buyer of a fishing vessel claiming economic loss.

It concerned the statutory certification of a fishing vessel which, pursuant to the Safety Provisions Act 1970 and the Regulations 1975 as regards British fishing vessels designed to ensure their seaworthiness. The vessel was inspected by a surveyor appointed by the DOT and a certificate was issued, the validity of which was extended twice every four years. No British registered fishing vessel could put to sea unless she carried a certificate issued by the DOT.

When the claimants bought the fishing vessel, she carried such a certificate, but it was based on an erroneous stability calculation made by the DOT's surveyor, which was discovered after the purchase. The certificate was then withdrawn as the expenditure required to be incurred by the purchasers to rectify the faults, improve her stability and satisfy the minimum statutory requirements was beyond their means. They sued the DOT for breach of the common law duty of care alleged to be owed to them and claimed damages for the economic loss suffered. The issue was whether the DOT owed a duty of care to purchasers of fishing vessels when issuing certificates of compliance.

The judge held that the requisite degree of proximity between the plaintiffs and the DOT was established taking into consideration the following factors:

(a) there was a virtual certainty that the certificate would be communicated to prospective purchasers such as the plaintiffs;
(b) there was an extreme likelihood that such prospective purchaser would rely on the certificate in deciding whether to purchase;
(c) there was overwhelming probability that the purchaser would do so without independent verification;
(d) these facts were all facts known actually or inferentially to the DOT.

In addition the plaintiffs did not appear to have a remedy against anyone other than the DOT; applying the criteria of fairness, justice and reasonableness, it was possible to set an acceptable limit or control mechanism which substantially avoided the mischief in question; this would be to confine the duty to persons who actually purchased the relevant vessel during the currency of the certificate. The DOT appealed.

The Court of Appeal reversed this decision because it thought that the judge had made a significant extension to the ambit of the tort of negligence. With regard to the relationship of proximity it said:

> When a British fishing vessel certificate was issued those who might in the future place reliance on that certificate when deciding whether to purchase the vessel did not form part of a class that was capable of definition and delimitation by identifiable characteristics; not only did potential future purchasers not form an identifiable class when the certificate was issued, the certificate was not issued for the purposes of providing information to assist

them in deciding whether or not to purchase the vessel; and foreseeability that the information might, or probably would be relied on by others than those for whom it was provided did not suffice to constitute such persons part of a class in a proximate relationship with those providing the information.

It would always be open to a party entering into a commercial transaction in relation to a certificated vessel to take steps such as surveying the vessel or stipulating for contractual warranties that would provide protection against the risk that the certificate did not reflect the true condition of the vessel.

With regard to the third characteristic of the test whether a duty of care should be imposed, the Court of Appeal said:

> The statutory framework was one designed to promote safety at sea. The protection of those whose commercial interests might foreseeably be affected by unseaworthiness of vessels formed no part of the purpose of the legislation and no part of the purpose for which the fishing vessel certificates were issued.

It would not be fair, just and reasonable to impose a duty of care on a body like the DOT, charged with the duty of certifying with a view to promoting safety at sea; the DOT when performing its regulatory functions under the MSAs performed a similar role to that of classification societies, that is, they existed for the purpose of further safety at sea rather than for the protection of commercial interests; and the learned judge erred in finding that the DOT had owed a duty of care to the purchasers, Mr and Mrs Reeman. The appeal was allowed. It is odd that the clear judgment of first instance was reversed since this case concerned the statutory certification of a fishing vessel which could not go to sea without it. The certificate was, therefore, a seaworthiness certificate, which is distinguished from the classification certificate issued by class.

It should be noted that the American approach to liability of a classification society towards third parties for economic loss is similar to the English approach. In the following case, a claim in damages was made by the owner of a ferry which was converted into a cruise ship and was approved by the classification society appointed by the Flag State in accordance with the International Convention for Safety of Life at Sea (SOLAS) 1974. It is important to note that the court held that the classification certificate was not a guarantee to the owner of the ship that the ship has been safely constructed; the responsibility for maintenance and seaworthiness remains with the owner who has a non-delegable duty in this respect.

The Sundancer[133]

Sundance bought a passenger car ferry and converted it into the luxury cruise ship, named *Sundancer*. The vessel was registered in the Bahamas.

---

133 [1994] 1 Lloyd's Rep 183.

Under the Bahamian MSA the vessel required, *inter alia*, a safety certificate representing compliance with the SOLAS 1974 Convention and a certificate showing compliance with the Load Line Convention.

The defendant classification society, ABS, was nominated under the Bahamian Regulations as one of six classification societies authorised to perform surveys on behalf of the Bahamian Government. ABS undertook SOLAS and Load Line surveys of *Sundancer*.

Acting on behalf of the Bahamian Government, ABS issued a five month provisional Load Line certificate and a SOLAS passenger ship safety certificate to the vessel. Shortly thereafter, ABS issued a provisional classification certificate to the vessel.

Sundancer struck an underwater rock off the coast of British Columbia. Her hull was breached below the waterline and, while only two watertight compartments were initially flooded, progressive flooding of other compartments occurred when water passed through two holes in bulkhead 124 and through the unvalved grey-water system. As a result of the progressive flooding, the vessel listed heavily and eventually sank at a nearby pier. There had been some violations of SOLAS regulations and ABS rules, neither of which had been reported by ABS. No lives were lost. The buyer sued ABS for negligence and/or gross negligence for the loss of the ship.

It was held that:

> A shipowner was not entitled to rely on a classification certificate as being a guarantee to the owner that the vessel was soundly constructed; the great disparity between the fee charged by ABS for its services and the damages sought by Sundance was strong evidence that such result was not intended by the parties. The shipowner, and not ABS, was ultimately responsible for and in control of the activities aboard ships; Sundance had full responsibility for the conversion and repair and maintenance of the vessel and their ongoing responsibility was supplemented by the requirement that the shipowner had a non-delegable duty to furnish a seaworthy vessel; ABS could not be said to have taken over such obligations by agreeing to inspect and issue a classification certificate. The purpose of a classification certificate was not to guarantee safety, but merely to permit the owner to take advantage of the insurance rates available to a classed vessel.

Such judicial statements, insofar as safety of life at sea is concerned, should now need to be qualified after the implementation of the International Safety Management Code (ISMC). Classification societies are delegated by Flag States to audit ships and ensure compliance with the requirements of the ISMC. Although such new obligations move towards the obligations of an aviation association, they are not yet the same.

Had there been loss of life in the aforesaid case caused by violation of the SOLAS regulations by the classification society, the question under English law would have been whether a duty of care ought to be imposed upon the class. A comparison with the regulatory regime applied to the air industry for the certification of aircraft is discussed in the next case.

Perrett v Collins[134] concerned physical injury of a passenger of an aircraft. Both the judge and the Court of Appeal decided in favour of the plaintiff who was injured while flying as a passenger in an aircraft, which had been certified as fit to fly.

Mr Collins, the first defendant, purchased an aircraft construction kit from which he constructed the aircraft. During construction, he exchanged the gearbox provided with the kit with another, which was not suitable.

The second defendant, an inspector of the Popular Flying Association (PFA), certified that the aircraft was fit to fly and issued the certificate of fitness for flight, valid for one month.

Mr Collins took the aircraft on a test flight from Rochester Airport. The plaintiff was his passenger. The first flight was very short consisting only of taking off, flying to a height of about 20 ft. and then landing. On the second flight the aircraft was taken up to 150 ft. As it descended, it went out of control hit the ground with the result that the plaintiff was injured.

The plaintiff's case was the personal injuries that he suffered when the aircraft crashed were caused by the negligence of one or more of the defendants, and alleged that the aircraft had a propeller, which did not match the gearbox fitted to the engine of the aircraft.

The preliminary issue for decision was whether (a) the third defendants (PFA) being approved by the Civil Aviation Authority (the CAA)/the Authority), pursuant to Art 110 of the Air Navigation Order 1989, as qualified to furnish reports to the Authority in connection with flying permits, owed a duty of care in tort to the plaintiff; and (b) the second defendant being a person to whom the third defendant had delegated the inspection of the aircraft with a view to enabling it to furnish such a report, owed a duty of care to the plaintiff.

It was held by both the judge and the Court of Appeal that it was foreseeable that, if the second and third defendants granted a certificate of fitness to fly in respect of this aircraft with an inappropriate gearbox, there was likely to be an accident, and they ought reasonably to have had in contemplation a person travelling as a passenger on the test flight in the aircraft as being so affected when they were directing their minds to the acts or omissions which were called into question

Also, that greater injustice would be done to a person injured in circumstances such as those that arose in this case, by not imposing a duty on those responsible for issuing a fitness to fly certificate than would result to the defendants in imposing such a duty; the first and second defendants had

134 [1998] 2 Lloyd's Rep 255.

undertaken to discharge the statutory duty for the protection of the public and no injustice was done by imposing such a duty on them in respect of a negligent act. The regulatory framework provided by the Civil Aviation Act 1982 was designed, at least in substantial part for the protection of those who might be injured if an aircraft was certified as being fit to fly when it was not.

This was a case of a personal injury in which it was obvious that, as a matter of common sense and justice, as well as because of a statutory duty, a duty of care was imposed. The balance of justice came down firmly on the side of imposing a duty, and the members of the public would expect to be protected from injury by careful operation of the regulatory system and to be compensated for injury sustained by its negligent operation. Hobhouse LJ (as he then was) said, in refusing to apply *The Nicholas H* to this case:

> What the second and third defendants seek to achieve in this case is to extend decisions upon 'economic' loss to cases of personal injuries. It represents a fundamental attack upon the principle of tortious liability for negligent conduct which had caused foreseeable personal injury to others.[135]

Swinton Thomas LJ focused on the distinction with *The Nicholas H* when he said:

> The regulatory framework recognises the dangers that are inherent in flying. That is the very purpose lying behind the prohibition on taking airplanes into the air without a certificate of airworthiness and a permit to fly, and the appointment of the CAA or those authorised by them to issue such certificates. The whole purpose is one of air safety. In my judgment, any reasonably well informed member of the public, although not in possession of the detailed framework, would expect there to be such a regulatory system in force to ensure his safety when flying and would rely upon it. Furthermore, a member of the public would expect that a person who is appointed to carry out these functions of inspecting aircraft and issuing permits would exercise reasonable care in doing so. The third defendants, and those appointed to act on their behalf, are experts in their field the first defendant is an amateur and inevitably will rely on the second defendant as an expert. The amateur who builds his own aircraft is unlikely to rely on any expertise other than that provided by the PFA. In relation to a ship, as in the *Marc Rich* case, the owners are likely to employ their own experts to ensure that the ship is seaworthy. In the case of a small private airplane, the only expertise which is supplied is that of the inspector, the second defendant. Until the certificate of fitness is granted, the aircraft cannot fly. That is in contradistinction to the position in the *Marc Rich* case where there was no such inhibition on the shipowners. The surveyor acting on behalf of NKK did not issue a permit to sail allowing the ship to go to sea in contradistinction to the second defendant in this case who did issue such a permit enabling the aircraft to fly. The primary purpose, as I see it, of the intervention of the CAA or its appointees is the safety of persons who fly in the aircraft which has been granted the certificate. Moreover, the primary purpose is to prevent physical injury as opposed to damage to property.[136]

---

135 [1998] 2 Lloyd's Rep 255, pp 257, 258.

The distinction between the certification of an aircraft and the certification of a ship was made clear, in that the former is a certificate of fitness for flying while the latter is not a permit to sail.

However, the position of a classification society may now be precarious under the requirements of the ISMC under which the class is delegated to do more than just issue a class certificate.

Given the reasoning in *Perrett* and the distinction made between economic loss cases, such as *The Nicholas H*, and personal injury cases, there must be a real prospect of establishing that class owes a duty of care to third parties as far as personal injury or death is concerned in circumstances not dissimilar from those assumed in *The Nicholas H*. But, if class came to be under a duty of care in respect of personal injuries, could there be two distinct rules – one for personal injury and a different rule for physical damage to property?[137]

Whether a new rule can be inferred from the *Perrett* case, that such a duty ought to be extended to class, is far from clear. There is not yet an equivalent legislation with regard to certification of vessels as that applicable to aircraft. Perhaps, similar mandatory statutory regulations as those existing in the aircraft industry could be considered for implementation in the shipping industry to make classification societies accountable, as far as human life is concerned in circumstances in which causation is proved.

There is a recent move by the European Commission to impose more controls upon class by its proposed amendment to Directive (94/57/EC) concerned with inspections of ships by classification societies. This directive was thought to provide inadequate safeguards. The proposed one addresses the need for classification societies to obtain recognition from the Commission and from the Flag States. The criteria for recognition include good safety record and pollution prevention. Both the Commission and the Flag State will have power to suspend or withdraw recognition, there will be greater disclosure of information to the Flag State and mandatory use of exclusive surveyors. It is proposed that financial liability be imposed on class which will be limited to ECU5 m for claims for personal injury or death caused by negligence of the classification society, ECU2.5 m for claims for property damage or loss and unlimited liability for such claims caused by gross negligence. Agreement has to be reached by the European Council of Ministers over the precise limits of liability.

Having discussed principles of ownership, registration and management of British ships, how the finance is provided and what are the mortgagee's rights and obligations, how a ship is acquired, either as a new building or as a

---

136 [1998] 2 Lloyd's Rep 255, p 272.

137 Extract from a paper delivered by Gross, P (QC), 'Duties owed by class and to whom?', the London Shipping Law Centre, 21 February 2001.

second hand ship, the natural sequence in the following chapters would be the ship's trading and the contractual arrangements involved. Trading is, however, a vast area and is deferred to a future date by the author when it is anticipated that a separate book in the series of risk management will be published.

PART III

SAFETY REGULATIONS IN
NAVIGATION AND LIABILITIES

OVERVIEW

This part, comprised of Chapter 12 alone, deals with safety regulations in navigation and liabilities arising from breach of the collision regulations and the statutory provisions of the Merchant Shipping Act 1995. Both criminal and civil liabilities of owners, managers, officers and crew are examined, after an outline of the Collision Regulations.

Incidents caused by negligent conduct of employees or officers are an inevitable part of business life, but steps can be taken to prevent or control their occurrence. The examples given in this part illuminate the circumstances in which negligence has resulted in detrimental legal consequences so that, it is hoped, they will provide a useful tool for guidance in the future.

CHAPTER 12

COLLISIONS AT SEA AND LIABILITIES

INTRODUCTION

This chapter is divided into three sections: Section A deals with Collision Regulations and their application (details of the regulations governing conduct at sea can be found in other notable works);[1] Section B deals with criminal liability for breach of these regulations; and Section C covers civil liability arising from collisions between ships, or ships with other objects, at sea. As the aim of this book is to present a cohesive overall view of the major topics of admiralty law, general principles are drawn together in this chapter, also giving a fairly detailed account of important decisions.

SECTION A

1 THE COLLISION REGULATIONS AND THEIR APPLICATION

1.1 Origins of the regulations

Briefly, the rules regulating prevention of collisions at sea, developed from the practice and custom of seamen, are applied by the Admiralty Court. Gradually, these practices and customs formed part of maritime law and are the foundation of the rules in force today. In 1840, there was a landmark development. For the first time, the London Trinity House set out the existing practice and custom in a form of regulations, adding two rules for steamships: first, the crossing position of steamships being on a different course, and second, the passage of two steamships in a narrow channel. In either situation, each vessel would put to port, so as always to pass on the starboard side of each other. Notwithstanding the non-statutory force of these regulations, they were enforced by the Admiralty Court as an authoritative yardstick of seamen's conduct in navigation. Later, the Trinity House rules of steamship were enacted by the Steam Navigation Act (SNA) 1846 giving them a

---

1   See *Marsden on Collisions at Sea*, 12th edn, 1998, Sweet & Maxwell.

statutory force for the first time and imposing penalties upon masters of ships for disobeying them. Although this Act was short lived, being repealed by the SNA 1851, the Merchant Shipping Act (MSA) 1854 replaced and expanded these rules conferring power to make regulations with respect to steam and sailing ships regarding lights and signals. Infringement of the rules, as enacted by these Acts, which caused a collision would, contrary to the old admiralty rule of division of loss, prevent the owner of the ship which infringed the rules from recovering any recompense for any damage sustained, even if the other ship was also to blame for the collision. Thus, if one ship infringed any regulations and the other did not, but still contributed to the collision by its own fault, there would be no division of loss.

1.2 Statutory presumption of fault and its subsequent abolition

All the existing regulations were repealed and a complete code was created by the Merchant Shipping Amendment Act 1862. The old admiralty rule of division of damages, where both ships were to blame, was restored by s 29 of this Act. A deeming provision of presumption of fault was made statutory, if it was proved that the collision was occasioned by non-observance of any of the code's regulations, unless the guilty party proved that the circumstances made a departure from the rule necessary. This was re-affirmed by the MSA 1873, and was re-enacted with some significant amendments by s 419(4) of the MSA 1894, which read:

> Where, in case of a collision, it is proved to the court before which the case is tried that any of the collision regulations have been infringed, the ship by which the regulation has been infringed shall be deemed to be in fault, unless it is shown to the satisfaction of the court that the circumstances of the case made departure from the regulation necessary.

The 1894 Act significantly amended the rule by not requiring proof that the collision was occasioned by the infringement of the relevant regulation, which s 29 of the 1862 Act had required. The effect of the amendment was to enable the court to adjudicate fault in collision cases without the necessity of determining whether or not the infringement of the collision regulation did, in fact, contribute to the collision. The statute placed the burden of proof, that the infringement could not possibly have contributed to the collision, upon the vessel which had infringed the regulation in question.

Apparently, such a rule of presumption of fault by reason of mere breach of a collision regulation was arbitrary in that it imposed an obligation upon the court to find fault for the collision without proof of negligence.[2] Thus, 17

---

2   For example, see *The Englishman* (1877) 3 PD 18: the trawler, which was not carrying sidelights and, therefore, was not seen by the other colliding ship, was held not at fault, while the other ship was held alone to blame for the collision on the ground of no lookout.

years later, by s 4 of the Maritime Conventions Act (MCA) 1911, the presumption of fault rule was abolished. Since then, a causative link between non-compliance with a collision regulation and the collision must be established, whether the breach was partial or the sole cause of the collision and the damage resulting from it. In addition, s 1 of the MCA 1911 established the division of loss rule in proportion to the degree to which each vessel was at fault, instead of 50/50 as was the position previously in every case of joint fault. The MCA 1911 was passed to implement the Brussels Convention on Collisions, in 1910, relating to collisions and salvage, and survived the passage of time until the enactment of the MSA 1995.

1.3 The law and regulations at present

Section 4 of the MCA 1911 made a significant amendment by abolishing the arbitrary rule of presumption of fault of s 419(4) of the 1894 Act.

In the middle and latter part of the 20th century, with continuous advancements in technology affecting ships and specialist craft, there were three sequential amendments to the Collision Regulations. The 1910 regulations were superseded by the 1948 regulations, then by the 1960 regulations and, finally, by the 1972 regulations.

The International Regulations for the Prevention of Collisions at Sea 1972 – adopted under the auspices of the International Maritime Organisation (IMO) – revised the 1960 Collision Regulations. The British Parliament adopted them in 1977. Since then, the 1972 Regulations have had the force of law with regard to all British ships on the high seas and all waters connected therewith navigable by sea-going vessels and to foreign ships coming within the UK territorial waters. These regulations were subsequently amended in 1983, 1989, and 1991. The current UK Merchant Shipping Regulations of 1996 revoked and replaced the Merchant Shipping (Distress Signals and Prevention of Collisions) Regulations of 1983, 1989 and 1991. They are subject to the MSAs which have been consolidated by the MSA 1995.

By s 306 of the MSA 1995, the Secretary of State has power to make regulations, orders or rules exercisable by statutory instrument and such instrument shall be subject to annulment pursuant to a resolution of either House of Parliament. With regard to collisions, he may make regulations as to the steps to be taken to prevent any collision involving a ship (s 85(3)(k) or a collision between seaplanes on the surface of water and between ships and seaplanes (s 85(4)).

1.4 Ships being subject to the Collision Regulations

The Collision Regulations apply to all British ships wherever they may be and to all foreign ships within UK waters. Her Majesty's ships are exempt from the provisions of the MSA 1995 to which the Collision Regulations are subject (s 308(1)), but obedience to Collision Regulations by the Royal Navy is provided by the Queen's Regulations, which are published to the world at large and are not only issued as a matter of departmental discipline.[3]

The current regulations, by reg 1(c), now allow the government of any State to make special rules regarding signal lights, shapes or whistle signals for ships of war and vessels proceeding under convoy, so that these lights, shapes or signals cannot be mistaken for any others authorised under the rules. Also, by reg 1(e) compliance with the Collision Regulations is excused, if a government so determines for special construction vessels for which other provisions can be made so as to provide for the closest possible compliance by them with the rules.

Non-naval government ships are not subject to the regulations, but power is given by s 308 of MSA 1995 for such ships and any ships held for the benefit of the Crown, that they might, by Order in Council, be registered as British ships, so that the Act will apply. Hence, the Collision Regulations being subject to it will also apply with exceptions and modifications, as the Order in Council may provide. Section 309 extends the application of such Order in Council to ships in the service of the government by a demise charter to the Crown. No orders have yet been made under these provisions. Nevertheless, the prevailing view is that, as a matter of good seamanship, such ships, which are not obliged by statute to comply with the regulations, will conform to them.

As has been seen in the first part of this book, no action *in rem* may be brought against Crown vessels (s 29 of the Crown Proceedings Act 1947), but only an action *in personam* against the relevant Government department as is provided by s 24(2) of the Supreme Court Act 1981.

1.5 Definition of vessel and ship

The rules define a vessel as including every description of water craft, including non-displacement craft and seaplanes,[4] used or capable of being used as a means of transportation on water (reg 3(a)). The Merchant Shipping (Distress Signals and Prevention of Collisions) Regulations 1996 (reg 2(2)) provides: 'ship' includes hovercraft; reg 2(1) provides for the application of

---

3   *HMS Truculent* [1951] 2 Lloyd's Rep 308 and, also, *The Albion* [1953] 1 Lloyd's Rep 239.
4   'Seaplane' includes a flying boat and any other aircraft designed to manoeuvre on the water (Civil Aviation Act 1982, s 97(6)).

the Collision Regulations to seaplanes registered in the UK and on the surface of water anywhere; also, on other seaplanes on UK waters. Special provisions for lights and shapes to be exhibited by seaplanes are made.

Section 313 of the MSA 1995 defines a ship as including every description of vessel used in navigation.[5] Section 310 makes the Act applicable to hovercraft.[6] By s 311 of the MSA 1995, the Secretary of State has power to declare anything designed or adapted for use at sea to be a ship for any purpose of the MSAs. This power is yet to be exercised.

There is no definition under the MSA 1995 of the words 'used in navigation'. Therefore, reference must be made to the definition given in decided cases.

Steedman v Scofield[7]

The plaintiff was riding a jet-ski when he was involved in a collision with a speedboat being driven by the first defendant. The first defendant was towing a water-ski on which the second defendant rode. The collision was caused by the negligence of the first defendant while acting as agent or servant of the water-skier. The plaintiff instituted proceedings against the defendants for his personal injuries. It was contended that the action was time barred by the time the writ was issued under the provisions of the s 8 of the MCA 1911. The issue for decision was whether the jet-ski (upon which the plaintiff rode when he was injured) was a 'vessel used in navigation' for the purposes of the MSA 1894. Section 742 of this Act defined 'vessel' as including any ship or boat or any other description of vessel used in navigation; and defined a 'ship' as including every description of vessel used in navigation not propelled by oars.

If a jet-ski was 'a vessel used in navigation' for the purposes of the MSAs, it was also a 'ship' because it was not propelled by oars. If s 8 of the MCA 1911 did not apply, the claim was brought within the three year time limit applicable to a claim for personal injuries caused by negligence.

The admiralty judge Sheen J held:

> To come within the definition of 'ship' as used in the MSAs the jet-ski had to be a vessel used in navigation; a vessel was usually a hollow receptacle for carrying people and the word 'vessel' was used to refer to craft larger than rowing boats and it included every description of watercraft used or capable of being used as a means of transportation on water; a jet-ski was not a vessel

---

5   Judicial interpretation of what constitutes a vessel has been given in various decisions; see, *op cit*, Marsden, fn 1, paras 1-6–1-18 and 6-34 with regard to mobile offshore drilling units; see, also, Chapter 1, above.

6   The enactment and instrument with respect to which provision may be made by Order in Council under s 1(1)(h) of the Hovercraft Act 1968 shall include this Act and any instrument made thereunder. See, also, the Hovercraft (Civil Liability) Order 1986 (SI 1986/1305) as amended.

7   [1992] 2 Lloyd's Rep 163.

The phrase 'used in navigation' conveyed the concept of transporting persons or property to an intended destination; navigation was not synonymous with movement on water but was planned or ordered movement from one place to another; a jet-ski was capable of movement on water at very high speed but its purpose was not to go from one place to another; it might be possible to navigate a jet-ski but it was not a vessel used in navigation

This was not an action to enforce a claim against the owners of a vessel in respect of personal injuries suffered by a person on board another vessel within the meaning of the MSAs 1894–1988; the action was not subject to the limitation imposed by s 8 of the MCA 1911.

1.6 Types of Collision Regulations

1.6.1 General

The International Regulations for Preventing Collisions at Sea (Colregs) 1972 as amended have international application, but are subject to variations of local rules of States giving effect to them, that is rules relating to harbours, rivers, inland waters.[8] See reg 1(b): '... such special rules shall conform as closely as possible to these rules'.[9]

As the scope of this work does not allow a detailed account of the rules, their full text, as amended, can be found in the 12th edition of Marsden. The rules contain five parts, A–E, with four annexes. They are a code of good practice rather than a code of law.

In Pt A, the rules deal with general matters such as application, responsibility for non-compliance and definitions. Part B deals with steering and sailing rules and Pt C with lights and shapes. It is these two latter parts that are discussed below with reference to decided cases.

The rules adopt a common sense approach and provide that regard shall be had to all dangers and special circumstances, which may allow departure from the rules necessary to avoid immediate danger.

1.6.2 Steering and sailing rules (Pt B, Section I)

It is stressed by reg 4 that the rules from 5–10 pursuant to Section I of this part must be complied with in any condition of visibility.

---

8   In *The Esso Brussels* [1972] 1 Lloyd's Rep 286, it was held that the Colregs and unwritten rules of good seamanship were only applicable insofar as the law of the place of the collision made them so.

9   In *The Genimar* [1977] 2 Lloyd's Rep 17, the principle of good seamanship applied, despite the fact that the Traffic Separation Scheme had not been given effect in Liberian law.

Regulation 5 (as amended): proper lookout

Every vessel shall at all times maintain a proper lookout by sight and hearing as well as by all available means appropriate in the prevailing circumstances and conditions so as to make a full appraisal of the situation and of the risk of collision.

A faulty lookout has contributed or has been the sole cause of many collisions. Whether or not it has been faulty is judged objectively. It involves an appreciation of what is taking place and it is not just the responsibility of one officer.[10]

The Maritime Harmony[11]

The collision between *The Anna Bibolini* and *The Maritime Harmony* occurred in waters connected with the high seas and accordingly, the Collision Regulations 1972 were applicable. At the time of the collision, *The Anna Bibolini* was on her way to Antwerp loaded with cargo but with only one of her two radar sets working. *The Maritime Harmony* was outbound from Antwerp also loaded with cargo, but with two operational radar sets. There was heavy tide and the tidal stream was quite forceful. Visibility was also reduced due to fog. Although *The Maritime Harmony* was on the correct side, she was not maintaining a proper or efficient radar watch. She had two radars, but the pilot was only making intermittent use of them. It was found that her lack of a proper watch could not justify the speed at which she was moving. It was also held that *The Anna Bibolini* did not maintain a proper radar watch either, or else the collision would have been prevented. As she had crossed into wrong waters and remained there until the collision, she was found 75% at fault.

The marking of successive radar plots of an approaching ship on the radar display gives the relative track of an approaching ship.[12] It may sometimes be necessary to use information from shore-based radar facility.[13] A proper lookout will depend at all times upon all circumstances.

Regulation 6: safe speed

Every vessel shall at all times proceed at a safe speed so that she can take proper and effective action to avoid collision and be stopped within a distance appropriate to the prevailing circumstances and conditions.

In determining a safe speed the rule further provides that all vessels should take the following factors into account:

---

10 *The Golden Polydinamos* [1993] 2 Lloyd's Rep 464.
11 [1982] 2 Lloyd's Rep 406.
12 *The Maloja II* [1993] 1 Lloyd's Rep 48, p 55, *per* Sheen J.
13 *The Nordic Ferry* [1991] 2 Lloyd's Rep 591.

(a) the state of visibility;

(b) traffic density;

(c) the manoeuvrability of the vessel with special reference to stopping distance and turning ability in the prevailing conditions;

(d) at night, the presence of background light such as from shores, etc;

(e) the state of the wind, sea and current, and the proximity of navigational hazards;

(f) the draught in relation to the available depth of water.

Further, vessels with operational radar shall take into account the following:

(a) the characteristics, efficiency and limitations of the radar equipment;

(b) any constraints imposed by the radar range scale in use;

(c) the effect on radar detection of the sea state, weather and other sources of interference;

(d) the possibility that small vessels, ice and other floating objects may not be detected by radar at an adequate range;

(e) the number, location and movement of vessels detected by radar;

(f) the more exact assessment of the visibility that may be possible when radar is used to determine the range of vessels or other objects in the vicinity.

In the pre-1972 rules the requirement was for a 'moderate speed' which had to be maintained in conditions of restricted visibility. A 'safe speed' requirement is adopted under the 1972 rules. An unsafe speed involves a speed that is slow as well as one that is excessive depending on the circumstances. Safe speed is a matter of good seamanship and is a relative term requiring various factors to be taken into account in any given case.

The Roseline[14]

Both *The Roseline* and *The Eleni V* were equipped with two operating radar sets. The vessels were proceeding in opposite directions, *The Roseline* at a speed of 14 knots and *The Eleni V* at a speed of about 13 knots. There was dense fog with poor visibility. Both vessels became aware of the presence of each other when they were at least six miles apart but neither of them reduced their speed. When only a few miles apart, *The Eleni V* put hard-a-port, bringing her across the track of *The Roseline* and a collision occurred. *The Roseline* struck *The Eleni V* in a way that severed *The Eleni V* into two parts, thus, resulting in the loss of a substantial quantity of her cargo of fuel oil.

It was held that the two ships were at fault, as they were obviously not being navigated in accordance with the Colregs 1972, or in accordance with seamanlike prudence. Both vessels were under a duty to comply with the regulations. Amongst the faults attributed to both vessels was unsafe speed.

---

14 [1981] 2 Lloyd's Rep 410.

The learned judge, Sheen J, put questions to the Trinity Masters. One of the questions was what a safe speed would have been for each vessel within the meaning of reg 6. The answer was that, in the prevailing circumstances and conditions, for *The Eleni V* a safe speed would have been 6 knots, and for *The Roseline*, 8 knots.

There are numerous examples of collisions cases which have occurred due to unsafe speed. While the reader is advised to refer to Marsden's recent edition, it suffices for the purpose of this book to mention two more. In *The Coral I*,[15] a collision occurred on a clear night with an anchored vessel due to high speed of the proceeding vessel in a crowded anchorage area with lack of a straight passage. The judge found that half manoeuvring speed ought to have been maintained in those circumstances. In *The ER Wallonia*,[16] the fault of the colliding vessels lay in their respective failure to reduce speed when visibility began to be restricted.

Regulation 7: risk of collision

(a) Every vessel shall use all available means appropriate to the prevailing circumstances and conditions to determine if risk of collision exists. If there is any doubt such risk shall be deemed to exist.

(b) Proper use shall be made of radar equipment if fitted and operational, including long range scanning to obtain early warning of risk of collision and radar plotting of equivalent systematic observation of detected objects.

(c) Assumptions shall not be made on the basis of scanty information, especially scanty radar information.

This rule suggests a sensible approach to determining the risk of collision which might exist. The second part of the rule is new. What is a proper use of radar was explained in *The Roseline* (above). In determining if risk of collision exists, para (d) of the rule gives guidelines to be considered: (i) if the compass bearing of an approaching vessel does not appreciably change; (ii) even if an appreciable bearing change is evident, a risk may exist when approaching a very large vessel or a tow or when approaching a vessel at close range.

A remarkable situation arose in a collision between *Selat Arjuna* and *Contship Success*,[17] in which the latter performed a major and wholly unexpected alteration to starboard when the vessels were starboard to starboard passing. Her master thought that he saw an echo on the radar on his port bow, which was in fact false. By altering to starboard, he placed the other vessel ahead and, becoming more confused, proceeded to alter more and more to starboard, whereupon he collided with and sank the other ship. *Contship Success* was found wholly to blame.

---

15 [1982] 1 Lloyd's Rep 441.
16 [1987] 2 Lloyd's Rep 485.
17 [2000] 1 Lloyd's Rep 627.

Regulation 8: action to avoid collision

The gist of the six paragraphs of this rule is that any action to avoid a collision shall be positive, made in ample time and with due regard to observance of good seamanship and the provisions of regs 5 and 6 shall be observed in avoiding collision.

Regulation 9: narrow channels

    (a) A vessel proceeding along the course of a narrow channel or fairway shall keep as near to the outer limit of the channel or fairway which lies on her starboard side as is safe and practicable.

The remaining six paragraphs of this rule give guidelines on safe crossing in narrow channels or fairways, limit the scope of overtaking unless necessary to permit safe passage with appropriate sounding signals, stress the need of particular alertness and caution when navigating near a bend, and prohibit anchoring in a narrow channel.

    A few examples illustrate this rule.

The Toluca[18]

A channel about 18 km long had been dredged through the mud in order to enable vessels to get to the city of Bangkok by river, situated about 25 miles above the mouth of Mae Chao. No local rules relating to the navigation of the channel had been passed, therefore, for every vessel navigating the channel, reliance had to be placed on the Colregs, the 1960 version. Regulation 25 of those rules provided that:

> In a narrow channel every power driven vessel when proceeding along the course of the channel shall, when it is safe and practicable, keep to that side of the fairway or mid-channel which lies on the starboard side of such vessel.

The Visahakit 1 loaded with petroleum products was heading for Bangkok, while *The Toluca* was leaving Bangkok laden with cargo. *The Toluca* was 3 ft longer than the longest ship normally permitted to enter the port of Bangkok so that she had to obtain special permission to enter. At night, in excellent visibility, a collision occurred between the vessels resulting in slight damage to *The Toluca*, but heavier damage to *The Visahakit 1*. It was found that the collision took place in the middle of the eastern half of the main channel, therefore, both vessels were bound to comply with reg 25 governing navigation of vessels in narrow channels. The admiralty judge held that, on the balance of probabilities, *The Toluca* was hampered by the limits of the channel and the effect of her speed. There was no fault on the part of *Visahakit 1*, even in starboarding at the last minute, as that was a decision made in the 'agony of the moment' in an attempt to avoid the collision, for which the

18 [1984] 1 Lloyd's Rep 131.

master could not be blamed. The Court of Appeal affirmed the decision and added:

> *Toluca* was not entitled to expect *Visahakit 1* to wait for her to come round the bend; *Toluca* was negligent in respect of her speed in approaching the bend and in her reduction of speed at the bend; the way in which the accident could have been avoided was by *Toluca* keeping on her own side of the channel as *Visahakit 1* had done ...

In particular, Slade LJ said:

> There is no dispute that *Toluca* would have had to go into the centre of the channel when rounding the bend. This would risk a collision if *Visahakit 1* was on the bend at the same time. In my opinion in these circumstances *Toluca* should have given way so that the two vessels passed in part of the channel that was straight. But *Toluca* did not slow down to avoid this situation, she approached the bend at 10 knots and it was too late to slow down when she realized that she was going to meet *Visahakit 1* on the bend. In answer to a question from us our assessors were of opinion that *Toluca* should have approached the bend at 6 knots and indeed that her speed should not have exceeded 6 knots in this channel. I agree with and accept this opinion. In my opinion the judge came to a correct conclusion and I would dismiss this appeal.[19]

Therefore, *The Toluca* was solely to blame for the damage caused.

In ***The Koningin Juliana***,[20] the collision with *The Thurokini* occurred in Harwich harbour, when the former was outward bound and the latter inward bound. The pilot of *The Koningin* having misunderstood that *The Thurokini* was not moving, created a crossing situation. The issue was whether *The Thurokini* was in the correct position on the dividing line to starboard and this depended on the meaning of mid-channel; did it mean the centre line of the whole navigable channel or of the dredged channel? The answer was – confirmed by the Court of Appeal – that 'narrow channel' meant the whole width of the navigable water and that in Harwich harbour the line to starboard of which each vessel shall keep is the centre of the dredged channel. Both ships were at fault.

Regulation 10: traffic separation schemes[21]

This rule is regulating opposing streams of traffic and vessels passing along the entire length of the scheme by establishing traffic lanes. The rule is new and has been amended by the recent amendments to the Colregs. The improvements have been based on examination of collision incidents and

---

19 [1984] 1 Lloyd's Rep 131, p 136.
20 [1974] 2 Lloyd's Rep 353 and [1975] 2 Lloyd's Rep 111 (HL).
21 For full details and interpretation of the individual paragraphs of this scheme, the reader is referred to *op cit*, Marsden, fn 1, paras 6-92–6-106.

indeed have reduced the number of these incidents, particularly in the Dover Straits.

A recent example[22] of breach of reg 10 occurred in Bosporus where *The Hagieni* (a bulk carrier proceeding southward) and *The Barbarossa* (a chemical tanker, proceeding northward) collided. *The Barbarossa* was largely at fault failing to keep her position in her own northbound lane. In addition, she increased her speed and caused confusion to the other vessel, her lookout was defective. The collision occurred at an angle of 80 degrees where the bow of *The Barbarossa* struck the starboard side of *The Hagieni*.

It was held by the admiralty judge that: *The Hagieni* failed to cope with the embarrassment of *The Barbarossa*'s approach. Her alteration to port was however an imprudent and unannounced close range option. But, the overriding consideration on this case was that *The Barbarossa* was at all material times persisting in navigating in the southbound lane or separation zone. She created a situation of danger and inevitably instilled the maximum of confusion as to her intentions. Therefore, she was 80% to blame.

1.6.3 Conduct of vessels in sight of each other (Pt B, Section II)

While Section I (regs 4–10) apply in any condition of visibility, regs 11–18 of Section II deal with conduct of vessel in sight of one another, and reg 19 of Section III applies to conditions of restricted visibility.

In particular, reg 12 refers to sailing vessels when they are approaching one another and which of them should keep out of the way to avoid a risk of collision. For example, the vessel which has the wind on the port side shall keep out of the way of the other.

Regulation 13 deals with overtaking situations stressing that any vessel overtaking any other shall keep out of the way of the vessel being overtaken.

Regulation 14 gives guidelines when vessels are on a head-on situation, whereupon each shall alter her course to starboard so that each shall pass on the port side of the other.

The rule provides, in particular, that:

When two power driven vessels are meeting on reciprocal or nearly reciprocal courses so as to involve risk of collision each shall alter her course to starboard so that each shall pass on the port side of the other.

Such a situation shall be deemed to exist when a vessel sees the other ahead or nearly ahead and by night she could see the masthead lights of the other in a line or nearly in a line and/or both sidelights and by day she observes the corresponding aspect of the other vessel.

---

22   *The Hagieni and Barbarossa* [2000] 2 Lloyd's Rep 292.

When a vessel is in any doubt as to whether such a situation exists she shall assume that it does exist and act accordingly.

An illustration of such a situation is given in the following case.

The Argo Hope[23]

The Argo Hope was outward bound from Runcorn, partly laden, navigated along the Manchester Ship Canal by a pilot, while *The Bebington* was bound from Stanlow to Manchester. They collided port to port at a 30 degree angle in the Manchester Ship Canal. The vessels were in a head-on situation and would have passed side by side if they had kept their correct headings. It was found that *Argo Hope* was not navigated with caution, the immediate cause of the collision being that she suddenly changed her heading to port. She was found 85% to blame. The master of *The Bebington* was also at fault having misjudged the speed of *Argo Hope* and did not keep well on the starboard side.

Regulation 15: crossing situation

When two vessels are crossing so as to involve risk of collision, the vessel which has the other on her own starboard side shall keep out of the way and shall, if the circumstances of the case admit, avoid crossing ahead of the other vessel.

The Nowy Sacz[24]

The Olympian and *The Nowy Sacz* were both proceeding northwards parallel to each other in the Atlantic Ocean, when a collision occurred between them at night in fine weather and good visibility. The vessels had been in sight of each other for a considerable period of time before the collision occurred. The plaintiffs, owners of *The Olympian*, contended that the crossing rules applied, and that under them, it was the duty of *The Nowy Sacz* having *The Olympian* on her starboard side, to keep out of the way of *The Olympian*. The defendants however, owners of *The Nowy Sacz*, said that the overtaking rules applied and it was the duty of *The Olympian* under those rules, as the overtaking ship, to keep out of the way of *The Nowy Sacz*. The judge held on the facts that the two ships were in sight of one another, and that the risk of collision between them had already arisen. The situation in this case (being subject to 1960 rules) was a crossing situation and not an overtaking one. Therefore, it was the duty of *The Nowy Sacz* to keep out of the way of *The Olympian*, and the duty of *The Olympian* to keep her course and speed. Also, *The Nowy Sacz* was at fault in failing to take early and positive action to keep out of the way of *The Olympian*, and in failing to reduce her speed in good time so as to allow *The Olympian* to pass ahead of her.

---

23 [1982] 2 Lloyd's Rep 559.
24 [1976] 2 Lloyd's Rep 682.

Regulation 16: action by give-way vessel

Every vessel which is directed to keep out of the way of another vessel shall, so far as possible, take early and substantial action to keep well clear.

In a collision between *Mineral Dampier* and *Hanjin Madras*,[25] the latter failed to take correct avoiding action as a give-way vessel in a crossing situation as soon as the vessels came into sight of one another. She should have altered her course to starboard. When it appeared clear to *Mineral Dampier* that she did not turn to starboard, *Mineral Dampier* turned to port in desperation and the bow of *Hanjin Madras* struck her aft starboard side at an angle of 50 degrees leading aft on *Mineral Dampier*. The apportionment of blame was 80%. and 20%, respectively.

Regulation 17: action by stand-on vessel

Whether one of two vessels is to keep out of the way, the other shall keep her course and speed.

The latter vessel may however take action to avoid collision by her manoeuvre alone, as soon as it becomes apparent to her that the vessel required to keep out of the way is not taking appropriate action in compliance with these Rules.[26]

Regulation 18: specifies responsibilities between vessels

For example, a power driven vessel shall keep out of the way of a vessel not under command, or restricted in her ability to manoeuvre, or engaged in fishing or sailing.

1.6.4 Conduct of vessels in restricted visibility (Pt B, s III)

Regulation 19

(a) The rule applies to vessels not in sight of one another when navigation in or near an area of restricted visibility.[27]

(b) Every vessel shall proceed at a safe speed adapted to the prevailing circumstances and conditions of restricted visibility. A power driven vessel shall have her engines ready for immediate manoeuvre.

(c) Every vessel shall have due regard to the prevailing circumstances and conditions of restricted visibility when complying with the rules of s I of this part.

---

25 [2000] 1 Lloyd's Rep 282.

26 See *The Estrella* [1977] 1 Lloyd's Rep 525 and *The Angelic Spirit* [1994] 2 Lloyd's Rep 595.

27 This paragraph extends the rules applicable to vessels navigating in restricted visibility to vessels navigating near an area of restricted visibility too (see *op cit*, Marsden, fn 1, p 225).

(d) A vessel which detects by radar alone the presence of another vessel shall determine if a close quarters situation is developing and/or risk of collision exists. If so, she shall take avoiding action in ample time, provided that when such action consists of an alteration of course, so far as possible the following shall be avoided: (i) an alteration of course to port for a vessel forward of the beam, other than for a vessel being overtaken; (ii) an alteration of course towards a vessel abeam or abaft the beam.

(e) Except where it has been determined that a risk of collision does not exist, every vessel which hears apparently forward of her bean the fog signal of another vessel, or which cannot avoid a close quarters situation with another vessel forward of her beam, shall reduce her speed to the minimum at which she can be kept on her curse. She shall of necessary take all her way off and on any event navigate with extreme caution until the danger of collision is over.

The Ercole[28]

A collision occurred between *The Embiricos* and *The Ercole*. The ships were approaching each other in opposite directions.

Each ship was observed by the other on the radar during the approach period. *The Ercole* was steering 230 degrees. and substantially making good that course at 13 knots. *The Embiricos* was on a course of 40 degrees doing about 15 knots. The visibility was restricted. The second officer, on watch on *The Embiricos,* first saw *The Ercole* at 18 miles some two to three degrees on the starboard bow. *The Ercole* then changed slowly to six degrees at eight miles and to eight degrees at five miles, when she ceased to be visible because of rain. The second officer estimated that, if the two ships maintained their courses they would pass each other on parallel courses at about mile and switched from automatic to manual steering. Meanwhile the master of *Ercole* first saw *The Embiricos* on radar on the 24 mile range bearing six degrees at 20 miles on her port bow. As she approached, he changed to the 12 mile range and when *The Embiricos* was some three miles distant, her echo disappeared into the clutter round the centre of the radar screen and he formed the view that the two ships would pass port to port at one to two miles. He altered course 10 degrees to starboard when some three miles distant. He next saw a group of white lights from *The Embiricos*, but before seeing her side lights he put the Ercole hard to starboard. *The Embiricos'* wheel was put hard to port and the collision then took place.

It was held that both ships were at fault.

On the above findings *The Embiricos* was at fault in two respects: first, as regards defective appreciation of the situation on the radar; and, second, for not reducing her speed substantially when the visibility lessened. *The Ercole*

---

28 [1977] 1 Lloyd's Rep 516.

was at fault in four respects: first, as regards defective appreciation of the situation on the radar; second, for not stopping her engines and then navigating them with caution when she lost the echo of *The Embiricos* in the clutter; third, for altering course 10 degrees to starboard at an improper time; and fourth, for going hard to starboard at the last instead of putting her engines full astern, and all these faults on either side were causative

Brandon J commented on the situation:

> If plotting is necessary in order to enable a navigator to ascertain correctly the course of an approaching ship, then either he should make a plot, or he should not draw conclusions about the course of that ship which are unwarranted without one.

1.6.5 Lights and shapes (Pt C)

Regulations 20–27

Regulation 20: applies to all weather conditions between sunset and sunrise and in restricted visibility and in addition when the use could reasonably be considered necessary.[29]

Regulation 21: defines each type of light.

Regulation 22: explains a new rule about visibility of lights.

Regulation 23: specifies the type of lights to be exhibited by power driven vessels underway.

Regulation 24: covers the situation of lights during towing.

Regulations 25 and 26: provide the requirements for sailing vessels, vessels under oars and fishing vessels.

Regulation 27: covers lights for ships not under command.

In *The Djerada*,[30] the judge said in relation to these rules:

> First, as to lookout. I find that the lookout on *The Djerada* was extremely bad, as a result of which the lights of *The Ziemia* were not properly observed, nor her course and speed properly appreciated, during the period of 45 minutes leading up to the collision.
>
> Second and third, as to lights. I find that *The Djerada* was not justified in carrying not under command lights and should in any case not have carried a white masthead light as well as such lights. I find that she was in both these respects in breach of reg 1(b) of the Collision Regulations, which forbids the exhibition of lights other than those prescribed by such rules.

---

29 See *The Coral* [1982]1 Lloyd's Rep 441.

30 [1976] 1 Lloyd's Rep 50.

The Albion[31]

A collision between the plaintiff's steamship, *Maystone*, and an uncompleted aircraft carrier, *Albion*, occurred in southerly gale, at night, in North Sea. *The Albion*, with skeleton crew on board, was being towed northwards by three tugs and *The Maystone* was southward bound. While the tugs of *Albion* safely passed by *Maystone* port to port there was an impact between stem of *Maystone* and port side aft of *Albion*, at approximately a right angle. *Maystone* sank after unsuccessful manoeuvres to clear *Albion*. An action was brought by the owners of the sunk ship against the admiralty, as owners of *Albion* and against SH (shipbuilders) who until acceptance by admiralty, were responsible for the care and efficient protection of the vessel and against FF (tugowners) who had contracted with SH to be responsible for the tow.

It was held:

> ... that the port light of *Albion* was defective and that no blame attached to *Maystone* for failing to see *Albion* lying across her course; that the number and disposition of the tugs, the failure to obtain a long range weather forecast, and the absence of warnings issued by *Albion* to shipping in the vicinity, together constituted a negligent failure to conduct the towage in a seamanlike manner; in addition, *The Albion* had suffered an accident and she was not in command, therefore she should display the 'non-under command lights'.

Regulations 28, 29, 30 and 31 specify the type of lights to be shown by vessels constrained by their draught, pilot vessels, anchored vessels and vessels aground, as well as seaplanes, respectively.

1.6.6 Sound and signals (Pt D)

After definitions of sound signals, reg 34 deals with manoeuvring and warning signals, reg 35 with signals for restricted visibility, reg 36 with signals to attract attention and reg 37 with distress signals. Part E exempts vessels under construction from displaying certain lights.

---

31 [1953] 1 Lloyd's Rep 239.

SECTION B

2 CRIMINAL LIABILITY

2.1 General

Maritime offences have been dealt with by the MSAs and are now to be found in the MSA 1995 as well as in regulations. By s 85, the Secretary of State has power to make regulations relating to safety and health on ships, which may provide that a contravention of those regulations shall be an offence punishable on summary conviction by a fine or on indictment by imprisonment for a term not exceeding two years and a fine.

Intentional or reckless damage to property of another, without lawful excuse, is covered by the Criminal Damage Act (CDA) 1971, which also includes endangering or threatening the life of another. Where a collision between ships or between a ship and a fixed or floating object is caused deliberately or recklessly, this criminal behaviour will now fall to be dealt with under the offences applicable generally to wilful damage of property.[32]

Apart from specific offences created by statute, the general principles of criminal law would apply in cases of loss of life by criminal gross negligence. A brief account of statutory offences under the MSA 1995 is given below. Then, criminal liability for involuntary manslaughter is briefly looked at, but the reader is also referred to Chapter 8.

2.2 Statutory offences under the MSA 1995

2.2.1 Disobeying the Collision Regulations

Failure to comply with Colregs, whether the breach causes a collision or not, has been made a criminal offence under the MSAs.

Section 419 of the MSA 1894 was the first statutory provision which made the infringement of a collision regulation a criminal offence if the infringement was caused by the wilful default of the master or owner of the ship. The effect of s 419(2) was that the offence was not absolute.[33] So the prosecution had to

---

32 See *op cit*, Marsden, fn 1, p 641; as to an offence of criminal damage committed by a British subject on a foreign ship on the high seas, see *R v Kelly, The Winston Churchill* [1981] 3 All ER 387 (HL).

33 *Bradshaw v Ewart-James (DC)* [1983] QB 671.

prove wilful default. If any damage occurred from non-observance, there was a deeming provision that the damage was caused by the wilful default of the person in charge of the deck of the ship at the time, unless it was shown that a departure from the regulation was necessary by the circumstances. This offence was amended by the amendments to the Colregs in 1983, 1989 and 1991.[34]

The current Collision Regulations of Merchant Shipping (Distress Signals and Prevention of Collisions) Regulations 1996, provide as follows.

Regulation 5

(1) Where any of these regulations is contravened, the owner or the vessel, the master and any person for the time being responsible for the conduct of the vessel shall each be guilty of an offence, punishable on conviction on indictment by imprisonment for a term not exceeding two years and a fine, or on summary conviction:

(a) in the case of any infringement of reg 10(b)(i) (duty to proceed with traffic flow in lanes of separation schemes) of the international regulations[35] and by fine not exceeding £50,000; and

(b) in any other case by a fine not exceeding the statutory maximum.

(2) It shall be a defence for any person charged under these regulations to show that the took all reasonable precautions to avoid the commission of the offence.

In addition, the vessel may be detained by any commissioned naval or military officer, any officer of the Department of Transport, any Customs and Excise Officer and any British Consular Officer, under s 284 of the MSA 1995.

There are two differences between this offence and that under s 419:

(a) first, no longer is it required that the prosecution proves wilful default of the master or owner of the ship. For example, the prosecution of the master for breach of the traffic separation scheme in *The NF Tiger*,[36] when he had delegated the task of bridge watch to the chief engineer, was unsuccessful, since the prosecution could not prove the requirement of the offence under s 419 of *mens rea*. The offence was not an absolute criminal offence. This case necessitated the change of the law and the requirement of proof by the prosecution of wilful default has been eliminated;

---

34 These were issued by the Secretary of State pursuant to his powers given under the then MSAs – the MSA 1894, s 418 and, subsequently, by the MSA 1979, s 21, which has now been repealed and replaced by the MSA 1995, s 85. Statutory instruments made under the MSA 1894, s 418 continue to be in force until superseded by new regulation made under the MSA 1995, s 85.

35 This offence corresponds to the offence under the MSA 1894, s 419(2).

36 [1982] 2 Lloyd's Rep 564; in *The Nordic Clansman* [1984] 1 Lloyd's Rep 31, the court applied *The Tiger*, but the master was convicted on proof of *mens rea*.

(b) second, the current provision includes any other person responsible for the conduct of the vessel at the time that can be prosecuted, and also that the master and the owner of the ship will not be exonerated from being prosecuted for that offence, even if the task of the watch on the bridge is delegated to another person, who commits the breach. For the owner to avoid conviction, he must show that he took all reasonable precautions to choose a competent master and that there was a system to supervise the master and ensure that he knew the regulations.[37]

However, this may not be sufficient now, bearing in mind the international regulations imposed on shipowners to ensure maritime safety. In particular, the adoption in July 1995 of substantial amendments to the International Convention on Standards of Training, Certification and Watchkeeping for Seafarers (STCW) together with the International Safety Management Code (ISMC) system of transparency of the company's practices will provide evidence as to whether the master and crew had been sufficiently trained and qualified in accordance with international standards.

As shipowners are corporate bodies, the corporation as well as the director, manager, secretary or similar officer may be found guilty of an offence, if it is proved that the offence has been committed with the consent or connivance of, or to be attributable to any neglect on the part of a director, manager, secretary or other similar officer of the body corporate or any person purporting to act ion such a capacity (s 277 of the MSA 1995).

2.2.2 Not giving assistance to vessels after collision or to vessels or persons in distress

Section 92 of the MSA 1995 (which replaced s 422 of the 1894 Act) provides that:

(1) In every case of collision between two ships, it shall be the duty of the master of each ship, if and so far as he can do so without danger to his own ship, crew and passengers (if any)

  (a) to render to the other ship, its master, crew and passengers (if any) such assistance as may be practicable and necessary to save them from danger caused by the collision, and to stay by the other ship until he has ascertained that it has no need of further assistance.

  (b) to give to the master of the other ship the name of his own ship and the names of the ports from which it comes and to which he is bound.

Although failure to do so does not raise any presumption of law that the collision was caused by his wrongful act, neglect or default, such failure is a criminal offence, which applies to masters of British ships and to masters of

---

37 *The Lady Gwendolen* [1965] 2 All ER 283.

foreign ships when in UK waters. In case of failure to comply with sub-s (1)(a), without reasonable excuse, he is liable (i) on summary conviction, to a fine not exceeding £50,000 or imprisonment for a term not exceeding six months or both; (ii) on conviction on indictment, to a fine or imprisonment for a term not exceeding two years or both. In case of failure to comply with sub-s (1)(b), he is liable to a fine. In either case, his certificate may be cancelled or suspended upon inquiry on his conduct.

By s 93(1), (2) of the MSA 1995, (which derived from s 22(1)(2) of the Merchant Shipping (Safety Convention) Act 1949), the master of a ship has a duty – upon receiving a signal of distress at sea or information from any other source that a ship or aircraft is in distress – to proceed at all speed to the assistance of the persons in distress, unless he is unable, or in special circumstances of the case considers it unreasonable or unnecessary to do so, or unless he is released from this duty in case of requisition as provided by sub-ss 4 and 5. Failure to do so is a criminal offence punishable on summary conviction to a term not exceeding six months or to a fine (not exceeding the statutory maximum) or both; on conviction in indictment up to two years imprisonment, or to a fine or both. Compliance by the master with these provisions shall not affect his right or the rights of others to salvage.

2.2.3 Breach of documentation and reporting duties

Section 77 of the MSA 1995[38] provides that, except as required by regulations under this section, an official logbook shall be kept in every UK ship. Regulations made under this section may prescribe the particulars to be entered in the official logbooks, and may require the production or delivery of official logbooks in circumstances as may be specified. They may also provide for exceptions of some ships from such requirements. Regulations under this section may make a contravention of any provision of this section an offence punishable with a fine. If a person intentionally destroys or mutilates or renders illegible any entry in an official logbook shall be liable on summary conviction to a fine.

Section 90[39] requires charts and other information to be carried on board when a ship goes to sea, as may be required by rules made by the Secretary of State under this section. If a ship goes to sea or attempts to go to sea without copies of charts, directions or information, which it is required to carry by rules under this section, the master or the owner shall be liable on summary conviction to a fine.[40]

---

38 Section 77 derives from the MSA 1970, s 68 and the Criminal Justice Act 1982, Sched 6, Pts III, IV, para 4 and s 46(2).

39 Section 90 derives from the MSA 1970, s 86 and the MSA 1979, Sched 6, Pt III.

40 *The Huntingdon* [1974] 1 WLR 505.

Section 91[41] requires the master of any UK ship to report dangers to navigation to ships in the vicinity and to authorities on shore, otherwise he shall be liable to a fine.

2.2.4 Dangerously unsafe ships and unsafe operation of ships

The MSA 1995 regulates the consequences of operating dangerous or unsafe ships in ss 94–107. **Section 94** (which derived from s 30 of the MSA 1988, as amended by the Merchant Shipping Maritime Security Act 1997) defines when a ship is 'dangerously unsafe' (see Chapter 8, para 5.6.1).

Section 95 gives power to the inspecting officer of an UK port to detain such a ship, whether she is British or foreign.

The provisions, which are relevant to the prevention of collisions, are contained in ss 98 and 100. Under **s 98** (which derived from s 30 of the MSA 1988), both the master and the owner of a dangerously unsafe ship (or any other person who has assumed responsibility for safety matters, such as charterers and managers) shall be guilty of an offence.[42] A defence to such an offence is specified under s 98(4), (5), (6) which states broadly that the accused must prove that at the time of the offence arrangements had been made to ensure the ship's fitness to go to sea as required.

Under **s 100** (being equivalent to s 31 of the MSA 1988) a duty is imposed upon the owner of any UK ship, or any ship registered under the laws of any other country and which is within the UK waters, to take all reasonable steps to ensure that the ship is operated in a safe manner. If the owner of such a ship fails to discharge such a duty, he shall be liable on summary conviction to a fine (up to £ 50,000), on conviction on indictment to imprisonment for a term up to two years or a fine, or both. In the event that the ship is chartered by demise or is managed, either wholly or in part, by any person other than the owner, the same duty is imposed on such a person as the case may be.

By contrast to s 98, this offence does not extend to the master of the ship.

With regard to officers of corporate bodies reference should be made again to s 277 of the Act.

The first case that was decided on the application of the former equivalent to this section was *The Safe Carrier*.[43] The ship-managers were charged with an offence for failing to secure that the vessel was operated in a safe manner when the chief engineer was given less than three hours to familiarise himself with the machinery. Within the next 24 hours, the engine broke down and the

---

41 This section derives from the Merchant Shipping (Safety and Load Line Convention) Act 1932, s 24, which was enacted after concerns caused by *The Titanic* disaster; the MSA 1964, s 16 added the information which has to be sent.

42 The details of this long section should be read from the Act.

43 [1994] 1 Lloyd's Rep 589 (HL).

vessel drifted at sea requiring the assistance of towage, but no damage occurred. Although the Court of Appeal held that the section has created a strict liability offence and no criminal state of mind was required, the House of Lords held that it was not helpful to categorise the offence as either one of strict liability or not. The prosecution must prove that the accused owner, manager, or demise charterer had failed to take all reasonable steps (which must be reasonable to him sub-s (4)(iii)) to ensure that the ship was operated in a safe manner. Although the test is objective, it has a subjective element. The fault of the employee below the senior management level was not to be taken into account for attributing liability to the corporation. The act or omission must have been of the directing mind and will of the relevant corporate owner or manager following the direction in the *Tesco v Nattrass* case.[44] The duty imposed is personal to the owner or charterer or manager.[45] The senior manager who has failed to operate a safe system will also be charged with the offence in accordance with s 277. Under the requirements of the ISMC will be easier to show that the senior management failed to operate a safe system, particularly as it requires that new personnel should be given sufficient time to familiarise themselves with the ship.[46]

The defective condition of hull or equipment or the improper loading or undermanning of a lighter or a barge which is used or is permitted to be used in navigation by any person, endangering human life by its unsafety, is made an offence by **s 99** of the MSA 1995. Equally, the Act contains provisions for the manning, qualification of officers and seamen, equipment and management of vessels the infringement of which carries penalties.

Relevant to danger to or safety of ships is the Dangerous Vessels Act 1985 which by s 1 authorises the harbour master to direct the removal from the harbour of any vessel the condition of which or the nature/condition of anything it contains might involve, in his opinion, a grave and imminent danger to the safety of any person or property; or it might involve a grave and imminent risk of preventing or seriously limiting the use of the harbour by its sinking or foundering.

2.2.5 Conduct endangering ships, structures or individuals

This offence was originally created by s 220 of the MSA 1894 as amended by s 27 of the MSA 1970 and was substituted by s 32 of the MSA 1988. The

---

44 The Identification Theory, see, further, in Chapter 8, paras 5.2 and 5.6.1, above.

45 It should be noted that other statutory offences may not be worded in the same way as s 100, so as to make the duty personal to the senior management of a company, and the special rule of attribution, as applied in *Meridian Global Funds Management Asia v Securities Commission* [1995] 3 All ER 918 (PC), may apply to attribute liability to the company when an employee below the senior management is found guilty of the offence; see, further, Chapter 8.

46 See Chapter 8.

amendments by s 32 became necessary after the sinking of the *Herald of Free Enterprise* (see later). It now appears in **s 58** of the MSA 1995. It refers to the master or any seaman of an UK ship, or a foreign ship being within UK waters.

Sub-section 2 provides that if such a person is on board the ship or in its immediate vicinity and does any act which causes or is likely to cause loss or destruction of or serious damage to his ship, machinery, navigational or safety equipment, or to any other ship, or the death of or serious injury to any person, he shall be guilty of an offence. The act must have been deliberate or have amounted to a breach or neglect of duty; or the master or seaman was under the influence of drink, or drugs at the time (sub-s (3)).

The same applies to an a omission of such a person to preserve his ship, etc, from being lost, destroyed or seriously damaged; or to preserve any person on board from death or serious injury; or to prevent his ship from causing loss or destruction or serious damage to any other ship or any structure, or the death of or serious injury to any person not on board his ship.

The offence extends by sub-s (4) to a situation in which the person performs his duties in relation to operation of his ship in such a manner as to cause, or to be likely to cause, any such loss, destruction, death or injury as mentioned above; also when he fails to discharge any of his duties, or to perform any such function, properly to such an extent as to cause, or to be likely to cause, any of those things.

The offence is punishable on summary conviction by a fine or on conviction on indictment by imprisonment (two years' maximum) (sub-s (5)).

There is a defence available to the accused as provided by sub-s (6) that he took all reasonable steps to discharge the duty imposed by sub-s (2) or that he was under the influence of drugs medically prescribed and he had no reason to believe that the drug might have the influence it had. In the case of an offence under sub-s (4), proof of reasonable precautions taken and exercise of due diligence to avoid committing the offence will excuse the accused.

While there is no defence when the act or omission was deliberate, there is a further defence under both subsections if the avoidance of the offence would involve disobeying a lawful command, or that in all the circumstances the loss, damage, death or injury in question could not reasonably have been foreseen or avoided by the accused.

It should be noted that under the original provision there was no defence and the court had to consider the gravity of the conduct in order to determine whether or not the offence had been committed. But, the words of the previous statutory provision did not include neglect of duty, for example, want of proper care in the discharge of the master's or seaman's duty. So, in the collision between *The Gladys* and *The Prome*[47] which resulted in the

---

47 [1911] 1 KB 571.

sinking of *The Prome* with her crew, poor lookout due to simple negligence of the master did not amount to a criminal offence. After this case, there were no further criminal prosecutions until 1980, when the court in *The Harcourt*[48] reached a decision (confirmed on appeal) which widened the scope of s 27 of the MSA 1970. The master was ill in bed but had left an experienced mate with instructions to keep watch during the night. While his vessel was anchored off the main navigational channel in the Hull West Roads, the mate left an experienced deckhand on watch after sunset, who omitted to turn on the forward anchor light creating a potentially dangerous situation. The mate noticed this when he returned for watch before midnight. The master became aware of the event by police officers when they boarded the vessel a few days later. Having accepted responsibility, he was found guilty.

It seems from this decision that the master' duty is non-delegable. He will only discharge his responsibilities under the statute if he checks personally whether or not those delegated by him carried out their responsibilities properly and the same will apply under the present statute, s 58. In addition, it follows from this decision that actual loss need not occur by reason of breach of the provisions of the statutory offence.

A further offence is provided by **s 59** of the MSA 1995 in relation to disobedience of lawful commands and neglect of duty by seamen.

2.2.6 Offence in relation to lighthouses, buoys or beacons

In addition to the general criminal law offences for damage to property provided by the Criminal Damage Act (CDA) 1971, the MSA 1995 includes specific offences in relation to criminal damage to lighthouses. **Section 219** is worded in similar language to s 1 of the CDA 1971 and makes it an offence when a person, without lawful authority, intentionally or recklessly damages any lighthouse, or its lights or buoy or beacon or removes, casts adrift or sinks, conceals or obscures any of the same. A person who is guilty of such an offence shall, in addition to being liable for the expenses of making good any damage so occasioned, be liable, on summary conviction, to a fine. Further, **s 220** gives power to the lighthouse authority to issue and serve 'a prevention notice' upon any person who exhibits a light on a place in such a manner as to be liable to be mistaken for a light proceeding from a lighthouse. If the person who is served with such a notice fails, without reasonable excuse, to comply with the directions contained in the notice, he shall be liable, on summary conviction, to a fine.

2.2.7 Breach of duty to give directions after shipping casualties

Under the MSA 1995, criminal sanctions attach also to oil pollution incidents which extend beyond pollution incidents arising out of collisions. **Section 136**

---

48 [1980] 2 Lloyd's Rep 589.

imposes a duty upon the owner or master of a ship to report the occurrence of discharge of oil mixture from a ship into a harbour in the UK waters, or escape of oil from a ship into any UK waters, to the harbour master or authority. Failure to comply with such a duty shall be punishable, on summary conviction, by a fine.

In addition, by **s 137**, the Secretary of State has wide powers to issue directions when an accident occurs to or in a ship and, in the opinion or the Secretary of State, oil from the ship will or may cause pollution on a large scale in the UK waters.

It will be an offence if a person to whom a direction is duly given under s 137 contravenes, or fails to comply with, any requirement with the direction (s 139).

2.3 Involuntary manslaughter for breach of duty

A breach of the Colregs, or of the provisions of the MSA 1995 relating to dangerously unsafe ships, ss 94, 98, and unsafe operation of ships, s 100 (seen earlier), which result in loss of life, will give rise to a prosecution for manslaughter if the elements of the offence for criminal negligence as stated at common law exist. The principles of criminal negligence were re-examined fairly recently in the following case.

R v Adomako[49]

The appellant, was the anaesthetist in charge during an eye operation in Mayday Hospital. During the operation, the supply of oxygen to the patient had been disconnected, but the appellant did not notice until the patient had a cardiac arrest a few minutes later and died. It was admitted that the appellant had been negligent, but the question was whether his actions were criminal. A jury convicted him of manslaughter after the death of the patient. The Court of Appeal, Criminal Division, dismissed his appeal and the same question was referred to the House of Lords. The question was stated as follows: in cases of manslaughter by criminal negligence not involving driving but involving a breach of duty, is it sufficient direction to the jury to adopt the gross negligence test without reference to the test of recklessness, as defined in *R v Lawrence*, or as adapted to the circumstances of the case? The House of Lords considered the authorities on the point and Lord Mackay, delivering the judgment, said:

> In my opinion the ordinary principles of the law of negligence apply to ascertain whether or not the defendant has been in breach of a duty of care towards the victim who has died. If such breach of duty is established the next

---

49   [1994] 3 All ER 79.

question is whether that breach of duty caused the death of the victim. If so, the jury must go on to consider whether that breach of duty should be characterised as gross negligence and therefore as a crime. This will depend on the seriousness of the breach of duty committed by the defendant in all the circumstances in which the defendant was placed when it occurred. The jury will have to consider whether the extent to which the defendant's conduct departed from the proper standard of care incumbent upon him, involving as it must have done a risk of death to the patient, was such that it should be judged criminal.[50]

Therefore, in reply to the question posed to the House, he stated:

> In cases of manslaughter by criminal negligence involving a breach of duty, it is sufficient direction to the jury to adopt the gross negligence test set out by the Court of Appeal in the present case following *R v Bateman* (1925) 19 Cr App R 8 and *Andrews v DPP* [1937] 2 All ER 552, [1937] AC 576 and it is not necessary to refer to the definition of recklessness in *R v Lawrence* [1981] 1 All ER 974 ... although it is perfectly open to the trial judge to use the word 'reckless' in its ordinary meaning as part of his exposition of the law if he deems it appropriate in the circumstances of the particular case.[51]

In the case of corporations, however (as discussed in Chapter 8), it has been difficult to convict the corporation itself for criminal negligence, unless it is found that the individuals, who can be identified as the 'directing mind and will' of the corporation, are themselves guilty of gross negligence. It is worth repeating in this context the following case.

Herald of Free Enterprise (R v East Kent Coroner ex p Spooner and Others)[52]

The vehicle ferry ship *Herald of Free Enterprise* capsized outside Zeebrugge harbour resulting in loss of life of a large number of passengers. A formal investigation carried out, pursuant to s 55 of the MSA 1970, by Sheen J, confirmed that the immediate cause of the vessel's loss was that she sailed with her bow doors open and trimmed by the head. In addition, it was found that the capsize was caused by the negligence of the assistant bosun, the chief officer, the master, the superintendent and the directors of the company who did not appreciate their responsibilities for the safe management of the ship (the company, from top to bottom, was criticised for sloppiness).

The incident was subsequently considered by a coroner, Turner J, who directed the jury that, as a matter of law, there was no sufficient evidence to convict the individuals. As regards the company, he said that, as a matter of law, a corporate body could not be guilty of manslaughter, unless one of the individual defendants who could be identified with the company could have

---

50 [1994] 3 All ER 79, p 86–87.

51 *Ibid*, p 88.

52 [1989] 88 Cr App R 10.

been guilty of manslaughter. He ruled against the adoption of the principle of aggregation of the faults of the individuals involved in order to convict the company. He said that where the acts or omissions of employees or managers of a corporate body were not sufficient to render them guilty of manslaughter, those acts or omissions could not be aggregated so as to render the corporate body guilty.

On an application for judicial review of the decision, Bingham LJ, in Queen's Bench (Divisional Court) held that:

> ... on appropriate facts the *mens rea* required for manslaughter can be established against the corporation. I see no reason in principle why such a charge should not be established.[53]

He further stated that:

> Whether the defendant is a corporation or a personal defendant, the ingredients of manslaughter must be established by proving the necessary *mens rea* and *actus reus* of manslaughter against it or him by evidence properly relied on against it or him. A case against a personal defendant cannot be fortified by evidence against another defendant. The case against a corporation can only be made by evidence properly addressed to showing guilt on the part of the corporation as such. On the main substance of his ruling I am not persuaded that the coroner erred.[54]

After *The Herald of Free Enterprise*, a new statutory offence was created by s 31 of the MSA 1988, making the owner, demise charterer or the ship-manager of a ship (upon whom responsibility for her safe operation lies at a particular time) criminally liable for unsafe operation, punishable upon summary conviction, with fine up to £50,000 or on indictment with two years' imprisonment. This offence is now repeated in s 100 of the MSA 1995, mentioned previously.

This section applies also to non-UK ships which are within UK territorial waters to take reasonable steps to ensure that the ship is operated in a safe manner, but it is not applicable to non-UK ships if they only came within the UK territorial waters due to weather or unavoidable circumstances.

However, the problems in relation to involuntary manslaughter may only be resolved by an enactment of the Law Commission's proposals for reform of this area of the law, which the British government has recently shown an interest to enact.[55]

---

53 (1989) 88 Cr App R 10, p 16.
54 *Ibid.*
55 See Chapter 8.

SECTION C

3 CIVIL LIABILITY

3.1 Introduction

It was explained in Section A of this chapter that there is no longer a presumption of fault by the mere breach of the Colregs. To establish civil liability resulting from a collision between ships or a ship and another object, the burden of proof is upon the claimant to prove the facts that have given rise to liability incurred due to negligence or want of good seamanship. Breach of the Colregs will be part of the evidence to be adduced by the claimant for the court to make an assessment of the blameworthiness of the defendant and evaluate the causative potency of the fault.

The principles of the law of negligence will be applicable (apart from one instance where no proof of negligence is required under s 74 of the Harbours, Docks and Piers Clauses Act (HDPCA) 1847 – this creates strict liability for damage to a harbour's property by a vessel). In all other instances, the claimant must establish that there was a duty of care, breach of that duty by the defendant, which caused the collision, and also that the breach caused the damage claimed which is subject to the remoteness rule.

For the court to identify whether there is a duty of care in negligence cases, a three stage test was developed in 1990.[56] These are: reasonable foreseeability of damage, a relationship of proximity between the parties, and that in all circumstances it was fair, just and reasonable to impose a duty of care upon the defendant. Although the three stage test applies universally to all cases whether the claim is for physical damage or economic loss, the proximity requirement of the test varies according to the circumstances and the type of damage claimed.

In straightforward cases of direct infliction of physical injury by the act of the defendant, the three stage test is easily satisfied. There may be no need to look beyond the foreseeability test in order to establish that the defendant had been in a 'proximate' relationship with the claimant.[57] In most claims in respect of physical damage to property or to a person, the question of the existence of a duty of care does not give rise to any problems, because it is

---

56 *Caparo Industries plc v Dickman* [1990] 1 All ER 568, or [1990] 2 AC 605 (HL).
57 *Murphy v Brentwood DC* [1990] 2 All ER 908, or [1991] AC 398 (HL), pp 486–87.

self-evident that such a duty exists and the contrary view is unarguable.[58] This is applicable to collision cases in which it is self-evident that a duty of care exists by a vessel towards other vessels navigating the same seas.[59] The same applies to consequential financial or economic loss resulting from the inflicted physical damage. When, however, a claim is for pure economic loss it is more difficult to satisfy the second and particularly the third stage tests. This aspect is examined in the context of damages and it relates in particular to claims by time or voyage charterers for financial loss.[60]

Since a duty of care exists in determining civil liability of a defendant in collision cases for physical loss and consequential economic loss, the other elements of the burden of proof will be examined later.

There are special rules for division of loss in collisions at sea, which became statutory by the MCA 1911. These are now consolidated in the MSA 1995, s 187.

3.2 Who may be liable?

3.2.1 The employer of the wrongdoer in personam

The employers of those on board whose negligent act caused the collision will be vicarious liable for the collision. The employer may be either the owner of the ship or the charterer by demise, who takes possession and control of the ship and employs the crew. A charterer under a time or voyage charter does not normally employ the crew. The act, or omission, giving rise to negligence must be that of the servant acting within the scope of his employment. In collision cases it will be the negligent act in navigation.

An interesting question arising in the context of vicarious liability is whether an employer or principal can be held liable to an innocent party when damage is caused due to a malicious, or criminal, act of the employee, or agent. In an old decision, *The Druid*,[61] the master of the ship deliberately rammed another vessel and caused damage to it when the master of the other

---

58   *The Hua Lien* [1991] 1 Lloyd's Rep 309 (PC); contrast *The Nicholas H* [1994] 1 WLR 1071 (HL), in which proof of foresight and proximity were not enough in a physical damage case where the claim was for economic loss. Instead, the third stage test, namely whether it would be fair, just and reasonable to impose such a duty, restricted the possibility of recovery by cargo-owners who sued the classification society of the ship, which was allowed to sail before permanent repairs to some defects had been carried out. The cargo on board the ship was lost when the ship sank due to unseaworthiness; (see, further, the analysis of decisions in this area in Chapter 11, para 9.

59   As developed originally by the landmark decision of *Donoghue v Stevenson* [1932] AC 562 (HL).

60   See *The Mineral Transporter* [1986] AC 1 (PC).

61   (1842) 1 W Rob 391.

ship refused to engage *The Druid* into a towage contract. The judge held the employer not liable for the criminal act of his employee because the act was not within the scope of the master's employment.

In later, non-admiralty, cases, however, concerning a fraudulent act of an agent,[62] or a theft of goods held under bailment by an employee of the bailee,[63] it was held that the agent, or the employee, acted in the course of his agency or his employment and, therefore, the principal or employer was liable. On the facts of these cases, it was the duty of the principal or the employer to exercise due care to see that no fraud or theft was committed. In a recent decision of the House of Lords,[64] it was held that before there can be vicarious liability, all the features of the wrong which are necessary to make the employee liable have to have occurred in the course of the employment. But the employer will not be liable for acts of an employee committed in the course of his employment which were not in themselves tortious and only became so when linked to other acts outside the course of his employment.

These are complex issues and the outcome will depend on the facts of each case. What is meant by the words 'occurred in the course of employment' is that the employee or agent had authority to do certain things on behalf of his employer or principal. Obviously, unless the employer or principal connives with the employee or agent to do the wrong, the wrongful act by the employee or agent should not be in the course of employment, or within the scope of agency. The cases of bailment mentioned earlier, or the cases in which a fiduciary duty is owed, differ from other cases because it is within the terms of bailment, or the fiduciary relationship, that due care should be exercised to employ honest servants, or to safeguard against the wrong.

Considering the facts of *The Druid* (above), the malicious act of the master, committed in a fit of temper, was not within the scope of his employment because it did not derive from actual or implied authority of his employer, although the authors of *Marsden* argue that the decision may not be good law today.[65] The master, and not his employer, will be personally liable for the criminal damage caused to an innocent party, but the employer cannot be held vicariously liable for such a criminal act, as it may be derived from the above House of Lords decision. In this connection, the rules of attribution of liability to a company for acts of employees are relevant (see Chapters 8 and 16).

---

62 *Lloyd v Grace Smith* [1912] AC 716 (HL); *Uxbridge Permanent Benefit Building Society v Pickard* [1939] 2 KB 248 (CA).

63 *Morris v CW Martin & Sons Ltd* [1966] 1 QB 716 (CA); *Port Swettenham Authority v T Wu & Co* [1979] AC 580 (PC).

64 *Credit Lyonnais Bank Nederland v Export Credits Guarantee Department* [2000] 1 AC 486 (HL).

65 See, *op cit*, Marsden, fn 1, para 12-05.

3.2.2 Persons responsible for the management and operation of the ship

Liability of a shipowner, or charterer by demise, or manager of the ship, for collision damage may arise from negligent management and operation of the ship and it is distinct from vicarious liability. Failure in ensuring that the ship is in a condition that she may be navigated safely by being properly equipped, manned and maintained, by reason of which the collision occurs, is negligence for which the persons responsible for the management will be answerable.

If the ship is properly maintained by the shipowner, or demise charterer, or the manager, but due to defective repairs, for example, in the steering gear, a collision occurs causing damage to a third party, the relevant person (shipowner, charterer by demise, or manager) will have to show in detailed particulars that: (a) he exercised due care to appoint competent repairers; (b) due attention had been given to any signs of possible malfunctioning of the steering gear, or defective equipment; and (c) no reasonable care and skill could have discovered the defect. In such circumstances, the repairer or supplier of the defective equipment will be joined as a second defendant, or as a third party to the proceedings under s 1 of the Civil Liability (Contribution) Act (CLCA) 1978 for contribution to liability, which may be a complete indemnity.[66]

The employer, shipowner, or demise charterer, will be liable to their own employees who may be injured on board the ship due to defective equipment. Under s 1 of the Employer's Liability (Defective Equipment) Act 1969, the employer is liable to any employee who suffers personal injury in the course of his employment in consequence of a defect in equipment provided by his employer, even if the defect is attributable to the fault of a third party, whether identified or not. A ship for this purpose is 'equipment'.[67] The Act provides for a right of contribution against the third party, who is really at fault. The third party, however, may not exist or may not be worth suing, so this is another policy reason behind the statutory liability of the employer, that is, for the protection of employees.

In practice, liability insurers will indemnify the relevant assured under the respective insurance policy for liability incurred by the collision to third parties.

3.2.3 Liability attaches on the ship

Leaving personal liability aside, liability *in rem* attaches to the ship for the damage caused by the collision, since damage caused by the ship is a maritime lien. This is irrespective of the fact that her owner may not be the

---

66 See para 3.11, below.
67 *The Derbyshire* [1987] 3 All ER 1068, see, also, discussion of the case in Chapter 2.

employer of the master and crew at the time of the negligence if the ship is under a demise charter. It is the voluntary entrusting of the possession of the vessel to the demise charterer, for a temporary period, that has been held not to relieve the ship from being arrested as security by the claimant, even though her owner would not be in such a case vicariously liable for the negligence of those employed by the demise charterer.[68]

3.2.4 Master and crew

The wrongdoer by whose negligence the collision occurred will also be liable. This includes any person in control of navigation, the master, pilot, seaman on watch, and the helmsman, who might have directed a wrong course resulting in the collision. The master is not vicariously liable for the wrongdoing of the crew, without fault of his own, but he may be liable if he gave negligent instructions to a helmsman, or if he allowed the pilot who was under the influence of drink to take charge of the ship. The master and crew can, under the 1976 Limitation of Liability Convention, limit their liability being included in the persons who can limit.[69] The pilot, who may be negligent during navigation of the ship, could limit his liability either under the 1976 Convention because he is treated as the employee of the owner or manager and operator *pro tempora*, or under s 22 of the Pilotage Act (PA) 1987.

3.2.5 Tug or tow

Under a towage[70] contract, it is common to have an express term that the master and crew of the tug are deemed to be the servants of the hirer of the tug. Although the effect of this clause is to impose vicarious liability on the hirer for negligent acts or omissions of the tug, such a provision regulates only the liabilities of the parties to the contract.[71]

The question whether the tug or the tow will be liable for a collision to a third party depends on who was in control of navigation at the time of the act or omission which caused the collision. The theory that the tow and the tug always comprise one unit, so as to render the tow always liable for negligence of the master or crew of the tug, has been implicitly overruled by *The Devonshire*,[72] in which the House of Lords explained the concept of the control theory.[73] Whether or not the tug is solely in control of the tow for all aspects of navigation is a question of fact.

---

68 *The Lemington* (1874) 2 Asp MC 475 and *The Father Thames* [1979] 2 Lloyd's Rep 364.
69 See Chapter 16, below.
70 For definition and nature of a towage contract, see Chapter 14, below.
71 See, eg, *The President Van Buren* (1924) 19 LlL Rep 185 and other authorities referred to in Chapter 14, below.
72 [1912] AC 634 (HL).
73 See Chapter 14, para 8.2.2, below.

The tug in this case was towing a dumb barge when a collision between the barge and *The Devonshire* took place due to negligence of the tug and *The Devonshire*. When the tow, which on the facts was an innocent party, sued the owners of *Devonshire* for the collision damage, the defence of contributory negligence was raised on the ground of the tug's negligence – being considered as the negligence of the tow on application of the 'unit' theory. The defence failed because the tow in this case had no control in navigation.

An instance of sole control by the tug arises when the tow is unmanned or in a condition in which she is incapable of navigation. In most situations, however, navigation will be shared between the two, whereupon the tug and the tow will each be responsible for their respective negligent acts or omissions which may cause or contribute to a collision and resulting damage thereof.[74] It will all depend on whose fault caused the collision.

Similarly under US law, in third parties' claims, the fault of the tug and the tow are considered separately in proportion to their individual fault. But, as regards navigation rules a tug and a tow are considered one vessel that must observe the rules as a unit. When damage is caused by a casualty involving the tow or the whole flotilla, the courts employ the concept of 'dominant mind' to place liability on the tug and to absolve the tow from liability. The rule is not absolute, however; at best it is only a presumption that the tug in control is responsible as the dominant mind.[75]

3.2.6 Salvors

Salvors are independent contractors and invariably take full control of navigation depending on the state of the vessel to be salved. They owe a duty of care not only to the salved property, but to third parties as well. Breach of such a duty during the salvage operation, resulting in damage, will expose them to liability. They can limit such liability under the provisions of the Limitation Convention 1976, as enacted by the MSA 1995.[76] As regards liability towards the salved property, an award of damages for negligence will be a set off against the salvage award earned.[77]

3.2.7 Pilots

Pilots are professionals and act as independent contractors although a port authority licenses them. Mere licensing does not create liability of the port authority, s 22(8) of the PA 1987. Sometimes, a port authority may employ a pilot, but even so, the authority will not be vicariously liable for his fault in

---

74 *The Panther and The Ericbank* [1957] P 143, see Chapter 14, below.
75 See Schoenbaum, TJ, *Admiralty and Maritime Law*, 2nd edn, 1994, West, p 689.
76 See Chapter 16, below.
77 See Chapter 13, below.

navigation of the ship.[78] Section 16 of the PA 1987, replacing s 15 of the PA 1913, has been construed as rendering a shipowner vicariously liable for negligent acts or omissions of the pilot on board his ship. The pilot, whilst on board a ship, is considered to be the employee of the shipowner, *pro tempora*, whether pilotage is compulsory or voluntary.[79] However, a port authority may be liable for its own faults, for example, by not providing for the attendance of sufficient and experienced pilots according to by-laws. The shipowner will have a cause of action to sue the pilot or the port authority, each for their own faults, but their respective liability is limited, by s 22 of the PA 1987, to £1,000 plus whatever dues the pilot was to earn on the relevant assignment.

3.2.8 Port authority

A port authority may incur liability to ships using its facilities if it has been careless in providing navigational safety in breach of its statutory duties. There is also a common law duty of care to make the port safe for users. Obstructions may cause ships to collide or strike an unlit object. When a ship sinks and becomes a wreck, there are statutory obligations imposed by the MSA 1995, local Acts and by-laws upon the authority to take certain steps in order to ensure the prevention of accidents.[80]

The question that frequently arises is whether the owner or the port authority will be liable for damage caused to third parties by a sunken wreck. It was held in *The Utopia* (below) that the owner's liability would depend on whether or not he divested himself from possession or control of the wreck.

Port or harbour authorities are given wide statutory powers to deal with sunken ships in their area. It is only when the port authority has, under its statutory powers, taken possession and control of the vessel, that the shipowner may be absolved from liability. But the Court of Appeal[81] has held that this only applies to cases where the shipowner or his servants were not negligent at common law. A defendant cannot avoid his common law liability for negligence, which cannot be wiped out by abandoning the thing that caused damage. Mere abandonment of the vessel after a collision for which the ship was at fault will not relieve her owner from liability arising afterwards; nor will mere delegation of control to a third party relieve the owner from liability.[82] The Privy Council, however, in the following case placed the blame on the port authority on the facts of this case.

---

78   *The Esso Bernicia* [1988] 2 Lloyd's Rep 8 (HL).
79   *The Cavendish* [1993] 2 Lloyd's Rep 292, see Chapter 15, below.
80   See Chapter 15, para 3.2, below.
81   See, later, *Dee Conservancy Board* [1912] AC 634.
82   *The Snark* [1900] P 105.

The Utopia[83]

Subsequent to a collision with *HMS Anson*, *The Utopia* sunk and lay with her hull submerged in the Gibraltar Bay. Her owners lighted the wreck at each masthead. The acting captain of the Port of Gibraltar then complained to the manager for the owners of *The Utopia*, that the lights were not sufficient, and were not properly looked after. He instructed a boarding officer to have a hulk moored in the vicinity of the wreck in order to warn vessels in accordance with the Board of Trade Regulations. The regulations required that these marking vessels, when so employed and fitted, should not show the ordinary riding light. The hulk was accordingly placed in a position near the wreck exhibiting the lights described in these instructions. It was the duty of those employed by the port to see that the positions of the lights relative to the wreck were preserved. *The Primula* entering the bay at about 8 pm on 31 March 1891, claimed to have only seen two lights visible on board of the hulk before the collision. Therefore, they were ignorant that they were approaching *The Utopia* till they saw her masts and funnel, and so came into collision with her. In proceedings brought by the owners of the steamship *Primula*, it was held that the port authority, and not the owners of the wreck, was liable for the collision which ensued. The control and management of the wreck insofar as it related to the protection of other vessels from her, had legitimately been transferred by the owners to the port authority, acting within the apparent scope of its powers.

Thirty-five years later, the Court of Appeal stated the respective duties of a port authority and of the owners of the wreck in the following case, and commented upon the ruling of the Privy Council in *The Utopia*.

Dee Conservancy Board v McConnell[84]

The first plaintiffs, the conservators, sued the defendants for expenses incurred in the removal of the defendants' ketch, which sunk in the river alongside the second plaintiffs' wharf. The wreck had been caused by the negligence of the defendants' servants. Immediately after the sinking of the ketch, the defendants had given notice of abandonment to their underwriters who refused the notice. Both plaintiffs paid for the removal of the ketch, as it became an obstruction to operations in the river. In the Court of Appeal, Sankey LJ, relied on the case of *Brown v Mallet* (1848) 5 CB 599 and *White v Crisp* (1854) 10 Ex 312 to lay down the duties of the ketch owners and the duties of the port authority respectively. The duty of the defendants was to use their vessel (of which they had control and management) on the navigable river; to use reasonable skill and care to prevent mischief to others; this liability was the same whether their vessel was in motion or stationary,

---

83 [1893] AC 492 (PC).
84 [1928] 2 KB 159.

floating or aground. The port authority on the other hand, was under a duty at common law to take reasonable care, so long as they kept the port open for the public use of all who chose to navigate it, that the public could do so without danger to their lives or property. The Court of Appeal held that the defendants, who by their negligence had sunk their vessel, which obstructed the navigation, were liable at common law for the expenses for its removal. They could not escape liability by abandoning the wreck. Sankey LJ explained the decision in *The Utopia* by stating that, in that case, although the owner of the wreck remained in possession, the port authority undertook the duty of indicating its position so as to ensure that other ships do not suffer damage by collision. The owners were, therefore, not liable for the resulting collision, because they had legitimately transferred that duty to the port authority, and duly indicated to the latter the position of the wreck. The Court of Appeal however questioned the *dictum* of Sir Frances June in *The Utopia* where he had stated, p 498:

> ... the owner of a ship sunk whether by his default or not, has not, if he abandons the possession and control of her, any responsibility either to remove her or to protect other vessels from coming into collision with her.

Thus, it is not the mere abandonment of the wreck after a collision by its owners that will absolve him of a subsequent liability incurred to third parties by the wreck. It is only when the port authority has clearly undertaken to deal with it and take care of safety precautions that the owner may be found not liable.

It is the duty of those in charge of a vessel sunk in the fairway to mark its position according to regulations. Thus, the owner of a wreck, who has given notice to an authority having power to remove wrecks, will not be liable for a collision caused by reason of an unlit wreck.[85]

An omission by a port authority to raise a wreck sunk in their jurisdiction, which results in other vessels colliding with the wreck, is regulated by statute and common law principles. Section 252 of the MSA 1995 gives powers to the authority to deal with the wreck for the protection of those using the area. Section 2(2) of the Occupiers' Liability Act 1957 imposes a duty of care to occupiers (including port or harbour authority) of premises to see that the premises are reasonably safe to visitors.[86] If the port is not safe for any reason, a warning notice should be displayed.[87]

---

85 *The Douglas* (1882) 7 PD 151; contrast *The Snark* [1900] P 105. If the owner does not abandon a sunken wreck but employs independent contractors to raise her, he will be liable for the fault of the contractor, even if he exercised due care in selecting him.

86 *St Just SS v Hartlepool Port Harbour Commissioners* (1929) 34 LIL Rep 344.

87 *The Moorcock* (1889) 14 PD 64; *The Bearn* [1906] P 48.

Sufficient mooring at a port or harbour for vessels using it is within the province of the authority and proper typhoon precautions must be taken.[88] If damage is sustained or done by a vessel by going adrift due to insufficiency or parting of the moorings, the authority would be in breach of its duty of care in this respect and, hence, wholly or partially liable.

A port, harbour or dock authority may also be vulnerable to potential liability if their servants are negligent in navigation when a harbour or dock master directs the movements of a ship in the harbour or dock as empowered to do so by statute.[89] They may be found wholly or partially liable for damage done to or by the ship.[90]

3.2.9 Shipbuilders and ship-repairers

As mentioned earlier, defects in building of, or repairs to a ship, or defective equipment, by reason of which a collision or death or personal injury occurs, will amount to liability for negligence under common law, or by statute (under s 2 of the Consumer Protection Act 1987, covering liability of manufacturers and repairers for defective products). As far as pure economic loss caused by manufacturer's defective products is concerned, see Chapter 11, para 8, above.

3.3 Actionable negligence

The duty owed to other vessels at sea is based on the principles of the tort of negligence and, as early as 1823, Lord Stowell in *The Dundee*[91] stated the essential elements of actionable negligence in collision cases as follows:

> Want of that attention and vigilance which is due to the security of other vessels that are navigating the same sea, and which, if so far neglected as to become, however unintentionally, the cause of damage of any extent to such other vessels, the maritime law considers as a dereliction of bounden duty, entitling the suffered to reparation in damages.[92]

Seven years earlier, Lord Stowell – presiding in the Admiralty Court at that time – stated, in *Woodrop Sims*,[93] that there are four possibilities in which a collision may occur:

---

88 *The Hua Lien* [1991] 1 Lloyd's Rep 309 (PC).
89 See Chapter 15.
90 See *The Zeta* [1893] AC 468; and *Mersey Docks Trustees v Gibbs* (1866) LR 1 HL 93.
91 [1823] 1 Hagg Ad 109.
92 *Ibid*, p 120.
93 (1815) 2 Dod 84, p 1423.

(a) without the blame being imputable to any party to it, that is, by a storm or without human error – in such a case the loss is borne by the party upon whom it happens to fall;

(b) both parties are to blame for want of due diligence and skill, whereupon the loss will be apportioned in accordance to the proportion of fault;

(c) misconduct of the suffering party only, who must bear his own loss;

(d) fault of the ship which ran the other down – the innocent party is entitled to recover compensation.

As there is no absolute presumption of fault by mere breach of the Colregs, since s 4 of the MCA 1911, which repealed the deeming provision of fault of s 419(4) of the MSA 1894, and has now been replaced by s 187(4) of the MSA 1995, a breach of the Colregs is only one factor to be taken into account in determining fault, and no civil liability will arise by a mere breach, unless the infringement was causative to the collision. The question to be asked in each case is essentially this: did the failure to observe the particular regulation set in motion or contributed to a chain of circumstances which resulted in the collision, or was there an intervening factor which broke this chain and that factor was in fact the real cause of the collision incident? The onus of proof[94] is on the party alleging negligence to discharge three elements of the burden in order to establish liability of the defendant, namely:

(a) breach of duty of care;

(b) that the breach caused or contributed to the collision (causation in fact); and

(c) it caused the damage claimed, which must not be too remote (causation in law and remoteness of damage).

These elements are examined in the following paragraphs.

3.4 Breach of the duty of care

3.4.1 Standard of care and burden of proof

A defendant would have fulfilled his duty of care if he behaved in accordance with the standard expected of a reasonable and careful person. It is an objective standard and disregards the idiosyncrasies or the opinion of the defendant. If there is a breach of that duty, it will be the servants of a shipowner, or demise charterer, who ought reasonably to have foreseen that carelessness on their part would be likely to cause harm to those navigating the same seas.

---

94 *Heranger v Diamond* [1939] AC 94 (HL), *per* Lord Wright.

Prior to s 4 of the MCA 1911 (which is now found in s 187(4) of the MSA 1995), and even until 1939, it had been held by the President, Sir Boyd Merriman, in *The Aeneas*[95] that it was for the defendant, who had been in breach of a Colreg, to exonerate himself and show affirmatively that his default did not contribute in any degree to the collision, or to the resulting damage.

The defendants' vessel *A*, while tying up to the bank in the Suez Canal to allow the plaintiffs' vessel *B* to pass, was exhibiting lights, which were more consistent with her not having finally been tied up than with that operation having been completed so as to enable the *B* to pass in safety.

In answer to the plaintiffs' allegation that they were misled by the lights, the defendants contended that if the *B* had kept a better lookout she would not have been misled.

The court held that the mere fact that if the *B* had been keeping a better lookout, she might have appreciated the situation sooner, was not sufficient to exonerate the defendants; that the burden was on the defendants, who had broken, not indeed one of the international regulations, but a rule of an accepted code laid down for canal pilots, to prove not only that the breach ought not to have misled the *B*, but that it did not in fact mislead her; and the court, being of opinion that the *B* was to some extent misled, found the *A* one-fifth to blame and the *B*, which was coming too fast and took drastic helm and engine action causing her to sheer into the *A*, four-fifths to blame.

A few years later, however, this case was overruled by the House of Lords in *Heranger v Diamond*.

Heranger v Diamond[96]

In an action arising out of a collision in the Thames between *The Diamond* and *The Heranger*, Bucknill J and the Court of Appeal (Scott LJ dissenting) held that *The Diamond* was the more seriously to blame, but that *The Heranger* was also to blame by failing to take effective action earlier by reducing her speed, and was, therefore, liable in the proportion of one-third. *The Diamond* was a small steamship in ballast and failed to comply with the Port of London river by-laws. *The Heranger* was a twin screw motor vessel, partly laden, and bound down the river in charge of a Trinity House pilot. The collision occurred at night at a point where the width of the river was about half a mile. *The Diamond* was expected to show her red light around the bend, but she did not do so and, thus, confused *The Heranger*, which did not take action sufficiently early to avoid the collision.

---

95 [1935] P 128.
96 [1939] AC 94.

On appeal to the House of Lords by the owners of *The Heranger*, the defendant, it was argued that *The Diamond* was solely to blame.

The court held that *The Heranger* left it too late to reverse her engines and thus reduce her speed, and was, therefore, in part liable for the collision. Two important issues were resolved by the House of Lords (*per* Lord Wright): (a) that the question whether a vessel is justified in maintaining her speed and relying on another vessel taking action to avoid the possibility of collision is a question of fact and not of law; (b) that whatever the admiralty law on the matter was before the MCA 1911, it is now clear that the onus is on the party setting up a case of negligence to prove both the breach of duty and the damage. This, the ordinary rule in common law cases, is equally the rule in admiralty.[97]

The decision of the courts below were affirmed.

Thus, the same rule of common law pertains also in admiralty that the claimant has to make out, by adducing evidence, a *prima facie* case of negligence by the defendant.

There are some situations, however, in which the burden of proof will shift to the defendant, when the facts speak for themselves and there is a *prima facie* evidence of negligence (as is shown below).

3.4.2 Res ipsa loquitur

Sometimes, the claimant may not have difficulty in discharging the burden of proof that there was a breach of duty because it may be obvious from the facts that there was a breach. In these situations, the facts provide a *prima facie* evidence of negligence, and the rule of *res ipsa loquitur* ensures that the burden of proof shifts to the defendant. It is then upon the latter to rebut that presumption of fault by adducing strong evidence that no amount of reasonable care and skill would have prevented the collision. Nothing short of the defence of inevitable accident will suffice to relieve him from liability. The test is that of reasonable explanation.

This was emphasised in **The Merchant Prince**.[98]

In broad daylight, the plaintiff's steamer was lying at anchor in the Mersey, when *The Merchant Prince*, belonging to the defendants, which was coming down the river, struck the plaintiff's steamer a heavy blow doing considerable damage to her. According to the defendants, the collision and damage were caused by a latent defect in the steering gear, leading to the jamming of the wheel, so that the collision could not be avoided. In the Court Appeal, the Master of the Rolls, Lord Esher, stated the plain rule laid down by the courts after long experience:

---

97 [1939] AC 94, p 104.
98 [1892] P 179.

> Unless you can get rid of it, it is negligence proved against you that you have run into a ship at anchor ... the only way for a man to get rid of that which circumstances prove against him as negligence is to shew that it occurred by an accident which was inevitable by him – that is, an accident the cause of which was such that he could not by any act of his have avoided its result. He can only get rid of that proof against him by shewing inevitable accident, that is by shewing that the cause of the collision was a cause not produced by him, but a cause the result of which he could not avoid.[99]

It was found that a probable cause of the accident was that the chain that goes around the leading wheel had stretched and become too loose. Therefore, the chain failed to respond and resulted in the wheel jamming. The Court of Appeal held that the defendants had not discharged the burden to support the defence of inevitable accident.[100] The stretching of the chain was something, which they could have foreseen. They had not shown that they took measures to prevent the accident by making provision for the immediate use of hand, instead of steam, steering gear. To discharge the burden of proof of inevitable accident the defendants must show all the possible causes of the effect produced and, further, with regard to every one of these possible causes, that the result could not have been avoided. Inevitable accident means that which cannot be avoided by the exercise of ordinary care and caution and maritime skill. Therefore, the cause of this accident was one, which could have been avoided.

In a later case, **The Kite**,[101] it was explained by Langton J that the defendant must give a reasonable explanation of the cause of the accident which, if it were accepted, would be an explanation showing that the accident happened without his negligence. He did not even need to go so far as that, because, if the reasonable explanation was equally consistent with the accident happening without his negligence as with his negligence, the burden of proof would shift back to the plaintiff to show that it was the negligence of the defendant that caused the accident.[102]

The plaintiffs' goods, while on board one of the lighterers' barges, which with others was in tow of a tug, were damaged through the barge colliding with one of the abutments of Cannon Street railway bridge. The plaintiffs brought an action against the tugowners, framing it entirely in tort. There being a *prima facie* case of negligence against the tug, the plaintiffs called no evidence on this point, and the defendants called one witness only, the master in charge of the tug, who did not see the actual contact but heard the blow and saw the barge 'flared out,' owing, in his opinion, to the breast rope not having been properly made fast by the lighterers' servants not the tug's servants:

---

99 [1892] P 179, 187–88.
100 See, para 3.7.1, below.
101 [1933] P 154.
102 *Ibid*, p 170.

Held, that there was no greater probability that the accident happened through negligence on the part of the tugowners' servants than on the part of the lighterers' servants, and that, following Lord Dunedin's *dictum* in *Ballard v North British Rly Co* 1923 SC (HL) 43, p 54, that '... if the defenders can show a way in which the accident may have occurred without negligence ... the pursuer is left as he began, namely, that he has to show negligence'. The plaintiffs failed on the issue of fact.

It will be seen that the discussion of this topic is linked to causation and to what defences the defendant can raise, of which there will be more examples below.

3.5 Causation in fact

Once the claimant proves breach of duty of care by the defendant he must also prove that the breach caused the collision. In other words, the collision would not have happened but for the defendant's breach.[103] Nautical assessors, who explain technical evidence, assist the judge in matters of navigation.[104]

The Humbergate[105]

In the middle of the river just above the Ocean Lock, were situated two sunken wrecks substantially blocking the navigable channel. In accordance with the 'Notice to Mariners' issued by the Conservation Authority, the dock master gave a light signal which signified that the plaintiff's vessel *Haskerland* was leaving the Ocean Lock and entering the tideway. In such circumstances, no other vessel was allowed to pass into a certain prescribed area. The defendant's vessel, *The Humbergate*, in spite of the unlocking signal, had entered and was proceeding through the prescribed area, rapidly getting closer to *The Haskerland*, as the latter was making her way. A wreck marking vessel (a barge) restricted the navigable channel and *The Humbergate* attempted to pass through between *The Haskerland* and the wreck marking vessel. A collision resulted at that point between the two vessels. It was held that, although the 'Notices to Mariners' did not have any apparent statutory effect, they should nevertheless be taken into account when considering the dictates of good seamanship. On the facts, the breach of duty by *The Humbergate* was causative to the collision and she was to blame for not

---

103 The principle is most aptly explained under the general law in *Barnett v Chelsea and Kensington HMC* [1969] 1 QB 428: the hospital was held not liable although the doctor employed by it had breached his duty of care to the plaintiff's husband by having failed to examine him, but the breach was not causative to his death, as he would have died by arsenic poisoning even if the doctor had examined him.

104 PD 49F, para 16.2.

105 [1952] 1 Lloyd's Rep 168.

holding back. But for her negligence, the collision would not have happened. No negligence was found against *The Haskerland*.

The House of Lords, in *The Statue of Liberty* (see facts later), distinguished causative from non-causative faults and held on the facts of this case that the failure to keep a proper lookout was not causative to the collision.

The Andulo was at fault in not taking more accurate observations at an earlier stage but that fault had no causative effect and should be left out of account in the assessment of blame.

There are many other cases exemplifying the point that the breach must have caused the collision; for example, in *The Estrella*[106] the fact that one vessel was travelling the wrong way in the traffic separation zone was left out of account as it was not causative of the collision. Similarly, in *The Tempus*,[107] failure by the defendant's vessel to blast a sound signal on turning her helm to port the last minute to avoid collision, was held to be non-causative, as the collision would have happened even if the signal had been given.

In *The Homer*,[108] the negligence of the pilot of the other ship to take a swift action to avoid a collision danger in a crossing situation was found to be non-causative to the collision. *The Homer* was solely to blame.

In *Selat Arjuna v Contship Success*,[109] in which the latter made an unexpected turn to starboard when the ships were passing starboard to starboard, sinking the former, she was found solely to blame. While *Selat Arjuna* might have gone hard to port, failure to do so was not characterised as negligent or in breach of duty of care. Her master could not have known what *Contship Success* would or might do, and while he should have appreciated earlier than he did that *Contship* was altering to starboard, even if he had, he would not be blamed for standing on. Similarly, in *The Hagieni* and *Barbarossa*,[110] the fault of *Hagieni* ordering half-ahead had minimal causative significance. She failed to cope with the embarrassment of *Barbarossa*'s approach, which created a situation of danger and instilled confusion as to her intentions. The apportionment was 80/20 in favour of *Hagieni*.

Even if the claimant establishes that the defendant was negligent, it is rarely the case in a collision between two or more ships that the collision occurred just by the fault of one ship. The court, therefore, will evaluate the blameworthiness of the fault of each vessel and deduce their causative potency.

---

106 [1977] 1 Lloyd's Rep 525.
107 [1913] P 166; see, also, *The Stella Antares* [1978] 1 Lloyd's Rep 41.
108 [1973] 1 Lloyd's Rep 501.
109 [2000] 1 Lloyd's Rep 627.
110 [2000] 2 Lloyd's Rep 292.

The Statue of Liberty[111]

A collision occurred at about 2 am between *The Statue of Liberty* and *The Andulo* some miles off Cape St Vincent while both vessels were on crossing courses. There were breaches of duty on the part of both vessels. It was the duty of *The Andulo* to maintain her course and speed when she saw *The Statue of Liberty* some miles away on her port bow. *The Statue of Liberty* was guilty of gross negligence for amongst other things, not giving way to *The Andulo*. The learned trial judge had apportioned 70% of the blame to *The Statue of Liberty* and 30% to *The Andulo*. The Court of Appeal varied the proportions to 85% and 15%, respectively. On appeal to the House of Lords, the appellants claimed that *The Andulo* was not to blame at all while the respondents sought to have the apportionment made by the learned trial judge at first instance restored. The House of Lords evaluated the blameworthiness of each party's fault. It was held that the fault of *The Andulo* in not taking more accurate observations at the earlier stage when *The Statue of Liberty* was sighted some miles away had no causative effect and would be left out of account in the final assessment of the degree of blame. It was held, however, that *The Andulo* could not be totally absolved from blame, because according to the assessors, it was bad seamanship on her part to change her course to port, the way she did, after she had seen the green light of *The Statue of Liberty*. Lord Reid said:

> One must consider both the 'causative potency' and the blameworthiness of the faults. I must confess that I find some difficulty in assessing causative potency in terms of percentages. But it is sufficient here to adopt the view of Brandon J at first instance that the failure by *The Statue of Liberty* to give way early was, to my mind, by far the most causative fault on either side ... [112]

In *The Devotion II*,[113] the Scottish Court of Session held that the collision was caused by the failure of both skippers to keep even a minimal lookout and liability was equally apportioned.

On causative potency the Court of Appeal will not normally disturb the judge's finding. While altering course to port at a distance of about 9 miles was wrong, the Court of Appeal said in *The Maloja II*,[114] such fault would only have added a small percentage to her share of the blame and the judge's assessment should not be disturbed.

An illustration of evaluating blameworthiness and apportioning fault can be found in a recent decision, ***The Mineral Dampier***[115] (which sank with all crew after a collision and was only 20% to blame).

---

111 [1971] 2 Lloyd's Rep 277.
112 *Ibid*, p 282.
113 [1979] 1 Lloyd's Rep 509.
114 [1994] 1 Lloyd's Rep 374.
115 [2000] 1 Lloyd's Rep 282.

While irrelevant factual causes are eliminated with the 'but for' test, this test does not apply where there are several successive causes of the accident, to which other rules apply. Invariably, in collision cases, the claimant himself, or a third party, may have contributed to the collision, or there may have been an intervening cause, which broke the chain of causation of the defendant's negligence. When there are multiple successive causes the view taken by the courts is to look at which of these was the most probable cause either solely or in operation with other causes.

3.6 Causation in law

After the elimination of irrelevant factual causes, the court has then to ascertain which of the relevant causes is to be regarded as the cause in law for the loss or the damage suffered. In other words, it has to answer the question whether the defendant is legally liable

For example, when subsequent, or successive, damage occurs after the first incident of collision by another cause, which is not related to the previous negligence, the defendant, whose fault caused the collision may be able to escape liability, if the damage caused by his fault is subsumed by the subsequent damage. This rule was laid down in *The Carslogie*[116] by the House of Lords, although the case is more relevant to measure of damages.

A ship damaged in a collision through the fault of another ship received temporary repairs, which rendered her seaworthy, but on the way to a port where permanent repairs were to be effected she encountered heavy weather and thereby suffered damage rendering her unseaworthy and requiring immediate repair. Both sets of repairs were effected concurrently, the work occupying 30 days. Ten days would have been required for the collision damage if executed separately: it was held that the owners of the ship at fault in the collision were not liable for damages in respect of the 10 days' detention, since the heavy weather damage was not a consequence of the collision. The owners of the damaged ship sustained no loss of profitable time by reason of the fact that for 10 out of the 30 days occupied in repairing the heavy weather damage she was also undergoing repairs necessitated by the collision.

On the facts of this case, the 10 days of detention needed to repair the collision damage were also needed to repair the heavy weather damage (see later on measure of damages). The heavy weather damage was an independent cause. But there can be cases in which the subsequent damage would not have occurred had it not been for the first accident, the effect of which continued for some time (see, for example, *The Calliope* later).

---

116 [1952] AC 292; see also under para 4.3.4, below.

Various scenarios of causation (both factual and legal) are examined below while considering the defences that may be available to the defendant. Principles of remoteness of damage are examined under para 3.12, below.

3.7 Defences available to the defendant

The defences are inextricably linked to questions of both causation in fact and in law.

3.7.1 Inevitable accident

Inevitable accident is one which the party charged with the damage could not possibly prevent by the exercise of ordinary care, caution, and maritime skill.[117]

The claimant must first make out a *prima facie* case of negligence or of want of good seamanship and then the burden shifts on the defendant.[118]

The defendant pleading inevitable accident must show that the proximate cause of the accident was some external event, which was totally unavoidable. The question is not whether all that could be done was done as soon as the danger of the collision arose, but whether sufficient precautions had been taken much earlier. Any negligence at any time will override the defence of inevitable accident. The burden of proof for this defence is heavy and has been successful only in a few cases.

The Marpesia[119]

In this case, a collision took place between *The Marpesia* and *The America* in the morning, but in such dense fog that the vessels could only discern each other at a very short distance. One vessel was proceeding up the Irish Channel and the other down the Irish Channel. Only about a minute elapsed between the vessels' sighting of each other and the collision. It was found that *The Marpesia* had failed to execute the proper manoeuvre which, after sighting *The America*, it was competent for her to have executed. The defence relied on by the appellants was that the collision was the result of inevitable accident.

The judge (Sir Robert Phillimore) held that *The Marpesia* was solely to blame, as she ought to have hauled aft her head sheets and let go all the lee braces, and pronounced *The Marpesia* to blame for the collision.

---

117 *The Virgil* (1843) 2 W Rob 201.
118 *The Marpesia* (1872) LR 4 PC 212.
119 *Ibid.*

The appeal from this decree was to the Judicial Committee, which reversed the decision, after considering the facts and the circumstances of the case. It was stated that:

> Here, we have to satisfy ourselves that something was done or omitted to be done, which a person exercising ordinary care, caution and maritime skill, in the circumstances, either would not have done or would not have left undone, as the case may be ... Considering the admitted time which elapsed after the two vessels had sighted each other to have been not more than a minute, and the state in which *The Marpesia* was, in attempting to go about, (we) have failed to come to the conclusion that the Captain was to blame for having omitted to do that which the judgment seems to find that he might have done. It is a question entirely of navigation ... the nautical assessors confirmed ... that the time was so short that the omission to do that which has been said ought to have been done with the rigging and the sails cannot be imputed as negligence, or anything approaching to negligence, in the master of *The Marpesia*.[120]

Defence succeeded.

After a *prima facie* case of negligence is made out, Fry LJ said in **The Merchant Prince**[121] that:

> The defendants had failed to sustain the plea of inevitable accident, as it was necessary for them either to shew what was the cause of the accident, and that though exercising ordinary care, caution, and maritime skill, the result of that cause was unavoidable, or to enumerate all the possible causes, one or other of which might have produced the effect, and shew with regard to every one, that the result was unavoidable.

That the defendants were liable, as they had not satisfied the burden of proof, for, in order to support the defence of inevitable accident, and disprove the *prima facie* evidence of negligence, it was necessary for them to shew that the cause of the accident was one not produced by them, and the result of which they could not avoid, but the defendants knew of the tendency of new chain to stretch, and, therefore, that an accumulation of links at the leading wheels might possibly cause jamming, and, considering the crowded condition of the river where the accident occurred, the use – or readiness for immediate use – of hand, instead of steam, steering gear, was a means by which the result could have been avoided.

This should not be misunderstood as altering the rule that the burden of proving fault lies on the person alleging it. It rather seems to elaborate that the defendant will have a difficult task in discharging the burden of proof to succeed in the defence of inevitable accident.

---

120 (1872) LR 4 PC 212, p 220.
121 [1892] P 179.

Inevitable accident – which implies no negligence – will not work as a defence in the event of damage to a harbour's property, being caught by the statutory strict liability provision of s 74 of the HDPCA 1847. Even act of God would be irrelevant to such liability, unless the ship was not under the control of human agency.[122]

3.7.2 Contributory negligence

At common law, in non-admiralty cases, there was a rule – until the Law Reform (Contributory Negligence) Act (LR(CN)A) 1945[123] – of no recovery of damages from the defendant if there was contributory negligence on the part of the plaintiff. By contrast, in admiralty cases concerning collisions caused by the fault of two or more ships, the admiralty law rule of division of loss until 1911 was equal division of loss without consideration of their respective degrees of culpability.

3.7.2.1 The proportionate fault rule

The MCA 1911 (by s 1), which enacted the Brussels Convention on Collisions 1910, altered the equal division of loss in collision cases to a rule of proportionate blame according to the degree of each ship's fault, even in cases where a vessel was to blame in a small proportion.

Now the division of loss rule in terms of proportion of fault is found in s 187 of the MSA 1995 which replaced s 1 of the MCA 1911. Sub-section (1)(a) states:

> Where, by the fault of two or more ships, damage or loss is caused to one or more of those ships, to their cargoes or freight, or to any property on board, the liability to make good the damage or loss shall be in proportion to the degree in which each vessel was in fault.

3.7.2.2 When and how does the rule apply?

(a) The apportionment of loss pursuant to this rule applies only to damage or loss caused by the fault of two or more ships. Apportionment applies only to those vessels at fault and their cargo on board. Thus, when there is a collision between a ship and a non-ship, the rule of contributory negligence under the LR(CN)A 1945 will apply.

(b) The ships at fault do not have to be in collision with each other. It will suffice if by the fault of ships A and B, for example, a collision occurs

---

122 See *The Mostyn* [1928] AC 57 (HL); and *River Wear Commissioners v Adamson* (1877) 2 App Cas 743 (HL), see Chapter 15, Section A on port authorities.

123 This Act intended to bring the common law rules regarding contributory negligence broadly in line with the admiralty rules: *Davies v Swan Motor Co* [1949] 2 KB 291, p 319, *per* Evershed LJ.

124 *The Cairnbahn* [1914] P 25; *The Betavier III* (1925) 42 TLR 8.

between B and C.[124] If C sues B, the latter will join A in the proceedings and the faults of all will be apportioned by assessing the faults of each, so that B can recover from A the adjudged proportion of what she has to pay C as well as her own damage.

(c) No liability will be attached to a ship whose fault has not contributed to the loss or damage at all (sub-s 4).

Section 187, sub-s 2, allows an equal division of loss only in cases where it is not possible to establish different degrees of fault. But the effect of sub-s 1 is mandatory. The judge should not decide too readily that the vessels are equally to blame merely because it is difficult to assess the degree of blame of each ship. Only when it is not possible to establish different degrees of fault, having regard to the circumstances of the case, will the liability be apportioned equally.

The Appeal Court will not normally interfere with the actual apportionment of blame fixed by the trial judge, who will have made his judgment having heard all the evidence and assisted by nautical assessors and the Elder Brethren, unless there is mistake in law.

The Anneliese[125]

A collision occurred in the English Channel, at daytime, between plaintiffs' steam tanker *Arietta S Livanos* (*Arietta*) and the defendants' motor vessel *Anneliese*. *Arietta* was on a course of 050 degrees (true) with engines at stand-by. Anneliese was on a course of 235 degrees (true) with engines at full ahead (15 knots) when *Arietta* was sighted (visually and by radar) bearing ahead distant about 6 miles. *Arietta* was, thereafter, watched visually and by radar (true motion on six mile range). Four minutes later, *Anneliese* altered course to 239 degrees (true), bringing *Arietta* fine on port bow, distant about four miles. Three minutes later, visibility deteriorated and *Anneliese* altered course to 250 degrees (true) to increase passing distance between vessels. Half a minute later Arietta disappeared from view and Anneliese commenced fog signals. Two minutes later Anneliese altered to starboard over a period of about two minutes until on a course of 267 degrees (true). During this time, *Anneliese*, realising from her radar that *Arietta* was altering to port, stopped her engines and, seeing *Arietta* visually distant half to a quarter of a mile and bearing 45 degrees on the port bow, put her wheel hard-a-port and ordered engines emergency full astern, sounding a two-short-blast signal and then a three-short-blast signal.

Arietta's case was that visibility was restricted by fog to about three-quarters to one mile and she was sounding regulation signals. Her relative motion radar was on eight mile range and the echo of *Anneliese* was seen distant about eight miles bearing five degrees on the starboard bow. A little

125 [1970] 1 Lloyd's Rep 355.

later, when *Arietta* saw that *Anneliese* had altered to starboard, *Arietta*'s wheel was put hard-a-port. *Arietta* saw *Anneliese* visually distant a quarter to one half of a mile bearing 60 degrees on starboard bow, and sounded two-short-blast signals. *Arietta*'s wheel was ordered hard-a-starboard, but collision occurred between stem of *Anneliese* and starboard quarter of *Arietta* at angle of about 59 degrees leading forward on *Arietta*.

Both vessels were criticised for not keeping a proper lookout and for using excessive speed in those conditions. Brandon J, at first instance, found himself unable to establish different degrees of fault and ordered that the liability should be apportioned equally. He expressed his approach to the MCA 1911, thus:

> ... on the whole, I have come to the conclusion that with such serious faults on both sides, it is impossible to say that there is any clear preponderance of blame on the *Arietta* ...[126]

The expression 'clear preponderance of blame' was derived from Lord Atkinson in *The Peter Benoit*[127] where he had said that a clear preponderance of culpability must be proved. Since then, the courts had used that approach. But Davies LJ in his judgment in *The Anneliese* (on appeal) stated, thus:

> With the greatest respect to the learned Lord, the section does not say that there must be proved a clear preponderance of culpability. What it says is: ... the liability to make good the damage or loss shall be in proportion to the degree in which each vessel was in fault, subject of course to the proviso that if, having regard to all the circumstances of the case, it is not possible to establish different degrees of fault, the liability shall be apportioned equally ... Now that section, as I read it, is mandatory. It does not say that the liability shall be apportioned equally unless different degrees of fault are shown. It is the other way round. It says that the court must apportion the liability in proportion to the degree in which each vessel was at fault unless it is impossible so to do. Of course, the different degrees of fault must be proved, like anything else in a court of law.[128]

It was held that it was possible to distinguish between the degrees in which each vessel was at fault. *Anneliese* was not at fault in making a succession of alterations to starboard nor was she at fault in failing to react more promptly to *Arietta*'s turn to port. Thus, *Arietta* was two-thirds to blame and *Anneliese* one-third.

As mentioned earlier, for the assessment of fault in a collision, it is not necessary for there to be a physical impact between two vessels, nor navigational fault.[129] In the event that one vessel responds foolishly to a deliberate action of another, the latter vessel may bear a greater degree of fault

---

126 [1969] 2 Lloyd's Rep 78, p 93.
127 (1915) 13 Asp MLC 203, p 207.
128 [1970] 1 Lloyd's Rep 355, p 363.
129 *The Norwhale* [1975] 1 Lloyd's Rep 610.

than the one which responded foolishly. This is illustrated in *Miraflores v Abadesa*.

Miraflores v Abadesa[130]

The George Livanos was proceeding up the river Scheldt behind *The Miraflores*. *The Abadesa* was proceeding down the river at the same time. When the vessels reached the narrows on the river, *The Abadesa* negligently failed to hold back to give way to *The Miraflores*. As a result, *The Miraflores* could not deal properly with the difficulties she met owing to a cross-current present at the time. She reacted foolishly steering first to starboard and then to port and continued to port until she was hit by *The Abadesa*. Both vessels, blocking the channel at the time, caught fire due to the leakage of burning oil. *George Livanos*, being behind *The Miraflores*, acted rather in a confused way and did not take immediate action to avoid danger. *George Livanos* ran aground, sustaining damage. The owners of *The Miraflores* brought an action against the owners of *The Abadesa* in respect of the collision, and the owners of *The George Livanos* brought a separate action against the owners of both *The Miraflores* and *The Abadesa* in respect of her grounding. The actions were heard together by Hewson J, who held in respect of the collision action that *The Miraflores* had been one-third and *The Abadesa* two-thirds to blame for the collision. In respect of the grounding action, he held that *The George Livanos* had herself been negligent. He treated the negligence which led to the collision as 'one unit' and the negligence of *The George Livanos* in respect of the grounding as the other unit. He found it impossible to distinguish between the degrees of fault of the two units and, therefore, held that *The George Livanos* was 50% to blame for the grounding and entitled to recover the remaining 50% from *The Abadesa* and *The Miraflores* in the proportions of two-thirds and one-third, respectively. The Court of Appeal varied the apportionment of liability, attributing 45% to *The Abadesa*, 30% to *The Miraflores* and 25% to *The George Livanos*.

On appeal to the House of Lords, Lord Wilberforce held that in investigating 'fault' under s 1(1) of the Act the 'unit approach'[131] was wrong, since it might be misleading to substitute for a measurement of the individual fault of each contributor to the accident, a measurement of the fault of one against the joint fault of the other two.

It was further held that, on the evidence, the same proportions of fault as between *The Miraflores* and *The Abadesa* fixed by the judge in respect of the collision should be adhered to in respect of the grounding but the proportion of fault attributable to *The George Livanos* should be altered, the final

---

130 [1967] AC 826.

131 The 'unit approach' did not require assessment of the degree in which each vessel was at fault. Such an approach was also disapproved by the House of Lords again in *The Koningin Juliana* [1975] 2 Lloyd's Rep 111, in which, also, a mathematical 'composite faults' approach was rejected.

proportions being assessed at two-fifths to *The Abadesa*, two-fifths to *The George Livanos* and one-fifth to *The Miraflores*.

> A person who embarks on a deliberate act of negligence should, in general, bear a greater degree of fault than one who fails to cope adequately with the resulting crisis thus thrust upon him; and further:

> ... the driver who deliberately goes round a corner on the wrong side should, as a rule, find himself more harshly judged than the negligent driver who fails to react promptly enough to the unexpected problem thereby created. For all humans can refrain from deliberately breaking well known safety rules; but it is not in mortals to command the perfect reaction to a crisis; and many fall short at times of that degree which reasonable care demands.[132]

The alteration of apportionment of loss from the finding of the trial judge was made with great caution and was stressed, repeating the rule of *The MacGregor* case[133] that, in matters of apportionment, even more than as regards finding of fact generally, the decision of the trial judge should be interfered with only where some clear error of law or principle can be shown to have influenced his decision.

3.7.2.3 The effect of subsequent negligence by the claimant – multiple causes

When the claimant's servants act reasonably in response to an accident for which the defendant was at fault, any negligence of the former in trying to mitigate the loss will not break the chain of causation.[134]

What is a reasonable act by the master and crew whose vessel suffers damage from a collision accident is a question of fact depending on the circumstances of a case, for example, in **The Oropesa**.[135]

Two steam vessels, the *MR* and *The O*, came into collision. Although the *MR* was badly damaged her master thought that she could be salved. He had sent 50 of his crew in two of his boats to *The O*, and, about an hour and a half after the collision, he decided himself to go to *The O* and confer with her master on the measures to be taken. The master launched another lifeboat in which he embarked with 16 men, including the sixth engineer. The weather was rough and it got worse, and before the boat could reach *The O* it capsized and nine of the men in it, including the sixth engineer, were drowned. *The MR* subsequently sank. In an action by the owners of *The MR* against the owners of *The O*, the parents of the deceased sixth engineer were joined as plaintiffs as his personal representatives suing for his lost effects. The court found *The MR*

---

132 [1967] AC 826, p 848, *per* Lord Pearce.
133 [1943] AC 197 (HL).
134 *The City of Lincoln* (1890) 15 PD 15.
135 [1943] P 32 (CA).

four-fifths to blame and *The O* one-fifth, and, accordingly, the parents of the sixth engineer were held to be entitled to recover against the owners of *The O*. in respect of the loss of his effects. The parents now brought an action against the owners of *The O* under the Law Reform (Miscellaneous Provisions) Act (LR(MP)A) 1934, as administrators of the estate, claiming damages in respect of the loss of expectation of their son's life, and also, in their own right, damages as part-dependants under the Fatal Accidents Acts (FAA):

The Court of Appeal, affirming the decision of Langton J below, held (i) the master of *The MR* had acted reasonably in the emergency and that the death was not the result of a *novus actus interveniens*, but was directly caused by the collision; (ii) that the cause of action under the LR(MP)A 1934 was different from that on which the plaintiffs' claim in the collision action had been founded, and that they were entitled to damages under that Act as well as under the FAAs.

Similarly, in **The Hendrick**,[136] when a trawler sank after a collision, there were criticisms of her crew by the defendant that they were inactive in seeking to preserve the trawler which was flooding with water due to the collision damage. Hewson J said, about judging what was reasonable in the circumstances:

> Placed suddenly in the situation in which they found themselves, the French crew must not be too harshly judged, and they must certainly not be judged in the light of theories, but in the light of the conditions and circumstances at the time. In reflecting upon that I must have in mind their lack of training in damage control and the absence of effective damage control gear on board their vessel. It may well be that a trained salvage crew, provided with all the necessary equipment ready at hand, would have prevented the inflow of water and probably saved the vessel; but this French crew, or any trawler crew, must not be judged by that standard. They must not be too critically examined from an armchair.

Invariably, however, difficult questions arise when further damage occurs by a separate and successive cause of damage following an earlier incident of collision. The courts consider whether either the strength of the subsequent event or lapse of time has interrupted the connection between the original collision and the subsequent damage.

Not infrequently are there situations in which there is a collision between A and B – for which either A is solely to blame, or they are both to blame – and there is further damage taking place at a different time and place, which may or may not be a consequence of the first incident. Would A's further collision damage, claimed as a second head of damage, fail altogether if A's subsequent negligence contributed to his further loss?

---

136 [1964] 1 Lloyd's Rep 371, p 379.

In 1927, the House of Lords, by majority of 3:2, held that the claimant's subsequent negligence broke the chain of causation. The claimant's negligence was not even considered to amount to contributory negligence.

The Paludina[137]

The Paludina, The Singleton Abbey and *The Sara* were moored by their sterns to the quay in Valetta Harbour, Malta, in the order named from east to west, and the vessels had their anchors down forward. There was a strong wind blowing from ENE and there was a swell in the harbour. At 8 am, *The Paludina* dragged her anchors and the fore part of the vessel fell down upon *The Singleton Abbey* and remained in contact with her. In endeavouring to get free from *The Singleton Abbey, The Paludina* broke away from her moorings and fell bodily upon *The Singleton Abbey* causing the parting of her moorings. In turn, *The Singleton Abbey* fell down upon *The Sara* and cast her adrift. *The Singleton Abbey* and *The Sara* then manoeuvred in the harbour under their own steam to keep away from the shore. Twenty minutes later *The Sara* got under the starboard quarter of *The Singleton Abbey*, when the revolving propeller of *The Singleton Abbey* struck *The Sara*, with the result that *The Sara* was sunk and the propeller was damaged. *The Paludina* was clear of both ships at the time. In an action by *The Singleton Abbey* against *The Paludina*, there being no appeal from the decision of the President that *The Paludina* was liable for the earlier collisions, the only question now at issue was whether she was also liable for the final collision between *The Singleton Abbey* and *The Sara*. The President, acting on the advice of two of the Elder Brethren of the Trinity House, found that the final collision was directly caused by the negligence of *The Paludina*, but his decision was reversed on appeal. The nautical assessors in the Court of Appeal advised (1), agreeing with the Elder Brethren, that there was no fault on the part of *The Sara*, and (2), differing from the Elder Brethren, that the master of *The Singleton Abbey* was guilty of want of reasonable care in not stopping his engines in time to avert the collision:

Lord Sumner, Lord Carson, and Lord Blanesburgh; Viscount Dunedin held (Lord Phillimore dissenting) that the final collision was not directly caused by the negligence of *The Paludina*, but that the action of *The Sara* constituted a *novus actus interveniens*. At the point in time of the second collision, the ships which broke away were free agents and, having not being in the 'agony of the moment', they could have taken reasonable steps to avoid the collision. The majority distinguished the facts of this case from those in *The City of Lincoln*[138] with regard to the actions of her captain, in which, it was

---

137 [1927] AC 16 (HL).

138 In *The City of Lincoln* [1890] P 15, the defendant's vessel negligently collided with and caused damage to the plaintiff's vessel, whose master attempted to reach port in safety. But the vessel grounded accidentally before he did so, and was lost. In the absence of negligence by the master, the defendants were liable not merely for the collision damage, but for the subsequent loss.

said: 'The hand of the original wrongdoer was still heavy on his ship and his own navigation was not the sole human agency determining her fortune.' The majority did not find that *Paludina*'s negligence was still operating.

The dissenting minority thought that there was no break in the chain of causation from the original negligence of *The Paludina*, which obliged the other ships to adopt the alternative of a dangerous leap, or to remain at certain peril.[139]

By contrast, Brandon J took a more robust view in *The Calliope* and sub-apportioned the subsequent damage between the parties at fault for the original collision, the effect of which was found to be continuous.

The Calliope[140]

The defendants' vessel *Calliope* collided in the river Seine with the plaintiffs' vessel *Carlsholm*, ran aground and was damaged. In view of the damage caused by the collision and the time lost, the master of *The Calliope* decided to proceed up river to Villequier and to lie there over the ebb tide. Next day, whilst executing a turning manoeuvre in the river, she grounded twice and collided with a tug which was assisting her, sustaining further damage. In an action between the plaintiffs and the defendants, it was agreed that *The Carlsholm* was 45% at fault and *The Calliope* 55% for the collision, and that the damage sustained by *The Calliope* as a result of the first grounding was a direct consequence of the collision. The question of law for decision was this: if there was negligence, and it was causative, is the court bound to hold that the damage due to the groundings is too remote to be recoverable?; or can it, if the facts warrant it, hold that this later negligence and the original collision were both causative, and, on that basis, make a further or sub-apportionment of liability in respect of that head of damage?

Brandon J observed that: 'The question of law so raised is interesting and difficult. It also seems to me to be of some general importance in the law of tort, not only in maritime cases but in other cases as well. It involves the interrelationship of the doctrines of contributory negligence and remoteness of damage.'[141]

---

139 [1890] P 15, p 32.

140 [1970] 1 Lloyd's Rep 84.

141 *Ibid*, p 96. Of particular interest is his reference to older cases, which he examined to see whether their effect was really (as the plaintiff put it) that, as far as recovery of such damage was concerned, it was all or nothing, or whether there was room for an intermediate position. In all but three of the 13 cases he mentioned, the court had found that there was no causative intervening negligence. It followed that the claim for consequential damage succeeded wholly, and there was no question of apportionment. The three cases in which there was causative intervening negligence were: *The Glendinning* (1943) 76 LlL Rep 86 (concerning subsequent grounding); *The Egyptian* [1910] AC 400 and *The Fritz Thyssen* [1968] P 255 (where the ship later sank). In these cases, the claim for consequential damage failed.

It was held that:

(1) it was open to the court as a matter of law, in cases like the present, to find that the alleged consequential damage was caused partly by the original casualty and partly by the claimants' own intervening negligence and to make a further apportionment or sub-apportionment of liability accordingly;

(2) on the facts, the two later grounding were not caused solely by the negligence of *The Calliope* in executing the turning manoeuvre, but partly by such negligence and partly by the joint negligence of that vessel and *The Carlsholm*, which led to the collision and the effect of which was still continuing when the two later grounding took place, from which it followed that a further or sub-apportionment for that head of damage must be made and that a further apportionment of liability for such head of damage on a 50/50 basis would be just;

(3) the question in a situation like this was not whether the negligence, which caused the collision, is continuing, but whether the effect of the collision – which such negligence caused – is continuing. The learned judge further stated that sub-s (1)(b) of the MCA 1911, referring to damage or loss caused by the fault of two or more ships, supports his approach, saying:

> This sub-section refers to damage or loss being caused by the fault of two or more vessels to one or more of them. It does not refer to a casualty, or event, being so caused. This is logical, for it is damage or loss resulting from a casualty or event which gives rise to a cause of action in negligence, and not the casualty or event itself.[142]

He went further to explain:

> The effect of the collision was obviously continuing in one sense in that, but for the collision, *The Calliope* would never have been at Villequier at all. But that is not, of course, enough. It is necessary to consider whether it was continuing in the further sense, that, at the time when the chief officer was negligent, the hand of the negligent navigator on board *The Carlsholm* was still heavy on *The Calliope*; or that those on board *The Calliope* were not, by reason of the hard necessities imposed on them by the collision, free agents; or that those on board *The Calliope* were still in the grip of the collision.

> In support of the view that the effect of the collision was continuing in such a way as to make it a *causa causans* and not merely a *causa sine qua non* the following points were taken. First, that the turning manoeuvre was a difficult one which no ship would choose to undertake unless compelled to do so by some emergency or unforeseen circumstances. Second, that even if executed in clear weather, it was an exceptionally difficult manoeuvre to carry out successfully, and involved a risk of grounding even without negligence on the part of those on board. Third, that it was, in fact, executed in the worst possible conditions, namely in dense fog with visibility virtually nil, which greatly

---

142 [1970] 1 Lloyd's Rep 84, p 99.

increased the difficulty of the operation and the risks inherent in it. Fourth, that negligence in the execution of the manoeuvre was itself foreseeable human conduct, and should not necessarily and by itself be regarded as breaking the chain of causation. In this connection it was rightly, I consider, that the negligence of *The Calliope*, even assuming it to be established, was in no way wilful or gross.[143]

Approaching the questions of causation which arise in this case from that point of view, I have reached the conclusion that the groundings were not caused solely by the negligence of *The Calliope* in executing the turning manoeuvre, but partly by such negligence and partly by the joint negligence of the plaintiffs and the defendants, which led to the collision and the effect of which was still continuing when the groundings took place.[144]

How can the judgment of Brandon J, who opted for an intermediate position to the question whether the subsequent damage is recoverable by apportionment or sub-apportionment of fault, be reconciled with two previous House of Lords' decisions, which had opted for the all or nothing approach?[145] Brandon J treated the matter as not being expressly decided previously, as a matter of law. The reasons for this, he said, were, in his view: (i) that the development of the concept of multiple causes or damage, and the elimination of the last opportunity rule, had been part of an historical process, which extended over many years. The process was greatly accelerated by the passing of the LR(CN)A 1945; (ii) that in certain cases the facts pointed towards the 'no recovery option' when there was an *actus novus interveniens*. Thus, where there is a substantial time interval between a casualty and alleged consequential damage, and intervening events occur which include further causative negligence of the party making the damage claimed, the case for finding on the facts that such further negligence was the sole cause of the damage tends to be very strong.

In a later decision, *The Vysotsk*,[146] Sheen J held that the negligence of the vessel, which largely caused the first collision, set in a chain of events which led to the second collision with a third vessel. As this chain had not been broken by an intervening negligence, the parties would be liable for the damage caused by the second collision in the same proportion as for the first.

3.7.3 *Actus novus interveniens*

As seen in *The Paludina* earlier, there will be no sub-apportionment of liability where the chain of causation is broken, in the case of a *novus actus interveniens*. A clear example is shown below.

---

143 [1970] 1 Lloyd's Rep 84, p 101.

144 *Ibid*, p 102.

145 *The Paludina* [1927] AC 16 (albeit not a unanimous decision) and *The Metagama* (1928) 29 LlL Rep 253 (HL).

146 [1981] 1 Lloyd's Rep 439.

Fritz Thyssen[147]

The plaintiff's motor vessel *Mitera Marigo* collided with the defendant's motor vessel *The Fritz Thyssen* off the north-west coast of France. The collision was quite severe and *The Mitera Marigo* suffered serious damage. She was also carrying a large amount of cargo at the time. Immediately after the collision, it was found that water was entering both No 1 hold and No 1 double bottom tank. From that moment, pumps were kept working continuously to pump water out of the No 1 hold. However, water continued to increase in the No 1 hold. A salvage tug was called from Falmouth to assist *The Mitera Marigo*, by which time the water in the No 1 hold had reached about four or five feet. The master, however, refused the assistance of the tug, merely engaging the tug as an escort. The vessel safely arrived at the Falmouth harbour, but a few hours later began to sink. The master called for the assistance of the tug, which had been standing by, but it was too late and *The Mitera Marigo* sank in deep water. The defendants alleged that the loss of the ship was wholly due to the negligence of her own master. The trial judge held that it was for the defendants to prove that the sinking was due to a *novus actus interveniens*. That, he held, involved proving first that *The Mitera Marigo* omitted some precaution required by good seamanship, and secondly that, if that precaution had been taken, the loss of the ship would probably have been averted. The Lords Justice in the Court of Appeal agreed with the judge's conclusions that the negligence of the master had broken the chain of causation. Willmer LJ emphasised the need not to judge the situation on the basis of hindsight in the light of what was now known, but to view the situation as it would have appeared to the master of *The Mitera Marigo* himself in the emergency with which he was faced. It was held that the master's omission to accept salvage assistance was a reckless gamble putting at risk a vessel and cargo worth about £800,000, the loss of which was attributable to that negligence.

By contrast, the decision of the master of ***The Guildford***,[148] to await tugs for assistance after a collision instead of accepting assistance from the colliding vessel, was on the facts of this case justified because there was no change for the worse in the situation of the *Guildford* during the waiting time. Accordingly, the sinking of *Guildford* was a consequence of the collision in respect of which she was entitled to recover her loss caused by the proportionate fault of the other vessel.

---

147 [1967] 2 Lloyd's Rep 199.
148 [1956] 2 Lloyd's Rep 74.

3.7.4 Exceptions to the proportionate fault rule

If both vessels are at fault, it will be right to apportion the blame. However, there are special circumstances where the rule of division of loss in proportion to blame cannot be applied.

3.7.4.1 Alternative danger

The claimant's master may have acted under the stress of circumstances forced upon him by the defendant's servants and may do some act which helps to bring about the collision. It would then be open to the party pleading 'alternative danger' or 'agony of the moment' as a counterdefence to contributory negligence to show how the danger arose. The alternative danger plea is also available where the actions of the claimant's master or crew force the defendant to act in the agony of the moment to avert a peril resulting from the negligence of the claimant's servants.

The sound rule is, that: a man in charge of a vessel is not to be held guilty of negligence, or as contributing to an accident, if in a sudden emergency caused by the default or negligence of another vessel, he does something which he might under the circumstances as known to him reasonably think proper; although those before whom the case comes for adjudication are, with a knowledge of all the facts, and with time to consider them, able to see that the course which he adopted was not in fact the best.[149]

Where one ship has, by wrong manoeuvres, placed another ship in a position of extreme danger, that other ship will not be held to blame if she has done something wrong, and has not been manoeuvred with perfect skill and presence of mind.

Brett LJ in the *Bywell Castle*[150] put the reasoning behind this as follows:

I am of the opinion that when one ship by her wrongful act suddenly puts another ship into the position of difficulty of this kind, we cannot expect the same amount of skill as we should under other circumstances. The captains of ships are bound to show such skill, as persons of their position with ordinary nerve ought to show under the circumstances. But any court ought to make the very greatest allowance for a captain or pilot suddenly put into such difficult circumstances, and the court ought not, in fairness and justice to him, require perfect nerve and presence of mind enabling him to do the best thing possible.[151]

---

149 *The Bywell Castle* (1879) 4 PD 219, p 228, *per* Cotton LJ.
150 *Ibid.*
151 *Ibid*, pp 226, 227.

The Bywell Castle

The Princess Alice, a paddle-wheel steamer of 158 tons register and 220 ft long, had come up the river under the south shore till near Tripcock's Point. She then starboarded her helm so as to keep close to but clear a powder hulk which was moored just above Tripcock's Point, and then cross to Bull Point on the north shore. She was struck on the starboard bow by *The Bywell Castle*, in consequence of the porting of the helm of the latter. *The Princess Alice* was struck on the starboard bow and soon afterwards sank. More than 500 of her passengers and many of the crew, including the captain, were drowned.

It was found in the lower court that *The Princess Alice* was navigated in a careless and reckless manner, without due observance of the regulations with respect to lookout and speed and that the Bywell Castle appeared to have been navigated with due care and skill until within a very short time of the collision.

The evidence certainly established that having seen the green light of *The Princess Alice*, *The Bywell Castle* put hard to port. There was no doubt that this was not only obviously a wrong manoeuvre, but the worst which she could have executed. The only defence offered for it was that it was executed so very short a time before the collision.

It was held at first instance that although *The Princess Alice* was to blame for the collision, *The Bywell Castle* made a wrong manoeuvre for which she would carry some blame. Had the wrong manoeuvre not been made by *The Bywell Castle*, *The Princess Alice* would still have received some injury, but would not have sunk and would not have lost so many lives. The Court of Appeal, overruled that *The Bywell Castle* was to blame at all. It held that *The Princess Alice* was solely to blame and said that a ship has no right by its own misconduct to put another ship into a situation of extreme peril, and then charge that other ship with misconduct. James LJ stated:

> My opinion is that if, in that moment of extreme peril and difficulty, such other ship happens to do something wrong, so as to be a contributory to the mischief, that would not render her liable for the damage, inasmuch as perfect presence of mind, accurate judgment, and promptitude under all circumstances are not to be expected.[152]

3.7.4.2 When a clear line can be drawn between two separate negligent acts

Section 187 of the MSA 1995 provides that nothing in the section shall operate so as to render any vessel liable for any loss or damage to which her fault has not contributed. Otherwise, the admiralty rule is for division of loss.

---

152 *The Bywell Castle* (1879) 4 PD 219, p 223.

If it is, in fact, the act of the claimant, unprotected by the alternative danger plea, which is the direct/proximate cause of loss, the defendant may escape liability. Most times however, it is difficult to establish a clear line rule as to when the second negligent act was sufficiently removed from the first to enable the party first at fault to escape liability. The courts consider whether the negligence of both parties is contemporaneous or whether the act of the claimant was in fact much later in time. As has already been mentioned, a usual consideration is whether there is sufficient separation of time, place, or circumstance between one negligent act and the next. However, strong evidence is required to show this separation as the following case shows.

Admiralty Commissioners v SS Volute[153]

The Volute was a leader of a convoy under the charge of two destroyers, *The Radstock* and another, (*The Radstock* being on the starboard hand). She had instructions when to alter her course and, being responsible for the alteration, she was to sound the necessary short blast helm signals when altering course. She was directed to alter course to port a little before midnight, and she starboarded her helm and blew the appropriate signal of two blasts, which was answered as intended by the other vessels of the convoy, and the course was altered without mishap. On this altered course, N 44 degrees W, the vessels then proceeded till a particular bearing, when it would be right for the course to be altered about seven points to starboard, from N 44 W to N 32 E, and this *The Volute* proceeded to do. She ought to have signified this very striking alteration by the blowing of a short blast of her whistle. Whether she did so was a serious matter in dispute at the trial. The night was dark, and no lights were being carried except that each vessel in the convoy carried a shaded stern light. *The Radstock*, whose officer and crew said that they heard no whistle, did not alter course when *The Volute* ported her helm and the result was that a position of danger arose. Only the master of those on board *The Volute* was examined, and he, though awake and in the chart room, was not on the bridge till the last moment. On discovering *The Volute*'s change of course to starboard, *The Radstock* went hard a port, but her helm jammed, and she then increased her speed from 8 to 18 knots, with the result that a collision occurred, notwithstanding that *The Volute stopped* and reversed her engines. In the opinion of the House of Lords on the evidence (reversing the finding of the trial judge), *The Volute* did not sound the appropriate helm signal before porting:

It was held that the collision was caused partly by *The Volute*'s omission to signal and partly by *The Radstock*'s going full speed ahead after the position of danger brought about by *The Volute*'s negligence, and that both vessels were to blame.

---

153 [1922] 1 AC 129 (HL).

The decision of the Court of Appeal holding *The Radstock* alone to blame was reversed.

The statement of principle of the rule in admiralty expounded by Viscount Birkenhead LC is important in this respect:

> Upon the whole, I think that the question of contributory negligence must be dealt with somewhat broadly and upon common sense principles as a jury would probably deal with it. And while no doubt, where a clear line can be drawn, the subsequent negligence is the only one to look to, there are cases in which the two acts come so closely together, and the second act of negligence is so much mixed up with the state of things brought about by the first act, that the party secondly negligent, while not held free from blame under *The Bywell Castle* rule, might, on the other hand, invoke the prior negligence as being part of the cause of the collision so as to make it a case of contribution. And the MCA with its provisions for nice qualifications as to the quantum of blame and the proportions in which contribution is to be made may be taken as to some extent declaratory of the admiralty rule in this respect.[154]

The above can be summarised as follows:

(a) where the negligence of both parties is contemporaneous and causative, the loss is divided according to the degree of fault;

(b) where the counterdefence of alternative danger, or agony of the moment, is successful, the other party bears the whole loss (for example, when C sues D, who raises the defence of contributory negligence, and C pleads alternative danger with success, D bears all the loss);

(c) where the claimant's negligence is subsequent to the defendant's negligence and is the sole cause of the collision (independent cause), the claimant cannot recover.

3.7.4.3 When an innocent third ship claims against one of the tortfeasors

It should be remembered that the division of loss rule under s 187 of the MSA 1995 is applicable to a situation when two or more ships involved in a collision are at fault. When an innocent third ship is involved in a collision caused by the fault of two other ships and then it proceeds to recover its damage from one of the tortfeasors, the common law rule will apply. In other words, he can claim the whole of his damage from either or both joint tortfeasors.[155] The paying tortfeasor can claim contribution, under the CLCA 1978, from the other tortfeasor for any excess amount – over and above his proportion of liability – paid to the innocent party, or alternatively their respective liability can be apportioned as between themselves in accordance with s 187. If only one tortfeasor is sued, the other can be joined as a third party, or as a second defendant later (see, further, para 3.11, below).

---

154 [1922] 1 AC 129 (HL), p 144.
155 *The Devonshire* [1912] AC 634; *The Cairnbahn* [1914] P 25.

3.7.4.4 Claims for personal injury or loss of life

Section 187 expressly provides for division of loss concerning property damage, while ss 188 and 189 deal with this category of claims. This is discussed later under para 3.8, below.

3.7.5 The defence of necessity

This may avail the defendant to escape liability in circumstances in which an action, which would otherwise have amounted to actionable negligence, might have been justified because of necessity to choose between two perilous situations, either in the interest of its own ship or in the interest of third parties.[156] The Colregs, by reg 2(b), also provide for departure from them in cases of necessity. But the defendant cannot avail himself of this defence if the necessity was brought about by his own fault.[157]

3.7.6 Time bar defence[158]

Section 190 of the MSA 1995 provides for a period of two years within which any claim or lien can be enforced against a ship or her owners. It covers all claims for property damage or loss caused by the fault of that ship to another ship, its freight, or any property on board. It also covers claims for damages for loss of life or personal injury caused by the fault of that ship to any person on board another ship.

The section, which derives from s 8 of the MCA 1911, does not apply when the collision is not between ships, but between a ship and another object.[159] In the latter case, the normal six years' time limit provided under the Limitation Act (LA) 1980 applies to property damage claims. In this connection the importance of defining a ship becomes apparent, as was discussed in Chapter 1.

As regards claims for personal injury or loss of life of persons on board the carrying ship, such claims are not covered by s 190 (which refers in sub-s (1)(b) to claims by persons on board another ship – the non-carrying ship). These are subject to the normal three years' time limit as provided under the LA 1980, as amended by the Latent Damage Act 1986, or, if the Athens

---

156 See *The Koursk* (1920) 2 LlL Rep 244 (HL), the defence that a reversing action would be fatal and, hence, the trust to port helm saved the ship, succeeded; *The Hessa* (1921) 9 LlL Rep 271, the defence succeeded: what is demanded of a man who has to choose between two perils is to exercise judgment as a prudent seaman.

157 *Southport Corp v Esso Petroleum Ltd* [1954] 2 QB 182.

158 This is a procedural type of defence, the time may be extended by agreement. For other procedural defences, such as *res judicata* or issue estoppel, see, *op cit*, Marsden, fn 1, pp 397–400.

159 See a recent decision, *The Nlase (formerly Erica Jacob)* [2000] 1 Lloyd's Rep 455.

Convention applies, two years' time limit is provided by Art 16 (see the end of this chapter).

The time commences from the date of the incident (that is, when the damage or loss was caused or the loss of life or injury was suffered) and stops running from the date of the issue of the claim form.

In sub-ss 5 and 6 of s 190, it is provided that any court having jurisdiction may, in accordance with rules of court, extend the period allowed for bringing proceedings to such extent and on such conditions as it thinks fit. In addition, if any such court is satisfied that there has not been – during the period allowed for bringing proceeding – any reasonable opportunity of arresting the ship within the jurisdiction of the court, or the territorial sea of the country to which the plaintiff's ship belongs, or in which the plaintiff resides or has his principal place of business, shall extend the period allowed for bringing proceedings to an extent sufficient to give a reasonable opportunity of so arresting the ship. It should be noted that when the claim form has been issued, the time limit is interrupted but because the validity of the *in rem* claim form lasts for one year,[160] it will need to be extended if the ship does not come within the jurisdiction within the year to be arrested. So, the provision under s 190(6) is useful with regard to the renewal of the *in rem* claim form.

3.8 How claims for loss of life and personal injury are dealt with

The rule of division of loss in s 187 of the 1995 MSA does not apply to cases of liability for death or personal injury. Sections 188 and 189 of the Act deal with such liability.[161] In particular, s 188 provides:

> Where loss of life or personal injuries are suffered by any person on board a ship owing to the fault of that ship and of any other ship or ships, the liability of the owners of the ships shall be joint and several.

That means that the claimant may claim his full damages from any one of the tortfeasors.

The origin of this rule lies at common law.

The Bernina[162]

A collision having occurred between the steamships *Bushire* and *Bernina* through the fault of the masters and crews of both, two persons on board *The Bushire*, one of the crew and a passenger, neither of whom had anything to do

---

160 PD 49F, para 2.1(6) being subject to CPR, r 7.6 (general provision of extension of time by the court).
161 MSA 1995, ss 188, 189 have substantially reproduced the MCA 1911, ss 2 and 3.
162 (1888) 13 App Cas 1 (HL).

with the negligent navigation, were drowned. The deceased's representatives brought, in the Admiralty Division, actions *in personam* against the *The Bernina*'s owners for negligence under Lord Campbell's Act (9 & 10 Vict c 93).

The court held, affirming the decision of the Court of Appeal (12 PD 58), that the deceased persons were not identified in respect of the negligence with those navigating *The Bushire*; that their representatives could maintain the actions; and could recover the whole of the damages. The admiralty rule as to half damages was not applicable.

If one of the joint tortfeasors bears all the loss, he has a right to contribution against the other as provided under s 189. No contribution would be available if by reason of any statutory or contractual limitation of, or exemption from, liability, or which could not for any other reason, have been recovered in the first instance as damages by the persons entitled to sue (sub-para 3).

A claim to enforce any contribution under ss 187–89 may be brought by way of an action *in rem* and must be brought within one year from the date of payment to the claimant (s 190(4)).[163]

As mentioned under para 3.7.6, when the claimant for personal injury or loss of life sues the non-carrying vessel, the action must be commenced within two years of the incident. This derives from s 190(1)(b). The time may be extended. The court has a discretion to grant the extension, which may be exercised depending on the length of the delay, or on whether the delay was excusable and beyond the party's control, or on whether justice would be done if the extension was granted. The time limit to bring an action for this type of claims against the carrying ship is three years.[164]

Where persons are killed, their estates have an action against the vessel at fault and her owners under the LR(MP)A 1934, and their dependants under the FAA 1976,[165] as amended by the Administration of Justice Act 1982.

3.9 Claims in relation to cargo damage

At common law, in tort, the position for recovery of loss or damage suffered by an innocent third party due to the fault of two joint tortfeasors is that he can recover the whole of his loss against either tortfeasor. As has been discussed under para 3.5.4.3, this common law rule applies to an innocent third ship involved in a collision and to claims for personal injury or loss of life.

---

163 Previously, the MCA 1911, s 8.
164 The limitation period provided for by the LA 1980 applies to this type of claim.
165 See *The Esso Malaysia* [1974] 2 Lloyd's Rep 143.

By contrast, the admiralty law doctrine of division of loss applies to the innocent cargo-owner, whose cargo is damaged or lost on board the carrying ship due to a collision between this ship and another for which both ships are at fault. Students of shipping law usually question this rule. An explanation as to the origins of the rule and whether or not it is 'just' can be found in the extracts of the following judgment. Since the questioning of the rule seems to be important, large extracts are quoted, so that a comprehensive answer may be found.

The Drumlanrig[166]

The plaintiffs, owners of cargo, had their goods on board the steamship *Tongariro*. This vessel collided with the steamship *Drumlanrig*, and it was not disputed that both vessels were to blame. Accordingly, the plaintiffs claimed against the owners of *The Drumlanrig* for the whole of the damage to their goods sustained by the collision. The question for the court was only as to damages: could the plaintiffs recover the whole of their loss, or only 50% of it?

Sir Samuel Evans (President) held that they were entitled to a moiety only of the fund lodged in court by the defendants to limit their liability, and decreed accordingly. This decision was affirmed by the Court of Appeal (Vaughan Williams, Fletcher Moulton, and Buckley LJJ). An appeal to the House of Lords followed in which the Lords affirmed the decisions of the lower courts. Each of the Lords, who – despite their comment that the rule may be unfair – thought they did not have a choice to alter the wording in the Judicature Act (JA) 1873, which was the subject matter for construction, and opined as follows:

Lord Loreburn LC[167]

Under the JA of 1873, s 25, sub-s 9: 'In any cause or proceeding for damages arising out of a collision between two ships, if both ships shall be found to have been in fault the rules hitherto in force in the Court of Admiralty, so far as they have been at variance with the rules in force in the courts of common law, shall prevail.'

In order to apply this statutory direction, let me first see what is the rule at common law. In 1873, when the Act was passed, the supposed rule was that the owner of goods in such a case could recover nothing at all, because he was imagined to be identified with the ship in which his goods were stowed, and, she being in fault, he also was disabled by her disability. There was really nothing to say either in principle or good sense for this metaphysical view, and it was finally exploded by the decision of this House in *The Bernina*,[168] which

---

166 [1911] AC 16 (HL).
167 *Ibid*, pp 18, 19.
168 (1888) 13 App Cas 1 (HL), concerning loss of life on board a ship.

decided that so far from recovering nothing the owner of cargo could recover the full amount of his loss.

The law of admiralty was different. In admiralty, the rule had been for a long time that, in case of collision between two ships where both were to blame, each shipowner could recover from the other one half his loss. In 1861, in *The Milan*,[169] Dr Lushington directly decided that the owner of cargo in one of the ships could in like manner recover only one half of the loss from the other ship. And he expressly repudiated the supposed doctrine of common law, relying upon the uniform practice in admiralty. How old that practice may have been in regard to cargo is not quite certain. Dr Lushington spoke of it as uniform 49 years ago.

My Lords, the question before us is, to my mind, very simple. It is this: was this admiralty rule in 1873 a rule 'hitherto in force,' or was it not? That is to say, was it a rule under which the court regularly acted? I think it clearly was. Accordingly, it prevails over the common law rule, whether we take that to be the erroneous practice which obtained before the decision in *The Bernina* or the sound law which obtained after it ...

That practice as to the cargo-owner only receiving one half his loss may have been based upon the similar and long settled practice as to shipowners. Perhaps the analogy was a false one and the practice not really fair. Indeed, that is my own opinion, and I should be very glad if I could award to these plaintiffs the full amount of their claim. But we must obey the Act of Parliament, and when once it is made good that the rule as to recovering one half only was in 1873 'hitherto in force', we have no choice. If this state of the law is to be remedied, the remedy must be provided by the legislature.[170] It is no valid argument to say it ought not to have been ever established.

Lord Atkinson[171]

My Lords, the sole question for decision in this case is this: whether the rule of law in force in the Courts of Admiralty in this country in the year 1873, to the effect that when two ships collide, each being found to blame, the innocent owner of the cargo carried by one of them is only entitled to recover half the damages he has sustained from each ship in default, is still in force. This again depends upon two considerations – first, whether this rule is in reality based on the principle that the cargo carried is identified with the ship which carries it, according to the principle laid down in the case of *Thorogood v Bryan*, and second, whether, even if this be so, the rule is stereotyped and continued in force by the provision of s 25, sub-s 9 of the JA 1873. Your Lordships, in the case of *The Bernina*, undoubtedly held that the case of *Thorogood v Bryan* was wrongly decided, and that the principle laid down in it was erroneous in law, and Sir Robert Finlay (for the appellants) contends that because of this the rule of law based upon the principle so held to be erroneous must, in the

169 (1861) Lush 388.
170 The subsequent MCA 1911and the present statute, MSA 1995, s 187, however, have perpetuated this rule.
171 [1911] AC 16, pp 21–25.

construction of the above-mentioned provision of the JA, be treated as non-existent, since the rules mentioned in the subsection mean true rules of law, not rules laid down in misapprehension of what the law on the subject really is.

When, therefore, the law laid down by such a tribunal as the Court of Admiralty, no matter how often, or over what a period of time, is declared by your Lordships' House to have been laid down erroneously, the rule must be treated as if it had never existed – treated as a mere misrepresentation or misstatement of the law, which, this being once authoritatively pointed out, goes for nothing. I shall presently consider whether Sir Robert Finlay's contention as to the foundation of this rule be sound or not; but, even assuming that it is sound, I do not think that the rule, however erroneous, can be thus got rid of. The words of the sub-section are: 'The rules hitherto in force in the Court of Admiralty, so far as they have been at variance with the rules in force in the courts of common law, shall prevail.' The words 'hitherto in force', or words equivalent to them, do not occur in sub-ss 10 or 11 of the same section dealing with the conflict between the rules of the common law and the rules of law as administered by the Court of Equity. The words 'so far as they have been' are also peculiar to this sub-section. They point apparently to the past, and it certainly would appear to me that both these phrases have been introduced in order to stereotype and perpetuate the rules of law in force in the Court of Admiralty

The question remains, is this rule in reality based upon the principle of *Thorogood v Bryan*? If not, its authority is untouched by the case of *The Bernina*. Well, in the first place the cargo is not completely identified with the ship that carries it, for its owner, though he, like the owner of that ship, is only entitled to recover half the damage sustained from the owner of the other ship, is entitled to recover the other half from the owner of the carrying ship. Again, Dr Lushington in *The Milan* case discusses this rule, first, from the point of view of its abstract justice, and, secondly, from that of the principles on which the admiralty practice is founded. As to the first, he says: 'The only inference I can draw from this view of the matter is that beyond all doubt an action would be maintainable by the owners of cargo against the owners of either vessel, but to what extent damages should be recoverable against one party only is left an open question.'

He then proceeds to deal with the rule of the Admiralty Courts, and, after pointing out that *Hay v Le Neve*, decided that the owner of the cargo is only entitled to recover half the damages from the ship which does not carry it, he says: 'Abstract justice might give a remedy to the owner of the cargo against the owner of each vessel in proportion to the culpability of each, but as it is impossible, where both of these are in fault, strictly to apportion the blame, by an equitable though arbitrary rule, or, as it has been called, a *judicium rusticorum*, the opposing ship is made liable to one half only of the damage, and the innocent owner of the cargo is left, as to the other half, to sue the owner of the ship on board which his goods were carried. I do not see injustice in this arrangement; on the contrary its purpose is equity.' He then proceeds to repudiate in most explicit terms the authority of *Thorogood v Bryan* and refuses to be bound by it. He says: 'It is difficult to conceive how it can be contended that he, that is, the owner of the cargo, is *particeps criminis* when he is not so either as principal or agent. It is argued that he shall be so considered, and deprived of his remedy because he himself or his agent selected the ship by which his goods were carried. But there is, in my judgment, in the mere selection of the ship for the conveyance of his cargo, none of the ingredients which constitute any kind of responsibility for a collision, for I cannot conceive a responsibility for an act done where the individual has not, either by himself or his agent, any power of interference or control.'

This would appear to me to be the precise line of reasoning which led the Court of Appeal and your Lordships' House in the case of *The Bernina* to decide that *Thorogood v Bryan* was wrongly decided, and to overrule it and the case of *Armstrong v Lancashire and Yorkshire Rly Co* which followed it ...

It would appear to me, therefore, that the rule applied in *The Milan* case is not based upon the principle of *Thorogood v Bryan* at all, and was not so regarded, but that it is based rather on some supposed principle of equity and justice to the effect that, as the innocent owner of the cargo suffered by the negligence of each of the ships found to blame, each should compensate him for a portion of his loss; and that, as it was found impossible to measure these respective portions according to the relative culpability of the two wrongdoers, the portions were made equal, the owner of each ship being thus made liable for half the damage.[172]

Lord Shaw[173]

Dr Lushington lays down, and I think he rightly lays down, that it has become the admiralty practice. He suggests a very plausible reason for it; he suggests that the Court of Admiralty looked upon the two ships as two tortfeasors, and divided the responsibility equally between them so that the owner of cargo recovered one half from one ship, and the other half from the other ship ...

I do not think that the rule started with the judgment of Dr Lushington in *The Milan* case. It was affirmed in *Hay v Le Neve*,[174] decided in 1824, and applicable not to ship alone, but also to cargo; and the judgment of Lord Gifford takes the admiralty practice back to the year 1789, and to the judgment and important *dicta* of Lord Stowell to which reference is there made. But, my Lords, *The Milan* case is important, not because it contains a *dictum* in the year 1861, to the effect that, in the opinion of Dr Lushington, the rule of equal apportionments should apply as well to damage to cargo as to damage to ships, but on account of the decision of that most learned and experienced judge, to the effect that the practice of the admiralty in that sense had been a uniform practice.

It may be observed from this decision that the theory of treating the innocent cargo-owners, whose cargo was carried on the one colliding ship at fault, as being tainted with fault as well, and therefore providing justification for the

---

172 The equal division of loss was made by the MCA 1911, s 1, an alternative option only if assessment of proportionate faults cannot be established

173 [1911] AC 16, pp 28, 29.

174 (1824) 2 Shaw's Scotch Appeals 395.

division of loss rule, was rejected. Whether the rule of division of loss with regard to cargo carried on board is fair or not, it appears to have been part of the traditional practice in the Admiralty Court, and it has been incorporated in the legislation of the 20th century. The purpose of this rule was to establish several (not joint) liability for the proportion of the damage to or loss of cargo carried on board any of the ships at fault.[175] Most maritime nations, which have ratified the Brussels Collision Convention 1910, apply this rule.

By contrast, in USA, where this Convention has not been ratified, the rule is joint and several liability, which can cause problems when cargo interests sue the non-carrying colliding ship for damages in US courts. The result is that the cargo-owners can recover in full from the non-carrying ship in US courts. Then, the non-carrying ship may recover from the carrying ship the amount proportionate to the latter's degree of fault.[176] This circumvents the right of the carrying ship to rely on the exceptions from liability against the cargo claimant under the contract for errors in navigation.[177]

To rectify this anomaly created by US law, a clause known as 'both to blame collision' clause is inserted in charterparties and bills of lading. The effect of this clause is that the carrying ship can claim back from the cargo interests the amount paid to the non-carrying ship in respect of its own proportionate cargo liability. The cargo underwriters, who usually agree to indemnify their assured under a 'both to blame' collision clause inserted in the insurance contract, will pay its assured for the refund made to the shipowner, provided they are given the opportunity to defend their assured against a claim under such clause. A further complication, however, is that, in the USA, the 'both to blame' collision clause in bills of lading has been regarded invalid.[178]

If, however, the liability issue between the two ships at fault is determined in England, after a determination of the cargo liability of the non-carrying ship in the USA, the exception from liability of the carrying ship will be taken into account in the apportionment, in order to give affect to the 1910 Convention.[179] This may leave the non-carrying ship worse off, but, if it also carried cargo, the respective liabilities of both ships as well as exceptions from liability will be adjusted during the apportionment of damages to each other.

---

175 See *The Giacinto Motta* [1977] 2 Lloyd's Rep 221, in which the purpose of the 1911 Act was explained.

176 *The Sucarseco* (1935) 51 LlL Rep 238 (US Sup Ct).

177 Hague-Visby Rules, Art IV, r 2(a), but not under the Hamburg Rules.

178 See details of this in *O'May on Marine Insurance*, 1993, Sweet & Maxwell, pp 185, 186.

179 *The Giacinto Motta* [1977] 2 Lloyd's Rep 221.

3.10 Claims in relation to collision between a ship and other objects

Whilst contributory negligence in a collision between ships is governed by s 187 of the MSA 1995 by which their respective faults are apportioned, contributory negligence in the event of collision between a ship and another object is governed by the LR(CN)A 1945. The purpose of this Act has been to bring the rules of common law more or less in line with those of admiralty. However, unlike the admiralty rule, where there is an individual assessment of the fault of each ship liable for damage caused to each other or to a third ship, as opposed to a 'unit approach'[180] assessment, the 1945 Act does not require individual assessment when there are multiple faults. The claimant's conduct is contrasted with the totality of the defendants' conduct (the 'unit approach') in the liability proceedings in which the claimant's contributory negligence is taken into account. Then, the extent of each of the defendants' responsibility *inter se* is determined in the contribution action under the CLCA 1978, which may be joined with the main action or be determined in separate proceedings.

Fitzgerald v Lane[181]

A plaintiff successfully sued more than one defendant for damages with regard to personal injuries. Contributory negligence by the plaintiff was established in the liability proceedings. Apportionment of liability between the plaintiff and the defendants, pursuant to s 1 of the LR(CN)A 1945 was kept separate from apportionment of contribution between the defendants *inter se* under s 2 of the CLCA 1978. Assessment of the plaintiff's share in the responsibility for the damage he had sustained did not involve the determination of the extent of the individual culpability of each of the defendants:

> In the contribution proceedings, whether or not they are heard during the trial of the main action or by separate proceedings, the court is concerned to discover what contribution is just and equitable, having regard to the responsibility between the tortfeasors *inter se*, for the damage which the plaintiff has been adjudged entitled to recover. That damage may, of course, have been subject to a reduction as a result of the decision in the main action that the plaintiff, by his own negligence, contributed to the damage which he sustained.[182]

In cases where no contribution between tortfeasors is involved, the apportionment of fault is determined in the liability proceedings.

---

180 *Miraflores v George Livanos* [1967] 1 AC 826.
181 [1988] 3 WLR 356 (HL); also, *op cit*, Marsden, fn 1, para 14–17.
182 *Ibid*, p 362, *per* Lord Ackner.

The Ellen M[183]

The Ellen M, was moored along side other vessels head up river about 300 yds down river from the Haven Bridge. About 0715 hours the bridgemaster of the Haven Bridge had verbally informed the master of *The Ellen M* that the bridge would be opened for those vessels at 0735 hours. A good lookout was being kept on *The Ellen M*.

About this time, all aft moorings of *The Ellen M* were cast off and a blue flag was exhibited from a flagstaff on the east pier of the bridge indicating that the bridge was about to be opened to allow vessels to proceed northward. *The Ellen M* began to come off the quay under the influence of the flood tide. Very shortly afterwards, the engines of *The Ellen M* were put half astern.

Immediately afterwards a strong gust struck *The Ellen M*, catching her port bow and turning her to starboard, whereupon the rudder of *The Ellen M* was put hard-a-port and her engines were worked variously ahead and astern in an attempt to straighten her on to an up-river heading. Despite those manoeuvres, *The Ellen M*, under the influence of wind and tide, was carried across the river angled to starboard. Very shortly afterwards, *The Ellen M*, as a result of her port quarter being in contact with and sliding forward on another vessel, straightened up to an up-river heading, from which position *The Ellen M* could have been safely manoeuvred up river and through the open bridge.

When, very shortly afterwards, *The Ellen M* was about to go ahead on her engines so as to proceed towards and through the bridge, the bridge was seen to begin to close to river traffic. Immediately afterwards, the starboard anchor of *The Ellen M* was let go and three short blasts were sounded on her whistle in accordance with local practice to indicate to those operating the bridge that the bridge should be kept open. The arms of the bridge stopped at an angle of about 45 degrees from the upright, apparently indicating that the bridge was going to reopen, whereupon the engines of *The Ellen M* were put full ahead.

Immediately afterwards, the arms of the bridge again began to lower, closing the bridge, whereupon the starboard anchor chain of *The Ellen M* was again veered, her engines were stopped and her wheel was put hard-a-starboard in an attempt to turn her round to starboard head to tide.

The engines of *The Ellen M* were worked variously ahead and astern in an attempt to keep her stern clear of a coaster moored up river and her bows clear of craft moored at Town Hall Quay while she was carried up-river, turning to starboard dragging her anchor.

Nothing further was or could be done to prevent *The Ellen M* from colliding in quick succession with (1) the offside of a motor cruiser moored alongside; and (2) other craft at Town Hall Quay closer to the bridge.

---

183 [1967] 2 Lloyd's Rep 247.

In proceedings by the owners of *The Ellen M* against the owners of the bridge, it was alleged that the collision was caused by the defendant's negligent operation of the bridge. The defendants alleged that the collision was caused by *The Ellen M* allowing herself to get out of control.

It was held by Brandon J: (1) that the bridgemaster was negligent in closing the bridge; (2) that *Ellen M* was negligent in reversing her turning manoeuvre and attempting to pass through the bridge in belief that it was opening again; (3) that the negligence of *Ellen M* was an immediate cause of casualty; that, although the bridgemaster's negligence would not have caused casualty, without the subsequent negligence of *Ellen M*, no clear line could be drawn between earlier negligence of bridgemaster and later negligence of *Ellen M* and that, accordingly, both acts of negligence should be regarded as causative, and both parties were equally to blame. Brandon J explained (at p 258):

> It seems to me that the second act of negligence was so close to the first and so mixed up with the state of things brought about by the first that both acts of negligence should be regarded as causative, and I so hold.

> That leaves me with the task of apportioning the blame between the two sides. Apportionment of blame in a case of this sort is governed by the LR(CN)A 1945. Under that Act, the same principles are to be applied as under the MCA 1911, that is to say, the court is to take account of both culpability and causative potency. I do not find this an easy case in which to apportion the blame. The original trouble was due to the negligence of the bridgemaster; the subsequent negligence of the master of *The Ellen M* was committed in the situation of difficulty caused by that original negligence and allowances must obviously be made for that. But, after making all allowances for that, I consider that the master's decision to reverse his turning manoeuvre in order to make for the bridge again was a rash decision. It was the duty of the master of *The Ellen M* to put the safety of his ship first in a crisis of that kind and not to 'chance his arm', as I think he did. On the whole I have come to the conclusion that the fair apportionment in this case is to hold both sides equally to blame.

There may be occasions when a ship strikes an object, that is, a pier, as a consequence of taking an evasive action to avoid a collision with another ship, which is at fault. If they are both at fault, s 187 of the MSA 1995 will apply between the two ships for apportionment of fault even if there had been no actual physical contact between them.

An example of such a situation is shown below, although on the facts of this case only one ship was found to have been at fault.

The Belle Usk[184]

The plaintiffs paddle steamship *Brittania* was in collision with the steamboat pier in her manoeuvre to avoid a collision with the defendants' vessel *Belle*

---

184 [1955] 2 Lloyd's Rep 421.

Usk. The Belle Usk had been lying on at the passenger pontoon to which *The Brittania* was bound. She was, however, required to move out from the pontoon at the times passenger vessels were required to use the pontoon. *The Brittania* was a passenger vessel, and at the time in question, was due at about 7 pm that evening. As *The Brittania* approached her berth, *The Belle Usk* was seen to be moving out of there and both vessels seemed to be safely clear of each other. However, *The Belle Usk* suddenly came ahead across the path of *The Brittania*, causing *The Brittania*, in an attempt to avoid a collision, to stop her engines, suddenly, and put full speed astern, her wheel being turned to starboard. In an attempt to regain her position, so that she could still make it into the berth, *The Brittania* got caught by the westerly wind and a slight set of tide, and was carried against bullnoses causing damage both to the vessel and the pier. It was held that the damage was due to the bad seamanship of *The Belle Usk* in crossing ahead of *The Brittania* rendering collision with the pier inevitable. Therefore, *Belle Usk* was alone to blame, and had to recompense the Brittania for damages paid to the pier owner.

The risk of contact between arriving or departing vessels and shore cranes is a matter of notoriety, particularly when ships berth in close proximity to each other and under the influence of cross wind. A recent example of such a situation worth reading is **The Maersk Colombo**,[185] which came into contact with a shore crane by the overhang of her bow while berthing and caused the crane to topple over and collapse. The admiralty judge found that, although *Maersk Colombo* created a situation of danger by trying to berth in cross wind without yet having the tug made fast forward, the crane manager and the berth master were negligent also. In accordance with regulations, cranes should be positioned close to midships for a vessel manoeuvring on and off a berth. In this case, however, there was not enough time to move the crane when *Maersk Colombo* arrived. Bearing in mind also, the negligence of the berth master, the contributory negligence of the crane owners amounted to 15%.

3.11 Contribution between joint tortfeasors

3.11.1 The common law rule in non-admiralty cases

Under common law, in non-admiralty cases, the liability of joint concurrent tortfeasors is joint and several. Payment by one in full and final settlement bars the claimant from making a claim against the other tortfeasors. The cause of action for damages is extinguished against all of them.[186] Contribution between joint tortfeasors was not permitted until the Law Reform (Married

---

185 [1999] 2 Lloyd's Rep 491.
186 *Jameson and Another v Central Electricity Generating Board* [2000] 1 AC 455 (HL).

Women and Tortfeasors) Act 1935, which was subsequently superseded by the CLCA 1978. These Acts provided that if one tortfeasor had paid damages in full, or more than the damages caused by his fault, to the injured party, he could later claim (in a separate action) contribution from the other guilty party.

3.11.2 Property claims in admiralty

It has already been mentioned that when one incident of damage or loss occurs concurrently through the fault of two or more wrongdoers, the wrongdoers are joint concurrent tortfeasors. In admiralty law, where there is property damage through the fault of two or more ships, there is division of loss and apportionment of liability by assessing the blameworthiness and causative potency of the faults of each wrongdoer. Each wrongdoer contributes to the loss caused to each other's property, including the property carried on board, and to consequential losses, in proportion of its fault. This right of contribution existed at common law for admiralty claims only[187] and was made statutory later by s 1 of the MCA 1911,[188] now being enshrined in s 187 of MSA 1995.

3.11.3 Non-property claims in admiralty

The common law rule of joint and several liability also applied to claims for personal injury or loss of life. These claims are now regulated by s 188 of the MSA 1995, and the right of contribution between the tortfeasors is governed by s 189 (previously ss 2 and 3 of the MCA 1911).

3.11.4 When the common law rule applies in admiralty

Where there is an innocent third ship, which suffered damage due to the fault of two other ships, the innocent third party is entitled to recover his damage of loss in full[189] from either tortfeasor. The liability is joint and several as it is under common law in non-admiralty cases, therefore, the common law rules apply.[190] If one of the tortfeasors paid the whole damage to the innocent party, his right of contribution would be based on the CLCA 1978. This Act is available as an alternative right of contribution to the MSA 1995 (see under para 3.7.4.3, above).

In some cases, the 1978 Act may be beneficial to the party entitled to claim contribution in two respects. First, the time limit to claim contribution is two

---

187 *The Frankland* [1901] P 161.
188 See Chapter 14, para 8.2.4, *The Cairnbahn* [1914] P 25.
189 Since the innocent ship was not at fault, MSA 1995, s 187, will not apply to it.
190 See *The Devonshire* [1912] AC 634.

years, commencing from when the claimant either is held liable, or he agrees to pay the innocent party, while the time limit under s 190(4) of the MSA 1995 is one year. Second, the 1978 Act, s 1(4), prevents the defendant in contribution proceedings from challenging the issue of the plaintiff's liability to the original claimant.[191]

In other cases, where ss 187–89 of the MSA 1995 do not apply, as when there is a collision between a ship and a non-ship, or a ship and property in a harbour, or a pier, the common law rule and the relevant statutes will apply. The LR(CN)A 1945 deals with contributory negligence if there is fault also on the part of the non-ship, and the right of contribution between concurrent joint tortfeasors is governed by the CLCA 1978.

3.12 Remoteness of damage

It has been explained earlier that the claimant bears the burden of proof to show, not only that the defendant's act or omission caused the collision (causation in fact, para 3.5, above), but that it was also one of the causes that caused the damage claimed (causation in law, para 3.6, above).

The first and earliest rule of the common law was that the defendant was liable for damage which 'in the ordinary course of things would flow from' his wrongful act.[192] It was also recognised, however, that the law was concerned with what were called direct, rather than remote, consequences, for otherwise the defendant could be held liable for increasingly remote consequences stretching indefinitely into the future.[193] It was wrong to hold that the defendant in a tort claim would be liable for all consequences that could be described as 'direct and natural'.

3.12.1 General principle

Since 1960, the general rule which has been accepted about 'remoteness' of damage is that the defendant would only be liable if he could reasonably have foreseen the kind of damage suffered by the claimant. The claimant must prove, therefore, that the breach of duty by the defendant caused the kind of damage claimed, which must not be too remote. The breakthrough for the establishment of this rule, started with *The Wagon Mound (No 1)*[194] (decision of the Privy Council).

---

191 See, also, *op cit*, Marsden, fn 1, paras 14-33, 14-34.
192 *The City of Lincoln* [1890] P 15, p 18, *per* Lindley LJ, quoting from *Mayne on Damages*.
193 As Lord Wright said in *Liesbosch Dredger v SS Edison* (1933) 45 LlL Rep 123 (HL), p 129; [1933] AC 449, p 460.
194 [1961] AC 388 (PC).

Prior to this decision, however, the Court of Appeal had decided in *Re Polemis*[195] that the defendant would be responsible for the direct consequences resulting from his negligence, whether or not the actual damage sustained was reasonably foreseeable.

Readers familiar with English law are, of course, well aware of the distinction. For the benefit of those who are unfamiliar, it is important to summarise and compare these two cases.

Re Polemis

Under a time charterparty contract between the shipowner and the charterer, damage caused by fire either to cargo on board or to the ship was mutually excepted.

Besides other cargo, the charterers loaded in the hold a quantity of benzine and/or petrol in tins in cases. During the voyage the tins leaked and, in consequence, there was a considerable quantity of petrol vapour in the hold. At one of the ports of call it became necessary for the stevedores, who were employed by and were the servants of the charterers, to shift some of the cases of benzine. For that purpose, the stevedores placed a number of heavy planks at the forward end of the hatchway, which they used as a platform for transferring the cases from the lower hold to the 'tween deck. Owing to the negligence of the stevedores, when the sling containing the cases of benzine was being hoisted up it knocked a plank into the hold. The fall was immediately followed by a rush of flames, the result being the total destruction of the ship.

The shipowners claimed the value of the ship as damages from the charterers. The charterers disputed liability, and the dispute was referred to arbitration under a clause in the charterparty. The arbitrators found that: the ship was lost by fire; the fire arose from a spark igniting the petrol vapour in the hold; the spark was caused by the falling board coming into contact with some substance in the hold; and the causing of the spark could not reasonably have been anticipated from the falling of the board, though some damage to the ship might reasonably have been anticipated.

Subject to the opinion of the court on any questions of law arising, the arbitrators awarded that the owners were entitled to recover from the charterers a sum assessed by the arbitrators. The judge on appeal affirmed the award and the charterers appealed to the Court of Appeal.

The charterers contended: (1.) that they were protected from liability by the exception of 'fire' in the charterparty; (2.) that the damages were too remote, as it could not reasonably have been anticipated that the falling of the board would have caused a spark.

---

195 [1921] 3 KB 560 (CA).

It was held, (1) that the exception clause did not protect the charterers against loss by fire caused by the negligence of their servants, there being no express stipulation to that effect; and (2) that, as the fall of the board was due to the negligence of the charterers' servants, the charterers were liable for all the direct consequences of the negligent act, even though those consequences could not reasonably have been anticipated; and they were, therefore, liable for the loss of the ship by fire.

Referring to previous authorities, the principle applicable was summarised by Scrutton LJ as follows:

> To determine whether an act is negligent, it is relevant to determine whether any reasonable person would foresee that the act would cause damage; if he would not, the act is not negligent. But, if the act would or might probably cause damage, the fact that the damage it in fact causes is not the exact kind of damage one would expect is immaterial, so long as the damage is, in fact, directly traceable to the negligent act, and not due to the operation of independent causes having no connection with the negligent act, except that they could not avoid its results. Once the act is negligent, the fact that its exact operation was not foreseen is immaterial.[196]

It should be noted that the claim in *The Polemis* case was made for breach of contract based on negligence committed in the performance of contractual obligations, namely the negligence of the servants of the charterers, the stevedores. The arbitration case was, in fact, concerned with the construction of an exemption clause in the charterparty contract.[197] The conduct of the stevedores in the course of their employment was in question in determining whether their principals, the charterers, should be held liable for the actual damage caused. The case reached the Court of Appeal, as a special case. Warrington LJ said that it was clear that the act causing the plank to fall was, in law, a negligent act, because some damage to the ship might reasonably be

---

196 [1921] 3 KB 560 (CA), p 577.

197 The distinction of *The Polemis* case had carefully been pointed out by the appellants' counsel (Ashton Roskill QC) in *The Wagon Mound (No 1)* who said: 'The first submission on *Polemis* is that the issue was one of contract, namely, the construction of the exceptions clause in a time charterparty ... If that be so, it is difficult to regard the case as a satisfactory authority on the tort of negligence or on what constitutes a cause of action in negligence. That submission may be elaborated under three heads. First, negligence is read by implication into the exceptions clause: it does not, in the context of the exceptions clause, mean the same as the tort of negligence. The exceptions clause means that the charterers were not responsible for the fire unless caused by their carelessness. It is doubtfully correct to say, as Warrington LJ said, that the claim was based on the tort of negligence ...' (p 393). It is tentatively submitted that for this reason *The Polemis* case has caused confusion, and in any event it is misleading to refer to it as a decision against the stevedores, as it is stated in *op cit*, Marsden, fn 1, para 13-10.

anticipated. If this was so then the charterers were liable for the actual loss, that being the direct result of the falling board on the arbitrators finding.[198]

What, then, did *Polemis* decide? That was the question posed by Viscount Simonds in *The Wagon Mound (No 1)* discussed next. He said that their Lordships did not propose to spend time in examining whether the issue there lay in breach of contract or in tort. That might be relevant for a tribunal for which the decision was a binding authority but, for their Lordships, it was not. It may, however, be observed, he said, that in the proceedings there was some confusion. The case arose out of a charterparty and went to arbitration under a term of it, and the first contention of the charterers was that they were protected from liability by the exception of fire in the charterparty. But it was clear from the pleadings and other documents that alternative claims for breach of contract and negligence were advanced, and it was clear, too, that before Sankey J and the Court of Appeal, the case proceeded as one in which, independently of contractual obligations, the claim was for damages for negligence. It was upon this footing that the Court of Appeal held that the charterers were responsible for all the consequences of their negligent act even though those consequences could not reasonably have been anticipated. The negligent act was nothing more than the carelessness of stevedores (for whom the charterers were assumed to be responsible) in allowing a sling or rope by which it was hoisted to come into contact with certain boards, causing one of them to fall into the hold. The falling board hit some substances in the hold and caused a spark: the spark ignited petrol vapour in the hold: there was a rush of flames, and the ship was destroyed. The special case submitted by the arbitrators found that the causing of the spark could not reasonably have been anticipated from the falling of the board, though some damage to the ship

---

198 Aspects of causation and remoteness in contract, claims for indemnity and in the tort of negligence were contrasted by Evans LJ recently in *The Sivand* [1998] 2 Lloyd's Rep 97 (CA), p 105 (see para 3.12.5, below): 'These two situations [breach of contract and indemnity] have in common what a claim in tort does not, namely, a pre-existing legal relationship, almost invariably contractual, between the parties. It must follow, therefore, that the legal aspects of causation and remoteness must depend upon that legal relationship also. For example, the basic rule that the wrongdoer is liable for the "direct and natural" consequences of his act is applied by reference to a person situated as the contracting parties were when the contract was made, rather than to a reasonable man at the time of the wrongdoing. The same considerations arise, in my judgment, in relation to the questions whether the liability of the wrongdoer is affected by negligence of the other party (the same duty to mitigate damage arises) or of a third party. In the indemnity cases, such negligence, far from breaking the "chain of causation", may be the very event against which the promise to indemnify was given ... The present case resting solely in tort, it is unnecessary for present purposes to consider these questions further.' (*The Sivand*, p 105.) See, also, how Staughton LJ contrasts issues of causation and remoteness in claims for breach of contract, claims for indemnity and in tort: *Total Transport Corporation v Arcadia Petroleum Ltd (The Eurus)* [1998] 1 Lloyd's Rep 351 (CA), a breach of contract case: 'Although the foreseeability test is a handmaiden of the law, it is by no means a maid-of-all-work. To my mind, it cannot serve as the true criterion when the question is, how was the damage caused? It may be a useful guide, but it is by no means the true criterion' (p 362). See, also, Treitel, GH, *The Law of Contract*, 9th edn, Butterworths, p 880.

might reasonably have been anticipated. They did not indicate what damage might have been so anticipated.

As it seemed that the decision of the Court of Appeal in *The Polemis* might have stated a general principle to the effect that when a defendant – being sued in tort – is guilty of negligence he is liable for all the consequences, whether reasonably foreseeable or not, the Privy Council disapproved of it in *The Wagon Mound (No 1)*. The events of this case are seen below.

The Wagon Mound (No 1)

The plaintiffs were shipbuilders and repairers and owned the Sheerlegs Wharf in Sydney for their business. The defendants were demise charterers of the vessel *Wagon Mound*, an oil burning vessel which was moored 600 ft from Sheerlegs Wharf and was taking in bunkering oil in Sydney Harbour. A large quantity of the oil was, through the carelessness of the defendants' servants, allowed to spill into the harbour. During that and the following day, the escaped furnace oil was carried by wind and tide beneath the wharf owned by the plaintiffs, at which was lying a vessel which they were refitting, and for which purpose their employees were using electric and oxyacetylene welding equipment. Some cotton waste or rag on a piece of debris floating on the oil underneath the wharf was set on fire by molten metal falling from the wharf. The flames from the cotton waste or rag set the floating oil afire either directly, or by first setting fire to a wooden pile coated with oil. Thereafter, a conflagration developed which seriously damaged the wharf and equipment on it.

In an action by the shipbuilders to recover from the defendants compensation for the damage by fire, it was found by the trial judge, on the evidence, that the defendants 'did not know and could not reasonably be expected to have known that the furnace oil was capable of being set afire when spread on water'. Apart from the fire damage, the plaintiffs had also suffered some damage from the fact that the oil had congealed upon and interfered with the use of their slipways.

The judge concluded, however, that on the basis of the decision in *In Re Polemis v Furness Withy & Co*, the defendants were liable for all damage suffered because it was the direct consequence of their negligence. On the defendants' appeal to the Full Court of the Supreme Court of New South Wales the main heads of appeal were, first, that *The Polemis* was wrongly decided, and, secondly, that if it was right, the damage by fire was not the direct consequence of the defendants spilling the oil. The judgment of the Full Court contained a critical analysis of the decision in *Polemis*, and the conclusion was reached that it would not be proper to regard that decision otherwise than as binding on them. Manning J, however, giving the judgment of the court, said that it would be a gross understatement to say that he was able to apply that decision with any degree of confidence, and he expressed the hope that the House of Lords, or the Judicial Committee of the Privy Council, would pronounce on it in the near future.

The Supreme Court of New South Wales allowed an appeal by the defendants (the appellants) to the Privy Council. Their Lordships were concerned to displace the proposition that 'unforeseeability is irrelevant if damage is direct'.

Viscount Simond, commenting on *The Polemis* case, said:[199]

> Before turning to the cases that succeeded it, it is right to glance at yet another aspect of the decision in *Polemis*. Their Lordships, as they have said, assume that the court purported to propound the law in regard to tort. But up to that date, it had been universally accepted that the law in regard to damages for breach of contract and for tort was, generally speaking, and particularly in regard to the tort of negligence, the same. Yet *Hadley v Baxendale* was not cited in argument nor referred to in the judgments in *Polemis*. This is the more surprising when it is remembered that in that case, as in many another case, the claim was laid alternatively in breach of contract and in negligence. If the claim for breach of contract had been pursued, the charterers could not have been held liable for consequences not reasonably foreseeable ... Their Lordships refer to this aspect of the matter not because they wish to assert that in all respects today the measure of damages is in all cases the same in tort and in breach of contract, but because it emphasises how far *Polemis* was out of the current of contemporary thought. The acceptance of the rule in *Polemis* as applicable to all cases of tort directly would conflict with the view theretofore generally held.

Examining all relevant authorities, they came to the conclusion that the *Polemis* case should not be applied and the test of foreseeability was reinstated.

It was held that on the footing that the damage was the direct result of the escape of the oil, and applying the test of foreseeability, the defendants (appellants), who could not reasonably be expected to have known that the oil would catch fire, were not liable for the damage.

In particular, Viscount Simonds stated:

> There is not one criterion for determining culpability (or liability) and another for determining compensation; unforeseeability of damage is relevant to liability or compensation – there can be no liability until the damage has been done; it is not the act but the consequences on which tortious liability is founded ...[200]

> ... the essential factor in determining liability is whether the damage is of such a kind as the reasonable man should have foreseen. This accords with the general view, thus, stated by Lord Atkin in *Donoghue v Stevenson* ...[201]

---

199 [1961] AC 388 (PC), p 419.
200 *Ibid*, p 425.
201 *Ibid*, p 426.

It is a departure from this sovereign principle, if liability is made to depend solely on the damage being the 'direct' or 'natural' consequence of the precedent act. Who knows or can be assumed to know all the processes of nature? But if it would be wrong that a man should be held liable for damage unpredictable by a reasonable man because it was 'direct' or 'natural', equally, it would be wrong that he should escape liability, however 'indirect' the damage, if he foresaw or could reasonably foresee the intervening events which led to its being done ... thus, foreseeability becomes the effective test – the 'direct' consequence test leads to nowhere but the never-ending and insoluble problems of causation.[202]

The defendant escaped liability for the fire damage caused to the wharf in Sydney harbour, because on the judge's finding of facts, the fire damage was not reasonably foreseeable, although it was a direct damage from the defendant's negligence. The damage, which was foreseeable, was the fouling of the harbour by the escaped oil.

In the sequel to this decision, *The Wagon Mound (No 2),*[203] the Privy Council explained in great detail the application of the foreseeability test and applied the same to both cases of nuisance and negligence claims.

In this case, the claimants were the owners of the two vessels undergoing repairs at the wharf in Sydney Harbour. They sued the demise charterers of *The Wagon Mound* for damages on the basis of negligence and nuisance.

Walsh J, in the Supreme Court of New South Wales, accepted that the most probable explanation of the fire was that a hot piece of metal fell on some object supporting a piece of inflammable material in the oil-covered water which was ignited. He found that the damage to the claimants' vessels was 'not reasonably foreseeable by those for whose acts the defendants were responsible.' Further findings were that reasonable people in the position of officers of *The Wagon Mound* would regard furnace oil as very difficult to ignite upon water and that if they had given attention to the risk of fire from the spillage they would have regarded it 'as a possibility, but one which could become an actuality only in very exceptional circumstances'. Having made these findings, Walsh J held that liability in nuisance did not depend on forseeability and that the defendants were liable in nuisance but not in negligence. Judgment was accordingly given for the claimants on the claim based upon nuisance and for the defendants on the claim based on negligence. The defendants appealed against the judgment based on nuisance, and the claimants cross-appealed, on the issue of negligence.

It was held by The Privy Council that (1) that creating a danger to persons or property in navigable waters (equivalent to a highway) fell in the class of nuisance in which foreseeability was an essential element in determining liability and that it was not sufficient that the injury suffered by the

---

202 [1961] AC 388 (PC), p 426.
203 *Overseas Tankship (UK) Ltd v The Miller Steamship Co* [1967] 1 AC 617 (PC).

respondents' vessels was the direct result of the nuisance if that injury was in the relevant sense unforeseeable.

(2) That, on the facts, a reasonable man having the knowledge and experience to be expected of the appellants' chief engineer would have known that there was a real risk of the oil on the water catching fire and the fact that the risk was small did not, in the circumstances, justify no steps being taken to eliminate it. Accordingly, both the appeal on the claim based on nuisance and the cross-appeal upon the claim based on negligence would be allowed.

Lord Reid, who delivered the judgment, distinguished *The Wagon Mound (No 1)* from the findings in this case by saying:[204]

> In *The Wagon Mound (No 1)* the finding on which the board proceeded was that of the trial judge: 'the defendant did not know and could not reasonably be expected to have known that [the oil] was capable of being set afire when spread on water.' In the present case, the evidence led was substantially different from the evidence led in *The Wagon Mound (No 1)* and the findings of Walsh J are significantly different. That is not due to there having been any failure by the plaintiffs in *The Wagon Mound (No 1)* in preparing and presenting their case. The plaintiffs there were no doubt embarrassed by a difficulty which does not affect the present plaintiffs. The outbreak of the fire was consequent on the act of the manager of the plaintiffs in *The Wagon Mound (No 1)* in resuming oxyacetylene welding and cutting while the wharf was surrounded by this oil. So, if the plaintiffs in the former case had set out to prove that it was foreseeable by the engineers of the *Wagon Mound* that this oil could be set alight, they might have had difficulty in parrying the reply that this must also have been foreseeable by their manager. Then there would have been contributory negligence and at that time contributory negligence was a complete defence in New South Wales.

The vital parts of the findings of fact (in the present case) which have already been set out in full are (1) that the officers of *The Wagon Mound* 'would regard furnace oil as very difficult to ignite upon water' – not that they would regard this as impossible; (2) that their experience would probably have been 'that this had very rarely happened' – not that they would never have heard of a case where it had happened; and (3) that they would have regarded it as a 'possibility, but one which could become an actuality only in very exceptional circumstances' – not, as in *The Wagon Mound (No 1)*, that they could not reasonably be expected to have known that this oil was capable of being set afire when spread on water. The question which must now be determined is whether these differences between the findings in the two cases do or do not lead to different results in law.

Further extracts from his judgment illuminate the issues involved in defining the words 'reasonably foreseeable' by comparison to facts of other cases:

---

204 [1967] 1 AC 617, pp 640–44.

In *The Wagon Mound (No 1)* the board were not concerned with degrees of foreseeability because the finding was that the fire was not foreseeable at all. So Lord Simonds had no cause to amplify the statement that the 'essential factor in determining liability is whether the damage is of such a kind as the reasonable man should have foreseen'. But here the findings show that some risk of fire would have been present to the mind of a reasonable man in the shoes of the ship's chief engineer. So, the first question must be: what is the precise meaning to be attached in this context to the words 'foreseeable' and 'reasonably foreseeable'?

Before *Bolton v Stone*,[205] the cases had fallen into two classes: (1) those where, before the event, the risk of its happening would have been regarded as unreal either because the event would have been thought to be physically impossible or because the possibility of its happening would have been regarded as so fantastic or far fetched that no reasonable man would have paid any attention to it – 'a mere possibility which would never occur to the mind of a reasonable man' (*per* Lord Dunedin in *Fardon v Harcourt-Rivington*)[206] – or (2) those where there was a real and substantial risk or chance that something like the event which happens might occur, and then the reasonable man would have taken the steps necessary to eliminate the risk.

In *Bolton v Stone*, a member of a visiting team drove a cricket ball out of the ground onto an unfrequented adjacent public road and it struck and severely injured a lady who happened to be standing in the road. That it might happen that a ball would be driven onto this road could not have been said to be a fantastic or far fetched possibility: according to the evidence it had happened about six times in 28 years. And it could not have been said to be a far fetched or fantastic possibility that such a ball would strike someone in the road: people did pass along the road from time to time. So, it could not have been said that, on any ordinary meaning of the words, the fact that a ball might strike a person in the road was not foreseeable or reasonably foreseeable – it was plainly foreseeable. But the chance of its happening in the foreseeable future was infinitesimal. The House of Lords held in *Bolton v Stone* that the risk was so small that, in the circumstances, a reasonable man would have been justified in disregarding it and taking no steps to eliminate it.

But, it does not follow that, no matter what the circumstances may be, it is justifiable to neglect a risk of such a small magnitude. A reasonable man would only neglect such a risk if he had some valid reason for doing so, for example, that it would involve considerable expense to eliminate the risk

In the present case, there was no justification whatever for discharging the oil into Sydney Harbour. Not only was it an offence to do so, but it involved considerable loss financially. If the ship's engineer had thought about the matter, there could have been no question of balancing the advantages and disadvantages. From every point of view, it was both his duty and his interest to stop the discharge immediately.

---

205 [1951] AC 850 (HL).
206 (1932) 146 LT 391 (HL).

It follows that in their Lordships' view the only question is whether a reasonable man having the knowledge and experience to be expected of the chief engineer of *The Wagon Mound* would have known that there was a real risk of the oil on the water catching fire in some way: if it did, serious damage to ships or other property was not only foreseeable but very likely. Their Lordships do not dissent from the view of the trial judge that the possibilities of damage 'must be significant enough in a practical sense to require a reasonable man to guard against them' but they think that he may have misdirected himself in saying:

'... there does seem to be a real practical difficulty, assuming that some risk of fire damage was foreseeable, but not a high one, in making a factual judgment as to whether this risk was sufficient to attract liability if damage should occur.'

In this difficult chapter of the law decisions are not infrequently taken to apply to circumstances far removed from the facts which gave rise to them and it would seem that here too much reliance has been placed on some observations in *Bolton v Stone* and similar observations in other cases.

In their Lordships' view, a properly qualified and alert chief engineer would have realised there was a real risk here and they do not understand Walsh J to deny that. But he appears to have held that if a real risk can properly be described as remote it must then be held to be not reasonably foreseeable. That is a possible interpretation of some of the authorities. But this is still an open question and, on principle, their Lordships cannot accept this view. If a real risk is one which would occur to the mind of a reasonable man in the position of the defendant's servant and which he would not brush aside as far fetched, and if the criterion is to be what that reasonable man would have done in the circumstances, then surely he would not neglect such a risk if action to eliminate it presented no difficulty, involved no disadvantage, and required no expense [emphasis added].

In the present case, the evidence shows that the discharge of so much oil onto the water must have taken a considerable time, and a vigilant ship's engineer would have noticed the discharge at an early stage. The findings show that he ought to have known that it is possible to ignite this kind of oil on water, and that the ship's engineer probably ought to have known that this had in fact happened before. The most that can be said to justify inaction is that he would have known that this could only happen in very exceptional circumstances. But that does not mean that a reasonable man would dismiss such a risk from his mind and do nothing when it was so easy to prevent it. If it is clear that the reasonable man would have realised or foreseen and prevented the risk, then it must follow that the appellant is liable in damages. The learned judge found this a difficult case: he says that this matter is 'one upon which different minds would come to different conclusions'. Taking a rather different view of the law from that of the judge, their Lordships must hold that the respondents (claimants) are entitled to succeed on this issue.

The judgment appealed from is in the form of a verdict in favour of the respondents upon the claim based upon nuisance, a verdict in favour of the appellants on the claim based upon negligence, and a direction that judgment be entered for the respondents ... The result of their Lordships' findings is that the direction that judgment be entered for the respondents (claimants) must stand but that the appeal against the verdict in favour of the respondents and the cross-appeal against the verdict in favour of the appellants must both be allowed.

3.12.2 The kind of damage

It derives from the decision of the Privy Council that no matter how small the foreseeable risk seems to be, it is the kind of damage that a defendant should put his mind to as a possibility of happening, if he continued his act. So, the limitation of recovery imposed by its previous decision in *Wagon Mound (No 1)* was explained in terms of different findings of fact stated by the judge in each case.

By later decisions, which adopted the principle of *The Wagon Mound*, foreseeability is said to be relevant to the kind of damage and not to the exact way in which it occurred. Lord Pearce, in the well known case of the House of Lords, *Hughes v Lord Advocate*,[207] put it succinctly that to demand great precision on the test of foreseeability would be unfair to the pursuer since the facts of misadventure are innumerable. The defendants are, therefore, liable for all the foreseeable consequences of their neglect. When the result is of a different type or kind from anything that a defendant could have foreseen, he is not liable for it.

The Trecarrell[208] is a good shipping case showing that the exact way in which the damage could occur is irrelevant to the test of foreseeability.

The motor vessel *Trecarrell* was undergoing specialist repairs at a ship-repairers' yard. The work involved was coating her deep tank with vinyl lacquer. This work was to be carried out by specialist contractors. While the contractors' employees were transferring drums of the highly inflammable vinyl lacquer from the drydock to the ship, one of them dropped a drum which fell on and cut a temporary electric cable. As a result, the drum broke, the lacquer escaped and was ignited by sparking caused by a short circuit. Both the ship and the yard were damaged by the fire.

The shipowners sued the contractors, who joined the ship-repairers as a third party. The latter counterclaimed in third party proceedings against the contractors.

Brandon J held that the employee of the contractors could reasonably have foreseen that dropping the drum would create a fire hazard, even if he could not reasonably have foreseen the particular source of ignition; that, therefore, in a situation where a high degree of care was needed, the employee was negligent and that negligence caused the fire.

---

207 [1963] AC 837 (HL), p 857.
208 [1973] 1 Lloyd's Rep 402.

Judgment was given for the shipowners and the repair yard in the third party proceedings.

Foreseeability depends on the facts of each case. In *The Daressa*,[209] the kind of damage suffered was in question.

Brandon, J said:

I accept that a question of reasonable foreseeability is a question of fact, but it does not follow that a court always needs evidence to decide it. If the question arises in a field of common human experience, such as crossing a road or driving a motor car, a court can plainly decide it without evidence. If, on the other hand, the question arises in a technical field, as in *The Wagon Mound* cases, evidence is equally plainly needed. In between these two extremes there are intermediate cases where, although evidence might well assist a court by supplementing its own knowledge and experience, it is not essential to enable the court to reach a conclusion.

The master of *The Daressa* could reasonably have foreseen that any ship with which he collided might be operating with the assistance of a Government operating subsidy and that such operating subsidy might be lost during detention of the vessel for repairs.

3.12.3 Extent of damage

It does not matter if the extent of the damage resulting from the negligent act is greater than expected provided the consequences were foreseeable. This, however, may lead to extreme results, but it is a matter of common sense and experience of the courts as to what extent of damage may be awarded.[210] For example, the defendant may not be found liable for all damage if there was contributory negligence on the part of the claimant, or not liable at all if the chain of causation was broken by a *novus actus interveniens*.

In *The City of Lincoln*,[211] the defendant's vessel negligently collided with and caused damage to the plaintiff's vessel, whose master attempted to reach port in safety. But the vessel grounded accidentally before he did so, and was lost. In the absence of negligence by the master, the defendants were liable not merely for the collision damage but for the subsequent loss.

In *The Metagama*,[212] the House of Lords approved and adopted the same approach as Lindley LJ in *The City of Lincoln*. The defenders admitted liability

209 *The Daressa* [1971] 1 Lloyd's Rep 60, pp 63, 64.
210 It may appear, from the decision of *Warren v Scruttons* [1962] 1 Lloyd's Rep 497, that the extent of the damage awarded was rather remarkable, namely for the eye infection of the claimant, which resulted from blood poisoning after his finger was pricked by a poisonous wire due to defendant's negligence. It was said by Paull J, p 499, that: 'It is sufficient to say that one of the consequences of getting his finger poisoned was that he got a further ulcer in his eye, and the result of having that further ulcer in his eye is that the eye has become far more misty ...'
211 [1890] P 15.
212 (1928) 29 LlL Rep 253; [1928] SC 21 (HL).

for a collision in which the pursuers' vessel was damaged, but they alleged that the damage was increased by the improper handling of the vessel by those in charge of her after the collision had taken place. It was held by the majority that those responsible for the damaged vessel were not guilty of negligence, and it followed that the defenders were liable for the whole of the damages claimed.

In *The Oropesa*,[213] the Court of Appeal presided over by Lord Wright adopted the same approach. Two vessels came into collision. The master of one of them launched a lifeboat so that he and some others could go across to the other vessel to confer with her master, despite the rough weather conditions. The lifeboat capsized and some of the crew members were drowned, including the sixth engineer, whose parents claimed damages from the owners of the other vessel, which was partly responsible for the collision. The owners of the other vessel alleged that the master's act was *novus actus interveniens*. This was rejected. The master's actions were reasonable. Lord Wright said: '... the hand of the casualty lay heavily on [his vessel] and the conduct of the master and of the deceased was directly caused by and flowed from it.'[214]

In a recent Court of Appeal decision, *The Sivand*[215] (see para 3.12.5, below), the physical condition of the soil in a seabed, which caused the capsize of a barge (belonging to contractors who were repairing the harbour works) having been damaged by the fault of a colliding tanker, was not a *novus actus interveniens*. Evans LJ said:

> ... 'reasonable foreseeability' does not limit the extent of damages when the kind or type of damage could be reasonably foreseen. This is, in effect, for the purposes of legal analysis a 'thin skull' type of case. The factor which increased the cost of repairs and therefore the amount of damages cannot be regarded as an independent, supervening cause. It follows that the reasonable cost is recoverable in full.[216]

And on causation he said:

> To break the chain of causation it must be shown that there is something, which I will call ultroneous, something unwarrantable, a new cause which disturbs the sequence of events, something which can be described as either unreasonable or extraneous or extrinsic.[217]

The issue of contributory negligence, which was considered in determining causation in law and the extent of damage recoverable, was explained in the following case.

---

213 (1943) 74 LlL Rep 86; [1943] P 32.
214 *Ibid*, p 92; p 37.
215 [1998] 2 Lloyd's Rep 97 (CA).
216 *Ibid*, p 106.
217 *Ibid*, p 102.

The Arzew[218]

The defendants' vessel *Arzew* arrived at her berth alongside the wharf in Cotonou, Benin Republic, and commenced discharge of the gas oil she was carrying. The plaintiffs' fishing trawlers were lying on a northerly heading starboard side towards the wharf and welding operations were being carried out. An oil fire broke out in the vicinity of one of the plaintiffs' trawlers and spread, doing damage to their other trawlers. The plaintiffs alleged that the fire was caused by the negligence of the defendants in allowing gas oil to escape. The defendants alleged that the plaintiffs were guilty of contributory negligence in allowing the welding operations to be carried out at a time when there was gas oil on the surface of the water. It was found that the cause of the ignition was heat from a piece of molten metal, which dropped from a welding rod being used to weld one of the plaintiffs' vessels. On the issue of contributory negligence, the question the judge addressed was whether those in charge of the welding were aware, or ought to have been aware of the gas oil on the surface of the water. It was held by Sheen J that:

> ... on the evidence there was no negligence in continuing the welding operations at the relevant time in that since gas oil was colourless it would have been very difficult to notice its presence ... no one noticed the smell of gas oil before the fire.

There was judgment for the plaintiffs.

3.12.4 Mitigation of loss or damage

It is said that there is a duty upon a claimant to mitigate his loss if he can reasonably do so. The test is how a prudent uninsured would have acted following the collision. The master and crew must take reasonable steps to minimise the damage[219] and preserve the ship, cargo or passengers on board from further loss. There are many cases on this issue, some of which are already discussed earlier in the issues of causation. Other cases are linked to the measure of damages (see later).

As much as the foreseeability rule, this issue is also inextricably linked to causation, to the remoteness rule and to measure of damages. In the following extracts from *The Metagama*,[220] Viscount Dunedin, with whom Viscount Haldane agreed, stated the issue as follows:

> But it is always the duty of the person who is damaged to do his best to minimise his loss. This is really the same thing as to say that, if he might reasonably have avoided any part of the damage he has suffered, to that extent

---

218 [1981] 1 Lloyd's Rep 142.
219 *The Egyptian* [1910] P 38.
220 (1928) 29 LlL Rep 253 (HL), p 256.

the damage is not such as arises directly from the act complained of. In many cases, the question is stated as to whether, after the original fault which started matters, there has been a *novus actus interveniens* which was the direct cause of the final damage. *Novus actus interveniens* may be the act of a third party, so that in this case, I think the best way of stating the question is: was the pursuer guilty of such negligence after the collision as to make that negligence the direct cause of the final damage?

Caution should be exercised when using this quotation with regard to 'damage ... as arises *directly* from the act'. The case was decided a long time before the test of foreseeability of damages was settled in 1960. But the point made in this case is that, in the event of multiple causes, the 'direct' or 'predominant' cause will be taken into account, and if the claimant has made his damage worse by unreasonable conduct, he cannot claim that part of damage.

The burden of proof is on the defendant to show that the claimant failed to mitigate his loss.

3.12.5 The idiosyncrasy of the claimant, remoteness and mitigation of damages

Sometimes, a claimant in a collision case may suffer further loss, which may be due to his financial inability to mitigate damages.

Under common law, the defendant must take his victim as he finds him (the 'thin skull' rule).[221] The principle applies, in particular, to personal injury cases, in which the claimant's physical characteristics at the time of the injury may have the effect of increasing the scale or extent of physical damage caused to him by the defendant's negligence.[222]

How the House of Lords treat the impecuniosity of the claimant, which aggravated his loss, is shown below.

The Edison[223]

The Edison fouled the moorings of a dredger, *The Liesbosch*, owned by the appellants, and carried her out to sea. Thereafter, she sank and was lost. The owners of *The Edison* (the respondents) were solely liable for the loss. The dredger had been engaged in construction work with the Patras Harbour Commissioners. There was evidence that one or more dredgers were available in Holland for purchase by the appellants to replace the lost one, but they did

---

221 *Smith v Leech Brain & Co Ltd* [1962] 2 QB 405 (HL), where Lord Parker, CJ re-asserted the common law rule that the defendant takes the plaintiff 'as he finds him'. This is exemplified by 'thin skull' cases.

222 A feature of 'thin skull' cases is that the plaintiff's physical characteristics are already in existence when the negligence occurs. The defendant cannot seek to reduce the damages on the ground that the extent of the claimant's injury was unforeseeable; see *McGregor on Damages*, 16th edn, 1997, paras 200ff.

223 [1933] AC 449 (HL).

not have the money, as most of their liquid resources were engaged in the contract of dredging. As a consequence of the loss of *The Liesbosch*, the Patras Harbour Authorities threatened to cancel the contract and forfeit the deposit unless it was replaced within a certain time. It was therefore necessary for the appellants to hire one, and they did hire *The Adria* from Italy. The rate of hire was very high because she was somewhat larger than *The Liesbosch* and more expensive to work. Along with her, and due to her size, the appellants were compelled to take also on hire a tug and two hopper barges.

The appellants claimed all their losses from the owners of *The Edison*. Both the registrar and the judge awarded all damages, but the Court of Appeal disagreed and reversed the judgment.

The substantial issue for the House of Lords was what, in such a case as the present, was the true measure of damage?

Lord Wright, affirming the Court of Appeal decision, held as follows on this issue:

> It is not questioned that when a vessel is lost by collision due to the sole negligence of the wrongdoing vessel the owners of the former vessel are entitled to what is called *restitutio in integrum*, which means that they should recover such a sum as will replace them, so far as can be done by compensation in money, in the same position as if the loss had not been inflicted on them, subject to the rules of law as to remoteness of damage.

> I think it desirable to examine the claim made by the appellants, which found favour with the registrar and Langton J, and which in effect is that all their circumstances, in particular their want of means, must be taken into account and hence the damages must be based on their actual loss, provided only that, as the registrar and the judge have found, they acted reasonably in the unfortunate predicament in which they were placed, even though but for their financial embarrassment they could have replaced *The Liesbosch* at a moderate price and with comparatively short delay. In my judgment the appellants are not entitled to recover damages on this basis. The respondents' tortious act involved the physical loss of the dredger; that loss must somehow be reduced to terms of money. But the appellants' actual loss insofar as it was due to their impecuniosity arose from that impecuniosity as a separate and concurrent cause, extraneous to and distinct in character from the tort; the impecuniosity was not traceable to the respondents' acts, and in my opinion was outside the legal purview of the consequences of these acts. The law cannot take account of everything that follows a wrongful act; it regards some subsequent matters as outside the scope of its selection, because 'it were infinite for the law to judge the cause of causes', or consequences of consequences. Thus, the loss of a ship by collision due to the other vessel's sole fault, may force the shipowner into bankruptcy and that again may involve his family in suffering, loss of education or opportunities in life, but no such loss could be recovered from the wrongdoer. In the varied web of affairs, the law must abstract some consequences as relevant, not perhaps on grounds of pure logic but simply for practical reasons. In the present case, if the appellants' financial

embarrassment is to be regarded as a consequence of the respondents' tort, I think it is too remote, but I prefer to regard it as an independent cause, though its operative effect was conditioned by the loss of the dredger.[224]

With reference to whether the defendant should take his victim as he finds it, Lord Wright said:

> The appellants' financial disability was not to be compared with that physical delicacy or weakness which may aggravate the damage in the case of personal injuries, or with the possibility that the injured man in such a case may be either a poor labourer or a highly paid professional man. The former class of circumstances goes to the extent of actual physical damage and the latter consideration goes to interference with profit-earning capacity; whereas the appellants' want of means was, as already stated, extrinsic.[225]

Recently, similar questions came before the Court of Appeal in *The Sivand*, mentioned earlier under extent of damage, which is a very important decision because it is relevant to both issues of causation and remoteness of damages including mitigation. Evans LJ restated the principles, thus:

> The defendant to a claim in tort was liable for what the law regarded as the consequence of his wrongful act, identifying its consequences on a common sense basis and distinguishing in particular between what had caused rather than provided the occasion of the plaintiffs' loss, subject to reasonable foreseeability of the particular kind of loss and subject also to loss which resulted from negligence of the plaintiff or those to whom he was responsible in breach of his duty to mitigate his loss; when it was alleged that the loss had been caused by the intervening act of a third party, or other *novus actus interveniens*, then the inquiry was whether there was such an independent cause, not limited to whether the third party's act was negligent or not.[226]

The facts of the case are as follows. As a result of negligence, the defendants' vessel damaged the harbour installations belonging to the plaintiffs. The latter engaged contractors to carry out repairs. While carrying out the work of

---

224 [1933] AC 449 (HL), p 460.

225 *Ibid*, p 461.

226 *The Sivand* [1998] 2 Lloyd's Rep 97 (CA), p 105. In cases of breach of contract and indemnity claims he said: 'These two situations have in common what a claim in tort does not, namely, a pre-existing legal relationship, almost invariably contractual, between the parties. It must follow, therefore, that the legal aspects of causation and remoteness must depend upon that legal relationship also. For example, the basic rule that the wrongdoer is liable for the "direct and natural" consequences of his act is applied by reference to a person situated as the contracting parties were when the contract was made, rather than to a reasonable man at the time of the wrongdoing. The same considerations arise, in my judgment, in relation to the questions whether the liability of the wrongdoer is affected by negligence of the other party (the same duty to mitigate damage arises) or of a third party. In the indemnity cases, such negligence, far from breaking the "chain of causation", may be the very event against which the promise to indemnify was given (*cf The Island Archon* [1994] 2 Lloyd's Rep 227, pp 234–36). The present case resting solely in tort, it is unnecessary for present purposes to consider these questions further.'

reconstructing one of the dolphins, the contractors encountered unforeseen conditions in the soil strata of the seabed; this caused the legs of the jack-up barge, which was at the time being used as a platform from which to transfer a concrete soffit onto one of the dolphins, to sink into the seabed and capsize the barge. The condition of the seabed was unforeseen and could not reasonably have been foreseen by an experienced contractor. There had been no intervening negligence on the part of the contractors.

Under cl 12 of the standard form contract conditions in the contract between the plaintiffs and the contractors, the contractors were entitled to, and recovered, extra payment from the plaintiffs for unforeseen physical conditions, as was this event. The plaintiffs, in turn, sought to recover the amount they had paid to the contractors from the defendants. The other costs for repairs were paid, but there arose a dispute concerning this extra payment.

The defendants contended that the extra payment was the result of extra loss caused by an unforeseen event, the nature of the soil, and that, therefore, the capsize of the contractors barge did not constitute foreseeable damage resulting from their own initial negligence. They alleged that there was in law an intervening event (a *novus actus*) which broke the chain of causation.

It was held that:

> Where the plaintiff acted in mitigation of his loss the sole relevant criterion was the reasonableness of the steps which he took in mitigation; provided he had acted reasonably he was entitled to recover the cost of mitigation as the correct measure of his loss; the defendants owed the plaintiffs a duty of care not to damage their property and it was at all times reasonably foreseeable that if they did so, the damage might need to be repaired and that contractors might be engaged to do the necessary work on an ICE form of contract; and the learned judge was right to find that it was foreseeable that the cost of repair might include the payment of remuneration which covered the risk of the relevant contractor encountering unforeseen physical conditions which added to the cost of the work and that all this was within the risk created by the defendants' negligence.

Evans LJ distinguished *The Edison* (*Liesbosch Dredger*) case on the ground that, in that case, there was an extraneous cause. *The Edison* case provided, he said, a further example of what Lord Wright described as an 'ultroneous' cause, notwithstanding that it was an attribute of the claimant himself and not involving any inquiry into whether he was negligent or not. There was a line to be drawn between what has caused, rather than provided the occasion for, the plaintiff's loss. The repair costs arising out of the contract was not an extraneous cause:

> ... no part of the total cost resulted from some other factor, which should properly be regarded as a *novus actus interveniens* – an independent, supervening event. That would be the case, as the respondents concede, if the repairs were disrupted by some unexpected natural event, such as an earthquake. A separate example is suggested by the *Liesbosch Dredger* case;

suppose the contractors became bankrupt and others had to be employed to complete the works. Nothing of that sort arises here. Clause 12 operated in the kind of circumstances for which it was designed. The occurrence of such circumstances was within the ordinary scope of such a contract, notwithstanding that the precise circumstances were not reasonably foreseeable or foreseen. Implicitly, it seems to me, the conclusion must be that no extraneous or 'ultroneous' cause arose, such as to prevent the total cost from being the proper measure of the respondent's loss.[227]

He further said about the 'thin skull' cases:

In my judgment, therefore, the answer to the submission is that causation is established in the present case ... and that 'reasonable foreseeability' does not limit the extent of damages when the kind or type of damage could be reasonably foreseen. This is, in effect, for the purposes of legal analysis a 'thin skull' type of case. The factor which increased the cost of repairs and therefore the amount of damages cannot be regarded as an independent, supervening cause. It follows that the reasonable cost is recoverable in full.[228]

The point to be borne in mind from what Evans LJ said is that a defendant in such circumstances ought to have foreseen that a contractor might be engaged under a contract providing for an indemnity for loss from an unforeseen physical condition of the soil of the seabed, while in *The Edison*, the impecuniosity of the claimant was not foreseeable but an extraneous cause.

A comparison between *The Edison*, a House of Lords decision, and this case, however, gives rise to this question: what would have happened in *The Edison* case if the dredger had not been lost but seriously damaged? Assuming that as a result of a prolonged repair period, the claimant was obliged to hire the same substitute dredger, if nothing else similar to the damaged dredger was available in the market, and incurred high costs in hiring her and the tug and barges that were necessary. In such a situation, would it not be right to say that the defendant ought to have foreseen that the claimant had a dredging contract to perform and that the claimant ought to recover the consequential loss of hiring another dredger which resulted from the damage caused due to the defendant's fault? It is submitted that the answer would be in the affirmative.

The law does not oblige the victim of damage to buy a substitute vessel to be able to continue his contractual commitments. On the contrary, the wrong doer ought to have foreseen that the victim might have had contractual undertakings to complete and, if damage or loss was caused to his tools by the negligence of the wrongdoer, the victim would be unable to carry on with contractual deadlines suffering consequential loss. Had he not done anything, the owner of the dredger would have been liable to pay damages for breach of

---

227 *The Sivand* [1998] 2 Lloyd's Rep 97 (CA), p 106.
228 *Ibid*, p 106.

the undertaking to the Patras harbour authority, which would have been greater than the loss suffered by the hire of the substitute dredger. It should be the necessity to hire a dredger to complete the contract caused by the defendant's wrongdoing that ought to be considered, regardless of the subsidiary reason of the claimant's lack of liquid funds to buy a new dredger. This reason, when put into perspective, differs greatly from the result of bankruptcy or loss of livelihood of the claimant, which the House of Lords considered as extreme consequences of the wrong and which would be irrelevant to the consideration of foreseeability.

The *Edison* case is a House of Lords decision, but it may not come as a surprise if another equivalent decision in the future disapproves of the result. It may be of assistance to quote what Hobhouse LJ said in *The Sivand*, who treated the issue as an issue of mitigation rather than causation:

> This is a claim for damages for the negligent damaging of the plaintiffs' property. Once the causation of physical damage to the plaintiffs' property is complete, the only remaining question is the assessment of that damage in monetary terms, *prima facie* the difference between the value of the undamaged property and the value of the damaged property quantified as the cost of repair or reinstatement. Where the plaintiff acts in mitigation of his loss the sole relevant criterion is the reasonableness of the steps which he took in mitigation. Provided he has acted reasonably, he is entitled to recover the cost of that mitigation (even if unsuccessful) as the correct measure of his loss. Questions of foreseeability are not relevant, save so far as they may enter into the question of the reasonableness of what the plaintiff did in mitigation ... The defendants cannot, and do not, deny that they owed the plaintiffs a duty of care not to damage their property. It was, further, at all times reasonably foreseeable that if they did so the damage might need to be repaired and that contractors might be engaged to do the necessary work on an ICE form of contract.[229]

A recent case of the Privy Council, *Alcoa Minerals of Jamaica v Broderick*,[230] may also be of assistance, where a house was damaged by nuisance for which the defendant was liable and the claimant could not repair it until the damages were paid. It was held that the claimant acted reasonably.

Since the claimant in *The Edison* did not have any other option but to hire another dredger to complete his contractual commitments, which were disrupted by the defendants breach of duty of care, and there was no issue whether he acted unreasonably, the defendant should have been liable for at least a part of the hire costs as consequence of his breach, in addition to the value of the dredger at the time of the loss, which was very low.

The registrar, when he awarded the damages to the owner of the dredger, made this finding:

---

229 *The Sivand* [1998] 2 Lloyd's Rep 97 (CA), p 108.
230 (2000) *The Times*, 22 March (PC).

... having regard to all the existing circumstances, such as the severe terms of their contract in regard to penalties and their want of liquid resources, they had acted reasonably, and that the hiring of *The Adria* to complete an important contract with a public body was a direct and natural result of the collision.

It should have been argued before the House of Lords that the decision of the dredger owner, in the circumstances, was in accord with what a prudent uninsured would have done, were he in the same circumstances.

4 ASSESSMENT OF DAMAGES

4.1 General principle: *restitutio in integrum*

The principles for recovering damages in collision cases are based on the general principles of damages under common law. The objective is to place the claimant in the same pecuniary position as he would have been in but for the defendant's breach of duty which caused the collision. It is known as the principle of 'restitutio in integrum', for example, the right to a full and complete indemnity.

The principle was laid down by Dr Lushington, in *The Clarence*,[231] as follows:

> The party who has sustained a damage by collision is entitled to be put, as far as practicable, in the same condition as if the injury had not been suffered.

In *Morrison Steamship Co Ltd v Greystoke Castle*,[232] Lord Porter said:

> One method of ascertaining the damages in an action in tort is to ask what loss would a reasonable man anticipate as a result of a wrongful act.

However, in admiralty law, the principle of *restitutio in integrum* is affected in the following ways: First, the right of the defendant to limit his liability by establishing a limitation fund[233] will inevitably affect the amount recoverable by various claimants. All claimants will take from the fund *pari passu*, or in the priority the court determines, and their recovery will depend on the amount of the fund. Second, when the division of loss is applied to damages, the ship which received the greater damage will be awarded the difference between the damage caused to the other ship and the damage received, while the ship that received the less damage will be awarded nothing. Limitation of liability,

---

231 (1850) 3 W Rob 283, p 285.
232 [1947] AC 265, p 295 (HL).
233 See Chapter 16, below.

if applicable, will be applied to the remaining balance, after deduction.[234] Third, exception from liability for negligent navigation provided in the contract of carriage affects full recovery by the cargo-owner, whose cargo was damaged or lost on board the carrying ship. Under English law, he can only recover from the other ship at fault in proportion to the degree of its fault.

Commonly, in collision cases, the defendant also assumes the role of a claimant by virtue of a counterclaim against the claimant for his loss, if they are both to blame.[235]

The registrar determines the assessment of damages after the court has determined the issues on liability.

4.2 Total loss of a ship

4.2.1 Value of the ship (how is it ascertained)

If the kind of loss is foreseeable, the claimant is generally entitled to the market value of the ship at the time of the collision. If there is no market value, he will be entitled to the value of the ship to her owner as a going concern, that is, what the ship was worth from a business point of view. In the following case, the court overruled the measure of damages awarded to the owners of a sunken ship by the registrar.

The Harmonides[236]

A collision occurred between *Harmonides* and *Waesland* resulting in the sinking of *The Waesland* with all her cargo. *The Harmonides* was found solely to blame for the collision, and in a later action, her owners obtained a decree limiting their liability. The owners of *The Waesland* in the limitation suit claimed to have the vessel valued at certain figure. The cargo-owners, however, contested that the value was too high as a result of which their share in the limitation fund would be considerably reduced. The question arose as to what value to be placed on *The Waesland*. The judge, Barnes J, said:

> The best evidence is that of those who know the ship, and the next best evidence that of those who have experience of the market, but who do not know the vessel except from the shipping records. There are other criteria, such as the amount of capital invested, the amount of depreciation, the amount of profits, and so forth. All these matters have to be considered, to my mind, where it is impossible to say that there is a real market test of the value of such a vessel as this. If one goes to the root of the matter, it is obvious that what the

---

234 *The Khedive* (1882) 7 App Cas 795 (HL); see, also, Art 5, Sched 7 to the MSA 1995.
235 For procedure in collision cases see: Meeson, N, *Admiralty Jurisdiction and Practice*, 2nd edn, 2000, LLP, paras 7-030–7-073.
236 [1903] P 1.

shipowners lose if a vessel like this is run into and sunk is what it would cost to replace them in the position they were in before the accident. But where a ship like this has gone to the bottom you cannot, speaking from a business point of view, replace them in the position they were in before, because you cannot replace the vessel which is at the bottom of the sea; you cannot buy another like her in the market; you cannot get another made immediately, and if you bought another ship she would be new, and consequently more valuable, because she would start as a new ship from that day, and, therefore, you would have to discount her value down. So that the real test, where there is no market, is, as counsel on both sides agree, what is the value to the owners, as a going concern, at the time the vessel was sunk? You cannot get at this with any great certainty, for you cannot get at it from the market value. Possibly, for such a ship at such a time there would be no buyers and she would have to be sold for old iron. You cannot deal with it like an ordinary commodity being sold every day. You must look at it and see what is the loss to the owners. It has been pointed out that you may look at the original cost, plus the money expended on her, and so forth. That is of assistance, but it is not complete assistance, because it is a rough and ready method. You may look and see also how the ship is paying. That, however, is not a complete test, because you cannot be sure that the way she has been paying will continue. But one thing is absolutely certain – you cannot say the test is her market value.[237]

4.2.2 Loss of a profitable charterparty

In 1849, Dr Lushington examined the issue of damages when a ship was lost due to a collision while she was performing a profitable charter, in *The Columbus*.[238]

In a collision off Dungeness a smack was sunk, and her owner claimed not only the value of his vessel but further sums, first, for wages, which it was said he would have earned as master of the smack, and, secondly, for profits which it was supposed the smack would have made had it not been for her loss by the collision. Both these further claims were rejected

He stated about the assessment of damages:

It has been argued ... that the principle upon which this court proceeds in all matters of this kind is *a restitutio in integrum*; in other words, the principle of replacing the party who has received the damage in the same position in which he would have been, provided the collision had not occurred. As a general proposition, undoubtedly, the principle in question is correctly stated; and not only in this court, but in all other courts, I apprehend the general rule of law is, that where an injury is committed by one individual to another, either by himself or his servant, for whose acts the law makes him responsible, the party receiving the injury is entitled to an indemnity for the same. But although this is the general principle of law, all courts have found it necessary

---

237 [1903] P 1, p 6.
238 (1849) 3 W Rob 158.

to adopt certain rules for the application of it; and it is utterly impossible, in all the various cases that may arise, that the remedy which the law may give should always be to the precise amount of the loss or injury sustained.

However, by comparison to partial loss of the ship, the House of Lords, in *The Argentino*,[239] conclusively held that the loss of earnings in an employment contracted for is not too remote to constitute an element to be considered in the assessment of damages in the case of a partial loss. In later decisions, such as in *The Northumbria*[240] and *The Kate*,[241] it was expressly held that, in the case of a vessel being totally lost by collision while under a charter, the proper measure of damages against the vessel solely liable for the collision was the value of the vessel at the end of the voyage, plus profits lost under the charterparty. It was commented that, in *The Columbus*, the difficulty of the admiralty judge was that the claims seemed to be speculative.

It is not disputed that a proper measure of damages to satisfy, as closely as possible, *restitutio in integrum*, should include a net sum of loss of earnings. This is subject to the proviso that such sums are proved and are not speculative.[242] In *The City of Rome*,[243] Lord Hannen refused to allow a claim for the value of the fish which it was alleged would have been taken. An attempt was made there to introduce an uncertain and speculative profit. Where, on the other hand, there is a definite contract for the employment of the vessel the charter is to be taken into account whether there is one or more consecutive charters.

There is, however, a conflict between the authorities as to whether the value of the ship is to be the market value at the time of the collision together with the proper net sum in respect of her existing charters, subject to allowances for contingencies,[244] or her value that she would have had at the end of the voyage as enhanced by the loss of her earnings (see *The Northumbria* and *The Kate*, earlier). If the latter was correct, there might be some wear and tear or depreciation of the ship at the end of the voyage. In reconciling the authorities, it seems that the best time taken in assessing her value as a going concern should be the time of the collision when the wrongdoer caused the loss.

---

239 *The Argentino* (1888) 14 App Cas 519 (HL).
240 (1869) LR 3 A&E 6.
241 [1899] P 165.
242 *The Kate* [1899] P 165; *The Argentino* (1888) 14 App Cas 519 (HL).
243 (1887) 8 Asp 542.
244 *The Philadelphia* [1917] P 101 (CA).

4.3 Partial loss of the ship and incidental losses

4.3.1 Cost of repairs

The owner is entitled to such costs of repairs as to put his vessel in substantially the same state as she was in before the damage occurred. He must act as a prudent uninsured and mitigate his losses.

There is no subtraction from the sum awarded on the basis of new for old, and this is something the wrongdoer must accept. The repairs must be carried out at a reasonable expense and must be satisfactory. Permanent, instead of temporary repairs would be reasonable.

4.3.2 Loss of profit

If the vessel was under a charterparty and after the collision damage she needs repairs, the owner can claim the loss of freight or hire, less the disbursements already paid, and an allowance for wear and tear saved may be made. The claimant can only claim loss of use of the ship at the time of her repairs at a rate which is arrived at based on an average figure earned over a number of charterparties.

The Naxos[245]

The Aliartos was damaged as a result of a collision with *The Naxos*. *The Naxos* was entirely to blame for the collision. *The Aliartos* was surveyed and the surveyor made recommendations for permanent repairs to be done. Since the damage to the ship was not serious, he advised that the permanent repairs could be deferred until later at the owners' convenience. The owners carried out temporary repairs for two days, thereafter, the vessel continued to trade under a series of charterparties. *The Aliartos* spent two days in drydock and five days doing the permanent repairs. The plaintiffs put in a claim for several items, including a claim for detention during permanent repairs. The vessel had lost five days trading during the permanent repairs. The defendants contended that the plaintiffs had failed to mitigate their loss. In particular, that the permanent repairs could have been carried out while the vessel was trading, and therefore had lost trading time unnecessarily; that the rate of profit at which the plaintiff was claiming for the loss was much higher than usual and that a fairer method would be to take the average of the rates of profit over a number of voyages.

Brandon J held that the mitigation point was a question of fact and, in the circumstances, the plaintiffs had not acted unreasonably. On the rate point, he

---

245 [1972] 1 Lloyd's Rep 149.

held that the court should take an average of the voyages before and after the detention in order to arrive at a representative figure for the earning capacity of the vessel at the period. It would be unfair to the defendants if the higher figure of the charterparty subsequent to detention was only taken into account.

The shipowner can only claim profit lost under an immediate or consecutive charterparty, not under a speculative employment. He cannot claim special damages if there was no prospect of the vessel being employed.

The Hebridean Coast[246]

In the collision between The Hebridean Coast and The Lord Citrine, the owners of The Hebridean Coast admitted liability. The issue that arose was the amount of damages due to The Lord Citrine. The vessel belonged to the Central Electricity Authority and was one of the vessels used to bring coal to London from various ports. The owners claimed loss of the use of the vessel for coal carriage due to detention for the period when the vessel was undergoing repairs. During the detention period none of the appellants' ships was idle. The appellants were using a number of chartered ships at the time, but no specific ship could be said to have taken the place of The Lord Citrine. The registrar held that the appellants had failed to show that they had chartered tonnage to replace the ship and that interest on capital was therefore the only available measure of damages, but he adopted a rate of interest of over 30% on the agreed value of the ship. Lord Merriman, P, whose decision the Court of Appeal affirmed, held that interest on the capital value was the true measure of damages, but that the rate adopted was inordinate and should be reduced to 7%. On appeal to the House of Lords it was held that the measure of damages should be based on interest on the value of the ship and not on a calculation of the cost of carrying in chartered tonnage the coal, which The Lord Citrine would have carried.

It was not proved that the loss of use of the ship resulted in the appellants having to use chartered tonnage. The finding that none of the appellants' ships was idle did not exclude the possibility that they were not being used to their full capacity and so were able to carry the very small proportion of the total coal carried during the remainder of the relevant period, which The Lord Citrine would have carried during the detention period.

4.3.3 Out of pocket expenses and financial loss

The shipowner or demise charterer can recover not only the immediate costs of repairs, but any other loss foreseeably resulting from the collision, which is

---

246 [1961] AC 545 (HL).

incidental or consequential to the collision, including financial loss. Financial loss includes loss of profit, survey costs, the cost of drydocking, and out of pocket expenses, such as payment for salvage services, towage services, dock dues are recoverable.[247] It does not include pure financial or economic loss.[248]

The owner or demise charterer of the damaged ship will, however, be able to recover the type of financial loss, which results from the damage to their property in which they have proprietary or possessory rights. The issue of non-recoverable pure financial loss arises when a time or voyage charterer claims loss of profit by the non-use of the ship, or incidental expenses, after the collision damage.

A time or voyage charterer, is not entitled to recover for pecuniary loss resulting from damage caused by a third party because a time charterer has no proprietary or possessory right in the chartered vessel.

Hewson J held in *The World Harmony*:

> There is no reported case, so far as I am aware, in the long history of chartering where a time charterer has recovered damages for pecuniary loss because of damage by a third party to the chartered vessel.[249]

The courts generally will not give redress to any party claiming loss of income, wasted expenditure or loss of profits, being purely economic losses, when they are merely based on loss of contractual rights by reason of the collision and not on loss of proprietary or possessory rights.[250] This issue arose in the following case, which is worthy of noting, particularly because the time charterer was in fact the owner of the ship that suffered damage by collision, but he was claiming loss of profit (financial loss) in his capacity as a time charterer of the ship.

---

247 For further details, see *op cit*, Marsden, fn 1, Chapter 15.

248 The principles applicable to recovery for pure economic loss have been explained in the previous chapter, under liability of classification societies, and Section C, para 3.1, below.

249 [1965] 2 WLR 1275; [1965] 2 All ER 139, p 155.

250 It should be noted, however, that the cargo-owners in *The Nicholas H* lost against the classification society despite their proprietary interest in the lost cargo. They claimed economic loss for damage to their cargo carried on the ship at the time of its loss, contending that the classification society owed them a duty of care when its surveyor negligently allowed the ship to sail without permanent repairs being carried out first. The main reason of the House of Lords for not recognising a duty of care in such a case was that, upon the application of the third ingredient of the test in negligence, it would not be fair, just and reasonable to impose such a duty to classification societies, particularly because the cargo interests have redress against the owners of the ship, whose duty to make the ship seaworthy is non-delegable. See, also, Chapter 11, para 8, above and para 3.1 of this chapter.

The Mineral Transporter[251]

By a bareboat charter, the first plaintiff (owner) let *The Ibaraki Maru* to the second plaintiff (the demise charterer) and, by a time charter of the same date the second plaintiff, let it back to the first plaintiff. Under the bareboat charter, the bareboat charterer would be liable for the cost of repairs if occasioned by a collision, and under the time charter the daily hire payable by the time charterer to the bareboat charterer would be reduced while the vessel was undergoing repairs. While the vessel was at anchor off Port Kembla, New South Wales, *The Mineral Transporter* owned by the defendant negligently collided with *The Ibaraki Maru* causing her damage. Temporary repairs to *The Ibaraki Maru* were delayed by 32.79 days by a union ban in support of its campaign to persuade foreign vessels trading regularly to Australia to have repair and maintenance work done in Australia. Final repairs were effected in Japan. On the plaintiffs' claim for damages for negligence against the defendant in the Supreme Court of New South Wales Admiralty Division, it was held that the time charterer was entitled to recover the amount of hire paid whilst the vessel was not operational and the profits it lost during that period, and that the bareboat charterer was entitled to recover the total cost of repairs and the amount by which the hire had been reduced, and in quantifying the damages the days lost by reason of the union ban should be included.

On appeal to the Privy Council it was held, allowing the appeal, that it was a principle of common law that, if a wrong was done to a chattel a person who merely had a contractual right in relation to the chattel and not a proprietary or possessory right could not bring an action against the wrongdoer for injury to his contractual right, and that principle had been applied so that it had become well established that a time charterer could not recover damages for pecuniary loss caused by damage to the chartered vessel by a third party. Therefore, the first plaintiff, suing as time charterer, and not as owner of the damaged vessel, was not entitled to recover from the defendant the hire paid to the bareboat charterer and loss of profits while the vessel was not operational.[252]

Although this case was decided before the re-examination of principles of the tort of negligence, the point made, that there should not be an extension of the common law duty of care in such cases, is consistent with the three stage test, applicable since 1990.

This principle would also apply to other parties, such as sub-charterers, stevedores, surveyors or agents of the damaged ship, claiming economic loss for loss of income or wasted expenditure.

---

251 [1986] AC 1.
252 *Ibid*, pp 15, 24, 25.

Liability for damage suffered due to oil contamination resulting from the escape of oil from a wreck is dealt with by the pollution legislation. Such liability, however, will not extend to pure financial loss. It was recently decided by the Scottish Court of Session in *P&O Scottish Ferries Ltd v The Braer Corporation*[253] that the claimants' claim for loss of passenger and freight revenue after the tanker *Braer* ran aground at Garths Ness, Shetland, resulting in extensive pollution in that area, was a pure economic loss. Applying the common law principles mentioned earlier, such loss was not recoverable for lack of the necessary relationship of proximity. Moreover, the losses claimed were no more than an indirect consequence of adverse publicity affecting the image of Shetland as a source of fish and fish products.

When a substitute vessel is hired until repairs are completed, the damages include cost of hire paid to the substituted ship, which is consequential financial loss of the owner or demise charterer. The claimant is entitled to recover from the defendant, not only the out of pocket expenses caused by the collision, but also substantial damages for the loss of the services of the damaged ship during the time her place was taken by the substituted ship.[254]

4.3.4 Detention time and dock charges

If the claimant has his routine repairs carried out at the same time as the collision repairs, he is entitled only to recover loss of use and dock charges for the time of detention needed to repair the collision damage. Loss of use caused due to detention in the shipyard to carry out owner's repairs should be deducted.[255] If the routine repairs are not necessary but are just brought forward, the wrongdoer will not be entitled to any credit for this in the sense that the claimant would have lost the use of the ship sometime later, provided the routine repairs do not take up extra time.[256]

In the following case, routine repairs, which were brought forward but were not necessary, were allowed without any credit of time being given to the wrongdoer. The costs of additional docking time, however, which was not required for the collision repairs, was excluded from the damages claimed.

The Admiralty Commissioners v SS Chekiang[257]

The Cairo collided with *The Chekiang*, for which collision *The Chekiang* was entirely to blame. *The Cairo* was temporarily repaired at Hankow, and she then proceeded to Hong Kong for permanent repairs. She was shortly due for

---

253 [1999] 2 Lloyd's Rep 535.
254 *The Mediana* [1900] AC 113 (HL).
255 *The Hassel* [1962] 2 Lloyd's Rep 139.
256 *The Ferdinand* [1972] 2 Lloyd's Rep 120.
257 [1926] AC 637 (HL).

her annual refit, and after her arrival at Hong Kong the Admiralty decided to do both sets of repairs at the same time. The combined operations occupied about eight weeks, but the registrar found that the time properly allocated to the collision repairs was 20 days, and, in respect of the loss of use of *The Cairo*, he allowed a sum per day being calculated on the basis of 5% per annum on the estimated capital value of the ship at the time of the collision:

It was held by the House of Lords that the fact that the Admiralty took the opportunity of the docking required for the collision repairs to do the refitment repairs, which had not become necessary at the time of the collision, was not a ground for reducing the liability of the respondents to make good the damage caused by the collision, and that the registrar had rightly allowed damages as for the total deprivation of the use of the vessel for the 20 days.

Lord Sumner said about measure of damages:

The measure of damages ought never to be governed by mere rules of practice, nor can such rules override the principles of the law on this subject.

When *The Chekiang* ran into *The Cairo* she imposed on the Admiralty, as the direct consequence of this wrong, the necessity for docking the Cairo at Hong Kong during the repair of the collision damage. Why should not *The Chekiang* pay for that docking? Her overhaul was not then due. It had not been determined upon for that time, and the programme of overhauls was itself liable to alteration. The overhaul imposed no extra burden on *The Chekiang* when it took place; in fact, the dock charges are claimed only to the end of the collision repairs and not till *The Cairo* left the dock. There is abundant authority for saying that the fact, that the owners of an injured ship take the opportunity of the docking required for collision repairs to do work on their own ship, which had not already become necessary at the time of the collision, nor was brought about by the owners' negligence contributing to the collision, is no ground for reducing the wrongdoer's liability to make good the damage his wrongdoing has caused. It is not, like *The Haversham Grange*, a case of both to blame and of a second collision following a first one, which had already made docking inevitable.[258]

The Haversham Grange[259]

In order to effect repairs necessitated by two collisions for which the owners of two wrongdoing vessels were liable, the plaintiffs, the owners of the damaged vessel, put her into drydock, and proceeded to repair, at the same time, the separate damage sustained in each collision. The defendants, the owners of the wrongdoing vessel in the second collision, objected to pay any portion of the dock dues on the ground that the repair of the damage caused by their vessel occupied a shorter time than that required for the repair of the

---

258 [1926] AC 637 (HL), pp 643, 645.
259 [1905] P 307.

damage sustained in the first collision, so that the plaintiffs had not been put to any additional expense.

The Court of Appeal, reversing the decision of Sir Gorell Barnes, President, held that the principle as to apportionment of expenses between owner and underwriter in respect of drydocking for simultaneous work on the vessel, laid down in *The Vancouver* (1886) 11 App Cas 573, and explained in *The Ruabon* [1900] AC 6 (HL), applied, and, therefore, the defendants were liable for a proportion of the drydocking and incidental expenses, excluding demurrage.

By contrast, if there had been a separate cause of damage, which necessitated repairs, detention time for the collision repairs, may be subsumed.

The Carslogie[260]

The plaintiff's vessel was damaged in a collision, underwent temporary repairs at Port Glasgow and was certified as authorised to be confirmed in her present class without fresh record of survey, subject to certain permanent repairs at the owner's convenience. She then sailed for New York and during the Atlantic crossing she sustained heavy weather damage, which necessitated 30 days of repair time in New York. During 10 days of that period, the repairs to the collision damage were also carried out. The claim for loss of use during that 10 day period to complete her collision repairs failed because the vessel would, in any event, be incapable of gainful use taking into account the repairs for the heavy weather damage, which were carried out at the same time. Viscount Jowitt was willing to assume that the collision was a cause of her detention in New York, but he held that she would have been detained for that period in any event.

4.4 Pollution damage

Liability incurred by pollution after a collision will also be part of damages claimed or apportioned.

Although oil pollution is beyond the scope of this book,[261] it is worth noting briefly that the Civil Liability Convention (CLC) 1969, as amended by the 1992 Protocol, is now known as the International Convention on Civil Liability for Oil Pollution Damage 1992 and entered into force 30 May 1996 for those States which have ratified it. The UK has done so and the Convention is

---

260 [1951] 2 Lloyd's Rep 441 (HL), pp 445, 448.

261 The reader should refer to specialist books on the subject, see, for example, De La Rue and Anderson, C, *Shipping and the Environment*, 1998, LLP and Oya Oscayir, Z, *Liability for Oil Pollution and Collisions*, 1998, LLP. With regard to new proposals in relation to prevention of oil pollution and liabilities initiated by the European Commission, see Chapter 17, below.

to be found in Pt VI, Chapter III of the MSA 1995. The Fund Convention 1971 (International Convention on the Establishment of an International Fund for Compensation for Oil Pollution Damage) was also amended by a further Protocol in 1992 and is now known as the Fund Convention 1992, being in force in the UK. The previous MSA 1974, which enacted the Fund Convention, has been replaced by the MSA 1995 and the provisions of the Fund Convention are found in Pt VI, Chapter IV of the Act.

The CLC regulates liability of owners of tankers for oil pollution. It imposes strict liability, which may be limited (see Chapters 16 and 17), compulsory insurance against liability for pollution (s 163 of the MSA 1995, Chapter III) and gives a right of direct action by oil pollution victims against the insurers.

The Fund is applicable to compensation of victims for pollution damage caused to the territorial waters of a contracting state as well as to expenses incurred to prevent pollution. It is supplementary to the compensation recovered under the CLC system. It is also designed to relieve shipowners and their insurers of some of the financial burden imposed upon them by the CLC. The main aim of the Protocol was to raise the limits of liability.

The USA has not ratified these Conventions and liability for oil pollution incurred in USA waters is regulated by various Federal and State statutes relating to damage caused by pollution: the Clean Water Act; the Federal Water Pollution Control Act; the Comprehensive Environmental Response, Compensation and Liability Act; the Oil Pollution Act (OPA) 1990. Generally, the liability imposed by American statutes is strict or absolute with only limited defences. Limitation of liability under the OPA 90 is much higher than that provided by the Protocol 1992 and the right to limit may be defeated even in a case of gross negligence of a low level employee.[262]

The International Convention on Liability and Compensation for Damage in connection with Carriage of Hazardous and Noxious Substances by Sea 1996 has not yet been ratified, but it is contained in Sched 5A of the MSA 1995, which was inserted by Sched 3 of the Merchant Shipping and Maritime Security Act 1997. Chapter V of the latter Act, s 182B, gives power to Her Majesty to give effect to the Convention by Order in Council after its ratification by the UK. Section 14 of the 1997 Act, (which amended Pt VI of the MSA 1995) has given the Convention statutory effect being subject to a commencement Order in Council. The Convention applies to dangerous chemicals, often referred to as 'hazardous and noxious substances' (HNS) and, since there is no other Convention dealing with pollution damage from such substances, it is very important that the Convention is ratified as a matter of priority. It follows the same liability regime as the CLC.

The International Convention on Civil Liability for Bunker Oil Pollution Damage 2001 was finally agreed on 23 March 2001. It follows the same pattern

---

262 See Brice, G, *Maritime Law of Salvage*, 1999, Sweet & Maxwell, pp 452–56; also, *op cit*, De La Rue and Anderson, fn 261.

as the CLC, for example, it provides for strict liability limited, with compulsory insurance and a right of direct action against insurers. There is, however, no stand alone fund to top up the limited liability as is under the Fund Convention 1992, nor is there an industry top up fund, as there is under the HNS Convention. The Convention shall enter into force one year following the date on which 18 States have singed it, without reservation or have deposited instruments of ratification, etc, with the Secretary General.

4.5 Damages in foreign currency

In 1976, the House of Lords changed the old rule that the court did not have power to award damages other than in sterling.[263] If the claimant incurs expenses for the repairs to the ship after a collision in a number of currencies, the currency is which he normally conducts his business will be taken into account.[264] Thus, the claimant is entitled to damages measured not by the currencies immediately involved, but in the currency in which (he can prove) it was reasonably foreseeable he would have to incur the expenditure for repairs, or feel the loss. The yardstick is the currency in which he normally conducts his trading operations. This is not always easy because, in international shipping, there may be dealings in many currencies. This is illustrated in the following case, in which Bernard Eder QC and Belinda Bucknall QC enjoyed a contest.

Transoceanica Francesca and Nicos V[265]

The plaintiffs were given judgment by the admiralty registrar in Italian lire, so they appealed seeking to recover in US dollars.

On the date of the collision, *Francesca* was operating under a long term charterparty dated 1 March 1963, under which the charter hire was paid in US dollars. The plaintiffs owned four other ships, all of which were being operated by charterers under a charterparty under which the hire was also paid in dollars. The plaintiff company had obtained from the Ufficio Italiano dei Cambi two consents to maintain and operate accounts in US dollars. The maximum sum which the company was authorised to hold in US dollars was $1,105,000. If, at any time, the balance of the US dollar account at the banks exceeded the maximum, the bank would have automatically converted the excess into Italian lire and credited the company's Italian lire account with lire and transferred the dollars to the Government. The income which the plaintiffs received by way of charter hire of their ship was in dollars. Those dollars were paid into their dollar accounts. Dollars were used to make

---

263 *Miliangos v George Frank (Textiles) Ltd* [1976] AC 443 (HL).
264 *The Despina R* [1979] AC 685.
265 [1987] 2 Lloyd's Rep 155.

trading payments and included in those dollar payments were the cost of repairs. Mr Eder submitted that it is clear from this that the plaintiffs really felt their loss in dollars.

Miss Bucknall submitted that one must start from the fact that the plaintiffs are an Italian company carrying on business in Italy. She pointed out that it is usual to agree charter hire rates in US dollars and that the sole purpose of the dollar accounts was to avoid the need to make frequent applications to the exchange control authority to cover individual items of expenditure in currencies other than lire. The significant feature of the dollar accounts, she said, was the maximum holding placed upon the consents to maintain and operate those accounts. The plaintiffs did not bear the risk of fluctuations in dollar value if their income exceeded the limit placed on the dollar accounts. Miss Bucknall also submitted that the plaintiffs would have kept only lire if there had been no problem arising on conversion to other currencies.

Sheen J held that the Admiralty Registrar was right to award damages in lire.

5 LIMITATION OF LIABILITY

The wrongdoer will be able to limit his liability on the basis of international conventions. The current law in the UK is the 1976 Convention, which is incorporated in the MSA 1995 (see Chapter 16).

6 LIMITATION PERIODS FOR COMMENCEMENT OF CLAIMS[266]

The following time limits apply when there are two or more vessels are at fault. If a vessel collides with a non-ship, the time limit is six years as provided by the LA 1980.

Legal proceedings by cargo interests or for personal injury against the non-carrying vessel must commence within two years from the time when the cause of action arose, s 190 of the MSA 1995 (previously, s 8 of the MSA 1911).

Claims for personal injury and loss of life against the carrying vessel must commence within three years. *Navaro v Larrinanga*.[267] See, also, the FAA 1976 and the LA 1980.

---

266 See, also, the defence of time bar under para 3.1, above, and Chapter 5.
267 [1965] P 80.

When the Athens Convention 1974 applies, Art 16 provides that claims for damage arising out of the death or personal injury to a passenger or for the loss of or damage to luggage shall be time barred after a period of two years. The commencement date with regard to personal injury is the date of disembarkation; with regard to death, from the date the passenger should have disembarked, or, if he was injured and died later, from the date of death, provided this period does not exceed three years from the date of disembarkation; with regard to claims for loss of or damage to luggage, the commencement date is the date of disembarkation, or when disembarkation should have taken place, whichever is later.

Other claims for damage to or loss of cargo carried on board the ship at fault must be brought within the limitation period provided in their contract.

The two year time limit of s 190 applies also to claims of the vessels at fault against each other for their respective damage suffered by the collision.

Claims for contribution against the other ship at fault must be brought within one year from the date of establishment of liability to third parties, or settlement of claims for loss of life or personal injury, s 190(4) of the MSA 1995. Claims for contribution based on the CLCA 1978 can be brought within two years.

Claims under the CLC for Oil Pollution Damage 1992 can be brought not later than three years after the claim arose, or six years after the occurrence or first of the occurrences resulting in the discharge or escape of oil (s 162 of the MSA 1995).

7 INSURANCE ISSUES AND RISKS ARISING FROM COLLISIONS

Damage to or loss of a ship caused by collision is insured by the hull and machinery (H&M) insurance under perils of the sea. This is separate from liabilities incurred to third parties due to the fault of the colliding insured ship.

Such liabilities are, commonly, damage to or loss of the other colliding ship, cargo or any other property on board any of the colliding ships including freight earned on the voyage in question. Personal injury or loss of life on board any of the colliding ships is a third party liability.

The liability of a vessel, which collides with the insured vessel, is a matter of subrogation. When the insured vessel is lost or damaged by collision, her insurers, having settled the claim on the physical loss or damage sustained, will be subrogated to the rights of the assured as against the colliding vessel, to the extent that she is liable. There is also the liability of the assured vessel to the other colliding vessel, which is covered by a clause in the Institute Clauses for H&M, known as the Running Down Clause (RDC).[268] The RDC covers three-fourths of the proportionate liability of the assured, including legal costs if the liability is contested. It expressly does not cover cargo claims, or loss of life or personal injury claims, or claims in respect of liability incurred to harbours, piers, etc, or for removal of obstruction consequent on such collision.

Cargo underwriters cover loss of or damage to the cargo insured and carried on board a colliding ship under the Institute Cargo Clauses. When a cargo claim has been settled by the cargo insurer, he, too, is subrogated to the rights of the assured cargo-owner as against the non-carrying colliding ship, to the extent of her proportionate fault. A cargo claim against the carrying ship will be subject to exemption from liability under the contract of carriage for negligent navigation.

P&I mutual insurance (P&I associations) cover the liabilities of their assured shipowner incurred to third parties, which include cargo claims, pollution liabilities, damage to harbours, piers, etc, and personal injury or loss of life claims, which are all excluded from the RDC clause. In addition the P&I association insures the remaining one-fourth of the assured's liability under the RDC clause. Legal costs in defending such claims are covered as well.

Insurance is a contract of indemnity, which means that once the assured has paid for the damage or loss incurred to a third party, he will be indemnified by the insurer subject to the terms of the insurance contract.

The collision liability clause makes the underwriters' liability to the assured contingent not only to liability but also to payment by the assured. Also, under the rules of a P&I association, there is a rule known as 'pay to be paid', which means that the assured has to pay the third party first in order to be indemnified. The requirement of payment by the assured creates difficulties to third parties under the Third Parties (Rights against Insurers) Act 1930 in case the assured becomes insolvent before payment to the third party, discussed in Chapter 16 in the context of personal injuries.

Once the insurer has paid his assured, he will be entitled to pursue the rights of the assured, which he might have against third parties pursuant to the doctrine of subrogation.

The adjustment of claims for collision damage is complex. At law, there are two methods of assessment when two vessels are both to blame for the collision. The first is the 'single' liability method by which the respective liabilities are assessed, a set off is made, and then there is a single payment by the vessel with the balance to pay. The second method, which is included in

---

268 See, *op cit*, O'May, fn 178, Chapter 7.

the RDC, is the 'cross' liability by which the claim on underwriters is assessed as if each side actually made payment of their respective liability to the other side.[269]

In the Pt IV, assistance of vessels at sea and in ports is examined, covering salvage, towage, ports and pilots.

---

269 See, further, *op cit*, O'May, fn 178, p 241.

PART IV

ASSISTANCE AT SEA AND IN PORTS

OVERVIEW

Not infrequently, ships find themselves in need of assistance at sea due to various incidents that might affect their safe navigation alone. Assistance may be required whether or not a ship is in danger. An engine breakdown, for example, may be serious enough to put a ship in danger so as to call for a salvage tug and, if the other prerequisites of salvage exist, the special admiralty law rules of salvage will apply, which are different from those applicable to rescuers in land. If there is no danger but, nevertheless, a ship needs some assistance to reach its destination, a tug engaged for this purpose will be contracted under special terms of a towage contract. When reaching or leaving a port, a ship needs guidance from a harbour master or a pilot to navigate through other ships or obstructions, for berthing or departing. Harbour owners or administrators of public ports are under statutory obligations to keep the ports safe from any obstructions to navigation and provide pilotage and other services, which are regulated by specialised statutes and by-laws.

These three unique areas of admiralty law, salvage (Chapter 13), towage (Chapter 14) and harbours/pilots (Chapter 15) will be examined in this part.

There have been recent developments in salvage to overcome problems arising out of the wording of Art 14 of the Salvage Convention 1989, in relation to compensation of salvors with regard to prevention or minimisation of pollution. Such problems were unveiled by the House of Lords decision in *The Nagasaki Spirit*.

The opportunity is taken again in the following chapters to discuss risk management, particularly in relation to towage contracts, while in many areas it transpires, from cases discussed, that risk management should be viewed as a new way of proactive thinking in any business activities.

CHAPTER 13

SALVAGE

The maritime law of salvage is based on principles of equity.

(Lord Wright in *The Kafiristan.*)

This of course does not mean that a sort of 'justice under the palm tree' or 'justice under the mast' is to be substituted for legal principles.

(Salmon LJ in *The Tojo Maru.*)

1 INTRODUCTION

The law and practice of salvage used to be very simple in olden times, but mammoth developments have occurred in this area of law in recent years. For a century the principle of 'no cure no pay', enshrined in the Lloyd's Open Form (LOF) agreements, ensured that success in saving property was generously rewarded but failure could even leave salvors out of pocket. There had been a widespread acceptance of these forms, but that was so at times when ships were not so sophisticated as they are today and professional salvors had not emerged. The advent of very powerful modern tugs, standing by ready to assist in disasters, has meant time and money for the salvors, particularly with the rise of concern in recent years about environmental damage and pollution to marine life which has occurred after major casualties. Thus, it has been recognised that salvors should be encouraged, even if no property was saved by their efforts, when minimisation or prevention of damage to the environment was successful. These developments will be discussed at the end of this chapter. It is first important to state the basic principles of salvage.

Two comprehensive 'Bibles' exist on the law of salvage in our times, that of Brice[1] and Kennedy.[2] The scope of this book does not permit the same indulgence into the details of salvage as have been admirably analysed in the successive editions of these works. The intention in this chapter is to state the basic principles as supported by leading decisions. This way the reader has

---

1 Brice, G, *Maritime Law of Salvage*, 3rd edn, 1999, Sweet & Maxwell. It is an admirable achievement that the author delivered this new edition, which greatly contributes to our knowledge in the subject, just in the year in which he sadly died.

2 Steel, DW and Rose, FD, *Kennedy's Law of Salvage*, 5th edn, 1985, British Shipping Law Series, Stevens.

the option to glance first at the basics and then use the 'Bibles' as reference guides for further research.

2 THE CONCEPT OF SALVAGE UNDER MARITIME LAW

Brice[3] defines salvage as a right in law, which arises under English law when a person, acting as a volunteer (that is, without any pre-existing contractual or other legal duty so to act) preserves or contributes to preserving at sea any vessel, cargo, freight or other recognised subject of salvage from danger. This is known to be the 'civil salvage' as opposed to military, which is the rescuing of property from the enemy at a time of war for which a reward is made by the Court of Admiralty sitting as a Prize Court.

In Kennedy,[4] salvage is defines as a service which confers a benefit by saving or helping to save a recognised subject of salvage when in danger from which it cannot be extricated unaided, if and so far as the rendering of such service is voluntary in the sense of being attributable neither to a pre-existing obligation, nor solely for the interests of the salvor.

The origins of salvage are ancient and exist in ancient legal systems. Its fundamental principles were established in the early part of the 19th century. It was then recognised that there was a need to administer justice and to proceed according to equitable principles of fairness in the varying and unsettled cases that had arisen when property at sea was in danger. These principles were continually refined and developed by judges of the Admiralty Court. But, not until 1910, were these principles unified by the first salvage Convention to apply internationally.[5]

The right to reward, rather than remuneration, arises from the fact that salvage is a mixed question of a private right and public policy. Its purpose is not merely to compensate the salvor for the benefit he has conferred to the salved property. It is also to provide a positive incentive to seafarers to take risks for the purpose of assisting others in danger. Although the parties involved may regulate, if they wish, the rendering of salvage services by agreement, the right to reward for salvage at sea under common law is based both on equitable principles and public policy and is not in origin contractual.[6] The law seeks to do what is fair and just both to the owners of property and to the salvor. Each interest that has received a benefit from the salvage services provided must contribute.

---

3   *Op cit*, Brice, fn 1, p 1.
4   *Op cit*, Kennedy, fn 2, p 8.
5   *Op cit*, Brice, fn 1, pp 3–5.
6   Goff (Lord) and Jones, G, *On Restitution*, 5th edn, 1998, Sweet & Maxwell, Chapter 18, pp 483–85.

In *The Five Steel Barges*,[7] the underlying concept was put succinctly:

> The jurisdiction which the court exercises in salvage cases is of a peculiarly equitable character. The right to salvage may arise out of an actual contract; but it does not necessarily do so. It is a legal liability arising out of the fact that property has been saved, that the owner of the property who has had the benefit of it shall make remuneration to those who have conferred the benefit upon him, notwithstanding that he has not entered into any contract on the subject.

Also, Sir John Nicholl in *The Industry*[8] examined the policy underlying the amount of the salvage reward:

> ... there are various facts for consideration – the state of the weather, the degree of damage and danger as to ship and cargo, the risk and peril of the salvors, the time employed, the value of the property; and when all these things are considered, there is still another principle – to encourage enterprise, reward exertion, and to be liberal in all that is due to the general interests of commerce, and the general benefit of owners and underwriters, even though the reward may fall upon an individual owner with some severity.

Thus, the foundation of salvage is necessity when the subject of salvage has been in danger and services are rendered, even without request, in circumstances that a reasonably prudent owner would have accepted them.

3 SALVAGE UNDER CONTRACT

Salvage, in olden times, used to be rendered by persons or ships using personal skill and efforts chancing their lives in undertaking to rescue property from danger without a specific contract. The salvor did not assume any obligation to continue the services and he could withdraw at any time, yet claim a reward if his services had contributed to the successful saving of the ship. Before 1875, professional salvage contractors did not exist and express contracts were unknown.

When, near the end part of the 19th century, there was an increase in steamships, salvage was rendered under agreements on a 'no cure no pay' basis, which developed into LOF. In the latter half of the 20th century, most salvage services, other than that of 'standing by' a vessel in distress, are performed by professional salvors under a salvage agreement in LOF.[9]

With the availability of powered tugs, modern means of communication and more readily available facilities for salvage, salvage is rendered more commonly by professional salvors under contract, with each party having

---

7 (1890) 15 PD 142, p 146.
8 (1835) 3 Hagg 203, p 204.
9 *The Tojo Maru* [1971] 1 Lloyd's Rep 341 (HL), p 362, *per* Lord Diplock.

rights and duties governing the relationship. Under it, the salvage contractor undertakes a continuing obligation, until the ship is brought to a safe port, to use his best endeavours to salve her and to provide the equipment and labour which, in the circumstances, it would be reasonable for him to use for this purpose. These professional salvors keep tugs and equipment, waiting for an opportunity to provide assistance and earn large salvage reward.

Contracts are usually entered into on the LOF (1980, 1990, 1995 and now the 2000 LOF). Under these contracts, the salvors receive no salvage award in cases where no property is salved. However, the concept of special compensation to recover expenses for efforts made to prevent or minimise damage to the environment with an increment of those expenses in the event of succeeding to prevent or minimise such damage, whether or not property is saved, has developed in recent years.[10] This was a major reason for the new International Salvage Convention 1989.[11]

4 THE SALVAGE CONVENTIONS[12]

As was earlier mentioned, the first attempt to unify the principles on the law of salvage was the Brussels Convention 1910, at the initiative of the International Maritime Organisation (IMO). It was enacted only in parts into English law by the Maritime Conventions Act (MCA) 1911. The Convention was amended by the Brussels Convention on Salvage of Aircraft 1938 to extend the law of salvage to salvage by or to seaborn aircraft.

The provisions of the 1910 Convention, however, proved to be inadequate to cover the needs of modern times, particularly with regard to problems arising from big disasters which resulted in damage to marine environment.[13] There was a need, therefore, to encourage salvors with some incentive to prevent or minimise such losses. The first initiative to this effect was an inclusion in the LOF 1980 of a novel concept providing for an 'enhanced award', when the salvor, in addition to saving property, also prevented pollution from oil tankers, and for a 'safety net' in a form of compensation for the salvor's expenses in the event that he failed to earn an award because the tanker sunk, but he prevented pollution to the coastline. In effect, the safety net was a deviation from the general principle of 'no cure no pay' but it provided an incentive to salvors to undertake salvage involving oil tankers. The enhanced award was part of the 'property salvage' (payable by the

---

10 See, further, under paras 7–13, 16.

11 For a historical background to LOFs 1980 and 1990 and the reasons behind the 1989 Convention, see Darling, G (QC) and Smith, C, *LOF 90 and the New Salvage Convention*, 1991, LLP.

12 See commentary on the 1989 Convention by Shaw, R, [1996] LMCLQ 202.

13 Such as *The Torrey Canyon*, *The Amoco Cadiz* and *The Exxon Valdez*.

underwriters of the ship and cargo) but the safety net became known as the 'liability salvage' (payable by the Protection and Indemnity (P&I) insurers of the shipowners).

A draft Convention was prepared by the Comité Maritime International (CMI) in 1981, which was discussed by the legal committee of the IMO and, finally, at a diplomatic conference, in London on 28 April 1989, the new Salvage Convention 1989 was concluded. It replaced the Brussels Convention for the Unification of Certain Rules of Law Relating to Assistance and Salvage at Sea, 1910. The concepts of enhanced award and safety net enshrined in the 1980 LOF, were adopted by the new Convention. The former is taken into account when the assessment of the award is made by the arbitrators under Art 13(1)(b) and the latter is known as the 'special compensation' provision under Art 14. They apply, not only to environmental damage from oil pollution, but to substantial physical damage to human health, or to marine life, or resources in coastal or inland waters or areas adjacent thereto by pollution generally, contamination, fire, explosion or similar major incidents (Art 1(d)).

The preamble to the Convention illustrates the need for such a move:

The States Parties to the present Convention,

Recognising the desirability of determining by agreement uniform international rules regarding salvage operations,

Noting that substantial developments, in particular the increased concern for the protection of the environment, have demonstrated the need to review the international rules presently contained in the Convention for the Unification of Certain Rules of Law Relating to Assistance and Salvage at Sea, done at Brussels, 23 September 1910,

Conscious of the major contribution which efficient and timely salvage operations can make to the safety of vessels and other property in danger and to the protection of the environment,

Convinced of the need to ensure that adequate incentives are available to persons who undertake salvage operations in respect of vessels and other property in danger.

The 1989 Convention (referred to as 'the Convention' in this chapter) came into force internationally on 14 July 1996, but, in the meantime the UK enacted it into English law by the Merchant Shipping (Salvage and Pollution) Act (MS(SP)A) 1994[14] and it came into force in the UK on 1 January 1995. With the consolidation of the Merchant Shipping Acts (MSAs) by the MSA 1995, the 1994 Act was repealed, and the Convention is found in Sched 11 of the MSA 1995.

---

14 For a detailed exposition of English statutes, historically, which have affected the law of salvage see: *op cit*, Brice, fn 1, pp 1–32.

Article 6(1), Sched 11, Pt I of the MSA 1995, provides that the Convention shall apply to any salvage operations save to the extent that a contract otherwise provides expressly, or by implication. Therefore, parties are free to contract out of the Act, or parts of it, by an express term in their contract.

The substantive changes to salvage law brought by the Convention were first incorporated in the LOF 1990. However, before the Convention had the force of law, these changes – as incorporated in the LOF 1990 – had only a contractual effect. Once the Convention became part of English law by statute,[15] its provisions have had the force of law since 1 January 1995, whether or not the parties enter into a contract, unless the parties to the LOF choose to contract out of some provisions of the Convention.

It should also be noted in this context that the International Convention on Oil Pollution, Preparedness, Response and Co-operation 1990 (OPPRC Convention) was concluded at a diplomatic conference in London at the IMO in November 1990. The OPPRC Convention is in force internationally and provides for salvage policy, contingency plans and reporting of casualties. Briefly, it requires harbour authorities and ships to have oil pollution emergency plans and provides for oil pollution reporting procedures, including national contingency plans, as well as exhorting international co-operation to take action on receiving information about oil pollution incidents. Pursuant to powers under s 128(1)(d) of the MSA 1995 to give effect to the OPPRC Convention, the Merchant Shipping (OPPRC) Order 1997 enables the OPPRC Convention to be given effect by the making of regulations, the Merchant Shipping (OPPRC) Regulations 1998 (SI 1998/1056).

5 PRECONDITIONS OF SALVAGE

Before examining the essential elements of salvage, the geographical limits in which salvage can take place and the subject matter of salvage are looked at, as some important changes have been brought by the Convention.

5.1 The relevant waters for salvage prior to the salvage Convention 1989

For the services rendered to be considered as salvage services there was a precondition that the salvage should have occurred in tidal waters.[16] That

---

15 First by the MS(SP)A 1994, s 71(1), and now by the MSA 1995, s 224(1), the provisions of the Convention (Pt I, Sched 11) shall have the force of law in the UK.

16 Although the Salvage Convention 1910 by Art 1 provided that all salvage services in whatever waters the services had been rendered were subject to that Convention, this provision had not been enacted into English law.

requirement was an essential ingredient to the cause of action of salvage and had its basis on s 546(1) of the MSA 1894 (now repealed), which provided:

> ... a salvor had a right to remuneration for salvage services rendered to any vessel wrecked, stranded or in distress at any place on or near the coast of the UK or any tidal water within the limits of the UK.

Section 742 of the same Act defined tidal waters as meaning any part of the sea and any part of the river within the ebb and flow of the tide at ordinary spring tides not being a harbour.

The problem created by this statutory definition became apparent in the amusing factual situation of *The Goring*, a notorious case, which reached the House of Lords, but now belongs to the past.

The Goring[17]

The Goring, a passenger vessel owned by the respondents, broke free of her moorings before midnight, 14 September 1984, in the river Thames, up-river of Reading bridge. Being unmanned, she began to drift towards other vessels, which were moored close by, and she was at risk of colliding with these vessels, or of being otherwise carried away. The appellants, employees or members of the Bohemian Club, which was situated on an island in the middle of the river, were enjoying themselves. With the help of the club's ferry boat, they managed to get someone on board *The Goring*, thereby making it possible to get a line from her to the island and to haul her to a vacant mooring where she was made fast. They claimed salvage reward, which was at first instance granted to them by Sheen J. All the elements of salvage being present, the question for decision in the House of Lords was whether the appellants were entitled to salvage, bearing in mind that the Thames above Reading bridge is not tidal.

Lord Brandon of Oakbrook said:

> Section 458 (of the 1854 Act) is important because in it the legislature for the first time prescribed the places in which it was necessary for services to a ship, her cargo or her apparel to have been rendered in order to qualify as salvage services within the UK. It was necessary that they should have been rendered on the shore of any sea or tidal water in the UK. If the legislature had intended that services rendered in non-tidal inland waters of the UK should also qualify as salvage services, it would surely have expressly so provided. It did not do so, however, and the inference which I draw is that the legislature did not have that intention.[18]

> The definitions of the expressions 'harbour' and 'tidal water' in s 742 create a problem when applied to ascertain the meaning of the expression 'tidal water' in s 546. The result of applying the very wide definition of 'harbour' to the

---

17 [1988] 2 WLR 460; [1988] AC 381 (HL).

18 *Ibid*, p 465.

definition of 'tidal water', and then applying the definition of 'tidal water' so produced to interpret s 546, is to exclude from the meaning of 'tidal water' in that section numerous localities which might be expected to be included in it. It is fortunately not necessary to solve this problem in this appeal. The significance of s 546 is the same as that of s 458 of the MSA 1854. It prescribes the places in which services must be rendered in order to qualify as salvage services in the UK, and does so in such a way as to exclude non-tidal inland waters.[19]

It was held that there was no cause of action for salvage in respect of services rendered to a ship in danger in navigable non-tidal inland waters. The provisions of the statute had the effect of limiting the scope of salvage to tidal waters and extension of that scope should be left to the legislature. Therefore, the appellants were not entitled to salvage.

As a result of this decision, there was later an attempt to amend s 546(2), by the MSA 1988 (Sched 5, para 3) which defined tidal waters[20] as follows:

(a) any water within the ebb and flow of the tide at ordinary spring tides; or

(b) the waters of any dock which is directly, or (by means of one or more other docks) indirectly, connected with any such waters.

It was meant to extend salvage to events which occurred in harbours, by redefining tidal waters as including the waters of any dock directly or indirectly connected with tidal waters. In the following case, the question was whether there could be a right to salvage when services were rendered in a harbour.

The Powstaniec Wielkopolski[21]

The vessel laden with cargo at the time was moored in Gravesend Reach, within the port limits of the Port of London (which was tidal) awaiting a berth. During the evening, her moorings began to part and later she drifted to the north side of the river and was obviously in danger of colliding with other vessels moored along her side. Although she made no call for assistance, three tugs set off to assist her. Subsequently, the tugowners together with officers and crew brought an action *in rem* against her for salvage remuneration. The defendants contended that on the facts, as the services were rendered within a harbour, they did not give rise to salvage. Salvage was governed by s 546, and since it requires salvage to occur in tidal waters, the latter should be construed in accordance with s 742.

Section 742 of the Act of 1894 provided:

---

19   [1988] 2 WLR 460, p 466.

20   Note now that s 255(1) of the 1995 Act defines tidal waters as meaning 'any part of the sea and any part of a river within the ebb and flow of the tide at ordinary spring tides, and not being a harbour'.

21   [1988] 3 WLR 723.

> In this Act, unless the context otherwise requires, the following expressions have the meanings hereby assigned to them; (that is to say) ... 'harbour' includes harbours properly so called, whether natural or artificial, estuaries, navigable rivers, piers, jetties, and other works in or at which ships can obtain shelter, or ship and unship goods or passengers; 'tidal water' means any part of the sea and any part of a river within the ebb and flow of the tide at ordinary spring tides, and not being a harbour ...

The problem obviously arose from the last sentence of this section.

Sheen J held that, in the reality of things and bearing in mind previous cases in the last 94 years which had recognised salvage in harbours, it would be absurd to require that the word 'harbour' in the definition of 'tidal water' under s 742 should be given the meaning assigned to it by this section. Instead, the word 'harbour', where it appears in the definition of tidal waters must be given its ordinary and natural meaning and a tidal harbour was not excluded from being a place in which salvage could occur. The place where the services were rendered was tidal. It was unnecessary for him to decide the meaning of tidal waters in s 546 because of the amendment by the 1988 Act mentioned earlier. Therefore, the plaintiffs were not precluded from claiming a salvage award based on a geographical limitation.

5.2 The law under the Salvage Convention 1989

Now Art 1(a) of the Salvage Convention 1989 defines that, for the purpose of the Convention, salvage operation means any act or activity undertaken to assist a vessel or any other property in danger in navigable waters, or in any other waters whatsoever.

But Art 30 of the Convention permits any State to reserve the right not to apply the provisions of the Convention *inter alia* when the salvage operation takes place in inland waters and all vessels involved are of inland navigation. The UK has made such a reservation. Schedule 11, para 2(1), Pt II of the MSA 1995 stipulates that the provisions of the Convention do not apply to:

(a) salvage operations which take place in 'inland waters' of the UK and in which all the vessels involved are of inland navigation, and

(b) to a salvage operation which takes place in 'inland waters' of the UK and in which no vessel is involved.

It is thereafter stated that 'inland waters' do not include any waters within the ebb and flow of the tide at ordinary spring tides or the waters of any dock which is directly, or indirectly, connected with such waters (that is, tidal waters).

This leads to an examination of the next precondition of salvage.

5.3 What is a recognised subject of salvage

5.3.1 The law prior to the Convention

A vessel or craft had to qualify as a ship before it was recognised as a subject of salvage. Section 742 of the MSA 1894 defined 'vessel' as any ship or boat, or any other description of vessel used in navigation; and 'ship' as including every description of vessel used in navigation not propelled by oars.[22]

The Gas Float Whitton (No 2)[23]

The Gas Float Whitton was shaped like a boat and used for purposes connected with navigation in the same sense as a lighthouse, or as a buoy. It was moored as a beacon or to warn vessels off a shoal. It could not be used for navigation and it was next to impossible to tow it. In December 1894, in a moderate gale, it got adrift and the plaintiffs helped to secure it. They claimed salvage remuneration. Both learned judges in both the county court and in the Admiralty Division held that the gas float was a ship or vessel and a wreck within the MSA 1894. They stated that the jurisdiction of the admiralty was not limited so closely 'as to exclude a structure used in connection with navigation, and exposed in the ordinary course of its use to the perils of the sea'. The Court of Appeal reversed this decision. On appeal to the House of Lords, the judgment of Lord Esher MR was affirmed: that there are no proper subjects of a maritime claim for salvage other than vessels or ships used for the purpose of being navigated, and goods which at one time formed the cargoes of such vessels, whether found on board, or drifting on the ocean, or cast ashore. The Lords rejected the view of the admiralty court.

5.3.2 The law after the Convention

Neither the 1989 Convention, nor the MSA 1995 has greatly improved the definition of a ship. Article 313(1) of the MSA 1995 defines 'ship' as including every description of vessel used in navigation. The Convention, by Art 1(b) defines vessel as meaning 'any ship or craft, or any structure capable of navigation'. If in ordinary parlance, as Brice says, one would not refer to a particular structure as a 'vessel' or a 'boat', then it will not be a 'ship'. He also says that the use of a comma after 'craft' is of significance in that the words 'capable of navigation' may only refer to structures. Therefore, sunken or

---

22 For more details, see Chapter 1; by the Merchant Shipping (Registration etc) Act 1993, an amendment to s 742 dropped the phrase 'not propelled by oars' and under the new definition a ship includes every description of vessel used in navigation, which has been adopted by the MSA 1995, s 313.

23 [1897] AC 337.

derelict vessels, which are not capable of navigation, could be subjects of salvage.[24]

Article 1(a) defines salvage operations as including services rendered to vessels, or to any other property in danger. Property means any property not permanently and intentionally attached to the shoreline and includes freight at risk (Art 1(c)). The Convention does not apply to fixed or floating platforms or mobile offshore drilling units when they are on location engaged in the exploration, exploitation or production of seabed mineral resources (Art 3). This suggests that oil rigs and offshore installations which are not fixed or floating on location, or are not engaged in activities described above, would probably be recognised subjects of salvage. Gas floats and landing stages not attached to the shoreline[25] may well be included under Art 1(c) of the Convention. 'Shore line' is defined in the *Oxford English Dictionary* as the line where shore and water meet. So, if a vessel or a buoy were attached to the seabed or moored at sea, it would not be included in the definition of 'property'.[26]

All merchandise being carried on the vessel could be subject to salvage except personal effects of the crew, master and passengers.[27]

By Art 4, of Sched 11 of the MSA 1995, the Convention does not apply to warships or non-commercial vessels owned or operated by the State and entitled, at the time of salvage operation, to sovereign immunity under international law, unless that State decides otherwise. Section 230 of the MSA 1995 deals with salvage claims against and by the Crown.

5.3.3 Hovercrafts/aircraft

The Hovercraft Act 1968, ss 1(1)(h)(ii)[28] and 2(2) provide that rules of law relating to ships apply to hovercrafts as if references to ship included reference to hovercraft. Also, by Art 8 of the Hovercraft Order 1972, salvage services to hovercraft are treated as if they were salvage services to a ship. Similar provisions are made in s 87 of the Civil Aviation Act 1982, extending salvage to aircraft.[29]

---

24 *Op cit*, Brice, fn 1, p 211; by the MSA 1995, s 311, the Secretary of State has power to decide that a thing designed or adapted for use at sea is or is not to be treated as ship for the purposes of the provisions of the Act.

25 *The Gas Float Whitton* was attached to the shore bed.

26 *Op cit*, Brice, fn 1, p 212.

27 See *op cit*, Brice, fn 1, Chapter 3, further details of salved property.

28 The MSA 1995 applies to enactments and instruments with respect to which provision may be made by Order in Council pursuant to the Hovercraft Act 1968, s 1(1)(h).

29 Thus, *Watson v Victor* (1934) 22 LlL Rep 77, where a claim for salvage of cinematography equipment from a wrecked seaplane failed, is now not good law after the Civil Aviation Act 1982.

5.3.4 Bunkers

Save when the ship is on time charter, when the bunkers will be the property of the charterers, the bunkers are usually a valuable element of the salved value. The House of Lords, in *The Span Terza*[30] has made it clear that the position of the shipowner in relation to the bunkers, when the ship is time chartered, is that of a bailee and the charterers remained the owners of the bunkers until re-delivery.

5.3.5 Cargo

Property in Art 1 of the Convention naturally includes goods or merchandise being carried on the vessel excluding personal effects of the crew or master and passengers' luggage. Salvors removing cargo during the course of salvage are in a position of bailees of the cargo-owners.[31]

5.3.6 Freight

Article 1(c) of the Convention refers to freight at risk. Freight in this context is the remuneration due and payable for the carriage of cargo and not hire for the use of the ship.[32] Obviously, it does not cover freight paid in advance. The freight may be at the risk of the shipowner or charterer.[33]

5.3.7 Life salvage

Prior to the 1989 Convention, there was no pure life salvage as such, but it depended on whether property was salved. If there was no property salved, remuneration for mere life salvage was not recoverable in the Admiralty Court. The MSA 1854 (ss 458–60) provided for liability to pay a reasonable amount of salvage to life salvors by the owners of cargo as well as the owners of the ship, but such liability was limited to the value of the property saved from destruction. There should have been something more than life saved by salvors for the property to contribute to life salvors' award.

Cargo ex Sarpedon[34]

The S was abandoned at sea in a sinking condition. A Spanish vessel, *The C*, saved part of the cargo belonging to the vessel, as well as 88 people on board the ship. The court had already awarded salvage remuneration, which the

---

30 [1984] 1 Lloyd's Rep 119.
31 *The Winson* [1982] 1 Lloyd's Rep 117.
32 *Op cit*, Brice, fn 1, pp 220–25.
33 *The Pantanassa* [1970] 1 Lloyd's Rep 153.
34 (1877) 3 PD 28.

owners of the salved cargo paid. The cargo-owners subsequently called upon the owners of the lost vessel asking them to contribute payment to the salvage award because of the lives that were saved. They contended that the master of the lost vessel was bound to contract, and did contract, by implication, with the master of *The C* for the saving of these lives. It was held that since no property belonging to the owners of *The S* had been salved, they could not be held personally liable to pay any portion of the sum awarded. The learned judge held:

> I consider it to be now a fixed principle of salvage law that, in the absence of any special contract, some property in the ship or cargo must be saved in order to found the liability of the owners of the ship or cargo to the payment of salvage remuneration.[35]

In the following case, however, the court deviated from a strict construction of the statutory provisions. It held that it was immaterial whether or not the property saved from destruction had been saved by the salvors who saved the lives on board.

Cargo ex Schiller[36]

Whilst the cargo and the ship were in danger, the plaintiff salvors saved the lives of 15 persons, some of whom were passengers and others crew members. But, the ship and cargo sunk in deep water and was abandoned after all the attempt to save both. Sometime afterwards, the defendants who were owners of part of the sunken cargo, engaged divers and workmen and, at great expense, raised part of the sunken cargo. The plaintiffs, as life salvors, instituted a suit against the defendants, although the plaintiffs were not the ones who salved the cargo eventually. Affirming the decision of the trial judge, the Court of Appeal held that the MSA 1854 was passed to remedy the injustice of the existing laws and practice insofar as they failed to provide reward for the saving of life, when unaccompanied by a saving of property. Baggallay LJ held:

> ... under the provisions of that Act the owners of all property saved, whether ship, cargo, or apparel, and however saved, are rendered liable, to the extent of the value of the property saved, for a reasonable amount of salvage in respect of life saved, even though the life salvors have in no respect assisted in the salvage of either ship or cargo ... it would follow that in the present case the claim of the plaintiffs for salvage is well founded, and that the decision of the judge of the Admiralty Court should be affirmed.[37]

Nevertheless, by reason of lack of clear statutory provisions to encourage the saving of life at sea, there still existed an uncertainty with regard to rewarding

---

35 (1877) 3 PD 28, p 34.

36 (1877) 2 PD 145.

37 *Ibid*, p 158.

life salvors. Thus, a Mercantile Fund was established by s 544 of the MSA 1894 and voluntary organisations, such as the Royal National Lifeboat Institution (RNLI) and the HM Coastguard, were formed to help those in danger at sea.

The MS(SP)A 1994 repealed the relevant sections of the MSA 1854, and by Sched 2, s 6(3)(b), saving life was included in salvage services. Now, life salvage is dealt with by Art 16 of the Convention (Sched 11, Pt I of the MSA 1995). The article provides that no remuneration is due from persons whose life is saved but leaves national laws unaffected on this subject (Art 16(1)). On the occasion of an accident giving rise to salvage (see in the next paragraph) a salvor of human life is entitled to a fair share of the payment awarded to the salvor of property (Art 16(2)). Although an independent right to remuneration for saving life is established, it is linked to the saving of property. In Pt I of Sched 11, para 5(2) the Secretary of State, if he thinks fit and when the sum under Art 16(2) is less than reasonable, may pay the salvor saving life what he thinks fit in respect of the services rendered. The jurisdiction of the Admiralty Court is entertaining claims for life salvage under s 20(2)(j) of the Supreme Court Act (SCA) 1981.

6 ELEMENTS OF SALVAGE

From the definitions given by Brice and Kennedy at the beginning of this chapter, there seem to be four elements or ingredients that there must exist for the right to salvage reward to arise, namely: (i) there should be a recognised subject matter; (ii) the object of salvage should be in danger at sea; (iii) the salvors must be volunteers, that is, without a pre-existing relationship or obligation to the object to be salved; (iv) there must be success by either preserving or contributing to preserving the property in danger.

Since what is a recognised subject of salvage has been dealt with, the three central elements of salvage are examined below.

6.1 Danger

6.1.1 General principles

There must be some real danger, which is likely to expose the property to destruction or damage. An apprehension of danger will suffice as long as it is not a fanciful danger and it does not need to be immediate or absolute. The following examples illustrate these points.

The Phantom[38]

> I am of the opinion that it is not necessary that there should be absolute danger in order to constitute salvage service; it is sufficient if there is a state of difficulty, and reasonable apprehension.

The Charlotte[39]

The vessel was proceeding on a voyage from Bombay to Liverpool. The master of the vessel missed the harbour he was aiming for and the vessel was caught up in a violent gale, with fog and rain, which drove the ship towards the rocks. After a day of effort to board her, the salvors took the ship in tow with great exertion and labour having to force their way through a heavy sea before they could get the vessel towed in. Then, they claimed salvage remuneration. The owners' defence was that no salvage services had been rendered because during the whole time of the towing of the ship, the weather was fine and that there was an agreement for towage at the cost of 20 shillings each. It was held that, on the facts, it was undisputed that the vessel's masts and all her sails had been cut away, and that in her dismasted state she was towed into Long Island Channel, and that, *prima facie*, salvage services had been rendered. Dr Lushington said:

> According to the principles which are recognised in this court in questions of this description, all services rendered at sea to a vessel in danger or distress are salvage services. It is not necessary, I conceive, that the distress should be actual or immediate, or that the danger should be imminent and absolute; it will be sufficient if, at the time the assistance is rendered, the ship has encountered any damage or misfortune which might possibly expose her to destruction if the services were not rendered.[40]

It does not matter if the danger is slight, but it is important that danger can be said to exist. The extent of the danger is only relevant in determining the extent of the award.

The Helenus[41]

The Helenus, fully laden, was to sail for Rotterdam, but the voyage was cancelled as a gale began with mighty and forceful winds that afternoon. It gradually became stronger causing the stern ropes of *The Helenus* to part. Her master made a call for assistance. The vessel, surging under the influence of the wind and tide, came into collision with *The Motagua* which was lying close to *The Helenus*. As a result *The Motagua* rendered her own moorings. Both vessels drifted north and rubbed up against *The Imichil* pushing that vessel's

---

38 [1866] LR 1 A&E 58, p 60, *per* Dr Lushington.
39 (1848) 3 W Rob 68.
40 *Ibid*, p 71.
41 [1982] 2 Lloyd's Rep 261.

bows to port pressing it up against a large dockyard crane. The crane was lifted off its feet on one side, so that it was leaning over dangerously. This was the dangerous position the vessels were in when the tugs arrived. The tugs made fast to *The Helenus* and pulled her away. They were unable to reach *The Motagua* but, once *The Helenus* was removed, *The Motagua* was in a less dangerous situation and was assisted to her berth. A salvage award was claimed. Sheen J examined the dangers in the circumstances:

> But having regard to the fact that it was night, there was a very high wind; they were in a very confined space; the tide was ebb; there were dangers of damage to the side of the vessel from ranging against *The Motagua* and the danger to both vessels from that source. There was the possibility, if they tried to move, of fouling other vessels or doing more damage or even possibly damaging their propellers if they got too close to the wharves.[42]

It was held that salvage services had been rendered to *The Helenus*, but the services rendered to *The Motagua* was to be treated as a comparatively minor service.

Would a temporary difficulty amount to danger on the above criteria?

The North Goodwin (No 16)[43]

On 15 September 1976, the defendants' light vessel *North Goodwin* was in tow of the Trinity House vessel *Mermaid* and had been towed to a position about a mile east of the entrance to the River Tyne where it was anticipated that the light vessel would be handed over to the tugs *Northsider* and *Ironsider* so that the light vessel might be taken to Smith's Dock berth at North Shields. The tugs were employed under the UK Standard Conditions for towage. On the morning of 15 September, gale force winds caused such a heavy swell that *Northsider* moved up-river. When the tugs arrived at the bar, the Tyne pilots considered the weather conditions too bad to allow the pilot cutter to leave the harbour entrance, but *Northsider* continued out through the piers and turned to the north, towards *Mermaid*. *Mermaid* decided to take her tow into the river and hand over to *Northsider* when the vessels had protection from the piers and in order to do this the wheel of *Mermaid* was put to port. The master realised that he was too close to the coast and decided to turn to starboard.

While *Mermaid* was engaged in turning to starboard, the towing hawser parted and the light vessel was free to drift down wind. *Northsider* seeing what had happened immediately went to the assistance of the light vessel and managed to pass a towage connection to those aboard and then towed her to an anchorage about a mile and a half from the coasts.

Sheen, J held that although the light vessel was drifting downwind, she was equipped with three anchors and if *Northsider* had not reacted so

---

42 [1982] 2 Lloyd's R 261, p 265.
43 [1980] 1 Lloyd's Rep 71.

promptly to the parting of the tow rope, *Mermaid* would have been alerted to the danger presented by the lee shore and given orders for an anchor or anchors to be let go which would have held the light vessel until *Mermaid* could have manoeuvred to put a line aboard; and if *Northsider* had come up with the light vessel and offered her services on salvage terms, there was no doubt that that offer would have been declined and the light vessel was not in danger.[44]

6.1.2 Future or contingent danger

In a recent decision, it was held that there would be a reasonable future apprehension of danger even when the swing of the ship by the wind had stopped temporarily.[45]

The Troilus' danger, as is known, illustrates what kind of future danger the court will be prepared to take into account in assessing the existence of danger, but each case will be judged on its own facts. There is no rigid rule about it

The Troilus[46]

The vessel was carrying cargo from Australia to Liverpool. She fractured her tail shaft and dropped her propeller in the Indian Ocean, but, otherwise, she was unimpaired. She was towed to Aden where she anchored. This admittedly constituted salvage services. There being no facilities for repairs, nor for storage of cargo at Aden, the damaged ship was towed by another vessel to the UK, since repair in the Mediterranean would have been difficult and would have involved considerable delay. The cargo-owners contended that this constituted ocean towage, not salvage services, since the ship was in perfect safety when she reached Aden.

The court held that, although the ship and cargo were in physical safety at Aden, the services in question were salvage services. The master of a damaged ship must do his best to preserve the ship and cargo and bring them to their destination as cheaply and as efficiently as possible, bearing in mind expense and the effect of delay on both and considering the possibility of transshipment or of repair at some convenient port. Salvage lasts so long as the master acts reasonably for the combined benefit of ship and cargo. A salvage award held to be reasonable in the case of a ship would be held reasonable in the case of the cargo also, unless it were established that the master neglected its interests.

---

44 [1980] 1 Lloyd's Rep 71, p 74.
45 *The Hamtun and St John* [1999] 1 Lloyd's Rep 883.
46 [1951] AC 820.

The decision of the Court of Appeal (*sub nom The Troilus*) [1950] P 92 was affirmed.

Lord Porter added:

> The solution of the question whether a ship and cargo have reached a place of safety must, I think, depend upon the facts of each case, one of which is the possibility of safely discharging and storing the cargo and sending it on to its destination and the danger of its deterioration. It is not a sufficient answer to say that she can lie in a particular position of physical safety. It must be remembered that in every voyage of a merchant ship carrying cargo the interests of both ship and cargo have to be borne in mind.[47]

> In the present case the whole of the facts and law were carefully considered by the learned President, and, unless the appellants could establish that salvage services always end where the ship can be in physical safety and where the cargo also can remain at least for some time without danger or damage, he appears to me to have reached the right conclusion upon ample and adequate grounds. He carefully considered the opportunities for repair at each port on the voyage, the risks and delay involved and the possibilities of safe towage. Amongst others, he had in mind those of drydocking *The Troilus* without discharging her cargo and the imprudence of tipping a Liberty ship sufficiently to fit a propeller. On the last two points the Court of Appeal took the advice of their assessors, who thought that either expedient would be unsafe, and your Lordships' assessors took the same view.[48]

Therefore, the services still constituted salvage services.

6.1.3 Effect of danger on a towage contract[49]

The existence of danger is a question of fact. The master's decision that the ship is in danger must be reasonable. If his decision was unreasonable, there would be no danger for salvage no matter how honestly his decision was made. It is not unusual for danger to arise during performance of a towage contract.

Towage may be converted to salvage if the circumstances that occurred had not reasonably been contemplated by the parties when they entered into the towage contract.

The Aldora[50]

It was standard practice for ships of *The Aldora*'s size to be met at the harbour by a pilot and tugs to help her navigate into her berth. Due to a misunderstanding about the time of her arrival, the tugs and pilot were not

---

47 [1951] AC 820, p 830.

48 *Ibid*, p 836.

49 See definition and details of towage contracts in Chapter 14, below.

50 [1975] 1 Lloyd's Rep 617.

yet at the buoy when *The Aldora* arrived. The master of the vessel decided to proceed out to sea again when, due to the master's error, the ship ran aground on a sandbank outside the dredged channel leading to the harbour. Four tugs were engaged to help to refloat her. With the help of these tugs and the ship's own engines, and under the direction of the pilot, the vessel was refloated. Thereafter, she was taken up the channel and into the harbour and to her berth with the help of the pilot and the tugs. The tugowners and crew and the pilot claimed salvage remuneration from the defendants – owners of *The Aldora*. The latter contended that the refloating of the vessel constituted salvage, but the subsequent service of assisting the ship back to the harbour was towage. The pilots and tugowners contended that they were entitled to a salvage award and that the salvage services were completed when the vessel was safely berthed in the harbour. Brandon J laid down the general principle governing claims for salvage by a pilot engaged to pilot a ship, or a tug engaged to render towage services:

> ... they are only entitled to claim salvage if, first, the ship is in danger by reason of circumstances which could not reasonably have been contemplated by the parties when the engagement to pilot or tow was made, and, secondly, risks are run, or responsibilities undertaken, or duties performed, which could not reasonably be regarded as being within the scope of such engagements. This principle is, in my view, a continuing principle in the sense that, where a salvage situation arises by reason of the existence of the two factors referred to above, it only remains in being so long as those factors continue to exist to some extent at least. [51]

It was held that *The Aldora* was exposed to dangers which could not reasonably have been contemplated within the scope of the original engagements of the pilot and tugs. But, having refloated her and returned her to the dredged channel, the ship was no longer in any unexpected danger, and the responsibilities of the pilot and tugs were exactly the same as those to be undertaken under their original engagements.

Also in the *North Goodwin (No 16)* the judge said that:

> Since *Northsider* (the tug) came out of the protection of the piers pursuant to the terms of her towage contract, it could not properly be said that the risks were incurred or duties performed which were not within the scope of the contract.[52]

The Convention also provides, by Art 17, that no payment is due under the provisions of the Convention unless the services rendered exceed what can be reasonably considered as due performance of a contract entered into before the danger arose.

---

51   [1975] 1 Lloyd's Rep 617, p 623.
52   [1980] 1 Lloyd's Rep 71, p 74.

6.1.4. Threat or danger to the environment

What if there is a threat of damage to a third party? Article 8 of the 1910 Convention considered only the danger run by the salved vessel, her passengers, crew and cargo as a criterion for fixing salvage remuneration. By contrast, Art 13(1)(b) of the 1989 Salvage Convention lists the relevant factors for the assessment of the award amongst which is 'the skill and efforts of the salvors in preserving or minimising damage to the environment'. Also, Art 14 allows special compensation to salvors who prevent or minimise damage to the environment. The 'safety net'[53] concept of LOF 1980 was very different from the special compensation under Art 14 of the present Convention:

> Damage to the environment means substantial physical damage to human health or to marine life or resources in coastal or inland waters or areas adjacent thereto, caused by pollution, contamination, fire, explosion or similar major incidents [Art 1(d)].

This aspect of salvage will be considered later.

6.2 Voluntary services

'Voluntary' means that the services are not rendered under a pre-existing agreement or under official duty, or purely for the interests of self-preservation. As long as the persons are recognised in law as volunteers and they render salvage services, they are entitled to salvage remuneration. Subject to this rule, there is no limit to the class of persons that can be considered as volunteers. Clarke J in *The Sava Star*[54] said:

> There are no rigid categories of salvor. They include any volunteer who renders services of a salvage nature.

The 1989 Convention does not refer to voluntariness but states in Art 17 that no payment is due under the Convention unless the services rendered exceed what can be reasonably considered as due performance of a contract entered into before the danger arose.

6.2.1 Pre-existing agreement preventing salvage

This relates to agreements entered into prior to the time of the existence of danger. It includes the ship's master and crew who have pre-existing employment agreements with the shipowner and, therefore, have a duty to preserve the ship and cargo. They cannot convert themselves into salvors,[55] although it is not impossible.

---

53 See Brice, G, 'Safety net' [1985] 1 LMCLQ 33.
54 [1995] 2 Lloyd's Rep 134, p 141.
55 Contrast the situation in *The Telemachus* [1956] 2 Lloyd's Rep 490, where the master and crew of a ship owned by the same owner as *The Telemachus* received a salvage reward for valuable personal services.

In *The Neptune*,[56] it was held that a salvor is a person who, without any particular relation to a ship in distress, confers useful service and gives it as a volunteer adventurer without any pre-existing covenant connected with the duty of employing himself for the preservation of the ship.

Lord Stowell explained:[57]

> ... the crew of a ship cannot be considered as salvors. What is a salvor? A person, who without any particular relation to a ship in distress, proffers useful service, and gives it as a volunteer adventurer without any pre-existing covenant that connected him with the duty of employing himself in the preservation of that ship; not so the crew, whose stipulated duty it is (to be compensated by payment of wages) to protect that ship through all perils, and whose entire possible service for the purpose is pledged to this extent. Accordingly, we see in the numerous salvage cases that come to this court, the crew never claim as joint salvors although they have contributed as much as (and perhaps more than) the volunteer salvors themselves.

In *The North Goodwin (No 16)*, Sheen J said:

> ... the master and crew of *Northsider* were not volunteers in that they were employed to work aboard *Northsider* whenever the tug was rendering towing services as she was on this occasion.[58]

The Albionic[59]

During bad weather and rough sea, the vessel *A* caught fire and was completely out of control. The master shouted for all hands to jump overboard in the lifeboats, which had been made ready to pick them up. Some of the crew and the master did so, but the chief officer, who had now taken control, forbade the rest of the crew from abandoning the ship. Those who remained on board rendered valuable assistance in getting the ship to port and keeping the fire under control. The wireless operator of the ship claimed salvage for the services rendered after half the crew had left the ship. He contended that the circumstances in which they left the ship amounted to abandonment.

Lord Greene MR, delivering judgment, said that the mere order of the master to abandon the ship was not enough to constitute abandonment. Whether or not there had been abandonment depended on the facts of each individual case. His Lordship also found, as in the opinion of the trial judge, that the master did not give an order in the ordinary sense of the word, but 'a

---

56 (1824) 1 Hagg 227.
57 *Ibid*, p 236.
58 [1980] 1 Lloyd's Rep 71, p 74.
59 [1942] P 81.

piece of advice' given in a state of panic. It was, therefore, not an order which the men were bound to obey or having terminated their contract of service. The conclusion was, thus, that those who remained on the ship did so in the ordinary discharge of their duty and were not entitled to any salvage.

6.2.2 Exemptions

Despite a pre-existing agreement, the circumstances that arose in the following cases allowed salvage award.

6.2.2.1 When would the services of the master and crew qualify for salvage award?

The San Demetrio[60]

The vessel *The S* was proceeding with a convoy from Halifax to a UK port heavily loaded with petrol, when an enemy warship attacked the convoy. The ships in the convoy were hit, some sunk, or left disabled. *S* was severely damaged and her captain gave orders to abandon the ship. The crew left in three boats one of which was manned by the plaintiffs. *The S* was hit again and burst into flames. Two days later, the plaintiffs boat still at sea spotted *The S* which was still in flames. Everything on her was destroyed except her engines. There were no navigational instruments whatsoever. The plaintiffs got on board, extinguished the fires and after many days, with the help of tugs, took the vessel to Clyde safely with 10,000 tons of cargo still on the ship. Langton J found that the four requisites laid down by Dr Lushington in *The Florence*[61] to justify a reasonable abandonment of the ship had been fulfilled. The ship was properly abandoned under the orders of her master. It was held that the plaintiffs had rendered a magnificent service and a salvage award was given.

6.2.2.2 When would the services of tugs under towage qualify for salvage award?

Similarly, the obligations of a tug contemplated under a towage contract (see Chapter 14) normally prevent the rise of salvage for the services rendered by the tug to the tow unless there are exceptional circumstances not being contemplated by the contract.

In what circumstances, then, if any, could tugs engaged in towage claim salvage?[62]

---

60 (1941) 69 LIL Rep 5.
61 (1852) 16 Jur 572.
62 See *The Aldora* [1975] 1 Lloyd's Rep 617.

Hill J in *The Homewood*[63] outlined the circumstances in which a towage contract can be converted into salvage.

> To constitute a salvage service by a tug under contract to tow two elements are necessary: (1) that the tow is in danger by reason of circumstances which could not reasonably have been contemplated by the parties; and (2) that risks are incurred or duties performed by the tug which could not reasonably be held to be within the scope of the contract.[64]

The following case provides an example of circumstances, which did not qualify for salvage in the view of the Court of Appeal.

The Texaco Southampton[65]

As a result of a switchboard fire, the defendants' vessel *Texaco Southampton* was without power and was drifting in a westerly direction. The master of the vessel requested Fenwicks, who were Texaco's sole suppliers of tugs, to place tugs on standby. The tugs were supplied under a towage document. Fenwicks sub-contracted with another company, Wallace Tugs Pty, to place tugs on standby. *The Kembla 11* tug was supplied. *The Texaco* was disabled, and the crew of *The Kembla 11* had little experience towing a disabled tanker. Although they were paid wages and overtime allowances for their effort, both the ship and they claimed salvage remuneration. The defendants contended that, since their services had not been voluntary, the plaintiffs were not entitled to salvage remuneration. It was held that the work performed by the plaintiffs did not go outside the scope of their normal duties and exposed them to no risks, which were not within the contemplation of their contract of employment. The fact that the tug had been sub-contracted made no difference to the conclusion.

Article 17 of the Convention provides:

> No payment is due under the provisions of this Convention unless the services rendered exceed what can be reasonably considered as due performance of a contract entered into before the danger arose.

In the above cases, the services rendered would probably be considered under the provisions of the Convention as qualifying for salvage. The same would apply in the following cases concerning pilots.

6.2.2.3 When would the services of pilots qualify for salvage award?

Pilots are in a different situation but these, too, cannot claim salvage, unless the services rendered were exceptional – that is, not within the normal

---

63 (1928) 31 LlL Rep 336; see Chapter 14, below, on towage for full facts.

64 *Ibid*, p 339.

65 [1983] 1 Lloyd's Rep 94.

services expected from the pilot. The following cases show the exceptional circumstances in which such an award can be made.

The Sandefjord[66]

The defendants' motor vessel, *Sandefjord*, being in charge of a pilot, was stranded on Goodwin Sands after a breakdown of steering gear. Lifeboats and tugs were standing by. Upon recommendation by the pilot that tugs should not be engaged, a kedge anchor was laid out by lifeboats and the ship was refloated by hauling on anchor.

Willmer J held, that although the courts would never encourage a pilot (in possible anticipation of big reward) to take undue risks in advising against the use of tugs, in the particular circumstances of this case the pilot took no more than a fair risk as, with tugs standing by, there would still have been time for them to have been engaged before the position became critical, and that the pilot was entitled to a substantial award, though not approaching a sum which might have been awarded to tugs had they been employed – salved values £655,500, award £500.

> He brought his personal knowledge of the local conditions and his seafaring skill to bear on the problem created by the grounding of *The Sandefjord*; He gave the master advice (which events proved to be good advice); and he gave one more thing of a rather intangible nature, as to which I have had an opportunity of forming some judgment, having seen him in the witness box: he gave, I have no doubt, a great deal of encouragement to this foreign master, whose ship was stranded in waters with which he was not familiar.[67]

Akerblom v Price[68]

On her way to Barrow-in-Furness, the vessel was driven by the violence of the wind and sea to Morecambe Bay, and later was driven to dangerous sands. The locality was strange both to her captain and crew, and therefore she was in danger of being lost. Seeing the peril, the pilots put to sea to assist her. By preceding and signalling to her, they led her to a safe anchorage in the bay. The question put to the Court of Appeal was whether the amount paid to the pilots was only for pilotage services, or was it to be treated as payment for salvage services.

Brett LJ put it rhetorically: would a fair owner have insisted in requiring the necessary services for ordinary pilotage fees, or even a higher rate of pilotage payment? Would a fair pilot have refused to perform the necessary services unless upon the terms of a salvage reward? The question, thus, turned on whether the acts of the pilots, by reason of the weather and the

---

66 [1953] 2 Lloyd's Rep 557.
67 *Ibid*, p 561.
68 (1881) 7 QBD 129.

position of the ship, were so different in danger or responsibility from the ordinary acts of service of pilots, so that no fair and reasonable owner would have insisted on requiring such service for other than a salvage award. The rule of law was held to be as follows:

> ... in order to entitle a pilot to salvage reward he must not only shew that the ship is in some sense in distress, but that she was in such distress as to be in danger of being lost, and such as to call upon him to run such unusual danger or incur such unusual responsibility, or exercise such unusual skill, or perform such an unusual kind of service, as to make it unfair and unjust that he should be paid otherwise than upon the terms of salvage reward. [69]

It was held that the payment to the pilots ought to be considered as payment for salvage.

The Hudson Light[70]

The Hudson Light was lying at anchor in Gravesend Reach in a position near the southern edge of the channel just above Denton Wharf. There was a strong ebb tide and shortly before evening hours, she began to drag her anchor under the influence of the tide. Despite attempts to combat the drag, she continued to move down river and eventually went aground. Efforts to refloat her with her engines were unsuccessful. Tug assistance was called, and in response, five tugs came to her rescue, but were unable to move her as she was aground on the bottom of sand and gravel covered by a thick layer of mud. A pilot was requested and the plaintiff was first on turn at the pilot station. As soon as he was on board, he took charge of the operations for refloating the ship, giving instructions to each of the tugs. The plaintiff displayed a very considerable degree of skill both in planning and executing the refloating operation. The ship was eventually refloated and safely moored at a buoy in Gravesend, at about midnight. The plaintiff claimed a salvage reward for his services contending that a high degree of skill and care was needed bearing in mind especially the congested area of the operation. The defendants, rejecting the claim, said that only ordinary skill and care were needed and that the method to be used for refloating the vessel was obvious.

It was held that, not only did the plaintiff display considerable skill, but the responsibility which he undertook in rendering the services and running the risks involved were commendable. He was entitled to salvage reward. It was also held that in assessing the reward, it was necessary to consider the merits of the contribution made by the plaintiff to what were in effect joint services rendered by the tugs and him.

---

69   (1881) 7 QBD 129, p 135, *per* Brett LJ.
70   [1970] 1 Lloyd's Rep 166.

6.2.2.4 Would cargo-owners be able to claim a salvage award for services rendered?

Prior to the following case there had been no authority that the owners of cargo on board a ship in need of salvage, who render assistance and advice as to how a particular cargo on board should be handled and, therefore, contribute in the salvage of ship and cargo, could claim salvage. The issue that was recently before the court was that cargo-owners, as put by counsel for the shipowners on whose ship the cargo was carried, should not be entitled to a salvage award because of self interest or because they have a motive for self-preservation.

This interesting point was dealt with by Clarke J (as he then was) as a preliminary issue.

The Sava Star[71]

The plaintiffs were the owners of complex fertiliser NPK in bulk which was being carried on board the defendants' vessel *Sava Star* from Heroya in Norway to Immingham in England. The charterers of the vessel under the voyage charterparty were the plaintiffs' parent company.

The master noticed smoke and gas escaping from the holds. On finding that the cargo was decomposing, the master called the charterers who gave practical advice over the telephone regarding cooling of the cargo. The master had further contact with the charterers overnight. The decomposing cargo could not be discharged overboard. The plaintiffs were informed of the incident and, thereafter, they initiated a crisis plan which included, *inter alia*, contacting the Humberside Fire Brigade, arranging a helicopter overnight to make an inspection, constructing fire lances and providing chemists to take gas tests on the north and south banks of the Humber.

The plaintiffs' general manager gave advice to the dock master at Hull and to the Skuld P&I surveyor. United Towing Ltd (they later became contractors under Lloyd's Form of Salvage Agreement) were informed of the casualty and decided to mobilise one fire-fighting tug. The contractor's tug departed carrying eight firemen, the plaintiffs' technical manager (Mr Martin) and their chief fire fighting officer (Mr Hay), together with specialised fire-fighting equipment provided by the plaintiffs. A meeting took place on board the contractors' tug and the plaintiffs' representatives advised on the use of fire lances and the need to avoid breathing the fumes released by the burning cargo. After preparations and briefings, the crew of *Sava Star* and Mr. Hay, directed by the salvage master fought the decomposition using water lances and thermocouples provided by the plaintiffs.

---

71   [1995] 2 Lloyd's Rep 134.

In consultation with the salvage master, Mr Martin and Mr Hay recommended that one of the two fire-fighting tugs use their fire monitors to set up a water curtain in an attempt to knock the fumes down to the sea water so that some of the noxious gases might be absorbed. Mr Martin and Mr Hay also identified that the fire monitor might be used to cut through the encrusted product and reach the seat of decomposition. The fire-fighting team monitored the condition of the cargo overnight with the salvage master and Mr Hay, extinguishing one instance of decomposition. The salvage of vessel and cargo was completed within two days and the plaintiffs claimed salvage remuneration, although, admittedly, cargo-owners had not historically claimed salvage, presumably because the occasion had not arisen.

The defendants contended that neither principle nor authority supported the proposition that cargo-owners were or should be permitted to claim salvage from owners of the ship carrying the cargo. Cargo-owners were not within the recognised categories of salvor and they were bound up in the maritime adventure with the shipowners; as such they owed a duty to render such assistance as they could to salve ship and cargo. Further, or alternatively, a cargo-owner who rendered what would otherwise be salvage service acted in self preservation of his own property and as such ought not to be treated as a volunteer. Considerations of public policy pointed to the exclusion of cargo-owners as salvors.

Clarke J held that the submission that cargo-owners were not volunteers would be rejected and stated that the reason why persons with contractual duties or persons like the master and crew of the ship cannot recover is because they are performing services ordinarily to be expected of them.

He reviewed the principles of cases with regard to salvage services rendered to sister ships where the owner of the salving tug and the owner of the salved are the same and, nevertheless, salvage has been rewarded against both the salved ship and the cargo on board her. He did not see any logical reason why, if a shipowner was entitled to claim salvage against the owners of cargo carried in his ship, a cargo-owner should not be entitled to claim salvage against a ship carrying his cargo.

The judge concluded, thus:

> I have reached the clear conclusion that there is no reason based in principle or authority why cargo-owners should not be able to claim salvage from shipowners in an appropriate case. Considerations of public policy support that conclusion. Moreover, I doubt whether this conclusion will open any floodgate. In any event, cargo-owners may now be able to render valuable salvage services in circumstances where they would not have been able to do so in the past. For example, a large oil company might own tugs or tankers. I can see no reason why salvage services rendered by such tugs or tankers should not attract a salvage award from the owner of the salved ship. In order to qualify, the services would have to be in the nature of salvage services and voluntary in the sense that they were not rendered pursuant to a duty owed to

the shipowners and not part of what might ordinarily be expected of a cargo-owner such as providing advice about the characteristics of the cargo. For these reasons, my answer to the question posed at the outset, namely whether on the assumed facts the plaintiffs are entitled to salvage remuneration from the defendant shipowners, is in the affirmative.[72]

Although the facts of this case were unusual there might be occasions when a chemical cargo on board necessitates the special expertise of handling it by the provider, shipper, but the terms of the bill of lading or charterparty ought to be checked, in case the shipper has an obligation under contract to assist.[73] In any event, the analysis by the judge of the principles applicable in analogous situations appeals to common sense and is supported by a leading author in this field, who has stated that the fact salvage services are rendered out of moral obligation to go to rescue of those in distress, or self-interest on the part of the salvor, does not bar recovery.[74]

6.2.3 Could performance of duties arising under statute or official duty be a bar to salvage award?

6.2.3.1 Duty to assist after a collision

It has been discussed in the chapter on collisions at sea (Chapter 12) that the MSA 1894, s 422, now replaced by s 92 of the MSA 1995, imposes a duty upon the master of a ship involved in a collision to stand by and render assistance after the collision. Failure to comply with such a duty without reasonable excuse is a criminal offence, s 92(4).[75] The issue whether compliance with such a duty bars the marines from claiming salvage award was for the first time affirmed by the House of Lords in the following case.

The Melanie v The San Onofre[76]

In a collision, which occurred in the Bristol Channel between the S and the M on a foggy morning in December 1916, the S struck the M on her starboard side and made a large hole in her, with the result that the engine room and one of the holds filled with water. The master of the M believing that he was in immediate danger of sinking, he and most of the crew climbed on to the S, and the rest of the crew boarded the U, an armed steam trawler which was escorting the S. As the M did not sink, the master of the S proposed, with the assistance of the U, to tow her to Barry, and the crew of the M returned to her

---

72   [1995] 2 Lloyd's Rep 134, p 144.
73   See Commentary on Current Statutes, the MSA, Chapter 21, Art 17 of the Convention.
74   *Op cit*, Brice, fn 1, para 1-208, the principle derives from older authorities cited therein.
75   See Chapter 12.
76   [1925] AC 246 (HL).

and lashed her to the S on the starboard side and to the U on the port side. After towing for three-quarters of an hour, all three vessels inadvertently grounded on a ledge of rocks near the shore. The S and the U got off soon after and left the M on the rocks. When the tide fell, the water in the M drained out of her, and the master, by closing a watertight door between the hold and the engine room, was able to prevent the water coming into the hold. Both the S and the M were badly damaged by the grounding. The M was successfully towed to Barry by two tugs on the following day.

A series of litigation resulted from the incident. First, it was found in the collision action that the M was solely to blame for the collision. Later this action was brought by the owners of the S claiming salvage against the M which was disputed on the ground that the M was left abandoned in the rocks after the grounding and, thus, in a greater danger than she was originally. In any event she was ultimately saved by other tugs.

Bailhache J, acting on the advice of his assessors, decided that the towage had not materially contributed to the ultimate safety of the M and dismissed the claim, but the Court of Appeal, on the advice of their assessors, came to the contrary conclusion.

The House of Lords reversed the Court of Appeal and restored the judge's decision on the ground that the services rendered were not meritorious.[77]

Lord Phillimore stated on the point of the duty of mariners to assist after a collision:

> The counsel for the appellants rightly insisted upon the importance of s 422 of the MSA 1894, which runs as follows: 'In every case of collision between two vessels, it shall be the duty of the master or person in charge of each vessel, if and so far as he can do so without danger to his own vessel, crew and passengers (if any), to render to the other vessel, her master, crew and passengers (if any), such assistance as may be practicable.' He did not, however, as I understand desire to contend that the duty to assist in certain cases deprived the assisting vessel of the right to salvage. This is, I believe, the first opportunity which this House has had of pronouncing upon a question which has, I imagine, long been treated as settled in the courts below. Ever since the judgment of Sir Robert Phillimore in *The Hannibal* and *The Queen* accepted, I think, in the Privy Council, though there was another ground on which the decision was confirmed – it has been taken as law that the duty cast by the MSAs upon one of the two colliding vessels to stand by and render assistance, does not prevent that vessel if she renders assistance from claiming salvage. That particular judgment was given upon the construction of the MSA of 1862; but there is no material difference in the section which must govern this case. I am glad that your Lordships have the opportunity of giving your adhesion to this doctrine.[78]

---

77 See para 6.3, below.
78 [1925] AC 246, p 262.

Even when the fault of the vessel, which stands by after the collision, was causative to the collision will not prevent her to earn salvage.[79]

6.2.3.2 Duty to assist others in distress

In addition to the statutory duty to stand by after a collision, there has also been a duty upon masters of ships to help others being in distress at sea. This was first imposed by Art 11 of the Brussels Convention 1910. The provision was enacted into English law by s 6 of the MCA 1911, which was replaced by the MS(SP)A 1994 (Sched 2, para 2). It is now found in the consolidating statute, s 93 of the MSA 1995. Article 10 of the present Salvage Convention reinforces that duty.

By s 93,[80] a master of a ship is obliged to give assistance to persons in distress, upon receiving information that a ship or aircraft is in distress, failure of which is a criminal offence (s 93(6) and Sched 11, Pt II, para 3 of the MSA 1995). However, it has expressly been stated in this section (para 7), and in its predecessor, that compliance with this provision shall not affect his right, or the right of any other person, to salvage. An example is provided by the following decision.

The Tower Bridge[81]

The *TB* got into an ice field and she was totally surrounded by a pack of ice being in a very dangerous situation with the possibility of sinking. An SOS message was sent out and *The Newfoundland* (*N*) hastened to her assistance. She had just contrived to get out of the ice herself earlier on. It was however found that the *TB* was not in so desperate a position as it had seemed, and by the time the *N* came in sight of the *TB*, she had managed to get things under control to an extent. The *TB*, thus, requested that the *N* merely stand by and see the *TB* into port. The captain of the *N* thought this was unnecessary, and intimated that he was not ready to stand by, indefinitely. Instead, he gave the chief officer of the *TB* definite information on what to do to get into clear water. On compliance with the advice, the *TB* got out of the ice field. It was held that a very material service was rendered by the *N*. One of the arguments put forward by the *TB* was that the master had not, in fact, rendered any salvage service as he was only complying with his duty under the statute. It was held that the provision of the then Merchant Shipping (Safety and Load Line Conventions) Act 1932 clearly stated that compliance by the master with the provisions of this section shall not affect his right, or the right of any other person, to salvage.

---

79 See *The Kafiristan* [1938] AC 136, at para 9.5, below.
80 Previously, the Merchant Shipping (Safety Convention) Act 1949, s 22 (repealed).
81 [1936] P 30.

6.2.3.3 *Salvage by officers under orders of a naval commander of the Royal Navy*

Confusion may arise as to whether salvage is earned when the services are rendered under orders of a naval commander, which are rendered under an official duty. Exclusion from salvage would arise if the duty were owed to the vessel to be salved[82] and not when the duty was to obey orders of a naval commander. The test of voluntariness in these situations was laid down in *The Sarpen*[83] as follows:

> The test of voluntariness is only applicable between salvor and salved, and if the services are voluntary in relation to the salved, that is, not rendered by reason of an obligation towards him, it is quite immaterial that the salvor has been ordered by someone who has control of his movements to render them.

In this case, which involved the issue of both public duty and voluntariness, the admiralty, acting under its powers requisitioned tugs to be despatched to Sheerness Dockyard. *The Simla* was so despatched and eventually went up to Kirkwall Bay. While lying there, *The Sarpen*, a Norwegian steamship ran ashore on the rocks. The master of *The Simla* obtained permission from the commander of *The Northern Patrol* under whose orders he was, and proceeded to assist *The Sarpen*. She succeeded in towing *The Sarpen* off the rocks and brought her into Kirkwall harbour. The plaintiffs claimed salvage remuneration but s 557 of the MSA 1894 provided as follows:

> Where salvage services are rendered by any ship belonging to Her Majesty or by the commander or crew thereof, no claim shall be allowed for any loss, damage, or risk caused to the ship or her stores, tackle, or furniture, or for the use of any stores or other articles belonging to Her Majesty by reason of that service ...

The trial judge held that *The Simla*, being in the service of the Crown and in the positions of a King's ship, was precluded from making any claim for salvage. Also, that the master and crew of the vessel were not entitled to have their claim for salvage finally adjudicated upon, unless the consent of the admiralty to the prosecution of that claim had been taken. In the Court of Appeal one of the questions was whether *The Simla* was to be considered a King's ship for the purposes of that provision. It was held that, since the vessel was taken by the Admiralty upon the terms of the owners paying wages and health insurance of crews, providing and paying for the necessary equipment and taking marine risks on the crew and vessel, the admiralty were not at risk in the matter, and the vessel could not be regarded as a King's ship. She was, therefore, not precluded from a salvage award. On behalf of *The Sarpen*, it was

---

82 In *The Carrie* [1917] PDA 224, the crew of two HM trawlers claimed salvage successfully for saving cargo of munitions belonging to the allies from a German submarine, which was about to sink the carrying ship. Although they had a duty to the allies, they did not owe an official duty to the ship itself.

83 [1916] P 306, p 315.

contended that there could be no award as the services rendered were not voluntary on the part of the tug, since she had been directed by the naval officer in command at Kirkwall to proceed to the assistance of the vessel. It was held that the material thing was that the services were rendered voluntarily as between the salvors and the salved.

Prior to 1947, officers of the Royal Navy were regarded as being under a duty by standing orders to carry out salvage services. The courts did not favour claims by them for salvage, but only for special services rendered of substantial importance at personal risk outside their normal duties.

Since s 8(2) of the Crown Proceedings Act 1947 (CPA), there has been no bar on claims for salvage by or against the Crown in relation to services in the nature of salvage rendered by or to the Royal Navy. This position has been confirmed and clarified by s 230(1), (2) of the MSA 1995. Save for the exclusion of *in rem* proceedings against the Crown, salvage claims against or by Her Majesty's ships shall be subject to the same law as with respect to any other private person. However, para 3 provides that no claim for salvage by the commander or crew of any HMS vessel shall be finally adjudicated upon without the consent of the Secretary of State.

In *The American Farmer*[84] the crew of an RAF aircraft was awarded salvage, although the services were not considered meritorious because the ship in danger would have been found by the other tugs sent for help, nevertheless, the action to send an aircraft across was not a usual risk to be taken by Royal Air Force planes. The judge said:

> I have no doubt whatsoever that if the Royal Air Force had never been in a position to send this Liberator to find her and had never given the position which they did give, this salvage would have taken exactly the same course as it has taken. At the same time one must remember ... that the risk involved in dispatching an aircraft to go over 700 miles of sea is a very different risk to that which is involved in dispatching a salvage tug to a vessel requiring assistance.[85]

Article 17 of the Convention deals only with contractual pre-existing relations precluding salvage. Salvage services rendered pursuant to a public duty is dealt with by Art 5, of which see below.

6.2.3.4 Salvage operations controlled by public authorities

Article 5 of the Salvage Convention, Sched 11, Pt I of the MSA 1995, states that the Convention shall not affect any provisions of national laws or any international convention relating to salvage operations by or under the control of public authorities, (Art 5(1)). The extent to which a public authority under a

---

84 (1947) 80 LlL Rep 672.
85 *Ibid*, p 689.

duty to perform salvage operations may avail itself of the rights and remedies provided for in this Convention shall be determined by the law of the state where such authority is situated (Art 5(3)). For example, English law by statute forbids a Fire Authority, which may assist in fire fighting in salvage, to charge for its services (s 3(4) of the Fire Services Act 1947).

Section 252 of the MSA 1995 (replacing s 530 of the MSA 1894) gives the harbour authority the power to remove any vessel sunk, stranded or abandoned in water under the control of the harbour authority which vessel is likely to be or is an obstruction or danger to navigation. It does not seem to impose a duty, but harbour authorities have a common law duty to ensure that the harbour is safe for navigation. The authorities also have a statutory charge of recovery of expenses for removal of the wrecks. Therefore, they may not be entitled to salvage remuneration unless they did more than what is expected of them under their statutory power.

The Gregerso[86]

The ship grounded in the river Witham leading to the port of Boston. She could not free herself and in that position completely obstructed all entry to and exit from the port. She called for assistance from the port authority and a tug was manned and taken to the scene. The dock and harbour master had to spend the whole night on board her because the tug could not free the ship by towage that night as the tide had fallen. In the morning, when the tide was higher, the vessel was freed without much difficulty. The tug rendered further assistance by getting her a short distance down the river away to a position where she could proceed safely on her own. The port authority, the dock and harbour master, and the master and crew of the tug claimed salvage from the owners of the ship.

It was held that the casualty had given rise to needs, one of which was, in the interest of the port, to clear the channel of the obstruction created by her. The measure appropriate to meet this need was the same as the measure required to meet the need of the owners of the ship in order to free their vessel to enable her to proceed on her voyage. This measure was the provision of a tug to assist her. It was, therefore, held that the authority and its employees were not entitled to salvage, their services not being voluntary but in discharge of their duties. The corporation owed a duty to all users of the port and to the owners of this ship, which duties could only be performed through its employees. Considering the circumstances, there was nothing exceptional in terms of difficulty or danger in the work done by their tug. It was also held that the port authority had no power to deal with the situation by entering into an LOF contract to salve the vessel.

---

86 [1971] 1 All ER 961.

By contrast, such a claim was successful in the circumstances of *The Mars*.[87]

This was a salvage claim by three employees of the Port of London Authority, who, as crew, manned *The Boy Mark*, a patrol motor vessel, and claimed to have rendered salvage services to 11 drifting dumb barges in Northfleet Hope, River Thames, on the early morning of 16 May 1946. The barge owners contended that the services were rendered in the ordinary course of claimants' employment by the Authority, to whom the barge owners had paid a sum for the services, and that, therefore, there could be no claim for salvage.

It was held that the mere existence of the statutory duty imposed by s 431(2) upon the Port of London Authority did not, of itself, automatically exclude the possibility of a claim for salvage, and that where, as here, the plaintiffs rendered services which went beyond their ordinary every day duties as servants of the Port of London Authority, they were entitled to an award; but that, the claim being in respect of personal services, the award would be small.

6.2.3.5 Salvage operations and HM coastguards

Section 250 of the MSA 1995 provides for the remuneration of coastguards for services rendered in watching or protecting property at sea, payable by the owner of the property on a scale fixed by the Secretary of State. Being part of the marine division of the Department of Environment and Transport, they perform a public duty and are, therefore, unlikely to be able to claim salvage award, unless they render services far and above those duties expected of them.[88]

6.2.3.6 Salvage by lifeboat crews of the RNLI

The duty of a lifeboat crew is to go out and save lives and the RNLI rewards them on a scale basis provided they make no claim for salvage. The RNLI is supported by voluntary contributions. Lifeboat crew are not supposed to render services to save property, if other vessels are on the spot. If no other vessel is standing by, then the crew may accept salvage engagement whereupon they become hirers of the lifeboat and, if they succeed, they must pay to the RNLI expenses incurred in respect of the boat in accordance with the RNLI's regulations.[89]

A good example of the courts' attitude towards life boat crew is provided in the decision of Hewson J, in *The Viscount*:[90]

---

87 (1948) 81 LlL Rep 452.
88 See examples referred to in *op cit*, Kennedy, fn 2, pp 253–55.
89 See *op cit*, Brice, fn 1, Appendix 7, para 15-29, for the regulations of the Institute.
90 [1966] 1 Lloyd's Rep 328.

Services were rendered by the plaintiff crew of the RNLI lifeboat *Henry Blogg* to the defendants' motor vessel *Viscount* which ran aground on the Norfolk coast. *Henry Blogg* arrived at 10.00 hours and stood by until the tide began to make, when she went along the starboard side of *Viscount*. While she was manoeuvring on to *Viscount*'s port quarter, a carton of 200 cigarettes was thrown on board from *Viscount*. *Henry Blogg* was asked to come back and take a rope in an hour, but as the tide was setting strongly to the SE, the plaintiffs insisted on taking rope then (15.15 hours). *Viscount* was refloated in a few minutes. The plaintiffs claimed salvage award, but *Viscount* denied that *Henry Blogg* rendered any material assistance, and contended that the plaintiffs agreed to render any assistance necessary for 200 cigarettes. Salved values were: *Viscount*, £45,000; cargo, £15,848; freight, £450; total, £61,298.

Hewson J held that, although there was little danger, *Henry Blogg* acted as an 'animated drogue' in helping to hold up *Viscount*'s stern against the flood tide and those services were rendered at the critical few minutes between the time she became lively and the time she went astern into deep water; that cigarettes were not accepted as prepayment for assistance which was requested; and that, therefore, plaintiffs were entitled to salvage award of £250. And, he added a general comment:

> In making this award I want to make it quite clear that the primary duty of lifeboatmen manning lifeboats owned by the RNLI is the saving of life. It must be clearly understood that in the course of standing by to save life this court is giving no encouragement to lifeboatmen to get a line on board a disabled vessel at all costs; but, nevertheless, they must be encouraged to stand by and to give such assistance, without unduly risking their craft, when necessary.[91]

The weight of judicial opinion with regard to the crews of RNLI lifeboats has been to favour an award for personal risk, local knowledge and highly meritorious services by those men, for which they should be rewarded for future encouragement.[92]

6.3 Success

6.3.1 Meritorious services

Without success or meritorious services there will be no award. The cause of action of salvage, which is available in the Admiralty Court, is quite distinct from a *quantum meruit* available in the common law courts.[93]

---

91 [1966] 1 Lloyd's Rep 328, p 333.
92 *The Boston Lincoln* [1980] 1 Lloyd's Rep 481; *The Africa Occidental* [1951] 2 Lloyd's Rep 107; *The Geertjie K* [1971] 1 Lloyd's Rep 285.
93 *Op cit*, Brice, fn 1, para 1-102.

The principle was laid down by Dr Lushington in *The India*:[94]

> ... unless the salvors by their services conferred actual benefit on the salved property, they are not entitled to salvage remuneration.

Article 12 of Sched 11 of the consolidating MSA 1995 provides that a salvor will be entitled to a reward if the salvage operations had a useful result. The exception to this is contained in Art 14, which gives salvors the right to recover special compensation for salvage services rendered to a vessel, or its cargo, when by itself or its cargo threatened damage to the environment.[95]

Lord Diplock in *The Tojo Maru*[96] examined certain characteristics of salvage contracts which differentiate them from ordinary contracts for work and labour. He said:

> The first distinctive feature is that the person rendering the salvage services is not entitled to any remuneration unless he saves the property in whole or in part. This is what is meant by 'success' in cases about salvage.[97]

The following examples illustrate what would not amount to 'success'. If after the service is actually rendered, the ship is in as grave a danger as it was originally, then no award will be given. Also, services which rescue a vessel from one danger but end by leaving her in a position of as great, or nearly as great, a danger, though of a different kind, are held not to contribute to the ultimate success and are not entitled to salvage reward.

The Cheerful[98]

On her way from London to Liverpool, *The Cheerful* (C) lost her propeller in the English Channel. The H came to her rescue and proceeded to tow her to port when, near the Shambels lightship, both the hawsers parted and the C at this time got into a position of considerable danger in adverse weather conditions. In an attempt to get the hawser on board again, the H got out of command, became unmanageable and eventually collided with the C, causing damage to both vessels. Eventually, the H bore away for Portland, as she was in danger herself. Two tugs finally came to the assistance of the C and towed her to Portland roads in safety. The H claimed salvage alleging that at the time she came to the C's rescue, the weather was bad, that there was a heavy sea with squalls and gale and that the C was in danger of going on to the coast and becoming a total wreck if no vessel had come to her rescue. The defendants, owners of the C, on the other hand, alleged that she was in no immediate danger and that the H had by her actions left the C in a worse

---

94 (1842) 1 Wm Rob 406.
95 See, later, para 12.
96 [1972] AC 242 (HL).
97 *Ibid*, p 293.
98 (1855) 11 PD 3.

position than she found herself in and should not be awarded salvage. They also counterclaimed for damages for the injury done to the *C* as a result of the negligence of *H* at the time they were attempting to get the hawser on board again. Since no actual benefit was conferred on the *C* by the services of the *H*, no salvage would be awarded. In the opinion of the Elder Brethren, however, the *H* was not negligent in her actions or omissions, therefore, the counterclaim for injury to *C* due to *H*'s negligence failed.

In the Melanie v The San Onofre[99]

The defendants claimed that the plaintiffs had left the *M* in a position of greater comparative danger than she was in before the *S* began to tow her, and, therefore, no salvage was due. It was held that services which rescue a vessel from one danger, but end by leaving her in a position of as great, or nearly, as great danger, though of another kind, do not contribute to the ultimate success and do not amount to salvage. The mere fact that the claimant has brought the ship to a position or spot where the ultimate salvor has found her does not of itself show that bringing her to that spot was a contribution to the ultimate success.

Where many vessels were involved in the salvage operation of a ship, only those vessels that could be considered as having 'materially assisted' the rescue of the ship or cargo would be entitled to any salvage reward.

The Killeena[100]

The Killeena had been abandoned by her master and crew on her way to Liverpool from New York during a heavy gale which affected the vessel badly. She drifted about in the Atlantic till she was sighted by *The Nora* a Norwegian vessel. The crew of *The Nora* boarded *The Killeena* until they became frightened. They decided to abandon the vessel and hoisted an ensign, union down. This attracted the attention of those on board *The Beatrice*, which, with the assistance of the *L*, brought *The Killeena* into Falmouth. The court held that the master and crew of *The Nora* unlike the others, were not entitled to any salvage reward. Sir Robert Phillimore quoted a passage from *The Undaunted* (1860) Lush 90 which summarises the principles of law applicable to the question whether *The Nora* was entitled to a salvage reward:

> Salvors who volunteer, go out at their own risk for the chance of earning reward, and if they labour unsuccessfully, are entitled to nothing. The effectual performance of salvage service is that which gives them a title to salvage remuneration. But if men are engaged by a ship in distress, whether generally or particularly, they are to be paid according to their efforts made, even though the labour and service may not prove beneficial to the vessel.

99 [1925] AC 246, see para 6.2.3.1 for a summary of the facts.
100 (1881) 6 PD 193.

And then Sir Robert Phillimore continued:[101]

> Now, there is no doubt that where a set of salvors have done some acts which tend to the ultimate salvage of a vessel they are usually entitled to some remuneration, but there is a circumstance in this case most material to consider. The four men and the boy who were put on board from *The Nora* deliberately, according to the evidence, when *The Beatrice* had answered their signal, abandoned and deserted *The Killeena*. It appears to me, therefore, that *The Killeena* was again a derelict vessel. As the men on board her deliberately determined to leave her, four men were found with better heart and courage to take the places of these men, and to do what was necessary for the preservation of *The Killeena*.

> It appears to me that it would be contrary to the principles upon which salvage remuneration is awarded, to allow *The Nora*'s people to appear as salvors in this case, inasmuch as they were, according to the evidence, turning their backs and running away from the danger to which the vessel was exposed. The men from on board *The Beatrice* had as much reason to be alarmed, but they persevered, and their courage deserves to be rewarded. I am clearly of opinion that the owners, master, and crew of *The Nora* are not entitled to claim salvage.

6.3.2 Salvage services by standing by a vessel in danger

Meritorious services can also be rendered merely by standing by as long as the property is ultimately saved.

In *The Tower Bridge*,[102] it was held that the N rendered most valuable assistance in showing the TB how to get out of the ice field. It was not necessary to define the precise moment at which the service began or to quantify the moral support afforded to the TB when the only available ship in the North Atlantic came ploughing her way through the ice. Each separate item of the proceedings could not be regarded in isolation. The whole of the circumstances that existed at the time must be looked at.

6.3.3 Salvage and engaged services

Before the emergence of sophisticated salvage agreements, there used to be salvage services rendered at request – as contrasted with volunteer salvors – and, even if there was no contribution to success, there would be salvage remuneration, as an exception to the general rule that the right to salvage accrues only upon success. That exception was affirmed by Dr Lushington, in *The Undaunted*:[103]

> There is a broad distinction between salvors who volunteer to go out, and salvors who are employed by as ship in distress. Salvors who volunteer, go out

---

101 (1881) 6 PD 193, p 198.
102 [1936] P 30, see para 6.2.3.2.
103 (1860) Lush 90, p 92.

at their own risk for the chance of earning reward, and if they labour unsuccessfully, they are entitled to nothing; the effectual performance of salvage service is that which gives them a title to salvage remuneration. But if men are engaged by a ship in distress, whether generally or particularly, they are to be paid according to their efforts made, even though the labour and service may not prove beneficial to the vessel. Take the case of a vessel at anchor in a gale of wind, hailing a steamer to lie by and be ready to take her in tow if required; the steamer does so, the ship rides out of the gale safely without the assistance of the steamer: I should undoubtedly hold in such a case that the steamer was entitled to salvage reward ...

Almost 40 years later, in *The Dart*,[104] Sir Robert Phillimore summed up three distinct situations within which engaged services may fall:

If a salvor is employed to do anything and does it, and the property is ultimately saved, he may claim a salvage award, though the thing which he does, in the events which happen, produces no good effect. If a salvor is employed to complete a salvage and does not, but, without any misconduct on his part, fails after he has performed a beneficial service, he is entitled also to a salvage award. If a salvor is employed to do a thing and does not do it, and no doubt uses strenuous exertions and makes sacrifices, but does no good at all, then it seems to me he is not entitled to salvage.

A later example of engaged services falling within the first category of Phillimore's classification is apparent in *The Alenquer and Rene*.[105] *Alenquer*, having done the thing she was asks to do by *The Rene* (that is, to respond to a distress signal and stand by *The Rene*) would have entitled her to an award, had it not been for her negligence which deprived her right to it.

There have been a few other cases in which salvage was awarded on that basis, which are mentioned by Brice,[106] but, in modern times of salvage requirements and facilities available, such services will either be covered by a specific agreement for towage or salvage, or will be considered as salvage operations falling within the definition of Art 1(a) of the Convention.

7 SALVAGE AGREEMENTS

7.1 General

Ordinary salvage arises out of the fact that aid has been given voluntarily at the time of danger and if there has been benefit to the subject of salvage from

---

104 (1899) 8 Asp 481, p 483.

105 [1955] 1 Lloyd's Rep 101.

106 *Op cit*, Brice, fn 1, paras 1-393–1-402, argues that, although such services come within the Convention definition, there is no legislative purpose to exclude them in English law.

the services rendered to the subject matter, an award will be made. There is no need for an actual contract between the parties. Unless the parties expressly agree to contract out of the Act, all salvage operations will be governed by the statute (Art 6(1), Sched 11 of the MSA 1995).

If the services were already rendered prior to any agreement, a subsequent agreement will cover only future action. The salvor has vested rights prior to the agreement.[107]

Similarly the new Convention and the 1995 Act protect salvors in respect of any salvage operations with a useful result. (Art 12).

Formal salvage agreements came to be used in late 19th century, with the first standardised form dated 1892, on basis of 'no cure no pay'.[108] Professional salvors render services under an agreement entered into at the time of danger. These agreements are made on the 'no cure no pay' basis, on the LOF and the remuneration is fixed by arbitration. The parties to the agreement retain their common law rights. During the writing of this book, the LOFs commonly in use were the 1990 and 1995 forms and a new salvage 2000 became operational in September 2000. Both the 1990 and 1995 forms were long, including procedural rules about the conduct of arbitration and incorporated most articles of the Convention either directly or by reference. By contrast, the latter is made simple and contains only the most essential terms, corresponding to LOF 1995, in one sheet excluding the procedural provisions, which are separately provided in the Lloyd's Standard Salvage and Arbitration Clauses and are incorporated by reference. As will be seen later, problems of salvors' compensation for protecting the environment from pollution which arose from difficulties in the interpretation of Art 14 of the Convention, led to commercial pressure exerted by the salvage community for improvement of the wording of Art 14. After consultation and negotiations between the International Salvage Union, property underwriters and P&I clubs, there has been the birth of a new clause, known as the SCOPIC (Special Compensation of Protection and Indemnity Clause). This, in fact, is a form of guaranteed remuneration to salvors payable by the P&I club of the shipowners, whose vessel needed salvage, to encourage the salvor to proceed to a casualty, whether or not there is a threat of damage to the environment. It can be incorporated into any LOF, if the salvors so choose (of which see later). The previous LOFs may still be used if the parties so desire. Unless the parties wish to contract out of some of the provisions of the Convention, or, as far as English law is concerned, the provisions of the MSA 1995, which incorporates the 1989 Salvage Convention, the Convention shall apply. If there is no contract, the rules of the Convention shall apply to all salvage operations, save where the law applicable to a salvage operation is of a State that has not ratified the Convention.

---

107 See *The Inchmaree* [1899] P 111, pp 116–17.
108 For the history of Lloyd's forms, see, *op cit*, Brice fn 1, Chapter 8.

The contract is for supply of services. Therefore, the Supply of Goods and Services Act 1982, ss 13–16 would apply, particularly regarding implied terms of reasonable care and skill, to provide a tug fit for the purpose and complete the services within a reasonable time.

The Unfair Contract Terms Act 1977, apart from s 2(1) regarding no exclusion of liability for death or personal injury, has no application to marine salvage contracts, but there is an exception in case the owner of the salved property is dealing as a consumer and this could arise if there is a salvage of a private yacht.

There may be salvage agreements with fixed amounts for specific services, as mentioned earlier, but with the passing of the Salvage Convention, the scope of these sorts of contracts have been limited. If the amount is not agreed upon, the remuneration will be adjudged by the court, which has jurisdiction under s 20(2)(j) of the SCA 1981. There is, however, a lump sum agreement, the 'Salvom' International Salvage Union Agreement with detailed clauses about the parties' rights and obligations.[109]

7.2 Court's intervention

Unlike ordinary contracts under English law, the courts can reopen salvage contracts even in the absence of economic duress, misrepresentation or operative mistake. This is more common where the contracts are fixed sums salvage agreements[110] rather than open form agreements. It is in the nature of salvage that agreements have to be entered quickly and under pressure because of the danger the property is involved. There is, inevitably, inequality of bargaining, which does not always mean that the salvor is taking undue advantage, so as to render the agreement voidable on the basis of economic duress.[111]

The 1989 Convention, Art 7, also provides that a contract may be annulled or modified if it has been entered into under undue influence or the influence of danger and its terms are inequitable, or if the payment under the contract is in an excessive degree, too large or too small, for the services actually rendered. The LOF 2000 expressly prohibits undue influence prior to entering into the agreement.

---

109 The full text is provided in *op cit*, Brice, fn 1, Appendix 7, Pt II.

110 See, eg, *The Mark Lane* (1890) 15 PD 135; *The Crusader* [1907] P 15.

111 *Huyton SA v Peter Cremer* [1999] 1 Lloyd's Rep 620, in which the ingredients of economic duress were re-evaluated by the English court. It was held that it was the deflection rather than the coercion of the will of the innocent party that the court will be looking for in considering whether the contract is voidable. The illegitimate pressure must be a significant cause, which must have induced the innocent party to enter into the contract, but the court will take in to account other possible choices available to the victim and assess them objectively.

The circumstances in which the English courts have interfered with a salvage agreement in the past are examined next.

7.2.1 When the agreement is reached by extortion or overbearing conduct

The Port of Caledonia[112]

During a southwesterly gale, the *P* and the *A* were heading to the wind and fully exposed to the ground swell. The *P* was dragging towards the *A*, both vessels being in danger of fouling one another. The master of *P* called for a tug and pilot and the *S*, being close by, responded to the signal. The master of *P* asked how much it would cost to hire the tug. *S* replied '£1000', but *P*'s master offered to pay £100. The master of *S* rejected *P*'s smaller offer and the latter's proposal to leave the matter to be settled between their respective owners. At this point, as the master of *P* was in a great difficulty, he accepted to pay the greater amount and hailed *S* to take the tow. *S* towed the *P* to a safe berth and claimed the sum of £1000 as well as a reasonable sum for salvage from *A*. The learned judge considered the value of the services to be less than £1000 and the question was whether the bargain was so inequitable and unreasonable that the court could not allow it to stand. It was held that, as one party *S* was in a position to insist upon his terms, and the other party had to put up with it being in a desperate situation, the agreement was inequitable, extortionate and unreasonable.

A failure to perform the agreed services may not destroy the right to remuneration. The courts may intervene to determine the rate of remuneration even though a fixed sum had been agreed.[113]

7.2.2. Misrepresentation and non-disclosure

The general principles of common law and statute will apply, if either party to the agreement has misrepresented the true facts so as to cause prejudice to the other party's position, who relied on the facts as represented. Liability in damages may lie under the Misrepresentation Act 1967, s 2(1).[114]

In addition, the Admiralty Court has inherent jurisdiction to interfere with salvage agreements and the following case is an example of the court's approach when the salved misled the salvor about the danger.

---

112 [1903] P 184.

113 See *The Westbourne* (1889) 14 PD 132.

114 See, also, *Howard Marine and Dredging Co Ltd v A Ogden & Sons Ltd* [1978] QB 574 (CA); *The Unique Mariner* [1978] 1 Lloyd's Rep 438, pp 454–55, *per* Brandon J; and see Chapter 14, para 4.4.

The Kingalock[115]

At the entrance of the river Thames, *The K* met with extremely bad weather and suffered considerable damage. *The K*'s master entered into an agreement with the master of a steamer to tow *The K* to London for a fixed sum of £40, but he did not disclose the fact that *The K* had encountered such difficulty and had been damaged. A short time after the towage began, the hawser broke and the master of the steamship discovered what had previously happened to *The K*. He immediately declared the agreement at an end, but, nevertheless, towed the vessel to London, as though no agreement had been made. With much difficulty, the vessel was towed safely to London. The salvors claimed a salvage reward, but the owners of *The K* contended that the original agreement was still valid and subsisting. Dr Lushington stated, thus:

> An agreement to bind two parties must be made with a full knowledge of all the facts necessary to be known by both parties; and if any fact which, if known, could have any operation on the agreement about to be entered into is kept back, or not disclosed to either of the contracting parties, that would vitiate the agreement itself. It is not necessary, in order to vitiate an agreement, that there should be moral fraud; it is not necessary, in order to make it not binding, that one of the parties should keep back any fact or circumstance of importance, if there should be misapprehension, accidentally or by carelessness; we all know that there may be what, in the eye of the law, is termed equitable fraud.[116]

It was held that the omission to state the undisclosed facts would vitiate the agreement because those facts would have affected the service to be performed. The lack of ground tackle on the ship may have been important, particularly during weather so tempestuous as this was. This might have to a certain extent governed the manoeuvres of the steamer. Therefore the agreement was null and void *ab initio*. The owner of *The K* was ordered to pay an additional sum suitable in the circumstances because the tug had been misled that this was an ordinary towage. Dr Lushington stressed that if there had been an agreement for extraordinary towage, with full knowledge of the state of the vessel, no addition would have been made.

---

115 (1854) 1 Spinks E&A 265.
116 *Ibid*, p 265.

8 THE MASTER'S AUTHORITY TO ENTER INTO SALVAGE AGREEMENTS

The master of a ship has authority to act on behalf of the owners in various circumstances arising from being in command of the ship. Such authority is derived mainly from his contract of employment and it is actual authority express or implied depending on the circumstances. Actual authority will exist in most cases when the owner issues standing orders, or gives such authority through wireless communications. Implied authority derives from the nature of the contract of employment in respect of acts which are necessary to be done in the performance of that contract and fall within the usual scope of his position, as for example the act of signing bills of lading, or engaging other agents to provide necessary materials and provisions for the running of the ship. On some occasions, the authority may be implied by the operation of law, as for example when the master acts as an agent of necessity. While it is not difficult to trace the root of the master's authority *vis a vis* the owner of the ship through the principles of agency law, a problem has arisen, particularly in the context of signing salvage agreements, with regard to whether the master can bind third parties, such as the owners of the cargo carried on board. Prior to the Salvage Convention 1989, the issue was dealt with in accordance with the principle of agency of necessity, but this proved to be problematic in certain circumstances where the criteria of that agency were not satisfied, as the examples of cases will show.

8.1 Master's authority at common law

The essential characteristic of agency is the power of the agent to affect the legal position of the principal as regards third parties.[117] In a situation of salvage, the master of the ship will be acting as agent of the owners of the properties to be salved with the view to binding them into an effective contract of salvage with the third party, the salvors. There are two sets of triangular relationships to be examined, first as between the master, his employers, and the salvors; and, second, as between the master, the owners of cargo (or of other property on board) and the salvors.

---

117 Markesinis, B and Munday, R, *An Outline of the Law of Agency*, 3rd edn, 1992, Butterworths, pp 52–54.

8.1.1 The basis of the master's authority to bind his principal to a salvage contract[118]

It has been established that the master of a ship, which needs salvage assistance, has implied actual authority to bind his principal, the shipowner, to the contract of salvage.[119]

The Unique Mariner (No 1)[120]

The master, under the mistaken belief that a tug which approached him when his vessel ran aground had been sent on behalf of his owner, signed an LOF salvage agreement. He later discovered that it was another tug that had been retained by the owners and, therefore, dismissed the prior salvors in favour of the latter. The question before the trial judge was whether this was a valid contract binding on the owners. Counsel for the owners contended that, although the master had implied actual authority to accept the services of a tug, such authority did not extend to his entering into a special contract, such as the LOF. Brandon J stated:

> The implied actual authority of a master, unless restricted by such instructions lawfully given, extends to doing whatever is incidental to, or necessary for, the successful prosecution of the voyage and safety and preservation of the ship.[121]

He continued, thus:

> I do not think that the implied actual authority of the master of a stranded ship to accept the services of a suitable tug is limited to his accepting them subject to the ordinary maritime law of salvage. I think, on the contrary, that it extends to accepting such services on the terms of any reasonable contract.[122]

It was held that the LOF has been both used and accepted as being reasonable and fair.

8.1.2 The basis of the master's authority to bind cargo interests to a salvage contract[123]

The master could bind them to the contract as an agent of necessity, if the means of communication in the time available to respond to an emergency would put his ship and cargo on board at a greater risk. The same would apply in case of freight being at charterer's risk.[124]

---

118 See, also, Chapter 14, para 4.1, below.

119 *The Unique Mariner (No 1)* [1978] 1 Lloyd's Rep 438.

120 [1978] 1 Lloyd's Rep 438, as the ship was in ballast there was no issue of the master's authority vis à vis cargo-owners.

121 *Ibid*, p 449.

122 *Ibid*, p 450.

123 See, also, Chapter 14, para 4.2, below.

Agency of necessity arises by operation of law in certain circumstances where a person is faced with an emergency in which the property or interests of another person are in imminent jeopardy and it becomes necessary, in order to preserve the property or interests, to act for that person without his authority.[125]

There should exist four elements for the agency to arise:

(i) an emergency;
(ii) inability to obtain instructions, or failure by the cargo interests to give any instructions when appraised of the situation;[126]
(iii) the master of the salved acts *bona fide* for the interest of all; and
(iv) it is reasonable for the master or shipowner to enter into the particular contract.[127]

The court in the following case examined the agency of necessity in the context of salvage together with principles of bailment.

The Winson[128]

The Winson, a bulk carrier, was chartered by Food Corporation of India (the cargo-owner) to carry full cargo of wheat from US Gulf ports to Indian ports under a voyage charterparty. In the course of the voyage, she stranded on the North Danger reef in the South China Sea. Professional salvors (China Pacific) were quickly on the scene and a salvage agreement in the LOF was entered into, signed by the master on behalf of the shipowner and cargo-owner. During the salvage operations, it was necessary to lighten the vessel by off-loading part of her cargo into barges provided by the salvors and carrying it to a place of safety. This was done, and some 15,429 tonnes of wheat were off-loaded and carried to Manila which was a proper place of safety. The carriage was in six separate parcels that arrived in Manila at various dates between 10 February and 20 April 1975. The salvage operations at the site of the stranding were temporarily suspended on 15 April 1975, owing to fighting in the vicinity having broken out between the forces of North Vietnam and South Vietnam. On 24 April 1975, the shipowner gave notice to cargo interests that he had abandoned the chartered voyage. By that date, it was obvious that the completion of the carriage of the cargo in *The Winson* to its destination under the charterparty, even if it were to become physically possible (which, in the

---

124 *The Pantanassa* [1970] 1 Lloyd's Rep 153.

125 *Bowstead and Reynolds on Agency*, 15th edn, 1996, Sweet & Maxwell, p 84.

126 Lloyd J at first instance in *The Winson* [1982] AC 939 (HL) thought that the first element of the agency of necessity was inability by the master to obtain proper instructions.

127 The fourth criterion was added by Slade LJ in *The Choko Star* [1990] 1 Lloyd's Rep 516, see below.

128 [1982] AC 939 (HL).

event, it did not), would involve such long delay as would frustrate the contract.

It was not disputed that it never became practicable thereafter to resume the salvage operations and, on 20 May 1975, the salvors gave formal notice of termination of their salvage services. *The Winson* with the remainder of the cargo of wheat still on board her eventually became a total loss.

Upon arrival of each parcel of salvaged wheat at Manila, where the salvors had no storage premises of their own, it became necessary for it to be stored in suitable accommodation under cover, until a decision was reached what to do with it. The salvors arranged for the storage of part of the wheat in a vessel, *The Maori*, lying in Manila Harbour, and as to the remainder in a bonded warehouse ashore. In doing so, they incurred expenses for stevedoring and charter hire of *The Maori* and warehouse charges ashore. The stored wheat was held to their order by those in whose vessel and warehouse it was stored ('the depositaries'). These expenses which the salvors became personally liable to pay under the contracts that they made as principals with the depositaries continued to be incurred by them until the cargo-owner had completed taking possession of the wheat – which did not happen until 5 August 1975.

The storage expenses incurred after the termination of the contracted voyage (24 April 1975) were paid by the cargo-owners. The salvors brought this action against the cargo-owners to recover the storage expenses up to that date. The cargo-owners contended that by virtue of the contract of carriage, the immediate right to possession of the goods before it was terminated rested with the shipowner, and the salvors were, thus, under a duty to deliver the cargo to the shipowner. Therefore, it was the shipowner that was liable to reimburse the salvors for the expenses incurred before the termination of the contract of carriage. They did not dispute the payment from 24 April. Such a proposition was rejected by Lloyd J at first instance but accepted by the Court of Appeal.

The decision of the House of Lords

Apart from the importance of this decision on issues of bailment, the relevant issue in this context was the legal nature of the relationship between the master of the ship and the owner of the cargo when the salvage contract was signed. The issue of payment of the salvors' expenses was solved on the basis of bailment.

It was held that, where in the course of salvage operations cargo is off-loaded from the vessel by which the contract of carriage was being performed and conveyed separately to a place of safety, the direct relationship of bailor and bailee is created between the cargo-owner and the salvor as soon as the cargo is loaded on vessels provided by the salvor to convey it to a place of safety. All the mutual rights and duties attaching to such a relationship at common law become binding. The relationship continues to exist until the cargo-owners take possession of the cargo from the warehouse. The cargo-owner, therefore, had to pay for all expenses incurred.

It is important to quote how Lord Diplock analysed the problem:

> My Lords, it is not suggested that there is any direct authority on the question of law that is posed in this appeal. In my opinion the answer is to be found by applying to the unusual circumstances of the instant case well known and basic principles of the common law of salvage, of bailment and of lien.[129]

> ... with modern methods of communication and the presence of professional salvors within rapid reach of most parts of the principal maritime trade routes of the world, nearly all salvage of merchant ships and their cargoes nowadays is undertaken under a salvage contract in Lloyd's Open Form. The contract is one for the rendering of services; the services to be rendered are of the legal nature of salvage and this imports into the contractual relationship between the parties to the contract by necessary implication a number of mutual rights and obligations attaching to salvage of vessels and their cargo under common law, except insofar as such rights and obligations are inconsistent with express terms of the contract.

> Lloyd's Open Form is expressed by cl 16 to be signed by the master '... as agent for the vessel her cargo and freight and the respective owners thereof and binds each (but not the one for the other or himself personally) to the due performance thereof'. The legal nature of the relationship between the master and the owner of the cargo aboard the vessel in signing the agreement on the latter's behalf is often though not invariably an agency of necessity. It arises only when salvage services by a third party are necessary for the preservation of the cargo. Whether one person is entitled to act as agent of necessity for another person is relevant to the question whether circumstances exist which in law have the effect of conferring on him authority to create contractual rights and obligations between that other person and a third party that are directly enforceable by each against the other. It would, I think, be an aid to clarity of legal thinking if the use of the expression 'agent of necessity' were confined to contexts in which this was the question to be determined and not extended, as it often is, to cases where the only relevant question is whether a person who without obtaining instructions from the owner of goods incurs expense in taking steps that are reasonably necessary for their preservation is in law entitled to recover from the owner of the goods the reasonable expenses incurred by him in taking those steps. Its use in this wider sense may, I think, have led to some confusion in the instant case, since where reimbursement is the only relevant question, all of those conditions that must be fulfilled in order to entitle one person to act on behalf of another in creating direct contractual relationships between that other person and a third party may not necessarily apply.

> In the instant case, it is not disputed that when the Lloyd's Open Form was signed on 22 January 1975, the circumstances that existed at that time were such as entitled the master to enter into the agreement on the cargo-owner's

---

129 [1982] AC 939 (HL), p 957.

behalf as its agent of necessity. The rendering of salvage services under the Lloyd's open agreement does not usually involve the salvor's taking possession of the vessel or its cargo from the shipowner; the shipowner remains in possession of both ship and cargo while salvage services are being carried out by the salvors on the ship. But salvage services may involve the transfer of possession of cargo from the shipowner to the salvors, and will do so in a case of stranding as respects part of the cargo, if it becomes necessary to lighten the vessel in order to refloat her. Where in the course of salvage operations cargo is off loaded from the vessel by which the contract of carriage was being performed and conveyed separately from that vessel to a place of safety by means (in the instant case, barges) provided by the salvor, the direct relationship of bailor and bailee is created between cargo-owner and salvor as soon as the cargo is loaded on vessels provided by the salvor to convey it to a place of safety; and all the mutual rights and duties attaching to that relationship at common law apply, save insofar as any of them are inconsistent with the express terms of the Lloyd's open agreement.

On parting with possession of cargo to the salvor the shipowner loses any possessory lien over it to which he may have been entitled for unpaid freight, demurrage or general average. Whether the lien in respect of liabilities of the cargo owner that had already accrued due at the time of parting with possession would revive upon the shipowner's recovering possession of the cargo for on-carriage to its contractual destination is a question on which there appears to be no direct authority; but it does not arise for decision by your Lordships in the instant case. The shipowners neither obtained nor even sought repossession of any part of the salved wheat after it had been off loaded from *The Winson* into the barges provided by the salvors on and before 24 April 1975 ...[130]

My Lords, as I have already said, there is not any direct authority as to the existence of this correlative right to reimbursement of expenses in the specific case of a salvor who retains possession of cargo after the salvage services rendered by him to that cargo have ended; but Lloyd J discerned what he considered to be helpful analogous applications of the principle of the bailee's right to reimbursement in *Cargo ex Argos* (1873) LR 5 PC 134, from which I have taken the expression 'correlative right,' and in *Great Northern Rly Co v Swaffield* (1874) LR 9 Ex 132. Both these were cases of carriage of goods in which the carrier/bailee was left in possession of the goods after the carriage contracted for had terminated. Steps necessary for the preservation of the goods were taken by the bailee in default of any instructions from owner/bailor to do otherwise.[131]

In the instant case the cargo-owner was kept informed of the salvors' intentions as to the storage of the salved wheat upon its arrival in Manila; it made no alternative proposals; it made no request to the salvors for delivery of any of the wheat after its arrival at Manila, and a request made by the salvors to the cargo-owner through their solicitors on 25 February 1975, after the

---

130 [1982] AC 939 (HL), pp 958–59.
131 *Ibid*, p 960.

arrival of the second of the six parcels, to take delivery of the parcels of salved wheat on arrival at Manila remained unanswered and uncomplied with until after notice of abandonment of the charter voyage had been received by the cargo-owner from the shipowner.

The failure of the cargo-owner as bailor to give any instructions to the salvors as its bailee although it was fully apprised of the need to store the salved wheat under cover on arrival at Manila if it was to be preserved from rapid deterioration was, in the view of Lloyd J, sufficient to attract the application of the principle to which I have referred above and to entitle the salvors to recover from the cargo-owner their expenses in taking measures necessary for its preservation. For my part, I think that in this he was right and the Court of Appeal, who took the contrary view, were wrong. It is, of course, true that in English law a mere stranger cannot compel an owner of goods to pay for a benefit bestowed upon him against his will; but this latter principle does not apply where there is a pre-existing legal relationship between the owner of the goods and the bestower of the benefit, such as that of bailor and bailee, which imposes upon the bestower of the benefit a legal duty of care in respect of the preservation of the goods that is owed by him to their owner.[132]

Lord Simon agreed with Lloyd J, the judge at first instance, that when the LOF was signed, the circumstances that existed were such as to have entitled the master to enter into the agreement on the cargo-owner's behalf as its agency of necessity. On the issue of agency of necessity, Lord Simon commented:

One of the ways in which an agency of necessity can arise is where A is in possession of goods the property of B, and an emergency arises which places those goods in imminent jeopardy: If A cannot obtain instructions from B as to how he should act in such circumstances, A is bound to take without authority such action in relation to the goods as B, as a prudent owner, would himself have taken in the circumstances. The relationship between A and B is then known as an 'agency of necessity', A being the agent and B the principal. This was the situation descried by Lloyd J and denied by the Court of Appeal.

Issues as to agency of necessity generally arise forensically when A enters into a contract with C in relation to the goods, the question being whether B is bound by that contract. The purely terminological suggestion that, in order to avoid confusion, 'agent of necessity' should be confined to such contractual situations does not involve that other relevant general incidents of agency are excluded from the relationship between A and B. In particular, if A incurs reasonable expenses in safeguarding B's goods in a situation of emergency, A is entitled to be reimbursed by B: see *Bowstead on Agency*, 14th edn, 1976, Art 67; *Chitty on Contracts*, 23rd edn, 1968, Vol 2, para 119; *Petrinovic & Co Ltd v Mission Fraèaise des Transports Maritimes* (1941) 71 LlL Rep 208, p 220.

To confine 'agent of necessity' terminologically to the contractual situations is justified by the fact that the law of bailment will often resolve any issue between alleged principal and agent of necessity, as it has done here. But, sometimes, the law of agency will be more useful: for example, if available

---

132 [1982] AC 939 (HL), p 961.

here it would obviate any problem about the correlation of performance of a duty of care with a claim for reimbursement, since an agent is undoubtedly entitled to an indemnity for expenses incurred reasonably to benefit his principal.

However, I respectfully agree with the Court of Appeal [1981] QB 403, p 424, that:

> 'The relevant time, for the purpose of considering whether there was a necessity, or an emergency … is … the time when the existence of the supposed emergency became apparent. The emergency would be the arrival, or expected arrival, of salved cargo at Manila, with no arrangements for its off loading or for its preservation in proper storage having been made or put in hand. There never was, so far as one can ascertain from the evidential matter here, such an emergency.'

In addition to the factual difficulty in treating the case as one of agency of necessity, there are legal difficulties in the way of the salvor. For an agency of necessity to arise, the action taken must be necessary for the protection of the interests of the alleged principal, not of the agent; the alleged agent must have acted *bona fide* in the interests of the alleged principal: *Bowstead on Agency*, 14th edn, 1976, p 668: *Prager v Blatspiel, Stamp and Heacock Ltd* [1924] 1 KB 566, pp 571, 572, 573. The Court of Appeal [1981] QB 403, p 425, held that the salvor's purpose in storing the salved cargo was to maintain his lien on it. This was assuredly at least in part the salvor's purpose. The law does not seem to have determined in this context what ensues where interests are manifold or motives mixed: it may well be that the court will look to the interest mainly served or to the dominant motive. In view of the opinion I have formed on the rights arising by implication from the Lloyd's Open Form and from the common law bailment, it is unnecessary to come to any conclusion on these issues …[133]

Although the general principle of what is required for agency of necessity to arise is clear, in practice, even if there may be a possibility for the master to communicate with the cargo interests before signing a salvage contract, he may not do so because of pressures to respond quickly to protect the interests of his ship and property on board. He may not think of it, or he may have not been so advised, that he has to obtain the cargo-owners' approval. The problem of the master's authority to bind the cargo interests to a salvage contract came to a head a few years later in

The Choko Star[134]

The C, on charter from ports in the Argentine to Italy, grounded in the river Parana and was stranded. At the time, she was loaded with cargo consisting of soya beans and sunseeds in bulk. As the master could not refloat the vessel

---

133 [1982] AC 939 (HL), pp 965–66.
134 [1990] 1 Lloyd's Rep 516.

without assistance, he entered into a salvage agreement in the LOF 1980, whereupon the vessel was successfully refloated and the salvors claimed salvage remuneration. The shipowner settled their part of the remuneration, but the cargo-owners contended that the master had no authority to engage salvors on their behalf. After arbitration, they paid the amount due, though under protest. They commenced proceedings against the salvors claiming restitution of the monies on the ground that the salvage contract was not done in their own best interests and that it was also unreasonable because the salvors employed were European instead of local ones, who would have been better equipped, and would have had more experience of that river. The issue was the master's authority to bind them to the salvage contract.

The question was whether the master would have authority to bind the cargo-owners by contract in circumstances where it was reasonably practicable to communicate with cargo-owners and obtain their instructions before signing the contract on their behalf. (The master here had not so communicated with the cargo interests in this case.) Would the law imply a term in the contract of carriage binding the cargo-owners even though the circumstances that existed did not give rise to an agency of necessity?

The learned trial judge held that when cargo was loaded on a ship, the cargo-owners must recognise that circumstances may exist in which the ship or cargo would require salvage services. Therefore, if the master had implied authority to enter into salvage agreements on behalf of the shipowner, he must also have implied authority to enter into the same reasonable contract on behalf of the cargo-owner. The master's implied authority arose out of the contract of carriage and was not given by necessity. It was being necessarily implied. On appeal by the cargo-owners, the Court of Appeal was not convinced that it was necessary to imply such a term in order to give the contract of carriage business efficacy.[135] Slade LJ stated, thus:

> Until an emergency arises, such as to give rise to an agency of necessity, there is no question of the shipowner or master being an agent for the cargo-owners. Accordingly, it is not possible to spell out authority for either of them to bind the cargo-owners to a salvage contract, as merely incidental to his pre-existing general authority as an agent ...

> Merely because the authority conferred by shipowners on their agent, the master, is deemed to extend to engaging salvors on reasonable terms on behalf of the shipowners, it does not follow that the master has the like implied authority to bind cargo-owners to salvage contracts, in the absence of circumstances giving rise to an agency of necessity.[136]

Regardless of the correctness of statement of principle of the incident of agency in those circumstances, this decision caused confusion in practice, particularly because of the invidious situation the master of a ship finds

---

135 In the sense laid down by the House of Lords in *Liverpool v Irwin* [1977] AC 239.
136 [1990] 1 Lloyd's Rep 516, pp 525–26.

himself in when there is an emergency whereupon quick decisions have to be made to save his ship and cargo on board. Unnecessary haggling over reaching an agreement has caused in practice more problems in saving a ship and its cargo from danger.

However, with the speed of modern means of communication nowadays, it has been accepted that it would be possible to obtain such authority from the cargo-owners, if they are easily identifiable and accessible, as opposed to a situation where there is general cargo on board belonging to various widely spread cargo-owners. Nevertheless, the obligation upon the master to consult the cargo owners before entering into a salvage agreement introduces practical problems in situations when immediate response would be highly desirable.[137] Obstinate cargo-owners can cause more harm by not granting their authority and injustice to salvors, who may not get remunerated despite their contribution to save the cargo as was shown in the following case:

The M Vatan[138]

On 5 July 1985, *The M Vatan* was almost fully laden with crude oil, the property of the National Iranian Oil Company, the charterers and cargo-owners. At the time, she was engaged on a shuttle service between Kharg Island and Sirri Island when she was struck by a missile which caused a great fire. The explosion caused a large hole in the side of the ship, crude oil flowed from the vessel and the fire grew in intensity. The salvors offered there services and were engaged under the LOF agreement under which the master had added a note to the effect that the cargo-owners did not authorise the master to give instructions regarding cargo salvage. The salvors salved the ship and necessarily most of her cargo. The cargo-owners were aware of the salvors' rights to remuneration for the services they had rendered. In accordance with custom, the matter was referred to arbitration for fixing of the salvage award, but by reason of the endorsement, which was a departure from the standard terms of Lloyd's salvage agreement, the remuneration for salving the cargo was not referred to the original arbitrator. It is well established law that the owners of the ship are generally not liable to pay for the salving of her cargo; the owners of the cargo are not liable to pay any part of the ship's proportion of the salvage reward. Each property owner is liable to pay his due proportion to the total salvage reward depending on the value of his property. This principle is called the *pro rata* rule. The original arbitrator considered the merits of the services as a whole and decided the total amount due to the salvors. However, in assessing how much the shipowners were to pay the salvors, he added an additional sum which was actually a part of the liability of the cargo-owners. The appeal arbitrator held that the original

---

137 Munday, R, 'The Choko Star' [1991] LMCLQ 1.
138 [1990] 1 Lloyd's Rep 336.

arbitrator had erred in principle in departing from the long established *pro rata* rule, and there was no justification for such a departure in this case. The question in the Admiralty Court was whether the fact that the salvors had not recovered a reward from the owners of the cargo could be a good reason for ordering the owners to pay more than their *pro rata* share of the proper reward. Counsel for the salvors submitted that since the circumstances of this case were abnormal, it was justified for the arbitrator to hold that this case falls outside the normal rule as to contribution. Sheen J held in his judgment:

> I know of no principle of equity which entitles a court to order the owners of one part of the salved property to pay more than its liability calculated *pro rata*, merely because the salvors appear to be having difficulty in recovering a salvage reward from the owners of the other salved property.[139]

The judge was very critical of the cargo-owners, the National State Oil company of Iran for their inequitable conduct and hoped that they would follow what was recognised by all maritime nations to be just and fair, otherwise no salvors would come to their assistance in the future.

8.2 Master's authority under the Convention

The practical problems arising from these decisions led to a recognition that the question of the master's authority to bind the cargo interests to a salvage contract ought to be solved by an international Convention. Article 6(2) of the 1989 Convention has put an end to these problems and clearly provides that:

> The master shall have the authority to conclude contracts for salvage operations on behalf of the owners of the vessel. The master or the owner of the vessel shall have authority to conclude such contracts on behalf of the owner of the property on board the vessel.

Before the Convention had the force of law, this provision had been inserted in the LOF 1990, cl 14, but it had only contractual force and there were still questions as to whether the consent of the cargo owners was necessary to be obtained expressly. Since 1 January 1995, however, when the provisions of the MS(SP)A 1994 came into force giving effect to the Salvage Convention 1989, the authority of the master was clothed with statutory force insofar as English law was concerned. The subsequent LOF of 1995 incorporated Arts 1, 6, 8, 13 and 14 of the Convention on the back for information. To avoid any doubt, cl 16 of LOF 1995 restated the master's authority to bind the respective owners of the properties to be salved to the agreement which he signs on their behalf.

It can be inferred from the wording of Art 6(2) of the Convention, 'the master shall have the authority', that it is obligatory. It does not allow the

---

139 [1990] 1 Lloyd's Rep 336, p 344.

parties to provide otherwise in the contract, as the previous para 6(1) does.[140] The policy reason behind it is to prevent delays in signing the contract for the interests of the salved property.

However, problems may still arise with regard to master's authority in particular circumstances[141] when the law of a country which has not ratified, or enacted, the Convention applies to the contract. A recent decision, *The Pa Mar*,[142] in which the events occurred before the Convention had the force of law, provides a good example of the considerations that should be borne in mind by both a shipowner and a salvor when the master signs a salvage agreement to bind the cargo interests.

On 9 June 1993 the tug *Leopard* took the motor vessel *Pa Mar* – whose generators had failed – in tow in the Red Sea. She did so pursuant to the terms of LOF 90, which had been agreed by her master. That contract was subsequently varied by the managers of *Pa Mar* ('Kappa') on behalf of her owners. The variation concerned the place of delivery of the properties after salvage. The contractors under the LOF, both in its original form and as varied, were Tsavliris Salvage International Ltd ('Tsavliris'). It was common ground that both the master and Kappa purported to contract on behalf of the owners of *Pa Mar*, her cargo, freight, bunkers, stores and other property on board her. However, at a comparatively early stage, before the vessel left Singapore and while security was being negotiated, the owners of the cargo took the point that neither the master nor Kappa (or, indeed, the shipowners) had any authority to contract on their behalf. The principal question for decision in these actions was whether the owners of cargo were bound by the LOF apparently entered into on their behalf, either in its original form or as varied.

It was held by Clarke J:

> The evidence showed that no towage assistance was available on commercial terms so that unless the vessel and her cargo were to be left indefinitely immobilised prudence dictated the engagement of the tug on LOF; it was true that the vessel was at anchor in the Red Sea and that her anchor was not dragging, but she could not fairly be said to be in a place of safety; she was exposed to both the winds and the swell and her exposed position together with the fact that she was indefinitely immobilised was sufficient to satisfy the requirement that it was necessary to take salvage assistance; Tsavliris had shown that it was necessary for the master to take salvage assistance.
>
> In entering into the original contract, that is, without a Dubai/Colombo option, the master and indeed Kappa were acting reasonably; the master was acting both *bona fide* and reasonably in the interests of both ship and cargo when he

---

140 Cf Gaskell, N, 'LOF 1990' [1991] LMCLQ 104.
141 See *op cit*, Brice, fn 1, p 326.
142 [1999] 1 Lloyd's Rep 338.

entered into the unamended LOF on 9 June; and the cargo-owners were bound by the contract in that form.

However, as to the variation of the agreement with regard to final destination the judge held that:

> No reasonable shipowner would have committed the owners of cargo to a LOF which involved a long tow on salvage terms without carrying out further investigations; Tsavliris had failed to discharge the burden of proving on the balance of probabilities that Kappa acted *bona fide* and reasonably in the interests of cargo in agreeing to a variation of the LOF by adding the Dubai/Colombo option.

What was needed was that the owners should have asked both the ship's Classification Society and the Salvage Association surveyor to investigate the position at the first stop, Aden. It would be prudent, therefore, if owners and salvors did bear this in mind in future similar cases.

LOF 2000 expressly provides not only that English law shall apply to the contract, but it also defines the scope of the master's authority, namely, cl K provides:

> The master or other person signing this agreement on behalf of the property identified in the contract enters into this agreement as agent for the respective owners thereof and binds each (but not the one for the other or himself personally) to the due performance thereof.

9 DUTIES AND CONDUCT OF SALVORS

Under ordinary maritime law of salvage, there is no obligation on the salvor to complete salvage. He can discontinue the salvage services without incurring any liability. Under Lloyd's standard forms and the Convention, there are certain obligations upon the salvor which are examined next:

9.1 Best endeavours

All LOFs, 1980, 1990, 1995 by cl 1(a) and LOF 2000 by cl A, provide that the contractor (salvor) shall use his best endeavours to salve the property and take it either to a place agreed or to a place of safety. In addition, LOF 1990, 1995, cl 1(a)(ii), and 2000, cl B, provide that while performing salvage operations the contractor shall also use his best endeavours to prevent or minimise damage to the environment.

There is no absolute obligation of success but that the contractor will do his best, not second best.[143] There has been no definition of 'best endeavours'

---

143 *Op cit*, Brice, fn 1, p 528.

in salvage cases.[144] The phrase has been defined in a few cases concerned with obtaining a licence for sale of goods. It has been held that, whatever phrase is used, the seller must show that he has done his best,[145] and that the practice of other exporters will be taken into account in determining whether the seller exercised due diligence in obtaining an export licence.[146] By analogy, it would seem that in salvage cases it could equally be said that to determine whether a salvor exercised his best endeavours the standard of reasonable diligence should apply. The standard of reasonableness is that of a prudent salvor acting properly in the interests of the salved property, and his duty is what can reasonably be done in the circumstances.[147] Whether there is an element of subjectivity, in other words what the salvor believes, in his capacity, to be reasonable in the circumstances, is not clear. It is submitted that, if the practice of other salvors possessing the same expertise possessed by the salvor in question is taken into account, the standard is an objective one. Support that there should be an objective standard may be gained from cl G of LOF 2000, which grants a right to both the salvor and the owner of the vessel to terminate the salvage when there is no longer a reasonable prospect of useful result. Such right was given only to the owner of the vessel in the 1990 and 1995 LOFs (see para 10.2, below).

On proof that best endeavours were not used, there would be a breach of contract.

9.2 Due care

Under the Convention, Art 8(1)(a), (b), it is provided:

1   The salvor shall owe a duty to the owner of the vessel or other property in danger:

(a) to carry out the salvage operations with due care;

(b) in performing the duty specified in sub-paragraph (a) to exercise due care to prevent or minimise damage to the environment.

Not only does the salvor owe a duty to the owners of the property in danger to carry out the salvage operations with due care, but also to exercise due care to prevent or minimise damage to the environment. The salvor also has a duty

---

144 In the glossary to *Current Statutes*, MSA 1995, Chapter 21, para 21-390, it is said that the difference between 'best endeavours' and 'due care' may be that a higher standard is required by the former phrase and that the salvor under LOF 1995 may not be excused if he decides for commercial reasons, in an uneconomic salvage, that it may not be worthwhile continuing.

145 *Oversea Buyers Ltd v Granadex SA* [1980] 2 Lloyd's Rep 608, *per* Mustill J (as he then was).

146 *Malik Co v Central European Trading Agency Ltd* [1974] 2 Lloyd's Rep 279, *per* Kerr J, applying the principle in *Anglo Russian Merchant Traders Ltd v Batt (John) & Co Ltd* [1917] 2 KB 679.

147 *Terrell v Mabie Todd & Co* [1952] 2 TLR 574.

under Art 8(c), (d) – when circumstances reasonably require – to seek assistance from other salvors, and to accept intervention of other salvors, when requested to do so by the owner or master of the vessel or the property in danger.

The reason why the term 'due care' has been used in the Convention may be that it is easily understood internationally.[148] The standard to be applied to due care is that of reasonableness taking into account the standards applied by the salvage industry.

Article 8 has been incorporated into LOF 1990 by reference (see cl 2) while it has been incorporated into LOF 1995 fully as information. If there is a different standard to be applied to 'best endeavours' and to 'due care', there is a potential conflict in the LOF 1990 and LOF 1995 which incorporate Art 8.[149] The 2000 LOF does not expressly include what are the duties of the contractor, while it expressly includes the duties of the property owner. However, the fact that cl J provides expressly that the contract shall be governed by English law, the duties of the salvor will be found in Art 8 of the Convention, as incorporated into English law.

The consequences of the salvor's misconduct are laid down in Art 18: he will be deprived of the whole or part of the payment due under the Convention to the extent that the salvage operations have become necessary or more difficult because of fault or neglect on his part, or if the salvor has been guilty of fraud or other dishonest conduct.

Wilful or criminal misconduct will forfeit the right to claim award.

9.3 Negligent misconduct

The English courts have for many years recognised that negligence of salvors who respond to an emergency of a ship in distress at risk to themselves should be judged leniently. It was considered that deduction from the award of an assessed sum of the damage done would be sufficient,[150] or in more serious cases of negligence the deduction would be in proportion to the

---

148 However, in Art 21 'best endeavours' is used in relation to the obligation of the owner of the vessel to ensure that security is provided to the salvors by the cargo interests before the cargo is discharged. This raises the question why this term was incorporated in the Convention if consistency was intended, unless it was due to an oversight.

149 See, also, *op cit*, Gaskell, fn 140, pp 111–14: since LOF 1990 has incorporated Art 8, there may be a potential contradiction as to which shall apply, unless the standard for both terms is a requirement of reasonableness judged objectively.

150 *The Dwina* [1892] P 58; *The Queenforth v Royal Fifth* (1923) 17 LlL Rep 204.

misconduct,[151] or the misconduct could forfeit the award.[152] The courts have been reluctant to award damages against salvors even in cases in which the misconduct may have led to the loss of the ship.[153] Mistake or misconduct, other than criminal, which had diminished the salved value used to be taken into account in the amount of the award. But, wilful or criminal misconduct would work an entire forfeiture of the award.[154] The question whether or not a salvor would be liable in damages to the owner of the property arose in 1874 in the *CS Butler*[155] case, where *The Butler* responded to a distress signal sent by the Baltic and agreed to tow her upon a fixed sum. During the services, *The Butler* came into collision with *The Baltic* three times causing much damage to her, but eventually *The Butler* brought her to a place of safety. The concept of *crassa negligentia* was adopted by Sir Phillimore who stated:

> … gross want of proper navigation, which certainly would, in my judgment, render her liable for damage that she, thus, caused, notwithstanding that she was acting as salvor.

The Baltic recovered damages assessed in the usual way and *The Butler* was awarded the amount agreed upon as salvage remuneration.

In the 20th century, the courts have been more robust in considering awarding damages to the owner of the salved property for salvors's negligence. In *The Delphinula*,[156] the Court of Appeal (reversing first instance decision) held that if the salvor is guilty of misconduct not only may a reduction in value of the salved property caused by his negligence be taken into account in assessing the award, but also a counterclaim or cross-claim, or an independent action for damages, will lie. In *The Alenquer*,[157] no salvage award was made but the damage claim had to be paid in full although the judge adhered to the general principle of policy by saying:

> It seems to me that I have to pay regard to the general principles of policy in relation to salvage which have been laid down over the years by this court.

---

151 *The Cape Packet* (1848) 3 W Rob 470; *The Perla* (1857) Swab 230; *The Magdalen* (1861) 31 LJ (Adm) 22, the reduction of the award to one salvor of the two who was negligent was said to be not as a punishment but was by way of indemnifying the owner.

152 See *The Neptune* (1842) 1 W Rob 297; *The Kendal* (1948) 81 LlL Rep 217.

153 *The Yan-Yean* (1883) 8 PD 147, due to salvor's negligence the ship sank, but was later raised by her owners. No award of salvage was made nor of damages. As the loss arising from the misconduct of the salvors was probably equal to that from which the Y was first rescued, no salvage reward was due. If the Y had been ultimately saved such misconduct would have worked a partial forfeiture of the reward only. It was laid down by the Privy Council in the case of *The Duke of Manchester* (1847) 6 Moo PC 91, that if by the negligence of the salvors a ship is led into peril as great as that from which she has been rescued all claim to salvage is forfeited.

154 *The Atlas* (1862) Lush 518.

155 (1874) LR 4 A&E 178, p 183.

156 *Anglo-Saxon Petroleum Co Ltd v The Admiralty (The Delphinula)* (1947) 80 LlL Rep 459.

157 [1955] 1 Lloyd's Rep 101, p 112.

Those general principles of policy require that this court, in judging the conduct of salvors, should err, if anything, on the side of leniency towards salvors insofar as their behaviour is criticised ... quite contrary to the public interest, if the result of the decisions of this court were such as to discourage salvors from taking risks and showing enterprise when rendering services at sea. The matter is summed up in a passage in Kennedy LJ's book on the *Law of Civil Salvage* (3rd edn), to which I was referred in the course of the argument. There, at p 162, the learned author says:

> 'In considering whether a salvor has shown such a want of reasonable skill and knowledge as ought materially to affect the court's award, or is guilty only of an error of judgment, the court will incline to the lenient view, and will take into favourable consideration any special circumstances which tend to exonerate the salvor from blame, such as, for example, a request for help, the suddenness of the emergency, or the absence of more efficient means of succour.'

That appears to me to be the correct approach to the matter, and I gladly adopt that paragraph as part of my judgment.

In 1971, the House of Lords affirmed that a claim in damages will lie against the salvors for their negligence by way of a counterclaim, independently of merely taking salvors' negligence into account in the assessment of the salvage award.

The Tojo Maru[158]

Subsequent to a collision with an Italian ship in the Persian Gulf, *The Tojo Maru* entered into a salvage agreement under the standard LOF, 'no cure no pay' basis. In order to cover the aperture left by the collision, a large plate had to be bolted to the hull. This was done by firing bolts from a cox bolt gun, but the adjoining tank had to be made gas free first for safety reasons. The respondents' (salvors) chief diver however, contrary to the orders he had received, fired a bolt through the shell plating of the vessel. The result was an explosion which caused extensive damage and caused a fire on the vessel. Eventually, after obtaining additional help to put out the fire and make the vessel seaworthy, she was towed to Singapore and then Kobe where she was repaired. Before the arbitrator, who had jurisdiction to fix the award of salvage, the owners counterclaimed damages suffered due to salvor's negligence. They argued that the salvors had by the contract undertaken to 'use their best endeavours' to salve the vessel, but in breach of that contract, they had negligently caused damage to the vessel, and were therefore liable in damages for the loss caused to the owners by their negligence.

The salvors argued that the rules of maritime law were that a successful salvor could not be liable in damages to the owner for the result of any

---

158 [1972] AC 242, or [1971] 1 Lloyd's Rep 341 (HL).

negligence on his part, but such negligence would only allow the court to reduce or forfeit the salvage award and, thus, did not give rise to a claim for damages. The reason, they said, was that the salvage services resulted in an overall benefit to the owner. That is, that the salvor has done more good than harm and no counterclaim in respect of the harm is possible.

The arbitrator found, on the facts, that the salvors were negligent and the owners were entitled to recover damages. He took the net salved value after deduction of the damage suffered by the owners and on the basis of that figure he calculated the salvage award. Then he deducted the amount of the award from the damage amount (which was higher) leaving a balance to be paid by the salvors to the owners. But, then he applied, on this balance, limitation of liability based on the tonnage of the salvor's tug, diminishing the amount of damages due from £206,767 to £10,725.

He stated the case as a special case for the court to determine the issues of whether the owners were entitled to a counterclaim and whether the salvors could limit their liability. Willmer LJ sitting as a judge agreed with the arbitrator with regard to the counterclaim for damages, but disagreed with him on the limitation. (Briefly, under the then prevailing limitation of liability statute, s 503 of the MSA 1894, he did not consider that the criteria of this section were met because the diver who caused the damage was not acting 'in the management of the ship'.)[159]

On appeal to the Court of Appeal,[160] the then Master of the Rolls, Lord Denning, took pains to explain – by analysing all previous relevant authorities – that the issue whether the owners were entitled to full damages could only be determined by the maritime law of the world which the English Admiralty Court had done so much to form and not strictly by the common law of England. The principle established in the authorities, where there was more good than harm done by the salvors,[161] shows, he said, that:

> In assessing the amount of salvage remuneration, the conduct of the salvor is a material consideration. He is rewarded highly for great service, poorly for bad service. If he has behaved in a violent or overbearing manner, it may diminish the amount of his reward, even though he has done no damage (*The Marie* (1882) 7 PD 203). So also if he has been negligent and, by so doing, damaged the vessel he is seeking to save, it may diminish the amount of the reward,

---

159 Analysis of this principle together with the present law on limitation is examined in Chapter 16. Suffice to mention that under the present law the salvors would be able to limit in the circumstances that arose in this case.

160 [1969] 2 Lloyd's Rep 193 (CA).

161 *The Cape Packer* (1848) 3 W Rob 122; *The Perla* (1857) Swab 230; *The Atlas* (1862) Lush 518; *The Yan-Yean* (1883) 8 PD 147; *The Dwina* [1892] P 58; *The Queenforth v Royal Fifth* (1923) 17 LlL Rep 204 (these cases established that the most grave misconduct, gross negligence or wilful, would only forfeit the award, while other negligence would just diminish it).

according to how much he is to blame; but not necessarily to the full extent of the damage done.[162]

Save for three authorities[163] which were distinguished by Lord Denning because there was more harm than good done by the salvors, he further said:

> The long line of cases represents the maritime law of England and of the world on this subject. They apply whenever the salvor has done much good in saving a vessel in distress, but, in the course of the salvage operation, has damaged her somewhat by his negligence. The damage is taken into account in two ways: first, the salvage award is calculated on the salved value and is, therefore, less on account of the damage; second, it may be further reduced by deducting some part of the damage, or even the whole of it, from the salvage reward. But, save to this extent, the salvor is not liable for the damage done. In particular, he is not liable to a counterclaim for damages.[164]

Lord Denning MR distinguished *The Delphinula* on the basis that the comments made there by the Court of Appeal were *obiter dicta* and, in any event, he disagreed with that decision in which English common law was applied instead of English maritime law, which was quite different.

To the lucid judgment of Lord Denning, Salmon LJ added most persuasively why *The Delphinula* was different from the present case. First, it was not a claim for salvage but for damages, as the vessel – having stranded in port at the time – blew up due to the negligence of the superintendent of salvage operations at the port. The case was for damages because the salvors conferred no benefit. He did not read the judgment of Scott LJ in that case as meaning that, if at the end of the day the ship had been saved, the owners might successfully have claimed a sum due to salvor's negligence. He drew a dichotomy of two categories derived from previous authorities, although none was binding on the Court of Appeal. The first category was cases in which the ship had been in dire danger of becoming a total loss and was saved from that danger, but due to salvor's negligence some damage was done (the 'dire danger' cases). In all such cases, negligence by the salvors has been taken into account in assessing the salvage reward, the effect of which has been a reduction in the amount of the reward to the extent of the negligence. The second category was where the total loss danger did not exist and in which, by reason of negligence by the salvor, no benefit was conferred (the 'non-dire danger' cases). In this second category, the owners, at the end of the day, were worse off than they would have been, but for the salvors' negligence. In such circumstances, an award in damages would not be inconsistent with the principle that:

---

162 [1969] 2 Lloyd's Rep 193 (CA), *per* Lord Denning MR, p 199.

163 *The Thetis* (1869) LR 2 A&E 365; *The Butler* (1874) LR 4 A&E 178; *The Alenquer* [1955] 1 Lloyd's Rep 101.

164 [1969] 2 Lloyd's Rep 193 (CA), p 200.

On grounds of public policy it is of the greatest importance for the safety of shipping that salvors should come to the assistance of vessels in distress and especially that professional salvors should be encouraged to invest capital and incur expenses in maintaining salvage tugs and services to enable them to come to the assistance of ships in distress.[165]

The Court of Appeal, unlike the House of Lords (see below), dealt also with the question as to when limitation should be applied, that is, before or after a set-off. The salvors were not entitled on the facts of the case to limit under s 503 of the MSA 1894, but, if they were, then there would be no set-off before limitation was applied. If, on the other hand, they were not entitled to limit, the salvage reward should first be calculated as if no damage had been done by their negligence; then the counterclaim should be calculated on the cost of repairs, delay and loss of profit; then a balance should be struck.[166]

The House of Lords reversed the decision of the Court of Appeal, which appealed to salvage specialists as being fair and reasonable in the context of salvage at sea, and has left issues unresolved (see later). Lord Reid compared volunteers who save land property from danger with professional salvors contrasting the effect of their respective negligence.

Lord Reid said:

The maritime law of England has a long history. It differed in many respects from the common law; statutory amendment of the common law has removed some of these differences but by no means all. So, if examination of the authorities led me to the conclusion that any such rule or principle as that for which the salvors contend has been established, I would have no hesitation in giving effect to it. But after hearing full argument I have come to the clear conclusion that no such rule exists.

It is said that public policy requires and always has required that every proper encouragement should be given to salvors. With that I agree. In older times, it was highly desirable to encourage the master and crew of any vessel which encountered another in distress to do their utmost to save that other vessel. And, today, it is equally desirable to encourage professional salvors to maintain salvage vessels in a wide variety of situations. Just as courts are very slow to hold that errors of judgment in emergencies amount to negligence, so too courts are slow to impute negligence to salvors. But, here the arbitrator has found against them on that matter and the respondents do not seek to challenge his finding.

It is said that it will be most discouraging to salvors if they have to contemplate the possibility of heavy awards of damages against them by reason of their vicarious liability for their employees, and that it is not easy for them to cover their liability by insurance. But the rule for which the respondents contend would not prevent such awards. The rule is only said to apply where the

---

165 [1969] 2 Lloyd's Rep 193 (CA), p 205.
166 *The Tojo Maru* [1969] 2 Lloyd's Rep 193 (CA), pp 203, 207.

salvage has been successful. It is not disputed that if, by reason of the negligence of the salvors' employees, a ship which they are trying to salve is lost, then the salvor can be sued for that negligence and he must pay damages. To serve the public interest the encouragement of salvors must operate on their minds before they begin salvage operations. But, at that stage, the salvor cannot know whether, if negligence of his employees occurs in the course of salvage operations, it will merely cause damage, or will cause total loss of the vessel. I could understand a rule that a salvor can never be liable for the damage caused by negligence in trying to salve a vessel. And there may be a very good case for extending the limitation provisions with which I shall deal later so as to prevent large awards against salvors. But the rule for which the respondents contend would not be a satisfactory solution of the problem viewed as a whole.

My noble and learned friends have dealt with the authorities in detail and I do not think it would be useful for me to go over the same grounds again. On this matter, I am in full agreement with them.

But, there is a second argument which was accepted by the Court of Appeal. It was said that the salvors' operations should be considered as a whole. We should consider the position when the salvors began their operations. If the actual salved value, notwithstanding the damage done by the salvors' negligence, exceeds the value which the vessel had in its perilous and damaged condition when the salvors began their operations, then the salvors have done more good than harm to the owners and they ought not to have to pay damages. It may be proper to forfeit any award of salvage but it would be unjust to go farther.

There is little or no authority for such a principle. But this case presents some novel features, and I would not reject this approach merely because it is new. There would be much to be said for it in certain circumstances. This is not only a question of maritime law. Suppose a house is on fire. It contains a valuable collection of, say, china. There is little or no hope of saving the collection but a passer-by, with or without the consent of the owner, goes in and brings most of the collection to safety. But owing to some gross negligence on his part some of the china is smashed. On land, a person who interferes to save property is not in law entitled to any reward. But it would be most unjust in my view if, although he benefited the owner by saving the bulk of the property, he were held liable for his negligence in destroying the rest. Of course, in such a case the court would be very slow to find that the rescuer was guilty of negligence, but the circumstances might be such that such a finding could not be avoided. Similarly, if a passing ship lends assistance to a vessel in dire distress, when without such assistance the vessel would almost certainly be lost, and the salvor succeeds in saving the vessel but by gross negligence causes much unnecessary damage to it, it might be quite proper to forfeit any salvage award, but I would think it most unjust that the salvor should have to pay damages. Taking the salvor's operations as a whole he would have done much more good to the owner than harm. Could it be right that the owner need not even say thank you for the good, but should recover damages because the ship which, without the salvor's efforts he would never have seen again, is of less value when returned to him than it would have been if the salvor had not caused damage by negligence?

But any such exception from the general rule would have to be confined within reasonable limits. Take the volunteer who saves property from the burning house. The case would look very different if others on the spot would almost certainly have saved all the property if the volunteer had not officiously interfered. Or suppose that there is no immediate emergency. The owner of a house is advised that it is likely to collapse soon and he engages professional removal contractors to remove the contents. If they do damage to the furniture by their negligence they could not possibly be allowed to plead that if nothing had been done the furniture would have been destroyed when the house fell a week later.

Even if such a principle were accepted I do not think it could be applied in this case. This was not a case of a sudden emergency. There is nothing to suggest that *The Tojo Maru* would have become a total loss if the respondents' tug had not offered her services. The respondents offered their services as professional salvors, time was taken to arrange a contract, then they made elaborate preparations to do the necessary repair work before the vessel could be towed away and it was only several weeks later in the course of that repair work that the negligence of the diver caused this damage. It would require a very strong case to convince me that in such circumstances it is unjust to apply the ordinary law.[167]

While Lord Reid felt uncomfortable in accepting the proposed solution of Salmon LJ as an exception to the general rule of common law negligence, he was minded to consider the application of the 'more good than harm' principle in very exceptional cases, where there is emergency and assistance is given to a ship in distress by a passing vessel when there is no hope that the property would be saved without assistance. Although he was not convinced that there was any support in previous authority for the theory advanced by Salmon LJ, he was open-minded not to reject this approach because it was new. The case before him, however, was not at all within such a category of 'dire danger'. Lord Diplock was more robust in his conviction that the general rule of negligence applicable at common law should apply here as well. He found support for his view on the following basis.

Comparing salvage contracts with contracts for work and labour, **Lord Diplock** said:

The first distinctive feature is that the person rendering the salvage services is not entitled to any remuneration unless he saves the property in whole or in part. This is what is meant by 'success' in cases about salvage ... In my view there is nothing in it which ought in principle to displace the general law as to the liability of a party to a contract for work and labour for negligence in the performance of it.[168]

---

167 [1972] AC 242 (HL), p 267–69.
168 *Ibid*, p 293.

He then phrased the ordinary rule of English law to be, thus:

> The special characteristics of salvage remuneration payable for salvage services whether rendered under Lloyd's standard form of salvage agreement with professional salvage contractors, or volunteered by a passing vessel and accepted without any express contract, would not appear in themselves sufficient to oust the ordinary rule of English law that a person who undertakes for reward to do work and labour upon the property of another owes to the owner of the property a duty to exercise that care which the circumstances demand and, where he holds himself out as carrying on the business or profession of undertaking services of that kind, to use such skill in the performance of them as a person carrying on such a business may reasonably be expected to possess.[169]

Lord Diplock thought that there was no justification for treating salvage services as excluded from the general principles of English law of liability for negligence[170] as it has developed in the twentieth century. He further said:

> It is not in this but in an entirely different situation that the converse of the concept of 'more harm than good' has previously been applied in salvage law. That is: where one salvor has performed salvage services to a vessel in distress but has not completed her rescue and she has been ultimately brought to a place of safety by a different salvor. The right of the first salvor to share in the salvage reward depends upon his showing that he has contributed to the saving of the vessel. This has often turned upon whether, when his own services ended, he had left the vessel in less peril than that in which he found it, that is, whether his services had done 'more good than harm' … I have endeavoured to show that the conclusions sought to be drawn from judgments given in the mid-19th century cases, upon which this proposition is founded, are based upon a misunderstanding of the historical use of the expression 'negligence', upon a failure to take into account of the supposed limitations upon the jurisdiction of the Court of Admiralty and upon a misapprehension of the kind of situation in which it was relevant to inquire whether a salvor had done more good than harm.[171]

The House of Lords rejected the approach of the Court Appeal on the basis of 'more harm than good' principle, in other words that damages would be recoverable from the salvors only if the measure of the harm done by the salvors exceeded the measure of the good. Such a principle was not to be found in any of the previous authorities.[172]

---

169 [1972] AC 242 (CA), p 293.

170 The general principle of negligence had been applied in the *Anglo Saxon Petroleum Co v Lords Commissioners of the Admiralty (The Delphinula)* [1947] KB 794 (CA), or (1947) 80 LlL Rep 459, which was criticised by the Court of Appeal as being inappropriate to salvage cases.

171 *The Tojo Maru* [1971] 1 Lloyd's Rep 341 (HL), p 367.

172 This principle was deduced by the Court of Appeal from old decisions, which reflected justice and fairness in the cases of salvage in which well established principles of maritime law had been applied for a long time. It was accepted that these authorities were not binding upon the Court of Appeal as none had reached the House of Lords but, nevertheless, they had not been wrongly decided.

Therefore, reversing the Court of Appeal decision, it was held permissible to entertain the owners' counterclaim for damages, which could be set off against the award. It was stressed, however, that damages would be allowed only by a counterclaim to a claim for an award with respect to successful salvage services. If there was no success, there would be no award, and no separate claim for damages. Thus, the arbitrator's decision was restored except with regard to the method of assessment of the salvage award. Lord Diplock objected to the arbitrator's assessment of the salvage award on the basis of her damaged state, the effect of which would be to account for the salvor's negligence twice, and he remitted the award to the arbitrator to make the adjustment.

Their Lordships held that the owners should be put in the same position they would have been in had there been no negligence. In particular, had the salvage operation been conducted without negligence the owners would not have had to spend money for repairs and would not have suffered loss. On the other hand, they would have to pay salvage. The proper measure of damages was the difference between what would have been the value of the ship upon completion of the salvage if there had been no negligence (undamaged salved value) and her actual value at the place of termination in the state in which she was as a result of the negligence. With regard to salvage remuneration, it was held that it was to be assessed on the assumption that there had been no negligence (no deduction of costs for repairing the damage). Then, the figures arrived at would be set off against each other.[173] The result would seem to be that either a salvage award would be due to the salvor, or an award for damages would be due to the shipowner depending on which figure was the highest.

Article 8(1) of the 1989 Convention imposes a duty of care on salvors but it does not address the issue of damages. The Salvage Convention 1910 did not do either. Article 18 provides for the consequences of salvors' misconduct, in that the salvors may be deprived of the whole or part of the payment due under the Convention to the extent that the salvage operation has become necessary or more difficult because of fault or neglect on his part, or if the salvor has been guilty of fraud or other misconduct.

9.4 Unresolved issues

In the light of the decision in *The Tojo Maru* and the fact that the Convention does not deal with the issue of damages, there are some unresolved issues concerning salvors' negligence. Brice[174] has been critical of the decision and

---

173 [1971] 1 Lloyd's Rep 341, pp 355, 367, 368.
174 Paper given at a debate on salvage held by the London Shipping Law Centre on 19 June 1997

suggested that the formula of assessment of damages and of the award of salvage adopted by the House of Lords may not be appropriate in all cases and commented, as follows:

(a) In *The Tojo Maru* there was an isolated incident of negligence by the diver of the salvors causing damage to the ship during the salvage services, which were otherwise competently performed.

(b) He questioned the way salvage remuneration was proposed to be assessed, which might not be appropriate particularly in cases where the whole planning and execution of a salvage operation was negligent. In such cases, he commented, to assume a non-negligent salvage service in the assessment of the award would be to create a fictional state of affairs. One could not assume a successful service for the purpose of assessing the award when the ship was rendered of little value due to the salvor's negligence. Perhaps, he suggested, in those cases the 'no cure no pay' principle should be applied and the damages should be assessed on the actual damage done; a fictional state of affairs and an assumption that a successful service was rendered could not be contemplated.

(c) On the assumption that there were two salvors and the ship, although saved, was of little value due to the negligence of the one, for the purpose of arriving at an award for damages against the negligent salvor in accordance with the formula of *The Tojo Maru*, his salvage remuneration would have to be assessed on a notional ship value. The non-negligent salvor, however, would receive no reward as this would be the consequence of the negligence of the other. It would be absurd, he said, if the assessment of damages with regard to the negligent salvor were arrived at on the basis of the formula of *The Tojo Maru*. Presumably, he pondered, the non-negligent salvor would have a cause of action in tort against the negligent one.

In his book, Brice[175] proposes a solution and compares American with English law on the question of salvors' negligence. American salvage law is, in general, the same as English law and the Salvage Convention applies in both systems. There is, however, a significant difference in approach. It is interesting to note that American courts, Brice says, have developed the doctrine of a liability restricted to 'distinguishable and independent damage'. A distinguishable damage is other than that which the salved would have suffered, had the salvors efforts not been undertaken. In *The Tojo Maru*, for example, the damage was 'distinguishable', in that it was not the type which was inherent in the situation. He concluded that, perhaps, the English courts may consider to adopt the American approach of distinguishable and independent damage done by salvors, in cases where they assisted a ship in dire peril. Considering that the property would have been lost in any event, but for the salvors services, the proper approach would have been that the

---

175 *Op cit*, Brice, fn 1, pp 510–22.

salvor would be made liable for damage only if the damage was distinct and independent of the immediate peril, that is, it would not have occurred in the absence of assistance. The court, he proposes, should exercise greater leniency in cases where the salvors are not professionals and also in cases where the circumstances are very perilous for the would be rescuer. (This proposal is close to what Lord Reid was prepared to accept.) But, in the more run of the mill cases, he says, the degree of leniency would be less and the ordinary principles for recovery of damages in tort or breach of contract should apply.

It seems that this solution is similar to the two categories (the 'dire danger' and the 'non-dire danger' cases) distinguished by Salmon LJ in the Court of Appeal in *The Tojo Maru*. It varies the 'Salmon' solution only to the extent of the 'run of the mill cases', as Brice put it. Brice urges that there should be flexibility in application of the general rule of negligence at common law to salvage cases since salvage is a distinct area of the law and, historically, is not just only part of common law.

Whether limitation of liability by the salvor should apply before or after the set-off was left unanswered by the House of Lords. Thus, one may assume that the answer given by the Court of Appeal on this issue, albeit *obiter*, that limitation of liability must be applied first to the damages award before the set-off between the damages and the salvage awards, should be good law, but these *dicta* were not essential to the decision, since limitation was refused.

9.5 Negligence occurring before salvage services were rendered

This can occur when there is a collision between two ships and salvage services are rendered afterwards to the one ship, which has been put in danger by the fault of the other ship. It has already been seen that there is a statutory duty upon masters and crew of colliding ships to offer assistance to each other after the collision and that that duty is no bar to earning a salvage award.

A question in law has arisen when the salvage services are rendered to one of the colliding ships by a vessel, which is a sister ship of the other colliding ship. The argument advanced in such a case was, in the past, that the law should not permit a sister ship of a ship at fault to take the benefit of a salvage award. However, there is no principle of law that prevents a ship from obtaining a salvage award, merely because she belongs to the same owner[176] as the owner of the vessel that caused, or was partly responsible for, the damage giving rise to the necessity for the salvage services. So, it was held by the House of Lords in the following case.

---

176 Article 12(3) of the 1989 Convention expressly states that the provisions of the Convention shall apply notwithstanding that the salved vessel and the vessel undertaking the salvage operations belong to the same owner.

Beaverford v Kafiristan[177]

This was an appeal from a decision of the Court of Appeal[178] which had affirmed a decision of Bucknill J.

On 16 June 1935, the Canadian Pacific Railway Company's liner *Empress of Britain* was in collision in the Gulf of St Lawrence with the steamship *Kafiristan*. The latter was badly damaged, and *The Empress of Britain* stood by her until *SS Beaverford*, another ship belonging to the Canadian Pacific Railway Company, came up and took *The Kafiristan* in tow. *The Beaverford* towed for about 100 miles and then handed *The Kafiristan* over to tugs which took her to Sydney. A writ was issued by the owners, master and crew of *The Beaverford* claiming salvage remuneration, but it was subsequently agreed that the case should go to arbitration and that Lloyd's standard form of salvage agreement should be signed. When the arbitration was held, liability for the collision had not been settled, and the point was raised whether, in the event of *The Empress of Britain* being found wholly or partly to blame, her owners, as owners of *The Beaverford* would be entitled to salvage. The salvage arbitrator held against awarding a salvage award.

When the case reached the court, the collision liability had been settled on the basis that both vessels had been at fault. The trial judge, upholding the arbitrator's decision, held that *The Beaverford* was not entitled to a reward basing his decision on the principle that no man could profit by his own wrong, in that the negligence of the servants of *The Empress* prevented them from claiming any advantage from the salvage services, which the servants of the same owners rendered from the sister ship. The Court of Appeal upheld that decision. On appeal to the House of Lords, Lord Wright said:

> Where ... both colliding vessels are to blame, the fixing of the salvage remuneration would seem to be a necessary step in setting off the items of damage on the one side or the other so as to ascertain the final balance of account. It is true that the owners of the other colliding vessel are in law responsible for the damage caused by negligence of their servants including the amount of any salvage awarded to the salving vessel which they also own, but the equities are best worked out by making the salvage award without regard to the fact of common ownership, leaving the incidence of what is awarded to depend on the relative proportions of blame.[179]

> It is, I think, in accordance with the ideas of maritime law to treat in a case like this for purposes of salvage the vessels concerned as separate entities and to

---

177 [1938] AC 136 (HL); *The Glengaber* (1872) LR 3 A&E 534, approved; *Cargo ex Capella* (1867) LR 1 A&E 356, distinguished. *Dictum* of Lord Phillimore in *The Melanie* [1925] AC 246 (HL), p 262, that 'the duty cast by the MSAs upon one of the two colliding vessels to stand by and render assistance, does not prevent that vessel, if she renders assistance, from claiming salvage', approved.

178 Decision of the Court of Appeal [1937] P 63, reversed.

179 [1938] AC 136, p 148.

disregard at that stage the aspect of common ownership and the consequences of the rule of vicarious liability. Thus, the owner of the salving ship is dissociated from himself as owner of the wrongdoing ship.[180]

Lord Atkin added:

> As far as the agreement is concerned at this stage after the accident the question of fault seems to be irrelevant. Is it possible to imagine the master of the injured vessel saying to the master of the proposed salvor, I want you to agree to do your best to salve me? You may have to risk your own ship and cargo and to deviate from your voyage and delay your adventure; but it is understood that if either you or any vessel of your owners is in any degree responsible for any damage you will get nothing. The obvious result would be no agreement, no attempt at salvage, other than the ordinary assistance given from humane motives, or sense of statutory duties under the MSA.[181]

The 1989 Convention expressly states in Art 12(3) that the provisions of the Convention shall apply notwithstanding that the salved vessel and the vessel undertaking the salvage operations belong to the same owner.

10 THE POSITION OF SEVERAL SALVORS

10.1 Dispossession of one salvor by another under maritime law salvage

Under maritime law salvage, the master of the vessel is the sole judge of whether or not to accept salvage services. If, after the master has accepted the services of a salvor, a subsequent salvor supersedes the first against the wishes of the master, he will earn no remuneration. Thus, the principle at common law is that, unless there are special circumstances, a subsequent salvor is not entitled to dispossess a prior salvor, provided that the prior salvor has a reasonable prospect of accomplishing the salvage service himself and is not endangering the safety of the salved property.[182]

An example of special circumstances is shown in the following case:

The American Farmer[183]

After a collision with another American steamship, *The American Farmer* was abandoned badly holed in the North Atlantic Ocean. She had been on a voyage from New York to England laden with a general cargo and mail. An

---

180 [1938] AC 136, p 149.
181 *Ibid*, p 141.
182 *The Fleece* [1850] 3 W Rob 278.
183 (1947) 80 LlL Rep672.

SOS message sent was picked up by various vessels including *The E*. *The American Farmer* was partly submerged with a large hole in her port side and she was a danger to navigation. Her crew had been rescued earlier and taken off the vessel. *The E* came up to her and began to take her in tow at about 3.45 pm that day. At about 4.30 pm, the ropes of *The American Farmer* parted. As a new rope was about to be connected to her, another vessel *The AR* came up and offered to assist. Although *The AR* was informed by the chief officer of *The E* that no assistance was required, nevertheless, *The AR* got her engineers and crew on board *The American Farmer*. The master of *The E* once again refused the assistance of *The AR*, but the crew stayed on, and her engineers worked in the engine room of the derelict vessel. As night began to fall, *The E* decided to stop and resume towage in the morning. The crew of *The AR* left and returned to their vessel. In the early hours of the morning, towage operations resumed again. *The AR* returned and its crew immediately started working on *The American Farmer* to get up her steam and to get the steering engine into commission as most of the oil in the steering gear had run out. The crew of *The AR* were more familiar with that steering gear than the crew of *The E*, so *The AR* managed to get the engine of the vessel working again. A naval vessel, which had come to the scene and was standing by, tried to persuade the *The* to cast off his tow ropes and let *The AR* get the vessel going, but *The E* refused. *The E* began to tow the vessel, succeeding in getting her some distance ahead. About halfway through the towage, *The AR* threatened to cut away the tow ropes of *The E* which were fast to *The American Farmer*. *The E* was finally persuaded to cast off her tow ropes and her crew returned to their vessel. *The American Farmer* was manoeuvred slowly in company with the naval ship (*P*) and *The AR* towards England. As the vessels proceeded in charge of the master of *The AR*, two salvage tugs came by and at the request of the master of *The AR*, stood by. *The American Farmer* was eventually safely anchored in Carrick Roads. The naval ship (*P*) left when the tugs arrived and *The E* proceeded on her voyage to Barry. *The E*, *The AR*, the salvage tugs and the master and crew of these vessels made salvage claims against *The American Farmer* and her cargo.

The court considered whether the master of *The AR* was justified in dispossessing the master of *The E* of his prize by threatening to cut her towropes off *The American Farmer*. On the facts, it was held that there was not, in fact, any reasonable probability of *The E* being able to accomplish the service unaided. *The E* would undoubtedly have had to hand over to the salvage tugs before she could have brought the vessel to a place of safety. Upon the findings of the Elder Brethren, the only method which held out any prospect of the vessels remaining in towage connection for any substantial period was by using *The American Farmer*'s wire, a method which the master of *The E* had not thought of applying. Therefore, the master of *The AR* had acted with perfect proprietary. *The E* would never have been able to do the job, although her effort and work were commendable. Both *The E* and *The AR* were entitled to salvage rewards. The other salvage tugs had merely given moral support to the other salvors but also helped in the anchoring of *The American Farmer* in Carrick Roads. They were entitled to a smaller reward.

10.2 Dismissal of a salvor under contract by the master of the vessel being salved

Dispossession of a salvor by way of dismissal by the master of the ship being salved has different consequences under (a) maritime law salvage where there is no contract, and (b) where there is a salvage contract. (The consequences of dismissal under the Convention are set out in para 10.3, below.) The contrast between these situations is illustrated by the following case, the facts of which are not uncommon.

The Unique Mariner (No 2)[184]

During a voyage from Port Kelang in Malaysia to Samarinda, Indonesia, *The UM* ran aground on the Western edge of the Nipa Shoal. All attempts to refloat her being unsuccessful, her owners in Hong Kong appointed a company in Singapore as its agents for the purpose of retaining a suitable tug to be despatched from Singapore. After contacting a tug company, the agents sent a telegram to the master informing him that a tug was being despatched. In the meantime, the captain and crew of a tug called *The Salvaliant*, noticed *The UM* aground in the vicinity and offered salvage assistance. The master, mistakenly believing that *The Salvaliant* was the tug which had been sent from Singapore, signed a salvage agreement under the LOF. While *The Salvaliant* was preparing to refloat *The UM*, the master of the latter received a further telegram from the agents of his principals about the other tug and realised his error. Consequently, he instructed the master of *The Salvaliant* to stop work immediately. Her crew got off *The UM* and *The Salvaliant* stood by. The tug hired by the agents arrived the following day and finally succeeded in refloating *The UM* and towed her to Singapore. The owners of *The Salvaliant* claimed damages for breach of contract and/or salvage remuneration under the LOF in arbitration. They contended that, had their tug not been dismissed, she would have made a refloating attempt by towage and would probably have been successful.

The arbitrator awarded the contractors US$75,000. The shipowners appealed against this award and the appeal arbitrator allowed the appeal, reducing the award to US$35,000, on the ground that the original arbitrator had erred in his approach to the assessment of the sum to which the contractors were entitled.

---

184 [1979] 1 Lloyd's Rep 37.

This was a special case for the decision of the court stated by Mr Barry Sheen QC the appeal arbitrator.

The question for the court was how to assess the award for salvage services which had been wrongfully interrupted by the master and whether the contractors were, in addition to an award, entitled to *restitutio in integrum* as compensation, or as damages for breach of contract, or both. The contractors contended that as superseded salvors, the compensation should be assessed at an amount which they would have earned by way of salvage remuneration, had they been allowed to complete their services successfully, less deductions for risks not run, expenses not incurred and operating time saved, including an allowance of a discount for the possibility that they might have been unable to complete the services successfully, even if they had been allowed to do so.

Brandon J stated the general principles applicable to: (1) salvage under the general maritime law (where there is no salvage contract); and (2) salvage under contract to be as follows:

> (1) Under maritime law salvage, the owners of the property to be salved were under no obligation to allow the salvors to complete their services but were entitled if they wished to dismiss them and supersede them by other salvors.

> However, it the salvors were later dismissed by the master of the ship and superseded by other salvors, they were entitled to remuneration in the nature of salvage (a) as a reward for the services which they had actually rendered before they were superseded and (b) by way of some compensation for the loss of opportunity to complete their services.

The justification for the compensation, he said, was to be found on reasons of public policy referred to by Lord Merriman P in *The Hassel* and implicit in the passage from Kennedy adopted as a correct statement of the law by Willmer J in *The Loch Tulla*. The reasons of public policy were the encouragement of salvors to be willing and ready to render salvage services even though they may, after entering upon them, be deprived, as a result of being superseded, of the opportunity to complete them successfully.

He concluded that salvors, in such cases, were not entitled to full compensation, assessed like damages, for breach of contract or duty, on the basis of *restitutio in integrum*; and the right to compensation for being superseded was not dependant on any prior benefit having been conferred.

> (2) By contrast, where the salvors were engaged under an express salvage agreement in the terms of Lloyd's form, as was in the present case, it was an implied term that the owners of the property to be salved would not act in such a way as to prevent the salvors from performing the services, so long as they (the salvors) were willing and able to do so. The obligation not to act in such a way so as to prevent performance included an obligation not to dismiss or supersede.[185]

185 [1979] 1 Lloyd's Rep 37, p 51–52.

With particular reference to the facts of this case he held that:

> As the appeal arbitrator had found that the salvors were willing and able to perform the services which they had undertaken and the act of the master of *Unique Mariner* in superseding *Salvaliant* with *Asiatic Gala* was a breach of contract, such a conduct was a breach of obligation of such a character as to constitute a repudiation of the contract which was accepted on behalf of the salvors.

On the basis that the shipowners repudiated the salvage agreement and the salvors accepted such repudiation, the salvors were entitled to the usual remedy in damages, which a party to a contract had in such a case. It ought to be assessed on the usual principles of *restitutio in integrum*. However, they were not also entitled to recover payment for services that they had actually rendered.

Summary of the principles

(a) Under ordinary maritime law salvage, there is no obligation not to dismiss. There will be payment for salvage rendered and some compensation for lost opportunity.
(b) Under contractual salvage the master of the salved has a duty not to prevent salvors from doing their work and a dismissal by him will be breach of contract answerable in damages for repudiation of the contract. No award in this case would be due.

Both LOF 1990 and 1995 contain a new provision (not being in the Convention) in cll 18 and 4, respectively, about termination of the agreement by the owner of the vessel, when there is no longer any prospect of a useful result leading to salvage reward in accordance with Art 13, by giving reasonable notice to the contractors. Clause G of LOF 2000 grants a right to termination to both the owners of the vessel or the contractor by giving reasonable prior written notice to the other, when there is no longer any reasonable prospect of a useful result in accordance with Arts 12 and 13 of the Convention.

The expression 'useful result', which is borrowed from Art 12 of the Convention has not been defined, although in obvious cases it may be easily understood. There are potential problems, however, if there is no agreement between the parties to the contract concerning whether the ship is economically salvable where repair costs have not been properly assessed.[186]

---

186 Buckley, M, 'Salvage: LOF 2000' (2000) *International Maritime Law*, May, p 99.

10.3 The position of several salvors under the Salvage Convention 1989

Article 8(1)(c) imposes a duty on a salvor, whenever circumstances reasonably require, to seek assistance from other salvors; and Art 8(1)(d) imposes a separate duty on a salvor to accept the intervention of other salvors when reasonably requested to do so by the owner or master of the vessel or other property in danger; provided, however, that the amount of his reward shall not be prejudiced should it be found that such a request was unreasonable.

Thus, prior salvors cannot refuse assistance from subsequent ones, nor exclude them. Any misconduct by a salvor will be taken into account to reduce the award or, depending on the seriousness of the misconduct, deprive him of any payment under the Convention (Art 18). The Convention does not deal, however, with whether the salvor will be liable in damages if such conduct causes damage to the property being subject to salvage. The problems arising from such an omission were discussed under paras 9.3 and 9.4, above.

There is also a general duty imposed by Art 8(2)(a) on the owner and master of the vessel or the owner of other property in danger to co-operate fully with the salvor during the course of the salvage operations. No provision for remedies to the salvor is found in the Convention in the event that his success is impeded by the non-co-operation of those in charge of the property to be salved. Thus, as far as English law is concerned, principles of common law will apply, of which see next.

11 DUTIES OF THE SALVED

11.1 Duty to co-operate

Under common law, the master and owner of the ship in danger have a duty to co-operate with and not to mislead salvors.[187]

The Valsesia[188]

The *V* grounded upon rocks at Friars Point on 25 August 1926. Two tugs belonging to the plaintiffs were engaged to render her assistance. The tugs were expected to get the *V* to the beach in Whitmore Bay but after some hours' work, the *V* grounded again due to the negligence of her crew, who had failed to slip the cable at the time agreed between the parties that the

---

187 *The Kingalock* (1854) 1 Spinks E&A 265.
188 [1927] P 115.

cable should be slipped. The plaintiffs' tugs were, therefore, unable to complete the salvage operation and the ship, *V*, grounded again. She was then in a worse position than before the tugs got hold of her. The plaintiffs claimed damages from the owners of *V* on the ground that they were deprived of the opportunity to earn the stipulated sum due to the negligence of the latters' servants. They also contended that, since the tugs had performed the services except for completing the salvage, which was not due to their fault, they should be treated as if they had performed the contract and were, thus, entitled to recover the stipulated salvage sums.

Hill J said:

> In my view this case falls to be decided according to the ordinary principles of common law and no question peculiar to the law of salvage is involved. I think there was a mutual obligation implied in such an agreement as this, at least, to act with ordinary skill and care in carrying out the respective parts in the combined work. It was the duty of the tugs to obey the orders of those who were in command of the ship and to use skill and care in the handling of the tugs, and it was equally the duty of those in charge of the ship to use ordinary skill and care in carrying out their part of the contract, which was the slipping of the cable at the right time. This indeed, was the essential part which the ship was to play in the combined operation.[189]

He later continued, thus:

> I find a difficulty in saying that anybody can recover a lump sum to be paid in respect of a completed work, when in fact, that work has not been completed. But if the plaintiffs were prevented from completing it by the negligence of those on board the ship, and if they were thereby deprived of the opportunity of earning the stipulated sums, then they are entitled to damages for the breach ... and in this case the damages would be exactly commensurate with the stipulated sums because the plaintiffs had in substance completed the whole of what they had undertaken to do.[190]

Under the 1989 Convention, Art 8(2)(a), there is an express duty upon the owner of the property in danger and the master of the vessel to co-operate fully during the course of the salvage operations.

The previous Salvage Convention did not provide for duty of care owed by either the salvor or the salved to each other during salvage operations, but common law principles applied. The present Convention spells it out in Art 8, which provides in para 2:

> The owner and master or the vessel or the owner of other property in danger shall owe a duty to the salvor:
>
> (a) to co-operate fully with him during the course of the salvage operations;

---

189 [1927] P 115, p 118.
190 *Ibid*, p 119.

(b) in so doing, to exercise due care to prevent or minimise damage to the environment; and

(c) when the vessel or other property has been brought to a place of safety, to accept re-delivery when reasonably requested by the salvor to do so.

Nothing is said, however, about recoverable damages in the event of breach, limitation of liability, contributory negligence or duty to mitigate with respect to which national law should apply, as Brice suggests.[191]

Under LOF 1990 and 1995, both contracts provide, by cl 3, that the owners their servants and agents shall co-operate fully with the contractor in and about the salvage, including entry to a place named or the place of safety. The equivalent clause of LOF 2000 'duties of property owners' is more extensive; in particular cl F spells out in detail what the co-operation is about:

(i) the contractors may make reasonable use of the vessel's machinery gear and equipment free of expense provided that the contractors shall not unnecessarily damage abandon or sacrifice any property on board;

(ii) the contractors shall be entitled to all such information as they may reasonably require relating to the vessel or the remainder of the property provided such information is relevant to the performance of the services and is capable of being provided without undue difficulty or delay;

(iii) the owners of the property shall co-operate fully with the contractors in obtaining entry to the place of safety stated in the contract or agreed or determined in accordance with the contact.

11.2 Obligation to provide security to salvors

The Convention by Art 21 and both LOFs 1990 and 1995, by cll 4 and 5, respectively, impose a dual obligation on the owner of the salved vessel: first to provide satisfactory security for the salvage claim, including interest and costs in respect of the vessel and, second, to use their best endeavours to ensure that the cargo-owners provide satisfactory security including interest and costs before the cargo is released.[192] It is submitted that 'best endeavours' in this context also, as under cl 1(a) of LOFs 1990 and 1995 (discussed under para 9.1), means the exercise of due diligence. The salved property shall not be removed from the port or place of arrival after completion of salvage without the consent of the salvor, until such security is provided.

A provision for salvage security is included as an important notice in the LOF 2000. It states:

---

191 *Op cit*, Brice, fn 1, para 7–57.

192 When satisfactory security for the salvor's claims is duly provided or rendered, including interest and costs, the salvor may not enforce his maritime lien (Art 20(2)).

As soon as possible the owners of the vessel should notify the owners of other property on board that this agreement has been made. If the contractors are successful the owners of such property should note that it will become necessary to provide the contractors with salvage security promptly in accordance with cl 4 of the Lloyd's Standard Salvage and Arbitration Clauses (LSSA) clauses. The provision of general average security does not relieve the salved interests of their separate obligation to provide salvage security to the contractors.

Common law principles will apply as to the amount of the security, which must be reasonable.

The Tribels[193]

The motor vessel *T* took the ground at Muscat in the course of a liner service to Indian ports as she was entering the harbour and turning to starboard. Three harbour tugs which had been present for the purpose of helping her into her berth went immediately to her rescue and commenced pushing. The master agreed to employ the tugs on the standard LOF salvage agreement form and the tugs performed the services for a period of nine hours. The salvors demanded £3,323,000 as security, and the plaintiffs applied for an injunction to restrain the salvors from requiring security exceeding £1m. It was held that it is an implied term of the salvage contract that the contractor would not ask for unreasonably high security. The salvors were entitled to demand security for a sum that would secure payment of a top level award which they could reasonably anticipate to obtain including the arbitration costs. The plaintiffs were granted the injunction.

12 ASSESSMENT OF THE AWARD AND SPECIAL COMPENSATION

The Convention provides (Art 12(1), (2)) that if the salvage operations have had useful result the salvor will be rewarded and, except as otherwise provided, no payment is due under the Convention, if there is no useful result. Article 13 refers to the assessment of award for property salvage, Art 16 is relevant to life salvage and Art 14 deals with special compensation (liability salvage).

12.1 The underlying principles and developments

Before the details of assessment of the award and of special compensation are analysed, it would be appropriate to refer to the relevant passage of the

---

193 [1985] 1 Lloyd's Rep 129.

judgment in *The Nagasaki Spirit*[194] in which Lord Mustill summarised the history most succinctly:

> My Lords, the law of maritime salvage is old, and for much of its long history it was simple. The reward for successful salvage was always large: for failure it was nil. At first, the typical salvor was one who happened on a ship in distress, and used personal efforts and property to effect a rescue. As time progressed, improvements in speed, propulsive power and communications bred a new community of professional salvors who found it worth while to keep tugs and equipment continually in readiness, and for much of the time idle, waiting for an opportunity to provide assistance and earn a large reward. This arrangement served the maritime community and its insurers well, and the salvors made a satisfactory living. It was, however, an expensive business and in recent years the capital and running costs have been difficult for the traditional salvage concerns to sustain. A number of these were absorbed into larger enterprises, less committed perhaps to the former spirit, and unwilling to stake heavy outlays on the triple chance of finding a vessel in need of assistance, of accomplishing a salvage liable to be more arduous and prolonged than in the days of smaller merchant ships, and of finding that there was sufficient value left in the salved property at the end of the service to justify a substantial award. At about the same time, a new factor entered the equation. Crude oil and its products have been moved around the world by sea in large quantities for many years, and the risk that cargo or fuel escaping from a distressed vessel would damage the flora and fauna of the sea and shore, and would impregnate the shoreline itself, was always present; but so long as the amount carried by a single vessel was comparatively small, such incidents as did happen were not large enough to attract widespread attention. This changed with the prodigious increase in the capacity of crude oil carriers which began some three decades ago, carrying with it the possibility of a disaster whose consequences might extend far beyond the loss of the imperilled goods and cargo. Such a disaster duly happened, at a time when public opinion was already becoming sensitive to assaults on the integrity of the natural environment. Cargo escaping from the wreck of *Torrey Canyon* off the Scillies caused widespread contamination of sea, foreshore and wild life. The resulting concern and indignation were sharpened when *Amoco Cadiz* laden with 220,000 tons of crude oil stranded on the coast of France, causing pollution on an even larger scale, in circumstances which rightly or wrongly were believed to have involved a possibly fatal delay during negotiations with the intended salvors.
>
> To this problem the traditional law of salvage provided no answer, for the only success which mattered was success in preserving the ship, cargo and associated interests; and this was logical, since the owners of those interests, who had to bear any salvage award that was made, had no financial stake in the protection of anything else. This meant that a salvor who might perform a valuable service to the community in the course of an attempted salvage, by, for example, moving the vessel to a place where the escape of oil would be less

---

194 [1997] 1 Lloyd's Rep 323 (HL), pp 326–28.

harmful, would recover nothing or only very little, if in the end the ship was lost or greatly damaged. Something more was required to induce professional salvors, upon whom the community must rely for protection, to keep in existence and on call the fleets necessary for the protection of natural resources in peril. Some new form of remuneration must be devised. It is with an important aspect of the scheme worked out during long and hard fought negotiations between the shipowning and cargo interests and their insurers on the one hand and representatives of salvors on the other, with participation by governmental and other agencies, that the present appeal is concerned.

It is important to make clear at the start that the solution devised in the 1980s was not to create a new institution: a kind of free standing 'environmental salvage'. The services performed remain, as they have always been, services to ship and cargo, and the award is borne by those standing behind ship and cargo. The difference is that the sum payable to the salvor may now contain an additional element to reflect the risk of the environment posed by the vessel for which the services are performed.

This element of 'special compensation' is based on the salvor's 'expenses' (as defined) and may be enhanced in cases where the salvage operations have actually prevented or minimised environmental damage. The reward for the salvage itself is assessed and apportioned between the vessel and other property interests as before, and the difference if any between the amount so awarded (or nil, if there is no award) and the amount of the special compensation is due to the salvor from the shipowner alone.

Before turning to the relevant provisions of LOF 1990, a little of its history must be given. The move towards the evolution of what has been called a 'safety net', designed to provide an additional incentive for salvors to keep fleets on station, began during the late 1970s with two parallel initiatives. These first bore fruit in the 1980 revision of the Lloyd's Open Form, so as to make cl 1(a) read as follows:

> 'The contractor agrees to use his best endeavours to salve the [vessel] …
> and/or her cargo bunkers and stores and take them to … or other place to
> be hereafter agreed or if no place is named or agreed to a place of safety.
> The contractor further agrees to use his best endeavours to prevent the
> escape of oil from the vessel while performing the services of salving the
> subject vessel and/or her cargo bunkers and stores. The services shall be
> rendered and accepted as salvage services upon the principle of 'no cure
> no pay' except that where the property being salved is a tanker laden or
> partly laden with a cargo of oil and without negligence on the part of the
> contractor and/or his servants and/or agents (1) the services are not
> successful or (2) are only partially successful or (3) the contractor is
> prevented from completing the services the contractor shall nevertheless
> be awarded solely against the owners of such tanker his reasonably
> incurred expenses and an increment not exceeding 15% of such expenses
> but only if and to the extent that such expenses together with the
> increment are greater than any amount otherwise recoverable under this
> agreement. Within the meaning of the said exception to the principle of
> "no cure no pay" expenses shall in addition to actual out of pocket

expenses include a fair rate for all tugs, craft, personnel and other equipment used by the contractor in the services and oil shall mean crude oil fuel oil heavy diesel oil and lubricating oil.'

The history of this revision to the common form of salvage contract does not appear from the materials before the House, but it is possible to give an account of the contemporaneous efforts to reach an international solution, in the shape of a replacement for the Salvage Convention of 1910. Within a few months of the *Amoco Cadiz* disaster the International Maritime Organisation (IMO) had taken the matter in hand and prepared an initial report. The problem was also addressed by the Comité Maritime International (CMI) which agreed to co-operate in a study of the private law principles of salvage. The outcome was the establishment of a sub-committee under the chairmanship of Professor E Selvig, which prepared a draft convention accompanied by a report. These documents were placed before a conference of CMI in Montreal during May 1981, by which time LOF 1980 with its safety net provision had come into force. The debates at Montreal led to a final draft, together with a report by Mr B Nielsen. For a time, there was little further progress, but eventually a diplomatic conference led to the agreement of the International Convention on Salvage 1989 (the Convention). This did not come into force internationally until July 1996, when the necessary ratifications were achieved. So far as English domestic law is concerned the Convention was given the force of law in the UK by the MSA 1995, s 224. But the Act did not affect rights and liabilities arising out of operations started before 1 January 1996. Accordingly, the claim now under consideration is a private law claim, based on LOF 1990. The Convention is relevant only because having partly been inspired by LOF 1980 it is now incorporated by reference into LOF 1990.

12.2 The criteria of assessing the salvage award and special compensation

The criteria for assessing the award under the Convention and English law are set out in Art 13(1) and reflect the common law position. Both Arts 13 and 14 are incorporated in the LOF 1990 and 1995 by reference. LOF 2000 is made subject to English law. Every interest salved contributes according to its salved value. Relevant factors under the Convention (Art 13(1)) are:

(a) value salved: every interest salved contributes according to its salved value;

(b) the skill and efforts of the salvors in preventing or minimising damage to the environment;

(c) the measure of success obtained by the salvors;

(d) the nature and degree of danger;

(e) salvor's skill, effort in salving the vessel, other property and life;

(f) the time used and expenses and losses incurred by the salvors;

   (g) the risk of liability and other risks (including equipment) run by salvors or their equipment;

   (h) the promptness of the services rendered;

   (i) the availability and use of vessels and equipment intended for salvage operations;

   (j) the state of readiness and efficiency of the salvor's equipment and the value thereof.

Article 14(1)

If the salvor has carried out salvage operations in respect of a vessel which by itself or its cargo threatened damage to the environment and has failed to earn a reward under Art 13 at least equivalent to the special compensation assessable in accordance with this article, he shall be entitled to special compensation from the owner of that vessel equivalent to his expenses as herein defined.

Article 14(2)

If, in the circumstances set out in para 1, the salvor by his salvage operations has prevented or minimised damage to the environment, the special compensation payable by the owner to the salvor under para 1 may be increased up to maximum of 30% of the expenses incurred by the salvor. However, the tribunal, if it deems it fair and just to do so and bearing in mind the relevant criteria set out in Art 13(1) may increase such special compensation further, but in no event shall the total increase be more than 100% of the expenses incurred by the salvor.

Article 14(3)

'Salvor's expenses' for the purpose of paras 1 and 2 means the out of pocket expenses reasonably incurred by the salvor in the salvage operation and a fair rate for equipment and personnel actually and reasonably used in the salvage operation, taking into consideration the criteria set out in Art 13, para 1(h), (i), (j).

Article 14(4)

The total special compensation under this article shall be paid only if and to the extent that such compensation is greater than any reward recoverable by the salvor under Art 13.

Skill and efforts to minimise damage to the environment will be taken into account in assessing property salvage by way of an enhanced award (Art 13(1)(b)). In addition to the enhanced award, the salvor will get his expenses paid by way of special compensation, under Art 14(1), if he made efforts to protect the environment. He will even get his expenses regardless of whether property was saved or whether his efforts to minimise or prevent damage to the environment were ultimately successful. But, he will not get Art 14 compensation, if the award under Art 13 is higher than the total special compensation (Art 14(4)). In particular, Art 14(1) provides for special compensation being equivalent to the salvor's expenses, in the event he has not earned an award under Art 13 at least equivalent to special compensation, when the vessel, or its cargo, threatened damage to the environment. In addition, if by his salvage operations the salvor has, in fact, prevented or minimised such damage, the special compensation will be increased up to 30% of the expenses incurred by the salvor. Such compensation may be further increased, taking into account the factors under Art 13, but no more than 100% of the expenses incurred (Art 14(2)). Negligence on the part of the salvor will deprive him of the whole, or part, of any special compensation under this article (Art 14(5)).

12.3 The decision in *The Nagasaki Spirit*

The principal issue in *The Nagasaki Spirit* was concerned with the definition of 'expenses' in Art 14(3) and, in particular, that part of it which refers to 'fair rate of equipment'. In other words, the point was whether in assessing a 'fair rate' for the salvor's own craft, equipment personnel, etc, it was permissible to include a market or profitable rate, or whether the salvor was entitled solely to reimbursement of expenditure. Article 14(3) reads:

> Salvor's expenses for the purpose of para 1 and 2 means the out of pocket expenses reasonably incurred by the salvor in the salvage operation and a fair rate for equipment and personnel actually and reasonably used on the salvage operation, taking into consideration the criteria set out in Art 13, para 1(h), (i), (j).

The facts and the award

Briefly the case involved a collision between *The Nagasaki Spirit* and *The Ocean Blessing* in the northern part of the Malacca Straits. Following the collision, about 12,000 tonnes of crude oil flowed from *The Nagasaki Spirit* into the sea causing an enormous fire. Both vessels were engulfed in the fire and all crew on *The Ocean Blessing* lost their lives. Two members of the crew on board *The Nagasaki Spirit* survived. The next day, professional salvors agreed to salve *The Nagasaki Spirit* and her cargo under the LOF 1990, which contained Arts 13 and 14 of the 1989 Convention. With the help of a number of tugs, the fire on *The Nagasaki Spirit* was extinguished. Her cargo was transshipped and the vessel was safely redelivered to her owners.

The award was made on the basis of Art 13 and the arbitrator, in fixing special compensation, stressed the need for encouragement. In order to arrive at a fair rate, he took into account some contribution to future investment so that professional salvors were encouraged to stay in business. The appeal arbitrator disagreed; he increased the award under Art 13 and took a different line on Art 14, taking into account the type and scope of the job in assessing the fair rate, which would be reflected in the costs to the salvors. Since his assessment of the award was higher than that of the special compensation, no compensation under Art 14 was payable.

The admiralty judge, on appeal from the award, concluded that, although fair rate imported the idea of remuneration, which normally would include an element of profit, the appeal arbitrator was right to reject this. The words read in their context meant recompense for expenditure, because the Convention drew a distinction between remuneration or reward and compensation.

The Court of Appeal agreed with the judge and, reading Art 14 in context with Art 13.1, concluded that fair rate means a rate of expenses, which is to be comprehensive of indirect or overhead expenses and taking into account the additional costs of having resources instantly available. So, fair rate, in the view of the Court of Appeal, was not to be salvage reward, or anything like it. Article 14 does not refer to skill and effort of the salvors, etc, as does Art 13(1).[195]

Evans LJ dissented only to the extent that these expenses did not necessarily exclude any profit element and, in this respect, he preferred the approach of the appeal arbitrator, Mr Willmer. In particular, he said:

> I agree with the judgment of Staughton LJ on the 'fair rate' issue in rejecting the concept of salvage remuneration or reward and in limiting the salvor's claim under Art 14(3) to the expenses which he has incurred. I would not go on to hold, however, that these expenses necessarily exclude any profit element or that they are confined to costs, including overheads, as the learned judge held. The appeal arbitrator, Mr JF Willmer QC adopted an approach which is distinct both from that of the arbitrator, Mr RF Stone QC, and that of the judge. In summary, I would hold that the judge was wrong to exclude altogether a possible 'profit' element and that Mr Stone erred in assessing the 'fair rate' as if it was a form of remuneration or reward. Broadly speaking, in my judgment, Mr Willmer was correct to have regard to commercial or, where relevant, market factors as well as to the salvor's costs.[196]

The House of Lords, with Lord Mustill delivering judgment, held that 'fair rate', under Art 14(3), meant fair rate of expenditure and did not include any element of profit. The first half of Art 14(3) covered out of pocket expenses and the second half covered overhead expenses. The word 'rate' was the appropriate word to use when attributing or apportioning general overheads to equipment and personnel reasonably and actually used in the particular salvage operation. 'Expenses' denoted amounts either disbursed or borne, not earned as profits. The fact that Art 14(3) requires fair rate to be added to the out of pocket expenses made it clear that it contained no element of profit. Also, Art 14(2) twice makes use of the expression 'expenses incurred' by the salvor. The word 'incur' obviously showed that it is not something that

---

195 [1996] 1 Lloyd's Rep 449, p 455, *per* Staughton LJ.
196 *Ibid*, p 457.

yielded him profit. Lord Mustill concluded that Art 14(3) was not concerned with remuneration and described the intention of the legislation, thus:

> Furthermore, and in my view decisively, the promoters of the Convention did not choose, as they might have done, to create an entirely new and distinct category of environmental salvage, which would finance the owners of vessels and gear to keep them in readiness simply for the purpose of preventing damage to the environment. Paragraphs 1, 2 and 3 of Art 14 all make it clear that the right to special compensation depends on the performance of 'salvage operations' which, as already seen, are defined by Art 1(a) as operations to assist a vessel in distress. Thus, although Art 14 is undoubtedly to encourage professional salvors to keep vessels readily available, this is still for the purpose of a salvage for which the primary incentive remains a traditional salvage award. The only structural change in the scheme is that the incentive is now made more attractive by the possibility of obtaining new financial recognition for conferring a new type of incidental benefit. Important as it is, the remedy under Art 14 is subordinate to the reward under Art 13, and its function should not be confused by giving it a character too closely akin to salvage.[197]

13 PROBLEMS ARISING FROM THE DRAFTING OF THE CONVENTION

Professional salvors reacted strongly to the decision of the House of Lords in *The Nagasaki Spirit*. From their point of view, the decision disregarded the loss suffered by salvors in maintaining sophisticated tugs and equipment (which invariably may have to be made available by borrowing a large capital) in readiness during salvage operations until the danger to the environment is eliminated. Such advance capital provision cannot be compensated, in their opinion, without allowance of an element of profit in the 'fair rate' of Art 14.

In reply to this, Lord Mustill defended his judgment – at a debate held by the London Shipping Law Centre on 19 June 1997 – that ' he was only the pianist who had to perform the music composed by someone else', referring to the draftsmen of the Convention being the composers.

During the same debate, the appeal arbitrator of the decision, John Willmer QC highlighted the problem arising from the drafting of the Convention and, in particular, with regard to special compensation, as follows.[198]

---

197 [1997] 1 Lloyd's Rep 323, pp 332–33.

198 The paper delivered at the seminar is available from the office of the London Shipping Law Centre, UCL Law Faculty.

13.1 Territorial limits

Article 1 provides:

> For the purpose of this Convention: ...
>
> (d) Damage to the environment means substantial physical damage to human health or to marine life or resources in coastal or inland waters or areas adjacent thereto, caused by pollution, contamination, fire, explosion or similar major incidents.

Considerable concerns had been expressed by professional salvors as to the territorial limits of Art 1(d). If salvage of a major disaster on the high seas was required, Art 14 would not apply. Undoubtedly, oil or other chemicals would be transported to the coastal areas, but unless a special agreement was reached between the owners' liability insurers to cover the expenses of salvors as they would be covered had Art 14 applied, there would be no incentive to salvors to act.

It might be possible, however, in a given case, Mr Willmer said, to prove that, having regard to the prevailing wind and current, a ship spilling thousands of tons of oil or noxious chemicals, even though far out to sea, nevertheless, threatened damage to marine life or resources in coastal waters or areas adjacent thereto has arisen. Questions would, however, arise as to the meaning of coastal waters. Could they be equated to the economic zone? Should the waters over the continental shelf be regarded either as coastal or adjacent waters? Unless these questions were authoritatively answered, uncertainty would prevail for salvors and P&I clubs as to the ambit of the special compensation provision.

13.2 Substantial physical damage

The second difficulty arising from the wording of Art 1(d) has been that the damage must be substantial and physical. Minor damage to a tourist beach or mere economic loss would not be enough. The historical context in which the provisions of the Convention have to be construed, said Mr Willmer, indicated that the word 'substantial' had to be considered 'seriously' and must mean something more than 'not trifling'. However, he continued, the imprecision of the word 'substantial' would be likely to lead to continued argument as to its application to the facts in particular cases.

13.3 Threatened damage

The next drafting ambiguity for the application of special compensation has been the word 'threatened' in Art 14(1). Lloyd's arbitrators treat it as indicating that for the salvor to succeed in a claim for special compensation there ought to be reasonable apprehension, rather than actual danger of damage to the environment. The main reason for that approach, he said, was that the incentive or encouragement to salvors intended by the Convention would not be promoted by too rigid an interpretation of this word. To wait until it could be seen that there was actual danger would increase the risk that help would arrive too late.

In this connection, Brice had commented that the distinction between the two words used by the Convention 'danger' in Art 13, and 'threatened' in Art 14, was significant. This was because there might be cases when a threat of damage to the environment may not materialise as, for example, when there was change in wind force and direction. However, this approach was not universally acceptable by P&I clubs and it was important that parties to a salvage agreement knew where they stood.

13.4 Fair rate

How the arbitrator was to ascertain the fair rate has posed a real practical problem. Staughton LJ in the Court of Appeal (*Nagasaki Spirit*) concluded that this was a mater of judgment for the tribunals of fact and not necessarily the result of any mathematical calculation. Lord Mustill said in the same case that:

> Your Lordships were pressed with a submission that the meaning given to Art 14(3) by the judge and the Court of Appeal would be unworkable in practice. I cannot accept this, for it seems to me that the ascertainment of the fair rate must necessarily be performed with a fairly broad brush, albeit not so broad as the fixing of the reward under Art 13, and the uplift under Art 14(2). Quite sufficient information for such purposes could be derived from the salvor's books, as indeed became clear when reference to materials from that source was made in the course of argument.[199]

Mr Willmer explained during this debate that, from his experience as an appeal arbitrator, the real problem here was that professional salvors were very reluctant to disclose books which they would regard as highly confidential. Involvement of accountants would increase the costs of the arbitration and delay matters.

13.5 The increment

Another problem arising in arbitration has been whether for Art 14(2) entitlement to increment the salvor had to prove that, but for the services performed, an escape of oil would have occurred and would have caused the

---

199 [1997] 1 Lloyd's Rep 323, p 333.

requisite damage. Mr. Willmer disagreed with such a construction, which would be illogical in the context of the Convention.

13.6 Security for special compensation

The last point of difficulty raised during this debate was the issue of security for special compensation. Under the Convention, Art 21, there is an obligation upon the owner of the ship to provide security. However, if there was no ship salved, it could be difficult to enforce this obligation under the Convention. Even if the ship was saved, there would be no maritime lien attached to the ship for special compensation. An arrest in this jurisdiction is allowed, but there will be other claims in priority of payment. The co-operation of liability insurers (P&I clubs) would be required in order to obtain security for special compensation.

13.7 The solution provided by the SCOPIC – government intervention

The marine salvage industry faced with these problems, appointed a committee of experts which worked for two years since 1997 and proposed a new solution, the SCOPIC (Special Compensation of Protection and Indemnity Clause). This clause leaves the fundamental principles of special compensation unchanged but puts in place a more workable framework for calculating remuneration, which is based on pre-agreed rates for vessels, personnel and equipment. It provides a greater financial security to salvors. It dispenses with the problematical special 'triggers' required under Art 14. Instead, the salvor may invoke SCOPIC at any stage during a salvage operation, but only in appropriate circumstances, including high risk, low value cases. So, it reinforces the salvor's ability to deliver a swift response.[200] The implementation of the SCOPIC, which came into effect in August 1999, was the result of lengthy negotiations and required 'give and take' on the part of all interested parties; it represents a balance of everyone's interests.[201]

The parties to a salvage contract may agree to incorporate SCOPIC into any LOF contract by reference, therefore contracting out of Art 14 of the Convention.

Briefly the SCOPIC is supplementary to a 'no cure no pay' LOF, as an adjunct to it (cl 1). The clause clears the problems arising from Art 14

---

200 Walenkamp, H (President to International Salvage Union), 'SCOPIC: a new solution now available for us' (2000) 14(7) P&I International, July, p 166.

201 Paper by A Bishop (of Holman Fenwick and Willan), who has been the consultant to the International Salvage Union in respect of the drafting of this clause.

discussed earlier.[202] Whether or not there is a threat of damage to the environment, the salvor has an option to invoke the clause by sending a written notice to the shipowner (cl 2). However, if services to protect the environment were already rendered prior to the written notice, the compensation for them would not come under the SCOPIC. Therefore, it is important for the salvor to exercise his option as soon as possible in order to maximise his recovery.[203]

SCOPIC provides tariff rates for compensation with regard to personnel, tugs, other craft, portable salvage equipment (assessed on a time and material basis), out of pocket expenses and a bonus of 25%. The out of pocket expenses mean money paid by the contractor, or on his behalf, to third parties for hire of men, tugs, other craft and equipment, as well as other expenses reasonably necessary for the operation. These expenses may be agreed at cost, or on tariff rates if the hire is from another ISU (International Salvage Union) member (cl 5). The SCOPIC compensation is only payable to the extent that it exceeds the total Art 13 salvage award (cl 6). If the Art 13 award proves to be in a sum greater than the compensation assessed under SCOPIC, the contractor agrees (in cl 7) that the Art 13 remuneration shall be discounted by 25% of the difference between Art 13 and the SCOPIC compensation. This would, in effect, be the consequence of opting for SCOPIC when it was not necessary, for example, if there were prospects of an adequate salvage award.[204] The liability for SCOPIC compensation is that of the shipowner and his P&I club provides the security.

The P&I clubs agree through a Code of Conduct (which is basically a gentleman's agreement between the International group of P&I clubs and the International Salvage Union) to provide any security required for SCOPIC compensation by a Standard Guarantee Form ISU 5. Clause 3 of the SCOPIC sets out a timetable for the provision of the security and if it is not provided, cl 4 permits the salvor to withdraw from the SCOPIC. The P&I clubs have the opportunity to get involved in the salvage operations, because the shipowner can appoint a casualty representative (SCR) from a panel to attend.[205] The hull and cargo underwriters may each appoint a special representative, a technical man, to attend the casualty and report on the salvage operations. The salvage master, the shipowners and the SCR are obliged to co-operate with the special representative. It is intended that no more than these experts

---

202 See Brice, G, 'Salvage and the role of the insurer' [2000] LMCLQ, February, pp 26–41, which includes the clause and Code of Practice between property underwriters and P&I clubs, as well as Code of Practice between P&I clubs and the International salvage Union.

203 Browne, B, 'Salvage – LOF and SCOPIC' (1999) *International Journal of Shipping Law*, June, Pt 2, pp 113, 120.

204 *Op cit*, Brice, fn 202, p 31.

205 *Op cit*, Brice, fn 202.

can have access to the casualty in attempt to prevent endangering the salvage operation.

Immediately after the SCOPIC was completed, the Government accepted Lord Donaldson' proposal in his report – 'Review of Salvage, Intervention, Command and Control' – for a Government official (SOSREP) to represent the Secretary of State in maritime emergency situations in UK territorial waters. While the SOSREP will not intervene when he accepts the salvage plan, he has power to resume operational control and determine the salvage plan with the salvage master. The idea to limit the control to two key persons developed after the disaster of *The Sea Empress* spill, at Milford Haven, in which miscommunication between port master and the pilot contributed to the exacerbation of damage caused to the environment. However, potential conflicts may arise when the SCR and the special representatives of the property underwriters have conflicting views with the SOSREP. The aspect of how to resolve conflict was not thought through, due to lack of consultation between the committee, which drafted the SCOPIC, and the advocates of the SOSREP.[206] It was, however, thought very important and urgent to provide a mechanism by which the Government could use its intervention powers in appropriate circumstances.

It should be noted in this connection that the Merchant Shipping and Maritime Security Act 1997 which amends the MSA 1995, extends the powers of the Secretary of State and of fire authorities to deal with emergencies and safety at sea. In particular, there are powers of intervention where a shipping accident threatens pollution; powers of intervention in cases of pollution by substances other than oil; and powers of fire authorities to use fire brigades and equipment at sea (amending s 3 of the Fire Services Act 1947).

Clause 9(i) gives the option to the contractor to terminate the services under the SCOPIC if the sums to be incurred exceed the sum of the value of the property capable of being salved, and all sums to which he will be entitled as SCOPIC compensation. However, by cl 9(iii) termination may be hindered if the Government, or a port authority, or any other officially recognised body having jurisdiction over the area where the services are being rendered, restrains the contractor from demobilising his equipment. This provision may give rise to difficulties for salvors, whose security may prove not to be sufficient to maintain his services. It is suggested that cl 9(i) be amended, so as to provide flexibility and enable the contractor to obtain further security should the circumstances of cl 9(iii) arise. Subject to cl 9(iii), the shipowner, by cl 9(ii), has also the option to terminate SCOPIC compensation provided he gives five clear days' notice to the contractor to demobilise his equipment. Time for demobilisation shall be included in the compensation should it exceed the five clear days' notice.

---

206 *Op cit*, Browne, fn 203.

The duty of the contractor throughout the salvage operations to protect the environment is to use his best endeavours (cl 9). In other words, he must show that he did his best, which will be determined on the basis of standards applicable to other salvors possessing the same expertise (see para 9.1)

The potential exposure of salvors and port authorities to criminal prosecution after the successful prosecution of the Milford Haven port authority in *The Sea Empress* case, which was made to pay a fine of £4 m imposed under a strict liability statute,[207] has caused concern to salvors and port authorities. Thus, steps have been taken recently by the ISU to proceed with a formula for responder immunity, which is yet to be implemented.[208]

14 APPORTIONMENT

The apportionment of the reward, under Art 13, between salvors shall be made on the basis of the criteria contained in that article in accordance with the parties' contribution to salvage. In apportioning the crew's proportion of award, their basic pay (excluding bonus) would be taken into account. Article 15 of the Convention, Sched 11, Pt I of the MSA 1995, provides that the apportionment between the owner, master and other persons in the service of each salving vessel shall be determined by the law of the flag of that vessel. If the salvage has not been carried out from a vessel, the apportionment shall be determined by the law governing the contract between the salvor and his servants.

The 1995 LOF contains provision for the protection of rights of subcontractors (cl 18) by which the head salvors can claim salvage and enforce any award on their behalf (unless the sub-contractor acts in performance of public duty, for example, fire brigades: see Brice, para 1–245). A similar provision is incorporated in cl 13 of the Procedural rules of the LOF 2000.

15 LOF 2000 OVERVIEW

Each clause of this LOF has been referred to in paras 7–11. To recapitulate, cll A and B provide that the contractor agrees to use best endeavours to salve the property and to prevent or minimise damage to the environment. By cl C, the SCOPIC provisions may or may not be included. Clause E expressly states that services rendered prior to the agreement are included, and clause F spells out the duties of the property owners.

---

207 See Chapter 16, below.

208 'Salvors consider the need for responder immunity' Report from a Conference held by the International Salvage Union (1999) 13(5) P&I International, May, p 117.

The right of termination under cl G depends on whether there is no prospect of useful results, but the right is given to both parties, the contractor and the shipowner.

The deeming provision of a place of safety, where the services could be terminated, as in LOF 1990, has been clarified by inserting an agreed place of safety in LOF 2000. The duty of co-operation by the owners of the property has been clarified in cl F by stating what kind of information the salvors should expect from the owners.

In practice, salvors have been frequently faced with a situation when local authorities of a port, where the salved property was taken, demanded a large sum of money as a security for alleged, or possible contamination of the territorial waters. Salvors have been put into a position of having either to negotiate terms or to seek to protect their interests by obtaining insurance cover in the event their efforts to salve failed due to delays ensued by reason of such demands. Clause H is a novel clause which could protect salvors in such situations, by providing for a deemed performance of the services. The clause states:

> ... the contractors' services shall be deemed to have been performed when the property is in a safe condition in the place stated or agreed ... in accordance with cl A. For the purpose of this provision, the property shall be regarded as being in safe condition notwithstanding that the property (or part thereof) is damaged or in need of maintenance if (i) the contractors are not obliged to remain in attendance to satisfy the requirements of any port or harbour authority ... and (ii) the continuation of skilled salvage services from the contractors or other salvors is no longer necessary to avoid the property becoming lost or significantly further damaged or delayed.

Unfortunately, the wording under proviso (i) may still cause problems for salvors in some ports because it does not define in what circumstances the requirements of the port authority would be satisfied and this may give an opportunity to some port authorities to abuse their powers.

The LOF 2000 is supplemented by the LSSA clauses and Procedural Rules which are incorporated by reference (cl I).

The governing law is English (cl J), but even so, cl K reiterates the master's authority to sign the contract on behalf of all respective owners of the property. Inducement to sign the agreement is prohibited by cl L.

16 AN OVERVIEW OF ENVIRONMENTAL SALVAGE

The long standing principle in salvage law of 'no cure no pay' changed, first, with the introduction of the novel concept of 'safety net' by the LOF 1980, the purpose of which was to encourage salvors to protect the environment from oil pollution. But this concept related only to damage to the environment by oil pollution.

A significant improvement to the LOF 1980 was made in favour of salvors by the Convention and, consequently, by the LOFs 1990 and 1995 in terms of incentives. The new concept of special compensation has widened the scope of encouragement, in that it applies to prevention of any pollution not just oil pollution. However, damage to the environment is limited to substantial physical damage to human health or to marine life or resources in coastal or inland waters or areas adjacent thereto (Art 1(d)).

In a nutshell, to use the words of Lord Mustill, there is no longer 'no cure no pay' salvage because of the fallback on Art 14, but no profit is allowed by it. However, the Convention has not introduced a 'pure environmental salvage'. Article 14(3) is not concerned with remuneration, which implies a profit element, but with reimbursement of reasonable incurred expenses and overheads. Giving the words used in this article their natural meaning and considering its context as a whole, Art 14 is subordinate to Art 13. It is an uplift to Art 13 only if the compensation under Art 14 is higher than the award under Art 13.

Its novelty lies on the provision for compensation in respect of expenses incurred by reason of the efforts made during salvage operations to protect the environment, even though no property is saved, or even when damage to the environment is not prevented (Art 14(1)).

However, not all problems were resolved by the Convention and perhaps more were created, as has been discussed earlier. For example, under LOF 1980 the safety net was applicable even if the salvor's efforts to minimise or prevent damage to the environment took place on the high seas, as opposed to near coastal or inland waters or areas adjacent thereto only (Art 1(d)).

A solution has now been found for these problems by the SCOPIC, which can be incorporated to any LOF, but it will become operative only when the salvor opts to invoke the clause.

In practice, there are insuperable problems that salvors are faced with particularly when there is a risk to the environment, which unfortunately is being valued higher than the dangers to human life, that is the crew of either the salved or the salvor. A marine casualty becomes a political matter and international law does not yet oblige coastal states to render assistance to salvors by providing a refuge. This issue was recently highlighted in the salvage of *The Castor* off the coast of Spain. This case was an unusually difficult salvage and, for this reason, extracts from the press release of the salvors, who successfully salved this ship, are included here with their permission, hoping that swift steps will be taken by the international maritime community to progress in the matter of ports of refuge.

Successful saving of *The Castor* and related problems (Press Release, 16 February 2001)

In recent days, a marathon six week battle to salve the product tanker *Castor* and her cargo of about 30,500 tonnes of unleaded gasoline was brought to a successful conclusion with the safe transshipment of the fuel in Malta and the towage of the tanker to Greece. Under tow by the 10,000 hp *Megas Alexandros*, escorted by another Tsavliris tug, *Atlas*, *The Castor* arrived at anchorage this week in Piraeus roads.

One of the most memorable salvage operations of recent times, carried out under the glare of daily publicity from the international maritime press as well as general media, has now come to an end, although it highlighted numerous important issues that will be debated in shipping and political circles for years to come.

For the duration of the operation, there was unprecedented co-operation between the salvors, the vessel's classification society – the American Bureau of Shipping, and maritime officials in Cyprus, the vessel's Flag State, to whom we owe our thanks. We also enjoyed an excellent level of co-operation with the managers of the tanker, Athenian Sea Carriers. Deserving of a special mention are the owners and operators of the tankers *Giovanna* and *Yapi*, who were willing to offer their vessels for the discharge of cargo at normal time charter rates when many other shipowners were prone to believe hysterical assessments of the dangers involved or else sought to take advantage of the crisis by demanding exorbitant payments.

Most of all, however, our company wishes to express its appreciation and gratitude to our own crews and technicians who succeeded in this uniquely challenging and risky operation. In particular, Tsavliris thanks the crew of the salvage vessel *Nikolay Chiker*, commanded by Captain Victor Pilipchuk, that was carrying out its first major salvage operation for the group. Their professionalism was in the finest salvage traditions and their skills on at least one occasion directly prevented a major catastrophe. Last, but not least, we express our thanks and admiration to the company's gallant salvage team on site, headed by project manager Nan Halfweeg and senior salvage engineer Nicolas Pappas.

By contrast, no thanks whatsoever are due to the Mediterranean coastal States that flatly refused to grant the vessel access to sheltered coastal waters, and, in the process, turned a challenging salvage job into a nightmare that added significantly to the risks faced by salvage personnel and the environment. *The Castor* is not the first vessel to be turned into a 'leper of the sea', a trend that has worried the salvage industry increasingly in recent years. But to our knowledge, *The Castor* has set a dismal new record in being refused assistance by no less than eight different countries.

From the beginning, Tsavliris offered a sound salvage plan, including detailed and painstaking safety precautions, supported by a wealth of independent technical analysis, to show that *The Castor* could be swiftly rendered safe, hence the threat to the environment would be defused. Each of the national authorities that were approached chose to ignore this solution, with apparent disregard to the possibility that the vessel might eventually sink, with the inevitable result of her cargo causing destruction to the marine eco-structure. Their assessment of the risks has now, of course, been proved wrong. In Tsavliris' view, however, none of the Government agencies that denied the ship the traditional courtesy of a sheltered area did so because they believed she represented an unacceptable hazard. It is our belief that the vessel was seen rather as an unwanted political encumbrance. The fact that in a number of instances our detailed salvage plan and the accompanying technical analyses went unread points to this conclusion.

Even worse, in our company's view, were the reported remarks of some maritime officials that seemed to suggest that the element of a profit motive in salvage operations, somehow, made safety of life in our profession a matter of lesser significance. During this operation, we read, aghast, suggestions by maritime officials that while rescuing other seafarers is 'a duty' of the international community, salvage personnel, by implication, are expendable. As a company, Tsavliris deplores this stance and we can only hope that remarks in this vein were uttered idly, perhaps under the pressure of the moment, and that they do not form any part of the considered policy of any nation with sea borders.

In reality, *The Castor* case yet again demonstrated the importance of having qualified and courageous salvage crews, as well as powerful, well kept salvage vessels, available to protect life, property and the environment. This conclusion was supported by a meeting on 21 January of 'experts' in Cyprus, including environmental bodies, that considered contingencies in the ongoing drama. That meeting failed to identify a satisfactory alternative way of disposing of the problem posed by the gasoline cargo, while endorsing our salvage operation as 'the best hope' of preventing damage to the environment.

With the successful completion of the Castor operation, the international salvage industry can add another job well done to its long, proud record of serving shipping – and the shore based community. In the past, many independent reports, commissions and salvage judgments have highlighted the important public role played by salvors as a last line of defence when things go wrong at sea. It would be a matter of great regret if – in the face of all the most learned and informed opinion – *The Castor* case were to become a precedent for treating the salvage industry with prejudice or discourtesy whenever it seems expedient to do so.

In the light of the *Castor* incident, the debate on 'places of refuge' was at its peak at the IMO when the writing of this book was completed.

---

209 In *The Lake Avery* [1997] 1 Lloyd's Rep 540, the issue was whether there was an effective agreement to arbitrate and this depended on whether the salvage services were rendered under LOF 1995 which the defendants disputed. The salvors had appointed an arbitrator and applied to court to confirm that there was a valid appointment. If there was a valid agreement, there would be no issue as to the validity of the appointment of the arbitrator; the proceedings were ancillary to arbitration proceedings, so Art 1(4) of the Brussels Convention applied and the case was outside the Brussels Convention which does not apply to arbitration (*The Atlantic Emperor* [1992] 1 Lloyd's Rep 342, applied).

17 JURISDICTION

Under the LOF contracts, the parties submit to the jurisdiction of a Lloyd's arbitrator to determine the award.[209] But salvage is also a remedy that arises independently of contract. The Admiralty Court has both an inherent jurisdiction to protect the interests of salvors during the course of salvage operations[210] and a statutory jurisdiction under s 20(2)(j) of the SCA 1981 for any claims under the Salvage Convention, or any contract in relation to salvage services, or in the nature of salvage not falling within the above. A claim against salvors for negligence is within both para 2(j) and (h).[211] Also, a claim by salvors against the shipowner for breach of the clause in the LOF contracts in relation to his obligation to ensure that the cargo interests provide security before the discharge of the cargo comes within para 2(j).[212]

A salvage claim is enforceable *in personam* (s 21(1)) and *in rem* (s 21(3)). A property salvage attracts a maritime lien against all property salved, but environmental salvage under Art 14 does not. The Convention, by Art 20(1), does not affect the salvor's maritime lien under national or international law, so it will be up to the law applicable to a particular salvage claim whether a maritime lien is permitted for environmental salvage. In practice, the salvors' rights to compensation for environmental salvage depends on the co-operation of the liability insurer, the P&I club, and his right can be protected by obtaining security for such claims from the liability insurer. The intention behind the SCOPIC clause is that such co-operation will be forthcoming; the will to co-operate will be shown in future cases.

A sister ship arrest under s 21(4) is available if the requirements are satisfied, but the maritime lien is not transferable to the sister ship. A maritime lien enjoys certain priorities.[213]

18 TIME LIMITS

Article 23(1) of Sched 11 of the MSA 1995 provides for two years' time limit for claims in relation to payment under the Convention within which to commence arbitral or judicial proceedings. The limitation commences on the date on which the salvage operations are terminated. The person against whom a claim is made may, at any time during the running of the limitation period, extend that period by a declaration to the claimant. The period may in the like manner be further extended (Art 23(2)). An action for indemnity by a

---

210 *The Tubantia* [1924] P 78.

211 See *The Eschersheim* [1976] 1 WLR 430; [1976] 2 Lloyd's Rep 1 (HL), discussed in Part I, above.

212 Contrast *The Tesaba* [1982] 1 Lloyd's Rep 397; Chapter 2, paras 3.8.4 and 3.10, above.

213 See Chapter 4, paras 8 and 9, above, on maritime liens and priorities.

person liable may be instituted even after the expiration of the limitation period of the preceding paragraphs, if brought within the time allowed by the law of the State where proceedings are instituted, Art 23(3).

It would seem from the wording of Art 23(1) that the time limit applies only to claims for payment under Art 13 and 14 and not to claims for damages.[214] However, since claims for damages against the salvors for negligence can be brought by way of a counter-claim, a wide meaning of the word 'payment' ought to be given.

---

214 See, also, commentary in *Current Statutes*, MSA 1995, Chapter 21, p 426.

CHAPTER 14

TOWAGE

1 INTRODUCTION

Towage is known in shipping parlance as the service provided, usually by special tugs, to assist the propulsion, or to expedite the movement of another vessel (the tow) which is not in danger. Danger is an element of salvage, as discussed in the previous chapter. Tugs can range from ocean-going ships to coastal or harbour tugs that are designed with special equipment to push or pull the tow.

The purpose of this chapter is to examine the basic principles relating to the operations of tug and tow under a towage contract governed by English law. Particular attention is given to areas where the law seems to be unsettled. With the evolution of the standard form contracts, the relationship between the parties is primarily governed by the terms and conditions contained in those contracts. Standard form contracts are: the United Kingdom Standard Towage Conditions of 1986 (UKSTC); the Baltic and International Maritime Council (BIMCO) forms designed for International Ocean Towage (Towcon and Towhire); and the BIMCO Supplytime 1989 Form.[1] While the UKSTC is heavily in favour of the tugowner, Towcon and Towhire contain more balanced terms of division of liability, as between tow and tug and their respective liability to third parties. Major issues are dealt with by express terms of the contract. Common law principles and principles derived from relevant statutes will apply to fill the gaps in the contract. A comparison is made in this chapter between common law principles and contractual terms where is appropriate. Examples of drafting problems in certain clauses of contracts are shown for purpose of risk management.

2 DEFINITIONS

Unlike salvage, which does not always depend upon a contract, towage services are rendered always under contract concluded between a tug and tow for specific services or purpose at a fixed price. It is a contract for services.

---

1   For a detailed treatment of the subject, see Rainey, S, *The Law of Tug and Tow*, 1996, LLP; for American law, see Parks, A and Cattell, E, *The Law of Tug, Tow and Pilotage*, 3rd edn, 1994, Cornell Maritime Press and Schoenbaum, T, *Admiralty and Maritime Law*, 2nd edn, 1994, West.

Therefore, like any other contracts, towage is governed by the basic principles of contract law, but its particular features have led, over the years, to it being regarded as a specialised maritime law subject.

Towage was defined in *The Princess Alice*[2] as:

> ... the employment of one vessel to expedite the voyage of another, when nothing more is required than the accelerating of her progress.

The UKSTC 1986, cl 1(b)(i) defines 'towing' as

(i) ... any operation in connection with the holding, pushing, pulling, moving, escorting or guiding of or standing by the hirer's vessel and the expressions 'to tow', being towed' and 'towage' shall be defined likewise;

(ii) 'vessel' shall include any vessel, craft, or object of whatsoever nature (whether or not coming within the usual meaning of the word 'vessel') which the tugowner agrees to tow or to which the tugowner agrees at the request, express or implied, of the hirer, to render any service of whatsoever nature other than towing;

(iii) 'tender' shall include any vessel, craft or object of whatsoever nature which is not a tug but which is provided by the tugowner for the performance of any towage or any service;

(iv) the expression 'whilst towing' shall cover the period commencing when the tug or tender is in a position to receive orders direct from the hirer's vessel to commence holding, pushing, pulling, moving, escorting, guiding or standing by the vessel, or to pick up ropes, wires or lines, or when the towing line has been passed to or by the tug or tender, whichever is the sooner, and ending when the final orders from the hirer's vessel to cease holding, pushing, pulling, moving, escorting, guiding or standing by the vessel or to cast off ropes, wires or lines has been carried out, or the towing line has been finally slipped, whichever is the later, and the tug or tender is safely clear of the vessel.

Dr Lushington in *The Kingalock*[3] gave the definition of ordinary and extraordinary towage:

> ... there are two species of agreement that may be entered into by a vessel whose usual occupation is to tow vessels from one place to another. One is, where she meets with a vessel disabled, and ... undertakes for any sum agreed upon between the parties to perform the service of bringing the vessel from one port to another or place of safety. This may be called extraordinary towage ... ordinary towage is that which takes place for the purpose of expediting a vessel on her voyage either homeward or outward.

---

2   [1849] 3 W Rob 138.

3   (1854) 1 Ecc & AD 264.

3 TOWAGE VERSUS SALVAGE

Although towage is distinguishable from salvage because a salvor is generally a volunteer, sometimes there seems to be an overlap or, as has been seen in the previous chapter, the towage may be converted into salvage in exceptional circumstances.

Article 17 of the 1989 Salvage Convention makes it clear that:

> No payment is due under the provisions of this Convention unless the services rendered exceed what can be reasonably considered as due performance of a contract entered into before the danger arose.

Also, cl 6 of the UKSTC 1986 provides:

> Nothing contained in these conditions shall limit, prejudice or preclude in any way any legal rights which the tugowner may have against the hirer including, but not limited to, any rights which the tugowner or his servants or agents have to claim salvage remuneration or special compensation for any extraordinary services rendered to vessels or anything aboard the vessels by any tug or tender ...

By comparison, cl 15 of Towcon and Towhire does not expressly provide for a possible right of the tugowner to claim salvage, but it should be implied in the first sentence (see below) that any extraordinary services, which are not contemplated by the agreement, will qualify for salvage. The second paragraph deals mainly with a warranty of authority by the tow when it is necessary for the tug to accept or seek salvage assistance from other vessels. In particular, the clause provides:

> Should the Tow break away from the tug during the course of the towage service, the tug shall render all reasonable services to reconnect the towline and fulfil this agreement without making any claim for salvage.

> If at any time the tugowner or the tugmaster consider it necessary or advisable to seek or accept salvage services from any vessel or person on behalf of the tug or tow, or both, the hirer hereby undertakes and warrants that the tugowner or his duly authorised servant or agent including the tugmaster have the full actual authority of the hirer to accept such services on behalf of the tow on any reasonable terms

At common law, the issue of when a towage contract is converted into salvage has been analysed in decided cases some of which have been discussed in the previous chapter. The general principles, as have been established in those decisions, are summarised in the following examples:

The *dicta* of Lord Kingsdown in *The Minnehaha*[4] illustrate when towage can become salvage:

---

4   (1861) 15 Moo PC 133 (HL), pp 153, 158.

... if in the discharge of this task, by sudden violence of wind or waves, or other accidents, the ship in tow is placed in danger, and the towing vessel incurs risks and performs duties which were not within the scope of her original engagement, she is entitled to additional services if the ship be saved, and may claim as a salvor, instead of being restricted to the sum stipulated to be paid for mere towage ... In the cases on this subject, the towage contract is generally spoken of as superseded by the right to salvage ...

... they [the tugowners] must show that, the ship being in danger from no fault of theirs, they performed services which were not covered by their towage contract, and did all they could to prevent the danger.

Sir Samuel Evans considered the same issue in *The Leon Blum*:[5]

Where salvage services (which must be voluntary) supervene upon towage services (which are under contract) the two kinds of services cannot co-exist during the same space of time. There must be a moment when the towage service ceases and the salvage service begins; and, if the tug remains at her post of duty, there may come a moment when the special and unexpected danger is over, and then the salvage service will end, and the towage service would be resumed. These moments of time may be difficult to fix, but have to be, and are, fixed in practice.

This, however, raises the question as to how the tugmaster is supposed to know when salvage has superseded towage and what to do in circumstances where there is uncertainty as to whether the duties to be performed are within the contemplation of the parties to the contract.

In *The Annapolis*,[6] the learned judge laid down the rules that may assist the parties involved to recognise the situation in which there may be a conversion from towage to salvage as follows:

... a contract for mere towing does not include the rendering of any salvage service whatever. If it happens by reason of unforeseen occurrences in the performance of the contract to tow that new and special services are necessary, the contract is not at once rendered void, nor is the tug at liberty to abandon the vessel, for that would be most detrimental; nor, on the other hand, is the tug bound to perform the new service for the stipulated reward agreed for the original service; but the law requires performance of the service and allows salvage reward.[7]

And Hill J, in *The Homewood*,[8] considered the elements that should exist for the tug to be able to claim salvage.

To constitute a salvage service by a tug under contract to tow two elements are necessary: (1) that the tow is in danger by reason of circumstances which could not reasonably have been contemplated by the parties; and (2) that risks are

5   [1915] P 90.
6   (1861) Lush 355.
7   *Ibid*, p 361.
8   (1928) 31 LlL Rep 336.

incurred or duties performed by the tug which could not reasonably be held to be within the scope of the contract.[9]

In this case, the steamship had previously been in tow of the tug under a towage contract. Due to bad weather, she broke away and drifted. The crew were rescued and taken off by a lifeboat. The vessel was lying in an exposed position with no one on board. The tow was an empty shell with no means of propulsion and could not anchor. The tug resumed towage services without knowledge of the tow's crew. When the tug claimed remuneration for salvage, the question was whether the events that arose during the towage were within the contemplation of the contract.

It was held that the risk of interruption and prolongation by bad weather, the possibility of the hawser parting, and the fact that there was a need to anchor the tow were reasonably within the scope of the contract. However, the contract did not contemplate that the lifeboat would take off the crew or that the vessel would be let at anchor with no one on board. The element of danger to the tow was present. The crew of the tug was, therefore, entitled to remuneration for salvage.

Similarly, the facts of *The Aldora*[10] are worth noting for the purpose of defining the boundary between towage and salvage.

The defendants' ship, *The Aldora*, was on a voyage with a full cargo to be delivered at a terminal in Blyth Harbour, which was approached from the sea by a dredged channel the seaward limits of which were marked on the north side by a buoy. It was standard practice at the harbour for a ship of *The Aldora*'s size to be met outside the harbour and to be navigated into her berth in the harbour by a pilot with the assistance of four tugs. Due to a misunderstanding as to the time, *The Aldora* arrived earlier than had been anticipated by the pilot, or the tugs which had been engaged to render assistance to her at a position about two miles from the buoy, and *The Aldora* continued on her inward journey towards the buoy at reduced speed, expecting to be met by the pilot and the tugs at any moment. On reaching the buoy and finding that the pilot and the tugs had still not arrived, the master of *The Aldora* turned her around in order to proceed out to sea again. In the process of that operation, the ship ran aground on a sandbank. The pilot and the tugs arrived soon afterwards and succeeded in refloating the ship. Thereafter, the pilot, with the assistance of the tugs, navigated *The Aldora* to her berth in the harbour.

The plaintiffs, the pilot, and the tugowners, masters and crew brought an action *in rem* against the owners of *The Aldora* claiming remuneration for salvage services and contended that such services lasted until *The Aldora* was safely berthed in the harbour. Brandon J held that the salvage services

9   (1928) 31 LlL Rep 336, p 339.
10 [1975] QB 748.

terminated near the buoy before the ship proceeded inward into the harbour and that, thereafter, the plaintiffs were entitled to be paid for towage services only.

This part of their service was contemplated by the towage contract.

A contrast between *The Albion* and *The North Goodwin* (below) can illustrate the boundary between towage and salvage: In *The Albion*,[11] the contract simply provided for towage. While the towage services were being performed and after a temporary anchoring of the tow, a strong gale rose which forced the tug to seek shelter nearby. The gale blew the tow into sea resulting in the loss of equipment and anchors. Upon moderation of the weather, the tug went searching for the tow. After considerable effort, the tow was found and was towed back to safety. The tug was awarded salvage for her efforts to find the tow and tow her back.

By contrast in *The North Goodwin*,[12] this lightship was in tow of *The Mermaid*. Having reached close to River Tyne, about a mile distance, it was anticipated that two other tugs, *The Northsider* and *The Ironsider*, would take over the towage under the UKSTC. However, gale force winds caused heavy swell and it was considered dangerous to allow the pilot boat to leave the harbour. Despite this blowing gale and swell, *The Northsider* went out to meet the tow, being still under tow of *The Mermaid*, which was trying to bring the lightship into the river for more protection and then handed her over to the other tugs. At this point, the towing hawser parted and the lightship drifted away, whereupon *The Northsider* went immediately to her assistance and managed to pass a towage connection and tow her to an anchorage about a mile from the coast. The owners, master and crew of *The Northsider* claimed salvage in respect of these services. Sheen J held that there was no salvage in these circumstances:

> It is implied in all such contracts that the tug will do her duty in case of accident and do all she can to take care of and protect the ship. From time to time towing ropes do part. If *Northsider* had already taken the light vessel in tow and the tow rope had parted in precisely the same position as that in which it parted, and thereafter *Northsider* had made fast again, I do not think it would have been arguable that the tow was in danger by reason of circumstances which could not reasonably have been contemplated by the parties, or that risks were incurred or duties performed by the tug which could not reasonably be held to be within the scope of the contract. In these circumstances, it being conceded that *Northsider* had come out of the protection of the piers pursuant to the terms of her contract, I do not think it can properly be said that risks were incurred or duties performed which were not within the scope of the contract.[13]

---

11 (1861) Lush 282.
12 [1980] 1 Lloyd's Rep 71.
13 *Ibid*, p 74 .

Although each case must be looked upon on its own facts, the facts of this case indicate that it ought to be regarded as a borderline case and perhaps another judge may have held a different view. A clearer case than this on the issue that there was no immediate danger other than some unexpected difficulty in the performance of the towage was *The Glaisdale*.[14] This involved an engine defect developed unexpectedly in the tow after the engagement of towage. The weather conditions were not such as to impose danger. It was held that there was nothing to indicate that the circumstances were so different and the risk to the ship such that the towage contract should be changed retrospectively into a salvage service.

4 THE MAKING OF A BINDING CONTRACT

Towage contracts are invariably entered into directly between the owner of the tow and professional tug owning companies. There are, however, circumstances where the master of the ship may have to sign the contract as an agent of the owners and, if there is cargo on board, as an agent for the cargo-owners provided the requirements of agency of necessity are met. It is necessary first to examine how the master's authority to bind these parties to the contract arises.

4.1 Authority of the master to bind the shipowners

The basic principles of principal and agent and the sources of authority are to be found in *Bowstead*[15] from which the following extract illustrates the position of principal and agent by way of a general definition:

> Agency is the fiduciary relationship which exists between two persons, one of whom expressly or impliedly consents that the other should act on his behalf so as to affect his relations with third parties, and the other of whom similarly consents so to act or so acts. The one on whose behalf the act or acts to be done is called the principal. The one who is to act is called the agent. Any person other than the principal and the agent may be referred to as a third party. In respect of the acts which the principal expressly or impliedly consents that the agent shall so do on the principal's behalf, the agent is said to have authority to act; and his authority constitutes a power to affect the principal's legal relations with third parties. Where the agent's authority results from a manifestation of consent that he should represent or act for the principal expressly or impliedly made by the principal to the agent himself, the authority is called actual authority, express or implied. But the agent may also have authority resulting

---

14 (1945) 78 LlL Rep 403.
15 Bowstead, FMB and Reynolds, W, *Bowstead and Reynolds on Agency*, 16th edn, 1996, Sweet & Maxwell.

from such a manifestation made by the principal to a third party; such authority is called apparent authority.[16]

By virtue of his employment contract, the master of a ship has an implied actual authority to enter into towage contracts, only when it is reasonably necessary and the terms are reasonable. This is an additional authority to what is necessary for, or incidental to, effective execution of his express authority in performing his duties for the preservation of the ship and safe prosecution of voyages. The general principle was laid down in *The Ocean Steamship v Anderson*,[17] *per* Brett MR, when he said:

> A captain cannot bind his owners by every towage contract which he may think fit to make: it is binding upon them only when the surrounding circumstances are such as to render it reasonable to be made, and also when its terms are reasonable.

Brandon J referred to this authority in **The Unique Mariner**,[18] holding that the implied actual authority of the master, unless is restricted by instructions lawfully given by his principal, extends to doing whatever is incidental to, or necessary for, the successful prosecution of the voyage and the safety and preservation of the ship. Although actual implied authority is distinct from ostensible or apparent authority, they can co-exist or overlap only when the restriction of the actual implied authority is not brought to the attention of a third party who deals with the agent, in this case the master. This was the situation in *The Unique Mariner*.[19]

With the modern means of communication, however, the master will normally be able to communicate with his principals (unless he genuinely misunderstands instructions) and an express authority may be given to him. Sometimes, when the third party (the tugmaster) enters into the contract of towage with the apparent agent of the owner of the tow, the latter may be estopped[20] as against the tugowner from denying that the master of the tow acted as his agent. If, in fact, the master had no actual authority, he may be liable for breach of warranty of authority,[21] unless his principal ratifies the contract.

---

16   *Op cit*, Bowstead and Reynolds, fn 15, para 1-001.

17   (1883) 13 QBD 651, p 662.

18   [1978] 1 Lloyd's Rep 438, pp 443, 449; see, also, Chapter 13.

19   *Ibid*, pp 450–51; see, also, *Freeman and Lockyer v Buckhurst Park Properties* [1964] 2 QB 480, p 503; and *op cit*, Bowstead and Reynolds, fn 15, p 105 ('ostensible or apparent authority is the authority of an agent as it appears to others'); and discussion of ostensible and actual implied authority see in Markesinis, B and Munday, R, *An Outline of the Law of Agency*, 3rd edn, 1992, Butterworths, pp 21–52.

20   *Op cit*, Bowstead and Reynolds, fn 15, p 101 and para 8-029: 'Ostensible or apparent authority is merely a form of estoppel, indeed, it has been termed agency by estoppel, and you cannot call in aid an estoppel unless you have three ingredients (i) a representation (ii) a reliance on the representation and (iii) an alteration of your position resulting from such reliance.'

21   *Op cit*, Bowstead and Reynolds, fn 15, para 9-065.

In circumstances in which the hirer is not the owner of the tow, there is an express warranty of authority given by the hirer to the tug in all standard terms towage contracts that the hirer has such an authority to bind the owner of the tow to the contract. In particular, cl 2 of the UKSTC (and cl 22 of the Towcon and Towhire) provide:

> If at the time of making this agreement or of performing the towage or of rendering any service other than towing at the request, express or implied, of the hirer, the hirer is not the owner of the vessel referred to therein as the 'hirer's vessel', the hirer expressly represents that he is authorised to make and does make this agreement for and on behalf of the owner of the said vessel subject to each and all of these conditions and agrees that both the hirer and the owner are bound jointly and severally by these conditions.

Another type of agency, agency of necessity, which arises by the operation of law, is referred to below but it has also been discussed in Chapter 13, para 8.

4.2 Authority of the master to bind the cargo-owners

The relevance of the authority of the master in this respect is with regard to binding the cargo-owners to pay to the owners of the carrying vessel their pro rata proportion of the towage costs, if the towage comes properly within the provisions of general average.[22] Unless there is agency of necessity,[23] the master would not have authority to bind the cargo-owners to the towage contract, except when the cargo-owners give express authority to him. Neither the owners of the ship nor their master have authority to bind the goods or the owners of the goods by any contract.[24] The master is always the agent of the ship and, in special cases of necessity, the agent of the cargo.[25]

---

22 See the York-Antwerp Rules 1994. General average is part of the law of carriage by sea. It arises when sacrifices are made or expenditure is incurred for the preservation of ship, freight and cargo, the loss of which is insured under marine insurance policies. Section 66(1) of the Marine Insurance Act 1906 defines a general average loss as a loss caused by or directly consequential on a general average act. It includes a general average expenditure as well as a general average sacrifice. Section 66(2) states that there is a general average act where any extraordinary sacrifice or expenditure is voluntarily and reasonably made or incurred in time of peril for the purpose of preserving the property imperilled in the common adventure. Rule A of the York-Antwerp Rules 1994 has extended the definition of general average act, thus: 'there is a general average act when, and *only when*, any extraordinary sacrifice or expenditure is *intentionally* and reasonably made or incurred for the common safety for the purpose of preserving *from peril* the property involved in a common adventure' (emphasis added to indicate differences). Rule D is important because it makes the rights to contribution in general average independent of fault of one of the parties to the adventure. This rule, however, does not prejudice any remedies or defences that the other party may have against the party guilty of fault. The rules specify events that will qualify as general average. See, generally, Rose, F, *General Average – Law and Practice*, 1997, LLP.

23 See Chapter 13, above, para 8.1.2.

24 *Anderson v Ocean Steamship* (1884) 10 App Cas 107, p 117, *per* Lord Blackburn.

25 *The Onward* (1874) LR 4 A&E 38, p 51.

Agency of necessity has been discussed in the previous chapter but it would be useful to repeat its elements here as well. It has been defined by Bowstead[26] in the following terms:

> A person may have authority to act on behalf of another in certain cases where he is faced with an emergency in which the property or interests of the other are in imminent jeopardy and it becomes necessary, in order to preserve the property or interests, so to act. In some cases this authority may entitle him to affect his principal's legal position by making contracts or disposing of property. In others it may merely entitle him to reimbursement of expenses or indemnity against liabilities incurred in so acting, or to a defence against a claim that what he did was wrongful as against the person for whose benefit he acted.

Following the decision in *The Winson*[27] defining this type of agency, the principle was elaborated more extensively in **The Choko Star**[28] in relation to salvage:

> Until an emergency arises, such as to give rise to an agency of necessity, there is no question of the shipowner or master being agent for the cargo-owners. Accordingly, it is not possible to spell out authority for either of them to bind the cargo-owners to a salvage contract, as merely incidental to his pre-existing general authority as an agent.

It derived from these authorities that the rules applicable to the exercise of this authority must be in circumstances when it would be impossible or impracticable to communicate with the principal in question. This could include situations where there are too many principals to consult (for example, owners of cargo shipped under bills of lading on liner terms). The agent must have acted *bona fide* in the interests of the principal; the action must be necessary for the benefit of the principal and the authority could not prevail against the express instructions of the principal.[29]

4.3 Authority of the tugmaster

A tugmaster of a professional tug company will be acting within the scope of his employment contract when he enters into a towage contract and his authority will be actual, express or implied to do what is necessary and reasonable to bind his employers to the contract. In cases where the master of a merchant ship decides to tow a vessel without the express authority of his employer, it could not be said that he could bind the owners of his ship to a towage contract because the scope of his usual employment would not

---

26   *Op cit*, Bowstead and Reynolds, fn 15, p 145.
27   See Chapter 13, above.
28   [1990] 1 Lloyd's Rep 516, pp 525–26, *per* Slade LJ.
29   See Chapter 13, on salvage.

encompass entering into such contract. Only if the circumstances of a case are such as to justify him to assist a vessel in distress by towing, it could be held that the master would have implied authority to bind his principals, but this situation would be more likely to amount to salvage services.[30]

4.4 Pre-contractual duties

Under English contract law, the governing principle is that negotiating parties are under a duty not to mislead each other by positive misrepresentation of fact. There is no pre-contractual obligation or positive duty upon the parties to make full and frank disclosure of all material facts. The parties are free to make their own investigations. However, there are limited classes of contracts known as contracts of *uberrimae fidei* (utmost good faith). For example, contracts of insurance are contracts of utmost good faith, which impose upon the negotiating parties the additional duty to disclose all material facts (which are, or ought to be known, by a party to the contract and are material to the formation of the contract). A party to a contract of insurance is also under the ordinary duty to avoid making material misrepresentations before the contract is concluded. Sections 17–20 of the Marine Insurance Act 1906 have codified these principles. Failure to comply with the duty of utmost good faith by one party entitles the other to avoid the contract.[31]

Whether contracts for salvage or towage fall within the class of contracts of *uberrimae fidei* was discussed in *The Unique Mariner*, in which the contractor argued that they did. Reference was made to *The Kingalock*[32] decided over 100 years earlier.

In this case, a tug came to the assistance of *The Kingalock* and entered into an agreement to tow her from Newfoundland to London for £40. In the course of the towage, the hawser broke and the master of the tug discovered for the first time that the tow had previously suffered heavy weather damage. He declared the contract at an end and continued to tow her as if no contract had been made. He brought her safely to port and claimed salvage remuneration, which was resisted on the ground that there was an agreement to tow for £40. Dr Lushington decided in favour of the tug holding that the towage agreement was null and void *ab initio*, because the master of *The Kingalock* had failed to disclose the weather damage to the master of the tug before the agreement was made, which was material to the arduousness and difficulty of the towage. He dealt with the claim on the basis of salvage and rewarded the tug salvage remuneration of £160 explaining, thus:

---

30 *The Thetis* (1869) LR 2 A&E 365.

31 See Merkin, R, *Insurance Contract Law*, 2000, Kluwer, loose-leaf section A5; and, for the test of materiality, *Pan Atlantic Insurance Co v Pine Top Insurance Co Ltd* [1994] 3 All ER 581 (HL).

32 (1854) 1 Spinks E&A 265.

An agreement to bind two parties must be made with full knowledge of all the facts necessary to be known by both parties; and if any facts which, if known, could have any operation on the agreement about to be entered into is kept back or not disclosed to either of the contracting parties, that would vitiate the agreement itself. It is not necessary, in order to make it not binding, that one of the parties should keep back any fact or circumstance of importance, if there should be misapprehension, accidentally or by carelessness; we all know that there may be what, in the eye of the law, is termed equitable fraud.

However, as was accepted by Brandon J, in *The Unique Mariner*, *The Kingalock* is not an authority which establishes a general principle that all contracts relating to salvage services are contracts of *uberrimae fidei*. This case was just one example of the exercise by the Admiralty Court of its equitable power to treat that kind of salvage agreement as invalid on the ground of serious unfairness. The Admiralty Court has always exercised an equitable jurisdiction to declare invalid, and refuse to enforce, an agreement of this kind if it considers that the agreement, in all the circumstances of the case, is seriously inequitable to one side or the other. There is no reason why these contracts, which are commercial contracts for work and labour, should be regarded as contracts of *uberrimae fidei*. Insofar as misrepresentation is concerned, Brandon J did not see any reason why the ordinary principles of law relating to rescission of contracts for fraudulent or innocent misrepresentation (including the relevant provisions of the Misrepresentation Act (MA) 1967) should not apply to contracts for the rendering of salvage services, including contracts on the terms of Lloyd's form, in exactly the same way as they apply to all other contracts. Thus, there should be no reason for the exercise by the Admiralty Court of any additional equitable jurisdiction to treat such contracts as invalid by reason of misstatement.[33]

4.5 Unfair contract terms

Towage contracts are entered into usually between commercial companies with fairly equal bargaining power. The provisions of the Unfair Contract Terms Act (UCTA) 1977 generally do not apply to any contract of marine salvage or towage, unless the tow-owner (of small boats or a yacht) is dealing as a consumer. However, the Act imposes, by s 2(1), a total ban in all contracts on exception clauses which exempt liability for death and personal injury.[34] The Act applies to contracts when the owner of the tow is dealing as a

---

33 *The Unique Mariner* [1978] 1 Lloyd's Rep 438, pp 454–55.

34 Cases dated prior to the Act, in which exclusion clauses from liability for loss of life or personal injury were held to be valid, are no longer good law. Eg, towage contracts, even on the basis of standard forms, contained such clauses, see *Great Western Rly Co v Royal Norwegian Government* (1945) 78 LlL Rep 152. As a result, neither the exclusion from liability clause nor the indemnity clause of the UKSTC 1986 contain a reference to loss of life or personal injury.

consumer and prohibits exception clauses for negligence (by the tug) if the clauses are unreasonable. If they are, they may be struck down. There may be occasions when a yacht owner or a small boat owner will need towage or salvage and enter into such contracts as individuals and not in the course of business (s 12(1)). An additional protection for consumer yacht owners may be found in the EC Directive on unfair contract terms, which was given statutory force in the UK by the Unfair Terms (Consumer Contracts) Regulations in 1994, came into force on 1 July 1995 and they are now superseded by the 1999 Regulations. There is, however, very little that this Directive can add to the UCTA 1977, as far as English law is concerned. An interesting variation introduced by this Directive is that a term would be unfair (if it has not been 'individually negotiated', that is, the consumer was not able to influence its substance), when it is contrary to the requirements of good faith. As such, it causes a significant imbalance in the rights and obligations of the parties to the detriment of the consumer, taking into account the nature of the services and the circumstances in the making of the contract. As it is not the scope of this chapter to analyse its complex provisions, the reader is advised to look at the standard contract law textbooks.[35]

5 COMMENCEMENT OF TOWAGE, INTERRUPTION AND TERMINATION

5.1 Commencement

At common law, the towage contract commences when the ropes have been passed between the vessels. Under the UKSTC 1986, commencement can occur at an earlier stage, when the tug is ready to receive orders from the hiring vessel. The Towcon and Towhire contracts specify the place from which the contract commences.

The duration of the towage operation under the UKSTC is written in much wider terms than at common law. For the purpose of the UKSTC 1986, cl 1(b)(iv) provides that:

> The expression 'whilst towing' shall cover the period commencing when the tug or tender is in a position to receive orders direct from the hirer's vessel to commence holding, pushing, pulling, moving, escorting, guiding or standing by the vessel or to pick up ropes, wires or lines, or when the towing line has been passed to or by the tug or tender, whichever is the sooner, and ending when the final orders from the hirer's vessel to cease holding, pushing, pulling, moving, escorting, guiding or standing by the vessel or to cast off ropes, wires

---

35 See, eg, Halson, R, *Contract Law*, 2001, Longman.

or lines has been carried out, or the towing line has been finally slipped, whichever is the later, and the tug or tender is safely clear of the vessel.

It is very important to know when a towage contract commences, how long it lasts, when is interrupted or terminated for the liabilities and obligations of the contracting parties, as well as the operation of exception clauses or indemnity, will be determined accordingly.

The following examples of cases illustrate situations of different wording of clauses with regard to commencement and their effect on the operation of exemption from liability of the tug in the event of negligence, or indemnity from the tow to the tug for liability incurred by the tug.

The Clan Colquhoun[36]

Clause 1 of the agreement provided:

> ... the towage or transport shall be deemed to have commenced when the tow-rope has been passed onto the tug and to have ended when the tow-rope has been finally slipped.

The two vessels *Beam* and *Sirdir* belonged to the plaintiffs (the Port of London Authority). They contracted with the defendant to tow the vessel *Clan Colquhoun* (*CC*). *Sirdir* was ahead of *CC* while *Beam* was behind. As they went through the lock into the dock, *Beam* was struck by the revolving propeller of *CC*, and was damaged. The collision was due to the negligence of those on board the tug *Beam*. The plaintiffs contended that, by cl 4 of the towage contract, the defendants were obliged to pay for any damage to their property arising from collision, even though it was due to the contributory negligence of the plaintiffs' tugs. The defendants contended that the clause was inapplicable, as the towage contract had not commenced because, under cl 1 of the agreement, the contract was deemed to commence when the tow-rope had been passed. As the ropes had not yet been passed to the tug *Beam*, the contract had not commenced.

It was held that cl 1 could fairly be interpreted as meaning that the towage shall be deemed to have commenced when the tow-rope or ropes have been passed to each of the two tugs asked for by the owner of the tow. This provision not having been satisfied, the plaintiffs could not take advantage of the terms and conditions of the agreement. Thus, the exception clause did not apply at the time of the collision.

The Uranienborg[37]

The 'commencement' clause in this case stated that:

For the purpose of these conditions, the phrase 'whilst towing' shall be deemed to cover the period commencing when the tug is in a position to receive orders direct from the hirer's vessel to pick up ropes or lines or when the tow-rope has been passed to or by the tug, whichever is sooner ...

The towage contract was to commence at 11 am. The tug arrived a few minutes earlier, but was travelling so fast that she was unable to reverse her engines in time. As a result, she struck and damaged the tow. At the time of the collision, the crew of the tow were not ready to give orders as they were still discharging the ship. Also, the crew of the tug were not expecting such orders. The question was whether the towage conditions had begun to apply to enable the tug to take advantage of the exemption provisions.

It was held that 'in a position to receive orders' does not refer to physical readiness. It means, not only that the vessel is within hailing distance, but that the vessel is ready in herself to receive orders, which the tow was not. Sir Boyd Merriman said:

I doubt whether the word 'position' is only used in the sense of local situation, I think it involves also the conception of the tug being herself in a condition to receive and act upon orders. But, however, that may be, the orders which she is to be in a position to receive are orders to pick up ropes or lines, not orders generally, but those specific orders, and I think that that must have some reference to the intention of those on board the ship to give those orders, and to the readiness of those on board the tug to receive them.[38]

By contrast, in *The Glenaffric*,[39] upon construction of the same clause, towage had commenced on the facts of this case. The agreement was subject to the UKSTC, cl 1 of which provided:

For the purpose of these conditions, the phrase 'whilst towing' shall be deemed to cover the period commencing when the tug is in a position to receive orders direct from the hirer's vessel to pick up ropes or lines, or when the tow-rope has been passed to or by the tug whichever is the sooner ... Clause 3 provided: the tugowner shall not whilst towing, bear ... damage of any description done ... to the tug and the tugowner shall not, whilst at the request expressed or implied of the hirer rendering any service other than towing, be held responsible for any damage done to the hirer's vessel and the hirer shall indemnify the tugowner against any claim by a third party ...

On 5 April, at about 6 am the tugs in performance of the agreement approached within 20 or 30 ft of the steamship which was at anchor with her anchor lights burning in the Barry Roads about one mile from the Barry Dock. Those in charge of *The Glenaffric* hailed the tug, *Standard Rose*: 'We are not ready. Clear away or keep away.' The master of the tug dropped astern, but kept his engines working to stem the tide until he saw the anchor lights of the

---

38 [1936] P 21, p 27.
39 [1948] P 159, or [1948] 1 All ER 245 (CA).

steamship replaced by the navigation lights. He then steamed within about 20 ft of the steamer. He was then hailed: 'Don't want you yet. Wait till we get in a bit.' The tug stood off again, and when the steamer had drawn nearer to the dock he approached again all ready to receive ropes or lines and take the ship in tow. He was told that no rope would be passed then and was ordered to take a message to the dockmaster to say that the ship would not dock that tide. In dropping astern to obey that order his tug struck the ship and sustained damage to herself, for which the tugowners claimed to be indemnified under the conditions of the towage agreement.

It was held that, on the true interpretation of the agreement and the application of it to the facts of the present case, the plain meaning of the words in cl 1 were not susceptible of modification by implying the additional words: '... and the ship is ready to give orders'. It was expressly provided that 'whilst towing' was deemed to cover a period of time before the towing proper actually began. The tug was in that position and the plaintiffs were entitled to be indemnified in respect of damage to the tug by virtue of the provision of cl 3 of the conditions.

Scott LJ distinguished the judgment of Sir Boyd Merriman in the previous case which was the only one on the same point. He said:[40]

> That was quite a different case. There the tug was employed to go to a wharf in the Thames where the vessel was discharging, in order to tow her from her wharf after discharge or to assist her in her passage from the wharf by towing. The tug arrived before the vessel was ready, at a time when the discharging was still going on. In my view, one answer to the question, which was raised in that case indirectly, is that the primary condition precedent to the whole business of towing, namely, that the ship was ready to be towed, had not come into operation, and the learned President so held. He deals, on p 28 of his judgment, with an additional reason which I think I ought to read ... Mr Bateson argues that *The Tanga* quite plainly was in a position to receive orders to pick up ropes or lines. This is true in the sense that she was within 300 ft and within hailing distance, but in no other sense; she knew that the time was not ripe and was acting accordingly. There is not a shred of evidence from *The Kenia* that anybody, from the master downwards, was even thinking in terms of ropes and lines at the material time. Certainly, they had come there in order to be available for the towing whenever the towing began.

A wide commencement clause used in *The Ramsden*,[41] 'whilst tug is in attendance upon or engaged in any manoeuvre for the purpose of making fast', was held to cover the negligence of the tugmaster when he was proceeding towards the tow in order to make fast.

---

40 [1948] P 159, p 166.
41 [1943] P 46.

The criteria of when a tug is ready to receive orders were laid down in *The Apollon*.[42] The usual commencement clause provided that:

> ... the period commencing when the tug is in a position to receive orders direct from the hirer's vessel to pick up ropes or lines or when the to-rope has been passed to or by the tug, whichever is the sooner ...

The owners of *The Apollon* had ordered two tugs. The first tug commenced towing. While the second tug was manoeuvring towards *The Apollon*, she struck a dock gate and sustained damage. The tugowners claimed an indemnity under the conditions providing for the hirer to pay for damages sustained whilst towing.

Brandon J laid down the general principles extracted from the earlier cases:

> It seems to me that, for a tug to be in a position to receive orders direct from the hirer's vessel to pick up ropes or lines, three conditions must be fulfilled. The first condition is that the situation is such that those on board the tug can reasonably expect the ship to give the tug an order to pick up ropes or lines. The second condition is that the tug is ready to respond to such orders if given. The third condition is that the tug should be close enough to the ship for the order to be passed direct: in other words, that the tug should be within hailing distance.[43]

It was held that all three conditions had been fulfilled in this case, even though the tug had to make a further manoeuvre in order to carry out the pilot's instructions. She was, nevertheless, in a position to receive that order.

In *The Blenheim v The Impetus*,[44] there was no need for the tug to be able to perform at the time the orders were given provided she was ready to receive the orders. When the collision occurred after orders had been given, but before they were carried out, the tug was protected by the exclusion of liability clause.

5.2 Interruption of towing

Where the towage is interrupted, the principle is that it is the tug's duty to return to the tow and resume towage, or if this cannot be done, it must not leave the tow until she is safe or other assistance is sought. If neither of these duties is performed, the towage terms will cease to operate, as there will be an interruption of the towage amounting to a breach of contract.

---

42 [1971] 1 Lloyd's Rep 471.
43 *Ibid*, p 480.
44 [1959] 2 All ER 354.

The Refrigerant[45]

The towage contract provided that:

> During the towage service the master and crew of the tugboat become the
> servants of the owners of the vessel in tow, and are under the control of the
> master or person in charge of the vessel in tow, the company only providing
> the motive power. The company will not be liable for any damage or loss to or
> occasioned by the vessel in tow ... or any damage or loss to any person or
> property whatsoever, although such damage or loss may be caused or
> contributed to by the acts or defaults of the master or crew of the tugboat, or by
> any defect in or breakdown of or accident to the ... equipment or towing gear
> of the tugboat.

It was also expressly stated that the tugowners (the plaintiffs) would provide
a towing hawser sufficient for the purpose, and that the tow should have
steam available.

During the towage, the hawser parted when the weather was bad. The tug
left the tow and went to Falmouth in search of a new rope. The master of the
tug sent another tug to assist the tow, but the tow refused assistance, unless
the master of the new tug was ready to make an agreement. Eventually, the
tow had to hire and pay for the services of another vessel up to Plymouth,
before the plaintiffs returned and completed the towage. When the plaintiffs
claimed remuneration, the tow counterclaimed for the amount paid to the
other vessel. The tugowners sought to rely on the terms of the contract
excluding liability for losses or damage to the tow, or any person or property
during the towage service.

It was held that the tugmaster had acted improperly by leaving the tow, as
the master ought to have stood by the tow throughout. Bateson J stated that

> In my opinion the words 'during the towage service' mean while the service is
> being conducted – not while it is being interrupted, in the sense that the master
> of the tug leaves the ship altogether and goes into port and sends out
> somebody else to do his work.[46]

The judge in this case relied on the *dictum* of Lord Sterndale in *The Cap Palos*
(see below) and held that the exceptions from liability in the contract did not
apply to an interruption of towage, but were confined to a time when the
tugowner was doing something in the actual performance of the contract, and
not when he had abandoned his duties.

---

45 [1925] P 130.
46 *Ibid*, pp 140–41.

The Cap Palos[47]

The plaintiffs entered into contract with the defendants for the latter to tow their vessel on a round voyage. A very wide exception clause was agreed to protect the defendants for damage done, otherwise than by collision to the vessel being towed, or having been towed, by reason of the default of the tugowner. The defendant got another tug to assist in the towing. Both tugs lost their hawsers during the tow. The plaintiff's vessel could not make her way out of the bay, and the defendants' tugs left her there, at which time, a moderate breeze was rising. The defendants erroneously thought that the Salvage Association would provide tugs to assist the tow, but three days later, still unable to get out, she drifted onto the rocks and became a constructive total loss. When the plaintiffs brought an action for loss of their vessel, the defendants pleaded the exception clause under the contract. The question was whether the exception could cover the period of time where the defendants had left the tow, in breach of his obligations under the contract. Lord Sterndale MR, in the Court of Appeal, reversing the judge's decision, said:

> I think that the whole clause points to the exceptions being confined to a time when the tugowner is doing something or omitting to do something in the actual performance of the contract, and do not apply during a period when, as in this case, he has ceased even for a time to do anything at all and has left the performance of his duties to someone else. In other words, I think the exception extends to cover a default during the actual performance of the duties of the contract, and not to an unjustified handing over of those obligations to someone else for performance.[48]

5.3 Termination of towing

The towage operations will terminate upon the occurrence of one of the following events: either (i) when the final orders by the tow to cease holding, pushing, pulling, moving, escorting, guiding or standing by, or to cast off ropes wires or lines have been carried out; or (ii) when the towing line has been finally slipped. The latest of either of these events will be taken into account, provided the tug is safely clear of the tow. Whether the lines have been finally slipped does not refer to accidental parting of the towline.

In *The Walumba,*[49] which involved the refloating of a grounded vessel outside Melbourne, the tug, engaged under the UKSTC, was carried away by the tide and the tow-line parted, whereupon the tug's propeller was fouled and the tug obtained salvage assistance. When the costs of the salvage were claimed from the owners of the tow by way of an indemnity pursuant to cl 3(b)

---

47   [1921] P 458.

48   *Ibid*, p 468.

49   *The Walumba (Owners) v Australian Coastal Shipping Commission* [1965] 1 Lloyd's Rep 121.

of the UKSTC (which provides for an indemnity to the tug for any loss or damage and any claims of whatsoever nature, or howsoever arising or caused (whilst towing) suffered or made against the tugowner), the issue was whether the clause applied. It was argued on behalf of the tow that since the towage had been terminated when the tow-line parted, the clause did not apply. The judge of the Supreme Court of Victoria, Australia, held that the word 'slipping' of the tow-line in the clause did not refer to accidental parting of the line, and up to the time of fouling of propeller there was no question of abandoning towing operation; therefore, fouling of propeller occurred 'whilst towing' and the liability incurred by the tugowner for salvage services, when in peril, was a direct consequence of damage sustained whilst towing. Thus, clause 3(b) did apply. An appeal to the High Court of Australia by the owners of the tow was dismissed.

6 DUTIES OF THE TUGOWNER

The mutual relations of tug and tow are governed by the express terms of the contract and, in the absence of express terms, certain terms will be implied provided they are not inconsistent with the express terms or have not been expressly excluded.

6.1 Fitness of the tug for the purpose for which she is required

This obligation is usually an implied term of the contract. It includes an obligation that the crew, tackle and equipment are what might reasonably be expected of a vessel of the particular class.

Whether such an obligation amounts to an absolute warranty – like the undertaking by the common carrier to provide a seaworthy ship in a carriage of goods contract[50] – has not been definitively decided. Judgments decided before the Court of Appeal decision in *The West Cock* (see below) seemed to favour the view that it was an absolute warranty or undertaking. A breach of an absolute warranty can have two consequences. First, the party complaining of a breach by the tugowner with respect to fitness of the tug would not be obliged to prove the tugowner's negligence. Second, breach of such an

---

50 *Steel v State Line Steamship Co* (1877) 3 App Cas 72 (HL); Lord Blackburn said, p 86: 'I take it my Lords, to be quite clear, both in England and in Scotland, that where there is a contract to carry goods in a ship, whether that contract is in the shape of a bill of lading, or any other form, there is a duty on the part of the person who furnishes or supplies that ship, or that ship's room, unless something be stipulated which should prevent it, that the ship shall be fit for its purpose. That is generally expressed by saying that it shall be seaworthy; and I think also in marine contracts, contracts for sea carriage, that is what is properly called a warranty, not merely that they should do their best to make the ship fit, but that the ship should really be fit.'

absolute obligation may deprive the tugowner from relying on a contractual exception from liability, if upon construction of the relevant exception clause the parties intended that the scope of the exception should not extent to cover such a breach.

6.1.1 Cases in favour of an absolute warranty of fitness

Butt J in *The Undaunted*,[51] in which the tug had insufficient coal for the voyage, said:

> ... there being an implied obligation on the tugowners to supply an efficient tug, that is to say, one properly equipped and properly supplied with coal, and as I have found that the tug was deficient in the latter respect, the plaintiffs would be liable. Notwithstanding the exception contained on the card ...the plaintiffs had not properly fulfilled their contract.

In *The West Cock*[52] (1st inst), the decision of the President is important not only because it was confirmed by the Court of Appeal as to the result, but also because the comments made by the Court of Appeal disapproving the view of the President as to an implied warranty of fitness in towage contracts were only *obiter*.

The defendant's tugs were engaged to tow the plaintiff's vessel to Liverpool. During the towage, the towing gear of one of the tugs carried away and fell overboard, causing the plaintiff's vessel to be driven against the knuckle of the pier head at the entrance to the dock. The plaintiff's vessel was damaged. It was found that the accident was due to weakness, fatigue and a defective condition in the rivets of the tug, resulting in the tug's inefficiency to perform the towage services contracted for. Also, that this inefficiency could have been ascertained by the reasonable care, skill and attention on the part of the tugowners, but they had made no proper inspection of the tug before the towage contract was entered into. The defendants relied on an exemption in the contract, under which they were not responsible for any damage to the tow arising from accidents of the seas, rivers 'or arising from towing gear (including consequences of defects therein or damage thereto)'.

The President, Sir Samuel Evans, at first instance, made the following findings of fact:

> Without going in further detail into the evidence, I will state the conclusions at which I have arrived as to the cause of the accident. I find that the accident was due to the weakness, fatigue, and defective condition of the eight rivets, and that at the time of the contract, and of the commencement of the towing operations, the tug *West Cock* was inefficient on this ground to perform the towage services which the defendants contracted to perform ... I further find

---

51 (1886) 11 PD 46, p 48.
52 [1911] P 208; [1911] P 23 (CA), pp 30–34.

upon the evidence ... that this inefficiency could have been ascertained by reasonable care, skill, and attention on the part of the tugowners; that no proper inspection of the tug was made by them or their servants before the towage contract was entered into; and that the last inspection before the contract was only an ordinary and perfunctory one, and did not extend to an examination of the rivets or fastenings between the towing gear and the bulkhead casing.

He referred to authorities that he thought supported his view that there was a warranty of fitness:

The primary obligation of a tugowner under a towage contract may be described as a duty to provide a tug which, at the time of the contract or at the commencement of the operations of towage under the contract, is efficient to perform the towage services which the tug undertakes to perform in circumstances reasonably to be expected; or as a representation, or an engagement, or a contract, or an implied engagement that the tug is reasonably efficient for that purpose. If my findings of fact in this case are justified, it matters not whether this primary obligation is an absolute one, so as to amount to a warranty of fitness or efficiency, or whether the obligation is satisfied by the tugowner proving that the unfitness or inefficiency was not discoverable or preventable by any care or skill, or by his proving that he was not aware of the unfitness or inefficiency, and that it could not be discovered by an ordinary inspection ...

In my opinion it is not sufficient for a tugowner in an action like the present to prove that he was not aware of any unfitness or inefficiency or that it could not be discovered by an ordinary inspection. At the lowest, I think his obligation is to prove that the unfitness or inefficiency was not preventable or discoverable by care and skill. But is not the obligation at the outset greater than this? Is it not an obligation which is absolute and which, therefore, amounts to a warranty? I think it is. It is well established that the obligation under a charterparty or a bill of lading to provide a vessel which is 'seaworthy', in the commercial and legal sense, is an absolute one and amounts to a warranty of seaworthiness; and this obligation has been described as 'a representation and an engagement – a contract – by the shipowner that the ship ... is at the time of its departure reasonably fit for accomplishing the service which the shipowner engages to perform' (*per* Lord Cairns in *Steel v State Line Steamship Co.*); and as 'a duty on the part of the person who furnishes or supplies the ship ... unless something be stipulated which should prevent it, that the ship shall be fit for its purpose. That is generally expressed by saying that it shall be seaworthy; and I think also in marine contracts, contracts for sea carriage, that is what is properly called a "warranty", not merely that they should do their best to make the ship fit, but that the ship should really be fit ...'

It is as important that a tug which undertakes to tow a vessel in some cases for long distances and in varying circumstances, with lives and property at risk, should be efficient for the accomplishment of its work, as it is that a cargo laden ship should be seaworthy, and in this sense fit for the purposes of the services undertaken under a charterparty. The foundation of the obligation is the same in either case, namely, the fitness of the tug or the ship for the purpose of the services to be performed ...

In *The Minnehaha*, Lord Kingsdown, in giving the decision of the Privy Council, said:

'When a steamboat engages to tow a vessel for a certain remuneration from one point to another, she does not warrant that she will be able to do so, and will do so, under all circumstances and at all hazards; but she does engage that she will use her best endeavours for that purpose, and will bring to the task competent skill, and such a crew, tackle, and equipments, as are reasonably to be expected in a vessel of her class. She may be prevented from fulfilling her contract by a *vis major*, by accidents which were not contemplated, and which may render the fulfilment of her contract impossible, and in such a case, by the general rule of law, she is relieved from her obligations. But she does not become relieved from her obligations because unforeseen difficulties occur in the completion of her task; because the performance of the task is interrupted, or cannot be completed in the mode in which it was originally intended, as by the breaking of the ship's hawser.'

This, I think, means, or at any rate is consistent with the construction, that there is, in a towage contract, first a warranty that at the outset the crew, tackle and equipments are efficient, and afterwards an implied obligation that competent skill and best endeavours should be exercised in the performance of the work.

I see no reason whatever why the same kind of obligation as to efficiency or fitness should not attach to a marine contract of towage as attaches to a marine contract of carriage. But whether the ordinary contract be (as I think it is) a warranty of fitness, or an implied obligation to provide a tug in a fit and efficient condition, so far as skill and care can discover its condition, a serious question remains, namely, whether, under the special terms of exemption in the contract in this case, the defendants are relieved from liability. Whatever the exact obligations of the tugowners may be, there are exceptions under which they seek to avoid, restrict, or minimise those obligations, and they must clearly make out that they are protected by these conditions. I think that the canon of construction to be applied is similar to that which has so frequently been applied in 'seaworthiness' cases.

Before looking at the reasoning of the Court of Appeal in *The West Cock*, which belongs to the next category (that is, not in favour of a warranty of fitness), it is important to see how Sir Samuel Evans had dealt with the same issue in his next decision, decided in the same year, although he was there more concerned with whether the tug would be entitled to salvage.

The Marachal Suchet[53]

The contract was to tow the vessel from Falmouth to London by a tug to be supplied by the plaintiffs. The vessel while in tow of the tug took the ground.

53   [1911] P 1.

This was due to a strong wind encountered, which caused the tug and the tow to drift. The vessel remained aground for several days until lifeboats, boatmen and other tugs belonging to the plaintiffs, came to her assistance. Claims for salvage awards by all parties involved were separately considered. With regard to the owners, master and crew of the tug engaged under the towage contract, it was held that the owners had failed to prove that they had supplied a tug efficient for the purpose for which she was engaged. The President, Sir Samuel Evans said:

> The contract ... was for the towage of the *Marachal Suchet* by a tug to be supplied by the plaintiffs. This being so, the owners of the tug must be taken to have contracted that the tug should be efficient, and that her crew, tackle, and equipment should be equal to the work to be accomplished in weather and circumstances reasonably to be expected; and that reasonable skill, care, energy, and diligence should be exercised in the accomplishment of the work. On the other hand, they did not warrant that the work should be done under all circumstances and at all hazards, and the failure to accomplish it would be excused if it were due to *vis major* or to accidents not contemplated, and which rendered the doing of the work impossible.[54]

Scrutinising the claim for salvage, he stated that

> The burden of proof is upon the plaintiffs [tugowners]. It is a twofold burden. They must shew that they were not wanting in the performance of the obligations resting upon them under the towage contract.; and they must also account for the stranding of the vessel by shewing something like *vis major*, or an inevitable accident.[55]

The plaintiffs proved neither of these.

Having failed in the towage contract, the tugowners could not in the circumstances claim as salvors. It was also held that while the special conditions in the towage contract could not avail the plaintiffs in the salvage claim, they had a defence to the counterclaim for damages for breach of contract. The court was left in doubt as to whether the accident was due solely to the inefficient condition of the tug and its equipment. Thus, it cannot really be stated that this decision is a positive authority supporting the view that the obligation to provide a fit tug amounts to an absolute warranty.

In 1992, the Court of Appeal in Hong Kong decided the issue in *The Sumi Maru 9001*,[56] by preferring the comments of the President in *The West Cock* that there was an implied absolute warranty as to fitness of the tug and adopting what he said.

---

54 [1911] P 1, p 12.

55 *Ibid*, p 12.

56 *Wiltops (Asia) Ltd v Owners of the Tug Sumi Maru 9001* 1993 1 SLR 198. (I acknowledge my gratitude to Bernard Eder QC for bringing this case, in which he acted as counsel for the tug owners, to my attention.)

The Sumi Maru

The respondents (tugowners) undertook the towage of tow vessels belonging to the appellants from Eleusis Bay, Greece, to Taiwan at an agreed price of $530,000 in four instalments, the first being paid in advance. The contract contained a very wide exception clause (which will be discussed later). The tugowners were obliged to provide bunkers and all necessary provisions. Due to an increase in bunker prices, the tugowners were unable to pay for them at the increased price and after negotiations the appellants agreed to pay the second instalment, although it was not yet due. In return, the tugowners agreed to commence towing on 9 July 1979, but, in fact, did on 25 August. Thereafter, the tugowners pressed for early payment of the third and fourth instalments and a further bunkers surcharge. The third, and part of the fourth, were paid, but the rest was refused. At Cape Town, the tugowners failed to provide bunkers for the next stage of the voyage and were only provided after the appellants agreed to an increase of $170,000 towage fee on a 'no cure no pay' basis of which $60,000 was paid, together with the balance of the fourth instalment. The tug, however, deviated to Mauritius instead of sailing direct to Singapore, because it did not have sufficient bunkers. *En route*, she encountered bad cyclonic weather and the tugowners demanded a further sum of $103,500 as demurrage for delays, which was refused by the appellants. The cyclonic conditions worsened and the portside main wire snapped, resulting in the parting of the tug from the tows on 28 January. She did not retrieve the tows, but sailed for Colombo to begin another assignment. Subsequently, the tugowners went into liquidation.

The Lords Justice held that there was an implied absolute obligation in the towage contract on the part of the tugowner to provide a tug efficient for the operation of the towage at the commencement of each stage of the voyage in the same way as in contracts of affreightment.[57] They considered that the implied obligation was fully consistent with the obligations of a tugowner as laid down by Lord Kingsdown in *The Minnehaha*[58] and disregarded the *obiter* comments made by the Court of Appeal in *The West Cock* (see below).

The factual position, however, in this case speaks for itself and indicates the level of pressure that can be exerted by some tugowners upon tow-owners, who find themselves in a very unequal bargaining position. From a legal point of view, the question is this: can a general principle be drawn from

---

57 *Thin & Another v Richards & Co* [1892] 2 QB 141; *The Vortigern* [1899] P 140 (CA); *Northumbrian Shipping Co v Timm* [1939] AC 397 (HL).

58 (1861) 15 Moo PC 133, pp 152–55: when a steamship engages to tow a vessel for a certain remuneration from one point to another, she does not warrant that she will be able to do so and will do so under all circumstances and at all hazard, but she does engage that she will use her best endeavours for that purpose, and will bring to the task competent skill, and such a crew, tackle, and equipment as are reasonably to be expected in a vessel of her class.

the decision of the Hong Kong Court of Appeal with regard to the nature of the tug's obligation to provide a tug fit for the purpose?

It may be doubtful that it can for the following reasons: first, this was a case of a deliberate conduct of the tugowner. Not only did he not meet the standard of reasonable skill and care expected of him, but received all instalments by exercising undue pressure and still abandoned the contract, the company finally becoming insolvent. Second, it is doubtful whether *The Minnehaha* established the same principle, as held by the Court of Appeal (HK). In *The Undaunted,* the judge did not address the issue, other than having confirmed that there was an implied obligation. Third, the analogy drawn from the contracts of carriage of goods authorities is misplaced because these are different contracts from the contracts of towage. Fourth, the owner of the tug is not a bailee of the tow, nor is he a bailee of the cargo carried aboard the tow. The rights and duties between the parties are governed by the law of towage, being a unique blend of the law of contract and tort, and the common carrier rules of liability do not apply.[59]

It is submitted that the correct approach should be that there is no absolute warranty as to tug's fitness, but the tug should be reasonably fit for the service required, as far as reasonable care and skill can make her.[60] The obligation may be modified by express or appropriate terms in the contract. Such was the view held by the Court of Appeal in *The West Cock,* referred to next.

6.1.2 The view that there is no absolute warranty of fitness of the tug

The West Cock[61]

The Court of Appeal (Vaughan Williams, Farwell, and Kennedy LJJ) affirmed the decision in the court below, that the defendants were liable, but for a different reason from that of the judge. That was that the defective condition of the rivets of the tug was not covered by the exemptions in the contract, the conditions of which only applied to circumstances occurring after the commencement of, and during, the towage, and not to the state of things existing before the towage began.

The Court of Appeal implicitly disapproved of the President's view at first instance, that the obligation to provide a fit tug was an absolute one. Both Farwell LJ and Kennedy LJ did not wish to extend the category of common law absolute warranties by adding another one to them, that is, by adding to tugs and tug service to ships the same liability as for carriage of goods. Although the Court of Appeal did not have to decide the point, it is important

---

59   *Op cit,* Schoenbaum, fn 1, p 676.
60   The same view is suggested by *op cit,* Rainey, fn 1, p 33.
61   [1911] P 208 (CA).

to state the views (albeit *obiter*) expressed in the course of the judgment on this issue.

Vaughan LJ said[62] that the President, Sir Samuel Evans, referred to his own decision in *The Marachal Suchet* and claimed that his observations there were based upon the House of Lords decision in *The Ratata*.[63] However, both *The Ratata* and the Privy Council's decision in *The Minnehaha*, on which the President relied, pointed the other way, rather than supporting the statement that there was a common law warranty or condition of fitness at the commencement of the risk. As regards all other cases claimed by the President to support his proposition, they were cases dealing with different contracts entirely, namely contracts of carriage. Vaughan LJ did not agree that the same principle applying to contracts of affreightment should also apply to towage.

The question as to what is the liability of the tugowner was answered by Farwell LJ by quoting Lindley J in *Hyman v Nye*,[64] which was dealing with a contract of carriage by coaches and horses. He paraphrased the test of that case – which was a test of reasonable care and skill – and adopted it to the situation of tug hire.

> His duty appears to me to be to supply (a tug) as fit for the purpose for which it is hired as care and skill can render it; and if whilst (the tug) is being properly used for such purpose it breaks down, it becomes incumbent on the person who has let it out to shew that the breakdown was in the proper sense of the word an accident not preventable by any care or skill ... As between him and the hirer the risk of defects in (the tug), so far as care and skill can avoid them, ought to be thrown on the owner of (the tug). The hirer trusts him to supply a fit and proper (tug), the lender has it in his power not only to see that it is in a proper state, and to keep it so, and thus protect himself from risk, but also to charge his customers enough to cover his expenses. [65]

Although Kennedy LJ reserved his final opinion, he was inclined to support[66] the law as laid down in *Hyman v Nye* and the alternative view pointed out by the President, which was:

> ... an implied obligation to provide a tug in a fit and efficient condition so far as skill and care can discover its condition.

Since the Court of Appeal did not have to decide the issue and the comments made by the Lords Justice were only *obiter*, the practitioner is none the wiser

---

62 [1911] P 208 (CA), p 225.

63 [1898] AC 513 (HL), p 517. Lord Halsbury said: 'The fact that it was an inefficient tug ... is proved by the defendants themselves, when they shew how on other occasions it had properly and efficiently performed its functions. If it was suggested that it was some extraordinary and unusual event, and as this was not a contract of warranty, the defendants would have been entitled to insist on that as a defence; it was for the defendants to prove it.'

64 [1881] 6 QBD 685, p 687.

65 *The West Cock* [1911] P 208 (CA), p 227.

66 *Ibid*, p 232.

as to the answer to this problem. However, contractual terms provide for an obligation on the part of the tugowner to exercise reasonable care to provide a seaworthy tug, as is seen next.

6.1.3 What do the contractual terms of standard towage contracts provide?

Clause 4(c)(i) of the UKSTC provides that the exceptions from tug's liability under cl 4(a) and the indemnity given by the tow to the tug under cl 4(b) shall not apply to the following:

> All claims which the hirer shall prove to have resulted directly and solely from the personal failure of the tugowner to exercise reasonable care to make the tug or tender seaworthy for navigation at the commencement of the towing or other service. For the purpose of this clause the tugowner's personal responsibility for exercising reasonable care shall be construed as relating only to the person or persons having the ultimate control and chief management of the tugowner's business and to any servant (excluding the officers and crew of any tug or tender) to whom the tugowner has specifically delegated the particular duty of exercising reasonable care and shall not include any other servant of the tugowner or any agent or independent contractor employed by the tugowner.

The duty of the tugowner under this contract is to exercise reasonable care to make the tug seaworthy for navigation at the commencement of the towing. The duty is personal upon the persons having the ultimate control and chief management of the business (the *'ego'* of the company).[67] The duty may be specifically delegated by the tugowner to any of his servants, other than the officers and crew of the tug. To that extent, only, the duty is delegable, but the tugowner cannot delegate it to independent contractors or any other servant or agent employed by him. Therefore, the rule of *The Muncaster Castle*,[68] which is applicable to contracts of carriage of goods by sea to which the Hague-Visby Rules have been incorporated, applies partially. Personal failure to exercise reasonable care to make the tug seaworthy will contractually deprive the tugowner from relying on the clause exempting him from liability for negligence, or relying on the indemnity provision with respect to claims which have directly and solely resulted form such personal failure. The burden of proof for breach of this obligation and that such breach was the sole and direct cause of the claim is upon the hirer. Then the burden will be on the tugowner to show that he personally exercised reasonable care to meet his obligation.

Similarly, **cl 13 of the Towcon and Towhire** provides that:

---

67 See the definition of *'ego'* and *alter ego* or how liability is attributed to a company in Chapters 8 and 16.
68 [1961] 1 Lloyd's Rep 57.

The tugowner will exercise due diligence to tender the tug at the place of departure in a seaworthy condition and in all respects ready to perform the towage, but the tugowner gives no other warranties, express or implied.

This clause again reduces the obligation of the tugowner to that of reasonable care, but it is silent as to whether or not the obligation is personal of the tugowner. It is unclear, therefore, whether the duty to exercise reasonable care is delegable or not.

6.2 The position of fitness when a specific tug is requested

When a particular tug is known in the market for its strength and specific equipment, a tow-owner may request it for an ocean towage. Whether or not, in such a case, there is an implied absolute obligation on the tugowner to provide a fit tug, the position is not clear. There are again two strands of judicial view.

6.2.1 One school of thought: no absolute warranty of fitness

It is said that there is no warranty of fitness because if the tow-owner chose the tug he would not be able to argue that he had relied on the skill and judgment of the tugowner to choose a suitable tug. It is said in those cases that the tow-owner would have assumed the risk of a possible inefficiency of the specific tug chosen and the consequential damage or loss arising thereof. In this connection, there are some *dicta* in old cases:

Robertson v Amazon Tug and Lighterage Co[69]

The plaintiff, a master mariner, contracted with the defendants for a lump sum to take a specified steam tug, *V*, belonging to the defendants to tow six sailing barges. The steam tug had just been bought by the defendants but, unbeknown to both parties, the vessel had been kept sunk in water for sometime and her boilers and engines were damaged and out of repair. Subsequently, she performed the voyage very slowly, costing the plaintiff more than usual because he had to pay the crew and make provisions for all on board for the duration of the journey. The plaintiff alleged that there was an implied contract that *V* should have been reasonably fit for the purpose for which she was hired. By majority of 2:1, the Court of Appeal disagreed with this view and reversed the first instance judgment. **Brett LJ** said:

> The larger vessel, *The Villa Bella*, was named to the plaintiff at the time of the contract, and, although I do not think it is material, the plaintiff had an opportunity of seeing it. That at once makes the contract a contract with regard to that specific vessel.

---

69 (1881) 7 QBD 598 (CA).

Now the plaintiff, being a skilled mariner and master, undertook by this contract to take the command of the expedition to the Brazils, and to conduct the large tug, *The Villa Bella*, and the barges across the sea. He was to be supplied of course with the means of working the large tug and also the smaller vessel, but he undertook amongst other things to provision the crews, and further, he undertook to conduct this expedition for a fixed sum. It, therefore, was most material to him to calculate what would be the time in which he should in all probability perform the voyage. The larger tug, *The Villa Bella*, at the time when the contract was made, had been kept during the winter in a state which is not infrequent, that is to say, sunk in the water, which may not be so bad for the vessel itself, but it certainly is very deleterious to the engines. She was, in fact, a vessel with engines considerably damaged, but she was the vessel, which the plaintiff undertook to conduct across the Atlantic.[70]

... when there is a specific thing, there is no implied contract that it shall be reasonably fit for the purpose for which it is hired or is to be used. That is the great distinction between a contract to supply a thing which is to be made and which is not specific, and a contract with regard to a specific thing. In the one case you take the thing as it is, in the other the person who undertakes to supply it is bound to supply a thing reasonably fit for the purpose for which it is made ...

If there had been evidence in this case that, after the contract was made, the machinery from want of reasonable care by the defendants had become in a worse condition than it was at the time of the contract, I should have thought that there would have been a breach of contract for which the defendants would have been liable. But I find no such evidence. The only misfortune about the tug was that the machinery at the time the contract was made was in such a condition that the vessel was not reasonably fit for the purpose of taking these barges across the Atlantic. Therefore, the misfortune which happened was the result of a risk which was run by the plaintiff, and of which he cannot complain, and consequently he has no cause of action as regards *The Villa Bella*.[71]

Cotton LJ, following the same line of argument, added:

This inefficiency was attributed to the fact that the boilers of *The Villa Bella* were not sufficiently powerful for the engines, and principally to the fact that the boilers were in a bad condition ...

The evidence shewed that at the time of the contract the defendants were proposing to send out *The Villa Bella*, and that this was known to the plaintiff. The contract must, therefore, be dealt with as one made with reference to an ascertained steam vessel. Though the contract contains no warranty in terms, the question remains whether there are in it expressions from which, as a matter of construction, any such warranty as that relied on by the plaintiff can be inferred. In my opinion this is not the case ...

70 (1881) 7 QBD 598 (CA), p 605.
71 *Ibid*, pp 606–07.

If the vessel were not at the time of the contract ascertained and known to both parties, probably the contract would imply such a warranty as relied on by the plaintiff. But a contract made with reference to a known vessel, in my opinion, stands in a very different position. In such a case, in the absence of actual stipulation, the contractor must, in my opinion, be considered as having agreed to take the risk of the greater or a less efficiency of the chattel about which he contracts ... He may examine the chattel and satisfy himself of its condition and efficiency. If he does not and suffers from his neglect to take this precaution, he cannot, in my opinion, make the owner liable. He must, in my opinion, be taken to have fixed the price so as to cover the risk arising from the condition of the instrument which he might have examined if had thought fit so to do.[72]

The two Lords Justice relied upon no authority. However, **Bramwell LJ**, dissenting, relied on common sense, thus, he said:

The plaintiff's complaint was that he had agreed upon a lump sum to take this vessel towing several lighters to the Brazils, that it was important to him that the vessel and apparatus should be efficient, as the faster he went the more he gained, and the slower he went the less he gained or the more he lost. He proved as a fact that the boilers were out of order, that they were sufficient in themselves, but needed repairs, and that in consequence it took him much longer to perform his undertaking than it otherwise would have done. The defects, the want of repair, were obvious – obvious to anyone who had looked at or tried the boilers.

The question is, if this gives a cause of action. I am of opinion that it does. The contract of the defendants was to deliver to the plaintiff the tug and barges, with and in relation to which he was to perform a certain work, or bring about a certain result, for the profitable doing of which the efficiency of the tug was all important. The case seems to me the same as a contract of hiring, and as all contracts when one man furnishes a specific thing to another which that other is to use. The man so letting and furnishing the thing does not, except in some cases, undertake for its goodness or fitness, but he does undertake for the condition being such that it can do what its means enable it to do. Thus, if a man hired a specific horse and said he intended to hunt with it next day, there would be no undertaking by the letter that it could leap or go fast; but there would be that it should have its shoes on, and that it should not have been excessively worked or unfed the day before. If I am asked where I find this rule in our law, I frankly ... cannot discover it plainly laid down anywhere. But it seems to me to exist as a matter of good sense and reason, and it is I think in accordance with the analogous authorities. I am afraid that the nearest is the *dictum* of Lord Abinger in *Smith v Marrable*: 'No authorities were wanted'; 'the case is one which common sense alone enables us to decide'.[73]

How did later decisions treat this case?

---

72   (1881) 7 QBD 598 (CA), pp 607–09.
73   *Ibid*, p 603.

The Privy Council in *The Mary Francis Whalen*[74] preferred to support the view of the majority in the *Robertson* case in an appeal from the Supreme Court of Canada arising out of an action brought against this tug, which caused the loss of the tow (a scow) and its cargo on board by abandonment.

The Mary Francis Whalen had been described by its owners to the tow-owners as exactly the same as another tug known to them. On evidence, it was found that this tug was insufficient and lacked capacity to accomplish the task undertaken by it in the weather encountered. Without giving much thought to the issue, the Privy Council held that:

> ... it was a contract for a named vessel, which brings the case within the authority of *Robertson v The Amazon*, followed by Kennedy in *The West Cock*, and excludes any implied warranty.

The *ratio decidendi* for their decision of no liability of the tug was, however, based on the fact that it had not been explained to the tugowner that the 'scow' would be so difficult to tow as it was.

In another towage case, *Fraser & White Ltd v Vernon*,[75] it was held by the judge that since the contract was one for the supply of specific tugs, there was, accordingly, no implied warranty as to the fitness of the tugs. The hiring over the telephone of two named and specific tugs was distinguished from the case where there was a general contract for towage services.

6.2.2 Second school of thought: there can be no general rule about absence of a warranty of fitness

There is another string of cases, where the hire of a chattel was treated the same as the hire of a tug, in which a general rule as to the absence of a warranty of fitness without qualification was disapproved of. The Court of Appeal in *Yeoman Credit Ltd v Apps*[76] (concerning a hire purchase agreement of a car which was unusable) was surprised at the decision of the majority in the *Robertson* case and did not feel bound by it. It held, instead, that in the ordinary hiring agreement of a specific chattel there was an implied obligation that the chattel should be fit for the purpose for which it was hired, except in the case where the defect was apparent to the hirer and he did not rely on the skill and judgment of the owner.[77]

---

74 (1922) 13 LlL Rep 40 (PC).

75 [1951] 2 Lloyd's Rep 175.

76 [1962] 2 QB 508.

77 It applied a previous Court of Appeal decision, *Karsales (Harrow) Ltd v Wallis* [1956] 1 WLR 936; also, it considered *Reed v Dean* [1949] 1 KB 188 as correct. (It concerned the hire of a named motor launch. Due to an unexplained cause the launch caught fire. The defendant's failure to provide proper fire-fighting equipment was a breach of the implied warranty of fitness which was subject to the exercise of reasonable skill and care.)

6.2.3 Tug fitness and risk management

The apparent conflict between the decisions discussed is unsatisfactory. It appeals to common sense that the proper rule to be applied to such cases should be that the tug or chattel should be fit for the purpose for which it is hired, as far as skill and care can make it. Robertson's case may be limited to its own factual situation, which was unusual. It is submitted that the *Yeoman Credit* case makes more sense in the reality of commercial relations. The only exception to this rule should be when the tow-owner has actual knowledge of the condition of a specific tug he has requested for hire and accepts it as it is, recognising that there may be a risk which might arise from that condition. In such a situation, there would be a conscious commercial decision made about allocation of risk between the parties matched with an appropriate price for the service. A distinction between a contract for the hire of a specific tug and contracts to perform towage services, in which the tugowner selects one of his tugs for the purpose, may be artificial and cause more confusion than offers a solution.[78]

It is important that parties who engage the services of a tug bear these issues in mind as a risk management exercise and, because the law is unsettled, make it clear in their contract what they expect from the tug and tugowner as to fitness of the tug or tugs and services to be provided.

6.3 To use best endeavours to complete the towage

The standard forms of contract do not mention that the tugowner will use best endeavours to complete the towage, but common law will fill this gap.

In *The Minnehaha*,[79] Lord Kingsdown laid down the principle governing the duty of a tug to complete the towage services by his well known statement in this case:

> When a steamboat engages to tow a vessel for a certain remuneration from one point to another, she does not warrant that she will be able to do so and will do so under all circumstances and at all hazards; but she does engage that she will use her best endeavours for that purpose, and will bring to the task competence, skill, and such a crew, tackle and equipment as are reasonably to be expected in a vessel of her class.

> She may be prevented from fulfilling her contract by a *vis major*, by accidents which were not contemplated and which may render the fulfilment of her contract impossible; and in such case, by the general rule of law, she is relieved from her obligations.

---

78 See, also, *op cit*, Rainey, fn 1, pp 35, 36; and, for the American view, *op cit*, Parks and Cattell, fn 1, p 127.

79 (1861) 15 Moo PC 133, p 153.

... but she does not become relieved from her obligations because unforeseen difficulties occur in the completion of her task; because the performance of the task is interrupted, or cannot be completed in the mode in which it was originally intended, as by the breaking of the ship hawser.

Best endeavours means that the tug did its best (reasonable efforts)[80] in the circumstances to complete the towage. The tug will only be excused by the intervention of unforeseen incidents, which were not contemplated when the contract commenced and which rendered the fulfilment of the contract impossible. But it will not be excused if an unforeseen event made the contract more difficult than expected.

6.4 The duty to exercise proper skill and diligence throughout

Unless the contract otherwise specifies, ss 13 and 15 of the Supply of Goods and Services Act (SGSA) 1982 apply to the towage contracts which are contracts for supply of goods and services. Section 13 provides:

In a contract for the supply of a service where the supplier is acting in the course of a business, there is an implied term that the supplier will carry out the service with reasonable care and skill.

Section 14 deals with the time for the service to be carried out if it is not fixed by the contract. There is an implied term to carry out the service within a reasonable time; what is a reasonable time is a question of fact.

In fact, these implied terms existed at common law prior to the statute. The Privy Council in an old case had given a comprehensive analysis of these duties.

The Julia[81]

A steam tug entered into an engagement to tow a vessel. By the misconduct of the master and crew of the vessel in tow, who acted contrary to the directions of the pilot on board the vessel, a collision occurred whereby the tug received damage. The owner of the tug brought an action to recover damages from the owners of the tow on the grounds that the negligent acts of the master and crew of the towed vessel had caused the collision. It was held that the collision had, indeed, been caused by the negligent acts of the tow, and the tugowners were entitled to recover. On the duties of both parties to the contract, Lord Kingsdown stated:

When the contract was made, the law would imply an engagement that each vessel would perform its duty in completing it; that proper skill and diligence

---

80 See Chapter 13, para 9.1, that the suggested standard to be applied is objective, ie, proof of exercise of reasonable diligence.

81 (1861) 14 Moo PC 210.

would be used on board of each; and that neither vessel, by neglect or misconduct, would create unnecessary risk to the other, or increase any risk which might be incidental to the service undertaken. If, in the course of the performance of this contract, any inevitable accident happened to the one without any default on the part of the other, no cause of action could arise. Such an accident would be one of the necessary risks of the engagement to which each party was subject, and could create no liability on the part of the other. If, on the other hand, the wrongful act occasioned any damage to the other, such wrongful act would create a responsibility on the party committing it, if the sufferer had not by any misconduct or unskilfulness on her part contributed to the accident.[82]

In line with this principle was the House of Lords' decision in *The Ratata*,[83] in which Lord Halsbury stated:

My Lords, no written contract between the parties has been put in evidence, but your Lordships are invited to infer what the contract was from the ordinary course pursued between shipowners and contractors for towage. Looking at the facts, I should infer that, while on the one hand there is no warranty by the contractors that the vessel shall arrive in time to avoid grounding, on the other hand, I think it is clear that they undertook to exercise reasonable care and skill in the performance of the obligation which they have taken upon themselves for hire and reward in conducting the business of the towage to its consummation. Looking at the nature of the thing to be done, I should say they were bound to have reasonable knowledge of the state of the tide, inasmuch as they are to give the signal for the starting of the operations; reasonable care and skill in conducting the operation itself, where, as in this case, a number of vessels have to be brought up during the same tide; and reasonable care in providing adequate steam power to accomplish the object in question.

7 DUTIES OF THE TOW

7.1 Duty to specify what is required and to disclose the condition of the tow

It was discussed earlier, under pre-contractual, duties (para 4.4) that the tow-owner ought to give all necessary information about the tow before the contract commences, so that the tug can make the appropriate arrangements for the towage services required. The court has an equitable jurisdiction to open agreements, which were entered into without full knowledge of the condition of the tow, if, for example, a non-disclosure of material facts would

---

82 (1861) 14 Moo PC 210, p 230.
83 [1898] AC 513, p 516.

render the job of the tug more difficult than was contemplated and reflected in the remuneration. The court may award damages for breach of contract, or fix a price that would be fair in the circumstances. Any untrue representation of material facts about the tow would be subject to the provisions of the MA 1967.

Elliot Steam Tug Co v New Medway Steam Packet[84]

The defendants called the plaintiff's tug company to tow an 800 ton concrete lighter from the mudbank where she was lying. Nothing was disclosed to the plaintiffs showing that this was anything other than an ordinary towing job. But in fact, the lighter had been lying in mud for some years and the berth was not easy to get to unless the vessel was very small. It was not, therefore, in a position in which the plaintiff's tug could reach it. Consequently, the tugmaster abandoned the tow attempt. The parties entered into a second agreement whereby the plaintiffs supplied a smaller tug. However, they were still unable to shift the lighter. The plaintiffs claimed damages for breach of contract. It was held that the defendants were in breach of their duty to put the lighter in a position where she could be reached, and in not disclosing that the contract was anything but a simple towage contract.

Whether the tow should be in a seaworthy condition for towage will depend on the circumstances, which have necessitated the towage. There can be no general rule that there must be an implied obligation on the part of the tow-owner to provide the tow in a seaworthy condition to be towed as some cases seem to be taken as suggesting.[85] The obligation that the tow should be in a fit condition to be towed is obviously different. Provided the position and condition of the tow has been made clear, towage services may be needed because the tow has run into difficulties and may not be considered seaworthy to reach her destination in a damaged condition.[86]

The Towcon form, in cl 12 which has the title 'Tow-worthiness of the tow', provides that:

---

84 (1937) 59 LlL Rep 35.

85 See *op cit*, Rainey, fn 1, pp 47–48. In *Elliott Steam Tug Co Ltd v Chester* (1922) 12 LlL Rep 331, Hill J commented that, under a contract for the towage of an obsolete ship, there must be an implied obligation on the part of the tow that she is in a reasonably fit condition to be towed. (This case did not decide that the tow should be 'seaworthy' but 'fit to be towed' which is different. The statement by Rainy that there is an implied term that the tow must be seaworthy while referring to this case is misleading). *The Smjeli* [1982] 2 Lloyd's Rep 74 was about transporting cargo of sections of a steel oil rig on a barge under tow. The sections of steel oilrig were lost due to negligence of both tug and tow in making the arrangements for the towage of the barge. Sheen J said that there was a common law duty upon both tug and tow in this case to use reasonable care to send their vessels to sea in a seaworthy condition. (It is submitted that this case was clearly about transportation of cargo with the assistance of a tug and the obligation of the tow-owner to carry the cargo on a seaworthy barge was an important obligation owed to the owner of the cargo for this purpose.)

86 *Gamecock Steam Towing Co Ltd v Trader Navigation Co Ltd* (1937) 59 LlL Rep 170.

(a) The hirer shall exercise due diligence to ensure that the tow shall at the commencement of the towage be in all respects fit to be towed from the place of departure to the place of destination. (b) The hirer undertakes that the tow will be suitably trimmed and prepared and ready to be towed at the time when the tug arrives at the place of departure and fitted and equipped with such shapes, signals, navigational and other lights of a type required for the towage.

The obligation of the tow-owner under this clause is understandably that of exercising due diligence to make the tow tow-worthy. It is submitted that the words 'tow-worthy' and 'fit to be towed' signify something different from a requirement to make the tow seaworthy, in the sense known under contracts of affreightment.[87] In other words, the tow must be fit with reference to the requirements of the towage needed and is assessed at the commencement of the towage.

As evidence of the tow's tow-worthiness, the clause further requires that the hirer shall supply to the tugowner or the tugmaster on arrival of the tug at the place of departure an unconditional certificate of tow-worthiness issued by a recognised firm of marine surveyors, provided always that the tugowner shall not be under any obligation to perform the towage until in his discretion he is satisfied that the tow is in all respects trimmed, prepared, fit and ready for towage. The tugowner shall not unreasonably withhold his approval.

7.2 The tow to exercise due care and skill during the towage

This is an implied term in the contract and has been explained in *The Julia* case (summarised at para 6.4, above) but situations in towage vary and, in some instances, it may be that the tow is powerless to do anything depending on who is in control of towage, as will be seen later. However, even if the tow is not in control of navigation, there is still a duty of care and skill to be exercised in the planning of towage, in navigation, and in co-operating with the tug throughout towage, unless the tow is an unmanned barge.[88]

7.3 To pay remuneration to the tug

Towage is a service contract. Therefore, payment is done on completion of the service. Failure to perform towage, which has been fixed for a lump sum on arrival, will result in no remuneration. If the contract provides for payment 'per running day', then the tug, which has used best endeavours to complete, but failed to do so, will be remunerated for the work actually completed.

---

87 Seaworthiness is an innominate term: *Hong Kong Fir v Kawasaki* [1961] 1 Lloyd's Rep 159.
88 Eg, see *The Devonshire* [1912] P 21 (HL); *The Abaris* (1920) 2 LlL Rep 411; *Minnie Sommers* (1921) 6 LlL Rep 398; *The Valsesia* [1927] P 115 .

If, on the other hand, the contract is frustrated by an unforeseen and supervening event which had not been anticipated by the parties, but payment was made before the time of discharge as a result of a contractual obligation to pay, such sum shall be recoverable. Sums payable after the time of discharge shall cease to be payable. If the tugowner, however, had incurred expenses for the performance of the contract before the time of discharge, the court may, if it considers it just to do so, allow the tugowner to retain or recover the whole or part of the sum so paid or payable (s 1(2) of the Law Reform (Frustrated Contracts) Act 1943).[89]

8 RELATIONHIP BETWEEN TUG AND TOW AND THEIR LIABILITIES TO THIRD PARTIES

8.1 Tug and tow

The obligations and liabilities between the tug and tow are governed by express or implied terms of the contract. In standard form contracts, it is usually provided that the crew of the tug are deemed to be the servants of the tow. For example, **cl 3 of the UKSTC** states:

> Whilst towing or whilst at the request, express or implied, of the hirer, rendering any service other than towing, the master and crew of the tug or tender shall be deemed to be the servants of the hirer and under the control of the hirer and/or his servants and/or his agents, and anyone on board the hirer's vessel who may be employed and/or paid by the tugowner shall likewise be deemed to be the servant of the hirer and the hirer shall accordingly be vicariously liable for any act or omission by any such person so deemed to be the servant of the hirer.

This clause effectively transfers the risks – arising from negligence of tug's officers and crew, or other employees of the tugowner – whilst towing (see cl 1(b)(iv)) or whilst rendering any other services at the request of the hirer, upon the tow. Under ordinary common law principles, an employer is, by law, vicariously liable for the negligence of his servants. By contrast, in towage situations under UKSTC, the tow will be vicariously liable for the negligence of the tug's master or crew during towage because they are temporarily made the servants of the tow by agreement.

However, this contractual provision is only relevant between the parties to the contract. For example, if damage occurs to the tow due to the negligence of the tug's servants, the tow-owner cannot claim damages sustained by his

---

89 Generally, as to principles of frustration and *force majeure* clauses see McKendrick, E (ed), *Force Majeure and Frustration of Contract*, 2nd edn, 1995, LLP.

vessel against the tug (cl 4 (a)). Moreover, if damage occurs to the tug due to the negligence of those on board it, the tow-owner will be liable to the tugowner for such damage (cl 4 (b)).

In *The President Van Buren*,[90] decided before the use of the UKSTC, a similar clause in the contract was construed to have the foregoing effect.

S was one of the tugs engaged to tow the American steamship belonging to the defendants. A collision occurred between S and *The President Van Buren*. The defendants alleged that the collision was the result of the negligence of the tug S. The plaintiffs claimed that by the terms of the contract, they were not liable for any damage done by reason of the negligence of those in charge of the S, but that, on the contrary, they were entitled to claim against the defendants for the damage done to their own vessel S. It was held that the clause in the contract achieved what it set out to do, which was to make the master and crew of the tug the servants of the owners of the tow for the purposes of towage and for all other purposes connected thereto. It was also clear from the contract that the owners of the tow undertook to pay for any damage caused to property belonging to the tugowner.

By contrast to the 'blanket' exception from all liability of the tugowner under the UKSTC, the Towcon provides for a balanced distribution of risk and back to back indemnity in cl 18(1), first for liabilities in relation to deaths or personal injuries occurred during the towage to those engaged in the towage services. Second, by cl 18(2), the contract allows each party to bear its own loss in respect of loss of or damage to each other's property caused by their respective negligence, as well as to third parties. In addition, both the tugowner and the hirer will be entitled to an indemnity from each other in respect of liability adjudged to be due to a third party.

8.2 Tug, tow and third parties

Third parties who may suffer damage or loss due to negligence of the tug's master or crew will not be concerned with the allocation of risk between the contracting parties by their contractual terms. Clause 3 has no effect upon third parties' rights to claim for damage or loss caused by the negligence of the servants of either tug or tow. The usual rules of liability arising from breach of duty of care at common law will apply, as between third parties and tow or tug. The tow and tug are seen as separate or joint tortfeasors. Ultimately, liability would depend on who was in control of navigation or of the towage operations when the cause of action arose, which is a question of fact. Should it be found on the facts that the tug had been in control at the time of the incident and liability to the third party is adjudged against it, then the

---

90   (1924) 19 LlL Rep 185.

tug can invoke the indemnity clause of the contract (cl 4 of UKSTC) to recover from the tow in respect of its liability to the third party.[91] Under the Towcon whoever is liable to a third party will seek indemnity from the other (cl 18).

8.2.1 Tug in control of a particular manoeuvre

The Panther and The Ericbank[92]

The steam barge *The Trishna* came into collision with the tug of *The Ericbank* as she was proceeding inward-bound up the Manchester Ship Canal, *The Ericbank* failed to signal to her tug that they were passing *The Trishna*, and the tug without orders from the tow made a manoeuvre resulting in a collision with *The Trishna*. The tug's propeller, which was improperly left revolving, struck *The Trishna* repeatedly, after which *The Trishna* sank. The contract between *Ericbank* and her tug deemed the crew of the tug to be the servants of the tow. It was found that the damage done to both vessels by the actual collision was minimal, but the cause of the eventual damage to the *Trishna* was the continuous revolving of the tug's propeller. The tugowners sought to rely on the contractual term in order to escape liability to the third party.

Willmer J stated the effect of the House of Lords decision in *Mersey Docks and Harbour Board v Coggins and Griffiths*[93] to be as follows:

> … as between themselves, these parties agreed that the crew of the tug should be deemed to be the servants of the owners of the tow. But, as against a third party who is injured by the act of a servant, the question which of two possible masters is liable (the regular employer or the temporary employer to whom the servant is loaned) does not depend on the terms of the contract made between the respective employers; it depends upon which employer has the right to control the servant, not only as to what he is to do, but as to the way he is to do it. Moreover, it has been held that where the servant of one employer is temporarily loaned to another, it requires cogent evidence to prove that the latter has acquired such a degree of control over the servant as to render him, rather than the regular employer, liable in the event of negligence on the part of the servant.[94]

He stated further:

> Here, however, the faulty manoeuvre of failing to stop the port propeller in time was a matter which concerned the tug alone and not the tow, and in such circumstances, I hold that the liability for the negligence of the mate of *The Panther* [the tug] rests with his regular employers, the owners of *The Panther*.[95]

---

91 *The Atlantic and The Wellington* (1914) 30 TLR 699; see para 9.2, below.

92 [1957] P 143.

93 [1947] AC 1 (HL).

94 [1957] P 143, p 147.

95 *Ibid*, p 149.

8.2.2 Contrast between the 'unit' and the 'control' theories

There have been two theories under common law on the question of liability of tug and tow to third parties: the 'unit' and the 'control' theories. Under the unit theory, both tow and tug are regarded as being one unit, so that the faulty navigation of the tug is attributable to the tow in accordance with the rule of undivided command. The control theory is based on which of the two is in control of the particular act of navigation resulting in the damage, as seen in the case above.

The unit and control theories have been explained in Chapter 12, but it is appropriate to refer to them briefly here in the context of towage.

8.2.2.1 The unit theory (the notion of identity)

Cases decided on the basis of this notion produced peculiar results. For example, in *The Singuasi*,[96] in which the tug negligently caused a collision by turning to port without orders from the pilot on board the tow, the tow was held liable because the tug was regarded as the servant of the tow. This concept was elaborated in the following leading authority.

The Niobe[97]

The (tug) *Flying Serpent*, while towing *The Niobe*, came into collision with *The Valetta* resulting in severe damage and ultimate sinking of *The Valetta* with two members of her crew being drowned. *The Niobe* also collided with *The Flying Serpent*, but no damage resulted from that collision. It was found that the collision was partly caused by a bad lookout on the part of *The Niobe*, and her failure to warn the tug that she was on a collision course. It was held that the collision was due to the fault of both the tug and *The Niobe*. The latter had failed to keep a lookout and guide her tug.

Sir James Hannen said:

> But it appears to me that the authorities clearly establish that the tow has, under the ordinary contract of towage, control over the tug. The tug and tow are engaged in a common undertaking, of which the general management and command belongs to the tow, and in order that she should efficiently execute this command it is necessary that she should have a good lookout and should not merely allow herself to be drawn, or the tug to go, in a course which will cause damage to another vessel.[98]

He later stated that:

---

96   (1880) 5 PD 241.
97   (1888) 13 PD 55 (HL).
98   *Ibid*, p 59.

> If it had been shewn that *The Flying Serpent* had, by some sudden manoeuvre, which those on board *The Niobe* could not control, brought about the collision, I should have held *The Niobe* blameless.[99]

In the House of Lords,[100] the owners of *The Niobe* sought to recover under their insurance policy. *The Niobe* was insured from Clyde to Cardiff and/or Penarth till she arrived at Singapore. The insurance provided that, if the insured vessel came into collision with any ship, and the insured became liable to pay persons interested, the assured would be indemnified by the insurer a certain proportion of the sum so paid. The owners of *The Niobe* paid the owners of *The Valetta* and sought to recover this from their insurers. One of the underwriters refused to pay on the ground that the insurers would only be liable if the damage arose from a 'collision' with *The Niobe* itself. They contended that the words in the policy imported the meaning that there must be contact between *The Niobe* and the other ship, not just a collision between the tug and the other ship.

The majority of the Lords held that *The Niobe* was, in the contemplation of the law, one and the same ship with her tug for all purposes of their joint navigation. Therefore, within the meaning of the insurance policy, the collision between the tug and *The Valetta* must be taken to have been a collision of *The Niobe* with *The Valetta*. The underwriters were liable. Lord Watson said:

> A sailing vessel, and the steam tug which has her in tow, have frequently been described by eminent judges as, for certain purposes, constituting 'one ship', an expression which has been borrowed by text writers, and is familiar to persons conversant with maritime law. The expression is figurative, and must not be strained beyond the meaning, which the learned judges who have employed it intended that it should bear. As I understand their use of the expression, it signifies that the ship and her tug must be regarded as identical, insofar as the two vessels, with their connecting tackle, must be navigated as if they were one ship, and, the motive power being with the tug, must, in order to comply with the regulations for preventing collision at sea, be steered and manoeuvred as if they formed a single steamship; and also, insofar as the ship towed, when she has (as in this case) the control of the tug, and the duty of directing the course of the tug in accordance with these regulations, is responsible for the natural consequences of the tug being wrongly steered, through the neglect of her officers or crew to perform that duty.[101]

Although the judge in the collision action had found the tow liable on the ground that it was in control of the towage operation, the House of Lords in the insurance claim arrived at the same conclusion by applying the notion of the 'unity' between tug and tow. It should be noted that this decision of the

---

99 (1888) 13 PD 55 (HL), p 60.
100 [1891] AC 401.
101 *Ibid*, p 407.

House concerned liability of the insurers under the insurance contract, but it caused some confusion. Thus, the House of Lords found the opportunity 20 years later in *The Devonshire* (below) to analyse the position of tug and tow liability to third parties by taking into consideration which of the two, on the facts, was in control of navigation at the particular time. The artificial notion of a unity between tug and tow regardless of who was in control was rejected. The question of who was in control would be a question of fact in each case.

8.2.2.2 The control theory

The control theory emerged from a pragmatic view of towage situations and allows the court to look upon the facts of each case instead of ascribing control to the tow as a matter of presumption for reasons of expediency and avoidance of a divided command.

The Devonshire[102]

The tug was towing a dumb barge, *The Leslie*, which had no propelling apparatus, the control and management of the navigation being entrusted to the tug. *The Leslie* sank after coming into collision with another ship, *The Devonshire*. The owners of *The Leslie* sued the owners of *The Devonshire* claiming damages. It was found that the collision was caused by the faulty navigation of both the tug and *The Devonshire*. The owners of the barge were neither actually nor constructively to blame. The tug was in sole control of the navigation and her crew were not in the position of servants to the owners of the barge. Lower courts held that the dumb barge – being an innocent ship – could recover the whole of her loss from either one of the two other ships that had caused the collision. The owners of *The Devonshire* were, therefore, ordered to make good the whole of the damage in accordance with the common law rule of no contribution between joint tortfeasors as was applicable at that time. On appeal to the House of Lords by the owners of *The Devonshire*, one of the questions was whether the tow was to be regarded as being one entity with the tug and, therefore, guilty with her of faulty navigation.

Viscount Haldane LC, in enunciating the control theory, relied on the judgment of Butt J, and Sir James Hannen in the case of *The Quickstep*.[103]

This case involved the paddlesteamer *Charles Dickens*, which was proceeding down the River Tees. When she was almost off the graving dock entrance, she saw the masthead and red light of *The Quickstep*, which, with the hopper barge in tow, was heading up the river, having come out from the buoys on the south shore with the intention of straightening down. Owing to the absence of a second masthead light to indicate that *The Quickstep* was

102 [1912] AC 634.
103 (1890) 15 PD 196.

towing, *The Charles Dickens* came into collision with the hopper barge, and sustained such injuries that she had to be beached. The hopper barge carried a proper light, had two men on board, and had a rudder. It was admitted that there was no interference by those on board the hopper barge with the navigation of the tug.

The county court judge found that the collision was caused by the negligence of those on board the tug, *The Quickstep*, and that there was no negligence on the part of those in charge of *The Charles Dickens*, or of the hopper barge; but he held the owners of the hopper barge, as well as the owners of *The Quickstep*, liable on the ground that the owners of the hopper barge, having employed *The Quickstep* to tow the barge, those on board *The Quickstep* were, as matter of law, at the time of the collision the servants of the owners of the hopper barge.

Butt J, in the Divisional Court, said:[104]

No doubt in many cases of towage the negligence relied on as making the owners of the vessel in tow liable for a collision has been the negligence of those on board the tug; and where, as in most of such cases, the navigation was under the direction of those on board the vessel being towed, such negligence has been rightly held to be in law the negligence of her owners. In one or two cases in the Court of Admiralty, Dr Lushington seems to have intimated that the inexpediency of having a divided command and direction of the vessels would in itself be a sufficient reason for attaching liability to the vessel in tow. In all such cases, however, the real question is whether or not the relation of master and servant exists between the defendants, the owners of the vessel towed, and the persons in charge of the navigation of the steam tug. Unless that relation exists, considerations of expediency cannot avail to impose liability on the owners of the vessel in tow...

The truth is, no general rule can be laid down. The question whether the crew of the tug are to be regarded as the servants of the owner of the vessel in tow must depend upon the circumstances of each case.

There would seem to be no better reason for holding the master of the tug, in the present case, to be the servant of the owners of the barge, than there is for saying that the master of a ship engaged in carrying cargo is the servant of the charterer, and so may render the latter responsible for a collision caused by the negligence of the master of the vessel.

It would be a hopeless task to attempt to reconcile the numerous decisions bearing on the subject in our English courts. Nor are the American cases more uniform in their result. We think the right view of the law is that stated by Lord Tenterden and Littledale J, in the case of *Laugher v Pointer* adopted and approved by the Court of Exchequer in *Quarman v Burnett*. Both those cases were actions for negligence in driving a carriage. In the earlier case, Lord Tenterden said:

---

104 (1890) 15 PD 196, 199–201.

'If the temporary use and benefit of the horses will make the hirer
answerable, and there be no reasonable distinction between hiring them
with or without a carriage, must not the person who hires a hackney coach
to take him for a mile, or other greater or less distance, or for an hour, or
longer time, be answerable for the conduct of the coachman? Must not the
person who hires a wherry on the Thames be answerable for the conduct
of the waterman? I believe the common sense of all men would be shocked
if anyone should affirm the hirer to be answerable in either of these cases
… If the case of a wherry on the Thames does not furnish an analogy to
this subject, let me put the case of a ship hired and chartered for a voyage
on the ocean to carry such goods as the charterer may think fit to load, and
such only. Many accidents have occurred from the negligent management
of such vessels, and many actions have been brought against their owners;
but I am not aware that any has ever been brought against the charterer,
though he is to some purposes the *dominus pro tempore*, and the voyage is
made not less under his employment, and for his benefit, whether he be on
board or not, than the journey is made under the employment, and for the
benefit of the hirer of the horses. Why, then, has the charterer of the ship,
or the hirer of the wherry, or the hackney coach, never been thought
answerable? I answer, because the shipmaster, the wherryman, and the
hackney coachman, have never been deemed the servants of the hirer,
although the hirer does contract with the wherryman, and the coachman,
and is bound to pay them, and the pay is not for the use of the boat, or
horses, or carriage only, but also for the personal service of the man …'

Adopting this reasoning, Viscount Haldane LC said in *The Devonshire*:

In the case of *The Quickstep*, Butt J, in delivering the judgment of Sir James
Hannen and himself, laid down that, where a tug and its tow came into
collision with an innocent ship, the question whether the owners of the latter
can recover damages against the owners of the tow depends on whether the
relation of master and servant obtains between the owners of the tow and
those of the tug. Unless this relation is established, he said that there was no
liability on the part of the tow. I think that, as the doctrine of identification as
enunciated in *Thorogood v Bryan* has now been swept away, the principle so
laid down was right, and that it is a simple application of the rule established
in the well known case of *Quarman v Burnett*. No relation such as that of master
and servant was established in the present case, and the tow was therefore an
innocent ship, and its owners are at common law entitled to recover the whole
of their damage from the owners of *The Devonshire*.[105]

8.2.2.3 Application of the control theory for risk management

When a contract, such as the UKSTC, provides that, whilst towing, the master
and crew of the tug will be deemed to be the servants of the tow, the question
of control is answered by the terms of the contract as between the tug and
tow. As regards third parties, who may suffer damage or loss caused by a

---

105 [1912] AC 634, p 645.

collision between either the tug or the tow or both and another vessel, the question of control will be determined by the court judging from the circumstances of the particular case. The principle that derives from *The Devonshire* is as follows:

(a) when a tug has undertaken towage of an unmanned boat or craft and there is a collision between either the barge or the tug and a third vessel, the tug, which must, in such circumstances, have been in control of the situation, will be responsible, if it can be established that the negligence of those on board the tug caused or contributed to the collision;

(b) when the tow has officers and crew on board, they should be able to be in control of navigation and warn the tug of dangers in compliance with the collision regulations and seamanship skill. Equally, those on board the tug will have a duty to exercise due care in navigation and will be in control of towage operations depending on the circumstances. To determine which of the two was in control of a particular manoeuvre, which caused a collision, will be a question of fact and the particular circumstances in each case;

(c) a third innocent party who has suffered damage due to the negligence of the other two can sue either of them for the whole loss. This issue is explained further below.

The Collision Regulations of 1972 apply to tugs and tow and both have a duty to observe them.[106] In addition to the regulations which apply generally to all vessels, there are special provisions dealing with towage situations, for example, r 21 deals with 'towing lights'; or r 27 specifies additional lights to be displayed by certain towing vessels.[107] Although there is no presumption of fault for breach of these regulations by any vessel, failure to observe the regulations constitutes evidence on which the plaintiff may rely in showing breach of the duty of care owed to other vessels at sea.[108]

8.2.3 Joint tortfeasors (the common law rule)

At common law, prior to 1935 (that is, the Married Women and Joint Tortfeasor's Act, being replaced by the Civil Liability (Contribution) Act 1978), there was no contribution between joint tortfeasors, each was liable for the entire damage inflicted on an innocent third party by their joint wrong. By contrast, in admiralty there has been the rule of division of loss between two ships at fault.

---

106 There are numerous cases of breach of the collision regulations (lookout rule, speed, warning on danger, etc); see, eg, *The Basis* (1950) 84 LlL Rep 306, when both tug and tow were in breach of the duty to obey those regulations.

107 For a more detailed discussion of collisions involving tugs and tows, see Kovats, LJ, *The Law of Tugs and Towage*, 1980, Chichester and London: Barry Rose.

108 See Chapter 12, above.

The question put to the House of Lords in **The Devonshire** was whether the admiralty law rule as to division of loss was applicable to cases when the victim was innocent.[109]

The owners of *The Devonshire* contended that they could only be held liable for half of the loss. Also, that since the tow had committed its navigation to the tug, it could not be treated as a wholly innocent ship. The submission was that *The Leslie* should be precluded from recovering more than half of its damage from the owners of the other delinquent ship (*Devonshire*). The House of Lords considered whether there was an admiralty rule displacing the common law rule and **Lord Atkinson** analysed the issue referring to some relevant previous authorities and explained, thus:

> [In *The Niobe*] the contest in the Court of Admiralty was as to whether *The Niobe* was to blame. The tug admitted her liability, but the significance of the decision in relation to the general principle contended for in the present case is that full damages were awarded against tug and tow jointly, and the rule as to the limitation of damages applicable in admiralty cases where the ship of the plaintiff collides with the ship of the defendant, and both are to blame, was not applied. The two tortfeasors were held liable for all the damage caused as they would have been in a court of common law.[110]

> In the following year, 1891, the case of *The Avon and Thomas Joliffe*[111] came up for decision. In that case *The Avon*, while in tow of tug, came into collision with another vessel named *The Thomas Joliffe*. The crews of both the tug and tow were held to have been to blame, and the crew of *The Thomas Joliffe* was held to have been blameless. Sir Charles Butt was pressed to divide the damages between the two wrongdoers on the authority of two American cases, *The Sterling and The Equator* and *The City of Hartford and The Unit*. He refused to do so on the distinct ground that the rule of limitation of damages only applies in admiralty law to cases where the ships of the plaintiff and the defendant have been in collision and have both been found to blame.[112]

> In the several cases subsequent in date to 1891 referred to in the judgment of the learned President in the present case, the same principle appears to have been acted upon, and no instance has been found where it was departed from in this country. On the question of the identity of the tow with the tug it is only necessary, I think, to refer to two additional authorities; the first preceded *The Quickstep* in date, and the second was quite recent. The first is the case of *Union Steamship Company v Owners of the Aracan*, decided by the Privy Council in 1874.

---

109 See Chapter 12, paras 3.11.3 and 3.7.4.3, above.

110 That was the result of applying the unit theory in that case by which the tow was found to blame for the negligence of the tug.

111 [1891] P 7.

112 Thus, the admiralty division of loss rule could not apply as between two colliding ships one of which was innocent, but only to the two ships at fault.

There, a disabled steamer, *The Syria*, was being towed home from Ascension by another steamer, *The American*. Both belonged to the same owners. On the voyage, *The American* came into collision with and sank the sailing vessel named *The Aracan*, belonging to the plaintiffs. The learned judge of the Admiralty Court said that, in fact, neither of the crews of *The Syria* or *The American* were to blame, but that the crew of *The American* was solely to blame; but notwithstanding these findings, *The Syria* must, he thought, be pronounced to blame on the ground that she must in intendment of law be treated as one vessel with *The American*. The Privy Council, after considering several American authorities, reversed this decision, on the ground that there was no evidence of *The American* having been hired by the captain of *The Syria* or having acted in any way under the control of the latter; that on the contrary it appeared that the governing power was wholly with *The American*.

The second is the case of the lightship *Comet* (*The WH No 1 and The Knight Errant*.) There the lightship, moored at the mouth of the Mersey, was run into and sunk by a hopper barge, *WH No 1*, which was coming up the river in tow of the tug *Knight Errant*. The owners of the lightship sued both the owners of the barge and the owners of the tug for the damages caused by the negligent navigation of the tug and tow, or alternatively of one of them. The then President, Lord Mersey, held that both the tug and tow were in fact to blame. He treated them, he said, expressly as joint tortfeasors, each being liable for all the damages that followed from their wrongful act. The owners of the hopper barge alone appealed. On behalf of the appellants, *The Quickstep* was relied upon, and it was urged that, as the barge had no motive power of its own, the crew of the tug were necessarily in sole control of the navigation, that the crew of the tug were not, therefore, the servants of the owners of the barge, and the crew of the latter not, in fact, guilty of any negligence.

The Court of Appeal, consisting of Lord Halsbury and Fletcher Moulton and Farwell LJJ, came to the conclusion that the crew of the hopper barge were not, in fact, guilty of any negligence, and allowed the appeal with costs. The plaintiff appealed to this House, when it was again held that the crew of the barge were not, in fact, guilty of negligence, and the appeal was dismissed on this ground. It must therefore, I think, now be taken as conclusively established that the question of the identity of the tow with the tug that tows her is one of fact, not law, to be determined upon the particular facts and circumstances of each case.

Now, in the present case, the President has on the authority of *The Quickstep* found that the owners of the barge were neither actually nor constructively to blame; in other words, that the tug was in sole control of the navigation, and that her crew were not in the position of servants to the owners of the barge ... This case resolves itself into one where two vessels belonging to two different persons, not being plaintiff and defendant respectively in a suit, both ships having been negligently navigated, have inflicted damage on a third vessel by and through their joint wrongful act. In my view the appellants have wholly failed to shew that there ever was any general principle of law administered in the Court of Admiralty, according to which the owners of the vessels in default were, in such circumstances, not treated in the same way as joint tortfeasors are treated at common law, and each made liable for all the damage he helps to inflict. [113]

The House of Lords stressed that this type of case was different from cases in which two or more ships collide and all are found to be at fault. Only in those cases would the admiralty law rule of division of loss apply pursuant to s 25(9) of the Judicature Act (JA) 1873, which was applicable at the time. A couple of years later, when the admiralty law rule was by then enacted by the Maritime Conventions Act (MCA) 1911, the division of loss rule applied between two vessels at fault in an action for contribution after payment had been made to the innocent third party by the one wrongdoer (*The Cairnbahn*, below).

8.2.4 Contribution between joint tortfeasors by statute

The Cairnbahn[114]

This case was concerned with an action between two tortfeasors for contribution. A collision took place between an innocent barge in tow of a tug and a steamship. The steamship and the barge were damaged. The collision was due to the fault of the tug (*Nunthorpe*) and the steamship (*Cairnbahn*). The barge recovered the whole of her damage against the steamship. The owners of the steamship sought to recover half of the damage from the tugowners. The question was whether the admiralty rule as to division of loss applied between the two vessels at fault. It was contended on behalf of the owners of the steamship that the tug, *Nunthorpe*, would have to bear half the loss sustained by the owners of the steamship, including half the amount of damage sustained by the owners of the barge, which had been paid by the owners of the steamship. The owners of the tug, *Nunthorpe*, contended that as both the steamship and the tug were at fault, the owners of the steamship were not entitled to call upon the owners of the tug to bear any share of the loss, because the two vessels were in the position of joint tortfeasors. It was argued that as the two vessels at fault were not 'colliding vessels', the admiralty rule, preserved by s 25(9) of the JA 1873, would not have applied before the MCA 1911 came into operation and that the Act did not alter the law in this respect. Therefore, they argued, the common law principle, that there could be no contribution between joint tortfeasors, governed the case.

However, the President, **Sir Samuel Evans**, held that:

The wording of s 1(1) of the 1911 Act is quite different from that of the repealed sub-section. Its language, appears to me to be quite plain. Reading the words of the section which are applicable to the circumstances of this case, it enacts

---

113 [1912] AC 634, pp 653–57.
114 [1914] P 25.

that, where by the fault of two vessels damage or loss is caused to one or to both of those vessels, the liability to make good the damage or loss shall be in proportion to the degree in which each vessel was in fault (subject, of course, to the proviso). There is nothing in the section about the two vessels in fault being themselves in collision with each other. Translate the words into the facts of this case, then the enactment would read thus: 'Where by the fault of the tug *Nunthorpe* and the steamship *Cairnbahn* damage or loss was caused to the *Cairnbahn*, the liability to make good such damage or loss shall be in proportion to the degree in which the tug *Nunthorpe* and the steamship *Cairnbahn* were in fault, namely, in equal degree.' As has been said, the damage or loss caused to *The Cairnbahn* was admitted to include the sum which *The Cairnbahn* was adjudged to pay to the innocent barge, as well as the damage caused to the steamship herself.[115]

On appeal, the Court of Appeal upheld the view that s 1 of the MCA[116] applies even where the damage to be apportioned does not arise from a collision between the vessels at fault. **Lord Parker** of Waddington said:

The section, then, being applicable to the present case, we have to consider its true meaning and effect. It provides for the apportionment in a certain way of the 'liability for the damage or loss' referred to, that is to say, the damage or loss caused by the fault of two or more vessels to one or more of those vessels, to their cargoes or freight, or to any property on board.

Before the passing of the Act there was at common law no liability on the part of anyone to make good the damage caused to *The Cairnbahn*, both she and *The Nunthorpe* being to blame, and, according to the admiralty rule referred to in s 25, sub-s 9, of the JA 1873 (if such rule were applicable), the only liability to make good this damage lay on *The Nunthorpe*, but to the extent only of a moiety thereof. Having regard to the strange results which would otherwise follow, I think that the section must be construed not as apportioning any existing liability, but as providing that the whole of the damage or loss referred to is to be borne in proportion to the degree in which each vessel is in fault, and if it be impossible to establish different degrees of fault, then equally.

I do not think that there is anything in proviso (c) to preclude the adoption of this construction. The fact that *The Nunthorpe* was not by common law under any liability, or, if the admiralty rule would have applied, was liable for a moiety of the damage only, could not, in my opinion, entitle her to say that she was, within the meaning of the proviso, wholly or partially exempted from liability by some provision of law. Further, I think that though the section refers to damage or loss caused to one or more of the vessels in fault, to their cargoes or freight, or to any property on board, this is only a figurative way of referring to the damage or loss caused to the persons interested in the vessels, their cargoes or freight, or any property on board. Loss cannot, with any propriety of language, be said to be caused to a vessel or other property,

---

115 [1914] P 25, p 29.
116 Now, see the MSA 1995, s 187 (Chapter 12).

though it may well be said to be caused to those interested in the vessel or property in question.[117]

It was made clear that the MCA 1911 dealt with the question from the point of view of the guilty parties only. The rights of the innocent party were not in issue in this case as they were in *The Devonshire* because this case was for contribution between the tortfeasors in a separate action.[118]

9 EXCLUSION FROM LIABILITY AND INDEMNITY CLAUSES (RISK MANAGEMENT ISSUES)

At common law, the tugowner will be liable for damage to the tow caused by the tug's negligence. Under the UKSTC 1986, the tugowner is protected by an exemption from such liability, as well as by an indemnity for liability that might be incurred by negligence of the tug to third parties. It has been explained earlier that the UCTA 1977 does not apply to towage contracts except insofar as the tow owner deals as a consumer. By contrast, the Towcon form of contract places the parties at an equal footing and each one will bear its own loss. There is also a mutual indemnity provision for liability incurred to third parties.

Their respective liabilities to each other and to third parties are insured. Collision cross liabilities with regard to damage caused to tug and tow respectively are insured up to three-fourths by hull and machinery (H&M) insurers and one fourth by the Protection and Indemnity mutual insurance (P&I clubs) depending on the particular rules of the club to which the owner is a member. Physical damage to or loss of the tug or tow under towage will be covered by their respective insurers (under the Institute Marine clauses for H&M) who will be subrogated to the rights of their assured against the other party or third parties once payment under the insurance contract has been made (see insurance issues and collisions in Chapter 12).

Liabilities to third parties, such as cargo damage on board the tow or loss life or personal injury are covered by the P&I insurance of the tow. The P&I insurer will be subrogated – after payment to its assured – to any rights the tow might have in respect of such liability against the tug (subject to the terms of the towage contract) or against a third party who caused or contributed to such liability.

---

117 [1914] P 25, pp 30–31.
118 See, further, Chapter 12, paras 3.7.4.3 and 3.11, above.

9.1 The ambit of the exception from liability clauses

Exclusion from liability clauses must be drafted in clear terms, or else, the tugowner may discover that he cannot take advantage of them because, under the rules of construction of contract terms, vague and wide clauses will be construed against the person claiming benefit from them.

The Carlton[119]

The terms of the towage contract between the plaintiff and the Port Authority (the defendants) contained a clause stating:

> ... the owners of the ship ... so being towed or transported hereby agree and undertake to indemnify and hold harmless the Port Authority against all claims for or in respect of ... loss or damage of any kind whatsoever and howsoever or wheresoever arising in the course of and in connection with the towage or transport, and whether such loss, injury or damage be caused or contributed to by any negligence, default or error in judgment on the part of any officers or servants whatsoever of the Port Authority ...

The plaintiff's steamship suffered damage when in tow by the defendant Port Authority's tugs due to wrong signals negligently given by the defendants' lock foreman. The lock foreman had signalled to the plaintiff's ship in tow of the defendants' tugs to enter into the Cutting. About the same time, he also signalled to another tug to enter the Cutting from the opposite end. In an attempt to avoid a collision, the plaintiff's steamship made a wrong move. As a result, she got out of position and struck the walls of the Cutting and suffered damage. When sued by the plaintiff, the Port Authority sought to rely on the above clause alleging that if their servants were guilty of negligence, they were under no liability to the plaintiffs. They counterclaimed for the damage done to the side of the Cutting.

It was held by Bateson J that the defendants' lock foreman was negligent. The clause was not an indemnity against party and party claim, but only against third party claims. Also, that the damage did not arise in connection with the towage or transport and that accordingly the plaintiffs were entitled to recover the amount of the damage caused by the negligence of the defendants' servant. Clearer terms would be required in the contract to protect the Authority from such negligence.[120]

Tugowners may be lulled into a false sense of security if they rely on a contract in which the exception clauses have been drafted in very wide and unclear terms. The following two examples demonstrate that exception of liability clauses will not assist the tugowner if he does not do the thing

---

119 [1931] P 186.
120 *The Carlton* was later approved by the Court of Appeal in *The Lindenhall* [1945] P 8.

contracted for (*The Cap Palos*) or if the exception clause attempts to negate the object of the contract (*The Sumi Maru*).

The Cap Palos[121]

The defendant contracted to tow the plaintiffs' schooner *CP*. on a round voyage of which the first stage was Immingham to Hartlepool. Through the negligence of the defendant's tugmaster the vessels got into Robin Hood's Bay on the night of 23 October. The tugs got aground and lost their hawsers and the *CP* came to anchor. The tugs got afloat on the early morning of 24 October and proceeded to Hartlepool, leaving the *CP* in the bay with a rising north east wind. The *CP* remained in the bay making vain attempts to get out until 26 October, when at about 3 pm. she drifted onto the rocks and became a constructive total loss. It appeared that the defendant had ordered another tug to go to the *CP*, but cancelled the order, as he thought (erroneously) that the Salvage Association had sent tugs to her assistance. In an action by the plaintiffs for the loss of their vessel by reason of the defendant's breach of contract or duty the defendant pleaded the exception clause in the towage contract whereby the tugowner was not responsible (*inter alia*) for 'any damage or loss that may arise to any vessel or craft being towed, or about to be towed, or having been towed ... whether such damage arise from or be occasioned by any accident or by any omission, breach of duty, mismanagement, negligence, or default of the steam tugowner, or any of his servants or employees ...'

It was held by the Court of Appeal, reversing Hill J, that as the defendant had at any rate temporarily given up any attempt to continue the towage and had left the performance of his duty to others, he could not avail himself of the words 'default of the steam tugowner', which only extended to cover defaults during the actual performance of the duties of the contract. It was not clear enough to cover 'not doing the thing contracted for in the way contracted for'.

In **The Sumi Maru**,[122] the exclusion of liability clause was very wide and it is important to quote it in full:

> Tugowners shall not be responsible for any loss, damage or delay whatsoever to the tow or any of the cargoes on board or for failure to undertake and/or complete the towage services however caused whether due to any unseaworthiness or defect in or breakdown of the tug or to the unfitness of any gear employed, shortage of fuel, bunkers from whatever cause, or other unforeseen circumstances or to the act of God, perils of the sea, fire, snow, ice barratry or negligence of the master or crew, arrest or restraint of princes, rulers or people, strikes, labour disturbances or civil commotion, explosion, bursting of boilers, breakage of shafts, or any latent defect in hull, machinery, gear or appurtenances, collision, stranding or other accidents of navigation

---

121 [1921] P 458 (CA); see, also, para 5.2, above.
122 1993 1 SLR 198; see, also, para 6.1.1, above.

even when occasioned by the negligence, default or error in judgment of the pilot, master or crew of the tug or any other servants of tugowners or for any personal injury or loss of life to persons on the employ of contractor or any third party; and contractor shall relieve tugowners from and indemnify them against all such loss, damage, injury or liability and against all claims whatsoever arising out of or in respect of such matters including any costs, charges or expenses which tugowners may incur or may be put to in defending any such claims.

The Court of Appeal held that the clause should not be construed in such a way as to render the whole contract nugatory or defeat the object, which both parties had in view, or to make the contract to become nothing more than a statement of intent.

Failure to undertake and/or complete the towage services, however caused, cannot possibly extent to and include an intentional and deliberate failure or refusal to perform an obligation under the contract.

The UKSTC have a wide and fairly clear clause of exclusion of liability. Clause 4(a) provides:

Whilst towing, or whilst at the request, either expressed or implied, of the hirer rendering any service of whatsoever nature other than towing:

(a) the tugowner shall not (except as provided in cl 4(c) and (e) hereof) be responsible for or be liable for

  (i) damage of any description done by or to the tug or tender, or done by or to the hirer's vessel or done by or to any cargo or other thing on board or being loaded on board or indented to be loaded on board the hirer's vessel or the tug or tender or to or by any other object or property; or

  (ii) loss of the rug or tender or the hirer's vessel or of any cargo or other thing on board or being loaded on board or indented to be loaded on board the hirer's vessel or the tug or tender or any other object or property; or

  (iii) any claim by a person not a party to this agreement for loss or damage of any description whatsoever;

arising from any cause whatsoever, including (without prejudice to the generality of the foregoing) negligence at any time of the tugowner his servants or agents, unseaworthiness, unfitness or breakdown of the tug or tender, its machinery, boilers, towing gear, equipment, lines, ropes or wires, lack of fuel, stores, speed or otherwise.

Paragraph (c) qualifies the foregoing and renders the tug liable in certain limited occasions (see para 9.3, below), while para (e) prohibits the tug's exception from liability for death or personal injury.

Although cl 4(a) has a very broad spectrum, it is not ambiguous. The question whether a serious breach of the contract by the tugowner will render exception clauses inoperative depends on the construction of the contract as a whole.[123]

It was once thought that a fundamental breach gave the court power to declare that such a breach overrode express contractual terms exempting the guilty party from liability under the contract. Such a rule was overruled by the *Photo Production v Securicor* (as aforesaid) and, since 1980, it has been definitively settled that there is no such a thing as a fundamental term, or a fundamental breach, which is not excludable by an exception clause. The parties are free to put what they like into their contract. If they agree that a breach should not be actionable, the agreement is binding.[124] The rule now, briefly, is that the court should look at the intention of the parties, as it can be deduced from the wording of the clause viewed in the context of the contract. The construction of exclusion clauses in some old decisions, such as, for example, *The Refrigerant, The Cap Palos, The Carlton* (discussed previously) would be in line with the present principle.

The parameters of the exception cl 4(a) of UKSTC are, however, limited by the first two lines of the clause, and the tugowner must show that the incident took place 'whilst towing' or, 'whilst at the request'. In *The Impetus*,[125] when the tug had come along on a parallel course to the tow for the purpose of receiving the tow lines, a collision occurred. The argument was that it was not ready to receive orders so the exception from liability did not cover the tug as the collision was outside the scope of 'whilst towing'. It was held that the tug was in a position to receive orders. The fact that no orders were given until after the collision was irrelevant. Therefore, the tug was protected by the exception clause.

The wording of the clause shows fairly clearly what the parties intended to exclude from liability. If there is an interruption of towage, the question whether or not the exclusion from liability will avail the tug will depend on whether he can show that he had not abandoned the tow, (that is, that he did not stop doing what he had been contracted for) as in *The Cap Palos* (above).

Clause 4(d) stipulates that the tugowner shall under no circumstances whatsoever be responsible for or be liable for any loss or damage caused by or contributed to or arising out of delay or detention of the hirer's vessel or of the cargo on board.

Clause 7 also contains a clause exempting the tugowner from liability for the consequences of war, riots or other unforeseen conditions or delays of any description even if caused by the negligence of the tugowner or his servants.

---

123 *Photo Production Ltd v Securicor Transport Ltd* [1980] AC 827 (HL).

124 See Atiyah, PS, *An Introduction to the Law of Contract*, 5th edn, 1995, Clarendon Law Series (paperback 1996), pp 178, 303.

125 [1959] 1 Lloyd's Rep 269, it applied *The Glenaffric* (1948) 81 LlL Rep 174, see para 5.1, above.

9.2 Indemnity clause

In all contracts, the importance of clear language used in the drafting has been stressed throughout this book. This is more so with respect to exception or indemnity clauses. Parties claiming the benefit of such clauses may find themselves victims of clumsy and ambiguous drafting. The following case illustrates the consequences of lack of clarity.

The Devonshire and The St Winifred[126]

A laden barge whilst in tow of a tug, owned by the Manchester Ship Canal Company, was sunk in the Mersey after a collision with a steamship, and the owners of the lost cargo commenced an action for damages against the steamship and the tug. The tugowners brought in the owners of the barge as third parties. They claimed a declaration that they were entitled to be indemnified by the barge owners under the terms of a 'towage requisition' in respect of any sum to which they (the tugowners) might be liable to the cargo owners.

The 'towage requisition' contained a long clause excepting the tugowners from any liability and provided as follows:

> The tugowners were not to be responsible or liable for damage or injury to any ship vessel or craft, or the persons or goods on board any ship vessel or craft, of which the company may undertake the towage or docking in the river Mersey ... or which may be piloted by any of their servants to or from any place in the river Mersey ... or for any loss sustained or liability incurred by any one by reason of such damage or injury, or for any loss or liability incurred in consequence of any such ship, vessel, or craft colliding with or otherwise damaging any other vessel or thing, or for any loss or liability of any kind whatsoever arising from the towing, docking or piloting whatever may be the cause or causes of such damage, injury, loss or liability, or under whatever circumstances such damage, injury, loss or liability may have happened or accrued, even though arising from or occasioned by the act, omission, incapacity, negligence or default, whether wilful or not, of the company's servants or agents or any other persons, or any defect, imperfection, or insufficiency of power in or any delay, stoppage or slackness of speed of any tug or vessel, her machinery or equipment engaged in towing or docking any ship, vessel or craft, whether such defect, imperfection or insufficiency of power be in existence at the beginning of or during the said towing or docking.

The argument for the tugowners was that they were relieved by the contract from all liability and from all loss, however incurred or caused, while the towing was carried out; and that consequently there was in their contract with the barge owners an implied term that they should be indemnified from all

---

126 [1913] P 13.

liability and loss whatsoever. Authorities like *Hamlyn v Wood*,[127] *The Moorcock*,[128] and *Kruger & Co v Moel Tryvan Ship Co*[129] were relied upon.

Sir Samuel Evans held:[130]

In my view the contract in this case is an ordinary business contract which speaks for itself, and which does not require any implied term to give it efficacy, or to give it the effect which was intended by the parties. Dealing with contracts of indemnity and third party procedure, Bowen LJ in *Birmingham and District Land Co v London and North Western Rly Co*.[131] says as follows:

'I think it tolerably clear that the rule' – that is, the third party rule – 'when it deals with claims to indemnity, means claims to indemnity as such either at law or in equity. In nine cases out of 10, a right to indemnity, if it exists at all as such, must be created either by express contract or by implied contract: by express contract if it is given in terms by the contract between the two parties; by implied contract if the true inference to be drawn from the facts is that the parties intended such indemnity, even if they did not express themselves to that effect, or if there is a state of circumstances to which the law attaches a legal or equitable duty to indemnify, there being many cases in which a remedy is given upon an assumed promise by a person to do what, under the circumstances, he ought to do. I say in nine cases out of 10, for there may possibly be a 10th. Thus, there might be a statute enacting that under certain circumstances a person should be entitled to indemnity as such, in which case the right would not arise out of contract, and I do not say that there may not be other cases of a direct right in equity to an indemnity as such which does not come within the rule that all indemnity must arise out of contract express or implied.'

The contract in this case is between A (the tugowners) and B (the barge owners). It means that A is not to be responsible or liable to B for damage, injury, or loss however occasioned: not that A is not to be responsible or liable to any one. In the circumstances of this case A was responsible and liable to, and suffered judgment at the suit of, other persons, namely, the cargo-owners, for the negligence of A. A seeks to say, not merely 'I shall not be responsible or liable to you, B, for any damage, injury, or loss, which may in any way arise out of the towage', but, further, 'You, B, are responsible and liable to me, A, for any such damage, etc, for which I may be responsible or liable to the rest of the world'. The contract does not say so. I do not believe that the parties intended that it should impliedly mean that. To make such an implication is not in any sense necessary for the efficient performance of the contract. To introduce such an implied term would, I think, be to make a wholly different contract from that which was made, or which the parties intended to make.

---

127 [1891] 2 QB 488.
128 (1889) 14 PD 64.
129 [1906] 2 KB 792, or [1907] AC 272.
130 [1913] P 13, pp 19–20.
131 [1886] 34 Ch D 261, p 274.

An attempt was made therefore by cl 4(b) of UKSTC to define the circumstances in which the tugowner can claim an indemnity from the hirer. **Clause 4(b)** of UKSTC provides:

> The hirer shall (except as provided in cl 4 (c) and (e)) be responsible for, pay for, and indemnify the tugowner against and in respect of any loss or damage and any claims of whatsoever nature or howsoever arising or caused, whether covered by the provision of cl 4(a) hereof or not, suffered by or made against the tugowner and which shall include, without prejudice to the generality of the foregoing, any loss of or damage to the tug or tender or any property of the tugowner even if the same arises from or is caused by the negligence of the tugowner his servants or agents.

This clause, albeit that it strikes an unfair commercial bargain, is very wide and covers in fairly clear terms liabilities incurred by the tugowner to third parties, as well as damage to or loss of the tug, or any other property of the tugowner, regardless of his servants negligence. The words 'claims of whatsoever nature or howsoever arising' include a salvage claim by a third party for his efforts to save the tug, if due to its negligence such salvage assistance became necessary.[132]

By contrast, an equal bargaining is struck by the Towcon contract in which neither the tugowner nor the hirer will have recourse against each other for either damage or loss to themselves or damage or loss to third parties caused by the negligence of their respective servants or agents, as provided by cl 18.

9.3 Limitations to exclusion and indemnity clauses

Under the UKSTC, the risk of towage is put on the tow and the period of towage defined in cl 1(b)(iv) is quite wide, continuing from the prescribed instances of commencement to the instances of termination: '"whilst towing" shall cover the period commencing when the tug or tender is in a position to receive orders direct from the hirer's vessel to commence holding, pushing, pulling ... or when the towing line has been passed to or by the tug or tender, whichever is the sooner, and ending when the final orders from the Hirer's vessel to cease holding, pushing ... or the towing line has been finally slipped, whichever is the later ...'

An attempt has been made by cl 4(c)(ii) to exclude the effect of the exception from the tug's liability under cl 4(a), and the indemnity given by the tow to the tug under cl 4(b) in circumstances which may give rise to interruption of towage. **Clause 4(c)(ii)** limits the tug's right to claim exception from liability or indemnity:

---

132 In *The Walumba* [1965] 1 Lloyd's Rep 121, a salvage claim was recoverable under the indemnity clause which provided indemnify the tugowner against all consequences thereof.

All claims which arise when the tug or tender, although towing or rendering some service other than towing, is not in a position of proximity or risk to or from the hirer's vessel or any other craft attending the hirer's vessel and is detached from and safely clear of any ropes, lines, wire cables or moorings associated with the hirer's vessel. Provided always that notwithstanding the foregoing, the provisions of cl 4(a) and (b) shall be fully applicable in respect of all claims which arise at any time when the tug or tender is at the request, whether express or implied, of the Hirer, his servants or his agents, carrying persons or property of whatsoever description (in addition to the officers and crew and usual equipment of he rug or tender) and which are wholly or partly caused by, or arise out of the presence on board of such persons or property or which arise at any time when the tug or tender is proceeding to or from the hirer's vessel in hazardous conditions or circumstances.

The length of the clause needs to be broken down. The first criterion in determining whether this clause applies so as to render the exception from liability and indemnity clauses inoperative, is to decide whether or not the tug was in a 'position of proximity or risk to or from the hirer's vessel or any other craft attending' at the critical point in time in which a liability arose. If it was not in a position of proximity or risk, it must also have been detached from and be safely clear of any ropes, etc. The words 'is detached from and safely clear' may indicate (but it is not certain) that although the towage period might have not been terminated, there may have been an incident of interruption, other than the parting of ropes due to 'hazardous conditions or circumstances' (final words of the clause). The qualification of the clause provided by the second long sentence limits the exclusion of the operation of cl 4(a) and (b) when the incident described in the first sentence is due to request, express or implied from the tow or his agents to carry persons or property or equipment. A further limitation to this is that such persons or property must have been on board (presumably meaning the tug) or the necessity of their carriage must have arisen from hazardous conditions or circumstances.

It is fairly easy to imagine the difficulties involved in interpreting such a clause. Clear and plain language would greatly assist those who are involved in treacherous towage operations.

An example of criticism by the Court of Appeal about bad drafting is provided by *The Salviva*,[133] in which Parker LJ said: 'The dispute between the parties arises out of an unusual and very ill drafted towage.'

That contract, being under the Norwegian ocean towage form, provided, principally, for the towage of APA's crane barge *Montasser* from Kegoya, Japan, to Alexandria, Egypt, by Goliath's ocean-going tug *Salviva*.

---

133 [1987] 2 Lloyd's Rep 457.

Clause 10 provided who would be responsible for the seaworthiness of the tow as follows:

> The tow to be prepared for towage by the tugowner and to the satisfaction of the tugowner and/or their master and provided with the necessary documents required for towage issued by a competent classification society [or Nippon Kaiji Kentei Kyokai]. If the tow becomes unseaworthy during the voyage for any reason whatsoever the seaworthiness to be re-established by the company and a new seaworthy certificate to be issued on tugowner's request.

Clause 17 dealt with liabilities as follows:

> **Damage and loss**
>
> Provided the tugowners shall exert due diligence to prepare the tug before departure from Kegoya in a fit, seaworthy and perfect condition in all respects to perform the voyage and provided the tugowner prepares the tow for this towage in accordance with [Nippon Kaiji Kentei Kyokai's] surveyor's requirements the tugowner shall not be responsible for any loss, damage or delay whatsoever to the tow or any of the cargoes on board or for failure to undertake and/or complete the towage services however caused whether due to any unseaworthiness or defect in or breakdown of the tug or to the unfitness of any gear employed, shortage of fuel bunkers from whatever cause or other unforeseen circumstances or to the act of God, perils of the sea, fire, snow, ice, barratry or negligence of the master or crew, arrest or restraint of princes, rulers or people, strikes, labour disturbances or civil commotion, explosion, bursting of boilers, breakage of shafts, or any latent defect in hull, machinery, gear or appurtenances, collision, strandings or other accidents of navigation even when occasioned by the negligence, default or error in judgment of the pilot, master or crew of the tug or any other servants of the tug, tugowner or for any personal injury or loss of life to persons in the employ of the company or any third party, and the company shall relieve tugowner from and indemnify them against all such loss, damage, injury, loss of life or liability against all claims whatsoever arising out of or in respect of such matters including any costs, charges or expenses which tugowners may incur or may be put to in defending any such claims.

The tug and tow departed from Kegoya on 16 October 1981 and shortly thereafter it deviated from her course to avoid the typhoon Gay. The deviation lasted from 0300 GMT on 19 October to 0400 on 24 October. In respect of this, Goliath claimed US$5000 per day for three days extra steaming time pursuant to cl 24 of the contract. The learned judge upheld this claim and no issue now arises in respect of it. Its only present materiality is that roughish, but by no means abnormally rough, weather conditions were encountered both during and after the deviation.

Some time later, probably on 29 October, the crew of the tug inspected the tow and found that some of the sea fastenings consisting of steel wire, which were supposed to immobilise the crane's jib, boom and counterweight during the voyage, had loosened and that they and other sea fastenings had suffered damage. As a result it was necessary to put in to Singapore for repairs. The repairs were carried out at a cost of US$84,027.18 and were paid for by Goliath. Tug and tow departed from Singapore on 4 December. Goliath claimed to be entitled under the contract to recover (a) the amounts expended by them on repairs, and (b) demurrage amounting to US$110,310.41 in respect of the time spent in Singapore. The judge upheld both claims. APA contended that he erred in so doing.

Between Singapore and Port Said the sea fastenings and lashings suffered further damage necessitating the carrying out of further repairs in Port Said. In respect of the cost of those repairs no claim was made, for they were paid by APA's insurers. Goliath, however, claimed demurrage amounting to US$50,821.90 in respect of the time spent in Port Said while repairs were being effected. This claim also was upheld by the learned Judge. APA contended that in so doing he also erred.

APA's basic case was that under the terms of the contract, express or implied, Goliath warranted the tow-worthiness of the tow. In other words, it warranted that the materials and workmanship of the sea fastenings were reasonably fit for the purpose of immobilising the crane during the course of the voyage. These were not so fit because steel wire was used for the primary lashings, such lashings would inevitably stretch in foreseeable weather conditions and, having stretched, would allow movement which would set up loads leading to damage and the necessity for repairs.

APA contended in the alternative that Goliath contracted to prepare the crane barge for towage and to procure her survey. Although they were entitled and expected to sub-contract the work of preparation, they are vicariously liable for any negligence on the part of the sub-contractor or surveyor. It was, they submitted, negligent to use wire lashings.

Goliath, on the other hand, contended that under the contract their obligation was merely to procure and pay for the preparation of the tow for towage to the reasonable satisfaction of themselves and/or the tugmaster, to comply with the recommendations of the towage approval surveyor, and to obtain a certificate of fitness to tow from such surveyor. With those obligations they complied and, having done so, they were, under the terms of the contract, entitled to recover the amount claimed. The judge upheld these contentions.

There was nothing wrong with the steel wire lashings as such. They were unstretched, but the plan did not provide for stretched wire. There was nothing wrong with the workmanship of Kegoya in applying the lashings. APA's case was simply that wire should not have been used at all, but that, instead, chain, or structural steel rods or tie bars should have been employed.

Parker LJ proceeded to construe the contract and said:

Clause 17 and other clauses throw light upon the meaning and intent of the opening words of cl 10 ...

The two provisos upon which the wide relief accorded to the tugowner depend are of considerable significance. So far as the tug itself is concerned, the exercise of due diligence to make it seaworthy must be shown, but with regard to the tow it is sufficient to show that it has been prepared in accordance with, in the event, NK3's requirements. If cl 10 imposes on the tugowner not merely an obligation to exercise due diligence in the preparation of the tow, but a positive unqualified warranty of seaworthiness and suitability of materials and workmanship, it appears to me unlikely in the extreme that APA would have agreed to relieve the tugowners from all loss, damage or delay to the tow, and indemnify the tugowner against all such loss and damage on the mere proof that the tow had been prepared in accordance with NK3's requirements, albeit that such requirements were insufficient to produce a seaworthy tow, provided for unsuitable materials and were grossly negligent. If the second proviso stood alone, it would in my view point strongly to the mutual intent of the parties that the tugowner's obligation under cl 10 being the limited one found by the learned judge. The indication is even stronger when the second proviso is contrasted with the first proviso. Mr Sumption submits that to derive a limited meaning to cl 10 from the wording of cl 17 is to cut down by an exemption clause the extent of the obligation in cl 10, but this submission in my view fails for two reasons: first, because the problem is to find out by reference to the contract as a whole what is the meaning of cl 10; secondly, because it is of the essence of an exemption clause that it should cut down a liability that would otherwise exist.[134]

The lesson to be learned from this case is that the intention of the parties particularly with regard to exception clauses ought to be made clear. This of course will depend on the parties' respective bargaining powers as well as on the skill of the draftsman.

10 THE SUBSTITUTION AND HIMALAYA CLAUSE OF THE UKSTC

10.1 Substitution

In particular, **cl 5 provides** that:

The tugowner shall at any time be entitled to substitute one or more tugs ... for any other tug ... or tugs ... The tugowner shall at any time ... be entitled to contract with any other tugowner ... to hire the other tugowners's tug or tender and ... it is hereby agreed that the tugowner is acting ... as the agent of the hirer, notwithstanding that the tugowner may in addition, if authorised ... act as agent of the other tugowner at any time and for any purpose including the making of any agreement with the hirer ... It is hereby agreed that such

---

134 [1987] 2 Lloyd's Rep 457, p 461.

contract is and shall at all times be subject to the provisions of these conditions so that the other tugowner is bound by the same and may as principal sue the hirer thereon and shall have the full benefit of these conditions in every respect expressed or implied herein.

It purports to give authority to the tug to act as an agent of the tow and, at times, of another tugowner for the purpose of substituting another tug, if necessary, binding the tow and the substituted tug to the terms of the contract.

This provision was drafted as a result of the circumstances that existed in the case below.

The Conoco Arrow[135]

In this case, the substitution clause stated as follows:

The tug may substitute one tug for another and may sub-let the work, wholly or in part to other tugowners who shall also have the benefit of and be bound by these conditions.

P & Sons, tug supplies company, agreed to supply tugs to the defendants under the then applicable UKSTC. The contract also contained an indemnity provision in favour of the tug-owner. The tug let to the defendants belonged to the plaintiffs and not to P & Sons. A collision occurred between the tug and the defendant's vessel as a result of which the tug sank. The plaintiffs claimed damages from the defendants' vessel on the basis of negligence, and also damages in contract based on the agreement between P & Sons and the defendants. They contended that under the UKSTC agreement, the company had sub-let the work of supplying tugs to them, and that they were therefore entitled to the same remedies by way of indemnity as the company would have had. The admiralty registrar struck out the claim based on contract.

On appeal to the High Court, Brandon J held that the admiralty registrar had rightly struck out the alternative claim based on contract. Without any evidence of agency or trusteeship, the plaintiffs could not obtain rights under a contract between the defendants and the head contractors. The claim was bound to fail in the Court of Appeal and House of Lords unless the House of Lords was inclined not to follow its earlier decisions holding that a party could not succeed upon a claim based on a contract to which he was not party.

10.2 The Himalaya provision and the Contracts (Rights of Third Parties) Act 1999

The doctrine of privity of contracts under English law has meant that third parties can neither take the benefit nor be imposed with obligations arising under a contract made between two other parties.[136] However, sometimes, a

---

135 [1973] 1 Lloyd's Rep 86.

contract and its performance can affect third parties. This has caused difficulties, over many years, particularly with regard to the extent to which third parties may benefit from exclusion or limitation of liability clauses in a contract for loss or damage arising through their negligence. Civil law systems provide in their codified law that, in some circumstances, rights or obligations under a contract may be conferred to third parties. Although vicarious immunity was accepted by the House of Lords in *Elder, Dempster Co Ltd v Paterson, Zochonis Co Ltd*,[137] demonstrating a desire by the judiciary to find ways around the doctrine of privity, the majority of the House of Lords later, in *Midland Silicones Ltd v Scruttons Ltd*,[138] did not accept that a general principle could be drawn from the *ratio decidendi* in its previous decision. To overcome this problem, parties to a contract have used techniques to enable third parties to take benefit of exclusion clauses when the circumstances require that third parties involved in the performance of the contract should be protected. Such clauses have been known as the 'Himalaya'[139] clauses and an encouragement for their use was given by the majority of the Privy Council in *The Eurymedon*.[140] This involved the performance of unloading of goods from a ship by stevedores, who sought to rely on the exclusion from liability clause in the contract of carriage agreed between the shipper and the carrier for the latter's benefit. Lord Wilberforce said:

> [The contract] ... brought into existence a bargain initially unilateral but capable of becoming mutual, between the shipper and the [stevedores], made through the carrier as agent. This became a full contract when the [stevedores] performed services by discharging the goods. The performance of these services for the benefit of the shipper was the consideration for the agreement by the shipper that the [stevedores] should have the benefit of he exceptions and limitations contained in the bill of lading.[141]

Although this decision has been criticised for providing an artificial analysis, the policy reason behind it was to discourage actions against the servants, agents or independent contractors in order to get round the exceptions in the contract. The Privy Council, again in *The New York Star*,[142] re-affirmed the principle of *The Eurymedon*, and stressed that it should not be confined to its own facts. Lord Goff, fairly recently at the Privy Council, reviewed the

---

136 For example, in the towage context, when a towage contract had been entered into between the time charterers and the tug, no claim of indemnity could be enforced against the owners of the vessel: *The Basis* (1950) 84 LlL Rep 306.

137 [1924] AC 522 (HL).

138 [1962] AC 446 (HL).

139 It derived the name from the name of the vessel in *Adler v Dickson* [1955] 1 QB 158 (CA), which involved a claim by passengers of a ship against the master of the ship, in tort, in order to avoid the limitation of liability clause in a passenger ticket (see, also, Chapter 8, contracts of management of ships, BIMCO SHIPMAN 98)

140 [1975] AC 154 (PC).

141 *Ibid*, p 167.

142 [1981] 1 WLR 138.

function of the Himalaya clauses in *The Mahkutai*;[143] following this decision, the view has been that the Himalaya clauses are developing towards becoming a full fledged exception to the doctrine of privity.[144]

In UKSTC, cl 5 combines the substitution with a Himalaya clause and effectively shows the intention of the parties that a substituted tug will enjoy the benefits of and be subject to the obligations for the performance of the contract, the conditions of which should be binding between the substituted tug and the hirer.

In addition, for extra protection of the servants and agents of the tugowner, or any tugowner whose tug has been sublet to the hirer, the hirer undertakes by cl 8 (the non-suit clause) not to bring proceedings against them in respect of any negligence, breach of duty, or other wrongful act.

The Towcon expressly regulates the rights of the tug's servants or agents to rely on the exceptions, defences, immunities, limitation of liability, indemnities, privileges and conditions granted or provided by the main agreement between the tugowner and the hirer by a separate Himalaya clause (cl 19).

The doctrine of privity has recently been reformed at the initiative of the Law Commission, which published its report on *Privity of Contracts: Contracts for the Benefit of Third Parties* in 1996,[145] as a result of which the Contracts (Rights of Third Parties) Act C(RTP)A 1999 received Royal Assent on 11 November 1999. Section 10(2) provided for it to come into force six months thereafter, so contracts made before 11 May 2000 are not subject to the Act while contracts made after that date are.

One of the reasons why there should be reform was said to be (by the Law Commissioner, Andrew Burrows)[146] injustice to third parties. In particular, he put it that:

> The privity rule causes injustice to a third party where a valid contract has engendered in the third party reasonable expectations of having the legal right to enforce (as it does, for example, where the contract contains an express term to that effect). The injustice is heightened where the third party has relied on the contract to regulate his or her affairs or has accepted it by communicating assent to the promisor. Indeed, where such heightened injustice is present, we believe that it outweighs the general right of the contracting parties to change their original intentions. That is, the parties' right to vary or cancel the contract

---

143 [1996] 3 WLR 1; he did not accept that the principle extends to exclusive jurisdiction clauses.

144 For full review and analysis of the privity doctrine, as well as the 1999 Act, see Merkin, R, *Privity of Contract*, 2000, LLP (Himalaya clauses, p 158).

145 See Law Commission Report No 242, *Reforming Privity of Contract* [1996] LMCLQ 467, p 468, for the background to the problems existed by reason of the doctrine of privity.

146 *Ibid.*

should be overridden once the third party has relied on, or accepted, the promise.

Where English law applies to a towage contract the 1999 Act enhances the protection of third parties intended to be protected by the terms of the contract, providing an alternative to the Himalaya clauses. Section 1 of the Act grants to a third party the right to enforce a term of a contract if either the contract expressly provides he may, or if the term purports to confer a benefit upon him. Section 1(5) of the Act stipulates the enforcement of rights of third parties (as provided by s 1): 'There shall be available to the third party any remedy that would have been available to him in an action for breach of contract if he had been a party to the contract.'

11 LIMITATION OF LIABILITY[147]

The 1976 Limitation of Liability Convention was enacted by the MSA 1979. This Act has been repealed and its provisions have been incorporated in the MSA 1995. Article 1 of the 1976 Convention provides for the parties who can limit liability: shipowners and salvors. Shipowner includes owners, charterers, managers and operator of a sea-going ship. This means that both shipowners involved in the towage contract can limit their liability by reference to the tonnage of their vessel. Liability is limited by reference to a limitation fund calculated on the basis of the vessel's tonnage (Arts 11–14).

One main issue dealing with limitation of liability in relation to tugs and tows has been whether or not their tonnage should be aggregated in order to provide higher limitation fund. The question of aggregation is usually referred to as 'the flotilla issue'.[148] If the theory that tug and tow is one unit were correct, the aggregated tonnage of the two might be considered for purpose of limitation. In most collision cases, however, a collision is caused by the faulty navigational manoeuvre of the one that has been in control. That may be either the fault of the tug, or of the tow, or of both. In accordance with the control theory, the limitation fund will be calculated on the basis of the tonnage of the particular vessel or vessels at fault. This is of particular concern to claimants who may have suffered loss caused by the negligent navigation of a small tug towing a great liner. The small tug has comparatively small value and it would have a correspondingly low measure of liability if limitation were to be calculated on the basis of its tonnage alone, as opposed to calculation based on an aggregate tonnage of both tug and tow.

In the following cases only the tug's tonnage was taken into account for the calculation of the limitation fund.

---

147 For an outline of the principles of limitation of liability, see Chapter 16.
148 *Op cit*, Rainey, fn 1.

The Bramley Moore[149]

M and another dumb barge were in tow of *The Bramley Moore* when a collision occurred between M and a motor vessel E. M brought an action against the E and the tug (*Bramley Moore*) as third party. The trial judge found the vessel E and the tug equally to blame and entered judgment against the owners of the E. He also entered judgment for the E against the owners of the tug for half of the damage. The owners of the tug brought a limitation action and claimed to limit their liability by reference to the tonnage of their tug alone. They contended that the calculation would be based on combined tonnage only if the tug and tow had common ownership. The counter argument was that the limit should be calculated with reference to the combined tonnages of the tug and one or both of the barges, whether or not they belonged to the same owners. The trial judge held that the tugowners were entitled to limit based on the tonnage of the tug alone. The Court of Appeal held that after the MSA 1958, which amended the limitation provisions of the MSA 1894, where damage was caused by a tow, owing to the negligence of those on the tug and not of those on the tow, the damage was caused by the negligence of the person on board the tug and the tugowners could limit their liability according to the tonnage of the tug alone. The flotilla was not to be taken as a unit.

Even when both the tug and the tow belonged to the same defendant the calculation of limitation was not done on the basis of the aggregate tonnage.

The Smjeli[150]

A tug towing a dumb barge, both belonging to the defendants, damaged the groynes of the District Council of Shepway, which claimed damages against the defendants, tugowners. The defendants contended that they were entitled to limit their liability pursuant to s 503 of the MSA 1894 as amended by the 1958 Act. The plaintiffs however contended that if the defendants were entitled to limit their liability, the amount was to be calculated by reference to the aggregate tonnage of both vessels belonging to the defendants. Sheen J held that as the plaintiffs' claim depended solely on an allegation that there was negligence in the navigation of the tug, so the limit of the defendants' liability must be calculated by reference to the tonnage of the tug alone.

Issues and principles of limitation of liability are examined in Chapter 16. In the next chapter, the rights and liabilities of port authorities and pilots are explained.

---

149 [1963] 2 Lloyd's Rep 429.
150 [1982] 2 Lloyd's Rep 74.

CHAPTER 15

HARBOURS AND PILOTAGE

INTRODUCTION

With the ever-increasing demands for safer ships, cleaner seas and prevention of environmental damage in coastal waters by marine casualties, the role of harbour authorities in ensuring that such demands are met is very important. It is equally important for them to maintain their ports in a safe condition and with adequate facilities, so that accidents to ships using them can be prevented. Manoeuvring in or out of a port can be quite difficult without the guidance of expert pilots, or harbour masters, who know local waters. There are various statutes and by-laws, which regulate the rights and obligations of harbours in making ports safe, preventing accidents and dealing with dangerous or unsafe ships, taking care of environmental safety and many other functions. Not only has the British Government charted a new course on port marine operations[1] – which includes accountability of port authorities, contingency plans and emergency response, management of navigation and pilotage – but parallel proposals towards a coherent policy on ports and maritime infrastructures have also been made by the European Commission.[2]

The Secretary of State is given powers of intervention by s 137 of the Merchant Shipping Act (MSA) 1995, as amended by s 2 of the Merchant Shipping and Maritime Security Act (MSMSA) 1997, when an accident has occurred to, or in, a ship and, in the opinion of the Secretary of State, oil from the ship will, or may, cause significant pollution on a large scale in the UK, the UK waters, or a part of the sea specified by virtue of s 129(2)(b). For the purpose of preventing, or reducing, oil pollution, he, or his representative, may give directions as respects the ship, or its cargo, or the risk of oil pollution, to the owner of the ship, master, salvor and to the harbour master, or to the harbour authority. The Secretary of State, or his representative, is able to override the powers of harbour masters and harbour authorities where this is necessary in order to prevent, or minimise, pollution.[3]

---

1   See 'A guide to good practice on port marine operations', 30 January 2001 and 'Review of trust ports', following *The Future of Transport*, White Paper, www. shipping.detr.gov.uk.

2   Proposal for a Directive (2000/35/EC) on Market Access to Port Services; and a Directive (2000/179/EEC) (OJ 2001/C14/08) to harmonise procedures for the safe loading and unloading of bulk carriers.

3   A representative of the Secretary of State may be appointed (SOSREP) in maritime emergency situations in UK territorial waters, as proposed by Lord Donaldson in his report 'Intervention powers, command and control', March 1999, www.shipping.detr.gov.uk.

The Merchant Shipping (Oil Pollution Preparedness, Response and Co-operation Convention) Regulations 1998 require the harbour authorities to have approved oil pollution emergency plans.[4]

A Port State, whose port a ship enters voluntarily, must ensure that international conventions, with regard to protecting the marine environment from vessel-source pollution, are complied with. The Port State Control is a recent development and is part of an international regulatory regime.[5] It monitors observance of international standards and inspects ships entering its ports, reports to the Flag State, if there are any deficiencies, and may impose penalties. In Europe, a unique system of Port State Control emerged from the Paris Memorandum of Understanding (MOU) 1982 under which 15 States originally agreed, on a co-operative basis, to inspect vessels entering their ports and check whether they complied with the requirements of international conventions. Its purpose is to ensure that sub-standard ships of whatever flag do not enter or leave ports with consequent risk to safety of life, the preservation of property and the protection of the environment. Its role is like a police force that provides an effective deterrent to those owners who might, otherwise, have considered too lightly the risks involved in allowing a 'rust bucket' to leave a port and endanger lives at sea.[6] It became necessary, in the light of evidence that the Flag States were failing to enforce compliance with international conventions rigorously enough.[7] The MOU has been adopted by States in other regions as well.

This chapter concentrates on duties, rights and liabilities of harbour authorities and pilots, as well as on the legal relations between pilots and ship's master, the question of who employs the pilot when on board the ship and liabilities to third parties. It is not within the confines of this chapter to examine all aspects of this topic the treatment of which can be found in Douglas and Geen.[8] First, the law relating to harbours' duties and liabilities is examined (Section A) and, secondly, the law of pilotage (Section B).

---

4 The Secretary of State in exercise of the powers conferred by Art 2 of Merchant Shipping (OPPRC) Order 1997 (SI 1997/2567) issued the 1998 Regulation (SI 1998/1056). This implemented the Oil Pollution Preparedness, Response and Co-operation Convention 1990 (OPPRC) which is about salvage policy, contingency plans and reporting of casualties, see Chapter 13, para 4.

5 For its origin and the background to it see Kasoulides, M, *Port State Control and Jurisdiction*, 1993, Kluwer. See, also, Chapter 8 of this book where recent developments of the regulatory regime in its totality are discussed in context.

6 Sir Anthony Clarke 'Port state control or sub-standard ships: who is to blame? What is the cure?'[1994] LMCLQ 202.

7 See further developments in this respect and initiatives taken by the European Commission in Chapters 8 and 17

8 Douglas, R, Lane, P and Peto, M, *Douglas and Geen on the Law of Harbours, Coasts and Pilotage*, 5th edn, 1997, LLP.

SECTION A – ASPECTS OF LAW AFFECTING HARBOURS

1 SOURCES OF POWERS AND DEFINITIONS

1.1 Statutes and regulations regulating harbours' powers

Legislation about harbours and pilots is very important to harbour authorities, so that they can regulate their affairs and the activities of other persons using the harbours. There exist numerous statutes and local legislation, some of which have been repealed by subsequent legislation. Reference is made to statutory provisions, which have caused problems in their interpretation. The following statutes are the basic applicable statutes at present:

(a) the Harbours, Docks and Piers Clauses Act (HDPCA) 1847 (10 Vict c 27), which is 'the mother statute' containing a comprehensive code of operational powers of the authorities governed by statute, and sections of it are usually incorporated in special legislation of harbour authorities;

(b) the Harbours Act (HA) 1964 was passed after recommendations of the Rochdale Report and was the first Act concerned with the central organisation of harbours, it included provisions for subordinate legislation;

(c) the Docks and Harbours Act 1966, which conferred some new powers on the harbour authorities, including power to carry out harbour operations;

(d) the Health and Safety at Work Act 1974;

(e) the Water Resources Act (WRA) 1981;

(f) the Dangerous Vessels Act (DVA) 1985;

(g) the Pilotage Act (PA) 1987, referred to under pilotage law later;

(h) the Environmental Protection Act 1990;

(i) the Aviation and Maritime Security Act 1990;

(j) the Ports Act 1991 provides for the privatisation of port trusts;

(k) the Transport Works Act 1992, basically amends some parts of the HA 1964;

(l) the Environment Act 1995;

(m) the MSA 1995 consolidated all the previous MSAs and some provisions of the HA 1964 – it is relevant in this context with respect to wrecks, lighthouses, pollution and relevant powers of port authorities.

(n) the MSMSA 1997 contains important provisions in relation to environmental protection and emergency situations in UK territorial waters. It includes powers of the Secretary of State to make regulations. A representative of the Secretary of State (SOSREP) may be appointed to perform the functions of the Secretary of State under the MSA 1995 (s 293) in relation to marine pollution.

The following regulations are also relevant:

- the Dangerous Substances in Harbour Areas Regulations (DSHA Reg) 1987;
- the MS (Dangerous Goods and Marine Pollutants) Regulations 1990;
- the Control of Major Accident Hazard (COMAH) Regulations;
- the MS (Reporting Requirements for Ships Carrying Dangerous or Polluting Goods) Regulations 1995;
- the MS (Port State Control) Regulations 1995;
- the MS (Prevention of Pollution) Regulations 1996;
- the MS (Port Waste Reception Facilities) Regulations 1997;
- the MS (Prevention of Pollution by Garbage) Regulations 1998;
- the MS (Oil Pollution Preparedness Response and Co-operation) Regulations 1998;
- the MS (Carriage of Cargoes) Regulations 1999.

Harbour authorities have a duty to make proper use of powers to make bylaws, and to give directions (including pilotage directions) to regulate all movements in their waters. The powers should be exercised in support of policies and procedures developed in the authority's safety management system. They should have clear policies on the enforcement of directions and should monitor compliance.[9]

1.2 Definitions

A 'harbour' is defined by s 313 of the MSA 1995 for the purposes of this Act as including 'estuaries, navigable rivers, piers, jetties, and other works in, or at which, ships can obtain shelter, or ship and unship goods or passengers'.

In relation to pollution matters, the Act, in Chapter II, Pt VI defines harbour in the UK as meaning 'a port, estuary, haven, dock or other place the waters of which are within the UK national waters and, in respect of entry into or the use of which by ships, a person or body is empowered by an enactment (including a local enactment) to make any charges other than charges in respect of navigational aids or pilotage'.

The definition of harbour by s 57(1) of the HA 1964 for the purpose of this Act is wider, including, 'any harbour, whether natural or artificial, and any port, haven, estuary, tidal or other river or inland waterway navigated by sea-going ships, and includes a dock, wharf, and in Scotland a ferry or boat slip being a marine work ... Dock is a dock used by sea-going ships and wharf is

---

9   DETR, *Guide to Good Practice on Port Marine Operations*, 20 January 2001, s 8, 'Management of navigation'.

any wharf, quay, pier, jetty or other place at which sea-going ships can ship or unship goods or embark or disembark passengers'.

The PA 1987 and the Ports Act 1991 adopt this definition, so it is very relevant to the discussion in this chapter.

'Harbour operations' are defined by s 57(1) of the HA 1964 as:

(a) the marking or lighting of a harbour or any part thereof;

(b) the berthing or drydocking of a ship;

(c) the warehousing, sorting, weighing or handling of goods on harbour land or at a wharf;

(d) the movement of goods or passengers within the limits within which the person engaged in improving, maintaining or managing a harbour has jurisdiction, or on harbour land;

(e) in relation to a harbour (which expression for the purposes of this paragraph does not include a wharf);

(f) the towing, or moving of a ship which is in or is about to enter or has recently left the harbour;

(g) the loading or unloading of goods, or embarking or disembarking of passengers, in or from a ship which is in the harbour or the approaches thereto;

(h) the lighterage or handling of goods in the harbour; and

(i) in relation to a wharf, the towing or moving of a ship to or from the wharf, the loading or unloading of goods, or the embarking or disembarking of passengers at the wharf in or from a ship

2 TYPES OF HARBOUR AUTHORITIES

Harbours may be classified by the type of functions they perform and by the nature of their organisation. Most major ports perform the following broad categories of functions:

(a) provision and maintenance of harbour facilities and pilotage services;

(b) carrying out harbour operations and taking precautions about navigational safety;

(c) regulating the movement and berthing of ships and preventing pollution.

The major ports in the UK are either Port Trusts[10] created by statute for the management of a harbour without share capital, or statutory companies created by local Acts of Parliament. A number are managed by local authorities (municipal port authorities), while others are re-constituted under

---

10 The Government has proposed the 'Review of Trust Ports', *A New Deal for Transport, Better for Everyone*, 1999, White Paper, www. shipping.detr.gov.uk.

the name 'Associated British Ports' by virtue of the Transport Act (TA) 1981, and they are controlled by a company. The TA 1981 allowed the investment of private capital in the development of harbour facilities. Nationalised ports (that is, ports serving the British railway system, south and east coasts) are controlled by the Association of British Ports. There are also ports registered as limited privately owned companies which are subject to the Companies Acts 1985.[11]

3 POWERS, DUTIES AND LIABILITIES
OF HARBOUR AUTHORITIES

3.1 Powers of harbour authorities

Harbour masters appointed by harbour authorities run harbours.

Reference must be made to the local Acts and orders. Powers are derived either from special Acts of Parliament, mentioned earlier, or from general Acts of Parliament relating to harbours and enabling them to make bylaws. The MSA 1995 contains several powers of the harbour authorities. If these powers are exceeded, the acts of the harbour authority will be *ultra vires*.[12] Similarly, if a company is registered by an Act of Parliament to operate public services (as, for example, for railway and market services), the company cannot abandon its objects without statutory sanction, even if the services are no longer required.[13]

The major Acts under which harbour authorities have received their powers are those referred to above, having amended or repealed previous Acts. The DVA 1985 empowers harbour masters to give instructions to refuse entry, or to require the removal of dangerous vessels. However, it also enables the Secretary of State to countermand the directions of harbour masters, if he considers that this is necessary to secure the safety of any person or vessel.[14]

In addition to the 1985 Act, harbour authorities have powers to regulate the activities of other persons at harbours and give directions to a casualty and to ships involved in salvage operations in order to ensure safety and prevention of pollution.[15]

---

11 For more details, see *op cit*, Douglas and Geen, fn 8, Chapter 2.

12 *Dundee Harbour Trustees v Nicol* [1915] AC 550.

13 *Re Salisbury Rly & Market House* [1969] 1 Ch 349.

14 Donaldson (Lord), *Command and Control, op cit*, fn 3, DETR, Appendix 4, 'Specific intervention powers'.

15 See *op cit*, Douglas and Geen, fn 8, Chapter 6.

The Merchant Shipping (Prevention of Pollution) Regulations 1996, together with the provisions of the MSA 1995, give powers to harbour authorities to regulate the discharge of oil into the sea. Section 131 of the MSA 1995, as amended by s 7 of the MSMSA 1997, created a criminal offence if any oil or a mixture containing oil is discharged from a ship into UK national waters which are navigable by sea-going ships. Both the owner and the master of the ship shall be guilty of the offence. Section 144 of the MSA 1995 gives power to the harbour master to detain the ship. The general responsibility is in the hands of the Secretary of State. General powers of the Secretary of State derive from s 137 of the MSA 1995, as amended by the MSMSA 1997.[16]

Apart from statutes, additional powers of harbour authorities derive from EC Directives, which are implemented by regulations. Directive 93/75/EEC 'The Hazmat Directive', requiring reporting of ships carrying dangerous or polluting goods, was implemented by Merchant Shipping (Reporting Requirements for Ships Carrying Dangerous or Polluting Goods) Regulations 1995. This directive is due to be amended by a new proposed directive to extend powers of reporting (see Chapter 17). The Merchant Shipping (Port State Control) Regulations 1995 implemented Port State Control. There is currently a proposal to amend Directive 95/21/EC on Port State Control to step up inspections in ports. The main point of the proposal is the banning of sub-standard ships (see, generally, Chapter 17).

3.2 Duties and rights of harbour authorities

3.2.1 Duty to operate the port

Section 33 of the HDPCA 1847, which is incorporated, or substantively contained, into local legislation of commercial harbour authorities, imposes the duty on harbour authorities to operate harbours, keep them open for anyone wishing to use them and offer facilities. In particular, it provides that:

> Upon payment of the rates made payable by this and the special Act (that is, the Act which incorporates s 33) and subject to the other provisions thereof, the harbour, dock and pier shall be open to all persons for the shipping and unshipping of goods and the embarking and landing of passengers.

A wide construction should be given to the interpretation of this section of the Act, said the House of Lords in the following case.

---

16   See, further, *op cit*, Douglas and Geen, fn 8, Chapter 9, 'Prevention of Oil Pollution'.

LNER v British Trawlers Federation Ltd[17]

The appellants were owners of a railway, a harbour and dock. They operated a fish market on their dock quays. The respondents were fish merchants and owners of fish trawlers. The appellants sought to impose, as a condition of admitting the respondents' vehicles to their harbours and docks for the purpose of removing fish landed at or purchased in the fish markets, a restriction as to the manner in which or place to which the fish was to be utilised or removed. There had been carried on by the appellants and their predecessors on the dock quays, since at any rate before 1852, a market or markets for the sale of fish landed at the port. The position of the markets was such that they could only be reached by the private roads and approaches which formed part of the appellants' estate. The question was how far the appellants in exercise of their statutory powers, or of their powers as proprietors, were entitled to impose restrictions upon the access to the fish market by those desiring to buy fish thereat, or remove fish therefrom. The appellants were seeking to exclude all vehicles the owners of which would not take from the appellants a form of licence, some of the conditions of which were directed to securing the removal by rail, and not by road, of all fish consigned to places beyond a radius of 12 miles from Lowestoft, in the county of Suffolk.

The action out of which this appeal arose was begun by the respondents, claiming certain declarations to the effect that the appellants were not entitled to impose any restriction as to the manner in which or the place to which, after removal from the appellants' premises, the fish was to be utilised or removed, and claimed also an injunction and damages. The appellants argued that, in their capacity as proprietors, they were entitled to exclude altogether, or admit upon such terms as they arbitrarily determined, any person who sought access. Section 33 of the HDPCA 1847 was the issue for construction.

The House of Lords held in favour of the respondents. Lord Tomlin, referring to s 33, said:

> First, I think that upon the true construction of the Acts governing the statutory undertaking ... the carrying on and control of the fish markets is either expressly or by necessary implication authorised as part of or incident to the harbour and docks undertaking ... In fact, they (the harbour) have been authorised by statute to acquire lands for the extension of the markets and to exercise powers in relation to them beyond those which they could exercise as mere proprietors. The result, in my opinion, must be that as long as they do carry on the markets (and it is not necessary to determine whether they are bound to carry them on) there is necessarily implied a right of access on the part of those who *bona fide* desire to resort to the markets, subject only to such regulation as may be imposed by valid bylaws duly confirmed by the competent authority.

---

17 [1934] AC 279.

Secondly, it may fairly be said that, having regard to the terms of the definition of HDPCA 1847 and s 12 of the Special Act of 1865, and to the fact that under the Special Acts the fish markets are part of the works authorised to be carried on by the appellants, the marketing of the fish when landed must be regarded, for the purposes of the Special Acts, as part of the unshipping process, access for which is given by s 33 of the Clauses Act [HDPCA]. I do not think that the words 'shipping' and 'unshipping' are to be confined to the narrow operation of lifting goods from the quay to the ship or from the ship to the quay, nor do I think that the access under the section can be limited to access in person without any vehicle. It must, I think, be such access with such vehicle as the party seeking it *bona fide* deems necessary, but it is an access always subject to be controlled by valid and operative bylaws.[18]

For the purpose of s 33, the harbour authority must make facilities for the operation of tugs, which may be necessary for the loading, or unloading, of cargo.

JH Pigott & Son v Docks and Inland Waterways Executive[19]

The defendants were the administrators of Immingham docks under delegation from the British Transport Commission. They were subject to statutory restrictions including that in s 33 of the HDPCA 1847. By that section, the harbours, docks and piers are to be kept open to all persons for the shipping and unshipping of goods upon the payment of dues. The defendants also owned two tugs, which performed most of the towage services required at the docks. However, the defendants' towage services came under increasing competition from the plaintiff's tugs, and the defendants tried to exclude the plaintiff's tugs from providing tug services for vessels entering and leaving their docks. The question was whether the defendants, as the body responsible for the dock undertaking, were entitled to exclude tugs of the plaintiffs and others, and reserve towage services to their own tugs, or such as they wished to hire to assist the services.

It was held that the defendants were not entitled to exclude other tugs. Following the decision in *LNER v British Trawlers*, Sellers J (as he then was) held that s 33 was not to be narrowly constructed. He stated, thus:

> In interpreting the section, I would hold that any of the persons providing any of the facilities which I have mentioned and the persons engaged in such activities are persons to whom a dock must be open if it is to be open for the shipping and unshipping of goods. I can see no real distinction between the contractor who, by his vehicles, brings in the goods for shipment or removes them after discharge, the tugowner who, by his tugs, brings in and takes out vessels engaged in the shipping and unshipping of goods, and the shipowner who brings his ship to the port aided or unaided by tugs. They are all

---

18 [1934] AC 279, pp 297, 298.
19 [1953] 1 QB 338.

performing services without which goods cannot be shipped or unshipped by vessels using the port; and the section makes no discrimination between persons. Provided they resort to the docks for the shipping and unshipping of goods, they are on an equality, and the shipowner does not appear to have any greater or better right than a stevedore or a haulage contractor, or, I could add, a tugowner, though the rights of all are subject to the payment of the appropriate dues which the dock authority may prescribe and subject to any regulation and control which the authority may have power, expressly or impliedly, to exercise.[20]

With regard to special rights given to users by a contract, Donaldson J (as he then was) said, in *Thoreson Car Ferries Ltd v Weymouth and Portland BC*,[21] that, under s 33, a harbour authority is obliged to keep their harbour open to any person. Subject to rights of others to use it, it was possible to grant regular use to some persons by contract, such as the right to use a specific berth, to an operator who needs access regularly. A provision can be included in the local legislation by which a harbour may set aside or appropriate part of the port or equipment for the exclusive or preferential use for a certain trade or by certain people. No other person may use the facilities of the appropriated part without the consent of the harbour master.[22] Any appropriation must be narrowly construed to derogate as little as possible from the freedom enshrined in s 33. If there is a berth available, then s 33 dictates that the authority must allow a lawful user to use it.[23]

Whether a port authority has power to restrain lawful trade in order to prevent unlawful protest came for judicial review in *R v Coventry CC ex p Phoenix Aviation and Others*.[24]

It concerned the issue whether public authorities – operating air and sea ports – were entitled to ban the flights or shipment of livestock by animal exporters and, if so, whether they could properly refuse to handle that trade so as to avoid the disruptive consequences of unlawful protest by animal rights protesters. Two applications were made by livestock exporters, who relied on statutory provisions relating to availability of facilities for lawful trade on equal terms to all without discrimination: Art 78(3) of the Air Navigation Order 1989 and s 33 of the HDPCA 1847, respectively. The third application was by the local authority for judicial review of the decision of a statutory body not to ban the export of livestock. It relied on the ground that the local authority had discretion, under s 40 of the HA 1964, to refuse the use of dock services to those engaged in a particular trade for the reason that a substantial police force was needed to control animal protesters. The first two

---

20 [1953] 1 QB 338, p 348.
21 [1977] 2 Lloyd's Rep 614.
22 Dover Harbour Revision Order 1969.
23 *R v Coventry CC ex p Phoenix Aviation and Others* [1995] 3 All ER 37, p 54.
24 *Ibid.*

applications were granted and the third was refused on the following grounds:

(a) the public authority had no general discretion under their respective statutory powers to distinguish between different lawful trades;

(b) the rule of law did not allow public authorities to respond to unlawful protest and threats from pressure groups by surrendering to their dictates, but required them, in co-operation with the police, to safeguard the right of others to go about their lawful business without disruption.

It is important to note the principles that emerged from this case so that future users of ports know where they stand and harbour authorities do not repeat the same mistake when there is a disruption in the port by protesters, which is not an infrequent occurrence nowadays.

3.2.2 Statutory duty to provide navigational safety, and other safety procedures

Each harbour authority is accountable for managing operations within the port safely and efficiently and its board members should hold themselves responsible for ensuring that it does so. The code of good practice on port marine operations represents the national standard against which the policies, procedures and performance of harbour authorities may be measured. Executive and operational responsibilities for marine safety must be clearly assigned and those to whom they are entrusted must be held accountable for their performance. Harbour authorities must have a 'designated person' to provide independent assurance about the operation of its marine management systems, who has direct access to the board.[25]

Lighthouses, beacons and buoys[26] for marking channels and providing warning of dangers to users of the port, as well as removing any obstructions, are functions of utmost importance. Now, the MSA 1995, Pt VIII has consolidated all provisions included in the previous MSAs and the HA 1964, as well as the Port Act 1991, concerning powers, functions, division of duties between general and local lighthouse authorities, rights and liabilities. Section 195 of the Act imposes responsibility on the harbour authority for the management and superintendence of lighthouses and general maintenance of all property vested in them. Sections 197 and 198 deal more specifically with the duties of lighthouse authorities in this respect.

Part IX, Chapter I allocates rights and duties with respect to salvage and wrecks; Chapter II deals with vessels in distress and the duties of harbour

---

25 *Op cit*, DETR, fn 9, s 2, 'Accountability of the duty holder'.

26 See definitions in s 223 of the MSA 1995; s 77 of the HDPCA 1847 is incorporated in special legislation of harbour authorities and requires the harbour authority to lay down buoys for guidance of vessels.

authorities in dealing with wrecks.[27] The power to remove wrecks causing obstruction is granted by s 252 of the Act in Chapter III, which grants extensive powers to the authorities even to destroy the wreck, as well as provides for rights in claiming wreck removal expenses.[28] In addition, s 56 of the HDPCA 1847, which is incorporated in almost all special legislation of harbour authorities, empowers the authority and the harbour master to remove wrecks or other obstructions impeding navigation. Intervention is justified when the wreck causes an obstruction to navigation and, hence, a hazard to other ships, or a threat to the environment. The conservancy duties of a harbour authority have been stated in several decisions (see paras 3.2.3 and 3.2.4, below).

While maritime States may have legislation dealing with wrecks in their territorial waters, immense problems can arise when the wreck is on the high seas posing a risk of pollution to coastal waters. There is, as yet, no power permitting States to force the owners of wrecks to incur the expenses of wreck removal in international waters.[29] In this respect, there is a draft Wreck Removal Convention (still under consideration by a legal committee of the International Maritime Organisation (IMO)) purporting to fill that gap by giving rights to States to intervene, if their interests are threatened.[30] It is envisaged that shipowners will be made liable for the removal of wrecks in international waters. The draft covers risks to the safety of navigation and the risk of damage to the marine environment, or to the coastline. It should apply to all types of danger to navigation, especially the danger posed by drifting ships and other ships which may reasonably be expected to result in wrecks.

Under the Merchant Shipping (Port State Control) Regulations 1995, Pt 1, reg 15(3), if a port authority, in exercising its normal duties, learns that a ship within its port has deficiencies which may prejudice the safety of the ship or pose an unreasonable threat of harm to the marine environment, the authority must inform the Maritime Safety Agency. Failing to do so, will result in the port authority being guilty of an offence.

It is important to refer also to the Merchant Shipping (Carriage of Cargoes) Regulations 1999, which came into force by a statutory instrument[31] on 15 March 1999. They consolidate the previous 1997 regulations, which implemented Chapter VI of the International Convention for Safety of Life at Sea (SOLAS) 1974, and its Protocol 1978, as amended in 1996. Basically, these

---

27 For interests in wrecks, see Palmer, N and McKendrick, E (eds), *Interests in Goods*, 2nd edn, 1998, LLP, Chapter 7.

28 There can be forfeiture of the right to claim expenses if the obstruction was caused by the fault of the harbour authority: *The Oxbird* (1937) 58 LlL Rep 346. Here, the authority had no defence under statute because it had contracted with the owner of the wreck to raise it, but due to its negligence in failing to light the wreck a collision occurred.

29 Gaskell, N, 'Interests in wrecks', para 3.2, in *ibid*, Palmer and McKendrick.

30 IMO, document LEG 76/5.

31 SI 1999/336.

regulations require the master of the ship and the terminal representative to agree a loading plan prior to the loading of bulk cargoes to ensure safe loading and unloading of ships.[32]

At the European Commission level, there are other newly proposed safety procedures for monitoring, control and information with regard to traffic in European waters and with regard to inspection of ships at European ports and prevention of oil pollution. Also, increased controls are proposed to be imposed upon ship inspection organisations and administrations.[33]

3.2.2.1 Abandonment of wreck by its owner and powers of harbour authorities

Sometimes, the owner of a sunken ship may abandon his ownership rights of the wreck by showing a positive intention to relinquish his rights in the property. But by doing so, the owner cannot relinquish accrued liabilities.[34]

A problem connected with the removal of a wreck, which has been abandoned by its owners, has been the recovery of the expenses incurred by the authority. The authority has statutory powers to sell the wreck and in that way recover its expenses, but very often the wreck removal expenses may exceed the value of the wreck.

Although the problem of port authorities recovering their surplus expenses is now being dealt with local legislation, it is important, by way of background, to explain how the courts, in the light of old legislation, had dealt with this issue.

The problem, which arose from the wording of s 56 of the HDPCA 1847, was this: unless there was a statutory provision expressly granting the authority a cause of action to sue the relevant owner, who was the owner of the ship at the time of the sinking and before abandonment, the expenses could not be recoverable because the right to claim them against the owner would not have accrued at the time of sinking, but after the owner had abandoned the wreck, or ceased to be its owner.

Thus, in the following case, the House of Lords decided against the claiming authority because the expenses were incurred after the abandonment by the owners of the wreck, who were not the owners within the meaning of s 56 of the HDPCA 1847.

---

32 See, also, a newly proposed European Commission Directive (2000/179/EEC) to enhance procedures for safe loading and unloading of bulk carriers at European ports.

33 See, further, Chapters 8, 11 and 17.

34 See *op cit*, Gaskell, fn 29, Chapter 7, para 2.2, in *op cit*, Palmer and McKendrick, fn 27.

The Crystal[35]

Subsequent to a collision with another vessel near the approach to the harbour, *The Crystal* sank and she became an obstruction to navigation. There was no evidence of negligence on her part and her owners gave notice of abandonment to their underwriters and to the harbour authorities. The harbour authority, acting under the HDPCA 1847 and the Removal of Wrecks Act 1877, took possession of the wreck, destroyed it by explosives, and sold part of her cargo that had been raised. After deducting the proceeds of the cargo from the expenses, they sued the owners for the balance under s 56 of the 1847 Act. That section provides that the harbour master may remove any wreck, or other obstruction to the harbour, which impedes the navigation thereof; and the expense of removing any such wreck or obstruction shall be repaid by the owner of the same, etc. The owners of the vessel when she sank argued that the section did not attach any personal liability on them as they were not the owners of the wreck within the meaning of the section when the expenses were incurred. One of the issues was whether the expression 'the owner' of the wreck in s 56 meant the owner of the ship at the time of sinking, or the owner of the wreck at and during the time of its removal. The House of Lords decided that it meant the former.

Lord Watson, referring to an earlier (Court of Appeal) decision on this point, *Earl of Eglinton v Norman*,[36] rejected the construction adopted by the Lords Justice that a right to remove a wreck at the expense of the then owner accrues to the harbour authority at once and cannot be affected by any subsequent change or loss of ownership. Instead, he did not think that it was reasonably possible to arrive at that conclusion, except by holding that the legislature, in using the words 'owner of the wreck', meant to designate the owner of the ship at the time when she became a wreck. If it meant the latter, nothing could be easier than to give it expression. He further stated:

> The only thing which the harbour master, under the clause in question, has authority to deal with is the wreck, and not the ship; and the only charges which, in any view, he can have right to recover are those which may be duly incurred by him for the purpose, and in the course of its removal. It is clear to my mind, that, *prima facie*, the owner of the wreck must be the person to whom the wreck belongs during the time when the harbour master chooses to exercise his statutory powers. That appears to me to be the primary and natural meaning of the words. It may, of course, be displaced by force of the context. But I can find nothing in the context to suggest that the words were intended to have any other than their natural meaning.[37]

---

35 [1894] AC 508.
36 Referred to in the judgment.
37 *The Crystal* [1894] AC 508, p 522.

It was held that expenses could not be recovered from the owner for the additional reason that the wreck had been removed by destruction and the Act only gave the harbour authority power to 'remove' and not to 'destroy'.

Obviously, the draftsman of the section had not envisaged the situation of abandonment of the wreck, nor the possibility that there may be a need to destroy the wreck. Thus, the construction of the section could not, in the Lords' view, be stretched to mean what was said in the previous Court of Appeal case, although, admittedly, a fairer result would have ensued. Much later, in 1988, the problem was rectified by an amendment to the old statutes.[38]

A further House of Lords decision, in *Barraclough v Brown*,[39] considered the same point with regard to the construction of s 47 of the Aire and Calder Navigation Act 1889. It followed the same line of argument and Lord Herschell said:

> I think the words 'the owner' at the end of cl 47 do not mean the person who was owner of the vessel at the time she sank, if he had ceased to be owner before the expenses were incurred. The clause does not impose upon the owner the duty of removing his vessel; it only renders it lawful for the undertakers to remove her if he does not. And in the latter part of the clause the words used are 'the owner,' not 'such owner', which one would have expected to find if the intention had been to refer to the same person throughout. I think the latter part of the clause refers to the person who was owner at the time the expenses were incurred, and not to the person who was owner when the vessel sank, if his ownership had ceased.

Section 77 of the Thames Conservancy Act 1894, which had similar wording to s 56 of the HDPCA 1847, but with the added words 'the owner of such vessel', was construed by the judge, in *The Wallsend*,[40] to mean the owners of the vessel so sunk, who should pay the authority's expenses.

After considering s 77, Bargrave Deane J construed the section and said:

> As the section stands, it says that when a vessel is sunk the owner of such vessel shall pay. It does not say, and I do not think I am entitled to read into it, 'the owner of such vessel at the time such expenses are incurred, or at the time that such demand is made'. It is plain simple language: 'the owner of such vessel' so sunk. It is the owner at the time she is sunk, and it seems to me that I can only draw one inference, and that is that the Thames conservators are to have this means of recouping themselves the cost of raising a vessel by recourse to the owner of the vessel so sunk, and, as I read it, to the owner of the vessel at the time that she was so sunk. I do not think the owner of a vessel can get rid of his vessel under this section by quietly saying, 'I abandon'. I do not

---

38 Eg, the MSA 1894, s 531, which dealt with wrecks, was amended by the MSA 1988, Sched 5, para 2 which created a personal debt of the wreck-owner and changed the test of ownership.

39 [1897] AC 615.

40 [1907] P 302.

think he is allowed to do that under this section. It would be so simple for the Thames Conservancy to be left in the lurch if that were to be read into the section. In my opinion this liability is a liability which attaches by law ...[41]

The learned judge was not satisfied that there was abandonment in this case.

How the words 'owner of the sunken ship' were construed under a different Act, namely s 13 of the Victorian Marine Act (VMA) 1890, for the purpose of expenses incurred for raising the wreck, is seen in the following case.

William Howard Smith v Wilson[42]

The appellants were the registered owners of the SS *Gambier*, which was run into and sunk by the SS *Easoby* within the limits of the harbour of Port Phillip, in the Colony of Victoria. On the same day, the appellants gave due notice to their insurers with whom the sunken vessel was insured, that they abandoned all their interests insured and claimed payment under their policies for a total loss. The insurers admitted the claim and paid to the appellants the full amount of the policies. Later, the certificate of registration of *The Gambier* was cancelled in consequence of her having become a wreck. The insurers, therefore, had become, at common law, the owners of the wreck. Section 13 of the VMA 1890 provided that:

> If any ship be sunk stranded or run on shore in any port within Victoria, or having been sunk shall be permitted so to remain, and the owner or master shall not clear such port of any such ship and of every part of the wreck thereof within such time as the port officer harbour master or in their absence the proper officer of customs of or at such port shall by notice in writing require, or shall not give security to the satisfaction of such port officer harbour master or officer of customs for the removal of such ship and wreck within such further time as the said port officer, harbour master or officer of customs may appoint, any two justices are hereby authorised and required, upon the complaint of the said port officer, harbour master or officer of customs, to issue their warrant for the removing such ship or wreck in such manner as such port officer, harbour master or officer of customs shall direct, and for causing the same to be sold and out of the money arising from such sale to defray the expenses of such removal, paying the overplus (if any) to the owner of such ship or if he cannot be found to the Treasurer of Victoria on behalf of such owner; and if the money arising from such sale shall not be sufficient to defray the expenses aforesaid, the excess thereof beyond the proceeds of such sale shall be chargeable to the owner of the ship; and if not paid within 20 days after having been demanded by the authority of the justices aforesaid shall be recovered as hereinafter mentioned.

---

41 [1907] P 302, p 308.
42 [1896] AC 579 (PC).

The respondent, an officer of the port, served a notice upon the appellants requiring them – as owners of *The Gambier* at the time she was sunk – to clear the port of the wreck. The appellants took no action. Later, the respondent claimed for the expenses the port had incurred for the removal of the wreck. The appellants argued that they were not the owners of the ship within the meaning of s 13 of the VMA 1890 and that, by their abandonment, ownership of the ship had passed to the underwriters. Lord Watson sitting in the Privy Council distinguished the VMA 1890, in this case, from the HDPCA 1847, which was the subject matter of *The Crystal* (in which he was sitting in the House of Lords). The distinction noted was that the expressions used in the 1847 Act were 'wreck', and the 'owner of the same'. Unlike the clear wording in the 1890 Act, there was no mention of the word 'ship' in the 1847 Act. Under the 1890 Act, the duty upon the owner to clear the port attached at once, and was made equally imperative whether or not the ship continued to be a ship. The duty was imposed upon the owner or master of the ship. Therefore, the registered owner of the ship at the date of the occurrence could not escape liability by abandoning the wreck to the underwriters who, although they became, at common law, owners of the wreck, were not the owners within the terms of the section.

3.2.2.2 Legal risks management in drafting

It is obvious from the aforesaid that any drafting, whether of statutes or clauses in contracts, requires the skill of being able to foresee the legal risks that may arise by an unclear wording, or a wording which does not cover all possibilities for recovery of what would be right and due.[43]

The MSA 1995, which repealed and replaced the previous statutory provisions about wrecks, including Sched 5, para 2 of the MSA 1988 – by which the problem of who would pay the port authority's expenses had been rectified – gives very wide powers by ss 252–55 to the harbour authority for the removal or destruction of a wreck.[44] A power of sale of the wreck and reimbursement for the expenses incurred in respect thereof out of the

---

43 In this connection, it should be noted that a similar problem of recovery of wreck removal expenses arose under a charterparty (*The Fajal* [2000] 1 Lloyd's Rep 473), in which the parties had agreed that 'in the event of the vessel becoming a wreck or obstruction to navigation the charterer shall indemnify the owner against any sum whatsoever which the owner shall become liable to pay and shall pay in consequences of the vessel becoming a wreck or obstruction to navigation'. Upon arrest of the ship, being the ship of the bareboat charterer, by the owners to recover indemnity, Rix J decided that when the owners became liable to pay the wreck removal expenses after the sinking of the ship the charterers had ceased to be the charterers of the ship. In the light of this decision, the clause should contain express words that the charterers' liability to indemnify the owners shall accrue at the time of the sinking and irrespective of when the owners pay such expenses.

44 Similar powers are given to lighthouse authorities by s 253.

proceeds of sale is also included.[45] But the section does not give the relevant authorities a personal cause of action against the owners of the sunken ship to recover their expenses. However, local legislation provides who is the owner who will compensate the port authority of its wreck removal expenses. In particular, s 46(6) of the Medway Ports Authority Act 1973 supplements s 252 for the purpose of raising wrecks and defines 'owner' as the person who was the owner of the vessel at the time of the sinking, stranding or abandonment.

3.2.2.3 The duty to mark wrecks and liability to third parties arising from unmarked wrecks – risk management issues

When a ship sinks and becomes a wreck, questions of liability for resulting damage to third parties whose ships navigate the area of the sunken wreck will arise. Wrecks present a risk to navigation and, unless they are properly dealt with will, sooner or later, cause damage to others navigating territorial waters within which the harbour authorities can exercise their statutory powers. There are certain statutory provisions which provide that the authority should place the appropriate light and use the appropriate shape of a buoy in such a distance so as to give a sufficient warning to others that there is a sunken wreck at that position.

Issues with respect to risk management of these liabilities merit consideration in raising awareness of what must be done and by whom in order to prevent possible liability to third parties.

The question that has arisen from olden times is in what circumstances the owner of the wreck, or the harbour authority, can be made liable for damage caused to a vessel which comes into contact with the wreck. The owner of the wreck would be liable if, having control over his sunken ship, he did not place a warning light or a buoy and did not warn the harbour authority.[46] But, if the harbour authority had undertaken to buoy the wreck, the authority, and not the owner, would be liable, as is shown in the following case.

The Douglas[47]

This ship, in consequence of the sole default of her master and crew, had sunk in the Thames, and had become a wreck obstructing the navigation of the river. Her mate sent a message to the harbour master to inform him of the accident, who said that he would cause the wreck to be lighted. The crew were taken off by a lifeboat. A few hours afterwards, the wreck not having been lighted, a vessel, without any fault on the part of those on board her,

---

45 With regard to a statutory right to detain the *res* and power of sale of the port authority to recover its expenses and priority of claims, see *The Sea Spray* [1907] P 133; *The Queen of the South* [1968] P 449, Ch 4, Pt I.

46 See *Harmond v Pearson* [1808] 1 Camp 515.

47 [1882] 7 PD 151.

came into collision with the wreck and sustained damage. An action for damages having been instituted on behalf of the owner of the damaged vessel against the owners of *The Douglas*, the judge at the trial refused to admit the evidence showing that the mate of *The Douglas* had sent a message to the harbour master, and that the latter had promised to light the wreck.

The Court of Appeal held that the evidence was wrongly rejected, that the collision had not been caused by the negligence of the owners of the wreck and that they were not liable for the damage done. The giving of notice of the event to the harbour authority, which undertook, in this case, to do the rest, fulfilled the obligation of the owners of a wreck. As long as they did that, the owners were not liable for the collision that occurred afterwards.

The principle arising from the above case, that once the port authority has, under its statutory powers, undertaken control and management of the wreck, the shipowner will be absolved from liability, was confirmed by the Privy council in *The Utopia*.

The Utopia[48]

The case arose out of a collision between *The Utopia*, which was lying sunk in Gibraltar Bay, and *The Primula* entering that bay. *The Utopia* had been sunk by collision with HM ship *Arson* and, thereafter, lay with her hull submerged. For a few days, her owners lighted the wreck at each masthead. The harbour master gave orders that the wreck should be lit properly, according to regulations and the authority undertook this. On the question whether the owners of the wreck were liable for the damage to *The Primula*, the court below held they were, because they remained in possession of the wreck. The Privy Council, approving the decision in *The Douglas*, summarised the principles as derived from previous authorities, thus:

> The owner of a ship sunk whether by his default or not (wilful misconduct probably giving rise to different considerations) has not, if he abandons the possession and control of her, any responsibility either to remove her or to protect other vessels from coming into collision with her. It is equally true that, so long as, and so far as, possession, management and control of the wreck be not abandoned or properly transferred, there remains on the owners an obligation in regard to the protection of other vessels from receiving injury from her. But, in order to fix the owners of a wreck with liability, two things must be shewn, first, that in regard to the particular matters in respect of which default is alleged, the control of the vessel is in them, that is to say, has not been abandoned, or legitimately transferred, and, secondly, that they have in the discharge of their legal duty been guilty of wilful misconduct or neglect.

> In the present case, *The Utopia* was certainly not abandoned by her owners in the sense that they gave up all rights of property and possession in her. On the

---

48 [1893] AC 492 (PC).

contrary, they, no doubt, always intended to raise her if they could and, in fact, either before or soon after the collision with *The Primula*, they commenced the construction of a coffer-dam, and by its means eventually recovered the vessel.

It is clear, however, that before the collision with *The Primula* the port authority of Gibraltar, represented by the acting captain of the port, took from the owners, and itself assumed, the task of protecting other vessels from the wreck by means of the signals which it directed to be employed for the purpose. The owners of *The Utopia* yielded to the action of the port authority, and thenceforward stood aloof from the operation of lighting the wreck. In these circumstances, it appears to their Lordships that the control and management of the wreck, so far as related to the protection of other vessels from her, and of her from them, was properly transferred to the port authority. Further, their Lordships are unable to see how any part of the conduct of the owners of *The Utopia* can lay them open to a charge of negligence. Neither in allowing the port authority to take on itself the control of the lighting, nor in abstaining from interfering with the subsequent action of the port authority in the matter, do their Lordships think that any default can be imputed to them. It would be dangerous if an owner of a wreck were compelled, in order to avoid a personal responsibility, to interfere with the action taken by a public authority constituted for such purposes to ensure the safety of other vessels navigating those waters.[49]

It should be noted that a common law liability for negligence could not be wiped out by abandoning that which has caused the damage and doing nothing else to prevent accidents.[50] If the owner of the wreck employs an independent contractor to raise the wreck, he cannot be absolved from liability to third parties caused by the negligence of he contractor. In *The Snark*,[51] the Court of Appeal held that the owners of the wreck, who had not abandoned it nor transferred management or control, were bound to see that the necessary precautions were taken to prevent danger to the public, and could not escape from liability by throwing the blame on the contractor employed by them to do the work.

When a harbour authority, in the exercise of its statutory powers, assumes responsibility for marking the wreck, it owes a duty of care to all persons lawfully using the port to carry out that marking with reasonable skill and care.[52] Provided that such duty is discharged, the authority will not be liable for an accident caused due to the negligence of a third party by not keeping a good look out or by not appreciating the message conveyed by the warning.

---

49 [1893] AC 492 (PC), pp 498–99.

50 *Dee Conservancy Board v McConnell* [1928] 2 KB 159, a ketch sank through the negligence of her owners who became liable at common law for the damage caused by the obstruction to the navigation of the river and the blocking of the approach to the wharf. They could not escape liability for that damage by abandoning the wreck.

51 [1900] P 105.

52 *The Tramontana II* [1969] 2 Lloyd's Rep 94.

Causation issues of course will also be relevant depending on the facts of each case.[53]

3.2.3 Statutory duty to maintain the port in good condition and risk management

Port authorities are surely aware that they are exposed to liabilities to shipowners and others, if there is no compliance with their statutory duty to make the port safe. Fortunately, there are statutory controls but, as will be seen later, such liability is also dealt with at common law, if there is a breach of their duty to exercise reasonable care. The following decision illustrates that a warranty of accessibility of the port will be implied from an advertisement by the port authority that the port has a certain depth or other characteristics.[54]

Bede SS v River Wear[55]

Where harbour commissioners, who were authorised and required by statute to execute works of improvement and maintenance in a harbour, and were empowered to make and maintain docks in connection therewith, and to take harbour and dock tolls and dues in respect of the use of the harbour and docks, advertise that there is a certain depth of water on the sill of a dock belonging to them, they thereby incur, towards shipowners who send their ships to the dock on the faith of that advertisement, the obligation of at least using reasonable care to provide for an access from and to the sea to and from the dock with a sufficient depth of water under the normal conditions of the time of year for all ships of such draught as to enable them to pass over the dock sill.

Therefore, where in such a case the commissioners had not used such care, but had allowed silt to accumulate at the entrance of their harbour, and a ship had consequently been detained for four days in the dock, the commissioners were liable to the shipowners in damages for the detention of their ship.

A warranty of the accessibility of a dock may be implied from such an advertisement, for ships of such draught, as before mentioned, so far as that accessibility depends on the condition of places within the harbour works or so situated that their condition is within the commissioners' powers of inspection and control.

---

53 *The Tramontana II* [1969] 2 Lloyd's Rep 94.
54 By contrast, the issue of information and charts indicating a minimum depth of water does not give rise to a representation or warranty: see *The Neptun* [1938] P 21 (para 3.2.4, below).
55 [1907] 1 KB 310.

3.2.4 Common law duty of care to make
the port safe for users and risk management

Apart from the statutory duty of harbour authorities to keep the port safe for navigation, public authorities are subject also to the common law duty of care in making the port safe. Failure to take reasonable care will result in liability to pay damages. An example of this is *Mersey Docks Trustees v Gibbs*,[56] in which, by reason of accumulated mud in the port, the port was unfit to be navigated. The principle with regard to the common law duty of the port authority was restated referring to previous authorities:

> When such a body is constituted by statute, having the right to levy tolls for its own profits, in consideration of making and maintaining a dock or a canal, there is no doubt of the liability to make good to the persons using it any damage occasioned by neglect in not keeping the works in proper repair ... And the common law in such a case imposes a duty upon the proprietors to take reasonable care, so long as they keep it open for the public use of all who may choose to navigate it, that they may do so without danger to their lives or property.

It did not make any difference that, in this case, the trustees did not collect tolls for their own profit, but merely as trustees for the benefit of the public.

Failure by the trustees in whom a harbour had been vested by statute to examine whether a berth was safe, was breach of the duty to take reasonable care. They could not shift this duty to the local pilots who were not their servants.

The Bearn[57]

The owners of the steamship sued the harbour trustees, in whom a harbour was vested by statute with the usual rights as to tolls, and duties as to maintenance, for damage to their vessel due to the defective condition of the berth. They also sued the owners of the wharf, alongside which the berth was located. The trustees argued that as they had not received any report from the local pilots, upon whom the duty was imposed by by-laws to make periodical inspections and take soundings, they had not been negligent in being unaware of the defective condition of the berth. The owners of the wharf argued that, as the responsibility of keeping the berth in proper condition rested with the trustees, they were not negligent in being unaware of a defect which was due to a breach of the harbour by-laws by persons unknown.

The Court of Appeal held, affirming the decision of the court below, that both defendants were liable – the trustees because they had negligently omitted to perform the duty laid down in *Mersey Docks Trustees v Gibbs*, of

---

56   (1866) LR 1 HL 93.
57   [1906] P 48.

taking reasonable care to see whether the harbour, including the berth in question, was in a fit condition and they could not shift this duty on to the local pilots who were not their servants, and whose duty to take soundings was for the purpose of enabling them to navigate the vessels employing them efficiently. The railway company was liable under the rule in *The Moorcock*,[58] because, as wharfowners, they had invited the plaintiffs' vessel alongside for profit to themselves, and could not rely upon the pilots performing the duty cast upon them by the trustees, for, in their capacity as wharfowners, they had the opportunity of ascertaining the condition of the berth, and should, therefore, have either satisfied themselves that it was reasonably fit, or warned those in charge of the vessel that they had not done so.

Even when no dues are charged, the duty to use reasonable care exists. There is a general benefit derived from the use of the port.

In *The Grit*,[59] the plaintiffs' motor barge received damage by taking the ground on some large stones in a berth alongside the defendants' wharf at K, where she was loading a cargo of slag. The defendants, a railway company, owned the wharf, but not the bed of the river alongside the wharf, and they charged no dues in respect of the use of the wharf. The arrangements for the cargo to be loaded into the barge at the wharf were made by W, who was the collector of dues for the Humber Conservancy Board at K, and had an office on the wharf. W acted as agent for both the plaintiffs and the shippers of the cargo, and told the defendants' stationmaster at K that the barge was coming to load a cargo of slag. The cargo was carried over the defendants' line of railway to K. A year previously, W had warned the defendants that the berth might be dangerous to vessels using it, because stones had been placed to protect the river bank from falling into the bed of the river. The defendants took some soundings, but did nothing else.

It was held that: (1) although the defendants did not charge dues for the use of the wharf, they derived benefit therefrom by reason of the freight earned for the land carriage of the cargo, and that they were in the position of persons who had invited vessels to use the wharf; that they owed a duty, therefore, if they had not taken steps to see that the berth alongside the wharf was safe for vessels to ground in, to warn that they had not done so; (2) although the person to whom the warning should have been given was W, he was entitled to assume that the defendants were satisfied with their soundings and that the risk of stones reaching the berth had not passed from risk to fact; that, accordingly, the plaintiffs, through W, were still entitled to a warning that the defendants had not taken reasonable care to see that the berth was safe, and that such knowledge and apprehension as W had, did not

---

58 (1889) 14 PD 64.
59 [1924] P 246.

affect the plaintiffs' right to recover from the defendants the amount of the damage sustained by the barge.

In the succeeding case, *The Neptun*,[60] it was explained that the liability of the Humber Conservancy Board depended on the special relationship, which arose through their taking dues. Although this relationship was not exactly that of invitor and invitee, it imposed duties analogous to the common law duties existing between invitor and invitee to take reasonable care.[61]

The Neptun

The plaintiffs' steamship, outward bound from Goole, became a total loss through stranding a little below the Middle Whitton lightship in the Upper Humber, for which the defendants, the Humber Conservancy Board, were the buoyage and beaconage authority.

The plaintiffs alleged that the defendants levied dues as a buoyage and beaconage authority and that, as such, it was their duty and/or their contract with the owners of vessels to exercise reasonable care in the performance of their functions to keep the channels safe for vessels to navigate in and to place lightships in such positions as would indicate to vessels where the deep water channels were; that the information supplied by the defendants indicated a minimum depth of 3 ft at low water ordinary spring tides throughout the Whitton channel; that, from time to time, the defendants issued notices indicating a shallower depth, and that, no such notice having been issued, the information given raised a representation or warranty that a depth of 3 ft could be relied on. The plaintiffs calculated that, on this information, there would be a minimum depth of 16 ft, 6 in, while navigating the channel, and that, on the draught of the vessel, they would have a margin of between 1 ft 2 in and 1 ft 6 in.

It was in evidence that the channels in the Upper Humber changed their course frequently and rapidly, that the lightships had constantly to be moved, and that the Upper Whitton lightship had been shifted before the accident happened.

It was held that the liability of the defendants depended upon the special relationship which arose through their taking dues; that this relationship, though not exactly that of invitor and invitee, imposed duties analogous to the common law duties existing between invitor and invitee to take reasonable care; that the issue of the information and charts did not give rise to a representation or warranty that a minimum depth of 3 ft would be found on any given date in a bed of a river which was constantly changing; that the

---

60 [1938] P 21.

61 *Maclenan v Segar* [1917] 2 KB 325; *St Just Steam Ship Co Ltd v Hartlepool Port and Harbour Commissioners* (1929) 34 LlL Rep 344.

defendants had not been negligent as regards the frequency, or extent of their soundings, or in the placing of the lightships; and that the action failed.

Vessels using ports are invitees and, today, the Occupiers' Liability Acts 1957 and 1984 will also apply.

The place and method of mooring vessels within a port are within the authority of the harbour master or port captain. Where, by a harbour master's orders, two vessels were removed from moorings and negligently re-moored and retained in new positions, so that, on the occurrence of an extraordinary flood, both were carried away and lost, it was held by the Privy Council that the harbour board, constituted by the Cape Colony Act 36 of 1896, were liable for the acts of their officer.[62]

Limitation of liability of owners or trustees of harbours, docks and piers will be seen in the Chapter 16, on limitation.

3.2.5 Contractual duty to make the port reasonably safe

In cases where a private dockowner invites shipowners to use his dock, there is a warranty attached to the contract between the parties: that the dockowner has taken reasonable steps to see that the berth offered to the boat is safe and to see that it is safe. If it is not safe, the dockowner will give notice of the fact to the shipowner.[63]

The dockowner may exempt himself from liability for negligence by a notice placed at a visible place in clear and unambiguous language, as the following example shows.

The Ballyalton[64]

While lying aground at a berth which was under the defendants' management and control, the plaintiffs' vessel sustained serious damage by reason of the unevenness of the berth. The plaintiffs brought an action alleging negligence, breach of contract and breach of warranty by the defendants.

The defendants claimed to be protected by the terms of a notice, of which the plaintiffs had had knowledge (*inter alia*) as follows:

> Notice is hereby given that vessels ... have to take the ground after high water, and it must be understood that, while the corporation take steps to keep [berths] in order, they do not ensure the berths always being level ...
>
> ... vessels ... must be and are at the risk of the owners ... AND NOT OF THE CORPORATION, who will not be responsible for and will repudiate any

---

62 *East London v Caledonian Shipping* [1908] AC 271.

63 *The Moorcock* (1889) 14 PD 64.

64 [1961] 1 WLR 929.

liability in respect of any damage ... to vessel ... resulting from using [a berth], or taking ground thereat ...

... owners must satisfy themselves that the vessels both in their construction and the disposition in them of the cargo, may safely take the ground and lie in the berths, and of the condition of the berths, as the corporation will not be responsible for and will repudiate any liability in respect of any damage ... to vessel ... resulting from using the quays or river diversion, or either of them, or taking the ground thereat or therein, or from the berths thereat or therein ...

It was held, that, since the only liability to which the defendants were exposed to was that for negligence by their servants, the defendants were protected by the notice excepting them from liability for damage to vessels. Not only were the words of the exemption clause wide and unambiguous enough to cover negligence, but they were meaningless on any other interpretation.

Exception clauses will be subject to the test of reasonableness of the Unfair Contract Terms Act 1977 and of course liability cannot be excluded for death or personal injury, under s 2(1) of that Act.

3.2.6 The duty to provide efficient pilotage services

Following the accident of *The Sea Empress* at Milford Haven in 1997 and the comments made by the Marine Accidents Investigation Branch about the role of the port authority in the handling of the accident, it was thought necessary to review the functions conferred to harbour authorities by the PA 1987.[65]

The main points emphasised in the report of the review were that:

(a) pilotage ought to remain a harbour authority function and become fully integrated with other port safety services under the control of the authority;

(b) harbour authorities should use their powers to ensure that there is a clear practical assignment of responsibility for the safety of piloted vessels;

(c) harbour authorities should keep under formal regular review the specific powers and duties by the 1987 Act, relating to use of powers and direction, as well as the recruitment, authorisation, examination, employment status and training of pilots;

(d) harbour authorities should be made more accountable for all their port safety functions, with a new reserve power for the Secretary of State to direct improvements where neglect of safety duties may cause a danger to public navigation.

The principal proposal of the report is that a Marine Operations Code for Ports should be developed, covering all port safety functions, and not just

---

65 *Review of the Pilotage Act 1987*, Consultation Paper, 27 July 1998, updated 7 March 2001. Some of the recommendations require legislation which will be taken forward at the earliest opportunity for the consideration of a Shipping or Transport Bill.

pilotage. This should serve as a national standard, among other things, for training and examination of pilots, a guide to best practice, and a framework for the preparation of published policies and plans by harbour authorities.

The recommended good practice Marine Operations Code for Ports, incorporating the points of the report, was published at the end of January 2001.[66] It also requires the harbour authority to have available competent pilots and properly certified boats or their use. It must also ensure that the assigned pilot to every ship is fit and appropriately qualified for the task and that, under the PA 1987, pilotage services provided by a harbour authority should be based upon a continuing process of risk assessment. Authorised pilots should be accountable to their authorising authority for the use they make of their authorisation and harbours should have contracts with authorised pilots, regulating the conditions under which they work, including procedures for resolving disputes.[67]

Section 2 of the PA 1987 states the duty of a competent harbour authority which is to provide pilotage services where they are needed, and to designate areas, which in the interests of safety, would be compulsory pilotage areas. Section 4 provides for the employment of pilots by the authority, either under contracts of employment, or under a contract for services. Section 22(3) provides for limitation of liability of the authority where an authorised pilot – without any personal act or omission of the authority – has caused any loss or damage. Section 22(8) provides that the harbour authority shall not be liable for any loss or damage caused by any act or omission of a pilot authorised by it, merely because of a fault simply in authorising the pilot. On the issue of liability of harbour authorities for acts of pilots, see Section B of this chapter. In the light of the recommendations of the review of pilotage services, ss 4 and 22 of the Act will need to be amended.

It is important at this point to mention that the harbour authority may be criminally liable for permitting the pollution of waters, under s 85(1) of the WRA 1981, which provides for strict liability, namely: 'A person contravenes this section if he causes ... any ... polluting matter to enter any controlled waters.' This may arise in connection with an inexperienced pilot, as it did arise in *The Sea Empress*.[68]

Briefly, the ship was laden with light crude oil when she struck the mid-channel rocks in the entrance to Milford Haven, North Wales, due to negligent navigation of her pilot, who had been trained and authorised by the Milford Haven Port Authority. Then she grounded in Mill Bay, causing a large scale oil spill in the area. The port authority was prosecuted under this section, pleaded guilty without admission of fault, and the case came before the

---

66 See para 3.2.2, above.
67 *Op cit*, DETR, fn 9, s 9, 'Pilotage'.
68 [1999] 1 Lloyd's Rep 673.

admiralty judge, David Steel, to determine the application of the section to the facts and the fine. Assisted by a House of Lords authority[69] in the interpretation of this section, the judge said that the section would apply if there was a positive act, not an omission, by the defendant, which need not be the immediate cause of the oil escape. With regard to causation, the section would apply if the defendant produced a situation in which the polluting matter could escape, but a necessary condition of the actual escape was also the act of a third party. If that act were a matter of ordinary occurrence, as opposed to an extraordinary, it would not negative the causal effect of the defendants' act, even if it were not foreseeable.

Having analysed the scope of the section, the judge had no difficulty in concluding that the port authority, being the operator of the port of compulsory inward pilotage, which trained and authorised the pilot, whose experience for this type of vessel was sketchy, did something which caused pollution, bearing also in mind that the pilot's negligence was a normal occurrence. He made no finding of fault, but on the basis of strict liability he fined the authority £4 m, reflecting the genuine and justified public concern.

The Sea Empress prompted the British Government, in addition to the review of the functions and accountability of harbour authorities, to take other measures as well. It accepted a proposal made by Lord Donaldson for an official representative of the Secretary of State (SOSREP) to have powers of intervention and agree a salvage plan with the salvage master to prevent situations arising, such as in *The Sea Empress* case, where the local pilot cannot have such powers (see Chapter 13, para 13.7, above).

4 LIABILITY OF SHIPOWNERS FOR DAMAGE CAUSED TO HARBOURS

In England and Wales, ports or harbours, whether privatised by an Act of Parliament, or publicly owned, are regulated by statutes and bylaws. Their obligations and their rights for damage caused to their property are to be found in statutory provisions.

Under the old statute, HDPCA 1847, cl or s 74, there is strict liability imposed upon shipowners whose ship causes damage to any of the property of the harbour or port authority. In other words, the shipowner will be liable, whether or not the damage was caused by his or his servants' negligence. This means that the port authority does not have to prove that the damage was caused by negligence. There may be a defence that the damage was caused by the intervention of a non-human agent when, for example, the ship was a

---

69   *Empress Car Co v National Rivers Authority* [1998] 1 All ER 481.

derelict, or had been abandoned by her crew because of tempestuous weather. As it will be seen in the following cases, the courts had a great deal of difficulty in construing this section. It is important to quote fairly large parts of these decisions in order to show the distinction between the liability created by this section and liability at common law.

River Wear Commissioners v Adamson[70]

The defendants' ship was driven on shore by a storm in endeavouring to make the port of Sunderland. The crew were taken off with difficulty, and the ship, being a complete wreck, was afterwards driven by the winds and waves against the pier belonging to the harbour and did damage to it, for which the commissioners brought an action under s 74 of the HDPCA 1847.

The question was whether the defendants were liable to pay the commissioners for the damage suffered. This depended on the interpretation of s 74, which reads:

> The owner of every vessel or float of timber shall be answerable to the undertakers for any damage done by such vessel or float of timber, or by any person employed about the same, to the harbour, dock, or pier, or the quays or works connected therewith, and the master or person having the charge of such vessel or float of timber, through whose wilful act or negligence any such damage is done, shall also be liable to make good the same; and the undertakers may detain any such vessel or float of timber until sufficient security has been given for the amount of damage done by the same: provided always, that nothing herein contained shall extend to impose any liability for any such damage upon the owner of any vessel where such vessel shall, at the time when such damage is caused, be in charge of a duly licensed pilot, whom such owner or master is bound by law to employ, and put his vessel in charge of.[71]

The issue was whether it was the intention of the legislature that the owner was not to be excused even for liability caused by such tempestuous weather amounting to act of God. **Mellish LJ**, at the Court of Appeal, said that:

> I think, looking at the language of the section, it clearly was the intention of the legislature to extend the liability of the owners of vessels, in favour of the owners of piers and harbours, beyond the liability which is imposed on them by common law: because, if that is not the intention, it is not easy to see the object of the section at all. Looking at the pointed language in which negligence or wilful act is brought in, looking to the fact that the section goes on to speak of the master, or the person having the charge of the vessel, it seems to shew clearly that the owner is intended to be liable even in the case

---

70 (1876) 1 QBD 546 (HL).

71 The proviso of s 74 (last sentence) has been overruled by the provisions of the PAs since 1913, which made the owner answerable to any damage caused by pilot's negligence while he is in control of navigation of the ship whether or not pilotage is compulsory, see para 8, below.

where neither the master nor the crew had anything to do with it. But the question arises, because we may decide, on the language used, that the owner may be made liable where it is not proved that he or the master was guilty of negligence, are we bound to hold that in every case whatever, where the vessel physically damages the pier, etc, the owner is so liable? I am of opinion that the statute only contemplates the case where either directly or indirectly, through the act of man, the vessel is caused in some way or other to run against the pier. It is quite consistent with our law that in certain cases a person may be made liable as insurer against the acts of all the men whom he may have under his control.[72]

Denman J sitting at the Court of Appeal also said:

I am of the same opinion. No doubt, taking the words of s 74, it is possible to hold that they impose an absolute liability to the dockowner on the part of the owner of the vessel. The words are strong, intelligible, and grammatical (referring to the first part of the section). But I am of opinion, taking the rest of the section, some qualification must be put on those words, not by introducing fresh words into the Act of Parliament, or supposing a clause to exist in it which does not exist, but by qualifying those words by the principle of law which is so well known, and which must be taken to override the language of an Act of Parliament. I apprehend that there is no principle of law better established than this, that in an Act of Parliament words are not to be construed to impose upon individuals as liability for an act or acts done, if those acts are not done by the individual, or not caused by his property or his servants, but are acts which are substantially caused by a superior power, such as the law calls the act of God. In this case, there can be no doubt, from the facts, that the injury occasioned by the vessel was not the result of any neglect on the part of the owner, or on the part of any person having charge of the vessel, or, indeed, of any human being, but it was really the effect of the violence of the winds and waves overcoming all control on the part of the master or owner of the vessel, and forcing the vessel against the pier. Under those circumstances I apprehend, on the general principle that every statute is to be so construed as to leave untouched a principle of common law which applies to all similar cases, we are not bound to hold – and ought not to hold – that the damage was done by the vessel within the meaning of the Act of Parliament; but that, on the contrary, it was damage occasioned by the act of God, and therefore no action lies.[73]

Therefore, the defendants (respondents) were held not liable because, as the Court of Appeal thought, the statute intended to excuse the owner, in the same way as common law excuses the common law carrier, when act of God was the cause of the damage.

On appeal to the House of Lords,[74] although the House disagreed with the broad and liberal construction given to the words of the statute by the Court

---

72 (1876) 1 QBD 546, p 553.
73 *Ibid*, p 555.
74 (1877) 2 App Cas 743.

of Appeal, their Lordships affirmed its judgment for different reasons. The majority held that a strict liability was created by the statute and there was no intention in the statute to excuse the owner for act of God in the same way as the common law carrier is. The liability under the statute is different from that under common law. From careful reading of what the majority said, it seems that they were prepared to excuse the owner when the damage to the pier had been occasioned by a vessel, through the violence of the winds and waves, at a time when the master and crew had been compelled to escape from the vessel, and had, consequently, no control whatever over it.[75]

In particular, the **Lord Chancellor (Lord Cairns)** explained that:

In my opinion, these expressions (stated above by the Court of Appeal) are broader than is warranted by any authorities of which I am aware. If a duty is cast upon an individual by Common Law, the act of God will excuse him from the performance of that duty. No man is compelled to do that which is impossible. It is a duty of a carrier to deliver safely the goods entrusted to his care; but, if in carrying them with proper care, they are destroyed by lightning, or swept away by a flood, he is excused, because the safe delivery has by the act of God become impossible. If, however, a man contracts that he will be liable for the damage occasioned by a particular state of circumstances, or if an Act of Parliament declares that a man shall be liable for the damage occasioned by a particular state of circumstances, I know of no reason why a man should not be liable for the damage occasioned by that state of circumstances, whether the state of circumstances is brought about by the act of man or by the act of God. There is nothing impossible in that which, on such an hypothesis, he has contracted to do, or which he is by the statute ordered to do, namely, to be liable for the damages. If, therefore, by the section to which I have referred, it is meant that the owner of every vessel shall, independently of whether anything has happened which would, at Common Law, give a right of action against anyone, pay to the undertakers the damage done by a ship to the pier, I should be unable to see any reason why the payment should not be made in the manner required by the statute.

I cannot, however, look upon this section of the statute as intended to create a right to recover damages in cases where, before the Act, there was not a right to recover damages from some one. The section and those which follow it are in an Act which collects together the common and ordinary clauses that it was the habit of Parliament to insert in the private bills authorising the construction of piers and docks.[76]

Confusion arose in the interpretation of this judgment because Lord Cairns elaborated further that there was no new substantive right created by the statute, but a new procedure. In other words, as a matter of procedure, a claim

---

75 Lord Gordon, dissenting, said: 'On the ground that the intention of the legislature in passing the Act must be decided by the ordinary meaning of the words used, and here the words used in the first portion of the section were words creating a liability without any restriction whatever.'

76 (1877) 2 App Cas 743, p 750.

could be brought against the owner under s 74 and there was no need to prove negligence, but by reason of the defence of compulsory pilotage, as provided at the end of the section, the owner could recover over what he would have to pay to the port authority, if the damage was caused by the negligence of the pilot.[77]

Lord Hatherley, concurring, delivered a more crisp judgment[78] of what the construction of s 74 should be:

> When we look at the whole construction of the clause, it appears to me that it speaks, in the first place, of damage done by a vessel without regard to anyone being on board or not; then it speaks in the second place of damage done by any person employed about the vessel; and then it says that the master or person in charge of a vessel is to be liable if damage is done through his wilful act or negligence; and then the excepted case occurs of the pilot, because he had been compulsorily, and against any power of resistance on the part of the owner, placed on board and in charge.

> Now, my Lords, we have to see whether or not damage arising from the act of God, that is to say in the particular case a tempest, should be held to be excepted. There might be other cases which would be similar to this of a tempest; the vessel might have been driven on the pier in some other way, or have been injured and become unmanageable by lightning, or the like. However it occurred, if the pier was damaged by the vessel in the way which was called, by the learned judge in the court below, the act of God, is there anything in the Act of Parliament to say (and this clause seems to contain all that is said in the Act about it) that the owner of the vessel shall not be responsible for the damage, but that there shall be an exception in respect of damage so caused?

> One can easily conceive that the legislature might think it desirable that those who provide this great accommodation for the navigation of the country, those who provide harbours of refuge and the like, which are greatly wanted in many parts of the coasts of the UK. should be indemnified against the possible damage which may accrue to their docks, or to other works which they construct in discharge of the duties in question, and in the exercise of those powers which they have for making docks and other works. Those promoters might say, 'We offer protection to the public at all times, only, in consideration of the benevolent hospitality which we so afford, protect us from having our works damaged.' There is nothing, as it appears to me, utterly unreasonable in such a proposition reasonably carried out. It is quite true that many cases, put by the learned judges in the court below, are cases in which it would seem to be a very rigid enactment indeed that damage to a very large and extensive amount, exceeding the value of the vessel itself, should be compensated by the

---

77　He meant that the owner would have to prove negligence of the pilot, which if proved would have the effect of surpassing the strict liability element of his liability to the port authority. The defence of compulsory pilotage that was applicable under s 74 of this Act became obsolete by the PA 1913 (see under Section B, 'Pilotage', paras 6 and 8), so there is no longer an issue in this respect.

78　(1877) 2 App Cas 743, pp 752–54.

persons whose vessel has done this damage, being made answerable to make it good to the full amount of the damage done, which might even go to the destruction of the principal works, and might therefore result in the ruin of those persons whose vessel had been so forced against them. But, on the other hand, if there was any intention at all of giving a relief of this kind, which must be sought of course in the words of the Act, then I apprehend that the exception of a storm or tempest would be a very singular one, because it is a probable case to happen.

Lord Blackburn gave the substantive reasons that existed behind this legislation by saying:

My Lords, reading the words of the enactment, and bearing in mind what was the state of the law at the time when it was passed, it seems to me that the object of the legislature was to give the owners of harbours, docks, and piers more protection than they had. It seems to have occurred to those who framed the statute, that in most cases where an accident occurs, it is from the fault of those who were managing the ship – and in most cases those are the servants of the owners – but that these were matters which in every case must be proved, and consequently that there was a great deal of litigation incurred before the owner, though he really was liable, could be fixed: and with a view to meet this, the remedy proposed was that the owner, who was generally really liable (though it was difficult and expensive to prove it), should be liable without proof either that there was negligence, or that the person guilty of neglect was the owner's servant, or proving how the mischief happened, and this is expressed by saying that the owners shall be 'answerable for any damage done by the vessel or by any person employed about the same' to the harbour …

My Lords, on reading the words of the enactments, I am brought to the conclusion that such was the scheme of legislation adopted by Parliament; the mischief being the expense of litigation; the remedy that the owners should be liable without proof of how the accident occurred.[79]

There is no doubt from the above extracts that the majority decided that the words used in the statute imposed strict liability and did not generally give any indication of an exception to strict liability for damage caused by act of God. The variation made to this general principle – taking into account the facts of this case – was that the only exception to liability would arise when there was no human agency on board the ship at the time of the tempest, as it happened in this case. Lord Gordon, who dissented from the majority as to the outcome of the decision with great hesitation, was of the view that the owners, even on the facts of this case in which the crew were forced by the tempest to abandon ship, should not be excused from liability. He agreed with the judge and concluded:

I am humbly of the opinion, which I entertain with very great hesitation after the opinions which have been expressed by your Lordships, that the statute

---

79   (1877) 2 App Cas 743, pp 768–69.

ought not to be construed as if it contained an exemption from liability for damage where it occurred from the act of God. The words of the statute appear to me to be express and unambiguous, and being so, I think they should be read according to their ordinary construction. But in accordance with the opinions expressed by your Lordships, the judgment will fall to be affirmed.[80]

Although the decision of the majority was not obscure, it was thought, nevertheless, by shipping lawyers and judges, that it created an ambiguity arising from the *dicta* of Lord Cairn that no new substantive right of action was created, whether or not human agency was involved in the accident and the result was lack of guidelines for the courts below, as was shown in *The Mostyn*. The House of Lords felt the need to interpret it, in its later decision, *Great Western Rly Co v Owners of SS Mostyn (The Mostyn)*.[81]

The Mostyn

The appellants, who were the owners of the docks at Swansea, brought this action against the respondents, the owners of the steamship *Mostyn*, to recover an agreed sum by way of damages for negligence, or alternatively an amount for which the respondents were liable under s 74 of the HDPCA 1847, for the damage done by *The Mostyn* to the Swansea docks, or the works connected therewith. In a masonry chaseway at the bottom of a communication passage leading from King's Dock to the Prince of Wales' Dock, electric cables were laid for lighting purposes and the supply of power. On the night of 26 October 1923, while *The Mostyn* was proceeding along this communication channel to the Prince of Wales' Dock, her port anchor fouled and damaged some of these cables, with the result that the docks were plunged in darkness. The cables were part of the dock works.

The President came to the conclusion on the evidence that no negligence was proved against the respondents, and held, on the authority of the decision of the House of Lords, in *River Wear Commissioners v Adamson*, that, where negligence was disproved, liability, under s 74 of the Act of 1847, did not lie upon an owner whose vessel had damaged a dock or works in connection therewith. He, therefore, gave judgment for the respondents. Evidently, the President misapplied the *Adamson* case.

The Court of Appeal (Bankes, Atkin and Sargant LJJ) affirmed the judgment of the President.

The House of Lords dealt with the question in more detail and in broader terms drawing a general principle for guidance in subsequent cases and the majority held:

Under s 74 of the HDPCA 1847, the owner of a vessel doing damage to a harbour, dock or pier, or works connected therewith, is responsible to the

---

80 (1877) 2 App Cas 743, p 780.
81 [1928] AC 57 (HL).

undertakers for the damage, whether occasioned by negligence or not, where the vessel is at the time of the damage under the control of the owner or his agents. [Viscount Haldane, Lord Shaw of Dunfermline, and Lord Blanesburgh; Viscount Dunedin and Lord Phillimore dissenting].

When commenting on the *River Wear v Adamson*, **Viscount Haldane** said, in particular:

> My Lords, the massive legal intelligence even of Lord Cairns does not seem to me to have wholly disposed of the question before us. He was dealing with a case in which human agency had been superseded. Here, we are dealing with one in which there was human agency, although there was no breach of duty. I think that he meant to go further, and to suggest that, even if there was human agency, there would be no liability created provided that there was no breach of duty at common law. But that question was not before him, and what he suggests was not necessary for the decision of the *Adamson* case. It is, therefore, important to see whether his suggestion was concurred in by the other noble and learned Lords who took part in the decision.

> The very power of rhetoric which Lord Cairns commanded when stating his conclusions about matters of legal principle makes it the more desirable to see that we are following the substance rather than the form of his propositions. Even if we accept his view that the section is one creating a new procedure, that of suing the owner while giving him a right to recover over, I am quite unable to see how this leaves the existing substantive law intact and relates to procedure alone. The owner could not be sued under that law unless he had violated some duty. If he can be sued at all, even with a right to recover over, it must be because some new substantive liability has been imposed on him by the statute. *I think, therefore, that it follows that the common law has been altered and that a new right of action has been created depending on the alteration* [emphasis added]. This is much more than mere procedure. Did his colleagues who heard the appeal with him accept his view as I interpret it? I think they did not.

> Lord Hatherley was a very careful judge. I think that his disposition here was to hold that the words of the Act were so free from ambiguity that they covered cases in which there was no human agency, though he did not say so in terms. He was content to express his general agreement with the view of Mellish LJ that the statute only applied where human agency had intervened, and that it was because it was absent in the *Adamson* case, that he concurred in the judgment of the Court of Appeal. I doubt whether Lord Hatherley himself was ready to accept even this restriction of its scope, but he thought it at least a possible one, and if true it was enough to take the circumstances in the case before him, where there was no human agency, outside the language of the Act. That Lord Hatherley did not in terms dissent from the general result reached by the majority I cannot regard as an important circumstance in ascertaining his opinion.

Lord Gordon expressly dissented. At the conclusion of an elaborate judgment, he expressed the opinion that the statute ought not to be construed as if it contained any exemption from liability where it occurred even from the act of God. The words appeared to him to be express and unambiguous, and being so, he thought that they ought to be read according to their ordinary construction.

Lord Gordon:

My Lords, there remain to be considered the opinions of Lord O'Hagan and Lord Blackburn, with a view to ascertaining whether these noble and learned Lords concurred in the view which had been expressed by Cairns LC, that no new right of action at all was created, whether or not human agency was present.

My Lords, upon scrutiny of the words used by Lord O'Hagan, I have come to the clear conclusion that he did not concur in the *dictum* of the Lord Chancellor, so far as it went beyond the facts of the case before him, that the statute created no new right of action, but was confined in its scope to procedure only. The language, Lord O'Hagan thought, was *prima facie* sufficient to cover all cases, including those in which no human agency came in. But he was of opinion that, reading the whole of the section, and particularly the reference to 'such' vessel in the words declaring the liability of the master or person having charge of it, an intention was expressed to confine the liability of the owner to vessels 'in charge of a master or somebody else'. On this point he expressed his concurrence with Mellish LJ. The owner is therefore placed in a worse position than he would have been at common law, but not so bad as that in which he would have been had he been made liable when no one had charge on his behalf ...[82]

My Lords, when the expressions used by Lord Blackburn are considered. I cannot find in them concurrence with the *dictum* of Lord Cairns that no new right of action was created, even where human agency came in, and that the wide words at the beginning of the section were intended to introduce nothing more than what Lord Cairns had spoken of as a new form of procedure, which would indeed assist the dockowner to pursue a new kind of remedy, but conferred on him no fresh substantive right. On this point, the opinions delivered appear to me to leave us under the duty of deciding, unfettered by authority, whether when the vessel which caused the damage was under the control of the owner's agents, he is liable notwithstanding that there was no breach of the duty not to be negligent on their and his part. *I do not think that River Wear Commissioners v Adamson settles the point of non-liability where the vessel was in charge, at the time of the accident, of the owners' agents. It seems to me that the words of the statute are too clear to admit of this conclusion, and that the decision of this House in the earlier case is not in truth any authority for it* [emphasis added]. We do not know enough of the facts in *Dennis v Tovell* to enable us to say whether that case was one of a derelict or whether any one remained in charge of the vessel. If there was no human agency, then what I have said does not apply in that case. I comment on the decision in the *Adamson* case on the assumption that, notwithstanding what was said by Lord Blackburn, there was no such human agency. For, if there was, that in my view brings the case within the uncontrolled words, and would render it analogous to the present case. But, on the facts set out in the report, I think that the vessel must be taken to have become out of human control.

---

82 [1928] AC 57, pp 67–69.

> *It appears to me to be bound by the authority of the Adamson case to hold that the section in question is not to be read literally, but as applying when the damage complained of has been brought about by a vessel under the direction of the owner or his agents, whether negligent or not. The decision further exempts the owner when the vessel is not under such control but is, for instance, derelict. When there are facts to which it applies, it effects an alteration in the common law which imposes a new liability to be sued on the owner, and to that extent changes not merely procedure but also substantive law* [emphasis added].

> My Lords, if these things are true I think that, on the facts established in the present case, we must find the owners liable, reverse the judgment of the court below in their favour, and give judgment for the appellant railway company for damages, the agreed amount of which is 226*l*.[83]

The difference on the facts between the *Adamson* and the *Mostyn* cases was that, in the former, the ship had been abandoned because of the extreme weather while, in the latter, the ship was in control of its master and crew when the accident happened.

The issue of strict liability was questioned again later in the context of damage suffered by the harbour authority, which was due partly to its fault. The House of Lords had another opportunity to clarify the application of s 74 in this context in ***The Towerfield***[84] (which is seen fully later under shipowners' liability for pilot's negligence).

The facts were briefly these. In 1941, a ship in charge of a compulsory pilot, approaching an English harbour through a channel, went aground on an undredged accumulation of river silt, sustaining damage. It was conceded on behalf of the shipowners that she had also caused damage to the harbour. The harbour authority was found, on the facts, partly negligent for not having maintained the approaches to the harbour clean, which contributed to the casualty. The pilot on board the ship, which stranded, was also found partly negligent for the stranding of the ship and the damage caused to the property of the harbour.

On the issue of whether the application of strict liability of the owner was excluded because of the fault of the harbour authority, it was held that contributory negligence by the harbour authority was no defence to a claim by them under s 74 of the HDPCA 1847, for damage caused by the ship to the harbour (Lord Porter, Lord Normand, Lord Morton of Henryton and Lord Radcliffe; Lord Oaksey dissenting).

Applying *The Mostyn*, **Lord Potter** said:

> ... the majority of their Lordships took the view that the shipowner was responsible for damage done to harbour works whether he was in fault or not, save in a case similar to that decided in the *River Wear* judgment. Accordingly, where the ship had been abandoned and was therefore out of the control of its

---

83 [1928] AC 57, pp 71–72.
84 *Workington Harbour Dock Board v Towerfield (Owners)* [1951] AC 112.

owners, they agreed that no liability attached under the section. But save for that concession they decided in terms, as I think, that the only exception from liability was that afforded to an abandoned ship.

My Lords, until *The Mostyn* decided the true effect of the wording of the section a profound difference of view as to its construction was to be found amongst those who practised in that branch of the law which is devoted to shipping matters, but that dispute has now been decided on broad lines and, like Lord Dunedin, who, though he was of the other opinion, expressed his satisfaction that a clear rule for future cases had been laid down, I cannot think that fine distinctions should be introduced which would limit the generality of the decision which has been reached.[85]

In short, the effect of the interpretation of the *Adamson* decision, given by the Lords in *The Mostyn,* is that shipowners will be liable for any damage caused by their ship to the property of public harbour, or dock authorities, whether caused by negligence of their servants or not, or even if it is caused by act of God, unless the ship is abandoned because of tempestuous weather by reason of which the ship is not under human direction. Since s 74 imposes strict liability in this respect, *The Towerfield* case added to this principle that the fault of the port authority contributing to the loss would not be a defence for the shipowner. This is, however, irreconcilable with the statutory and common law duty of port authorities to maintain the port in a safe condition. Bearing in mind that the events of *The Towerfield* occurred before the Law Reform (Contributory Negligence) Act (LR(CN)A) 1945 came into operation, contributory negligence is nowadays taken into account as a matter of causation. In other words, although the port authority does not have to prove negligence for the damage caused by the ship to its property, it should be open to a shipowner, in an action against him, to show that the predominant or contributory cause of the damage was the breach by the port authority to maintain the port in a safe condition. It is submitted that this view on causation is not in conflict with *The Mostyn* because no issue of causation was before the House of Lords in *The Mostyn*, nor for that matter in the *Adamson* case.[86]

The damages and loss that can be claimed by a jettyowner or pier where ships frequently load can range from physical damage to the property to dead freight payable to a carrier under a contract, whereby the carrier has agreed to furnish to the jettyowner a number of vessels for the carriage of a cargo from the jetty and, perhaps, demurrage payable to vessels delayed at the jetty by reason of damage to it and the consequential delay for its repair.[87]

---

85 *Ibid*, p 136.

86 In the writer's view, the comments of Lord Potter in *The Towerfield* [1951] AC 112 with regard to contributory negligence (see under para 7, Section B of this chapter) should nowadays be disregarded.

87 *Texada Mines Ltd v The Ship Afovos* [1974] 2 Lloyd's Rep 168.

5 HARBOUR DUES

The harbour authority has a right to arrest a ship and have it sold, if port dues are not paid.[88] The authority's claim for their expenses of removal or conservation of a wreck has priority over other claims, even those giving rise to maritime liens, such as collision damage and salvage. The reason for this is that, had the authority not preserved the *res*, there would be no property left for the satisfaction of these claims, provided the proceeds are sufficient.[89]

The Veritas[90]

The Veritas was in distress outside the Mersey Docks. Salvage services were rendered to her, bringing her into the Mersey. Thereafter, a collision occurred between *The Veritas* and another steamship. Salvage services were again rendered to her by two tugs and she was brought alongside the dock wall. However, she drifted against a landing stage, doing damage to the stage and, finally, she sank. The Mersey Docks and Harbour Board, under the statutory powers conferred upon it, removed her. An action was instituted by the salvors against the *V* in respect of the salvage services rendered. The board intervened in the action and the vessel was released to the board, which sold it. After deducting its expenses, it paid the proceeds of the sale into court. The present action was to determine priorities between the judgment creditors. It was held that the claim of the board took priority over that of the salvors. This was because the lien of the board was one which arose *ex delicto* as opposed to one arising *ex contracto* or quasi *ex contracto*. Gorell Barnes J stated that:

> It is also clear that liens arising *ex delicto* take precedence over prior liens arising *ex contracto*. The principal ... [reason is] that the person having a right of lien *ex contracto* becomes, so to speak, a part-owner in interest with the owners of the vessel. He has chosen to enter into relationship with the vessel for his own interests whereas a person suffering damage by the negligent navigation of a ship has no option. Reparation for wrongs done should come first.[91]

SECTION B – PILOTAGE LAW

1 INTRODUCTION

The term 'pilot' refers to a person with specialised knowledge of local conditions and navigational hazards who is generally taken on board a vessel

---

88 *Corps & Corps v The Queen of the South* [1968] 1 Lloyd's Rep 182.
89 *The Sea Spray* [1907] P 133.
90 [1901] P 304.
91 *Ibid*, p 313.

at a specific place for the purpose of navigating or guiding a ship through a particular channel, river, or other enclosed waters to or from a port.[92] His functions are to guide vessels form open sea into port, or vice versa; to guide a ship from anchorage to a berth or from berth to a terminal within a port; or to help a ship to dock or undock within a port.

The history of pilotage in the UK can be found in Douglas and Geen.[93] The authors say that in 1514 Henry VIII granted a charter to the Trinity House giving it powers to control the operations of ships, pilots and mariners throughout the country. This charter was confirmed by the succeeding Tudors. In 1604, James I gave Trinity House a more comprehensive charter, but this was dissolved by Parliament in 1647, being considered as having Royalists tendencies. Charles II restored this charter and in 1685 there was a new charter under James II, which strictly stated that no person would be permitted to act as a pilot unless he had first been appointed and authorised by the Trinity House. There have been various successive Acts of Parliament relating to London Trinity House, of a general nature, since the 18th century. It became apparent in the early 20th century that a confusion had been created by the variance between the general statute law and the special provisions of local Acts regulating the business of pilots. As a result, the PA 1913 was passed to consolidate and amend the law relating to pilotage.

This was amended by the MSA 1979 upon recommendations of an Advisory Committee on Pilotage, which established the Pilotage Commission to act as an advisory body. But, in 1983, both the 1913 Act and the pilotage provisions of the MSA 1979 were repealed and replaced by the PA 1983. The responsibility of administering a pilotage district was upon a pilotage authority, which licensed pilots for its district and, where there was a compulsory pilotage, it granted pilotage certificates to masters. Its other functions were the making and enforcement of bylaws, pilotage charges and approval of pilots' boats. It could also employ pilots, but the majority of pilots, however, were self-employed.[94]

Finally, a new statute was passed in 1987, which came into force in 1 October 1988 to simplify the law of pilotage. It made radical changes to the provision of pilotage services by transferring the functions of pilotage from a pilotage authority to the harbour authorities. Nevertheless, there are still some provisions in this Act which fall short of a demand for clarity, which perhaps contributed to the problems encountered by the Milford Haven port authority in *The Sea Empress*, resulting in the review of pilotage and the duties of the harbour authorities in relation to pilotage services as mentioned under Section A of this chapter.

---

92 See Schoenbaum, T, *Admiralty and Maritime Law*, 2nd edn, 1994, West, p 697.

93 *Op cit*, Douglas and Geen, fn 8, Chapters 19 and 20 for detailed history and development of legislation in pilotage law.

94 *Op cit*, Douglas and Geen, fn 8, Chapter 19.

By s 1 of the PA 1987, the responsibility for provision of pilotage services was placed upon a class of harbour authorities, which manage their harbours under statutory powers, designated as 'competent harbour authorities', the functions of which will be seen later.

A pilot is defined in s 31(1), as amended by the MSA 1995, as 'any person not belonging to a ship who has the conduct thereof'.[95]

2 DUTIES OF A COMPETENT HARBOUR AUTHORITY IN RELATION TO PILOTAGE

2.1 Consideration and provision of pilotage service

The primary duty of a competent harbour authority imposed by s 2(1) of the PA 1987 is to consider whether pilotage services are needed to be provided to ensure the safety of ships entering the port, and whether pilotage should be compulsory at any part of the harbour in the interests of safety. Such duty cannot be delegated, even to another competent authority, but it can be to a joint committee which is specifically established to carry out the pilotage functions of two or more competent harbour authorities.

Section 11, however, allows that the duty of providing pilotage services – as considered to be necessary by a competent harbour authority under s 2 – may, by arrangement, be provided on its behalf by another competent harbour authority or an agent.

The designation of an area as a compulsory pilotage area is left at the discretion of the competent harbour authority, by s 7 of the Act, if it considers that it would be necessary in the interests of safety. Unlike the 1983 Act, the present statute does not contain any classes of ships which would be exempt from compulsory pilotage, such as Her Majesty's ships and ferryboats. The only exempt ships are small boats of less than 20 m long or fishing boats registered as having less than 47.5 m length (s 7(3)).

These duties should now be read in conjunction with the Code of Good Practice for Port Marine Operations, seen earlier.[96] The principle of

---

95 Detailed provisions relating to pilot ladders and safety issues can be found in Merchant Shipping Notice (MSN 1716) which includes the IMO Resolution on Pilot Transfer Arrangements, amplifying SOLAS 1974, Chapter V, reg 17. The Merchant Shipping (Pilot Transport Arrangements) Regulations 1999 (SI 1999/17) replaced the Merchant Shipping (Pilot Ladders and Hoists) Regulations 1987 and implemented SOLAS 1974, Chapter V, reg, 17. It came into force on 10 February 1999 and includes duties of the shipowner, master and officers of the ship in relation to safety providing for penalties in the event of contravention of its provisions, which is made a criminal offence.

96 See Section A, para 3.2.6, above.

accountability, which has been the main objective of the review of pilotage services, applies to the discharge of the authority's statutory duties. The harbour authority's duty relates to safety of navigation and regulation of marine operations. Safety of navigation is a public right; provision of pilotage is a specific duty to facilitate the public right. But, harbour authorities are not publicly accountable at large.

However, a harbour authority which fails to provide adequate services of pilots might incur liability to the owner of a ship which sustains damage in consequence of the absence of pilots in the port.[97] The question whether the authority will be liable to the owner for damage sustained by his ship, in the event that the pilot provided is incompetent, has caused problems, because of the interpretation given to s 22(8) of the PA 1987 and to the exception of compulsory pilotage defence by the shipowner (as will be seen later under paras 7 and 8). But, in the light of the review of the duties of the harbour authorities after *The Sea Empress* and the recent Code of good practice, harbour authorities should guard against such risks by proper risk management and seek to obtain insurance cover.

2.2 Authorisation of pilots

There has been a major change by the new Act in the engagement of pilots. By contrast to the PA 1983, which gave power to a pilotage authority to license pilots, now, by s 3 of the 1987 Act, it is the harbour authority that has power to authorise (instead of licensing) persons to act as pilots in their harbour. Although, under each Act, the purpose has been to ensure that pilots have the necessary qualifications, the difference is that, in the past, a licence enabled the pilot to act in the district in which he was licensed, while, under s 3 of the present Act, the authorisation must be coupled with a contract of employment or otherwise enable him to act as an authorised pilot in a particular harbour.

The employment status of pilots has been a contentious issue. Whatever arrangements are made for the use of pilots, they must safeguard the authority's position of control. Employment is a default option and the easier way of integrating pilotage services. Pilots should become direct employees of the port authority and not of a subsidiary of the authority, as was the Milford Haven Pilotage Ltd.[98]

An authorisation must specify the area within which it has effect and it may limit his authority to certain parts of the harbour or types of ships. The authority determines the qualifications, skill, age, fitness, local knowledge and

---

97 *Anchor Line (Henderson Bros) Ltd v Dundee Harbour Trustees* (1922) 38 TLR 299; the case is still good law under the present statute.

98 *Op cit*, Consultation Paper, fn 65.

other qualities of the pilot.[99] The authorisation may be suspended if the pilot is found guilty of misconduct or has ceased to have the relevant qualifications, or when the number of pilots required exceeds the needs of the area.

Section 8 allows a competent harbour authority to issue exemption certificates, upon the application of a master or mate of a ship, where a pilotage is compulsory, to enable him to navigate that ship in the area concerned without a pilot, if it is satisfied that his experience, skill and knowledge of the local area and of the English language are sufficient.

All of these duties have been reviewed by the recent pilotage services Consultation paper (see under para 3.2.2 of Section A above) and an emphasis has been placed on the duty of the harbour authority properly to train pilots and keep pilotage and safety procedures under constant review. The recommendation stated that a national minimum standard of pilot training and examination in the UK should be prepared. The sub-committee at the IMO dealing with standards of training certification and watchkeeping of seafarers is also developing provisions for certification of pilots.

3 CHARGES BY THE COMPETENT HARBOUR AUTHORITY

The authority is authorised by s 10 of the PA 1987 to make reasonable charges for the services of pilots authorised by it; for expenses reasonably incurred in connection with pilot's services; for costs in providing, maintaining and operating boats for the area; for other costs and penalties. There is no right to a maritime lien. The charges are recoverable as a debt, which is enforceable under s 20(2)(i) of the Supreme Court Act 1981 by an *in rem* claim form.

4 DUTIES OF MASTERS AND PILOTS IN A COMPULSORY PILOTAGE AREA

Once a compulsory pilotage area is designated, a ship navigated in that area must be under the pilotage of an authorised pilot, accompanied by an assistant, if that is required, or the master must hold an exemption certificate (s 15). A master who navigates in a compulsory pilotage area, without notifying the competent harbour authority that he proposes to do so, will be

---

99   *Op cit*, Douglas and Geen, fn 8, p 270.

guilty of an offence and liable of summary conviction (s 15 (3)).[100] If any ship is not under such pilotage after an authorised pilot has offered to take charge of the ship, the master will be guilty of an offence, liable on summary conviction (s 15(2)).

It is not an offence, nor is it prohibited, to be in a compulsory pilotage area without a pilot if an offer has not been made, but the master has to look out for one.[101]

What constitutes an offer by a pilot? The offer must be clearly communicated in relation to the particular movement of the ship and it is a question of fact.[102] Mere display of the pilot flag may not be sufficient to constitute an offer (s 15). An offer made on the basis that the pilot would return next morning, instead of offering his services during the evening tide, would not be a reasonable offer, as the example below shows.

The Ignition[103]

The vessel was navigated in a compulsory pilotage area. The master requested the services of a licensed pilot in the district who boarded the vessel shortly after that. Sunset was imminent and the pilot, therefore, suggested that he would return early the next morning, as it would be unsafe to proceed at the time when the tide was flooding. The master navigated his ship along the river out to the sea in the evening tide, without a pilot, and without any problems. The master was charged with navigating in a compulsory pilot district without a pilot, after a licensed pilot of the district had made an offer. This was an offence under s 11 of the PA of 1913, as amended. The question was whether the pilot had made a reasonable offer. On the basis of the pilot's evidence that 'it would be unsafe to sail on the evening tide' the court decided that this was unacceptable and, accordingly, held that a licensed pilot had not offered to take charge of the ship within the meaning of the Act. Therefore, no offence had been committed.

The master of the ship is also under an obligation, by s 50, to display a pilot signal in a compulsory area. When the offer is accepted, the master has an obligation to provide information about the ship (s 18) and facilitate the pilot boarding and leaving his ship (s 20).

---

100 See, also, *Muller v Trinity House* (1924) 20 LlL Rep 56; *Clayton v Albertsen* [1972] 2 Lloyd's Rep 457, the master was prosecuted because he failed to be under pilotage and failed to display a pilot signal in circumstances in which pilotage was compulsory in the Tyne Pilotage District for the purpose of entering and making use of the Port of Tyne in that the ship was carrying passengers, contrary to the PA 1913, ss 11 and 43. The charges were dismissed because it was found, on the facts, that the drivers of the lorries carried on the ship were not passengers.

101 *Muller v Trinity House* (1924) 20 LlL Rep 56; *Rindby v Brewis* (1926) 25 LlL Rep 26.

102 *Babbs v Press* [1971] 2 Lloyd's Rep 383.

103 [1983] 1 Lloyd's Rep 382.

An authorised pilot has a right to supersede an unauthorised one. It would be an offence if the master has an unauthorised pilot on board, without first notifying the harbour authority, or if he continues to employ him after an authorised pilot made an offer (s 17).

5 PILOT'S AUTHORITY AND DIVISION OF CONTROL BETWEEN MASTER AND PILOT

Who is a pilot? Section 742 of the MSA 1894 (now repealed) provided that: 'A pilot is a person not belonging to a ship who has the conduct of her.' The same definition is adopted by s 31(1) of the PA 1987.

The master remains in command of the vessel.[104] The pilot's duties are confined to navigation and he does not supersede the master. But the pilot is the person best qualified to appraise the situation in the particular area in which he has been authorised. Co-operation and assistance, in looking out for danger, in guiding the pilot how to handle the ship and ensuring that the crew carry out the pilot's instructions is expected from the master.[105]

Under the Merchant Shipping (Reporting Requirements for Ships Carrying Dangerous or Polluting Goods) Regulations 1995, reg 12, the master of a ship before entering port in the UK, or a port of another Member State of the European Union, must complete a checklist giving details of the ship, her equipment, crew and survey certificates and also make that list available to any pilot boarding the ship.

Under reg 13, if the pilot engaged in berthing or unberthing a ship in UK waters learns of deficiencies in the ship, which may prejudice its safe navigation, he must immediately inform the port authority. If he boards a ship, knowing or believing that she has defects which may prejudice her safe navigation, he shall notify the master. Upon the master failing to notify the port authority of the defects in question, the pilot must himself notify the port authority (reg 14). Failure to comply with these regulations, or the deliberate making of false statements, is a criminal offence (reg 15). The same duty of reporting defects in a ship by a pilot authorised by the PA 1987 to berth or unberth a ship applies under the Merchant Shipping (Port State Control) Regulations 1995 (reg 15).

The respective duties of a pilot and master were clearly defined as long ago as 1850, in *The Christiana*,[106] by Baron Parke:

---

104 MSA 1995, s 313(1).

105 *Owners of SS Alexander Shukoff v SS Gothland* [1921] 1 AC 216 (HL); *The Nord* [1916] P 53; *The Hans Hoth* [1952] 2 Lloyd's Rep 341.

106 (1850) 13 ER 841.

The duties of the master and the pilot in many respects are clearly defined. Although the pilot has charge of the ship, the owners are most clearly responsible to third persons for the sufficiencies of the ship and her equipments, the competency of the master and crew, and their obedience to the orders of the pilot in everything that concerns his duty, and under ordinary circumstances we think that his commands are to be implicitly obeyed. To him belongs the whole conduct of the navigation of the ship, to the safety of which it is important that the chief direction should be vested in one only.

The master is entitled to rely on the pilot's guidance, and he cannot interfere with the pilot's actions except in extreme necessity, for example, when there is a danger to his ship.[107] Otherwise, he may be held liable for negligence. However, situations of conflict or misunderstanding are not uncommon and they may vary from master to master and their underlying personalities.

The Prinses Juliana[108]

The P and the E came into collision in the entrance to Harwich Harbour. Shortly before the collision, the master of the P took the navigation of the vessel out of the hands of the compulsory pilot and countermanded his order. Bucknill J stated succinctly that:

> If the master sees fit to take the navigation out of the hands of the pilot and countermand his orders, he must satisfy the court that he was justified in so doing, and that the action which he took was at all events more calculated to avoid a collision than the manoeuvre which he countermanded.[109]

It was held that, on the facts of the case, the master of the P wrongly and without any justification took the matter of out of the pilot's hands and without the pilot's consent. He also gave a wrong order without which the collision would not have occurred.

Before the abolition of the defence of compulsory pilotage (by s 15 of the PA 1913) – on which a shipowner could rely to disclaim liability for damage caused by his ship while she was under compulsory pilotage – the pilotage authority had to prove that there was negligence on the part of the shipowner's servants. It was necessary, therefore, to distinguish between the duties of the pilot and the master. Since the above Act came into force (and the subsequent Acts, which replaced it), such need does not arise as far as English law is concerned. It will be seen later, in detail, how the courts have construed this section to impose liability for the negligence of the pilot upon the shipowner.

---

107 'If the pilot is intoxicated, or steering a course to the certain destruction of the vessel, the master, no doubt, may interfere and ought to interfere, but it is only in urgent cases.' *The Peerless* (1860) 167 ER 16, p 17, *per* Dr Lushington.

108 [1936] P 139.

109 *Ibid*, pp 149–150.

It suffices at this point to mention that, even in compulsory pilotage areas, the duties of the master and crew remain the same, namely, to give assistance to the pilot to navigate the ship. The Federal Court of Canada dealt with this issue, in *The Irish Stardust*,[110] in which Dube J said:

> The House of Lords' decision in *Workington Harbour & Dock Board v Towerfield (Owners) (sup)* establishes that the word 'answerable' in s 15 of the PA 1913, means 'responsible' and the liability of the owner exists where the damage is sustained by his own ship. as well as where the damage is done to other property.

> At first blush it does appear to be harsh for owners of a ship to be liable for damage occurring to their ship while she is being navigated by a pilot who has been imposed upon them and who is not one of their servants. But the role of the pilot is to provide local knowledge about areas foreign to the master of the ship; he does not relieve the master of his responsibilities. The officers and crew on the bridge are there for a purpose, to be on guard, alert and ready to provide quick assistance. That rule is well illustrated in a House of Lords' decision, *Owners of SS Alexander Shukoff v SS Gothland* [1921] AC 216, p 223:

>> '... this rule, which is intended as a measure of security, does not mean, and must not be taken to mean, that a pilot when once he is in charge of a vessel is so circumstanced that the master and crew owe him no duty to inform him of circumstances which, whether he has noticed them himself or not, are material for him to know in directing the navigation of the vessel. The master and crew are not mere passengers when a pilot is on board by compulsion of law. The pilot is entitled to their assistance, and to apply the defence of compulsory pilotage to a case where the accident would have been averted if such assistance had been given, though in fact it was not, would defeat the policy which has created the defence, and so far from increasing the safety of navigation would actually increase its risks.

> And Lord Birkenhead goes on to quote Lord Alverstone (p 224):

>> In *The Tactician* Lord Alverstone CJ, stated the rule in these terms: 'The cardinal principle to be borne in mind in these pilotage cases ... is that the pilot is in sole charge of the ship ...', and he expressed his agreement 'with the opinions of the very learned judges, from Dr Lushington downwards. ... as to the danger of a divided command, and the danger of interference with the conduct of the pilot; and that if anything of that kind amounts to an interference or a divided command serious risk is run of the ship losing the benefit of the compulsory pilotage ... But side by side with that principle is the other principle that the pilot is entitled to the fullest assistance of a competent master and crew, of a competent lookout, and a well found ship ...'

---

110 [1977] 1 Lloyd's Rep 195.

6 LIABILITY OF A PILOT

Under s 21 of the PA 1987, a pilot may be guilty of an offence and be summarily convicted to imprisonment for a term not exceeding six months, or a fine, or convicted on indictment to imprisonment for a term not exceeding two years, or to a fine, or both, if:

(a) he does any act which causes, or is likely to cause the loss or destruction of, or serious damage to, the ship or its machinery, navigational equipment or safety equipment, or the death of, or serious injury to, a person on board the ship; or

(b) he omits to do anything required to preserve the ship or its machinery, navigational equipment or safety equipment from loss, destruction or serious damage, or to preserve any person on board the ship from death or serious injury; and

(c) the act or omission is deliberate or amounts to a breach or neglect of duty, or he is under the influence of drink, or a drug, at the time of the act or omission.

The pilot must exercise reasonable skill and care in the performance of his duties and acquaint himself with the local conditions. Whether performing voluntary or compulsory pilotage, he will be liable for his own negligence. His liability may be limited to £1000 and the amount of the pilotage charges in respect of the voyage during which the liability was incurred (s 22(2)). Obviously, there is not much point in suing him to recover that little.

The target for a claimant who sustained damage or loss by a ship due to negligence of the pilot on board is the shipowner, even if the ship was navigated by the pilot in a compulsory pilotage area. By the passing of the PA 1913, the defence of compulsory pilotage was abolished because s 15 made the owner, or the master of the ship, answerable[111] for any loss or damage caused by the vessel or by any fault of the navigation of the vessel in the same manner as he would if pilotage were not compulsory.

There is a policy reason that the statutes on pilotage law following the 1913 Act have adopted the same provision.

It will be seen shortly that the courts have consistently held the shipowner liable not only to third parties, but also for damage sustained by his ship due to the pilot's negligence whether or not the pilot is an independent contractor or a person whose general employer might be the harbour authority. They have held that a pilot is the employee of the shipowner *pro tempora* during the time of the navigation of the ship.[112]

---

111 'Answerable' means responsible in terms of damage sustained by the ship due to pilot's negligence, or of damage done to third parties: *Towerfield v Workington Harbour & Dock Board* (1950) 84 LlL Rep 233 (HL).

112 *The Cavendish* [1993] 2 Lloyd's Rep 292.

7 LIABILITY OF HARBOUR AUTHORITIES WITH RESPECT TO PILOTAGE

The duty of the authority under the 1987 Act is to provide adequate pilotage services and qualified pilots to do the job, who are usually independent contractors.

Section 22(8) expressly provides that the harbour authority shall not be liable for any loss or damage caused by an act or omission of a pilot authorised by them by virtue only of that authorisation. The PA 1983 had a similar provision (s 17).

Licensing, as it was under the older statute, or authorising pilots, as it is under the present statute, does not involve the authority in any liability for negligence of pilots so authorised. The reason given in decided cases is that the authority is not the principal in the piloting of ships, nor is it involved in the conduct of management of the particular ship which sustained damage.[113]

Upon reading s 22(3), however, which entitles the authority to limit liability for the negligence of a pilot whom they employ, it seems that this sub-paragraph may be in conflict with sub-para 8. The reconciliation of these paragraphs may be settled by distinguishing the duty of mere authorisation by the harbour authority from the duty to provide adequate pilotage services with qualified pilots. While the authority will not be liable for the negligence of a properly qualified pilot who is authorised by the harbour authority to act, it is submitted that it will be liable for physical damage arising from the lack or inadequate pilotage services, or caused due to the negligence of a pilot who is non-properly trained and qualified to act in a particular area, as this would amount to inadequate pilotage services.

If a pilot is not properly qualified or trained but he is, nevertheless, authorised by the harbour authority, the latter should be accountable and liable for the damage caused, at least, to the ship, or for loss of life or personal injury caused due to the negligence of a non-properly qualified pilot. Support for such a proposition is gained from the Code of good practice, as it seems to be the intention derived from the Consultation paper, mentioned earlier,[114] that the duty of the authority will be to ensure that pilots are properly qualified and trained for the job. The review of the duties of harbour authorities under the PA 1987, as stated in the Code of practice, will have the effect of making the authority assume responsibility for safe pilotage.[115] The question whether a duty of care might be owed to third parties by the harbour

---

113 *Fowles v Eastern and Australian Steamship Co Ltd* [1916] 2 AC 556 (PC); *The Esso Bernicia* [1989] AC 643.

114 See para 3.2.6, above.

115 See Section A, para 3.2.6 and Section B, para 2.1. Lord Jauncey in *Esso Bernicia* [1989] AC 643 (see para 8) said that, theoretically, it is possible that the general employer, port authority, may be liable if it assumes responsibility for safe pilotage.

authority for negligence of a non-properly qualified pilot causing economic loss will be met with the same legal considerations as those in relation to classification societies, discussed in Chapter 11.

The limitation of harbour authorities' liability is governed by s 191 of the MSA 1995.

8 LIABILITY OF THE SHIPOWNER FOR NEGLIGENCE OF THE PILOT

Under common law, owners of vessels were always held liable whenever they took on a pilot in a non-compulsory pilotage area. But where pilotage was compulsory, the owners were not liable because the pilot could not be regarded as the owners' servant or someone for whose acts and omissions the owners should be liable. This rule was enshrined in s 633 of the MSA 1894, which provided:

> An owner or master of a ship shall not be answerable to any person whatever for any loss or damage occasioned by the fault or incapacity of any qualified pilot acting in charge of that ship within any district where the employment of a qualified pilot is compulsory by law.

By contrast, Art 5 of the Brussels Collision Convention 1910 provided that the liability imposed by the articles of the Convention attached in cases where the collision was caused by the fault of a pilot, even where the pilot was carried by compulsion of law. This provision had effect only in collision cases, but it was not enacted in the Maritime Convention Act 1911, which brought the Collision Convention into English law.

However, the defence of compulsory pilotage (as mentioned under para 6) was first abolished by s 15 of the PA 1913, which provided:

> Notwithstanding anything in any public or local Act, the owner or master of a vessel navigating under circumstances in which pilotage is compulsory shall be answerable for any loss or damage caused by the vessel or by any fault of the navigation of the vessel in the same manner as he would if pilotage were not compulsory.

Section 15 was wider than Art 5 of the Collision Convention. Next came the repeal of the 1913 Act by the consolidating Act of Pilotage 1983 and s 35 of this Act was identical to s 15 of the PA 1913.

Problems of construction of the wording of this section gave rise to interesting decisions, which perhaps provided the ground for the amendment of the same provision by the equivalent section of the 1987 Act, s 16. It was thought that the new Act intended to change the law, but this was not so (see later).

It will help to consider, first, how the courts construed s 15 of the 1913 Act and then see whether Art 16 of the 1987 Act brought any change.

The Towerfield[116]

The case involved a ship in charge of a compulsory pilot, which was approaching an English harbour and went aground on undredged accumulated river silt. She sustained damage and also caused damage to the harbour. It was found, on the facts, that both the harbour authority and the pilot were negligent and their negligence contributed to the casualty. The harbour authority were negligent in that they failed to discharge their duty to ascertain the condition of the channel and to communicate the relevant information either to the master or to the pilot. The duty to give warning to the master arose from the relation of invitor and invitee. The argument by the harbour board that the pilot was intimately acquainted with the port and that he knew, or at any rate they were entitled to assume that he knew, the port's exact condition was rejected.

Regarding the pilot's negligence, the House of Lords held the shipowner responsible, not only for the damage which his ship sustained, but also for the damage to the harbour on the basis of s 15 of the PA 1913.

In particular, the issue was whether 'answerable' meant more than the damage just done by the ship to the harbour, so as to include damage suffered by the ship.

The owners' submissions were that, on the language of the section, the effect of the change of the law was that they would be liable for any loss or damage to other persons, in case the negligence of the pilot was imputed to them, but, on the other hand, the section did not prevent them from claiming damage done to their ship.

Although **Lord Norman** criticised the clumsy drafting of this section, he said:

> The wording of s 15 is not happy. The word 'answerable' is not the cause of the difficulty, and it is merely the equivalent of 'responsible'. But the words 'answerable for any loss or damage caused by the vessel', though apt when the claim is against the owner of a ship, are incapable of applying when the claim is by the owner for damage done to his ship. The words 'answerable for any loss or damage caused … by any fault of the navigation of the vessel' are ill chosen and clumsy, but they are capable of applying to the shipowner's claim.[117]

Despite the admission by Lord Norman that, in his view, the words used in the section were incapable of applying to the shipowners' claim, his final conclusion may be seen as arbitrary for lacking any substantial support.

---

116 [1951] AC 112.
117 *Ibid*, p 145.

The majority of the Court of Appeal had accepted that while the liability of a shipowner for the negligence of the pilot was applicable to a claim in tort, it held that it had no application in a contractual situation. In their view of this case, the harbour had offered to receive any ship on the terms that the channel was safely dredged and by entering the port *The Towerfield* had accepted such an offer.

The House of Lords did not accept this and reversed the decision. **Lord Potter** said robustly in this respect:

> My Lords, for the purpose of this decision and without staying to consider its accuracy, I am prepared to accept the suggestion that such a contract was so formed. But I do not find myself able to agree with the contention that the withdrawal of the protection given to ships employing a compulsory pilot affects only cases where a claim in tort is made.

> Taking the view which I do, that upon the true construction of the Act a shipowner is, after the beginning of 1918, to be responsible for the acts of a compulsory pilot, I do not find myself influenced by a consideration of the history of the negotiations leading to a change in the law. The provisions of the Act, as I think, themselves plainly attribute to shipowners liability for the fault of a compulsory pilot in all cases and I can, therefore, see no reason for differentiating between contract and tort, more particularly as this appears to have been accepted as the correct view from the time when the Act came into force until the present day.[118]

Lord Porter gave the following answer to the owners' submissions, and also dealt with the effect of the port authority's negligence in the light of the strict liability of the owner under s 74 of the HDPCA 1847 (which was mentioned under para 4 of Section A of this chapter):

> My Lords ... the section says that the owner or master shall be answerable for any loss or damage caused by the vessel, or by any fault of the navigation of the vessel. In the present case, the damage to *The Towerfield* was undoubtedly caused by faulty navigation, but when the Act says that the owner shall be answerable for that faulty navigation, it has to be determined whether 'answerable' means more than that the damage, whether done to or done by his ship, is his responsibility or is confined to damage done by the ship. Either view no doubt is theoretically possible but I do not think that read in its context the use of the word 'answerable' would naturally convey the suggestion that, though the shipowner is liable for any damage done by the pilot's fault, yet he can recover his own damage in full. 'Answerable', as I think, simply means responsible, and a shipowner who through a compulsory pilot is responsible for faulty navigation is responsible for damage to his own ship as well as for injury to the property of another...[119]

> There remains, however, to be determined the contention put forward by the harbour board that though their negligence may be one of the causes of the

118 [1951] AC 112, p 134.
119 *Ibid*, p 133–34.

disaster, yet they can recover by reason of the terms of s 74 of the HDPCA 1847.

The section has, my Lords, been considered at least four times and has twice been fully discussed ...

In *River Wear Commissioners v Adamson* ...where the matter was fully discussed, Lord Gordon took the first view and Lord Cairns the second. The other noble Lords agreed with Lord Cairns in holding the shipowner not liable, but with considerable doubt and in the case of the majority, as I think, because that liability only attached where the ship was still in charge of and controlled by some person. This, at any rate, seems to have been the reasoning upon which the Court of Appeal acted and your Lordships' House approved their judgment.

The next case to reach your Lordships' House was *Great Western Rly Co v Mostyn (Owners)*, but before that case was considered Roche J (in *Det Forenede Dampskibs Selskab v Barry Rly Co* followed the decision in the *River Wear* case in holding a shipowner not absolutely liable, but excused in a case where the damage to the harbour works was, in part at least, caused by the fault of the harbour authority. As I read the decision in *The Mostyn*, however, the majority of their Lordships took the view that the shipowner was responsible for damage done to harbour works whether he was in fault or not, save in a case similar to that decided in the *River Wear* judgment. Accordingly, where the ship had been abandoned and was therefore out of the control of its owners, they agreed that no liability attached under the section. But, save for that concession, they decided in terms, as I think, that the only exception from liability was that afforded to an abandoned ship ...

I would only add that, like those of your Lordships who are of the same opinion, I would limit the damages to those directly caused to the harbour, in which, as the shipowners concede, are to be included the restoration of the channel to the condition in which it was before the stranding of *The Towerfield*, but I would not embrace amongst them any loss of revenue to which the harbour board have been put thereby. Save to this extent I think the claim and counterclaim fail.[120]

It was discussed earlier, under s 74,[121] that when the incident occurred in this case the LR(CN)A 1945 was not in force, albeit that the case was decided in 1951. If the case on these facts was decided today, it is submitted that the shipowner would be able to plead contributory negligence on the ground of breach of statutory duty by the port authority to maintain the port in a safe condition, which contributed to the damage suffered by both the ship and the harbour. This would be consistent with the principles enunciated both under common law and the statutory duty of the harbour authority to maintain the port in a safe condition (see para 3.2.3 and 3.2.4 of Section A). It should be noted that the defence of contributory negligence does not affect the position

---

120 [1951] AC 112, pp 135–136.
121 Section A, para 4, above.

of the harbour authority to claim its damage without having to prove negligence on the part of the ship on the basis of the strict liability under s 74. In any case, it is time that this old section is reconsidered for amendments to clarify matters.

The construction of s 15 was again examined, almost 40 years later, by the House of Lords in the following case, but the issue in this case, *inter alia*, was purely concerned with s 15 and it did not involve negligence of the harbour authority to make the port safe for navigation, as the previous case did.

The Esso Bernicia[122]

In 1978, *Esso Bernicia* with a pilot on board was being berthed at a jetty in an oil terminal (a compulsory pilot area) in Shetland Islands with three tugs in attendance. A tow-line had been secured by one of the tugs, S. At about midnight, a coupling blew out of a hydraulic pipe above the engine exhaust of the tug. The escaped hydraulic oil caught fire and the tow-line was cut off. *Esso Bernicia* was no longer under the control of the other two tugs and came into contact with mooring dolphins, whereby she and the dolphins sustained damage. Large quantities of bunker oil escaped. The tug S had been designed and built by Hall Russell Co Ltd for the purpose of berthing tankers at the oil terminal. The owners of *Esso Bernicia* brought an action against the ship builders, Hall Russell, on the ground of negligence in the building of the tug, for an indemnity with respect to oil pollution liabilities incurred to third parties and for damage to the jetty. The pilotage authority were joined as third parties to the action. The shipbuilders averred that the pilot on board the vessel had caused the accident, and that the pilotage authority was vicariously liable for his acts and omissions, being an employee of the authority. When the incident happened in 1983, the PA 1913 was, just, still in force.

Despite powerful previous authorities on the issue, counsel for the shipbuilders was not deterred from arguing that the pilotage authority, being the general employer of the pilot were vicariously liable. He maintained that while the owner was responsible throughout to third parties for the acts and omissions of the pilot, he was not the master of the pilot for the purposes of any damage which the pilot caused to him. Therefore, he could sue both the pilot (*Lister v Romford Ice and Cold Storage Co Ltd* [1957] AC 555) and, if he was employed by an authority, his employer. Thus, he argued, so far as the pilot was concerned it mattered not whether he fell to be treated as the servant of the owner, or an independent contractor for the purposes of a negligent act. In either event, the owner could recover from him subject always to any statutory limitation of liability.

122 [1989] AC 643, or 1 Lloyd's Rep 8.

Lord Jauncey took the opportunity to analyse both principle and policy:

The critical question is whether the owner can recover from a general employer of the pilot ...

The fact that he was an independent contractor did not alter the common law rule that when he had been engaged voluntarily by a shipowner he was, so far as any acts or omissions on his part were concerned, the servant of the shipowner. The rule operated whether he was in the general employment of a pilotage authority, or whether he was an independent contractor ... My Lords, nothing that has been said on behalf of Hall Russell persuades me that the rationale of the line of authority to which I have referred was wrong or that there is any exception to the general application of s 15 of the Act of 1913 to damage suffered by a ship under pilotage. Subject only to what I have to say in the context of Hall Russell's second submission, the pilot is to be considered for all purposes as the servant of the owner ... If Hall Russell's argument were correct, there would follow the curious result that the doctrine of *respondeat superior* would apply to two different masters in respect of two different claims of damage arising out of a single act of negligence. It is a well recognised principle, exemplified in cases involving crane drivers, that a servant in the general employment of A may, for a particular purpose, be treated as in the *pro hac vice* employment of B. However, there is no principle which permits a servant to be in the *de jure* employment of two separate masters at one and the same time.[123]

The shipbuilders' second argument was that the pilotage authority had assumed the responsibility of piloting ships and had held themselves out as undertaking pilotage services as principals of the pilot.

Lord Jauncey rejected this argument also and concluded by stating a general rule:

My Lords, it may be stated as a general rule that the employer of a qualified licensed pilot is not vicariously responsible to the owner of a ship damaged by his negligence while under pilotage. All the authorities support such a rule and none appear to controvert it. The basis of the rule is twofold, namely: (1) the pilot is an independent professional man who navigates the ship as a principal and not as a servant of his general employer, and (2) s 15(1) makes him the servant of the shipowner for all purposes connected with navigation.

In stating this rule, I am not going so far as to say that an employer of a licensed pilot could never be responsible for his negligent navigation. It is theoretically possible that such an employer could himself assume the obligation of safe pilotage although, at the moment, I have very great difficulty in envisaging a situation in which such an event could occur. However, it is unnecessary to speculate further since there is nothing in the present case to take it out of the general rule.[124]

---

123 [1989] AC 643, pp 685–86.
124 *Ibid*, pp 690–91.

The third significant case in the line of these authorities, which is particularly important because it was decided after the 1987 Act was in force, is *The Cavendish*. The relevant sections were ss 2 and 16 of this Act. **Section 2** provides:

2(1) Each competent harbour authority shall keep under consideration:

(a) whether any and, if so, what pilotage services to be provided to secure the safety of ships navigating in the approaches to its harbour; and

(b) whether in the interests of safety, pilotage should be compulsory for ships navigating in any part of that harbour or its approaches and, if so, for which ships and in which circumstances and what pilotage services need to be provided for those ships.

(2) without prejudice to the generality of sub-s (1) above, each competent harbour authority shall in performing its function under that subsection have regard in particular to the hazards involved in the carriage of dangerous goods or harmful substances by ships.

(3) Each competent harbour authority shall provide such pilotage services as it considers need to be provided as mentioned in sub-s (1)(a) and (b) above.

Section 16 provides:

The fact that a ship is being navigated in an area and in circumstances in which pilotage is compulsory for it, shall not affect any liability of the owner or master of the ship for any loss or damage caused by the ship or by the manner in which it is navigated.

The Cavendish[125]

Briefly, the defendants, Port of London Authority (PLA), provided pilotage services under the PA 1987. They had directed that pilotage be compulsory for ships navigating in the approaches to the River Thames. The plaintiffs requested the services of a pilot to pilot *The Cavendish* from the seaward limit of their pilotage jurisdiction. A pilot was duly provided and took charge of the vessel. About 40 minutes later, the vessel struck the Sunk Head Tower and/or buoy, in the approaches to the Thames, resulting in damage to her. The plaintiff sought to recover their loss and expense from PLA. For the purpose of determining a preliminary issue about the effect of ss 2 and 16 of the new Act, the parties agreed that it was to be assumed, without being admitted, that the loss suffered by the plaintiffs was caused by the negligence of the pilot.

The first issue was whether s 2 of the 1987 Act imposed a positive duty upon the authority to pilot ships, therefore, becoming vicariously liable for the negligence of the pilot. The second issue was whether PLA was liable to the plaintiffs in contract, having contracted to supply pilotage services subject to a statutory common law implied term that such services would be performed

---

125 [1993] 2 Lloyd's Rep 292.

with reasonable skill and care and that the claim was not precluded by s 16 of the Act.

Clarke J (as he then was) held on the first issue that the effect of s 2 of the 1987 Act was not to impose duties upon competent authorities to pilot ships, but to require them to supply properly authorised pilots for ships.[126] If the law had intended to provide for this new duty upon an authority, it could have been done in clear and unequivocal terms. In essence, s 2 gave statutory definition to duties which were, in practice, assumed by pilotage authorities under the earlier legislation. Therefore, PLA were not vicariously liable in tort for the negligence of the pilot.

On the second issue, he held that there was no basis for holding that a contract existed between the parties.[127] It was no more than an arrangement between PLA and the plaintiffs for the discharge of the shipowner's statutory obligation by taking a compulsory pilot and paying a fee provided by the regulations made under the Act.

Finally, on s 16, the plaintiffs argued that this section has changed the law in that it prevents the shipowner from relying on the negligence of a compulsory pilot in resisting claims by third parties, but it restores the common law position so far as claims by the shipowner against the general employer of the pilot is concerned. The judge held that s 16 replaced the similar provision of the 1913 Act and it was not intended to alter the meaning of the earlier provision but to put it into more modern language. It imposed liability for negligence of a compulsory pilot on the shipowner in respect of claims by third parties. If this was so, there was no reason for holding that the pilot was the servant of the shipowner for that purpose but not for the purpose of making them liable to bear their own loss.

A pilot could not have two masters and once it was held that the pilot was, for some purposes, the servant of the shipowner he could not be at the same time the servant of his general employer, the competent authority.

This case seems to have closed any further debate on these issues, although the wording of s 16 of the 1987 Act has still not made the position clearer than its predecessor. For example, the words 'any loss or damage caused by the ship' which Lord Norman in *The Towerfield* criticised as being clumsy drafting and not capable of applying when the claim is by the owner for damage done to his ship, have been copied without any additional words referring to damage done or caused to the ship.

New issues for consideration by the courts may, however, arise in the future when the application of the code of good practice on port marine

---

126 The judge applied the principle of *Fowles v Eastern and Australian Steamship Co Ltd* [1916] 2 AC 556.

127 The judge applied the principle in *Oceanic Crest Shipping Co v Pilbara Harbour Service Ltd* (1985) 160 CLR 626.

operations is enforced by a regulation made under the powers of the Secretary of State, which should clearly apportion responsibility between harbour authorities and shipowners in order to clarify the unhappy wording of s 16 and delineate the responsibility of harbour authorities in the event of providing unsafe pilotage.

The defence of compulsory pilotage may be available by the law of the country where the wrong was committed, as in the following example.

The Waziristan[128]

The *S* grounded in the Shatt el Arab (in Iraqi territorial waters). The grounding was caused by an obstruction to the channel by *The Waziristan*, which had gone aground by negligent navigation of those on board while proceeding down the channel ahead of *S*. The owners of the *S* claimed damages from *W*'s owners. *W* claimed that the grounding of *S* was due solely to *S*'s negligent navigation, and that, as there was a compulsory pilot in charge on board her, they were not responsible.

Willmer J found, on the evidence, that the *W* was not at fault for taking the ground. No negligence had been shown. He, however, went on to discuss the issue of compulsory pilotage. The question was whether the presence of a compulsory pilot on board the *W* could be relied upon as a defence by the defendants. In Iraq, there was no equivalent provision to s 15 of the UK PA 1913 making the shipowner responsible for the negligence of a compulsory pilot. It was found that the state of the law in Iraq was such that the defendants could not be liable in this case for such negligence.

In the USA, a shipowner will be liable for the negligence of a pilot who is engaged voluntarily, but not if he is engaged in a compulsory area because the pilot will be forced by operation of law and not by choice, so as to create a relationship of a master and servant. Therefore, neither the master nor the owner of the vessel is liable *in personam* for the negligence of the compulsory pilot, provided the pilot has been solely at fault and there is no negligence on the part of the ships' personnel, or the owner, in failing to make the ship seaworthy. However, the ship itself, being regarded as a legal entity under admiralty law, is chargeable with fault for the wrong of the pilot and is subject to a suit *in rem*. The harbour authority, also, being the employer of the pilot, will be liable for the negligence of a pilot under the doctrine of *respondeat superior*.[129]

Limitation of liability of shipowners and others is examined in the next chapter.

---

128 [1953] 2 Lloyd's Rep 361.

129 See Parks, A and Cattell, E, *The Law of Tug, Tow and Pilotage*, 3rd edn, 1994, Cornell Maritime Press Inc, pp 1022–29.

PART V

MISCELLANEOUS

OVERVIEW

This final part includes Limitation of Liability (Chapter 16), developments at the European Commission in relation to maritime safety (Chapter 17) and an epilogue of the book relating to the development of a culture for risk management by shipping companies.

The civil liabilities discussed in this book are brought to a happy ending for those who are entitled to limit liability. Various aspects of it are looked at in the following chapter, commenting on some problems in the interpretation of the 1976 Convention, and the risks involved in the right of limitation being lost. Consideration is also given to the implications of the International Safety Management Code on the issue of breaking the right to limit.

In the light of new and urgent proposals that have been made by the European Commission with regard to enhancing safety at sea, it was thought important to include an overview of such proposals as emerged after the sinking of *The Erika* tanker.

In the Epilogue, it is endeavoured to bring the salient features of this book together, with emphasis on risk management issues.

CHAPTER 16

EXCLUSION AND LIMITATION OF LIABILITY

1 INTRODUCTION

Historically, for 250 years, limitation of shipowners' liability for maritime claims has been designed to encourage and protect trade. It encourages shipowners to stay in business and their insurers to be able to insure risks for liability to third parties, which would, otherwise, be uninsurable.[1] Limitation of liability is not a matter of justice, but of public policy which has its origin in history and its justification in convenience.[2] It is regulated by separate regimes of limitation implemented by international conventions.

The Hague Rules 1924, the Hague-Visby Rules (HVR) 1968 and the Hamburg Rules 1978[3] regulate the carrier's obligations and liabilities with respect to the carriage of goods by sea and provide for limitation of the carrier's liability for loss of or damage to cargo 'carried on board' (known as the 'package or unit' limitation). The Athens Convention 1974, as amended by the 1976 and 1990 Protocols,[4] relates to the carriage of passengers and their luggage by sea and provides for limitation of liability in this respect. The Limitation Convention 1976, as amended by the 1996 Protocol,[5] provides for 'tonnage' limitation of liability for maritime claims which may arise, not only in relation to carriage, and will be seen later. The original Civil Liability Convention 1969 and the Fund Convention 1971, which have been superseded by the respective Protocols 1992 (the CLC and Fund 1992), cater for liability and its limitation with respect to oil pollution.[6]

---

1   *Limitation of Shipowners' Liability: The New Law*, 1986, Southampton University.

2   *Alexander Towing Co v Millet (The Bramley Moore)* [1964] P 200, *per* Lord Denning; Read, also, a thoughtful address to the British Maritime Law Association in 1993, Mustill (Lord), 'Ships are different – or are they?' [1993] LMCLQ 490, and the reply by Steel, D, QC, 'Ships are different – the case for limitation of liability' [1995] LMCLQ 77.

3   The Hamburg Rules have not been adopted by the UK, nor do they have international application, although they have been ratified by 26 countries, but not by major maritime nations.

4   The 1976 Protocol stated limits in SDR, instead of Gold Francs used in the original text, and the 1990 Protocol, which is not yet in force, increased the limits.

5   The 1996 Protocol increases the limits, but it is not yet in force. It has been implemented by SI 1998/1258, which adopts the amendments and will be in force once the Protocol has been ratified.

6   See Trew, J and Seward, R, *The Britannia Guide to Oil Pollution*, 1999, The Britannia Steamship Insurance Association Ltd; and De La Rue, C and Anderson, C, *Shipping and the Environment*, 1998, London: LLP.

The rationale for shipowners' limitation of liability was put in a nutshell by Mr Justice Staughton (as he then was) in *The Garden City*:[7]

> The reasoning behind the Convention may now be that shipowners should be encouraged to insure against liability, and limitation makes it easier for them to do so; but that limitation should not be tolerated in the case of outrageous conduct, such as deliberately or recklessly causing loss.

> However, the historical reason for the introduction of limitation appears to have been to enable British ships to trade on equal terms with those of other nations.

Some argue that limitation of liability is anachronistic and overprotective to shipowners and their insurers.[8] While, however, the original reason for limitation was to increase the number of ships and to prevent any discouragement to merchants, limitation has been encouraged and maintained over the years because it has evolved into a system for the support of a whole series of infrastructures. There is an undercurrent utilitarian philosophy for its perpetuation. Politicians and legislators would not be prepared to protect the interests of a minority (the shipowners) by legislation if, by doing so, it were not for the benefit of the community at large. In other words, the fact that the system of limitation of liability is built in to a viable insurance system facilitates trade and boosts the employment of a large part of the workforce and, consequently, allows a series of infrastructures of the service industries to operate.

While it is easy for the objectors to limitation to see only the benefit to the shipowners, derived from the fact that the law allows them to limit their liability, it should not be overlooked that, had it not been for limitation, freight and fuel prices would not be competitive, insurance would be scarce – hence, there would be no guarantee for payment of claims – and the movement of goods would be slower or more difficult. It takes little imagination to envisage that the dependant and related services would suffer, which would have a knock-on effect on the prosperity of a country and, generally, on employment. This is a major reason for the consensus that has been reached internationally in favour of limitation, hence, the limitation conventions have been ratified by most of the maritime nations.

However, the trends and mood internationally in recent years are changing and questions of ethics have been posed with regard to overprotectionism of shipowners and their insurers, by comparison to other industries and their insurers. Limitation is now regarded as not being fair to victims. This is true, insofar as passengers' claims are concerned, for loss of life or personal injury and, perhaps, a different approach should be adopted with

---

7   [1982] 2 Lloyd's Rep 382, p 398.
8   See Guici, G (Dr), 'Limitation of liability in maritime law: an anachronism' (1995) 19(1) *Marine Policy* 65, pp 65–74.

regard to those claims. Efforts are being made to amend the Athens Convention.[9] But the tides are changing course more rapidly in relation to limitation with respect to environmental damage by oil pollution. The problems in this area have been highlighted by the recent sinking of *The Erika* and the subsequent sinking of *The Kristal* off the territorial waters of Spain. In consequence of *The Erika* incident, the Transport Department of the European Commission has taken the initiative to reform the law pertaining to liability and limitation for oil pollution caused in European waters by proposing the implementation of a regulation by which it is aimed to bring the shipping industry into line with the other industries involved in transport, where liability incurred to third parties is unlimited in cases of gross negligence.[10]

Such a move may have a justification, but, regrettably, too great a concern is shown by regulators on property damage than victims of personal injury or loss of life. In reality, if shipowners are driven out of business because their insurers either will charge very high premiums, or will no longer find it viable to insure if there is no sufficient market capacity, trade will be restricted, the service industries will suffer and the infrastructures supported by shipping and trade will be shaken. It is beyond the bounds of this book to discuss the ethics of the limitation system and the conflicting community interests further. It suffices to say that it is to be hoped that a compromise will be reached in order to maintain a reasonable balance. A compromise is, indeed, needed to help trade to continue and encourage shipowners to budget for the maintenance of their ships, so that big disasters are prevented by constant improvement in quality. The measures being taken recently to improve quality in ships and eliminate sub-standard shipping (discussed in Chapter 8) stand out as the most significant event in shipping history. These need to be rigorously enforced. Improvement of limitation, in respect of passengers' vessels is, however, urgent. The proposed amendment to the Athens Convention will be mentioned briefly later.

2 THE SCOPE OF TONNAGE LIMITATION OF LIABILITY UNDER THE 1976 CONVENTION

In this chapter, the law relating to limitation of liability under the 1976 Convention, which concerns tonnage limitation in relation to maritime claims, is examined. It is known as 'tonnage' limitation because it is based on the size of the liable ship, by contrast to its value, as was before the Merchant Shipping

9 See, later, para 3.3, a discussion of the problems with regard to passengers' claims and recent trends.
10 See Lalis, G, Director of Transport of EC, paper delivered at the Third Cadwallader Memorial Lecture of the London Shipping Law Centre, 14 September 2000, available at the Centre's office, UCL Law Faculty; and the measures proposed by the EC in Chapter 17, below.

Act (MSA) 1894. This limitation is also referred to as 'global' because it is designed to deal with disasters in which the owner faces claims from a variety of claimants and seeks to create one overall maximum limit in relation to them.[11] The details of limitation under other Limitation Conventions applying to individual contracts, such as carriage of goods by sea under the HVR, or transportation of passengers under the Athens Convention 1974 (Art 183 of the MSA 1995) can be studied in the specialist books dealing specifically with carriage of goods or passengers by sea. Separate limits exist for oil pollution under the special regime of the CLC 1992 (Art 157 of the MSA 1995). The limits of the 1976 Convention are due to be increased when the Protocol 1996 comes into force.

2.1 Reasons of acceptance of the 1976 Convention

The predecessor to the 1976 Convention was the International Convention Relating to the Limitation of Liability of Owners of Sea-going Ships 1957, which had not been wholly adopted by the UK, but some of its provisions were used to amend the previous regime on limitation enshrined in s 503 of the MSA 1894. This was done by the Merchant Shipping (Liability of Shipowners and Others) Act (MS(LSO)A) 1958. Limitation under these provisions could not avail the shipowner if he could not show that the incident giving rise to the claims took place without his 'actual fault or privity'. It was a difficult burden for the shipowner to discharge in the frequent litigation that ensued. This issue, coupled with a demand for a higher limitation figure, led to the International Conference for Limitation of Liability held in London in 1976, under the auspices of the International Maritime Organisation (IMO), which resulted in the adoption of the 1976 Convention. This Convention was a compromise in order to strike a balance between successful claimants and shipowners. It achieved the increase of the limitation fund to a sufficiently high level, so that the claimants could reasonably be compensated, but not so high as to make the shipowners' liability uninsurable. As a *quid pro quo* for the increase of the fund, the article providing for the breaking of limitation became tighter, so that it is almost impossible for the claimants to break the right to limit (discussed later).

The new Convention was wholly adopted by the UK for reasons of international uniformity and was given domestic effect first by s 17 of the MSA 1979. The consolidating MSA 1995 contains the Convention in Sched 7, Pt I and, by s 185 of the same Act, the Convention applies to English law, subject to certain reservations contained in Pt II, Sched 7. The Convention came into force on 1 December 1986. Countries which have not ratified the

---

11 See 'Glossary', *Current Statutes*, MSA 1995, Chapter 21, p 221.

1976 Convention may have their own national system of limitation, or may apply the 1957 Convention.

2.2 Application of the Convention and limitations

Article 15 of the Convention (Sched 7, Chapter IV of the MSA 1995) provides that the Convention shall apply whenever any person entitled to limit (per Art 1) seeks to limit his liability before the Court of a State Party or seeks to procure the release of a ship, or other property, or the discharge of any security given within the jurisdiction of any such State.

Article 15(2) of the Convention allows the State Parties to make their own provisions of limitation to be applied to vessels which, according to the law of that State, are ships intended for navigation on inland waters, or ships of less than 300 tons. On the other hand, the Convention forbids the Courts of a State Party to apply the Convention to ships constructed for, or adapted to, and engaged in, drilling:

(a) when that State has established under its national legislation a higher limit of liability than that otherwise provided for in Art 6; or

(b) when that State has become party to an international convention regulating the system of liability in respect of such ships.

2.2.1 Limitation to sea-going ships

The Convention applies to sea-going ships. However, the UK has made no alteration to the previous regime applicable under English law and the right to limit has been reserved to apply to any ship[12] whether sea-going or not (Pt II para 2 of Sched 7 and s 185 of the MSA 1995). Reference to a ship in the Convention in para 12 of Pt II includes reference to any structure (whether completed, or in the course of completion) launched and intended for use in navigation as a ship, or part of a ship.

The provisions of limitation which have the force of law under s 185 shall also apply to Her Majesty's ships, which are defined by s 192(2) as ships of which the beneficial interest is vested in Her Majesty in right of Her Government in the UK, or are registered as Government ships, or which are for the time being demised, or sub-demised to, or in the exclusive possession of the Crown.

---

12 'Ship' is defined in the MSA 1995, s 313, as including any description of vessel used in navigation.

2.2.2 Hovercraft not included in the Convention

Since the provisions of the MSA 1995 apply to hovercraft (Sched 13, para 42 of the MSA 1995), the Limitation Convention under English law applies to hovercraft to the extent that it shall not apply to the baggage of hovercraft passengers to which the Carriage by Air Act (CAA) 1961 applies.[13]

2.2.3 Minimum tonnage

Subject to variations from State to State with respect to minimum tonnage, as is allowed by the Convention, there is a single minimum limit for all ships of no more than 500 tons, but the UK has varied this position. There is a new minimum level of limitation for ships of less than 300 tons in respect of all claims within Art 6, not just for loss of life or personal injury claims, as was the position under s 1 of the 1958 Act. With respect to passengers' claims, the number of passengers which the ship is certified of carrying is relevant and not the tonnage, according to Art 7 of the 1976 Convention.

2.2.4 Floating and drilling platforms excluded

By Art 15(5), the Convention does not apply to floating platforms constructed for the purpose of exploring or exploiting the natural resources of the seabed, or the subsoil thereof.

Since the UK has not incorporated this limitation to the MSA 1995, whether such platforms are to be regarded as ships for the purpose of limitation will depend on whether the Secretary of State, who has powers by virtue of s 311 of the MSA 1995 to order that a thing designed or adapted for use at sea may be treated as a ship, so orders. Equally, the provision of the Convention (Art 15(4)) excluding drilling units from limitation does not have the force of law in the UK. So, if a drilling unit satisfies the definition of a ship, it will qualify for limitation under the MSA 1995.

3 PERSONS ENTITLED TO LIMIT

Article 1 provides:

(1) Shipowners and salvors, as hereinafter defined, may limit their liability in accordance with the rules of this Convention for claims set out in Art 2.

(2) The term 'shipowner' shall mean the owner, charterer, manager or operator of a sea-going ship.

---

13   Civil Liability Order 1986 (SI 1986/1305).

(3) Salvor shall mean any person rendering services in direct connection with salvage operations. Salvage operations shall also include operations referred to in Art 2, para 1(d), (e) and (f)

(4) If any claims set out in Art 2 are made against any person for whose act, neglect or default the shipowner or salvor is responsible, such person shall be entitled to avail himself of the limitation of liability provided for in this Convention.

(5) In this Convention the liability of a shipowner shall include liability in an action brought against the vessel herself.

(6) An insurer of liability for claims subject to limitation in accordance with the rules of this Convention shall be entitled to the benefits of this Convention to the same extent as the assured himself.

(7) The act of invoking limitation shall not constitute an admission of liability.

3.1 Shipowners and others

3.1.1 Owner, manager or operator

Under the old regime of limitation, the right to limit liability was only given to actual registered or beneficial owners of a ship, by s 503 of the MSA 1894. That right was extended to persons other than shipowners by s 3 of the MS(LSO)A 1958, which amended the earlier section (pursuant to the 1957 Convention, Art 6) to include 'charterers, any person interested in or in possession of the ship,[14] a manager or operator of the ship, and the master, crew or other servants of the owner ... acting in the course of their employment'.

Under the 1957 Convention, a person merely in possession, but not in operation of the vessel, for example, a mortgagee, or ship-repairer, was allowed to limit his liability by s 3(1) of the 1958 Act.[15] By eliminating the words 'any person interested in or in possession of the ship' in Art 1(2) of the 1976 Convention, it is clear that the right is not given to a mortgagee, unless the mortgagee upon default by the owner takes over the management and operation of the ship, nor is it given to other persons who merely hold possession of the ship, such as a ship-repairer, at a given time. The right is restricted to the shipowner which, for the purpose of the Convention, means the owner, charterer, manager or operator of a sea-going ship. The word

---

14 'Any person interested in ... the ship' meant a person having a legal or equitable interest in the ship: *McDermid v Nash Dredging & Reclamation Co Ltd* [1987] AC 906 (HL).

15 *Mason v Uxbridge Boat Centre* [1980] 2 Lloyd's Rep 592; the judge followed the precedent of the House of Lords' decision in *The Ruapehlu* [1927] AC 523 (HL), which decided in favour of a dockowner acting as a ship-repairer under the previous statute of limitation, the MS(LSO)A 1900, s 2.

'manager' does not include the crewing agent but a manager who is involved in the technical management of the ship, or in the ship's operation.[16]

3.1.2 Charterer

A charterer can limit liability for claims for which he is liable. A slot charterer was recently included in the category of a 'charterer' under the provision of the Supreme Court Act 1981 in relation to the arrest of a ship,[17] so presumably he may now be included in the class of charterers as having the right to limit liability. The authors of limitation of liability, Griggs and Williams, suggest that since the slot charterer uses only part of the ship, and there is no provision which allows a slot charterer to limit liability proportionately, the choice would seem to be between allowing him to limit according to the full tonnage of the ship, or not at all. But the authors prefer the former view which is in line with the aim of the Convention.[18]

Until recently, it was not clear whether a charterer could limit liability with respect to claims for indemnity pursued by the owners. This issue arose in *The Aegean Sea*,[19] in which Thomas J decided against such limitation upon a claim by the owners against the charterers, for an indemnity in respect of cargo and pollution claims made against the owners, by reason of the loss of the ship, which had been sent by the charterers to an unsafe port. His reasons were these:

(1) From the development of the limitation prior to the 1976 Convention and the way in which the 1976 Convention was structured and its language, the 1976 Convention did not provide (and was not intended to provide) an entitlement to charterers to limit where the shipowner brought the types of claims the owners were bringing against the charterers; such claims could not be reasonably brought within its language;

(2) it could not have been intended that either the limitation amounts or the fund be reduced by direct claims by the owners against the charterers for the loss of the ship, or the freight or the bunkers; it was intended for claims by cargo interests and other third parties external to the operation of the ship against those responsible for the operation of the ship; to permit the claims of the type advanced by the owners against the charterers for the direct losses they suffered to come within the scope of the limitation amount or the fund would diminish what was available to others;

(3) on the assumption that the 1976 Convention covered claims by the shipowner against the charterer, the loss of the ship was not the loss of 'property ... occurring in direct connection with the operation of the ship' in

---

16 For types of management of ships, see Chapter 8.
17 *The Tychy* [1999] 2 Lloyd's Rep 11 (CA); see Chapter 3, para 4.2.
18 Griggs, P and Williams, R, *Limitation of Liability for Maritime Claims*, 3rd edn, 1998, LLP, p 9; and [1997] IJSL 118–21.
19 [1998] 2 Lloyd's Rep 39.

Art 2(1)(a), because it was the operation of the very ship that must cause the loss of property; the ship could not be the object of the wrong.

3.1.3 Any person for whose act, neglect or default the shipowner or salvor is responsible

The wording of Art 1(4), '... any person for whose act, neglect or default the shipowner or salvor is responsible, such person shall be entitled to avail himself of the limitation of liability provided for in this Convention', can potentially cause problems of interpretation as to the extent of persons for whose acts, etc, the shipowner is responsible. It should be borne in mind, however, that the provision is mainly concerned with granting an independent right of limitation to those people for whose act, neglect or default the shipowner, or charterer, or manager, or operator, or salvor will be vicariously liable. These people were, before the 1957 Convention, potentially exposed to be sued separately from the shipower, if the claimants wished to bypass the owner's right to limit.

It may be that the provision is intended to include persons other than merely the master or crew, other servants of the owner, etc, acting in the course of their employment. Such a wording was used in the 1957 Convention. Was it necessary to change it? The answer to this may be that it was done just for purpose of clarification or, in order to expand the list of people in this class. The most obvious category of those people is the stevedores who, although they are generally independent contractors, must show that, in the particular case in which they seek to limit liability, they were employed by the shipowner or the charterer as the case may be. There can be no further extension to this category, so as to include independent contractors who were, for example, engaged to repair the ship and due to their negligence the ship was rendered unseaworthy causing the loss or damage claimed.[20] Although the shipowner will be constructively liable for the loss caused by the unseaworthiness of the ship, if the unseaworthiness was due to the negligence of independent contractors (*The Muncaster Castle*),[21] it does not mean that the independent contractor is a person for whose act, etc, the owner will be vicariously liable. The owner is liable in such cases because he owes a direct duty to the person who suffers the loss, and the duty is non-delegable.[22] The word 'responsible', in Art 1(4), must mean, it is submitted, that the owner

---

20 Cf *op cit*, Griggs and Williams, fn 18, p 11; the authors say that independent contractors may be included in the category, although they explain, p 111, that it may be more difficult for the independent contractor to prove that he is a 'person for whose act ... the shipowner is responsible'.

21 [1961] 1 Lloyd's Rep 57 (HL).

22 See *Salsbury v Woodland* [1970] 1 QB 324, pp 336–37, *per* Widgery LJ: 'It is trite law that an employer who employs an independent contractor is not vicariously responsible for the negligence of that contractor. He is not able to control the way in which the independent contractor does the work, and the vicarious obligation of a master [contd]

or salvor is vicariously liable, for the person seeking to limit to have an independent right to limit.[23]

3.2 Salvors

The new Convention introduced the right of limitation for salvors, as well as any person rendering services in direct connection with salvage operations (Art 1(3)). Art 1(1) of the Convention provides that salvors, '… may limit their liability in accordance with the rules of the Convention for the claims set out in Art 2 of the Convention'. This new development was a direct consequence of *The Tojo Maru*. It should be noted briefly what happened in this case with regard to limitation.

The Tojo Maru[24]

A salvage agreement was signed on the Lloyd's Open Form on the 'no cure no pay' basis. During the salvage operation, the salvors' diver, who was trying to repair a crack at the bottom of the ship being salved, negligently fired a bolt through the shell plating of the ship and through a gas-filled cargo tank. This resulted in an explosion causing substantial damage to the vessel. When the salvors claimed salvage remuneration, the shipowners counterclaimed damages for the damage to be set off against any remuneration the salvors might have been entitled to. The salvors sought to limit their liability under s 503 of the MSA 1894, if they were liable to damages. This section restricted limitation to acts, or omissions (which caused the damage or loss) in the navigation or management of the ship, or through the act, or omission, of any person on board the ship, the owners of which were seeking to limit liability. The central issue with regard to limitation was whether the negligent act of their diver which caused the explosion took place in the management of their tug or, alternatively, whether it took place on board the tug. While the owners' counterclaim for damages was upheld, even though the salvors' operation was successful and had overall done more good to the vessel than bad, it was held that the salvors were not entitled to limit their liability under

22 [contd] for the negligence of his servant does not arise under the relationship of employer and independent contractor. I think that it is entirely accepted that those cases – and there are some – in which an employer has been held liable for injury done by the negligence of an independent contractor are, in truth, cases where the employer owes a direct duty to the person injured, a duty which he cannot delegate to the contractor on his behalf.'

23 Under contracts of carriage, in which the Hague Rules apply, there is no equivalent independent right given to the carrier's servants to limit liability, unlike under the HVR; so Art 1(4) of the 1976 Convention will be useful to them for the purpose of limitation, although it is common in such contracts to include a Himalaya clause. When English law applies to such contracts, the Contracts (Rights of Third Parties) Act 1999, which applies to contracts made after 11 May 2000, enhances the protection of third parties to the contract intended by the terms of the contract to be protected in the same way as the parties to the contract (see, further, Chapter 14, para 11).

24 [1972] AC 242 (HL) (see Chapter 13, 'Salvage').

s 503(1) of the MSA 1894. The salvors' contention that the negligent act of their diver was done either in the management of, or on board, the tug was rejected. Lord Reid stated, quite sympathetically:[25]

> But a court must go by the provisions which have been agreed and enacted. If the special position of salvors was unforeseen, then we must await alteration of those provisions if those concerned see fit to make some alteration.

Now, the wording of Art 2(1) of the Convention specifically covers the circumstances of this case, namely that limitation applies to claims in respect of loss of life, or personal injury, or loss or damage to property occurring on board, or in direct connection with the operation of the ship, or with salvage operations, and consequential loss resulting therefrom.[26]

In addition, Art 1(4) includes the servants of the salvor in the list of people with the right to limit, if any claims under Art 2 are made against any person for whose acts neglect or default the salvor is responsible.

3.3 The liability insurer

The Convention has innovated by including, in Art 1(6), for the liability insurer to be entitled to the benefits of this Convention to the same extent as the assured himself. This will work in the event the insurers are sued directly by injured persons, or the dependants of those whose life was lost on board, or in connection with the operation of the ship, or with salvage operations.

3.3.1 When is there a right of action against the insurer?

The right of action against insurers was first introduced by the Third Parties (Rights Against Insurers) Act 1930, which, in essence, provides for a statutory subrogation entitling the victim of the wrongdoer (the assured) to bypass the privity of contract barrier and take the benefits of the contract of insurance between the liability insurer and the assured. The rights of the assured against the insurer under the contract in respect of the liability are transferred to, and vest in, the third party to whom the liability was so incurred (s 1(1) of the 1930

---

25 [1972] AC 242 (HL), p 270.
26 In Chapter 13, paras 9.3 and 9.4, above, issues of setting off damages for salvor's negligence against the salvage award and when a salvor can limit are discussed.

Act). This statutory subrogation arises in the event of insolvency or bankruptcy of the assured, in other words when he is unable to satisfy the claim.

There are two preconditions that have to be fulfilled before the third party can claim against the insurer. First, the third party must obtain a judgment, or an arbitration award, on liability against the assured and become a judgment creditor. He cannot sue the insurer unless the assured's liability to him is first established because the assured himself cannot claim his indemnity from his insurer, if such liability has not been established.[27] Second, since the assured (defendant) is insolvent and cannot satisfy the judgment debt, the judgment creditor must obtain a winding up order of the company of the assured in England.

To obtain a winding-up order when a company is foreign, as in most cases shipowning companies are, the claimant must establish jurisdiction in the UK. Although doubts existed in the past, it is now possible that such an order can be obtained if the company has assets within the jurisdiction. Insurance proceeds, payable in England under the Protection & Indemnity (P&I) cover, have been regarded as such an asset for this purpose.[28] The court has discretion whether or not to grant the order. The question that still arises, in the case of P&I clubs that are registered as offshore companies, is whether the insurance proceeds would be regarded as an asset within the jurisdiction for the purpose of the winding-up order, if the responsible party was paying from abroad. Would it matter, in fact, where the insurer was incorporated, or would it be sufficient that the responsibility for payment of the proceeds to the assured lay upon the managers of such P&I clubs, operating in England, or their London agents? To the writer's knowledge, there has been no judicial answer to this question as the situation has not arisen, but the making of a winding-up order is discretionary.

Once these two preconditions (a judgment on liability and a winding-up order) are satisfied, the judgment creditor 'steps in the shoes' of the assured and takes over the assured's rights against the insurer under the contract in respect of the liability incurred to the creditor (s 1(1) of the 1930 Act).

---

27 *Post Office v Norwich Union Fire Insurance Co* [1967] 1 Lloyd's Rep 216: Lord Denning MR said in this case, p 219: 'I think the right to sue for these moneys does not arise until the liability is established and the amount ascertained. How is this to be done? If there is an unascertained claim for damages in tort, it cannot be proved in the bankruptcy, nor in the liquidation of the company. But, nevertheless, the injured person can bring an action against the wrongdoer. In the case of a company, he must get the leave of the court. No doubt, leave would automatically be given. The insurance company can fight that action in the name of the wrongdoer. In that way, liability can be established and the loss ascertained. Then the injured person can go against the insurance company.'

28 *The Allobrogia* [1979] 1 Lloyd's Rep 190; *The Vainqueur Jose* [1979] 1 Lloyd's Rep 557; *Re Compania Merabello San Nicholas SA* [1973] Ch 75.

3.3.2 'Pay to be paid rule' under the rules of the liability insurer[29]

Assuming that a claimant obtained a judgment and an English winding-up order against the debtor was granted, there is another impediment for the claimant before he can obtain payment from the insurer. First, liability insurance is subject to the terms of the contract between the assured and his P&I insurer, contained in the club rules, which require that, for an indemnity to be paid to the assured, the latter must have first paid the third party, known as the 'pay to be paid' rule.[30] This rule prohibits the third party creditor stepping into the shoes of the assured, since the reason why he needs to claim from the assured's insurer is that the assured has not paid him.

Were he, the assured, claiming indemnity from his insurer, he should first have paid the creditor, and, in this case, it would mean that the creditor should pay himself. It has been suggested that the creditor may devise ways to pay himself (pretending to be two different entities at the same time, for example, the assured, on the one hand, who hands over the money, and, on the other hand, the creditor, who receives the money due).[31] Then he may claim to be indemnified from the liability insurer, who will be entitled to limit his liability under Art 1(6).

However, while cargo claimants who are supported by cargo underwriters may use this device, it is not feasible for personal injury claimants to find the money to pay themselves. The Law Commission, therefore, has made recommendations to amend the 1930 Act, so as to enable claimants of personal injury, or loss of life, to claim directly from the liability insurers.

3.3.3 Insurer's contractual and statutory defences

Since the creditor claiming against the insurer will be in the shoes of the assured, he will be faced with another possible difficulty in recovering from the insurer, which may arise if the assured was in breach of the contract of insurance and, in particular, of ss 39(5) and 55(2)(a) of the Marine Insurance Act (MIA) 1906.

Section 39(5) provides that the insurer is not liable for any loss attributable to unseaworthiness, if the ship was sent to sea in an unseaworthy condition with the privity of the assured. Similarly, by s 55(2)(a), the insurer is not liable for any loss attributable to the wilful misconduct of the assured. On the hypothesis that the insurer could provide evidence to show that the assured was guilty of such conduct, the creditor – stepping into the assured's shoes – would be faced with the same defences that the P&I insurer would have had against the assured under the contract of insurance.

---

29   Hazelwood, S, *The Law and Practice of P&I Clubs*, 3rd edn, 2000, LLP.
30   *The Fanti and The Pandre Island (No 2)* [1990] 2 Lloyd's Rep 191 (HL).
31   *The Vainqueur Jose* [1979] 1 Lloyd's Rep 557.

3.3.4 Implications for claimants in respect of personal injury, or loss of life

The implications of the law in the latter respect are enormous in cases of loss of life, or personal injury, where the victims may be left without any remedy other than gratuitous payments. It is worth noting such implications, at this point, in the hope that the law will be changed in the foreseeable future and without delay through the admirable work being undertaken by international organisations, such as the IMO and the CMI (Commité Maritime International).

Briefly, the liability of the carrier for passengers' claims is dealt with by the Athens Convention 1974,[32] the text of which is included in Sched 6 to the MSA 1995, and has been incorporated into UK law by s 183 of this Act. Article 3 provides for liability of the carrier with regard to damage suffered as a result of the death, or personal injury, to a passenger and the loss of, or damage, to luggage in the course of the carriage and being caused due to the fault or neglect of the carrier, or of his servants, or agents acting within the scope of their employment.

There is a presumption of fault or neglect of the carrier or his servants or agents, unless the contrary is proved, if the claims in respect of loss of life, or personal injury, or the loss of, or damage to cabin luggage arose from, or in connection, with the shipwreck, collision, stranding, explosion or fire, or defect in the ship. In respect of loss or damage to other luggage, such fault or neglect shall be presumed, unless the contrary is proved, irrespective of the nature of the incident, which caused the loss or damage. In these cases, therefore, the claimant would not have to prove negligence but the burden shifts onto the carrier to prove otherwise. In all other cases, for example, for loss or damage to vehicles of passengers, fault must be proved by the claimant.

The liability of the ferryowner may be limited by Arts 7 and 8 of the Convention, provided that the right to limit is not barred by such conduct as provided by Art 13, namely, if it is proved that the damage resulted from an act or omission of the carrier done with intent to cause such damage, or recklessly and with knowledge that such damage would probably result.

When the carrier is guilty of such misconduct, his insurer will rely on the statutory defences to avoid liability, as discussed earlier. Assume the following scenario: there is a one-ship company owning a ferry which sank, causing personal injuries, or loss of life, to passengers carried on board. The circumstances in which it sank raise questions as to the conduct of the carrier with respect either to breach of international regulations or safety standards, such as the International Safety Management Code (ISMC), or to being reckless in the performance of the carriage, having knowledge that such damage would probably result. Although the latter conduct[33] would have the effect of

---

32 See 'Glossary on the application of the Athens Convention', *Current Statutes*, MSA, Chapter 21, pp 360–61.
33 See Chapter 8, para 5.5, above, the effect of the ISMC on limitation and, later in this chapter, under para 8.4.

breaking limitation under Art 13, so that his liability would be unlimited, the fact that he had already limited his liability up to the only asset of the company, being a one-ship company, would not be good news for the victims, unless there was fraud, in which case the corporate veil would be pierced. Even if the victims were able to surpass the difficulties posed by the Third Parties (Rights Against Insurers) Act 1930, the liability insurer would not pay, otherwise than gratuitously.

3.3.5 *What the future holds for passengers*

It is feasible to resolve these problems by an amendment to the Athens Convention, which is long overdue. Indeed, there has been such an initiative by the Legal Committee of the IMO, proposing that a revised draft Protocol to the Athens Convention be put to a Diplomatic Conference in 2000–01. The Committee met in October 1999 and delegates of Member and non-member States to IMO attended, including the CMI. The core of the proposed amendments had been to impose compulsory insurance, or financial security, as an alternative to liability insurance. The CMI had proposed that a Personal Accident Insurance (PAI) could be bought by the shipowner for passengers. Such insurance would provide adequate protection to passengers because they could have a direct action against the insurers providing financial security, thus, bypassing the problems posed by the 1930 Act, as well as the defences the liability insurer could have against his assured.

There were, however, objections by some delegates at this session and a compromise was reached to require the carrier, who performs the carriage, to insure without restricting the possible choices as to the different types of insurance available.

Another suggestion made was to bring the Athens Convention into line with the 1999 Montreal Protocol to the Warsaw Convention, thus, change the structure of liability and limitation. The Montreal Protocol provides for a two-tier system of liability for air passengers' claims, namely: (a) strict liability under the first tier, but limited on a *per capita* basis; (b) unlimited liability under the second tier, unless the carrier proves that the accident occurred without his fault, or that of his servants or agents.[34]

This was subject to further discussions, and the Committee met again in March 2000, but no draft was agreed. The preponderance of delegations was in favour of limited changes to the Athens Convention, for example, to increase the limit sufficiently high and provide a right of direct action against liability insurers. The International Group of P&I Clubs proposed that the insurers should be directly responsible to the claimant up to a certain limit, but above that limit the insurers would only be liable to the shipowner by way

---

34 *CMI Newsletter* (1999) No 4.

of indemnity. It was also felt that compulsory insurance, up to a certain limit should not be sacrificed in order to obtain the right of direct action.[35]

It was unfortunate that the CMI initiative for a PAI, or compulsory financial security, was put on one side and, instead, compulsory liability insurance was preferred with an attached right of direct action against the insurer in favour of passengers. This form may resolve only the problems posed by the 1930 Act, but not the problems posed by the MIA 1906. The liability insurers quite understandably, do not wish to derogate the protection given by the MIA 1906.

There was another meeting of the delegates in October 2000, the 82nd Session. It was hoped that a draft text would be agreed for a Diplomatic Conference.[36] (The 83rd Session is due in October 2001.)

3.4 Harbour authorities

Although the Convention does not include harbour authorities, or conservancy authorities, or the owners of docks or canals, in the class of persons who are entitled to limit their liability, s 191 of the MSA 1995 grants them the right of limitation in the UK in respect of claims for damage caused to ships,[37] goods, merchandise or other things whatsoever on board the ship. The basis of limitation is by reference to the tonnage of the largest UK ship, which has been within the area over which the authority discharges any functions at the time of the loss, or within the last five years before the relevant incident. According to s 191(5), the limit of liability shall be ascertained by applying the method of calculation specified in para 1(b) of Art 6, Pt II, Sched 7, read together with para 5(1)(2), Pt II. Dock includes wet docks and basins, tidal dock and basins, locks, cuts, wharves, piers, stages, landing places and jetties (s 191(9)).

---

35 *CMI Newsletter* (October 2000); for the concerns of the liability insurers regarding the proposed increase of limits, see Gaskell, N, 'International News' (2000) *International Maritime Law*, March, p 47.

36 At that time, there was the sinking of *Express Samina* on 26 September 2000 in the Aegean Sea. Although the Athens Convention did not apply to domestic carriage in Greece, it was hoped that this example and other ferry disasters – such as *The Herald of Free Enterprise* in the English Channel, *The MS Estonia* in the Baltic Sea, and *The Marchioness* in the Thames – would urge the delegates to speed up the process of amending the Athens Convention. Perhaps, the European Commission will be sufficiently interested to give priority and speed up the reform to the liability regime in relation to passengers of ships, rather than to oil pollution from tankers.

37 Limitation will, presumably, still apply even if the dock incurs liability by discharging its function of repairing a ship within its area The majority of the House of Lords held that the right was not confined to acts done in their capacity as dockowners but extended to acts done in their capacity as ship-repairers: *The Ruapehlu* [1927] AC 523 (HL).

4 CLAIMS SUBJECT TO LIMITATION

Article 2 provides:

(1) Subject to Art 3 and 4 the following claims, whatever the basis of liability may be, shall be subject to limitation of liability:

    (a) claims in respect of loss of life or personal injury or loss of or damage to property (including damage to harbour works, basin and waterways and aids to navigation), occurring on board or in direct connection with the operation of the ship or with salvage operation, and consequential loss resulting therefrom;

    (b) claims in respect of loss from delay in the carriage by sea or cargo, passengers or their luggage;

    (c) claims in respect of other loss resulting from infringement of rights other than contractual rights, occurring in direct connection with the operation of the ship or salvage operations;

    (d) claims in respect of the raising, removal, destruction or the rendering harmless of a ship which sunk, wrecked, stranded or abandoned, including anything that is or has been on board such ship;

    (e) claims in respect of the removal, destruction or the rendering harmless of the cargo of the ship;

    (f) claims of a person other than the person liable in respect of measures taken in order to avert or minimise loss for which the person liable may limit his liability in accordance with this Convention, and further loss caused by such measures.

(2) Claims set out in para 1 shall be subject to limitation of liability even if brought by way of recourse or for indemnity under a contract or otherwise. However, claims set out under para 1(d), (e) and (f) shall not be subject to limitation of liability to the extent that they relate to remuneration under a contract with the person liable.

4.1 All claims whether for damages or for a debt or indemnity (Art 2(1), (2))

Article 2(1) provides that subject to excluded claims, specified in Art 3, and when there are reasons for barring limitation, as stated in Art 4, limitation shall apply to all claims outlined in sub-paras (a)–(f) whatever the basis of liability may be. Furthermore, it is emphasised in Art 2(2) that claims set out in para 1 shall be subject to limitation of liability, even if brought by way of recourse, or for indemnity under a contract, or otherwise.

This article has altered the position under the UK old regime of limitation when, by s 503 of the 1894 Act, as amended by the 1958 Act, limitation was applicable only to claims for which the shipowner was liable in damages and not for a debt or for an indemnity under contract.[38]

The result is a considerable extension of claims being subject to limitation, which is reinforced for clarification purposes by express provisions, as seen below. It is convenient to start with the express provision regarding limitation for wreck removal expenses and the reservation made by the UK in this respect, and then contrast it with claims brought by way of consequential loss.

4.2 Expenses incurred for wreck removal imposed by law (not being incurred contractually) (Art 2(1)(d), (e))

The predecessor to the 1976 Convention, the 1957 Limitation Convention, (Art 1(1)(c)), had extended the right of limitation of liability imposed by law for expenses relating to removal of wreck. Despite the incorporation of this provision into UK law by the 1958 Act, a reservation had been made by the same Act restricting that provision from coming into force until such a date as the Secretary of State appointed by a statutory instrument, which he did not do. Therefore, the previous limitation statutes were consistent with the common law position.[39]

Similarly, the 1976 Convention preserves the owners' right to limit with respect to claims for expenses incurred for raising, removal, destruction or rendering harmless of a ship which sunk, wrecked, stranded or abandoned, including anything that is or has been on board such a ship (Art 2(1)(d), provided the liability does not relate to remuneration under a contract (Art 2(2)).

The Convention, by Art 18, however, allows States to make reservations. The UK has continued to reserve the position against limitation of liability for claims of harbour authorities (as provided by s 201 of the MSA 1995 and s 56 of the HDPCA 1847) whether or not the expenses have been incurred under contract. Schedule 7 of Pt II, para (3) states that Art 2(1)(d) shall not apply unless provision has been made by an order of the Secretary of State for the setting up of a fund to be used for making payments to the harbour or conservancy authority, as a compensation for the reduction of their expenses by reason of Art 2(1)(d). The reason for this reservation is to protect the public authority's right to recover its expenses in relation to the raising of wrecks in full,[40] but, paradoxically, not in relation to the raising of cargo under para (1)(e). There may have been an oversight in the drafting of the reservation, which is only made in relation to para (1)(d) of Art 2 and not in relation to para (1)(e). The latter refers to claims in respect of the removal,

---

38 *The Kirkness* [1956] 2 Lloyd's Rep 651, in which the owners of the tug, which suffered damages whilst it was towing under a contract of towage containing the usual covenant of indemnity, claimed against the owners of the tow to be indemnified. The latter could not limit their liability.

39 See *The Stonedale (No 1)* [1956] AC 1.

40 See Art 2(2).

destruction or the rendering harmless of the cargo on board the ship. The odd result of this may be that, while a shipowner will not be able to limit, under para (1)(d), for the expenses in relation to the removal, etc, of 'anything that is or has been on board such ship', which might include the cargo on board, he may technically be able to limit under para (1)(e). Whether he will be able to limit only when the cargo is removed from a stranded ship before it has sunk, as has been suggested by Griggs and Williams,[41] is not clear, but it would still seem strange that this fine distinction was intended by the draftsman.

4.3 Claims occurring on board or in direct connection with the operation of the ship or with salvage operations (Art 2(1)(a))

Claims under Art 2, which are subject to limitation, may arise either in contract, or in tort, or through any other cause. Article 2(1)(a) covers claims for loss of life or personal injury when, for example, the crew or passengers of one ship claim damages caused due to negligence of another ship involved in a collision. Similarly, property claims including damage to harbours are included.

As explained earlier, Art 2(1)(a) was primarily drafted this way to overcome the difficulties the salvors had with regard to their inability to limit liability in *The Tojo Maru*.

Previously, only those claims which arose due to negligent acts or omissions done by persons on board, or in the navigation or management of the ship, or in the loading, carriage or discharge of its cargo, or the embarkation, carriage or disembarkation of its passengers, were subject to limitation.

Article 2(1)(a) of the present Convention has widened the scope of limitation quite considerably. The wording 'directly connected with the operation of the ship' is capable of encompassing claims arising from neglect or default of a person (for whose acts or omissions the shipowner is responsible) ashore, such as the superintendent, while he is performing duties in connection with the operation of the ship. It is suggested, by Griggs and Williams, that such claims may encompass claims for personal injury or property damage caused by a person for whose acts, neglect or default the owner is responsible when the vessel is in drydock, and the damage is caused by such a person in performance of an act ashore being directly connected with the operation of the ship. They even suggest that it might encompass damage caused by external repairs and maintenance work and also that it

---

41   *Op cit*, Griggs and Williams, fn 18, p 18.

would probably cover claims arising from the provision of bunkers or supplies, since such services are directly connected with the operation of the ship.[42]

For the purpose of clarification, it is submitted that, while claims for damage caused by negligence during repairs and maintenance work carried out by the crew are clearly within this provision, claims arising from the negligence of independent contractors engaged in drydocking would lie against the contractors and would not fall within the provisions of the Convention.[43] In the case of claims made against the owner or manager for damage caused by defective bunkers supplied to the ship, the ship will be the noxious instrument of damage. The owner or manager should be able to limit his liability if Art 2(1)(a) is construed liberally. The question for construction will be this: do the words 'in direct connection with the operation of the ship' in Art 2(1)(a) mean strictly faulty navigational or managerial operation? Of course, defective bunkers can cause a mechanical fault during the operation of the ship, which then may cause damage to third parties. In that sense, claims against the owner or manager arising from such an incident ought to qualify for limitation.

4.4 Claims for consequential loss under Art 2(1)(a), and a possible anomaly

Real problems arise from the wording of Art 2 and, in relation to other provisions, in the following respects which should be noted carefully. With regard to the reservation made by the UK for unlimited liability for wreck removal expenses of the harbour authority, and with regard to Art 2(2) (providing for no limitation with respect to contractual remuneration under Art 2(1)(d), (e), (f)), unfair results can occur in the light of the wording in Art 2(1)(a), which includes 'consequential loss' without limiting its extent.

An example referred to by the authors of Marsden[44] illustrates the position. Assume that, after a collision incident, a wreck removal becomes necessary; the expenses incurred will be 'consequential loss' of the owner of the wreck against the colliding ship. While the owner of the colliding vessel will be able to limit his liability as against the entire collision liability, including the wreck removal expenses (paid by the owner of the wreck), under Art 2(1)(a), the owner of the wreck will not be able to limit his liability

---

42 *Op cit*, Griggs and William, fn 18, p 16.

43 Claims against the owner caused by unseaworthiness, which was due to the negligence of independent contractors, would be subject to limitation – see paras 3.1.1 and 3.1.3, above.

44 Marsden, *On Collisions at Sea*, 13th edn, 1998, London: Sweet & Maxwell, p 540.

vis à vis the harbour authority, nor his liability to his own contractor engaged to remove the wreck, according to Art 2(2).

Similar situation can arise with Art 2(2) (allowing claims of indemnity to be subject to limitation), Art 2(1)(a) (consequential loss) and Art 3(a), which excludes salvage or contribution in general average from limitation.

For example, the shipowner, in *The Breydon Merchant*,[45] was able to limit liability when the cargo-owners claimed compensation against him with respect to the amount their insurers had to pay to the salvors, who were engaged and successfully salved the ship and cargo in the English Channel when fire broke out on board. The claim was based in damages for breach of contract and the cargo's contribution to the salvage award was regarded as a consequential loss resulting from the fire damage to their property for which salvage was necessary. The judge stressed that it was not a salvage claim against the shipowner, which is only allowed by salvors, so as to be excluded from limitation by Art 3.

It seems highly unlikely that the draftsman of the Convention intended these anomalies in the application of the Convention, when one claimant can limit liability through the 'consequential loss' or indemnity provisions, while another claimant is caught by the exclusions to limitation for a claim of the same nature. Ideally, Art 2(1)(a) should have included expressly, after the words 'consequential loss', that such loss is subject to limitation provided its nature does not fall within those claims for which other provisions of the Convention exclude limitation. It is submitted, therefore, that Art 2(1)(a) should be construed in the light of the other provisions of the Convention. It should be observed that, in the preamble to Art 2(1), it is stated that 'subject to Art 3 and 4 the following claims, whatever the basis of liability may be, shall be subject to limitation of liability'.

4.5 Claims for loss resulting from delay (Art 2(1)(b))

This new provision, under Art 2(1)(b), may be of particular help to the shipowner seeking to limit liability for loss suffered by the cargo-owner due to delay in delivery of the goods under the contract of carriage, as it is not certain whether Art IV, r 5(a) of the HVR includes such claims. However, this would create a conflict between the provisions of the two limitation regimes.

4.6 Claims for rights which have been infringed (Art 2(1)(c))

Claims in respect of other loss, resulting from infringement of rights which occur in direct connection with the operation of the ship, or salvage

---

45 *The Breydon Merchant* [1992] 1 Lloyd's Rep 373.

operations, are subject to limitation, provided they do not arise from contractual rights. This may include rights of access into a port by other ships, or the rights of the port itself, if the port is obstructed by a stranded ship which prevents a right of passage or use of the port facilities.

4.7 Claims in respect of measures taken in order to avert or minimise loss (Art 2(1)(f))

Sub-paragraph 1(f) should be read together with the second sentence of Art 2(2) which makes it clear that limitation will not apply to claims relating to remuneration under contract with the person liable. It is also made clear, by the insertion of the words 'claims of the person other than the person liable', that claims under para (f), which incur by reason of the steps taken to prevent or minimise loss, are only claims made against the shipowner (the person liable). An example of loss 'for which the person liable may limit liability' is a claim made by a cargo-owner whose cargo is in peril of loss and measures are taken by a third party to minimise such loss of the cargo on board for which the shipowner would be liable and able to limit his liability. The costs of those measures when paid in full by the cargo-owner to the salvor can be claimed against the shipowner who can limit his liability under this sub-paragraph, but he cannot limit if he took those measures himself. He could also limit his liability to the cargo-owner if further damage was caused to the cargo in the course of taking such measures to avert or minimise loss.[46]

5 CLAIMS EXCEPTED FROM LIMITATION (ART 3(a)–(e))

Article 3 provides:

The rules of this Convention shall not apply to:

(a) claims for salvage or contribution in general average;

(b) claims for oil pollution damage within the meaning of the International Convention on Civil Liability for Oil Pollution damage ...;

(c) claims subject to any international convention or national legislation covering or prohibiting limitation of liability for nuclear damage;

(d) claims against the shipowner of a nuclear ship for nuclear damage;

(e) claims by servants of the shipowner or salvors whose duties are connected with the ship or salvage operations, including claims of their heirs, dependants or other persons entitled to make such claims, if under the law governing the contract of service between the shipowner or salvor and such servants the shipowner or salvor is not entitled to limit his liability in

---

46 See, also, *op cit*, Griggs and Williams, fn 18, pp 19, 22.

respect of such claims, or if he is by such law only permitted to limit his liability to an amount greater than that provided for in Art 6.

5.1 Salvage and contribution in general average claims

Claims excluded from limitation under Art 3(a) are direct claims against the shipowner (as defined in Art 1(2)) by salvors, or by a party who has incurred a general average loss or sacrifice. But, as has been discussed earlier, if a cargo-owner has paid his proportion of salvage, or of general average, to the party entitled to it, he can claim that amount by way of damages or indemnity against the shipowner, in which case limitation of liability will apply to that claim.

A new Protocol 1996, amending the 1976 Convention, has been agreed, which intends to increase the potential liabilities of shipowners and their insurers when it comes into force. One of the amendments in this connection is of Art 3(a) as follows:

> Claims for salvage, including, if applicable, any claim for special compensation under Art 14 of the International Convention on Salvage 1989, as amended, or contribution in general average.

This provision has already been given effect in the UK by para 4(1), Pt II of Sched 7 to the MSA 1995, so the compensation due to salvors under Art 14, or equivalent contractual provision, is not subject to limitation for the obvious reason of providing encouragement to salvors.

5.2 Claims for oil pollution

Claims for oil pollution damage, within the meaning of the Civil Liability Convention (CLC) as amended by the 1992 Protocol, are excepted from limitation under this Convention (Art 3(b)) because they are dealt with separately by the specialised Convention and, insofar as the UK is concerned, by s 153 of the MSA 1995. In this connection, it should be noted that, while under the 1976 Convention the owner, charterer, manager or operator of a ship may limit liability, under the CLC, only the owner can. Having excluded limitation for oil pollution from the 1976 Convention, it means that the ship-manager or operator of a ship, the charterer, or the salvor are unable to limit, unless domestic legislation addresses this gap.

Insofar as the UK is concerned, para 4(2), Pt II, Sched 7 to the MSA 1995 expressly limits the exclusion from limitation with regard to oil pollution to 'claims in respect of any liability incurred under s 153 of the MSA 1995', which refers to pollution liability of the owner of the ship. Thus, it seems that the liability for oil pollution of a ship-manager or operator, as well as of a charterer and of a salvor, may be limited under the 1976 Convention.

Similarly, since the CLC does not deal with bunker spills, nor does Art 3(b) of the 1976 Convention exclude that liability from limitation, it follows that losses from bunker spills and consequential financial losses are subject to limitation under Art 2(1) of this Convention. A new Convention on Civil Liability for Bunker Oil Pollution was agreed on 23 March 2001, which will permit limitation under the general law of limitation, whether this is applicable by national law, or by international convention.

5.3 Nuclear damage claims

Claims subject to any international convention for nuclear damage (under Art 3(c)) are excluded from limitation, to the extent that there is an international convention dealing with these claims. However, under UK law, para 4, Pt II, Sched 7, stipulates that such claims are claims made by virtue of ss 7–11 of the Nuclear Installation Act 1965. The 1965 Act allows limitation in certain circumstances. With regard to Art 3(d), nuclear damage done by a nuclear ship is outside the scope of the 1976 Convention, but, in the UK, such damage is dealt with by a separate statute, the Liability of Operators of Nuclear Ships Act 1962.

5.4 Claims by the master and crew against employers

Claims under Art 3(e) are not, strictly speaking, excepted from limitation as the title of this article indicates. Article 3(e) refers to the law governing the contract of employment of the master and crew. If that law is the law of any part of the UK, s 185(4) of the MSA 1995 has re-enacted s 35 of the MSA 1979 and exercises the option of Art 3(b) of unlimited liability for claims by the master and crew against their employer. Section 185(4) provides that the provisions of the Convention shall not apply to any liability for loss of life, or personal injury caused to, or loss of or damage to any property of, a person who is on board the ship in question, or employed in connection with that ship, or with the salvage operations in question if (a) he is on board or employed under a contract of service governed by the law of any part of the UK; and (b) the liability arose from an occurrence that took place after the commencement of this Act (that is, 1 January 1996).

If the law of the contract is foreign, one has to find out whether the law governing the contract provides for unlimited liability, or for limitation which is lower than that provided by Art 6 of the Convention. If the former is provided, then the limitation of the Convention shall not apply; if the latter is provided, then the limitation of the Convention shall apply. If the limitation is greater than that of Art 6, then the greater limitation shall apply to crew claims.

A very important House of Lords' decision, regarding the duty owed by the employer to their employees and limitation of liability, should be mentioned in this connection, albeit that it was decided under the old system of limitation: *McDermid v Nash Dredging.*[47]

The plaintiff was employed by the defendants as a deckhand. In the course of his employment, he worked on board a tug owned by a Dutch company and under the control of a Dutch captain employed by them. The plaintiff's work included untying ropes mooring the tug fore and aft to a dredger. The system used by the captain was that, when the plaintiff had untied the ropes and it was safe for the captain to move the tug, the plaintiff would give a double knock with his hand on the wheelhouse. While the plaintiff had untied the aft rope but was still in the course of untying the forward rope, the captain, without waiting for the plaintiff's signal, put the engine of the tug hard astern. As a result, the rope snaked round the plaintiff's leg causing him serious injury. On his claim against the defendants for damages for, *inter alia*, negligence, Staughton J held that his injuries had been caused by the captain's negligence and that, therefore, the defendants were vicariously liable for his negligence to the plaintiff. He also held, however, that the defendants were entitled to limit their liability by virtue of s 503 of the MSA 1894 as extended by s 3 of the MS(LSO)A 1958. The Court of Appeal dismissed an appeal by the defendants on the question of liability and allowed a cross-appeal by the plaintiff on the limitation point.

On appeal by the defendants, the House of Lords held, dismissing the appeal, that: the defendants owed the plaintiff a duty of care to devise a safe system of work for him and to see that that system was operated; that, assuming that the captain's system of waiting for a double knock on the wheelhouse before putting the tug in motion could be called a safe system, it had not been operated at the time of the plaintiff's accident and the captain's negligence in not operating it had not been casual or collateral, but had been central to the operation of the system; that the defendants' duty of care was non-delegable in the sense that they were personally liable for its performance and could not escape their liability, if it was delegated and not

---

47 *McDermid v Nash Dredging & Reclamation Co Ltd* [1987] AC 906 (HL).

properly performed; and that, accordingly, although they had delegated the performance of their duty of care to the captain, they could not thereby avoid their own liability to the plaintiff.

5.5 Claims by harbour authorities for expenses in relation to wreck raising or removal in the UK

This is covered by para 3, Pt II, Sched 7 of the MSA 1995, which is concerned with the reservation made by the UK against limitation of liability with respect to harbour or conservancy authorities' claims, whether contractual or otherwise, for expenses in connection with the raising of a sunk ship, including anything that is, or has been, on board. The reservation will prevail until provision is made by an order of the Secretary of State for the setting up and management of a fund to be used for the making of payments to such authorities to compensate them for the reduction in consequence of limitation under Art 2(1)(d).

5.6 Claims of contractors with shipowners in respect of steps taken to avert or minimise loss

It was seen in para 4.7 (above), that claims of a person (other than the person liable) in respect of measures taken in order to avert or minimise loss, for which the person liable may limit his liability in accordance with this Convention, and further loss caused by such measures, are subject to limitation by Art 2(1)(f). However, Art 2(2) excludes from limitation claims for remuneration of contractors who have taken such measures.

6 EXCLUSION OF TOTAL LIABILITY

With regard to British ships, the old statute, s 502 of the MSA 1894, provided for exclusion of shipowners' liability for any loss or damage to property (such as cargo) caused by *fire on board, or to valuables by reason of theft, provided the nature and value of valuables had not been declared to the owner at the time of shipment.* An overriding qualification to exclusion from liability was that the loss or damage did not result from the owner's actual fault or privity. Damage by fire includes damage caused by smoke or water to put the fire out.[48]

This section was repealed and replaced by s 18(1)(a) of the MSA 1979, which maintained the exclusion for the same claims but adopted the test for breaking the right of exclusion from Art 4 of the 1976 Convention. The same provision is now found in s 186(1) of the MSA 1995. This section applies to property so damaged or lost on British ships (except passenger vessels[49] and claims for loss of, or damage to property of persons employed on board, or in connection with the ship, or with salvage operations).[50] Paragraph 3, s 186, adopts the same test for breaking the right to exclude liability as provided in Art 4 of the Convention (examined below). Therefore, the position with these claims for fire or theft of valuables is either total exclusion, or a bar to exclusion, if there is proof of the conduct required by Art 4 of the Convention.[51]

While the following case was decided under the old law with regard to the provision barring the exclusion, it is still relevant to the question whether the fire needs to be the direct cause of the loss or not.

---

48 *The Diamond* [1906] P 28: the crew on board the vessel caused an outbreak of fire by negligently overheating a stove. The plaintiffs' bags of flour and bran on board the vessel were damaged by the fire, smoke and the water used to extinguish the fire. The plaintiffs alleged that the vessel was unseaworthy because the stove was placed too near a bulkhead without any means of insulation and the defendant was privy to the position of the stove. Therefore, they alleged, the defendant was not entitled to exclude his liability on the basis of the MSA 1894, s 502(2). Also, that damage by smoke and water used to extinguish the fire were not within the scope of the statute. It was held that the stove was not placed in an improper position rendering the vessel unseaworthy. Therefore, there was no actual fault or privity on the part of the owners. The judge also held that the water and smoke were matters which occurred by reason of the fire, thus, they were covered under provisions of the statute.

49 The MSA 1995, para 13, Pt II, Sched 6, which incorporates the Athens Convention 1974, expressly states that s 186 shall not relieve a person of any liability imposed on him by the Athens Convention.

50 For such claims, limitation is not allowed either by s 185(4) (and previously by s 35 of the MSA 1979).

51 With regard to contracts for the carriage of goods by sea, to which the HVR apply, there is no exclusion from liability, but s 6(4) provides that the right of the British shipowner under the MSA 1995, s 186, is to be treated as a matter of limitation of liability. HVR, Art VIII states that these rules shall not affect the rights and obligations of the carrier under any statute, for the time being in force, relating to limitation of the liability of owners of sea-going ships.

Louis Dreyfus v Tempus Shipping[52]

The plaintiffs' ship left Cardiff with a cargo of coal under charter for the Plate, and there entered into a charterparty to load grain for ports in the UK and the continent. The defendants were indorsees of the bill of lading issued under the latter charterparty.

In the course of the voyage, fire broke out on board in the coal bunkers and a quantity of grain had to be discharged into a lighter. In consequence of the fire, damage was caused to the grain, as the court found, 'owing to incandescence of the coal and later owing to the coal being actually on fire before discharge'.

The shipowner claimed a general average contribution, but the court found that the coal was unfit for the voyage and that the vessel was unseaworthy. The then applicable York-Antwerp Rules 1924, r D, being incorporated in the charterparty, provided that, 'rights to contribution in general average shall not be affected though the event which gave rise to the sacrifice or expenditure may have been due to the fault of one of the parties to the adventure; but this shall not prejudice any remedies which may be open against that party for such fault'.

It was held that the shipowners could not avail themselves of the rule, there being no express words to exclude the warranty of seaworthiness.

With regard to the defendants' counterclaim for damage to the grain, the shipowners sought to rely on s 502 providing for exclusion of liability. The defendants contended that the plaintiffs could not rely on this provision, as there was no evidence of fire on board, but only heating, so far as the goods were concerned. It was held that the damage or loss of the grain in the lighter was the direct and necessary consequence of the coal on board being on fire. For while the section requires a causal connection between the loss or damage and the fire on board, this need not be by actual contact, if it is operative in fact. As the fire occurred without the actual fault or privity of the shipowners, they were freed from liability.

As far as theft of valuables on board is concerned, the exclusion of liability under s 186 of the MSA 1995 will be operative, if neither the nature nor the value of valuables carried on board were declared at the time of the shipment. The justification for this exclusion is that it would be unfair to make the shipowner liable for highly expensive cargo for which he did not have an opportunity, if its value was not declared, to charge higher freight. Again the exclusion shall not apply if the conduct required under Art 4 of the Convention is proved (s 186(3)).

---

52 [1930] 1 KB 699.

The following case, although it was decided under the previous law, illustrates the kind of declaration that needs to be made for the exclusion not to be applicable.

Williams v The African Steam Ship Co[53]

The plaintiff delivered four bags and one box of gold dust of the value of 2,000*l* on the defendant's vessel to be delivered in London. Upon discharge, they claimed that the defendants failed to deliver one bag and one box of the gold dust and that their loss was due to the improper care and conduct of the defendants. The defendants averred that the valuables were stolen out of the ship without their own actual fault or privity. They also contended that the plaintiff did not insert into the bill of lading, nor declare in writing to the master or owner, the nature and value of the goods on board. It was held that the nature of the gold was sufficiently stated (that is, 'gold dust'), but an exact statement of the quantity shipped was missing. Even an estimation of the quantity was unstated. Therefore, the shipowner was not liable for the loss. The judge added that:

> The only case where the description would be sufficient without an express statement of the value, seems to me to be where the shipment consists of coin; there it may be enough to state the number and description of the coins.[54]

Section 186 does not mention whether limitation of liability will apply when the nature and value of such valuables have been declared and loss or damage occurs, as it is expressly stated under the Athens Convention. By comparison, Art 5 of the Athens Convention provides that the carrier shall not be liable for valuables, unless they have been deposited with the carrier for the purpose of safekeeping, in which case the carrier shall be liable up to the limit provided for by this Convention.

7 CONDUCT BARRING LIMITATION OR EXCLUSION OF LIABILITY

Limitation provisions have rules defining when the right to limit is lost, apart from the Hague Rules which do not attempt to restrict the carrier's right to

---

53 [1856] H&N 300.
54 *Ibid*, at p 305.

limit under Art IV, r 5, where it is stated that: 'Neither the carrier nor the ship shall in any event become liable for any loss or damage to or in connection with the goods in an amount exceeding ... unless the nature and value of such goods have been declared by the shipper before shipment and inserted in the bill of lading.'

Under the 1976 Convention, it is difficult, if not impossible, to break the right to limit. The Party States to the Convention agreed this stringent test in exchange for higher limits. Article 4, provides:

> A person liable shall not be entitled to limit his liability if it is proved that the loss resulted from his personal act or omission, committed with the intent to cause *such loss*, or recklessly and with knowledge that such loss would probably result.

The Athens Convention 1974, Art 13 provides, similarly:

> The carrier shall not be entitled to the benefit of the limits of liability prescribed in Arts 7 and 8 and para 1 of Art 10, if it is proved that the damage resulted from an act or omission of the carrier done with intent to cause such damage, or recklessly and with knowledge that *such damage* would probably result

Article IV, r 5(c) of the HVR has almost the same wording:

> Neither the carrier nor the ship shall be entitled to the benefit of the limitation of liability provided for in this paragraph if it is proved that the damage resulted from an act or omission of the carrier done with intent to cause damage, or recklessly and with knowledge that *damage* would probably result.

The Warsaw Convention 1929 as amended by Art 13 of The Hague Protocol 1955, hence, the CAA 1961, similarly provides by Art 25:

> The limits of the liability specified in Art 22 shall not apply if it is proved that the damage resulted from an act or omission of the carrier, his servants or agents, done with intent to cause damage, or recklessly and with knowledge that damage would probably result; provided that, in the case of such act or omission of a servant or agent, it is also proved that he was acting within the scope of his employment.

While, under the 1976 Convention, 'loss' is only mentioned and in the other three Conventions (the Athens Convention, the HVR and The Warsaw Convention) reference to 'damage' is only made, Art 8 of the Hamburg Rules provides more certainty by referring to *loss, or damage, or delay*:

> The carrier is not entitled to the benefit of the limitation of liability provided for in Art 6 if it is proved that the loss, damage, or delay in delivery resulted from an act or omission of the carrier done with intent to cause such loss, damage or delay, or recklessly and with knowledge that such loss, damage or delay would probably result.

There are slight but not insignificant differences in the wording of these provisions, which may have material effect on the test of breaking limitation to some extent, as will be discussed later.

The test for breaking limitation is, however, strict under the above provisions.

7.1 Comparison between the 'fault and privity' system and the present systems of limitation

7.1.1. Burden of proof

Under ss 503 and 502 of the MSA 1894, as amended by the MSA 1958 following the 1957 Limitation Convention, the claimant was entitled to full compensation unless the shipowner, who claimed that he was entitled to limit, or be excluded from liability, discharged the burden of proof that the loss was caused without his 'actual fault or privity'. Many cases were litigated and it was usually difficult for the shipowner to discharge this burden.

Under the 1976 Convention, the philosophy underlying the new system, as reflected in the wording of Art 2(1) ('subject to Arts 3 and 4 the following claims ... shall be subject to limitation of liability'), is that the right to limit shall apply automatically, unless it is proved by the claimant that the party seeking to limit is guilty of the misconduct barring limitation under Art 4. The court is not obliged to investigate whether or not the person liable is guilty of conduct barring limitation when that person commences a limitation action.[55] The effect of Art 4 is that, once the person liable has established that the claim falls within the claims mentioned in Art 2, he is entitled to a decree of limitation, unless the claimant proves the facts required by Art 4[56] (for example, that the loss resulted from the personal act or omission of the shipowner, or other person liable, committed with the intent to cause such loss, or recklessly and with knowledge that such loss would probably result).

It is obvious that not only is the burden of proof difficult to discharge, but also it is now upon the claimant and not upon the shipowner, as it used to be under the old law.[57] The same applies under the other Conventions mentioned earlier but with the following differences.

(a) *Whose act or omission?* It is the carrier's act or omission under the Athens Convention, the HVR and the Hamburg Rules, while under the 1976 Convention it is emphasised that it is the personal act or omission of the person liable as referred to therein (see, further, para 7.1.2, below). Under the Warsaw Convention, it is the act or omission of the carrier his servants or agents.

---

55 *The Bowbelle* [1990] 3 All ER 476, *per* Sheen J.
56 *The Capitan San Luis* [1994] 1 All ER 1016, *per* Clarke J.
57 *The Norman* [1960] 1 Lloyd's Rep 1 (HL).

(b) *Whose conduct?* Article 1 of the 1976 Convention defines the persons who are entitled to limit and who have a separate right from each other, that is, the 'person liable'. It is the conduct of that person (as regards a corporate body, see para 8, below). The other Conventions define who is the carrier whose conduct is important. Under the HVR, Art 1, the 'carrier' includes the owner or the charterer who enters into a contract of carriage covered by a bill of lading, or similar document of title. Under the Athens Convention, Art 1, 'carrier' means the person in whose name the contract is concluded. He remains responsible, by Art 4, even if the performing carrier performs the contract. The performing carrier means a person other than the carrier, who may be the owner, or the charterer, or the operator of the passengers' ship. Under the Hamburg Rules, the 'carrier' is the person named in the contract of carriage, and 'actual carrier' is the person entrusted by the carrier to perform the contract. The carrier remains responsible for the acts or omission of the actual carrier and of his servants and agents.

(c) *In relation to what loss or damage?* The conduct mentioned in the 1976 Convention is related to 'such loss' and in the Athens Convention is related to 'such damage' that occurred. The Hamburg Rules, more explicitly, refer to 'such loss, damage or delay'. The HVR and the Warsaw Convention refer to 'damage' (for the interpretation of these words, see para 7.1.5, below).

7.1.2. Personal act or omission versus acts or omissions of others

Section 503 of the 1894 Act, as amended, provided that:

(1) The owners of a ship, British or foreign, shall not, where all or any of the following occurrences take place without their actual fault or privity ... be liable beyond the following amounts.

It is important to set out para (c) of this section in order to compare it with the present Convention in relation to 'act or omission'.

(c) Where any loss of life or personal injury is caused to any person not carried in the ship through the act or omission of any person (whether on board the ship or not) in the navigation or management of the ship in the loading, carriage or discharge of its cargo or in the embarkation, carriage or disembarkation of its passengers, or through any other act or omission of any person on board the ship.

Similar wording had been adopted in relation to loss of or damage to property under para (d). It is to be noted that under the old law, it was the 'act or omission of any person', and not the 'personal act or omission' of the person claiming limitation, that was taken into account for limitation purposes.

On the construction given to this wording by the courts, the owners were not able to limit their liability incurred by the fault of a person to whom a task had been delegated by them, unless they could show that the particular occurrence took place without their actual fault or privity.

By contrast, Art 4 of the 1976 Convention has restricted the 'act or omission' or the 'fault of any person' to the 'personal act or omission' of the person liable. For example, even if the act or omission which causes the loss is that of the master of the ship, or any of the crew members acting in the course of their employment, the owner, or salvor, or the charterer or the manager or operator of the ship, whoever was vicariously responsible for the acts or omissions of those servants, would still be able to limit his liability, even if the employee was guilty of the misconduct described in Art 4. Also, if the act or omission is that of the owner's agent, for example, the manager of the ship, the owner will be able to limit, whilst under the old law he was not able to limit for the fault of his agents or servants, if he could not prove that the damage occurred without his actual fault or privity.[58]

The manager or operator, or the master and crew will be able to limit independently, provided their act or omission which caused the loss was not committed with intent to cause such loss, or recklessly and with knowledge that such loss would probably result.

If, however, the manager or operator is not a third party ship-management company, but is integrated within the owner's corporate structure, questions may arise with regard to who was the 'directing mind'[59] of the owning and managing companies, as, invariably, the mind and control of both companies may be the same.

A material difference exists in the wording of Art 25 of the Warsaw Convention stating that it is also the misconduct of the carriers' servants or agents which will disqualify the carrier from limitation.

The other Conventions do not require 'a personal' act or omission of the carrier, but just 'act or omission of the carrier'. However, it can be derived from the *travaux preparatoires* to these Conventions that it is only the misconduct of the carrier himself which will defeat the right to limit. This interpretation has been accepted by the English courts in relation to the HVR and the Athens Convention.[60]

7.1.3 'Fault or privity' versus 'intent or recklessly and with knowledge'

The words 'fault or privity' under the old system of limitation were interpreted by Lord Denning MR in *The Eurysthenes*,[61] which concerned the

---

58 *The Marion* [1984] 2 Lloyd's Rep 1.

59 The concept of the *alter ego* is discussed in para 8.

60 *Op cit*, Griggs and Williams, fn 18, p 27; Diamond, A (QC), 'The Hague-Visby Rules' [1978] LMCLQ 225; *The European Enterprise* [1989] 2 Lloyd's Rep 195; *The Lion* [1990] 2 Lloyd's Rep 144.

61 [1976] 2 Lloyd's Rep 171 (CA).

interpretation only of the word 'privity' under s 39(5) of the MIA 1906, but the historical development of these words, as used in the MSAs in relation to limitation, was analysed, thus:

> I have looked into the history of the word 'privity' in this context and find it to be as follows: according to the old common law, the master of a servant was only responsible for the acts of his servant if they were done 'by his command or with his privity'. But, if the acts were done by the servant in the course of the master's service, and for his master's benefit, they were presumed to be done by the authority of the master 'although no express command or privity of his master was proved', see *Turberville v Stamp* (1697) Raym 264; *Huzzey v Field* (1835) 2 CM&R 440, in which the judgment was written by Baron Parke. On the other hand, the owner of a ship was absolutely liable for the loss of goods, because he was a common carrier and liable by the custom of the realm, even though they were stolen without his fault or privity. That was settled in 1674 in the great case of *Morse v Slue* (1674) 1 Vent 190, p 238. That operated so harshly on shipowners that in 1734 Parliament passed the first of the MSAs (7 Geo 11 c 65) saying that a shipowner was not to be held liable for any loss or damage occasioned by the master or mariners 'without the privity and knowledge' of the owner to an amount greater than the value of the ship. This was followed by a succession of MSAs, all of them directed to limiting the responsibilities of the shipowner for the acts or defaults of his servants. He was not to be liable for acts done 'without his fault or privity' beyond the value of the vessel. The object of these Acts was to limit his liability for his servants on the basis of *respondeat superior*, but to leave him fully liable for faults done by himself personally or with his privity – see *Wilson v Dickson* (1818) 2 B&A 2, *The Spirit of the Ocean* (1865) B&L 336, p 339, *per* Dr Lushington; *Asiatic Petroleum Co v Lennard's Carrying Co* [1914] 1 KB 419, p 432, *per* Buckley LJ. This distinction underlies the provision of the MSA 1894, which limits the liability of a shipowner for damage or loss of goods which takes place 'without his actual fault or privity' but leaves him fully liable for acts done by his actual fault or with his privity.

> This historical survey shows to my mind that, when the old common lawyers spoke of a man being 'privy' to something being done, or of an act being done 'with his privity', they meant that he knew of it beforehand and concurred in it being done. If it was a wrongful act done by his servant, then he was liable for it if it was done 'by his command or privity', that is, with his express authority or with his knowledge and concurrence. 'Privity' did not mean that there was any wilful misconduct by him, but only that he knew of the act beforehand and concurred in it being done. Moreover, 'privity' did not mean that he himself personally did the act, but only that someone else did it and that he knowingly concurred in it. Hence, in the later MSAs, the owner was entitled to limit his liability if the act was done without his 'actual fault or privity'. Without his 'actual fault' meant without any actual fault by the owner personally. Without his 'privity' meant without his knowledge or concurrence.

> Such is, I think, the meaning we should attach to the word 'privity' in s 39(5). If the ship is sent to sea in an unseaworthy state, with the knowledge and concurrence of the assured personally, the insurer is not liable for any loss

attributable to unseaworthiness, that is, to unseaworthiness of which he knew and in which he concurred.

> To disentitle the shipowner, he must, I think, have knowledge, not only of the facts constituting the unseaworthiness, but also knowledge that those facts rendered the ship unseaworthy, that is, not reasonably fit to encounter the ordinary perils of the sea. And, when I speak of knowledge, I mean not only positive knowledge but also the sort of knowledge expressed in the phrase 'turning a blind eye'. If a man, suspicious of the truth, turns a blind eye to it, and refrains from inquiry – so that he should not know it for certain – then he is to be regarded as knowing the truth. This 'turning a blind eye' is far more blameworthy than mere negligence. Negligence in not knowing the truth is not equivalent to knowledge of it.[62]

Thus, under the old limitation system without his 'actual fault' meant without any actual fault by the owner, personally, and without his 'privity' meant without his knowledge and concurrence, but not necessarily amounting to willful misconduct. The present system clearly requires either willful misconduct ('intent') or 'recklessness' and, in addition to recklessness, the person liable must have had particular 'knowledge that such loss would probably result'.

These words have been interpreted in criminal law and, in the context of Art 25 of the Warsaw Convention, in connection with claims by air passengers. The latter interpretation is relevant here and it is important to look at it in some detail, after examining the definition given to 'recklessness' in criminal law by way of a contrast.

Under criminal law 'intent' means the subjective intent (*mens rea*) of the person liable. 'Recklessly' had been interpreted to encompass both an objective and a subjective test. Lord Diplock defined the test in *R v Caldwell*:[63]

> ... to decide whether someone has been 'reckless' as to whether harmful consequences of a particular kind will result from his act, as distinguished from his actually intending such harmful consequences to follow, does call for some consideration of how the mind of the ordinary prudent individual would have reacted to a similar situation. If there were nothing in the circumstances that ought to have drawn the attention of an ordinary prudent individual to the possibility of that kind of harmful consequence, the accused would not be described as 'reckless' in the natural meaning of that word for failing to address his mind to the possibility; nor, if the risk of the harmful consequences was so slight that the ordinary prudent individual upon due consideration of the risk would not be deterred from treating it as negligible, could the accused be described as 'reckless' in its ordinary sense if, having considered the risk, he decided to ignore it.[64]

---

62 [1976] 2 Lloyd's Rep 171, pp 178–79.

63 [1982] AC 341 (HL).

64 *Ibid*, p 354.

Although Lord Hailsham expressed his distaste, in **R v Lawrence**,[65] at the excessive use of the words 'objective' and 'subjective', he agreed with Lord Diplock's definition of recklessness by saying:

I share the distaste for the obsessive use of the expressions 'objective' and 'subjective' in crime. In all indictable crime, it is a general rule that there are objective factors of conduct which constitute the so called *'actus reus,'* and a further guilty state of mind which constitutes the so called *'mens rea'*. The necessity for this guilty state of mind has been increasingly emphasised of recent years (see *R v Sheppard* [1981] AC 394) and this I regard as a thoroughly praiseworthy development. It only surprises me that there should have been any question regarding the existence of *mens rea* in relation to the words 'reckless,' 'recklessly' or 'recklessness'. Unlike most English words, reckless has been in the English language as a word in general use at least since the eighth century AD, almost always with the same meaning applied to a person or conduct evincing a state of mind stopping short of deliberate intention, and going beyond mere inadvertence, or in its modern, though not its etymological and original sense, mere carelessness ... It is, of course, true that in a legal context, the state of mind described as 'reckless' is discussed in connection with conduct objectively blameworthy, as well as dangerous.[66]

'Recklessness' in the context of criminal law is a subjective realisation that something done, which is objectively blameworthy, is wrong, but there is indifference as to its consequences by the person who does it.

However, the Court of Appeal, in **Goldman v Thai Airways International**,[67] cautioned against construing an international Convention on the basis of English statutes and Eveleigh LJ said:

When conduct is stigmatised as reckless, it is because it engenders the risk of undesirable consequences. When a person acts recklessly he acts in a manner which indicates a decision to run the risk or a mental attitude of indifference to its existence. This is the ordinary meaning of the word, as I understand it, and, as it seems to me, Lord Diplock and Lord Hailsham of St Marylebone LC understood it in the quotations above referred to. One cannot, therefore, decide whether or not an act or omission is done recklessly without considering the nature of the risk involved. In the present case, the omission relied upon was the failure to order seat belts to be fastened. The risk with which we are concerned, therefore, is the risk of injury to the passenger whose belt should have been fastened. If the article had stopped at the word 'recklessly', I would have been prepared to say that, on the judge's findings, the plaintiff had proved his case. This is because, on those findings, the pilot had deliberately ignored his instructions which he knew were for the safety of the passengers, and, thus, demonstrated a willingness to accept a risk. Also, it might be said that he thought that he knew better than those responsible for the manual and, while this might mean that he in his own mind saw no risk, he was, in fact,

---

65 [1982] AC 510 (HL).

66 *Ibid*, pp 520–21.

67 [1983] 1 WLR 1186.

taking the risk that his judgment was better than that of other experts. If this is so, I would be prepared to say, as did the judge, that a deliberate disregard of the rule must be considered recklessness in the circumstances of the case. I shall consider later whether or not a deliberate disregard of instructions has been proved. However, the doing of the act or omission is not only qualified by the adverb 'recklessly', but also by the adverbial phrase 'with knowledge that damage would probably result'. If the pilot did not know that damage would probably result from his omission, I cannot see that we are entitled to attribute to him knowledge which another pilot might have possessed or which he himself should have possessed. I appreciate that, when introducing an English version to coincide with a French text, there is naturally an inclination to follow the pattern of that text and where possible to avoid a free translation. Even so, I cannot believe that lawyers who intended to convey the meaning of the well known phrase 'when he knew or ought to have known' would have adopted 'with knowledge'.[68]

... An act may be reckless when it involves a risk, even though it cannot be said that the danger envisaged is a probable consequence. It is enough that it is a possible consequence, although of course there comes a point where the risk is so remote that it would not be considered reckless to take it. We look for an element of rashness which is perhaps more clearly indicated in the French text '*temerairement*', Art 25, however, refers not to possibility, but to the probability of resulting damage. Thus, something more than a possibility is required. The word 'probable' is a common enough word. I understand it to mean that something is likely to happen. I think that is what is meant in Art 25. In other words, one anticipates damage from the act or omission.[69]

The modified definition of 'recklessness' by the Court of Appeal in the context of the Convention, being interpreted not in isolation but with the additional words 'and with knowledge that damage would probably result', makes the test subjective. So, a person acts recklessly in relation to a particular risk when he anticipates that damage would be likely to happen from his act or omission.

Lord Eveleigh continued:

I say at once that, reading Art 25 as a whole for the moment and not pausing to give an isolated meaning to the word 'recklessly', the article requires the plaintiff to prove the following: (1) that the damage resulted from an act or omission; (2) that it was done with intent to cause damage; or (3) that it was done when the doer was aware that damage would probably result, but he did so regardless of that probability; (4) that the damage complained of is the kind of damage known to be the probable result.[70]

The provision of barring limitation requires, therefore, that there must be either actual knowledge or a deliberate shutting of the eyes to a means of

---

68   [1983] 1 WLR 1186, p 1194.
69   *Ibid*, p 1196.
70   *Ibid*, p 1194.

knowledge, which if used, would have produced the same realisation. The 'shut eye' or 'blind eye' knowledge does not include constructive knowledge.[71] In other words, there is a clear distinction in the legislature between what a person ought to (or should) have known and what a person must have known (or did know).[72] The move to identify actual knowledge and to reject imputed knowledge is an indicator of the narrow scope intended for the provision by the 1955/56 Hague Conference which amended Art 25 of the Warsaw Convention. The greater the obviousness of the risk, the more likely the tribunal is to infer recklessness and that the defendant, in so doing, knew that he would probably cause damage.[73]

A similarity of reasoning is exhibited in another context, in marine insurance, in which the word 'privity' had to be construed. The Court of Appeal, in *The Star Sea*,[74] defined the kind of knowledge that a person of the shipowning company – responsible in seeing that the ship was seaworthy before she was sent to sea – ought to possess in order for the insurer to be able to discharge the burden that the ship was sent to sea in an unseaworthy condition with the privity of the assured, under s 39(5) of the MIA 1906, and said on this issue:

> However negligent it might have been not to learn lessons from the previous fires on *Centaurus* or *Kastora*, or to fail to give proper instructions in fire-fighting, what the underwriters had to establish was a suspicion or realisation in the mind of at least one of the relevant individuals that *Star Sea* was unseaworthy in one of the relevant respects and a decision not to check whether that was so for fear of having certain knowledge of it ... To succeed, the underwriters would have to establish that one or other of the individuals, Lou Kollakis, George Kollakis or Mr Faraklas, suspected that the master was incompetent in lacking the knowledge as to how to use CO_2 and that that rendered *Star Sea* unseaworthy, but that he decided not to check for fear of having certain knowledge and allowed the ship to go to sea anyway.[75]

Leggatt LJ, in particular, stressed that:

> An allegation that they ought to have known is not an allegation that they suspected or realised, but did not make further enquiries.[76]

The House of Lords recently approved the decision of the Court of Appeal and Lord Clyde said:

---

71 See, also, the same construction given in the context of Art 5(a) of the HVR, in *op cit*, Diamond, fn 60, p 246.

72 See, also, *Rolls Royce v HVD* [2000] 1 Lloyd's Rep 653, p 659.

73 *Nugent v Goss Aviation* [2000] 2 Lloyd's Rep 222 (CA), pp 227, 232: 'As a matter of proof, the two will often stand or fall together.'

74 [1997] 1 Lloyd's Rep 360 (CA).

75 *Ibid*, p 377 (the House of Lords recently (18 January 2001) approved the decision of the Court of Appeal).

76 *Ibid* (CA), p 378.

Blind eye knowledge requires a conscious reason for blinding the eye. There must be at least a suspicion of a truth about which you do not want to know and which you refuse to investigate.[77]

As there has not yet been a decision on the interpretation of Art 4 of the 1976 Convention, the construction of the wording of Art 25 of the Warsaw Convention by Eveleigh LJ has been accepted as a guide for interpretation of the equivalent provision under the 1976 Convention and the other Conventions, save for minor differences discussed under para 7.1.5, below.

7.1.4 Faults of ship-managers under the old system as compared with the present

The extent of managerial duties of owners and managers, especially in relation to the supply of navigational information and publications to their vessels, was in issue in some cases from 1960. The House of Lords, in *The Norman*,[78] threw a new light in the duty of managers and it was, since then, no longer permissible for managers to wash their hands of all questions of navigation or to leave everything to the unassisted discretion of the masters. Any company which embarks on the business of shipowning must accept the obligation to ensure efficient management of its ships, if it is to enjoy the very considerable benefits conferred by the statutory right to limitation.[79]

In 1984, there was the famous limitation of liability case, *The Marion*.[80] The vessel was owned by a Liberian company and was managed by professional managers, an English company, who were insured for third party liabilities with the same P&I club as the owners of the ship.

It is important to note in what way the managers were at fault, which prevented limitation by the owners under the old system. What was said in this judgment sounds like the prelude to the kind of supervision needed under the ISMC today. Such conduct will be relevant when the shipowners' and managers' system of management is scrutinised under the ISMC, but it may or may not amount to the conduct required under Art 4 of the 1976 Convention for purpose of limitation.[81]

The Marion

The vessel's anchor fouled an oil pipeline on the seabed causing damage to it due to the master's negligence, who was relying on out of date charts. It was the managers' duty to oversee that there were up to date charts on board and that the master used them. There was evidence that the master was in the

---

77 Transcript, 18 January 2001, p 1.
78 [1960] 1 Lloyd's Rep 1.
79 *The Lady Gwendolen* [1965] 1 Lloyd's Rep 335, pp 345, 346, *per* Sir Gordon Willmer; and in *The England* [1973] 1 Lloyd's Rep 373, p 383.
80 [1984] 2 Lloyd's Rep 1.
81 See Chapter 8, para 5.5.1, above.

habit of being superficial in this respect and, had he used the new charts, he would have seen the position of the pipeline, so the accident would not have happened. Upon a claim made by the pipeline owners for $25 m, the shipowners admitted liability but sought to limit their liability under s 503 of the MSA 1894, as amended. The issue for the court was whether the damage occurred without the owners' actual fault or privity. The questions for decision of the court were: (1) what action should have been taken by the managers as reasonably prudent ship-managers to ensure that *Marion* was supplied with up to date charts? (2) If the answer to the first question showed that there was fault on the part of the managers, was that fault a fault for which that company was liable upon the footing *respondeat superior*, or was it the fault of somebody for whom the company was liable because his action was the very action of the company itself? The judge held that, on the evidence, there was no fault on the part of the managers, so he allowed limitation, but he was overruled by the Court of Appeal. The shipowners appealed to the House of Lords. The thrust of the issue was whether the managers had, in their management and operation of *The Marion*, a system by which the managing director ensured that an adequate degree of supervision of the master to keep and observe the up to date charts was exercised, either by himself or by his subordinates. Although in the absence of the director from the office, his subordinate had written to the master to follow the new charts, as had been pointed out by the report on the ship by the Flag State, Liberia, he omitted to follow this up and ensure that the master, in fact, did so. The director was in communication with the office but he was not informed about this report. The inference by the House of Lords was that his instructions in this respect to his subordinates were insufficiently clear, so his system of supervision was defective.

Confirming the decision of the Court of Appeal, Lord Brandon said:

> My Lords, in the result, I conclude that there were two actual faults of the appellants: first, in Mr Downard's (director of the managers) failure to have a proper system of supervision in relation to charts; and, secondly, in failing, when he departed to Greece, to give to Mr Lowry and Mr Graham (his subordinates) instructions with regard to the matters about which he required to be kept informed which were sufficiently clear, precise and comprehensive.[82]

In order to break limitation under the new system, it would be the managers, separately from the owners, who would seek limitation. The owners would be able to limit because the failure of Mr Downward, which should qualify for a personal omission under Art 4, would not be the personal omission of the owners.[83] However, whether or not the managers would be able to limit

---

82 [1984] 2 Lloyd's Rep 1, p 8.
83 See the identification theory, para 8.2, below.

under the 1976 Convention, it must be proved by the claimants that such personal omission amounted to a reckless conduct, as defined in *Goldman*, and, also, that the person liable was aware that such loss would probably result from his omission.

While the information in the system of management, which will now be transparent because of the ISMC, will assist the claimants in the burden of proof under Art 4, it will be a matter of degree as to whether the conduct of the person liable in a particular case amounts to recklessness and with the required knowledge. On the facts of *The Marion*, it would be reckless under the present system not to have dismissed a master of a ship who was known to be in the habit of being sloppy in following instructions about charts and navigation matters, but such conduct would not in itself amount to knowledge that such loss would probably result? The interpretation of 'such loss' is examined below.

7.1.5 'Loss' and 'such loss'

Under the old system of limitation, s 503, as amended, referred to occurrences with respect to which the owner would not be liable beyond certain limits, and then referred to 'such loss, damage, or infringement' in relation to which the conduct, 'actual fault or privity', barring limitation would bite.

Under the 1976 Convention, the word 'loss' in Art 4 must refer to loss of or damage in relation to various claims outlined in Art 2 (see p 904), although it is curious why the word 'damage' has been omitted, perhaps inadvertently, from Art 4. By contrast, the word 'damage' is used in both the HVR, Art IV, r 5(e), and in Art 13 of the Athens Convention.

Although the provisions of limitation under the various Conventions are not identical, it must have been intended that the bar to limitation would be applicable to either 'loss' or 'damage', otherwise, it would not make sense if the bar to limit applied only either to 'damage' or to 'loss', as the case may be under the aforesaid Conventions.

Similarly, a difference exists between the Conventions with regard to loss or damage that relates to the mental element. For example, the 1976 Convention refers to 'with intent to cause such loss, or recklessly and with knowledge that such loss would probably result'; the Athens Convention refers to 'such damage'; while the Hamburg Rules refer to 'such loss, damage or delay'. By contrast, the HVR and the Warsaw Convention, as amended, link the misconduct generally to 'damage' without using the word 'such'. This may, or may not, be of a material significance when reading the interpretation given to these words by Eveleigh LJ, when he said, in *Goldman*:

> It is with rather less confidence that I have said that the damage anticipated must be of the same kind of damage as that suffered. I have reached my conclusion because Art 25 is designed to cover cases of damage both to the

person – in other words, injury – and to property ... There may be occasions when an act can be said to be done recklessly in regard to one possible kind of damage, although morally wholly justified as the price of averting some other more serious hurt. Perhaps, one could resolve this matter by saying that recklessness involves an element of moral turpitude. If all that can be anticipated is the spilling of a cup of tea over someone's dress, it does seem wrong that the pilot should be blamed for unexpected personal injuries. Whether or not I am right in this, I am satisfied that the pilot must have knowledge that damage will result from his omission. With respect to the judge, I cannot see that the fact that a wine glass may slip from a tray and cut a passenger's leg should make the carriers liable for unlimited damages in respect of an injury suffered because there was no seat belt to protect him. The damage, whether it is referred to as 'the damage' or merely 'damage,', refers to something which results from the omission. The French text, by the use of the word 'en', clearly establishes this.[84]

Puchtas LJ said that 'damage' involves probable damage contemplated by the article.[85] It is established from this case that the damage anticipated must be the result of the act or omission and not any other kind of damage generally. The kind of damage, under the fourth limb of the test of Eveleigh LJ (see earlier, under para 7.1.3), is used because the Convention applies to both personal injury and property damage, as the 1976 and the Athens Conventions also do. It may be that the word 'such', under the latter Conventions, emphasises that the loss suffered must be the kind of loss that had been anticipated, for example, either personal injury or property loss, in order to violate limitation. It has been suggested, however, by Griggs and Williams[86] that a more restrictive interpretation of the word 'such', that is, meaning the 'same' loss is arguable, thereby importing an added safeguard to the person liable. The present writer is more inclined to accept that the additional word is inserted by way of emphasising the loss of the sort contemplated in Art 2, as it would be impossible to be precise. For example, when the guilty person expected that some personal injury would probably result from his act or omission, and it did result, why should the right to limit be inviolate if the injury is in fact that of a broken neck rather than just of a bruise? By contrast, if he anticipated that his act might result in a property damage, or loss, but, in fact, there was an unexpected personal injury, there should be no reason to make the person liable to the extent of unlimited liability. As Lord Eveleigh illustrated in the *Goldman* case, provided that there was a causative link between the act or omission (committed with conscious realisation of the probable result) and the claim complained of, it would not make any difference whether the word 'damage' refers to 'the damage' or

---

84 [1983] 1 WLR 1186, p 1196.

85 *Ibid*, p 1202.

86 *Op cit*, Griggs and Williams, fn 18, p 30.

merely 'damage'. It is submitted, therefore, that 'such' loss in Art 4 refers to the kind of loss (and not the same loss) complained of, which the person liable had anticipated would be the probable result of his act or omission.

8 CORPORATE PERSONALITY AND WHOSE MISCONDUCT SHOULD BE ATTRIBUTED TO THE COMPANY

The owners, managers or operators, or charterers of ships are corporate bodies. In law, a personality is attributed to a corporation by a fiction. Since a corporation is not a living person with mind and hands to carry out its intentions, the attribution of liability to a corporation was originally solved by the development of a concept known as the *'alter ego'*. Later, this was better expressed as the 'identification' doctrine. However, since in certain circumstances, the identification of key people in a company, who are commonly described as the 'brains and nerve centre' of the company, has not given satisfactory answers to all questions of attributing liability to a company, a new approach to the 'rules of attribution' has developed. This is known as 'the *Meridian* rule of attribution', derived from the name of the case in which it was developed.[87] By this approach, the court has to interpret the substantive rule of law under which liability is sought in order to determine whether the policy or the intention of the substantive rule, which is usually a statute or convention, requires the court to attribute liability to the company in question, even if the damage or loss claimed of, or the breach of duty, was caused or committed by a person lower in the hierarchy of the company's directing mind.

It is important to recapitulate, in this context, how these concepts developed over the years and which rule of attribution would seem to be appropriate in the context of limitation of liability under the 1976 Convention, while also making a comparison with the old system of limitation.

8.1 The concept of the *'alter ego'* of a corporation

The *alter ego* concept was first developed by English judges to ascribe a mind to a corporation. In 1915, the issue arose in relation to the 'fault or privity' of the owner, under s 502 of the 1894 MSA, in the following case.

---

87   See a summary of these principles in Chapter 8, para 5.2, and *Meridian Global Funds Management Asia Ltd v Securities Commission* [1995] 3 All ER 918, under para 8.3, below.

Lennard's Carrying Co Ltd v Asiatic Petroleum Co Ltd[88]

A cargo of benzine was carried on board the British steamship *Edward Dawson*. During the voyage, the vessel met with heavy weather, stranded and then caught fire and the cargo was destroyed. The shipowners were a limited company and the managing owners, JM Lennard & Sons Ltd, were another limited company. The managing director of the latter, John Lennard, was the registered managing owner and took the active part in the management of the ship on behalf of the owners. The purchasers of the cargo made a claim for non-delivery of the cargo based on breach of contract, on the ground of unseaworthiness of the ship by reason of the defective condition of her boilers. The defendants (owners) admitted their failure to deliver but relied on s 502, seeking to exclude their liability. The judge found that the ship was unseaworthy, that the fire and the loss of the cargo were due to that unseaworthiness and that the loss did not happen without the owners' actual fault or privity. At the Court of Appeal, the defendants contested the finding about the cause of the fire and, in any event, submitted that the fire and the loss of the cargo were caused without their actual fault or privity. The majority of the Court of Appeal affirmed the judge's decision.

The owners appealed to the House of Lords, the question for decision being a general question of law as to whether the fault of the managing owner was the fault of the company itself for the purpose of s 502. In other words, did what happened take place without the actual fault or privity of the owners of the ship who were the appellants?

Lennard was director of both companies entrusted with the management of the vessel. He appeared to be the spirit in the joint stock company. So, Lennard knew or had the means of knowing of the defective condition of the boilers, but he gave no special instructions to the captain or the chief engineer regarding their supervision and took no steps to prevent the ship putting to sea with her boilers in an unseaworthy condition.

Viscount Haldane stated:[89]

> A corporation is an abstraction. It has no mind of its own any more than it has a body of its own; its active and directing will must consequently be sought in the person of somebody who for some purposes may be called an agent, but who is really the directing mind and will of the corporation, the very ego and centre of the personality of the corporation. That person may be under the direction of the shareholders in general meeting; that person may be the board of directors itself, or it may be, and in some companies it is so, that that person has an authority co-ordinate with the board of directors given to him under the

88 [1915] AC 705.
89 *Ibid*, pp 713–14.

articles of association, and is appointed by the general meeting of the company, and can only be removed by the general meeting of the company ... For, if Mr Lennard was the directing mind of the company, then his action must, unless a corporation is not to be liable at all, have been an action which was the action of the company itself, within the meaning of s 502 ... It must be upon the true construction of that section in such a case as the present one that the fault or privity is the fault or privity of somebody who is not merely a servant or agent for whom the company is liable upon the footing *respondeat superior*, but somebody for whom the company is liable because his action is the very action of the company itself. It is not enough that the fault should be the fault of a servant in order to exonerate the owner, the fault must also be one which is not the fault of the owner, or a fault to which the owner is privy; and I take the view that when anybody sets up that section to excuse himself from the normal consequences of the maxim *respondeat superior* the burden lies upon him to do so.

In the unique case, *The Lady Gwendolen*, in 1965, the Court of Appeal crossed the borderline between those on the board running the company and those below the board, in tracing the fault, which caused the liability, upwards from the marine superintendent through the traffic manager to the assistant managing director, and barred the company from limiting liability under the old system. It is still important to note the failures of the ego of the company to provide a safe management system that led to unlimited liability in this case, so that a comparison can be made with what is required today under the ISMC, in terms of risk assessment and implementation of a safe management system.

The Lady Gwendolen[90]

This was an appeal by the plaintiffs, Arthur Guinness Son & Co (Dublin) Ltd, owners of the motor vessel, *The Lady Gwendolen*, from a decision by Mr Justice Hewson dismissing their claim for a declaration limiting their liability for damages arising out of a collision between *The Lady Gwendolen* and the motor vessel *Freshfield* which was at anchor in the Crosby Channel of the River Mersey in thick fog.

It was held by the Court of Appeal, confirming the judgment below, that the causes of the collision were, briefly: inadequate use of radar and excessive speed in fog; the master, who took command of *The Lady Gwendolen* (which was fitted with radar), had had no experience in radar and was given no instructions as to its use or misuse.

The assistant managing director (Williams) was responsible for the plaintiffs' vessels and was the *alter ego* of the plaintiff company. The radar problem merited his personal attention. Although the plaintiffs' main business was that of brewers, in their capacity as shipowners they were to be judged by

90   [1965] 1 Lloyd's Rep 335.

the standard of conduct of the ordinary reasonable shipowner in the management and control of vessels. The primary concern of a shipowner was safety of life at sea, and that involved a seaworthy ship, properly manned and safely navigated. Insofar as high speed in fog was encouraged by radar, the installation of radar required particular vigilance of shipowners through the person (in this case W) who was responsible, in the capacity of the owners, for the running of the ships. The plaintiffs had failed in that vigilance and had failed to consider or appreciate the problems which had arisen through the use of radar and to impress their master with the gravity of risks he was taking. Therefore, they failed to prove that the accident happened without their actual fault or privity.

It is interesting to note the chain of responsibility in this case, as it may be relevant in cases where similar duties are delegated to a designated person under the ISMC.[91] That does not mean to say, however, that the delegation will necessarily extend the class of persons (whose acts are to be regarded in law as the personal acts of the company itself) beyond those who, by the articles of association, are entitled to exercise the powers of the company.[92] It will be seen later what impact the ISMC may have on limitation under the 1976 Convention.

The marine superintendent in *Lady Gwendolen*, Mr Robbie, had perused the logs in the performance of his duty, but failed to detect the master's habit of navigation in such dangerous circumstances, or if he did, or suspected it, he failed to warn the master, or deter him from this practice, or take any step to see that the regulations were complied with. He also failed to inform his employers, who, throughout, seemed to have been unaware of the risks the master of this ship was taking. The superintendent did not supervise properly, though the judge was satisfied that he knew enough to enable him to do so.

With the obvious sources of fault lying with the master and the marine superintendent, why did the judge and the Court of Appeal attribute the fault and privity of the superintendent upon the company for the purpose of barring the owners from limiting liability?

The Court of Appeal answered this as follows:

It is on account of the introduction of radar and the learned judge's view of an owner's obligation with regard to the supervision of its use. Reliance on a competent master and an efficient marine superintendent has been held by him not to be enough to exonerate the owners.

Mr D Williams was the assistant managing director of the plaintiff company. He had previously been the head brewer. Later, he took charge of the traffic department, whose function it was to manage and control the ships owned by

---

91 See the reference to delegation by Lord Reid in *Tesco v Nattrass* [1972] AC 153 (HL), para 8.2, below.

92 As Lord Diplock said in *Tesco v Nattrass* [1972] AC 153 (HL): 'Insofar as there are *dicta* to the contrary in *The Lady Gwendolen* [1965] P 224, they were not necessary to the decision and, in my view, they were wrong.'

the company for the purpose of distributing its product. Mr DW Boucher was the traffic manager, but his training and experience had not been with ships, but with railways. He was no doubt expert in arranging the dispatch of the cargo. The highest in the management who had any real knowledge of ships was Mr Robbie, the marine superintendent.

On these facts, **Willmer LJ** explained (pp 344, 345):

> I think the true view is that where shipowners delegate the performance of a duty of the kind conveniently described as 'non-delegable' they are held constructively guilty of fault of its non-performance. This means that, so far as liability is concerned, they cannot escape. But such fault falls short, in my view, of what is meant by 'actual fault' within the meaning of s 503 of the Act. Constructive fault goes only to liability, and leaves untouched the question whether there is such actual fault on the part of the shipowners themselves as will defeat their right to limitation. This seems to me to accord with the view expressed by Lord Justice Buckley in *Asiatic Petroleum Company Ltd v Lennard's Carrying Company Ltd*, p 432, as follows:
>
> > The words 'actual fault or privity' in my judgment infer something personal to the owner, something blameworthy in him, as distinguished from constructive fault or privity such as the fault or privity of his servants or agents ...
>
> It follows that in my view the question of actual fault or privity cannot be determined on the artificial basis contended for by the defendants. On the contrary, I think it is necessary to examine in detail the facts of each particular case in order to see what, in fact, the shipowners did, or omitted to do, which could fairly be said to constitute actual fault on their part. Where, as here, the owners are a limited company, it is almost inevitable that difficult questions will arise. It is necessary to look closely at the organisation of the company in order to see of what individual it can fairly be said that his act or omission is that of the company itself. The decision in *Lennard's* case, of course, affords valuable guidance in the conduct of this inquiry.
>
> ... But neither in the Court of Appeal nor in the House of Lords was said that a person whose actual fault would be the company's actual fault must necessarily be a director. Where, as in the present case, a company has a separate traffic department, which assumes responsibility for running the company's ships, I see no good reason why the head of that department, even though not himself a director, should not be regarded as someone whose action is the very action of the company itself, so far as concerns anything to do with the company's ships. In the present case Mr Boucher was not only the head of the traffic department, but he was also the registered ships' manager.
>
> ... On the principles stated in these cases, I should be disposed to say that actual fault on the part of Mr Boucher, as registered ship's manager and head of the traffic department, would be sufficient in the particular circumstances of the present case to constitute actual fault or privity of the company. But I do not find it necessary to reach any final conclusion upon this point – for it seems to me that, in the particular circumstances of this case, all concerned, from the members of the board downwards, were guilty of actual fault, in that all must

be regarded as sharing responsibility for the failure of management which the facts disclose.

Although constructive knowledge was said to be relevant only to liability and not to the question of actual fault or privity for the purpose of limitation, an aggregation of faults was taken into account. The *dicta* of this decision (albeit *obiter*) are closer to the special rule of attribution of *Meridian Global Funds v Securities Commission* (see para 8.3, below) where the fault of a manager, a person lower in ranking than a director of the company, was attributed to the company for the purpose of the statute which was interpreted in this case.

As seen earlier (para 7.1.3), in 1976, Lord Denning MR, in *The Eurysthenes*,[93] unraveled the meaning of 'privity' in relation to the *alter ego* and said:

> The knowledge must ... be the knowledge of the shipowner personally, or his *alter ego*, or, in the case of a company, its head men or whoever may be considered their *alter ego*. It may be inferred from evidence that a reasonably prudent owner in his place would have known the facts and have realised that the ship was not reasonably fit to be sent to sea. But, if the shipowner satisfies the court that he did not know the facts or did not realise that they rendered the ship unseaworthy, then he ought not to be held privy to it, even though he was negligent in not knowing.[94]

In 1989, Mustill LJ (as he then was) did not wish to draw a general rule restricting *alter ego* to the board of directors, in *The Ert Stefanie*.[95] In particular, he said

> The board of directors of a corporation may not always comprise the whole of the group of people who together constitute the governing mind and will of the corporation, for the cases show clearly that the fault of a senior manager below board level may on occasion be included in the group. Nevertheless, it seems to me that any director must necessarily be a member of the group unless formally dis-seized of responsibility in the manner just described.
>
> Thus, I would prefer to steer clear of generalisations about the constituent elements of the *alter ego*. Each case must turn on its own facts.[96]

8.2 The 'identification' doctrine

In 1944, three justices of the Divisional Court, in *DPP v Kent and Sussex Contractors Ltd*,[97] overruled the court below in a criminal case in which the

---

93   [1976] 2 Lloyd's Rep 171.
94   *Ibid*, p 179.
95   [1989] 1 Lloyd's Rep 349.
96   *Ibid*, p 352.
97   [1944] KB 146.

court was of the opinion that the company could not, in law, be guilty of the offences charged. It was explained by Viscount Caldecote CJ that:

> [In the present case] the offences created by the regulation are those of doing something with intent to deceive or of making a statement known to be false in a material particular. There was ample evidence, on the facts as stated in the special case, that the company, by the only people who could act or speak or think for it had done both these things.[98]

Furthemore, Hallett J said:

> With regard to the liability of a body corporate for torts or crimes, a perusal of the cases shows, to my mind, that there has been a development in the attitude of the courts arising from the large part played in modern times by limited liability companies. At one time, the existence, and later the extent and conditions of such a body's liability in tort was a matter of doubt, due partly to the theoretical difficulty of imputing wrongful acts or omissions to a fictitious person, and it required a long series of decisions to clear up the position. Similarly, the liability of a body corporate for crimes was at one time a matter of doubt, partly owing to the theoretical difficulty of imputing a criminal intention to a fictitious person and partly to technical difficulties of procedure.[99]

In 1957 the concept of identification of the relevant persons in a company hierarchy was clearly defined when Denning LJ (as he then was) approved the approach of the court in the last case and tried to merge the same principle in both civil and criminal cases. He said, in *HL Bolton (Engineering) Co Ltd v TJ Graham & Sons Ltd*:[100]

> A company may in many ways be likened to a human body. It has a brain and nerve centre which controls what if does. It also has hands which hold the tools and act in accordance with directions from the centre. Some of the people in the company are mere servants and agents who are nothing more that hands to do the work and cannot be said to represent the mind or will. Others are directors and managers who represent the directing mind and will of the company and controls what it does. The state of mind of these managers is the state of mind of the company and is treated by the law as such. So you will find that, in cases where the law requires personal fault as a condition of liability in tort, the fault of the manager will be the personal fault of the company. That is made clear in Lord Haldane's speech in *Lennard's Carrying Co Ltd v Asiatic Petroleum Co Ltd*. So, also, in the criminal law, in cases where the law requires a guilty mind as a condition of a criminal offence, the guilty mind of the directors or the managers will render the company itself guilty.

---

98 [1944] KB 146, p 156.

99 *Ibid*, p 157.

100 [1957] 1 QB 159, p 172, relating to the intention of a limited company owning property and managed by its directors.

In 1972, the identification doctrine was adopted by the House of Lords in *Tesco Supermarkets v Nattrass*, in the context of offences under the Trade Descriptions Act (TDA) 1968, and in which the concept of the *alter ego* was, for the first time, questioned.

Tesco Supermarkets v Nattrass[101]

The defendants, a body corporate owning supermarket stores, were charged with an offence, under the TDA 1968, for failing to display the correct prices on goods at a branch. They sought to raise a defence under s 24(1) on the grounds that the commission of the offence was due to the act or default of another person, namely, the manager of the store at which the offence was committed, and that they had taken all reasonable precautions and exercised all due diligence to avoid the commission of such an offence. The shop manager was not a person within s 20, carrying out functions as a director, manager, secretary or other similar.

Lord Reid said:

I must start by considering the nature of the personality which by a fiction the law attributes to a corporation. A living person has a mind which can have knowledge or intention or be negligent and he has hands to carry out his intentions. A corporation has none of these: it must act through living persons, though not always one or the same person. Then the person who acts is not speaking or acting for the company. He is acting as the company and his mind which directs his acts is the mind of the company. There is no question of the company being vicariously liable. He is not acting as a servant, representative, agent or delegate. He is an embodiment of the company or, one could say, he hears and speaks through the persona of the company, within his appropriate sphere, and his mind is the mind of the company. If it is a guilty mind then that guilt is the guilt of the company. It must be a question of law whether, once the facts have been ascertained, a person, in doing particular things, is to be regarded as the company, or merely as the company's servant or agent. In that case, any liability of the company can only be a statutory or vicarious liability ...

Normally the board of directors, the managing director and perhaps other superior officers of a company carry out the functions of management and speak and act as the company. Their subordinates do not. They carry out orders from above and it can make no difference that they are given some measure of discretion. But the board of directors may delegate some part of their functions of management, giving to their delegate full discretion to act independently of instructions from them. I see no difficulty in holding that they have thereby put such a delegate in their place, so that within the scope of the delegation he can act as the company.[102]

In some cases, the phrase *alter ego* has been used. I think it is misleading. When dealing with a company the word *alter* is I think misleading. The person who

101 [1972] AC 153 (HL).
102 *Ibid*, pp 170–72.

speaks and acts as the company is not *alter*. He is identified with the company. And when dealing with an individual, no other individual can be his *alter ego*. The other individual can be a servant, agent, delegate or representative, but I know of neither principle nor authority which warrants the confusion (in the literal or original sense) of two separate individuals ...

I have said that a board of directors can delegate part of their functions of management so as to make their delegate an embodiment of the company within the sphere of the delegation. But here, the board never delegated any part of their functions. They set up a chain of command through regional and district supervisors, but they remained in control. The shop managers had to obey their general directions and also take orders from their superiors. The acts or omissions of shop managers were not acts of the company itself.[103]

Viscount Dilhorne and Lord Pearson suggested that one has to determine who are in actual control of a company, which may vary from one company to another.[104] **Viscount Dilhorne** said, in particular:

If, when Denning LJ referred to directors and managers representing the directing mind and will of the company, he meant, as I think he did, those who constitute the directing mind and will, I agree with his approach.

These passages, I think, clearly indicate that one has, in relation to a company, to determine who is or who are, for it may be more than one, in actual control of the operations of the company, and the answer to be given to that question may vary from company to company depending on its organisation.[105]

Similarly, **Lord Pearson** said:[106]

In the case of a company, the ego is located in several persons ... in similar position of direction or general management. A company may have an *alter ego*, if those persons who are or have its ego delegate to some other person the control and management, with full discretionary powers, of some section of the company's business. In the case of a company, it may be difficult, and in most cases for practical purposes unnecessary, to draw the distinction between its ego and its *alter ego*, but theoretically there is that distinction.

[In this case] Mr Clement, being the manager of one of the company's several hundreds of shops, could not be identified with the company's ego, nor was he an *alter ego* of the company. He was an employee in a relatively subordinate post. In the company's hierarchy, there were a branch inspector and an area controller and a regional director interposed between him and the board of directors.

It was suggested in the argument of this appeal that, in exercising supervision over the operations in the shop, Mr Clement was performing functions of management and acting as a delegate and *alter ego* of the company. But supervision of the details of operations is not normally a function of higher

---

103 [1972] AC 153 (HL), pp 174–75.
104 This approach is similar to that followed by the CA in *The Star Sea* [1997] 1 Lloyd's Rep 360.
105 *Tesco v Nattrass* [1972] AC 153 (HL), p 187.
106 *Ibid*, p 193.

management: it is normally carried out by employees at the level of foremen, charge hands, overlookers, floor managers and 'shop' managers ...

What this case decided is that the person acting as the company is not a delegate but the embodiment of the company. If directors of a company delegate, provided the delegate is given full discretion to perform certain tasks and he acts within the scope of delegation, the delegate can act as the company. The person who acts as the company is not an 'alter ego' but the 'ego' of the company. 'Alter ego' is a servant, unless the 'ego' has given him the control to act with full discretionary power. Supervision of details of a function by a manager is not making him the 'alter ego' in that sense.

Lord Diplock emphasised, in the following passage, that no extension of the class of people identified with a company should be made beyond those who are entrusted with the control of the company by the articles of association:

> There has been in recent years a tendency to extract from Denning LJ's judgment in *HL Bolton (Engineering) Co Ltd v TJ Graham & Sons Ltd* [1957] 1 QB 159, pp 172, 173, his vivid metaphor about the 'brains and nerve centre' of a company as contrasted with its hands, and to treat this dichotomy, and not the articles of association, as laying down the test of whether or not a particular person is to be regarded in law as being the company itself when performing duties which a statute imposes on the company.

> In the case in which this metaphor was first used, Denning LJ was dealing with acts and intentions of directors of the company in whom the powers of the company were vested under its articles of association. The decision in that case is not authority for extending the class of persons whose acts are to be regarded in law as the personal acts of the company itself, beyond those who by, or by action taken under, its articles of association are entitled to exercise the powers of the company. Insofar as there are *dicta* to the contrary in *The Lady Gwendolen* [1965] P 294, they were not necessary to the decision and, in my view, they were wrong.[107]

In 1994, *The Safe Carrier*[108] concerned the duty of shipowners, charterers and managers to take reasonable steps to ensure the safe operation of their ships. Breach of this duty is a criminal offence by statute, s 31 of the MSA 1988 and now s 100 of the MSA 1995.

The House of Lords held that the duty consisted simply in failure to take steps which, by an objective standard, were held to be reasonable steps to take in the interests of the safe operation of a ship and the duty which it placed on the owners, charterers or managers was a personal one; the owner, charterer

---

107 *Tesco Supermarkets v Nattrass* [1972] AC 153 (HL), p 200.
108 [1994] 1 Lloyd's Rep 589 (HL).

or manager would be criminally liable if he failed personally in the duty, but would not be criminally liable for the acts or omissions of his subordinate employees, if he himself had taken all such reasonable steps. The identification doctrine was applied as was clarified in the *Tesco* case.

It is clear from these decisions that, as a general rule, the embodiment of a company is its directors (the 'ego'). Depending on the policy of a company,a person below the level of directors may be given control and full discretionary power to perform certain tasks, whereupon he will, exceptionally, be the 'alter ego' of the company for those specific tasks. His acts or omissions will be those of the company for the purpose of attributing liability to the latter. When a duty is imposed upon the company by statute, the question of law is whether or not that duty is personal to the company.

What is important is to look at the overall scheme and purpose of the statute or the Convention, or the rule of law, which is the subject matter for interpretation. This latter approach was followed in the middle 1990s, as is explained next.

8.3 The *'Meridian* rule of attribution' by interpretation of the substantive rule of law

In 1995, a new direction was taken in the search for the relevant person in the corporate structure, when the Privy Council considered, in **Meridian Global Funds Management Asia Ltd v Securities Commission**,[109] the principle of the identification theory and introduced flexibility in approach as to what acts or omissions can be attributed to a corporation. It was emphasised that it was not merely a question of identifying the relevant person in the company hierarchy, but the rule of attribution was a matter of interpretation or construction of the relevant substantive rule of law in each case.[110] The rule of attribution was defined by **Lord Hoffmann**, thus:

> ... [When] the court considers that the law was intended to apply to companies, although it excludes ordinary vicarious liability, insistence on the primary rules of attribution would, in practice, defeat that intention. In such a case, the court must fashion a special rule of attribution for the particular substantive rule. This is always a matter of interpretation: given that it was intended to apply to a company, how was it intended to apply? Whose act (or knowledge or state of

---

109 [1995] 3 All ER 918 (PC).

110 The identification theory was not applied to the following statutory criminal offences: in *Re Supply of Ready Mixed Concrete* [1995] 1 All ER 135 (HL), the company was held guilty of contempt of court for breach of an injunction due to the act of junior management despite specific instructions having been given by senior management not to act in the manner it did; in *Regina v British Steel plc* [1995] 1 WLR 1356 (CA), the senior management was held criminally liable for the death caused at work by negligence of their employees upon construction of the relevant statute, the Health and Safety at Work Act 1974. It was said, p 1363: 'He will only be exposed to the risk if the system (if any) designed to ensure his safety has broken down and it does not matter for the purposes of s 3(1) at what level in the hierarchy of employees that breakdown has taken place.' For this reason the *Tesco* case was distinguished.

mind) was for this purpose intended to count as the act, etc, of the company? One finds the answer to this question by applying the canons of interpretation, taking into account the language of the rule (if it is a statute) and its content and policy.[111]

It is derived from this statement that the issue is one of choice of the appropriate attribution rule for corporate liability. In the case of attribution of liability to the company itself of a tort committed by employees of a company in the course of their employment, the choice of the attribution rule will be the general rule of vicarious liability. In cases where a particular law (or otherwise the substantive rule of law with which the court is dealing) imposes liability to a company on the basis of a personal fault and a kind of conduct which is either wilful misconduct or more than just mere negligence, requiring a mental element of intention or a personal knowledge of the facts that would be likely to result in the harm inflicted, the articles of association, or board decisions, of the company will assist in finding the person who is the directing mind of the company. If, however, the scheme of, or the purpose behind, the substantive rule of law under which liability is sought to be imposed requires one to look at persons other than the directors of the company, the court will fashion a special rule to be applied to the particular substantive rule of law.[112]

The *Meridian* approach suggests that the choice of attribution rule depends on the purpose behind the rule of substantive liability.[113] The purpose will vary from one substantive rule of law to another. When statutory criminal offences are considered, the conduct of persons in managerial as opposed to directorial position might be taken into account with regard to the liability of the company for the offence committed, if that intention was derived from the policy behind the statute. When the substantive rule of law is, for example, an international convention, the court would have to look at the overall purpose of the Convention as may be found at the *travaux preparatoires*, so that there is a uniform application of the Convention. For example, the interpretation of the provision as regards limitation of liability under the 1957 Convention will be differently construed from Art 4 of the 1976 Convention. In this connection, it is now relevant to interpret these provisions in the context of the ISMC.

8.4 The effect of the ISMC on limitation and risk management

Applying the principles enunciated in the relevant authorities, it is submitted that the interpretation of the substantive rule of law and policy behind the 1976 Limitation Convention will not permit the extension of the class of

---

111 *Meridian Global Funds Management Asia Ltd v Securities Commission* [1995] 3 All ER 918, p 924.

112 This is very close to what Mustill LJ said in *The Ert Stefanie*, fn 95.

113 See, further, Armour, J, 'Corporate personality and assumption of responsibility'[1999] LMCLQ 246.

people who, under the articles of the company's association, or decisions of the Board pursuant to those articles, are entrusted with the control of the company or of particular functions of it. It is the philosophy and purpose behind the 1976 Convention that does not permit the rule of attribution to cross the board level. Although constructive knowledge is, in certain circumstances, taken into account in determining liability when the duty imposed by law is non-delegable, such knowledge, will be insufficient for the purpose of limitation under this Convention.[114]

It follows that the delegation of supervision of safety matters, in a ship or the shore management, to the designated person, appointed pursuant to the Code, will not make the designated person a person whose acts or omissions will be those of the company, unless he is delegated with full discretionary powers and control for the tasks.[115]

Unlike the 1957 Limitation Convention, the misconduct of the designated person will not bar limitation of his employers under Art 4 of the 1976 Convention. This requires proof that the loss resulted from the personal act or omission of the 'controlling mind and will' of the company committed with intent to cause such loss, or recklessly and with knowledge (actual or of a 'blind eye' kind) that such loss would probably result. In other words, the 'ego' of the company must have consciously anticipated the kind of loss claimed.

By contrast, it should be observed that, for the purpose of barring limitation, Art 25 of the Warsaw Convention takes into account not only the personal act or omission of the carrier, but of his servants or agents as well.

In the event that the designated person is sued personally in tort, however, will not be able to limit, if such misconduct amounts to that under Art 4. If he has been insured separately, his insurers would be likely to deny liability unless a special cover has been obtained for reckless conduct of the kind described in Art 4.

The direct access of the designated person to the senior management and his duties of reporting to them, will undoubtedly expose the senior management and their system of management practices to questions as to how and why the particular incident causing liability could not be prevented.

In this connection, it is important to refer to a relevant recent decision of the English court, *Rolls Royce plc v Heavylift-Volga Dnepr Ltd*,[116] concerning limitation of liability, again under Art 25 of the Warsaw Convention. The liability arose in relation to damage caused by the negligence of Servisair's employees to a Rolls Royce engine being unloaded from Rolls Royce's lorry with a 10 ton forklift truck at East Midlands Airport. Similar

---

114 See, also, Chapter 8, para 5.5.1, above.
115 See the author's earlier article: 'The International Safety Management Code in perspective' (1996) 10(6) P&I International, June, p 107, pp 109–10.
116 [2000] 1 Lloyd's Rep 653.

provisions of safety regulations apply to cargo handling operators in airports to those applicable to onshore management of ships. Breach of those regulations, in particular with regard to monitoring and providing a co-ordinated system of safety, as well as negligence, was found on the part of the company's safety and security manager, on the part of the designated 'competent' person and on the part of the employee involved in the unloading. The right hand was apparently unaware of what the left hand was doing, and the designated person had failed to ensure that all his staff were aware of all risks which they might encounter. It was pointed out that someone responsible in the company's safety systems should have picked up his failures. It was even commented by the court that any competent management would have foreseen the need to make sure that their staff did not operate this vehicle if it was not in proper condition. Nevertheless, the court held that:

> For the finding of wilful misconduct the court must find on a balance of probabilities that the acts (or omissions) alleged to constitute the misconduct must not only fall below the standards to be expected of persons acting reasonably, but be sufficiently below such standards as to be capable of being regarded as 'misconduct', and not just as careless, or very, or grossly careless. Second, the person must know that he is misconducting himself when he does (or fails to do) the acts complained of and does them intentionally or recklessly as to the consequences.

> Overall, Servisair were guilty of negligence. What might have avoided the accident would have been proper training on the heavier forklift truck. The company's failure to have a proper system of work which would have ensured that only properly trained and qualified people operated such vehicles was causative of the accident. However, neither separately nor in the aggregate did the failures of the various persons identified as being at fault amount to misconduct or to recklessness with knowledge under the Convention.[117] Thus, limitation was allowed.

This decision may be borne in mind in limitation cases under the 1976 Convention, when similar failures in the system of safe operation of ships may arise under the ISMC, but, as this case indicates, it may still be difficult for the claimant to break limitation.

There may well be limitation cases in the future to test this in the light of the ISMC, but it will be a matter of degree and extent of the deficiencies of the management system which, in a particular case, may amount to a bar of the right to limit.

Different criteria apply to cases of criminal liability arising from breach of statutory offences, as specified by the statutory instrument making the ISMC

---

117 [2000] 1 Lloyd's Rep 653, p 659.

part of English law, because of the wording of those offences, being the substantive rule of law for interpretation according to the attribution rule.[118]

However, the person who may seek to limit ought to be warned that the factual situations of *The Lady Gwendolen*,[119] *The Marion*,[120] *The Garden City*,[121] *The Anonity*[122] are situations to be avoided at all costs. Were these cases to be decided today, questions would be raised as to how and why the directing mind of the company was not able to ensure that a proper safety system was in operation. This inquiry may lead to a train of inquiries, which may reveal that the directing mind of the company, suspecting that a loss of the kind sustained would probably result, 'shut his eyes' to a means of knowledge provided by the ISMC and, recklessly as to the consequences, went ahead with the act or omitted to do the thing that would have prevented the kind of loss claimed. But to ascertain the knowledge of the person seeking to limit will depend on skilful cross-examination in each case.

---

118 See Chapter 8, para 5.6.2, above.

119 *Lady Gwendolen* [1965] 1 Lloyd's Rep 335 (defective radar lookout coupled with excessive speed in fog). The evidence disclosed a serious failure in the management of the ships which contributed to the collision. It was noted, at first instance, on the facts that: 'If the marine superintendent is put upon inquiry for an obvious disregard of the regulations, he should take steps about it, and if his steps fail, he must go higher until something is done about it.' This may be relevant under the ISMC to the extent of showing how far the questioning of the practices of the directors in the management of the ships might go.

120 [1984] 2 Lloyd's Rep 1: There were two types of faults noted here which may be relevant to the questioning of directors of shipowners or managers by virtue of the ISMC: first, failure of the managing director to have a proper system of supervision, and second, failure to give instructions on what matters he would like to be kept informed. Although such failures alone, without more in the conduct of directors, will not break the limit under Art 4 of the 1976 Convention, as it did under the old system, they are, however, worth keeping in mind.

121 [1982] 2 Lloyd's Rep 382: where Staughton J (as he then was) said that the top management of every shipowning company ought to institute a system for the supervision of navigation and detection of faults. Although there was a system here providing for two officers to be on the bridge when the vessel was navigating in fog, the master did not keep to it. In this case, however, no fault of the director was found. Under the ISMC, today, the director would be questioned why such a habit of the master had not been detected, but, to break the limitation under Art 4, there must be evidence of a conscious realisation (drawn from previous collision incidents that might have been caused by the master's same disregard of instructions) that the loss suffered was anticipated as very likely to happen and, nevertheless, recklessly, no preventative measures were taken.

122 [1961] 1 Lloyd's Rep 203: the issue on the facts was whether adequate instructions were given by the shipowners to their servants as to extinguishing of galley fires when the ship was lying alongside an oil jetty. The sparks that escaped caused fire to the jetty, which was destroyed. On the evidence, circular instructions about galley fires had been sent by the marine superintendent to the master. The *alter ego* of the company, Mr Everard, was very strict about compliance by the crew in all matters, but the master, who had been at the employ of Mr Everard for 16 years, was disobedient and perhaps sloppy. He filed the circular instructions in his desk and forgot about it, after a brief discussion with the chief and second officers. Under the old system of limitation, the owners could not limit liability because the circular was not enough; there ought to have been instructions from the owners exhibited by a notice next to the galley fire prohibiting its use at oil berths.

9 ESTABLISHMENT OF THE LIMITATION FUND

9.1 Procedural matters under the Convention

Article 11 of the 1976 Convention provides for the establishment of a limitation fund, which will be distributed by the court to satisfy the claims being subject to limitation:

> Any person alleged to be liable may constitute a fund with the court or other competent authority in the State Party in which legal proceedings are instituted in respect of claims subject to limitation.

Paragraph 8(3), Pt II, Sched 7 gives the court, in which the fund has been constituted, discretion to stay any proceedings, relating to any claim arising out of that occurrence, which are pending against the person by whom the fund has been constituted.

Article 13(1) provides that, when a limitation fund has been constituted, any person having a claim against the fund shall be barred from exercising any right in respect of that claim against other assets of the person on whose behalf the fund has been established. Paragraph (2) of Art 13 allows the release of a ship – by an order of the court – arrested within the jurisdiction where the fund has been constituted and belonging to the same person who has constituted the fund. Such a release is mandatory if the limitation fund has been constituted either:

(a) at the port where the occurrence took place; or
(b) at the port of disembarkation (in respect of loss of life, or personal injury claims); or
(c) at the port of discharge in respect of cargo claims; or
(d) in the State where the arrest is made;

provided always that the rules of the above paragraphs shall apply only if the claimant may bring a claim against the limitation fund and the fund is actually available and freely transferable in respect of that claim.

Any person who has a claim arising out of the same incident may, nevertheless, pursue to break limitation. Regardless of whether a claimant contends that he can prove that the shipowner was guilty of conduct barring limitation, the combined effect of Arts 2 and 13 of the 1976 Convention is that a person liable can only be compelled to constitute one fund, in accordance with Art 11, and not be also compelled to put up bail for the release of his ship.[123]

Once the release of the ship has been ordered, there is a bar to other actions but the person whose ship has been released shall be deemed to have submitted to the jurisdiction of the court (para 10, Pt II).

---

123 *The Bowbelle* [1990] 3 All ER 476.

The law applicable to the constitution and distribution of the fund shall be the law of the State in which the fund is constituted (Art 14).

No lien or other right in respect of any ship or property shall affect the proportion in which, under Art 12, the fund is distributed among several claimants (para 9, Pt II).

9.2 Counterclaims

Article 5 of the Convention provides:

> Where a person entitled to limitation of liability under the rules of this Convention has a claim against the claimant out of the same occurrence, their respective claims shall be set off against each other and the provisions of this Convention shall only apply to the balance, if any.

Thus, limitation of liability applies after the respective claims of the parties have been set off. The limits provided by the Convention apply to the balance.

In the same way, the House of Lords had decided, as far back as 1882, in *The Khedive*.[124]

Two ships *V* and *K* came into collision and the owners of the *V* brought an action *in rem* in the Admiralty Court against the owners of the *K*, who counterclaimed. Both ships were held to blame. The owners of the *K* brought an action to limit their liability under the then Merchant Shipping Amendment Act 1862 and paid the amount of their liability into court. The damage to the *V* was greater than that to the *K*, and the fund in court was not sufficient to satisfy all the claims for which the owners of the *K* were answerable in damages

It was held that limitation of liability applied to the balance remaining after deducting the smaller from the larger claim. The owners of the *V* were entitled to prove against the fund their damage, less the damage sustained by the *K*, and to be paid in respect of the balance due to them (after such deduction) *pari passu* with the other claimants out of such fund.

9.3 Amount of limitation

The general limits for claims other than passenger claims (Art 7) arising on any distinct occasion are calculated on the basis of a sliding scale depending on the size of the vessel's tonnage (Art 6(1)). It is the gross tonnage of the ship that is relevant. For hovercrafts, however, limitation is calculated by reference to the maximum operational weight.

Claims for personal injury or loss of life are treated preferentially to other claims. Up to 500 tons of a ship the limit is 333,000 units of account; from

---

124 (1882) 7 App Cas 795 (HL).

501–3000 tons another 500 units of account per ton are added; from 3001–30,000 tons, 333 units of account per ton are added; from 30,001–70,000 tons 250 units of account per ton are added; and, in excess of 70,000 tons, 167 units of account are added.

The limit in respect of any other claims starts at 167,000 units of account per ton for vessels below 500 tons. For a ship in excess of 500 tons, there is again a sliding scale of tonnage to which more units of account are added per ton, in addition to that applicable to the first scale (501–30,000 tons, 167 units of account for each ton; 30,001–70,000, 125 units of account for each ton; in excess of 70,000 tons, 83 units of account per ton).

Two separate funds are provided for each category of claims, personal claims and other claims, but the fund for other claims is available to meet any unsatisfied balance of the personal claims which then rank rateably with the other claims (Art 6(2)).

The unit of account is defined in Art 8 and is stated in Special Drawing Rights (SDR) as defined by the International Monetary Fund (IMF). It is based on the daily value of a basket of currencies and is converted into the national currency of the State (Member of the IMF) in which limitation is sought, according to the value of that currency at the time. If the State is not a Member of IMF, the value of the national currency in terms of SDR shall be calculated in a manner determined by that State (Art 8 of the 1976 Convention and Art 7 of Pt II, Sched 7 of the MSA 1995).

Order 1998 (SI 1998/1258) contains the amendments made to the 1976 Convention by the 1996 Protocol, which is not yet in force, and details as to the determination of the unit of account into sterling. The order provides for the implementation of the 1996 Protocol, by which the limitation figures are significantly increased, and it will come into force upon the ratification of the Protocol. It has, particularly, provided for the avoidance of an overlap of limitation under the Athens Convention for claims to which the latter applies, as well as under the International Convention on Liability and Compensation for Damage in connection with the Carriage of Hazardous and Noxious Substances by Sea 1996, which is not yet in force.

The 1976 Convention provides for a global limit and applies to each distinct occasion of injury. The aggregate of claims that arise from any distinct occasion is taken into account, under Art 9 of the 1976 Convention.

Article 7 of the 1976 Convention provides for a separate limitation fund for passengers in the amount of 46,666 units of account multiplied by the number of passengers the ship is authorised to carry.

However, the Carriage of Passengers and their Luggage by Sea (UK Carriers) Order 1998[125] has increased the limit for death or personal injury claims to 300,000 units of account per passenger. It came into force on 1 January 1999 and applies only to carriers whose principal place of business is in the UK.

---

125 SI 1998/2917.

The Athens Convention 1974, as amended by the 1976 Protocol, came into force internationally on 28 April 1987 and, in the UK, by s 14 of the MSA 1979. Upon the repeal of this Act, the Convention has been incorporated into UK law by s 183 of MSA 1995 and is included in Sched 6 to the Act. It applies to each passenger and the limit stated is 46,666 units per passenger, which, by the 1976 Protocol, were stated to be in SDR. An attempt was made by the 1990 Protocol to the Athens Convention to increase the limitation fund per passenger to 176,000 units of account. Although the Protocol has been agreed, it has not yet entered into force.

The Athens Convention does not modify the rights or duties of the carrier, or performing carrier, and their servants or agents provided for in other International Conventions and relating to limitation of liability of owners of sea-going ships (Art 19). Therefore, a carrier, or performing carrier, may choose to limit under either Convention.

9.4 Procedure in the Admiralty Court in relation to limitation (brief account)

There are three ways of enforcing the right to limit: the admiralty Practice Directions provide that limitation may be relied upon by way of defence to any claim;[126] a limitation claim may be brought by counterclaim with the permission of the Admiralty Court;[127] a limitation claim is begun by the issue of a claim form in admiralty.[128]

If the defendant invokes the right to limit by way of defence and counterclaim and is found liable, the limit of that liability will apply only to that claim. Therefore, to avoid separate proceedings, if it is envisaged that many claims will be brought, the best method of proceeding would be to institute a limitation action, in which the limitation fund will be valid against all claimants who claimed against the fund.

There is no provision in the Convention as to the jurisdiction of limitation claims, nor a requirement that the limitation action must be brought in the court in which liability is determined. Thus, as it has been seen in Pt I of this book (Chapters 5 and 6), a limitation claimant may choose the forum of his choice (forum shopping). The only restriction on jurisdiction has been brought by Art 6A of the Brussels Convention, which provides that the court which has jurisdiction in actions relating to liability shall also have jurisdiction over claims for the limitation of such liability. This provision, however, applies when the liable party is sued in a Contracting State of the Brussels/Lugano Conventions.

---

126 PD 49F, para 9.1(1).
127 PD 49F, para 9.1(2).
128 PD 49F, para 9.1(3), Form No ADM15.

When a limitation fund has been constituted a caveat against arrest will be issued.

Once the limitation decree is granted, the Admiralty Court may order the stay of any proceedings relating to any claim arising out of the same occurrence; or order the claimant to establish the fund, if he has not done so; or give directions for the advertisement of the decree, if it is a general and not a restricted one.[129] Claimants against the fund are invited in the advertisement to submit their claims.

Any person other than a named defendant may apply to the admiralty registrar, within a time fixed in the decree, to set aside the decree.[130]

The limitation fund is distributed to claimants in proportion to their established claims against the fund (Art 12(1) of the 1976 Convention) and no lien or other right in respect of any ship or property shall affect the proportions in which, under Art 12, the fund is distributed among the several claimants (para 9, Pt II, Sched 7 of the MSA 1995).

129 See, further, PD 49F, para 9.3.
130 PD 49F, para 9.4.

CHAPTER 17

THE EUROPEAN COMMISSION AND MARITIME SAFETY

RECENT DEVELOPMENTS[1]

1 INTRODUCTION

Following the sinking of the oil tanker *Erika* in December 1999 off the coast of France, the European Commission set out a communication for general strategy on 21 March 2000[2] on the safety of 'seaborne oil trade' and made proposals for consideration by the Council and the European Parliament with a view to tightening up safety measures, so that the recurrence of this type of accident is prevented in the future. The proposals are part of an overhaul of the safety of the seaborne oil trade, being regulated by the International Maritime Organisation (IMO), and incorporate measures: to eliminate manifestly sub-standard ships; to increase inspection of vessels posing risk; to increase information obligations; to improve monitoring; to impose higher standards for inspection organisations; and to phase out single-hull vessels.

Apart from tankers, the Commission has also taken the initiative to propose a directive[3] with regard to requirements for loading and unloading of bulk carriers in order to increase their safety when calling at terminals in the Community for loading or unloading solid bulk cargoes. The directive, which has been approved by the European Parliament,[4] aims to reduce the number of bulk carrier casualties – being due to structural failures – by reducing the stresses and physical damage to the ship's structure during loading or unloading. In many cases, rapid loss of buoyancy leaves the crew with little chance of safety. Harmonised procedures for co-operation between ship and the terminals are proposed to ensure that terminal operators are required to comply with the IMO codes. Further, more recent, proposals include a directive on reinforcing quality services in sea ports and a directive on a minimum level of training for seafarers.[5]

At the time of writing, the post-*Erika*, first and second set of proposals were under consideration by the Council and the European Parliament, which

---

1 COM(2000) 802, Brussels, 6 December 2000.
2 COM(2000) 142, Brussels, 21 March 2000.
3 COM(2000) 179, 22 May 2000.
4 Resolution Ref: A5-0037/2001, 13 February 2001.
5 COM(2000) 35 and COM(2000) 313, respectively.

are summarised here. Mention will be made of those proposals which were later approved.

2 FIRST SET OF PROPOSALS

2.1 A proposed amendment to Directive (94/57/EC) on inspections of ships

This concerns common rules and standards with regard to the activities of ship inspection organisations and maritime administrations. The former organisations are the classification societies to which Member States delegate the verification of safety standards on ships and the latter are the Flag States. The proposed amendment intends to provide closer supervision of the activities of both classification societies and Flag States. The revision of this directive includes harmonisation of the legal regime for financial liability of classification societies in the event of non-performance or negligence. It also includes regular inspections of recognised classification societies by the European Community (EC) in conjunction with Member States. The proposal has been approved by the European Parliament, save for some recommended amendments.[6]

2.2 Phasing out single-hull tankers

The Commission has been determined to speed up the process of banning single-hull oil tankers and phase in double-hull, or equivalent design for single-hull oil tankers, by a regulation. The original proposal of 21 March 2000 was amended to take into account the amendments suggested by the European Parliament on 30 November 2000.[7] The Commission accepted the recommended amendment by the Parliament concerning the phase out schedule for single-hull tankers, the exclusion of tankers between 600 and 3000 tons deadweight from the phase out schedule and, also, agreed to withdraw its proposed system of financial incentives and disincentives based on differential charging of port and pilotage fees. It was accepted that a joint approach with the IMO with regard to amending the existing international MARPOL regulations (the International Convention for the Prevention of Pollution from Ships 1973) and to agreeing the dates of implementation was

---

6   Resolution Ref: A5-0342/2000; COM(2000) 849, 12 December 2000 containing the amendments the Commission accepts and those that it does not; see, also, Chapter 11, end of para 8.

7   Amended proposal COM(2000) 848 12 December 2000.

desirable. A compromise was reached at the 46th Plenary Session of the Marine Environment Protection Committee of IMO on 27 April 2001, as reported by Lloyd's List. MARPOL single-hull crude oil tankers of between 5,000–20,000 dwt, and product tankers under 30,000 dwt, will be withdrawn by 2015. Pre-MARPOL tankers will be phased out by 2007. A small number of single-hull tankers with double sides, or double bottoms, which do not comply with the definition of a double hull, will be permitted to operate until their 25th year, or up to 2017. However, it has been made clear by EU members that EU ports will bar entry to those tankers, so that they may be phased out voluntarily. Otherwise, the compromised deal about the dates of phasing out has been accepted by EU members.

2.3 Amending the directive on Port State Control

The Commission's work also involves the banning of sub-standard ships from European Union (EU) waters by imposing more stringent inspections of ships which pose risk to such waters. The EC has proposed to amend the existing Directive (95/21/EC) on Port State Control, concerning the enforcement of international standards for ship safety, pollution prevention and shipboard living and working conditions of ships using Community ports and sailing in European waters. The Commission proposes to step up inspections in ports so that certain ships which fail to meet international standards will be banned from European ports altogether.[8] The European Parliament adopted the proposed amendment making suggestions for refusal of access of substandard ships to all ports and mandatory guidelines relating to this refusal of access.[9]

3 SECOND SET OF PROPOSALS

In connection to the above directive, it is also proposed that the Directive (93/75/EEC), on monitoring of traffic within EU ports and reporting requirements, be amended by a new directive. The aim is to achieve extension of monitoring to all ships which sail in coastal European waters, or call at a Community port.

The monitoring and general supervision is proposed to be controlled by a Maritime Safety Agency.

The EC has also set out to improve the system of liability and compensation for damage to the environment in the event of accidental pollution.

---

8   COM(97) 416, re-amended by proposal COM(2000) 850.
9   Resolution Ref: A5-0343/2000.

The reason for these new proposals is that the Commission has recognised that the instruments put in place to cope with accidents or pollution caused by sub-standard ships in European waters are still inadequate. Sub-standard ships still escape inspection in the EU, even after the safety measures already taken.

This second set of proposed measures was confirmed at the Biarritz European Council on 14 October 2000 and are briefly summarised here, with the reasons of the Commission.[10]

3.1 The proposed directive for a Community monitoring, control and information system

Reporting requirements of dangerous or polluting goods and bunker fuels on board is already provided for by Directive (93/75/EEC) which has been in force since 1995 and is known as the Hazmat Directive. Pursuant to this Directive, the masters or operators of a ship carrying dangerous or polluting goods are required to provide information to the competent authorities designated by the Member States. However, this Directive is not so well understood and has limitations.

A major limitation is that it applies only to ships bound for, or leaving, a Community port and carrying dangerous or polluting goods.

The Commission's proposal is, therefore, to extend these provisions to all ships, whether or not they call at a Community port and whether or not they are carrying dangerous or polluting goods.

Another major limitation of this Directive is that there are no proper means of enforcement in that the only sanction upon a ship is refusal of access for failure to provide notification after leaving the port of departure outside the Community.

What is needed, the Commission proposes, is a system of financial penalties.

The monitoring of ships (posing a serious threat to marine safety and environment) and circulation of information among Member States in order to take any preventive action is an essential measure in the new proposal to amend the Hazmat Directive.

The monitoring will include a wider obligation upon ships entering European waters to declare their entry, and will require them to carry on-board automatic identification systems.

---

10   In COM(2000) 802, 6 December 2000.

The proposal also includes the further development of common databases and networking of centres responsible for managing the information received under the Directive, and the enhancement of powers of intervention of the Member States, as coastal States. With the information that it is hoped to be gathered by the implementation of the new proposed Directive, Member States would be able, before accepting high risk ships into their ports, to ask for additional information in order to check compliance by the ship with international conventions and, if necessary, to carry out on-board inspections under the Port State Control Directive (presently 95/21/EC).

A most revolutionary proposal, included in the monitoring, concerns the recommendation that ships calling at Community ports should carry 'black boxes' – similar to those applicable in the air industry – or voyage data recorders, in order to facilitate the investigation of accidents.

A much debated issue involves a requirement that Member States receive ships in distress in ports of refuge. The proposal aims to make it easier to seek a port of refuge in the event of trouble at sea and also to prevent the risk of accident by prohibiting ships from leaving ports of call in the Community if particularly bad weather and sea conditions increase the risk of an accident. The IMO has also taken a pro-active role in this respect, particularly after the recent incident of the gasoline carrying vessel, *The Castor* being in distress outside the Spanish waters (referred to in Chapter 13).

Once the new directive is adopted, the Council Directive (93/75/EEC) will be repealed, 24 months thereafter (Art 26 of the proposed directive). The new directive will enter into force on the 20th day following that of its publication in the Official Journal of the European Communities (Art 28).

Since this is a very important amending directive, it is surprising that procedures for it to come into force will take such a long time.

3.2 The proposed regulation for establishment of a Maritime Safety Agency

In addition, in order to control monitoring of ships' compliance with Community law and assessing the effectiveness of the measures in place, the Commission is proposing the establishment of a European Maritime Safety Agency by a regulation, which will facilitate co-operation between Member States and the Commission. The role and organisation of the agency, which will include assessment and auditing of classification societies, is proposed to be largely based on the Aviation Safety Agency.

3.3 The proposed regulation on the establishment of a fund for compensation for oil pollution damage in European waters and reform of the liability regime

The Commission recognises that the present system of compensation of oil pollution victims is workable and provides some important benefits, namely:

(a) there is no difficulty for the victims to identify who is the liable party:

(b) there is no need for them to prove fault on behalf of the shipowner;

(c) their compensation does not depend on the financial position of the shipowner in the light of compulsory liability insurance and the right of direct action against the insurer.

Nevertheless, with regard to major oil spills, such as those that occurred in European waters in recent years,[11] the Commission considers that the compensation procedures have been complex and slow, therefore unacceptable. In the Commission's view, this is due to insufficient limits of compensation rather than deficiencies inherent in the compensation procedures.

3.3.1 The present system of compensation for oil pollution[12]

When in 1967 the Liberian tanker *Torrey Canyon* ran aground off Land's End in the UK causing severe pollution to the coasts of southern England and northern France by spilling 119,000 tonnes of crude oil, it prompted the international community, through the IMO, to take measures to protect the marine environment.

The International Convention on Civil Liability for Oil Pollution (CLC) 1969 and the parallel Convention setting up the Oil Pollution Compensation Fund (Fund Convention) 1971 were passed and entered into force, in 1975 and 1978, respectively. The CLC regime provided for strict, but limited, liability of the registered tanker's shipowner, which is covered by the owner's insurance under the rules of its Protection & Indemnity club. The test for breaking the

---

11 *The Aegean Sea*, 1992, in Spanish waters; *The Braer*, 1993, in UK waters; *The Sea Empress*, 1996, in UK waters; *The Erika*, 1999, in French waters.

12 The provisions for prevention of pollution, generally, and oil pollution, specifically liability, limitation and compulsory insurance can be found in Pt VI, Chapters I, II, III and IV of the Merchant Shipping Act (MSA) 1995 and Scheds 4 and 5 to the Act. Chapter III deals with liability, limitation and compulsory insurance. The Oil Pollution (Compulsory Insurance) Regulations 1997 came into force on 1 September 1997. The most recent developments on pollution liability incurred by any hazardous and noxious substances carried on a ship and powers of intervention by the Secretary of State can be found in the Merchant Shipping and Maritime Security Act (MSMSA) 1997, which amends the MSA 1995 by inserting the Convention in Sched 5A. Power is given by the MSMSA 1997, s 182B, to Her Majesty to give effect to the Convention by Order in Council after ratification by the UK. The Hazardous and Noxious Substance Convention is not yet ratified.

right to limit under the 1969 Convention was 'actual fault or privity'[13] of the owner, while under the present system s 157(3) of the MSA 1995 follows a similar test to that of Art 4 of the 1976 Convention. Compulsory insurance to protect the rights of third parties who suffered loss due to oil pollution has been required. A direct action by oil pollution victims against the insurer has been allowed, being subject to the insurer's defence that the discharge, or escape, of oil was due to the wilful misconduct of the owner.[14] The Fund, financed by oil-receivers, provided a supplementary compensation to the victims.

The 1984 Protocol, by which an increase of the limits had been proposed, did not receive sufficient ratification by oil-receiving States. However, a second attempt in the 1990s resulted in the 1992 Protocols to the CLC and Fund Conventions, which entered into force in 1996.[15] While these Protocols maintained the broad framework of liability under the CLC system, they brought significant changes in both the limits of liability to compensate victims of oil pollution and the test by which the right to limit might be barred. The test, now, is similar to that applicable under the 1976 Limitation Convention, discussed in the previous chapter. There are, however, a couple of minor, but quite significant, differences. The proof required, under the new s 157(3) of the MSA 1995, to break limitation is that 'the discharge or escape or the relevant threat of contamination resulted from anything done or omitted to be done by the owner either with intent to cause any such damage or cost ... or recklessly and in the knowledge that any such damage or cost would probably result'. The insertion of the word 'any' before 'such damage' is intended to be in favour of the victims who may not be required to discharge the higher burden with regard to the owners' knowledge of the particular damage suffered. This section, unlike the equivalent section of the 1976 Convention, does not refer to the 'personal' act or omission of the owner.[16] Compulsory insurance and the right of a direct action against the insurer have been maintained.

Since 1998, it has not been possible for a Member State to belong to both regimes. All EU Members with a coastline, except Portugal, which is in the process of finalising ratification, are parties to both Protocols. The USA is not a party to this regime, but has established its own system by passing the Oil Pollution Act (OPA) in 1990, following the oil pollution disaster in Alaska caused by *The Exxon Valdez* in 1989.

---

13 MSA 1995, Sched 4, Chapter III, s 157(1).

14 See Sched 4, Chapter III, ss 163, 165 of the MSA 1995.

15 The Merchant Shipping (Salvage and Pollution) Act 1994, s 5, enabled the UK to ratify the 1992 Protocols and give them effect by this Act which was later consolidated into the MSA 1995 (the latter came into force on 1 January 1996).

16 See Chapter 16, above.

3.3.2 The Commission's proposals and reasons

The shortcomings of the present regime, in the Commission's view, are basically fourfold. First, the existing international liability and compensation regime is inadequate in terms of the current limits of liability and compensation. The sinking of *Erika* showed that victims of an oil spill may not be fully compensated, even if the validity of their claims has been established. Inadequate limits contribute to uncertainty and delays in payment.

Secondly, the right to limit liability is practically unbreakable.

Thirdly, the method of calculation, on the basis of the gross tonnage of the ship, ignores the nature of the cargo on board and the extent of oil spilled.

Fourthly, the prohibition of claiming for oil pollution damage against the charterer, manager and operator of the ship is restricting the victims' rights of recovering more compensation.

The *Erika* incident prompted the Commission to act quickly in order to create a mechanism whereby the limits of compensation will be raised in order to ensure that victims of oil spills in Europe will be adequately compensated. It also proposes to introduce penal sanctions for grossly negligent behaviour on the part of anyone involved in the sea transport of oil.

The specific concern of the Commission is that the current threshold for loss of limitation rights should be lowered, in order to bring it into line with other comparable regimes. It proposes that, at least, proof by the claimants of gross negligence on behalf of the shipowner should trigger unlimited liability.

The Commission recognises, however, that other comparable regimes of environmental liability do not provide for compulsory insurance, or for a direct action against the insurer by the victims. Such protection is necessary because of the nature of the shipping trade and the type of company structures common in shipowning. Nevertheless, the Commission proposes that it is possible to reconstruct the framework of limitation, so that the insurance requirement is restricted to the limits of the strict liability, whereas the fault based unlimited liability is borne by the owner himself.

Another problem posed by the present liability and limitation regime for oil pollution, as identified by the Commission, is that it is directed against the registered owner and protects the operators and managers or charterers of the ship, who may exercise as much, or even more, control over the operation and transport as the registered owner. Such protection of key players, the Commission considers, is counterproductive and it is of the opinion that the prohibition of claiming compensation from those categories of people should be removed from the present regime.

The aim of the Commission is that the reform of the present regime of liability and limitation, as proposed, must be reviewed and implemented at an international level. If, however, this in not likely to be agreed, the Commission will make a proposal for adopting Community legislation introducing a Europe-wide maritime pollution liability and compensation regime. Should this take place, it would mean that, for the Commission to impose additional individual liabilities on shipowners or any of the protected parties, Member States would have to denounce the present international Convention regime before they could implement the proposed Community regime.

In the meantime, the Commission hopes that, by way of interim measures, the creation of a supplementary 'third tier' fund, (the COPE fund), covering compensation up to ECU1 billion, will top up the financial means provided by the international Oil Pollution Compensation Fund in relation to valid claims for oil spills in European waters. This fund will be financed by oil-receivers.

3.3.3 A brief commentary on the Commission's proposal

The changes to oil pollution liability and the limitation regime by the 1992 Protocols has been implemented fairly recently and became acceptable by Member States because it provided a compromise. The limits were increased in return for a higher threshold in the test of breaking limitation. In this way, it became possible to insure the limited liability of the shipowner and, hence, there has been certainty of recovery rather than no recovery at all.

The Commission's proposal, if it were to be adopted only as a Community law, will pose rather insuperable problems. It suffices to mention five major problems arising from this proposal that are capable of showing its futility. These concern:

(a) the inevitable conflict that would arise if there were two separate regimes on oil pollution liability;
(b) loss of tonnage;
(c) possible increase of pollution risks
(d) trade problems; and
(e) problems of enforcement of high compensatory claims.

Conflict

A Community liability regime would require Member States to denounce the international liability and limitation regime, which will cause obvious and insoluble problems.

For example, if Member States had to denounce the international regime in order to comply with the Community liability regime, which system of liability would apply when a ship of a Member State caused an oil spill outside European waters? Conversely, if a ship of a non-Member State caused pollution within European waters, theoretically, both systems would apply. However, how would the two systems be reconciled, since the international regime prevents any additional liabilities from being imposed. Perhaps, an answer to this problem may be offered by the Commission, but there has no thought being given to it in the communication made to the Council and the European Parliament.

Loss of tonnage

Member States have been making efforts in various ways to increase the number of ships registered with their respective flags. Such efforts include the enforcement of international safety standards. A separate system of Community law on pollution liability would place Member States in great difficulty if they had to denounce the international regime. A significant consequence, which should not be ignored, would be the transfer of registered EU Member States ships to other Flag States, or the non-registration of new tonnage in registers of EU Member States.

Increase of pollution risks

While there is acceptance that some States of flags of convenience must be closely observed because they are lax in the enforcement of international safety regulations and, therefore, contribute to risks of pollution, the Commission's proposal to impose a Community law on oil pollution will have an undesirable and reverse consequence. Shipowners will find ways of survival and will easily opt for the already attractive option of registering their ships with flags of convenience, thus the risk of pollution will increase.

Trade problems

If the issue is not resolved internationally, a major problem for the EU States will be inhibition of trade of oil products in Europe, which will result in severe financial losses to Community States, as well as in havoc to ordinary living.

Enforcement

The fifth problem concerns the enforcement of additional liabilities and arises from the nature of shipowning structures, the legitimacy of one-ship companies. An unlimited liability regime, which cannot be covered by insurance, will be impracticable in terms of enforcing full compensation against the one-ship registered owner. Even if the new law was extended to operators and managers, and to charterers of tankers, as the Commission correctly proposes that it should, neither group would have the capacity for unlimited liability, which is not insurable anyway, nor visible assets against which compensation claims could be enforceable. It is, however, imperative that these protected players are included in the present liability and limitation for oil pollution damage regime, as they are, indeed, included in the 1976 Limitation Convention.

Finally, it may be possible to envisage that the devastating accidents that caused pollution damage in the last three decades will not recur. The accidents that prompted the Commission to take steps in proposing unlimited liability of shipowners for gross negligence causing oil spills occurred at such a time that the international regulations on safety and monitoring of sub-standard ships were being tested. It is possible that, with the proper enforcement of the ISM system and the campaign of quality shipping by rigorous monitoring and control, such accidents may be eliminated in the future. At present, the regulations are not yet rigorously enforced by all players and, sadly, at the time of revising the final draft of this book, another tanker, *The Kristal*, carrying molasses, broke into two outside Spain, which reinforced the Commission's view to proceed with its proposals without delay.

The other initiatives of the Commission, however, concerning the extension of monitoring of all ships and the establishment of a Maritime Safety Agency, as well as steps taken to ensure a closer supervision of the activities of classification societies are – to the credit of the EC – very important proposals and are capable of achieving the desired objectives for safety at sea.

RISK MANAGEMENT CULTURE
AND COLLECTIVE RESPONSIBILITY

1 INTRODUCTION

In order to understand risk management, discussed in various parts of this book, it is important to understand the infrastructures involved in the setting up, operating and trading of shipping companies. The complexities of the interrelations between such infrastructures are enormous and they would require a separate study from sociological, psychological and economic perspectives, with examples of case studies if that were feasible. Therefore, it is only intended, in this epilogue, to present a framework against which risk management can be evaluated and highlight the areas in which legal risk management, which has been misunderstood, would need to be practised more systematically.

What is a risk? In common parlance, 'risk' generally means taking a chance in the hope that everything will turn out to be either safe or profitable, depending on the circumstances of risk taking, or it may turn out the other way. Many factors, such as personality traits, experience or knowledge, financial incentives or needs and statistics, determine whether or not a person is prepared to take risks, other than the ordinary risks of everyday living. Although this definition of risk is commonly understood to be applicable to all strata of life, private or business, risk also carries an additional connotation of a hazard that needs to be covered by insurance in the event of its happening.

In business life, in particular, risk is understood as the chance of an incident happening that may result in danger to life, property, the environment, or in a commercial dispute, or in litigation. That being so, it needs to be evaluated in terms of its significance to the business, probability of occurrence and tolerance of its consequences. The method of evaluation is based on experience, statistical analysis of frequency, other information systems, and the environment in which a particular risk might occur.

The phrase 'risk management' has been used in different contexts. It may signify to a layperson the management of risks by, simply, good housekeeping, while it may mean to a professional, broadly: a systematic approach of taking safety precautions in all levels of business, managing financial and commercial risks and obtaining insurance cover for risk exposure. Legal risk management is the area which is the least thought of, although it may be thought as being included under the umbrella of insurance.

If one were to break down the categories of risks into their various components, the exercise would produce a long list of risk items, which business people may take into account either consciously or sub-consciously every day. The difference between this exercise and one of proper risk management is that, in the latter, a system of identification, evaluation and assessment of risks is set up for the purpose of taking prophylactic measures to ensure prevention, or minimisation and control, of identified and potential risks, which would be beyond the level of tolerance of a particular business management.

The broad categories of risks concern: (a) risks inherent to particular forms of corporate structures; (b) risks regarding the safety of people or property; (c) financial risks; (d) risks of liabilities to third parties; and (e) criminal liabilities. More specifically, they all concern risks, which, if taken or ignored, have legal consequences, thus, the term 'legal'.

A corporation may be exposed to legal proceedings either for non-compliance with statutory provisions (see Chapters 8 and 12), or for accidents occurring by non-compliance with regulations (Chapter 12), or due to unwise corporate structures (Chapter 3), or contractual arrangements (Chapters 9, 10, 11, 14), or, generally, for incidents arising from the operation and trading of ships (Chapters 12, 13, 15). Risks in relation to carriage of goods by sea, or under insurance contracts, are the subject of separate books in this series.

The common element in all these types of risks is that the lack of a systematic approach to the probability of their occurrence, and the lack of a system being in place for reduction or minimisation of their recurrence, will result in undesirable legal consequences with financial repercussions. The proper approach to risk management, therefore, whether shipping or non-shipping, is (apart from the pure commercial risks) to classify them as 'legal', instead of looking at legal risks as a marginalised area of risk management.

2 UNDERSTANDING INFRASTRUCTURES OF SHIPPING COMPANIES

Without wishing to state the obvious, shipping is a very competitive service industry and it operates to make profit for those who are brave enough to take on the risks involved in this business. Risk management cannot be understood without understanding how the infrastructures of the business as a whole interrelate. As one writer[1] on managing risks in shipping has put it: 'Commercial pressures are ever present and, for every constructive improvement, risks are taken to innovate and exploit opportunities.'

---

1   Parker, CJ, *Managing Risks in Shipping: A Practical Guide*, 1999, The Nautical Institute, p 2

The infrastructures are divided for simplicity into: internal, relational and external.

2.1 Internal infrastructures

A company is made up of the aggregate of personalities of people who are working in it. It is very important that, at the selection and recruitment level, employees, or those who hold managerial positions, are chosen very carefully to reflect the culture of the company and meet the objectives set by it.

2.1.1 Vertical and horizontal structures

People employed at the top, who are the 'mind and will' of the organisation (see Chapters 8 and 16), determine the safety culture and the risk tolerance of the company. The staff employed in the technical operation, in the shore management, and in the navigation of ships are performing the core of the business and are invariably the source of risks, if communication between themselves and their superiors, motivation and training afforded to them by their superiors are not consistent. Without clear communication and training, which have become even more essential for compliance with the International Safety Management Code (ISMC) and Standard of Training Certification and Watchkeeping Convention, the company is at risk, at least, of being labelled as suffering from the 'disease of sloppiness' from top to bottom (see Chapter 8).

An effective management is one that implements the following objectives: clear communication, leadership and benchmarking of areas in need of improvement; consistency in approach and rewarding excellence; cultivating co-operation and defusing conflict.

The staff's trust, co-operation, commitment and identification with the company for the fulfilment of its objectives can be gained in various ways that are beyond the scope of this book. To maintain levels of co-operation and efficiency from top management to the floor, is a study of behavioural science,[2] but it is crucial for the image of the company and the results the company aims to achieve, from both financial and risk management perspectives.[3]

---

[2] Elementary reading: Cowling, A, Stanworth, M, Bennett, R, Curran, J and Lyons, P, *Behavioural Science for Managers,* 2nd edn, 1988, Edward Arnold; Armstrong, M, *How to be an Even Better Manager,,* 4th edn, 1994, Kogan Page; Mulling, L, *Management and Organisational Behaviour,* 2nd edn 1989, Pitman.

[3] The author has researched in and written on behavioural patterns in complex organisations, but her book on the subject is not relevant in this context.

2.1.2 Safety culture

A safety culture of a company aims for transparency of management and operational practices and the minimisation of all possible risks that are due to human factors (see Chapter 8). Regular audits, risk assessment and evaluation, as well as implementation of plans to control risk exposure should lead to a safety culture and a company almost free from risk incidents. In an ideal shipping world, all infrastructures should be able to work in harmony with each other. But, in the real world, there are factors of safety that are not within the control of the shipowning, or managing, companies.

2.1.3 Risk tolerance

Risk tolerance is the level of acceptance of risks, which depends on the nature of risks and on various other factors. First and foremost are the commercial pressures to engage the ships in profitable markets. Freight fluctuations, overcapacity creating more supply than demand, financial commitments to the mortgagee, internal pressures from partners, staffing costs and venture capital are influential to risk tolerance. Therefore, the management of a company may be more tolerant in accepting a certain level of risks and, thereby, it may economise in employment of high quality trained crew, or in maintenance of its ships. If a risk is insurable, there may be a tendency to take it (provided the conduct is not such as to prejudice the insurance contract) and respond to a loss or liability incurred reactively, instead of pro-actively.

On the other hand, the need to observe regulations and consider the consequences of non-compliance, is a factor of reducing risk tolerance. Little regard may, however, be paid to consequences arising from breach of contract.

2.2. Relational infrastructures

2.2.1 Corporate interrelations

Shipowning companies are complex organisations. The simplest form of a corporate structure is the one-ship company. The next stage of simplicity is the owner who owns two to five ships, each registered under one-ship companies. A parent company may control these subsidiaries and the management of all these ships may be in the hands of the same people under a management company. Some of these ships may have been chartered to a bareboat charterer who charters them down the line to different time charterers. The control may, or may not, remain with the parent company. The next stage of corporate structure is a complex one and may involve a venture of multinational companies, where it may be difficult to ascertain easily whether there is congruence of opinion in policy and safety matters. Many ships may be owned by various subsidiary companies, owned and controlled by one or two parent companies. The ships may be entered into pools or consortia and may be let via bareboat charterers, having financial interest in the owning companies, to various time charterers, etc.

The distance created between the real owners, through complex corporate structures, is a legitimate method of limiting liability and, thus, controlling risk exposure (see examples of legitimate corporate structures in Chapter 3).

However, intercorporate relationships are a crucial factor to influencing the risk profile of the shipowning companies. Differences of opinion as regards policy objectives and orientation between the top people in each company, as well as the inevitable reduction of effective communication down the line of the hierarchy, may give rise to incidents of accidents the cause of which may not be easily noticed by the top people, so that an inefficient system of assessment and evaluation of risk may result.[4] Pinning responsibility upon the 'directing mind' of the company for the purpose of attributing liability, or for breaking the limit under Art 4 of the 1976 Convention, is almost impossible (see Chapters 8 and 16). On the other hand, the availability of more resources and access to financial capital markets ought to facilitate the implementation of a viable safety system in each company.

2.2.3 Owners and others

Owners and their bankers may involve a very delicate relationship, which may have a significant impact upon the company's risk profile, for better or for worse.

There is also a delicate relationship between owners and professional managers. Experienced owners may not easily delegate full management to professional managers, as they would wish to oversee technical and operational matters themselves, as well as control the cost of maintenance of ships for the purpose of compliance with regulations, unless they want to remove the name of their company from the ISMC requirements (see Chapter 8).

The nationality and experience of owners, and the nationality of the crew used may affect the acceptance of their ships by charterers.

The relational infrastructure includes, also, the owners' relationships with Flag State, Port States, the classification society of its ships, shipbuilders or repairers and Government representatives, all of which affect the risk profile of a particular company.

---

4   Perhaps that may have been a hidden factor in the accident of *The Herald of Free Enterprise* (see Chapter 8).

2.3 External infrastructures

While external infrastructures seem to overlap with the previous category to a certain extent, what is outlined under this category is the effect of external pressures upon risk exposure of a shipowning or management company and the 'third parties' factors' to it.

2.3.1 Regulatory and fiscal

Regulations are here to stay and their importance has been stressed throughout this book. A lot depends, however, not only on whether the owners or managers have a system of compliance in place (Safety Management System (SMS)) but also on those who inspect a ship. A very original proposal was recently made by a speaker at the London Shipping Law Centre,[5] that a solution to this problem may lie in the implementation of a new Code of Honesty, Respectfulness and Integrity of Surveyors in their Tasks (CHRIST), which, if it were to be adopted internationally, should have severe repercussions for breach. This is not to be treated as a light joke, because the role of a surveyor, whether it be that of a classification society, or of any other professional body, is most crucial in enhancing safety at sea. It has, fortunately, in recent years, been recognised that controls should be imposed upon the activities of classification societies and also of Flag States in the inspection of ships (see Chapters 8, 11 and 17).

Equally, Flag States that neglect procedures in the enforcement of international regulations should be more rigorously controlled. But, one major reason why shipowners have chosen registration of their ships with flags of convenience is that governments of most respectable registers have encouraged 'flagging-out' to tax havens by having, themselves, a disadvantageous taxation system for corporations or directors (Chapter 5).

2.3.2 Third parties' factors

Shippers, charterers, port authorities, shipbuilders, classification societies, brokers and insurers are all to be regarded as sharing responsibility for risk exposure of owners and managers, insofar as the external infrastructures are concerned. Dangerous cargo can do more harm to a ship and to the environment than the ship can do to a cargo. Charterers disregarding safety matters, either with respect to cargo, or choice of substandard ships to cut costs, or choice of unsafe ports, equally can do more harm than is usually perceived. Terminal operators accustomed to unsafe practices would also

---

5   Coutroubis, A, 'Flag States, Port States, classification societies and shipowners', lecture in the series On Corporate Structures, held at the London Shipping Law Centre, 18 October 2000.

need to exercise risk management to minimise risks to ships and to the environment. Port States may not always be consistent in their policies of inspecting and penalising ships for deficiencies, which inevitably leads to confusion and discrimination. Classification societies have a greater role to play now, as they are even entrusted to guard the implementation of international regulations. If there is going to be a significant change in the culture of safety it is important to bear in mind this question: *Quis custodiet custodes*? There is a tendency to blame the owners, but perhaps little regard is still paid to other participants, mainly because they are more difficult to target (see Chapter 8).

Shipbuilders, who may construct defective hatch covers or weak bulkheads, or ship-repair yards, who may repair defects superficially,[6] cannot be left out of the equation of a global safety culture. Brokers and insurers insuring dangerous cargo or sub-standard ships, should be taken into account in this equation. Insuring sub-standard ships, or allowing the shipment of insured cargo on sub-standard ships may, hopefully, now be a phenomenon of the past.

2.3.3 Market forces

What drives the management of a company are the objectives of: enhancing the company's position with profitable engagements of the ships; placing the company in a favourable competitive position by long term plans of employment; and ensuring the good reputation of the company externally and with its financiers. Such a perspective of the management is interwoven with market forces, demand and supply, overcapacity and quality.

When there is quality of services provided by ships, which do not cause problems to the contracting parties or to the environment, and the owners/managers have a good reputation of dealing with third parties, there will be a positive correlation between employment and demand. Quality marketing and public relations will strengthen the company's position. Apart from quality, however, other factors such as overcapacity of other good quality ships of the same type, demand for particular commodities, technological advancements, and the like, will affect the matrix of correlation between demand and employment of a company's ships.

Survival in this competitive business may lead owners or managers to cut down the budget required for maintaining quality performance in order to be able to accept lower rates of freight or hire and overlook what may result in risk exposure. In the long run, however, it should be remembered that due diligence and a systematic approach to risk management will pay dividends. There are several examples given in this book of cases which reached the courts to resolve disputes that arose due to these underlying factors and, not

---

6   *The Muncaster Castle* [1961] 1 Lloyd's Rep 57 (HL).

infrequently, due to bad management practices, or lack of knowledge of legal risks.

3 COLLECTIVE RESPONSIBILITY AND COMMITMENT

The objectives of safety of people, property and the environment, as well as prevention of liabilities to third parties are a matter of collective responsibility and commitment, not only of the company concerned from the top of the hierarchy to the workplace, but also of all players involved in the complex infrastructures. Congruency in policy and approach to risk management of the owner or manager will enable the company to surpass most problems posed from the outside. In particular, if the framework of procedures, discussed below, becomes part of the company's practices, a reduction in accidents and an increase of risk control will result. It is recognised, however, that it is not possible to eliminate all marine casualties. In this respect, a Lloyd's underwriter[7] speaking at a conference on risk management said: 'Because of the nature of the business in which we operate, accidents and losses will continue to happen in the most safety conscious environments. But we all have a collective responsibility to work together in order to ensure that these losses are reduced to the lowest possible level.'

3.1 Risk exposure

Failing to identify a potential risk, its frequency, probability of recurrence and its consequences would be a sloppy way of running ships. The company will be exposed to criminal or civil liabilities resulting in enormous financial loss.

It would be impossible to enumerate the situations of risk exposure. The matter lies with the experience of each operator or shipowner who should diligently carry out with experts an audit of incidents that they have encountered and be aware of other incidents which do frequently happen in commercial shipping.[8]

A few examples of those can conveniently be divided into three categories: 'the transportation' category, the 'human factor' category and the 'contractual' category. In relation to transportation of goods, there is the risk of fraud in the shipment or destination of goods consigned on board; charterers' credibility and reputation, hazardous cargo, piracy, stowaways, and unsafe ports risks, are common. In relation to the human factor category, in which the owner or

---

7   Redmond, S, 'The apparent cyclical nature of marine insurance and its effect on risk assessment and management', IBC Conference on Maritime Risk Assessment Management and Control, 1997.

8   See an analysis of common occurrences of risks in *op cit*, Parker, fn 1.

manager may be, more or less, in control in the preparation for a voyage, good inspection and maintenance of the ship,[9] as well as training of the crew in navigational matters[10] are the core areas of risk exposure. Failure to comply with international regulations will certainly be caught at the next visit to a Port State Control. However, as it has been stressed in this book, it should not be ignored that non-compliance may arise from a combination of factors. In relation to the contractual category, risk exposure depends, a great deal, on both the choice of a particular contracting party and on the negotiating or drafting of contracts, examples of which have been looked at in this book.[11] Invariably, disputes result from bad drafting, inequality of bargaining power, commercial or corporate pressures, and when people fixate themselves to one inflexible position being unwilling to see the broad picture of a problem, in order to seek other options through negotiation or mediation.

3.2 Risk profile

A company can become aware of its risk profile by identifying and evaluating the risks that it has experienced, or it may encounter. It can develop a programme for the monitoring and control of risks.[12] This process involves the listing of identified risks, counting their frequency and assessing their consequences on individual tables or bar charts. Then an assessment of risk acceptability can be made for the purpose of setting priorities as to which risks need to be monitored or controlled by taking the appropriate action plan.

With the requirement for an SMS, it will now be easier for a company to carry out its risk management profile and assessment of risks. By way of a summary of what was explained in Chapter 8, the SMS obliges the company to have in place: (i) the company's policy on safety; (ii) implementation of that policy with a well designed documented system; (iii) regular review and reassessment of its effectiveness.

With this system in place, the company can establish its objectives and targets, improve performance by evaluating results and taking corrective action, communicate progress and develop action plans for individual responsibilities of key people and of its staff.

However, not all kinds of risks are assessable. Assessment invariably depends on the subjective perception of its assessors, or a risk may become apparent with the benefit of hindsight. The way in which the SMS assists in

---

9   While there are a number of examples in this area, it suffices to note the well known case, *The Torenia* [1983] 2 Lloyd's Rep 210.

10 See, eg, *The Makedonia* [1962] 1 Lloyd's Rep 316.

11 See, in particular, Chapters 10, 11 and 14.

12 Woodcock, J, Sedgwick Risk Consulting, IBC Conference on Maritime Risk Assessment, Management and Control, 1997.

this respect is that it imposes an obligation upon the management of a company, first, to have a system of recording incidents and the situation in which they have occurred, second, to make a conscious observation and graphic analysis of how they occurred, third, to take action to prevent their recurrence and, fourth, to visualise unsuspected exposure. The requirement of team work by the ISMC, headed by the designated person and the operations manager, is bound to ensure that a systematic risk assessment and evaluation is made, so that it is likely that a subjective element of risk assessment will be reduced and risk awareness will be increased.

3.3 Risk management standards for risk control

Standards derive from policies and policy objectives for a safe management system and procedures, supported by guidelines on each individual aspect and stage of risk management. The stages at which risk management standards should be implemented for risk control, following the exercise of identification, evaluation and assessment explained earlier, are examined below, by way of illustration only.

3.3.1 At the incorporation stage

It has been discussed in Chapter 3 that properly constituted corporate structures are a legitimate way of limiting liability when a distance is kept between companies in the same group through careful formation of one-ship companies. The formation of this type of corporate structure is even more advisable now, since the effect of *The Indian Grace*[13] is that it creates a personal jurisdiction against the defendant, interested in defending the claim in the *in rem* proceedings, from the service of the proceedings. This means that a judgment obtained, even in default of appearance, will be executable against the other ships in the fleet, if they are under the ownership of the same company.

Care must be taken to avoid transfer of a ship within the same group of companies, or by forming a new company after claims have arisen, as the court may find such a transfer to be a sham transfer. While separate corporate structures provide a shield to lifting or piercing the corporate veil, it should be borne in mind that an incident of proven fraud is a good reason to pierce the corporate veil.

While making provisions through third party liability insurance to meet legitimate claims, a ship arrest is a disruption of business. It may be thought prudent to keep separate accounts, separate stock, separate directors and officers, separate operations, separate financial statements and tax returns

13 See Chapter 3.

between a parent and subsidiary companies to protect exposure of the assets held by the subsidiaries, in case a ship owned by them calls in jurisdictions where associated arrest of ships is favoured by the legal system.

However, above all this, the safest way to prevent risk exposure would be to have a system in place by which care is taken to control or minimise liabilities for which claims could be made. What follows is a guide for such a system.

3.3.2 At the technical and operational stage

The right choice of personnel and, in particular, of the designated person, marine superintendent and of the crew is paramount. No matter how much training or instructions were given, if members of the crew were not able to absorb what is taught or what is expected of them, the human factor element to risk exposure would not be in control. Equally, the captains of the ships, the designated person and marine superintendent must be committed and able to obey instructions, as well as understand the importance of recording and reporting incidents, which need the managers' or directors' attention.

Incidents of collisions at sea, discussed in Chapter 12, as well as incidents where the company was not able to limit liability under the 1957 Convention, discussed in Chapter 17, are examples of inattention to the collision regulations, or disobedience with instructions. If the circumstances of such incidents are systematically plotted and evaluated, followed by an assessment of the liability exposure of the company and by an action plan for their monitor and control, the company will save money, not only in terms of minimising liabilities to third parties, but also in terms of insurance premiums and legal costs.

Routine maintenance, fire drills, training facilities and prevention of work fatigue of the crew are essential practices of a well functioning management in this respect. Lack of these practices may result in loss of life and criminal liabilities (Chapter 8).

3.3.3 At the contract stage

As has been discussed in this book, negotiating and drafting contracts are frequently the root of risk exposure. Examples of clauses in contracts unfavourable to the owners have been seen in various chapters. For example, in the drafting of mortgage covenants, care should be taken to limit the mortgagee's right of possession to occasions of financial default (Chapter 9); in the area of ship building, skilful negotiations are needed before the standard terms of contract offered by shipbuilders are accepted (Chapter 10). As regards sale and purchase of used ships (Chapter 11), there are many examples of cases that ended up in litigation either because the parties, through their brokers, did not make their intentions clear, or because the standard terms of Norwegian Sale Forms are very much in favour of the seller, or contain ambiguous clauses. The buyers' attention has been drawn to when an undertaking or an indemnity is given in the contract by the seller for encumbrances or claims, which may be worth only the value of the paper that it is written on.

In contracts of towage (Chapter 14), there is a need to spell out in the contract clearly what the parties expect from each other. As regards salvage contracts (Chapter 13), the recent changes with respect to special compensation for protection of the environment have brought some clarity in the expectations of the parties and safeguards for the salvors. A great deal of effort has been made to produce this result through negotiations and careful drafting. Yet, it is still early to say whether the Special Compensation of Protection and Indemnity Clause (SCOPIC) will be without teething problems.

It has been seen, in Chapter 15, that the area of harbour law is burdened with old statutes containing obscure wording. Care needs to be taken when copying such clauses into local legislation.

There are numerous other areas of contracts that have been beyond the scope of this book. The same principles discussed in this epilogue can be applied to contracts of affreightment from which most disputes arise.[14]

There is further the risk of a disappearing debtor, which must be borne in mind at the stage of contracting. There will be very little that the law can do if a party, appearing to contract for another, disappears leaving no undisclosed principal behind. Checking the solvency and credibility of a would be contracting party is more important than just succumbing to market forces.

3.3.4 At the performance stage

While due diligence should have been exercised at the technical and operational stage to make the ship seaworthy in all respects, in order to prevent risks from arising at the performance stage, many other risks can arise at this stage. Such risks may either stem from badly drafted clauses in the contract (contract stage), or may be linked to the inherent dangers of the sea voyage, or be due to human factors. Although some of them might be minimised, or controlled, complete elimination would be impossible.

This stage concerns the physical handling of the ship by those on board, and also the directions given from the shore, during a voyage, on how to handle loading or discharge, deal with unexpected situations and port authorities, shippers, charterers, stevedores, or those who have come to assist

---

14 Risk management aspects of this area of maritime law will be the subject of the next book in this series.

the ship in an emergency. Several judicial decisions in this book provide examples of such incidents.

While, again, the human factor can considerably be reduced by equipping seafarers with the knowledge and skills required at this stage, 'seafarers have an innate ability to understand and assess the risks that the job places before them and undertake intuitive risk analysis'.[15] However, it is the management of the company itself that must have clear goals and policies about safety, regardless of commercial pressures, so that confusion does not arise.

The following (non-inclusive) areas are of paramount importance as part of the risk management of the company:

(a) Has it made sure that: there has been a voyage planning; there are up to date navigational charts[16] and notices on board, weather forecast, tidal forecasts; draught restrictions are obtained, collision regulations are observed[17] with particular reference to the voyage planning; watchkeeping is not impaired by fatigue of the watch on duty, or that a new member of crew is given sufficient time to familiarise himself with the ship.[18] Have there been sufficient bunkers for the voyage and procedures to be followed, should the ship need to take further bunkers to prevent pollution, or to check the quality of bunkers?

(b) Has the management set clear instructions on what it expects from the master and crew during loading to have the ship ready to receive the cargo, during stowage and lashing of the cargo, as well as when signing bills of lading?[19]

(c) Stowaways are a frequent and costly risk for owners and their Protection & Indemnity (P&I) clubs. Although it is not always easy to detect their entry into the ship, extra watch and vigilance should be exercised to look in suspected places and, in case of container ships, to investigate non-sealed containers.

(d) Port restrictions, weather conditions and manoeuvering the ship out of or into port will depend on the knowledge of and co-operation between the pilot and crew of the ship. Their co-operation and understanding of the circumstances and of each other are crucial in avoiding accidents. The management must stress the importance of it to the master and crew.

(e) Proper training of the crew at the operational stage will ensure their knowledge of how to check the cargo for lashing, temperature, ventilation, or any possibility of water ingress, or any leakage of cargo, or any overheating which may result in combustion or fire in the holds.

---

15 Bailley, T (Captain), 'Managing risk on board ship', in *op cit*, Parker, fn 1, Chapter 3.

16 *The Marion* [1984] 2 Lloyd's Rep 1, see Chapters 8 and 16.

17 See Chapter 12.

18 *The Safe Carrier* [1994] 1 Lloyd's Rep 589, see Chapter 8.

19 See Cook, J *et al*, *Voyage Charters*, 1993, LLP (the second edition is expected in 2001).

Fire drills and exercises will ensure how the crew should be able to deal with unexpected fire on board.

(f) The test of whether the cargo has been properly stowed and securely lashed will be when the ship encounters heavy storms, particularly a tropical cyclone. Although a well maintained and securely loaded ship with well trained crew and an experienced master will be able to withstand bad weather, the unpredictability of sea conditions should not be underestimated, even if meteorological information is of the highest standards. Most accidents reported in Lloyd's List are due to severe weather conditions, which perhaps hit a less well maintained, or prepared, ship. It should be noted, however, that not all of these accidents are preventable, although their effect may be minimised with careful voyage planning. Only seafarers are experts to talk from their own experience of how difficult it is to handle the ship in a severe tropical cyclone.

(g) Grounding accidents, perhaps, could be prevented if an up to date chart and publications of local waters are observed. Engine failures during the voyage could equally be preventable if, at the operations and preparation stage of the voyage, sufficient care is taken. But these do occur due to other reasons, perhaps a latent defect, or a survey that has failed to detect faults. In the same vein of argument, bulkhead failures and stresses may depend either on construction, or survey faults, or miscalculation of the stresses on the ship, with a particular cargo on board.

(h) Although a systematic risk management practice will be capable of reducing risk exposure to a significant extent, it would be naive for one to believe that all will be 100% perfect. What is important, however, is whether the company's policy or approach to the eventuality of accidents is proactive or how the management reacts to the happening of such occurrences. For example, fear of losing the co-operation of insurers may lead the owner to invent some, not so plausible a cause of the accident, while it would be better to keep to the facts as they occurred. Nevertheless, it is crucial in this respect that the insurers, themselves, adopt a collective responsibility attitude, as has been stressed in this chapter. Sometimes, overzealousness of insurers, or their lawyers, make things worse and their respective trust between the insurer and the assured is undermined, resulting in protracted litigation. There are numerous examples in marine insurance claims (which are not within the scope of this book) in which the approach of insurers and their lawyers has been such as to alienate the assured, instead of endeavouring to resolve or minimise the impact of the accident by co-operation.

(i) Finally, but not least, the voyage may be completed uneventfully but there may be problems at the discharge port. The owners' P&I clubs provide extensive guidelines on how to deal with various circumstances, such as obnoxious receivers, or threats of arrest of the ship for alleged shortage of cargo, or demand for delivery without production of, or without the correct bills of lading, which should be referred to and followed. Clear communications and instructions at this stage are important, as well as obtaining professional advice and resolving disputes in the best way possible. If not, then the next stage would inevitably follow.

3.3.5 At the dispute resolution stage

Litigation can be bedevilled at times by procedural entanglements, either because procedural rules may appear to have more than one interpretation, or because they are unskillfully drafted, or because the litigants make procedural mistakes. Examples of these have been encountered in Pt I of this book.

It would be better to avoid reaching this stage if a systematic process of risk management were to be practised in the first place.

Whatever form is chosen for resolution of disputes, the parties may include, as part of their risk management system, the choice of advisors and experts.

Forum shopping, regardless of a jurisdiction agreement, or on the criteria of special advantages in a particular forum, will not be looked upon favourably by English judges. The criteria of an appropriate forum, for the interests of all parties and for the ends of justice, and the consequences of breach of jurisdiction agreements have been examined in Chapters 5, 6 and 7. Forum shopping by way of limitation actions has been discouraged by the English courts. Litigants have been warned not to waste litigation costs by such forum shopping, but to follow the clear guidelines laid down by the House of Lords in *The Spiliada*. The rules applicable under the Brussels Convention have been looked at in Chapter 6 and the principles, when anti-suit injunctions may be granted, are discussed in Chapter 7. Neither England, nor another forum, will be a good place to shop in if the interests of justice and comity to other nations' jurisdiction are not observed.

3.4 Enhanced safety culture

3.4.1 Adopting a systematic process

It derives from the foregoing and from what other experts in risk management have advocated, that it is first imperative to establish a systematic approach to risk management and change the company's philosophy to quality and safety. As part of the system of establishing a risk profile by identifying, evaluating and assessing risks, there should be a process for monitoring and reviewing risk exposure. Such a system should be enhanced by increased dialogue, training and further education for the purpose of increasing awareness of potential risks and their management. The London Shipping Law Centre offers such opportunities throughout the year with an educational programme tailored on risk management.

3.4.2 Funding risks

It is common sense that, if investment is made to control risks proactively, the cost of prevention or minimisation of risks will be less than the costs of reacting to risks after their occurrence to meet the liabilities or losses resulting from them. While it may seem more time consuming and cost inefficient to devote resources for a systematic audit of risk exposure of a company, to assess, analyse and control risks, when other priorities are pressing, it is false to assume that the result will be less cost efficient.

3.4.3 Commitment to change and collective responsibility

Quality shipping is a matter of collective responsibility as has been stressed throughout this book. It can be presented like a ring, with the owners and managers of ships in the centre, their internal infrastructure of personnel and related companies in the next ring, and all other players mentioned earlier in extended surrounding rings, as is shown in the following diagram.

Quality shipping is a worthwhile objective with long term rewards. It will make the company more competitive, it will have the effect of lower insurance premiums, it will enhance freight returns, and it will open other opportunities.

LEGAL RISK MANAGEMENT

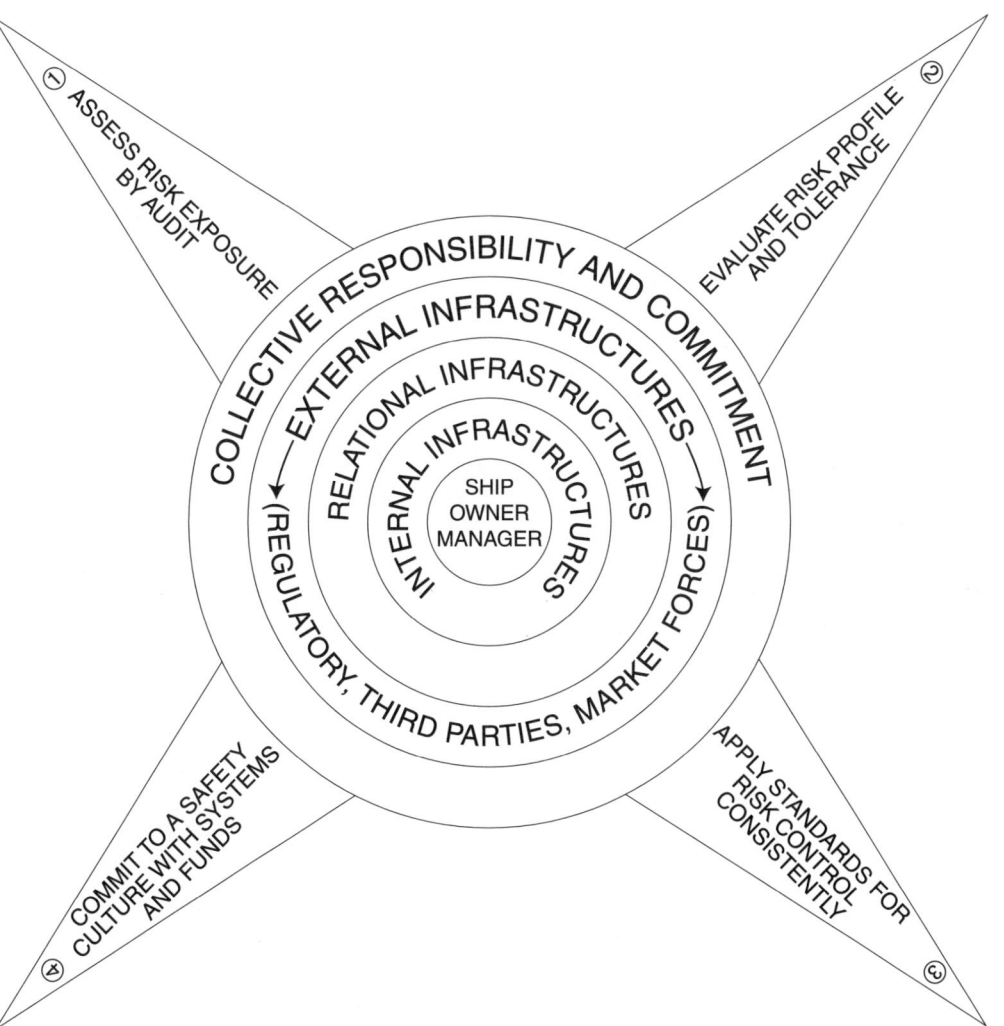

INDEX

C

G